EVANGELICALISM IN MODERN BRITAIN

By the Same Author

Patterns in History
Leicester: Inter-Varsity Press, 1979

The Nonconformist Conscience
Chapel and Politics, 1870–1914
London: Allen & Unwin, 1982

The Baptists in Scotland
A History
(Editor)
Glasgow: Baptist Union of Scotland, 1988

Evangelicals led to charges by eighteenth-century opponents that they were subjecting the Bible to arbitrary interpretation under the alleged illumination of the Holy Spirit. The opponents, often maintaining a doughty tradition of Anglican apologetic, claimed to be the more scriptural party in appealing to the bare text.[92] Yet Evangelicals were certain they understood the Bible clearly. Hence the nineteenth-century Scottish revivalist Brownlow North 'spent hours every day in hard and prayerful study of its pages'.[93] A contemporary evangelist, Henry Moorhouse, was similarly devoted. 'He would not suffer anything, not even a sheet of paper, to be laid upon his Bible. There alone, apart, it must lie, unique, matchless, wonderful, the very mind and presence of the infinite and eternal God.'[94] Evangelicals revered the Bible.

Respect for the Bible did not necessarily lead them into far-fetched views. The passage from the book of Hebrews about a rock following Israel through the wilderness came up for discussion at a conversation party for Cambridge undergraduates led by Charles Simeon. Did the rock really move? 'Oh yes, of course', replied Simeon, 'with a hop, skip and a jump!'[95] Here was no wooden literalness. It is true that doctrinal preoccupations often encouraged an instinct for turning to the New Testament letters in preference to the gospels.[96] Yet Evangelicals did not normally concentrate on obscurities. For the end of the nineteenth century, when the age of the questionnaire was just dawning, we possess a detailed breakdown of texts taken by preachers in a variety of Evangelical pulpits on a Sunday in March 1896. The survey came about because, intriguingly, the journal *Tit-Bits*, on receiving a complaint from a reader about the length of sermons, launched a competition to find the longest – it was, it turned out, a sermon preached at a Primitive Methodist chapel lasting one hour eighteen minutes. *The British Weekly*, an interdenominational paper, repeated the survey and also investigated texts. Three-quarters were drawn from the New Testament. John's gospel was the most popular source, followed closely by the first letter of John and then by the other three gospels. In the Old Testament, most texts came from Psalms, Genesis and Isaiah. None was taken from Philemon, 2 or 3 John, Lamentations, Obadiah, Micah, Nahum, Habakkuk or Zephaniah. The single verse that inspired most sermons was Galatians 2:20 about being crucified with Christ.[97] Certainly there is no evidence here of the deliberate searching out of obscure texts.

There was agreement among Evangelicals of all generations that the Bible is inspired by God. When it came to determining the implications of inspiration, however, there were notable divergences. Henry Venn of Huddersfield referred incidentally in 1763 to 'the infallible word of God' and the Countess of Huntingdon's Connexion confessed its belief in 1783 in 'the infallible truth' of the scriptures.[98] 'The Bible is altogether TRUE', wrote Edward Bickersteth in his extremely popular *A Scripture Help* (1816). 'It is truth without any mixture of error.'[99] Yet in the period up to that date there was no attempt to elaborate any theory of infallibility or inerrancy.

On the contrary, there was remarkable fluidity in ideas about the effects of inspiration on the text. The overriding aim of early Evangelicals was to bring home the message of the Bible and to encourage its devotional use rather than to develop a doctrine of scripture. A body of Evangelical opinion, however, began to insist from the 1820s onwards on inerrancy, verbal inspiration and the need for literal interpretation of the Bible.[100] In reaction against the publication of *Essays and Reviews* (1860), a Broad Church manifesto for studying the Bible in the manner of any other book, the newer dogmatic school of thought became more vocal.[101] 'To us', wrote the Baptist C. H. Spurgeon, 'the plenary verbal inspiration of the Holy Scripture is a fact and not a hypothesis.'[102] From the chair of the Congregational Union in 1894, by contrast, G. S. Barrett repudiated the 'crude and mechanical theory of verbal inspiration'.[103] Attitudes to the Bible drew apart until, in the wake of the First World War, the Evangelical world divided into conservatives and liberals primarily on that issue. The importance attributed by Evangelicals to the Bible eventually led to something approaching schism in their ranks.

CRUCICENTRISM

The doctrine of the cross, fourthly, has been the focus of the gospel. The Evangelical movement, in the words of Gladstone, 'aimed at bringing back, and by an aggressive movement, the Cross, and all that the Cross essentially implies'.[104] Nothing in the Christian system, according to John Wesley, 'is of greater consequence than the doctrine of Atonement. It is properly the distinguishing point between Deism and Christianity.'[105] The reconciliation of humanity to God, that is to say, achieved by Christ on the cross is why the Christian religion speaks of God as the author of salvation. 'I am saved', wrote an early Methodist preacher, 'through faith in the blood of the Lamb.'[106] There is a cloud of witnesses on the theme. An eighteenth-century Scottish theologian, John Maclaurin, like many subsequent Evangelicals, preached on 'Glorying in the cross of Christ'.[107] 'The death of Christ', according to the clerical manual of 1830, 'in this scriptural and comprehensive view, includes the whole Christian system.'[108] Representative twentieth-century Evangelicals in the Church of England said much the same.[109] Theologians elaborated the point: R. W. Dale, with telling reasonableness in 1875; James Denney, with scrupulous clarity in 1902; John Stott, with contemporary awareness in 1986; and, greatest of all, P. T. Forsyth in a series of vibrant treatises in the early twentieth century.[110] Critics deplored what they saw as an obsession. The Quaker statesman John Bright, having heard G. B. Bubier, a Congregational divine, is said to have murmured to himself, 'The atonement, always the atonement! Have they nothing else to say?'[111] Even those who professed a liberal version of Evangelical belief in the twentieth century like the Methodist W. R. Maltby felt compelled to lay great stress on the cross.[112] 'If men are Evangelical Christians at all', declared the Congregationalist Alexander Raleigh in 1879, 'they can say without a shadow of insincerity, "God forbid we should glory, save in the cross of our Lord Jesus Christ . . . "'[113]

Looking back on an interwar childhood in the Brethren, Anne Arnott recalled trying on Christmas Day to escape in imagination to Bethlehem from the ministry which, as always, centred on the crucifixion.[114] The atonement eclipsed even the incarnation among Evangelicals. In 1891 Charles Gore, a rising young Anglo-Catholic, inaugurated a central tradition in Anglican thought by arguing in the Bampton Lectures for the incarnation as the heart of Christian theology.[115] The warning issued to Methodists in the following year is instructive:

> We rejoice in the prominence which is being given to the doctrine of the Incarnation, with all its solemn lessons and inspirations. But we must be careful lest the Cross passes into the background, from which it is the glory of our fathers to have drawn it. Give to the *death* of Christ its true place in your own experience and in your Christian work – as a witness to the real and profound evil of sin, as an overwhelming manifestation of Divine love, as the ground of acceptance with God, as a pattern of sacrifice to disturb us when life is too easy, to inspire and console us when life is hard, and as the only effectual appeal to the general heart of men, and, above all, as the Atonement for our sins.[116]

To make any theme other than the cross the fulcrum of a theological system was to take a step away from Evangelicalism. The Congregationalist James Baldwin Brown, to the dismay of many co-religionists, had already followed the Broad Churchman F. D. Maurice along that path, and by 1897 a Methodist, J. Scott Lidgett, was doing the same.[117] Christopher Chavasse was still urging caution on Anglican Evangelicals about this trend of thought in 1939. 'Let us', he told them, 'keep close to Scripture, and allow the Atonement to explain the Incarnation – Christ was born in order to die . . . '[118] Michael Ramsey, Archbishop of Canterbury, showed he knew his Evangelicals when, in addressing their Keele Congress in 1967, he urged them to recognise that other Anglicans also upheld, in different ways, the 'supreme assertion that in the Cross of Christ alone is our salvation'.[119]

The standard view of Evangelicals was that Christ died as a substitute for sinful mankind. Human beings, they held, were so rebellious against God that a just penalty would have been death. Yet, as Thomas Scott the commentator discovered to his delight, 'Christ indeed bore the sins of all who should ever believe, in all their guilt, condemnation, and deserved punishment, in his own body on the tree'.[120] Belief in a substitutionary atonement originally distinguished Evangelicals from even the strictest divines of other schools. William Law, an outstanding devotional writer drawn on by Scott, among many others, explicitly repudiated the idea that Christ suffered in our stead.[121] Probably the greatest sermon by Robert Hall, Baptist minister in Cambridge at the opening of the nineteenth century and the ablest preacher of his day, was a defence of the doctrine of substitutionary atonement.[122] Its argument was still being repeated, with due acknowledgement of Hall, in a statement of Evangelical principles by the Anglican W. R. Fremantle in 1875.[123] By the 1870s, however, the fear was expressed that substitution was being discarded, and even the leading Wesleyan theologian W. B. Pope was equivocal on the subject.[124] The humanitarian tone of public opinion was veering against this understanding of the death of Christ. George Bernard Shaw voiced the newer attitude in characteristically searing fashion. 'I detest the doctrine of the Atonement', he once wrote, 'holding that ladies and gentlemen cannot as such possibly allow anyone else to expiate their sins by suffering a cruel death.'[125] In the early years of the twentieth century the teaching was fading from the Methodist pulpit.[126] It survived nevertheless in conservative Evangelical circles, enshrined, for instance, in the statement of faith of the Inter-Varsity Fellowship of Christian Unions. Jesus Christ was there described as dying not only as our representative but also as our substitute.[127] Belief that Christ died in our stead was not uniform in the Evangelical tradition, but it was normal.

The implications of the cross for life were also important for Evangelicals. There was a bond between the atonement and the quest for sanctification. 'All treatises', wrote Henry Venn, '. . . written to promote holiness of life, must be deplorably defective, unless the cross of Christ be laid as the foundation . . . '[128] The motive for spiritual growth was gratitude for Calvary. Preoccupation with the cross led to some exaggerated forms of spirituality. Mrs Penn-Lewis, an early twentieth-century holiness advocate, for example, went about teaching that there must be a decisive experience for the believer of crucifixion of the self.[129] But it was also common for preachers to dwell, as did the Congregationalist David Thomas in the 1840s, on the 'relation of the Atonement to practical righteousness'.[130] By 1908 this line of thought had generated in the mind of the Wesleyan J. E. Rattenbury a sanction for socialism. The gospel declares that human beings are to be considered not for their station, rank or riches but for their potential as sons of God. Consequently, he contended, 'the theology of the cross . . . is well fitted to be the soul of the Collectivist movement'.[131] Richard Heath, an extreme proponent of the social gospel, went further. The vicarious suffering of Christ was for him a symptom of the never-ceasing fact of human solidarity in adversity. God was suffering with his creatures.[132] Attention to the cross could lead in diverse directions.

The *theologia crucis* gave rise to debate. For whom did Christ die? For the elect only, as Calvinist believers in particular redemption affirmed? Or for all, as Arminian advocates of general redemption insisted? The Evangelical ranks were riven in the eighteenth century by controversy between Methodists, who were Arminians, and most others, who were

Calvinists. By the beginning of the nineteenth century, however, this debate was dying down. Most Evangelicals were content to adopt a 'moderate Calvinism' that in terms of practical pulpit instruction differed only slightly from the Methodist version of Arminianism. Leading Anglican Evangelicals expressed the view in 1800 that redemption is both general and particular. Arminians were right to stress human responsibility to repent and Calvinists right to stress the need for divine grace.[133] 'I frankly confess', wrote William Wilberforce, 'that I myself am no Calvinist, though I am not either an anti-Calvinist.'[134] Discussion of the scope of the atonement became moribund. It was dismissed as mysterious, impractical, a subject ill suited to bringing about conversions. Hence denominations that had maintained a separate existence because of the issue eventually came together. In England the gap between General and Particular Baptists that went back to the early seventeenth century steadily narrowed during the nineteenth, and in 1891 the two bodies formally fused. In Scotland, the Congregational Union, professedly Calvinist, and the Evangelical Union, revivalist and Arminian in style, united in 1897. What Evangelicals agreed on seemed of infinitely greater importance than their disagreements, and their pre-eminent ground of agreement was the cruciality of the cross.

THE BACKGROUND

Evangelical religion displaying these four characteristics burst on western Christendom at an epoch when the fundamental division between Catholics and Protestants had become firmly established over two centuries. Although in 1770 there were some 80,000 Roman Catholics in England,[135] the state in Britain was Protestant. The crown was restricted to Protestants, and so were a number of other offices of state. The Church of England, the Established Church of England and Wales, had retained its bishops at the Reformation but emerged from the seventeenth century as an unequivocally Protestant body. Its establishment meant that the Church of England was intertwined with the state. The monarch was the supreme head of the church. Theoretically, all his subjects in England and Wales belonged to it. The bishops of the Church of England sat of right in the House of Lords. Parliament exercised as much authority in spiritual matters as in temporal affairs. With the decay of church courts, ecclesiastical cases increasingly came before the secular courts. More than half the patrons of livings who appointed parish clergymen were laypeople. For advancement in a clerical career the patronage of some member of the social elite was essential. Clergymen were expected to display the manners of the gentry, among whom they were educated at Oxford and Cambridge. Their pulpit ministry was partly designed to teach the lower orders their place in the order of things. Conscientious men there were in the Church of England, notably at episcopal level, but there was little effective check on clerical negligence. The church played a salient role in everyday life, but at the expense of imbibing a strong dose of secularity.[136]

Protestant Dissent, though possessing roots in the sixteenth century and perhaps earlier, was primarily indebted to the strength of the Puritan movement in the seventeenth century. In the 1650s, under Cromwell, the Puritans had enjoyed a brief spell of official favour, but with the Restoration of Charles II in 1660 their period in the sun came to an abrupt end. Some 2,000 ministers who refused to accept the Book of Common Prayer of 1662 in its entirety were expelled from the Church of England. Despite persecution, the Dissenting congregations survived to enter an era of toleration following the Glorious Revolution of 1688. Dissenters were allowed to practise their religion unmolested, but, with hardly any of the gentry in their ranks, were reduced to a marginal role in society. Most of them retained the Calvinist theology in the Reformed tradition of their Puritan forebears, though there were some General Baptists who held Arminian views and the more numerous Quakers professed a belief in an 'inner light'. This credal difference, together with distinctive clothes, language and even calendar, set the Quakers apart from their Dissenting brethren. The mainstream consisted of the 'three denominations'. Presbyterians, who numbered many merchants in their ranks, formed the section of Dissent that was to be least influenced by Evangelicalism. Adopting increasingly broad theological views as the eighteenth century advanced, many of them reached a Unitarian position by its end. Independents, also known as Congregationalists, believed in the independence from all external authority of the local congregation. Like the less numerous Particular Baptists, who were identical apart from holding that baptism should be by immersion and for believers only, the Independents generally remained orthodox during the eighteenth century. These bodies were to be swept along by the Evangelical Revival.[137]

In Scotland there was an entirely different situation. The seventeenth-century kirk had wavered between Episcopalianism and Presbyterianism, contriving to blend them both after the Restoration. With the Glorious Revolution, however, the Church of Scotland became definitely Presbyterian. Bishops were at last repudiated. Episcopalian congregations, which were numerous in the north-east, began a life outside the Established Church. The whole population of Scotland belonged in theory to the Church of Scotland, and in practice an effective form of social discipline was maintained in many parishes against notorious sins. There was a continuing appreciation of Puritan classics and every minister had to profess at his ordination an acceptance of the Reformed theology of the Westminster Confession. The more rigid adherents of traditional ways and doctrine, however, began to detect a relaxation of standards. Several were particularly dismayed that, following the Union of Scotland with England in 1707, lay patronage had been restored to the Church of Scotland. Discontent on this issue induced Ebenezer Erskine, one of the ministers of Stirling, to lead a secession from the church in 1733. Presbyterian Dissent became a feature of Scottish church life, and small Independent and Baptist groups followed soon after. The Puritan legacy in the eighteenth century was greater in Scotland than in England.[138]

The changing role of Evangelical religion in modern Britain forms the theme of the following pages. There is a pattern of overlapping chapters. Chapter 2 examines the nature of the movement in the first century of its existence up to about 1830. It enquires why the movement began and discovers the answer in the cultural mood impinging on the Protestant tradition. Contrary to the common view, Evangelicalism was allied with the Enlightenment. Chapter 3 deals with a change of direction in Evangelicalism that occurred in the 1820s and 1830s, tracing the shift of emphasis once more to its cultural roots – this time in Romanticism – and examining some of the consequences down to about 1860. In Chapter 4 there is a study of the impact of Evangelical religion on British society as a whole during the nineteenth century, when its influence was at its peak. Chapter 5 analyses a movement in late nineteenth-century spirituality that again helped to reorient the movement. Chapter 6 deals with the effects of earlier factors in dividing Evangelicals into conservative and liberal camps during the interwar years. The transforming effect of twentieth-century cultural trends on Evangelicalism is the subject of Chapter 7. Chapter 8 tries to pick up the threads by analysing developments since the Second World War and Chapter 9 reaches some general conclusions. It becomes clear that Evangelical religion in Britain, despite the four constant elements discussed in this chapter, has altered enormously over time in response to the changing assumptions of Western civilisation.

[2]

Knowledge of the Lord:
The Early Evangelical Movement

And they shall teach no more every man his neighbour, and every man his brother, saying, know the LORD: for they shall all know me, from the least of them unto the greatest of them, saith the LORD. (Jer. 31:34)

The decade beginning in 1734 witnessed in the English-speaking world a more important development than any other, before or after, in the history of Protestant Christianity: the emergence of the movement that became Evangelicalism. Priority in the British Isles must go to Wales. A young schoolmaster living near Brecon, Howel Harris, came to faith during the spring of 1735.[1] A few weeks later Daniel Rowland, curate at Llangeitho in Carmarthenshire, underwent a similar experience of forgiveness. Soon both began travelling round South Wales, gathering large audiences and preaching the arresting message that salvation could be known now.[2] England followed. George Whitefield, converted as an Oxford undergraduate in the spring of 1735, stirred both Bristol and London by his oratory two years later, exhorting his hearers to seek the new birth.[3] Charles Wesley, who at Oxford had been Whitefield's mentor in his religious quest, did not reach assurance of faith for himself until 1738. In the same week, on 24 May, his brother John felt his heart 'strangely warmed' as he trusted 'in Christ, Christ alone for salvation'. Prompted by Whitefield, John Wesley began his career of open-air preaching at Bristol in the following year.[4] Whitefield roused parts of Scotland in 1741, and in the next year there broke out at Cambuslang near Glasgow a revival in which men and women anxiously looked for pardon.[5] Already there had been a comparable phenomenon in the colony of Massachusetts. In 1734–5, exactly when Harris and Rowland were wrestling with their conviction of sin in Wales, Jonathan Edwards was involved in a revival in the town of Northampton, where he was minister. His published analysis of the revival had impressed Wesley between his experience of trusting Christ and the inauguration of his travelling ministry and was well known to the Scottish ministers most involved at Cambuslang.[6] The movement in America, which Whitefield fanned into a larger flame, is usually styled 'The Great Awakening'. But it was part and parcel of 'The Eighteenth-Century Revival',[7] a quickening of the spiritual tempo in Britain and beyond.

The quickening seemed desperately needed. The Dissenters, the immediate inheritors of the Puritan legacy in England, were at a low ebb. In the 1730s there was a proliferation of writings on 'the decay of the Dissenting interest'. Philip Doddridge, writing in 1740, believed that the decline was concentrated chiefly in the west and south of England,[8] but there it was acute. In the same year the Western Association of the Particular Baptists urged four fast days to repent of spiritual declension.[9] Fewer new Independent and Baptist places of worship were registered in the 1730s than in any other decade when the system of registration was in force.[10] Evangelicalism, however, transformed the situation. Later in the century, when the revival movement impinged significantly on the Old Dissent, numbers of Independents and Baptists rose steadily. It has been estimated that in 1750 there were about 15,000 Independent and 10,000 Particular Baptist church members. By 1800 the respective figures had risen to 35,000 and 24,000.[11] Although there was marked population growth in the period, this rate of church growth outstripped it. The number of churches in the Particular Baptist Western and Midland Associations approximately doubled between 1780 and 1820. Furthermore, the overall increase in membership per church doubled over the period. And the most spectacular change among Calvinistic Dissenters was a great rise in the number of those who attended regularly as 'hearers' without becoming members. One church, at Gold Hill in Buckinghamshire, was said in 1818 to have five hearers for every member.[12] So the Dissenters touched by the revival enjoyed far more success afterwards than before.

The Methodists made even greater progress. Their membership increased from 22,410 in 1767, the first year when it was recorded, to 88,334 in 1800 and 232,074 in 1830.[13] Round the core of loyal members Methodist 'hearers' formed a large penumbra. In the Church of England, by contrast, the number of communicants seems to have decreased during the eighteenth century. It continued falling relative to population until the 1830s.[14] Evangelicalism had made much less impact on the Established Church than among Dissenters. In the Church of Scotland, whose Evangelical strength was greater than that of the Church of England, communicant levels probably kept pace with population during the eighteenth century. But it was Presbyterian Dissent, much of it fired with evangelistic fervour, that grew most in Scotland. By 1835, only a century after the first secession, it enjoyed the allegiance of nearly a third of Edinburgh churchgoers.[15] It is clear that the appearance of Evangelicalism was the signal for a major advance by Protestant Christianity in the ensuing century.

The motor of expansion was the message of justification by faith. Lost sinners must trust Christ for salvation. In the classic compendium of Evangelical faith and practice, *The Complete Duty of Man* (1763), Henry

Venn, Vicar of Huddersfield, defines saving faith as 'a dependence upon Christ for righteousness and strength, as having paid to the justice of God full satisfaction for his broken law, and obtained acceptance for all believers in his name, to the reward of eternal life'.[16] Christ had done all that was needed to achieve salvation. It remained only for men and women to accept forgiveness at his hands. Faith was therefore seen as the gift of grace. It was 'simply to hang upon Him'.[17] To insist on faith as the way of approaching God was to reject certain popular alternatives. Venn condemns three. Our ground of hope, he explains, cannot be works, that is, the performance of good deeds, for even the best actions have flaws and so are unacceptable as an offering to a God of absolute holiness. Sincerity is equally inadequate. God expects perfect obedience (which only Christ could perform), not our good intentions. Nor will a mixture of faith and works help us. If we rely partly on our good deeds, the grand difficulty of their being tainted by sin remains.[18] 'Attempts to complete what grace begins', according to Venn's Baptist friend Abraham Booth, 'betray our pride and offend the Lord, but cannot promote our spiritual interest'.[19] Thus ordinary Methodists would go about urging that mere morality was of no avail in justification, for faith alone did everything.[20] They would swap texts with broader-minded Bible students. 'Whenever I read in St. Paul's Epistles on justification by faith alone', recalled James Lackington, then an apprentice shoemaker, 'my good mistress would read in the Epistle of St. James, such passages as suggest a man is not justified by faith alone, but by faith and works . . . '[21] It was a telling riposte, but scholarly Evangelicals were able to point out that while Paul writes of the condition of justification, James is discussing the nature of genuine faith.[22] If faith is real, it will automatically produce good works. Holiness is the fruit of faith. This explains the apparently paradoxical position of Wesley: 'we are justified by faith alone', he wrote, 'and yet by such a faith as is not alone . . . '[23] Faith is the only means by which we are made right with God; but faith, as soon as it exists, creates an impulse towards living a better life. Views differed about whether or not it was essential to understand the notion of justification by faith. Joseph Milner, a clergyman near Hull and the leading Evangelical historian, held the doctrine absolutely necessary to salvation.[24] Wesley, with his customary latitude in matters of opinion, supposed that those ignorant of the belief, or even hostile to it, might be saved.[25] But Evangelicals were united in holding that the reality of faith – as opposed to belief about it – is the sole condition of acceptance by God.

The bearers of the message did not always find a ready welcome. To be told that sincerity in the performance of the religious duties of one's station did not command the blessing of God was startling, if not insulting. To be assured that good works were as filthy rags seemed subversive of all morality. To hear faith lauded to the skies aroused suspicions of fanaticism, the 'enthusiasm' that the eighteenth century shunned because its seventeenth-century version had killed a king. Polite society was alarmed. It is true that Frederick, Prince of Wales, was so impressed that he was rumoured to be intending to use his powers as monarch to make Whitefield a bishop.[26] But Frederick was on bad terms with his father, George II, and in any case predeceased him in 1751. Evangelical penetration of high society, with the notable exceptions of the Countess of Huntingdon and the Earl of Dartmouth, was deferred until the aftermath of the French Revolution, when a high religious profile began to have welcome anti-revolutionary connotations. So the Evangelical movement laboured under severe disadvantages. Undergraduates were expelled from Oxford for Methodist practices in 1768;[27] young men suspected of Evangelical views were denied ordination in certain dioceses of the Church of England;[28] and unwelcome ministers of more sober outlook were imposed on parishes with Evangelical preferences in the Church of Scotland.[29]

There is a vivid fictional portrayal of resistance to Evangelicalism in George Eliot's tale, 'Janet's repentance'. Mr Tryan, a new Evangelical curate, arrives at a chapel-of-ease on the outskirts of the parish of Milby. His proposal to deliver Sunday evening lectures in the parish church of the town itself on the grounds that the resident clergyman does not preach the gospel arouses the ire of the town lawyer. A petition is organised to oppose the application to lecture. Tryan, according to the lawyer, preaches against good works. 'Tell a man he is not to be saved by his works', the lawyer declaims, 'and you open the floodgates of all immorality. You see it in all these canting innovators; they're all bad ones by the sly; smooth-faced, drawling, hypocritical fellows . . . '[30] When the lecture is eventually established, Tryan has to run the gauntlet of 'groans, howls, hisses, and hee-haws' on the way to church. Stories circulate about the minister and his hearers. Tradespeople among them are warned that they will lose good customers. 'Mr Budd harangued his workmen, and threatened them with dismissal if they or their families were known to attend the evening lecture; and Mr Tomlinson, on discovering that his foreman was a rank Tryanite, blustered to a great extent, and would have cashiered that valuable functionary on the spot, if such a retributive procedure had not been inconvenient.'[31] The storm subsides precisely because convenience triumphs. This narrative is set in the 1820s. At an earlier date resistance was commonly both fiercer and more sustained. Wesley endured mobbing when he first preached in Staffordshire in the 1740s.[32] His followers were violently assaulted. Christopher Hopper was the victim of 'invectives and lies, dirt, rotten eggs, brickbats, stones and cudgels'; Peter Jaco 'was struck so violently with a brick on the breast that the blood gushed out through my mouth, nose, and ears'; John Nelson's wife was beaten by a crowd of women 'so cruelly that they killed the child in her womb, and she went home and miscarried directly'.[33] Opposition was sometimes led by members of the elite and had a measure of local co-ordination. A clergyman fearful for his congregation or his standing might egg on a crowd to violence. Or else popular resistance might possess its own dynamic. It was rightly perceived that Evangelicalism threatened to divide community life. Customary ways were under attack and the mob retaliated in the only way available to the plebeian population of the eighteenth century.[34]

Evangelicals created their own community life. Methodism was famous – or notorious – for it. The weekly class meeting for the exchange of spiritual experience was the essence of Wesley's system for building up those who had been awakened by preaching. The pattern began almost accidentally at Bristol in 1742. A building debt had to be extinguished. Consequently the 'society', the body of all Methodists in the city, was broken down into short lists, to each of which was assigned a collector of weekly contributions. The collectors soon developed a pastoral role, and Wesley directed that members on each list should gather to seek their guidance.[35] To possess a quarterly ticket as a class member was the defining quality of a Methodist; to be noted as having 'ceased to meet' in class was to be no longer a Methodist. By 1783 in Bristol there were fifty-seven classes, each including from nine to eighteen members. The allocation to classes was on a purely geographical basis.[36] In addition to classes, however, early Methodism possessed other tight-knit groups. Only those professing justification were admitted to the bands, which also met weekly, and which were divided according to sex and marital status. This arrangement permitted greater intimacy. 'In the classes', it was recalled, 'they only confessed in general terms, that they have been tempted by the world, the flesh, and the devil. But in the bands they confessed the particular sins which they had been tempted to commit, or had actually committed.'[37] Those Methodists judged to be near or in the state of entire sanctification, at least in the larger societies, assembled in select bands. There were sometimes also penitents' meetings for backsliding band-members.[38] The plethora of preaching meetings, watch-nights, covenant services at new year and love-feasts, that is larger gatherings for the relating of testimonies while buns and water were handed round – all these bound Methodists strongly together in a hostile environment. 'Such was our love to each other', according to John Haime, the promoter of a Methodist society in the army, 'that even the sight of each other filled our hearts with divine consolation.'[39] Visits to the sick and dying brought genuine sympathy; substantial interest-free loans were available, at least in London, from a common fund; and Methodists looked after the businesses of sick brothers.[40]

Although the organisational structure was unique to Methodism, the spirit was characteristic of Evangelicalism as a whole. Jonathan Edwards knew the value of religious conversation as an antidote to spiritual melancholia.[41] The Yorkshire and Lancashire Particular Baptist Association, perhaps inspired by the Methodist example, urged in 1764 an increase of 'private meetings for mutual conference on the things of God'.[42] Samuel Walker, the Evangelical curate of Truro, organised societies for converts using material drawn from the Book of Common Prayer, less tightly controlled groups for religious conversation and a Parsons' Club, the prototype for many subsequent societies of Evangelical clergy, from about 1750.[43] Societies for prayer were promoted in and about Glasgow during the 1740s by John Maclaurin, minister of the North West Church there, and others.[44] Meetings for prayer became the hallmark of congregations touched by the revival. There was a natural tendency for Evangelicals to meet for religious purposes. The resulting fellowship was no ethereal thing but a strongly cemented form of social solidarity.

Who composed the Evangelical communities? The Methodist membership list for Bristol in 1783, which includes occupations, may be taken as an example. Of 790 names, only 99 are unidentified. The largest occupational group is the servants, of whom there are 55 of each sex. In addition, 26 women are concerned with laundry work, 24 with dressmaking – and so in many cases are probably more specialised servants. Shoemakers and members of related trades, together with their wives, form a group of 80 names. Apart from 29 gentlemen and gentlewomen and 25 classified as old, poor or almswomen, no other group contains as many as 20 names. There are only 13 labourers.[45] The list is fairly representative of evidence from elsewhere. The large number of servants, for example, is repeated in a sample of the converts in the Cambuslang revival of 1742, although not, apparently, among Evangelical Nonconformists in England.[46] More uniformly, a high proportion of shoemakers is found in Evangelical communities of the eighteenth and early nineteenth centuries. The most consistent finding has been that the artisan section of society, embracing shoemakers but also including a variety of tradesmen such as carpenters and coopers, was heavily over-represented in Evangelical ranks. Such skilled men and their families formed as high as 66 per cent of a Relief Church in Glasgow between 1822 and 1832.[47] A thorough trawl of evidence has shown that this social group was more than twice as numerous in eighteenth-century Methodism, at 47 per cent, as in society at large.[48] Unskilled men were few, at least among committed members of Evangelical bodies. There may well have been more of them among the 'hearers', the regular attenders who had not actually joined. Although artisans could be impoverished in bad times for their trade, Evangelicalism was rarely the religion of the poorest and outcast. Nor was it the religion of the prosperous and successful in the eighteenth century. The gentry may sometimes have been marginally over-represented in Methodism,[49] as the Bristol statistics illustrate, but the impact of the Evangelicalism of the Church of England on the elite was only just beginning when Hannah More and William Wilberforce composed their appeals to the great in the 1780s and 1790s.[50]

Women were numerous in the movement. 'I have heard Mr. Wesley remark', reported a rather jaundiced ex-Methodist, 'that more women are converted than men; and I believe that by far the greatest part of his people are females; and not a few of them sour, disappointed old maids . . . '[51] A measure of confirmation is provided by the discoveries that about 55 per cent of a sample of East Cheshire Methodists in the later eighteenth century were women and that nearly half of them were unmarried.[52] Religion may have provided psychological reassurance, even emotional outlet, for this section of the population. In any case, women were consistently found in larger numbers than men. Both Cambuslang converts in 1742 and Bristol Methodists in 1783 included two women for every man.[53] Nor were they necessarily kept in the background. Outside the formal setting of public worship, and even occasionally in it, women found opportunities for self-expression. In the proliferating cottage meetings of early Evangelicalism it was often women who took the lead in prayer and praise, counsel and exhortation.[54] In 1803 Wesleyans effectively prohibited female preaching for the sake of propriety, but the custom was restored by the Primitives. The Bible Christians of south-western England, too, put what they called 'female brethren' on the preaching plan.[55] In the upper echelons of society Hannah More, blue-stocking and Evangelical ideologue, played a no less significant role.[56] In an age when avenues for women into any sphere outside the home were being closed, Christian zeal brought them into prominence.

The places where Evangelicalism struck deepest root were usually of certain particular kinds. Where artisans were most numerous, vital religion was most likely to do well. Therefore, areas springing into life with proto-industrial employment for the skilled worker, townships like Paddiford Common in 'Janet's Repentance' with weaving and mining as the chief occupations, were ideal territory.[57] Methodism and Calvinistic Dissent as well as the Evangelical Anglicanism that George Eliot depicts thrived there. Growing industrial areas, including the big cities, were deliberately targeted by Wesley and his contemporaries, for there dwelt the most concentrated populations. In the countryside, patterns of settlement were highly significant determinants of Evangelical strength. Scattered dwellings of recent erection in large parishes or on parish boundaries, together with market towns, proved more receptive to the gospel than ancient nucleated villages of small size.[58] It was partly that in areas of scattered settlement the parish church was often far distant, so that when travelling preachers arrived they offered a monopoly of religious provision, whereas tight-knit communities usually clustered round the parish church. Only on the rare occasions when a clergyman of the Church of England held Evangelical convictions was this an advantage. Similarly in Scotland Evangelicals gained most ground in the vast parishes of the Highlands as well as in the new industrial regions.[59] Landownership also played a part. In so-called close parishes, where land was held by one or at most three proprietors, penetration by Evangelicalism was rare. Land for erecting a chapel was far more likely to be available in open parishes where landownership was fragmented.[60] Many of the determinants boil down to the issue of social control. Wherever authority could be exerted from above to encourage conformity to established ways, the innovations of popular religion would be resisted. Squire or parson, or both together, could publicise their distaste for enthusiasm. The mob would be conscious of their support – albeit normally tacit – for throwing the Methodist preacher in the duckpond.[61] Conversely, where the expectations of squire and parson could be ignored with impunity, gospel preaching would be sustained. In particular, artisans who prided themselves on avoiding dependence on the landed order for their daily bread would assert their self-reliance by giving the new message a hearing – and perhaps more. Evangelism was most effective where deference was weakest, whether in town or countryside. It is no accident that Yorkshire and Cornwall, with their large parishes and numerous artisans, were the fields of the greatest Methodist harvests.[62]

VARIETIES OF EVANGELICALISM

Despite its self-conscious unity, the Evangelical movement comprised several distinct strands. The Methodists were set apart from other groupings by both doctrine and discipline. They asserted a strong doctrine of assurance that will call for detailed scrutiny; and they believed in Christian perfection, which again deserves fuller attention.[63] The essence of their distinct doctrinal position, however, was Arminianism. Christ, they claimed, made salvation available to all who believed, and not just to the limited number of the elect. Such a rejection of Calvinism was not quite unique among Evangelicals, for a few of the clergy unconnected with Wesley shared Arminian beliefs.[64] So did the New Connexion of General Baptists, founded by an ex-Methodist, Dan Taylor, in 1770.[65] But Methodism was the chief bulwark of Arminianism. Charles Wesley filled many a hymn with anti-Calvinist polemic: 'The invitation is to all'; 'For all, for all, my Saviour died!'; 'Thy sovereign grace to all extends'.[66] His brother John called the connexional journal *The Arminian Magazine*. The first issue carried an article on Jacobus Arminius, the early seventeenth-century Dutch divine who drastically modified Reformed theology.[67] Yet John Wesley did not adhere closely to the structure of Arminius's thought. Nor was his theological system similar to the arid scheme of those rational Dissenters who treated Arminianism as a staging post to Unitarianism. Theirs, as Dr Nuttall has pointed out, was an Arminianism of the head; Wesley's was a version of the heart.[68] It was a dynamic message, a proclamation that the love of God is vast and free. No fatalism cast a shadow over the experience God wishes all to enjoy. Any man or woman can receive saving faith.

Wesley could not tolerate several aspects of the Calvinist scheme of salvation. It is true that he sometimes minimised the distance between his own and the Reformed position. 'I think on justification', he wrote to John Newton in 1765, 'just as . . . Mr. Calvin does.'[69] But Wesley rejected outright belief in predestination, the doctrine that some human beings are foreordained to salvation by God's decree. It was alien to his upbringing, for both parents stoutly denied it.[70] It was equally far removed from the ethical cast of his thought. If some are chosen and others are not, so that human beings cannot affect their destiny, the sanction for morality disappears. This was what Wesley meant by claiming that the teaching led to antinomianism. So he deplored the defection of a Cornish clergyman who had 'fallen into the Pit of the Decrees'.[71] A related objection was to the Calvinist doctrine of imputed righteousness. Reformed theologians held that God treats sinners as righteous by the legal fiction that Christ's merits are theirs. Wesley again held that this principle undercut the biblical summons to holy living. According to Calvinists, believers may commit sins and yet still be accepted by God for Christ's sake. According to Wesley, a person ceases to be a Christian as soon as he performs a sinful act. Calvinism was lulling people into a baseless sense of their security. Furthermore, Reformed theologians taught that any true believer would remain one until death – the doctrine of the perseverance of the saints. God would guarantee their ultimate salvation. Again, Wesley viewed such teaching as licence for immorality.[72]

Although he repudiated it, Wesley pursued no vendetta against Calvinism. Men holding Reformed views were admitted to his annual conference, and during the 1760s Wesley employed without examination a preacher, Thomas Taylor, who read little but Calvinist authors and leaned to imputed righteousness and final perseverance.[73] There was more eagerness for battle on the other side. The publication of the minutes of the 1770 Methodist Conference, referring to good works as a 'condition' of salvation, provoked an outcry by Calvinists such as Rowland Hill and Augustus Toplady. Wesley seemed to be rejecting no less a doctrine than justification by faith. In reality he did not. Good works, according to Wesley, were not the way to justification, but they were essential to final salvation. So the 'Calvinistic Controversy' of the 1770s that drove Methodism further apart from other Evangelicals was based in part on a misunderstanding.[74] There was, nevertheless, substantial theological disagreement between Wesley and the Reformed tradition. Evangelical Arminianism was a distinct body of thought.

Methodism was also differentiated from other strands of the Evangelical movement by its discipline. Wesley professed to be a loyal son of the Church of England, constantly resisting calls for separation.[75] Yet Methodism was an elaborate religious organisation that had no dependence, except for the sacraments, on existing ecclesiastical structures. Wesley personally supervised the whole massive machine. All the preachers were his 'helpers'; membership lists were revised by his decision, against which there was no appeal. Some suggested that 'the love of power seems to have been the main spring of all his actions'.[76] By and large, however, his authority was willingly accepted. The problems arose with his death in 1791. How was the machine to operate without Wesley's guiding hand? Some preachers, led by Alexander Kilham and inspired in part by the egalitarianism of the French Revolution, pressed for greater local autonomy and more lay power. They were routed, however, and forced to leave the Wesleyan body to set up the Methodist New Connexion in 1797.[77] By the 1810s another autocracy had been established. Less openly than Wesley but only slightly less firmly, Jabez Bunting shaped the policies of Wesleyan Methodism until the middle of the nineteenth century. It was Bunting who ensured, especially during the turbulent years following the Napoleonic Wars, that radicals were summarily cashiered from the movement.[78] Theoretically, the Wesleyan connexion was ruled after its founder's death by the so-called 'Legal Hundred' of travelling preachers who in law formed the conference. The hundred were those named by Wesley in 1784 and, as they died, their successors. In practice, far more of the travelling preachers participated. Conference was supreme in its decisions and on occasion it could overrule even Bunting; but the powers of conference were limited by its being in session for only three weeks or less each summer. It was conference that allocated preachers to circuits, the parts of the country where they were to itinerate, raising up and sustaining the societies. By 1791 there were 87 circuits in Britain, each with from one to three travelling preachers, who were normally changed each year.[79] Although under Wesley most of them were untrained laymen, the travelling preachers gradually evolved into the Methodist ministry. The title 'Reverend' was officially adopted in 1818.[80] Far more of the meetings, however, were conducted by local preachers. With class leaders and band leaders, stewards in charge of society funds and trustees in charge of society buildings, they formed a formidable army of lay workers. Methodism provided a host of opportunities for laymen to assume prominent public roles. If they lacked power, they possessed responsibility.

Methodism also arose in several Calvinistic forms. George Whitefield's preaching gave rise to societies that, like him, adhered to Reformed teaching. He established in the capital the Moorfields Tabernacle in 1741 and the Tottenham Court Chapel in 1756.[81] By 1747 there were 31 Whitefieldian societies and 27 preaching stations.[82] Selina, Countess of Huntingdon, converted in 1739, was sufficiently free of family duties by 1760 to devote herself largely to organising evangelism. She appointed gospel clergymen as her chaplains, directing them as firmly as Wesley treated his assistants, and erected chapels for their eloquence in fashionable resorts such as Brighton (1760), Bath (1765) and Tunbridge Wells (1765). In 1768 she created at Trevecca, under the superintendence of Howel Harris, a college to train candidates for the ministry, and in 1777 a chapel at Spa Fields, London, which soon attracted a wealthy congregation.[83] By her death in 1791 there were between 55 and 80 congregations supplied with preachers trained at Trevecca.[84] She had already, in 1782, reluctantly seceded from the Church of England, but she failed to make adequate provision for the government of the new denomination. Only seven chapels, as her personal property, were transferred to the continuing Countess of Huntingdon's Connexion.[85] Whitefield's connexion disintegrated even more catastrophically. He had begun as moderator of a Calvinistic Methodist 'association' in 1743, the year before Wesley held the first meeting of his equivalent conference.[86] With Whitefield frequently absent in America, however, his place was taken by John Cennick, but in 1745 he departed to the Moravians. His successor, Howel Harris, also withdrew in 1749, and central direction of the movement stopped. Because the Whitefieldian societies (if Moorfields is representative) permitted congregational decision-making, it was easy for them to develop into Independent churches.[87] Preachers were similarly attracted over the narrow dividing-line. In 1748, for instance, one Herbert Jenkins 'went off to the Independents'.[88] In 1764 the Moorfields Tabernacle and Tottenham Court Chapels were themselves registered as Independent.[89] Although a Gloucestershire Calvinistic Methodist Association was still functioning in 1784,[90] the connexion virtually dissolved following Whitefield's death in 1770. Only in Wales did Calvinistic Methodism become a permanent force. Howel Harris resumed his organisational work in 1763, but, making no headway with a plan for a 'General Union' embracing Wesleyans and Moravians, concentrated his efforts in the principality.[91] His legacy was a body which in the nineteenth century, as the Welsh Calvinistic Methodist Connexion, became the strongest single denomination in Wales.

Another strand consisted of Evangelicals in the Church of England, its ordained clergy and their associates. Few were Methodist converts or even touched by Calvinistic Methodism. Rather they normally discovered their vital faith by painful steps in seclusion. Thomas Scott, curate at Ravenstone and Weston Underwood in Buckinghamshire and subsequently the eighteenth-century Evangelicals' greatest commentator on the Bible, has left a classic account of such a spiritual pilgrimage during the 1770s, *The Force of Truth* (1779). Entering the ministry for the sake of preferment, he began with virtually Socinian views, holding Christ to be nothing but a man proclaiming enlightened doctrines. Struck by the conscientious pastoral care of the Evangelical, John Newton, his near neighbour, he was convinced by Bishop Burnet's book on the same subject that he must be more attentive to his duties. A reading of Samuel Clarke, the early eighteenth-century champion of a more liberal doctrine of the Trinity, paradoxically drew him back from Socinianism towards orthodoxy. William Law persuaded him to give far more time to devotion; Hooker attracted him to Reformed divines; from them he learned justification by faith. Strangely, as he puts it, 'my faith was now fixed upon a crucified Saviour (though I dishonoured his person, and denied his Deity)'.[92] Other reading eventually brought him to profess Calvinism. Scott, as he insists, changed his sentiments 'very gradually' and not because of the teaching of Evangelicals.[93] A similar process took place in many parts of the land. At St Gennys in Cornwall in 1733 or 1734, George Thomson was awakened by dreams of judgement and gained confidence of salvation through Romans, Chapter 3.[94] At Wintringham in

Lincolnshire, Thomas Adam, though corresponding with the Evangelical Thomas Hartley, was influenced during a perplexing decade chiefly by the mystical writings of Law before he reached settled convictions in 1748.[95] In London around 1750, 'like most others', according to his biographer, William Romaine probably 'grew clearer by degrees, through the word, prayer, and experience'.[96] By such means the number of Evangelical clergy increased. In 1769 Wesley knew of between fifty and sixty who preached salvation by faith. He wrote to them all inviting co-operation, but received only three replies. In a phrase long remembered, he dismissed them as 'a rope of sand'.[97] Although they were later to consolidate in clerical societies, in the early years of the revival the Evangelical clergy were few and scattered.

Respect for church order varied among them. Samuel Walker of Truro was at one pole of opinion, persuading others 'to keep close to the discipline of mother Church'.[98] He believed in 'regularity', that is, confining his work to the parish he served. Others, like John Berridge, of Everton, Cambridgeshire, felt bound to itinerate outside the parish – to 'go round the neighbourhood, preaching in the fields, wherever a door is opened, three or four days in every week'.[99] William Grimshaw, at Haworth in the West Riding, even acted as one of Wesley's stated 'helpers'.[100] There was a broad range of different degrees of 'irregularity', which ensured that the boundary between loyal Churchmen and their more flexible brethren was blurred. Thomas Haweis, finding the parish of Aldwincle, Northamptonshire, too small a sphere for his labours, put himself at the service of the Countess of Huntingdon from 1774.[101] The trend of opinion, however, was in the opposite direction. As Evangelical clergy became more numerous, the need for itinerancy seemed to lessen; and as criticism of Evangelicals mounted, it became valuable to be able to stress loyalty to the forms of the Church of England. Accordingly, Henry Venn, who at Huddersfield up to 1771 co-operated with the Wesleyans in field preaching, later became aware of what his son called 'the evils of schism' and dissuaded others from irregularity.[102] The views of Charles Simeon, Vicar of Holy Trinity, Cambridge, from 1783 to 1836 and mentor to generations of Evangelical ordinands, were decisive for the future course of the movement. 'A Preacher has enough to do in his own parish', he roundly declared.[103]

Concentration on a parochial ministry could be highly effective. At Aldwincle, for example, Haweis found no households maintaining family prayers, but by never leaving a house without praying soon ensured that family devotions became the rule.[104] The grand difficulty of the Evangelicals in the Church of England, however, was in sustaining an awakened congregation when the gospel minister left the parish. The next clergyman was unlikely to be an Evangelical. The flock might then disperse. More likely, it would go over to Independency, securing its own building and its own preacher of the gospel. This happened after Venn's departure from Huddersfield (with his sanction), and even in Truro after the death of

Walker, the arch–defender of parish loyalty.[105] The problem was a result of the patronage system that entrusted the choice of a clergyman to laypeople who were rarely sympathetic to the cause of the gospel. Hence many early Evangelical clergy were to be found in places of worship outside the normal patronage system: in proprietary chapels erected, especially in London, by converted notables; in daughter chapels where the appointment was in the hands of an Evangelical minister; and in lectureships, often survivals from Puritan days, where the choice was by some form of election. But it was Simeon who dealt most effectively with the problem of continuity. In order to achieve a sucession of Evangelical clergy in strategic parishes such as Cheltenham, he created, in 1817, a trust to purchase rights of patronage.[106] It expanded and was also imitated by other trusts. In this, as in many other ways, Simeon gave an assured place to what was becoming an Evangelical party in the Church of England.

The impact of Evangelicalism on orthodox Dissent in England and Wales did not become general until the last years of the eighteenth century. The delay is partly explained by factors that inhibited the effectiveness of Dissenters in mission. It was prudent for those outside the Established Church to posses licences for their places of worship, and licences would hardly be granted for the type of field preaching adopted so powerfully by Methodists, whether Arminian or Calvinistic. Dissenters in any case suffered from the reputation of being peculiar people, a disadvantage not shared by those operating at least nominally under the auspices of the Church of England. And Dissenting congregations, by and large, were isolated and introspective.[107] Non-involvement in the revival was a matter of deliberate choice. People proud of their traditions did not wish to associate with those who at best neglected the niceties of doctrine and discipline and often actually veered into what seemed to be theological laxity. The foibles and wild ways of the new evangelists startled and repelled.[108] Worst of all, the revival was divisive. Thomas Morgan, Independent minister at Morley, Yorkshire, lamented in 1765 the 'unhappy *Divisions* almost in all the Congregations in the Kingdom chiefly occasion'd by *Methodistical Delusions*'.[109]

Yet even in the early days inhibitions about the new movement were overcome by some. Risdon Darracott, Independent minister at Wellington, Somerset, was in close touch with Evangelical clergymen including Samuel Walker and Henry Venn.[110] Darracott's tutor, Philip Doddridge, co–operated fully with Whitefield.[111] Doddridge's pivotal role in turning orthodox Dissenters into friends of the revival was subsequently played by Thomas Gibbons, Independent minister at Haberdashers' Hall, London, and tutor at Mile End Academy.[112] Men converted through the Calvinistic Methodists soon swelled the ranks of Dissent. The Saviour, according to Whitefield, 'has inclined many converted unto him thro' his Grace by us, to join with the Dissenting Congregations . . . '[113] Baptists profited as well as the Independents. Henry Philips, converted through Howel Harris and later

Baptist minister at Salisbury, was preaching at Tiverton with 'freedom and affection' on the universality of the gospel invitation in 1765.[114] Robert Robinson and John Fawcett, two of the most influential Baptist ministers of the later eighteenth century, were both converted under Whitefield.[115] Furthermore, whole congregations sometimes joined the Dissenters, perhaps on the termination of an Evangelical ministry at a parish church or when a Wesleyan preacher turned Calvinist.[116] The New Connexion of General Baptists, which remained Arminian in theology and made marked headway in the East Midlands, was also the fruit of the revival. Its core churches, based on Barton-in-the-Beans, Leicestershire, arose from the evangelism of a servant of the Countess of Huntingdon. Its creation as a separate denomination, by fission from the older General Baptist Churches that in general had moved to a more liberal theology, was the work in 1770 of Dan Taylor, an ex-Wesleyan preacher who shared Wesley's genius for co-ordination.[117] Dissent gained a new vitality from the infusion of Evangelicalism.

Scotland was home to several strands of the movement. In the Established Church a substantial section of the ministry – how large we do not know – held Evangelical views. The leaders of this body of men, John Maclaurin, John Erskine and John Gillies among them, were highly respected in the Kirk. Maclaurin, an able Highlander in a Glasgow charge, corresponded with Jonathan Edwards and others in New England and so learned early of the revivals there. He urged concerted prayer to stir up similar awakenings in Scotland and rejoiced in the events at Cambuslang in 1742.[118] Erskine, who acknowledged his debt to sermons by Maclaurin, became minister of New Greyfriars Church, Edinburgh. During a long career he gave publicity to Cambuslang, defended Whitefield and edited some of Edwards's posthumous works.[119] Gillies, Maclaurin's son-in-law and a close friend of Erskine, became Whitefield's first biographer.[120] Such men identified wholly with the Evangelical cause. In the second half of the eighteenth century they became embroiled in party warfare in the Church of Scotland. The problem was fundamentally the same one that confronted their brethren in the Church of England: how was continuity of godly ministry to be obtained when parish ministers were appointed by patronage? Their solution was to join others in urging that congregations, or at least their leading lights, the elders and heritors, should have a right of veto over presentees to charges. The so-called Moderate party, insisting on the letter of church law, resisted resolutely and successfully.[121] Consequently non-Evangelical ministers were imposed on unwilling congregations. Quite frequently from 1761 onwards a congregation would respond by deserting the parish church to form a 'Relief Church'. So was born a wholly Evangelical body, Presbyterian in polity but outside the Established Church, that earned the nickname the 'Scots Methodists'.[122] They existed alongside the congregations of the Secession that in 1733 had also split off from the Church of Scotland on the patronage issue. It was the Secession

Church that originally invited Whitefield to Scotland in 1741, and, despite disillusionment when he would not embrace their distinctive principles, many of the more open-minded in the Secession remained Evangelical in thought and practice.[123] By the end of the century Presbyterian Dissent was a powerful force in Scotland, especially in urban Scotland. At Jedburgh, admittedly an extreme case, in the 1790s, more than 70 per cent of the adult population were Dissenters.[124] Despite the weakness of Methodism north of the border, Evangelical religion had put down deep roots there.

CONTINUITY WITH THE PAST

The multi-faceted movement that was the Evangelical Revival was to touch the lives of millions. But was it nothing new? Was it simply a massive expansion of pre-existent patterns of faith and practice, a popularisation of received forms of religion? With meticulous scholarship, Dr Geoffrey Nuttall has demonstrated that there was a large measure of continuity between elements of the Reformed tradition embodied in Dissent and the revival. He singles out a common eagerness for unity in Christian work, a consequent impatience with divisive doctrinal tests and a stress on personal experience in devotion to Christ. He discerns a tradition that runs from Richard Baxter in the mid-seventeenth century through Philip Doddridge in the early eighteenth to Evangelicals such as the Baptist, Andrew Fuller.[125] Baxter and Doddridge certainly fit his specification. So does Whitefield, whose division of opinion with the Secession in Scotland was the result of the overriding importance he attached to catholicity, comprehensiveness and heart work. Whitefield was aware of the affinity. He assured Doddridge that a recently published sermon of his 'contains the very life of preaching, I mean sweet invitations to close with CHRIST'. 'I do not wonder', he added, 'that you are dubbed a Methodist on account of it.'[126] Dr Nuttall can point to the assistance rendered to Whitefield by Thomas Cole, the Dissenting minister in the evangelist's home city of Gloucester, who was already in pastoral charge long before Whitefield's conversion.[127] He also draws attention to the experimental devotion of individual Dissenters, both laymen and ministers, especially in the west of England, in the early eighteenth century. 'These', he writes, 'were Evangelicals before the Revival . . . '[128] The thesis of continuity from the pre-revival period can be supported by evidence drawn from the Baptists, from Scotland and from Wales. Bristol Baptist Academy was producing a stream of ministers with vital spirituality, evangelistic concerns and a catholic outlook under the three principals who served from 1720 to 1791, Bernard Foskett, Hugh Evans and Caleb Evans.[129] In Scotland, John Maclaurin and his circle, those who welcomed the Cambuslang Revival in the 1740s, were already resisting liberal theological trends in the name of heart religion during the protracted Simson case of the 1720s.[130] And, for Wales, recent scholarship has stressed the circulation of literature, the Dissenting preaching and the gospel themes of both that anticipated the emergence of the revival in the 1730s.[131] It is clear that in many respects Evangelical religion prolonged existing lines of development.

Even Methodism, the new growth on Evangelical soil, had roots in Puritan tradition. Wesley's mother, Susanna, herself the daughter of one of the ejected divines of 1662, esteemed Baxter highly.[132] Although her son John was deliberately guarded from Dissenting literature when young, Susanna lived with him in the crucial years 1739–42 when his position was crystallising after the experience of 24 May 1738. Baxter, especially in his *Aphorisms of Justification*, became Wesley's mentor. Baxter's moderate version of Puritanism appealed almost as much to him as to Doddridge.[133] The fifty-volume *Christian Library* published by Wesley for his followers contains far more literature of a Puritan stamp than of any other ecclesiastical genre.[134] A Methodist convert so devoted to books that he saved money for their purchase by living on bread and tea assembled a collection overwhelmingly Puritan.[135] John Bunyan's *Pilgrim's Progress* and Joseph Alleine's *Alarm to the Unconverted* were particularly prized by the early preachers.[136] A clergyman trying to dissuade a parishioner from attending Methodist meetings had no doubt of the identification: 'he showed him several old Puritanical books, which treated on the new birth, &c., and told him, "It is a false religion, because it is an old religion!".'[137] The call for conversion, embracing an expectation of a period of conviction of sin preceding the crisis of the new birth, was reminiscent of seventeenth-century Reformed divinity. So was the constant appeal to scripture and what a visiting Swede noticed as Wesley's message of 'a crucified Saviour and faith in his merits'.[138] Three characteristic marks of Evangelicalism, conversionism, biblicism and crucicentrism, had been as much a part of Puritanism as they were of Methodism. It has been argued that the affinities go beyond such theological areas to include aspects of liturgy, pastoralia, family piety and ethics.[139] Although features of Methodism in these areas also had an ancestry elsewhere, it is true that Wesley originally met the practice of extempore prayer among Scots in America who were maintaining earlier Reformed practice; that the Methodist covenant service owed a great deal to the individual covenants beloved of Puritan authors; that class meetings resembled the fellowship groups fostered by the godly of the seventeenth century; that Wesley's pattern of family prayer was drawn from the Nonconformist Philip Henry; and that Wesley's rigorism, for all its High Church ascetic flavour, had parallels in Puritan moral teaching.[140] Methodists inherited a substantial legacy from the Puritans.

DISCONTINUITY WITH THE REFORMED TRADITION

The Evangelical Revival nevertheless does represent a break with the past. Apart from the emergence of new denominations, perhaps the most marked discontinuity was in the Church of England. The doctrine of justification by faith had well-nigh disappeared. Calvinism was at a discount after the Restoration. 'Puritan' had become a term of abuse. Professor Rupp has suggested that there must be a thread linking the Reformed tradition of the seventeenth century with the Evangelicals of the eighteenth.[141] Yet there is scant evidence for so inherently likely a hypothesis. The last Calvinist bishop, Hall of Bristol, died in 1710.[142] Among the clergy, it was said in the 1730s that some had abandoned the Reformation teachings of their youth. Richard Seagrave, an unbeneficed clergyman, was a lonely voice in the 1730s calling for allegiance to the doctrines of the Thirty-Nine Articles. He had no identifiable influence in bringing the early Evangelicals to their mature position.[143] Thomas Allen of Kettering (1714–55) was exceptional in retaining a Puritan stance and then being classified (by Simeon, for instance) as an Evangelical.[144] James Hervey, Rector of Weston Favell, Northamptonshire, the most popular *littérateur* among the first generation of Evangelical clergy, was aware of likeminded men in an earlier age. 'Is it Puritanical?' he asked. 'Be not ashamed of the name.'[145] But, as was usual, his faith had come independently – in his case through Oxford Methodism. Other Evangelicals, like James Bean at the beginning of the nineteenth century, were eager to repudiate all connection with the Puritans, who were so widely seen as virulent critics of the constitution of the Church of England. The Reformation he honoured, but not its dyspeptic successors.[146] Occasionally, there are traces of the persistence of Puritan faith and experience without benefit of clergy. For example, an early Methodist preacher came on a serious young man at Newark. 'It was evident that the Lord had graciously visited his soul, though he had never heard a gospel sermon in his life, and had solely the Bible, the Common Prayer-Book, and Milton's *Paradise Lost* to read.'[147] Pockets of lay piety were no doubt sustained in obscurity and nourished by old books. It remains true, however, that the men of eminence were now in their graves. The tide of Reformed teaching that continued to flow in the Church of Scotland and in English Dissent was at an ebb in the Church of England.

There were three significant symptoms of discontinuity. One was the stimulus given to the revival by the alternative High Church tradition of the *Ecclesia Anglicana*. The ideal of 'primitive Christianity', stripped of the decadent accretions of later centuries, had been popularised by William Cave, Vicar of Islington, in 1673. Five years later, under the guidance of Anthony Horneck, a German who had become preacher at the Savoy, there was created the first 'religious society'. Appealing chiefly to young men, the religious societies soon became the vehicle for spreading 'primitive Christianity' throughout the land. Members bound themselves to self-examination, directed prayer, monthly communion, fasting and the quest for holiness. Society meetings, normally weekly, were tightly controlled by clergymen, excluded controversy over theology and church government and were designed overall to ensure that the members should (as the model rules put it) 'keep close to the Church of England'. By 1714, 27 per cent of London places of worship in the Established Church received support from some religious society.[148] It was a body of this type that Wesley gathered round himself at Oxford from 1729 onwards. Attracting the nickname 'The Holy Club', it was designed to nurture the religious attainments of young men through guided reading, spiritual exercises and good works. Prison visiting, attendance on the sick and help for the poor formed part of the traditional discipline of the religious societies.[149]

The decoding of the diaries of Wesley and Benjamin Ingham, one of his associates, is revealing a more complex organisation in this Oxford Methodism than had previously been supposed. Wesley's care group spawned several sub-groups, which in turn created a number of other groups. The programme of pursuing the Christian ideal not according to any system of theology but by imitating the lives of Christlike people was evidently enjoying something of a vogue among successive cohorts of undergraduates.[150] Self-examination was taken to an extreme. Members were encouraged to test themselves hourly on various aspects of devotion and record their ratings on a scale from one (low) to nine.[151] Wesley carried forward the ascetic temper of the Holy Club into the mature Methodism of the revival. His followers were exhorted to pursue a regimen in exactly the manner of Horneck with a dedication to precise self-scrutiny, works of charity and attendance on the means of grace.[152] Methodists were to be found observing Lent and it was a standard practice to fast before watch-night services.[153] Furthermore, the existing religious societies of the Church of England formed a reservoir of zealots in earnest for their souls that the early evangelists could tap. Some societies went over virtually en bloc to the Methodists or the Moravians. Half the Moravian members in London in 1742 were believed to have come from the religious societies.[154] The revival owed an enormous debt to the methods and the personnel of this set of institutions.

There was also a debt to the teaching of the High Church tradition. The pursuit of holiness, Wesley's grand aim, was grounded in a number of esteemed devotional writers both ancient and modern. Foremost among them was Jeremy Taylor, once chaplain to Archbishop Laud and Charles I and, after the Restoration, a bishop in Ireland. His treatise on *Holy Living and Dying* (1650–1) made an immediate impact on Wesley in 1725 at the age of twenty-two. 'Instantly', he recalls, 'I resolved to dedicate *all my life* to God, *all* my thoughts, and words, and actions, being thoroughly convinced, there was no medium . . . '[155] Taylor urged a Laudian form of devotion, at once strict and sacramental. Wesley in his later Evangelical years adopted a rule of life based on Taylor's recommendations.[156] A year after discovering Jeremy Taylor he came on Thomas à Kempis's *Imitation of Christ*, the classic of fifteenth-century piety. Although he felt à Kempis exaggerates the need for renunciation, the *Imitation* illuminated for him what he called 'the religion of the heart'.[157] In the next couple of years two works by Wesley's contemporary William Law, his *On Christian Perfection* (1726) and *A Serious Call to a Devout and Holy Life* (1728), convinced Wesley more than ever (as he put it) of 'the absolute impossibility of being *half a Christian*'.[158] It was Taylor, à Kempis and Law who laid the foundation for the rigorism of the Holy Club.

Another strand of influence over Wesley, derived partly from Roman Catholic authors and in some tension with the teaching on obedience to constituted authority found in Taylor and Law, was the mystical element in the Christian inheritance. Wesley's mother Susanna valued the *Pugna Spiritualis* of Lorenzo Scupoli, an Italian work, and *The Life of God in the Soul of Man* (1677) by Henry Scougal of Aberdeen almost as highly as Baxter.[159] Growing up in this atmosphere, Wesley was naturally attracted to John Norris, the last of the Cambridge Platonists, who had contrived to blend intellectual analysis with mystical apprehension. He read fifteen works by Norris in the period 1725–35, more than the number from any other author.[160] A range of continental mystics was known and absorbed by Wesley. The most enduring mark was made by Jean Baptiste de Saint-Jure's *Holy Life of Monsieur de Renty*, a seventeenth-century French aristocrat of mystical temperament who became Wesley's most admired model of a Christian.[161] After 1736 Wesley turned away from mysticism itself as too passive, introspective and anti-institutional, but it continued to exercise a lifelong fascination over his brother Charles.[162] Certain eighteenth-century Evangelicals were drawn back towards the mystical, especially the forms propagated by Law in his later years, for the Evangelical and the mystic shared a common attachment to experiencing the divine.[163]

The patristic and liturgical preoccupations of High Church scholarship had less in common with the revival, yet they too played a part in preparing its way. Wesley imbibed a fascination for eastern Orthodoxy that reinvigorated his ideal of perfection at the fountainhead of monastic spirituality; and his zeal for the early centuries of the church eventually drove him back to the Bible as a uniquely authoritative account of primitive Christianity.[164] Many an individual Evangelical, especially among the clergy, had passed through a High Church phase of some type. It had served, they would later have said, as a schoolmaster to bring them to Christ.

A second symptom of discontinuity was the assimilation of influences from continental Protestantism. The decisive impulse to the brothers Wesley came from Luther: Charles was reading his commentary on Galatians and John was listening to his preface to the letter to the Romans when they first came to vital faith.[165] Yet neither subsequently rated Luther very highly, so that Lutherans of their own day came to be more important than the reformer. The experience of the Protestants in the central European regions where the Counter-Reformation had gained the upper hand was part of the context in which revival was born. There were anxieties about the future of the Protestant cause that encouraged a willingness to experiment with novel religious methods. In Silesia in particular, Protestants retained few places of public worship and so were forced back on informal techniques of open-air preaching and domestic meetings to sustain the faith. Again, in 1731, the Protestants of Salzburg were expelled by Austrian troops and had to seek refuge elsewhere. Charity sermons were preached on their behalf in London, and John Wesley sailed in 1737 alongside a vessel carrying a party of them to Georgia.[166] Their ministers, whom Wesley consulted about their convictions, were trained at Halle, which was the centre of the Lutheran movement that most affected Evangelical origins: Pietism. Philip Spener had written in 1675 the manifesto of the movement, *Pia Desideria*, urging the need for repentance, the new birth, putting faith into practice and close fellowship among true believers.[167] His disciple August Francke created at Halle a range of institutions for embodying and propagating Spener's vision. Chief among them was the orphan house, then the biggest building in Europe, with a medical dispensary attached. It was to inspire both Wesley and Whitefield to erect their own orphan houses and Howel Harris to establish a community as a centre of Christian influence at Trevecca. Francke printed Bibles and spiritual reading in huge quantities for dissemination in Germany and far beyond to the south and east, and at Halle there were trained ministers to carry the gospel even further.[168] Under the patronage of the King of Denmark, a mission was launched to India in 1705. Griffith Jones, the creator of the Welsh circulating schools, and his patron Sir John Philipps, an influential member of the Society for Promoting Christian Knowledge, were admirers of Francke who tried to imitate the missionary impetus of Halle in their native Wales. These two, clergyman and layman, were the closest approximation to Evangelicals in the Church of England before the revival. Francke's writings were to take their place in the spiritual biographies of Whitefield and both Wesleys.[169] Pietism had already achieved in Lutheranism a great deal of what these men were to undertake in the English-speaking world.

Even more decisive for the emergence of Evangelicalism were the Moravians. Beginning as the followers of Jan Hus in Bohemia in the early fifteenth century, this body, officially the *Unitas Fratrum* or Unity of the Brethren, had become accepted as Protestants after the Reformation. Their popular nickname was the result of their prominence in Moravia until they were harried into exile and decline by the advancing Counter-Reformation. A party of refugees settled in 1722 at Herrnhut in Saxony on the estate of Count Nicholas von Zinzendorf, a man who had been touched by Pietism but now identified wholly with the Moravians. Under Zinzendorf's guidance they were reorganised in 1727 as the Renewed Unity of the Brethren and became a dynamic missionary force.[170] Zinzendorf spread the message that true religion must be a matter of experience, not of speculation. Each for himself must accept the forgiveness made available by the Lamb of God sacrificed for sins. The cross, faith, forgiveness and assurance were the keynotes. Intense devotion, especially to the crucified Christ, was the result.[171]

Wesley encountered the Brethren on his missionary trip to Georgia. One of their number, Peter Böhler, was his chief guide in the months following his return in 1738 that led to his own experience of forgiveness. For more than two years Wesley was actually a member of a predominantly Moravian fellowship in Fetter Lane. Even after his withdrawal there were many comings and goings between the early Methodists and the Moravians, who developed their own itinerant missionary work in England and Wales. There were negotiations for reunion as late as 1785–6.[172] The initial obstacle to combined work was the common Moravian teaching on 'stillness', a denigration of prayer, Bible-reading, church attendance, receiving the sacrament and good works, in order 'wholly to rely on the blood and wounds of the Lamb'.[173] It was an exaggeration of Luther's insistence on faith alone as the instrument of salvation. There were other peculiarities caused by the German ethos and language of the movement, as when it was recorded that the unmarried sisters held 'a Heathen Love-Feast' – that is, a tea to encourage support for missions to the heathen.[174] Yet the Moravians had a special appeal for those seeking 'primitive Christianity': a threefold pattern of ministry, bishops, priests and deacons, whose orders were recognised by the Archbishop of Canterbury in 1737; a firm discipline, a warm fellowship and an apostolic zeal for missions; and, from 1746 at Fulneck in Yorkshire, and soon elsewhere, the community life of Herrnhut imitated in England.[175] Apart from a crucial element of their teaching whose importance will be discussed shortly, the Moravians transmitted a substantial legacy to the revival, especially in its Methodist variety. Their practice of an *ecclesiola in ecclesia* (a tight-knit religious fellowship within a broader church), their organisation in bands and their hymn-singing were taken over by Wesley – although each was blended with the inheritance of the religious societies. Perhaps the watch-night services and conference of Methodism were imitated from the Moravians; this is certainly true of the love-feast and the use of the lot for discerning the will of God, though the latter practice was discontinued by Wesley after the early 1740s.[176] Evangelicalism learned much from the Moravians.

The third of the striking symptoms of discontinuity was a new emphasis on mission. In the sixteenth and seventeenth centuries it was rare to find a Protestant divine commending the spread of the gospel beyond the bounds of Christendom. Richard Baxter was most unusual among the Puritans in expressing an eagerness for the conversion of the nations.[177] There were efforts during the Commonwealth to propagate the faith in 'the dark corners of the land', which effectively meant Wales, the north and the south-west, and subsequently certain Independents and Baptists engaged in itinerant evangelism in their areas.[178] But the evangelistic work of John Eliot among the Iroquois Indians of Massachusetts became celebrated precisely because it was exceptional. Protestant missionary effort was pitiably weak by comparison with the Roman Catholic record.[179] The Great Commission at the end of Matthew's gospel, 'Go ye therefore, and teach all nations', was given no expository comment in the Geneva Bible that was widely used among English-speaking Protestants of the seventeenth century.[180] The text, it was supposed, applied only to the early church. Cotton Mather, a leading Puritan of the New World writing early in the eighteenth century, regretted the scandal 'of so little having been done by the churches of the Reformation to spread the faith.[181]

The activism that, as we have seen, was an enduring hallmark of the Evangelical movement stood in stark contrast. It was still believed, by Jonathan Edwards for instance, that God exercises his sovereignty in men's salvation by bestowing the means of grace on one people but not on another.[182] Now, however, it was increasingly held that human beings could be the appointed agents of bringing the gospel to unevangelised nations. We know, wrote Edwards, 'that it is God's manner to make use of means in carrying on his work in the world . . . '[183] 'Means' was the key word signifying the whole apparatus of human agency. Like Edwards, the Baptist Abraham Booth argued in 1768 that such means were entirely legitimate in the furtherance of the purposes of God.[184] His co-religionist William Carey put the case more strongly in 1792 in a work entitled *An Enquiry into the Obligation of Christians to Use Means for the Conversion of the Heathen*. Means were now held to be obligatory, for, as Carey contended, the Great Commission is still binding on believers.[185] The new breed of Evangelicals practised what they preached. Edwards supported his friend David Brainerd in a mission to the Indians and at the end of his life undertook the same work himself.[186] Carey established the Baptist Missionary Society, the first foreign mission to spring from the revival, and by 1793 was pioneering its operations in India.[187] Mission was now held to be essential to Christianity.

The activism was at first most apparent among the Methodists. A Moravian devotee of stillness reported to Zinzendorf in 1740 that Wesley was 'resolved to *do* all things himself . . . I will let our Saviour govern this whirlwind'.[188] Wesley's preachers felt a similar gusting impetus from their conversions. 'Now the same spirit that witnessed my adoption', according to one of them, 'cried in me, night and day, "Spend and be spent for God!"'[189] The dynamic was soon equally evident among those Evangelicals who felt in conscience bound to stick to their parish work. Apart from taking Sunday services, Walker of Truro conducted prayers on Wednesdays and Fridays together with burials and baptisms, visited the sick, directed his converts, spent every evening from Monday to Friday speaking either publicly or privately and occupied Saturday in preparing Sunday's sermon.[190] Such men were far from the normal image of an easy-going eighteenth-century parson with plenty of time for diverting recreations and ample dinners. As the evangelistic impulse came to dominate orthodox Dissent in the last two decades of the eighteenth century it gave rise to a transformation of its organisation. Independents and Baptists began to imitate the Methodist itinerancy. In most English counties *ad hoc* societies or county unions were created to evangelise the villages.[191] In Scotland the Relief Church led the way and the brothers Haldane, Robert and James, with Christopher Anderson and others, followed in despatching travelling preachers to the Highlands.[192] Schemes for foreign missions were likewise in the air. Wesley, after all, had travelled to Georgia with the aim of evangelising the Indians even before his decisive experience of 1738. Yet in later life he discouraged missions to the heathen by Methodist preachers on the grounds that there were more immediate prospects of success at home. Consequently, no Wesleyan Missionary Society was set up until 1813. The Countess of Huntingdon toyed with the idea of a mission, again to the Indians of Georgia, and there was a plan for sending men from the Church of England to Bengal.[193] But it was Carey, fired by Captain Cook's account of the peoples of the South Seas, who first brought a mission to birth. His example roused others. In 1795 the London Missionary Society, undenominational at first but increasingly an Independent body, was set up with the South Seas as its chief target; in 1796, although the General Assembly of the Church of Scotland rejected an Evangelical overture for the foundation of a missionary society, interdenominational missionary bodies were founded in Edinburgh, Glasgow and elsewhere; and in 1799 the Church Missionary Society was established to spread the gospel on lines acceptable to the Church of England.[194] Overseas missions were to remain a permanent expression of the energy that characterised the Evangelical movement.

THE DOCTRINE OF ASSURANCE

The three symptoms of discontinuity in the Anglo-Saxon tradition of conservative Protestantism should not be seen in isolation from each other. They are bound together by an underlying factor, a shift in the received doctrine of assurance with all that it entailed. Those who pursued the High Church quest for holiness with single-minded devotion frequently felt a nagging doubt. For all their self-discipline, were they to be numbered among those finally saved? Their efforts gave them no certainty; sometimes their failures heightened their anxiety. So the novel assurance they discovered in Evangelicalism was greeted with relief. Again, continental Protestantism exercised its most decisive influence on the origins of Evangelicalism not in the sphere of practice but in that of doctrine. The Moravians taught that assurance is of the essence of faith. By embracing this principle for a while and approximating to it throughout his life, Wesley was one of those responsible for disseminating a newly enhanced doctrine of assurance.[195] And the dynamism of the Evangelical movement was possible only because its adherents were assured in their faith. Without assurance, the priority for the individual in earnest about salvation had to be its acquisition; with it, the essential task was the propagation of the good news that others, too, could know the joy of sins forgiven. All this is not to claim that assurance appeared for the first time in the Evangelical Revival. On the contrary, as Professor Rupp has pointed out, the doctrine was rooted 'deep within the Puritan tradition'.[196] There was as much desire for confident knowledge of one's own salvation in the seventeenth century as in the eighteenth. But if there was a common preoccupation with assurance, the content of the doctrine was transformed. Whereas the Puritans had held that assurance is rare, late and the fruit of struggle in the experience of believers, the Evangelicals believed it to be general, normally given at conversion and the result of simple acceptance of the gift of God. The consequence of the altered form of the doctrine was a metamorphosis in the nature of popular Protestantism. There was a change in patterns of piety, affecting devotional and practical life in all its departments. The shift, in fact, was responsible for creating in Evangelicalism a new movement and not merely a variation on themes heard since the Reformation. For that reason it demands close scrutiny.

Calvinists had faced a problem. They believed in predestination in a strong sense. God is sovereign in determining who should be saved. A favourite text, Romans 8:30, teaches that 'whom he did predestinate, them he also called: and whom he called, them he also justified: and whom he justified, them he also glorified'. God's purpose in predestination would certainly be fulfilled. Nobody chosen, called and justified by God could fall away so as not to share in heavenly glory. Yet it frequently happened that men and women professing to have become true Christians deserted the faith. Experience seemed to suggest that justification was no guarantee that believers would persevere to the end. The parable of the sower apparently supports this view by declaring that some 'receive the word with joy' but 'in time of temptation fall away' (Luke 8:13). A solution to the dilemma was found by the Elizabethan Puritan divine William Perkins in the doctrine of temporary faith. It was possible, he held, for a person numbered among the non-elect, those not chosen for salvation, to possess faith for a time but then for it to pass away.[197] Consequently, there was a doubt hanging over the faith of any individual. He could not be confident that he was elect and would therefore be saved. Ordinary Elizabethan Puritans experienced few difficulties in this area, for in the sixteenth century the notion of temporary faith held by Perkins had not yet been popularised.[198] But Perkins and a host of seventeenth-century divines in his wake insisted on its implications. A person, they urged, must question whether or not his faith is permanent. Already, in the sixteenth century, it had been mooted among Calvinists that saving faith does not necessarily include assurance.[199] Now it was taught that the lack of assurance is in some ways an advantage. The ignorance of the believer about his future destiny would drive him to scrutinise himself for signs of grace. He was told that he should 'rest not satisfied without a persuasion from the Spirit of Adoption that God is your Father'.[200] But self-examination was protracted. 'These things', wrote the Scot William

Guthrie in his immensely popular *The Christian's Great Interest* (1659), 'will keep a man in work all his days'.[201] Confidence in one's own salvation was the rare blessing of a mature faith. 'No Christian', wrote Perkins, 'attaineth to this full assurance at the first, but in some continuance of time, after that for a long space he hath kept a good conscience before God, and before men . . . '[202] Many might not reach the experience until after death.[203] The developed Puritan view of the subject is formalised in the Westminster Confession. Certainty of being in a state of grace is attainable in this life. But there is a major reservation. 'This infallible assurance doth not so belong to the essence of faith, but that a true believer may wait long, and conflict with many difficulties before he be partaker of it.'[204]

The difficulties were expected to be substantial, for the Christian life was conceived as a constant struggle. The conflict was partly with temptation. The believer must flee from sin. But equally there was an obsession with doubt. Perhaps the inclination to sin was itself a sign that God's grace had not yet been planted in the heart. The numerous Puritan works of casuistry were designed to deal with precisely this fear. Thomas Brooks's *Precious Remedies against Satan's Devices* (1669) enumerated among the diabolical methods for keeping souls in 'a sad, doubting, questioning, and uncomfortable condition' the suggestion that 'their graces are not true, but counterfeit . . . faith, is but fancy'. The remedy was rigorous self-examination. Brooks offers a checklist of ten particulars for distinguishing between sanctifying and temporary grace.[205] Perhaps it is no surprise that scrutiny according to so thorough a catalogue merely served to intensify the terrors about the fate of his soul felt by William Grimshaw in 1739, shortly before his conversion to an Evangelical faith.[206] Yet Puritans were convinced that this introspective technique was the kernel of the spiritual life. They appealed to the scriptural injunction to 'give diligence to make your calling and election sure' (2 Peter 1:10). High on the lists of the signs of grace – of which Baxter alone supplies at least four[207] – was the evidence of works. The Reformation had decried all reliance on works as a means of meriting salvation, but increasingly works were valued as an indication of the reality of divine grace.[208] To do good was a sign of sanctification, the Spirit's fruit in the life of the true believer. It was this concern with works that, according to the sociological pioneer Max Weber, drove Protestants to 'worldly asceticism', the disciplined lives in the secular world that gave rise to capitalism.[209] Certainly the attention paid to works generated an imperative to godliness. The individual was called upon to validate his faith by his works; but, finding his works to be imperfect, he was driven back to reliance on God. The quest for assurance, together with its non-attainment, created 'the internal spiritual dynamic of puritan religion'.[210] The style of piety persisted into the eighteenth century wherever Puritan divines continued in esteem. In 1716 John Willison, Minister of the South Church, Dundee, urged self-examination on intending communicants. 'I pity those poor trembling, and doubting souls, who cannot attain to any light or clearness about their condition', he declares. 'To such I would say, that you ought to wait on God, and hold on in the way of duty to your lives' end, and whatever discouragements you may meet with therein, God in his own time will let you know that your labour is not in vain.'[211] A persistent phase of gloom was a sign of true religion. Assurance was by no means the norm.

The doctrine among Evangelicals was far more robust. 'I *knew* that I was His child', wrote Howel Harris, the emphasis being his own.[212] 'My God! I know, I feel thee mine', echoed Charles Wesley.[213] His brother John, with characteristic thoroughness, set off to Germany shortly after his experience of 24 May 1738 to investigate the authentic Moravian view of the matter at its source in Herrnhut. His mentor Böhler had taught that a man cannot have peace with God without knowing that he has it. Wesley discovered at Herrnhut that, although certain Moravian leaders concurred with Böhler, others, including Zinzendorf and Michael Linner, the oldest church member, held that assurance may come long after justification. More usually, however, according to Linner, forgiveness and a full assurance of forgiveness come 'in one and the same moment'.[214] So Wesley returned from his visit believing that assurance is not intrinsic to faith but a distinct gift;[215] and yet that assurance is the normal possession of the believer. This position he maintained for life, though sometimes stressing the one side and sometimes the other.[216] Thus the first Methodist Conference of 1744 announced that no man can be justified and not know it; yet the Conference of 1745 admitted that there may be cases where a sense of God's pardoning love is not a condition of his favour.[217] We preach assurance, explained Wesley in old age, 'as a common privilege of the children of God; but we do not enforce it, under the pain of damnation, denounced on all who enjoy it not.'[218] Other Evangelicals likewise taught that assurance is the 'common privilege of the children of God', though the Calvinists, believing in the perseverance of the saints, necessarily held that the Christian is sure not only of his present state of grace but also of his future share in glory. The sermons of Romaine and Hervey seemed to suggest there is no true faith without assurance, and Grimshaw actually held this opinion.[219] Walker of Truro thought there was a risk in this direction of identifying faith with feeling, and preferred to rest assurance on the objective work of Christ.[220] The intermediate view that prevailed in the Church of England was that of Venn. Faith, he taught, must not be based on inward feeling only. Yet real faith produces a clear and permanent sense of dependence on Christ. 'No one can possess it', he contends, 'without being conscious he does so . . . '[221] Later Evangelicals in the Church of England admitted that the comforts of religion may sometimes be withdrawn, either by God or by Satan.[222] But the eclipse would be temporary and an awareness of the favour of God would return. 'It is not reasonable . . . to suppose a man to have the Spirit of God', according to Joseph Milner, a leading Evangelical author, 'if he have no evidence of it.'[223] Assurance, in the teaching of the fathers of the

Evangelical movement, is the normal experience of the believer from the
time of his conversion onwards.

Ordinary Christians touched by the revival enjoyed a new style of
piety. Converts seeing the glory of Christian truths, according to Jonathan
Edwards, could no more doubt them than doubt the existence of a blazing
sun in a clear sky.[224] There was no need for a plunge into anxious discouragement, Abraham Booth declared, for the Christian has as much warrant
to believe as the hungry to feed. Accordingly, for Booth, wrestling was no
longer with fears but with sins alone.[225] It is a dangerous error, asserted an
early Methodist preacher, to suppose that a man may be accepted by God
and yet be unaware of it. 'To be a real member of Christ's Church is to
feel Christ in us.'[226] Doubt over one's standing with God could arise only
when the sense of pardon was not incontestably clear.[227] For the most part
it was banished from Christian experience. There was still self-examination
with a view to discovering the marks of a real change made by the Spirit
of God.[228] Now, however, the process was, as it were, non-recurrent: it
was expected that the verdict would be favourable. If ever there appeared
gloom or fear that an individual had no part in Christ, he would be able
'to prove his [*sic*] self a believer, by proving his whole dependence for
salvation is on Christ alone'.[229] The difference from traditional teaching
was unmistakable. A Methodist preacher exhorted a Dissenter not to rest
till he was sure that Christ had died for him. 'I hate to hear people talk of
being assured of any such thing', was the retort.[230] Another Methodist,
Thomas Payne, had believed. 'But', he recounts, 'I had a Calvinian library,
which I often read. And hence I imbibed that miserable notion, that it was
absolutely necessary every believer should come down from the mount.
Hence I was persuaded that . . . I must doubt of my justification, which
those wretched casuists lay down as one mark of sincerity. For want of
knowing better, I listened to these, till I lost the witness of the Spirit.'[231]
The age of such Puritan casuists was passing.

There was an important consequence of their supersession by new
teaching. In the devotional life there was bubbling confidence. 'O! with
what joy', declared Whitefield, '– joy unspeakable – even joy that was full
of and big with glory, was my soul filled, when . . . a full assurance of
faith broke in upon my disconsolate soul!'[232] The radiant spirit was most
apparent in adversity. During the battle of Fontenoy in 1745 wounded
Methodist troops rejoiced to be going to Jesus; a preacher with both his legs
taken off by a cannon ball was laid across a cannon to die, but as long as he
could speak was praising God; another who suffered injuries to both arms
announced that he was as happy as he could be out of paradise and survived
to report to Wesley that it was 'one of the sweetest days I ever enjoyed'.[233]
Such striking exuberance was rooted in a settled inclination to be happy.
Sins were certainly forgiven; there could be delight in fellowship with Jesus.
There were, of course, exceptions among Evangelicals. The hymn-writer
William Cowper suffered from inveterate melancholy.[234] But in his case

the disposition was a result of anxieties that sometimes took him over the boundary of insanity. In general, Evangelicals turned from a spirituality that expected bouts of despondency to a calmer, sunnier devotional life.

The turning point between the two attitudes to assurance can be located precisely. It occurred in the work of Jonathan Edwards at Northampton, Massachusetts, during the revival of 1734–5. As he was at pains to stress, there was no novelty in the content of his teaching. His sermons consisted of 'the common plain Protestant doctrine of the Reformation'.[235] Nor was the phenomenon of revival new. There had been five similar harvests of souls at Northampton under his father-in-law and predecessor as minister, Solomon Stoddard, and another four or five under his own father at East Windsor.[236] What was fresh was the pastoral guidance Edwards offered to converts. Those who claimed to have undergone a decisive spiritual experience were interviewed by the minister. If he was satisfied that they had truly been converted, he assured them that they were real Christians. Received Puritan practice would have been to encourage them to wrestle through their own doubts and fears over a protracted period. Consequently, Edwards was sharply criticised for his departure from customary ways. He had two justifications. Guidance was essential to avoid the sheer distress that some would otherwise unnecessarily suffer; and the confident avowals of conversion that resulted from his practice stimulated an awakening of spiritual concern in others.[237] Edwards recounts the effect on those who had previously doubted if they were among the elect:

> Grace in many persons, through this ignorance of their state, and their looking on themselves still as the objects of God's displeasure, has been like the trees in winter, or like seed in the spring suppressed under a hard clod of earth. Many in such cases have laboured to their utmost to divert their minds from the pleasing and joyful views they have had, and to suppress those consolations and gracious affections that arose thereupon. And when it has once come into their minds to inquire, whether or not this was true grace, they have been much afraid lest they should be deceived with common illuminations and flashes of affection, and *eternally* undone with a false hope. But when they have been better instructed, and so brought to allow of *hope*, this has awakened the gracious disposition of their hearts into life and vigour as the warm beams of the sun in spring have quickened the seeds and productions of the earth.[238]

The better instruction Edwards subsequently systematised in his book *The Distinguishing Marks of a Work of the Spirit of God* (1741). He sets out a checklist of signs that conversion had been valid. Through it others in the Reformed tradition learned how to hearten new believers rather than throw them back into painful introspection. Edwards created an Evangelical framework for interpreting Christian experience.

How could he be so bold? It was because he was far more confident than his Puritan forefathers of the powers of human knowledge. A person, he held, can receive a firm understanding of spiritual things through a 'new sense' which is as real as sight or smell. Unbelievers might languish in ignorance of God, but at conversion the Holy Spirit originates 'a new inward perception or sensation of their minds'.[239] Assured knowledge of God is therefore possible. This was the capacity he encouraged among those touched by revival. Edwards's attention to epistemology, the theory of knowledge, was typical of his age. The emerging Enlightenment was generating an imperative to enquire into the nature of things. The philosophically inclined were reflecting in particular on how human beings acquire knowledge. John Locke was primarily responsible. In his *Essay concerning Human Understanding* (1690) he denies that the mind possesses innate ideas. Nobody, he teaches, is born with automatic knowledge, even of morality of God. All we know comes through the five senses from the external world. Experience is the source of all understanding.[240] Traditionalists were scandalised that the powers of the mind were held to be so circumscribed. Others felt they could not dispute Locke's premisses. But, while accepting his axiom that knowledge comes from experience, they set about explaining what human beings do know in terms that modified Locke's analysis. Thus, for instance, Francis Hutcheson taught that human beings possess a moral sense for discerning right and wrong.[241] Edwards's 'new sense' is analogous to Hutcheson's moral sense. Responding to the Lockean spirit of the age, he was postulating a capacity for religious knowledge acceptable to philosophers of his era.

The determining influence of Locke over Edwards has in the past been exaggerated.[242] He absorbed a variety of other recent authors including the Platonist Henry More, the scientist Isaac Newton and the French philosopher Nicolas Malebranche. Edwards's teaching in moral philosophy, logic and metaphysics differs from Locke's.[243] Yet it remains true that the debt to Locke in certain specific fields was substantial.[244] And there is a palpably Enlightenment tone about Edwards's form of expression. Although he is prepared to describe the soul's awareness of God in traditional theological language as a spiritual infusion or in phraseology derived from the Platonic tradition as illumination, he is generally eager to translate the older idiom into up-to-date terminology.[245] The new sense, he says, is 'what some metaphysicians call a new simple idea'.[246] Because philosophical discourse in his day was shaped so largely by Locke, Edwards inevitably speaks as his disciple. For Locke, knowledge derived from the senses is certain. Edwards was simply extending the range of senses available to a human being when he put the capacity to embrace the gospel in that category. Once seen in that light, knowledge of God is also indubitable. It is something not to be brooded over in solitude but to be joyously affirmed. Edwards derived his confidence about salvation from the atmosphere of the English Enlightenment.

The case of Wesley is similar. The issue of whether we can be certain of being in a state of salvation was raised for him by Jeremy Taylor in 1725. He found temporary solace in the belief that 'our sincere endeavours' guarantee us present acceptance by God.[247] Preoccupation with the question increased in the 1730s. Sincerity, good works and the contempt of the world[248] remained the rather sandy foundation for his hope of salvation. Responsible as he was for instruction in aspects of philosophy and diligent as he was in his reading, Wesley necessarily formulated his concern for assurance in intellectual terms. How is God known? A variety of sources was available. His favourite John Norris, for example, offered a theory of knowledge drawn from a blending of Platonic and Cartesian sources.[249] But Wesley, like Edwards, was affected by Locke. He read the philosopher in 1725 and gave the *Essay concerning Human Understanding* more extensive study in 1727 and 1732.[250] He later appealed explicitly to Locke's authority, propagated his writings and, while disagreeing on points like his low valuation of logic, concurred in the thrust of his argument about the processes of gaining knowledge.[251] Certainly Wesley agreed with Locke in rejecting innate ideas. Infants brought up without religious instruction, he contended, would have no more knowledge of God than the beasts of the field.[252] Understanding is the fruit of experience.

Probably the largest debt in the field of epistemology was owed by Wesley to Peter Browne, Bishop of Cork and Ross, whose work *The Procedure, Extent, and Limits of Human Understanding* (1728) Wesley abridged during three months in 1730 and followed closely in his own philosophical compendium in later life. Browne transposed Locke's *Essay* into a theological key. He also rejected Locke's doctrine that ideas may come from reflection, that is, the operation of the human mind on itself. The sole source of ideas is direct sensation of the external world. It followed, according to Browne, that knowledge of God, who as spirit is not part of the material external world, could only be indirect, the result of reasoning about experience.[253] The early influence of Browne upon Wesley was twofold. On the one hand, he was encouraged to adopt as his enduring point of view the appeal to experience shared by Browne with Locke. On the other, the tendency of Browne's teaching was to distrust any claims to immediate experience of God. But that was a position in which Wesley could not bear to abide. He craved assurance. 'I want that faith', he wrote in his journal early in 1738, 'which none can have without knowing that he hath it.'[254] He was driven towards seeking direct experience of God.

It was the Moravians who taught him that it is possible. One of them in Georgia enquired whether Wesley had the witness within.[255] Peter Böhler insisted that to know God he must lay aside 'that philosophy', no doubt Wesley's supposition, buttressed by Browne, that claims to direct contact with God are a symptom of enthusiasm – the eighteenth-century term for fanaticism.[256] Experience showed Wesley in 1738 that the pardon of God may be felt. It confirmed the conviction drawn from empiricist writers that knowledge is a matter of sensation. He characteristically describes faith in almost identical terms to Edwards. It is 'a supernatural inward sense, or sight'.[257] Faith in the spiritual world is what sight is in the natural. 'It is necessary', he writes, 'that you have the *hearing* ear, and the *seeing* eye, emphatically so called; that you have a new class of senses opened in your soul . . . '[258] Like other Enlightenment thinkers, Wesley teaches that the only valid source of knowledge is what is experienced by the senses, but he adds, as it were, a sixth sense. He agrees with Hutcheson, for instance, that there must be a moral sense for human beings to have awareness of right and wrong; but he diverges from Hutcheson in claiming that it is not natural to man. It is imparted as a supernatural gift of God.[259] The basis of Wesley's doctrine was still Browne's epistemology. Although he now held that direct knowledge of God is possible, it comes, as Browne claimed, through sensation alone: this he termed the 'Direct Witness'. Confirmation of the knowledge can be derived from reasoning about experience, the evaluation of the marks of a true believer: this he called the 'Witness of Our Own Spirit'. The two witnesses agree, but the first, because it is the work of the Spirit of God, is incontrovertible. Wesley was charged by critics with holding 'perceptible inspiration', the belief that the Spirit communicates his will infallibly to an individual. Although Wesley rebutted the charge by pointing to the need to evaluate the evidences of grace, it remains true that he propagated a strong view of the certainty instilled in the believer by the Spirit.[260] It often seemed the greatest novelty about Methodism. At Leeds, uproar was caused by a convert claiming to know that his sins were forgiven.[261] When Charles Wesley preached that 'we might know our sins forgiven in this life, yea, this very moment', an early Methodist recalled, 'it seemed to me new doctrine, and I could not believe it at all'.[262] The Methodist teaching about assurance was new because it was part and parcel of the rising Enlightenment. It was a consequence of Wesley's application of an empiricist philosophy to religious experience.

THE INFLUENCE OF THE ENLIGHTENMENT

To recognise the alignment of Edwards, Wesley and the revival with the Enlightenment has not been customary. The whole movement of eighteenth-century thought has been depicted as irreligious in tendency. Voltaire's assault on revealed and organised religion has been taken to be typical.[263] The trends within the Enlightenment, on this view, necessarily acted as a solvent of Christian orthodoxy. Reason was banishing superstition. The new prestige of science associated with the name of Isaac Newton inspired the ambition to investigate all aspects of the world with the aim of dispassionately establishing truth. As wisdom spread from the enlightened elite, it was believed, tyranny in church and state would be put down and humanity would progress towards a happier future. It is generally acknowledged that the temper of the age affected religion in Britain. Deists put themselves beyond the bounds of the churches by rejecting the very notion of revealed religion. Their slogan was the title of one of the chief works produced by this school of thought, *Christianity not Mysterious* (1695) by John Toland.[264] Within the Church of England the Latitudinarians attempted to meet the Deists on their own ground of reason. The clergyman cast by many in the role of Locke's successor as England's leading philosopher, Samuel Clarke, gained a Cambridge DD by arguing that 'no article of the Christian faith is opposed to right reason'.[265] Clarke's *Scripture Doctrine of the Trinity* (1712), though not endorsing unorthodoxy, contended that received Trinitarian doctrine had no explicit biblical sanction either. He persuaded many that Trinitarianism was a matter of abstruse metaphysics alien to the spirit of primitive Christianity.[266] John Simson, professor of divinity at Glasgow, taking his signal from Clarke, adopted a similarly liberal – though biblicist – position in theology.[267] Later in the century the Church of Scotland was to produce a crop of distinguished scholars who stood in the vanguard of the Scottish Enlightenment.[268] The intellectual leaders of English Dissent, nourished in their academies, were similarly swayed by the secular learning of the day. Unrestrained by subscription to articles or a confession of faith, they moved less equivocally towards the Socinian heresy that denies the divinity of Christ. Joseph Priestley, chemist as well as theologian, was perhaps the most eminent of these 'rational Dissenters'.[269] The effect of the Enlightenment on the churches was undoubtedly to liberalise thought. The Evangelicals, by contrast, were wedded to orthodoxy. It is hardly surprising that they should be supposed to have been exempt from the influence of the Enlightenment.

The revival, furthermore, has often been treated as a reaction against the tide of rationalism.[270] Certainly, Evangelicals treated reliance on reason as a grand cause of spiritual deadness. The gospel, according to the Baptist Abraham Booth, is 'contrary to every scheme of salvation which human reason suggests'.[271] Evangelicals in Scotland dismissed those influenced by Hutcheson as 'paganized' divines.[272] Learning could appear a dangerous snare. To one early Methodist the study of Latin and other scholarly languages was firmly set down as an alternative to Christian devotedness.[273] To another, the pursuit of education seemed the high road to heresy. 'I hoped my acquaintance with authors on most subjects might be of some use to me', he reflected; 'but I was greatly mistaken . . . If I attempted any such thing, I was instantly filled with my old deistical ideas again.'[274] Accordingly some seemed to turn from reason to emotion. One Methodist became 'the weeping prophet', another 'the *damnation preacher*'.[275] Conversion, according to an ex-Methodist, could be a matter of psychological self-indulgence. 'At last', he recalled, 'by singing and repeating enthusiastic amorous hymns, and ignorantly applying particular texts of scripture, I got my imagination to the proper pitch, and thus I was born again in an instant . . .'[276] Wesley himself appeared to encourage this withdrawal from the world of the intellect to the dispositions of the heart. In the preface to his *Sermons* of 1746 he famously remarked, 'I design plain truth for plain people'. He therefore avoided, he continued, philosophical speculations, intricate reasonings, show of learning, difficult words, technical terms and an educated manner of speaking.[277] Wesley can plausibly be represented as no more than a popular propagandist – or, if anything more, then as a 'believer in dreams, visions, immediate revelations, miraculous cures, witchcraft, and many other ridiculous absurdities, as appears from many passages of his Journal, to the great disgrace of his abilities and learning . . . '[278] This contemporary estimate has often been echoed subsequently. It is easy to depict Wesley the pedlar of quack medical cures such as marigold flowers for the plague[279] as credulous, uncritical, a champion of the ancients against the moderns. Voltaire seemed to him a 'consummate coxcomb'.[280] Wesley, together with the whole revival movement, can appear to be devoted to resisting the Enlightenment's march of mind.

This was not, however, Wesley's own estimate of the matter. 'It is a fundamental principle with us', he claimed, 'that to renounce reason is to renounce religion, that religion and reason go hand in hand, and that all irrational religion is false religion.'[281] On 11 June 1738, less than a month after the turning point of his life, he preached before the University of Oxford on 'Salvation by Faith'. There was no ranting or hectoring, but instead logical order, careful argument and a nearly total absence of exhortation.[282] Increasingly, Wesley is being recognised as an Enlightenment thinker in his own right.[283] The sceptical Enlightenment of the continent he certainly rejected, but the whole cast of his mind was moulded by the new intellectual currents of his time. Supremely he was an empiricist. He drew out the implications of his position in many fields alongside the area of epistemology that has already been examined. His beliefs in religious tolerance, freewill and anti-slavery have rightly been identified as Enlightenment affinities.[284] So was his antipathy to 'enthusiasm'. He spelt out his attitude in a letter to Thomas Maxfield, an early preacher who eventually led a secession from Methodism that laid extravagant claims to special revelations. 'I dislike something that has the appearance of *enthusiasm*', wrote Wesley: 'overvaluing *feelings* and inward *impressions*: mistaking the mere work of *imagination* for the voice of the Spirit: expecting the end without the means, and undervaluing *reason*, *knowledge* and *wisdom* in general.'[285] Likewise Wesley's loyal followers could appeal to 'rational, scriptural evidence'; favour a rational religion that deprecated visions and revelations; incur censure from Moravians for being 'so full of law and reason'; and accord the highest praise to a society by calling its members 'sincere, peaceable, humble, and rational Christians'.[286]

Other Evangelicals spoke in similar vein. Joseph Milner defended Adam of Winteringham as a teacher of divinity properly called rational; Walker of Truro advised his young converts to take a course in logic.[287]

The Independent Thomas Gibbons published verse entitled, 'A Religious, the only Reasonable Life; or Reason and Religion the Same'; the Baptist Abraham Booth condemned Socinianism as 'unphilosophical'.[288] Preachers on the Evangelical fringe could lapse into rationalist heresies that drifted towards Unitarianism.[289] Seceders from Wesley's connexion in north-east Lancashire actually formed a Methodist Unitarian movement.[290] Among the great majority who retained their orthodoxy, Evangelical religion was rarely chosen as an escape-route from the fearful illumination of modern thought. Only in upper social circles did a number of people, swayed by Latitudinarianism or Deism, begin to doubt the evidences of Christianity before embracing the gospel.[291] Rather, Evangelicalism was accepted along with many characteristic traits of the Enlightenment. Its emergence was itself an expression of the age of reason.

To recognise the early phase of Evangelicalism as an adaptation of the Protestant tradition through contact with the Enlightenment helps explain its timing, a problem that has baffled many commentators. Why should the revival have begun in the 1730s? The great French historian Elie Halévy offered the fullest proposed answer in 1906. The fusion of traditional Protestant piety with High Church loyalties, the achievement of the Wesleys, was possible, according to Halévy, because of the continental influence that led to their conversion and the Welsh example that stimulated field preaching. But an essential third condition explaining the warm reception given to the message was an industrial crisis in 1739 creating popular unrest that was directed into religious channels.[292] The problem with this hypothesis (apart from doubts about the extent of the alleged 1739 crisis) is that the economic conditions of the industrialising parts of England where distress prevailed were totally different from those in the backwoods of New England; and yet there, too, sustained revivalism broke out.

It is far more convincing to hold the high cultural environment to be the essential novel ingredient. Between 1727 and 1760 Locke's *Essay* appeared in nine separate English editions and four collected editions. Although it would be an error to identify the English Enlightenment with the philosophical influence of John Locke alone, these figures form one index of the rising ascendancy of a new idiom in the intellectual world. Before this period, Locke had been championed only by forward spirits like Joseph Addison in 1711;[293] from about 1730 an empiricism owing a great debt to Newton as well as Locke became the prevailing philosophical temper. In the 1730s both George Berkeley, with his *Theory of Vision* (1733), and David Hume, with his *Treatise of Human Nature* (1739), were pressing empiricist thinking towards more drastic conclusions. Classicism had made corresponding progress in the arts. Alexander Pope's *Essay on Criticism* of 1711 had been a radical summons to rigorous observance of classical literary models. By the 1730s his *Essay on Man* (1733–4), conforming to the ideals he had announced two decades before, enjoyed a great vogue.

The Enlightenment approach, whether in matter or manner, was becoming more general, at least among the educated. The Lockean mode in political theory may have been less prominent during the eighteenth century than was once supposed,[294] but in philosophy, and especially in epistemology, a fresh era was opening. It is hardly surprising that men immersed in the learning of the age such as Edwards and Wesley should recast Protestant thought in the new style and set about persuading others to do the same. The timing of their remoulding of the doctrine of assurance according to empiricist canons has to be understood as a result of the spread of a new cultural mood.

This analysis is confirmed by the attitude of those in the Reformed tradition who most welcomed the revival. They too were men of the Enlightenment. Although he held reservations about Whitefield, the Independent divine Isaac Watts was eager to promote a renewal of religious vitality. In 1737 he arranged the first publication of Edwards's *Narrative* of the revival in his parish; he had already begun corresponding with Walker of Truro following the clergyman's conversion.[295] Watts held Locke to be 'the ingenious Director of modern Philosophy' and many truths of his *Essay* to be 'worthy of Letters of Gold'.[296] Although he rejected Locke's opinion that matter may think and even his repudiation of innate ideas, Watts followed his method in its essentials.[297] The notion of relying on a 'clear and distinct idea', for example, is drawn direct from Locke.[298] He was persuaded by Locke to embrace universal religious toleration.[299] Watts shares the characteristic ideals of the *avant-garde* of his day: moderation, a concern for utility and an admiration for the classical in art. The obscure he could not abide, whether in philosophy or literature. His achievement in the modification of the Psalms for public worship he succinctly described as 'dark expressions enlightened'.[300] Likewise his friend Philip Doddridge made constant appeal to Locke in his lectures to students for the Dissenting ministry.[301] Doddridge was opposed to subscription to any creed for the sake of free enquiry; he used Latin rather than English as the medium of instruction for the sake of clarity.[302] The great seventeenth-century Puritan divines John Goodwin and John Owen he dismissed with the comment that he was not very fond of 'such mysterious men'.[303] Doddridge can appear a conundrum for having both favoured the revival and trained ministers who carried freedom of thought to new lengths. The conundrum is resolved, however, when it is recognised that Doddridge was as much an Enlightenment thinker as a Calvinist theologian. The 'enlightened' tone of his teaching could lead students either towards unorthodoxy or towards gospel preaching – for both were rooted in the Enlightenment. Men training for the ministry in contemporary Edinburgh, where Locke's *Essay* appeared in the curriculum in the 1730s, could similarly emerge either as Moderate literati or as Evangelical leaders like John Erskine and John Witherspoon.[304] When the Enlightenment impinged on Calvinism, the result was not necessarily a doctrinal downgrade. From the 1730s onwards it could generate the new light of the gospel.

RESISTANCE TO ENLIGHTENMENT

Since the adoption of revivalism was bound up with a whole new cultural mood, it is no wonder that it encountered deep-rooted resistance in the Reformed tradition. In America, as is well known, opponents of Whitefield in Presbyterianism denounced the new-fangled ways so vehemently that a schism occurred. The Old Side wished to reject candidates for the ministry infected by Whitefield's indiscriminate zeal or his neglect of traditional points of church order and, significantly, accused the New Side of holding over-rigid views of assurance.[305] Similar happenings in Scotland have been less noticed. The Seceders who had left the Established Church over patronage in the 1730s welcomed Whitefield to Scotland in 1741. But they were not content with hearing plain preaching of the gospel. They wished, as Whitefield complained, 'to set me right about the matter of church government and the solemn league and covenant'. The evangelist would not turn rigid Presbyterian or confine himself to Secession pulpits. He was 'determined to go out into the highways and hedges'.[306] The Seceders rated ecclesiastical punctilio above gospel outreach in the manner of the seventeenth century. Their ethos, even in the later eighteenth century, was that of the Puritans. They maintained terminological exactitude in doctrine, intense self-scrutiny in devotion. Conscious of their own imperfections and depravities, they frequently fell into doubts about their salvation. 'Hence they were often sorrowful, when they might have been glad . . . '[307] Yet there were signs of change. Some of their ministers began to pay less attention to approved patterns of piety from the past and turned to their own independent researches. New light, as it was actually called, was dawning. Both branches of the Secession, the Anti-Burghers and the Burghers, split as a result of the New Light controversies of the 1790s. The occasion for debate was whether ministers were still bound to hold, following the Westminster Confession, that the secular ruler had power over the church and that the solemn league and covenant taken by Scots in the seventeenth century was still binding. But the underlying issue was whether they should embrace Enlightenment attitudes. Knowledge, held the progressives, advances over time. Consciences should not be tied to earlier statements of faith. The Westminster Confession might err. They claimed that 'no human composition . . . can be supposed to contain a full and comprehensive view of divine truth; so . . . we are not precluded from embracing . . . any further light which may afterward arise from the word of God . . . '[308] They were rejecting, like Doddridge, the principle of subscription. The ranks of the 'New Lichts' swelled in the early nineteenth century, for they were active in evangelism. But a dwindling minority of Seceders continued in the traditional ways, faithful to their archaic testimony as the 'Auld Lichts', long into the nineteenth century.

The introspective piety of pre-Evangelical days lingered on elsewhere. Its strongest bastion was the Highlands of Scotland. On their fringe, at Rhu in Dumbartonshire, McLeod Campbell discovered this apparently joyless form of religion in the 1820s.[309] It was to survive into the late twentieth century in the Gaelic-speaking territory of the north-western coastline and the Western Isles. In the mid-nineteenth century, its heartland was still Ross-shire. Lowlanders criticised Highland religion for its expectation of a fictitiously high standard of spiritual experience. 'The Christian Highlander, they say, is employed in determining whether he is a true servant of Christ or not, when he should be proving that he is so by being "up and doing".'[310] Conversely, the Highlander was astonished at the ease with which the Lowlander adopted the language of assurance: 'he thinks the confidence with which his brother speaks cannot always be in his heart, and if it is not there, he cannot, he thinks, be right in using words which express it'.[311] Highland religion seemed marked by gloom and an extraordinary inhibition about receiving communion until the believer attained the rare confidence that he was a child of God.

Among the Calvinist Dissenters south of the border the old ways tended to pass away more rapidly. In 1814 a traditionalist was lamenting their loss of 'peculiarity of character' through 'laxity of principle, and indiscriminate zeal which distinguished the Methodists'.[312] Yet there was resistance among them to itinerancy as an unwarranted instance of being 'up and doing'.[313] In Wales 'the strange fire' of Evangelical preaching was held at bay by Baptists until late in the eighteenth century.[314] And in East Anglia tensions in the Norfolk and Suffolk Baptist Association culminated in schism in 1830.[315] The issues were closely related to those in America which in the 1820s spread an anti-mission movement among Baptists.[316] The evangelistic imperative was felt to be less important than testimony to the truth. For Baptists this meant an insistence on believer's baptism as a condition of communion. William Gadsby, minister at Manchester from 1805 to 1844, provided a rallying-point for those who adhered to this principle, the Strict Baptists.[317] As the nineteenth century wore on, this minority of Calvinistic Baptists emerged as a separate denomination. Their piety remained modelled on pre-Enlightenment patterns. The title of the biography of their minister at Trowbridge who died in 1857 is eloquent of an earlier world: *Mercies of a Covenant God, being an Account of Some of the Lord's Dealings in Providence and Grace with John Warburton*. It is replete with accounts of soul-searching anxieties. 'Where is your good hope now, that you have talked about? . . . O how I sank down into the very pit of despair, and could only whisper, "Let not the pit shut her mouth upon me".'[318] Frowning on decadent times, the Strict Baptists maintain their witness down to the present, chiefly in the rural nooks of the south-east.[319] In the 1970s their publications were on sale in the

Free Presbyterian book-room in Inverness. Although the Strict Baptists were touched by later Evangelical influences, the core of the religion they shared with the most traditional of Highland Christians was still the Puritan divinity of the seventeenth century.

ENLIGHTENMENT ASSUMPTIONS

The Evangelical movement, however, was permeated by Enlightenment influences. Its leaders would casually refer to the opinion of Locke as settling an issue or to his *Essay* as providing the best account of the human mind.[320] The empiricist method learned by the eighteenth century from Locke became equally habitual. Thomas Scott appealed to the joint authority of 'the Scriptures and universal experience and observation'; Henry Venn put together experience and scripture, in that order.[321] Edwards rejected all views built upon 'what our reason would lead us to suppose without, or before experience'.[322] This was to adopt the inductive method of science. Isaac Newton had shown the eighteenth century the power of scientific investigation to discover truth. Why should its methods not be applied elsewhere? Hypotheses should be put to the test of the facts. Moving from the particular to the general, the investigator could establish general laws. Thus Wesley was reluctantly forced to admit that errors about the Trinity could accompany real piety when he came across an instance of it because, he declared, 'I cannot argue against matter of fact'.[323] Consequently, there was in the eighteenth century and long into the nineteenth no hint of a clash between Evangelical religion and science. 'We can make no progress in any science', wrote Venn, 'till we understand its first principles. In religion it is the same, that science, in which we all are most deeply interested.'[324] Admittedly a few Evangelicals in the Church of England were attracted by Hutchinsonianism, a system of belief rejecting Newton's views on the ground that the Bible contains a complete system of natural philosophy. T. T. Biddulph of Bristol held this position, as did William Romaine in his earlier years. But it is significant that Romaine was weaned from Hutchinsonianism as his Evangelical convictions deepened and Walker of Truro tried to guard Oxford undergraduates against imbibing the system.[325] Far more common was a warm appreciation of Newton, such as that of Joseph Milner.[326] It is the context of a fascination with science that explains much of Wesley's apparent credulity. He actually published a book on electricity, a field then on the borders of knowledge, as a curative agency.[327] It was impossible to distinguish in advance between promising and unpromising areas for exploration, but investigation, he held, is essential. Experiments, he urged, were the foundation of success in medicine.[328] In the light of these assumptions, it is not surprising that Evangelicals frequently spoke of true Christianity as 'experimental religion'. It must be tried by experience. Wesley called his 1780 hymn book 'a little

body of experimental and practical divinity'.[329] Edwards summed up the
attitudes of his co-religionists. 'As that is called experimental philosophy',
he wrote, 'which brings opinions and notions to the test of fact; so is that
properly called experimental religion, which brings religious affections
and intentions, to the like test.'[330] Evangelicals held Newtonian method
in high esteem.

A number of consequences flowed from this position. Early Evangelicals,
like their educated contemporaries, had an anti-metaphysical bent. In the
past, it was generally held, philosophers, especially of the scholastic camp,
had spent their time spinning cobwebs of discourse that obscured reality.
Now investigation of the facts made antiquated theories superfluous. Thus
John Witherspoon, the organiser of the Evangelical party in the Church
of Scotland who crossed the Atlantic to become Principal of Princeton,
found there that teaching was 'tinctured with the dry and unedifying
forms of the schools . . . He introduced into their philosophy all the most
liberal and modern improvements of Europe'.[331] Venn, by concentration
on observation and scripture, avoided 'all abstract reasoning about the
nature of the soul'.[332] Josiah Conder, a learned and highly orthodox
Congregationalist of the early nineteenth century, preferred plain scripture
language to what he called the 'vain philosophy' of the Westminster
Assembly's catechism, by which he meant Puritan technical terms like
'effectual calling'.[333] 'Keep off metaphysical ground', declared Richard
Cecil, probably the leading thinker among Evangelicals in the Church of
England at the turn of the nineteenth century.[334] Aversion to imposing
theoretical structures on scripture probably grew over time, culminating in
Simeon's dictum, 'Be Bible Christians, not system Christians'.[335] Systems
were not only distant from the facts; they were also bound to generate
differences of opinion. Enlightenment Evangelicals were eager to avoid
disputation. Biddulph steered clear of 'controverted points of doctrine'.[336]
One of two grand criticisms made by Wesley against the Puritans was that
'they drag in controversy on every occasion, nay, without any occasion or
pretence at all'.[337] His desire for peace was echoed by an early follower. 'I
have always been averse to disputing', wrote John Mason. 'I remember how
much I suffered thereby in the beginning of my turning to God. And I believe
it would be happy if all the children of God would strive to agree as far as
possible . . . '[338] Methodism, it has been pointed out, was remarkably free
in its earlier years from internal doctrinal controversy.[339] It was a symptom
of a principled preference for harmony over exact theological definition.

The devotion to science, experiment and investigation nevertheless did
not lead to a rejection of all philosophy. On the contrary, it generated
its own philosophical stance. Like their contemporaries, Evangelicals saw a
law-governed universe around them. Order had been established by the
Creator. The natural world furnished material for praise. Thus once at the
seaside William Wilberforce broke out into exuberant delight that God, far
from erecting a granite wall to prevent incursions by the sea, appointed

its bounds by means of mere grains of sand.[340] Natural theology was important. There were abundant evidences in the world of God's design. The chief role of reason, according to the Evangelical leaders as much as their orthodox contemporaries, was to weigh up the evidences in the way popularised by William Paley.[341] Reason must conclude in favour of the existence of a God who could reveal his will. This was no mere hope: James Lackington, a bookseller who deserted Methodism for freethinking, was restored to his faith by a battery of books on the evidences.[342] In the early nineteenth century the task of welding this scientific apologetic into the body of Christian theology was triumphantly achieved by Thomas Chalmers.[343]

Chalmers built on a class of writing increasingly regarded as the foundation of Evangelical thinking, the works of the Scottish common-sense school of philosophers. The founder of the school, Thomas Reid, argued in his *Inquiry into the Human Mind* (1764) that human beings perceive not ideas, as Locke had supposed, but the real world direct. This realism, or common-sense view, allowed that certain basic axioms of thought are grasped intuitively.[344] It enabled Evangelicals to express in a fresh way their belief in the accessibility of God. Defenders of the validity of conversions at Cambuslang anticipated an aspect of Reid in asserting the trustworthiness of the senses.[345] In fact, John Witherspoon, the organiser of Scottish Evangelicals before his departure to Princeton, claimed to have done battle for the philosophy of common sense for a decade before Reid published his treatise.[346] Certainly Witherspoon expounded the views of Reid and his circle, 'some late writers', once he reached America: 'there are certain first principles, or dictates of common sense, which are either simple perceptions, or seen with intuitive evidence. These are the foundation of all reasoning, and without them to reason is a word without a meaning. They can no more be proved than you can prove an axiom in mathematical science . . . '[347] Like Reid, Witherspoon uses this premiss as a ground for repudiating unwelcome elements in the thought of Locke and Hume. He regards Locke's objections to innate ideas as 'wholly frivolous': human beings do possess, for example, a moral sense. Again, Hume had contended that, since all we know is in the form of ideas, there can be no guarantee that our ideas correspond to reality. His scepticism extended to questioning the very existence of causation. Witherspoon insists on the contrary that the condition of all understanding of the world is the belief that everything must have a cause.[348] The conviction that the pattern of cause and effect, the scientist's natural assumption, underlies all phenomena was to pervade Evangelical thinking long into the nineteenth century and, in many quarters, beyond that.[349] The academic citadel of such an approach was Scotland, but, as common-sense philosophy spread through the propagandism of Dugald Stewart and the Edinburgh reviewers, it increasingly became the standard supposition of the educated Englishman as well.[350] Evangelicals were integrating their faith with the rising philosophy of the later Enlightenment. They were in harmony with the spirit of the age.

OPTIMISM

Likewise Evangelicals reflected the later Enlightenment in their optimistic temper. The eighteenth century, and especially its second half, characteristically believed that humanity enjoyed great potential for improvement. It was the later eighteenth century that witnessed the emergence of the idea of progress, the conviction that human beings are steadily becoming wiser and therefore better.[351] The Arminianism of the Methodists can be seen as an equivalent 'optimism of grace', a theology that does not limit the possibility of Christian renewal to the narrow company of the elect.[352] There was also greater hope about the human condition among the Reformed who learned from Edwards to trust their quickened religious affections. One of Edwards's American disciples calculated that the proportion of the lost to the saved would eventually be in the ratio of 1 to 17,456 1/3.[353] All Evangelicals were animated in their outreach by the expectation that salvation was widely available.

They were also convinced that God wished human beings to be happy. 'Holiness is happiness' has been seen as the fundamental principle of Wesley's theology.[354] Many of his followers behaved as though it were. 'I was still happy', wrote one; 'but found a strong desire to be more holy that I might be more happy.'[355] But identification of happiness as the grand goal of humanity, a typical theme of more liberal moralists such as Hutcheson, was shared by Calvinists as well as Methodists. Maclaurin wrote a 'Philosophical Inquiry into the Nature of Happiness'; Venn contended that the children of God 'know more pleasure than any people on earth'; Wilberforce described happiness as the end of civil society.[356] Yet Methodists went further in embracing the perfectibility of man. Wesley disagreed with those enlightened thinkers who supposed that all human beings might attain perfection. For Wesley, only the regenerate possess the essential qualification. Experience taught him, however, as he explains in his *Plain Account of Christian Perfection* (1766), that believers may progress to a state in which they are free from all known sin. No aspect of Methodist teaching gave more openings for ridicule. There was much glee when a 'perfect' sister was detected stealing coal from a 'sanctified' brother.[357] Wesley sorrowfully noted such cases, concluding that the state could readily be lost, but he nevertheless insisted on its reality.[358] He criticised the Puritans for holding so low and imperfect a view of sanctification.[359] In this area, Calvinist Evangelicals remained loyal to their Puritan forefathers. Their arguments could nevertheless be cast in a new form. Walker of Truro, for instance, laid down that perfect holiness is necessary for perfect happiness; the perfect can be a work of God alone; it cannot be expected in this life; there can be progress only in the perfecting of the believer.[360] Even in rejecting Wesley's teaching, Walker commended progress towards the goal of happiness. As much as the Utilitarian school, Evangelicals elevated happiness into the primary place among human objectives. In seeing vital Christianity as the way to achieve it, they were differing from the Utilitarians about means, not ends.

The basis for optimism was the doctrine of providence. God, Evangelicals believed, is in active control of the world. Confidence in his government formed a larger part of their creed than might be supposed. For Biddulph, providence was pre-eminent among doctrines.[361] John Newton's hymns are full of the theme. 'There is no such thing as accident', he declared.[362] A distinction was normally drawn between general providence, the overall superintendence of the earth by its Creator, and particular providences, direct divine interventions in the course of events. Particular providences were of two kinds, displaying either the judgement or the mercy of God. In the first category were put such incidents as when the town clerk of Wincanton, after reading the Riot Act to disperse the hearers of a Methodist preacher, immediately started to bleed copiously from the nostrils, became a lunatic and soon afterwards died.[363] Judgement was expected on nations as well as individuals if they persisted in corporate sins like tolerating the slave trade.[364] Likewise mercies could be individual or national. Thomas Scott believed that God 'always steps in just at the crisis . . . I never prayed for money but I got it'.[365] One Methodist was brought to conviction of sin by deliverance from an overturning wagon; another saw divine mercy in a narrow escape from the fall of a building; another, in being preserved from the collapse of a roof in a Cornish tin mine.[366] The Eclectic Society of London ministers spent a meeting in 1801 cataloguing 'the signal interpositions of providence in favour of Britain during the late war'. The death of the Czar of Russia shortly after he had turned from opposing to supporting France was cited as one of many wonderful examples.[367]

If particular providences were sometimes dwelt on at the Eclectic, however, there was also a tendency to caution. In accordance with the canons of scientific investigation, alleged instances of special divine interference contrary to the course of nature should be treated with 'the most rigid suspicion'. The providential government was normally maintained by 'second causes', that is, through the regular course of events.[368] The very order of the Newtonian universe, in history as well as nature, glorified its divine architect. 'God has so assigned to things their general tendencies', according to Wilberforce, 'and established such an order of causes and effects, as . . . loudly proclaim the principles of his moral government . . . '[369] If Evangelicals were sometimes more forward than their contemporaries in detecting the hand of God in particular events, their general attitude to providence was close to that taught by central eighteenth-century thinkers such as Joseph Butler and Edmund Burke.[370] All alike saw the historical process as subject to the divine sovereignty. That was why all alike could look with confidence to the future.

Optimism was expressed in doctrinal form through belief in a millennium. In the eighteenth century millenarianism was no fanatical aberration of the social outcast but a common preoccupation of the intellectual. Expectation of a future state of unblemished happiness on earth was widely held by philosophically inclined theologians of the time.[371] Many Evangelicals shared the belief. It appeared to be founded on the statement in Revelation, chapter 20, that Satan would be bound for a thousand years. It drew extra support from passages predicting a future outpouring of the Spirit in the latter days. The particular version of the belief held in the Enlightenment era was uniformly postmillennial: the second coming of Christ, that is to say, would not take place until after the millennium. There would therefore be no sharp break from preceding history. Rather, the millennium would be the result of gradual improvement – a belief that shaded into the idea of progress. Evangelicals identified the future epoch as a time of peace and glory for the church that would follow on persistent mission.

They could draw on earlier Reformed writers who cherished a similar hope.[372] The outbreak of revival, however, quickened expectations of the imminent approach of the latter days. Erskine expressed such anticipations in his work on Cambuslang, *The Signs of the Times Consider'd* (1742).[373] More famously Edwards announced the same, but added, in a work of 1743, the speculation that the millennium would come to birth in America. 'The new world', he wrote, 'is probably now discovered, that the new and most glorious state of God's church on earth might commence there . . . '[374] Perhaps more congenial to British readers was his subsequent argument, in *An Humble Attempt* (1747), that unfulfilled prophecy is an incentive to prayer.[375] This work, influential in Britain after its republication in 1784, did much to foster millennial expectations. Its editor, the Baptist John Sutcliff, nevertheless expressed the hope that if a reader held different views of prophecy he would not withhold prayer for revival.[376] Doddridge had rejected the very notion of a millennium; Erskine's biographer excused him for his apocalyptic guesswork on the score of youth; and Conder, writing in 1838, treated millenarianism as an aberration.[377] It is clear that the Evangelical world was far from unanimous on the matter. Yet William Carey, explicitly appealing to Edwards, held that no fulfilment of prophecy would intervene before the conversion of the heathen that would usher in the millennium.[378] Similar expectations surrounded the foundation of the London Missionary Society.[379] John Venn, son of Henry, told the Eclectic Society that a future period of peace and glory for the church is clearly predicted in scripture. Scott and Cecil concurred.[380] A Scottish Secession Presbytery minuted in 1787 its anticipation of 'the iminent [sic] glory of the latter days'.[381] Thomas Chalmers wrote of 'that universal reign of truth and of righteousness which is coming'.[382] The postmillennial theory was evidently widespread. Evangelicals shared high hopes for the future with their contemporaries.

MODERATE CALVINISM

The substance of Reformed doctrine was also remodelled under Enlightenment influence. Apart from Methodists, General Baptists and a few avowedly Arminian clergy, some of the other Evangelical Anglicans, especially by the start of the nineteenth century, were beginning to disclaim Calvinist tenets.[383] The remainder of the Evangelical world, however, was professedly Calvinist. Yet there was also a certain reserve in their allegiance. Edwards was content to be called a Calvinist, 'for distinction's sake: though I utterly disclaim a dependence on Calvin'.[384] The influential Baptist Andrew Fuller similarly declared, 'I do not believe every thing that Calvin taught, nor any thing because he taught it'.[385] John Erskine was Calvinistic in doctrine, but his version, according to his biographer, was 'not the vulgar Calvinism, which exhausts itself on intricate and mysterious dogmas'.[386] In 1808 an Evangelical clergyman claimed to have heard only one sermon on predestination in twenty years.[387] 'Calvinism', according to John Newton, 'should be, in our general religious instructions, like a lump of sugar in a cup of tea; all should taste of it, but it should not be met with in a separate form.'[388] This diffuse doctrinal system was sometimes labelled 'moderate Calvinism'.[389] In its refusal to subordinate free inquiry to the authority of one man, in its repudiation of mysterious dogma, in its very moderation, it was a typical product of the eighteenth century.

This was supremely true of its moralistic tone. Because Evangelicals preached salvation by faith, they could on occasion be heard teaching that obedience to the divine law is humanly impossible or dismissing misrepresentations of Christianity as a 'mere system of ethics'.[390] A small number like Romaine so exalted faith that they seemed to depreciate law. Romaine was said to have made many antinomians – that is, to have propagated the view that the believer is not bound by the moral law.[391] This was the central charge thrown in the face of Evangelicals as a whole by their critics. They were condemned for subverting morality, at least at the theoretical level. But it was a judgement wide of the mark in nearly every case. With the possible exception of Romaine and a few others, Evangelicals urged only that obedience to the law will not avail for salvation unless preceded by faith. 'Christ the lawgiver', declares Venn, 'will always speak in vain, without Christ the Saviour is first known.'[392] Venn's *Complete Duty of Man* insists that faith is essential if the law is to be obeyed. Equally, however, it teaches that the law does apply to the believer.[393] Hence Evangelicals concentrated on ethical themes. Venn dwells on family duties. Of Erskine's published sermons it was noted that sound morality occupied by far the greatest part.[394] All true faith, according to a central plank of Scott's teaching, 'must and will prove itself by its fruits'.[395] The summons to holiness was constantly heard in the Evangelical pulpit. A preoccupation with moral instruction was quite as characteristic of Evangelicals as of other theological parties of the period.

Evangelical Calvinism was also moderate in that it rejected stronger views of God's control of human destiny. Evangelicals were not fatalists. Human beings, they emphatically taught, are responsible agents. Edwards supplied the intellectual tools for their approach in his treatise on *Freedom of the Will* (1754). He distinguishes between the natural necessity of human actions, which he rejects, and their moral necessity, which he commends. He means that human beings are not compelled by God to behave contrary to their wills. Rather, the freedom they possess to follow their wills is compatible with their actions being determined by preceding conditions. Free acts are not forced, though they are caused. This was to contend that human beings are part of an ordered universe, but to hold that they are nevertheless responsible for what they do.[396] Edwards was reinterpreting the sovereignty of God as an expression of the law of cause and effect. He was echoed in England by Scott, according to whom divine sovereignty is 'in perfect consistency with . . . free agency and accountableness'.[397] Hence human beings, not God, are responsible for their own damnation. Scott laid down, in the words of his biographer, 'that none fail of being saved . . . except by their own fault'.[398] Evangelicals generally repudiated the traditional Calvinist doctrine of reprobation, that God had destined certain souls to hell. Instead human beings were considered guilty of causing their own perdition by failing to respond to the gospel.[399]

A cardinal principle of the Evangelical scheme was 'duty faith'. 'It is the duty of men to believe', declared William Goode at the Eclectic.[400] Debate between Calvinists touched by enlightened thought and those who clung to older forms often revolved round whether believing in Christ can be considered a moral obligation. It was the so-called 'modern question'. The controversy first arose among Northamptonshire Independents in the late 1730s. It drew in John Gill, the Baptist systematic theologian, on the side of the traditionalists, while Doddridge supported the promoters of 'modern' thought.[401] Strict Baptists continued to repudiate duty faith in the following century.[402] The issue proved the dividing line between Evangelicals and unreconstructed Calvinists partly because it was highly practical. If believing was an obligation, preachers could press it on whole congregations. If it was not, they could merely describe it in the hope that God would rouse certain predetermined hearers to faith. Those on the modern side had a rationale for urgent evangelism, the so-called invitation system.[403] The logic of Evangelical activism was founded on the doctrine of duty faith. It was most systematically expounded by Andrew Fuller, the Baptist theologian who put his convictions into practice by becoming the first secretary of the Baptist Missionary Society. Fuller's *The Gospel Worthy of All Acceptation* (1785) is the classic statement of eighteenth-century Evangelical Calvinism. But the inspiration for Fuller's thinking can be traced back to Edwards, and especially his formulation of the distinction between moral and natural necessity.[404] Edward Williams, the Independents' equivalent of Fuller, owed the same debt to Edwards; Milner refers to Edwards's 'masterly treatise on Free-will'; and in Scotland Chalmers declared, 'My Theology is that of Jonathan Edwards'.[405] There can be no doubt that Edwards was the chief architect of the theological structures erected by Evangelicals in the Reformed tradition. That was sufficient to ensure that they were built on Enlightenment foundations.

PRAGMATISM

The spirit of the age – flexible, tolerant, utilitarian – affected Evangelicals as much in practice as in thought. Field preaching, an activity that lay near the heart of the revival, was an embodiment of the pragmatic temper. If people would not come to church, they must be won for Christ in the open air. Wesley was content to flout parish boundaries for the sake of souls. His justification was the effectiveness of open-air preaching in attracting large numbers, inducing conviction of sin and bringing about conversions.[406] His utilitarian approach to religious practice helps explain why Wesley quotes Proverbs and Ecclesiastes more than any other biblical books.[407] The same temper informed other Evangelicals. Typical was Charles Simeon's attitude to church buildings. Having acquired the living of Cheltenham in 1817, he set about planning a new church. It must be severely functional, like a Methodist chapel rather than a traditional parish church. In the style of Bentham's Panopticon, it was to be cheap and there were to be no obstacles to clear vision such as pillars. Supremely it was designed for preaching. Old churches, he wrote, were not built to preach in; 'and after the experience we have had of them it is folly & madness to raise for preaching any further edifices after their model'.[408]

Likewise the priorities of the gospel dictated the deployment of manpower. Although the most rigid of Evangelical churchmen remonstrated with Wesley on the matter,[409] the existence of Methodism depended on the use of preachers who were laymen. Their employment in church work became a hallmark of Evangelicals in the Church of England, so that their creation in 1836, the Church Pastoral Aid Society, was intended (to the disgust of High Churchmen) to support lay parish workers as much as additional parish clergy.[410] In the Church of Scotland, Chalmers's ministry was notable for the revival of the lay office of deacon;[411] and in English Dissent laymen were sent out in large numbers as preachers, either voluntary or salaried.[412] Justification for female preaching was expressed in terms of gospel pragmatism. 'If persons who exercise in the ministry are of good report', wrote the Primitive Methodist leader Hugh Bourne with particular reference to women, 'and the Lord owns their labours by turning sinners to righteousness, we do not think it our duty to endeavour to hinder them . . . '[413] It was an argument from success characteristic of Evangelicals in their Enlightenment era.

The relegation of principle relative to pragmatism was evident in church order. Methodism, as some of its nineteenth-century defenders delighted to insist, was totally flexible on this subject.[414] Wesley and his adjutants initially had 'no plan at all'.[415] He approved of bishops, but could see no reason for restricting certain powers to their office and so was prepared, in 1784, to ordain presbyters for America himself.[416] The Plan of Pacification of 1795 that settled connexional practice after Wesley's death was an avowed compromise between contesting parties.[417] Above all, Methodists did not have to be Christians. Admission as full class members was open to all who sought the forgiveness of sins and not just to those already converted. Thus a preacher could report 38 new members of a group of classes at the same time as 23 additions 'to the church of the living God'.[418] There was no correspondence between joining the Methodist organisation and entering the true church. The organisation was merely an environment suitable for gaining converts.

A similar utilitarian spirit modified ecclesiastical order among Dissenters, whose *raison d'être* had originally been the creation of church structures of pristine purity. The New Connexion of General Baptists could not contemplate merger with the Old partly because the traditionalists insisted on the imposition of hands at baptism and the obligation of abstaining from blood.[419] For the Evangelicals of the New Connexion these were matters of no importance. Particular Baptists shifted towards opening the Lord's Table to those not baptised as believers when Evangelicalism moderated their views.[420] Likewise, in the ecclesiastical strife of Scotland over patronage in the later eighteenth century, the Evangelicals of the Popular party, unlike their Moderate opponents, thought little of the letter of church law.[421] In England churchmen were prepared to co-operate with Dissenters. 'In this day of darkness and licentiousness', according to Walker of Truro, 'it becomes all the friends of the Gospel to bear with one another; and while they differ in opinion and denomination, to unite together in heart and endeavour for the support of the common cause.'[422] Although it has recently been pointed out that modern denominations were themselves the fruit of the revival, essentially agencies to promote evangelism,[423] it is nevertheless true that what Whitefield called a '*catholic spirit*'[424] was generated among Evangelicals. This was perhaps most true in the late 1790s when home mission was at its most vigorous. The interdenominational temper led to the establishment of a variety of organisations for joint endeavour, including the London Missionary Society, which drew supporters from many denominations in the early years, and the British and Foreign Bible Society, an enduring monument to the possibilities of co-operation.[425] Such bodies exemplified an abandonment of exclusive denominationalism, a certain practical empiricism.

LITERATURE

The Enlightenment mood affected the taste of Evangelicals. It is a mistake to suppose that they shunned literature. Theatrical performances they did deplore as tending to demoralise, but many of them enjoyed reading selected dramatic works in the privacy of their own homes. Fiction, a recent art form, was sometimes suspect, although Wesley abridged a novel for publication. Almost the whole Evangelical world read poetry.[426] Even among Dissenters there was an elite devoted to literature. The Pattisson family of Witham in Essex eagerly discussed the latest publications in the years round 1800.[427] After ordination to the ministry of the Church of Scotland in 1742, according to his biographer, John Gillies's 'fondness for literary amusements still continued'.[428] Taste was formed by the classics. Gillies could quote appositely (and 'sometimes with pleasantry and humour') from Horace and Virgil; Horace was likewise Wesley's favourite.[429] The Baptist divine Robert Hall declared 'that we should gain nothing by neglecting the unrivalled productions of genius left us by the ancients, but a deterioration of taste . . . '[430] Hence classical canons of literary decorum prevailed. '"What is it", asked Wesley, "that constitutes *a good style?*" Perspicuity and purity, propriety, strength, and easiness, joined together.'[431] Wesley commended Swift, with his ability to wield language like a rapier, as a model for imitation.[432] Swift's favourite genre, satire, was indulged in by Evangelicals, for were there not classical precedents? The most telling published assault on the Moderates in the Church of Scotland, John Witherspoon's *Ecclesiastical Characteristics* (1753), was no reasoned argument, but rather an unrestrained ridiculing of their legalistic zeal for church discipline.[433] Charles Wesley incorporated satirical sallies against Calvinism in many of his hymns.[434] It was all entirely in accordance with the temper of an age that regarded ridicule as the test of truth. Protestantism had passed through a Baroque phase but had emerged, in its Evangelical form, in the Augustan atmosphere of the Enlightenment.

There is a host of other symptoms. The prolix scholarship of the earlier era was no longer congenial. Although John Wesley prepared for the press his father's discursive *Studies in the Book of Job* (1735), he later commented that it 'certainly contains immense Learning, but of a kind which I do not admire'.[435] The number of headings in Independent sermons plummeted from the twenties or thirties to two or three.[436] Erotic themes, common in the religious verse of the Metaphysical school and still present in Watts, were eliminated by Charles Wesley and censured by his brother.[437] The Evangelicals were deeply imbued with the classicism of Pope. Thus, when their Unitarian friend Crabb Robinson tried to interest the Pattissons of Witham in Kant and Wordsworth, they resolutely adhered to a preference for Locke and Pope.[438] Reading as much as thinking was conditioned by the Enlightenment.

The Augustan tone is evident in the greatest literary achievement of the revival, the hymnody of Charles Wesley. Because his hymns express feeling in common vocabulary, they have sometimes been classified as anticipations of the Romantic era. The content and the manner, however, both bear testimony to their being characteristic expressions of Augustanism.[439] The themes are often the standard ones of the classical lyric poet. There is, for example, material on melancholy and pastoral retirement.[440] Because content is primarily dictated by Christian purpose, however, the manner is where the spirit of the age is most obvious. Classical metrical forms are drawn from near contemporaries. Dryden, Pope and Prior are the models for diction, and Cowley, the pioneer of classical correctness in verse, is admired.[441] While also esteeming poets of more traditional idiom such as Milton and Young, Charles Wesley is therefore a disciple of the *avant-garde* of the literary Enlightenment in its displacement of the Baroque. Emotion is present, but always carefully controlled, as in his meditations on the passion of Christ. The hymns are didactic, for their aim is to transmit doctrine to their singers. Yet this quality is as much a feature of the age as a consequence of their purpose. The language is clear, precise and succinct. Latin-derived words are strategically placed to embody a depth of meaning in a short space. In one line profundity can be mingled with paradox: 'Impassive He suffers, immortal He dies'.[442] John Wesley supplied the most apt comment on his brother's verse in his preface to the 1780 *Collection of Hymns* for Methodist use: 'Here are (allow me to say) both the purity, the strength, and the elegance of the English language – and at the same time the utmost simplicity and plainness, suited to every capacity'.[443] It was a fair statement of the Augustan ideal.

Hymns were part of a vast educational campaign undertaken by the Wesleys. As much as the circle around *The Edinburgh Review*, they aimed for the diffusion of useful knowledge. 'Reading Christians', according to John Wesley, 'will be knowing Christians.'[444] He designed *The Christian Library* (1749–55) in fifty volumes to convey practical divinity to his followers. It consisted of a range of spiritual classics, many of them abridged by the editor. In conformity with his canons of taste, Wesley believed in brevity: 'if Angels were to write books', he remarked, 'we should have very few Folios'.[445] Conciseness would increase circulation. His preachers dutifully absorbed the series, and in the 1820s there still existed sufficient demand to call for the reprint of one of the volumes every two months.[446] From 1778 Wesley issued the monthly *Arminian Magazine* to encourage the reading habit. By his death its monthly circulation was about 7,000.[447] One Methodist father presented each of his children with a copy of the magazine bound in calf.[448] Wesley tried to maintain a tight control over ideas circulating in the connexion. No preacher, on pain of expulsion, was to go into print without his approval, or, after 1781, without his correction.[449] 'There are thousands in this society', wrote a critic in 1795, 'who will never read anything besides the Bible, and books published by Mr Wesley.'[450] All preachers were to carry a stock of his writings to sell or give away; they must spend at least five hours a day in study; they were to ride with a slack rein so that, in imitation of Wesley himself, they could read on horseback; and when staying in a household above an hour, they should take out a book to read as a good example.[451] Wesley expected high standards of his men. In 1764 he read through the first edition of his work on philosophy with the London preachers.[452] Through the efforts of the preachers, through class meetings and reading circles, learning spread among the rank and file of his followers. Because they wasted little time but regularly heard sermons, poor Methodists, it was said, possessed far more knowledge than the poor in general.[453]

What was systematically organised in Methodism was pursued ad hoc in other branches of Evangelicalism. Yet a zest for understanding the faith, often nourished on libraries in church or chapel, did much to foster self-improvement. Dissenting colleges modelled on Trevecca multiplied, and their products, though rarely distinguished academically, at least imbibed a respect for knowledge.[454] From 1783 the Sunday School movement expanded rapidly, bringing basic instruction to thousands.[455] Tracts were distributed in huge quantities. From 1799 there existed the Religious Tract Society for their production.[456] In 1841 alone the Methodist Book Room sold 1,326,049 of them.[457] Evangelical religion was a force dedicated to the advance of education. The imperative of spreading Bible knowledge demanded it. But the fulfilment of religious duty was entirely in harmony with the goal of eighteenth-century progressive thinkers: the enlightenment of the masses.

HUMANITARIANISM

The Evangelical education enterprise has often been seen as a masked attempt at social control. The bulk of the population, growing in numbers and entering a phase of rapid social change induced by industrialisation, had to be kept in its place. Evangelical teaching was a suitable tool. Especially in the wake of the French Revolution, submission to the existing order was given a divine sanction.[458] A variant of the argument is the thesis of Ford K. Brown that Evangelicals with Wilberforce at their head were concerned to seize control of church and state in order to seek power through enforcing their own values on the nation at large.[459] It is true that the 'reformation of manners' was an Evangelical preoccupation. Wilberforce and his circle secured in 1787 a royal proclamation against crime and public immorality and formed a Proclamation Society to prod backward magistrates into enforcing it.[460] But this was not primarily designed to enhance the power of the rulers. Significantly, the measure came before the French Revolution had broken out. It was an expression of Evangelical hostility to sin coupled with a pragmatic preparedness to employ state power, as much as private exhortation or pulpit admonition, to do battle with it. Wilberforce's friend Hannah More composed a series of tracts in the 1790s that were intended to repress revolutionary tendencies and were circulated at government expense. *Village Politics* (1792), the first in the series, presents the homely counsel of Jack Anvil, the village blacksmith, to live contentedly in a well-ordered England under the wise dispensations of providence. But if Hannah More insisted on the duties of the poor, she had already written on the obligations of their superiors. In *Thoughts on the Importance of the Manners of the Great* (1788) she had castigated the gentry for neglect of their paternalist role.[461] Like many others in the eighteenth century, Evangelicals put the emphasis in social teaching on reciprocal duties, not exclusively on passive acceptance of their lot by the worse off.

Traditionalist they were, by and large, but Evangelicals believed in a conscientious performance of traditional responsibilities. With the growth of their influence in the following century, a much higher proportion of the gentry resided on their estates in order to take a personal interest in their tenants. It has been suggested that Evangelicalism is a cause and greater residence the effect.[462] Likewise ministers of religion were roused to greater zeal in the performance of their duties. Although in Scotland the custom of visiting the flock had been generally maintained, in England, as the clergy rose in income and social status during the eighteenth century, mixing with their inferiors became less expected of them. The hunting, shooting and fishing parson was a common type. It was the Evangelical movement that prompted the clergy to greater diligence, especially in cottage visiting.[463] Stirring the elite in church and state to care for the poor may have had the effect of reinforcing the social order, but its primary purpose was to ensure that the privileged took a humane interest in the welfare, secular and spiritual, of those committed to their charge.

Philanthropy was actively promoted by Evangelicals from the beginning of the movement. Wesley's generosity was legendary. He would scatter coins to beggars, he waded through snow in old age to raise money for the relief of the poor and he died worth virtually nothing because his considerable income from publications was given away.[464] Evangelicalism as a whole taught that good works are a fundamental element of Christian duty.[465] There was continuity between traditional teaching on concern for the poor, as expressed for instance in the religious societies of the Church of England, and the charitable work of Evangelicals. What the revival added was its characteristic zeal. There was a proliferation of local schemes for doing good. Wesley encouraged his followers to visit the sick, going in pairs.[466] The Calvinistic Methodist London Tabernacle ran a workshop for a while and later an employment exchange.[467] Perhaps most strikingly, there were the orphan houses. Halle provided the model. Both Whitefield and Wesley lavished their care on similar institutions, in Georgia and Newcastle respectively. Whitefield expended enormous energy on planning, organising, supporting and defending his orphanage. 'I called it Bethesda', he wrote, 'that is, the House of Mercy; for I hope many acts of mercy will be shewn there . . .'[468] The Evangelical impulse was to give rise to an empire of philanthropy in the nineteenth century,[469] but already before the eighteenth was over almsgiving was becoming systematically organised. Methodism gave rise to a number of Strangers' Friend Societies. The first existed in London by 1784. 'A few poor men', according to Wesley, '. . . agreed to pay each a penny a week in order to relieve strangers who had no habitation – no clothes – no food – no friends. They met once a week, and assigned to each his share of the work for the ensuing week; to discover proper objects (who, indeed, were easily found); and to relieve them according to their several necessities.'[470] Such charitable work can hardly be attributed to the Enlightenment. It was the spontaneous expression of a Christian movement. Yet it was entirely in harmony with the spirit of an age that set benevolence among its highest values.

On the other hand, the greatest example of Evangelical humanitarianism, the anti-slavery campaign, was undoubtedly the fruit of the Enlightenment. Anti-slavery was not intrinsic to Evangelicalism: some of the stoutest defenders of slavery in the American South were preachers of the gospel.[471] It was the tide of opinion running against slavery among the philosophical luminaries of the eighteenth century that prepared the way for British abolition of the slave trade in 1807 and the extinction of the institution in British dominions under an act of 1833. Benevolence, happiness and liberty, three leading principles of the time, all created a presumption in favour of abolition. Unless they had been thoroughly imbued with these values themselves, Evangelicals would not have taken up the cause. As it was, however, Wilberforce and the Clapham Sect, overwhelmingly though not exclusively Evangelicals of the Church of England, dedicated themselves to the elimination of what, with other progressive thinkers, they condemned out of hand. What Evangelicals brought to the campaign was not a fresh theoretical perspective but the dedication that compelled them to act.[472]

The ending of the slave trade did not come about (as was once held) because it had ceased to be profitable to Britain. Evangelicals were by no means pawns in the hands of economic interests.[473] There is nevertheless a tendency in contemporary historiography to play down the Evangelical contribution to anti-slavery. It is true that other groups took important parts. The Quakers, only beginning to be touched by Evangelical religion, supplied money, manpower and ideas, moving into action before the Evangelicals.[474] There was popular radical participation in anti-slavery from the 1790s onwards.[475] The slaves, by their frequent rebellions that created problems of colonial administration, helped free themselves.[476] Yet Evangelicals were central to the whole enterprise. Wilberforce contributed able leadership, his college friendship with Pitt, the Prime Minister, proving a huge advantage to the cause; information was assiduously collected by Thomas Clarkson and the James Stephens, father and son; missionaries fostered sympathy for the oppressed blacks; and in 1831–3 there was a mighty upsurge of Evangelical public opinion in favour of ending slavery.[477] A number equivalent to ninety-five per cent of the connexion's membership signed Wesleyan anti-slavery parliamentary petitions in those years.[478] It has been suggested that mass abolitionism was created not by Evangelicalism but by the vision of artisans whose ambience was also favourable to Evangelical Nonconformity. Yet contemporaries were in no doubt that arguments based on biblical principle did most to rouse anti-slavery feeling.[479] Although favourable parliamentary circumstances must also be taken into account – the Talents administration of 1806–7 was more sympathetic to abolition than its Pittite predecessor and the extension of the franchise in 1832 sounded the death-knell of slavery – it remains true that the main impetus against both trade and institution came from the religious public. Evangelicalism cannot be given all the credit for the humanitarian victory over slavery, but it must be accorded a large share.

POLITICS

Although anti-slavery swept a large proportion of the Evangelical public into exerting pressure on government, in general its leaders discouraged involvement in the political sphere. Here was an area of sharp contrast with their Puritan forebears, who for the most part saw the achievement of a holy commonwealth as one of their grand aims. Partisan endeavour now seemed a diversion from the one essential task of preaching the gospel. 'Politics', declared Thomas Jones of Creaton, a leading Evangelical clergyman, 'are Satan's most tempting and alluring baits.'[480] It is sinful, according to John Witherspoon in Scotland in 1758, for a minister 'to desire or claim the direction of such matters as fall within the province of the civil magistrate'.[481] Even Dissenters, who operated largely as a united political phalanx in the interest of civil and religious liberty, began to have doubts about the wisdom of pressing their cause. It is true that in the early 1790s Robert Hall was defending the freedom of the press and his fellow-Baptist William Winterbotham was imprisoned for preaching sermons allegedly sympathetic to the French Revolution.[482] Political activity in the wartime years that followed, however, was minimal. The Baptist Western Association, for instance, did little more than announce its opposition to military training on the sabbath.[483] Hall became so indifferent to political concerns that he scarcely ever read a newspaper.[484] Fuller was typical of the Evangelical sector of Dissent in deprecating strife between Whigs and Tories: 'it is not for the wise and the good to enlist themselves under their respective standards, or to believe half what they say'.[485] Wesley's legacy to his followers was a 'no politics' rule that forbade the agitation of controverted questions within the connexion.[486] It is clear that Wesleyan voters took no common line. At Bristol in 1784, for instance, they divided in approximately the same proportions as the electors at large.[487]

What vital Christianity entailed, according to many Evangelicals, was a blend of quietism and loyalism. 'I meddle not with the disputes of party', wrote John Newton, 'nor concern myself about any political maxims, but such as are laid down in scripture.'[488] He was no doubt thinking chiefly, as did Wesley, about commands to respect those in authority and pay taxes.[489] Wesley lamented popular participation in politics, discouraged sympathy for the Americans in the 1770s and helped ensure that after his death official Methodism steered a steady patriotic course.[490] Wilberforce eulogised 'the unrivalled excellence' of the British constitution.[491] Alongside his friends with reforming objectives in the Clapham Sect, there was a much larger bloc of Evangelical MPs from 1784 onwards with unqualified Tory views.[492] Likewise, after the French Revolution the Evangelical clergy were overwhelmingly Tory.[493] Most enfranchised Dissenters continued to prefer the Whigs. Nevertheless, attachment to the existing political order was the most prominent feature of attitudes to public affairs among all sections of Evangelical opinion down to the end of the French Wars.

There were, however, two areas apart from anti-slavery in which sections of the Evangelical world were more liberal. One was the American Revolution. Dissenters and the Popular party in the Church of Scotland generally backed the American cause. Caleb Evans of the Baptist College at Bristol rebutted Wesley's attack on the colonists as a revival of 'the good old Jacobite doctrine of hereditary, indefensible, divine right and of passive obedience and non-resistance'.[494] Most Baptist ministers in the provinces and all but two of them in London were believed to have taken the American side.[495] Scottish Evangelicals similarly upheld the colonists' case. John Erskine warned against conflict with the colonies as early as 1769 and in 1776 called for a compromise settlement.[496] John Witherspoon, the Scottish Evangelical who had become Principal of Princeton, so far forgot his earlier objections to ministers dabbling in politics as to be the only one to sign the Declaration of Independence.[497] The bonds between Presbyterians on the two sides of the Atlantic helped foster the sympathy for American resistance to George III. So did a dislike for oppression and a fear that true religion was under threat in North America from Catholics and Episcopalians.

Similar motives induced many Evangelicals to adopt another liberal stance in the era of toleration. It was to be expected that Dissenters such as Hall would approve of the principle of religious liberty.[498] But so did others. Thomas Scott wrote of 'the vast obligation' owed to Locke for his *Letters Concerning Toleration*.[499] Adam Clarke, admittedly the most Whiggish of Methodist leaders, broadened the principle into an Arminian constitutional axiom. 'Of all forms of government', he commented, 'that which provides the greatest portion of civil liberty to the subject, must be most pleasing to God, because most like his own.'[500] Wesley himself favoured religious tolerance. He opposed the removal of Catholic disabilities, it is true, but on the ground that the Roman Catholic Church was itself theoretically committed to persecution. He was not prepared to tolerate intolerance. Otherwise he was the foe of bigotry, the champion of entire liberty of conscience.[501]

Scottish Evangelicals, though convinced in the same way as Wesley that concessions to Catholics were too much of a gamble,[502] shared a favourable disposition towards religious toleration. It was part of that broad, humane, pragmatic outlook that characterised their attitudes in so many spheres.

THE RISE OF EVANGELICALISM

The Evangelical Revival represents a sharp discontinuity in the Protestant tradition. It was formed by a cultural shift in the English-speaking world, the transition from the Baroque era to the Enlightenment. In most spheres of taste and fancy a new phase opened early in the eighteenth century. The philosophy of Locke was the greatest motor of change, but literature and art, all forms of human expression, were affected. The prose of Addison and the verse of Pope marked a breakthrough to severe classicism from the greater exuberance of the previous age. The Third Earl of Shaftesbury censured Wren, an architect recently venerated, for having failed to follow classical or Italian models and so ruining the skyline of the City of London with buildings tainted by the Gothic.[503] Religion could not go unscathed by such a revolution in taste. It is a commonplace that much Protestant thought followed a path of religious liberalism that led through Latitudinarianism and Socinianism towards a Unitarian destination, though sometimes stopping far short of that goal. What has rarely been perceived is that other strands of Protestantism, despite being tenaciously orthodox, were equally affected by the Enlightenment atmosphere. The legacy of the Puritans, in both faith and practice, was modified by the temper of the new era without losing its grasp of central Christian tenets. The old introspective piety, with its casuistry and reflex syllogisms, and the old polemical divinity, with its metaphysical distinctions and ecclesiastical preoccupations, faded away before the preaching of a simple gospel. A rearguard action was fought by men like Adam Gib, the theologian of the Anti-Burgher Seceders in Scotland, who suffered from gloomy spiritual apprehensions, split his denomination on a fine point of principle and published in his seventy-third year a rambling theological work entitled *Sacred Contemplations in Three Parts* (1786).[504] But the future lay with those who heard or read Whitefield, Harris, Edwards or Wesley. The fulcrum of change was the doctrine of assurance. Those who knew their sins forgiven were freed from debilitating anxieties for Christian mission. Typical was Abigail Hutchinson, a young girl whose experience of conversion Edwards related. 'She felt a strong inclination immediately to go forth to warn sinners', according to Edwards; 'and proposed it the next day to her brother to assist her in going from house to house . . . '[505] The activism of the Evangelical movement sprang from its strong teaching on assurance. That, in turn, was a product of the confidence of the new age about the validity of experience. The Evangelical version of Protestantism was created by the Enlightenment.

[3]

A Troubling of the Water: Developments in the Early Nineteenth Century

. . . an angel went down at a certain season into the pool, and troubled the water. (John 5:4)

In the years around 1830 there was a change of direction in Evangelicalism. Not all sections of the Evangelical community were equally affected, but those that took the new path entered a phase in which many of their previous assumptions were superseded. It was not that their most fundamental convictions altered. Evangelicals continued to preach for conversions, to engage in ceaseless activity, to respect the Bible and to dwell on the theme of the cross. But fresh attitudes became characteristic of the movement towards the church and the world, towards public issues and even towards the purposes of God. A different mood was abroad. It was partly because a new generation was coming to the fore. The old leaders were going to their reward: Robert Hall, Adam Clarke, William Wilberforce, Hannah More, Rowland Hill and Charles Simeon all died between 1831 and 1836.[1] Their successors had risen within an Evangelicalism whose place in the world was assured. They were much less inclined towards a careful pragmatism that would recommend the movement to suspicious onlookers. Rather they expected their views to be given a hearing. They were more confident, more outspoken, more assertive. But the altered tone of much of the Evangelical world was far more than a matter of changing personnel. New influences and fresh circumstances directed currents of opinion into different channels. The shift of mood has often been detected but little analysed. Ford K. Brown notices the change, but his explanation hardly goes beyond the break between the generations.[2] Ian Bradley censures 'a new obscurantism and fanaticism' without diagnosing it further.[3] Alec Vidler, like many others, treats the shift as partly a reaction against the Oxford Movement.[4] In fact, however, the process was well under way before the Oxford Movement began; and the new Evangelical mood shared a great deal in common with the Oxford Movement. The fresh trends have recently been valuably summarised,[5] but they call for more detailed examination. Evangelicalism, it becomes clear, was far from a static creed.

THE STRATEGY OF MISSION

One of the reasons for the emergence of new views was doubt about existing methods of spreading the gospel. Organisations like the Bible Society might be at work, but were they proving sufficiently effective? Churchgoing was not improving significantly, if at all. During the decade 1811–21 population growth was extremely rapid. In those ten years, in fact, demographic expansion was at its highest rate in British history. Although Dissent was spreading, attendance at the parish churches was falling relative to population, especially in the developing urban areas.[6] Attention was drawn to the gulf yawning between the Church of England and the labouring masses by Richard Yates, chaplain to the Chelsea Hospital, with two works on the need for church extension published in 1815 and 1817. The public disorder provoked by economic troubles in the wake of the Napoleonic Wars induced politicians to take note. Church building was seen as the antidote to revolution, and so in 1818 parliament voted £1 million for new churches.[7] In this context Evangelicals were acutely conscious of the challenge to their strategy of mission. The people had not yet been won for Christ. Thomas Chalmers, serving as a parish minister in Glasgow from 1815, recommended fresh methods of re-Christianising the urban poor in a series of quarterly papers on the *Christian and Civic Economy of Large Towns* (1819–23). His technique concentrated on administering poor relief only through the churches.[8] Some of his proposals were to be widely heeded in subsequent decades.

Others were driven to believe that the sole remedy lay in an appeal for divine assistance. In 1821, James Haldane Stewart, a respected London Evangelical clergyman, issued a call to prayer for a special effusion of the Holy Spirit. The societies designed to advance the kingdom of Christ, he argued, had managed to achieve much less than they desired. That showed 'the inadequacy of means, even of divine appointment, without a peculiar divine agency accompanying these means'.[9] Stewart's summons, although in no sense hostile to the religious societies, was the first public questioning of their potential from within the Evangelical camp. Later in the decade, stimulated by news of awakenings in America, there was much prayer for revival.[10] Cries for supernatural aid began to seem preferable to the plodding methods of the societies. Foreign missions seemed no more effective than those working at home. The sharpest challenge to the existing approach came in a sermon preached before the London Missionary Society in 1824. Edward Irving, a celebrated young

Scottish minister in London, urged that missionaries, like the earliest apostles, should be sent forth 'destitute of all visible sustenance, and of all human support'.[11] They should be compelled to rely on God alone. Why should they need the bureaucratic organisation of a missionary society to back them? Spurning the hospitality of the LMS, Irving created a great stir by denouncing its system of operation. The circle of radicals that gathered round Irving went on to develop a coherent critique of religious societies in general as embodiments of worldly expediency. Pressure from Irving's party induced a number of organisations to symbolise the fact that they were more than business enterprises by opening their meetings with prayer. The Jews' Society first adopted the practice in 1828.[12] There was a powerful onslaught on existing patterns of mission.

THE REVIVAL OF CALVINISM

A second factor that contributed to altering the face of Evangelicalism in this period was renewed interest in Calvinism. In part this movement derived from contacts with Geneva. With the reopening of the continent to British travellers after the defeat of Napoleon, visitors were attracted to the city of Calvin. There, a revival was springing up from roots in Moravian piety. Robert Haldane, a Scottish Evangelical who had launched extensive home missionary work in his native land, turned his attention to Europe in 1816. He settled in Geneva, delivering regular lectures on the letter to the Romans with the intention of re-establishing Calvin's leading doctrines. The depth of conviction and the obvious vitality of the Genevan revival helped create in Britain an idealised vision of the meaning of Calvinism. It was less specific doctrines than 'a way of thinking and a quality of life' that inspired certain British Evangelicals.[13] The man most affected by Geneva was Henry Drummond, a banker who was to become closely associated with Irving. Drummond followed Haldane as spiritual mentor to the Evangelical community in Geneva and, when the state church looked askance on their new-found opinions, encouraged certain ministers to secede. In 1819 Drummond created a Continental Society to employ some of those who withdrew as itinerant missionaries, particularly in France.[14] These roving figures became the exemplars of the new style of missionary envisaged by Irving in his LMS sermon – men relying on providence for their support, spreading gospel light in a dark land. The separation of the Genevan Evangelicals from the state church prepared Drummond and ultimately others to contemplate the same step. And 'Calvinism' became the label for the ideal of a primitive, apostolic Christianity. 'I saw also in the history of the church', declared a speaker invented by Drummond as a vehicle for his own views, 'that in proportion as she became Arminian she relapsed into the world, and that in proportion as she became Calvinistic she came up out of the world.'[15] As in the early years of Elizabeth I, the example of Geneva stirred up reformers of the church in Britain to push ahead with their task.

Native traditions exercised a similar influence. A handful of champions of Calvinism survived from the controversies of the 1770s to sway the minds of the next generation but one. Chief among them was Robert Hawker, a redoubtable clergyman who had laboured at Plymouth since 1778.[16] Another high Calvinist, but in this case an eccentric Dissenter, was William Huntington, an ex-coalheaver who delighted to place the letters 'S.S.' after his name to indicate that he was a 'Sinner Saved'.[17] These were the men alluded to by Simeon in 1815 when he lamented, 'Five pious young men are running into Huntingdon's [*sic*] and Dr. Hawker's principles, and are leaving the Church'.[18] Simeon was referring to the so-called 'Western Schism'. A number of clergymen in the West Country, led by George Baring, seceded from the Church of England on reaching the conclusion that its principles were incompatible with their Calvinist views. One of them, James Harington Evans, was provided in 1818 with a London chapel by the munificence of Drummond, who no doubt saw this as a parallel enterprise to his efforts in Geneva. Evans had come to see, he wrote, that 'salvation is not of debt but of grace'.[19] Like Hawker, he held that since flawed human works can form no test of the reality of acceptance with God, faith is its sole evidence. Faith was exalted at the expense of works. Dismayed by teaching that he knew would open Evangelicals to censure and alarmed by its disruptive consequences, Simeon preached a sermon in Dublin condemning the Calvinist system as 'unfair and unscriptural'.[20] But the trend of the times was away from the views of men of the older generation like Simeon. In 1811 it was guessed that there were not as many as ten full-blooded Calvinists in the ministry of the Church of England.[21] By the late 1820s, however, Calvinism was the religious vogue among the young at Oxford. Their pulpit idol was Henry Bulteel, Curate of St Ebbe's from 1826, who had been influenced by Hawker.[22] He was in touch with Irving, who was calling his own convictions 'Calvinistical' and teaching that God's sovereignty is so absolute that he was responsible for the fall of man.[23] Simeon's repudiation of human systems was on the decline; there was a growing yearning after the primitive convictions of the Reformation divines.

EDWARD IRVING

Already it has emerged that the central figure in the ferment of the period was Edward Irving. His personal charisma played a remarkable part in changing the direction of Evangelicalism, even if his tragic career ended in an early death. In 1822 at the age of twenty-nine he arrived as minister of the Church of Scotland congregation in Hatton Garden, London. His capacity for self-dramatisation was enhanced by a striking physical presence – an athletic figure standing six feet two inches, with a strong, rich bass voice.

In his later years the hair, in the manner of an artistic genius, was parted right and left so as to hang down on his shoulders 'in affected disorder'.[24] During 1823 his eloquence attracted the cream of fashionable society, so that on one Sunday no fewer than thirty-five carriages bearing aristocratic coronets were counted outside his church. Fame changed to notoriety in 1824 with his sermon before the London Missionary Society denouncing its own missionary methods. Irving's reputation for erratic ways increased when, two years later, in *Babylon and Infidelity Foredoomed of God*, he announced his adoption of distinctive prophetic beliefs. Christ would soon return, he went on to declare, in glory and majesty. Suspicious eyes were turned in Irving's direction. Soon he was teaching that Christ at the incarnation assumed not human nature *per se* but fallen human nature. He continued to assert the sinlessness of Christ (the result of the power of the Holy Spirit), but charges were laid against him which culminated, in 1833, in his deposition from the ministry of the Church of Scotland for heresy on this question. Already the most controversial phase of his life had begun. In 1830 speaking in tongues was heard in two parishes in the west of Scotland, often identified as the first modern instance of the Pentecostal gift. Irving accepted the cases as genuine, and in the following year strange tongues were heard in his own congregation. The scandalised trustees excluded Irving from his own church, and so he established the so-called Catholic Apostolic Church, purveying a strange blend of adventism, tongues, elaborate liturgy and punctilio over ecclesiastical order. Its mentor, though remaining the 'angel' (minister) of a London congregation, lost control over the course of events when a prophet debarred him from appointment as an apostle.[25] Irving fell ill and died in Glasgow in December 1834 when still only forty-two.

What is the explanation of Irving's quixotic career? He was eager to present the full orbit of Christian doctrine in a fresh guise. 'We feel', he wrote in his first work, 'that questions touching the truths of revelation have been too long treated in a logical or scholastic method, which doth address itself to I know not what fraction of the mind; and not finding this used in Scripture, or successful in practice, we are disposed to try another method, and appeal our cause to every sympathy of the soul which it doth naturally bear upon.'[26] He intended to appeal to the heart. There was therefore a need to rouse his hearers by vigorous declamation on vivid themes. In the years of Walter Scott's greatest vogue, it helped if Irving's subject-matter could be tinctured by the atmosphere of an age gone by. 'He affected the Miltonic or Old-English Puritan style', recalled his friend Thomas Carlyle.[27] Anything venerable warranted his respect; anything modern was suspected of degeneracy. The ideal in oratory was not the recent notion of Augustan economy but rhetorical extravagance. The sermon before the LMS was so long that he had to pause twice during its delivery for a hymn to be sung.[28] Contemporary German thought held attractions. Although he disliked the infidelity of Schiller and Goethe, Irving

encouraged Carlyle in his study of Schiller and would allude as a matter
of course to Goethe's *Faust*.[29] It was Germany, he held, 'where alone any
powerful poetry exists'.[30] Nevertheless he was eager to discover any sign
that Wordsworth was appreciated.[31] Irving was being swept along by the
spirit of the age in its reaction against the manner of the Enlightenment.
Bentham, the toast of recent 'enlightened' opinion, was dismissed as 'the
apostle of expediency', perhaps the most limited philosopher of the day.[32]
Like the young John Stuart Mill in the same decade, Irving was freeing
himself from the ascendancy of the Utilitarian mode of thinking; but his
liberation was more complete than that of Mill. In short, Irving was a
Romantic. He owed his celebrity to a capacity for blending Evangelical
religion with the latest intellectual fashions.

THE INFLUENCE OF ROMANTICISM

The chief agent of Irving's liberation was S. T. Coleridge. Again like
Mill, Irving discovered in Coleridge a new world of thought and feeling.
The ripening friendship of the two men from 1823 to 1826, when, despite
continuing mutual esteem, they diverged on account of Irving's prophetic
studies, can be traced in Coleridge's correspondence. Coleridge adjudged
Irving 'the greatest *Orator*, I ever heard'.[33] For his part, Irving counted
Coleridge (as he declared to a surprised religious world) 'more profitable
to my faith in orthodox doctrine, to my spiritual understanding of the
Word of God . . . than any or all of the men with whom I have entertained
friendship and conversation . . . '[34] When taken by Irving to meet Coleridge,
a bewildered Thomas Chalmers discovered that there was 'a secret and to
me as yet unintelligible communion of spirit betwixt them, on the ground
of a certain German mysticism and transcendental lake-poetry which I am
not yet up to'.[35] From this intimacy Irving derived a Coleridgean reverence
for the ideal. The poet also confirmed in the preacher a developing contempt
for the expediency of the age that was to be the germ of much subsequent
Evangelical socio-political thought.[36] But most of all, as the Scotsman
avowed, Coleridge taught him a 'right conception of the Christian Church'.
By 1825 Irving was laying great stress on proper ecclesiastical order and
appealing to a typical Coleridgean rationale. 'The twofold nature of man,
body and spirit', he asserted, 'maketh it necessary that every thing by
which he is to be moved should have an outward form.' Thus 'the visible
Church is the sensible form of the heavenly communion'.[37] The substance
of his exalted ecclesiology was Coleridgean. Deep draughts of the teaching
of Coleridge fortified Irving to lead the adaptation of Evangelicalism into
the Romantic idiom of the day.

  Romanticism was well fitted to be a vehicle for religious thought.
The term is used here not in the narrow sense of the literary generation
that was fading by the 1820s but in the much broader sense of the whole

mood that was inaugurated by that generation and lasted throughout the nineteenth century and beyond. This was the movement of taste that stressed, against the mechanism and classicism of the Enlightenment, the place of feeling and intuition in human perception, the importance of nature and history for human experience. Goethe embodied the Romantic spirit in Germany, where the initial impact of the movement was strongest, while Wordsworth, Coleridge, Keats, Shelley and Byron represented its various expressions in English verse. Its quintessence was what has been called 'natural supernaturalism', the ability to discern spiritual significance in the everyday world.[38] Awe before the numinous in nature is the hallmark of Wordsworth's poetry, and a revelling in the strange, the uncanny and the mysterious runs like a thread through Romantic art and literature. There was immense potential affinity for religion. Broad and High Churchmanship in Britain were both deeply affected during the nineteenth century,[39] but the Evangelical tradition was no less touched by the new cultural style. This is not to argue that there was an intrinsic bond between the Romantic and the Evangelical. It has frequently been held that such a connection did in fact subsist. 'Now Evangelical Christianity', writes Dr Kitson Clark, 'seems to satisfy all the categories of romanticism, except the love of fancy dress.' The leading Romantic characteristics, as expounded by Dr Kitson Clark, were the importance of emotion and imagination, with a consequent emphasis on moments of intense experience, a profounder appreciation of the values of the past and a spirit of escape and revolt from present conditions.[40] All these, however, far from being part and parcel of the Evangelical Revival, were novelties in the years around 1830. Reason, not emotion, had been the lodestar of the Evangelicals; many of them looked to the millennium of the future, not to the past, for their ideal of a Christian society; and far from wishing to flee from existing conditions, they used normal contemporary methods, whether in business, politics or religion, to accomplish their aims. So the outburst of imaginative energy represented by Irving constituted a revolt against the conventions of the Evangelical world. There was a new appreciation of the dramatic, the extraordinary and the otherworldly element in religion. That is the key to the thought of Edward Irving. His mind bore the impress of a heightened supernaturalism.

MILLENARIANISM

A distinguishing feature of Irving and his circle was the advent hope. Many Evangelicals, as the previous chapter has illustrated, were expecting the millennium to be attained through the preaching of the gospel. Only after this period of prosperity for the church would Christ come again.[41] But an alternative millenarian view had frequently been held in Christian history. Christ would return, according to this alternative version, before the commencement of the millennium. The second advent, far from being deferred to the distant future beyond the triumph of Christ's earthly church, was to be expected imminently. This form of prophetic interpretation is usually called *premillennialism* (since Christ is to come *before* the millennium) to distinguish it from the *post*millennial view (according to which Christ is to be expected *after* the millennium). Premillennialism was taken up by Irving's new school of Evangelicals. They believed, as their prophetic journal *The Morning Watch* put it in 1830, 'that our Lord Jesus Christ will return to this earth in person before the Millennium'.[42] J. F. C. Harrison has recently attributed this premillennial view to the largely self-educated, characterising postmillennialism, by contrast, as a more intellectually sophisticated belief. Yet, as Professor Harrison himself admits, the distinction cannot be drawn rigidly along these lines. The premillennialists numbered the highly literate and extremely sophisticated Irving in their ranks. The postmillennialists had no monopoly on respectability or scholarship.[43] The distinction was not so much one of educational attainment as of period. Whereas in the first three decades after the French Revolution it was normal among students of prophecy to expect a steady spread of Christian truth, from the 1820s onwards there was a growth of the premillennial advent hope.

The seminal influence in drawing the attention of the Evangelical world to this alternative approach to prophecy was James Hatley Frere, with his work *A Combined View of the Prophecies of Daniel, Esdras, and St. John* (1815). William Cuninghame, a Scottish Presbyterian, had published a premillennial work two years earlier, and was to continue propagating his views in the 1830s,[44] but Frere enjoyed the prestige of predicting, shortly before Waterloo, the downfall of Napoleon. The second coming, he argued, would take place at the start of a phase in the millennium that would occur in 1822–3. In Frere, however, the second coming is treated merely as a metaphor – 'some extraordinary manifestation of the power of Christ'.[45] It is to be a spiritual, not a literal, event. Irving, who imbibed his opinions from Frere, agreed in a publication of 1826 that the advent is imminent, but not literal.[46] In the same year, however, Irving fell to translating from Spanish a strange work by a Chilean Jesuit masquerading as a converted Jew ('Ben-Ezra') entitled *The Coming of Messiah in Glory and Majesty*. It drove its translator to the conclusion that Christ would certainly return in person.[47] The publication of this book in 1827 marked the decisive re-emergence of the premillennialist tradition.

A receptive audience for 'Ben-Ezra' had been created by the growing desire for the conversion of the Jews. Organised missionary work concentrating on the Jews alone was a novelty of the early nineteenth century. The London Society for Promoting Christianity among the Jews was established in 1809 as an interdenominational body and in 1815 was reconstituted as an Anglican organisation.[48] Its prime mover, Lewis Way, was inspired by the prophecies of the return of the Jewish people to their own land and, noticing the connection drawn in the Bible between this event and the last things, came to believe in the nearness of Christ's coming again. Between 1820 and 1822, under the pseudonym 'Basilicus', Way ventured a series of speculations on the future prospects of the Jews in the society's journal *The Jewish Expositor*. Christ, he claimed in the course of the letters, would soon return in person.[49] Four years later the majority of the committee believed the doctrine of the imminent second coming.[50] Most crucially, Way's views had spread to Henry Drummond, who became a Vice-President of the Jews' Society in 1823. It was Drummond, 'abundant in speculations as well as money',[51] who set about exploring prophetic views in depth. He assembled twenty or so people, including Way and Irving, at his country estate in Surrey, Albury Park, for eight days during Advent 1826. It was the first of an annual series of prophetic conferences at Albury that lasted until 1830.[52] If the return of the Messiah is to be associated with the restoration of the Jews, they concluded, the millennium can be located only after the second coming. Conversation ranged over a variety of other topics – the dignity of the church, the iniquities of the religious societies, the political implications of these doctrines – but two of the six major points of agreement at the 1829 conference still concerned the Jews: the Christian dispensation, like the Jewish, would be terminated suddenly in judgements; and the Jews would be restored to their land during the judgements.[53] The gloomy expectations of the Albury participants grew out of their more sanguine hopes for the Jews.

THE ADVENT HOPE

The significance of the emerging premillennial position lay less in its expectation of a coming millennium than in its confidence in the imminent return of Christ. There was little, if any, dwelling on the status reversal of the millennium, whereby the great of the earth would be subject to the authority of the humblest believer. In that respect, the radical eschatology of the nineteenth century differed from what was typical of most millenarian movements.[54] It was, in fact, more concerned with the coming achievement of Christ than with any state of earthly beatitude, more adventist than millenarian. The kernel was what Irving called Christ's 'own personal appearance in flaming fire'. The return, it was often stressed, would be a literal coming. The reason is that previously belief in a visible return by Christ in the flesh had been no part of accepted doctrine. Many Protestants, Irving observed, 'start when you say that Christ will appear again in personal and bodily presence upon the earth'.[55] Like Frere when he wrote *A Combined View*, the most respected Evangelicals did not believe it. Thomas Scott declared in 1802 that in the future there would be 'no visible appearance of Christ'; and in 1830 Charles Simeon assured a correspondent that it was a matter with which he had not the slightest concern.[56] Certain early advocates of a premillennial eschatology spelt out the novelty of their belief in the return of Christ in the flesh.[57] Other writers like Haldane Stewart can be detected hesitating on the brink of deciding in favour of a personal advent.[58] The doctrine long continued to be rejected by the Evangelical mainstream. In a prize essay on missionary work selected by a panel of adjudicators drawn from five denominations in 1842, John Harris, President of Cheshunt College, contended that the coming of Christ would be 'in strange providences, and at critical junctures'.[59] Although he explicitly set aside discussion of whether the coming would be personal, he evidently did not believe it. In the 1840s, in fact, premillennialists sometimes claimed that expectation of a personal advent was confined to their ranks.[60] They were mistaken, but their case was plausible. The belief that Christ would come again in person was an innovation in the Evangelical world of the 1820s.

It was part of the Romantic inflow into Evangelicalism. Christ the coming king could readily be pictured by poetic imaginations fascinated by the strange, the awesome and the supernatural. 'To such minds', a critic of premillennialism argued, 'any other view of the subject is perfectly bald and repulsive, while theirs is encircled with the glory that excelleth. To them it carries the force of intuitive perception; they *feel* – they *know* it to be true.' The advent hope was far more than a bare doctrine. Because the content of the expectation was Jesus Christ himself, the hope became an object of devotion. 'Souls that burn with love for Christ' were 'ready to embrace it almost immediately *con amore*'.[61] To Lord Shaftesbury, for instance, it was something to 'delight in', 'a moving principle in my life'. His close friend Alexander Haldane, according to Shaftesbury himself, 'intensely loved' Christ, 'and ever talked with a holy relish and a full desire for the Second Advent'.[62] There was nothing anomalous, according to the new way of looking at the world, in expecting a divine figure to appear suddenly in the midst of the affairs of the nations. To minds nurtured on earlier ideas of cause, effect, order and gradualness, however, there was little appeal: 'whatever Scripture intimations regarding the future destinies of the Church and of the world involve events out of the usual range of human occurrences, or exceeding the anticipations of enlightened Christian sagacity, are almost instinctively overlooked or softened down'.[63] So the expectation of Christ's personal return attracted younger men in tune with the rising temper of the age, who were prepared to break with part of the legacy of the Enlightenment. But it was left to one member of the younger generation to incorporate the advent hope into an Enlightenment framework. David Brown, once Irving's assistant minister in London and eventually Principal of the Aberdeen Free Church College, published the most popular nineteenth-century restatement of the postmillennial scheme, *Christ's Second Coming: Will it be Premillennial?* (1846). Brown was a man of 'a poetical nature' who wrote verse in his youth, carried about with him a copy of Keble's *Christian Year* and had once been a premillennialist himself.[64] His book was persuasive precisely because, unlike earlier postmillennial advocates, his Romantic temperament led him to commend the personal return.[65] Brown constitutes an exception to the normal rule of the association of this doctrine with the premillennial position. But he well illustrates the cultural affinities of the reviving belief in the second coming as a personal event. Adventism was a symptom of Romanticism.

VARIETIES OF PREMILLENNIALISM

As prophetic interpretation settled into established grooves during the 1830s and 1840s, two schools of thought emerged. The dominant school was that normally called 'historicist', although at the time, because of its origins in Reformation polemic, its advocates usually preferred to style it 'the Protestant view'.[66] With this approach the book of Revelation and the prophecies of Daniel were to be interpreted as narratives that could be decoded by pairing symbols such as vials of wrath with remarkable historical events. The basic premiss was that prophetic references to days should be understood as years. There was great scope for debate about the proper starting point for calculation, but most commentators pointed to 1866–8 as the likely date for the second coming. A chart in *Horae Apocalypticae* (1844), a four-volume work of scholarly prophetic studies published by E. B. Elliott, a Fellow of Trinity College, Cambridge, clearly depicts the beginning of the millennium at a point two-thirds of the way through the nineteenth century.[67] After 1868 commentators nevertheless took the need for recalculation in their stride.[68] Although one of the best known exponents of historicist premillennialism was a Presbyterian, John Cumming, a self-professed populariser of the work of Elliott,[69] this form of the advent hope became most entrenched in the Church of England. It was propagated through the twice-yearly meetings of the Prophecy Investigation Society, begun in November 1842 at St George's, Bloomsbury.[70] H. M. Villiers, the Rector of St George's, promoted an annual series of published lectures that spread the message far and wide.[71] By 1854 the new prophetic convictions were sufficiently common to provoke a systematic rebuttal in the Bampton Lectures by Samuel Waldegrave, himself an Evangelical and shortly to become Bishop of Carlisle.[72] In the following year it was thought that probably a majority of the Evangelical clergy favoured premillennial views.[73] The great majority had embraced a version of prophetic interpretation that drove them to scan their newspapers for indications of 'the signs of the times'. Historicist premillennialism, as we shall see, was to encourage specific attitudes to the public affairs of the day.

The second school of thought, by contrast, fostered withdrawal from public concerns into an esoteric world of speculation about supernatural events still to come. This, the futurist school, held that the book of Revelation depicts not the course of history but the great happenings of the future. In 1826 there appeared a book arguing strongly for a futurist interpretation of Revelation in order to undermine all millenarian notions. The unintended effect of this work by S. R. Maitland, the future historian, was to inspire an alternative tradition of millennial thought.[74] At Albury, Maitland's theory that Revelation was yet to be fulfilled was already being canvassed, and by 1843 half a dozen other writers had taken the field in favour of the same principle.[75] Irving's Catholic Apostolic Church embraced a moderate type of futurism, teaching that many of the events predicted in Revelation were still to come.[76] But the most significant figure to adopt a form of futurist premillennialism was J. N. Darby, the fertile mind behind another adventist sect, the Brethren. Darby was an Irish ex-clergyman, originally trained as a lawyer, who in the early 1830s was a leading participant in a series of conferences held in imitation of Albury under the sponsorship of Lady Powerscourt near Dublin. He steadily elaborated the view that the predictions of Revelation would be fulfilled after believers had been caught up to meet Christ in the air, the so-called 'rapture'. No events in prophecy were to precede the rapture. In particular, the period of judgements on Christendom expected by other premillennialists, the 'great tribulation', would take place only after the true church had been mysteriously translated to the skies. The second coming, on this view, was divided into two parts: the secret coming of Christ *for* his saints at the rapture; and the public coming *with* his saints to reign over the earth after the tribulation. Darby's teaching is often termed 'dispensationalism' because it sharply distinguishes between different dispensations, or periods of divine dealings with mankind.[77] Although never the unanimous view among Brethren, dispensationalism spread beyond their ranks and gradually became the most popular version of futurism. In the nineteenth century it remained a minority view among premillennialists, but this intense form of apocalyptic expectation was to achieve much greater salience in the twentieth.

THE INSPIRATION OF SCRIPTURE

In addition to the advent hope, the radical Evangelicals of the 1820s bequeathed another enduring legacy to their successors, a more exalted estimate of scripture. In the earliest years of the nineteenth century Evangelicals shared the standard attitude of contemporary theologians to the Bible. Henry Martyn, the distinguished Cambridge scholar who abandoned his academic career to travel as a missionary to the East, was at one point closely questioned by a high-ranking official in Persia. Believing in the verbal inspiration of the Koran, the Persian enquired whether Martyn considered the New Testament to be the word spoken by God. 'The sense from God', Martyn replied, 'but the expression from the different writers of it.'[78] Martyn did not believe in verbal inspiration. Simeon, Martyn's mentor, while sometimes using language suggesting a strong view of inspiration, could also maintain that scripture contains 'inexactnesses in reference to philosophical and scientific matters'.[79] Similarly, Daniel Wilson, Vicar of Islington and subsequently Bishop of Calcutta, supposed that the Bible had been preserved only from 'every kind and degree of error relating to religion';[80] and T. H. Horne, the author of a four-volume *Introduction to the Critical Study and Knowledge of the Holy Scriptures* (1818), freely admitted that there are discrepancies in the text of scripture.[81] The chief court of appeal on the question of inspiration and its effects was Philip Doddridge.[82] Even the high Calvinist Robert Hawker treated the opinion of Doddridge on this subject as decisive.[83] Doddridge distinguished between different modes of inspiration, so that some passages were held to afford greater insight than others into the divine mind. It was Doddridge's view that predominated in the discussion of inspiration in 1800 by the Eclectic Society, the body consisting of London Evangelical leaders. Richard Cecil declared that 'there is some danger in considering *all* Scripture as *equally* inspired'. Although Henry Foster ('a plain and deeply pious man') propounded a theory of verbal inspiration, John Davies argued that the ideas, and not the words, of scripture are inspired.[84] Here were sober, experimentally minded men concerned to investigate the nature of the scriptures.

Such views began to be challenged by a much more robust attitude. It originated with Robert Haldane, the Scottish Evangelical who in 1816 found vital religion at a low ebb in Geneva. The Bible was neglected there, he soon concluded, because of misty Romantic notions to the effect that scripture is inspired in the same sense in which poetry is inspired. In reaction, Haldane contended for a much higher view of biblical inspiration. Parts of the Bible could not be accepted or rejected according to the judgement of human reason, he argued, for the whole, containing 'things evidently mysterious', was to be revered as divine teaching. This was to counter one Romantic attitude with another – the assertion that men should 'receive with adoring faith and love what they could not comprehend'.[85] Haldane elaborated his case in *The Evidence and Authority of Divine Revelation*, first published in the same year. The scriptures, he taught, make 'a claim of infallibility and of perfection' for their own inspiration. The Doddridgean view of different degrees of inspiration was dismissed as sophistry.[86]

Haldane's ideas might have made little impression but for the Apocrypha controversy that embroiled the British and Foreign Bible Society in the 1820s. For many years the society had been sponsoring versions containing the Apocrypha for use on the continent, where its inclusion was normal among Catholics and Protestants alike. Haldane protested that this policy was an adulteration of the pure word of God. Uninspired material was being mingled with inspired scripture. The secretaries of the society, supported by Simeon and others who held the traditional lower views of inspiration, were reluctant to abandon a means of increasing the acceptability of the Bible. It was a clash of principle against expediency. Although by 1826 the society had gone a long way towards meeting the demand for change (even agreeing to remove existing Bibles containing the Apocrypha from stock), the Edinburgh and Glasgow auxiliaries remained dissatisfied and withdrew.[87] The fundamental issue, the nature of inspiration, was raised explicitly when, in 1826, John Pye Smith, tutor at the Independent Homerton College, referred favourably to a preface inserted in Bibles furnished by the British and Foreign. The preface, by a French theologian, Dr Haffner, treated inspiration in the way that had so disgusted Haldane in Geneva: Ezekiel, for instance, was said to have possessed 'a very lively imagination'.[88] Pye Smith pointed out that there was nothing explicitly erroneous about Haffner's opinions and added a statement of his own views on inspiration, which closely resembled those of Doddridge. Haldane arranged for an impoverished Baptist pastor in Ulster, a man of strong dogmatic views, Dr Alexander Carson, to assault Pye Smith's position. Haldane himself threw in a treatise *On the Inspiration of Scripture* in 1828. Although the extremely able Pye Smith had the best of the arguments, the effect was to publicise the views of Haldane.[89] A new and stronger understanding of inspiration had been broached.

BIBLICAL LITERALISM

One of the chief reasons for the spread of the new attitude was its association with premillennialism. Haldane did not toy with prophetic speculation, but many of those who fought the Apocrypha battle at his side were among those whose concern for the Jews blossomed into expectation of the advent. There was a tight logical connection between high hopes for the Jews and a new estimate of scripture. Those who looked for indications in the Bible that God's chosen people would be gathered into his fold were inclined to take Old Testament prophecies literally.[90] By contrast, Evangelical commentators had customarily argued that the prophecies of the Old Testament should be read spiritually, not literally: they should be applied to the Christian church. The beginning of the innovatory interpretation can be located precisely. In a pamphlet called *The Latter Rain* (1821) Lewis Way, the sponsor of the Jews' Society, urged special prayer for the children of Israel on the ground that Old Testament prophecies had a '*primary* and *literal* reference to the Jews'.[91] The literal interpretation of scripture became a battle-cry of the radical Evangelicals of Albury. One anonymous student of prophecy was soon to assert that the highway of Isaiah and the chariots of Ezekiel were to be construed literally as having reference to 'railroads and railway conveyance by locomotive carriages'.[92] Literalism did not imply restraining the imagination. It is not surprising that, in the opinion of a contributor to *The Eclectic Review*, 'the most dangerous feature of Millenarian theology, is the erroneous method of Biblical interpretation . . . '[93] Innovations in the fields of prophecy and the understanding of scripture went hand in hand.

Different views of what literalism implied jostled each other during the 1830s and 1840s. Horatius Bonar, the chief Scottish premillennial champion, conceded that, 'No one maintains that *all* Scripture is literal, or that *all* is figurative'.[94] Historicists found it hard to be thoroughgoing advocates of literal interpretation. There was too great a gulf between the detail of biblical images and their alleged historical fulfilment to make any such claim plausible. Futurists did not suffer from this handicap. Consequently, they shouted louder for literalism – and, among the futurists, the dispensationalists shouted loudest of all. J. N. Darby was contending as early as 1829 that prophecy relating to the Jews would be fulfilled literally.[95] As his thought developed during the 1830s, this principle of interpretation became the lynchpin of his system. Because Darby's opinions were most wedded to literalism, his distinctive scheme enjoyed the advantage of taking what seemed the most rigorist view of scripture. Conversely, the preference for the literal over the figurative approach to biblical exposition drew growing popular support from the advance of millenarianism.[96] The rising prestige of biblical literalism in turn reinforced the stronger convictions about scripture propounded by Haldane and his circle.

TOWARDS FUNDAMENTALISM

The classic text setting out the new and more exalted doctrine of scripture was Louis Gaussen's *Theopneustia* (1841). Gaussen was a professor of theology at Geneva whose high doctrine of inspiration was originally derived from Haldane.[97] His book was directed against Schleiermacher and others who denied miraculous inspiration in whole or in part, but also against English authors influenced by Doddridge, such as Pye Smith. The English theologians, he points out, admitted the existence of unique divine in-breathing (the 'theopneustia' of the title) in the Bible, but not to the same degree in all parts.[98] Gaussen, by contrast, asserts the plenary inspiration of the whole Bible. The word 'plenary' was subsequently adopted by many advocates of his case, but its use was not confined to the new school. Followers of Doddridge employed it freely.[99] The distinctiveness of Gaussen's position can be characterised more accurately by two other terms – verbal inspiration and inerrancy. Verbal inspiration is professed in a section of his book directed to meeting what he calls an 'evasion', the belief that the ideas rather than the words of the Bible are inspired. He also offers a precise statement of inerrancy. 'Theopneustia' he defines as 'that inexplicable power which the Divine Spirit, aforetime, exercised upon the authors of Holy Scripture, to guide them even to the words which they have employed, and to preserve them from all error, as well as from any omission.'[100] He did not support any theory of divine dictation, as critics both at the time and subsequently have alleged.[101] On the subject of inspiration, he remarks in the book, 'Scripture never presents to us either its mode or its measure, as an object of study'.[102] It seems clear that he would have agreed with Haldane that full inspiration did not imply that 'the ordinary exercise of the faculties of the writers was counteracted or suspended'.[103] The verbal inspirationists, that is to say, believed in the possibility of simultaneous divine and human agency. If God gave the words, there is no implication that the human mind did not also give them. So Gaussen provided, for the first time, a carefully argued defence of the inerrancy of the Bible.

His effort was part of the intensified supernaturalism of the times. Gaussen was jealous for the divine honour. 'Is the Bible from God?' he demanded in the preface. 'Or, is it true (as has been affirmed) that it contains sentences purely human, inaccurate narratives, vulgar conceits, defective arguments . . . ?' The approach of Doddridge, and most contemporary British Evangelicals, was degrading to the miraculous documents provided by God. 'According to their view', he wrote, 'inspiration . . . would be unequal, often imperfect, accompanied with harmless errors, and meted out according to the nature of the passages, in very different measure, of which they constitute themselves more or less the judges.'[104] Such theologians were guilty of pitting their own reason against God's revelation. Gaussen's target is essentially the inductive method, the critical sifting of evidence to discover the nature of inspiration in any particular book. By this means, observing 'the Baconian rules of inductive reasoning', Pye Smith had concluded that the Song of Songs and Esther should probably be rejected from the canon.[105] So unpalatable a conclusion confirmed the diagnosis in the circles of Gaussen and Haldane that there was a flaw in the method. They therefore adopted what has justly been styled a deductive approach to the doctrine of inspiration. Beginning with the axiom that God in his perfect wisdom had inspired the writing of the Bible, they went on to deduce its qualities and then tried to match the results of empirical examination of the text with their *a priori* assumptions.[106]

It was too much for many who had been schooled to the Enlightenment values of free inquiry. Pye Smith's views did not change, although he knew Gaussen's book; his fellow–Congregationalist John Harris, lecturing as principal on 'The Inspiration of the Scriptures' at the opening of New College, London, in 1851, pointed out that 'the sacred writers nowhere claim for themselves immediate and universal verbal inspiration'; and two years later T. R. Birks, then a trusted leader of the Evangelical clergy, explicitly rejected dogmatic inerrancy on the ground that we should engage in inquiry into the mode of inspiration.[107] But the deductive method soon won converts. William Steadman at Bradford Baptist Academy abandoned Doddridge's system in favour of Haldane's, and Thomas Chalmers at Edinburgh used Haldane and even Carson as class-books on inspiration.[108] James Bannerman, who later wrote a treatise on *Inspiration* (1865), and Alexander Black, a colleague at New College, Edinburgh, both held by 1850 the new view that the whole Bible is 'fully and verbally inspired'.[109] There was a clear division of Evangelical opinion. With the backing of *The Record*,[110] inerrantism made progress among the Anglican clergy.

Nevertheless, at a representative clerical meeting in 1861 a majority still favoured the traditional view that there might be biblical inaccuracies on non-religious topics.[111] If Fundamentalism as a theological phenomenon is defined as belief in the inerrancy of scripture, Fundamentalism had not prevailed among Evangelicals by this date. The common supposition of historians that Evangelicals of the mid-nineteenth century and before held, as a deduction from the doctrine of inspiration, that the Bible must necessarily contain no error is quite mistaken. This conviction was a novelty, a Romantic innovation. In the middle years of the century there was no more than a rising tide of Fundamentalist opinion.

SUPERNATURAL INTERVENTION

The most vivid instance of the increasing supernaturalism that marked the Evangelical world of the 1820s and 1830s was the appearance of speaking in tongues. The traditional view was that such miraculous signs had been withdrawn from the church after its early years. At Albury it was suggested that they ended solely because faith had grown cold.[112] It followed that, as faith was rekindled, the gifts might be restored. A. J. Scott, Irving's assistant minister, reached this conclusion and, on holiday on the Clyde in 1830, opened his mind to Mary Campbell of Roseneath. It was she who, a few months later, first spoke in tongues. News of the manifestations in Scotland led to intense expectancy in London, where the earliest instance occurred in April 1831. By October Irving was permitting the exercise of tongues inspired by the Spirit in public worship. 'An awful stillness prevailed for about five minutes', wrote a critical visitor. 'Suddenly an appalling shriek seemed to rend the roof, which was repeated with heart-chilling effect. I grasped involuntarily the bookdesk before me; and then, suddenly, a torrent of unintelligible words, for about five minutes, followed by – "When will ye repent? Why will ye not repent?"'[113] Prophecies in English and miraculous healings were also known. In one year forty-six spiritual cures were reported among the Irvingites of England alone. These unfamiliar proto-Pentecostal happenings soon became confined to Irving's Catholic Apostolic Church, which, despite erecting some magnificent places of worship, never became a power in the land. Its numbers in the United Kingdom were estimated in 1878 to be under six thousand.[114] But for a while – probably significantly, in the years during and immediately after the great cholera outbreak of 1831–2 – the revival of spiritual gifts in the church was a subject of widespread attention among Evangelicals. It was an extreme sign of the new craving for the divine to break into the world.

A complementary tendency was the downgrading of natural theology. Evangelicals, as we have seen, had previously delighted in the scientific arguments that defended the faith on the basis of the Newtonian cosmology.[115] Now the radicals began to feel that their theology had been too

strongly marked by natural philosophy. They had left little or no room
for divine intervention in the present or future. Prejudice, confessed the
respected G. T. Noel, had previously prevented him from accepting
the possibility of miraculous intercourse between heaven and earth in a
millennial state.[116] The prejudice was identified and condemned at Albury
as a habitual looking at second causes rather than at first. 'Nothing can be so
opposed to the disposition of faith', ran the first conference report, 'as that
which is only to be convinced by external evidences. It is, in fact, saying that
we will not believe God unless He can bring a voucher for the truth of what
He says.'[117] The demolition of the structure of natural theology would leave
the way clear for the bare trust in divine revelation characteristically urged
by Irving and his friends. But to those who continued to see 'the mechanical
philosophy' as the main buttress of Christian truth it was highly alarming.
They remained convinced, as the Congregational theologian John Harris put
it, that 'the moral department of the Divine government is conducted on a
plan equally with the natural or the physical; that in the world of mind, as
well as of matter, certain causes produce certain effects'.[118] It was a clash
between those who inherited the eighteenth-century beliefs in order, design
and gradualness and those who, in the iconoclastic spirit of the nineteenth
century, wished to substitute the free, the dynamic and the cataclysmic. The
older school was to retain its hegemony at least until the debates stirred up
by Darwinism from the 1860s onwards.[119] But from as early as the 1820s
a new force was in the field.

DOCTRINAL REFORMULATION

The same novel influences were affecting central doctrines. One of the
most significant developments was a reaction against Calvinism in favour
of the belief that the atonement was general in its scope. A landmark was
the publication, in 1828, of *The Unconditional Freeness of the Gospel* by
Thomas Erskine, a Scottish Episcopal layman whose Romantic sensibility
was nourished by a love for works of art.[120] 'The Gospel', he writes,
'reveals to us the existence of a fund of divine love containing in it a
propitiation for all sins, and this fund is general to the whole race . . .'[121]
His views received a warmer welcome than might have been expected: Henry
Drummond approved the book, and even Chalmers, though dissenting
from its main conclusion, 'went cordially with its leading principles'.[122]
Most crucially, a Church of Scotland minister in the west of Scotland,
John McLeod Campbell, concurred wholeheartedly. McLeod Campbell,
who in 1856 was to publish a treatise on general redemption entitled *The
Nature of the Atonement*, was deposed from the ministry of the Church of
Scotland in 1831 for departing from Reformed orthodoxy. It was McLeod
Campbell who, in 1828, persuaded Irving of the truth of these views.[123]
It seems strange at first sight that Irving, who gloried in what he called

Calvinism, should adopt this anti-Calvinist kernel of an alternative scheme of theology. The apparent contradiction is resolved when it is recognised that Irving perceived an inadequate doctrine of redemption as the root problem of contemporary Evangelical thought.[124] If God is sovereign, he held, then his redeeming power must be totally effective and therefore encompass the whole of humanity. The conviction of Erskine, McLeod Campbell and Irving that Christ died for all rested on a sense of the absoluteness of divine authority. It was newly held that humanity enjoys a solidarity – a typical theme of nineteenth-century thought – because it is subject as a whole to Christ. Such themes were to be propagated by A. J. Scott, once Irving's assistant and later the first Principal of Owen's College, Manchester, and by F. D. Maurice, the leading Broad Church theologian of the mid-nineteenth century, who professed a deep debt to Erskine and Irving.[125] If it was formally condemned at the time, the broader view of the atonement adumbrated by Erskine was to enjoy increasing favour among Evangelicals and non-Evangelicals alike as the century advanced.

Another doctrinal field marked by innovation in the 1820s was Christology. Irving propounded the belief that at the incarnation Christ assumed not just humanity but sinful humanity. 'The point at issue is simply this', he explained: 'whether Christ's flesh had the grace of sinlessness and incorruption from its proper nature, or from the indwelling of the Holy Ghost. I say the latter.'[126] It was for his book arguing this case, *The Orthodox and Catholic Doctrine of our Lord's Human Nature* (1830), that Irving was excluded from the ministry of the Church of Scotland. The condemnation rested on the received doctrine of the union of the two natures of Christ in one person. If God and man were united, Irving's claim amounted to the assertion that a person who was God was capable of sin – a conclusion of definite unorthodoxy. Irving, however, insisted that he was speaking not of Christ as a person but of the humanity he assumed.[127] It is clear that Irving was not wishing to deviate from the mainstream of Christian teaching. He wished to contend that Christ was subject to all the influences of his day without in some sense being guarded by the coat-of-mail of intrinsic sinlessness. The incarnation was utterly real. This aligned Irving with tendencies gaining momentum in the early nineteenth century making for greater emphasis on the doctrine of the incarnation that, once again, came to fruition in the thought of Maurice. It was a distinctly Romantic trend.[128] To claim that the Holy Spirit was responsible for preserving Christ's sinlessness was to exalt the work of the third person of the Trinity, just as Irving did in explaining the manifestations in his congregation. He was contending once more for a higher estimate of divine involvement in the contemporary world. Underlying the Christology was his central preoccupation with the irruption of the supernatural into the human sphere.

For the discernment of the supernatural, faith was essential. One of the most enduring legacies of the ferment surrounding Irving was the idea that faith must be magnified if God is to be served aright. This, according to

Irving, is to be the governing principle of Christian mission. 'It was Faith they had to plant', he declared of the earliest apostles in his LMS sermon of 1824; 'therefore he made his missionaries men of Faith, that they might plant Faith, and Faith alone.' Faith entailed reliance on God for material as well as spiritual needs. Today's missionaries should therefore imitate the apostles in going out 'destitute of all visible sustenance, and of all human help'.[129] Similar convictions were maturing in other minds. A. N. Groves, an Exeter dentist, both preached and practised entire dependence on God in missionary service.[130] His brother-in-law, George Müller, established an orphanage at Bristol in 1835 on the same principles. Whenever money was exhausted, 'prayer and faith were again resorted to'. Part of Müller's inspiration derived from the example of August Francke,[131] but part was drawn from the atmosphere of radical devotion to God that Müller discovered in the circles around Groves that were developing into the Brethren movement. Müller's principle of living by faith was taken up later in the century by J. Hudson Taylor, another adherent of Brethren, and made the basis of his China Inland Mission in 1865. The CIM differed from previous missionary societies in possessing no structure of home support. Its backing came simply from those committed to praying for its agents in the field, who were thrown into dependence on God for their needs.[132] Hudson Taylor vividly illustrated an extreme version of this attitude to mission when, at a time when shipwreck seemed imminent on his first voyage to China in 1853, he gave away his life belt to assure himself that his trust was in God alone.[133] 'Living by faith' was to become the practice of an increasing proportion of full-time workers in the Evangelical world in later years. The origins of the policy can be traced back to the new desire to rely wholly on God that marked the juncture around 1830. If faith was strong, the reality of God's involvement in his world would be evident in the care he exercised over his servants.

HIGH CHURCHMANSHIP

A further feature of the new mood around 1830 was a stronger sense of churchmanship. It came to rapid fruition in the Albury circle, which hoped that a corporate awareness, 'a catholic, and universal spirit', would rescue Evangelicals from individualism. Churchmanship had suffered: 'we have almost forgotten that there is a church at all; . . . Christ, and the believer; that is all.'[134] Irving set out to retrieve the situation. He even claimed to doubt whether those who failed to give 'due reverence' to the church would reach the heaven that it symbolised.[135] But Irving and his immediate friends were not alone in publicising a higher view of the church. A. S. Thelwall, a young clerical graduate of Trinity College, Cambridge, was publishing similar ideas in his sermons.[136] It was also the burden of Henry Budd, the clerical secretary of the Prayer Book and Homily Society.

'Our Church is a glorious Church', he wrote in 1827, 'if it had but a soul.'[137] A sense of corporate solidarity had come into vogue. Coleridge, as we have seen, was a primary source. The whole movement of opinion was Romantic in inspiration.

The new school was also coming to fresh conclusions as a result of examining ecclesiastical tradition with more care. Irving derived something of his corporate sense from the seventeenth-century Scottish heritage of a covenanted nation.[138] Budd identified with 'the design of our Reformers', many of whose works he was responsible for reissuing.[139] There were appeals to the Thirty-Nine Articles and to the formularies.[140] This was part and parcel of the growing historical awareness of the age. Irving was glad the Church of England retained 'Baptismal and communion services, comminations, fastings, and festivals, ordinations, and all the other revered forms of the Latin Church'. They constituted a monument to past glories: 'like the ancient armour of our fathers, they mock their puny children'.[141] There was value as well in the church year, 'the various anniversaries which were instituted by the first Christians, in commemoration of different important events'.[142] By 1828 Drummond had reached the striking conclusion 'that the Popish practice of praying from a liturgy . . . *without preaching*, is nearer being a proper ceremonial for God's house, than making it a *mere preaching house* without prayer, as it is generally considered now'.[143] The whole trend culminated in the elaborate liturgy of the Catholic Apostolic Church, which moved ahead of all but the most advanced ritualists in the Church of England by introducing reservation of the consecrated elements in 1850, altar lights and incense in 1852, the mixed chalice in 1854 and holy water in 1868.[144] In this case High Churchmanship could hardly be higher.

There was a corresponding rise in the value attached to the sacraments. Drummond affirmed in 1828 that Catholic estimates of baptism and the Lord's Supper were nearer the truth than the idea that these sacraments 'are mere signs, as held by all the Dissenters, and by most of the Church of England Evangelicals'.[145] Drawing on such writers as Hugh of St Victor, a copy of whose medieval treatise on the sacraments he gave to Coleridge in 1829,[146] Irving adopted the same position. A sacrament, he held, is a 'sign containing the grace signified'. He scolded the church for its neglect of the Lord's Supper, which revealed, he contended, its unholy state.[147] Other Evangelicals were just beginning to adopt a loftier view of the sacrament. W. A. Shirley, who was eventually to become a bishop, commenced a Church Communion Society at about the same time.[148] The Brethren from their beginnings believed that the Christian community was constituted by its meeting to 'break bread' every week.[149] There was a growing appreciation of the holy communion in certain Evangelical circles.

In general, however, more attention was paid to baptism by the radicals. 'I know', wrote Irving, 'that amongst no class of the Church doth so much darkness and indifference exist upon the subject of baptism, as amongst the Evangelical, amongst whom I have hardly found one who hath even an idea of what is meant by this most excellent service of the Church.'[150] His *Homilies on the Sacraments* of 1828, in fact concerned entirely with baptism, were designed to make good the deficiency. Baptism, he teaches, 'involves a real ingrafting into Christ'.[151] It may well be that he adopted so strong a view partly because of emotional stress following the death of two infant children. Certainly he derived comfort from the doctrine in his affliction.[152] But it became a foundation stone of Irving's ecclesiology, 'the boundary of separation between the creature regenerate, and the creature unregenerate'.[153] Irving did not stand alone in magnifying the effects of baptism. Henry Budd, from the ranks of the Church of England, composed a thorough study of *Infant Baptism* (1827). Budd argues that infant baptism highlights the principle that God graciously fulfils his promises and therefore exalts the need for faith. 'We may then hope', he writes, 'that as faith pleads and acts on the PROMISE, God will bless his own mode of ameliorating the human character, and that our population shall not be a community of mere natural men, but a Communion of the Saints of God.'[154] Budd gained the approval of Shirley, of Drummond and, in some measure, of Maurice.[155] It was a time when, it has been suggested, belief in the innocence of childhood generated sentiment that could readily be transferred to the baptismal service.[156] Something of this kind was occurring among advanced Evangelicals.

Such developments, though highly reminiscent of the Tractarians, were proceeding before the Tractarian movement began at Oxford in 1833. The radical Evangelicals held in the 1820s views that sound characteristic of Newman, Pusey, Keble and their circle in the following decade. 'The communion of saints and the holy catholic church', recorded Drummond in 1827, 'are grown to be dead letters in the creed; their meaning is understood, their comfort felt, no more.'[157] Irving was using the phrase 'the idea of the Christian church' as early as 1825.[158] At Albury in 1827 the mark of unity in the church was valued so highly that attenders believed they had a duty to prove the Roman Catholic Church to be apostate in order to clear themselves of the sin of schism.[159] There was an associated high doctrine of the ministry. Irving was prepared to use the word 'priesthood' in 1828 when lamenting the growing disrespect for it.[160] 'The interference of laymen in ecclesiastical affairs is arrived at a fearful height', wrote Drummond (paradoxically a layman himself) in the same year.[161] He was glad to appeal to the Fathers.[162] The first Albury report concludes with a quotation from Keble, whose *Christian Year* is described as 'exquisite poetry'.[163] It becomes apparent that the radical Evangelicals were not just similar to the Tractarians but were actually an earlier phase of the same movement that in the 1830s proliferated into many strands – including Brethren and the Catholic Apostolic Church as well as Tractarianism.

Newman is a bond between the earlier phase and the Oxford Movement proper. During the 1820s, already a Fellow of Oriel, Newman was an Evangelical. He dabbled in prophecy, and as late as 1829 was elected co-secretary of the CMS auxiliary at Oxford.[164] He came to accept, like Irving, the doctrine of baptismal regeneration, and in 1826 noted in his diary that 'Pusey accused me the other day of becoming more High Church'.[165] Increasingly, Newman diverged from the extremists at Oxford around Bulteel, but he fully shared their heightened supernaturalism. Late in 1833 he published five letters in *The Record* urging Evangelicals to support the Oxford Movement.[166] The hope that they might rally to the cause was no chimera, for the influences affecting Newman were also playing on them. Similarly, the sons of William Wilberforce, with Henry Manning, found the transition from Evangelicalism to a much higher churchmanship a natural evolution.[167] Later, when the battle lines were drawn between Evangelical and Anglo-Catholic, the affinity was forgotten, but at the time it was substantial. Suspicion of the Tractarians soon arose among Evangelicals, and in 1838 it hardened into hostility on the publication of Hurrell Froude's *Remains* with its repudiation of Protestantism.[168] Admissions of links between the two sides became guarded. Budd's *Infant Baptism*, according to his biographer in 1855, 'gave the first hints of several reforms in the Church, which the Tractarians have caught up, and distorted'.[169] But when, in the second half of the century, the first wave of alarm at Tractarian innovation passed, many Evangelicals, as will appear, were prepared to alter their thinking, and especially their practice, in a more churchly direction.[170] They were returning to a tendency already marked in the Evangelical ferment of the later 1820s.

CHURCH AND DISSENT

Not all the changes that marked the period round 1830 can be attributed primarily to the changing cultural context. The diverging paths taken by Anglicans and Dissenters is an instance where other circumstances were more decisive. The increasingly secure position of Evangelicals in the Church of England was a factor distancing them from Dissent. There was a growing commitment to the Church of England as an institution. Edward Bickersteth, for instance, encouraged Evangelical churchpeople to make a point of attending the ministry of their parochial clergymen, in his *Christian Hearer* of 1826.[171] There were fewer scruples about the liturgy, and younger men were beginning to regard it as close to perfection. J. E. Gordon, an earnest Evangelical who entered parliament in 1831, was to praise its order of service as sublimely devotional.[172] It is not surprising that Gordon and many of his contemporaries displayed a higher regard for the establishment principle than had been customary among their predecessors.[173] The relations between church and state, furthermore, were brought to public attention by the so-called 'constitutional revolution' of 1828–32. With the national legislature no longer expressly Protestant and the church notoriously riddled with abuses, ecclesiastical reform seemed likely to come next after parliamentary reform. Lord Henley, an Evangelical, put forward his own proposals for church reform in 1832,[174] but, especially when the Whig government set out to restructure the Church of Ireland in the following year, the more wary began to fear the spectre of disestablishment.

The intellectual atmosphere, though undoubtedly secondary, did play its part in encouraging Evangelicals to a stouter defence of the Church of England as established. The radical Evangelicals were beginning to think, like Coleridge in *Church and State* (1830), about the complementarity of church and nation. 'It is the duty of the State to establish the Christian religion', declares an Albury conference report.[175] The rationale was that, just as the church represents Christ's priestly office, so the state represents his kingly office. In Parliament during 1831–2 Spencer Perceval, the son of the assassinated Prime Minister and later an apostle of the Catholic Apostolic Church, rose several times, Bible in hand, to summon the nation to greater dependence on God.[176] In 1834, R. B. Seeley, and an Evangelical publisher, issued a set of *Essays on the Church* in which he contends, in anticipation of Gladstone's book on *The State in its Relations with the Church* (1838), that the corporate personality of the state makes it competent to honour God by establishing the church.[177] Already William Dealtry had published *The Importance of the Established Church* (1832) and James Scholefield *An Argument for a Church Establishment* (1833). *The Record* gave its loud support to the establishmentarian position; groups of Evangelicals founded a Christian Influence Society and an Established Church Society in 1832 and 1834 respectively.[178] Under the auspices of the Christian Influence Society, in 1838 Thomas Chalmers delivered the most popular defence of the establishment of the decade to crowded audiences in London.[179] There was a marked trend of Evangelical opinion in the Established Churches in favour of active support for the union of church and state.

Naturally, the same trend was not apparent in the Dissenting churches. The repeal of the Test and Corporation Acts in 1828 was the result of their pressure. Dissenters had proved themselves to be loyal subjects of the crown for nearly a century and a half. Why, they asked, should they continue to be defined as unworthy of holding office in town corporations? Although in practice the legislation was virtually a dead letter, Dissenters felt that it made them the victims of social discrimination. So they successfully demanded that government should remove one of the leading stigmas of Dissent.[180] With the reform of Parliament enfranchising many Dissenters four years later, there was bound to be pressure for an end to their other grievances. In the winter of 1833–4 there was a remarkable upsurge of Dissenting feeling that adopted the disestablishment cry.[181] Permanent damage was done to relations between Evangelicals in church and chapel. It was long recalled (when his qualifications of the statement were forgotten) that Thomas Binney, a leading Congregationalist, had declared that the Established Church destroyed more souls than it saved.[182] Political battles over church rates and other questions of religious equality multiplied during the 1830s and 1840s. Co-operation in evangelism, as in the foundation of the interdenominational London City Mission in 1835, and in public work, as in the Evangelical Alliance from 1845, was fraught with bickering.[183] *The Christian Observer*, representing moderate Anglican Evangelicalism, claimed in 1843, a little disingenuously, not to have changed its former sympathetic attitude to Dissenters. Yet the Dissenters were showing a less kind spirit towards the Evangelicals of the Established Church than earlier in the century.[184] From the 1830s onwards, despite rapprochements from time to time, the gulf between church and chapel generally yawned much wider than before.

A DEFENSIVE POSTURE

Within the Church of England there developed a sense of being a bastion under assault. Like continental conservatives or Newman, Anglican Evangelicals identified the hostile force as Liberalism. They shared Newman's diagnosis of its primary assertion: 'No religious tenet is important, unless reason shows it to be so.'[185] Liberalism was any philosophy of life not built on divine revelation. Its adherents were called the 'Infidel, or indifferent party of our politicians . . . who separate the Policy of the state from the Supremacy of religion'.[186] The grand crime of the Dissenters was entering a coalition with such men and worshipping 'their idol liberalism'.[187] There were serious secular implications. Liberalism attacked primogeniture, the basis of landed property, and so threatened the social order with the 'evils of democracy'.[188] It insinuated that 'the people, and not God, are the source of legitimate power'.[189] The true foundation of political authority was, on the contrary, that kings hold power delegated by Christ. And political economy, fostered by Liberalism, denied the paternalist responsibility of Christian governments to care for the poor and oppressed.[190] So the effect of Liberalism was socially and politically disastrous. 'Liberalism', according to a report of Albury, 'is a system of unbindings, of setting free from all ties'.[191] Its anarchic individualism betokened revolution in the pattern of things ordained by God. Hence it was at all costs to be opposed. It is no wonder that exponents of such views turned towards whatever promised to resist the advances of Liberalism. During the 1830 most Evangelicals in the Church of England severed any previous links they might have had with Whiggery. *The Christian Observer* never supported the Whigs after 1834. Remaining Evangelical Whigs, in fact, became suspect.[192] Peelite Conservatism seemed a bulwark of true religion.

Infidelity, the apparent premise of Liberalism, seemed to be on the increase. The grand sin of these days, according to an Albury report, was 'scepticism, infidelity, the deification of the intellect of man, reasoning pride, disbelief in the Word of God'.[193] The tide of unbelief had swept in since the French Revolution; Voltaire, Rousseau, Diderot, Condorcet and other free-thinking writers were selling well in France; Tom Paine was influencing even the Reformed religion in Britain.[194] There had been an outburst of infidel propaganda during the Queen Caroline affair of 1820–1, some of it blasphemous and much of it scurrilous, that must have troubled Evangelicals.[195] Increasingly they lumped together what others naturally contrasted – the highly respectable Utilitarian body of social thought stemming from the Enlightenment and the popular printed material that poured scorn on the existing order in church and state. The former, whose advance was celebrated in the 1820s as 'the march of mind', was as much an expression of irreligion as the latter. Satan was manipulating both to ensure that people would accept nothing on the bare testimony of God's word, but only with reasons. 'This is the natural and inevitable consequence', it was said, 'of all education which is not founded upon the doctrines of Christianity . . . '[196] Hence the radical Evangelicals were vocal opponents of the creation in 1828 of London University, the institution that became University College, London. Nobody denounced this 'godless institution in Gower Street' where there was to be no religious instruction more vigorously than did Irving and Drummond. 'The Bible', wrote Drummond, 'does prescribe the mode in which youth shall be trained, namely, in the nurture and admonition of the Lord; and a system founded on the intentional neglect of, and disobedience to, that command, is an infidel system, or rather a system of premeditated and obstinate rebellion against God.'[197] The need to preserve the religious element in education became a standard characteristic of Evangelicals in the Established Church.

A corollary of this stance was that, even before the rupture between church and chapel, the circle around Irving and Drummond became fiercely hostile to co-operation with Unitarians. Evangelical Dissenters had retained their traditional links with the English Presbyterians who had adopted lower, more rationalist, 'Socinian' views of the person of Christ. William Smith, the leading Dissenting MP, shared these views and yet was a close colleague of Wilberforce and his parliamentary friends.[198] The new Evangelical school, however, regarded Unitarians with distaste as a species of infidel within the professing church. Socinianism, for Irving, was a form of apostasy.[199] Joint activities with Unitarians must therefore cease. In 1830–1 an attempt was made, with followers of Irving and Haldane in the van, to purge the Bible Society of its Socinian supporters.[200] In 1836 the orthodox Dissenters similarly determined to end their alliance with Unitarians, who were forced to withdraw from the representative General Body of Protestant Dissenting Ministers.[201] Orthodoxy was coming to be seen as a condition of co-operation.

ANTI-CATHOLICISM

The other grand threat to Evangelical values came from Roman Catholicism. Although its numbers had grown during the eighteenth century, the Catholic Church in Britain,remained in the 1820s a docile, unassertive body, eager to demonstrate the qualification of its members for the parliamentary franchise.[202] Evangelicals shared the common British aversion to popery as a compendium of all that was alien to national life, whether religious, political or moral. They inherited the Reformation identification of the papacy as Antichrist, the seventeenth-century fears that linked popery with continental autocracy and the popular suspicions that hovered round celibacy and the confessional. They added their own specific sense of the spiritual deprivation of Catholics. Yet the unobtrusiveness of the Catholic population and the predisposition to toleration of the early Evangelicals meant that virulent anti-popery was remarkably rare in the first three decades of the century. It was, after all, supposed that popery was a spent force, already tottering (since the French Revolution) to its ultimate fall, and so it seemed no threat.

Developments in the 1820s, however, began to point towards a more wholehearted anti-Catholicism. In Ireland Protestant–Catholic controversy took on a sharper edge following the provocative primary charge by William Magee, Anglican Archbishop of Dublin, in 1822.[203] Methodists were arousing Catholic resentment in Ireland by their evangelism and fuelling the growth of anti-Catholic feeling among their English co-religionists.[204] And in Britain the intense public discussion of the 1820s over whether or not to concede political rights to Catholics stirred up the ashes of ancient disputes.[205] Dissenters were divided among themselves on the question of Catholic emancipation, the more educated seeing the analogy with their own case against civil discrimination on grounds of religion, the rank and file a prey to traditional suspicions.[206] A similar fissure ran through the ranks of Evangelical Anglicans, though there were sophisticated figures such as Sir Robert Inglis and William Marsh who were devotedly opposed to the Catholic claims.[207] Irving was at first neutral, but later decided that a concession to Catholics would infringe his ideal of a state professing the true religion.[208] It was in his circle that the strongest anti-Catholic attitudes sprang up. In 1827 a Protestant Reformation Society for anti-Catholic propaganda was set up, with J. E. Gordon as secretary.[209] The church of Rome might be apostate, but its power to deceive had not disappeared. Catholicism was once more seen as a deadly foe.

The strongest stimulus to anti-Catholicism was the influx of Catholic Irish. Even before the famine of the mid-1840s brought a vast torrent from Ireland, the trickle of immigrants had swelled into a substantial flow. By the 1820s the pressures of over-population and cheaper rates for the passage to England stimulated a large-scale exodus. By 1851 half a million Irish-born had settled in England and Wales.[210] Apart from traditional disdain for the Irish, anti-Catholicism was fostered by fears of their revolutionary tendencies and a stereotype of poverty and laziness, barbarism and ignorance, which came close to the reality of immigrant existence in the urban 'rookeries'.[211] When these attitudes were mingled with inherited anxieties and enhanced by Evangelical fervour, the result was a heady and distasteful brew.[212]

It was most potent in the Anglican circles where premillennialism had taken hold. In the historicist scheme, there was no doubt that Antichrist was Rome. Thus the chief practical application of E. B. Elliott's massive four-volume work on the interpretation of Revelation was a warning that we should not 'seek nationally to identify ourselves with the Papal antichristian religion' or to 'abandon our distinctive Protestant character'.[213] But others untouched by the new prophetic movement also succumbed to a virulent anti-popery. Hugh Miller, editor of the newspaper of the Free Church of Scotland and a literary figure of some standing, was alarmed by the hordes of impoverished Irishmen crowding into the Edinburgh slums. 'We must employ betimes more missionaries and Bibles soon', he wrote, 'or we shall soon have to employ soldiers and cannon.'[214] The most politicised version of anti-Catholicism was the Protestant Association, founded in 1835 by J. E. Gordon. Its greatest strength was in Lancashire, where popular apprehensions about immigration were most intense, since Liverpool was the chief port of entry from Ireland. Hugh McNeile, once Drummond's vicar at Albury and now in Liverpool, set up in 1839 a Protestant Operative Society linked with the Association.[215] McNeile treated the Protestant cause as the defence of his country, argued explicitly for 'Nationalism in Religion' and declared that 'we cannot allow our spirituality as Christians entirely to supersede our patriotism as Britons'.[216] Inevitably, the Protestant Association and the strongest of the other anti-Catholics were firmly aligned with the Conservatives. Therefore the apparent betrayal of the Protestant cause by Peel in 1845, when he increased the government grant to the Catholic seminary at Maynooth, was an immense shock.[217] It provoked an upsurge of angry protest in the whole Evangelical community that was to be surpassed only once in the subsequent history of anti-Catholic opinion – the *levée en masse* in 1850–1 against the so-called papal aggression, when Pius IX restored the hierarchy of the Catholic Church in England and Wales.[218] By the middle of the century hatred of the papacy and all its works had. been powerfully reinforced in the Evangelical mentality.

AN OUTLOOK OF PESSIMISM

The assaults by infidels and papists on the truth of God and, for an increasing number, the onslaught by Dissenters on the establishment, made the prospects for Christianity seem dark. Expectations that the gospel would usher in a superior world order were dismissed by the new school as a sinister deception. 'Fye, oh, fye upon it!' exclaimed Irving, 'ye Christians have fathered upon the scriptures the optimism of the German and French infidels!'[219] Dreams of human improvement without decisive divine intervention were chimerical. The Brethren produced the most extreme version of the new pessimism with their assertions that the whole professing church, Protestant as well as Catholic, had lapsed into apostasy so that security lay in 'gathering to the name alone', that is, in withdrawing from existing ecclesiastical organisations to worship Christ in seclusion and simplicity.[220] Fears for the future were aggravated when the bastion of the Church of England turned out to be harbouring a fifth column. When, in the late 1830s, the Tractarians were perceived as crypto-Romanists, alarm scaled new heights. A typical comment was that Tractarians were 'working to poison' the education of the national church at its source in Oxford.[221] Prophecy added its seal by announcing the last days. Symptoms were all around. The prophetic writer J. W. Brooks censured 'the depraved taste of the age', citing '*Nicholas Nickleby*, abounding with the lowest vulgarity' as a good example.[222] The world seemed degenerate.

Resistance to the upsurge of gloom came from those who rejected premillennialism. Samuel Waldegrave still held in 1854 that the Old Testament predicted the blessings of gospel days.[223] John Harris, representing the predominant school of opinion among Dissenters, argued that hopes for the spread of the gospel must be sustained for the sake of encouraging support for foreign missions.[224] But the newer and darker view, propagated especially by *The Record*, was making headway. At some distance, *The Christian Observer* followed in its tracks. By 1844 this journal that had once been renowned for its humanitarianism was expressing doubts about the potential for reform. Social improvement through legislation and popular institutions was limited by the fallen state of man. Education might do something, but only regeneration could supply the remedy. In the field of social reform, 'men begin with expecting too much; and conclude with hoping for nothing'.[225] Francis Close, Vicar of Cheltenham and a leading exponent of the new attitudes, voiced the political implications of pessimism. 'In my humble opinion', he declared, 'the Bible is conservative, the Prayer Book conservative, the Liturgy conservative, the Church conservative, and it is impossible for a minister to open his mouth without being conservative.'[226] Evangelicals in the Church of England were turning into embattled defenders of the existing order.

The chief explanation for the transformation of Evangelicalism in the years around 1830 is the spread of Romanticism. Much must be attributed to the alarming political events of the times. The constitutional revolution in particular precipitated a revision of Evangelical attitudes. The changing religious situation, encompassing the immigration of the Catholic Irish, the rise of the Oxford Movement and the growing strength of Evangelicalism itself, played an essential part. But Evangelicals were most affected by the new cultural mood that in the 1820s spread beyond the small literary caste to a wider public. Before any of the shock-waves of repeal, emancipation and reform, a new world-view for Evangelicals had been fashioned by the radical coterie of Albury. Despite the retreat of Irving and Drummond to the private world of the Catholic Apostolic Church, they had already injected most of their attitudes into the mainstream of Evangelical life. An intensified sense of the supernatural spread in many forms and in many ways, revolutionising the inherited outlook.

Those who responded to the new ideas tended to be the young, and so they lived long to propagate their views. They were also drawn primarily from the social elite. The students of prophecy, it was noted as late as 1864, 'are not mere ignorant enthusiasts, but belong in considerable numbers to the respectable and educated classes of society'.[227] The Catholic Apostolic Church, embodying the full range of the new views, included in its ranks the seventh Duke of Northumberland, a viscount and four baronets; it was also disproportionately supported by lawyers, ex-clergymen, bankers, businessmen and physicians.[228] Likewise the well-to-do, including several peers, were attracted into the Brethren.[229] Because the new opinions had greater appeal for the upper and professional classes, they were much more widespread in the Church of England than outside. Dissenters were acting on the very Liberalism that Anglicans deplored, and so remaining loyal to the Enlightenment heritage. In the long run the new opinions of the years around 1830, and especially the prophetic and biblical convictions, were to reach a broader audience, percolating down eventually to the lower-class sectarian fringe. But in the middle third of the nineteenth century it was a section of the educated world that embraced the innovations. That is precisely because it was educated: it was more familiar with fresh ideas and more willing to accept them. The leaders of Evangelical opinion were swayed by the fashionable Romantic assumptions of their day. The gospel was being remoulded by the spirit of the age.

[4]

The Growth of the Word: Evangelicals and Society in the Nineteenth Century

But the word of God grew and multiplied. (Acts 12:24)

'Miss Drusilla Fawley was of her date, Evangelical.'[1] So Thomas Hardy describes the elderly aunt of the protagonist in his last novel, *Jude the Obscure*. While acidly implying that Evangelicalism, for all its claims to represent eternal truth, is entirely transient, Hardy incidentally points us to the period of Evangelical ascendancy in Britain. His novel, after publication in parts, appeared complete in 1895: the prime of Miss Drusilla Fawley must have been thirty to forty years before, that is, in the 1850s and 1860s. The cult of duty, self-discipline and high seriousness was at its peak in those decades. In 1850 the Lord Lieutenant of a Midland shire remembered a time when only two landed gentlemen in the county had held family prayers, but by that year only two did not.[2] When fast days were carefully observed during the Crimean War, there was satisfaction at the 'improved religious tone' of the age.[3] And sabbatarian opinion, a useful gauge of Evangelical social influence, reached its apogee in the campaigns of the 1850s to ensure the Sunday closure of the Crystal Palace and British Museum.[4] Evangelical attitudes were characteristic of the times as never before or since. The earliest favourable appreciation of Victorian civilisation, swimming against the tide of previous hostility to all things Victorian, G. M. Young's *Portrait of an Age*, fully recognised this broad ascendancy: 'Evangelicalism had imposed on society, even on classes which were indifferent to its religious basis and unaffected by its economic appeal, its code of Sabbath observance, responsibility, and philanthropy; of discipline in the home, regularity in affairs; it had created a most effective technique of agitation, of private persuasion and social persecution.'[5] Such 'Victorian values' should perhaps more accurately be styled 'high Victorian values', the social norms of the years immediately following the middle of the nineteenth century. Their dominance was primarily the fruit of Evangelical religion.

Not all mid-Victorians welcomed this development. To some more venturesome spirits the yoke of high Victorian values was irksome. A person, lamented J. S. Mill, 'who can be accused either of doing "what nobody does", or of not doing "what everybody does", is the subject of as much depreciatory remark as if he or she had committed some grave moral delinquency'.[6] Mill's *Essay on Liberty*, from which this quotation is taken, was an eloquent protest by the most distinguished English philosopher of his century against the forces making for conformity. It is the classic text of nineteenth-century Liberalism. But its shafts are directed less against the oppressive authority of the state than against what Mill calls 'the despotism of custom'. Completed in 1857 and published in 1859, the book is a condemnation of social pressures, and only secondarily of state interference. Mill was objecting to the power of opinion to wear down creative individuality to a uniform level of mediocrity. Although he never uses the word, Evangelicalism is his chief target. He criticises what he calls the theory of Calvinism, which is held, he suggests, by many who do not consider themselves Calvinists. According to Mill's caricature of the theory, human beings have but to submit to the divine will. All must bow to the same purposes, and so all must behave alike. The 'stricter Calvinists and Methodists . . . these intrusively pious members of society', in their passion for the improvement of morals, may well attempt the prohibition of popular amusements. Already they have launched three efforts to abridge personal liberty. There has been formed a United Kingdom Alliance to obtain the prohibition of the sale of liquor; there are outbreaks of sabbatarianism; and there is open hostility to Mormons.[7] All three of Mill's instances can be laid at the door of Evangelicals and their associates. Mill's powerful onslaught illustrates the extent to which popular Protestantism was (as it saw the matter) trying to be its brother's keeper. It is testimony to the mid-Victorian social influence of Evangelicalism.

Within the Church of England, as Gladstone pointed out in 1879, the Evangelical movement never became dominant, yet 'it did by infusion profoundly alter the general tone and tendency of the preaching of the clergy; not, however, at the close of the last or the beginning of the present century, but after the Tractarian movement had begun, and, indeed, mainly when it had reached that forward stage . . . of Ritualism'.[8] If the initiative had passed to the Oxford Movement and its offspring, the greatest influence of the Evangelicals as an Anglican party came in the period just after the middle of the century. The number of Evangelical clergy had been estimated in 1803 at five hundred.[9] In 1823 there had been 1,600 clerical subscribers to the Church Missionary Society.[10] By 1853 the Evangelical clergy were judged to embrace 6,500, that is, well over a third of the whole number.[11] The pace of change had increased in the 1830s and 1840s as a higher proportion of ordinands was drawn from the Evangelical camp. More young men were offering themselves for ministry, so that the balance of allegiance within the profession altered the more rapidly. By 1854 a majority of clergy had been ordained in the previous twenty years.[12] The younger men, even if outside the party boundary of Evangelicalism, had grown up in a world more favourable to vital religion, and its idiom, as Gladstone suggested, affected their preaching in particular.

The rising Evangelical tide was also evident in the episcopate. The first Evangelical bishop, Henry Ryder, was appointed to Gloucester in 1815 (and to Lichfield in 1824). The second and third, the brothers C. R. and J. B. Sumner, were elevated to Llandaff in 1826 (Winchester in 1827) and to Chester in 1828 respectively. Several clergy of Evangelical sympathies, if not firm party men, were consecrated during the 1830s.[13] In 1846 and 1848 W. A. Shirley and John Graham became Bishops of Sodor and Man and of Chester.[14] Between 1856 and 1860 six more Evangelicals were added to the bench: H. M. Villiers went to Carlisle (and later Durham), Charles Baring to Gloucester, Robert Bickersteth to Ripon, J. T. Pelham to Norwich, J. C. Wigram to Rochester and Samuel Waldegrave to Carlisle. This flurry of appointments owed more, it was said, to Shaftesbury's influence with Palmerston than to the candidates' merits. But that was unfair: Palmerston, like Shaftesbury, was looking for conscientious pastoral bishops and, not surprisingly, found suitable men among the enlarged ranks of the Evangelicals.[15] By this time, furthermore, there was an Evangelical Archbishop of Canterbury in J. B. Sumner (1848–62), who, if no striking personality, was as hard-working as his colleagues. The Evangelical school, dominant in the churches of Scotland and the chapels of England and Wales, had come into its own even in the Church of England.

THE 1851 RELIGIOUS CENSUS

It so happens that the Evangelical ascendancy coincided with the only official census of religion ever taken in Britain. It was calculated at the time that, of the population of England and Wales over the age of ten that could have attended, 54 per cent chose to be in church on census Sunday. A more recent recalculation has suggested that a minimum of 35 per cent of the total population attended church, or 47 per cent of the total population over the age of ten.[16] We can safely conclude that about half the available adult population went to church. Contemporaries were dismayed that attendance figures turned out to be so low, and historians have tended to echo them. In particular, they have drawn attention to the disparity between rural and urban churchgoing. The index of attendance (total attendances as a percentage of the population) was 71.4 for rural areas and small towns; but for large towns with a population of more than 10,000 it was 49.7. All eight London boroughs and Birmingham, Manchester, Liverpool, Leeds, Sheffield and Bradford recorded an index of attendance below 49.7. The figure for Preston was as low as 25.5. The cities of Victorian England seemed to be weak spots for the churches.[17] In the relatively static countryside they might have retained their hold on the population, but in the growing urban centres they appeared to be failing in their mission. Population growth, industrialisation and urbanisation had transformed the face of much of the country, and the churches had not adjusted to altered circumstances.

There is good reason, however, to call in question so pessimistic a verdict on the impact of the churches. For only half the available population to be churchgoers might trouble those mid-Victorians who assumed the whole nation should conform to religious worship. Yet that figure compares favourably with the statistics of the late twentieth century. In 1979 adult church attendance as a proportion of the adult population of England was 11 per cent.[18] By that yardstick mid-nineteenth-century congregations were flourishing. Furthermore, scattered evidence from the eighteenth century suggests that attendance was often low in a period long before the census. In thirty Oxfordshire parishes between 1738 and 1811 the number of communicants formed less than 5 per cent of the population. Likewise, communicant levels were poor in late eighteenth-century Cheshire.[19] Such findings are congruent with the torpor that commonly gripped the Georgian Church of England. Consequently, it is certain that the churches were facing no novel problem in the levels of abstention from worship in 1851.

On the contrary, the rates of attendance in that year represented a significant improvement on the pattern prevailing in the previous century. The churches had managed to recruit more effectively despite the immense growth in population of the early nineteenth century, despite industrialisation and urbanisation. Their success can confidently be attributed primarily to the hunger for souls of Evangelicalism. In the case of Methodism the process of growth can be documented from the careful membership statistics kept by the connexions. In 1801 Methodists formed 1.5 per cent of the adult English population; in 1851, 4.4 per cent.[20] Similarly, Congregationalists in England grew from an estimated 35,000 in 1800 to 165,000 in 1851 while population merely doubled.[21] In Scotland, the proportion of churchgoers in 1851 at congregations of the Free and United Presbyterian Churches, both wholly Evangelical bodies, was 51 per cent, and at the much more mixed Church of Scotland it was 32 per cent.[22] It can also be shown from the 1851 census that the Evangelicals of the Church of England had achieved more than their contemporaries of the same communion. Returns for a sample of Evangelical parishes belonging to the Simeon Trust have been compared with those for a sample of equivalent nearby parishes of unknown churchmanship. The index of attendance for the Simeon Trust parishes turned out to be 44, whereas for the equivalent parishes it was only 25.[23] Evidently Evangelical Anglicans shared fully in the large-scale recruitment of the early nineteenth century. Massive church growth underlay the Evangelical social influence of the mid-century.

If the 1851 religious census reveals overall success by the churches in winning men and women to Christian practice, it also shows great geographical variation in their support. A broad regional contrast existed between the south-east, where the Church of England was generally stronger, and the north-west, where it was weaker. The contrast reflected the division of England and Wales into a lowland arable zone, where greater prosperity had created smaller parishes and richer endowments centuries before, and an upland pastoral zone, where larger, less sought-after parishes had received less intensive pastoral care. The Old Dissent was most powerful in its historic heartland, a swathe of territory embracing East Anglia, the South Midlands and the West Country, together with Wales. The strength of Methodism lay primarily in the upland zone of the north and west where the Church of England had been least efficient. Local diversity was immense, having a great deal to do with how effective squire and parson could be in excluding Nonconformity from the parish.[24] Consequently rural churchgoing varied between an index of attendance of 104.6 in Bedfordshire (a result of frequent multiple attendances) and one of 37.3 in Cumberland. It is entirely mistaken to suppose that there was anything like monolithic religious conformity in the countryside.

The level and denominational balance of churchgoing in large towns resembled, though usually at a lower level, the pattern of the surrounding countryside. Migrants to the towns were preponderantly drawn from the adjacent villages and brought their religious preferences with them.[25] Urban churchgoing also tended to be lower where the town was larger and its economy more industrialised. The three large towns possessing an index of attendance above the rural average of 71.4, Bath, Colchester and Exeter, were centres of administration, commerce and leisure rather than of industry. There can be no doubt about where the greatest strength of Evangelicalism lay. The Methodists, far more numerous than the other Nonconformist bodies, gathered throngs of worshippers in several of the northern counties. In Stoke-on-Trent they actually attracted more attendances than all the other denominations put together. In Yorkshire they did almost as well, achieving a percentage share of attendances of 47.3 in the East Riding, 45.4 in the North Riding and 42.3 in the West Riding.[26] It is possible to assess the strength of Evangelicalism within the Church of England according to the percentage of congregations in a county supporting the Church Missionary Society. By far the highest figures relate to Yorkshire: 42.5 for the East Riding, 40.2 for the North Riding and 39.7 for the West Riding. The adjacent counties of Durham (27.2), Derbyshire (26.0) and Lancashire (25.3) come next on the list.[27] It is plain that the combined forces of Methodism and Evangelical Anglicanism had become firmly entrenched in the north of England, with Yorkshire as a huge bastion. There were many remote rural nooks in the county, but equally it contained several of the most important industrial cities. The gospel did not lack appeal in an urban, industrial environment.

SOCIAL CLASS

In addition, the religious census lays bare a correlation between churchgoing and social class. Large towns with a similar class structure possessed similar rates of churchgoing. Again, more detailed analysis of the returns has shown that where middle-class inhabitants were numerous, church attendance was higher. Conversely, in the poorer parishes, attendance was lower.[28] It seems that this pattern was general. Only in Liverpool, where some Catholic Irish showed conspicuous loyalty to their church, did predominantly working-class parishes record higher attendances than predominantly middle-class parishes.[29] The growth of class-specific suburbs in the later nineteenth century accentuated the tendency. By 1902 in London there was a close correspondence between levels of churchgoing and the position of a suburb in the social hierarchy. Thus, in Ealing, near the top of the social scale, 47 per cent of the population was in church, while in Fulham, near the bottom, only 12 per cent.[30] Where the social mix was more varied, the parish church might draw in different grades – though not necessarily to the same service. But this principle did not apply to Nonconformists. 'Class position amongst the Nonconformists goes very much by congregations', concluded an observer in 1902, 'the worshippers sorting themselves in this way much more than do those who attend parish churches.'[31] Throughout the century church attendance was most common at the highest social levels. The ability of the churches to attract those possessing wealth and power, it has been justly observed, was a significant achievement, a sign of the importance of religion in society.[32]

A consequence, however, was that some denominations were almost entirely middle-class in composition. Although this was truest of the non-Evangelical Unitarians and the only partly Evangelical Quakers, it was also commonly the case among Congregationalists. Their denomination, according to the same observer of London in 1902, was 'more than any other the Church of the middle classes, its membership being practically confined within the limits of the upper and lower sections of those included under that comprehensive title'.[33] During the second half of the century the middle-class proportion of the worshipping community increased, not least because of the growth in size of the lower middle classes in society at large. Between 1851 and 1911 the proportion of occupied males over 15 in clerical and similar posts increased from 2.5 per cent to 7.1 per cent.[34] Children from churchgoing families in the working classes, often giving promise of steadiness and reliability, thronged into this emerging sector. In 1902, even in predominantly working-class Bethnal Green, 34.6 per cent of worshippers in Congregational chapels and 24.0 per cent of those in their Baptist equivalents were clerical workers.[35] Nor were the Primitive Methodists, with their proletarian image, exempt. At Ashton-under-Lyne, between 1850 and 1870, 4 per cent of their worshippers were lower middle-class; for the period between 1890 and 1910 the proportion had risen to 21 per cent.[36] The process of embourgeoisement reinforced over time the tendency of the churches to be more successful further up the social scale.

This feature of churchgoing was so marked that it is sometimes suggested that the working classes abstained from Christian worship altogether. A pioneer historian of the subject has written of 'the general widespread alienation of the artisan classes from the churches'.[37] It is easy, especially on the hypothesis of urbanisation being intrinsically unfavourable to churchgoing, to reach too blanket a conclusion. In reality, the figures for the 1851 census show that there must have been extensive working-class attendance. Too many people went to church for religious practice to have been confined to the middle classes, which accounted for less than a quarter of the population. A majority of the working people did not attend, but a significant proportion did. More detailed research has shown that skilled workers, the artisans proper, were far more likely to enter a place of worship than unskilled labourers. In the early nineteenth century it was the skilled who were overwhelmingly attracted to Evangelical Nonconformity. Whereas artisans constituted some 23 per cent of society at large, they composed 59 per cent of Evangelical Nonconformist congregations.[38] The Secession churches of Glasgow made a parallel appeal to the skilled men of the city.[39] The great number of tiny contributions to the CMS suggests that Evangelicalism in the Church of England drew heavily on the same constituency.[40] Artisans were commonly to be found in church.

Unskilled workers, usually the majority and in some areas the great majority of the working classes, were drawn into places of worship in much smaller numbers. The case of the Primitive Methodists, normally supposed to have provided a religion for the poor, is instructive. It is true that in some areas they did penetrate the unskilled working classes. In part of Lincolnshire, for instance, 51 per cent of identified Primitive lay preachers in the mid-nineteenth century were agricultural labourers.[41] Generally, however, Primitive Methodist chapels catered for the skilled much more than for the unskilled. In a national sample of Primitive congregations in the first third of the century 16 per cent were labourers and another 12 per cent were miners, most of them unskilled; but 48 per cent were artisans.[42] An exhaustive study has shown that, although between 80 per cent and 100 per cent of nineteenth-century Primitive Methodists were manual workers, they were much more likely to be semi-skilled or craftsmen than labourers.[43] There was, of course, a natural tendency for converted characters to gain skills, find regular employment and so rise out of the lowest ranks of society. Evangelical religion, as many commented at the time, was itself an avenue of upward social mobility. Yet this process meant that the gospel abstracted individuals from their original setting rather than mingling with the lifestyle of the poor. So it can be concluded that although Evangelicalism enjoyed substantial working-class support it never secured the allegiance of the masses of the labouring population.

NON-CHURCHGOING

Why was there widespread alienation among the lower working classes from the churches? A primary factor was sheer poverty. Even at the end of the century, by which time the working-class standard of living had risen significantly, the family income could often be too low to buy the essentials of existence such as shoes and clothes. To appear at church was to court the contempt of neighbours for not being able to dress the family adequately. Nor could many families afford pennies for the offering.[44] And one of the chief deterrents was the pew rent system. Most nineteenth-century places of worship, apart from older parish churches, were financed at least in part by hiring out particular pews to those who would pay for them. Grades of comfort dictated price differentials. Consequently, variations in social status were imported into church. Cheap or free seating was normally made available for the poor, but often in inconvenient corners behind pillars. A working-class newcomer would be assigned what an Evangelical clergyman condemned in 1859 as 'a pauper's post outside the well-cushioned pew'.[45] Despite a chorus of criticism from many quarters, the system persisted in places long into the twentieth century. It was symptomatic of the barriers to church attendance erected by what a leading Congregational minister called 'the English caste system'.[46]

Unskilled workers outside Methodism, with its plethora of official posts, rarely found themselves involved in church administration or exercising church discipline. Conversely, discipline, as enforced by Nonconformists and all Scottish Presbyterians, tended to bear more heavily on the poorer section of the working classes whose offences were normally more public.[47] This factor should not be exaggerated, for discipline was exercised over even the eminent and prosperous: the affairs of Sir Morton Peto, a bankrupt building and railway contractor, were fully investigated and partly censured in 1867 by the Baptist church he had founded.[48] Furthermore, vigilance in exercising discipline declined in all churches during the last third of the century, so that by its end the practice could hardly be a grievance.[49] Although working-class resentment of failure by the churches to criticise the class system existed, it seems not to have been a major reason for absence from worship until the end of the century. Only then did wholesale condemnation of the churches for ignorance of industrial questions and contempt for the working people affect more than a small proportion of the population.[50] Class consciousness had by that time reached new heights. Yet a certain ecclesiastical insensitivity to proletarian self-respect had previously caused a diffuse but powerful indignation among the working classes. 'Let the poor learn', Bishop Robert Bickersteth declared in 1860, 'that there is a sympathy felt for them amongst the classes which, in social rank, are above them.'[51] Although the intention was kindly, a tone so patently *de haut en bas* was noticed and, by some, resented. The result was a reinforcement of traditional anticlericalism, 'antagonism . . . to the parson as a paid teacher of religion'.[52] Dislike for lazy clergy, incomprehensible worship and overbearing class assumptions could combine with the expense of involvement to deter many of the poor from churchgoing.

Perhaps the most widespread explanation within Evangelical churches for working-class non-attendance in the late nineteenth century was what the Congregational minister already quoted called 'the drink habit'.[53] Alcohol clouded the spiritual faculties, and its purchase (it was commonly held) was responsible for the poverty that kept people outside the church doors. Simplistic as this analysis undoubtedly was, it held a measure of truth. The consumption of alcohol probably mounted steadily until 1876 and, although it fell thereafter, it remained at high levels.[54] Alcohol was available from a vast array of outlets. In 1854 in Merthyr Tydfil there were 506 licensed drinking places, that is, one for every 93 of the population, and the town was not exceptional.[55] The public house, as it had done down the centuries, formed the chief alternative centre of community life to the church. 'Pub-going' was the only social activity to attract more people than churchgoing. So it represented a different use of leisure time that constantly posed a threat to the churches.

From the years around 1870 onwards, furthermore, there was a great expansion in organised leisure activities that rivalled the churches in drawing power. Traditional recreations had probably suffered less in the early industrial period than has been supposed, but now, with increasing middle-class patronage, they were turned into disciplined, rule-governed games that harnessed extensive popular enthusiasm. The general adoption of the Saturday half-holiday permitted a great expansion of football and cricket clubs in the 1870s. The churches, sensitive to the popular mood, realised the need to provide recreational facilities. At Bolton a third of the cricket clubs and a quarter of the football clubs had a religious connection; and in Birmingham at least a fifth of the cricket clubs and a quarter of the football clubs.[56] Although such agencies retained the allegiance of some young men, their creation was evidence of a recognition by churches of their potential power to draw away. Like the contemporary working men's clubs and music halls, they supplied communal enjoyments that an earlier generation might have found through religious outlets.

The counter-attraction of organised atheism was much less potent. Committed secularists numbered no more than about twenty thousand at any time in Victorian Britain, with the National Secular Society in 1880, near its peak, claiming only six thousand members.[57] Agnosticism was as yet merely a fashion of the intelligentsia. It may well be, however, that a stronger influence on the lower working classes was a folk religion heavily indebted to paganism. The survival of rural witchcraft is vividly illustrated in the novels of Hardy, but there is also a growing body of evidence suggesting widespread popular belief in esoteric remedies for misfortune, the sacredness of nature and the importance of ritual observances at turning points in personal life and the annual cycle. Such notions were not confined to the countryside. City churches, as in Lambeth, were thronged with working-class attenders at harvest festival and on New Year's Eve, the two occasions when church services regularly marked events in nature rather than in Christian story.[58] A deep-rooted though residual nature religion could only hamper the evangelism of the churches. But when all the obstacles to churchgoing have been reviewed, there remains a fundamental explanation for the alienation from the churches. As a recent historian has put it, the otherworldly preoccupations of the churches were too distant from the needs of day-to-day living.[59] Evangelicals were making a similar point when they contended that the heart of man is not naturally sympathetic to the truth of God. In view of this inevitable gulf, the wonder of the nineteenth-century Evangelical record is not its shortcomings but its degree of success.

REVIVALISM

Church growth was partly a steady, sustained process and partly a matter of short, sharp increases. The bursts of revival were most marked in Methodism, but also affected other denominations in some parts of Britain. In Wales, for example, there was a rhythm of booms and slumps in recruitment, with good periods in 1807–9, 1815–20, 1828–30, 1839–43 and 1849.[60] Such variations invite interpretation in terms of factors external to the life of the churches. The trade cycle, itself a sequence of booms and slumps, is an obvious explanatory candidate. There is evidence that economic adversity sometimes coincided with falls in Nonconformist recruitment rates.[61] Inability to make financial contributions may well have enhanced inhibitions about chapel-going at such times. On the other hand, during the cotton famine of the 1860s that blighted Lancashire's industrial heartland with depression, its Wesleyan circuits achieved remarkable results. The average recruitment rate for the whole connexion was 2.6 per cent, but for ten cotton towns it was 15.1 per cent.[62] At times, acute hardship could encourage resort to supernatural aid. No consistent correlation between economic and religious cycles emerges.

Discussion of an alternative hypothesis explaining patterns of church growth has emerged from E. P. Thompson's contention that popular religion was a form of stunted radicalism. Periods of religious revival, he argues, followed socio-political excitements.[63] Supporting evidence comes from the aftermath of the so-called Captain Swing riots, outbreaks of rural incendiarism in 1830–2. Primitive Methodist expansion was immediate and striking in the affected areas.[64] In other cases, however, political agitation and evangelism were rival activities (as in the north of England following the French wars) or else Evangelical religion dampened the potential for radical politics (as in Cornwall in the Chartist years).[65] The commonest relationship, it has been suggested, was that religious and political ferment were simultaneous. When religious and political issues became interwoven, churches could be mobilised for vigorous evangelism and political assertion at the same time.[66] The clearest instance is a late one, the upsurge of Nonconformist membership in 1902–6, when the chapels were roused to political indignation against the Conservative Education Act of 1902.[67] Other alleged instances, however, turn out to be invalid: there was no such thing as 'a massive popular disestablishment campaign' in 1875–6 to explain the high Nonconformist recruitment rate of those years.[68] So it appears that political stimuli could bring church growth either at the time or in their wake, but that there was no necessary connection.

Death has been proposed as another precipitant of large-scale recruitment. 'Terrible accidents and fearful deaths', it was said of South Wales, '[are] not uncommon in these iron and coal districts . . . [H]ence funeral sermons are frequent, and are often attended with good moral and religious effect.'[69] The most obvious spur to revival of the nineteenth century was the cholera epidemic of 1832 that killed thousands. The twelve months up to March 1833 saw the largest membership increase ever recorded in Wesleyan history, and other denominations also reaped a harvest.[70] In the most popular Evangelical tract, Legh Richmond's *The Dairyman's Daughter*, the heroine dies of consumption; and diaries regularly turn to spiritual issues on the death of friends and relations. The fall of the death rate in the later nineteenth century and its greater fall in the twentieth century must have been disadvantageous for recruitment. If it seems clear that the pattern of church growth was not controlled by external determinants, it seems equally clear that crises – whether economic, political or, most insistent of all, the crisis of death – could provide a favourable context for the propagation of the faith.[71]

A revival could be a form of spontaneous combustion. Typical was an outbreak at Burslem reported by a Wesleyan preacher in 1832:

Two colliers had been playing at cards all the night, and were . . . cursing and swearing in a dreadful manner; when as they thought lightnings began to dart upon them with a strong smell of brimston[e] . . . They began to cry for mercy. The neighbourhood was all alarmed . . . For several days and nights, nearly the whole population of the place which is considerable, were engaged in incessant prayer . . .[72]

Such currents of feeling could readily overflow the official channels dug by denominational functionaries and, for that reason, the Wesleyan authorities often looked askance on the more exuberant displays. In particular, they discountenanced the camp meeting, a technique of American frontier religion at which open-air preaching and prayer would go on deep into the night. The Wesleyan condemnation of a camp meeting held in 1807 on Mow Cop, a hill overlooking Stoke-on-Trent, led to the emergence in the Potteries of a new connexion, the Primitive Methodists, committed to revivalism.[73] The early years of the Primitives were marked by loud cries of emotion, exorcisms of the devil and vivid dreams. Women saw visions in which was revealed a sort of celestial pecking order of the leading revivalists of the day, with individuals moving up or down the league table: 'the head of the Church', it was recorded in 1811, 'now stands as follows: James Crawford 1, Lorenzo Dow 2, Mary Dunnel 3 . . . '[74] Strange new ways were part and parcel of the uninhibited expression of a spontaneous revival.

As the century wore on, however, spontaneity gradually gave way to arranged revivals. A landmark was the appearance in 1839 of Charles Finney's *Lectures on Revivals of Religion*, originally published in America in 1835, with its argument that conversions could be encouraged by the adoption of certain techniques – such as the isolated 'anxious seat' for the troubled sinner in search of salvation. Although the book was a major stimulus in 1839–43 to traditional, uncontrived revivals in Wales, it heralded a new age of revival planning.[75] In Scotland a wave of revivalism beginning at Kilsyth in 1839 led to enthusiasm for Finney's methods among young men, the expulsion of candidates for the ministry from the Congregational theological academy for 'self-conversionism' and the creation in 1843 of a new denomination, the Evangelical Union, designed to foment revivals. An American evangelist, James Caughey, toured British Methodism in the 1840s, relying on well-tried techniques to obtain converts.[76] It was but a short step to the end–of–century trumpeter-revivalist with his carefully contrived performance depicted by Arnold Bennett in *Anna of the Five Towns*.[77] By 1860, when revival broke out at Hopeman on the Moray Firth, the local newspaper felt bound to state that 'no attempts were made to "get up" this movement'.[78] There was a gradual transition during the century from folksy outbursts of anguished guilt to professionally planned occasions for much more conventional 'decisions for Christ'.

This distinction is the key to understanding what happened to British Evangelicalism in 1859–60. It has been argued by Edwin Orr, himself a distinguished evangelist, that in those years there began a nationwide and sustained revival, 'the second Evangelical awakening in Britain'. He adduces evidence from all over the country of revival activities in those years.[79] What he does not attempt, however, is to discriminate between spontaneous popular revival, deeply rooted in the community, and meetings carefully designed to promote the work of the gospel. His case faithfully reflects his chief source, *The Revival* magazine, set up by R. C. Morgan in 1859 to foster the cause. Morgan deliberately created the impression that a single phenomenon, revival, was already aflame throughout Britain. He was eager to extend the traditional variety to untouched areas.

In reality, however, its range was severely limited. The movement began in America in 1857–8, breaking out in Ulster early in 1859. It made a powerful impact, bringing about mass conversions and physical prostrations of a kind that would have been familiar to Wesley or the early Primitives. It was greatly hoped that revival, perhaps without the prostrations, would reach Britain. Parts of Scotland were affected. Scarcely a town or village between Aberdeen and Inverness, it was said early in 1860, had not been visited by the Spirit.[80] At Portassie in Banffshire for nearly three days and nights there was continuous praying, singing and exhortation of neighbours. 'Labour is totally suspended', it was reported. 'Even the cooking of victuals is much neglected . . . '[81] Revival was general in the Isle of Lewis, and at Greenock in Renfrewshire a thousand, chiefly working people, were said to have been converted in less than six months.[82] It is significant that the centre of revival meetings in Greenock was the Seamen's Chapel, for repeatedly fishermen were chiefly involved. At Portassie the five hundred engaged in religious exercises were 'purely seafaring' and at neighbouring Buckie crews came to shore already converted.[83] Fishing communities were tightly knit, often isolated and well aware of the high risk of death at sea. They were particularly likely to retain corporate expectations of turning to God. In Wales, too, there were similar outbreaks, beginning in remote Cardiganshire.[84] In England, however, instances were rare. One researcher has discovered only three.[85] There were more, but almost entirely in Cornwall and north Devon, where, again, fishermen were concentrated.[86] Community revivals in Britain, it is clear, were virtually confined to the periphery and were most likely within a single occupational group.

The hope that such movements would spread, on the other hand, was an inducement to redouble organised efforts for the spread of the gospel. *The Revival* was itself a novel technique, a magazine devoted to spreading information about the movement. Open-air preaching, already being adopted by Evangelical clergy in the 1850s, became common again. Iron mission halls were erected. Laymen entered careers as full-time popular evangelists, whether gentlemen like Brownlow North or working-class characters like Richard Weaver, 'the converted collier'. Even female ministry, justified as an exceptional measure for exceptional times, became common, just as it had done among the early Primitives.[87] The Methodist spirit of pragmatic, aggressive evangelism was spreading beyond the bounds of Methodism. A new ethos, negligent of denominational forms, emerged. The Brethren sect created much of the network responsible for the new temper and drew in many of the converts.[88] All the Evangelical denominations nevertheless felt the new winds, and the way was prepared for the arrival of the enormously influential undenominational evangelists Moody and Sankey in the 1870s.[89] It is therefore quite just to see 1859–60 as the threshold of a fresh phase in organised evangelism; but events of those years show that revival of the spontaneous variety was becoming marginal in Britain.

METHODS OF EVANGELISM

Most of the nineteenth-century impact of Evangelicalism, however, was achieved not through revivals but through regular methods of mission.

Ordinary Sunday services were fundamental. At the evening service, normally the second or third of the day, the pattern of worship and the style of preaching were adapted to the supreme task of implanting the gospel in the hearers, who by that hour would include domestic servants and (in the countryside) agricultural labourers. In the less inhibited denominations, evening service would be followed by a prayer meeting or after-meeting where a significant proportion of conversions would take place. Beyond Sunday gatherings, however, there was a battery of other activities designed to convince or sustain converts. Weekly prayer meetings, often on a Friday or Saturday evening, were intended primarily to seek God's blessing on the Sunday services. Two or three individuals might be asked by the minister to lead the prayer, or else free prayer might be permitted, the minister closing the proceedings.[90] A midweek preaching service, or else in the Church of England a meeting for communicants, would supplement the instruction given on Sunday. Cottage meetings, often in remoter parts of the district, would provide opportunities for guidance to smaller groups. Bible classes were held for special sections of the congregation: female servants, mothers from the working classes, working men, ladies, young men, candidates for confirmation or church membership and children.[91] Other gatherings such as monthly sewing meetings for the poor could subserve spiritual purposes. 'Associations of the promising young females of the higher or middle rank in our parishes are very desirable.'[92] Ideally each social group was catered for.

Perhaps most important, Evangelicals did not wait for people to come to their places of worship; Evangelicals went to the people. House-to-house visitation began on a significant scale with the formation of the Strangers' Friend Society in London in the 1780s,[93] but it received an immense fillip from the publication of the first volume of Thomas Chalmers's *Christian and Civic Economy of Large Towns* in 1821. Chalmers described the system of lay visitation he had set in motion in the inner-city parish of St John's, Glasgow, and soon he was widely imitated.[94] In 1825 London Nonconformists established the Christian Instruction Society. By 1832 it had assembled about 1,150 members who paid a Christian visit once a fortnight to nearly 32,000 families.[95] Its success made it a model for further similar efforts. Voluntary visitors, most of them women, would call on perhaps twenty families at frequent intervals, always delivering tracts, encouraging attendance at worship and reporting cases of need to the minister. There were risks of petty officiousness: district visitors were warned 'never to indulge in culinary curiosity and peep in the pot'.[96] Yet the technique ensured that there was a point of contact between the church and non-attenders. It was supplemented from 1857 by Mrs Ranyard's Bible women, full-time paid visitors of a lower social class.[97] With a multitude of organisations, subordinate clergy and district visitors to co-ordinate, the incumbent of a large urban parish could have charge of a huge administrative machinery. As Rector of St George's, Southwark,

William Cadman assembled nearly 200 voluntary parish workers in 1850.[98] Sustained evangelistic activity on such a scale could hardly fail to make inroads on religious indifference.

Local effort was supported by a large and heterogeneous machinery of organisations. Official structures could help. A sympathetic bishop such as C. R. Sumner of Winchester could back the exhortations to mission of his pastoral charges with bodies like the diocesan Church Building Society, founded in 1837.[99] The London Diocesan Home Mission, set up by A. C. Tait, provided special preachers of varied churchmanship, yet was valued by many Evangelicals.[100] Among Nonconformists, the Congregational and Baptist Home Missionary Societies placed evangelists in neglected areas or decayed causes.[101] The Baptists also operated a national Building Fund and a Metropolitan Chapel Building Fund that contributed greatly to their enduring strength in the capital.[102] The Methodists led the way in the central allocation of funds and were followed in Scotland by the Free Church, which defied prophets of financial disaster for the new denomination with its rapidly created and generously supported Sustentation Fund for ministers.[103] In the second half of the century the Congregational and Baptist Unions, though serving independent congregations, developed a central apparatus for augmenting stipends.[104] Foreign missionary societies stimulated evangelism at home not by financial backing but by providing an object lesson. Interest in foreign missions, it was cogently argued, 'stimulates, encourages, directs Christian life by calling attention to the example of converts from heathenism'.[105]

Much of the home missionary work was designed to grapple with the growing nineteenth-century problem of neglected inner-city areas where the non-churchgoing masses increasingly congregated. The difficulties of Manchester incumbents were becoming greater year by year, it was reported in 1858, because the more respectable parishioners were moving to the outskirts.[106] Similarly, the Minister of Shoreditch Baptist Tabernacle in East London recalled that his church possessed its share of the well-to-do until the mid-1890s, but then, because it was continually feeding suburban congregations, found it difficult to maintain its work on the offerings of the poor.[107] The Church Pastoral Aid Society, launched in 1836, came to the relief of Evangelical clergy by supporting extra staff in needy parishes. Though incurring High Church frowns for financing non-clerical workers and operating beyond episcopal control, the society expanded so that in 1858 it paid for 378 curates and 162 lay agents.[108] Its work was supplemented by the Scripture Readers' Association, begun in 1844 and consolidated as an Anglican body in 1849, supporting men who neither preached nor distributed literature.[109] Lay agents were also provided by the interdenominational city missions of which the largest and most successful was the London City Mission, founded in 1835. The LCM financed evangelists who were normally attached to particular congregations, but who sometimes ministered to particular ethnic groups like the Welsh or particular industrial occupations like the dockers. After half a century its staff reached 460. A slightly higher social group, consisting of shop assistants and their peers, was the special target of the Young Men's Christian Association, founded in London in 1844 and soon possessing branches in most cities.[110] A broad range of other bodies, similar but smaller, often local or specialised, existed to help with evangelism: the Evangelization Society (1864), the Christian Colportage Association (1874) and the Missions to Seamen (1856) are but three examples.[111] Behind them all stood the munificence of men such as Samuel Morley, a millionaire hosiery manufacturer who was a broad-minded Congregationalist. 'The distribution of his money', according to his biographer, 'was . . . the main business of his life.'[112] Christian mission benefited hugely from the organisations that brought to it some of the fruits of British economic prosperity.

PHILANTHROPY

The poor who were not attracted to church by the gospel were sometimes drawn in by charity. 'Neither Jesus nor his apostles', according to *The Christian* in 1880, 'ever separated the physical from the spiritual well-being of men. He and they fed and healed the bodies of the people, and the sympathy thus manifested won their attention, and enabled them to impart food and healing to their souls.'[113] The gospel and humanitarianism, even in this rather pietistic journal, were seen not as rivals but as complementary. Because God had created the body as well as the soul, argued the prince of philanthropists, Lord Shaftesbury, each body must be 'cared for according to the end for which it was formed – fitness for His service'.[114] Although the career of Shaftesbury was never forgotten, it is remarkable that the charitable theory and practice of the mass of nineteenth-century Evangelicals were to be minimised by many later commentators.[115] Probably the chief explanation is that Evangelicals of the nineteenth century have been tainted by the repudiation of Christian social obligation that marked certain of their successors in the following century.[116] In the nineteenth century, however, even if private philanthropy was common in all religious bodies and beyond, Evangelicals led the way. Among charitable organisations of the second half of the century, for instance, it has been estimated that three-quarters were Evangelical in character and control.[117] The prison reform work of Elizabeth Fry, a Quaker of Evangelical inclination, early in the century became celebrated precisely because it was held up as an inspiration to subsequent generations.[118] Dr Barnardo of the Brethren earned equivalent fame in caring for orphans later in the century.[119] The sick in body and mind, the blind, the deaf, the infirm, the elderly, vagrants, navvies, soldiers, prostitutes, and above all the poor received attention according to their particular needs. Evangelical activism carried over into social concern as an end in itself.

There was, however, a diffidence among many Evangelicals about certain aspects of relief work. Not all the needy deserved help; if at all possible, the poor should help themselves; and public assistance was to be rejected out of hand. This cluster of tenets flowed from the general acceptance, at least by the upper and middle classes, of the teachings of political economy. The great masters in the tradition of Adam Smith held that no disincentive to hard work could be permitted in a well-ordered society. Lesser figures such as Samuel Smiles in the mid-nineteenth century sang the praises of self-help. Christians of all traditions assimilated these opinions to a greater or lesser extent.[120] The result was a tight circumscription of the bounds of charity that sometimes has a harsh ring. Chalmers insisted that in no circumstances, high unemployment included, should the able-bodied poor have a right to relief. Poverty, following Malthus, he held to be the great spur to industry. Financial assistance for the destitute, furthermore, must never be the result of compulsory exactions. The poor should rely on the generosity of the better-off.[121] A leading exponent of similar, though marginally less rigid, views in the Church of England was J. B. Sumner, subsequently the first Evangelical Archbishop of Canterbury. Charity, he contended, should consist of private benevolence. Only in very rare instances where social evils were so deeply seated as to frustrate private action, should the state intervene.[122]

A leading Evangelical clergyman who later became a Dissenter, Baptist Noel, reveals the ambiguity that was the result. He urged the Christian duty of relieving those in need, but he also warned that the charitably disposed might turn the poor into greedy mendicants. Requests for money must be rejected because the worth of applicants could not be ascertained. 'It is painful', he admitted, 'to turn away from the request of those who *may* be suffering from extreme want . . . '[123] It became accepted wisdom that the poor should not be helped unless they were known to be 'deserving' and then only in kind, not in cash. 'Indiscriminate almsgiving is a great curse', declared John Clifford, a Baptist who was later to modify his views, 'Government relief is mostly lifting a man up by dropping him into a deeper abyss.'[124] Ideas shaped by political economy probably made greater progress among Evangelicals outside the Established Churches, for within them there were countervailing traditions of parochial responsibility for the poor. The most influential Evangelical clerical handbook nevertheless recommended giving only partial relief, leaving to the poor a stimulus to their own exertions.[125] The regiment of seven clergy and eleven scripture readers or city missionaries operating during the 1850s in the Evangelical parish of St Giles, Bloomsbury, was enjoined to concentrate on spiritual objects and so give no charity.[126] Resentment spread among the poor when they were spurned. The Evangelical record in the philanthropic field was not an unqualified asset for evangelism.

Yet there is no doubt that social concern did bring some of the less advantaged within the sphere of Christian influence. The philanthropic machinery of an individual congregation could be huge, especially as the century advanced. Kensington Congregational Church already possessed by the early 1820s, apart from schools and evangelistic agencies, a Benevolent Society run by ladies for visiting, instructing and relieving the sick poor; a Blanket Society, making free distributions in winter; an Infants' Friendly Society, through which ladies provided clothes and food for poor mothers and their children during their confinement; and collections in severe winters for the poor of the area.[127] A well equipped urban parish church at mid-century was expected to have a District Visiting Society, whose members could issue tickets for obtaining relief in kind from local tradesmen; a Provident Fund, collecting sums of not more than sixpence weekly, adding interest and returning coals or clothing in June or December; soup distribution at a penny a quart in winter; Maternal Charity tin boxes containing a Bible, Prayer Book, oatmeal, sugar, soap and sometimes linen for pregnant mothers; and (rather less popular) a Lending Library.[128] At Reading in the 1890s the various churches and chapels provided similar but even more numerous agencies: a Poor Fund in most chapels, Ladies' Visiting Associations, perhaps with paid sick visitors, Sunshine Funds attached to most Christian Endeavour groups, Dorcas Societies encouraging sewing for the poor, Soup Kitchens, Mothers' Meetings on behalf of the poor, Provident Clubs, Coal and Clothing Clubs, Loan Blanket Societies, Infants' Friends Societies, Penny Banks, maternity groups and much else. [129] All this battery of assistance amounted to far more than a minor palliative. Apart from the heartily disliked Poor Law, the churches were the most obvious source of help in a society which, until shortly before the First World War, lacked a state welfare system.

Local ecclesiastical provision was supplemented by the various societies that sprang up to channel funds from generous to the needy. Organisations like the Indigent Blind Visitation Society and the Destitute Children's Dinner Society proliferated. In the first half of the nineteenth century, it has been calculated, new philanthropic bodies were founded at an average rate of six a year.[130] With their annual gatherings entrenched among the May Meetings of the Exeter Hall, they held an honoured place in the Evangelical world. It was easy to satirise their blend of earnestness, business sense and bureaucratic officiousness. The annual meeting of the fictitious Society for the Distribution of Moral Pocket Handkerchiefs (Secretary: Soapy Bareface, Esq. Committee members: the Rev. Augustus Cant and the Rev. Nasal Whine) was gleefully chronicled by a High Church journal in 1860. The society's purpose was purchasing handkerchiefs, printing moral maxims on both sides and selling them to the poor. The annual accounts recorded committee expenses of £640, not entirely balanced by receipts from the sale of handkerchiefs: 3s. 4 1/2d.[131] Self-importance, incompetence and fraud were by no means absent from these bodies, but they did make inroads on the mass of deprivation, redistributing some of the country's wealth to those in most need. Whether locally or nationally organised, voluntary philanthropic societies were a monument to the activist temper of Evangelical religion.

EDUCATION

The traditional assumption that education fell within the province of the churches was reinforced among Evangelicals by an awareness of its moral value. Although it was no substitute for the gospel, it could subserve the gospel. 'Man', wrote John Venn in 1804, '. . . cannot by education be made a real Christian; but by education he may be freed from prejudices and delivered from the dominion of dispositions highly favourable to temptation and sin.'[132] Even more important, literacy was a precondition for reading the Bible. Reading skills had long been fostered primarily for that purpose throughout Protestant northern Europe, often by informal methods outside schools. By the mid–eighteenth century some 60 per cent of men in England and 65 per cent in Scotland were literate according to the gauge of the ability to sign their names, together with some 40 per cent of women in England and 15 per cent in Scotland.[133] Reading ability, however, was probably more widespread than ability to sign one's name. Certainly converts in the Cambuslang revival of 1742 for whom evidence survives could all read, male and female alike.[134] Around the year 1800 signing ability decreased in certain regions, often the most industrialised,[135] and so there was an extra reason for organised Christian effort to promote literacy.

Once reading skills had been achieved, they were used to promote understanding of the faith. The accepted method was catechising. Children and young people were required to learn their catechism (that of the Church of England or the Westminster Assembly), or else some equivalent, and were examined on their prowess, often in the afternoon service. Catechising, however, was steadily supplanted during the first half of the century by a combination of Sunday and day schooling,[136] though it was to survive long into the twentieth century in the Scottish Highlands. Sunday Schools had occasionally existed in earlier years, but it was in the 1780s that they became fashionable. Originally they were agencies for mass schooling largely independent of particular congregations, and their immense appeal was grounded on their free teaching of reading. Writing skills were sometimes taught as well, though stricter sabbatarians looked askance on the practice. Increasingly, Sunday Schools were attached to particular places of worship, the curriculum became more exclusively religious and general education was left to the better-trained day-school teachers.[137] In 1859 a typical Anglican Sunday School would meet twice, perhaps from 9.15 to 10.15 and from 3.00 to 4.30. In the morning the lesson would be the repetition of a hymn and text; in the afternoon, when attendance was normally higher, it would consist of the recitation of a collect, a New

Testament passage and an oral examination of the whole school by the superintendent.[138] The attenders were chiefly working–class, the teachers, at least in the first half of the century, often being the epitome of working–class respectability. Although children, especially the boys, rarely remained after the day–school leaving age of about 11, so that the Sunday School was inefficient as a direct recruiting agency, the proportion of the population reached was remarkably high. Of those aged 15 and above at twelve Manchester cotton mills in 1852, 90 per cent had at some time been to Sunday School.[139] And the legacy was lasting. According to a 1957 Gallup Survey of adults, 73 per cent had once attended Sunday School regularly.[140] The Sunday School established a point of contact with the working–class population at large that could sometimes be enlarged by subsequent evangelism.

Other branches of education also formed a bridge between the churches and the working people. Employers of strong Christian conviction sometimes provided a school for their own workers, as, for instance, did J. J. Colman, the Nonconformist mustard manufacturer of Norwich.[141] Night schools for adult workers on the pattern of Mechanics' Institutes but run by the churches drew significant numbers: in the heavily industrial diocese of Ripon there were 8,131 such attenders in 1870.[142] The Ragged Schools for the children of the streets, whose Union was founded under Shaftesbury's presidency in 1844, gave a rudimentary training to some of the most destitute.[143] More important in terms of the proportion of the population influenced were the elementary schools. At mid–century, the religious bodies sponsored schools providing for 1,049,000 out of the overall total of 2,109,000 pupils in day schools. Pride of place among the organisations promoting public education along Christian lines went to the National Society of the Church of England. In 1851, when other Anglican schools contained 336,000 pupils, National Schools educated 465,000. Launched in 1811 to propagate the schemes of Andrew Bell for cheap popular training in basic skills through monitors (senior pupils who passed on their lessons to the younger ones), the society relied entirely on local initiative. Evangelicals played a disproportionate part in the early years, but in 1853, dismayed by High Church leanings in its policy, a body of Evangelicals left to form a separate Church Education Society. Although it continued to function for many years, the new society never flourished, and Evangelical influence in the central counsels of the National Society was shattered.[144]

A parallel organisation was the British and Foreign Schools Society, founded in 1814 to support educational plans already begun by Joseph Lancaster, a Quaker. British Schools also initially adopted the monitorial system, but differed from National Schools in giving undenominational rather than distinctively Anglican instruction. Often attached to Nonconformist places of worship, British Schools nevertheless enjoyed the support of some Churchmen.[145] In 1851 they trained 123,000 pupils. The Congregationalists with 47,000 pupils and the Wesleyans with 37,000 also made valiant educational efforts,[146] but it was clear by the 1860s that voluntary schemes were failing to keep pace with population growth. The 1870 Education Act was the remedy, providing for rate-supported schools under local boards wherever there was a gap in voluntary facilities. Board Schools, like those set up, under the equivalent 1872 act consolidating the various Presbyterian schools in Scotland, did not exclude religious training, but concentrated on Bible teaching. There was less Christian content in the curriculum than in the first half of the century, when religious topics were introduced on every page of readers used in National Schools, but the Board Schools at the end of the century still exerted a diffuse influence in the direction of biblical religion on the whole of the rising generation.[147] In rural Church schools the clergy would still regularly appear, sometimes to teach the first half-hour's lesson every day.[148] The nature of public elementary education, even as it gradually came under state inspection and control, helps explain the continuing esteem for Christianity in the non-churchgoing population.

SOCIAL PRESSURES

Attendance at a place of worship was a public act open to scrutiny by social superiors. In the countryside an awesome power was potentially wielded by many landlords. Those not seen in church on Sunday, whether farmers or labourers, could face the displeasure of the squire and, ultimately, eviction. This power was ambiguous in its effects on Evangelical religion. On the one hand, where the incumbent clergyman was himself an Evangelical, the landlord's expectations could help create larger congregations under the sound of the gospel. Only when squire and parson fell out would parish discord be likely to weaken religious practice.[149] On the other hand, the hostility of landlords, who overwhelmingly adhered to the Established Churches, could imperil Evangelical Nonconformity. When the Ecclesiastical Commissioners acquired a Lincolnshire parish in 1862, the four chief tenants were evicted as Methodists.[150] In England Lord Salisbury's refusal to sell land for the Wesleyans to build a chapel at Hatfield was but one instance of a serious obstacle that in Scotland the Free Church also encountered in its early years.[151] Decisive opposition of this kind by landlords, however, was relatively rare. More common was traditional deference by country folk to the wishes of the gentry, a factor that tended to strengthen whatever churchmanship was on offer in the parish. Although deference was reinforced by 'attentions' like Christmas coal and summer treats, the extent of rural paternalism has probably been exaggerated in the past. Only 17 per cent of a sample of National Schools was found to have a landlord patron, and clergymen were usually left to their own efforts to raise money for church building.[152] Landlords frequently preferred their own pleasures to supervising the people of their parishes.

Yet if rural pressures making for social and therefore religious conformity have often been overstated, the equivalent urban pressures have sometimes been understated. The nineteenth-century city was no more a place of freedom from a sense of social obligation than a scene of constant industrial oppression. Employers in later Victorian Lancashire, it has been shown, fostered a community spirit of devoted loyalty among their workforce. Deference was willingly given.[153] In this setting, the social leaders were divided approximately equally between Church and Dissent.[154] Neighbourhoods took their religious tone from the leading local industrialist. Churchgoing offered prospects of employment or promotion. Thus, at Monkwearmouth it was known to be an asset when applying for work in the shipyards to be a member of the local Wesleyan Hall, for its leading spirit had built up the shipbuilding industry.[155] Some captains of industry, such as Sir Titus Salt at Saltaire or Lord Leverhulme at Port Sunlight, prided themselves on exerting no compulsion over their workers to attend the churches they had erected. But in both cases the silent example of the social leader ensured that his own Congregational church was packed.[156] On a smaller scale, an apprentice might be expected to attend the place of worship of his master. Thus the son of a Baptist deacon was temporarily compelled to conform to the Established Church when apprenticed to a Monmouthshire chemist in the 1850s.[157] And domestic servants were often denied independent religious choice. A Durham brewer and colliery owner, for instance, insisted that his servants, including the Methodists, should attend the Church of England.[158] Although such pressure might take employees away from a gospel ministry, its effect was equally commonly to strengthen the Evangelical cause.

Influence could be exerted more subtly but hardly less effectively by social peers. The wish for acceptance and esteem from one's fellows – in a word, respectability – was a powerful force in nineteenth-century Britain, closely bound up with Christian practice. Respectability, it was remarked in 1854, was to be found among the 'religious public'.[159] It was the kernel of high Victorian values – what Edward Baines, the Congregationalist newspaper proprietor of Leeds, itemised as education, religion, virtue, industry, sobriety and frugality.[160] Respectability remained the lodestar in the 1890s of Charles Pooter, the archetypal City clerk with social pretensions portrayed only a little larger than life in the classic satire by George and Weedon Grossmith. For Pooter, two peaks of beatitude were acting as a sidesman in the parish church and holding a conversation after morning service with the curate.[161]

Respectability, however, was no mere preoccupation of the greater and lesser bourgeoisie. It was an element in the artisan culture, an outward expression of economic and intellectual independence that permeated the working-class movements of the times.[162] It encouraged the adoption of personal conviction and, frequently in consequence, alignment with some branch of organised religion. To join a Dissenting church, it has been suggested, was to acquire a badge of social standing, not least because the congruence of daily practice with Christian profession was made the subject of inquiry.[163] Avoidance of drunkenness, gambling, debt and sabbath-breaking were the hallmarks of a disciplined life. Careful observance of such prohibitions inevitably permitted higher standards of clothing, better quality furniture and, for some, more commodious homes.[164] Upward social mobility was the reward of prudence. Working people of London who joined a church at the end of the century, it was noted, 'become almost indistinguishable from the class with which they then mix' and so there was a change 'not so much *of* as *out of* the class to which they have belonged'.[165] This was the goal of many, the fruit of perseverance in a policy of self-help. The Congregationalist Thomas Binney published a book for young men entitled *Is it Possible to make the Best of Both Worlds?* and gave a resoundingly affirmative answer. He set out his leading contentions in a logical train: 'the Evangelical form of Christian ideas, – best produces that religious faith, – which most efficiently sustains those virtues, – which, by way of natural consequence, secure those things, – which contribute to the satisfaction and embellishment of life'.[166] Many were swayed by such reasonings. Evangelicalism seemed to offer a passport to advancement in life.

ATTRACTIONS OF CHURCHGOING

The churches had other benefits to offer. Rites of passage were particularly important. Human societies in general create ceremonies to mark the great turning points of life – birth, marriage and death. In nineteenth-century Britain the churches held a virtual monopoly in this field. Infant baptisms were performed, especially in the Established Churches, even for children of families that had no previous church connection. In England and Wales between 1753 and 1836 no marriage was legally valid (Quakers and Jews apart) unless solemnised by the Church of England. Civil marriage was available from 1836, but, in 1851, 84.9 per cent of marriages were still conducted by the Church of England.[167] And although burial according to other rites in private grounds was legitimate, the Established Church possessed the sole right of interment in parish graveyards down to 1880. Custom, respectability and a popular association of church ceremonies with good luck ensured that each of these services was a regular part of the experience of all sections of the community.[168] A sense of church connection was created that an astute clergyman or district visitor could build on.

Furthermore, the churches could offer a great deal by way of fellowship to those who ventured within their doors. The dislocations created by demographic, industrial and urban development meant that the churches provided friendship and security at a time when traditional landmarks were being removed. The regular round of tea meetings, so characteristic of the chapels and so despised by Matthew Arnold, fulfilled an important need. Even in the countryside, compensation for increasing social distance stemming from agricultural prosperity could be discovered in the Methodist chapel.[169] Methodism, in fact, delighted in supplying a happy family atmosphere.[170] The Congregationalists, though more dignified in their ways, also created a community life for their members. Their very foundation principle of congregational independency demanded it.[171] And the strength of communal ties surrounding a Baptist chapel can be illustrated by a Sunday School reunion service at Bacup that attracted well over two thousand people.[172] Nonconformity fostered the spirit of fellowship much more consciously and much more effectively than most Anglican churches. Steadily, however, the clergy came to realise the importance of social activities, and by 1890 one Evangelical was recommending a village library with a club-room containing games, especially bagatelle, a temperance society and Band of Hope, a coffee or cocoa room, a recreation ground, a school treat, harvest home, choir supper, a parochial or communicants' tea – but *not* entertainments or any concession that would further 'the present mania for theatricals'.[173] A similar penumbra of facilities was created round congregations in Lowland Scotland.[174] Clearly the auxiliary side of church life was popular. The churches were catering for a substantial demand.

Women were undoubtedly attracted in greater numbers than men. Nonconformist membership statistics usually reveal disproportionate female strength. Between 58 and 68 per cent of nineteenth-century Cumbrian Congregationalists in different churches were women.[175] Nevertheless the proportions among churchgoers were normally much nearer equality in Nonconformity than in the Church of England. At York in 1901 there were 49 men for every 51 women in the chapels, but only 35 men for every 65 women in the parish churches.[176] In the borough of Lambeth at morning service in 1902 there were 1.2 adult women for every adult man among Nonconformists compared with 1.7 among the Anglicans, and in the evening 1.6 women per man compared with 2.0. The disparity was not, as some complained at the time, because Anglo-Catholics preyed on weak women with their parade of aesthetic delights and ecclesiastical millinery. In Lambeth, Evangelical parish churches on average attracted a higher proportion of women than those celebrating a more elaborate liturgy. The differential seems to have been more related to class than to theology. In places of worship that catered for working people, whereas men were numerous in morning congregations they were strikingly few in the evening.[177] This was partly because female domestic servants were generally released only in the evening, and partly because many mothers and housewives were effectively prevented by domestic responsibilities from attending in the morning.

Whatever the explanation, working-class women seem to have been more inclined to religious involvement than their menfolk. Religion was often regarded as part of the mythical world of childhood and so appropriate for women, the guardians of the young. Men, after all, had their own foci of sociability in the public houses and sport. Churches provided virtually the only equivalent for women. At a time when respectability (often reinforced by Evangelical arguments) closely circumscribed the role of women,[178] church work was one of their few outlets. Although Sunday School teachers were overwhelmingly male in the early nineteenth century, they were chiefly female by its end.[179] Philanthropy was a major channel for women's energies. Missionary support work, the YWCA, Christian Endeavour and the Student Volunteer Movement all springing from Evangelical soil, contributed to what one writer called the 'Epiphany of Women'.[180] Women could even occupy official positions – as deaconesses in the Church of England from 1862, as preachers among the Quakers, the Primitive Methodists and the Bible Christians and as officers in the Salvation Army.[181] It has been persuasively argued that Evangelical religion, despite its emphasis on the domestic role of women, was more important than feminism in enlarging their sphere during the nineteenth century.[182] In the churches women of all classes found much to satisfy their aspirations.

A STYLE OF LIVING

When, for all these reasons, Evangelicalism made its vast impact on British society, the strongest influence was felt in the home. Ronald Knox, the Roman Catholic son of an Evangelical bishop, recalled being brought up at the very end of the nineteenth century in an old-fashioned form of Protestant piety. Apart from its devotion to scripture, it was marked by 'a careful observance of Sunday; framed texts, family prayers, and something indefinably patriarchal about the ordering of the household'.[183] Prayers presided over by the paterfamilias erected the framework, morning and evening, within which life was lived. Henry Thornton of the Clapham Sect compiled one of the volumes most widely used on these occasions.[184] It was against such a hothouse atmosphere that those who discarded their Evangelical upbringing rebelled. Samuel Butler and Edmund Gosse, who wrote two celebrated accounts of rebellion, found it all too constricting. The problems of Butler and Gosse, however, seem to have derived more from their parents' personal idiosyncrasies than from anything intrinsic to Evangelicalism.[185] A pile of testimony can be put in the opposite scale. The most influential Evangelical handbooks on childcare, those written by Louisa Hoare, a sister of Elizabeth Fry, were full of sanity, warmth and affection. And she practised what she preached. One of her sons recalled the scripture readings at 7.15 each morning. 'Nothing can efface the lovely impression made on those occasions. There she used to be by a bright fire in her little room, in her snow-white dressing-gown . . . '[186] Evangelical homes were often happy homes.

The Evangelicals nevertheless attracted a disproportionate volume of contemporary criticism. Aristocrats might disdain their intensity, as when

Lady Palmerston, Shaftesbury's mother-in-law, 'spoke scornfully of every-one and everything which bordered in the least on serious views'.[187] Working-class radicals might hold that 'all Christians are sad bigots; Churchmen are among the worst, and Evangelicals are worst of all'.[188] Writers singled out hypocrisy for censure, whether through Dickens's shallow caricature of Chadband in *Bleak House* or George Eliot's devastating portrayal of Bulstrode in *Middlemarch*.[189] Such criticisms are inevitable, it has been pointed out by Professor Best, against those setting high standards of conduct; certain aspects of regularity of life were commercial virtues predating Evangelicalism; and the maintenance of a respectable public front was as general among High Churchmen or non-churchmen. Only in the unnecessary use of religious jargon, according to Professor Best, does the censure stick.[190] Even ministers at the time felt the same. Dr David Thomas, Congregational minister at Stockwell, inspired in 1880 the writing of a protracted satire of the Evangelical sub-culture, *The World of Cant*. 'Mr. Crayford', runs a typical passage, 'talked continually to Lorraine of the "light" that his wife enjoyed, and begged him in the most unctuous terms to accept her faith and to be "converted".'[191] Language once densely loaded with spiritual experience could be debased by over-use. Evangelicals were not immune to the risk of all tight-knit groups of generating their own argot that was well-nigh impenetrable to outsiders.

Criticism was also directed at Evangelicals as killjoys. There was no antago-nism, according to Wilberforce, between religion and any amusement that was *really* innocent. 'The question, however, of its innocence', he went on, 'must not be tried by the loose maxims of worldly morality, but by the spirit of the injunctions of the word of God . . . '[192] Behaviour not itself sinful could be dangerous if it diverted a believer from faithful religious practice, led him into bad company or gave any appearance of evil. Deciding what fell into any of these categories was no easy task. It is not surprising either that Evangelicals tended to shelter behind blanket prohibitions that avoided the need for careful evaluation in doubtful cases, or that the list of taboos varied over time. Evangelicals in the Church of England seem to have become more rigid during the early nineteenth century. Henry Venn, the secretary of the CMS at mid-century, excluded all but one novel from his house, whereas his father, John Venn of Clapham, had devoured Scott's novels avidly.[193] Among those influenced by premillennialism, it was axiomatic that there should be no trifling with the vain things of a world about to perish.

Other Anglicans, and Nonconformists generally, tended to broaden in their views in the later part of the century. Thus, when the theatre was condemned by members of the Eclectic Society in 1800, they were reflecting the unanimous opinion of the Evangelical community. The profaneness on stage, the low moral reputation of actresses and the specious appeal to the senses were the worst offences of the drama.[194] At mid-century it was still held that 'to sanction the representation of sin, is surely equivalent to mocking at it'.[195] When a United Presbyterian minister startled Edinburgh in 1883 by claiming that the drama could in principle be 'an educative force', he nevertheless conceded that its present unreformed state had prevented him from setting foot in a theatre.[196] But in 1894 the Chairman of the Congregational Union denied that it was wrong to see a play.[197] Resistance to the theatre was beginning to crumble.

A change of mind about musical performances took place more rapidly. The 1805 Wesleyan Conference prohibited recitatives and solos, but even at the start of the century it was recognised that music, as the handmaid of worship, had a certain value.[198] In the 1840s a young Congregational minister declined to attend a concert in deference to the convictions of others, but later in his career he felt no qualms of conscience on the point.[199] By the end of the century the chapels of Wales and the north had begun their tradition of regular choir festivals. Only rarely were there relics of resistance, as when in 1898 an 'ultra-Baptist' on a school board near Llandovery objected on principle to school concerts.[200]

To novels there was probably always more opposition in theory than in practice. The elite of Congregationalism gossiped to each other about their latest reading in the 1810s even though John Angell James, minister at Birmingham until 1859, 'could not endure fiction'.[201] *The Christian Observer* was urging resistance to novel-reading (fiction made light of sin, wasted time and had worldly associations) at a time when Sir Walter Scott was making inroads into pious households.[202] Attitudes broadened over time. The first Congregational novelist was probably Sarah Stickney, with her *Pictures of Private Life* (1833); by 1876 a Methodist novel was published and fiction was being serialised in *The Wesleyan Methodist Magazine*.[203] At the end of the century, a whole fictional genre, the so-called Scottish 'Kailyard School', existed to convey a Christian message, and the most popular novelist was Silas K. Hocking, a Methodist.[204] Like the concert, though unlike the theatre, the novel was Christianised.

Recreation was even more of a moral minefield than the arts. Contamination by associating with the unconverted was a greater risk. Although dinner parties were least suspect because restrained by the conventions of the home, they had their dangers – drowsiness after wine, splendid displays of plate and so on. The friend of a correspondent of *The Christian Observer* consequently abandoned 'the dinner system' as a violation of the moral law, 'pure Antinomianism'.[205] Balls could stir preachers to a frenzy of denunciation. Charles Clayton, Vicar of Holy Trinity, Cambridge, declaimed against the university Bachelors' Ball of 1857, contending that a murderer had once been prompted to his reckless crime by the sight of six clergymen at a ball.[206] Clerical standards of behaviour were fixed particularly high. J. C. Wigram, the Evangelical Bishop of Rochester, attracted some ridicule when, apart from censuring their beards and whiskers, he reprimanded his clergy for attending cricket clubs and archery meetings.[207] Henry Venn gave up cricket on his ordination in 1820, and football played by candidates for the Wesleyan ministry at Didsbury College attracted censure in the

early 1860s.[208] Marbles might be less fraught with danger: the venerable
Methodist Adam Clarke enjoyed playing – and winning – the game.[209]
Yet a boy in a Calvinistic Methodist home in Merthyr Tydfil in the 1820s
could have qualms:

> One of his schoolfellows remembers how wistfully he stood, on one occasion,
> watching the other boys as they played at marbles, a game which had much
> fascination for him, but in which, being perhaps at that time a Church member,
> or about to become such, he did not feel at liberty to indulge . . .[210]

A similar sensitive conscience fashioned the Evangelicals into opponents
of many forms of popular recreation. At Derby, pressure by Evangelicals
led to the abandonment of the races in 1835 and the suppression (by the
use of troops) of football in the streets in 1845 and the succeeding years;
at Cheltenham, Francis Close led a campaign directed impartially against
the theatre, undesirable literature, any breach of the sabbath and the local
races; at Bolton, the clergy sustained demands for the withdrawal of a
licence for a 'singing saloon'.[211] Such efforts were repeated all over Britain.
'Evangelicalism', George Eliot observes of the early nineteenth century,
'had cast a certain suspicion as of plague-infection over the few amusements
which survived in the provinces.'[212] It was not simply a middle-class
affair, as the unyielding Primitive Methodist hostility to popular sport in
the Potteries illustrates.[213] Nor was it merely an expression of the killjoy
spirit, for a strong element in the movement was opposition to cruelty,
whether to animals (as in cock-fighting) or to human beings (as in prize
fighting).[214] The essence of the campaigns was the belief that various
forms of popular recreation were occasions of sin. By the last thirty years
of the century, however, Evangelicals were to the fore in the general
shift in favour of providing organised leisure facilities for the working
people. Suspicion of amusements melted away as they came to be seen as
valuable adjuncts of church life.[215] It was another instance of a sphere
that early nineteenth-century Evangelicals had seen as worldly coming to
be recognised as having potential in the mission of the church.

PRESSURE FOR REFORM

The approach of Evangelicals to politics was also marked by a parade of
conscience. Some supposed political activity to be so corrupt as to exclude
Christians from participating. 'Thinks it wicked to vote', ran a note on an
elector in a mid-century Norwich canvassing book, ' – Leaves politics to
the world.'[216] Quietism of this order, though it persisted in some quarters
such as the Brethren movement, was a declining force among Evangelicals
as the century advanced. Increasingly, Evangelicals were drawn into mass
crusades against social evils. Only governments or local authorities held

sufficient power to remedy the moral blots on national life. By the 1832 Reform Act and the 1835 Municipal Corporations Act a large section of the Evangelical public was given a share in determining who held the power. Accordingly, beginning with the campaign for the emancipation of colonial slaves in 1832–3,[217] there were regular forays into public life.

There was a remarkable measure of consistency in the features of reform movements mounted by Evangelicals. It sprang primarily from their possessing a common target for attack: sin. George Stephen, the chief anti-slavery lecturer in the years 1830–3, found that he could best rouse the religious public against colonial slavery by branding it as 'criminal before God'.[218] Again and again in the rhetoric of subsequent crusades the object of attack was wickedness. This fundamental feature of the political campaigns should cause no surprise, for Evangelicals were, by definition, opposed to sin. As soon as they became convinced that they were responsible as citizens for a state of affairs that necessarily entailed sin, they considered themselves bound to act. Because the target was outright evil, the crusades cannot properly be labelled 'humanitarian', the traditional term used by historians to describe Evangelical socio-political attitudes.[219] It is true that the leaders often wished to eliminate suffering: Shaftesbury, with his strong sense of aristocratic responsibility for the poor, is a good example. It is also true, as in the case of anti-slavery, that the mass campaigns frequently had the effect of reducing suffering. That, however, was not their *raison d'être*. The Evangelical public was aware of the cruelties perpetrated by slaveholders long before the sudden upsurge of demands for the termination of slavery. Inhumanity in itself did not prod their consciences. Evangelicals did not display a blanket humanitarianism in politics. Rather, they mounted periodic campaigns against particular evils.

Three broad classes of wickedness stirred them into political action. The first is what may be called obstacles to the gospel. Anything that prevented human beings from hearing the gospel was a threat to their salvation that must be hateful to God. Slavery became the target of Evangelical assault in the early 1830s because it began to be seen, for the first time, as an absolute barrier to missionary progress in the Caribbean. Slaveowners suspected missionaries of having fomented the Jamaica slave rebellion of 1831 and determined to harry them from the island. Evangelicals concluded, in the words of John Dyer, secretary of the BMS, that 'either Christianity or slavery must fall'.[220] The 'Ten Hours' movement that campaigned to restrict the working day in the mills of the West Riding had a similar inspiration. Parson Bull of Byerley, an Evangelical, perceived that because the hands had too much work to attend religious meetings, the factory system must be subject to parliamentary regulation. It had become an obstacle to the gospel.[221]

A second class of evils attacked by Evangelicals consisted of what they saw as substitutes for the gospel. Alternative systems of belief, religious or secular, were condemned as affronts to the God who had revealed his truth in the Bible. Most threatening because most powerful was the Roman Catholic Church. Many of them did not scruple to label Catholic worship 'idolatry'.[222] The anti-Maynooth outburst of 1845 expressed the anxiety of Evangelicals that they, as taxpayers, would be promoting the soul-destroying errors of popery.[223] Likewise paganism, though normally less alarming, was an alternative to Christianity in the mission field. The British government was therefore successfully pressed to end official concessions to forms of Hindu worship in India.[224] Conflict about education was similarly fuelled by fears of forces hostile to Christianity in state schools. On the one hand, Anglican Evangelicals were anxious lest the Bible should be excluded from schools. 'I believe it were better almost for man that [education] were crushed', declared Hugh Stowell, 'than it were given unless it were christianised.'[225] On the other hand, Nonconformists were fearful of religious teaching with an Anglo-Catholic flavour, what they saw as indoctrination in sacerdotalism, as well as state support for the errors of Catholicism itself. 'Rome on the rates' was the war-cry of their opposition to the 1902 Education Act.[226] Doctrines alien to scriptural religion seemed to be preying on young minds, and their public endorsement made Evangelicals responsible for them.

Sins – in the most usual sense of the word – formed the third class of targets for Evangelical crusades. This is the category of infringements of the gospel code for living. Sexual wrongdoing came high on the list. In the 1870s even Christians who normally steered clear of politics – including undenominational evangelists and the Wesleyan authorities – were roused to agitate for the ending of health inspection of prostitutes under the Contagious Diseases Acts on the ground that it implied public sanction for sexual immorality.[227] Worries about sexual misbehaviour often turn out to underlie what at first sight were entirely different concerns. In 1842 there was an outcry by the religious public against conditions in the mining industry that enabled Shaftesbury to promote a bill prohibiting the employment of women and children underground. The cause of the high feeling, rather than being simple outrage at the inhuman treatment of the weak, was shock at the discovery, from an illustration in a Royal Commission report, that male and female children were being lowered to work together half-naked.[228] In the 1880s a chorus of voices, predominantly Evangelical, protested against overcrowded housing conditions in London. The explanation is that the Christian public had just been made aware that families living in single rooms were prone to incest.[229]

Next to sexual lapses as an object of attack was drunkenness. Although total abstinence became much more widespread among Nonconformists than among Anglicans, restriction of licensing hours and regulation of drink outlets were shared aims in national and local campaigns of the late nineteenth century. Associated with Hurdsfield Parish Church, near Macclesfield, the Evangelical vicar organised a Band of Hope for children, a Temperance Society for adults, a Teetotal Club with skittle alley and a Coffee Tavern.[230] From such agencies committed to 'moral suasion' of the population sprang hosts of dedicated workers eager to support any political measure tending towards prohibition.[231] Then there was a series of campaigns against cases of sabbath-breaking. So central was this issue to the Evangelical mind that when Henry Martyn undertook his missionary venture to India and Persia he set himself two objectives. He was intending to teach, together with the gospel of Christ, the observance of the sabbath.[232] In the mid-nineteenth century Sunday trains ran at their peril, proposals for the Sunday opening of the Crystal Palace met a wall of resistance and Shaftesbury secured, if only briefly, a cessation of Post Office work on the sabbath.[233] The dynamic of the Evangelical approach to politics was hostility to sin.

One consequence was that Evangelicals were committed to a negative policy of reform. Their proposals were regularly for the elimination of what was wrong, not for the achievement of some alternative goal. Their campaigns were often explicitly 'anti', as in the anti-slavery and the anti-Contagious Diseases Acts movements. Other pressure groups might advocate an innovation (like the six points of the Charter) or represent an interest (like the Trades Union Council), but Evangelical reform movements were designed to condemn features of existing policy. 'It was not his business', announced Arthur Guttery, the leading Primitive Methodist campaigner of the turn of the century, 'to propose schemes of redress or to suggest legislative measures. That was the duty of Statesmen and Cabinets. It was his business to denounce abuses and wrongs and shams . . . '[234] The campaigns were essentially protest movements. Their negative stance could in some cases be their strength: it is frequently easier for governments to abandon an old policy than to commence a new one. Slavery was abolished and the Contagious Diseases Acts were repealed. And even when the chief objective was not reached, the existence of mobilised Evangelical opinion sometimes prevented authorities from taking further steps in undesired directions. Repeatedly governments deferred proposals for a Catholic university in Ireland for fear of the reaction.[235] Governments had no desire to stir up a hornets' nest.

The policy of protest dictated a method of agitation. If the authorities were to be impressed by the strength of the movement, protest must be outspoken and widespread. Paid lecturers ('agitators') or voluntary speakers would address a series of public meetings up and down the country in an attempt to whip up a maximum pitch of outrage. William Knibb, a returned Jamaica missionary, carried round from gathering to gathering in 1832 a spiked iron collar to brandish in illustration of the punishment meted out to the slaves.[236] The grand 'indignation meetings', frequently the settings for the launching of petitions to Parliament or the approval of letters to MPs, constituted a spectacular form of entertainment. Furious denunciation of sin commonly degenerated into distasteful personal censure. This was (among other things) a poor political tactic, as Hugh Price Hughes, an embodiment of the late nineteenth-century 'Nonconformist Conscience', discovered when he tried to enlist the support of Lord Rosebery, the Liberal leader, for one cause after castigating him for backwardness in another. Rosebery refused because of Hughes's previous lack of charity.[237] Clamour could be counter-productive.

Another handicap was the stern moral absolutism of the crusades. Their demands were immutable, sacrosanct, certainly not open to negotiation. They were marked by an intransigence that is well illustrated by the policy of the United Kingdom Alliance, the chief prohibitionist pressure group. When a government offered legislation to restrict the consumption of alcohol that fell short of the Alliance's goal, the organisations condemned the proposals outright.[238] Half a loaf was often refused. While continuing to demand a whole loaf, Evangelicals commonly found themselves with no bread. Again, the same absolutism showed itself over the timing of reform. Change, Evangelicals regularly argued, must come urgently. Hence orators of the 1830s called for the *immediate* termination of slavery.[239] Sin, once identified, must not be tolerated. Policy, technique and style were all determined by the fundamental characteristic of mass Evangelical politics as a crusade against wrong.

The sharpest fissure that divided Evangelicals one from another during the nineteenth century and on into the twentieth was largely political. Church and chapel were at odds with each other on the establishment issue. Nonconformists felt branded as inferior by the alliance of the Church of England with the state. In the earlier days of the disestablishment movement they were roused because they saw the cause as another struggle for right against wrong on the pattern of the anti-slavery campaign. The union of church and state was condemned because it encouraged idle, unconverted men to enter the ministry of the Church of England for the sake of financial security and a certain social standing. Soon the development of the Oxford Movement raised the additional spectre of Romanising clergy within the Established Church. Furthermore, state aid for religion implied that the gospel could not bring in converts by itself – which seemed nothing less than an insult to the power of Christ.[240] So the disestablishment movement, organised from 1844 as the Anti-State Church Association and from 1853 as the Liberation Society, assumed the features of an Evangelical crusade.

In the same period the defence of the church as established was increasingly seen as a duty of Evangelical Anglicans. By 1856 a Committee of Laymen of Protestant inclinations was operating at Westminster to resist Nonconformist claims, and from 1859 the Church Institution, later the Church Defence Institution, existed to counteract the work of the Liberation Society.[241] The issue of the establishment principle was kept to the fore by the agitation of a variety of grievances by Nonconformists. They were compelled to pay any local rates that were levied for the upkeep of parish churches until 1868, excluded from degrees at Oxford and Cambridge until changes in the 1850s and 1871, and prevented from using their own forms of service in parish graveyards until 1880. Broader experience of social discrimination also helped to consolidate the traditional support of Nonconformists for the Liberal Party.[242] Celebrations in 1862 of the bicentenary of the Great Ejection and the controversy over Irish disestablishment during the 1868 election campaign drove church and chapel further apart.[243] In most parts of England, and even more fiercely in Wales, elections up to the First World War were commonly referendums on the relative strength of the Church of England and Nonconformity.[244] In Scotland too the disestablishment issue between 1874 and 1895 deeply divided the United Presbyterian and Free Churches on the one hand from the established Church of Scotland on the other.[245] Within the Free Church and the Church of Scotland there were significant minorities of Conservatives and Liberals respectively,[246] but in England and Wales polarisation was more complete. A handful of Evangelical Churchmen, including J. C. Miller and Robert Bickersteth, were Liberals,[247] and a small group of prosperous Conservatives existed among the Wesleyans and Presbyterians, strengthened after 1886 by opponents of Home Rule.[248] But the basic pattern was one in which political and denominational allegiance went hand in hand. Rivalry may have spurred the two sides to outdo each other in church growth. In general, however, the energy diverted into political feuding must have weakened the religious impact of Evangelicalism on society.

INTELLECTUAL ACHIEVEMENT

It is commonly supposed that there was little or no Evangelical scholarship. Newman in his *Apologia* remarked that the Evangelical party 'at no time has been conspicuous, as a party, for talent or learning'.[249] John Foster, a Baptist minister who retired to literary seclusion, penned an essay 'On some of the causes by which Evangelical religion has been rendered less acceptable to persons of cultivated taste' (1805), depicting and deploring the gulf between learning and gospel truth.[250] Contemporary opinion was certainly not wholly mistaken. It was a basic premiss of Evangelicalism that, in the last resort, scholarship must be counted as nothing when compared with the one thing needful. 'Without this knowledge of our want of Christ', an early Yorkshire Evangelical had declared, 'all human learning, all other knowledge whatever, is no better than florid nonsense and polite foolishness.'[251] The acquisition of human wisdom would not bring a person to heaven. On the other hand, it might so inflate his pride as to turn him aside from the heavenly path. It might even (especially if derived from Germany) be subversive of Christian truth.

The time of the believer, furthermore, had other calls upon it. Practical work so occupied Shaftesbury, who had gained a first-class degree, that he 'lost the art' of reading.[252] A zealous clergyman in particular, as an

Evangelical reminded a clerical audience in 1838, had more immediate duties: 'the Christian minister who can, in the present day, spend much time in the fields of literature and science, must either be ignorant of the dangers by which the flock is threatened, or heedless of the responsibilities by which he himself is bound.'[253] Many young Evangelicals fresh from achieving university laurels followed the example of Henry Martyn (senior wrangler at Cambridge in 1801) in devoting themselves to missionary work. Of forty-two Cambridge men enrolled by the CMS in the period 1841–61, twenty-eight had taken honours and nine had been wranglers (the equivalent of the first class in mathematics). R. B. Batty (second wrangler in 1852, Fellow of Emmanuel from 1853) took service with the CMS in 1860, only to die at Amritsar the following year.[254] Likewise F. W. Kellett (Fellow of Sidney Sussex, an able historian) abandoned the prospect of academic honours in England to join the Wesleyan Missionary Society in India.[255] Their distinction came not through scholarship but through service. Again, the Evangelical party could boast a fine array of colonial bishops, men such as Charles Perry, Bishop of Melbourne (1847–76), W. S. Smith, Bishop then first Archbishop of Sydney (1890–1909), and Robert Machray, Bishop then first Archbishop of Rupert's Land (1865–1904). But the fostering of the churches in the growing colonies was achieved at the expense of diverting such figures from the field of learning. Perry had been summoned to Trinity College, Cambridge, to assist Whewell, the Master, in his teaching; Smith had been a Fellow of Trinity as well as President of the Union; Machray had been Dean of Sidney Sussex.[256] The characteristic activism of Evangelicals made them chafe at the bit of reclusive scholarship.

Yet within Evangelicalism there was a leaven conducive to intellectual endeavour. The doctrinal preoccupations incumbent on a believer stimulated an early, sometimes precocious, capacity for abstract thought. The imperative to Bible study similarly accustomed him to reading. The role of Protestantism in encouraging popular literacy over the centuries has already been noted,[257] but it is important to insist that it could give rise to an intense bookishness. A rural Aberdeenshire minister of the Free Church possessing slender means was capable of purchasing, in a single and far from exceptional year, 518 volumes and 12 pamphlets and of reading 58 books in their entirety, with much of several others and 17 pamphlets.[258] It was impossible for a child reared in such an environment to avoid a taste for learning. Mill Hill, the Nonconformist boarding school, under the headship of Dr Weymouth, himself a translator of the New Testament, from 1869 to 1886, had twenty-three former pupils gain first-class degrees.[259] Even before Oxford and Cambridge opened their master's degrees to Dissenters in 1871, some Evangelical Nonconformists were entering Cambridge (as they were permitted to do) and carrying off academic honours including the senior wranglership.[260] Higher education was a preoccupation of many Evangelicals.

The University of Cambridge, or parts of it, became something of an Evangelical citadel. Trinity maintained a strong Evangelical presence from Simeon's day onwards. St John's was a particular resort of impoverished young men of ill breeding – called 'Sims' after Simeon – eking out their pittance in order to qualify for the ministry.[261] Other colleges served successively as havens for the sons of Evangelical parents, and consequently were bursting at the seams – Magdalene, Queens', Caius and Corpus Christi.[262] Simeon at Holy Trinity was assisted by eight wranglers, including James Scholefield, subsequently Regius Professor of Greek. The first three Jacksonian Professors of Natural and Experimental Philosophy (1783–1836) were Evangelicals: Isaac Milner, Francis Wollaston and William Farish.[263] There were distinguished men of the same party in the second half of the century including Edwin Guest, President of the Society of Antiquaries, chief founder of the Philological Society and Master of Caius (1852–80); and G. G. Stokes, Lucasian Professor of Mathematics (1849–1903), Master of Pembroke (1902–3), MP for the University and President of the Royal Society.[264]

Oxford, though much less fertile ground for Evangelicals, could boast a few men such as John Conington, Corpus Professor of Latin Literature (1854–69), who underwent a striking conversion from infidelity, and Sir Monier Monier-Williams, Boden Professor of Sanskrit (1860–87), who opened his home to undergraduates on Sunday evenings.[265] At London the first Professor of Divinity at King's College (from 1846) was Alexander McCaul, an Evangelical clergyman who had served the Jews' Society and had been offered the bishopric of Jerusalem; and the first Professor of History at University College (1834–43) was Robert Vaughan, afterwards Principal of the Lancashire Independent College.[266] The Scottish universities and theological colleges were replete with men of Evangelical conviction, of whom Robertson Smith, later Professor of Arabic at Cambridge (from 1889), is merely the best known.[267] There were Dissenters of high intellectual calibre outside the universities such as Robert Hall or John Pye Smith, and learned clergymen pursuing their studies in parish work such as Josiah Allport, of St James's, Ashted, near Birmingham, who translated the works of Bishop Davenant.[268] Ability, the spirit of inquiry and high attainments in the arts and sciences were by no means foreign to the Evangelical temper.

What was achieved in theology? The standard view, expressed equally by the German authority Otto Pfleiderer in 1890 and the most recent historian of nineteenth-century doctrine, Bernard Reardon, is that the Evangelical contribution was tiny. Only Thomas Erskine and McLeod Campbell among theologians drawn from any Evangelical tradition qualify for more than a sentence from Pfleiderer, and Reardon's survey follows broadly similar lines.[269] It was said at the time that there was a lack of Evangelicals qualified by their learning for the episcopal bench. Yet J. B. Sumner, who became Archbishop of Canterbury in 1848, had published *A Treatise on the Records of the Creation* (1816) which (before Chalmers's synthesis) reconciled the new learning of Malthus and the political economists with the teaching of scripture.[270] Both Charles Baring and Samuel Waldegrave held Oxford double firsts, and Waldegrave had delivered the Bampton Lectures in 1854.[271] So academic ability was by no means entirely absent from the Evangelical episcopate.

On the publication of *Essays and Reviews*, a correspondent of *The Record* suggested a counterblast from the Evangelical party. It is instructive to examine the names of established scholars that sprang to his mind as potential contributors.[272] Some, though advanced in years, had once made their mark. T. H. Horne had written the standard work on biblical criticism, Alexander McCaul had composed the most esteemed apologetic directed towards Jews, and Christopher Benson, the first Hulsean Lecturer at Cambridge in 1820, had published *A Chronology of Our Saviour's Life* in the previous year.[273] Joseph Baylee issued a privately printed work on the principles of scriptural interpretation, and J. B. Marsden, a student of Puritanism, had published a more general *History of Christian Churches* (1856).[274] T. R. Birks, who had been second wrangler in 1834, wrote *The Bible and Modern Thought* (1861), a single-handed riposte to *Essays and Reviews*, and later a series of solid works on ethics following his election to the Knightbridge Chair of Moral Philosophy at Cambridge in 1872.[275] William Goode, Dean of Ripon, though specialising in controversial theology, was undoubtedly a thinker of the first rank. His great assault on the Tractarians, *The Divine Rule of Faith and Practice* (1842), was argued, as an obituarist remarked, with 'logical justness'.[276] The final Evangelical notable, E. A. Litton, had shared the Oriel Senior Common Room with Newman in the 1830s and so was well qualified for his major work, *The Church of Christ* (1851), again a repudiation of Tractarian teaching.[277] Judged by the yardstick of this list of potential defenders of the faith, Evangelicals could justly claim to muster considerable intellectual power.

If the net is cast wider, the verdict is confirmed. Another Evangelical Anglican, Edward Garbett, delivered, as the Boyle Lectures for 1861, a lucid defence of Christianity as a body of revealed truth. As Bampton Lecturer for 1867 he took a similar theme, though admittedly making little impact on Oxford.[278] Robert Payne Smith, Regius Professor of Divinity at Oxford (1865–70) and Dean of Canterbury (1870–95), was an erudite Syriac scholar who worked on a thesaurus of the language for the last thirty-one years of his life.[279] Equally learned was Nathaniel Dimock, whose field was historical theology. His work on *The Doctrine of the Sacraments* (1871) was a particularly telling statement of an Evangelical position.[280] In Scotland there was much able scholarship. Patrick Fairbairn, Principal of the Free Church College, Glasgow, is a representative figure. Although his chief work was on the apparently pietistic theme of *The Typology of Scripture* (1845–7), it gave him an international reputation. He also ventured into the contested field of the interpretation of prophecy (1856) and wrote illuminatingly on the still vexed subject of biblical hermeneutics (1858). His academic reputation ensured him a place among those who translated the Revised Version of the Old Testament.[281]

There were many other unreconstructed Evangelicals in the Presbyterian north – men such as James Orr and James Denney.[282] One of the Scots whose theology was reconstructed on a Hegelian basis, and therefore hovers on the edge of the Evangelical category, was A. M. Fairbairn, who eventually became the founding Principal of Mansfield College, Oxford.[283] And the Evangelical world embraced two other Congregationalists of great distinction. The *oeuvre* of R. W. Dale, minister at Carr's Lane, Birmingham (1853–95), contains some slight pieces, but his work on *The Atonement* (1875) was a masterly restatement that was widely adopted for use in Anglican seminaries.[284] P. T. Forsyth, eventually Principal of Hackney College (1901–21), passed through a phase in which Evangelical formulations were irksome to another in which they formed the raw material for a series of passionately felt works on central theological topics – Christology, authority, theodicy and so on. Drawing on German sources far more than his contemporaries, Forsyth was a patently original thinker.[285] Originality, it must be admitted, was not the forte of most Evangelical theologians, who from the 1830s normally saw their task as essentially defensive. Yet Evangelicalism did generate academic theology. Its adherents did not spurn the task of reflecting on their faith.

THE DECAY OF EVANGELICAL ASCENDANCY

The prominence of Evangelicals in society shortly after the middle of the nineteenth century was never again to be repeated. Already by 1864 Shaftesbury was lamenting that the Protestant feeling of the nation was not what it was,[286] but the contraction of Evangelical influence was more marked from the 1870s. It was the era of the so-called 'Victorian crisis of faith' when young men began to discern insuperable objections to Christian belief. The proportion of graduates proceeding to ordination, and especially of first-class men, registered a sharp down-turn.[287] At Cambridge the characteristic attitude of the new academic vanguard to religion was 'indifference'.[288] An index of the changing national mood was its literature. In 1870 most new books were on religion, with fiction in fifth place; in 1886 most new books were fiction, with religion behind it in second place.[289] The belief was spreading that the greatest need of humanity was not rescue from its futile ways through salvation, but effort that would apply knowledge for the betterment of the world. The resulting stance has been labelled 'meliorism', the belief that, if only skills were exerted, the human race would make rapid progress. This widely diffused offspring of Enlightenment optimism seemed to fit the experience of industrial growth in the mid-Victorian years. It was systematised in a number of theories of which Herbert Spencer's so-called 'Social Darwinism' was the most popular.[290] A range of alternative worldviews to the Christian faith became available. At the same period several explicit assaults on Christianity were published. W. E. H. Lecky, for instance, depicted the steady advance of rationalism in European history as a dimension of human progress. Certain natural scientists of a polemical bent – T. H. Huxley and John Tyndall were prominent – did their best to show that science and religion were inveterate foes.[291]

The challenge of Darwin was part of the ferment. It is easy to mistake the consequences of the appearance of *The Origin of Species* in 1859. It did not give rise to immediate and sustained debate over the veracity of the early chapters of Genesis. The issue rarely resolved itself into a question of 'evolution or the Bible' until the following century. Rather, Darwin subverted what had seemed the most assured argument for Christian belief, the contention that the adaptation of particular species for their mode of life was evidence of a beneficent Creator. 'The old argument of design in nature, as given by Paley', wrote Darwin himself, 'which formerly seemed to me so conclusive, fails, now that the law of natural selection has been discovered.'[292] Animals and plants appeared to care for themselves. The divine hypothesis seemed redundant. To many Evangelical leaders trained up in Paley's apologetic, acceptance of evolution entailed rejecting a Guiding Intelligence. 'Then the universe will exhibit to us', wrote T. R. Birks, 'nothing but a Proteus without reason or intelligence, going through a series of endless changes, without conscious design, or any intelligible end or purpose in those changes.'[293] Other Evangelicals, however, willingly embraced the idea of evolution. Henry Drummond, a professor at the Glasgow Free Church College, even turned evolution into a vehicle for evangelism.[294] There was certainly no serious alarm among the occupants of the pews, but Darwinism did contribute to the shift in the fulcrum of educated opinion away from Christian belief. At least among the intellectual aristocracy, Evangelicalism was giving way to 'honest doubt'.

More widespread in their effects were changes in social circumstances. The second half of the nineteenth century was marked by an acceleration in the improvement of the standard of living. Between 1860 and 1900 there was an increase of some 60 per cent in the real wages of the average urban worker.[295] The quality and variety of food, longevity and health conditions all changed significantly for the better. With higher disposable income, the working population was able to turn to new activities outside the churches, ranging from cycling to the music hall. The provision of state education after 1870 meant that the churches rapidly lost their ascendancy in popular education. The new Board Schools might spread a general body of Bible teachings, but parents were less inclined to feel a need for churches as civilising agencies for their children. The creation of public welfare facilities had a comparable result. Libraries, baths and open spaces were provided by local authorities in the decades before the First

World War. Liberal legislation after 1906 made more elaborate provision, especially old age pensions and health insurance, that effectively superseded equivalent services previously offered by the churches. District visiting fell into decay.[296]

Paternalism was likewise becoming a thing of the past. With enlargement of company size, the end of family control and the appointment of anonymous managers, especially from the 1890s onwards, the solidarity of employer and workforce crumbled. No longer were employees at particular factories looked for at particular places of worship.[297] The other side of the coin was an upsurge of working-class consciousness. Better times fostered demands for higher wages, and in a series of waves – the early 1870s, 1888–92 and 1910–14 – working people increasingly banded together in trade unions to press their claims. Versions of socialism began to take root and the seeds of the Labour Party were sown.[298] The visionary idealism of the Independent Labour Party was far from anti-religious – indeed, it was an amalgam of the religious and the political – but the churches often seemed an irrelevance. 'I claim for Socialism', wrote Keir Hardie, the chairman of the ILP, 'that it is the embodiment of Christianity in our industrial system.'[299] All too often, according to a swelling chorus of working-class opinion, the churches ignored the appalling conditions of the poor along with 'the evils of competitive middle-class society'.[300] In these circumstances churchgoing was steadily eroded. By 1902 in London only 19 per cent of the population attended worship.[301] Some of the consequences will call for examination in Chapter 6, but it is clear that the churches were swimming against the social tide.

THEOLOGICAL CHANGE

At the same time the message of some of the churches was becoming less sharply defined. Despite the innovations of Irving's circle, the bulk of Evangelicals at mid-century retained their confidence in the Enlightenment appeal to evidences, scientific method and an orderly universe governed by cause and effect. At the beginning of 1863 *The Record* announced that 'the good sense of LOCKE, the analogies of BUTLER, and the "Common Sense" of REID, will preserve us from the vagaries of Prussian or German Rationalists . . .'[302] It was devotion to 'the inductive principles of the philosophy of Bacon and Newton' that buttressed T. R. Birks against Darwin.[303] The leaders of Evangelical Anglicanism were staunchly resistant to newer intellectual fashions. *The Record* saw Dr John Campbell, Minister of Whitefield's Tabernacle until 1866, as standing for the same traditional orthodoxies in Nonconformity.[304] Henry Rogers, author of *The Eclipse of Faith* (1852) and President of Lancashire Independent College from 1857 to 1864, was probably a more effective apologist in the traditional mould.[305] It was common, however, to draw a contrast: '*conservation* is the object of Evangelical Episcopalians, *progress* of Evangelical Dissenters'.[306] The inherited aversion of Nonconformists to creeds imposed by law predisposed them to look for fresh ways of stating Christian truth. The methods of science enjoyed particular prestige. And the idea of progress, so much in the air, became a normal assumption, especially among the better educated Congregationalists. Accordingly their organ, *The British Quarterly Review*, wished to adhere to orthodox truth and yet 'to encourage free and reverent enquiry'.[307] Investigation was seen as the motor of the advance of knowledge.

Devotion to this principle, itself an Enlightenment tenet, was, paradoxically, a corrosive of the Enlightenment version of Evangelicalism that prevailed among Nonconformists. At first it was held that research would not alter the framework of belief. Joseph Angus, Principal of Regent's Park Baptist College, taught in the 1860s that theology is an inductive science, with the texts of scripture as its facts and the rules of Francis Bacon as its method. Progress is possible, not through the appearance of new truth, but through better understanding of the old.[308] But by 1873, starting from the same premiss of the importance of inductive method in theology, it was being argued by a Nonconformist that no doctrines could be regarded as permanent. Any credal statement is an obstacle in the path to truth.[309] The implication was that, as Alexander Raleigh, a leading Congregational divine, put it in 1879, 'religious people have left the principle of authority, and have begun free inquiry, and the use of private judgment, and the practice of complete toleration'.[310] Fixed doctrines seemed outmoded. Starting with the same Enlightenment legacy as Evangelical Anglicans, several leaders in Congregationalism dwelt on its imperative to seek new knowledge, and so moved far along the path towards theological liberalism.

A second solvent of received theological opinion was Romanticism. Its influence was felt not only on particular doctrines, as the last chapter has shown, but also in due course on the whole temper of theology. German theology, the neology that Shaftesbury branded 'Christianity without Christ',[311] was one source. At the Congregational Spring Hill College, Birmingham, for example, D. W. Simon, who had spent ten years in Germany, dropped the traditional study of Christian evidences from the curriculum.[312] Another source was the English school of poetry. The feeling of one Congregational minister for Wordsworth 'amounted almost to a passion'.[313] Browning, himself brought up in Congregationalism, exercised an even stronger fascination.[314] Broad Churchmen, of whom F. D. Maurice and Charles Kingsley were chief, mediated the same influences. Some Evangelical Churchmen were affected, but, partly because of their inclination to free enquiry, Nonconformists imbibed Maurice more readily.[315] The blurring of the edges of doctrine, a characteristic symptom of the sub-Romantic influences, caused more than one stir in Congregationalism. In 1856 a collection of hymns entitled *The Rivulet* was condemned by John Campbell and other conservatives for its doctrinal vagueness. In 1877 a conference at Leicester of the most advanced ministers, men holding that religious communion depended on spiritual sympathy rather than theological agreement, provoked further alarm.[316] James Baldwin Brown, who defended the liberal stance in both these clashes, was the Congregationalist who did most to popularise Maurice in his denomination.[317]

Members of the new school, it was said in 1879, apart from treating all spheres of life as sacred, were distinguished 'by the milder views they take of the character of God; by the disuse of terror as an instrument of persuasion; by a timid denial of miracles; or, short of denial (which is a strong step), by keeping judicious silence about them . . . '[318] The Fatherhood of God was a typical theme, eternal punishment a typical omission. No specific doctrinal change was more marked than the decline of hell. Humble Methodist preachers might continue to excel in the 1870s at 'holding them over the pit', but even eminent Evangelicals in the Established Church, Birks and Samuel Garratt among them, departed from belief in everlasting retribution for the lost.[319] Edward White had led the way among the Congregationalists by arguing in *Life in Christ* (1846) that immortality is conditional on faith in Christ. The finally impenitent, on this view, face extinction, not punishment. Baldwin Brown went as far as the belief that all will ultimately be saved.[320] No consensus emerged within Congregationalism, let alone in the wider Evangelical community, but there can be no doubt that, under the sway of the sentiment of the age, opinion had been transformed.[321] A 'Christian humanitarianism' had come to dominate at least one denomination, the Congregationalists,[322] and sections of other bodies were not far behind. Something of the incisiveness of Evangelical theology had been lost.

The drift of opinion was sharply challenged in the Down Grade Controversy of 1887–8. C. H. Spurgeon, the pastor of the Baptist Metropolitan Tabernacle and by far the most popular preacher of the day, condemned the tendency to theological vapidity. In 1876 he had been dismayed to hear of a Congregational minister who did not preach the gospel. Modern culture, intellectual preaching and aesthetic taste, he claimed, were obscuring the truth.[323] He warned the Baptist Union in 1881 that some sermons were leaving out the atonement – 'and, if you leave out the atonement, what Christianity have you got to preach?'[324] Spurgeon's growing despondency about current trends culminated in 1887. He gave his backing to a series of anonymous articles appearing in his widely circulated church magazine under the heading 'The Down Grade'. Gaining little support, he withdrew from the Baptist Union, stigmatising such bodies that bound together the unorthodox with the orthodox as 'Confederacies in Evil'. His refusal to name individuals as guilty of error, as a result, probably, of earlier undertakings, aroused great resentment and few Baptist ministers followed him into isolation.[325]

Spurgeon was resisting the currents of thought that were running over from Congregationalism into Baptist territory. Theological investigations that might remould doctrine did not attract him. 'Rest assured', he wrote, 'that there is nothing new in theology except that which is false; and the facts of theology are today what they were eighteen hundred years ago.'[326] Hence he approved having creeds. In his scrapbook Spurgeon underlined two offending sentences in a sermon by J. G. Greenhough: 'Our preaching of hell wins none but the base and cowardly . . . Hopes are much larger than creeds.'[327] Another young minister whose utterances alarmed him, W. E. Blomfield, had been censured for appealing to non-Evangelical authorities like Maurice and Kingsley.[328] Spurgeon's protest against emerging liberal tendencies may not have carried many with him at the time, but the enduring esteem in which he was held in the whole Evangelical world ensured a wider hearing for conservative opinion in subsequent generations. He was widely applauded by Evangelical Anglicans, and his influence remained particularly powerful among the Baptists through men trained for the ministry at his college. The Down Grade Controversy helped prepare the way for sharper divisions among Evangelicals in the following century.

THE IMPACT OF HIGH CHURCHMANSHIP

The influence of the Evangelicals on society also suffered because of their displacement within the Church of England by men of higher churchmanship. Between 1865 and 1900 only six outright Evangelicals became bishops,[329] but moderate High Churchmen, heirs of Pusey's sober devotion to the forms of the Church of England, crowded on to the bench. Evangelicals themselves were more troubled by the 'advanced High Churchmen', the ritualists who indulged their Romantic taste by imitating the more elaborate features of medieval or contemporary Catholic practice. In the 1840s ritualism meant little more than intoning prayers, lighting candles on the communion table and preaching in a surplice. But bolder spirits steadily raised the level of display, adding full vestments, choral music and even incense, together with wafer or unleavened bread and a mixed chalice containing water as well as wine. To symbolise their status as priests, the clergy adopted the eastward position at communion, standing with their backs to the people so as to face the God who was believed to enter the elements. They began to hear confessions and declare absolution.[330]

Ritualism touched a raw nerve in Evangelicalism. Rome was within the gates. Acts like the elevation of the bread and wine for adoration seemed, in the full sense of the word, 'idolatrous'.[331] A service at St Alban's, Holborn, according to Shaftesbury, was outwardly 'the worship of Jupiter or Juno'.[332] Here was an outstanding target for a crusade. Ritual prosecutions in the ecclesiastical courts began in 1853 with an unsuccessful attempt to remove a high altar, its cross, candlesticks, coloured cloths and credence table from St Paul's, Knightsbridge. Protests against vestments at St George's-in-the-East in 1859–60 degenerated into brawls.[333] From 1865 there was an Evangelical organisation, the Church Association, designed to conduct legal cases against ritualists, and from 1874, under the Public Worship Regulation Act, there was a clear mode of procedure. Prosecution, however, failed to stem the advancing tide of ritual practices. Many blamed the bishops, who were permitted under the act to forbid the commencement of a case. When, in consequence, the wrath of the Church Association was turned in 1888 against the bishop observing the most advanced form of liturgy, the saintly Edward King of Lincoln, the result was an ignominious failure that convinced most respectable Evangelicals of the futility of legal action.[334] Only the Protestant Truth Society, founded in 1890 by John Kensit, sustained a continuing campaign, often taking direct action to disrupt obnoxious services. At All Saints, East Clevedon, the ritualist vicar issued brass knuckle–dusters so that members of his congregation could resist the Kensitites.[335]

It should not be supposed that the Church Association, let alone the Protestant Truth Society, enjoyed the support of all Anglican Evangelicals. Although J. C. Ryle, their leading figure, was a Vice-President of the Association until his elevation to the see of Liverpool in 1880,[336] many others agreed with Samuel Garratt, writing in the following year, that 'if there is one thing which, more than another, has injured the estimation in which Evangelical truth is regarded, by thoughtful and religious men, it is these prosecutions'. Yet the Evangelical body in the Church of England was so preoccupied with the ritualist menace that it neglected what Garratt called 'its old crusade against public evils'.[337] It was left largely to Nonconformists in these years to pursue campaigns on social questions. Anti-ritualism was an alternative form of an agitation against perceived evil. The energy poured into it was diverted away from other channels.

On the other hand, a higher churchmanship proved attractive to many Evangelicals. Their clergy, as Samuel Butler illustrates in *The Way of all Flesh*, discarded the old-fashioned gown and bands in the pulpit and introduced choral music into the service.[338] 'Churches now deemed decidedly Evangelical', it was remarked in 1883, 'would, thirty years ago, have been regarded as High Church.'[339] There are several reasons. For one thing, Evangelicals had never been uniformly Low Church in practice. Daniel Wilson introduced 8 a.m. communion, often thought a uniquely High Church practice, in 1824.[340] John Bickersteth, who always had salt fish on his table on Fridays, introduced a new organ, a choral service and the *Te Deum* after evening prayer soon after going to Sapcote, Leicestershire, in 1837.[341] There was therefore no entrenched bar to a higher liturgical pattern. For another, loyalty to the Book of Common Prayer could induce a punctilious observance of the rubrics. Thus from 1859 William Cadman obeyed the directive to daily prayer and weekly communion.[342] Again, Evangelicals participating in the life of the same church as High Churchmen could hardly avoid being affected by their attitudes. Clergy in particular necessarily rubbed shoulders from time to time. High Churchmen shared a similar spiritual discipline, often an identical religious vocabulary. There were men in the late nineteenth century such as G. H. Wilkinson who professed 'Evangelical-Catholic' principles, and by 1869 they were promoting a form of Anglo-Catholic revivalism.[343] Such High Churchmen were acceptable in certain Evangelical pulpits. Holding that the two parties had been moving together in belief ever since the Gorham Judgement, Edward Garbett announced in 1871 his conviction that they should actually combine.[344] Evangelicals had neglected the doctrine of the church 'as a visible organised society', he held, and the *Tracts for the Times* had done some good.[345] Copying High Church practice where it seemed to involve no sacrifice of principle was the result.

More elaborate services, furthermore, were partly a matter of following public taste. With all their poetic associations, flowers came back into use at funerals in the later nineteenth century. High Churchmen also used them to decorate their churches.[346] Evangelicals resisted for a while, the more conservative among them for a long while. In 1880, floral decorations lavished on altars, together with flower services, flower festivals and sepulchral flowers, were still being condemned as having a 'Pagan purpose'.[347] But most Evangelicals eventually succumbed. Again, they tried for a while to withstand the introduction of anthems, musical services and robed choirs. Bishop Waldegrave sternly insisted in 1868 that a service he was to attend should be 'of the simplest character – hymns or psalms (metrical) and chanting of the canticles – but no monotones, the rest of the service, both reading and responding, unmusical . . . '[348] It was in vain, however, and many Evangelicals gradually fell into line. By the early 1880s William Cadman at Holy Trinity, Marylebone, had extended the music to the responses and psalms and the choir was surpliced. He was ready to advance 'with the tastes of the times'.[349] It is clear that this is the fundamental explanation of the process, for similar developments were beginning to take place among the Presbyterians of Scotland and the Nonconformists of England. The pioneer of worship reform in Scotland, Dr Robert Lee, was at the broad end of the range of theological opinion, but through the Church Service Society, founded in 1865, Evangelicals were affected.[350] Chanting was begun at Union Chapel, Islington, in 1856 or 1857, F. B. Meyer was observing communion weekly before the end of the century and by 1906 one Congregational minister was even wearing a surplice.[351] So even where there was no heritage of liturgical worship, no Prayer Book and no Oxford Movement, the form and setting of the service were swayed by the Romantic temper of the age.

Change entailed friction. In Nonconformity there was some difference of opinion about architectural styles. Dissenting Gothic made swift strides in the later nineteenth century, especially in the suburbs.[352] Spurgeon, by contrast, erected his Metropolitan Tabernacle in the Grecian style of architecture. That, he believed, was the appropriate setting for the exposition of a New Testament written in Greek. He castigated congregations that put 'hobgoblins and monsters on the outside of their preaching houses'.[353] The loudest uproar in Methodism was about organs. The installation of an organ at Brunswick Chapel, Leeds, in the 1820s to meet the taste of a middle-class congregation actually precipitated the creation of a separate denomination, the Protestant Methodists.[354] Resistance to organs was also substantial in Scotland until the 1860s.[355]

In the Church of England, however, the great division of opinion among Evangelicals was over the surplice. Wearing the surplice to preach represented a preparedness to conform to the prevailing mode in the church. Evangelicals in the early nineteenth century ordinarily followed the customary procedure of discarding the surplice on entering the pulpit in order to preach in a black gown. Preaching in a surplice, however, was laid down in the Book of Common Prayer, and from the 1840s disciples of the Oxford Movement began to uphold the practice as a sign of submission to the authority of the church. The issue could generate enormous feeling, for it was a very visible shift in the 'popish' direction. When the High Church Bishop Philpotts directed the clergy of his diocese to adopt the surplice for preaching in 1844 there was serious rioting in Exeter.[356] Opposition was not merely a matter of vulgar prejudice. In 1867 Bishop Waldegrave was still describing wearing the surplice in the pulpit as 'in many cases but the first of a series of Romeward movements'.[357] The gown became the public badge of the Evangelical school. In 1871, however, the decision of the Judicial Committee of the Privy Council in the Purchas case was that the surplice must be worn in all ministrations. Evangelicals faced a dilemma. They wished to uphold the law in order to restrain ritualism; and yet the law commanded preaching in the surplice. A hardier soul like Garratt might persist in wearing the gown to the end of his parochial ministry,[358] but others wavered. In 1887 the surplice was introduced at Holy Trinity, Cambridge.[359] As in other respects, the trend was towards accommodation with the dominant practice of the Church of England. But the process divided the Evangelical party. When Ryle preached in a surplice while on holiday without his gown in 1876, he was much censured.[360] The tensions resulting from the growing preference for the decorous and the aesthetic in worship helped to blunt the impact of Evangelicalism as the century wore on. They also, once more, prefigured the division of the following century.

THE EVANGELICAL CENTURY

The hundred years or so before the First World War nevertheless deserve to be called the Evangelical century. In that period the activism of the movement enabled it to permeate British society. Righteousness, as Evangelicals might have put it, abounded in the land. Major inroads were made on the existing mass of religious indifference. Less impact was made on the lower working classes than on higher social groups, but it is quite mistaken to hold that the working classes as a whole were largely untouched by the gospel. Manners and politics were transformed; even intellectual life was affected far more than is normally admitted. If hypocrisy is the tribute vice pays to virtue, then the undoubted existence of hypocrisy is a sign of the Evangelical achievement in setting new standards of behaviour. Historians have sometimes been misled into minimising the role of popular Protestantism by the very omnipresence of an Evangelical atmosphere. The gospel conditioned unspoken assumptions. Historians have also been deceived by contemporary comments lamenting the scarcity of godliness. Shaftesbury's writings are full of them. Apart from Shaftesbury's dyspeptic temperament, the phenomenon can be explained by the scale of Evangelical ambitions. Nothing short of a nation united in the fear of the Lord was their aim. If achievements were great, expectations were always greater. Outsiders like Mill are the safer witnesses. So are those who broke away from the constraints of a pious home. The mind of Leslie Stephen, for instance, is inexplicable without analysis of his Evangelical inheritance.[361] Earnestness remained when Christianity faded.

The enduring power of the same legacy is evident in the group that gathered round Leslie Stephen's daughter, Virginia Woolf. The creed of Bloomsbury was a new revelation, a substitute for the gospel, but very similar to old-time religion in some of its characteristics. 'We are the mysterious priests of a new and amazing civilisation', wrote Lytton Strachey to Virginia's future husband, Leonard Woolf. 'We have abolished religion, we have founded ethics, we have established philosophy, we have sown our strange illumination in every province of thought, we have conquered art, we have liberated love.'[362] Strachey knew what their new set of values had to replace. His pungent polemic *Eminent Victorians* represents, according to his biographer, an 'onslaught upon the evangelicalism that was the defining characteristic of Victorian culture'.[363] Bloomsbury's attack was launched when Evangelicalism was well past its zenith. Social change, shifts within theology and alterations in the pattern of worship were already sapping the foundations of its ascendancy. Like British overseas trade or British power abroad in the same period, it stood so high relative to its rivals at mid-century that the only way was down. The initiative passed to other hands. But, at least for a while, Evangelicals had remoulded British society in their own image.

[5]

Holiness unto the Lord: Keswick and its Context in the Later Nineteenth Century

In that day shall there be upon the bells of the horses,
HOLINESS UNTO THE LORD. (Zech. 14:20)

From the 1870s onwards Evangelicalism was deeply influenced by a new movement. Advocates of holiness teaching urged that Christians should aim for a second decisive experience beyond conversion. Afterwards they would live on a more elevated plane. No longer would they feel themselves ensnared by wrongdoing, for they would have victory over sin. They would possess holiness, enjoying 'the higher life'. Initiates spoke 'a new spiritual language'.[1] They shared the belief that holiness comes by faith. Effort, conflict, endeavour were rejected as the path of sanctification. 'There is a mighty struggle going on in the Church of God between two doctrines', declared one advocate of the new views in 1874. 'Which will you have – sanctification by works or sanctification by faith?'[2] The sound Reformation principle, they could point out, was that salvation is the gift of God to the person who trusts him. They were simply pressing the principle further by contending that progress in the Christian life as well as its commencement can be had for the asking. God is as willing to give holiness as he is to confer salvation. The apostles of the new teaching were Robert and Hannah Pearsall Smith, an American couple who addressed gatherings 'for the promotion of scriptural holiness' at Oxford in 1874 and Brighton in 1875. In 1875 also there was held the first of the conventions at Keswick, in the Lake District, that were to become the focal point of the new spirituality. The message was taken up by many other bodies, including the Salvation Army, but the Keswick idiom became dominant. It shaped the prevailing pattern of Evangelical piety for much of the twentieth century.

The new style of devotion laid stress on 'the rest of faith'. With spiritual struggle over, trust brought calm to the soul. This attitude was clearly of a piece with the conviction of those who ran organisations or missions on the faith principle. As much as George Müller of the orphanage or Hudson Taylor of the China Inland Mission, the advocates of holiness by faith appealed to the trustworthiness of God. Just as human means must be laid aside in Christian mission, so human effort must be abandoned in the Christian life. Defence against temptation would be granted by a God who ensured a supply of funds. Hudson Taylor fitted naturally into the new world of holiness by faith, testifying that he had enjoyed the experience before it was widely proclaimed.[3] Furthermore, the new doctrine, with its strong dimension of supernaturalism, had a ready affinity for premillennialism. Those who believed in the imminence of the second advent, the decisive divine entry into history, were attracted by the idea that the power of God could already break into human lives. And when Christ returned, he would surely expect his people to be pure. Advent teaching was heard on its platform from the very first Keswick Convention, achieving greater prominence in the 1880s.[4] The consonance of the new teaching about sanctification with the faith mission principle and premillennialism betrays its origins. The holiness movement was another expression of the permeation of Evangelicalism by Romantic thought. The sensibility of the age (as it will appear) lay behind the new spiritual language.

The movement was partly a response to the circumstances outlined at the end of the previous chapter. By the early 1870s Evangelicalism was on the ebb. The rise in the standard of living was allowing the working classes to turn away from the churches for their leisure activities. Vital religion seemed threatened at the same time by the twin foes of rationalism and ritualism. When confronted with the choice of swimming with the tide or resisting it, some Evangelicals wished to escape from the dilemma. Accommodation to social trends by providing sport or entertainment for the masses was to erode the distinction between the church and the world. Watering down belief to make it acceptable to the contemporary mind was worse. Yet blank resistance to the social and intellectual currents of the times in the manner of Spurgeon seemed just as unacceptable. It stirred up controversy without achieving anything concrete. What was to be done? 'I came here', announced a clergyman at the Oxford holiness conference, 'because I felt a great want in my ministry. Crowds came and went, and yet with small result. I could not believe that all was right, and I came to see what was the secret of the spiritual power which some of my brethren possess.'[5] A more intense form of piety offered a fresh dynamic. A spirituality that harmonised with the thought of the age promised to reinvigorate evangelism. 'Above all', a historian of late antiquity has concluded, 'the holy man is a man of power.'[6] Rising above circumstance, he can control his destiny. Repeatedly, holiness advocates emphasised the availability of power. The attenders of the Oxford conference, it was said, had discovered 'a secret of power in service'.[7] The holiness movement offered what many late nineteenth-century Evangelicals wanted: a means of coping with the challenges of their era.

THE METHODIST HOLINESS TRADITION

The way was prepared for the assimilation of the fresh thinking by a wide range of background factors. There was, in the first place, the tradition in Methodism that Christian perfection is attainable on earth. John Wesley had taught that there is a second stage beyond justification in the Christian life when a believer 'experiences a total death to sin, and an entire renewal in the love, and image of God, so as to rejoice evermore, to pray without ceasing, and in everything give thanks'.[8] No Christian, Wesley held, commits sinful acts, but the perfect Christian is also freed from evil thoughts or tempers. He still makes mistakes for which Christ's atoning work is necessary, but involuntary mistakes of this kind are not properly sins. The only type of action that can reasonably be classified as a sin Wesley calls (in a phrase much quoted in later holiness debates) 'a voluntary transgression of a known law'.[9] So restricted a definition made it plausible for a number of the early Methodists, though not Wesley himself, to claim the state of Christian perfection or, as they usually preferred to call it, 'perfect love'. It was held to be gained instantaneously, although progress in holiness normally preceded and followed it; and it was received, Wesley insisted, by faith.[10] Here were many of the materials out of which the late nineteenth-century holiness movement was to forge its teachings. Before the 1870s, however, at least in Britain, these doctrines were almost entirely restricted to Methodism. After Wesley's death some of the preachers prized them as the sacred deposit of the connexion. Perfection, Disney Alexander pointed out at Halifax in 1800, is a divine command. 'If God gives us laws', he contended with a strict Enlightenment logic that Wesley had used in the same way, 'he gives us likewise an ability to keep them . . . '[11] But the tradition fell into decay. The more respectable in the connexion turned to a watered-down version of the tradition rendered by William Arthur in *The Tongue of Fire* (1856). In elegant phraseology the author, a Secretary of the Wesleyan Methodist Missionary Society, urged his readers to pray for a richer experience of the Holy Spirit. He denies, however, that there is any specific 'second blessing'. 'The difference between receiving the Spirit and being filled with the Spirit', he writes, 'is a difference not of kind, but of degree.'[12] This was to empty Wesleyan entire sanctification of its distinctiveness: indeed, one of Arthur's motives appears to have been to enhance the standing of the Wesleyans in the eyes of other denominations. Arthur's book gained considerable popularity and assisted in the natural process whereby the sharp outlines of Wesley's teachings were forgotten. By the 1860s the idea that there is a decisive second stage in Christian sanctification was at a low ebb among the generality of Wesleyans.

Yet in these years the legacy of Wesley's ideas continued to have an effect on Methodism. His *Plain Account of Christian Perfection*, a lucid apologetic work, encouraged some to seek the blessing.[13] The writings of John Fletcher of Madeley, Wesley's coadjutor and a claimant to the experience, were another source.[14] The lives of earlier Methodist preachers were similarly influential.[15] All these literary influences surrounded those growing up in the denomination in their most impressionable years. Candidates for the ministry were questioned as a matter of course on Christian perfection, and Wesley's sermons, including expositions of the subject, functioned as the subordinate standard of belief in the connexion.[16] Wesleyan theologians remained formally committed to their founder's doctrine. Agar Beet, who was to be appointed a tutor at Richmond College in 1885, published a book asserting instantaneous and entire sanctification by faith in 1880 despite remaining outside the reviving holiness movement; and W. B. Pope, the author of the magisterial *Compendium of Christian Theology* (1875), taught the possibility of the 'extinction of sin'.[17] Here and there entire sanctification retained zealous advocates. James Carr was still preaching it at Wesley Chapel, Nottingham, in the mid-1850s so that the young men fell to earnest discussion of the topic and some in the congregation, including the father of the founder of Boot's the Chemists, entered the experience.[18] A few well-placed men claimed 'full salvation'. Benjamin Hellier, classical tutor at Richmond between 1857 and 1868 and subsequently at Headingley College, was both an exponent and seemed an embodiment of the teaching.[19] Benjamin Gregory, who long before had startled those examining him as a candidate for the ministry by professing the experience, continued to testify to it as a connexional editor.[20] And Alexander McAulay, who was to become President of Conference in 1876 and Secretary of the Home Missions Department from then until 1885, was prepared to speak of his 'entire surrender to Christ' and, as though to substantiate it, was marked by a certain 'apartness'.[21] Such men were eager to welcome any sign of a revitalisation of the decaying tradition.

The thirst for holiness was resuscitated in Methodism by a small group of relatively obscure younger ministers. J. Clapham Greaves, W. G. Pascoe, I. E. Page and John Brash were drawn together in 1870 by a common experience of 'perfect love'. In 1871 they held several meetings to promote scriptural holiness in New Street Chapel, York, and during Conference that year there were informal discussions on the theme.[22] These were followed in 1872 by the first of an annual series of public meetings at Conference sponsored by Cuthbert Bainbridge, a wealthy Newcastle warehouse-owner. Bainbridge also provided the money to launch, in January 1872, *The King's Highway*, a substantial monthly periodical. The journal established a healthy circulation, secured more than seventy Wesleyan contributors in its first twelve years and was to last, under the care of Page and Brash, for twenty-eight years. It had some impact on other Methodist denominations, whose representatives were admitted to a share in its management.[23] Its influence extended even beyond Methodism. 'I have just got two copies of *The King's Highway*', reported a hyper-enthusiastic Baptist minister in 1872, 'and am eating them'.[24] By 1874 it was possible for the promoters to hold a conference devoted to holiness alone. Gathering at Wakefield, it attracted about fifty ministers and laymen.[25] By this point, however, a great deal of the eagerness to learn about the ways of holiness clearly derived from the stir made by the Pearsall Smiths, whose Oxford conference had just taken place. Robert Pearsall Smith, while still in America, had explained to the editor of *The King's Highway* that they had to be so careful not to confuse non-Methodists when talking of the experience 'that we may sometimes *seem* as though we did not mean the same thing practically as our dear Methodist brethren'. Nevertheless, he wanted to insist, their differences were no more than verbal.[26] In reviewing Pearsall Smith's new periodical, *The Christian's Pathway of Power*, soon to become the official organ of Keswick, the Methodist contributor agreed: 'THE CHRISTIAN'S PATH-WAY and THE KING'S HIGHWAY are different names for the same divine road to heaven – the old way of holiness.'[27] Consequently, it is not surprising that the new wind blowing from America gave fresh impetus to the holiness movement in Methodism. But it is equally clear that the reinvigoration of the Methodist inheritance was under way before the American breeze was felt. The wider holiness revival of the 1870s drew strength from the native tradition of British Methodism.

QUAKER SPIRITUALITY

Another indigenous influence was exerted by the Society of Friends. The Society, standing apart even from the Dissenting mainstream in the eighteenth century, had cherished its own highly distinctive spirituality, drawing heavily on earlier mystical and hermetic strands in European thought. The central notion in the early nineteenth century remained 'the light within', the guiding principle, to be distinguished from reason or conscience, that is given to each human being. Salvation depended on response to its illumination. As the Evangelical Revival remoulded Quaker life, however, doubts began to arise about the received spirituality. Could it be squared with belief in salvation through the atoning death of Christ as taught in the Bible? In 1835 Isaac Crewdson, a Manchester Evangelical Quaker, issued *A Beacon to the Society of Friends* to declare that it could not. He entirely repudiated 'the inward light', arguing that it was a barrier to the understanding of scriptural truth.[28] Although Crewdson left the Society in the following year, it became plain in the controversy surrounding the *Beacon* that the new generation of Quaker leaders was in fundamental sympathy with him.[29] J. J. Gurney, a Norwich banker and probably the chief figure in the Society in the 1830s and 1840s, found it hard to fit the idea of 'universal light' into his Evangelical way of thinking.[30] Evangelicalism became dominant in the Society, so that, for instance, from the 1870s Sunday evening home mission meetings, with hymn singing and an evangelistic address, were introduced alongside the traditional

Sunday morning meetings for worship, with their silence punctuated by contributions made under a sense of compulsion by the Holy Spirit.[31] Sharing in interdenominational work through agencies such as the Bible Society and the British and Foreign Schools Society, the Quakers had become accepted as part of the Evangelical world.

The older style of spirituality nevertheless lived on among Friends, an undercurrent or perhaps a backwater of Quietism. God, held the traditionalists, is to be discovered through passive acceptance of the influences he brings to play on the soul, through nature, humanity and interior reflection. They looked for their inspiration to the writings of the early Friends, and particularly those of George Fox, the founder of the Society, and Robert Barclay, the author of *An Apology for the True Christian Divinity* (1676). There they found extensive teaching about the development of the spiritual life. 'For looking down at sin, and corruption, and distraction, you are swallowed up in it', wrote Fox; 'but looking at the light which discovers them, you will see over them. That will give victory; and you will find grace and strength: and there is the first step of peace.'[32] The message of victory over sin bringing peace was to be the keynote of the Keswick Convention. Likewise, Barclay expounded the doctrine of Christian perfection. It is possible, he contended, 'to be free from actual sinning and transgressing of the *law of God*, in that respect *perfect*: yet doth this *perfection* still admit of a growth; and there remaineth always in some part a possibility of sinning . . . '[33] Both principle and qualifications would have found favour with the editors of *The King's Highway*. Such texts continued to mould nineteenth-century Quietists.

Much of the Quaker phraseology was to be taken up by the holiness movement. The 'baptism of the Holy Ghost', 'full surrender' and 'rest' were terms bandied around in holiness circles after 1870, but had long been in frequent use among Friends. There was often, however, some difference in meaning. Whereas the later movement used 'the baptism of/with the Holy Ghost' and 'full surrender' as descriptions of the moment of entire sanctification (or even of a subsequent experience), the Quaker practice was to apply them to a person's initial conversion. Similarly, 'rest' appears in an official Quaker statement of 1862 as a term describing the life of any true believer, not as a depiction of the state of someone who has received a second blessing.[34] For Quakers there was no decisive second stage in Christian experience, but it was certainly expected that believers would enjoy the condition of holiness. The whole Society, Hannah Pearsall Smith was to conclude, formed a sort of holiness organisation.[35] Evangelicals among the Friends, far from repudiating the call to advance in the spiritual life, were eager to endorse it. Their only wariness was that spiritual experience should be, as a Pastoral Epistle of the Yearly Meeting put it in 1883, 'grounded upon genuine conversion'.[36] With that assured, Evangelicals in the Society accepted much of the Quietist legacy of holiness teaching. They saw great value not only in Quaker texts but also in sources esteemed among Quietists like those by Fénelon and Mme Guyon – works that were to have a vogue in the holiness movement.[37] The assimilation of Quietist influences by Evangelicals within the Society of Friends was one of the ways in which alien ideas were sanitised, as it were, before reception by the broader Evangelical community.

Many of the Quaker influences were transmitted through the Pearsall Smiths. Hannah was brought up among Friends falling under the jurisdiction of the Philadelphia Yearly Meeting, which sustained distinctive Quaker customs and the Quietist spirituality with more natural vigour than in England. Despite a complicated subsequent history of religious exploration, Hannah was very much the Quaker on her arrival in Britain. Apart from retaining distinctive dress, she used 'thee' in correspondence, even to her husband, and insisted on receiving the approval of English Friends before undertaking public ministry.[38] Robert professed to be undenominational, but, as his critics noted, he too betrayed his Quaker background. The undogmatic call to holiness of living ('We did not come to Oxford . . . to discuss doctrines') bore the hallmark of Quakerism. So did the occasional unguarded idiom ('upon my light and guidance') and, most of all, the pivotal points in his teaching like 'the Rest of Faith'. The Quaker practice of meditation in stillness came over with the Pearsall Smiths. The Oxford conference included regular times of silence, 'an exercise which, as the congregations became more and more accustomed to it, proved increasingly acceptable'.[39] Quakers were naturally drawn to the ministry of the American visitors. During the communion service at the Brighton conference, about a hundred held their own 'spiritual observance' at the local meeting house; other less strict Friends were willing to participate in the communion.[40] One of the Quakers present was Robert Wilson, a gentleman from Broughton Grange, near Cockermouth in Cumberland. Together with T. D. Harford-Battersby, Vicar of St John's, Keswick, Wilson went on to organise the Keswick Convention. Although he took no part in public teaching, he chose the conference motto, 'All one in Christ Jesus', and set much of the tone.[41] Quaker spirituality was one of the foundations of the holiness movement.

BRETHREN TEACHING

A third Christian body, the Brethren, shared in the creation of the new ethos. Several strands in Brethren teaching contributed. There was the insistence on the 'heavenly calling' of the church. If true believers were about to be snatched away to meet the Lord in the air, the great task of the church was to prepare for that event. Holiness was one of the requirements taught in scripture for those who lived in the shadow of the second coming.[42] There was also the idea that underlay the whole movement of 'gathering to the Lord only'. Existing churches were condemned as organisations of human contrivance whose systems of government were a hindrance to the work of God. True assemblies, by contrast, were gathered by the Holy Ghost to Jesus as the only centre.[43] Brethren assemblies were therefore marked by a certain apartness that tended to encourage a desire for holiness by withdrawal. Furthermore, the main line of Brethren teaching on sanctification could readily lead on to a Keswick stance. Sanctification, according to the chief Brethren authorities, takes place in principle at conversion. What follows in the Christian life is merely the working out in experience of the reality already given. Hence, when seen from the point of view of the standing of the believer, sanctification is not progressive, but the immediate result of faith.[44] Both the immediacy and the stress on faith were to be characteristic of the holiness movement, especially in its earlier phases. The difference, however, is that whereas Brethren placed the crucial stage of sanctification at conversion, Keswick put it at a subsequent stage of 'full surrender'. Keswick teaching did enter Brethren circles, but it never became their orthodoxy. On the contrary, as late as 1919 the Brethren standpoint expressed in their most respected journal was that the second decisive experience taught at Keswick was illusory. 'When we hear of believers making a full surrender', ran the reply to a reader's question on consecration, ' . . . it generally means that they have by the Spirit been taught their sanctification through the blood . . . '[45] That is to say, they merely perceive that they have been wholly sanctified beforehand, at conversion. The difference between the dominant Brethren doctrine and the notions of the holiness movement was substantial. Yet the affinities were real. Already in the 1860s among Brethren the idea of instant and entire sanctification by faith was abroad.

Some were prepared to claim a distinctive spiritual experience. During the Oxford conference on scriptural holiness in 1874, one of the Brethren from George Müller's Bethesda Chapel, Bristol, rose at a communion service 'to say that he had lived in unbroken unclouded communion with Jesus for very many years'.[46] Others were ready to preach it. John Hambleton, 'the converted actor', one of the most popular Brethren evangelists of the 1860s, was propagating what has been identified as Keswick teaching in 1861.[47] In fact, it must have been the rather different holiness teaching of the Brethren, but holiness teaching it was. Consequently it is not surprising that critics should have seen Robert Pearsall Smith as having been 'led astray by Plymouth Brethren and other ill-instructed Christians'.[48] Pearsall Smith repudiated the charge, pointing out that 'the Plymouth Brethren or Exclusives' (he must have meant the Exclusives alone) had met his views with decided opposition.[49] Yet the Brethren of Philadelphia had been a significant influence on the developing thought of his wife. Although they were responsible chiefly for insisting on the importance of firm doctrinal convictions, they also asserted the centrality of faith as the way of justification – and, no doubt, in view of standard Brethren views, of sanctification.[50] So there was an element, albeit a small one, of Brethren teaching behind the Pearsall Smiths' doctrine of holiness by faith. Far more important, however, was the wider Brethren role in fostering expectations of higher attainments in practical holiness. In the wake of the 1859–60 revival they were expanding in numbers and seemed to be the *avant-garde* of keen Evangelicalism.[51] Consequently, they were heeded when they spoke about what one of their leading teachers called 'the blessed possibility of living in such unbroken communion with God . . . as that the flesh or the old man may not appear'.[52] Brethren influence helped cultivate the belief that entire consecration is possible.

THE MILDMAY CIRCLE

The Church of England, which was to be far more affected by Keswick ideas than the other denominations, had also anticipated aspects of the new wave of holiness convictions. Since 1856 there had been held, first at Barnet and then at Mildmay Park in north London, an annual (except in 1857) conference for Christian workers. William Pennefather summoned the conference while incumbent of Christ Church, Barnet, and transferred it to Mildmay Park when he moved to St Jude's there in 1864. Pennefather combined devotional intensity with remarkable energy: he also pioneered a number of other enterprises including an orphanage and the work of deaconesses in the Church of England. The conferences drew large numbers – some 1,000 by 1869[53] – to hear addresses from the leading evangelists of the day. Personal holiness was one of the central themes from the first; others, receiving varying degrees of emphasis from year to year, were foreign missions, home missions and the Lord's coming. The conferences were open to all who were in sympathy with these concerns. They were, in fact, assertively undenominational, designed as expressions of 'the great principle, often slighted, sometimes positively disowned by the Church of Christ, that her union in Christ, the living, glorified Head of all His members, is a *spiritual* union'.[54] Although the chief constituency always consisted of revivalist-inclined Evangelical Anglicans, likeminded groups were also represented. Outside influences spread into the Church of England at Barnet and Mildmay. Pennefather himself, who wrote of 'my love for Friends', drew a number of Quakers into the conference. Brethren also joined in.[55] And a third influence, usually repudiated by Evangelicals, probably left its trace on the conferences. William Haslam, Rector of Curzon Chapel, Mayfair, a regular speaker at Mildmay and an early promoter of the other holiness meetings, had once been caught up in the Tractarian movement, with its yearnings for holiness, until his dramatic conversion.[56] The High Church devotion to the holy life persisted in him. Mildmay introduced a section of the Evangelical party in the Church of England to higher spiritual aspirations than were normally entertained in the middle years of the century.

The tone of the Barnet and Mildmay conferences was set by Pennefather, who chose the speakers, and by his flock, who arranged hospitality. At Barnet, Pennefather wrote to a friend, 'the Church is very separate from the world'. He would rebuke worldly conformity from the pulpit. 'It was at a time when very small bonnets were in fashion', recalled a member of the congregation. 'Pausing and looking round the church, he said, with all the energy he could command, "Where is the shamefacedness of our daughters?"' But for all his attention to details of dress, Pennefather, unlike the Keswick school of the future, taught no particular path of consecration. The distinctive note in his instruction was the stress on the work of the Holy Spirit. The Saviour had promised to send the Comforter. 'Are we not then to look for the power of the Holy Ghost?'[57] Quite characteristically he opened the 1868 Mildmay Conference with an exhortation to seek the Holy Spirit.[58] All this was well calculated to stir up expectations that the holiness movement was later to satisfy. Furthermore, although Pennefather said nothing about a second blessing as such, his guidance could lead enquirers towards a decisive stage in Christian experience beyond conversion. One lady learned from him about what she called 'a second step of my Christian life . . . entire *consecration* to Christ'.[59] This was but a short distance from fully-blown holiness teaching. Nevertheless, Mildmay, which continued meeting into the twentieth century, long after Pennefather's death in 1873, never capitulated wholly to the characteristic message of the post-Pearsall Smith era. It permitted speakers on its platform who expounded holiness by faith, but, under the chairmanship of Stevenson Blackwood, it also invited speakers opposed to the new teaching – Grattan Guinness at a special conference in 1874 and Horatius Bonar at the regular one in 1875.[60] It never achieved the singleness of purpose of the Keswick Convention, and, though its attendance rose to 3,000,[61] it was destined to have a lesser sway than Keswick. But its role as a precursor was crucial. It injected a more intense form of piety into the bloodstream of Evangelical Anglicanism.

Mildmay quickened the zeal for holiness in the circle that was to sponsor the Pearsall Smiths. William Haslam gave Pearsall Smith his first public speaking opportunity in Britain in 1873; T. B. Smithies, the Primitive Methodist editor of *The British Workman*, was a Mildmay speaker who ran breakfast meetings for Nonconformists to hear Pearsall Smith; Stevenson Blackwood, later chairman of Mildmay, had been converted under Pennefather and proposed the Oxford conference of 1874; Alfred Christopher, Rector of St Aldate's, Oxford, and a close friend of Pennefather's, organised the Oxford conference; T. D. Harford-Battersby, who called together the early meetings of the Keswick Convention, had been a host to Pennefather in 1868; Admiral E. G. Fishbourne, a gentleman-evangelist and Pennefather's 'valued friend and constant counsellor', became Pearsall Smith's lieutenant in his work during 1875.[62] The Mildmay circle provided the core of personnel for the new movement of the 1870s. The chief institutional framework of the new phase also derived from this source. Barnet and Mildmay pioneered annual convention-going. Even before the advent of the Pearsall Smiths, imitations sprang up. By 1869 it was already being noted that certain villages had their annual gatherings.[63] But the chief conferences on the Mildmay pattern were at Perth and Clifton, both founded in 1863. The Perth conferences laid a foundation for the acceptance of convention-going in Scotland.[64] It was easy for Admiral Fishbourne to bring the views of Pearsall Smith to the Clifton platform in 1874.[65] From 1873 onwards, holiness conventions mushroomed – at Dover and Bath, Gloucester (moving to Salisbury) and Bristol, Aberdeen and Birmingham.[66] The distinctive message of holiness by faith usually rubbed shoulders with more traditional Mildmay views on sanctification. Keswick, unusual in insisting on holiness by faith alone, was but a drop in a mighty flood. The network of conventions was essential to the dissemination of the new ideas. They looked to Pennefather's conference as their model.

THE REVIVALIST BACKGROUND

The Christian workers drawn to Mildmay were usually part of the revivalist world. The heightened spiritual atmosphere of 1859–60 left a legacy of urgent evangelistic concern that prepared the way for the holiness movement. The work of laymen in preaching the gospel created a precedent for the ministry of the unordained Robert Pearsall Smith. Without the toleration of female preaching that emerged in the 1860s the role of Robert's wife Hannah would have been unthinkable.[67] The playing down of denominational allegiance, what one revivalist called 'the spirit of loving union of the present day',[68] led on to the undenominational temper of Keswick. The newspaper of popular evangelism, *The Revival*, carried articles by the Pearsall Smiths on holiness from 1867 onwards.[69] Its editor, R. C. Morgan, travelled in 1869 to America, attending one of the meetings of the burgeoning holiness movement there.[70] He republished a variety of works on 'the higher Christian life'.[71] From 1873 to 1875 all the events featuring the Pearsall Smiths were faithfully related in the newspaper, now called *The Christian*. The world of the revivalists provided a natural constituency for the assimilation of sanctification by faith. Their ideas also cleared a path for the new teaching. Their theological stance increasingly approximated in practice to Arminianism. The constant text of Henry Moorhouse, a leading revivalist, was John 3:16 and his message was summarised in the chorus 'Whosoever will may come'.[72] Calvinists remained Calvinists, but their version was no longer so high. William Pennefather, for instance, unconsciously influenced another clergyman, Clarmont Skrine, to modify his views on election. 'I found he was as strongly attached as I was to the doctrines of grace', wrote Skrine, 'but was not led to make them, as I believe I had done, a barrier to the free proclamation of Christ's gospel to the poor sinner.'[73] Calvinists were less prepared to look askance at Arminians. 'If a Methodist has begun work in a court', declared Reginald Radcliffe, 'and a Calvinist comes to the same place, let him ask for a blessing on his brother, and go on to the next court . . . '[74] There was less of a doctrinal barrier to co-operation. Consequently, too, Calvinists of the revivalist stamp had fewer inhibitions about embracing teaching that rejected traditional Reformed convictions on sanctification. The lower version of Calvinism in vogue among them was a more elastic worldview.

At the same time there was a shift of emphasis among revivalists away from theology towards ethics. Basic doctrine alone was important for evangelism. 'But if good is to be done', declared Baptist Noel in 1861, 'we must be holy ourselves.'[75] Manner of life impinged directly on the effectiveness of witness. With the burning low of revival fires that warmed the early 1860s, there was a widespread longing in the following years to recover the earlier intensity of religious experience. 'My heart has often been stirred with desires for holiness', R. C. Morgan confided to his diary in 1868, 'but the pressure of earthly cares seems to choke the Word, and it becomes unfruitful. Lord, cleanse me!'[76] The Pearsall Smiths spoke to this mood. They seemed to offer a short cut to a state of moral elation that would guarantee evangelistic success. 'Let us notice God's own way of revival', observed Pearsall Smith at Oxford. 'It did not commence with effort . . . but with cleansing.'[77] The ethical note of revivalism gave the message of sanctification by faith an immediate appeal. Likewise the very language of the revivalists pointed forward to a fulfilment in the holiness movement. They spoke freely of being 'filled with the Holy Spirit', usually of times when Christians were aware of converting power in their midst, but also of the state of believers who had made moral growth.[78] During the Evangelical Alliance week of prayer in 1860 there were petitions for 'our own entire sanctification' and 'an entire consecration of ourselves to God'.[79] The technical terms that would be employed in the new teaching of the 1870s were already in use during the revival period. In many ways the quickened tempo of revivalist religion in the 1860s was a precondition for the new frame of mind of the following decade.

Another expression of revivalism that favoured the reception of holiness teaching was the evangelistic work of the Americans Dwight L. Moody and his singing colleague, Ira D. Sankey. Moody and Sankey carried a simple gospel message round the British Isles between June 1873 and August 1875. Moody, who had spoken at Mildmay in 1872, was invited to Britain by William Pennefather and by Cuthbert Bainbridge, but both died before he arrived. Without official sponsors, campaigns in York, Sunderland and Jarrow turned out rather unspectacular affairs. In Newcastle, however, there was a breakthrough in attendances, conversions and popularity; success was far greater in Edinburgh; and the climax came with a stay in Glasgow from February to April 1874 that was to have enduring consequences for the life of the city. After an Irish interlude, Moody and Sankey returned to visit English cities, reaching London for a campaign from March to July 1874.[80] Moody's preaching has been adjudged 'Calvinist if anything'.[81] The Sunderland Wesleyan ministers withheld support because he seemed Calvinistic, while champions of Reformation orthodoxy in the Church of England rallied to his defence.[82] Moody preached the same brand of homely divinity, spiritual yet practical, that Pennefather had commended – entirely consonant with Calvinism, but erecting no barriers to free offers of the gospel. His anecdotal style, like the paraphernalia of inquiry rooms and all-day meetings, seemed excitingly unconventional. Even his sermon on the solemn theme of 'The Blood' was punctuated by illustrative stories in everyday speech: 'You go to a railway station, and you buy a ticket . . . There is a story told of the great Napoleon . . . A good many years ago, when the Californian gold-fever broke out . . . '[83] He cultivated the commercial image that came naturally to one who had originally been a shoe salesman. Sankey's singing drew in the crowds. Harmonium, solos, singalong choruses that stuck in the memory – all were new.[84] Evangelistic success gave the pair and their methods enormous prestige. Moody and Sankey encouraged an openness to novel techniques for wielding spiritual power.

According to Robert Pearsall Smith early in 1874, Moody was now preaching entire sanctification as definitely as the forgiveness of sins.[85] Pearsall Smith's over-eager temperament was leading him astray, for at no point did Moody endorse distinctive holiness teaching, let alone proclaim it. He stood close to it in his tendency to asceticism, which usually emerged not in his preaching but in his answers to questions at Christian conventions. 'A true Christian had no taste and desire for the world and its amusements', he declared at one of these; 'he was crucified to it, and it to him.'[86] But his conviction of the need for separation from the world was merely received Evangelical opinion, not a belief that carried him into the holiness camp. Again, he had enjoyed an experience in 1871 not unlike a second conversion, 'the *conscious* incoming to his Soul of a presence and power of His Spirit such as he had never known before'.[87] Thereafter he emphasised the importance of seeking such an 'enduement with power', publishing while in Britain a study called *Power from on High*.[88] Although this way of describing a second (or subsequent) blessing was common in holiness circles, it did not necessarily set its users within them. Moody could be found deprecating obsession with the higher Christian life, rebuking those who held (with extreme holiness teachers) that they had passed beyond a life of moral struggle and (in his farewell address at Liverpool) advising young converts that they would not lose their sinful natures until the end of their earthly pilgrimage.[89] In later years, although he welcomed Keswick teachers to America and spoke from the Keswick platform in 1892, he was to deny teaching entire sanctification as such.[90] It is clear that, though touched by currents of opinion similar to those that created the holiness movement, at no stage – least of all when in Britain – did he identify with it. Nor, however, did he condemn it; and he went out of his way to send a telegram to the Brighton convention of 1875 expressing the hope that great results would follow.[91] In such circumstances it was easy to suppose that the two pairs of visiting Americans were carrying the same – or at least complementary – teaching. Hence critics of the Pearsall Smiths, such as J. C. Ryle and Dean Close, were at pains to distinguish one pair from the other.[92] There can be no doubt that they were fighting an uphill battle. The Moody and Sankey campaigns greatly assisted the arrival of holiness teaching in Britain by making it generally believed for the first time among Evangelicals that sound innovations could come from America.

THE AMERICAN INFLUENCE

Stronger than any one of the native influences, and probably stronger than all of them put together, was what one Methodist holiness leader called 'the great wave from America'.[93] Its origins in the United States went back to the 1830s, when the Methodist doctrine of sanctification suddenly achieved unprecedented respectability. At Oberlin College, Ohio, Charles Finney, the leading revivalist of his day, and the principal, Asa Mahan, both claimed to pass through the crisis of sanctification in 1836. A furious controversy broke out as the various defenders of Calvinist orthodoxy vied with each other in condemning 'Oberlin heresy'. The advance of holiness teaching beyond the bounds of Methodism profited from the enormous publicity given by its opponents. It became one of the widespread features of mid-century American Protestantism.[94] Finney's *Views on Sanctification* (1840) achieved less circulation in Britain than his prestige as a revivalist might lead one to expect, but Mahan's *Scripture Doctrine of Christian Perfection* (1844) exercised more influence, chiefly (it seems) among Methodists.[95] The breakthrough into the non-Methodist world came with W. E. Boardman's work, *The Higher Christian Life* (1858). It was republished in London at a propitious time, when revival excitement was at its height in 1860, and it achieved considerable success in commending full salvation to the Reformed tradition.[96] Boardman brought his message to Mildmay in 1869, and, with Mahan, helped propagate holiness views in Britain during 1873–5.[97] Perhaps the most significant American before the Pearsall Smiths, however, was Phoebe Palmer, who taught 'a shorter way' to holiness. Christ, according to Mrs Palmer, is the altar that immediately cleanses anyone touching it in simple faith. Her writings and a protracted visit in 1859–64 rooted her message in British Methodism.[98] There were also to be echoes of her 'altar theology' in the teachings of the Pearsall Smiths.[99] Most important, she recruited to the holiness cause William and Catherine Booth, still a minister and his wife in the Methodist New Connexion but later the creators of the Salvation Army. Sanctification understood in Mrs

Palmer's fashion was duly embodied in the Army's doctrinal standards. In the early phase following its emergence in the 1870s, the Salvation Army was a vigorous holiness organisation, concerned to carry 'the fire of the Holy Ghost' into all its work. [100] Its message reflected the American influence on Britain.

The shock of the Civil War, supplemented by the centenary of American Methodism in 1866, drove Methodists in the United States to examine their basic convictions. Many of them saw in scriptural holiness, as interpreted by nineteenth-century commentators like Mrs Palmer, their *raison d'être*. John S. Inskip, a senior minister in New York City, received sanctification in 1864 and three years later launched a series of annual holiness camp meetings. Such outdoor gatherings, usually lasting several days, had long been a feature of frontier Methodism, but Inskip and his friends ran them near cities and gave holiness teaching only. It was the beginning of a vast expansion of the holiness movement that was to transform American religion. [101] The stir in America, Methodist-dominated but not wholly Methodist, played its part in rousing British Methodists to greater zeal in the cause of holiness. [102] The camp meetings provided a model for the British holiness gatherings. The Oxford meetings, the Americans were told, 'more nearly approach one of your National Camp Meetings than anything we have hitherto seen in England'. [103] The climate dictated the fundamental difference that British gatherings should be held indoors, but the camp meeting style stamped its mark on Keswick. Most important, however, was the effect of the holiness upsurge on the Pearsall Smiths. Hannah trusted for sanctification at a small-town Methodist meeting, Robert at a camp meeting in 1867. 'Suddenly', recalled his wife, 'from head to foot he had been shaken with what seemed like a magnetic thrill of heavenly delight, and floods of glory seemed to pour through him, soul and body, with the inward assurance that this was the longed-for Baptism of the Holy Spirit.' [104] The ideas that the Pearsall Smiths set out in the articles they transmitted to Britain and that were crystallised supremely in Hannah's *Holiness through Faith* (1870) and *The Christian's Secret of a Happy Life* (1875) were essentially those of the camp meetings in America. The British holiness movement depended for its very existence on the contribution of the United States.

THE CULTURAL CONTEXT

The movement has been seen as a religious equivalent of the secular cult of self-improvement. [105] Its classic embodiment was in *Self-Help* (1859) by Samuel Smiles. 'The highest object of life we take to be, to form a manly character', he declares, 'and to work out the best development possible, of body and spirit – of mind, conscience, heart, and soul.' Individuals, from whatever class they might originate, could rise to higher degrees of respectability and independence. To draw a parallel between self-help and holiness tendencies, however, would be mistaken. The summons of Samuel Smiles was to persevering effort. 'The battle of life', he writes, ' . . . must necessarily be fought uphill; and to win it without a struggle were perhaps to win it without honour.'[106] The holiness movement, in total contrast, encouraged its adherents to turn aside from struggle as a futile assertion of the self in order to discover the rest of faith. The secret of the way of holiness, according to an early exponent, was 'simply in ceasing from all efforts of our own, and trusting Jesus'.[107] Again, self-improvement normally entailed the provident laying aside of small sums of money on a regular basis over many years. The prospect of reward had to be deferred to the distant future. Holiness teachers, on the other hand, spoke of a crisis followed directly by the gratifications of the higher life. D. B. Hankin, Vicar of Christ Church, Ware, and one of the leading Anglican exponents of the holiness message in the 1870s, urged his hearers at the Oxford conference to 'an immediate and complete surrender of self-will and unbelief'.[108] The holiness movement represents a break with the spirit of self-help, not its expression in the religious sphere. The critics of 'Pearsall Smithism', in fact, had far more in common with the ethos of self-improvement. Bishop Perry of Melbourne, addressing the 1875 Islington Clerical Meeting after Hankin, explained his difference from the preceding speaker. 'He believed that the Christian life was one of progress, advance, step after step onwards; but Mr Hankin seemed to speak of something into which a believer might pass, as by a jump, all at once.'[109] Perry's belief seems an echo of Samuel Smiles. 'Great results', asserts Smiles, 'cannot be achieved at once; and we must be satisfied to advance in life as we walk, step by step.'[110] There is an evident affinity between the traditional Evangelical doctrine of sanctification and the contemporary spirit of self-help. The explanation is not far to seek. The primary intellectual source of the notions about effort, improvement and the goal of independence was the Enlightenment.[111] These notions constituted a variant, forged by the experience of industrialisation, of the idea of progress. Likewise the opponents of Pearsall Smith were defending an Enlightenment inheritance: the belief that sanctification is slow, steady, progressive.[112] Gradualism was the ideology of the social consensus of the high Victorian years, and it was this bastion that Pearsall Smith assaulted.

The kinship of the holiness movement was not with the legacy of the Enlightenment, but with the reaction against it that was gathering force at the time. Convictions were starting to be remoulded in many fields. In law, social theory and political economy there were shifts towards forms of developmental and organic thought, in response, largely, to the defects of the Utilitarian school. There was a new sense of historical relativism abroad. Patterns of evolutionary thinking, often crudely summarised as 'Social Darwinism', were coming into play.[113] There was 'a counterrevolution of values' stemming from dissatisfaction with simplistic notions of progress. Enterprise, technology and economic growth were seen as false idols whose veneration had led to the sacrifice of the aesthetic and the humane.

Industrial success had been purchased at too great a price. A point of view that in the first half of the century had been associated with a few names of brilliant but erratic genius – Carlyle and Pugin among them – became the orthodoxy of the educated. The mood is evident in Ruskin, Dickens's later novels, Mill's works of the 1850s and 1860s and, perhaps as obviously as anywhere, in Matthew Arnold.[114] 'The idea of perfection as an *inward* condition of mind and spirit', he argues in *Culture and Anarchy*, 'is at variance with the mechanical and material civilization in esteem with us . . . '[115] The holiness movement in America has rightly been diagnosed as an expression of the same cultural tendencies that generated the sentimentalised moralism of the New England Unitarian elite known as Transcendentalism. Emerson, its foremost exponent, taught the idea of 'communion with the oversoul', a milk-and-water version of the orthodox notion of fellowship with God described in language reminiscent of Mrs Palmer on entire sanctification.[116] Transcendentalism was the core of American Romanticism. All the currents of thought germane to the holiness movement – the relativism of social theory, the aestheticism of Matthew Arnold and the Transcendentalism of Emerson – were Romantic in form and substance. It is not surprising that holiness teaching bears the hallmark of Romanticism.

A ROMANTIC MOVEMENT

This is evident, first of all, in its atmosphere and associations. Critics over the years made great play with the charge that the holiness movement was all gush and no sinew. Pearsall Smith's strength, commented *The Record* disparagingly in 1875, lay in the 'emotional and sentimental'; a Scottish opponent in 1892 condemned its 'dreamy sentimental piety which only befits the cloister'; and the spirituality of Bishop Moule of Durham, the Keswick figure to rise highest in the ecclesiastical world, was said to be marked by 'a flavour of the sorry, syrupy stuff the world calls "pietism"'.[117] Many of the *habitués* of Keswick delighted in poetry. C. A. Fox, Pennefather's last curate, the most gifted orator of the Keswick platform, a devotee of Wordsworth and himself a poet with a special love for waterfalls, conferred on verse a high theological function. 'I believe the poetry of the spiritual', he wrote to another Keswick speaker, 'is one of the most purifying and elevating forces God has given us to lift us to Himself and out of self.'[118] When Wordsworth's poem *The Excursion* had been published in 1814, the Dissenting poet James Montgomery had contemptuously dismissed its portrayal of 'the study of nature as a sanctifying process',[119] but now Wordsworth was appreciated for this very quality. 'It was his interpretation of nature as a revelation of God', observed the biographer of J. B. Figgis, another leading Keswick figure, 'that inspired him to pen several verses of poetry.'[120] The great Mecca of the movement, Keswick, could not have been better placed to blend all the attractions of mountains and lakes, remoteness and grandeur, artistic associations and memories of Lake Poets. The setting was essential to the experience. 'The lovely face of nature's panorama in this valley', ran a report of the 1895 convention, 'if gazed upon with eyes sanctified by thankfulness to God for the gift and the vision to appreciate its charms, must ever have a chastening and purifying effect. The consecrated Christian of all men has a right to enjoy these outer garments of creation that speak so eloquently of God's power, and wish to make all things of the soul beautiful as well as new.'[121] It was as though Wordsworthian pantheism had become an additional article of the Evangelical creed. All was of a piece with the contemporary idealisation of the countryside in Thomas Hardy's early novels or Norman Shaw's 'Old English' architecture.[122] The educated public was turning to Romantic sensibilities as an escape-route from the urban, industrial present, and the holiness movement was part of the process.

Many of the *leitmotifs* normally found in Romantic thought were present in holiness teaching. There was, for instance, a stress on the power of the individual will, the force that according to many a Romantic such as Carlyle rules the world. Pearsall Smith was unusually explicit on this point, disagreeing with Jonathan Edwards's Enlightenment analysis of human psychology. 'President Edwards' teaching of the affections governing the will I believe to be untrue', he explained. 'The will governs the affections.'[123] A believer, according to Evan Hopkins, the chief mentor of Keswick, is placed in a state of perfect holiness 'by a decisive act of will'.[124] From the centrality assigned to the will, there followed a limited doctrine of sin. Only willed disobedience is sin. What Pearsall Smith calls 'an undesigned sin of ignorance' is not properly sin. That type of error cannot be escaped. Hence we, no more than the apostles, can claim 'an absolute holiness'.[125] This restriction of sin to particular known instances (a point on which he agreed with Wesley) enabled Pearsall Smith to rebut the charge of teaching sinless perfection. 'Faith's victory over *known* sin', he wrote, 'is not "Perfectionism".'[126] But there were other implications. The human capacity to commit sins is on this view conditioned by the extent of the individual's knowledge. Pearsall Smith offered the illustration of a newly converted heathen who may be observing the standards of morality to which he is accustomed and so, at one and the same time, be living in full communion with God and yet following practices that he will abandon through further knowledge of God's will.[127] The consequence is that there can be no objective morality. The standard for behaviour varies according to circumstances. Prebendary H. W. Webb-Peploe, one of the central circle of Keswick, declared that the rule for the man of God is 'the measure of light he had received'.[128] Such ethical relativism sounds strange on the lips of men professing new attainments in the paths of holiness, but in its context it is entirely comprehensible. Just as social theorists were concluding that the values of human groups vary according to their historical experience, so Evangelical teachers were reaching the position that duty depends on knowledge. Both views bear the stamp of the historical relativism associated with Romanticism that had come to dominate Germany and was spreading slowly into the Anglo-Saxon world.[129] The holiness movement was part of the most far-reaching cultural shift of the century.

OVERCOMING THE CALVINIST CRITIQUE

The contrast between the new holiness teaching and traditional views was probably most marked on the issue of whether sanctification is sudden or gradual. The distinctive note of the new school, as we have seen, was that it is sudden. They had come together, announced Pearsall Smith on the first day of the Oxford conference, 'to bring you to a *crisis* of faith'.[130] Such teaching was a world away from Hannah More's measured exhortation to sanctification from early in the century. 'Let us be solicitous that no day pass without some augmentation of our holiness', she writes, 'some added height to our aspirations, some wider expansion in the compass of our virtues. Let us strive every day for some superiority to the preceding day, something that shall distinctly mark the passing scene with progress.'[131] Such steady plodding was the received Evangelical view, hallowed by a long tradition of Reformed exposition. Hence it was the immediatism of holiness doctrine that drew the strongest fire. G. T. Fox, Vicar of St Nicholas, Durham, fulminated against instant sanctification in *Perfectionism* (1873); Horatius Bonar denounced it in *The Rent Veil* (1875). God is glorified, he argued in a subsequent letter, 'not in the instantaneous perfection of his redeemed, but in their gradual deliverance from imperfection'.[132] The whole idea of immediate sanctification seemed alien to minds nurtured on a belief in the orderly operation of a mechanistic universe: 'the notion of full consecration *per saltum*', wrote another Presbyterian critic in 1892, 'is inconsistent with the natural law of gradual development, which is the prevailing method in all the various departments of Divine activity. It were as reasonable that an acorn should all at once become a majestic oak . . . '[133] In the face of the barrage from Calvinist opponents, there was an increasing tendency to play down the crisis dimension until 'a manual of Keswick teaching' published in 1906 included scarcely a mention of the immediacy of receiving sanctification.[134] Outside Keswick circles there was less need to mollify critics, and in the Methodist and sectarian dimensions of the holiness movement the insistence on a moment of consecration retained its hold. Thomas Cook, for instance, the chief holiness preacher among the Methodists at the turn of the century, pressed believers to accept full salvation '*now*'.[135] The explanation of the initial popularity of sudden sanctification is an increasing acceptance that dramatic moments form a part of normal experience. That is simply another way of saying that the holiness movement appealed to spreading Romantic sensibilities.

Another battleground was the nature of Christian experience. Traditionally it was seen as a constant struggle against sin. One of the strongest selling points of the new teaching, by contrast, was its promise of rest for the weary. Christ has won our sanctification for us; our response is to accept it by faith; then we shall enjoy a calm repose. The catchphrase 'the Rest of Faith', though dating back to the Wesleys,[136] became a slogan of the holiness movement. It was part and parcel of the characteristic Romantic urge to escape – to flee the everyday world of strife in order to discover the secret of harmony. In literature the motif might find expression in fresh versions of the legend of the Holy Grail (discovered, significantly, by the pure). On the lips of Pearsall Smith it meant the continuing experience of the consecrated believer.[137] The champions of traditional Calvinism would have none of this. Bishop Perry repeatedly warned an Islington Clerical Meeting against the present-day danger of ignoring the fact that the life of the believer is 'a continual conflict'.[138] J. C. Ryle hammered away at the same theme by letter, pamphlet and, eventually, the treatise on *Holiness* (1877).[139] The theological issue, according to the traditionalists, was also a practical one. It was a favourite gibe that belief in the cessation of wrestling against sin was a sure path to the neglect of moral duties.[140] Rumours about the downfall of Robert Pearsall Smith seemed to vindicate the charge. During the Brighton Convention the apostle of purity allowed himself to whisper indiscretions to a young woman in his hotel bedroom. Although the matter was hushed up, his sponsors immediately packed him off to America.[141] Alarm spread again in 1884–6 about instruction given by two young men, Messrs Pigott and Oliphant, to the Cambridge Inter-Collegiate Christian Union during an outburst of holiness enthusiasm. Pigott eventually joined the notorious Agepomonites, who practised something approaching free love in a remote Somerset community, and was venerated there as Messiah.[142] The criticism that it encouraged antinomianism troubled the holiness school. The life of faith, its defenders increasingly conceded, is a matter of conflict, but whereas before full surrender defeat is a likelihood, afterwards victory is virtually assured. Moment-by-moment trust in Christ, it was explained, is the way to triumph over temptation. 'Victory' became probably the best known Keswick catchword. So the need for a measure of effort was introduced into the teaching of the holiness movement. Yet 'resting and rejoicing' remained the normative experience commended to the believer.[143] Even though the new school gradually came to accommodate the convictions of the old, the original debate between the two represented a fundamental clash of cultural styles.

Traditional Calvinists, especially in the Church of England, were equally critical of what they called the anti-doctrinal cast of holiness teaching. J. C. Ryle delivered a crisp paper to the 1878 Islington Meeting on 'The Importance of the Clear Enunciation of Dogma in dispensing the Word, with reference to Instability among Modern Christians'. The Pearsall Smiths, he contended, had disparaged theology.[144] The indictment was entirely just:

'We did not come to Oxford to set each other right', Pearsall Smith had declared, 'or to discuss doctrines . . . '[145] The difference between Moody and the Oxford conference, according to Ryle, was the difference between sunshine and fog.[146] The tradition stemming from the conference was markedly less concerned with didactic theology than Ryle and his school. 'The essence of Christianity seems to lie', wrote A. T. Pierson, a leading Keswick speaker, in 1900, 'not so much in doctrine, even historical, as in the surrender of the will . . . '[147] The Keswick stress on experience made dogmatic formulae remote and, to some, otiose. At the annual Broadlands conference, which began in 1873 and ran in parallel with Keswick until 1888, there was no dogmatism, but 'a gracious freedom that was like the air of open fields'.[148] Evan Hopkins, who did more to shape Keswick teaching than any other man, was drawn to Broadlands in Hampshire year after year.[149] There was no identity, but there was an affinity, between Broadlands and Keswick. William Cowper-Temple, the host at Broadlands, was seen as a Broad Churchman,[150] and other figures round and about the holiness movement were marked by a similar breadth of outlook. Hannah Pearsall Smith was a known universalist; Boardman and John Brash, an editor of *The King's Highway*, had both once been pantheists; Brash was an admirer of F. D. Maurice; and Harford-Battersby, not originally a professed Evangelical, had been chosen to go as curate to Keswick by a predecessor described as 'the Maurice of the north' who was 'dreamy, mystical, fond of German speculations'.[151] There is a danger, wrote Harford-Battersby himself, of 'leaving out too much the mystical element, if I may so call it, in our teaching and keeping to the hard, dry lines of scientific theology'.[152] Pearsall Smith spoke favourably of Roman Catholic mystics and published a selection of hymns by F. W. Faber, the Catholic convert and polemicist.[153] Pearsall Smith's eulogy of Faber, remarked Horatius Bonar, 'had introduced the whole of his idolatrous volumes into Protestant families, and . . . they lie side by side with Perfectionist works in London drawing-rooms. There must be some affinity between these hymns and Mr Smith's teaching . . . '[154] There was indeed, but it was not between Pearsall Smith and Faber's Catholicism. Rather it was between Pearsall Smith and Faber's tone, what Smith calls in the preface his 'sweet breathings'.[155] Any expression of Romantic devotion to God secured his approval. In a similar way the holiness school was drawn towards any version of intense piety, whether liberal or mystical. It is no wonder that many touched by Keswick were to move on in the years around the First World War towards a liberal form of Evangelicalism.[156]

REMODELLING THE METHODIST TRADITION

Perhaps what most troubled Calvinist critics of the holiness movement was that it might be nothing but Methodism renewed. They suspected that the holiness teachers would follow Wesley on the question of eternal security. Once a real Christian, stated the Reformed tradition, always a Christian. But Wesley had argued that someone performing a known sinful action forthwith ceases to be a Christian. Salvation can be lost.[157] At the Brighton conference, when a Methoist minister told people that if they were in a certain condition it was time to ask if they were Christians at all, a Calvinist jumped up to correct him by claiming that their Christian standing might be right even if they were in that condition. Care was taken to guard the movement against similar infringements of Reformed orthodoxy at Keswick.[158] The divergence in this area between the new holiness teaching and the Methodist tradition becomes apparent in their different interpretations of Romans 7. Here the apostle Paul laments his inability to do right. Whereas Calvinists never had difficulty in seeing this as a description of the lifelong struggle of the believer, Methodists argued that it must refer to Paul's sinful condition before his conversion. Pearsall Smith and the Keswick school adopted a third view. Paul recounts his own experience as a believer, according to Harford–Battersby, 'but not as one using and applying the all-conquering might of Christ, but rather as he is in himself, apart from Christ'.[159] The condition described is that of someone who has received justification but not sanctification. In reviewing these three positions, the Methodist learned journal concluded that its own stance was as different from the new holiness interpretation as it was from the old Calvinist opinion.[160] Although, as we have seen, the holiness movement was heavily indebted to Methodism, in no sense did it simply resuscitate the connexion's established opinions. John Brash had imbibed his holiness convictions from traditional Methodist sources, but later had been swept into the stream of the new movement. At Southampton a Methodist who stuck to the older presentation told him bluntly that he was 'very modern', meaning that he was not sufficiently definite. Looking back on his own early teaching, Brash found it 'very mechanical'. After prolonged exposure to Keswick, his view of sanctification became much more organic: 'the one central thought to me is living union with the living Saviour'.[161] The shift was therefore from the specific to the indefinite, from the mechanical to the organic – terms standardly applied to the transition from the classical to the Romantic. The Methodist tradition drew its sustenance from Enlightenment sources, but the new movement was shaped by Romantic sensibilities.

More specifically, how did the new school break the mould of the Arminian Enlightenment? In the first place, whereas Methodists had traditionally taught that the crisis of sanctification comes at the end of a long quest, the new view was that it is just the beginning of the quest. After justification, according to Wesley, a protracted period of self-discipline is necessary before death to sin comes.[162] In the era of Mrs Palmer, however, there was a reworking of the tradition. Sanctification, Catherine Booth came to believe, is not a matter of waiting for 'a great and mighty work' but an act of 'simple reception'.[163] God will give the needed faith whenever we want it; consequently holiness is available without waiting for it. Similarly, at Oxford and Brighton it was taught that sanctification is not a terminus but a departure. He proclaimed a crisis experience, declared Pearsall Smith, 'not as a finality, but as the only true *commencement* of a life of progress'.[164] The contrast between the older and the newer views reflects their cultural settings. The traditional Wesleyan position adopted the typical Enlightenment idea that there is a goal for humanity. We must struggle upwards towards holiness. The newer position assumed, with the Romantic age, that the crucial experience of life is possible here and now, with no delay. In the second place, whereas Wesley had expected very few to reach the goal,[165] the holiness school of the late nineteenth century believed the experience should be general among believers. It soon became fashionable to reject the phrase 'the higher Christian life' on the ground that the experience should be normal for the Christian. Webb-Peploe, who early in 1874 was content to use the term, repudiated it twenty years later for this very reason.[166] Holiness was being democratised. If (as Romanticism dictated) the experience of restful faith is immediately available to all, then it becomes 'the normal Christian life' from which anything inferior is an unnecessary declension.

In the third place, there was a shift from the established Methodist conviction that sin can be totally removed from the believer's heart to the view that in a holy life its operation is merely suspended. Although Wesley, in the empirical spirit of the eighteenth century, was not troubled about whether sin was described as suspended or destroyed so long as its absence was truly experienced, one of his conferences pronounced in favour of the eradication of sin at entire sanctification.[167] Methodists were properly called perfectionists, believing that perfection is possible before death. The chief holiness teachers, however, were eager to repudiate perfectionist views.[168] As Keswick teaching crystallised, it was most insistent that sin is never eradicated from human life on earth. Sinful tendencies always remain, even when they are repressed by the power of Christ.[169] Keswick was sensitive to the risk that eradicationism might lead to professions of sinlessness that would discredit the whole movement. It had to be on its guard because many Methodists, the Salvation Army and a number of fringe sectaries continued to uphold the belief that (as they put it) salvation is from *all* sin. In 1895 one of the sectarian leaders, Reader Harris of the Pentecostal League, rather melodramatically offered £100 if any Keswick speaker could supply scripture proof of 'the necessity of sin in the Spirit-filled believer'. Sin, replied R. C. Morgan in *The Christian*, is 'a *fact* in the Spirit-filled man . . . [but] *sinning* is not a *necessity* in a Spirit-filled man'.[170] Eradicationism was put to flight. The triumph of the idea of suspension, however, was not simply the result of guarding the flank against extreme teaching. It was also inherent in the logic of the mainstream holiness movement, for the notion that sin can be 'kept under' or 'repressed' (rather than excised or discarded) was bound up with a dynamic psychology, implying constant process in the human mind. Such a view fitted naturally into a Romantic estimate of the importance of the interior life, the growing, organic world within.[171] The favourite image of Keswick teachers to express the idea was significantly the organic one of the branch abiding in the vine of Christ.[172] Thus the Methodist inheritance was remoulded – and the process was one whereby Enlightenment assumptions gave way to those of the Romantic age.

AFFINITIES OF HOLINESS

Music bears its testimony to the same transformation. The holiness move-ment was bound up with a significant shift in musical taste. The primary symptom was simply that music was given unprecedented prominence. The Salvation Army had its marching bands and 'Hallelujah lasses' with tambourines.[173] Holiness Methodists stirred to mission work entered villages led by a singing band with 'an English concertina'.[174] There was large-scale hymn singing at the Brighton conference and it became a valued feature of the Keswick conventions.[175] The holiness movement, furthermore, became closely identified with the techniques of Sankey, Moody's singing companion. The revivalism that preceded the holiness era in the 1860s had already brought forth 'Richard Weaver's artless but powerful rendering of Revival melodies' and the similar style of Philip Phillips, the 'Singing Pilgrim',[176] yet it was Sankey who took the religious world by storm with his *Sacred Songs and Solos*. He filled a vacuum for popular participation in church music recently created by the abolition of traditional bands and folk choirs, a process just about complete by the 1870s.[177] The enthusiastic welcome for his style was a popular revolt against the respectability of the elaborate hymns and tunes preferred by organists. 'People want to sing, not what they *think*', argued R. W. Dale, 'but what they *feel*'.[178] Sankey catered for their taste. His style was valued by Moody because it was so close to that of the music hall.[179] Sankey's compositions were celebrated for their tunes, not their harmonies, as even their staunchest defenders were bound to admit.[180] But the melodious was what Romantic taste required. It also called for a devotional atmosphere. Consequently the settings for *Hymns of Consecration and Faith*, the Keswick hymn book, were 'generally soft and low'.[181] The new phase of piety adopted a musical idiom suited to the spirit of the age.

Something of the new ethos was a result of the larger part played by women in this stage of popular Protestantism. Keswick was seen as a landmark in the emancipation of women, at least in the religious sphere. Until the creation of the convention, it was claimed in 1907, few women had accepted the commission entrusted by Christ to Mary to deliver his message openly.[182] This was certainly a misrepresentation, both of the extent of female public ministry beforehand and of the degree of freedom given to women at Keswick. The growth of female preaching in the revivalist atmosphere of the 1860s and separate ladies' meeting at Mildmay from 1862 had created precedents.[183] At Keswick ladies were permitted to address female gatherings only, though at several subsidiary conventions the gender bar was abolished.[184] The Salvation Army went further, establishing equality of the sexes among its officers. By 1915 at least half were women.[185] Keswick definitely attracted women. Their proportion of the convention-goers increased over the years, and when a missionary call was first given at Keswick, it was women who were first to respond.[186] To a critic (albeit a friendly Methodist), the piety of the Oxford conference of 1874 'could have been more robust and manly'.[187] Women contributed a significant proportion of the hymnody of the holiness movement. Apart from Frances Havergal (who wrote more hymns in the Keswick collection than any other), there were Miss C. May Grimes, Fanny Crosby, Charlotte Elliott and Jean Sophia Pigott, who actually came in person to the convention.[188] What was the connection between Keswick spirituality and the larger share of female involvement? Romantic sentiment dictated that purity and love should be staple themes of the convention, and according to the stereotypes of the day, these were female qualities. Their prominence may owe a debt to female participation; and in turn the themes must have made an appeal to women. More concretely, the call to total surrender undoubtedly had attractions in an age when female submission was axiomatic. Frances Havergal liked thinking of Christ as 'Master'. 'It is perhaps my favourite title', she wrote, 'because it implies rule and submission; and this is what love craves. Men may feel differently, but a true woman's submission is inseparable from deep love.' A female friend concurred in preferring the title 'Master' and so did Jessie Penn-Lewis, the most accomplished lady speaker associated with Keswick.[189] This form of female piety was almost certainly the root of the growing practice at the end of the century of addressing public prayer to the Lord Jesus rather than to the Father through him.[190] Women were refashioning devotional practice through the holiness movement.

Patterns of behaviour were altered less. Holiness was so much an internal matter of personal consciousness, a trysting of the elevated soul with its God, that the practicalities of everyday living were generally passed over in silence. Dozens of Keswick addresses can be scanned in vain without discovering any detailed guidance. The rationale was that 'the teaching deals with great general principles rather than specific practices'.[191] When holiness teachers did descend from the highest planes, they would normally dwell on the need to abandon 'all doubtful things'.[192] This grey area contained every practice over which a question mark lingered in the mind. Its definition must have led to bouts of anguish for sensitive consciences. A barrier was effectively erected against playing cards for money, patronising the theatre, opera or ballroom and attending horse races (except to distribute tracts).[193]

It was very rare for anyone in the circle of readers of *The Christian* to raise a voice in favour of any of these activities, but in 1885 there was an isolated letter, emanating (significantly) from Grosvenor Mansions, Westminster, contending that at *some* theatres there was legitimate entertainment without any suggestion of evil.[194] In general, however, traditional Evangelical prohibitions were reinforced. Was it right, a perplexed enquirer asked H. F. Bowker at the 1880 Keswick, to play croquet, bagatelle, cards and so on to kill time? 'Shall I sit with Christ to judge the world', came the stern reply, 'and see anyone whom I have helped to kill time?' His partner on the platform, Pastor Stockmeyer, felt it necessary to add that an exception must be made for play with children.[195] Recreation was just about legitimate, but not in a state of heedlessness. 'Natural necessity', declared Page in *The King's Highway*, 'and the example of St John, who recreated himself with sporting with a tame partridge, teach us that it is lawful to relax and unbend our bow, but not to suffer it to be unready or unstrung.'[196] For all its emphasis on the inner life, holiness teaching did not blunt the Evangelical imperative to be prepared for action.

The chief innovation was the strengthening of temperance opinion. The coming of the American influences in 1873–5 coincided with an upsurge in temperance enthusiasm in the churches, at least in Nonconformity and Scotland, following the licensing legislation of Gladstone's government in 1872.[197] Pearsall Smith was very hot on this question. Should every Christian, he was asked at the Brighton conference, abandon alcohol? 'A thousand times, yes', he answered.[198] Moody also cast the mantle of his prestige over total abstinence.[199] A. T. Pierson, another American, was equally insistent that 'the wine–cup' bears the stamp of this world.[200] American revivalist opinion was more advanced on this question than British and through the holiness incursion of the 1870s reinforced incipient tendencies towards rejection of alcohol and, indeed, prohibitionism. The most borderline issue was smoking. There was relative little thought in the nineteenth century of injury to health, or else the fringe of the holiness movement that took up faith healing might have created a stir over tobacco.[201] Pierson claimed 'that those who accept Keswick teaching practically abandon tobacco, from an inward sense of its being promotive of carnal self–indulgence', but in 1892 one Keswick speaker commented that there had been smokers about, for he had noticed a great deal of odour that was not of sanctity.[202] Those who liked their pipe could appeal to the example of Spurgeon, who had declared that he smoked to the glory of God, and in the 1920s there were still vain attempts by enthusiasts to exhort convention–goers to perceive an inconsistency between smoking and holiness.[203] Over tobacco there was more resistance than over alcohol. So it was chiefly temperance attitudes that were fostered by the movement.[204] Previous taboos were undoubtedly reinforced, and that strongly, by the holiness impulse; but on the whole Evangelical attitudes to the world were not transformed by what was intrinsically an otherworldly movement.

THE BRITISH HOLINESS MOVEMENT

The appeal of the holiness message, notwithstanding the emergence of the Salvation Army and a number of other popular bodies, was overwhelmingly to the upper middle classes. The revivalist world that initially received it had an upper-middle-class, even an aristocratic, tinge. Pennefather, for instance, found on coming to his Barnet congregation 'many true Christians here among the upper classes';[205] gentry patronised full-time evangelists; peers even acted as revivalists themselves. Pearsall Smith's original *entrée* was to West End drawing rooms and country house parties. The sins he condemned were peculiarly suited to his audiences. 'Does the sudden pull of the bell', he asked, 'ever give notice in the kitchen that a good temper has been lost by the head of the household?'[206] In the years around 1870 the middle classes generally enjoyed longer hours of leisure, the fruit of economic prosperity. A whole literature sprang up discussing how it could legitimately be used.[207] Attendance at the conventions, which necessarily implied the possession of a good deal of leisure, provided a congenial answer for the conscientious Christian. It was sometimes claimed that Keswick attracted a wide social cross-section, but the resort was one that deliberately catered for the elite of Lakeland visitors.[208] Those who were of lower social standing were very obvious and called forth comment – like the camp of sixty to seventy who were 'mainly factory-workers, clerks and artizans' at the beginning of the twentieth century and the twenty from the Barnsley collieries in 1912.[209] In 1895 Keswick was criticised for becoming 'a Convention for the rich alone'.[210] The explanation of its social appeal is to be found in the nature of its message. The greater educational opportunities of the upper middle classes meant that they had commonly acquired a taste for Wordsworth, the poetic temper and elevating spiritual influences. The call to holiness, with all its Romantic affinities, was bound to have far more impact on them than on lower social groups. Although Keswick teaching was later to spread to a wider public, its initial constituency was drawn very largely from the well-to-do.

The varying attractions of sanctification by faith to different sectors of society help explain the denominational pattern of support. The new teaching made far more inroads among Evangelical Anglicans, with their higher average social standing, than among Evangelical Nonconformists. From the start the Church of England supplied the bulk of the convention speakers. Resistance at the Islington Clerical Meetings to Keswick teaching on sanctification was steadily eroded. In 1892 its doctrine was still being repudiated at Islington by Canon Hoare, but in that year Ryle, long an unyielding opponent and now Bishop of Liverpool, gave the movement a qualified imprimatur by offering prayer on its platform when Moody was the speaker.[211] By the dawning of the new century Keswick teaching went unchallenged at Islington and so had clearly triumphed in Anglican Evangelicalism.[212] Within the other denominations it did not achieve the same sway. Among Scottish Presbyterians there were house-parties including some fifteen to twenty ministers from each of the three main denominations at Keswick in 1900, but the overall contingent was not large.[213] Congregational and Baptist ministers had managed to muster a meeting of between fifty and sixty during the Brighton conference,[214] but Congregationalism was not to be deeply affected. Pearsall Smith was proud to have influenced a number of Baptists, including some members of Spurgeon's congregation,[215] but the only Baptist speaker to gain prominence on the Keswick platform before 1900 was F. B. Meyer, significantly the most urbane minister of his denomination. John Brash became a Keswick teacher and claimed that lots of Methodists attended, but even he felt rather out of place in so Anglican a gathering.[216] One Methodist minister who received the blessing at Keswick, W. H. Tindall, founded in 1885 a Methodist holiness convention at Southport, and one of its most incisive speakers, Dr E. E. Jenkins, had received entire sanctification at Brighton.[217] But Southport, while becoming a focus for holiness teaching in Methodism, had the effect of diverting members of the denomination away from Keswick. Apart from considerations such as time, Southport tolerated the eradicationism that Keswick ruled out of court.[218] So Anglican dominance in the mainstream of the holiness movement was assured.

Yet, as in America, the movement also created a tendency to separate from existing churches in order to teach holiness without reserve. 'Soon', wrote Page of the Methodist holiness movement in the early 1870s, 'the difficulty was to check the disposition to form separate organizations, and to discourage all movements which tended to the formation of a "Church within a Church" . . . '[219] The crucial decision, never rescinded, not to form a Methodist holiness organisation was taken at a conference at Wakefield in 1874.[220] To a large extent holiness enthusiasm was contained. The original ardour of the Salvation Army for 'the fire of the Holy Ghost' cooled. By the early years of the twentieth century, when General Booth was asked whether the Army taught entire sanctification as earnestly as formerly, he replied, 'When a man talks about full consecration, we say to him, "Go and *do* something"'.[221] The Army had none the less brought the experience of sanctification to the founders of two lesser holiness bodies, the Faith Mission in Scotland and the Star Hall in Manchester. But the Faith Misson was careful not to draw members away from their own churches, preferring to set up undenominational halls that would act as feeders for local congregations.[222] A similar policy was pursued by the Pentecostal League of Reader Harris, formed in 1891 'to spread Scriptural Holiness by unsectarian methods' from a London base, and later by the Overcomer League of Jessie Penn-Lewis. Both had their own magazines, *Tongues of Fire* and *The Overcomer* (founded 1909).[223] Yet the fissiparity of the American holiness movement that created twenty-five denominations by 1907[224] was also a British phenomenon. Already by 1884 there were thirteen independent congregations with their own magazine, *The Holiness Advocate*.[225] The International Holiness Mission

(1906) broke away from the Pentecostal League to set up separate churches; the Calvary Holiness Church separated (1934) from the IHM because it wished to permit faith healing; the Pentecostal Church of Scotland (1906) divided from the Parkhead Congregational Church over entire sanctification; and the Emmanuel Holiness Church (1916) was set up by an individual holiness teacher in Birkenhead.[226] This sectarian fringe was the context in which the Pentecostal movement was to spring to life in the first decade of the twentieth century.[227] Consequently, it was more important than it may appear. In itself, however, this phenomenon was remarkably small-scale. The strongest (apart from the Salvation Army) of the separatist bodies, the IHM, had only twenty-seven churches with about one thousand members when it merged with the Church of the Nazarene, based in America, in 1952.[228] Holiness separatism was weak in Britain both because the Methodists deliberately set their face against it and because of the remarkable hegemony of Keswick.

The holiness movement ushered in a new phase in Evangelical history. There was, it was said, between 1870 and 1876 'a change of religious climate'.[229] The holiness teaching that caught on in these years, though having many and various antecedents, was primarily an expression of the spirit of the age. It was a Romantic impulse, harmonising with the premillennialism and faith mission principle that had similar origins. It challenged the beliefs about sanctification held by both Calvinists and Arminians, creating a common Christianity of experience. The fresh spirituality revitalised congregations and induced many to offer for missionary service. In 1885 some 1,500 to 2,000 people attended the Keswick Convention; by 1907 there were between 5,000 and 6,000.[230] The success of Keswick led to a host of imitations, including Bridge of Allan as the main convention for Scotland and Llandrindod Wells for Wales. The message was spread by a battery of publications including Keswick's own journal, *The Life of Faith*. New Evangelical agencies of the late nineteenth century naturally took their colour from the movement. The Christian Unions at Cambridge and Oxford, the Bible Training Institute, Glasgow, for preparing Christian workers, and many obscure mission halls had intimate links with Keswick.[231] The undenominational tone they shared was to exercise a powerful influence on twentieth-century Evangelicalism. In part, the holiness movement exerted a broadening tendency. By shifting the fulcrum of Christianity from the head to the heart, it blurred ecclesiastical boundaries and softened the doctrinal inheritance. It is consequently not surprising that it was one of the forces behind the ecumenical movement of the twentieth century.[232] Yet at the same time it was a narrowing force. There was created, it was said, 'a new sect of "undenominationalists"'.[233] Keswick in particular fits all the standard criteria of a sect – a voluntary association, exclusiveness, personal perfection as the aim, and so on – and especially of a conversionist sect.[234] In no sense, as in the case of most sects, was it a refuge for the socially deprived, but otherwise the sectarian tendency was marked. It formed, wrote Webb-Peploe to Hopkins, 'a spiritual freemasonry which the outer world cannot apprehend'.[235] Secular society, and even the generality of torpid Christians, formed an alien and often hostile world. The adherents of Keswick were turning in on a shared but private experience. They were accepting that Evangelicalism, which had come so near to dominating the national culture at mid-century, was on the way to becoming an introverted subculture.

[6]

Walking Apart:
Conservative and Liberal
Evangelicals in the
Early Twentieth Century

Can two walk together, except they be agreed? (Amos 3:3)

The unity of Evangelicalism was broken during the 1920s. The movement had always been marked by variety in doctrine, attitude and social composition, but in the years after the First World War it became so sharply divided that some members of one party did not recognise the other as Evangelical – or even, sometimes, as Christian. Polarisation was by no means total, for co-operation between the two wings, liberal and conservative, continued in a number of organisations. Yet disagreement was sufficiently acute to cause schism in several Evangelical institutions including the Church Missionary Society. Many deeply regretted the partisanship. J. E. Watts-Ditchfield, Bishop of Chelmsford, wished to hear less and less of 'Evangelicals with a label', whether conservative or liberal.[1] But it was not to be. When a similar hope was expressed by a writer to *The Record* in 1934, another correspondent pointed out the scriptural injunction to withdraw from those teaching other than the truth. Only lately, he continued in disgust, an Evangelical in the daily press had urged that the feeding of the five thousand was merely a sharing of lunches.[2] Conservatives could not tolerate liberal views of this kind. The split became deep and permanent.

In the United States at the same period there was a comparable division. The Evangelical world erupted into violent polemic between Fundamentalists and Modernists. Both terms were used in Britain. Charges of Modernism were levelled in 1913 against George Jackson, a candidate for a theological chair, by his conservative opponents in Methodism. The word had already become familiar, not least because the Vatican had suppressed what was styled Modernism in the previous decade. Modernism, whether Protestant or Catholic, was an attempt to present Christianity in terms of modern thought, to translate traditional doctrines into a contemporary idiom. The word 'Fundamentalism' emerged later. It originated in America to describe the position of those who wished to defend the fundamentals of the faith. A series of booklets called *The Fundamentals* had been issued between 1910 and 1915 to affirm basic beliefs. Although a few of the authors were British, the booklets were an American venture that created far more of a stir on the other side of the Atlantic. In 1920 an American Baptist newspaper editor called for a conference of those ready 'to do battle royal for the Fundamentals' and the word Fundamentalism entered standard usage.[3] Four years later, as a Scottish commentator noted, the term was not yet naturalised in Britain. 'Yet', he went on, 'the thing which the uncomely word describes is not unfamiliar to us here. It denotes the position of those who tenaciously cling to traditional views of Bible inspiration, and who by the intensity of their convictions are compelled to oppose to the uttermost the more elastic teachings of many modern Biblical critics.'[4] There was some reluctance to employ the term in Britain, for it was felt to be alien, uncouth and pejorative. Yet some were prepared to wear the label. The journal of the Wesley Bible Union, for instance, changed its title in 1927 to *The Fundamentalist*.[5] There was sympathy for the American Fundamentalist struggle and some exchange of personnel. It is therefore quite mistaken to hold (as it sometimes has been held) that Britain escaped a Fundamentalist controversy. Evangelicalism in Britain as well as in America suffered from fiercely contested debates in the 1920s.

The issues, furthermore, were very similar. The conservatives made the status of the Bible central. Although, as will appear, they differed among themselves in their views of the inspiration and interpretation of scripture, they were united in treating it as uniquely trustworthy and authoritative. Many spoke of the verbal inspiration of the Bible and stressed its literal interpretation. They were concerned to defend certain doctrines, among which they normally placed the imminence of the second coming. Nearly all conservatives also embraced holiness teaching, generally in its Keswick form. Liberals, on the other hand, wished to be able to reinterpret theology in fresh terms. One of them pleaded in 1913 for 'the development of thought and doctrine'.[6] They were often eager to bring greater beauty and dignity into worship. Churchmanship in general, they considered, had been too much neglected in the past. Battle lines between conservatives and liberals stretched across a wide terrain of thought and action. Conservatives often saw the scientific principle of evolution as a threat to the proper interpretation of the Bible, whereas liberals dismissed their reservations as obscurantism. Conservatives blamed modern entertainments, particularly on church premises, for the decline in religious practice, but liberals saw theatricals, sport and the like as wholesome incentives to churchgoing. The 'social gospel' was condemned by conservatives as a diversion from the gospel for individuals at a time when liberals wanted to demonstrate their sense of responsibility for society. Each of these questions also divided American

Evangelicals. Although the balance of contentious issues was rather different – evolution, for example, being more prominent in the United States – the occasions of controversy in themselves were identical.

The rift in the Evangelical ranks appeared because of different responses to the same cultural mood. The liberals were rightly perceived at the time to be innovators. They wished to modify received theology and churchmanship in the light of current thought. Inevitably their ideas were swept along by the Romantic currents that had already been flowing powerfully in the later nineteenth century. Biblical inspiration, for example, was reinterpreted as of a piece with the uplifting power of the arts. It was defined by a Methodist college tutor as 'that which yields insight into beauty, truth, and goodness, and God.' Inspiration was said to make an impact comparable to that of Wordsworth's poetry, Bach's Mass in B Minor or the view of the Langdale Pikes.[7] In similar fashion, age-encrusted doctrine was to be recast in dynamic form, preferably with a scientific gloss. 'The unfolding purpose of redemption', the Dean of Manchester told a liberal Evangelical devotional conference, 'is also the unfolding purpose of creation. It is evolution on the highest and grandest scale.'[8] Leading Methodists, like their liberal Anglican contemporaries, were imbued with a new sacramental spirit as they realised they were the heirs of the treasury of Catholic practice. 'The past', wrote one of them, 'with its conquests, its fragrance, its saints, its immortal splendour, is ours . . .'[9] It was all consonant with the trends towards greater theological breadth and greater liturgical height that had begun to gather force before 1900. By the 1920s a Romantic gale was blowing across the Evangelical landscape.

Conservatives were by no means secure from the winds of change. It was supposed at the time, by friend and foe alike, that conservatives stood for traditional, received views. In *Letters to a Fundamentalist*, published in 1930 by the Student Christian Movement Press, Percy Austin confidently identifies his own Modernist position as 'the newer view-point', and his imaginary Fundamentalist correspondent as an upholder of 'the *traditional* interpretation of Christian truth'. 'In effect', he goes on, 'you say that what has been handed down to us from our forbears *is* truth, and we must cherish it, and pass it on unaltered to those who shall come after us.'[10] This estimate of the debate, however, was a total misperception. So-called 'conservatives' were in fact advancing causes of recent growth. Their views on verbal inspiration and literal biblical interpretation were derived, as Chapter 3 has shown, by the impinging of Romanticism on a section of Evangelical opinion in the early nineteenth century. Occasionally somebody would point out that conservative views of the Bible did not have a long ancestry. When in 1911 the issues surrounding inerrancy were given a protracted airing, one contributor reminded the participants that in 1853 only the Recordites, a minority of Evangelicals in the Church of England, believed in verbal inspiration.[11] Such voices were drowned in the welter of controversy. Conservatives maintaining premillennialism likewise supposed that their tenets were traditional. 'There has been', complained

one, 'a removal of the Evangelical centre of vision from the expectation
of the personal return of the King . . .'[12] In reality it was the doctrine of
the personal return that was the novelty among Evangelicals, going back
only to the knot of innovators around Irving. Belief in inerrancy may have
been spreading in the 1920s; premillennialism certainly was. Conservative
Evangelicals were as much swayed by Romantic attitudes as were their
opponents. The only contrast was that the conservatives were affected
in different ways.

THE RISE OF BIBLICAL CRITICISM

Among the causes of the divisions of the 1920s, a primary place must
be given to the emergence of conflicting estimates of the Bible. The rise
of the higher criticism – that is, broad analysis of the development of the
text, as opposed to the lower criticism, the close study of details such as
particular words – has usually been seen as the new factor in the late
nineteenth-century understanding of scripture. In reality, as will appear, the
progress of stronger views of inspiration, bolstering conservative opinion,
was of equal importance. Yet it is true that the importation of German
critical views by the more advanced scholars did much to foster liberal
Evangelicalism. In 1861, when *Essays and Reviews* first drew widespread
attention in the Church of England to critical methods and conclusions,
Evangelicals were numbered among the book's most convinced opponents.
Anyone leaning to its approach was by definition Broad Church.[13] The
premisses of critics were, after all, rooted in the intellectual milieu of
German philosophy. Nations, it was assumed, develop their distinctive
values gradually over time. When the principle was applied to the history
of Israel, it could only be supposed that the noble monotheism of the
Pentateuch arose at a late stage. The compilation of the first five books of
the Old Testament was therefore assigned to the seventh century BC at the
earliest. Analysis that distinguished different sources in the text underpinned
the theory. All this remained bound up, in the British view of the 1860s,
with the sceptical tendencies in religion that were summed up as German
neology.[14] It was foreign to Evangelicalism.

The contented sense that Britain was a bastion of reverence for the
Bible was first undermined in the later 1870s. William Robertson Smith,
the brilliant young Professor of Hebrew and Old Testament in the Free
Church College at Aberdeen, wrote an article on 'The Bible' for the
Encyclopaedia Britannica which assumed the validity of the most recent
German scholarship. His views attracted much uncomprehending censure.
Most serious, in the eyes of the Free Church committee that examined
his position, was his attitude to Deuteronomy. Sayings attributed there
to Moses were, according to Smith, the inventions of a later age. His sole
innovation, Smith submitted in his own defence, was to hold that scripture

'makes use of certain forms of literary presentation which have always been thought legitimate in ordinary composition, but which were not always understood to be used in the Bible'. The investigating sub-committee believed that the resort to a theory of 'dramatic personations, appropriate in poetry and parable' was too improbable in the case of Deuteronomy to be 'a safe position from which to defend the historical truth and inspired authority of the Bible'. The committee concluded that, although there was some cause for grave concern, there were no grounds for a charge of heresy.[15] After three years during which the issue rumbled through the complex Presbyterian legal machinery, the General Assembly in 1880 determined, by 299 votes to 292, that Smith should still be permitted to teach for the Free Church. A further *Encyclopaedia Britannica* article, however, appeared to be a flouting of the church's solemnly expressed concern over critical questions and in 1881 Smith was dismissed by a large majority. Two years later he found asylum as Reader in Arabic at Cambridge.[16]

Smith's purpose was clear. He was intending to remould the study of the Bible according to the Romantic canons generally accepted in Germany. As he testified, he was trying to reintroduce what had been lost in 'the epoch of Rationalism'. He believed that the loss had been the notion of revelation, which was 'never a mechanical, dead, unintelligible thing'. Rather 'the Biblical Literature' was 'an organic part of the history of the church in the ages of revelation'.[17] Religious truth, that is to say, had gradually been perceived through the ongoing experience of the people of God. His Evangelical contemporaries who had been brought up in an intellectual framework deriving from the Enlightenment, Smith's 'epoch of Rationalism', found the theoretical gulf from the young scholar's premisses too wide to bridge. Even the most thorough antagonist of Smith's views among English Nonconformists, Alfred Cave, did no justice to his views. The explanation is to be found in the title of one of Cave's later books: *The Inspiration of the Old Testament Inductively Considered* (1888). Cave was tied to Enlightenment categories such as induction that made constructive engagement with Smith impossible.[18] The appeal of the up-to-date approach to Old Testament scholarship was, however, irresistible. Smith himself was so patently free of scepticism and unorthodoxy as to inspire others to tread the same path. Already his teacher, A. B. Davidson, had taken some steps in that direction. Two further cases debated by the Free Church Assembly in 1890 raised questions of biblical criticism as well as of theological orthodoxy, and in both instances charges were dropped after investigation. In 1902 George Adam Smith, whose position on Old Testament criticism was substantially identical to that of Robertson Smith, was likewise effectively acquitted. In a solidly Evangelical denomination biblical criticism had become accepted.[19] In the Church of Scotland its inroads were just as great by the end of the century. John McMurtrie, editor of its magazine *Life and Work* and a noted Evangelical, would point to his extensive collection of German critical literature as 'my wicked library'.[20] At least among the ministers in Scotland, the new approach had come to stay.

The same was true in England. Fears that criticism was close to unbelief were allayed by the magisterial work of the so-called 'Cambridge Trio'. A. J. Hort, J. B. Lightfoot and B. F. Westcott, each in a different way, applied rigorous scholarly standards to the establishment and exegesis of the New Testament text, reaching conclusions that Evangelicals found generally unexceptionable – and even spiritually helpful.[21] The publication of *Lux Mundi* in 1889 announced the conversion of younger Anglo-Catholics to moderate critical opinions.[22] Two years later, S. R. Driver, Regius Professor of Hebrew at Oxford, presented a summary of recent Old Testament studies as entirely compatible with orthodoxy.[23] It was all reassuring to Evangelicals with intellectual aspirations. Congregationalists, with their predisposition to free inquiry, were foremost in the field. In 1893 a collection of essays by Congregationalists called *Faith and Criticism* was published. W. H. Bennett of Hackney and New Colleges unreservedly accepted the late dating of the Pentateuch in his Old Testament essay. If W. F. Adeney of New College was much more conservative in his study of the New Testament, the flair of P. T. Forsyth combined a zealous delineation of the person of Christ as redeemer with clear reservations about the 'old-Protestant theory of a book-revelation'.[24] Despite the best efforts of Alfred Cave, Congregationalists were evidently abandoning resistance to the modern approach. From 1892 summer schools held at their Mansfield College, Oxford, began to disseminate the new learning.[25] By 1895 the higher criticism had likewise been generally, though not universally, accepted by Wesleyan theological tutors, and had attracted a significant recruit in Driver's Primitive Methodist pupil, A. S. Peake.[26] It was surprising how rapidly Methodist ministers accepted critical conclusions. 'The trouble will come', it was rightly prophesied a few years later, 'when preachers are so absolutely honest as to say in the pulpit all they say to one another, and tell out all they believe and disbelieve.'[27] The first of the classic Fundamentalist controversies in Britain was to erupt when a Methodist did speak out.

OPPOSITION TO BIBLICAL CRITICISM

There were earlier signs of the coming storm. Spurgeon's charge that many ministers were on the Down Grade included, as a minor dimension, a protest against novel ideas about the Bible.[28] F. B. Meyer, then a rising Baptist, reviewed *Faith and Criticism* with expressions of dismay about the influence of its teachings on the next generation of Congregational ministers.[29] With certain exceptions, Baptists were certainly less inclined to critical innovations than other Nonconformists. Fringe Evangelical groups were most hostile. The tiny International Christian Mission, a holiness body based exclusively at 83–5 Queen's Road, Brighton, lamented among the signs of the times for 1898 that, 'The Word of God is assailed by professing Christians'.[30] This, more significantly, was the painful charge levelled against R. F. Horton, the cultured and spiritually minded minister of Lyndhurst Road Congregational Church, Hampstead, when he published *Inspiration and the Bible* in 1888. He had imbibed Driver's views at Oxford, where he had become the first Nonconformist to hold a fellowship. For his pains he was denounced by a host of assailants including Spurgeon and Joseph Parker of the City Temple. Even the aunt with whom he lived withdrew from his ministry in protest.[31] Among the Evangelicals of the Church of England there was an ominous calm. The standard case heard on their platforms was that the Christian estimate of scripture should be that of Christ himself.[32] Occasionally an adventurous analysis was put forward. As early as 1878 Edward Batty, of St John's, Fulham, declared at the Islington Clerical Meeting that they ought 'to admit that certain historical parts of the Bible were allegorical or open to different interpretations, and to show that they were fully alive to the importance of the claims of just, honest, reverential, and scholarly criticism'. But the cries of 'No, no' that greeted his suggestion that the authority of a passage in the gospel of John was open to challenge showed where majority feeling lay.[33] There was likely to be heavy weather ahead.

Opposition to the higher criticism first became organised in 1892. A Bible League was created, according to its object, 'to promote the Reverent Study of the Holy Scriptures, and to resist the varied attacks made upon their Inspiration, Infallibility, and Sole Sufficiency as the Word of God.'[34] Its immediate occasion seems to have been the appearance of *The Inspiration and Authority of the Bible* by John Clifford, a Baptist leader strikingly open to modern trends of thought, who, like Horton but more guardedly, was trying to popularise a newer understanding of the Bible.[35] Resistance was initially located on the Baptist fringe, around Spurgeon and the boundary with undenominational revivalism. Successive secretaries were John Tuckwell, a London Baptist minister; A. H. Carter, later Minister of Hounslow Undenominational Church and editor of the League's *Bible Witness*; and (from 1912) Robert Wright Hay, a former BMS missionary, Minister of Talbot Tabernacle, Notting Hill (an 'energetic Gospel centre') and an intimate friend of R. C. Morgan, editor of *The Christian*.[36] It was originally a small-scale affair, holding occasional rallies where Tuckwell might lecture on 'The Bible Right: confirmed by Babylonian archaeology',[37] but it gradually drew in more eminent figures from a wider range of denominations. Dinsdale Young, a well-known Methodist preacher, Dr C. M. Waller, a tutor in the CMS college at Highbury, and, crucially, Prebendary H. E. Fox, clerical secretary of the CMS from 1895 to 1910, were induced to identify with the organisation.[38] It was sufficiently strong by 1914 to hold a summer school at Littlehampton addressed by a dozen speakers.[39] Its essential message is summed up by the title of a publication three years later: *Christ or the Higher Critics*.[40]

The Bible League did much to stiffen opinion. Frequently its influence can be detected behind outbursts of opposition to the higher criticism. At Cambridge, for instance, a Bible League conference immediately preceded a schism in the Evangelical student movement in 1909–10 that anticipated the divisions in the wider ecclesiastical world fifteen or so years later.[41] A Cambridge Inter-Collegiate Christian Union (CICCU) had existed since 1877 for the promotion of evangelism, prayer and missionary commitment. A British College Christian Union had emerged in the 1890s to co-ordinate such bodies in higher education, taking the name of Student Christian Movement (SCM) in 1905. In the next two years the General Secretary of the SCM, Tissington Tatlow, received letters from Cambridge protesting against speakers in whom higher critical opinions blended with broader doctrinal views than were desired.[42] Nothing was done, for the settled policy of the SCM was to accept the new approach to the Bible. A great number of other issues, which were also to arise again on the wider scene in the 1920s, complicated the ensuing discussions within and around the CICCU. At the root of the debate, however, was the status of the Bible. When the CICCU disaffiliated from the SCM in 1910, it declared 'its first and final reference to the authority of Holy Scripture as its inerrant guide in all matters concerned with faith and morals'.[43] There were similar secessions from the other movements for young people. In 1916 the Aldersgate Street Young Men's Christian Association left its parent body and in 1921 a number of groups previously affiliated to the Young Women's Christian Association came together as the Christian Alliance of Women and Girls, standing for 'full allegiance to the Word of God and separation for His work'.[44] Strongly held views about the Bible were beginning to create institutional divisions.

VERBAL INSPIRATION AND INERRANCY

The strong views commonly included a belief in verbal inspiration. Critics might suppose that the Bible is merely the record of revelation, wrote Meyer in 1893, but 'we believe that God revealed Himself in the *words* of Scripture . . .'[45] Meyer stood in the verbal inspirationist tradition that went back to Robert Haldane and Louis Gaussen in the early nineteenth century. The Brethren, a body moulded at that time by the same influences that affected Haldane, formed a continuing citadel of the stronger view of inspiration. In an article published during 1921 in their magazine *The Witness*, its editor, Henry Pickering, enquired, 'Have we an inspired Word of God?' The answer was a ringing affirmative. The very letters, even the Hebrew punctuation marks, were inspired: had not Jesus confirmed that every jot and tittle of the law was eternal?[46] The cause had advanced steadily among the Evangelical clergy in the Church of England. J. C.

Ryle, Bishop of Liverpool from 1880 to 1900, undoubtedly represented the majority of clerical opinion in the party of which he was a trusted leader when he declared his unhesitating belief in verbal inspiration.[47] The same view was widespread in popular Evangelical apologetics. It was usually qualified by the statement that only the original documents were inspired in this way – a convenient proviso that made the hypothesis untestable.[48] The qualification, if sometimes securing greater intellectual respectability, could itself lead on to some strange inferences. It was held by one defender of plenary inspiration that every one of the original inspired words exists somewhere in the world, often in very ancient manuscripts.[49] There can be no doubt that belief in verbal inspiration had become common by the early twentieth century.

Yet it was rare for spokesmen, let alone scholars, in the Evangelical community to claim that the Bible is free from error. A. H. Burton, a non-practising doctor with a private income and a Brethren background, was one of the few to do so. In an article on 'The inerrancy of the Bible' he set out a simple antithesis between those who affirmed it and the higher critics who denied it.[50] An examination of the chief statements about scripture by Evangelicals in the first half of the twentieth century has revealed a remarkable absence of assertions of inerrancy. Only a couple, by D. M. McIntyre, later Principal of the Bible Training Institute, Glasgow, and W. E. Vine, a Brethren leader, were discovered. Even W. H. Griffith Thomas, Principal of Wycliffe Hall, Oxford, from 1905 to 1910, and a well-known Evangelical Anglican champion of a conservative view of scripture in the early twentieth century, though inclining towards inerrancy, avoided any explicit endorsement. Likewise G. T. Manley and T. C. Hammond, the leading exponents of the conservative position after the divergence of the 1920s, did not assert the inerrancy of the Bible. The problem, of course, was that the apparent discrepancies of scripture had been thoroughly canvassed for centuries and it was hard to fly in the face of them. Yet in America at the same time a stern repudiation of the possibility of error in a book given by a God of truth was massively elaborated by B. B. Warfield, so that the sparseness of British statements to the same effect is matter for comment.[51] Why did Evangelical leaders in Britain take this course?

One of the explanations is the restraining influence of Henry Wace. As a former Professor of Ecclesiastical History and then Principal at King's College, London, from 1875 to 1897, Wace was a scholar and ecclesiastical statesman of some weight. As Dean of Canterbury from 1903 until his death in 1924, he played a leading part in Evangelical counsels. At the Islington Clerical Meeting of 1911 he provoked considerable dissent among the more liberally inclined by avowing what he called the traditional theory of scripture. It included the axiom that in history as well as doctrine the Bible is free from error. Yet, for all the apparent conservatism of his position, he admitted there might be trivial mistakes of the text.[52] He held, as he often put it, the 'substantial truth' of scripture – and that fell short

of absolute inerrancy. 'Are there a few inaccuracies of detail?' he asked
at a conference in 1921. 'How could it be otherwise in a short sketch of so
many ages of development?'[53] The *Journal of the Wesley Bible Union* noted with
disappointment his willingness to surrender the detailed accuracy of Genesis.[54] To his friends he would commend Luther's attitude to the Bible, an
eagerness to grasp the leading truths 'without becoming a slave to verbal inspiration'.[55] He had originally been no party man, being drawn into the Evangelical ranks by a shared hostility to ritualism at the turn of the century, and
so he felt no initial sympathy for Ryle's rigidity about the words of scripture.
Rather the foundation of his position was a scholar's disdain for what he saw
as the aberrations of recent German study of the Old Testament. His remedy
for erroneous criticism was better criticism.[56] By involvement with the
Bible League, whose vice-president he became,[57] he made it impossible to
identify the conservative position on the Bible with wilder denunciations of
the higher criticism or rigid statements about inerrancy. Furthermore, his
intellectual premises reveal a deeper reason why it was uncommon to
deduce inerrancy from the trustworthiness of God. Whether the substantial
truth of the Old Testament, he wrote, 'involved minute exactitude in all
details is a matter partly for common sense, but chiefly for determination
by the facts . . .'[58] Appeal to common sense and the facts was the stock
in trade of a thinker whose mind was shaped by the familiar Anglo-Saxon
empiricism stemming from the Enlightenment. Wace was as wedded to
this tradition as was the Congregationalist Alfred Cave. The resistance to
the higher criticism was not grounded in a doctrine of inerrancy because,
at least among the educated, inerrancy held no more attractions than the
conclusions of the higher critics.

The motive force for the anti-critical movement came primarily, as in
America, from individuals and groups holding the advent hope. This was
no more an absolute rule than it was in America.[59] Nevertheless there was
a tight link between the premillennialist movement and the defence of the
Bible. 'Those who stood by the great truth of the Lord's return', it was
said at an Advent Testimony meeting in 1921, 'were firm on the authority
and infallibility of the Scriptures as the actual Word of God.'[60] The link
was literal interpretation. 'It is a principle of vital importance to the study
of Scripture', declared Fuller Gooch, a leading exponent of prophecy, in
1886, 'that the literal signification of words should be accepted in all cases
except where the obvious nature of the language employed necessitates
a figurative or symbolic sense. Only by a continuous violation of this
principle can the personal reign of Christ during the millennial era be
eliminated from revelation.'[61] Those who were tied to literalism could
hardly avoid believing in verbal inspiration. That is why the two trends
had grown up together during the nineteenth century. In the early twentieth
century, the denominations most affected by Fundamentalism were those
most touched by adventism – the Brethren, Anglican Evangelicals and the
Baptists. Conversely, Congregationalism was almost immune to both.

W. B. Selbie could be heard warning his fellow–Congregationalists in 1922 against the literal interpretation of scripture,[62] but his effort was hardly necessary. The case of Methodism is the exception that proves the rule. As will be seen, it was hardly touched by adventism. Yet the leader of the Fundamentalist party in Wesleyan Methodism, H. C. Morton, was by 1918 preaching the second coming.[63] In Morton's case, Bible defence came before adventism, but the association between the two is once more clear. The primary impetus for militancy on behalf of the Bible came from those who had embraced the advent hope.

THE CHRISTIAN HOPE

Another reason for the Evangelical divisions of the 1920s is therefore the rise of premillennialism. The rival version of the Christian hope, postmillennialism, had gone into serious decline. A few still held in the early years of the twentieth century that Christ would return in person once the preaching of the gospel had established his reign in all lands.[64] But interpretations of postmillennialism had commonly broadened with the years. 'Modern Methodism', it was said just after the opening of the twentieth century, 'has deliberately projected the second Advent into so distant a future that it is scarcely even named.'[65] High hopes for the far–off future merged imperceptibly with the idea of progress. By 1916 a leading Methodist was prepared to state that 'no visible return of Christ to the earth is to be expected'.[66] It was not only Methodists who followed this course. The editor of *Life and Work*, the magazine of the Church of Scotland, reaffirmed a Christian belief in progress despite the horrors of the First World War. Although apocalyptic speculation is fruitless, he claimed, 'there can be but one "evolution of society", one "social development"; it is the coming of the Kingdom of God'.[67] Likewise at Cromer, the devotional conference for liberal Evangelicals of the Church of England, a verse of a popular hymn was changed from:

> Brothers, this Lord Jesus shall return again
> With His Father's glory, with His angel train.

It appeared as:

> Brothers, this Lord Jesus dwells with us again
> In His Father's wisdom, o'er the earth to reign.[68]

Postmillennialism had become little more than an aspiration after the spread of Christian values.

Premillennialism, however, had made steady progress in the later nineteenth century. There was an annual conference for the Study of Prophetic

Truth at Clapham from 1884, and in the same year a session of the devotional Mildmay Conference was given over to the subject for the first time.[69] Crucially, advent teaching had early become intertwined with the Keswick message.[70] Association with the flowing tide of the holiness movement ensured that prophecy swept along increasing numbers. It became popular with the young. The Student Volunteer Movement for Foreign Missions, an international body launched in 1886 with the motto 'The Evangelisation of the world in this generation', gathered strength from the Keswick fringe.[71] Although there was no time for the conversion of the world, its members held, it was necessary to preach the gospel to every nation. That done, Christ would return. Missionary work would bring back the King. The Church Missionary Society was among the bodies feeling the benefit in a fresh wave of recruits.[72] Keswick and the new missionary enthusiasm alike disproportionately affected the Church of England. By 1901 a speaker at the Islington Clerical Meeting felt able to assume that all his hearers believed in the premillennial advent.[73] At least in the Church of England, prophetic teaching had become firmly established by the dawn of the new century.

The form of prophetic teaching making most headway was the futurist version. All the predictions of Daniel and Revelation, its advocates argued, were still to be fulfilled. The dispensationalism of J. N. Darby, the most systematic brand of futurism, captured many minds with its vision of a coming rapture of the church. It was the view generally accepted by Evangelical Churchmen who attended Keswick. 'Every day', remarked an incredulous Methodist, 'they are waiting for the saints to be caught up – the captain from his ship, the engine-driver from his locomotive, the mother from her family, &c.'[74] By 1892, the editor of *The Christian*, who had previously maintained neutrality between different schools, came down on the side of 'dispensational truth'.[75] Probably the greatest factor in favour of dispensationalism was the publication in 1909 of the Scofield Bible with footnotes expounding a Darbyite interpretation. Already four years later it was said to be 'so largely used by students and Christian workers'.[76] It accustomed its readers to seeing the biblical text through dispensationalist eyes. Although the writings of Henry Grattan Guinness, such as *The Approaching End of the Age* (1878), sustained the vitality of the alternative historicist version of premillennial teaching,[77] there can be no doubt that dispensationalism was the predominant form of the advent hope by the First World War.

The apocalyptic atmosphere of wartime encouraged prophetic speculation. At the outbreak of the First World War the only premillennialist organisation in Britain was the Prophecy Investigation Society, which exuded an air of rather musty erudition. About a hundred devotees assembled twice a year for the reading of arcane papers.[78] The war livened it up. 'The Rev. F. L. Denman', it was reported of one meeting, 'directed the attention of the members to the striking way in which several passages in Daniel xi. fit the character and conduct of the Kaiser.'[79] Hostilities in the Middle East created expectations in a wider constituency. The Jews might soon return to the Promised Land, a sure sign of the second coming. With British troops massing in Sinai for an advance on Jerusalem in the autumn of 1917, two ministers suggested to F. B. Meyer that there should be an effort to awaken Christians to the fulfilment of prophecy around them. Meyer secured the endorsement of other ministers known to be premillennialists, approached the Prophecy Investigation Society for its backing and launched the first of what was to be a permanent series of monthly London public meetings on 13 December. While preparations were going ahead, the government issued the Balfour Declaration announcing British support for the return of the Jews to Palestine. Four days after the first public meeting General Allenby received the surrender of Jerusalem.[80] The Advent Testimony and Preparation Movement enjoyed an auspicious beginning.

The message spread by a variety of means. Advent Testimony monthly meetings were widely reported in the Christian press; its magazine, *Advent Witness*, circulated extensively; and several of its members wrote books, of which E. L. Langston's *How God is Working to a Plan* (1933) was one of the most popular. The greatest publicity coup, however, was the conversion to the cause of Christabel Pankhurst, the ex-suffragette, who published a number of premillennialist works beginning with *The Lord Cometh* in 1923. In the autumn of 1926 she undertook a campaign tour for Advent Testimony, bringing, it was said, 'fresh inspiration' to the movement.[81] Douglas Brown, Baptist minister at Balham and a member of the Advent Testimony council, did a great deal to propagate premillennial teaching. In 1921 there broke out in East Anglia, especially among the fishermen, one of the last mainland revivals of the old-fashioned spontaneous type. Brown was the pivotal figure, delivering gospel addresses at Lowestoft and in the vicinity. The ingathering of converts, he reported to an Advent Testimony meeting, was 'largely through the preaching of the truth of the Lord's coming'. On thirty-one consecutive afternoons he spoke for fifty minutes on the second advent.[82] Others similarly discovered that premillennial enthusiasm helped evangelistic endeavour. The Pilgrim Preachers, for instance, a band of travelling young men drawn from the Brethren, proclaimed (according to their leader) '"the coming of the Lord draweth nigh", and that it is a case of *now or never* with the unsaved to decide for Christ'.[83] Association with gospel zeal helped in turn to propagate prophetic views. For the first time in many quarters they were being accepted as the orthodoxy of popular Evangelicalism.

The spread of the futurist version of the advent hope in the 1920s had important implications. By contrast with historicists, who paid a great deal of attention to public affairs, past and present, for the vindication of their views, futurists concentrated on the intricacies of scripture to the virtual exclusion of issues in the world. The sermons of Fuller Gooch on adventist themes were so incomprehensible to newspaper reporters that their accounts became gibberish.[84] There was little point in trying to identify the figures of prophecy since by definition they were future. At its fullest, interest in contemporary events was therefore a matter of looking out for signs of the emergence of a pattern of affairs similar to that predicted for the last days – like the combination of ten powers within the territory of the former Roman Empire to play the part of the toes of the statue in Daniel 2. Futurism encouraged the introversion that was a hallmark of interwar conservative Evangelicalism. There was another significant divergence of futurists from historicists in the identification of Antichrist. Historicists followed Protestant tradition in casting the papacy in that role. The Roman Catholic Church represented the great apostasy from the true faith predicted in scripture.[85] Futurists, on the other hand, believed that the Antichrist was still to come. They were consequently less inclined to militant anti–Catholicism. At the same time, however, they were expecting the Protestant world to lapse into unbelief on a vast scale. Higher criticism seemed a sinister symptom of the anti–Christian teaching subverting Christendom that had to be stoutly resisted. 'A falsely called Christian charity', declared an adventist magazine in 1919, 'has led many to temporize with these deadly doctrines, so that some have become swamped by the rising tide of apostasy.'[86] The fierce, denunciatory tone of Fundamentalism – in so far as it was heard in Britain – was largely spawned by the futurist prophetic school.

Futurism also created a gloomy worldview. Already, before the war, a Methodist had remarked that adventist clergymen were deeply pessimistic. 'Looking for our Lord's speedy coming', he explained, 'they expect things to go from bad to worse, and frankly tell me they have no hope of amelioration.'[87] The war and its aftermath confirmed and extended such attitudes. Premillennialists rejected the vision of 'the rosy Christian idealist – that honest, earnest, believer in the essential goodness of Humanity, who supposes that the Millennium is to be the automatic result of a gradual improvement in men and things'. God had revealed otherwise. 'He tells us plainly, not that the development of the Kingdom will bring the King, but that the King Himself must come to establish the Kingdom; and that He, not man, is to make the Kingdom fit for men to live in.'[88] Effort to reform the world was pointless, even perhaps an impious attempt to frustrate the purposes of God. Sympathy for progressive politics waned. Organised labour seemed a sinister force in both industry and politics. In the wake of the General Strike of 1926 readers of *The Life of Faith* were assured that this 'revolutionary plot . . . being hatched against the British Constitution . . . *was the rising of an Anti-Christ*'. 'I am not discussing politics', insisted the contributor, 'but as one who loves his Lord . . . I believe the time has come for Christians . . . to prepare themselves and their land for that which the Bible prophesies shall come to pass.'[89] Premillennialists, as in this case, normally proclaimed their distance from politics, yet rallied to the defence of the established order. Pessimism readily passed over into conservatism.

HEIGHTENED SPIRITUALITY

A further factor behind the interwar Evangelical schism was the holiness movement that has been discussed in Chapter 5. Its effects were ambiguous. The spirituality of the movement, as the Broadlands conference illustrates, could reinforce the trend towards softening doctrinal definitions. Keswick, as will be seen, was the setting for a tussle between more liberal and more conservative elements.[90] The outcome, however, could be in little doubt, for Keswick teaching was in general strongly associated with a non-critical understanding of the Bible and the advent hope. Its exponents, according to conservative Evangelicals, were beacons in the gathering gloom. 'I travel from Land's End to the Shetland Isles', wrote one in 1925, 'and I find wherever there is a real Keswick school minister there one finds the ungodly being awakened and led to Christ . . .'[91] More critical observers noticed the cultivation of the internal life, the camaraderie with the likeminded symbolised by the use of the adjective 'dear' in reference to Christian colleagues and commented that this ethos encouraged a narrowing of horizons.[92] The Keswick movement was still growing in size and influence in the 1920s, its message of 'fuller consecration' being disseminated by literature, lesser conventions and a variety of organisations. Its essentially Romantic spirituality was in itself too irenical to provoke adherents into militant Fundamentalism, but the Keswick allegiance did a great deal to glue together the conservative coalition.

The Methodist version of the holiness tradition played a similar role within the Wesleyan denomination. Its embodiment was Samuel Chadwick, a gifted devotional writer and from 1913 Principal of Cliff College, a denominational centre in Derbyshire for training lay workers. 'There is no Methodist doctrine of Inspiration, or of the Second Coming', he reminded a holiness meeting at the 1912 conference. 'But there is a distinctively Methodist doctrine of holiness.'[93] Among Wesleyans, therefore, entire sanctification was the potential rallying ground of theological conservatives. It had already been noticed that the holiness people for the most part did not embrace the higher criticism.[94] The leaders of the Fundamentalist faction that emerged in the Jackson affair of 1913, George Armstrong Bennetts and Harold Morton, were both advocates of entire sanctification.[95] So was Dinsdale Young, the most eminent Methodist to be drawn into the faction.[96] Samuel Chadwick, however, stood apart from the Fundamentalist campaign against individuals judged to hold erroneous views. In 1919 he called for an end to the 'wrangling and haggling' of the heresy hunt, condemning the 'heterodoxy of temper' displayed by the militant Wesley Bible Union a year later.[97] He ensured that *Joyful News*, the widely circulating weekly associated with Cliff College, remained aloof from controversy. Dinsdale Young was kept at a distance from the college and the Southport Convention, the main holiness platform.[98] Chadwick and his circle believed in the positive work of preaching the gospel, not in negative campaigns that aroused animosity.[99] The mildness and self-restraint of this approach were the natural fruit of teaching on personal sanctification. The Methodist holiness tradition, with a few exceptions, generated conservative Evangelicalism rather than Fundamentalism.

Other movements of opinion on the fringe of the holiness movement tended to stoke up spiritual fires to a more intense heat. From the early days there was a section, drawing inspiration from the American Dr Cullis, that believed physical healing, as well as victory over sin, to be available through faith in Christ.[100] 'When He has complete control in the fully surrendered life', it was said in 1921, 'He is responsible for directing our bodily lives – and is responsible for our health.'[101] This writer, like several others, did not shrink from the implication that illness is the result of sin. Only in exceptional cases, he contended when challenged by many dismayed correspondents, are the consecrated allowed to be invalids.[102] It was more normal to hold that sickness is not necessarily the result of want of faith, but occasional talk of 'bondage about doctors and nurses' was a sign of the anti-modern disposition of Fundamentalism.[103]

Another intensified version of holiness teaching pointed in the same direction. Some began to talk of a baptism of the Holy Ghost distinct from the experience of entire consecration. One source was the Pentecostal League of Reader Harris. Its leadership was taken over after his death in 1909 by Oswald Chambers, who a few years before had entered 'years of heaven on earth' through the baptism of the Holy Ghost.[104] Another source was the Japan Evangelistic Band, established in 1903, whose founder, A. Paget Wilkes, taught that sanctification is twofold, entailing cleansing from indwelling sin and then 'an incoming and indwelling of the Holy Ghost'.[105] But the chief source was the Welsh Revival of 1904–5. Spreading through much of Wales and affecting churches elsewhere in Britain, ordinary church life was suspended, whole communities anxiously sought salvation and some 100,000 people professed conversion.[106] A young candidate for the Calvinistic Methodist ministry, Evan Roberts, underwent a vivid spiritual experience that made him the central figure of the revival. Twelve years later he expounded his experience in a work written jointly with Jessie Penn-Lewis of the Overcomer League, *War on the Saints*. The remedy for the assault of deceiving spirits on the children of God was to be found in 'the Baptism of the Holy Spirit'.[107] Although such teaching was suspect at Keswick, from which Jessie Penn-Lewis had withdrawn in 1909, it was disseminated by fringe periodicals like *The Overcomer* and minor conventions at Matlock and elsewhere.[108] It helped ensure that a section of Evangelicalism, albeit a small one, remained firmly committed to the conservative side in the years after the First World War.

It was also in this atmosphere that Pentecostalism was born. Talk of the 'baptism of the Holy Ghost' in the holiness movement prepared the way. There were even thoughts of the possibility of the restoration of the gift of tongues, which was understood as the ability to speak other languages and so to evangelise the world.[109] The Welsh revival created fresh longings after the dynamic of the first-century church. The early leaders of two of the Pentecostal denominations, Daniel Powell Williams of the Apostolic Church and George and Stephen Jeffreys of Elim, were converted then together with many of the early rank and file.[110] A report on the Welsh Revival by F. B. Meyer contributed to the beginnings of Pentecostalism in San Francisco in 1905. Although there were earlier manifestations in the American mid-west, the movement usually traces the origin of its worldwide spread to what followed in San Francisco. Revival broke out in Azusa Street and speaking in tongues was heard.[111] Belief that a new outpouring of the Holy Spirit had begun soon reached Norway, where ecstatic utterances were witnessed early in 1907 by A. A. Boddy, Vicar of All Saints', Sunderland. At Boddy's request, T. B. Barratt, the Methodist minister who had brought the dramatic manifestations to Norway, now carried them to Sunderland, which became a major centre for their dissemination in the years up to the First World War. There were similar outbreaks elsewhere, and from 1909 Cecil Polhill, one of the 'Cambridge Seven' who had gone out as missionaries to China in 1885, organised regular meetings in Sion College, on the Thames Embankment in London, for 'all seeking Salvation, Sanctification, the Baptism of the Holy Spirit and Divine Healing'.[112] By July 1908 there were already thirty-two known centres in Britain where Pentecostal gifts were exercised.[113] A new dimension was added to the Evangelical world.

The pioneers Boddy and Polhill, as loyal Anglicans, tried to discourage the tendencies to separatism that soon appeared, particularly in Wales. The 'spoken word' movement began to teach that scriptural church government was through an elaborate hierarchy of apostles, prophets and others appointed through ecstatic utterance. Daniel Powell Williams, who received a call to apostleship in 1913, set about consolidating the Pentecostal assemblies that were springing up within this pattern. They became the Apostolic Church.[114] Another growing organisation was the Elim Evangelistic Band, led by the energetic George Jeffreys. First formed in Ulster in 1915, its work spread through Britain in the interwar years until, by 1939, the Elim Foursquare Gospel Alliance, as it had become known, claimed to have established 280 churches. Jeffreys, who was to leave Elim in a dispute in 1939–41, was the driving force. He would hold evangelistic and healing campaigns, usually in significant centres of population, and the converts would be gathered into a new cause.[115] Its connexional structure resembled the polity of Methodism. The Assemblies of God, by contrast, upheld the autonomy of local churches. It was formed in 1924 by small bodies eager to remain independent of the encroachments of the Apostolic Church.[116] It differed also from Elim in asserting that speaking in tongues is always the initial evidence of baptism in the Holy Spirit.[117]

Pentecostalism was united, however, in its advent teaching, which was often more prominent than its advocacy of tongues, and its summons 'back to the Bible'. 'This book, neglected by so many pulpits today', declared a short account of the denomination, 'is the basis of Elim's Fundamentalism.'[118] Yet ordinary conservative Evangelicals, and even other self-professed Fundamentalists, repudiated the whole movement. 'The question', announced *The Life of Faith* in answer to queries in 1922, 'as to the possibility of the periodical appearance of miraculous gifts during the course of this dispensation is one which still gives rise to acute differences of opinion. Fortunately, there is no need for us to come to any definite conclusion on this point in order to see how unscriptural, and, indeed, how utterly subversive of genuine spirituality, are the corybantic exhibitions associated with particular types of present-day "Pentecostalism".'[119] The position of the Pentecostalists in relation to Fundamentalism, it has been suggested, was similar to the position of the Quakers in relation to Puritanism: having similar origins, occupying much common ground and yet totally repudiated by the larger body.[120] Although spurned by others, Pentecostalists brought vigorous reinforcement to the conservative wing of Evangelicalism.

BROADENING THEOLOGY

The slackening doctrinal standards on the liberal wing also help explain the divisions of the 1920s. The principle of free inquiry coupled with a taste for the Romantic had begun to broaden the theology of Nonconformists in the later nineteenth century.[121] By the interwar years a typical publication of Congregationalists was *The Religion of Wordsworth* (1936), by the scholar-minister, A. D. Martin. It taught the religion of gratitude as illustrated by the poet.[122] Among younger Methodists such as Robert Newton Flew there were similar trends of thought. In 1918 Flew criticised the narrowness of the early Methodist preachers, who, he claimed, 'had not seen a vision of God affirming the world as good, as delighting in the colour and gaiety and many-sidedness of human life, ceaselessly operative as in Nature . . .'[123] A comparable widening of horizons is apparent in *Changing Creeds and Social Struggles* (1893) by Charles Aked, a Baptist minister at Liverpool eventually to be translated to the United States. But Aked was unusually broad for a Baptist, and Meyer was in due course to point out to him the limits of orthodoxy.[124]

The drift of opinion led to the New Theology controversy of 1907–10. R. J. Campbell, occupant of Congregationalism's premier pulpit at the City Temple, shocked the religious public with opinions so immersed in philosophical idealism as to verge on pantheism. Deity and humanity, he held in *The New Theology* (1907), are 'fundamentally and essentially one'.[125] The implications, worked out in a supplementary volume on *Christianity and the Social Order*, were no less alarming. 'The churches', he wrote, 'have nothing to do with getting men into heaven.' Their task was rather to hasten the kingdom of God, which was equated with the socialist order being championed by the Independent Labour Party.[126] As his leading opponent, P. T. Forsyth, insisted, Campbell had broken entirely with any theology of the cross. To the Evangelical press, the New Theology seemed so nonsensical – an 'extraordinary farrago' – as to pose little threat.[127] Campbell's supporters rallied in a Liberal Christian League, but by 1915 even ardent opponents could scent out few continuing followers.[128] In that year Campbell renounced his theology and was received into the Church of England.[129] While ministers who had abandoned Evangelical belief persisted in Congregationalism – indeed Bernard Snell of Brixton became Chairman of the Congregational Union in 1917 and T. Rhondda Williams of Brighton followed him in 1929[130] – by and large the Nonconformist denominations remained within the bounds of Evangelicalism.

There were comparable doctrinal developments in the Evangelical party of the Church of England. The time was fast passing, declared C. J. Procter, Vicar of Islington, in 1905, when religious people distrusted the increase of knowledge. 'Theological interpretation', he went on, 'like every other branch of knowledge, is a progressive science . . .'[131] When such sentiments were uttered from the chair of the Islington Clerical Meeting, very much the magisterium of the party, it is not surprising that others went further. In 1912, at the Ridley Hall reunion of old members, the vice-principal of the college, J. R. Darbyshire, delivered what was long remembered as 'that famous address' on 'Gospel and Culture'.[132] Darbyshire, then in his early thirties, voiced opinions in public that were held by many younger Evangelical clergy in private. An adequate philosophical basis for Evangelicalism was called for. The need was pressing because of the gathering strength of the Anglo-Catholic party, confident in its assertion of the authority of the church. Evangelicals sometimes appealed to the principles of the Reformation, 'but it is hard to see exactly to what this talk amounts' and Calvinism was not essential to Evangelicalism in any case. To claim authority for an infallible book was unacceptable, because (here Darbyshire follows the standard Anglo-Catholic case) it leads to individualism: each reader makes his own interpretation the final court of appeal. The proper Evangelical attitude is 'Experimentalism'. Theory is to be tested by religious experience through history. Thus the inspiration of the Bible 'lies in the intensity of the spiritual experiences recorded therein'. Varieties of religious experience (here the speaker echoes William James) must be recognised as valid. At present Evangelicals had fallen into the snare of renouncing the world. 'We must be for ever so presenting the Gospel to the unlearned in terms of a traditional phraseology if we are to be recognized as Evangelical, that we have no time to feed the thoughtful, inspire the ambitious, and shew the glory of consecrating the secular.' The remedy was a rapprochement between gospel and culture. There must be

Evangelical church music and belles lettres.[133] Darbyshire's views were eventually to take him beyond Evangelicalism and to the Archbishopric of Cape Town, but at the time he caught the mood of his hearers. Experience, not dogma, was to be exalted. The ablest young Evangelicals, swayed by the taste of the times, were looking for fresh ground to occupy.

Theological change at a popular level was accelerated by the First World War. The question of prayers for the dead, which had already been agitated in peacetime,[134] suddenly became a matter of pressing pastoral importance. The bereaved yearned to pray for those lost in the carnage. Public prayer for the departed, rare in 1914 in the Church of England, was sanctioned by authority in 1917.[135] Preaching at a united Free Church memorial service in the same year, a Wesleyan minister pronounced the practice legitimate.[136] Hopes about the eternal destiny of those who had died for their country furthered the erosion of the demarcation between heaven and hell. As early as 1914 Dean Wace, with studied ambiguity, wrote in *The Record* that 'we may confidently be assured that those who meet their death on the battlefields of this war in the spirit of faith in Christ, and in simple devotion to duty, will be received by Him in the sense of those gracious words, "Well done, good and faithful servant", and may hope to be admitted in some degree into the joy of their Lord'.[137] Salvation by death in battle was endorsed by many others in much less cautious terms.[138] The idea of a second chance of salvation after death entered Evangelical thinking. J. D. Jones endorsed the doctrine of probation in the after-life at the Congregational Union assembly in 1916 and published a book that teetered on the brink of belief in universal salvation.[139] The availability of salvation for those dying impenitent was rumoured to be preached in a few Wesleyan pulpits.[140] In a more general way, the war dissolved reservations about expressing views previously judged unorthodox. Speaking one's mind seemed to be a duty to the dead. Traditionalists were alarmed by daring opinions spelt out in the pulpit in the wake of the war.[141] In exactly the same way, traditionalists themselves felt bound to battle for the truth, especially against errors supposedly concocted by the theological professors of Germany.[142] Polarisation was encouraged by the war.

Doctrinal debate between the wings of Evangelical opinion centred on two areas, atonement and Christology. The understanding of the atonement handed down from the Evangelical fathers was expounded in a paper by Bishop Moule at the 1904 Islington Clerical Meeting. 'Substitution' and 'vicarious punishment', words expressing the belief that Christ took the place of guilty sinners at his death, were not in the Bible, Moule admitted, yet various passages left him wondering how else to articulate their meaning.[143] It was claimed by conservatives such as Langston in the 1920s that their opponents supposed the death of Christ to be 'not substitutionary, but exemplary'.[144] The more liberal usually preferred to describe the death of Christ as representative: his suffering was in some sense on our behalf. They wished to deny a whole series of notions surrounding substitution. Canon de Candole, a liberal Anglican leader, declared in a sermon in 1921 that God's anger was not appeased by the offering of his Son. The idea was revolting.[145] Likewise Leslie Weatherhead, then a Methodist *enfant terrible*, wished to deny the axiom stated in the Book of Hebrews that 'without the shedding of blood there is no forgiveness of sins'. 'In our modern view', he boldly asserted, 'this is simply not true.'[146] Conservatives insisted that the cross must be seen as a sacrifice in which the justice of God was satisfied; liberals wished to discard legalistic interpretations in which the love of God was obscured. For many of the more conservative including E. A. Knox, who retired as Bishop of Manchester in 1921, and Albert Mitchell, the leading lay liturgiologist among the Evangelicals, the doctrine of the cross was the heart of the debate between the two sides.[147]

Christology was also divisive. Again the more liberal made the running. Some contended that the omniscience of Christ must be given up.[148] That, however, was far from radical since it was a tenet championed by P. T. Forsyth, the foe of R. J. Campbell's New Theology. Others went further and treated Christ as primarily an example. If Christ were presented as the greatest exemplar, declared Canon Storr in 1933, people would be shamed into recognising their shortcomings.[149] Some were prepared to recast the traditional understanding of the person of Christ. Frank Lenwood disturbed Congregationalism with his avowal in *Jesus: Lord or Leader?* (1930) that he could not accept the divinity of Christ.[150] Weatherhead was barely less drastic. 'I think Christ's divinity', he wrote in 1932, 'was not endowed, but achieved by His moral reactions, so that He climbed to an eminence of character which the word human was not big enough to describe.'[151] The virgin birth, to many a buttress of the orthodox doctrine of the incarnation, was specifically assailed. Congregationalism had been troubled by this issue before the war,[152] and in 1935 Donald Soper, a young Methodist famous for his open-air speaking, was accused of denying that Christ was born of a virgin.[153] Evangelical Anglicanism was hardly afflicted with outright rejections, but it was thought worthwhile for *The Record* to carry a sermon devoted to the subject in 1925.[154] To the conservative, such vagaries were not mere theological speculations. They were a betrayal of the Christian faith itself.

The spread of liberal theology among Anglican Evangelicals had a measure of institutional support. A number of Merseyside clergy created in 1906 the Group Brotherhood for private discussion. Other groups were formed in imitation and from 1908 there was an annual conference. At first it was not specifically liberal. Rather its purpose was study and, it was hoped, the publication of books to inculcate Evangelical teaching.[155] Numbers grew following the war and in 1923 it was reconstructed as the Anglican Evangelical Group Movement (AEGM). Although it still deliberately avoided adopting the word 'liberal' in its title for fear of causing offence,[156] the movement was associated with a collection of essays entitled *Liberal Evangelicalism* and issued a set of fifty-three pamphlets to publicise the same position.[157] 'It is the mind of Christ, not the letter of Holy Scripture, which is authoritative', runs the introduction to *Liberal Evangelicalism*. 'The modern Evangelical is dissatisfied with some of the older and cruder penal substitutionary theories of the Atonement.'[158] At this stage Canon Vernon Storr was drawn into the organisation. Storr became its driving force and, from 1930, its president. He had not previously been identified with the Evangelical party, but the combination of intellectual breadth and spiritual experience that became the hallmark of the movement was very much Storr's creation. From 1928 it ran its own equivalent of Keswick, an annual devotional conference at Cromer that from the first year attracted more than a thousand.[159] In the 1930s it also planned its own retreats.[160] The movement was always largely clerical, never seeking to draw in the laity, but it achieved significant membership: some 200 clergy by 1923 and 1,500 by 1935.[161] Although certain members were connected with the Modern Churchmen's Union, an explicitly Modernist body,[162] it adopted a basis of recognisably Evangelical belief. Its members naturally attracted the criticism that they were 'claiming to be Evangelicals while wishing to enthrone Reason in place of Divine Revelation'.[163] It nevertheless did much to provide progressive clergymen with a shield of fellowship to defend them against the darts of enraged parishioners.

A parallel body called the Fellowship of the Kingdom emerged in Methodism. In 1917 a group of younger Wesleyan ministers in London began to meet for discussion and prayer. They discovered a number of like-minded cells, some of which went back as far as 1908. Groups sprang up elsewhere during 1919 and in the following year the first annual conference was held at Swanwick. Although non-Wesleyans were admitted and there were groups for lay preachers, the bulk of support, as in the AEGM, came from ministers.[164] The movement had three watchwords: Quest, Crusade and Fellowship. Quest was a desire for valid spiritual experience. The members felt the Methodist holiness tradition, with its particular jargon and shibboleths, to have 'passed beyond our horizon'.[165] A fresh start had to be made in the discovery of Jesus as a companion in the modern world. Crusade was the novel name for an evangelistic campaign. The organisation specialised in missions conducted by several ministers together. Fellowship was the mutual support of members in the groups meeting fortnightly. No group was permitted to have more than fifteen attenders because intimacy was essential.[166] Inspiration was drawn from W. Russell Maltby, Warden of the Wesley Deaconess Order, and J. A. Findlay, tutor in New Testament at Didsbury College.[167] Canon E. A. Burroughs, a leading figure in the AEGM, also provided some of the early vision through his book, *The Valley of Decision* (1916).[168] Bonds were forged with the AEGM from 1930 onwards.[169] The Fellowship of the Kingdom was the crucible in which was forged what the denominational history calls 'the typical "Jesus religion" school of recent Methodism'.[170] It was one of the chief expressions of liberal Evangelicalism.

RISING CHURCHMANSHIP

The parting of the ways between Evangelicals was hastened by the continued growth among some of High Church sympathies, attention to the eucharist and a desire 'for beauty in worship. Tensions in this area were already apparent at the Islington Clerical Meeting in 1883. P. F. Eliot, later Dean of Windsor, remarked that there was sometimes 'too much coquetting with Dissent'. He would not move an inch from 'Church principles' for the sake of co-operating with Dissent and there must be an end to the Evangelical neglect of sacramental teaching.[171] Others, on the other hand, felt that a common allegiance to the gospel made united work with Nonconformists advisable, a view often subsequently repeated at Islington.[172] The attractions of tradition nevertheless continued to draw erstwhile Evangelicals towards the High Church school. E. H. Pearce, Bishop of Worcester, who after an upbringing at All Souls', Langham Place, had taken that path, declared in 1924 that his generation had inadequately appreciated the 'spiritual procession that paces all down the ages'.[173] The centre of gravity within the Evangelical school undoubtedly shifted upwards. By 1909 it was noticed that a new Evangelical party was forming, which, apart from giving time to study, refused to stress ritual differences and firmly believed in church order.[174] The tendency crystallised in support for the idea of 'Central Churchmanship' propounded by J. Denton Thompson, shortly to be Bishop of Sodor and Man, in a book of that title in 1911. The AEGM entered into part of this heritage. That organisation, according to Storr, saw a larger place for ritual and held a greater sense of churchmanship than its Evangelical predecessors.[175] Loyalty to the forms of the Church of England was increasing.

The most tangible aspect was the trend towards more elaborate church decorations and tolerance of ritual practices once judged to be High Church. By the start of the twentieth century, the use of the surplice for preaching, though still resisted by a handful of diehards, had been accepted even by rigid opponents of ritualism.[176] At this stage to call a clergyman a liberal Evangelical was to refer to his views not on inspiration or theology, but on liturgical arrangements. On entering the church of such a liberal Evangelical in 1904, a correspondent of *The Record* discovered 'cross and flowers on the Table, Eastward Position adopted, Litany Desk and intoned service, black stoles with gold crosses'.[177] All was alien to Evangelical custom, but progressives were wishing to end the assumption that Evangelical theology and Low Church practice necessarily went together. Another correspondent reported that her church had the eastward position, flowers, a cross on the communion table and a surpliced choir, but sound teaching. Since homes were now 'more artistically beautiful' than in the past, why should not churches be so too?[178] Seventeen years further on the same issues were still under debate, but now for liberal Evangelicals it was the norm rather than the exception to wear white stoles at weddings and turn east for the creed.

They might be willing to have candles lit for 8 a.m. celebration, to speak readily of 'altar' and 'eucharist' and to use the word 'Catholic' freely.[179] As Anglo-Catholics were pressing forward with liturgical innovations such as incense and Italianate robes, they dragged progressive Evangelicals – at a very great distance – behind them. In the remoter parishes of Herefordshire it was still customary in the late 1930s to hold services without a surpliced choir, with prayers said rather than intoned and the 'Protestant type' of churchmanship firmly in place.[180] Such practices had by no means been banished from the city churches of conservative clergy either, but they had come to have something of a curiosity appeal.

The fiercest wrangling within Evangelicalism on a point of ritual was about the position adopted by the officiating clergyman at holy communion. The position that was to triumph in the later twentieth century, in which the clergyman faces the congregation from behind the holy table, was rare before the Second World War.[181] In most buildings it was physically impossible since the table stood against the east wall. A High Churchman would use the eastward position in which he stood with his back to the congregation facing the altar. It was intended to symbolise his role as a priest offering sacrifice to God on behalf of the people. Such an understanding was anathema to Evangelicals, for whom the sacrifice of Calvary could in no sense be re-enacted in the communion service. Hence, Evangelicals officiated at the north side of the communion table, the position that had been general before the innovations of the mid-nineteenth-century ritualists. Congregations were able to observe the clergyman's manual acts from the side so as to ensure that there was no sacerdotal mumbo-jumbo. For an Evangelical to employ the eastward position was 'a hoisting of the enemy's colours'.[182] Whenever the liberally inclined expressed a willingness to use the eastward position it caused a furore. To declare the practice allowable, as was done by Guy Rogers in a liberal manifesto of 1917, was to throw down the gauntlet.[183] For the Cromer convention communion services to employ the eastward position, as they did from 1935, was almost an act of secession from the Evangelical body.[184] The controversy was particularly troublesome to the Church Pastoral Aid Society. Conservatives constantly feared that its prohibition of grants to parishes adopting the eastward position would be rescinded. Its chairman and secretary nervously confirmed in 1917 that the society's views had not changed; the conservatives registered their satisfaction that the rule was being maintained in 1935; and debate on the question of a change of policy rumbled on even in the dark days of 1941.[185] The liturgical issue divided Evangelicals on substantially the same lines as the theological issue, though, if anything, liturgical conservatism was more powerful.

Public alarm at the ritual innovations of advanced Anglo-Catholics had led to the appointment of a Royal Commission on Ecclesiastical Discipline which sat from 1904 to 1906. It was Dean Wace who chose the ground on which Evangelicals were to rally in defence of Protantism. There was no hope of persuading the Royal Commission to recommend the enforcement of the rubrics of the existing Book of Common Prayer. There was doubt about their interpretation. In any case most Evangelicals were less than scrupulous in observing their provisions: few held services on holy days or used the prayer for the church militant on days when there was no holy communion.[186] Wace moreover wished to secure the support of moderates of all schools. He therefore appealed to the practice of the first six centuries of the church, urging that later developments such as the eastward position and the use of incense should be banned from the Church of England.[187] Despite protests from diehards like Samuel Garratt, who regarded certain sixth-century ceremonies with horror,[188] Wace attracted the signatures of most leading Evangelicals and more than 4,000 clergy altogether.[189] The division over the proper extent of opposition to ritual innovation was ominous for Evangelical unity.

A more serious division came later. Among the recommendations of the Royal Commission was the revision of the Book of Common Prayer to accommodate the more general High Church practices. In the decade after the First World War the final stages of the protracted process caused serious strains. Evangelicals were particularly dismayed at provisions for the reservation of the consecrated elements, since Anglo-Catholics would wish to worship them as the body and blood of Christ. They mounted a sustained campaign against the Revised Prayer Book, which will need to be considered again shortly. Most Evangelicals felt the issue intensely: how could loyal sons of the Reformation, asked one conservative, be accessories to 'an Act of National Apostasy'?[190] They demanded that the church, and subsequently Parliament, should reject the innovation. Once the new Prayer Book was officially endorsed by the convocation of the Church of England, however, the Evangelical representatives there accepted that the battle had been lost.[191] There was no question of asking Parliament to overturn the decision of the church. The AEGM concurred, holding a conference on how to come to terms with the new book.[192] The main body of Evangelicals, on the other hand, felt betrayed by the liberal wing.[193] The fact that several of the turncoats, but no continuing opponents of the Revised Prayer Book, were elevated to the episcopal bench in the years up to the Second World War kept the grievance fresh. The question of how far to go in resisting the Anglo-Catholic ascendancy in the Church of England fractured the Evangelical party.

The Free Churches, as Nonconformity now liked to be called, could not remain immune to the rising standard of churchmanship. The example of the Church of England, the attractions posed to educated young people by Anglican ceremony and the persistent Romantic atmosphere of middle-brow culture all dictated change in that direction. The phrase 'Lord's Supper' was discarded in favour of 'Sacrament of Holy Communion', the rationale being that the former pointed merely to the circumstances of its institution but the latter identified its nature.[194] The Fellowship of the Kingdom helped spread an appreciation of eucharistic worship. The Methodist Sacramental Fellowship, launched in 1935, encouraged the same trend.[195] More frequent communion, the use of service books and the observance of the Christian year were making headway among the Presbyterians of Scotland,[196] but some of the most significant liturgical developments there were undertaken by the Congregationalist John Hunter, Minister of Trinity Church, Glasgow. He loved to speak of 'the Holy Catholic Church', administered communion in Anglican style and compiled the often reprinted *Devotional Services for Public Worship*.[197] By 1925 another Congregationalist, W. E. Orchard, was conducting mass with wafers, incense and Catholic punctilio at the King's Weigh House in London.[198] He preached on how to make the most of Lent. 'On Ash Wednesday morning', he recommended, 'say to your wife, "My dear, is there any virtue you would like me to acquire?"'[199] Orchard was one of the Free Churchmen who took the path to Rome.[200] If such aberrations fed the flames of conservative Evangelical anger, they were infrequent. Far more typical of progressive interwar Nonconformity was the worship at Ealing Green Congregational Church under Wilton Rix. The minister wore cassock and gown and, like many of his congregation, preferred kneeling for prayer. Choir stalls for robed singers were introduced, the pulpit was balanced on one side by a lectern on the other, a communion table was central and eventually, in 1936, a cross was added.[201] It was a world apart from the plain unpolished services that were still usual among the more traditional.

The divergence between liberals and conservatives was apparent on a number of points of church order. One was the ministry of women. The spread of female higher education and the successful campaign seeking votes for women meant that demands were heard in the early twentieth century for female ordination. In the mainstream denominations it was permitted by 1930 only among Congregationalists and Baptists, whose decentralised polity would have made prohibition virtually impossible. The Wesleyan Conference determined in 1926 to accept female candidates for the ministry, but deferred action until later – which turned out to be 1973.[202] In the Church of England women could serve as deaconesses and, from the creation of the Church Assembly in 1920, could share in some aspects of the government of the church. Sterner Evangelicals such as Wace had resolutely opposed this development, arguing that the apostle Paul's prohibition of women speaking in church was 'absolutely decisive for Christian men'.[203] Prejudice against female ministry was said to be strongest 'in old-fashioned circles where the literalist doctrine of Scriptural inspiration still holds the field'.[204] On the other side, Hatty Baker, a Congregationalist who had acted as a minister without official recognition, argued that the churches should not bind themselves to Paul's pre-Christian rabbinic thought-world. It was wrong to discriminate against women, relegating them to the teapots, bread and butter; male and female qualities were both needed in the ministry; and 'none but a woman can understand the agony of a woman's heart'.[205]

Guy Rogers, a leader of the AEGM, put forward a comparable, though less distinctly feminist, case in the 1930s.[206] In general the tension was the usual conservative/liberal one, with a large body of uncommitted opinion in the middle. The question rarely pressed. It might be right in pure logic that women should be allowed to enter the ministry of the church, said *The Record* in 1936, but there was no demand for it.[207] The question of female ordination reflected rather than created the tendency to polarisation in the Evangelical world.

SCIENCE AND RELIGION

A factor that played a more active part in encouraging division was debate on the relation of science to religion. The focus was almost exclusively on evolution. Evangelicals had rapidly learned to live with Darwin's discoveries. Theologians took account of it in their schemes; scientists treated it as an assumption in their work. The Wesleyan W. H. Dallinger and the Anglican G. T. Manley both held that recent scientific developments that took evolution for granted tended to undercut the materialist philosophies of Spencer and Haeckel.[208] Evolution was by no means a bogey to the popular Evangelical press.[209] Only isolated individuals occasionally protested that Darwin's unproved views did contradict Christian teaching on the special creation of humanity.[210] In 1924 A. C. Dixon, the Baptist son of a frontier farmer-preacher in the American South who had risen to become one of Spurgeon's successors as the Minister of the Metropolitan Tabernacle, delivered a ninety-minute harangue against evolutionary theory under the auspices of the Bible League. *The Record* expected its readers to think Dixon was flogging a dead horse.[211] In the following year, when the anti-evolution campaign in the United States reached its climax, a spokesman for the Christian Evidence Society commented that, by contrast, there was now less interest in Europe in the relations of science and religion, 'owing to the fact that religious people do not oppose the findings of natural science to-day; and men of science do not attack religion'.[212] In 1926 *The Christian* deplored the foundation of an anti-evolution society in Georgia designed, intriguingly, to banish every teacher in the world who expounded Darwinism.[213] Many Evangelicals had no qualms about evolution.

Certain liberals went further, wishing to remould theology around the new scientific truth. The chief exponent of the need for doctrinal reconstruction in the light of evolution was Canon E. W. Barnes, a mathematician, sometime Fellow of Trinity College, Cambridge, and a Fellow of the Royal Society. He had been brought up to accept evolution as scientific fact, and, lacking ecclesiastical party loyalties, had little regard for Evangelical susceptibilities. Human evolution, he believed, meant steady development. The fall of man, he roundly declared in a sermon at the 1920 British Association meetings, was not a historical event but a parable explaining the origin of sin. Interpretation of biblical passages like the Genesis account of the fall, he explained in a subsequent sermon, must be revised in the light of scientific discoveries.[214] Bramwell Booth, who associated evolution with T. H. Huxley and his hostility to the Salvation Army, denounced Barnes's view unsparingly.[215] W. St Clair Tidsall, a supporter of the Bible League, criticised the sermons in two leading articles in *The Record*, and *The Christian* weighed in with the claim that Barnes 'not only surrenders the Fall but with it the doctrine of the vicarious Atonement'.[216] Here was the nub of the objections. It was feared that if humanity was not understood as fallen, there was no need for redemption. The Evangelical panorama of salvation was at risk. Barnes's critics were not so much defending the text of scripture as perceiving the thin end of a theological wedge. Evolution was not condemned outright. The first of a series of articles dealing with the subject in *The Christian* distinguished sharply between creative evolution, the validity of which was left to Barnes and his fellow-scientists, and moral evolution, the idea that human character makes progress over time.[217] Nevertheless, the 'monkey sermons' had made Barnes a symbolic figure, a champion of modern thought. Progressive Evangelicals eagerly co-opted him into the team that wrote *Liberal Evangelicalism* and had him address the AEGM.[218] Conservatives vigorously denounced his appointment as Bishop of Birmingham in 1924.[219] Barnes provoked a novel degree of polarisation on evolution.

After 1920 the undercurrent of popular hostility to evolution surfaced more frequently. Some conservatives were careful to go no further than a general wariness of evolutionary theory. It was still, according to Samuel Chadwick of the Methodist holiness tradition, no more than a hypothesis.[220] Others were far less reserved. Harold Morton of the Wesley Bible Union obtained an MA from the Intercollegiate University of Britain and America for a thesis published as *The Bankruptcy of Evolution*.[221] The Union's *Journal* was the periodical most committed in the 1920s to the anti-evolution cause, but the new antagonism spread to others. It was the opinion of a leading conservative Evangelical Anglican in 1933 that 'our Lord's personality, by its uniqueness, thrust evolution on to the dust-heap'.[222] Basil Atkinson, a Cambridge librarian and a rather eccentric champion of most conservative Evangelical causes, put forward a more popular apologetic line. 'The polar bear', he observed, 'has small hairs on its feet which prevent it from slipping on the ice. How could they have possibly evolved?'[223] He also insisted that no species had been known to pass over the border into another.[224] The contention that there was a missing link in the evolutionary chain separating humanity from the animal kingdom was frequently heard.[225] A small group including Basil Atkinson set up in 1935 an Evolution Protest Movement. Its figurehead was Sir Ambrose Fleming, Professor of Electrical Engineering at University College, London, and author of a number of anti-evolution books, and it set about corresponding with the Board of Education and the BBC about official endorsements of Darwinism.[226] That it existed is evidence for an element of anti-evolutionary thinking in conservative Evangelicalism; that it remained small is evidence for the weakness of the cause, even among conservatives.

THE USE OF LEISURE

Divergence between liberals and conservatives extended to the question of leisure. Wherever the influence of Keswick was felt, there was a tendency to reduce the circle of permitted activities. 'God was calling them', it was said at the 1930 convention, 'to an utter separation from everything that was questionable.'[227] Novelties such as the wireless were particularly suspect. Undesirable plays and operas were broadcast; there was little distinctive about Sunday programmes; and listening-in wasted time. On the other hand it was a blessing to the bed-ridden. 'Speaking generally', said one mediating contributor to a spirited debate in the weekly associated with Keswick, 'syncopated music, and programmes labelled "variety", are usually items that may well be excluded by the child of God, but much of the music of the old masters broadcast is sweet and ennobling . . . '[228] Cinema created wider differences. A contributor to *The British Weekly* reported in 1921 that news coverage had improved and the long 'film-story' had become customary. There was no hint of criticism, except that American films had virtually displaced domestic products.[229] To others, however, the cinema was simply a more alluring form of the theatre. Conservatives let loose a tirade of invective. There should be a crusade against 'nasty pictures in picturedromes'. The people should not be evangelised by Christian films, because the cinema is 'one of the devil's chief agencies for keeping them away from the Cross'. 'In many districts the cinema is synonymous with sin . . .'[230] Evangelicals divided between those who gave a discriminating welcome to new agencies of popular culture and those who viewed them with horror.

'Many look with dismay', commented a rather smug Brethren observer, 'upon young people flocking to the Theatre, Picture Palaces, and other places of amusement, yet at the same time are associated with the same *in miniature* in Churches and Chapels.'[231] No popular entertainments might sully the purity of a Brethren assembly, but it is true that they were becoming common on other church premises. The attempt to grapple with declining attendances by providing what the people wanted had gathered force with the years.[232] The First World War accelerated the trend. Returning troops demanded the use of premises for the dancing and other entertainments they had grown to expect on active service.[233] Since 'lads and lasses will want to meet each other while the world lasts', according to the magazine of the Church of Scotland, it was good that the church, rather than the streets or the picture houses, should provide their 'opportunities for harmless pleasure'.[234] Regular members of congregations, furthermore, wanted to use church facilities for their recreation. South London churches between the wars provided facilities for tennis, badminton and athletics, discussion, singing and drama, though churches in the Evangelical tradition normally drew the line at the whist drives promoted elsewhere.[235] There was always the evangelistic motive to supply justification. At mission services in the Brighouse United Methodist circuit, 'One pleasing feature has been the number of converts from the football teams associated with the three churches'.[236] Even churches in the Keswick orbit were advised that church sports clubs were appropriate if the aim was right.[237] Church-sponsored recreation was common across a broad Evangelical spectrum.

Yet worries were abroad. In 1912 H. C. Morton, later of the Wesley Bible Union, saw the decline in Methodist membership as a consequence of giving the young people amusements rather than training them in main church activities.[238] By 1935 a triumph had been won by the grumblers at denominational level, for the Methodist Conference passed a resolution against dramatic entertainment on church premises not in accordance with the spiritual life of the church.[239] For the tighter sects dancing was anathema and sport irrelevant.[240] Similar attitudes were promulgated by Advent Testimony. 'Antics of various kinds, such as smoking, drinking, dancing, theatricals, etc.', the vain efforts to fill the churches, were contrasted with the 'faithful preaching of the word', which alone brought people to Christ.[241] Most disturbingly, the worldliness of bazaars, concerts, clubs and billiards was ousting prayer. For about twenty years, it was said in 1932, weekly prayer meetings had become rare in Methodism. In nine months of regular preaching, a missionary deputation speaker had to announce only two week-night prayer meetings.[242] 'Restore the Prayer Meeting!', urged a *Life of Faith* leading article in 1926.[243] One method of recovering a spiritual atmosphere was to exclude the fun of entertainment from the duty of Christian giving. At Toxteth Tabernacle, Liverpool, for example, 'No bazaars, concerts, or other questionable methods of raising funds are countenanced.'[244] The same attitude, assisted by Keswick's influence and favourable treasurer's reports, spread through many Evangelical Anglican congregations during the 1930s.[245] Conservative opinion increasingly understood the world in dualistic terms. Entertainment was of the darkness, not of the light.

Darkest of all, in the eyes of many, was recreation that desecrated the sabbath. The Presbyterian churches appealed in 1919 to the people of Scotland for the observance of the weekly day of rest,[246] and in general sabbatarianism was stronger north of the border. Evangelicals throughout Britain, however, normally remained strict, refusing to take a Sunday newspaper ('the worst of all secularising influences').[247] The churches themselves deplored the decision of the London County Council in 1922 to open public parks for games on Sundays,[248] but it was the Lord's Day

Observance Society that led the battle against infringements of the sabbath. It protested against a Sunday evening radio debate between Bernard Shaw and Miss Madeleine Carroll on 'sex-appeal in cinematograph films' and achieved some minor successes like the suppression of a rodeo at the White City Stadium.[249] Divergence came over Sunday cinema opening. The Lord's Day Observance Society, supported by bodies such as the Evangelical Alliance, resisted a Sunday Entertainments Bill designed to legalise the showing of films.[250] The Council of Christian Churches on Social Questions, however, had declared in favour of localities being able to decide for or against Sunday opening, and the bill passed into law with that provision.[251] The liberal Evangelical Bishop of Croydon, E. S. Woods, gained a certain fame – which was notoriety among Evangelicals – by supporting Sunday opening locally, and was soon chairing a committee that selected films for showing on Sunday evenings.[252] He was almost alone in public advocacy of breaking with this Evangelical shibboleth, but there were other signs of greater flexibility on the question among the more progressive. One Bradford Wesleyan minister held that Christ intended much more latitude than the Old Testament on sabbath observance, and another that there would have to be give and take on its enforcement.[253] If sabbatarianism was still general, it was becoming more diluted in some quarters.

THE SOCIAL GOSPEL

A further cause of division among interwar Evangelicals lay in different attitudes to social reform. Many of the more conservative believed that liberals had turned aside from the true gospel to a 'social gospel'.[254] The impression was given at the time, and has often persisted down to the present, that the social gospel was an alternative to the Evangelical approach, an attempt to change human beings by transforming their environment rather than by touching their hearts. In reality, however, the social gospel was grounded in Evangelicalism. It was an application of the crusading style of reform (discussed in Chapter 4) to society overall. Sin was diagnosed in social structures, which therefore must be remodelled. Occasional social gospellers, such as the Congregationalist Fleming Williams, did profess to have abandoned (as he put it) 'theological metaphysics' for the sake of 'altering the condition of things', but men who thus departed from Evangelical belief were rare.[255] Scott Matheson, the United Presbyterian author of *The Church and Social Problems* (1893), was adamant in his priorities. 'Social reform', he declared, 'ought never to draw the Cchurch aside from her proper work of saving men.'[256] Campbell Morgan, known for his biblical exposition at Westminster Chapel, was quite prepared to devote a sermon on the eve of a London County Council election in 1919 to the need for the regulation of the drainage, atmosphere, smoke and traffic of the capital.[257] For the generation of Scottish and Nonconformist ministers at the height of their powers between the early 1890s and about 1920 a combination of social concern and evangelistic zeal came naturally.

The social gospel was generated primarily by practical experience of Christian work. It was a response to the difficulties of mission, particularly in the cities. Thus Hugh Price Hughes, its leading Methodist exponent, argued that 'evangelistic work has been too exclusively individualistic . . . we must do our utmost to promote the social welfare of the people'.[258] Likewise, Richard Mudie-Smith, a Baptist deacon and social investigator, contended that the gospel must affect the environment. 'If cleaner streets, better housing, sweeter homes do not come within the scope of our aim', he wrote, 'neither will those who are convinced that they have a right to these things come within the shadow of our places of worship.'[259] The social gospel was an evangelistic strategy for reaching the working classes. Intellectual influences naturally played a part in its formation too. The theology of F. D. Maurice stirred some to contemplate the divine pattern for the nation.[260] The teaching of T. H. Green and other idealist philosophers that the state has a duty to promote the moral development of its members had some effect.[261] Social Darwinism and the Romantic critique of industrialism in John Ruskin and William Morris, powerful intellectual currents of the time, swept along many in the Nonconformist ministry.[262] The challenge, real and imaginary, of revolutionary socialism also stirred greater attention to the welfare of the masses. 'There are two alternatives before us to-day', announced Hughes in 1887, '– Christianity or revolution.'[263] John Clifford, the other leading exponent of a Christian message for society, was taking up a phrase from *The Communist Manifesto* when in 1888 he launched the 'social gospel' as a campaigning slogan in an address to the Baptist Union.[264] The movement therefore represented a broadening of the horizons of Nonconformists, but it did not cut them off from their Evangelical roots.

An equivalent tendency existed among Evangelicals in the Church of England, but it remained weak. The participation of Evangelicals in the Christian Social Union, the Anglican body that took up social questions, was largely nominal: a few bishops and other dignitaries acted as presidents and vice-presidents of branches.[265] The predominant attitude, expressed in an editorial in *The Record* in 1904, was that social conditions might be important, but that conversion was the great remedy: 'surroundings will not save a soul'.[266] Few criticisms of the social structure, to which most were firmly wedded, entered their minds. Attitudes nevertheless partially altered during the first decade of the twentieth century, an unavoidable consequence of the greater attention paid by the public at large to social questions. An address on pastoral work by Denton Thompson to the Islington Clerical Meeting in 1898 had been fairly narrow in scope, but on the same subject in 1910 he gave much of his space to social problems.[267]

At Islington in 1913 Guy Rogers, a leading spirit of liberal Evangelicalism, cited Maurice's condemnation of capitalist competition with approval and looked forward to a more even distribution of wealth.[268] Most prominent among Evangelical Anglicans committed to social reform was J. E. Watts-Ditchfield, first Bishop of Chelmsford from 1914. Organised labour and organised Christianity, he contended in 1918, must combine to end preventible poverty, and his political sympathies had long been with Labour.[269] Significantly, however, Watts-Ditchfield's background was in Lancashire Wesleyanism, and he was ordained an Anglican clergyman only when the door to the Methodist ministry was closed.[270] When, in 1908, the Islington Clerical Meeting was devoted to social problems, it is equally significant that some of the speakers had to be drawn from outside the Evangelicals' ranks: George Lansbury, the Labour politician from Poplar, and A. J. Carlyle, Secretary of the Christian Social Union.[271] After Islington, correspondents of *The Record* expressed rank-and-file opinion: 'A Country Incumbent'asked why the clergy should take more interest now, when conditions were better, than they had in social questions twenty years ago; another opposed the stance of the Islington speakers, fearing that the church was being duped by the enemy of God into alliances inimical to Christianity.[272] The social gospel was not for them.

In the interwar years liberal Evangelicals in all denominations commonly believed that concern with social questions was a dimension of Christian mission. In a manifesto of 'Neo-Evangelicalism' in 1921, Frank Mellows, Vicar of Sparkhill, declared that its adherents preached a social as well as an individual gospel, attacking the evils of bad housing, inadequate wages and commercial tyranny as frequently as personal ones.[273] In Congregationalism, the venerable A. E. Garvie, Principal of Hackney and New College, took a leading part in interdenominational discussion of social issues, published a treatise on *The Christian Ideal for Human Society* (1930) and issued the more popular *Can Christ save Society?* (1933).[274] Methodism regularly made official pronouncements on social questions.[275] The Church of Scotland was responsible for an impressive array of institutions for orphans, the destitute and the elderly.[276] Yet even among the more liberal there was a tendency to withdraw somewhat from the vanguard of reform. The Methodist George Jackson believed that Christianity has social implications, but felt that the church should work at a deeper level than creating programmes for change. It should provide 'not so much the machinery of social reform as the spiritual driving power without which the best machinery is no better than so much scrap iron'.[277] Neither the Fellowship of the Kingdom nor the AEGM was forward with schemes of reconstruction. The initiative passed from the Nonconformist Conscience of prewar days to the Anglican heavyweights, Charles Gore, William Temple and R. H. Tawney. The Industrial Christian Fellowship, a drastic remodelling of the Christian Social Union, had the support of a number of Evangelicals including Guy Rogers, but they were overshadowed by others.[278] Evangelicals in general were keeping their distance from the pressing domestic public issues of the day.

The tendency to withdrawal was most marked among Evangelicals of a more conservative stamp. Anglicans of the Keswick school, by and large, needed little convincing that social reform lay beyond their province. The process of change was therefore more evident outside the Church of England. The Salvation Army was exceptional in remaining institutionally committed to a wide variety of social ministries.[279] Other bodies of conservative doctrinal inclinations shifted towards a more conservative stance on social questions. COPEC, the Conference on Politics, Economics and Citizenship promoted by Temple in 1924, attracted the sympathy of some conservative Evangelicals, but no general enthusiasm.[280] Instead they concentrated on questions which, unlike industrial relations or housing, could be analysed in terms of personal responsibility. In addition to the Sunday question, drunkenness and gambling were the great bugbears. The temperance campaign of Nonconformity was sustained after the war even in conservative circles. 'Alcohol', stated *The Journal of the Wesley Bible Union* unequivocally, 'is wholly evil when used as a beverage.'[281] The chief official Baptist social concern was about intemperance.[282] The Brethren were almost solidly teetotal, and some were even prepared to take political action, shunned by others in the sect, for the sake of putting down the drink scourge.[283] Gambling was also loudly condemned. Greyhound racing and football pools were the prime targets of censure.[284] Voices were occasionally raised on behalf of the unemployed,[285] but the trend among conservatives to deal with moral questions rather than broader social problems was a feature of the times. There was in Britain, just as there was in the United States, what has been called 'the great reversal':[286] a repudiation by Evangelicals of their earlier engagement with social issues.

THE GREAT REVERSAL

Why did a great reversal take place? One reason was a disenchantment with politics. Nonconformity had been highly politicised in the later nineteenth century. Its identification with the Liberal Party was never closer than at the 1906 election, when anger at a Conservative Education Act led to an unprecedented degree of electioneering by Nonconformist leaders. Disappointment followed. The Liberals, despite a huge Commons majority, failed to repeal the Education Act. Chapel membership began to fall, and some blamed the loss of spiritual power on over-absorption in public affairs. While Nonconformity 'has been making numerous and ardent politicians', it was complained, 'it has made scarce any saints'.[287] There was, furthermore, a growing trend for the most opulent and the most anti-Catholic among the Nonconformists to go over to the Conservative side.[288] Hence by the time of the 1910 elections many Free Church leaders became wary of close identification with Liberalism. The trend was encouraged by a parallel sense on the other side of the ecclesiastical divide that partisanship decreased the spiritual influence of the clergy.[289] The revulsion from politics was for many a distancing from social reform. 'Our fathers', commented *The Methodist Recorder* in 1912, 'were much more concerned about the glory of God and the dishonour done to him than about any social problems.' They dwelt on people's sins, not their rights. This was the spirit of the New Testament.[290] The recoil from politics was noticed and welcomed north of the border.[291] The process was nearly complete before the First World War, so that the accepted wisdom in the Free Churches in the 1920s was to keep political clamour at arm's length. 'It is not the business of the Christian Church to initiate legislation', stated a pamphlet issued by the Fellowship of the Kingdom, 'but it is the function of those who would follow Jesus to educate public opinion . . .'[292]

The eclipse of the social gospel is also partly explained by the belief that it was socialist. There was in fact no equivalence between the two. Hugh Price Hughes offered a social analysis that, when stripped of its bombastic rhetoric, was quite traditional. At a period when it was beginning to be recognised that poverty was more often the result of low pay and irregular work than of personal irresponsibility, Hughes still attributed it to laziness or vice.[293] Clifford, by contrast, was the leader of a short-lived Christian Socialist League in the mid-1890s[294] and wrote two Fabian tracts, *Socialism and the Teaching of Christ* (1897) and *Socialism and the Churches* (1908). From 1907 the Wesleyan J. E. Rattenbury attracted crowds to the West London Mission to hear denunciations of capitalist wrongs mingled with gospel addresses.[295] Socialism made most headway among the Wesleyans. By 1909 sixty-five of their ministers were members of a socialist Sigma Club led by S. E. Keeble, the author of *Industrial Day-Dreams* (1896).[296] Alarm was sufficient to bring about the creation of a Nonconformist Anti-Socialistic Union in 1909. It received little Free Church support, however, and a year later it had turned into an Anti-Socialist Union of Churches with Anglicans as the main speakers.[297] One of their number, Prebendary Webb-Peploe, represented the strong hostility to socialism that was the normal stance of Anglican Evangelicals.[298] It savoured too much of revolution, atheism and the subversion of the family to appear compatible with Christianity. The turbulence of the war, the Russian Revolution and the aftermaths of both made many Nonconformists more cautious. Clifford's own successor at Westbourne Park Baptist Church, Paddington, preaching in 1921, denounced materialistic demands for a social utopia that entailed the downgrading of religion.[299] Industrial unrest served to illustrate 'the subtle influence of Socialism, syndicalism and Atheism, helped . . . by funds from Moscow and elsewhere . . .'[300] The 'red scare' so widespread in the early 1920s made many feel that tampering with the social order was inopportune.

There were theological worries about the social gospel as well. It could seem over-optimistic about the possibilities of perfecting the human

condition. Hughes, in fact, was swayed both by the Wesleyan tradition and
by the Brighton holiness convention of 1875 towards the belief that human
beings need not sin. Hence it was possible to anticipate a day 'when justice
and love and peace will reign with unchallenged supremacy in every land;
and when men will literally do the will of God on earth as angels do it in
heaven'.[301] Although Clifford was influenced by the socialist contention
that human beings are moulded by the conditions of their environment, he
was careful to insist that outward changes could not do all for humanity.
According to Jesus, he explained, 'the inward is chief'.[302] Critics remained
unconvinced by such reservations. It was folly, declared a Wesleyan before
the First World War, to expect a better social fabric 'if human nature is
to remain what it is'.[303] The social gospel seemed to treat conversion
as superfluous. 'It treated man', declared the conservative Evangelical
Prebendary A. W. Gough in 1925, 'as one whose life could be made right
by the putting right of his circumstances, by the reordering of society, by
the pulling down of the existing structure and the setting up of something
else.'[304] Conversion, on the other hand, was 'a short cut to social reform'.[305]
Once a person was regenerate, relations with others would be changed.
Some good might come from COPEC, admitted the editor of *The Life
of Faith*, but 'we do not regret being old-fashioned enough to believe that
when once the human heart gets right with God, everything else falls into
line'.[306] It followed that Christian effort must be directed into evangelism
rather than social reform.

The most resounding condemnations of the social gospel came from
those with a sharper theological axe to grind. High hopes of reform, it
was argued, were bound up with a false eschatology. Social gospellers, in
the broadening postmillennialist tradition, expected the kingdom of God
to be realised on earth by the steady advance of Christian values. Thus
the vision of the perfected City of God in the Book of Revelation,
according to Hughes, would be realised at Charing Cross.[307] The key to the
teaching of Jesus, according to Clifford, is the kingdom of God, which is
to be identified with the divine will for the social order.[308] The growing
premillennialist school, however, rejected such ideas out of hand. It
looked for a king, not a kingdom. Only with the return of Christ would
human affairs be put right. The dominance of premillennialism among
Anglican Evangelicals goes a long way towards explaining their immunity
to the appeal of the social gospel before the First World War. The spread
of popular adventism from the end of the war was heavily responsible
for the retreat of non-Anglicans from social involvement. In its initial
manifesto, the Advent Testimony Movement asserted that 'all human
schemes of reconstruction must be subsidiary to the Second Coming of
our Lord, because all nations will then be subject to His rule'.[309] E. L.
Langston, a leading Anglican premillennialist, elaborated a critique of
COPEC on precisely this basis.[310] Even efforts for international harmony
now seemed futile. The Congregational Union autumn assembly of 1923

declared its faith in the League of Nations as the only way of securing peace. 'Students of the Word of God', growled the editor of *The Advent Witness*, 'have come to a different conclusion, for, is it not said that when the league of ten kings (Rev. xvii.12) is formed, their one all-absorbing and united aim will be to *make war with Christ*?'[311] Premillennialists distrusted the League. The advent hope supplanted all other Christian hopes for the future. Wherever it was held it ensured that the ideological gap between liberal and conservative Evangelicals was a yawning gulf.

FUNDAMENTALIST CONTROVERSIES

The strains within Evangelicalism snapped in a series of crises between 1913 and 1928. Although the various mutual suspicions that have been enumerated entered into the debates, the central issue in each case was the infallibility of scripture. Conservatives believed that loyalty to the Bible itself was under threat. The first crisis contained echoes of the New Theology controversy, which had been settled only a couple of years before, but it was different in kind.[312] Whereas R. J. Campbell had put himself outside the Evangelical school, the battle surrounding George Jackson in 1913 was over the future direction of Evangelicalism within the Wesleyan denomination. Were higher critical views acceptable? In 1912 Jackson was designated to occupy a chair at Didsbury College, Manchester, one of the four Wesleyan theological colleges, but in the same year he delivered a lecture that was expanded for publication as *The Preacher and the Modern Mind*. With the needs of educated young people in mind, he held that biblical criticism must be respected. Stiff opposition to the confirmation of his appointment gathered force just before the Wesleyan Conference of 1913. With masterly skill, Jackson convinced conference that his views on the Bible were by no means radical or extreme. A committee report exonerating his book from a charge of doctrinal unsoundness was accepted by 336 votes to 27. He took up office. That, however, did not end the debate. Jackson's opponents joined together as the Wesley Bible Union, issued a monthly journal and entered on a struggle to persuade conference to eliminate alleged heresy from the connexion. Their efforts were fruitless. The chief effect was to ensure that the conservative cause in Methodism was branded as the obsession of a few ill-tempered fanatics. The virulence of the Wesley Bible Union was counter-productive.[313]

Better known is the controversy of 1922 in the Church Missionary Society (CMS), 'the barometer of the Evangelical party'.[314] Some of its missionaries in Bengal expressed publicly their disquiet at the spread of higher critical views as early as 1907.[315] Conflict broke out when, in 1917, a party of the liberally inclined memorialised the CMS committee to tolerate candidates with broader opinions on topics including biblical research. The more conservative were outraged. Prebendary H. E. Fox, a former Secretary of the CMS and the President of the Bible League, took decisive action. At his instigation a counter-memorial was organised and partly through his pressure, a concordat was reached laying down belief in revelation, inspiration and the authority of scripture as essential in candidates.[316] It was Fox who demanded an explanation from a Hong Kong CMS missionary who in 1919 spoke of the Old Testament stories as myths; and it was Fox who called for action in solidarity with the Bible Union of China formed by conservative missionaries. 'Are we to sit still and do nothing?' he asked. 'Is respect for the Society to keep us silent, while its agents are preaching and teaching doctrines altogether inconsistent with those on which it was founded?'[317] Behind the CMS dispute lay the combative vigour of the Bible League.

Affairs came to a head following an address on the Old Testament at a CMS summer school in 1921. The earlier concordat, according to the conservatives, was not being observed. Their campaign was co-ordinated by D. H. C. Bartlett, Vicar of St Luke's, Hampstead, who acted as Secretary of the Fellowship of Evangelical Churchmen (FEC), a body formed in the wake of the 1917–18 debate.[318] At the December general committee meeting of the CMS, the subject of the summer school address was raised by S. H. Gladstone, treasurer of the society and president of the FEC, but inconclusively.[319] At the March general committee, Bartlett proposed a motion endorsing the authority of scripture, but action was deferred until after a private consultative conference of Evangelical leaders at Coleshill in June. The general committee reconvened for a trial of strength in July. Because membership was open to any clerical supporters, there were 614 recorded attenders. An amendment that CMS agents need adhere only to the Nicene Creed and article VI of the Church of England was followed by a compromise amendment suggested by a team of bishops. Although it was carried, Fox, Bartlett, Gladstone and their circle felt it was insufficiently firm on Christ's endorsement of scriptural authority. After consulting members of the FEC, they determined to set up an alternative to the CMS, which was dubbed The Bible Churchmen's Missionary Society (BCMS). A CMS sub-committee, followed by another committee meeting, failed to heal the breach. By March 1923 seventy-eight clergy had resigned their membership of the CMS and thirty remained undecided.[320] By its fourth anniversary in 1926 the BCMS had ninety missionaries and ten paid home staff.[321] The rift had the effect of weakening the conservative influence in the original society, but the BCMS, unlike the Wesley Bible Union, pursued a steady course of constructive work. Several redoubtable champions of a high view of the Bible, including E. L. Langston and G. T. Manley, remained with the CMS. The schism was caused by biblical conservatives, but the split it created was not straightforwardly between conservatives and liberals. The division was within the conservative ranks.

Controversy had already rocked the Keswick Convention, another seasoned Evangelical vessel. Evan Hopkins, the prophet of sound doctrine at

Keswick, died early in 1919.[322] In the same year Bishop Watts-Ditchfield, a believer in the annihilation rather than the punishment of the wicked after death and so suspect in more stringent quarters, was a speaker at Keswick, and Cyril Bardsley and H. L. C. V. de Candole, both broadening Anglicans, had already been on its platform.[323] So it seemed reasonable for R. T. Howard, Principal of St Aidan's College, Birkenhead, and a leading light of the body soon to become the AEGM, to give an address in which he dwelt on the presence of God at all times, in all places and in everything. A member of the audience rose indignantly to question whether so pantheistic a talk was in accordance with the word of God; the Keswick council declined to publish an account of it; and it was soon assailed in a pamphlet as being little different from R. J. Campbell's New Theology.[324] The pamphlet's writer, James Mountain, was a Keswick veteran in his late seventies who had been in the movement from its inception, a Baptist who was Minister of St John's Free Church, Tunbridge Wells, and a man of strong, if changeable, opinions.[325] Casting himself as a Mr Valiant-for-Truth, he led a band of folk from in and about Tunbridge Wells who were disgusted by the declension of the times. 'Shall the floods of German criticism', he asked, 'overwhelm the ripened fields of Keswick Truth, even as the hordes of German Huns overran the stricken fields of Belgium?'[326] He was particularly persistent in his hounding of Charles Brown and F. C. Spurr, two Baptists who also spoke at the 1920 Keswick, on the grounds that they had previously toyed with higher critical views.[327] It was an acrimonious affair that subsided only when Mountain turned his attention elsewhere.

While the consequences of Mountain's charges rumbled on, the ex-Chairman of the Keswick council and son of the convention's founder, John Battersby Harford, went into print in defence of critical views of the Old Testament entertained by Herbert Ryle, Dean of Westminster. D. F. Douglas-Jones, a retired colonel from Worthing and a Vice-President of the Bible League, was roused to ire, demanding that the other members of the council should dissociate themselves from such opinions.[328] An alarmed council did so, although pressure – from the Liverpool Keswick auxiliary, for instance – that Battersby Harford should resign from the council was ignored.[329] 'In view of the present unsettlement in respect of religious belief', announced the council, 'we are impressed with the necessity of maintaining the Keswick tradition of closest possible loyalty to the Word of God as the fully inspired and authoritative revelation of His Will, in all the ministry of the platform.'[330] There was to be a further crisis in the affairs of Keswick in 1928, when Stuart Holden was eased out of the chair after he and the council had been charged by *The Life of Faith* with going Modernist. That incident, however, was a response to Holden's proposal to sever the semi-official relation between *The Life of Faith* and the convention, and a reaction against his excessive personal dominance of the movement.[331] There was no chance by that stage of Keswick being lost to the conservatives. Indeed there never had been. In 1920–1 what happened was that the boundaries of Keswick were defined so as to exclude a more advanced section of Evangelical opinion than had hitherto been tolerated. Keswick perceptibly narrowed so as to become a rallying ground for conservatives, although conservatives of many shades. The characteristic noise of Keswick was still what was heard by listeners to a broadcast service in 1933: 'the sound of the rustling of the Bible leaves'.[332]

There were other jarrings. A proposal for the merging of Nonconformists into a Free Church Federation in 1919 was what first prompted James Mountain into militancy. It was feared that the Federation would adopt an inadequate creed and would lead on to incorporation with Anglican sacerdotalism.[333] Accordingly Mountain launched a Baptist Bible Union, which was to be his power-base for half a dozen years. In 1922 a body of the same title was to be formed in America that was eventually to emerge as a separate denomination.[334] Mountain's organisation showed similar tendencies. In 1923 it was reconstructed as a Bible Baptist Union to which churches could affiliate. If apostasy spread, it was to be the basis of 'an out-and-out Biblical Church'.[335] The precipitating factor leading to this development was the election of T. R. Glover, a Cambridge scholar and supporter of SCM, to be Vice-President of the Baptist Union in 1923. Glover was best known for his weekly religious column in *The Daily News*, in which, according to a Bible League speaker, he wrote, 'with flippant humour and half-contemptuous comment, on the Holy Scriptures'.[336] The election began a spillage of churches out of the Union that Mountain hoped to mop up. The scheme, however, rapidly fell apart, and in 1925 the organisation, by a fresh mutation, became the undenominational Believers' Bible Union.[337] A parallel attempt to create a Missionary Trust for supporting sound missionaries also collapsed.[338] Better piloted was the plan of E. J. Poole-Connor for a link between various undenominational mission halls and churches leaving their denominations. Begun in 1922, this project became the Federation of Independent Evangelical Churches, which was steadily to expand.[339] Disagreements also racked the Churches of Christ, among whom Modernism was scented at the new Overdale College between 1923 and 1927, and the Calvinistic Methodists of Wales, among whom Tom Nefyn Williams criticised received views in 1927 in a way more reminiscent of R. J. Campbell than of recent upsets.[340] The Baptists were again disturbed in 1932 by dispute about a booklet issued by Glover, in which he questioned the substitutionary nature of the atonement.[341] Britain was by no means immune to Fundamentalist controversies.

MODERATION

'There is no doubt', declared *The Life of Faith* in 1925, 'that the divergence between what are known, on the one hand, as the Fundamentalists, and, on the other, as the Modernists, exceeds, in the United States, anything known in this country . . .'[342] Although conservatives and liberals did pull in opposite directions in Britain, acrimony was less widespread and less drastic in its consequences than in America. With the exception of the CMS rift, controversies were contained. One explanation for the relatively moderate tone of debate is the institutional framework within which Evangelicals operated. It is true that the theological colleges tended to fragment the Evangelical school in the Church of England, with Ridley Hall leading the way in a liberal direction and, in 1929, only St John's, Highbury, and the BCMS College in Bristol receiving the approval of *The Fundamentalist*.[343] Yet all types met at the annual Islington Conference, where conservative and liberal speakers were often deliberately balanced. Although certain of the local clerical meetings fell into the hands of one grouping or another, they sometimes provided further common ground. The Evangelical Candidates' Ordination Council, established in 1925 to increase the supply of clergy, reflected every shade of opinion within the party.[344] There was similar diversity at the annual Conference of Evangelical Churchmen begun at Cheltenham in 1916 and moved to Oxford in 1929.[345] Its chairman at Oxford, Christopher Chavasse, used his prestige as first Master of St Peter's Hall, an Evangelical foundation, to keep the party united. Like certain others, he consciously adopted a centrist position. At an interdenominational level the Evangelical Alliance likewise tended to consolidate the tradition. At its conferences in the early 1920s eminent Fundamentalists, centrists and progressives spoke together in defence of the gospel. Among the centrists were J. D. Jones, the statesmanlike figure who helped hold Congregationalism together, and M. E. Aubrey, who, as Secretary of the Baptist Union from 1925, was to oppose tendencies to fissiparity.[346] Spurgeon's College, the one Nonconformist theological institution approved by *The Fundamentalist*, was steered back into Baptist denominational life by its principal, P. W. Evans.[347] The circuit system of Methodism meant that it was rarely possible for a congregation to build up an ethos widely different from the denominational norm. In Scottish Presbyterianism a conservative like Alexander Frazer of Tain frowned on anything other than full involvement in the life of the Kirk.[348] Denominational allegiance was a powerful brake on divergence.

In general, the Protestant cause had a similar effect. Anti-Catholicism still aroused powerful emotions in mainland Britain. The threat to the Protestant community in Ireland in the convulsions over Home Rule and independence between 1911 and 1924 tugged at Evangelical heartstrings. The Protestant Truth Society and its 'Wycliffe Preachers' were delighted to fan the flames of sectarian hatred, not least in Liverpool.[349] There was similar populist activity in Scotland during the interwar years.[350] Yet anti-Catholicism was part of the worldview of the most urbane. C. J. Cadoux, a scholarly Oxford Congregationalist and avowed Evangelical Modernist, could be contemptuous about Rome because of her repression of free enquiry.[351] The sustained struggle against the introduction of the

Revised Prayer Book bound together the popular and the educated strands of Protestant passion, eliciting an enormous volume of support. In 1918 a memorial against changes in the communion service was presented to the Archbishop of Canterbury signed by nine bishops, 3,000 clergy and 100,000 laymen.[352] The Church Association sprang into life, holding rallies and trying to co-ordinate political opposition. The National Church League, the result of a merger of smaller Protestant bodies in 1906, concentrated chiefly on issuing literature. The campaign proved victorious when, in December 1927, the House of Commons refused its sanction for the use of the Prayer Book and repeated its decision in the following year. Another bout of railing against Romish practices followed in 1932–3 with the denunciation of celebrations of the centenary of the Oxford Movement. Evangelical Churchmen in successive dioceses went into opposition to any official countenancing of the events.[353] The effect of all this rousing of the latent spirit of Protestant defence is clear. The attempt to turn the Church of England into 'an annexe of Rome', declared *The Record* in 1924, must lead all Evangelicals, whatever adjective they would insert before Evangelical, to make common cause against medievalising obscurantism.[354] In the following year the same newspaper ended a correspondence on the higher criticism because, it said, Evangelicals must unite against the sacerdotal challenge.[355] Notwithstanding the defection of the AEGM in 1927, the tendency of militant Protestantism was to inhibit divisions on other issues.

Another factor that minimised acrimony and schism was the restraint of the conservative Evangelicals as opposed to the Fundamentalists. Graham Scroggie, Minister of Charlotte Baptist Chapel, Edinburgh, was at pains to differentiate between the two. Apart from Modernists and the worldly, he argued, Christians could be divided into Fundamentalists and another class who, though sympathising with Fundamentalists, would not accept the label or 'contend for truth at the expense of charity'.[356] These, the moderate conservatives in the Evangelical range of opinion, included Scroggie and many others who would not reject biblical criticism out of hand. J. Russell Howden, one of the numerous Anglican clergymen in this category, used to distinguish between the right and the wrong kinds of criticism.[357] Likewise the Wesleyan Samuel Chadwick, guardian of the Methodist holiness tradition, believed that biblical criticism could not be ignored.[358] Several of these men – Stuart Holden, F. B. Meyer, Campbell Morgan and Scroggie himself – visited America and returned deploring the damage done to the gospel by raging Fundamentalism.[359] Scroggie insisted that premillennialism, although a tenet he embraced himself, should never become a condition of fellowship in Britain and thought the Apostles' Creed a sufficient declaration of orthodoxy.[360] Whereas in America the premillennial hope was the rallying cry of the Fundamentalists associated with the Bible Institutes, Principal McIntyre of the only fully fledged Bible Institute in Britain (in Glasgow) was not himself a committed premillennialist and, accordingly, his college lost favour with extremists.[361]

When *The Life of Faith* wished to resist the tide of liberalism, its answer was not vituperation but a weekly Bible School article contributed by McIntyre.[362] Of McIntyre it was later complained, 'We could never get him to denounce any one'.[363]

Most tellingly, the moderate conservatives struck at the power base of the militants, the Bible League. Its ex-secretary and editor, A. H. Carter, came back from the United States in 1923 breathing fire and brimstone, determined to imitate the tactics of American Fundamentalists.[364] The moderates pre-empted a fresh Bible League campaign by backing a new Fraternal Union for Bible Testimony. The committee, it was announced, felt strongly that 'it is futile to engage in mere declamation and denunciation, and that error can only be effectively countered by an intelligent and positive presentation of the Evangelical position'.[365] Annual Albert Hall rallies were supplemented by meetings up and down the country. Their organiser, a young Baptist minister named C. T. Cook, deplored the 'poisonous cloud of suspicion' emitted by irresponsible opponents of liberal theology.[366] The out-flanked Bible League vainly pointed to its thirty years of experience in the field, and Carter, on another visit to the United States, contented himself with lashing the Fraternal Union as open to Modernists.[367] The manoeuvre was decisive for the future course of Evangelicalism in Britain: moderates, not Fundamentalists, henceforward held the initiative on the conservative wing.

THE ANATOMY OF CONSERVATIVE EVANGELICALISM

What was the strength of conservative Evangelicalism? Snippets of local news reveal that enthusiasts could gather audiences in many parts of England. An interdenominational committee in Manchester held a convention on 'The Fundamentals of Bible Truth'; a similar convention was held at Uttoxeter, although all its attenders were contained in a garden; at Kingston upon Thames for sixteen days a local pastor conducted a campaign that began with a parade of scripture text carriers through the market square; Walworth Road Baptist Church in London held daily prayer meetings under the banner of the Sound Gospel Movement; and a Liverpool and Merseyside Fundamentals Fellowship held meetings in the 1930s.[368] Yet many of the attenders of these gatherings probably had only the haziest notions of whether their faith demanded vocal defence. A better gauge of commitment is the support for the various societies. The Advent Testimony Movement published a useful breakdown of its 1,103 members in September 1919, rather under two years from its inception; of these, 395 were male, 708 female. Two were bishops, 132 other clergy and ministers, and eighteen were military and naval officers; 367 lived in Greater London and 234 in the Home Counties, which together account for more than half the members.[369] The south coast resorts, perhaps Britain's Bible belt, contributed a particularly large number of supporters.[370] Membership figures were given for the last time in April 1922 – possibly because afterwards they fell – as 2,222.[371] The impression is of a small band of the well-to-do pursuing a good cause. Another body, the Fellowship of Evangelical Churchmen, had about 700 members in 1922 and 1,400 in 1934. In 1924 about ninety assembled for its annual conference.[372] Its supporters felt themselves to be isolated figures.

Neither Advent Testimony nor the FEC, however, were solidly Fundamentalist bodies, for both attracted numbers of the more moderate conservatives. The three most Fundamentalist organisations, enjoying mutual recognition, were the Bible League, the Wesley Bible Union and the Baptist Bible Union. Membership figures are available for none of them. At its height, in 1923–4, the Bible League was holding 330 meetings a year, but that gives little indication of committed support.[373] The Wesley Bible Union could muster only ten or twelve backers for its heresy hunts in the Wesleyan Conference. Although it reported the addition of 1,600 new members during 1930, its strength before that was not large and many of its supporters were elderly.[374] When the Believers' Bible Union, as the Baptist Bible Union had become, was wound up in 1928, a mere 130 subscribers to its magazine transferred, as recommended, to the Wesley Bible Union.[375] It seems clear that organised Fundamentalism in Britain was a weak force.

Financial stringency was both cause and effect of low membership. The collections at Advent Testimony monthly meetings, it was announced by Meyer in 1921, did not cover the costs. 'As believers in the Second Advent', he commented, 'they could not, of course, get into debt.'[376] Mountain's wife paid off the losses on the Believers' Bible Union *Bible Call* in its latter years, and Prebendary Fox enjoyed private means that may well have been channelled into the Bible League.[377] The Wesley Bible Union received a meagre regular income in 1917–18 and 1918–19: £258 and £382 respectively.[378] For a special venture the Union was able to secure promises of £1,000 and £500 from two members of the committee, one of them probably the wealthy businessman and ex-MP R. W. Perks.[379] This venture, however, was not pursued, and substantial sums were hard for any organisation to come by. Sometimes they came with strings attached. For example, £100 was given to the London City Mission to pay for evangelists on condition that they would proclaim 'Advent Truth and Testimony'.[380] The largest donor to Fundamentalist funds may well have been John Bolton, a Leicester manufacturer of children's wear whose advertisements for 'Chilprufe' studded the Evangelical press. His giving was the mainstay of the Baptist Bible Union and it is significant that he was invited to join the committee of the Wesley Bible Union at a time when it was looking for fresh injections of funds.[381] Noting the large gifts made to Fundamentalism in America, Morton complained in 1926 that the great need in England was money.[382] He was right: the contrast in this area goes a long way towards explaining the different trajectories of the Evangelical communities in the two countries. In Britain the extremists were starved of funds.

The conservatives, whether Fundamentalist or moderate, put their energies into a host of causes. The various faith missions provided an outlet for separatist tendencies without disturbing the peace of the existing denominations. Bodies imitating Hudson Taylor's China Inland Mission (1865) had multiplied. Missionaries were despatched without guaranteed stipends, relying in faith on the generosity of the Christian public. Grattan Guinness's Regions Beyond Missionary Union (1872) was followed by the Egypt General Mission (1897), the Sudan United Mission (1903), the Evangelical Union of South America (1911) and many others.[383] Undenominational missionary colleges sprang up to serve them, such as All Nations and Ridgelands. Other Bible colleges, primarily equipping Christians for service at home, also emerged, often ephemerally. One of the permanent institutions was the Bible College of Wales (1924), 'founded on faith and carried on by faith'.[384] There were also conference centres, like Slavanka, opened in Bournemouth in 1921 in connection with the Russian Missionary Society, which was to be the scene of many gatherings of keen Evangelicals.[385]

Other causes channelled their enthusiasms. There was the British Israel Movement, convinced that the ten lost tribes of Israel were to be identified with the Anglo-Saxon race. The esoteric 'science' of pyramidology was a fascinating occupation for leisure hours. It was supposed that the Great Pyramid of Egypt, built as it was by Hebrew slave labour, incorporated in its dimensions a prediction of the fortunes of the British Empire. An astonishing number of Evangelicals gave credence to this peculiar quasi-religious expression of imperial pride. They included James Mountain, Dinsdale Young and the Elim leader George Jeffreys.[386] Anti-semitism also fed on the Fundamentalist fringe. J. J. R. Armitage, a Liverpool incumbent and a British Israelite, was particularly virulent, supporting the driving of Einstein out of Germany because he was a Jew.[387] In a few isolated cases anti-semitism actually blended with fascism. G. H. Woods, a member of the Wesley Bible Union, was also a Divisional Officer of the British Fascists.[388] In general, however, the efforts of the International Hebrew Christian Alliance and sympathisers with the Jewish people minimised the growth of popular anti-semitism.[389] All these causes had the effect of turning conservative Evangelicals away from assaults on their liberal brethren. The diversity of the Evangelical mosaic inhibited the growth of power blocs.

If the liberals had gained the ascendancy in certain areas in the present, the conservatives adopted a grand strategy designed to give them control of the future. Mission to youth was a priority, often the overriding priority. 'Concentrate on young people', said Bishop Taylor Smith, an indefatigable conservative platform speaker, 'they will bring you in the biggest dividends . . .'[390] There were, of course, many long-standing youth organisations. In several cases, such as Christian Endeavour, they trained young people already associated with the churches.[391] The pressing need was now for pioneering evangelism to the unchurched. One of the chief organisations in the field was the Young Life Campaign begun in 1911 by Frederick and Arthur Wood. It specialised in missions for teenagers in towns where members of several churches co-operated. At Nottingham in 1921 there were reports of hundreds of decisions for Christ, more than four hundred new members and a continuing prayer fellowship with nine subsidiary district circles left behind.[392] The Children's Special Service Mission (1867) dealt with a younger age group, particularly through the seaside missions. Its offshoot the Scripture Union (1897) provided daily Bible reading notes for all ages.[393] Varsities and Public School Camps were another branch, catering for potential leaders. Eric Nash, a pertinacious bachelor clergyman always known as 'Bash', devoted himself to implementing his own prayer, 'Lord, we claim the leading public schools for your kingdom'.[394] Other bodies expanded in the interwar years: the undenominational Crusaders' classes (1906), providing camps and weekly Christian instruction for the children of the middle classes; the Covenanters, a rough equivalent normally aiming for a lower social grade and usually linked with the Brethren (1930); the Campaigners (1922), a conservative Evangelical version of Scouting based loosely on the Scottish clan system; and the Boys' Life Brigade (1899), rather less military in ethos than the Boys' Brigade.[395] There was dissatisfaction with other youth movements. Why, it was asked, should the church introduce 'the co-worship of Mars, Diana and the fairies through the formation of Boys' Brigades, Boy Scouts, Wolf Cubs, Girls Guildries, Girl Guides and Brownies'?[396] Organisations for the young had to be single-eyed. That was true also of the Inter-Varsity Fellowship (IVF), a body linking the university Christian Unions that will need further attention. 'To win a student for Christ', an IVF meeting was told in 1934, 'is to win what might be called "a keyman".'[397] That was the essence of the moderate conservatives' response to the defection from the truth, as they saw it, of the liberals in the interwar period. There was little point in denouncing their opponents. The task was to win the next generation for the truth.

THE INTERWAR DIVERGENCE

The disagreements of the interwar period had their roots in the impact of Romantic thought on Evangelicalism. Conservatives might appeal to the facts of common sense and reject the theories of the liberals as speculative,[398] but in reality their views were just as much affected by Romantic currents as those of their opponents. The liberals, on the other hand, might dismiss the ideas of the conservatives as outmoded notions unworthy of consideration by the educated, but the conservatives held their convictions precisely because they were influenced by movements of opinion within the intelligentsia over the previous century or so. If the broadening theology and heightened churchmanship of the progressives owed a debt to Romantic thought and taste, the crucial beliefs in verbal inspiration, the premillennial advent and holiness by faith held by the so-called traditionalists were of the same intellectual provenance. The divergence, however, was not solely a consequence of changing ideas. It also sprang from contrasting reactions to circumstances. How should the churches respond to the growing availability of leisure activities and social benefits and the resultant decline in churchgoing? The liberal formula was to follow the trends of secular society, to provide entertainments and promote reform, to insist on the relevance of the churches to everyday life. Guy Rogers, speaking in 1933, declared 'the Liberal Evangelical was interested in housing, whether cinemas should be opened on Sundays, . . . the perils facing the League of Nations . . . the establishment of a Christian civilisation'. He rejected 'the narrow views of the Gospel which thought of it simply in terms of individual life'.[399] Conservatives, it was true, took some pride in holding to a narrower view of the gospel, refusing to follow contemporary taste and being prepared to go into the wilderness for the sake of truth. Liberals clung to the integration of Evangelical religion with society that was the legacy of the nineteenth century; conservatives changed their approach because they judged society to have moved too far away from Christian values. In one sense, therefore, the liberals were traditionalists and the conservatives were radicals. In any case, from the blend of intellectual and practical influences there emerged alternative strategies: accommodation to the trends of secular society or resistance to them.[400]

Friction between the two parties, however, was less acute than it might have been. Fundamentalist controversies did exist in Britain, but they were storms in a teacup when compared with the blizzards of invective that swept contemporary America. Centrists helped to hold Evangelicalism together with the arguments of institutional loyalty and Protestant defence. Moderate conservatives, such as Russell Howden, Samuel Chadwick and Graham Scroggie, exerted a restraining influence. Energies were channelled into foreign missions and youth evangelism as well as into more recondite causes. Obsessional theories about conspiracies of Jews, Jesuits or Bolsheviks to corrupt civilisation through the spread of picture palaces, subversive literature and the teaching of evolution are to be found in the magazines of the Fundamentalist bodies,[401] but they were effectively marginalised. Those who believed that charity is Laodicaean lukewarmness were not allowed to dominate. Despite the divergence, crises were relatively few. A basic explanation is to be found in the nature of the fissures that appeared. The cleavage between conservatives and liberals was far from absolute. On different issues it was at different places along the Evangelical spectrum. Few believed in biblical inerrancy or opposed Darwinism outright, but many adhered to holiness teaching and retreated from the political implications of the social gospel. There was therefore a broadening continuum of Evangelical opinion in this period, rather than a simple separation into two camps. The denominations can usefully be located on the continuum. The Brethren, among whom there was no thought of a liberal pressure group and no need for a conservative one, were to be found near the Fundamentalist pole, along with several smaller sects. The Baptists, possessing no liberal group but having a conservative Bible Union, came next. The Church of England's Evangelical party, torn between the AEGM and the FEC but also having much centrist opinion, was in the middle. Methodism had an increasingly powerful progressive body, the Fellowship of the Kingdom, together with a weak Bible Union, and so stood marginally nearer the liberal pole. Congregationalism, with no need of a liberal group and no conservative one until after the Second World War, was closer to that point. The Presbyterians of Scotland and the Calvinistic Methodists of Wales were perhaps near the Church of England and Methodism. In many instances differences of opinion within the denominations had become as important as those between them. By the Second World War, Evangelicalism had become much more fragmented than it had been a century before.

[7]

The Spirit Poured Out: Springs of the Charismatic Movement

And it shall come to pass afterward, that I will pour out my spirit upon all flesh (Joel 2:28)

In 1963 charismatic renewal came to Beckenham. George Forester, Vicar of St Paul's, and a group of parishioners received 'the baptism of the Holy Spirit', started speaking in tongues and began to hold weekly fellowship meetings for the exercise of spiritual gifts. Beckenham was the first case to hit the headlines, but elsewhere in the Church of England others had already entered a similar experience.[1] Scotland was also affected. 'Strange new sect in Scottish kirk', reported the Glasgow *Sunday Mail*; the 'sect' was said to observe 'a form of worship bordering on the supernatural'.[2] An unfamiliar phenomenon was springing up. Speaking in tongues, the practice of glossolalia, had hitherto been confined to the Pentecostal tradition, but now there were outbreaks within the mainstream churches. It was not 'inarticulate gibberish', according to one Methodist recipient, but 'a beautiful flow of words' that expressed a sense of joyful praise.[3] Speaking in tongues was the most obvious feature of a movement that was beginning in many parts of the world during the early 1960s. It first received the label 'charismatic' – that is, 'of the gifts of the Spirit' – in the United States in 1962.[4] During the next quarter century it was to become a powerful force in British Christianity.

Its impact was chiefly felt in existing churches. Although from the start Anglo-Catholics were involved and from 1967 there was a renewal movement in the Roman Catholic Church, many recruits came from Evangelicalism. The first charismatic prayer meetings in the Church of England were held by an Evangelical clergyman in Burslem. The first parish to enjoy corporate renewal was St Mark's, Gillingham, served by a vicar who came from the Evangelical citadel of All Souls', Langham Place. The main propagator of renewal in the 1960s and early 1970s was Michael Harper, a curate at All Souls' when he received the baptism in the Spirit in 1963.[5] Renewal gained early footholds in the Revival Fellowships of the Methodists and the Baptists.[6] Harper and his circle, the leading figures in the early stages of the movement, adopted a strategy of permeating existing denominations and so were scrupulous to avoid appearing to rival old structures. The Fountain Trust, set up with Harper as general secretary in 1964 and *Renewal* as its magazine from the following year, had no membership, held no regular London meetings and encouraged people baptised in the Spirit to return to their own congregations. The Trust was to close down in 1980 precisely because it had achieved great success in implanting vigorous renewal movements in each of the main denominations.[7] The spread of renewal was nevertheless a painful business. Tensions between the renewed and the traditionalists in particular congregations arose frequently, especially over the conduct of worship. At one Methodist church in the North-West, when charismatics raised their arms during a chorus in a characteristic gesture of praise, the preacher stopped the singing to enquire whether they wished to leave the room. Despite subsequent discussions, the charismatics seceded from the congregation.[8] In other instances renewal triumphed and the traditionalists departed. By such adjustments the number of denominational congregations with a charismatic tone steadily increased.

Alongside renewal in the historic denominations there was a dimension of the charismatic movement outside them that is coming to be called Restorationism. Originally known as the 'house churches', because they met for worship in the homes of members, many congregations soon ceased to match their label when they outgrew private houses and so rented or bought more substantial accommodation. Some, like the Methodist group in the North-West, began as breakaway bodies of the charismatics who felt unwelcome in their previous churches. Yet Restorationism antedates renewal. Its origins have been traced to groups of independent Evangelicals, mostly Brethren in background, whose leaders held a series of conferences in Devon from 1958 to consider how to restore the pattern of church life found in the New Testament.[9] They were anti-denominational by conviction. Their ablest spokesman, Arthur Wallis, set out their mature views in *The Radical Christian* (1981), a denunciation of compromise with existing structures. 'The axe', he writes, 'is laid to the root of the tree.'[10] By the mid-1980s there were several categories of Restorationists. The churches led by Bryn Jones and based on Bradford formed probably the largest connexion, publishing *Restoration* magazine, selling Harvestime goods and running Bible Weeks that attracted thousands from 1976. A looser connexion, with Gerald Coates and John Noble as leaders and greater strength in the South-East, organised festivals from 1983.[11] Other connexions, sometimes included in the last category but in fact largely separate, were based on Basingstoke, Aldershot and elsewhere.[12] There were groupings professing distinctive beliefs: churches associated with Wally North held that the new birth differs in time from conversion and is to be identified with baptism in the Spirit and the coming of holiness; churches influenced by South Chard, Somerset, baptised in the name of Jesus only.[13] On the fringe of Restorationism there were other bodies such as the Icthus Fellowship of South London[14] that did not embrace its anti-denominational stance. It was a fluid pattern of rapidly growing congregations.

CHARISMATIC ORIGINS

Charismatics in the Church of England, according to one of their leaders, are best defined as those who have been influenced by classical Pentecostal teaching and practice.[15] The existing Pentecostal churches were undoubtedly a major source of charismatic experience. David du Plessis, a South African Pentecostalist who travelled the world propagating the baptism in the Spirit in the older denominations, made effective ecumenical contacts in Britain from 1959 onwards.[16] Speaking in tongues had spread from British Pentecostalists to isolated individuals in other denominations during the years, and the process seemed to be accelerating in the later 1950s.[17] Several of the early charismatics in the 1960s, including George Forester of Beckenham, received the baptism in the Spirit through the laying on of hands by Pentecostalists.[18] The Full Gospel Business Men's Fellowship International, an American body founded by a Pentecostal layman to organise Christian dinner gatherings, fostered the spread of spiritual gifts by holding a much publicised convention in London in 1965 and by establishing chapters in many parts of the country subsequently. David Wilkerson's *The Cross and the Switchblade* (1963), an account of his ministry as a Pentecostal pastor among New York drug addicts, did much to show the power of the baptism in the Spirit in transforming lives.[19] Restorationism drew some of its inspiration from the Apostolic Church, the Pentecostal body that set out to imitate the full range of church offices mentioned in the New Testament.[20] The charismatic movement owed a substantial debt to classical Pentecostalism.

Nevertheless, a gulf soon opened between the two. The Fountain Trust never invited Pentecostalists to address its meetings for fear of being tainted by their reputation for unwise behaviour.[21] Conversely, Alfred Missen, General Secretary of the Assemblies of God, left a Fountain Trust international conference in 1971 early because he did not feel at one with the participants. Pentecostalists generally were suspicious that the new movement emphasised testimonies at the expense of Bible teaching, compromised with the doctrinal errors of liberals and Roman Catholics and inexplicably failed to swell their own ranks.[22] Charismatics were also virtually unanimous in denying that speaking in tongues is the indispensable first sign of baptism in the Spirit, a position upheld by the Assemblies of God, though not by Elim.[23] There was even disagreement within the new movement about whether the breakthrough to a fresh experience of the Holy Spirit can properly be called 'baptism'. Harper was prepared to drop the term in deference to non-charismatics who argued that all true Christians are baptised in the Spirit.[24] There was a further divergence between charismatics and Pentecostalists about their attitude to receiving the 'baptism'. Traditionally, Pentecostalists had tarried for the experience with careful self-examination for moral shortcomings. It was a sign of their rootedness in the holiness tradition. Charismatics, by contrast, looked for a sudden sense of release rather than for any moral transformation.[25] That was symptomatic of an ethos that stressed immediacy, the human capacity for instant heightened awareness. For all its legacy from Pentecostalism, the charismatic movement had different cultural affinities.

A major influence in the formation of the movement, as part of the Pentecostal evidence has already illustrated, came from the United States. There, an initial centre of charismatic renewal was the Episcopal church of St Mark's, Van Nuys, California, whose rector received the baptism of the Holy Spirit in 1959 through two members of the congregation who had Pentecostal contacts.[26] A journal published by the renewed Episcopalians, *Trinity*, stirred interest in Britain, as did a favourable editorial in *Churchman* for September 1962. Passing visits in the following year by two ministers from California, Frank Maguire, an Episcopalian, and Larry Christenson, a Lutheran, helped establish a charismatic nucleus in London.[27] Subsequently, a steady stream of American literature and personnel did much to expand and consolidate the British movement. The renewal of the congregation at St Margaret's, Aspley, in Nottingham, for instance, was brought about in 1973 through an account of the events at Van Nuys.[28] The teaching of the Restorationists was reinforced between 1975 and 1977 by visits from Ern Baxter, one of the 'Fort Lauderdale Five' who in America asserted the importance of Christians submitting to the authority of apostolic figures.[29] Most significant were the visits in 1984–6 to England and in 1987 to Scotland by John Wimber, the author of *Power Evangelism* (1985). Drawing together denominational charismatics and Restorationists, Wimber proclaimed that signs and wonders were to be expected as agents of church growth.[30] Although a few drew back, his message gave fresh impetus to the charismatic cause in Britain. Repeatedly the new world was called in to bring vision to the old.

The charismatic movement was moulded most powerfully, however, by its context. Young people of the 1960s, in Britain as in America, were turning in large numbers to a counter-culture, the world of hippies and drop-outs, drugs and flower power. 'Make love not war' was the slogan of the day. In most aspects of the counter-culture, such as pop art or rock music, there was a deliberate violation of 'good taste'. Although in the 1970s these tendencies were contained, they were not reversed. Rather what had been fringe concerns became pervasive, the attitudes of the counter-culture rapidly infiltrating the social mainstream. The new stance was in revolt against a technocratic society dominated by scientific rationality. The traditional, the institutional, the bureaucratic were rejected for the sake of individual self-expression and idealised community. Religiosity, particularly with an oriental flavour, played its part in the revolt.[31] The official report on *The Charismatic Movement in the Church of England* (1981) pointed out that the rise of the counter-culture and of the charismatic movement were simultaneous. It diagnosed the movement as 'a form of Christianised existentialism'.[32] Just as the poet Allen Ginsberg explored the Eastern way of allowing his voice to utter sounds beyond his conscious direction, so the hallmark of the charismatic was glossolalia – 'the evangelical answer to mystical ecstasy'.[33] The new ethos formed a hospitable setting for the early days of the charismatic movement. 'The climate of opinion', as Harper put it, 'was against such a movement until the sixties.'[34] In that decade renewal created a Christian version of the counter-culture.

THE RISE OF CULTURAL MODERNISM

The cultural revolution of the 1960s was made possible by the broader circumstances of the times. The growth of international trade in the postwar world had created unprecedented affluence. The young, feeling that prosperity could be taken for granted, set out on a quest for higher values. Thrown together in the expanding institutions of higher education, they looked for something to replace the surrounding materialism. The Vietnam War increasingly symbolised for them the consequences of the capitalism against which they were rebelling. A sudden upsurge of radical attitudes was to be expected. Much of the vocabulary of revolt was supplied by the popular Marxism of the day. The opinions of the youthful *avant-garde*, however, drew their primary inspiration from deeper cultural currents. In the 1960s the ideas generated by an innovatory elite around the turn of the century began to impinge on a mass public. Before that decade twentieth-century novelties had been confined in most spheres to narrow groups of cognoscenti; now there was a rush by the rebels to embrace them as an alternative to the blended legacy of the Enlightenment and Romanticism that dominated public taste. The religious dimension of the counter-culture shared this genealogy. The charismatic movement was a product of the diffusion of cultural Modernism.

It is unfortunate that the same word 'Modernism' is applied to two different movements of opinion in the early twentieth century, one theological, the other cultural. Theological Modernism, the position of Bishop Barnes, was a desire to bring Christian doctrine up to date, an extension of theological liberalism. Modernism as a cultural phenomenon was something much broader, the result of a shift of sensibility as major as the transition from the Enlightenment to Romanticism a century before.[35] 'On or about December 1910 human nature changed', wrote Virginia Woolf, herself one of the leading exponents of the new mood. The date, though provocatively precise, refers to the opening of the first exhibition in London of Post-Impressionist art, one of the chief symptoms of the transition. 'All human relations shifted', Virginia Woolf went on, '– those between masters and servants, husbands and wives, parents and children. And when human relations change there is at the same time a change in religion, conduct, politics, and literature.'[36] The consequences for religion have been examined far less than the consequences for literature, but it is possible to set out some of the leading characteristics of the Modernist turn of mind. The movement was centrally concerned with self-expression. In German-speaking lands the desire to express whatever was in the artist's mind led the onset of Modernism to be dubbed 'Expressionism', whether in the form of Kafka's fiction or the architecture of the Bauhaus. Expressionism believed in giving vent to the undifferentiated mixture of thought and feeling that is the normal content of the human mind. It entailed delving beneath the surface of conscious reflection to explore the depths of the subconscious. Intense introspection was followed by frank revelation, not least of sexual feelings. The artistic movement clearly had affinities with the depth psychology of Freud and Jung that was emerging in precisely the same years.

Modernism, furthermore, delighted in the discovery by Nietzsche, perhaps the strongest single influence over the whole movement, of the arbitrariness of language. There is no fixed correspondence, it was beginning to be believed, between words and things signified. Only convention, for instance, dictates that verbs should not be used as nouns. All meaning was called into question and so the normal stood revealed as absurd. It was natural, therefore, for a theatre of the absurd to develop. Likewise it was thought unnecessary for there to be any correspondence between art and the external world. The Bloomsbury Group, the pace-setters of Modernism in Britain, embraced a non-representational theory of art – which is why they rejoiced over the French Post-Impressionists. Boundaries between areas of experience were characteristically dissolved, as in the novels of Virginia Woolf. And there was a revolutionary temper about Modernism. It believed in defying the customary, in shocking accepted taste, in destruction as well as in construction. Its culmination on the Continent was the Dada movement around the end of the First World War that carried anarchy into art, which was to be a form of absolute negation. This strain in Modernism could thrive in times of crisis, almost relishing the economic or military downfall of existing civilisation. Close human relations alone, many supposed, could be salvaged from the chaos. So multi-faceted a phenomenon resists definition, but certain common themes have been summarised: 'a loss of faith in objective reality and in the "word", established language; a fascination with the unconscious; a concern with the pressures of industrial environment and accelerating change; a desire to discover significant artistic structure in increasing chaos'.[37] From this matrix came the innovatory attitudes that were to sway youthful minds in the sixties.

THE OXFORD GROUP

Already in the interwar period the influence of cultural Modernism on Evangelical religion can be detected. There came to prominence in those years a body known as the Oxford Group. Teams of 'life-changers', often consisting chiefly of Oxford undergraduates, descended on a town or village urging their hearers to 'surrender' to God. Interested individuals were drawn into groups where there was frank admission of failures to attain the four ethical absolutes of the movement: absolute honesty, purity, unselfishness and love. Or else they were invited to 'house-parties' where more public 'sharing' of sins pointed them to the change that was possible in their lives also. Adherents were encouraged to spend 'quiet times' in which divine 'guidance' was to be expected in the form of 'luminous thoughts' that should be jotted down in a notebook.[38] The animating force was Dr Frank Buchman, a Lutheran minister from Pennsylvania, 'tall, upright, stoutish, clean-shaven, spectacled, with that mien of scrupulous, shampooed, and almost medical cleanness, or freshness, which is so characteristic of the hygienic American'.[39] It was he who directed the whole operation from small beginnings at Cambridge in 1920–1 until it made a remarkable impact on Britain in the years of deepest economic depression in the early 1930s.

The key to understanding the Oxford Group is to see that it was an exercise in maximum acculturation. Buchman had previously been a college evangelist in America. As the scope of his work widened to embrace the Far East and then Britain, he displayed a refined sensitivity to cultural variations. He was careful, for instance, to use 'lift' instead of 'elevator' when in Britain.[40] He recommended the young men of his international teams to observe the customs and social code of the lands they visited.[41] Even theological terminology was discarded because it formed a possible obstacle to evangelism. Life-changing alone is important, according to a book revised by Buchman. People needed to pass through the experience, 'whatever their various theological inheritance'.[42] Although this undoctrinal approach attracted suspicion from the Evangelical world,[43] for a while it held great appeal for Oxford undergraduates. In the early 1930s lunch-time meetings drew about a hundred and fifty daily. There were scholars as well as sportsmen. Three college chaplains gave their support.[44] Outside the university the main impact was on 'the well-to-do, the cultured, the leisured, and the intelligent'.[45] Indeed the Group earned censure as 'the Salvation Army of the upper classes'.[46] Buchman consciously aimed for leaders of opinion whose change of course would guarantee media attention and so fan the flame of the movement. He formulated a distinctive message that would attract the elite. Consequently Buchmanism was in the vanguard

of the evolution of taste. It appealed to those who prided themselves on
being up-to-date, to 'us moderns'.[47] The Oxford Group blended Evangelicalism with the first ripples of twentieth-century high culture. Symptoms
of Modernism can be recognised in many features of the movement.

SELF-EXPRESSION

A vein of joyful spontaneity ran through the whole Oxford Group. There
was no observance of the 'proper thing'. Speakers would lean against the
arm of a chair or sit on a table.[48] Meetings were scenes of 'laughter and
commonplace speech'.[49] 'It's such fun', was a pet phrase.[50] The 'sharing'
that was a feature of the movement meant testimony or confession in
public or in private. Public sharing could appear ridiculous. At a house
party a woman confessed to having allowed herself to think, 'Fancy Mavis
coming to communion in an orange blouse!'[51] Yet to a general practitioner
who identified himself with the Group, the mischief of *repression* could be
undone by 'free and unreserved self *expression*.'[52] The sharing of personal
sin was treated as 'the price of release'.[53] As critics were quick to point
out, personal sin was often sexual sin, especially among young men of
undergraduate age.[54] The medical practitioner reported that in an Oxford
house-party sex matters had frequently been discussed, always helpfully.[55]
One of Buchman's American aides coined a phrase that was daring for
its day: 'God-control is the best birth-control'.[56] Defenders of the Group
might contend that there was no preoccupation with sex and Beverley
Nichols might be disappointed at the reserve shown about the subject,[57]
but the eagerness with which prudery was cast to the winds was shocking
in interwar Britain. In its unstuffiness and frankness, the Oxford Group
was an innovative agent of self-expression.

All this was clearly bound up with psychological interests. It might not
be fair, remarked two commentators, to describe Buchman as a 'Freudian
Psychologist', but they were inclined to think the judgement not far wide
of the truth.[58] Groupers believed they were engaged in a form of therapy.
One of the Oxford chaplains who identified with the movement eulogised
'the pastoral side of the work, the process of deep cure, by which a sex
complex is cured, or an inferiority complex released into the perfection
of love which knows no fear'.[59] The practice of mutual confession was in
fact an anticipation of the technique of group therapy that developed in the
wake of the Second World War.[60] Groupers on the fringe of Buchmanism
began to speak of 'Divine Healing', pointing out the falsity of the antithesis
between soul and body.[61] Confession and reparation in at least one case led
to the disappearance of a nervous ailment.[62] The magazine *Groups* secured
for its readers the services of a consulting psychologist.[63] And there was
praise for the skills of Jesus in this field. 'It is evident', wrote L. Wyatt Lang,
'from the meaning underlying His parables that He had made careful research

into psychological processes, and was a very excellent psychologist.'[64] The two churchmen of the day who led the way in a rapprochement between psychology and religion, L. W. Grensted and Leslie Weatherhead, were both enthusiasts for the Group.[65] It was bound up with the rising tide of depth psychology that was a feature of the interwar period.

The Groupist quest for divine guidance was condemned in some quarters as another symptom of the supplanting of true religion by psychological dabbling. Adherents might penetrate only 'to the mysterious depths of the subconscious mind by relaxing the watchfulness of reason'.[66] Here was the essential stricture: irrationality. God does guide, argued Bishop Knox, but there is a need to test for false guidance by using our minds.[67] The Group on the other hand advocated the suspension of rational processes during the quiet time to ensure 'our absolute negation' to everything but the will of God.[68] It was a sign of the Group's participation in the general trend in European thought to downgrade reason, to diminish the claims of critical reflection.[69] Truth was perceived in moments of disclosure as self-validating as those in Proust. 'The age of miracles is still with us', announces the authoritative statement of Oxford Group methods in the section on 'Guidance'.[70] Hensley Henson, Bishop of Durham, made the same point in censuring the Group. 'It seeks the proofs of divine action', he wrote, 'in what is abnormal, amazing, even miraculous.'[71] Reason could be transcended by direct contact with God. The appeal of the idea in the early 1930s was an indication of a spreading attitude in twentieth-century civilisation.

COMMUNITY AND LIFESTYLE

'The first thing that struck me', wrote the Bishop of Calcutta about his initial experience of a house-party, 'was the wonderful spirit of fellowship which characterised the Group . . .'[72] It was the camaraderie which, as Grensted observed, made the movement particularly beneficial to solitary clergy and which, as others observed, attracted lonely students including isolated Rhodes scholars from the dominions.[73] A distinctive patois bound the Group together. To detractors it was all too closely related to current American slang.[74] Others noted Buchman's tendency to coin maxims like 'revival which continues in survival' and 'sin blinds, sin binds', reminiscent of American advertising technique but also of the habit common among Modernist artists of putting their programmes into slogans.[75] Buchmanite usage in everyday language is best caught by the fictional account of the movement in John Moore's *Brensham Village*, where the new Grouper rector uses expressions like 'scrumptious', 'ripping', and 'awfully jolly'. In this context first names were *de rigueur*. 'The Groupers', comments Moore, '. . . would have addressed the Holy Apostles themselves by their Christian names, or rather they would have abbreviated them and called Saint Peter Pete.'[76] So much help could be drawn from their tight-knit house groups that there were frequent complaints that Groupers neglected to attend regular church activities.[77] Commentators were right to discern in Group solidarity a reaction against individualism, although they were divided into those who praised (like Grensted) and those who deplored (like Henson).[78] J. H. Oldham, Secretary of the International Missionary Council, saw the Groupers as achieving 'life in community'. 'May it not be', he asked, 'that they are rediscovering the truth that the meaning of life is found in relations between persons?'[79] It was only with the Bloomsbury Group that this view became a commonplace in England. For Buchman's movement to represent the same principle was to align itself with a fundamental assumption of progressive thought in its day.

There was a certain holy worldliness about members of the Oxford Group. It is false, argued an editorial in *Groups*, to contrast the sacred and the secular. Religion is not 'a separate compartment of life', distinct from ordinary experience. On the contrary, Christianity is 'a way of living life', so that God approves of 'washing steps or keeping ledgers' as much as religious work.[80] 'Absolute Honesty in business', explained a Group manual, 'means our being level, our playing the game of business as cleanly as we would play any other game.'[81] Religion was to be embodied in every human activity, injecting a strong dose of happiness. Leisure was there to be enjoyed. There were grumbles about immodesty when a girl Grouper took a sun-bathe, and a rector reported sternly that the pleasure-loving Groupers desecrated the Lord's Day by country rambles and seaside trips at the weekend.[82] Smoking, like drinking, bridge and make-up, was rare in the Group. At a house-party of some five hundred, only three or four smoked.[83] Yet Groupers insisted that such matters of personal behaviour were left to the individual conscience, or, as they preferred to say, to guidance. The absence of rigid codes of prohibition is best illustrated by the Group's favourable attitude to that old Evangelical bugbear, the theatre. A girl of about twenty with a Fundamentalist mother who disapproved of theatres entered the movement. Far from abandoning theatre-going, the girl learned from the Group merely how to agree to differ with her mother.[84] By the 1936 national assembly, the Group was itself mounting a sketch, a minor anticipation of the movement's postwar purchase of the Westminster Theatre in order to put on uplifting productions.[85] Art could be God-controlled. In any and every sphere the changed life should reveal itself. By contrast with the conservative Evangelicals of their day, the Groupers did not believe in withdrawal. Far from shrinking from the world, they were out to conquer it.

ORGANISATION AND AUTHORITY

Groupism was a nebulous phenomenon. Membership was undefined by card or ceremony. A puzzled judge investigating whether the Group was a legal entity that could receive legacies enquired whether anything happened when a person joined. 'No', replied the ingenious counsel for Buchman, 'I think it is as invisible as joining the Church of England.'[86] The judge went on to hold that the Oxford Group was so lacking in organisation that in law it did not exist.[87] The same unstructured style was reflected in the Group's worship, or lack of it. A Methodist was struck by the absence of hymns at a London rally.[88] When Buchman conducted a Sunday morning meeting during a house-party to replace a church service, it would consist of only a quiet time and a Bible reading, with possibly a short prayer and a verse of a hymn.[89] An anti-ecclesiastical note crept into the movement's thinking. By contrast with the Group, the church seemed 'stale'.[90] Dwelling on this aspect of the movement, Hensley Henson insisted that, since the Group provided for all the spiritual needs of its members, other systems were superfluous and would naturally be abandoned. A sectarian logic was at work.[91] Buchman's aim, however, was permeation, not replacement. Groupers avoided holding meetings in church hours, encouraged participation in the sacraments of members' own churches and contended that they were not intending to supplant existing denominations.[92] 'Our only organisation', declared Buchman, 'is the Church.'[93] But that stance, while somewhat reassuring to existing churches, was itself anti-institutional. Ecclesiastical structures were matters of profound indifference. Planned activity for any purpose other than life-changing, whether registering members, observing worship or launching a church, was superfluous. The anti-organisational temper so marked among the Bohemian creators of Modernist art reappeared in the Oxford Group. It discarded the prayer and praise, kneeling and standing, of normal religious meetings, according to an apologist, 'in line with the present age'.[94]

So protean was the movement that it had to be held together by firm discipline. Henson was disgusted with 'the oracular despotism of "Frank"'.[95] Although Buchman often effaced himself at public meetings, he kept the whole Group on a tight rein. 'When guided', and the qualification is important, 'he would leave the leadership to another.'[96] In order to counter the charge that guidance was arbitrary, but also in order to control the movement, Buchman taught that guidance must be 'checked' with others – perhaps with a local group, but if necessary with the 'Inner Group'. How this mechanism operated is clear from occasions when it broke down. Methodist Groupers who undertook campaigns on their own initiative received correspondence from the leadership containing the repeated phrase 'You have not checked your guidance with us'. Dismayed by this 'new infallibility', they dropped the word 'Oxford' and developed their work as simple 'Groupers'.[97] Parallels began to be drawn between the Oxford Group and the Continental dictatorships.[98] Some substance was lent to the charge by the presence of two Nazi Groupers at the 1933 Oxford house-party, a visit by Buchman to the Berlin Olympics in 1936 and the change of direction in the movement from the mid-30s.[99] Buchman started to pay more attention to Continental Europe and national flags were carried at Groupist rallies.[100] The atmosphere became highly militaristic. 'After a silent period of communion', during the 1936 national assembly at Castle Bromwich, 'bugles were sounded and drums beaten as 1,000 young men marched to the front followed by a contingent of girls.'[101] Something verging on a personality cult was grafted on to the movement, with Buchman being installed in 'the world centre' at 45 Berkely Square, London, and international broadcasts by the leader.[102] The ethos had been transformed even before, in May 1938, Buchman announced the slogan that was to supersede 'Oxford Group' as the movement's title: 'Moral Re-Armament'.[103] In the postwar world, up to and beyond Buchman's death in 1961, it was to continue in its much more politicised form, but in Britain it would never repeat its impact of the early 1930s. For a while this strange chameleon-like body had matched its environment with remarkable success. It had led the way in absorbing elements of Modernist culture into the Evangelical bloodstream.

THE CHARISMATIC STYLE

The next radically new variant of Evangelical religion to strike Britain appeared in the 1960s in the form of charismatic renewal. It showed no particular awareness of a lineage deriving from the Oxford Group, but affinities were nevertheless substantial. The charismatic stress on the role of the Holy Spirit, for example, had been anticipated by the Group. At a house-party in 1934, an observer commented, 'the work of the Third Person of the Trinity received particular emphasis'.[104] 'One feels', declared a Groupist clergyman, 'the breath of the Spirit sweeping through the meetings, cleansing, convicting, empowering . . .'[105] The movement seemed in 1931 a channel for 'a fresh baptism of the Spirit'.[106] Nor did resemblances end there, for, as will appear, most of the chief characteristics of the Group that reflected the Modernist idiom were to resurface in the renewal movement. It was not a matter of continuity of personnel. Although Cuthbert Bardsley, a full-time Grouper in the 1930s, gave encouragement to charismatic activities as Bishop of Coventry in the 1970s, he was exceptional in spanning the chronological gulf between the popularity of the two movements.[107] Because both appealed particularly to the young, there was a gap of more than a generation between their chief constituencies. There seems to have been no direct transmission of influence from the one to the other. The explanation for the similarity is rather that each movement was closely adapted to its milieu. Although the cultural setting of the 1960s differed sharply from that of the 1930s, the relevant change during the intervening years was that an *avant-garde* outlook confined before the war to a small number had created by the 1960s an extensive counter-culture. The ideas of the few had reached a mass audience, even if in the 1960s it was a

youthful minority. The attitudes that clustered round Expressionism early
in the century had by the sixties become an 'Expressive Revolution'.[108] The
Oxford Group was an accommodation of Evangelicalism to the first, the
charismatic movement a comparable accommodation to the second.

The new style was obvious in worship. 'One of the clearest marks
of a true outpouring of the Spirit', according to Harper, 'is the free and
spontaneous worship which those affected offer to God, sometimes for
hours on end.'[109] Vibrant music, usually played on guitars, repeated
choruses, openness to interruption by worshippers praying, prophesying,
speaking in tongues or interpreting, and sheer length were typical of the
charismatic idiom. Loud celebration was normally varied by 'periods of
deep, soaring silence' or 'quiet verses of commitment'.[110] There was a
wealth of new songs, many of the earlier ones being collected in *Sound of
Living Waters* (1974) and *Fresh Sounds* (1976). Perhaps the most characteristic
feature was the use of the body in worship. 'The hands', it was said, 'as
well as the lips can be so expressive – as they are raised or clapped . . .'[111]
The lifting of hands in adoration became the party badge of those affected
by renewal, but hands could also be laid on other worshippers in prayer,
arms could be linked for corporate singing, hugs could show affection
and feet could tap. The London leaders of emergent Restorationism were
asked to leave their regular meeting place because of noise and threatened
damage to the floorboards through exuberant leaping and dancing.[112]
Headlines were attracted when, at the final eucharist of a pre-Lambeth
charismatic conference in 1978, '25 Anglican bishops led a dance round
the communion table half-way up the steps at the east end of the choir in
Canterbury Cathedral'.[113] The Oxford Group had delighted in spontaneity,
but, in a liturgically unbending era, had never ventured to carry it over
into public worship. In the more flexible 1960s and 1970s, the charismatic
movement dissolved the familiar contours of church services wherever it
appeared. For charismatics worship was expressive, not functional.[114] They
wished to lay bare what they felt for God, and so recovered what had long
been deficient in the Evangelical tradition, the priority of praise. It was a
Christian version of 'doing your own thing', a principle near the heart of
the expressive revolution.

The practice of healing, which charismatics saw as a gift of the Spirit,
reveals further affinities with contemporary secular culture. Interest in
divine healing, already fairly widespread, was the avenue for several
pioneers into the charismatic movement.[115] Renewal meetings, like one
at St Paul's, Hainault, in 1974, would sometimes concentrate on therapy.
A reporter described the queue stretching forward to where three clergy
offered prayer. 'A number prayed for keel over backwards. Well-positioned
experienced stewards ease them gently to the floor, where some lie
prostrate for five or ten minutes.'[116] Although physical healing was often
sought and sometimes evidently received, 'inner healing' was often the
focus of attention. This could sometimes mean deliverance from demonic

influence, and certain renewed churches specialised in exorcism.[117] More often it meant prayer counselling of individuals or else mutual confession reminiscent of the Oxford Group.[118] At Canford Magna Parish Church a team of thirty was set aside as counsellors; the Crusade for World Revival (1964) launched *The Christian Counsellor's Journal*; and institutions sprang up such as Briercliffe House, Lancashire, 'a home which seeks to minister the wholeness of the Lord Jesus Christ to those who are in need of prayer, Christian love, healing of mind, body or spirit'.[119] There was much preoccupation with 'release from tension and inhibitions', the 'shadow side of one's personality' and the 'collective unconscious of the human racial mind'.[120] Taking people deeper and deeper into 'psychological healing', admitted Harper, sometimes diverted the movement from evangelism.[121] It is clear that renewal was permeated by the assumptions of depth psychology, especially of the Jungian variety. It was part of a spreading tendency in later twentieth-century Britain.

INSIGHT AND EXPERIENCE

Insight was often exalted by charismatics against reason. The finest education, according to Harper, must yield to 'the utterance of wisdom or knowledge' that brings spiritual perception, 'a flash of inspiration'.[122] Just like Groupers, members of the new movement believed in direct messages from God. A Solihull house church was customarily exhorted to 'listen to what God is saying'.[123] A charismatic, it has been observed, will 'often confidently assert that "God told me"'.[124] Prophecy, according to the charismatic understanding, is a result of listening for the voice of God.[125] The transcendence of the rational, so scandalous to church leaders in the 1930s, was once more condemned by opponents . Does 'the true and living God ever deal with his people in ways that deliberately bypass their minds?', demanded a stern Reformed critic of the movement.[126] Charismatics were in no doubt that he does. There had long been, according to a leading Baptist adherent, an 'unbalanced emphasis on the intellect and the ability of human reason'.[127] The rationalist bias, Harper asserted, could be traced back to Aquinas, and through him to Aristotle. Aquinas spent his life showing that man has no direct contact with immaterial reality. It was reassuring, however, that 'Aquinas did have an overwhelming experience of God just before his death, which upset most of his theories'.[128] The Eastern church had avoided this bane of Western Christendom. 'The former has allowed much more scope for the Holy Spirit and His more direct ways of inspiration', wrote Harper, 'whereas the latter has emphasised reason and logic.'[129] Light could come from the East. The exaltation of the non-rational was of a piece with the desire for intensified perception that emerged in the sixties.

   Experience was likewise elevated above theology in the charismatic scale of values. When asked at an Evangelical theological college what renewal was about, Harper replied, 'It's about an experience of God'.[130] 'Theology of itself', he once wrote, 'does not provide strength. Bad theology can be more harmful than no theology at all.'[131] One charismatic who did ably undertake the theological enterprise was the Scot Thomas Smail, Harper's successor as Director of the Fountain Trust in 1975 and author of *Reflected Glory* (1975). Yet Smail illustrates the point. After four years in office he resigned to become a lecturer in doctrine[132] and eventually, disenchanted with the froth of the movement, he was to move outside renewal circles entirely. 'The stress on experience', Harper admitted, 'will not please some. It may be thought too subjective'.[133] That was the main burden of conservative Evangelical criticism, resulting in sharp polarisation during the 1960s.[134] Some kept up the barrage in the 1980s. Unconcern with theology, it was suggested, led to toleration of error: 'modernists and Roman Catholics are drawn in and do not cease to be modernists and Roman Catholics'.[135] Doctrinal diversity, as in the Oxford Group, had the function of ensuring that the movement was inclusive. Renewal could justly claim to be a unifying force among the churches. But avoidance of theological rigidity was more than a chosen policy. It was of the essence of the movement. Renewal, according to Harper in 1971, 'has no great theologians. Its teaching is varied and unsystematic'.[136] Dialogue with traditional Evangelicals later made Anglican charismatics wary of exalting the emotions at the expense of the intellect, but Restorationists continued to expect doctrine to be in perpetual flux as God revealed fresh themes.[137] Like the experience-oriented generation of the sixties as a whole, there was a tendency for charismatics to erect ideological fluidity into a virtue.

COMMUNITY AND CREATIVITY

Community became a watchword of the movement. Experience of the Spirit brought people together. Harper had previously seen the church as 'a collection of individuals . . . A religious club, if you like', but he came to recognise it as 'a living thing, an organism'.[138] David Watson, a powerful evangelist whose church at St Michael-le-Belfrey, York, became the showpiece of Anglican renewal, set out an influential communitarian vision in *I Believe in the Church* (1978). A high level of commitment to other church members was expected. It was common for adherents of renewed congregations to move house in order to be nearer the place of worship and each other.[139] Dinners, parties, picnics, away-days, weekends and church holidays fostered solidarity.[140] House groups for mutual care and evangelism became characteristic, forming another parallel with the Oxford Group.[141] And holism found expression in the creation of communities. Families would band together, as in the Post Green Community begun in 1975 in the home of Sir Thomas and Lady Lees at Lytchett Minster in Dorset.[142] A south coast Baptist church established Hunter's Moon, a home where six ladies of all ages could live communally; and the Sisters of the Jesus Way, a Methodist group, held their property in common.[143] Part of the motive for the communitarian approach was a desire to resist the pressures of a secularising society, and in particular to buttress Christian family life.[144] But it also reflected the paramountcy of personal relationships that the movement shared with Bloomsbury and the radicals of the 1960s. 'Everywhere', according to a minister of an Exeter house church, 'everything is based on relationships.'[145] Charismatics were aiming for the characteristic goal of the sixties counter-culture: 'purified community'.[146]

The new movement, rejoicing in its spiritual freedom, broke with many a shibboleth. Harper rejected the rigidity of what he called 'the evangelical code of behaviour'.[147] Wallis denounced sabbatarianism.[148] Members of a house church scandalised the Christian people of Aberdare by buying ice cream on Sunday, reading the Sunday newspaper and drinking wine at dinner.[149] Gerald Coates paraded his love of the cinema, the theatre and pop music, openly discussed masturbation and wore a canary yellow suit. His meetings at Cobham were dismissed as 'just religious show biz'.[150] The whole movement released a surge of creativity that included making banners, designing graphics, writing songs, playing instruments, moulding pottery and performing sacred dance.[151] Craft and coffee shops became a charismatic cottage industry.[152] Technical skills found an outlet in operating grand public address systems and the humble overhead projectors that permitted congregations to worship unencumbered with hymn books.[153] Drama, far from being condemned, was harnessed to Christian purposes, with acted presentations in worship, mime in the streets and evangelistic puppet shows. David Watson's congregation generated a full-time theatre company, Riding Lights.[154] There was an extraordinarily unEvangelical delight in symbol – 'a love of oil, candles, crosses etc.'.[155] The resulting artistic efflorescence was very reasonably labelled 'inchoate sacramentality'.[156] 'Verbal communication', a charismatic folk arts handbook declared, is 'clumsy and wearying'.[157] Although the disintegration of the Protestant tradition embodied in such a comment was real enough, the primary influence at work was not Catholicism. Rather the uninhibited exuberance, the penchant for the arts and the downgrading of the verbal all bear the stamp of Modernism.

STRUCTURE AND AUTHORITY

There was an anti-structural bias among charismatics. 'They reject altogether', declared Harper, 'the concept of the Church as an institution.'[158] New Testament structure, Wallis believed, was not about organisation but about people. Denominations are contrary to the divine will and worst of all is the 'religious hotchpotch' of the World Council of Churches.[159] 'Denominationalism', Coates roundly announced, 'is sin!'[160] Even churches in historic denominations found that ties with unrenewed congregations slackened.[161] Within the charismatic world informality reigned. As among Groupers, first names were standard: Lady Lees and her husband Sir Thomas, a member of the General Synod, became 'Faith and Tom'.[162] What was sometimes styled 'holy mirth' punctuated their meetings. God was saying, explained Wallis, 'Let laughter return'.[163] 'Let's chat a prophecy', was the approach of another Restorationist leader.[164] Early Fountain Trust conferences were largely unstructured. 'We have always found', wrote Harper, 'that when we have *not* organised, the Holy Spirit has worked more freely.' Shortly after his initial experience of the Spirit, Harper dropped the careful planning of sermons and a giant file of matters pending disappeared into the waste-paper basket.[165] People had to be flexible in the King's Church, Aldershot, 'since constant change is here to stay in our church'.[166] The ultimate rationale was that 'God is never stationary'.[167] Like so many radicals of the period, charismatics believed in dispensing with landmarks.

The fluidity of charismatic proceedings made it essential for leaders to impose discipline. A person who supposed himself to be prophesying but was in fact venting his own feelings would be instructed to sit down.[168] As leadership became more demanding, ministry teams emerged. Elders were commonly appointed in renewed Anglican, Methodist and Baptist congregations to provide kindly but firm pastoral guidance.[169] Harvestime churches regularly possessed a collective leadership.[170] Division arose within charismatic circles, however, over the role of apostles, that is, travelling teachers with 'translocal' responsibilities. Although contemporary figures might in certain respects exercise apostolic functions, stated the leading Evangelical Anglican charismatics, 'the apostles have no successors'.[171] The Restorationists around Bryn Jones, on the other hand, came to believe in the mid-1970s that today's apostles possess an authority to which elders of local churches should submit. From American teachers they learned that there is a 'structure of authority directly from the throne of God', passing down through apostles to elders and ultimately to ordinary believers.[172] Ron Trudinger of Basingstoke expressed a full-blooded version of this theory in *Built to Last* (1982). Denominational charismatics and many in the less tightly organised house churches were alarmed by the abrogation of Christian freedom entailed by the new 'shepherding principles', and cases of the abuse of power soon came to light.[173] A branch of Restorationism was becoming as authoritarian as the Oxford Group. Both, while denying legitimacy to existing Christian institutions in the growing spirit of the twentieth century, erected rigid structures of authority of their own.

SUPPORT FOR THE CHARISMATIC MOVEMENT

The social composition of the whole charismatic movement also resembled that of Buchmanism. Charismatics were overwhelmingly young and drawn from the middle classes. St Margaret's at Aspley in Nottingham, for example, which before renewal had few worshippers in the 18–50 age range, afterwards reflected far more closely the age structure of its parish because it drew in younger adults.[174] Restorationists were predominantly young, the first large wave of recruits to the house churches in the early 1970s having been mostly in their early twenties – the teenagers of the 1960s.[175] St Michael-le-Belfrey in York, it was reported, had a high turnover in its congregation because it 'tends to attract those who are in professions which move them on every few years'.[176] Likewise the arrival of a charismatic vicar in a rural parish in the Home Counties filled the church with commuters.[177] Restorationism also attracted small businessmen, civil servants, doctors, nurses, solicitors and accountants in abundance. Elders were commonly graduates, and Bryn Jones's church at Bradford included four holders of PhDs.[178] The contrast with Pentecostalism is total. In the 1950s Elim contained virtually no professionals, in fact few but working-class adherents.[179] 'While the sociological roots of the healthy movements of the Spirit in the past have been among the masses', admitted a leading Baptist charismatic, 'this is not so today . . . it appears we are largely a middle-class movement . . .'[180] The appeal was predominantly to the educated young – to those most affected by the new cultural currents flowing from the 1960s onwards.

The pattern of geographical spread was closely related to the social composition of the movement. Where young professionals were most numerous, on the outer rim of London and in the adjacent Home Counties, charismatics were thickest on the ground. Renewed congregations were also common on the edge of other cities. In the early stages up to 1965, the movement was strong relative to population in South-West England and there were smatterings in the Midlands, Yorkshire and Scotland, but the North-East, the North-West and Wales were hardly affected.[181] The North of England was still regarded as bleak territory twenty years later.[182] Most denominations were significantly affected by the new religious climate. By 1965 more than a hundred ministers were claimed to have received the baptism in the Spirit.[183] In 1979 it was estimated that 10 per cent of Anglican clergy and a rather smaller proportion of the laity, had entered the experience.[184] Promise for the future was guaranteed by the multiplication of diocesan renewal conferences from 1982 and the increase of charismatic ordinands – composing some 80 per cent of those in training at St John's College, Nottingham, by 1978.[185] Richard Hare, the Bishop Suffragan of Pontefract, an adherent from 1973, was for a long time the only episcopal charismatic, but in 1986 Michael Whinney, Bishop of Southwell, became an adviser to the Anglican Renewal Movement, and in the following year George Carey, already a charismatic, was consecrated Bishop of Bath and Wells.[186] The Methodist renewal magazine *Dunamis* published 6,000 copies by 1976, and 250 of the recipients were ministers.[187] The United Reformed Church, created by a Congregational–Presbyterian merger in 1972, had its

Group for Evangelism and Renewal, and the Baptists, whose charismatic congregations expanded markedly, were the most drastically affected of the Free Churches.[188] Alongside the historic denominations there was the rapid growth of the Restorationists, who by 1985 were guessed to number about 30,000.[189] The charismatic movement was poised to become the prevailing form of Protestantism in twenty-first-century Britain.

CHARISMATICS AND EVANGELICALS

Was the movement a prolongation of the Evangelical tradition? Its impact on Catholics, in the Roman as well as the Anglican communion, might suggest otherwise. At Canford Magna Parish Church the charismatic element, it was said, 'tends to cover over the more normal divisions of Catholic and Evangelical'.[190] When John Stott publicly disavowed the movement at Islington in 1964, charismatics were effectively distanced from the main body of Evangelicals.[191] Renewal could be condemned outright, especially for divisiveness. '. . . I have marked evidence', wrote a Cheltenham vicar, 'that Satan is active in and through it.'[192] In 1977 Stott was still doubting whether prophecy among charismatics was a genuine gift from God.[193] In that year, however, the publication of a report of discussions between charismatics and non-charismatics called 'Gospel and Spirit' reflected a rapprochement in the Church of England. 'We share the same evangelical faith', they declared; and they recognised that the worship and spirituality of Evangelicals and charismatics so overlapped already 'as to be almost indistinguishable'.[194] From 1979 Spring Harvest, an annual week-long training conference in evangelism, brought together keen charismatics and non-charismatics in a way reminiscent of Keswick in an earlier generation.[195] A study of Restorationism has located it firmly in the Evangelical Protestant tradition.[196] Furthermore, as a Scottish Roman Catholic bishop remarked, the effect of renewal on a Catholic was usually to give him 'something of the evangelical emphasis on Jesus as his personal Saviour'.[197] If the charismatic movement brought Christians of different backgrounds together, it did so on a basis that was discernibly Evangelical in appearance.

Conversion received fresh emphasis among most charismatics. 'The experience of the new birth', insisted Wallis, 'is more fundamental, more radical than that of receiving the Spirit.'[198] A Methodist office-holder explained that he was not born again until his contact with the charismatic movement.[199] Although in charismatic hymnody there was some shift away from concepts like 'sin' and 'salvation' to less abstract terms like 'healing' and 'life', an analysis has concluded that there was continuity in essentials between Evangelical and charismatic vocabulary.[200] There was a consequent accent on activism, especially in evangelism and counselling. 'Before this blessing', recalled a leader at a Bethnal Green mission, 'the young people would not go into the open air, but now, praise God, there is hunger for precious souls.'[201] There was, admitted Harper, a risk of downgrading the Word of God in the excitement of seeing 'spectacular manifestations'.[202] In all branches of the movement, however, a constant appeal to scripture prevented any retreat from biblicism. Harper also feared the removal of the death of Christ from its central position in the thought and experience of the believer.[203] It was in this area that some movement from the earlier Evangelical consensus was discernible, with the new life of the Christian frequently attributed to the resurrection as well as, or even instead of, the cross. The new emphasis on the resurrection, however, was just as evident in the non-charismatic as in the charismatic hymnody of the 1970s.[204] George Carey, writing on the atonement in 1986, reminded charismatics that even spiritual gifts are 'as much the gifts of Calvary as they are of Pentecost'.[205] Although crucicentrism was a little sapped, the substance of Evangelicalism found expression in the charismatic movement. It was altered, not superseded.

The charismatic upsurge represented another mutation in the Protestant tradition comparable to that which created Evangelicalism in the eighteenth century and that which modified it in the nineteenth. Once more a fresh cultural current impinged on popular religion. This time the spread of Modernism was behind the growth of renewal and Restorationism. Charismatics themselves sometimes noticed the affinity. 'When human words seem inadequate', wrote two Methodist adherents, 'the Holy Spirit inspires other, seemingly unintelligible words (rather like abstract art, some may say!) . . .'[206] The movement was rooted ultimately in the changed mood of the early twentieth century that gave rise to non-representational art, stream-of-consciousness literature and a preoccupation with the non-rational in all its forms. Many of the movement's features had been anticipated by the Oxford Group in the 1930s, when Buchman trimmed his sails to catch the new winds of secular influence. He remoulded Evangelicalism to suit the preferences of an elite already affected by the twentieth century's revolution in taste. By the 1960s the assumptions of a mass audience in and about the youth culture were shaped by Modernist canons. A religious movement sharing its ethos was likely to grow, and, as the counter-culture was assimilated to the mainstream culture during the 1970s, to become a major force in popular Christianity. That is what happened to renewal. Charismatics succeeded where the Groupers failed because their time had come. Both represented an adaptation of Evangelical religion to the trends of the twentieth century.

[8]

Into a Broad Place:
Evangelical Resurgence in the
Later Twentieth Century

. . . out of the strait into a broad place, where there is no straitness. (Job 36:16)

In 1967 a National Evangelical Anglican Congress was held at the University of Keele. It was the chief landmark in a postwar Evangelical renaissance that was gathering momentum well before the charismatic movement reinforced the process. Numbers, morale and impact all greatly increased. The place of Keele in the development of Evangelicalism in the Church of England has been compared to that of the Second Vatican Council in the Roman Catholic Church shortly before.[1] Repercussions were felt among all the Evangelicals of Britain, in the Anglican communion worldwide and in the whole of international Protestantism. There was at the time a sense of making history. 'The atmosphere', it was reported, 'was as exhilarating as on Derby Day.' Youth and ability were to the fore among 'the bright, thrusting, unsquashable men and women . . . who gave this congress an unmistakable glitter.'[2] At a time when the Church of England was in institutional flux, with canon law, liturgy and church government all in the melting pot, Evangelicals determined to be involved in its remodelling. The fourth of the six sections of the resulting Keele statement was devoted to 'The Church and its Structures'. No longer would other traditions be able to determine the terms of debate within the church. There was also a declaration that Evangelical Anglicans would participate in the church unity movement. 'We desire', announced the statement, 'to enter this ecumenical dialogue fully.' As subsequent letters to the press made plain, Evangelicals accepted that there was something for them to learn through ecumenism. It was an admission that they did not possess a monopoly of truth.[3] Perhaps most important, the statement endorsed social involvement. 'Evangelism and compassionate service', it said, 'belong together in the mission of God.' There was a commitment to give serious attention to the problems of society.[4] No longer would Evangelicals be able to regard their task as withdrawal from the world in the company, if possible, of other souls to be snatched from it. A decade later the significance of Keele was summed up as a symptom of a 'release from the ghetto'.[5]

It was no more than a symptom, for the trends consolidated at Keele had already been emerging beforehand. Ten years earlier, at the Islington Clerical Conference of 1957, Maurice Wood as chairman pointed out that Evangelicals were producing more ordination candidates than any other party: 'the future is ours', he concluded.[6] An Eclectic Society of younger Evangelical clergy existed from 1955 as a ginger group with growing influence.[7] There was a small number of Evangelical laymen who were prepared to give time to the Church Assembly.[8] One of their chief concerns was with church relations in the light of ecumenical progress. Social involvement was less prominent before Keele, but the Independent Evangelical Frederick Catherwood had already published *The Christian in Industrial Society* (1964). There was a steady widening of horizons that was sustained and accelerated after Keele. The process was unnecessary among liberal Evangelicals, who in general had long been committed to participation in the institutional life of their denominations, to advocacy of church unity and to concern with social issues. Rather, it was a broadening of the conservative Evangelical tradition. The postwar Evangelical renaissance was in fact a movement among those of firmly orthodox belief. Keele represents the triumph of the conservatives in the Evangelical party of the Church of England. Its chairman, John Stott, the Rector of All Souls', Langham Place, in central London, could draw attention afterwards to the fact that all its speakers were conservatives.[9] Although the most striking resurgence of the traditionalists was in the Church of England, there were similar developments in other existing denominations and in new church groupings. Those with attitudes to the Bible that had come to be labelled conservative in the interwar period gained greater prominence. They were responsible for something approaching an Evangelical Revival.

It seemed called for in the later twentieth century. However difficult it may be to conceptualise, secularisation was a stark reality. Church membership had been falling since the 1920s, and, although the process was arrested in the wake of the Second World War, there was a catastrophic collapse in the 1960s.[10] Adult church attendance dropped to a mere 11 per cent of the English population by 1979, to 13 per cent of the Welsh population by 1982 and to 17 per cent of the Scottish population by 1984.[11] Religion was increasingly marginal in people's lives. In 1966 two-thirds of marriages in England and Wales still took place in church; by 1980, the figure was fewer than a half.[12] The 1944 Education Act decreed that religious instruction and a daily act of worship should be compulsory in state schools.[13] By the 1970s both provisions were widely ignored with impunity. The television and the motor car dealt a drastic blow to Sunday School attendance in the 1950s.[14] Christian practice was ceasing to be buttressed by custom. Religious change was followed by moral change. In the 1960s traditional moral values based on the Christian ethic disintegrated. The pill heralded the permissive society in the field of sexual morality. The statute book was liberalised. Homosexual practice and abortion ceased to be crimes in 1967 and divorce by consent was permitted from 1969.[15] Even if church leaders often saw reason to condone or applaud such developments in the name of a more humane society, it was hard to disguise the shrinking of Christianity and its influence. A demanding task faced the churches: the turning of the religious tide.

THE RANGE OF EVANGELICAL OPINION

Four schools of thought coexisted in British Evangelicalism at the time of the Second World War. Although they shaded into each other, the bodies of opinion are clearly distinguishable. The liberal school, eager to welcome fresh light from modern thought and other Christian traditions, was powerful in the Church of England and Methodism, finding expression in the Anglican Evangelical Group Movement (AEGM) and the Fellowship of the Kingdom.[16] It was stronger in Congregationalism, weaker in the Church of Scotland and so weak as to be virtually absent from the Baptists. A second, centrist school tried to minimise the divide that had opened in the 1920s between liberals and conservatives. Typically, like Max Warren, General Secretary of the Church Missionary Society from 1942 to 1963, the centrists wished to hyphenate no word like liberal or conservative with Evangelical.[17] In the Church of England it was also the position of men such as Bryan Green, who was prepared to ignore differences of opinion with other Christians in his zeal for evangelism, and Bishop Christopher Chavasse, who wished to hold Evangelicals together for the defence of Protestantism.[18] This was the prevailing stance in the Church of Scotland and Methodism, while the influential 'Genevan school' of Congregationalists led by Nathaniel Micklem, orthodox, scholarly and liturgically minded, falls into the same category.[19] Ernest Payne, subsequently General Secretary of the Baptist Union, was one of a smaller number of Baptists who held similar views.[20] The liberals and the centrists together supplied the leadership in all the denominations except the smallest.

The third body of opinion inherited its moderate conservatism from the interwar debates. In the Church of England the bastion of conservatism, whether moderate or otherwise, was the Fellowship of Evangelical Churchmen, but, since the Anglican school was defined partly in terms of its liturgical practice, the Church Pastoral Aid Society, which still made grants only to parishes adhering to the north side position, must also be reckoned a conservative institution.[21] The Revival Fellowships of the Free Churches were soon to rally similar opinion: the Baptist body, formed in the 1930s, gathered strength and began annual conferences in 1954; the much smaller Congregational and Methodist equivalents began in 1947 and 1952 respectively.[22] 'Definite' Evangelicals, as the moderate conservatives sometimes preferred to call themselves, also existed outside such organisations. Equally these bodies included some who should be located in the fourth category, the Fundamentalists. The Advent Testimony Movement was one of several interdenominational organisations that contained a significant number of this persuasion, but articulate Fundamentalism remained weak in Britain. Conservatives like Stott were eager to repudiate the label when it became a matter of public debate in the mid-1950s.[23] They themselves, however, were by no means influential. The conservatives as a whole formed the obscurer section of a community that had been marginalised by the Catholic drift of religious life and the secular drift of national life during the earlier twentieth century. Despite numbering extremely powerful preachers such as the Methodist W. E. Sangster in their ranks, in the years around 1940 the conservative Evangelicals were probably at their nadir.[24] The remarkable resurgence symbolised by Keele demands explanation.

LIBERALS AND CENTRISTS

One factor is that the liberal impulse represented by the AEGM steadily lost its vigour. After the war it was regretfully recalled that Vernon Storr, 'our master', had died in 1940,[25] and no comparable figure took his place. The Cromer Convention, suspended in wartime, was revived in 1947 and 1948, only to fall victim to the rising costs of the period.[26] Steadily 'a less evangelical liberalism gained control'.[27] The movement became largely cerebral, issuing study outlines for group meetings and holding conferences. Numbers fell away, though there were still some 1,000 clerical members in 1950 and annual conferences were still being organised in the 1960s. The Methodist Fellowship of the Kingdom remained stronger, with about 1,800 members in 1950, and maintained more of a devotional temper.[28] The Union of Modern Free Churchmen, on the other hand, a preponderantly Congregational body, struck out on more advanced lines of thought and kept up something of its impetus into the 1960s.[29] The decay of organised liberalism was most marked in the Anglican body. It was partly a consequence of success. AEGM members were elevated to ecclesiastical office – in the single year 1946 the movement provided three diocesan bishops, one dean and at least three archdeacons – and so had less time or enthusiasm for sectional organisations. But it was also because its message was hardly electrifying: R. R. Williams, later Bishop of Leicester, declared in 1947 that its first purpose was to be a support of 'sober, central, Anglican churchmanship'.[30] In the 1950s one of its few advantages was that the editor of *The Church of England Newspaper and the Record*, formed by a merger of its two constituents in 1949, was a steady supporter – as well as being, from 1954, secretary of the Modern Churchmen's Union.[31] With his termination of office in 1959, the transfer of ownership to new hands in the following year and the appointment of a conservative as editor, liberalism lost one of its chief remaining props.[32] During the 1960s liberal Evangelicalism finally dissolved into the broad middle way of the Church of England.

Centrist Evangelicals possessed great dynamic in the later 1940s. Max Warren masterminded a series of schemes for putting Evangelicalism more obviously on the ecclesiastical map. In 1942 he launched the Evangelical Fellowship for Theological Literature (EFTL), a body designed to foster serious scholarship by younger members of the party in the Church of England. Numbering about 200 at its peak, it was by no means simply a liberal body, for its ranks in 1950 included conservatives such as T. C. Hammond and J. W. Wenham. From its membership were drawn the contributors to a series called the St Paul's Library, the first publication being *The Ministry of the Word* by Donald Coggan, subsequently Archbishop of Canterbury. Many EFTL members rose to the episcopal bench or theological chairs.[33] Warren was likewise behind a conference whose papers were published under the title *Evangelicals Affirm* (1948), urging the central importance of evangelism on the bishops of the Lambeth Conference, and a team statement of the Evangelical Anglican position, *The Fulness of Christ* (1950).[34] Warren's aim of welding together Evangelicals of all shades enjoyed some success. In 1951, for instance, it was agreed that the AEGM proctors in the Church Assembly should join the other group of Evangelicals for united action.[35] As time went by, however, there was a tendency for EFTL members to loosen their Evangelical moorings and sail off in a liberal direction.[36] A similar process took place in the interdenominational Student Christian Movement (SCM), which in the 1950s successfully continued its interwar role of drawing together speakers and students holding many types of theological opinion. In 1957 it had more than 7,000 members. In the 1960s, however, it became increasingly identified with radical stances and support melted away.[37] Centrism was probably most successful in Scotland, where D. P. Thomson and Tom Allan were leaders of an effective movement of co-ordinated lay evangelism, which began in 1947 and was known in the later 1950s as the 'Tell Scotland' campaign. Although the Church of Scotland took the lead, most of the other Protestant denominations participated. In the practical work of evangelism theological differences were ignored. Thomson, for instance, delighted in drawing personnel from both the SCM and the Inter-Varsity Fellowship.[38] Confidence in evangelistic campaigns, however, waned among the less conservative in the Scottish churches during the 1960s. In Britain as a whole, as the distance between the poles of theological opinion widened, the scope for centrist enterprise declined.

A CLIMATE OF SERIOUSNESS

Circumstances favoured conservative Evangelical growth much more than in the interwar period. The war itself was strangely beneficial. It is true, of course, that the churches suffered losses of manpower, premises and, in many cases, surrounding homes. On the other hand, the war generated an idealism of hope for the future, blended with a dedication to turning the dream into reality. The Dunkirk spirit had a spiritual dimension.[39] 'The amazing heroism', wrote a contributor to *The Advent Witness*, 'which has been displayed daily at sea, on land and in the air by those in the war makes us wonder whether we sacrifice enough for Christ in *our* war.'[40] In the ideological conflict of wartime and the ensuing Cold War, conservatives knew where they stood. If sin was the enemy within, according to Alan Redpath, Minister of Duke Street Baptist Church, Richmond, in 1953, 'Communism was the enemy without'.[41] Conviction ran deep and evangelism was in the air. In 1945 the Church of England published *Towards the Conversion of England*, the report to the Church Assembly of a commission on evangelism chaired by Bishop Chavasse. Although little official action followed, there was at least a London diocesan mission in 1949.[42] Maurice Wood believed there had been a swing from the prewar emphasis on pastoral work to a postwar stress on evangelism.[43] During his chairmanship of the Islington Conference, from 1952 to 1961, the theme was usually some aspect of gospel work, and conservatives came increasingly to the fore. In 1953, when John Stott addressed Islington for the first time, his subject was training the laity for house-to-house visitation.[44] In Scotland the same atmosphere was the backdrop to the Tom Allan campaigns, and evangelism received a fresh fillip from the most recent spontaneous revival movement in British history, the Hebrides Revivals of 1950 and 1952.[45] The Methodists organised a series of significantly named 'Christian Commando Campaigns' in the late 1940s; the Baptists sponsored an evangelistic 'Baptist Advance' in 1949–51; and the Congregationalists co-ordinated a Forward Movement in 1950–3.[46] At the Albert Hall the evangelist Tom Rees preached to packed audiences on undenominational lines, reaching his fiftieth rally there in 1955.[47] The legacy of war was a willingness to consider ultimate values in the population at large and a preparedness to respond on the part of the churches.

The prevailing theological tone of the 1940s and 1950s was also more sympathetic to conservative Evangelical preoccupations. A disappointed Congregationalist noted in 1942 the fashion of pronouncing Christian humanism and liberalism dead.[48] The biblical theology associated with C. H. Dodd, an attempt to think back into the minds of the biblical writers, was uncongenial to liberals.[49] So was the neo-orthodox systematic theology of Karl Barth. Conservatives could share in its repudiation of liberal nostrums, but that does not mean they endorsed its whole position. On the contrary, as J. Stafford Wright, Principal of Tyndale Hall, Bristol, explained in 1957, neo-orthodoxy seemed to them merely a 'newer liberalism'. Although rightly teaching an existential encounter with Christ, it was wrong in failing to base itself on the New Testament records as written down.[50] The divergence was so sharp as to occasion a schism in the Edinburgh

University Christian Union, which came under the influence of the Barthian theology of Professor T. F. Torrance and so was disaffiliated in 1953 by the Inter-Varsity Fellowship.[51] Neo-orthodoxy nevertheless provided a context in which conservative Evangelical opinions were not dismissed out of hand.

The radical theology that came into vogue in the 1960s also served, paradoxically, to strengthen the conservative position. Conservative Evangelicals were more prepared than most to denounce what they saw as departures from orthodoxy. *Honest to God* (1963), by J. A. T. Robinson, Bishop of Woolwich, was mildly deprecated by the Archbishop of Canterbury, but roundly dismissed by the conservative J. I. Packer as 'a plateful of mashed-up Tillich, fried in Bultmann and garnished with Bonhoeffer'.[52] An address to the Baptist Union assembly in 1971 by Michael Taylor, Principal of the Northern Baptist College, in which he questioned the divinity of Christ, led to an upsurge of conservative opinion that carried in the following year's assembly a fuller statement of belief than the Union had ever previously professed.[53] The views of Don Cupitt, Dean of Emmanuel College, Cambridge, especially in *The Myth of God Incarnate* (1975), and of David Jenkins, Bishop of Durham from 1984, were controverted equally firmly by Evangelicals with traditional beliefs. Conservatives gained credit for standing up for received Christian convictions.

THE ECUMENICAL MOVEMENT

One of the chief developments in the world church after the Second World War was the accelerating momentum of the unity movement. Its effects on Evangelicals were ambiguous, but they could not avoid it. The standard Evangelical view had been that external uniformity was unimportant and so there were risks of being too involved in the quest for reunion.[54] Students of prophecy were positively hostile. When the World Council of Churches (WCC) was set up in 1948, its purpose was to include all shades of thought, according to an editorial in *The Advent Witness*, and it would even welcome Roman Catholics and Greek Orthodox. Hence it was 'but a shadow of mystery Babylon, that great apostate body typified by the great whore of Revelation 17'.[55] Such attitudes were common on the Baptist fringe, racking the denomination in Scotland during the 1950s and leading the more conservative in England and Wales to demand the withdrawal of the Baptist Union from the WCC during the 1960s.[56] Principled opposition to ecumenical involvement led, as we shall see, to a schism in conservative Evangelical ranks in the late 1960s.[57] By 1974 disquiet had spread more widely at the interpretation by the WCC of the gospel in socio-political terms, particularly through the fund to combat racism,[58] and subsequently the Salvation Army actually ceased to be a full member. But the most outspoken opposition to the ecumenical trend was aroused by the scheme for Anglican–Methodist reunion put forward in 1963. It was to be expected that some Methodists would be unhappy, especially with the proposal that their ministers should submit to what could be interpreted as episcopal reordination. The validity of their earlier ministry was being slighted. Equally intransigent, however, was the bulk of the conservative Evangelicals in the Church of England, who objected not only to apparent reordination, but also to their exclusion from the commission that had drawn up the proposals. In alliance with Anglo-Catholics they ensured that the scheme was inadequately supported in 1969, 1971 and 1972, and so lapsed.[59] Conservative Evangelicals gained a reputation for opposing the ecumenical movement.

Those in the Church of England nevertheless insisted that they were far from being outright opponents of church unity. They wished to reunite with the Free Churches, but only on acceptable terms such as those that had created the Church of South India in 1947.[60] From 1955 many conservative Evangelicals joined the Weeks of Prayer for Christian Unity that sprang up around the country and usually participated in the local Councils of Churches that sponsored them. Growing contact with other Christians did a great deal to moderate their traditional anti-Catholicism. The changes of the Second Vatican Council made Rome less fearsome, and charismatic fellowship began to break down the Protestant–Catholic divide. Keele welcomed the possibility of dialogue with Roman Catholics on the basis of scripture; a decade later David Watson, to the scandal of some, was describing the Reformation as a tragedy.[61] Among Evangelical Anglicans, it was said in 1977, 'old-fashioned Protestants have died out'.[62] That was an exaggeration, for, especially in the Church Society that resulted from the merger of the Church Association and National Church League in 1950, there remained a phalanx for whom the defence of Reformation principles was the overriding priority. As high-level consultations between Anglicans and Roman Catholics steadily demarcated increasing common ground between the churches, Church Society threatened in 1986 that there would be a secession from the Church of England if it continued moving towards Rome.[63] Majority opinion had nevertheless shifted a long way. In 1970 leading Evangelicals and Anglo-Catholics were able to present a joint scheme for reunion in England.[64] The popular Protestantism that had made possible the defeat of the Revised Prayer Book in 1927–8 was in sharp decline.

Hence the traditional defiance of Anglo-Catholic liturgical practices faded away. During the 1950s there remained parishes such as St Mary-le-Port, Bristol, where the black gown was still worn for preaching, the sternly Calvinist *Hymns of Grace and Glory* were sung and collections went to the Irish Church Missions, the Trinitarian Bible Society and the Sovereign Grace Union. In 1952–3 there was a *cause célèbre* when the Bishop of London refused to ordain two Evangelicals who felt bound in conscience not to wear the white stole at the service.[65] North side celebration of communion was a conservative party badge; matins and evensong, which was often the better attended, were the main Sunday services; and there was strong attachment to the text of the 1662 Prayer Book interpreted in a Protestant sense. The 1961 Islington Conference was warned by its chairman of the perils of parish communion, which had already become normal outside conservative Evangelical circles.[66] During the 1960s, however, the new wave of Evangelical clergy was spilling out beyond the party's previous parishes, and some of them began to tolerate customary practices. At youth services there were concessions to modern language. And a number of junior clergy, with Colin Buchanan at their head, were beginning to contribute to the issues of liturgical revision in the church. In 1965 Series II was published as a modern alternative to the Prayer Book, and soon the more progressive Evangelical parishes were experimenting with it.[67] Even before the publication of *The Alternative Service Book* in 1980, most Evangelicals had ceased to use the 1662 order except for an early morning communion service. Keele went so far as to declare – though this was its most controversial pronouncement – that Evangelicals would 'work towards weekly communion as the central corporate service of the church'.[68] So drastic a reversal of policy represented a major rapprochement with the Anglo–Catholics. It issued in co–operation rather than conflict over liturgical matters in the General Synod during the 1970s.[69] More charitable church relations, both between and within denominations, were an important dimension of the increasing confidence of mainstream Evangelicalism during the period.

CONSERVATIVE EVANGELICAL STRENGTHS

Keswick remained a potent source of inspiration for conservative Evangelicals. At first after the Second World War its style did not change. 'It has been truly said', wrote a commentator in 1949, 'that the Keswick Convention is not a preaching festival. Its main purpose is to show from the scriptures how Christians may experience the *full* salvation which may be theirs in Christ.'[70] The message, however, was challenged from within conservative Evangelical circles during the 1950s. Leaders of the Rwanda Revival, a vigorous phase of African Christianity that attracted much attention, testified that there was no once-for-all experience of sanctification such as Keswick proclaimed.[71] In the manner of an angry young man of the time, J. I. Packer, from a Reformed standpoint, argued in 1955 that 'Keswick teaching is Pelagian through and through'.[72] Probably in response, 'a new breadth of vision' was evident at Keswick by 1960, with attention to the sins of the church, the role of the unconscious and the need for discipline as well as rest in the spiritual life.[73] By 1972 John Stott was delivering Bible 'studies' rather than the less expository Bible 'readings' that were traditional.[74] Keswick was becoming a preaching festival. The charismatic movement supplied an alternative mode of spirituality in keeping with the times. *The Life of Faith*, the newspaper associated with the convention, lost readers steadily until, in 1980, it was transformed into a magazine for Christian families without the note of victory by faith.[75] A devotional temper expressed in diffuse Romantic terms no longer appealed to the young. Keswick in its new form still helped to glue together Evangelicals from different denominations, but its most influential days as the power-house of the movement were over.

The conservative Evangelical tradition benefited from a range of other organisations. Youth work was maintained, not least because the interwar strategy of sowing seed for the future was showing its value by yielding a rich crop of leaders. In particular, the 'Bash Camps' for public schoolboys produced, among others, Michael Green, an able writer and evangelist, Dick Lucas, a powerful London preacher, and John Stott.[76] Scripture Union expanded its range of literature and activities, and an Inter-School Christian Fellowship was launched in 1947 to co-ordinate Evangelical groups in the education system.[77] To the interdenominational Crusaders, there was added, from 1953, a similar national youth organisation catering for Anglicans, the Pathfinder Movement.[78] From 1956 there was an annual 'Christian Holiday Crusade' at Butlin's Camp in Filey, beamed particularly at young people.[79] A resoundingly successful venture was the publication, in 1966, of *Youth Praise*, a collection of modern choruses designed to appeal to the burgeoning 'pop culture'. The undenominational missionary societies such as the Overseas Missionary Fellowship – the former China Inland Mission – did much to channel youthful enthusiasms into dedicated service. By their networks of officials, missionaries, literature and meetings they reinforced the zeal of conservative Christians. To their number was added, from 1962, Operation Mobilisation, an international body with roots in Spain designed to train and deploy young people in short-term evangelistic ventures.[80] For mission at home the Evangelical Alliance began to adopt a more active role. It produced an innovative glossy magazine, *Crusade*, from 1955; it issued a thorough study of evangelistic strategy, *On the Other Side* (1968); and it sponsored a short-lived annual assembly for Evangelicals of all denominations in 1965 and 1966.[81] All these activities expressed the evangelistic vitality of conservative Evangelicalism. They help explain both its effective recruitment and its acquisition of an increasingly up-to-date image.

Probably the most important factor in both these respects, however, was the impact of Billy Graham. In 1954–5, 1966–7 and 1984–5 the American evangelist held mass crusades in Britain. From the beginning huge numbers thronged in – 80,500 of them in the first week at Harringay in 1954.[82] Although there were widespread initial reservations, even among conservative Evangelicals, about importing an American with his razzamatazz, vast choirs and banks of technical equipment, Graham was brilliantly disarming. On arrival at Southampton in 1954, holding up a Morocco-bound Bible, he said, 'I am here to preach nothing but what is in this book, and to apply it to our everyday lives. I am not going to talk about your national problems or transgressions, as we have 10 times more in the United States.'[83] There were indeed criticisms, especially on his visits in the 1960s, that Graham failed to address public questions, including the Vietnam War.[84] There was also censure, normally rejected by actual attenders, on the ground that he was using techniques of mass suggestion.[85] Supposed converts, it was alleged, soon gave up church attendance. Ten months after the Harringay crusade, however, 64 per cent of the previous non-churchgoers who had come forward as 'enquirers' were still attending.[86] It was also asserted that 'the working classes . . . responded very little'.[87] An analysis of 1,317 enquirers in 1966, however, showed that 360 were unskilled or semi-skilled industrial workers. If skilled working people and members of working-class households are added, it is plain that Billy Graham was reaching extensively beyond the middle classes.[88] The crusades had enormous knock-on effects. 'Church life has been quickened', reported a Berkshire rector in 1955, 'several converts are worshipping keenly and winning others, finance has increased, study groups are thriving, and my own vision widened.'[89] Graham's imitators in mass evangelism – Eric Hutchings, Dick Saunders and Luis Palau among them – offered him the sincerest form of flattery. By declining to support him, many liberals eliminated themselves from the mainstream of Evangelical life in Britain. To those who supported him, a category extending beyond the conservative Evangelicals but having them as its core, he administered a powerful tonic.

THE REALM OF SCHOLARSHIP

Probably the most important single factor behind the advance of conservative Evangelicalism in the postwar period was the Inter-Varsity Fellowship (IVF). It had emerged during the 1920s and had been formally established in 1928 as a body linking the university students who followed the Cambridge Inter-Collegiate Christian Union in separation from the Student Christian Movement. Its basis of faith was resolutely conservative but by no means extreme: the first clause, for example, affirmed not the inerrancy of the Bible but the 'infallibility of Holy Scripture, as originally given'.[90] Students of diverse backgrounds, though few in most universities before the Second World War, were welded into tight-knit Christian Unions dedicated to zealous propagation of the faith under the watchful eyes of IVF travelling secretaries. The organising genius at the hub of the IVF for forty years from 1924 was Douglas Johnson, a London medical student of retiring disposition and studious habits who was particularly devoted to the weighty Reformed theologians of America. With the postwar expansion of higher education, the bodies affiliated to the IVF grew in numbers, scale and confidence. The collapse of the SCM gave them a clear field in the 1970s, by which time the title of the umbrella organisation was changed to 'Universities and Colleges Christian Fellowship' to mark its expanding role outside the university sector. Christian Union members naturally rose to positions of leadership in the various denominations. Thus, as Bishop of Barking, Hugh Gough, who had been a travelling secretary in 1927, gave crucial episcopal support to Billy Graham's first visit; J. Ithel Jones, IVF representative for Wales from 1933, became Principal of the South Wales Baptist College twenty-five years later; and Howard Belben, a CICCU member in the early 1930s, went on to be Principal of the Methodist Cliff College.[91] The Graduates' Fellowship (GF), consisting of ex-CU members, helped sustain their conservative theological convictions and encouraged them to express the faith in their professional lives. The proliferating branch organisations included the particularly large Christian Medical Fellowship (1949) and Research Scientists' Christian Fellowship (1944), whose members, swayed by the distinguished Brethren surgeon A. Rendle Short, took the lead in repudiating interwar conservative suspicions of evolution.[92] As early as 1948 a GF member, D. R. Denman, later Professor of Land Economy at Cambridge, was eager to study the problems raised by the social sciences for 'the Christian mind'.[93] The IVF was broadening the horizons of those with conservative theological views.

The work of the IVF was particularly noteworthy in biblical and related studies. So sparse did contemporary scholarship on acceptable lines seem in this field that, in 1943, the publishing arm of IVF was reissuing a work by the deceased D. M. McIntyre.[94] Already, in 1938, the IVF had formed a Biblical Research Committee designed to remove 'the reproach of obscurantism and anti-intellectual prejudice' from Evangelical Christianity. From 1942 there were academic Tyndale Lectures at the IVF's annual conference for theological students, in 1945 Tyndale House in Cambridge was opened as a centre for biblical studies and from the same year there was a Tyndale Fellowship for Biblical Research.[95] Thirty years later, between twenty-five and thirty of its members held teaching posts in British universities. The Old Testament specialist in the early years was W. J. Martin, Rankin Lecturer in Semitic Studies at Liverpool; his New Testament equivalent was F. F. Bruce, from 1959 to be Rylands Professor of Biblical Criticism and Exegesis at Manchester. Both were Brethren.[96] 'There is nothing', Bruce assured younger scholars in 1948, 'in the pursuit of source-criticism in the Biblical field which is necessarily incompatible with the outlook of the I.V.F. . . .'[97] Another enterprise, spearheaded by Douglas Johnson of the IVF, was the London Bible College, an interdenominational body for training graduates in Christian work that commenced classes in 1943. Like IVF and Tyndale House, the college owed much of its financial support to John Laing, an enormously successful Brethren building contractor.[98] The result of all these activities revolving in the orbit of the IVF was a resurgence, on a conservative basis, of Evangelical scholarship.

The transmission of scholarship to the public was another of Johnson's aims. 'A vital and up-to-date new Evangelical literature', he wrote in 1948, 'which will present truly biblical theology in the finest and simplest possible English style, is an essential need for this generation of Christian workers.'[99] The IVF undertook to fill the gap. It published, in addition to a growing list of other titles, a set of Bible study notes edited by G. T. Manley, entitled *Search the Scriptures* (1934–7); a digest of systematic theology, Archdeacon T. C. Hammond's *In Understanding be Men* (1936); the *New Bible Handbook* (1947), *New Bible Commentary* (1953) and *New Bible Dictionary* (1962); and a series of Tyndale commentaries on individual books of the Bible (from 1956).[100] When the Keele Congress Report recommended study material, more titles (30) were listed from IVF than from any other publisher. Second came Hodder and Stoughton (27), whose publications, though not as exclusively conservative as those of IVF, included many of that stamp. The Church Pastoral Aid Society issued 21, the Church Book Room Press 12 and the Marcham Manor Press, a recent firm concentrating on asserting the Evangelical position in Anglican debates, nine.[101] The Christian Brethren Research Fellowship, a group in which F. F. Bruce was prominent, published from 1963 a series of booklets that did much to stir hitherto rather introspective assemblies into facing similar issues to those raised at Keele.[102] *The Evangelical Quarterly*, founded in 1929 for the 'defence of the historic Christian faith', and the *Journal* of the Victoria Institute, a body concentrating on apologetic questions, especially in the area of science, were other vehicles for the dissemination of the conservative position. Both were edited for a while by F. F. Bruce.[103] There was a direct effect on the pulpit. The systematic exposition of the meaning of scripture came into fashion.[104] It was partly in imitation of the pulpit giants, particularly John Stott and Martyn Lloyd-Jones. But it was also because the intellectual tools were now available. Although the weightiest theological publishing in Britain remained in the hands of the SCM Press, it became increasingly difficult to dismiss conservative Evangelicals as disinclined to thought.

REFORMED AND SECTARIAN WINGS

The IVF graduates' magazine announced in 1950 that there was to be a conference at Westminster Chapel on 'the distinctive theological contribution of the English Puritans'. It was the beginning of a revival of interest in the Reformed theological tradition, especially in the seventeenth century. The prime movers were two Oxford students, one of them J. I. Packer. The Minister of Westminster Chapel, Martyn Lloyd-Jones, became the enthusiastic chairman of an annual Puritan Conference.[105] A Welshman who left medicine to enter the ministry, Lloyd-Jones awed packed congregations with his blend of logic, fire and close attention to the text of scripture. He functioned (in his own words) as 'the theologian of the IVF'.[106] For Lloyd-Jones the preoccupation with the Puritans was no reversion to the Baroque, but an engagement with their thought to discover what was applicable today. He was not a seventeenth-century man, as he put it, but an eighteenth-century man who believed in 'using the seventeenth-century men as the eighteenth-century men used them'.[107] Neo–Puritanism became a potent force. In 1963, at its height, the Puritan Conference attracted some 350 people, the majority young.[108] To students at the time Reformed doctrine seemed 'very novel, intoxicating to some, unnerving to many'.[109] It was disseminated by the Evangelical Library, an institution built on a collection of Puritan divinity made by Geoffrey Williams, a Strict Baptist bibliophile.[110] *The Banner of Truth*, a monthly magazine, was launched in 1955 and a publishing house under the same name two years later.[111] By 1960 there was a warning from the Islington platform that ultra–Calvinist views were straining the unity of Anglican Evangelicals.[112] With the encouragement of Lloyd-Jones, the Evangelical Movement of Wales crystallised in 1955 around a magazine and annual conference to rally individuals disquieted by the theological laxity within their denominations. Though not unanimously Calvinist, that was its predominant tone.[113] In Scotland another mixed Evangelical circle with Reformed leadership gathered about the figure of William Still, Minister since 1945 of Gilcomston South Parish Church, Aberdeen, and another prominent personality in the IVF. Resolutely attached to the Church of Scotland, they assembled annually at Crieff from 1971. Ten years later 170 attended.[114] In its various forms the Reformed revival was a sign of the theological appetite in sections of the conservative Evangelical world. It simultaneously bolstered the strength of the growing conservative movement and injected a divisive element into its ranks.

Sectarian expressions of Evangelicalism continued to grow in the postwar era, though in most cases at a rather slower rate than before the war. By 1979 there were nearly 550 Assemblies of God and 350 Elim churches in England alone.[115] The Apostolic Church, the third force in British Pentecostalism, enjoyed its greatest support in Wales and Scotland, where its congregations were more numerous than those of the Assemblies or Elim.[116] Ordinary Evangelicals had normally repudiated the Pentecostalists.'The usual line of attack is to use threadbare illustrations of "unfortunate incidents" . . .'[117] It was generally held that the supernatural gifts championed by the Pentecostalists had ceased with the passing of the early church, so that alleged modern instances were counterfeit. The rise of the charismatic movement made it difficult – though not impossible for the hard-liners – to sustain that line of argument. Upward social mobility among the Pentecostalists also made their acceptance into the Evangelical fold smoother during the 1960s and 1970s. A fresh Pentecostal sector, however, had risen through immigration from the West Indies. Few black newcomers found their way into existing congregations, even Pentecostal churches. Instead, they established their own sects: the New Testament Church of God (with 23 congregations in 1962), the Church of God of Prophecy (16), the Church of God in Christ (7) and several smaller groupings.[118] As in many other spheres, there was little integration into Evangelical church life. The one existing body to recruit heavily among West Indians, the Seventh-Day Adventists, was generally accepted in conservative circles, even if some suspected that it should be classified with the heretical cults.[119] Likewise the Church of the Nazarene, an American denomination which the main holiness churches had joined, shared in local inter-church activities.[120] The sect which gave most to pan-Evangelical work, however, was the Brethren. Although its narrowest segment, the Exclusives, gained notoriety in a succession of scandals,[121] the mainstream of the Open Brethren emerged increasingly as a denomination willing to change with the times. 'Assemblies' transformed themselves into 'Evangelical Churches'. The traditional resistance to full-time ministry crumbled, so that by 1980 34 per cent of 246 churches surveyed thought it a good idea.[122] Eminent Brethren, as we have seen, served and financed the IVF and its satellites. Conservative Evangelicalism derived a great deal of vitality from its sectarian dimension.

INTO THE WORLD

A consequence of the rise of the conservative Evangelicals was a change in their habits. Their introverted attitudes in the 1940s cultivated a distinctive style: 'unworldly, diligent in attendance at weekly prayer meetings, meticulous about quiet times, suspicious of the arts, missionary-minded, hostile to new liturgical ideas.'[123] The decline of the Keswick imperative gradually opened them to change. In 1947 J. W. Wenham, who was to go on to teach at Tyndale Hall, Bristol, urged in an IVF newsletter that ministers should drop their blanket prohibitions on the cinema, the theatre and tobacco. They were erecting false barriers that hampered the gospel. A wider onslaught on Evangelical taboos was launched for similar reasons in a Scripture Union book, *Culture, Class and Christian Beliefs*, by John Benington in 1973. Such criticisms slowly sapped inhibitions, but far more came about through the social change of the 1960s. Permissiveness was echoed, albeit dimly, among Evangelicals. At Keele half the congress erupted into laughter about some indiscreet remarks on contraception; ten years later, young Christian nurses were sometimes prepared to justify abortion on demand and a few Evangelicals were arguing that homosexual acts within a stable relationship are 'not a contravention of the biblical teaching'.[124] The youth culture was married to the gospel. The Salvation Army's Joystrings, a group of guitar-playing girls, led the way in 1964.[125] Cliff Richard, a converted pop singer who contrived to remain at the top of his career for decades, provided continuing inspiration.[126] From 1974 there was an annual Christian rock festival, Greenbelt. *Buzz* magazine, begun in 1964, attained a circulation of more than 30,000 in 1981 by catering for the gospel pop teenage market.[127] By 1976 Gavin Reid, evangelistic secretary of the CPAS, was opening a musical event for youth fellowships with the remark, 'Let's have a feeling of wrapped-around-ness.'[128] In the same year, during an Evangelical teaching conference session on a simpler life-style, a 'young man with a wispy moustache and tie-dyed jeans spoke poignantly of collecting waste-paper in Australia'.[129] The gulf that had once yawned between the church and the world had virtually disappeared.

Until well into the 1960s, social involvement remained under the cloud of suspicion it had attracted in the 1920s. It was typical that after an innovatory paper on the social implications of the gospel at the National Assembly of Evangelicals in 1966, 'some members were suspicious of a return to "the social gospel" and called for a more direct "witness"'.[130] Yet there were persistent traditions of social commitment. The Salvation Army, without compromising its beliefs, resolutely served the needs of the body as well as those of the soul.[131] Organisations with unimpeachable conservative Evangelical credentials such as the London City Mission maintained a philanthropic role.[132] Archdeacon Hammond, the IVF's early theologian, also wrote on social ethics.[133] George Duncan of St Thomas's, Edinburgh, declared in 1948 that some Evangelicals might 'find a greater place than they do for matters of social reform, such as housing, etc. Even a casual glance at the Old Testament prophets shows how clearly God was and is concerned in these matters.'[134] The greatest ideological obstacle to the more forthright expression of such views was adventism. The premillennial teaching so widespread in conservative Evangelical circles directly inhibited social action. His expectation of the second event, wrote W. G. Channon, a rising young Baptist minister, in 1949, made him realise that it was not the business of the church to Christianise society. Rather, the church was to evangelise until, when God had called out his people, Christ would return.[135] In succeeding decades, however, premillennialism went into decline. A milestone was the publication in 1971 by Iain Murray of *The Puritan Hope*, a reassertion on historical grounds of the postmillennial position. The premillennial message was already disappearing from the Keswick platform, and by the 1970s it was ceasing to be a feature even of the Brethren. Many conservative Evangelicals, while adhering to the belief in a personal second coming guarded by the IVF basis of faith, moved more or less unconsciously to an amillennial view. With the fading of the gloomy opinion that the world was under imminent sentence of death, effort to improve it seemed more worthwhile. A pent-up potential for social involvement was released.

The times seemed to call for action. The permissive society challenged Evangelical Christians at a traditionally sensitive point, their defence of sexual morality. Many rallied to the support of Mary Whitehouse, whose National Viewers' and Listeners' Association was established in 1965 to stem the tide of sex and violence that seemed to be overwhelming the media.[136] Eddy Stride, Rector of Spitalfields and a former shop steward, who had long been censuring the complacency of the 'middle-class, inward-looking Church', participated in several public protests against pornography in 1970.[137] Several eminent Evangelicals were recruited to Lord Longford's investigation of pornography in the following year,[138] a year that witnessed an upsurge of symbolic action against 'moral pollution'. Dubbed 'Festival of Light' by the recently converted broadcaster, Malcolm Muggeridge, an embryonic organisation held local rallies throughout the country to illuminate warning beacons. The culmination was a rally in Trafalgar Square on 25 September, followed by a march to Hyde Park. Although not wholly Evangelical in support, its orientation is clear from the evidence that 84 per cent of attenders at a follow-up rally five years later saw evangelism as a better remedy than legislation for Britain's moral decline.[139] The organisation became permanent as the Nationwide Festival of Light, which subsequently branched into CARE Trust (for research) and CARE Campaigns (for pressure group activity). A similar semi-spontaneous movement arose in 1985–6 to oppose what seemed another symptom of permissiveness, the deregulation of Sunday shop opening hours. Support extended well beyond Evangelical ranks and, remarkably, intended government legislation was defeated by a revolt of backbench Conservative MPs.[140] The widest enthusiasm for public campaigns, as in the nineteenth century, appeared when the target, in Evangelical eyes, was sin. Much of the renewed impetus for socio-political action sprang from an eagerness to take up broadly moral issues.

Sheer need did, however, play its part in prompting action. The dimensions of poverty in the Third World led, in 1968, to the creation of The Evangelical Alliance Relief (TEAR) Fund, which rapidly tapped funds from congregations that previously might have hesitated to give to Christian Aid. A symptom of changing attitudes was the supersession, around 1970, of the traditional vast arrays of produce at harvest festivals by token displays accompanied by collections for TEAR Fund. The Fund gave rise in 1974 to Tearcraft, an enterprise marketing goods from less developed countries, and that in turn to Traidcraft, an independent company with similar aims. Extremely influential in this field was R. J. Sider's *Rich Christians in an Age of Hunger* (1977), a biblical case for aid to the Third World originally aimed at an American audience. The multiple deprivation of the inner cities at home acted as a significant, if lesser, stimulus. David Sheppard, Warden of the Mayflower Centre in the East End of London and subsequently Bishop of Liverpool, set up a range of social programmes that he at first conceived as evangelistic bridges.[141] Subsequently his work *Built as a City* (1974) espoused and inspired more adventurous strategies of mission. The Frontier Youth Trust and later the Evangelical Coalition for Urban Mission pioneered fresh ventures. At the Nottingham National Evangelical Anglican Congress of 1977 a section not in the draft was added to the published statement on 'The gospel in urban areas'.[142] Inner-city issues were sufficiently salient to force themselves on the attention of at least a section of the Evangelical public.

Overseas influences helped to foster the new social awareness. Participation in ecumenical life made Evangelicals take up a stance on social questions, even if at first it was largely a repudiation of the policies publicised by the World Council of Churches. The 1968 Uppsala assembly of the WCC, by defining the mission of the church in partly socio-political terms, compelled self-scrutiny by those propounding an alternative view.[143] Dutch Reformed social thought stemming from Abraham Kuyper and Hermann Dooyeweerd was a more constructive factor. Its advocates in Britain were few, but in the late 1960s included Alan Storkey, a pioneer of Evangelical social analysis and subsequently the author of *A Christian Social Perspective* (1979). Influences from America were more widespread but more diffuse, tending to reinforce rather than initiate trends in British opinion. An exception must be made for writings from the Mennonite tradition. In particular, J. H. Yoder's work *The Politics of Jesus* (1972) fostered a new sympathy for a theologically grounded pacifism among British Evangelicals. The writings of Jim Wallis of the Sojourners' Community were also popular. From 1974, furthermore, there was international sanction for Evangelical social commitment. At Lausanne a congress on world evangelisation expressed repentance for previous Evangelical neglect in this field. The statement was partly a British achievement, a result of a strong rebuke by John Stott. Yet a Radical Discipleship group wished to go further in stating the social implications of the gospel. Led by Samuel Escobar, a South American who had grafted elements of liberation theology on to Evangelicalism, it called for a dedication to freedom, justice and human fulfilment.[144] The relationship between evangelism and social activity was more closely defined by a conference at Grand Rapids in 1982. 'They are like the two blades of a pair of scissors', its report declared, 'or the two wings of a bird.'[145] The British experience was part of a worldwide trend that steadily gathered momentum.

The increased emphasis on social responsibility also possessed its own national dynamic. The mushrooming of sociology in postwar British universities was bound to have consequences in a movement so strongly moulded by graduates. When IVF threw its weight behind social involvement, the trend was unstoppable. In this process the appearance of *Whose World?* (1970), a summons to formulate a Christian mind on all aspects of human affairs, was crucial. Its author, though cautiously employing a pseudonym, was Oliver Barclay, the IVF General Secretary. The Shaftesbury Project, designed to promote thought and action in every sphere of involvement, was developed by Alan Storkey on the fringe of the IVF from 1969 onwards. Its third director, John Gladwin, moved directly to become Secretary of the Board for Social Responsibility of the Church of England in 1982.[146] More systematic training in relating the faith to the forces at work in the modern world was provided by the London Institute for Contemporary Christianity, a brainchild created by John Stott after his retirement from All Souls' in 1975. Unfettered discussion of such questions was found from 1977 in the pages of *Third Way*, a fortnightly (then monthly) magazine that reached a circulation of more than 3,000 ten years later. Its readership breakdown in 1986 is illuminating: 52 per cent read *The Guardian* and 32 per cent *The Times*. By contrast, at the National Evangelical Anglican Congress in 1977, 60 per cent took *The Daily Telegraph*.[147] Evangelicals now included a liberally minded wing bearing no resemblance to the interwar stereotype of their forefathers. In expanding they had broadened.

GROWING PAINS

The diversity of the Evangelical movement created tensions. Several surrounded the figure of Martyn Lloyd-Jones, an Independent by temperament and conviction.[148] He was regularly prepared to pursue a distinctive line of policy, standing aside, for example, from Billy Graham's crusades as a cheapening of the gospel.[149] Partly through the Westminster Fellowship, an interdenominational ministers' fraternal that met in his chapel from the end of the war, Lloyd-Jones came to enjoy widespread and deeply felt respect.[150] The tercentenary in 1962 of the Great Ejection of Nonconformist ministers from the Church of England turned his mind to the issue of what unity Evangelicals should prize. In 1963 he spoke to the Puritan Conference about John Owen on schism.[151] On 18 October 1966 an incident took place that was to dramatise a fracture in the Evangelical world. Lloyd-Jones was invited to speak at the opening public meeting of the National Assembly of Evangelicals on the issue of unity. To the horror of members of his audience who valued their existing denominational allegiances, he urged that, although separation from liberals was no schism, separation from fellow Evangelicals was. Immediately afterwards John Stott rose from the chair to voice his belief that scripture was against the speaker – an act, though not an opinion, he subsequently regretted.[152] Lloyd-Jones's call for Evangelicals to leave their present churches was dismissed by nearly all those in the Church of England as being (in the phrase of their newspaper) 'nothing short of hare-brained',[153] and in other 'mixed denominations' he was little heeded. The appeal nevertheless reinforced the existing aversion of the Baptist Revival Fellowship to the ecumenical movement as an engine for compromising the truth and, during the next few years, just as Lloyd-Jones took Westminster Chapel out of the Congregational Union, so a number of Baptists withdrew from their Union. The Federation of Independent Evangelical Churches was immeasurably strengthened by Lloyd-Jones's support; the Evangelical Movement of Wales in 1967 permitted churches disenchanted with their previous denominations to affiliate direct;[154] and *The Evangelical Times* was launched in the same year as the monthly organ of principled separatism. A British Evangelical Council, formed in 1953 and also backed by Lloyd-Jones, acted as an umbrella organisation for the anti-ecumenical bodies. Enjoying the membership of the Free Church of Scotland, by 1981 it could claim to represent more than 2,000 congregations.[155] Predominantly but by no means exclusively Reformed in theological tone, it represented a significant force in the Evangelical World.

Some of the strains engendered by charismatic renewal have already been considered. Its separatist wing, the Restorationists, formed a rapidly expanding Christian presence in the 1980s.[156] But the assimilation of the renewal movement by existing churches was perhaps the more remarkable development. At Keele in 1967 there was no united opinion about whether charismatic manifestations were of the same sort as the New Testament 'gifts of the Spirit'.[157] By contrast, ten years later at the Nottingham Evangelical Anglican Congress, hands were raised in worship and charismatic leaders including Michael Harper and David Watson delivered addresses. Only a few jarring notes were heard. Gerald Bray, librarian of Tyndale House and subsequently editor of *Churchman*, for example, voiced continuing doctrinal misgivings about the movement. In general, however, as Harper remarked, 'the charismatic divide was given the last rites'. So deeply enmeshed in Evangelical Anglican life had the movement become between 1967 and 1977 that one commentator spoke, with perhaps a little exaggeration, of 'a dominating position for charismatics'.[158] Among Baptists, the Mainstream organisation formed in 1979 drew together traditional Evangelicals and charismatics in regular conferences.[159] One of its founders, Paul Beasley-Murray, went on to become Principal of Spurgeon's, the denomination's largest college, in 1986. Although there were many instances of local tension, overall the Baptists were adapting to the new influences. The British Evangelical Council could not manage the same feat. Sympathy for renewal was anathema to hard-line Reformed views, and, after strenuous efforts at containment, the issue eventually exploded with the seizure of *The Evangelical Times* by the anti-charismatics in 1986.[160] The new style represented by the charismatic movement proved acceptable to a majority of Evangelicals in the older denominations, but not to most of those who frowned on ecumenical involvement. Were the cultural forms of the twentieth century to be accepted or rejected? There were the makings of polarisation around this fundamental question.

There were signs of divergence around another issue, the interpretation of the Bible. If one consideration had been paramount among interwar conservative Evangelicals, it was the appeal to the text of scripture. In the postwar era, however, the proliferation of Bible versions meant that variations in the text were in widespread circulation. Although more than half the attenders at a Keswick youth meeting in 1970 still read the Authorised Version,[161] by that date the Revised Standard Version was in general use. The New English Bible attracted only a small following among Evangelicals, but the Good News Bible and then the New International Version achieved high popularity.[162] Discrepancies made it harder to settle issues by quoting biblical texts. Consequently, criteria were needed for establishing what the Bible meant. As was pointed out in 1974 by Tony Thiselton, subsequently Principal of St John's College, Durham, this was the question of hermeneutics. It was particularly acute when trying to tease out biblical teaching on ethics for application to the social problems of the day.[163] It was also a difficulty for Evangelicals as they took opposite sides on the question of whether women should be ordained in the Church of England.[164] Opponents pointed to the letter of scripture about women not having authority over men and keeping silence in church; supporters suggested that the statement about the barrier between male and female having been abolished in Christ took precedence. Hermeneutics was a pressing matter. The word was bandied about, with much ribald comment, at Nottingham in 1977.[165] Some were alarmed that the authority of scripture was being undermined. Dick Lucas, Rector of St Helen's, Bishopsgate, warned the 1979 Islington Conference that the new hermeneutic might prepare the way for a fresh bout of liberal scholarship.[166] The threatening storm burst in 1982 over two articles in *Churchman* by James Dunn, soon to be Professor of Divinity at Durham, propounding a view of the Bible that was too liberal for some of the journal's sponsors.[167] In the succeeding dispute, the editor was dismissed, a new editorial board formed and the dispossessed party founded a fresh journal, *Anvil*, in 1984. Thiselton, significantly, was on the Anvil Trust. In 1986 J. I. Packer was still having to give a steadying address to the Anglican Evangelical Assembly on hermeneutics.[168] The Bible was no longer treated as a simple unifying force in the Evangelical world. It had become a bone of contention.

Evangelicals in the Church of England faced another issue around 1980, but it was less a controversy and more a mood of self-doubt. It was labelled 'the Evangelical Anglican identity problem'. By the later 1970s traditional landmarks had been removed. An attempt by some older Evangelicals at Nottingham to insert a reference to the Thirty-Nine Articles and the Book of Common Prayer in the Congress statement came to naught.[169] Basics had already been brought into question. We need to ask, according to a leading article in *The Church of England Newspaper* on David Sheppard's *Built as a City*, 'whether the traditional evangelical understanding of the Gospel is in fact as biblical as it is often assumed to be'.[170] At Nottingham the statement admitted that 'we give different emphasis to the various biblical expressions of atonement': substitution was no longer central for all.[171] The party, as J. I. Packer commented in a booklet on the identity problem, was less cohesive at Nottingham than at Keele.[172] Although the number of self-professed Evangelicals in the General Synod increased from 1970 to 1980, their solidarity weakened.[173] '*The* great question-mark', according to Colin Buchanan, 'which had to be hung against the proposal that "we" should hold another Congress in 1977 was whether there existed any identifiable "we" to do it'.[174] John Stott's answer to such queries was unequivocal. They were committed to Bible and gospel, and so could not drop the title 'Evangelical'.[175] Yet debate continued for the next couple of years.[176] Institutional measures were taken to consolidate the party. Since 1960 a Church of England Evangelical Council had brought together representative leaders, and from 1980 there were broader consultations.[177] Since 1983 there has been an Anglican Evangelical Assembly with a combination of elected and nominated members, which at last supplanted Islington as the party's main forum.[178] The possibility of merging imperceptibly into the mainstream of church life seemed to have been averted.

LOOKING TO THE FUTURE

The heirs of the interwar conservative Evangelical tradition remained a distinctive movement, cutting across denominational allegiances, after the time of Keele. Though more fragmented, they were still conscious of an underlying unity. It is possible to locate their loyalties more precisely. Their greatest strength lay in the Anglican and Baptist denominations. At the first National Assembly of Evangelicals in 1965, Anglicans were reported to be easily the largest single group amongst them, with Baptists second.[179] At the same event the following year, about a quarter were Anglican and a quarter Baptist.[180] In 1985–6 readers of *Third Way* were 49 per cent Anglican and 22 per cent Baptist.[181] Attenders at the 1976 Festival of Light rally were 42 per cent Anglican and 22 per cent Baptist. Pentecostal churches and charismatic house fellowships contributed 9 per cent, Evangelical or Free Evangelical churches 6 per cent, Methodists 5 per cent and Brethren 3 per cent to this gathering.[182] All these figures are affected by – among other factors – their exaggerated reflection of the denominational balance in South-East England. A northern catchment area might have strengthened the Methodist presence: there had been since 1970 an organisation called Conservative Evangelicals in Methodism,[183] and many Methodists outside it remained Evangelicals. In Wales Anglicans would have been far less numerous, and in Scotland Presbyterians would have been significantly represented. The future of the Evangelical movement nevertheless lay disproportionately in the hands of two denominations. In 1986, for the first time, more than half the Anglican ordinands in residential colleges were said to be Evangelical.[184] Alone among the Free Churches, the Baptists reported growth in 1987.[185] The continuing expansion of the Restorationists would in due course affect the balance, the Church of Scotland possessed an increasing Evangelical sector, and the conservative bodies of the British Evangelical Council had emerged with a rugged tenacity. The kaleidoscope of Evangelicalism would turn again to create a new pattern. But growth was intended and expected. The movement was likely to occupy a more salient position within British Christianity in the twenty-first century than in the twentieth.

[9]

Time and Chance:
Evangelicalism and Change

. . . time and chance happeneth to them all. (Eccles. 9:11)

Evangelical religion in Britain has changed immensely during the two and a half centuries of its existence. Its outward expressions, such as its social composition and political attitudes, have frequently been transformed. Its inward principles, embracing teaching about Christian theology and behaviour, have altered hardly less. Nothing could be further from the truth than the common image of Evangelicalism being ever the same. Yet Evangelicals themselves have often fostered the image. They have claimed that their brand of Christianity, the form once delivered to the saints, has possessed an essentially changeless content so long as it has remained loyal to its source. In a Commons debate of 1850 a Unitarian referred to discoveries in theology since the reign of Elizabeth I. 'Discoveries in theology!' snorted Sir Robert Inglis, an Evangelical defender of the Church of England: '. . . all the truths of religion are to be found in the blessed Bible; and all "discoveries" which do not derive from that book their origin and foundation, their justification and their explanation, are worth neither teaching nor hearing.'[1] Such a claim to stability is a common feature of conservative Protestantism.[2] It is no wonder that outsiders, taking Evangelicals at their word, have often treated them as perversely impervious to change and so perennially old-fashioned. The germ of truth in that claim is that Evangelical religion has been consistently marked by four characteristics. Conversionism, activism, biblicism and crucicentrism have been transmitted down the generations. They have formed a permanent deposit of faith. Each of the characteristics, however, has found expression in many different ways, and one of them, activism, was a novelty that set Evangelicals apart from earlier Protestantism. Other features of Evangelical doctrine and piety, opinion and practice, have varied from time to time. Views on eschatology and spirituality have been particularly subject to change. So the movement did not manage a total escape to a world of eternal truths. It was bound up in the flux of events.

The reality was sometimes noticed by evangelicals themselves. The great nineteenth-century Congregationalist R. W. Dale was acutely aware of the changing theological fashions within the movement.[3] Occasionally it was recognised that change was not merely a matter of theology. 'To say that the Church has remained unaffected by influences permeating our national life', declared the Secretary of the National Sunday School Union in 1900 when analysing the altered tone of teaching during the previous half-century, 'would be to assert that we are independent of our social environment'.[4] But it was not until the Lausanne Congress of 1974 that it was commonly admitted by Evangelicals that the shape of their religion is influenced by the environment. Evidence from the mission field that the embodiment of the faith is deeply affected by its cultural setting seemed incontrovertible.[5] What this study has explored is the same interaction between Christianity and its setting in Britain.

Changing socio-economic and political conditions affected Evangelicalism and its potential recruits in ways that drastically moulded its size, self-image, strategy and teaching. When personally controlled firms became large-scale conglomerates, for example, it was no longer expected that employees would follow the religious preferences – often Evangelical – of their employers. New wealth permitted the state to provide educational and philanthropic facilities that had previously been supplied by the churches, and so to weaken the bonds between working-class people and evangelistic agencies. Such forces decreased church attendance around the end of the nineteenth century, sapped Christian confidence and so encouraged attempts to remodel Evangelicalism with a view to improving its impact. Again, political crises over Ireland, conjuring up the spectre of papist oppression, often stirred up the powerful spirit of anti-Catholicism. The First World War provoked heart-searching questions about doctrines surrounding the fate of the dead. Events in the public realm necessarily impinged on religious groups. Yet socio-economic and political developments fashioned Evangelical responses from the raw material of their existing attitudes. With other opinions they would have reacted differently. The cultural context, not economics or politics, does most to explain the shape of Evangelical religion. Conditions and crises in economic and political life might generate new phases of behaviour and even new expressions of belief, but rarely did they determine fundamental trends in Evangelical life. That role was normally reserved for the dominant ideas of the age.

The most influential bodies of thought were not distinctly religious. It is frequently assumed, especially by church historians, that theologians were the crucial innovators. Authors like F. D. Maurice are treated as the trend-setters for subsequent generations. Theologians, however, have usually been followers of trends set in other fields. Maurice, for instance, was deeply swayed by the organic view of society that was the hallmark of Romantic theorists.[6] Lay opinion was more affected by the general cultural atmosphere than by Maurice's expression of it. The basic trends in Evangelicalism were shaped by the shifts in cultural mood that eventually altered the orientation of the whole population. Changes in the intellectual climate have a significant impact on any social movement setting great store by ideas, whether political, educational or religious. Churches, which usually carry heavy doctrinal baggage, are particularly susceptible. Hence Christian beliefs and practices have reflected developments in high culture. The novelties of the philosophers and creative artists have been transmitted, often after some delay, to the Evangelical world. The crucial determinants of change in Evangelical religion have been the successive cultural waves that have broken over Western civilisation since the late seventeenth century. Popular Protestantism has been remoulded in turn by the Enlightenment of Locke, the Romanticism of Coleridge and the Modernism associated with, among others, the Bloomsbury Group. That is not to suggest that the currents of high cultural ideas have flowed clear and crystal between Evangelical shores. On the contrary, the streams have been muddied by other influences and at some stages have even run underground. The doctrines derived most clearly from shifts in taste in the intellectual *avant-garde* have subsequently been modified within Evangelicalism. Thus the holiness teaching of the later nineteenth century, very much a symptom of the Romantic inclinations of the period, was adapted to fit the Calvinist theological inheritance of its Anglican proponents. The resulting Keswick school was far from being simply a product of the contemporary intellectual climate. Yet what was distinctive about it did derive primarily from the spirit of the age, and can be understood only in that light.

The process of change can best be seen as a pattern of diffusion. Ideas originating in high culture have spread to leaders of Evangelical opinion and through them to the Evangelical constituency. By this means the novelties of one age have become the commonplaces of the next. Alongside the secular press, popular Protestantism has been among the chief agencies for the transmission of innovating ideas from the tiny cultural elite that forms them to the mass of the population that embraces them, often unaware of their origins. The diffusion has had two main dimensions, the social and the spatial. Ideas, that is to say, have spread downwards from the elite to the masses and outwards from the centre to the periphery. Groups higher in the social scale, usually enjoying higher standards of education, tend to absorb fresh attitudes earlier than lower groups.[7] They are the ones who usually read books and magazines first. But then the newer views seep down to lower social groups. Wilberforce, writing in 1797, recognised that 'the free and unrestrained intercourse, subsisting amongst the several ranks and classes of society, so much favours the general diffusion of the sentiments of the higher orders'.[8] The variation according to position on the social scale helps explain why, within Evangelicalism, Anglicans, with their strong support among the gentry and professionals, were normally more forward than Nonconformists in embracing new cultural attitudes.

Thus it was Anglicans, together with the socially superior Brethren and Catholic Apostolic Church, who disproportionately favoured the novel premillennialism of the nineteenth century. But the relation between elite and masses in the churches has never been founded on class distinctions alone. The ministry constituted a body of professional opinion-formers. Consequently, ideas would often reach a congregation first through the minister. Lower-class congregations could sometimes be charged with fresh enthusiasms before neighbours of more exalted social standing. Yet the general principle remains valid. Cultural diffusion within Evangelicalism was normally a matter of the percolation of ideas down the social scale.

The second dimension was spatial, the spread of new ideas outwards from cultural centres. Personal contacts, and especially addresses at conferences, were at least as important as literature in the dissemination of Evangelical novelties. Hence some areas would adopt new attitudes long before others. New teaching would normally be welcomed in London long before it was appreciated in the South-West or the North of England, let alone the remoter parts of Wales and Scotland. Although the difference between the regions was partly a matter of ingrained local preferences, which have survived the industrial and communications revolutions to a far greater extent than is normally recognised,[9] the spatial variation was far more the result of differing degrees of proximity to the sources of fresh waves of opinion, and especially to London. Most trends of thought seized the capital and its environs first – whether Hugh Price Hughes's social gospel or charismatic renewal. Metropolitan views took time to spread elsewhere. There was no direct correlation, however, between distance from London and the rapidity with which new opinion was taken up. The great cities functioned as subsidiary cultural centres, radiating outwards to their own hinterlands influences received from London, supplemented by occasional indigenous developments. Manchester, Bristol, Edinburgh and similar places ensured that trends spread in their own vicinities before they had affected areas nearer London that lacked a major urban focus – Suffolk, for example. There were also local centres of influence, often some sort of Evangelical training college (such as the Methodist Cliff College in Derbyshire), that spread particular messages in their own neighbourhoods. The general effect of spatial diffusion was to put more urbanised areas ahead of more rural parts, but that pattern was far from absolute since local centres or even individual enthusiasts could propagate new ideas in unexpected spots.[10] National variations were overridden in a pattern that straddled the boundaries between England, Wales and Scotland, so that developments usually affected Swansea before Herefordshire and Glasgow before Westmorland. It was in the periphery of Britain that the old ways lingered longest.[11] Traditional revivals in the twentieth century, for instance, have taken place chiefly in Wales, Cornwall, East Anglia, the Moray Firth coast of Scotland and the Hebrides. Spatial diffusion explains a great deal about the state of Evangelicalism.

The deepest divisions in the Evangelical world generally arose from the impact of the cultural waves. Denominational splits form an excellent index to the advance of fresh ideas. Repeatedly, new wine broke old bottles. Methodism, representing undiluted Enlightenment Protestantism, generated a momentum that carried it, despite John Wesley's wishes, beyond the bounds of the Church of England. The severance between New Lights and Old Lights in Scottish Presbyterian Dissent showed the impossibility of those who thought like Jonathan Edwards of remaining in fellowship with those adhering to the thought-world of the Westminster Confession. The same pre-Evangelical Calvinism was the ground from which certain Baptists in the South-East of England and Presbyterians in the North-West of Scotland refused to be dislodged. Hence there arose the Strict Baptists and the Free Presbyterians. The initial onset of Romanticism gave rise in the 1830s to two premillennialist bodies, the Catholic Apostolic Church and the Brethren. Its subsequent impact in the form of holiness teaching led to the foundation of bodies such as the Salvation Army and the Pentecostalists. Premillennialism, its associated attitude to the Bible and the holiness movement together created the matrix of interwar conservative Evangelicalism with all its tendencies to fission. And charismatic renewal, so largely an expression of cultural Modernism, could not be confined within existing structures, but also erected its own. That is not to say that every denominational split in the period can be traced back to a clash of cultural styles: on the contrary, several Methodist secessions and the Disruption of the Church of Scotland were the result of conflicts about control of institutions. Differences stemming from shifts of cultural mood can nevertheless be detected within and between congregations of the same denomination throughout the period. Deep-seated theological debates such as the Robertson Smith affair or the Down Grade Controversy were usually about whether truth was being compromised by the intellectual trends of the times. The assimilation of new ideas was naturally unsettling.

Because Evangelicalism has changed so much over time, any attempt to equate it with 'Fundamentalism' is doomed to failure. It is often assumed that the equation can be made; and a substantial treatise published by James Barr in 1977 identified the Fundamentalism of its title at least with the conservative variety of Evangelicalism in the postwar period.[12] Evangelicals, including conservatives, have generally repudiated the term in Britain.[13] If the word is used in a precise theological sense, then it defines a deductive approach to biblical inspiration, the belief that since the Bible is the word of God and God cannot err, the Bible is inerrant. That has been a current in Evangelicalism since the 1820s, but it never became unanimous and was weak in the early twentieth century, even among conservatives. Its greater popularity in the postwar period has been associated primarily with the esteem of the Reformed wing of Evangelicalism for B. B. Warfield and it has been treated with reserve by others.[14] If 'Fundamentalism' is taken in a social sense to describe a group so fanatically committed to its religion that it lashes out against opponents in mindless denunciation, there were only two stages when this unsavoury attitude disfigured Evangelicalism. Between about 1840 and 1890 many Anglican Evangelicals became obsessive in the desire to eliminate Romanising doctrines and ritual from their church; and in the aftermath of the First World War an extreme section of Evangelical opinion, though not the conservative leadership, attempted to take up the fight of their American cousins against 'Modernist' theological tendencies. In Britain such Fundamentalism – Evangelicalism with an inferiority complex – was at most times relatively weak. Only if Fundamentalism is defined in a third way, as the championing of fundamental Christian orthodoxies, can the term be applied to the Evangelical movement as a whole with any degree of plausibility. Even then, some of the more liberal thinkers within the movement would have been unhappy in that role. It is best to admit that Fundamentalism in any sense has been merely one feature among many, at some times and in some places, of Evangelical religion.

Lord Salisbury, the Conservative Prime Minister at the end of the nineteenth century, entertained a distaste for Evangelicalism. He wrote of its 'reign of rant' and 'nasal accents of devout ejaculation', and again of its 'incubus of narrow-mindedness . . . brooding over English society'.[15] The narrowness of Evangelical life has been a frequent reproach. It is true that its tendency to erect barriers against worldliness often did make it a restricted sphere. Its large claims and internal idiosyncrasies made it an easy target for cheap satire. Yet it has shaped the thought-world of a large proportion of the population. It has exerted an immense influence both on individuals and on the course of social and political development, particularly in the later nineteenth century. And it has shown a receptivity that goes some way towards modifying the charge of narrowness. Evangelical religion has been in contact with shifts in the mood of the intellectual elite. Like so many other aspects of British life, from political rhetoric to wallpaper design, it was affected by alterations in taste. In mediating high cultural changes to a mass public it brought its adherents into the mainstream of Western civilisation. Certainly Evangelicalism created its own backwaters, but overall it was no stagnant pool. The process of diffusion meant that the world of popular Protestantism was in flux. There was enormous variation in Evangelicalism over time; and at any particular moment there was an intricate pattern of beliefs, attitudes and customs. So there was an element of breadth – a broad range of opinion – that could be obscure to the eye of the contemporary observer and has all too frequently been overlooked by the historian. Moulded and remoulded by its environment, Evangelical religion has been a vital force in modern Britain.

Notes

ABBREVIATIONS USED IN THE NOTES

AFR	Anglicans for Renewal
AW	The Advent Witness
BC	The Bible Call
BW	The British Weekly
C	The Christian
CEN	Church of England Newspaper
CG	Christian Graduate
CO	The Christian Observer
CW	The Christian World
F	The Fundamentalist
JEH	The Journal of Ecclesiastical History
JWBU	The Journal of the Wesley Bible Union (which took the title The Fundamentalist in 1927)
KH	The King's Highway
LCMM	The London City Mission Magazine
LE	The Liberal Evangelical
LF	The Life of Faith
LW	Life and Work
MBAPPU	The Monthly Bulletin of the Advent Preparation Prayer Union
MR	The Methodist Recorder
MT	The Methodist Times
R	The Record
T	The Times
W	The Witness
WV	Wesley's Veterans, ed. J. Telford (London, n.d.)

CHAPTER 1: PREACHING THE GOSPEL

1 R. T. Jones, *The Great Reformation* (Leicester, 1985) G. Rupp, *Religion in England, 1688–1791* (Oxford, 1986), pp. 121, 125.
2 G. R. Balleine, *A History of the Evangelical Party in the Church of England* (London, 1951 edn), p. 40 n. Other general studies of Anglican Evangelicalism are: G. W. E. Russell, *A Short History of the Evangelical*

Movement (London, 1915); L. Elliott-Binns, *The Evangelical Movement in the English Church* (London, 1928); and D. N. Samuel (ed.) *The Evangelical Succession in the Church of England* (Cambridge, 1979). On the broader movement there is E. J. Poole-Connor, *Evangelicalism in England* (Worthing, 1966 edn).

3 Watts, preface to J. Jennings, *Two Discourses* (1723), quoted by G. F. Nuttall, 'Continental Pietism and the Evangelical Movement in Britain', in J. van den Berg and J. P. van Dooren (eds), *Pietismus und Reveil* (Leiden, 1978), p. 226.

4 The term is studiously avoided in Sir H.M. Wellwood, *Account of the Life and Writings of John Erskine, D.D.* (Edinburgh, 1818).

5 J. Milner, 'On Evangelical religion', *The Works of Joseph Milner*, ed. I. Milner, Vol. 8 (London, 1810), p. 199.

6 For example, T. Haweis to S. Walker, 16 July 1759, in G. C. B. Davies, *The Early Cornish Evangelicals, 1735–60: A Study of Walker of Truro and Others* (London, 1951), p. 174; cf. J. D. Walsh, 'The Yorkshire Evangelicals in the eighteenth century: with especial reference to Methodism', PhD thesis, University of Cambridge, 1956, appendix D.

7 The alternative usage of applying 'Evangelical' to the Anglican party and 'evangelical' to others of like mind outside the Church of England can be misleading. It has been adopted by E. Jay (*The Religion of the Heart: Anglican Evangelicalism and the Nineteenth-Century Novel* (Oxford, 1979), ch. 1, sect. 1, esp. p. 17) in order to deny the 'common spiritual parentage' of Anglicans and non-Anglicans in the movement. In reality, for all their divergences, their common inheritance was far more significant than this usage suggests.

8 E. Hodder, *The Life and Work of the Seventh Earl of Shaftesbury, K.G.* (London, 1888), p. 738.

9 H. Venn (ed.), *The Life and a Selection from the Letters of the late Rev. Henry Venn, M.A.* (London, 1835), pp. vii f.

10 J. C. Ryle, *Knots Untied* (London, 1896 edn), p. 9.

11 D. Voll, *Catholic Evangelicalism: The Acceptance of Evangelical Traditions by the Oxford Movement during the Second Half of the Nineteenth Century* (London, 1963).

12 G. W. E. Russell, 'Recollections of the Evangelicals', *The Household of Faith* (London, 1902), pp. 240 f., 245.

13 Wesley, 'The new birth', *The Works of John Wesley*, Vol. 2, ed. A. C. Outler (Nashville, Tenn., 1985), p. 187.

14 *Life of Ann Okely*, quoted by J. Walsh, 'The Cambridge Methodists', in P. Brooks (ed.), *Christian Spirituality: Essays in Honour of Gordon Rupp* (London, 1975), p. 258.

15 Milner, 'On Evangelical religion', pp. 201–5.

16 *R*, 2 May 1850.

17 R. W. Dale, *The Old Evangelicalism and the New* (London, 1889), p. 13.

18 Ryle, *Knots Untied*, pp. 4–9.

19 Garbett (ed.), *Evangelical Principles* (London, 1875), p. xiv.

20 *C*, 5 October 1888, p. 5.

21 Warren, *What is an Evangelical? An Enquiry* (London, [1944]), pp. 18–39.

22 J. R. W. Stott, *What is an Evangelical?* (London, 1977), pp. 5–14.

23 Packer, *The Evangelical Anglican Identity Problem*, Latimer House Studies, 1 (Oxford, 1978), pp. 20 ff.

24 G. W. McCree, *George Wilson McCree* (London, 1893), p. 20.

25 *WV*, Vol. 1, pp. 74 f.

26 *C*, 15 July 1875, p. 19.

27 N. G. Dunning, *Samuel Chadwick* (London, 1933), p. 54.

28 M. C. Bickersteth, *A Sketch of the Life and Episcopate of the Right Reverend Robert Bickersteth, D.D., Bishop of Ripon, 1857–1887* (London, 1887), pp. 27 f.

29 Edwards, 'The distinguishing marks of a work of the true Spirit', *Select Works*, Vol. 1 (London, 1965), p. 106. Walsh, 'Yorkshire Evangelicals', p. 290. J. Lackington, *Memoirs of the Forty-Five First Years of the Life of James Lackington* (London, 1795), p. 161.

30 T.D.B. in *CO*, January 1852, p. 3.

31 W. Hanna, *Memoirs of the Life and Writings of Thomas Chalmers, D.D., LL.D.*, Vol. 1 (Edinburgh, 1851), ch. 8.

32 Haslam, *From Death into Life* (London, n.d.), p. 48.

33 Venn, *The Complete Duty of Man*, 3rd edn (London, 1779), p. xi.

34 Russell, 'Recollections of the Evangelicals', p. 238.

35 Dale, *Old Evangelicalism and the New*, pp. 51–7.

36 *Evangel*, Summer 1987.

37 *The Journal of the Rev. John Wesley, A.M.*, ed. N. Curnock, Vol. 2 (London, 1911), pp. 333 f. (25 January 1740).

38 R. A. Knox, *Enthusiasm* (Oxford, 1950), ch. 21.

39 Warren, *What is an Evangelical?*, p. 26.

40 G. W. E. Russell, *Mr Gladstone's Religious Development* (London, 1899), p. 7.

41 C. D. Field, 'Methodism in Metropolitan London, 1850–1920: a social and sociological study', DPhil thesis, University of Oxford, 1975, p. 232.

42 *On the Other Side: The Report of the Evangelical Alliance's Commission on Evangelism* (London, 1968), p. 184.

43 A. T. Pierson, *Forward Movements of the Last Half Century* (New York, 1900), p. 207.

44 G. W. E. Russell, *Sir Wilfrid Lawson* (London, 1909), pp. 3 f. J. Burgess, *The Lake Counties and Christianity: The Religious History of Cumbria, 1780–1920* (Carlisle, 1984), pp. 88–95.

45 Edwards, 'A narrative of surprising conversions', *Select Works*, Vol. 1, p. 40.

46 Simeon, 'On the new birth', in A. Pollard (ed.), *Let Wisdom Judge: University Addresses and Sermon Outlines by Charles Simeon* (London, 1959), p. 51.

47 G. Redford and J. A. James (eds), *The Autobiography of William Jay*, 2nd edn (London, 1855), p. 22.

48 For example, *WV*, Vol. 4, p. 19 (J. Pawson).

49 *Revival*, 21 January 1860, p. 21.

50 R. Carwardine, *Transatlantic Revivalism: Popular Evangelicalism in Britain and America, 1790–1865* (Westport, Conn., 1978), p. 125.

51 M. Raleigh (ed.), *Alexander Raleigh: Records of his Life* (Edinburgh, 1881), p. 15.

52 J. Cox, *The English Churches in a Secular Society: Lambeth, 1870–1930* (New York, 1982), pp. 248 f.

53 J. Milner, 'The nature of the Spirit's influence on the understanding', *Works*, ed. I. Milner, Vol. 8.

54   Carwardine, *Transatlantic Revivalism*, pp. xiv, 63, 99.
55   Horton, *An Autobiography* (London, 1917), p. 37.
56   O. Chadwick, *The Victorian Church*, Vol. 1, 2nd edn (London, 1970), pp. 250–62.
57   D. M. Thompson, 'Baptism, Church and Society in Britain since 1800', Hulsean Lectures, University of Cambridge, 1984, pp. 12–17.
58   G. Bugg, *Spiritual Regeneration Not Necessarily Connected with Baptism* (Kettering, 1816). [C. Marsh], *The Life of the Rev. William Marsh, D.D.* (London, 1867), p. 131.
59   Sumner, *Apostolical Preaching Considered, in an Examination of St Paul's Epistles* (London, 1815), p. 137 n.
60   Walker, *The Gospel Commission* (Edinburgh, 1826).
61   W. Y. Fullerton, *C. H. Spurgeon* (London, 1920), pp. 305 ff.
62   *Auricular Confession and Priestly Absolution: Lord Ebury's Prayer-Book Amendment Bill* (London, 1880), p. 2.
63   *CEN*, 5 February 1965, p. 7.
64   Edwards, 'Narrative', p. 47.
65   J. Bull, *Memorials of the Rev. William Bull* (London, 1864), p. 248.
66   T. Waugh, *Twenty-Three Years a Missioner* (London, n.d.), p. 62.
67   *WV*, Vol. 1, pp. 99, 233; Vol. 2, p. 91.
68   J. Lawson, 'The people called Methodists: 2: "Our discipline"', in R. Davies and G. Rupp (eds), *A History of the Methodist Church in Great Britain*, Vol. 1 (London, 1965), pp. 189, 198.
69   Lackington, *Memoirs*, pp. 128 f.
70   S. Mechie, *The Church and Scottish Social Development, 1780–1870* (London, 1960), pp. 52 ff.
71   Dale, 'The Evangelical Revival', *The Evangelical Revival and other Sermons* (London, 1880), p. 35.
72   A. Russell, *The Clerical Profession* (London, 1980), chs 3 and 4.
73   C. Bridges, *The Christian Ministry*, 3rd edn (London, 1830), p. 477.
74   *CO*, March 1850, p. 213.
75   G. H. Sumner, *Life of Charles Richard Sumner, D.D.* (London, 1876), p. 212. Bickersteth, *Bickersteth*, p. 153.
76   'English Evangelical clergy', *Macmillan's Magazine*, 1860, pp. 119 f., quoted by W. D. Balda, '"Spheres of Influence": Simeon's Trust and its implications for Evangelical patronage', PhD thesis, University of Cambridge, 1981, pp. 196, f., 199.
77   R. P. Heitzenrater, *The Elusive Mr. Wesley: 1: John Wesley his Own Biographer* (Nashville, Tenn., 1984), p. 21.
78   H. Moore, *The Life of Mrs Mary Fletcher*, 11th edn (London, 1844), p. 150.
79   J. B. B. Clarke (ed.), *An Account of the Infancy, Religious and Literary Life of Adam Clarke, LL.D., F.A.S., &c., &c., &c.*, Vol. 1 (London, 1833), p. 191.
80   Field, 'Methodism in Metropolitan London', p. 46.
81   [Chalmers,] *Observations on a Passage in Mr Playfair's Letter* (Cupar, Fife, 1805), p. 10. I. H. Murray, 'Thomas Chalmers and the revival of the church', *Banner of Truth*, March 1980, p. 16.
82   *Evangelical Magazine*, 1803, p. 203, quoted by G. F. Nuttall, *The Significance of Trevecca College, 1768–91* (London, 1969), p. 7.

83 W. Selwyn, in H. Scholefield, *Memoir of the late Rev. James Scholefield, M.A.* (London, 1855), p. 335.

84 S. Neill, *A History of Christian Missions*, 2nd edn (Harmondsworth, Middlesex, 1986), pp. 213–16.

85 J. C. Pollock, *The Cambridge Seven* (London, 1955).

86 G. B. A. M. Finlayson, *The Seventh Earl of Shaftesbury, 1801–1885* (London, 1981), p. 322.

87 More, *An Estimate of the Religion of the Fashionable World* (London, 1808 edn), p. 146.

88 Heitzenrater, *Wesley*, Vol. 1, p. 149.

89 J. Dale, 'The theological and literary qualities of the poetry of Charles Wesley in relation to the standards of his age', PhD thesis, University of Cambridge, 1961, p. 145.

90 *WV*, Vol. 3, p. 57 (John Nelson).

91 ibid., Vol. 2, pp. 183 f. (George Shadford).

92 W. and T. Ludlam, *Essays Scriptural, Moral and Logical*, Vol.2 (London, 1817), p. 99, quoted by Walsh, 'Yorkshire Evangelicals', p. 14; cf. G. Reedy, *The Bible and Reason: Anglicans and Scripture in Late Seventeenth-Century England* (Philadelphia, 1985), ch. 5, pt III.

93 K. Moody-Stuart, *Brownlow North: The Story of his Life and Work* (Kilmarnock, [1904]), p. 185.

94 J. Macpherson, *Henry Moorhouse: The English Evangelist* (London, n.d.), p. 94.

95 H. E. Hopkins, *Charles Simeon of Cambridge* (London, 1977), p. 161.

96 For example, N. Anderson, *An Adopted Son* (Leicester, 1985), p. 289.

97 *BW*, 5 March 1896, p. 325; 26 March 1896, p. 379.

98 Venn, *Complete Duty*, p. 51. 'The fifteen articles of the Countess of Huntingdon's Connexion', in E. Welch (ed.), *Two Calvinistic Methodist Chapels, 1743–1811* (London, 1975), p. 88.

99 Bickersteth, *A Scripture Help Designed to Assist in Reading the Bible Profitably*, 17th edn (London, 1838), p. 2.

100 W. J. C. Ervine, 'Doctrine and diplomacy: some aspects of the life and thought of the Anglican Evangelical clergy, 1797–1837', PhD thesis, University of Cambridge, 1979, ch. 3; cf. below, pp. 86–91.

101 On Anglicans, cf. J. L. Altholz, 'The mind of Victorian orthodoxy: Anglican responses to "Essays and Reviews", 1860–1864', *Church History*, vol. 51, no. 2 (1982).

102 Spurgeon, *The Greatest Fight in the World* (London, 1896), p. 27, quoted by P. S. Kruppa, *Charles Haddon Spurgeon: A Preacher's Progress* (New York, 1982), p. 374.

103 Barrett, 'The secularisation of the pulpit', in *Congregational Year Book*, 1895, p. 27.

104 Gladstone, 'The Evangelical movement: its parentage, progress, and issue', *Gleanings from Past Years*, Vol. 7 (London, 1879), p. 207.

105 Wesley to Mary Bishop, 7 February 1778, *The Letters of the Rev. John Wesley, A.M.*, ed. J. Telford, Vol. 6 (London, 1931), pp. 297 f.

106 *WV*, Vol. 1, p. 118 (Christopher Hopper).

107 W. H. Goold (ed.), *The Works of the Rev. John Maclaurin*, Vol. 1 (Edinburgh, 1860), pp. 63–102.

108 Bridges, *Christian Ministry*, p. 320.

109   *R*, 12 January 1934, p. 15 (Stephen Neill). *CEN*, 5 March 1954, p. 8 (Bishop Joost de Blank).

110   Dale, *The Atonement* (London, 1875). Denney, *The Death of Christ* (London, 1902). Stott, *The Cross of Christ* (Leicester, 1986). Forsyth, *The Cruciality of the Cross* (London, 1909); *Positive Preaching and the Modern Mind* (London, 1907); *The Work of Christ* (London, 1910).

111   A. J. Davidson (ed.), *The Autobiography and Diary of Samuel Davidson, D.D., LL.D.* (Edinburgh, 1899), p. 64.

112   Maltby, *Christ and his Cross* (London, 1935); cf. W. Strawson, 'Methodist theology, 1850–1950', in R. Davies *et al.* (eds), *A History of the Methodist Church in Great Britain*, Vol. 3 (London, 1983), pp. 217 f.

113   Raleigh (ed.), *Raleigh*, p. 281.

114   Arnott, *The Brethren* (London, 1970 edn), p. 17.

115   Gore, *The Incarnation of the Son of God* (London, 1891); cf. A. M. Ramsey, *From Gore to Temple: The Development of Anglican Theology between 'Lux Mundi' and the Second World War, 1889–1939* (London, 1960).

116   'Annual address to the Methodist Societies', *Minutes of Several Conversations . . . of the People called Methodists* (London, 1892), pp. 374 f.

117   Baldwin Brown, *The Divine Life in Man* (London, [1860]). See also C. Binfield, '"No quest, no conquest." Baldwin Brown and Silvester Horne', *So Down to Prayers: Studies in English Nonconformity, 1780–1920* (London, 1977), p. 195. Scott Lidgett, *The Spiritual Principle of the Atonement* (London, 1897); cf. Scott Lidgett, *My Guided Life* (London, 1936), pp. 149–58.

118   *R*, 13 January 1939, p. 26.

119   *CEN*, 7 April 1967, p. 3.

120   Scott, *The Force of Truth* (Edinburgh, 1984 edn), p. 65.

121   Law, *A Serious Call to a Devout and Holy Life*, 20th edn (Romsey, 1816), p. 266.

122   Hall, 'On the substitution of the innocent for the guilty', in O. Gregory (ed.), *The Works of Robert Hall, A.M.*, Vol. 5 (London, 1839), pp. 73–103.

123   Fremantle, 'Atonement', in Garbett (ed.), *Evangelical Principles*, pp. 86–92.

124   E. Steane, *The Doctrine of Christ developed by the Apostles* (Edinburgh, 1872), p. viii. Pope, *The Person of Christ* (London, 1875), p. 51.

125   Shaw, 'What is my religious faith?', *Sixteen Self Sketches* (London, 1949), p. 79.

126   I. E. Page (ed.), *John Brash: Memorials and Correspondence* (London, 1912), p. 95. Strawson, 'Methodist theology', pp. 202, 215 ff.

127   D. Johnson, *Contending for the Faith: A History of the Evangelical Movement in the Universities and Colleges* (Leicester, 1979), p. 359.

128   Venn, *Complete Duty*, p. xiii.

129   M. N. Garrard, *Mrs Penn-Lewis: A Memoir* (London, 1930), pp. 26, 168, 197.

130   H. A. Thomas (ed.), *Memorials of the Rev. David Thomas, B.A.* (London, 1876), p. 37.

131   Rattenbury, 'Socialism and the old theology', *Six Sermons on Social Subjects* (London, [1908]), pp. 82 f.

132   M. R. Pease, *Richard Heath, 1831–1912* (n.p., [1922]), pp. 48 ff.

133   J. H. Pratt (ed.), *The Thought of the Evangelical Leaders: Notes of the Discussions of The Eclectic Society, London, during the Years 1798–1814* (Edinburgh, 1978), pp. 165 ff., 505 ff. For the background, see A. P. F. Sell, *The Great Debate: Calvinism, Arminianism and Salvation* (Worthing, 1982).

134 Wilberforce to Robert Southey, 5 December [?], 2519/63, National Library
     of Scotland, quoted by P. F. Dixon, 'The politics of emancipation: the
     movement for the abolition of slavery in the British West Indies, 1807–33',
     DPhil thesis, University of Oxford, 1971, p. 86.
135 J. Bossy, *The English Catholic Community, 1570–1850* (London, 1975), pp.
     184 ff.
136 N. Sykes, *Church and State in the Eighteenth Century* (Cambridge, 1954).
     G. F. A. Best, *Temporal Pillars: Queen Anne's Bounty, the Ecclesiastical
     Commissioners, and the Church of England* (Cambridge, 1964). J. C. D.
     Clark, *English Society, 1688–1832* (Cambridge, 1985).
137 M. R. Watts, *The Dissenters: From the Reformation to the French Revolution*
     (Oxford, 1978).
138 A. L. Drummond and J. Bulloch, *The Scottish Church, 1688–1843* (Edinburgh,
     1973). C. G. Brown, *The Social History of Religion in Scotland since 1730*
     (London, 1987).

CHAPTER 2: KNOWLEDGE OF THE LORD

 1 H. J. Hughes, *Life of Howell Harris, the Welsh Reformer* (London, 1892),
    p. 10; cf. G. F. Nuttall, *Howel Harris, 1714–1773: The Last Enthusiast*
    (Cardiff, 1965).
 2 G. E. Jones, *Modern Wales: A Concise History, c. 1485–1979* (Cam-
    bridge, 1984), p. 130. There is now D. L. Morgan, *The Great Awakening in Wales*
    (London, 1988).
 3 A. Dallimore, *George Whitefield: The Life and Times of the Great Evangelist of
    the Eighteenth-Century Revival*, Vol. 1 (London, 1970), chs 3–7.
 4 L. Tyerman, *The Life and Times of the Rev. John Wesley, M.A.*, Vol. 1
    (London, 1871), pp. 179 f., 233. Tyerman's is still the most authoritative
    biography. S. Ayling, *John Wesley* (London, 1979) is the most recent
    reliable study.
 5 Dallimore, *Whitefield*, Vol. 2 (Edinburgh, 1980), chs 5, 8. A. Fawcett,
    *The Cambuslang Revival: The Scottish Evangelical Revival of the Eighteenth
    Century* (London, 1971).
 6 Edwards, 'A narrative of surprising conversions' [1737], *Select Works*, Vol. 1
    (London, 1965). *The Journal of the Rev. John Wesley, A.M.*, ed. N. Curnock,
    Vol. 1 (London, 1909), pp. 83 f. (9 October 1738). G. D. Henderson, 'Jonathan
    Edwards and Scotland', *The Burning Bush: Studies in Scottish Church History*
    (Edinburgh, 1957), pp. 151–5. See also I. H. Murray, *Jonathan Edwards: A
    New Biography* (Edinburgh, 1987).
 7 Dallimore, *Whitefield*, Vol. 1, p. 14.
 8 Doddridge to Daniel Wadsworth, 6 March 1741, in G. F. Nuttall, *Calendar
    of the Correspondence of Philip Doddridge, D.D. (1702–1751)*, Historical
    Manuscripts Commission JP 26 (London, 1979), p. 130.
 9 R. Brown, *The English Baptists of the Eighteenth Century* (London, 1986), p. 77.
10 D. W. Lovegrove, 'The practice of itinerant evangelism in English Calvinistic
    Dissent, 1780–1830', PhD thesis, University of Cambridge, 1980, p. 54.
11 R. Currie *et al.*, *Churches and Churchgoers: Patterns of Church Growth in the
    British Isles since 1700* (Oxford, 1977), pp. 147, 151.

12   Lovegrove, 'Itinerant evangelism', pp. 247 f., 252.
13   Currie *et al.*, *Churches and Churchgoers*, pp. 139 f.
14   ibid., pp. 21 ff. A. D. Gilbert, *Religion and Society in Industrial England: Church, Chapel and Social Change, 1740–1914* (London, 1976), pp. 28 f.
15   C. G. Brown, *The Social History of Religion in Scotland since 1730* (London, 1987), p. 61. Baptists and Congregationalists, wrongly classified by Brown as Presbyterian Dissenters, are excluded from this proportion.
16   H. Venn, *The Complete Duty of Man*, 3rd edn (London, 1779), p. iii.
17   Wesley to Ann Bolton, 15 April 1771, *The Letters of the Rev. John Wesley, A.M.*, ed. J. Telford, Vol. 5 (London, 1931), p. 238.
18   Venn, *Complete Duty*, pp. vii ff.
19   A. Booth, *The Reign of Grace from its Rise to its Consummation* [1768], 8th edn (London, 1807), p. 17.
20   J. Lackington, *Memoirs of the Forty-Five First Years of the Life of James Lackington* (London, 1795), p. 48. Lackington's *Memoirs* are particularly revealing because their author had been zealous but had lapsed. He subsequently returned to the Methodist fold, as recounted in *The Confessions of J. Lackington* (London, 1804).
21   Lackington, *Memoirs*, p. 61.
22   [J. Bean], *Zeal without Innovation: Or the Present State of Religion and Morals Considered* (London, 1808), p. 87.
23   Wesley to Dr George Horne, 19 March 1762, *Letters*, ed. Telford, Vol. 4, p. 175.
24   Milner, 'On Evangelical religion' [1789], *The Works of Joseph Milner*, ed. I. Milner, Vol. 8 (London, 1810), pp. 203 f.
25   *Journal of John Wesley*, Vol. 5, p. 244 (1 December 1767).
26   Dallimore, *Whitefield*, Vol. 2, pp. 544 f.
27   S. L. Ollard, *The Six Students of St Edmund Hall Expelled from the University of Oxford in 1768* (London, 1911).
28   For example, F. K. Brown, *Fathers of the Victorians: The Age of Wilberforce* (Cambridge, 1961), p. 310.
29   R. Sher and A. Murdoch, 'Patronage and party in the Church of Scotland, 1750–1800', in N. Macdougall (ed.), *Church, Politics and Society: Scotland, 1408–1929* (Edinburgh, 1983), pp. 203–7.
30   G. Eliot, 'Janet's repentance', *Scenes of Clerical Life* [1858], ed. T. A. Noble (Oxford, 1985), p. 194.
31   ibid., p. 252.
32   Tyerman, *Wesley*, Vol. 1, pp. 406–15.
33   *WV*, Vol. 1, p. 121; Vol. 2, p. 12; Vol. 3, p. 86.
34   J. Walsh, 'Methodism and the mob in the eighteenth century', *Popular Belief and Practice*, Studies in Church History, vol. 8, ed. G. J. Cuming and Derek Baker (Cambridge, 1972). Lovegrove, 'Itinerant evangelism', ch. 5.
35   F. Baker, 'The people called Methodists: 3: Polity', in R. Davies and G. Rupp (eds), *A History of the Methodist Church in Great Britain*, Vol. 1 (London, 1965), pp. 222 f.
36   J. Kent, 'Wesleyan membership in Bristol, 1783', in *An Ecclesiastical Miscellany*, Bristol and Gloucestershire Archaeological Society Records Section, vol. 11, ed. D. Walker *et al.* (Bristol, 1976), p. 106.
37   Lackington, *Memoirs*, p. 70.
38   Baker, 'Polity', pp. 224 f.

39 *WV*, Vol. 1, pp. 25 f.
40 Lackington, *Confessions*, pp. 190 ff.; *Memoirs*, pp. 129, 149.
41 Edwards, 'Narrative', p. 50.
42 Brown, *Baptists*, pp. 87 ff.
43 G. C. B. Davies, *The Early Cornish Evangelicals, 1735–60: A Study of Walker of Truro and Others* (London, 1951), pp. 66–70, ch. 4.
44 W. H. Goold (ed.), *The Works of the Rev. John Maclaurin* (Edinburgh, 1860), p. xvii.
45 Kent, 'Wesleyan membership', pp. 107–11.
46 T. C. Smout, 'Born again at Cambuslang: new evidence on popular religion and literacy in eighteenth-century Scotland', *Past & Present*, no 97 (1982), p. 117. Gilbert, *Religion and Society*, p. 67.
47 Brown, *Religion in Scotland*, p. 150. The proportion should perhaps be higher, because textile trades are excluded. Artisan prominence here and elsewhere is clear despite such problems of definition. See also below, p. 111.
48 C. D. Field, 'The social structure of English Methodism: eighteenth–twentieth centuries', *British Journal of Sociology*, vol. 28, no. 2 (1977), p. 202.
49 ibid.
50 H. More, *Thoughts on the Importance of the Manners of the Great* (London, 1788). W. Wilberforce, *A Practical View of the Prevailing Religious System of Professed Christians in the Higher and Middle Classes in this Country Contrasted with Real Christianity* (London, 1797).
51 Lackington, *Memoirs*, p. 72.
52 G. Malmgreen, 'Domestic discords: women and the family in East Cheshire Methodism, 1750–1830', in J. Obelkevich *et al.* (ed.), *Disciplines of Faith: Studies in Religion, Politics and Patriarchy* (London, 1987), p. 60.
53 Smout, 'Born again', p. 116. Kent, 'Wesleyan membership', p. 107.
54 D. M. Valenze, *Prophetic Sons and Daughters: Female Preaching and Popular Religion in Industrial England* (Princeton, NJ, 1985).
55 W. F. Swift, 'The women itinerant preachers of early Methodism', *Proceedings of the Wesley Historical Society*, vol. 28, no. 5 (1952), and vol. 29, no. 4 (1953).
56 M. G. Jones, *Hannah More* (Cambridge, 1952).
57 Eliot, 'Janet's repentance', pp. 205 f.
58 A. Everitt, *The Pattern of Rural Dissent: The Nineteenth Century* (Leicester, 1972), ch. 2.
59 J. Macinnes, *The Evangelical Movement in the Highlands of Scotland, 1688 to 1800* (Aberdeen, 1951).
60 Everitt, *Rural Dissent*, pp. 20 ff.
61 For example, *WV*, Vol. 1, p. 184.
62 On regional distribution, see p. 109.
63 See pp. 42, 45–6, 48–50, 60, 153–5, 171–4.
64 J. D. Walsh, 'The Yorkshire Evangelicals in the eighteenth century: with especial reference to Methodism', PhD thesis, University of Cambridge, 1956, pp. 33 ff., 314.
65 Brown, *Baptists*, pp. 68 ff.
66 'A collection of hymns for the use of the people called Methodists', *The Works of John Wesley*, Vol. 7, ed. F. Hildebrandt *et al.* (Oxford, 1983), pp. 81, 123, 338.

67 *Arminian Magazine*, vol. 1, no. 1 (1778), pp. 9–17.
68 G. F. Nuttall, 'The influence of Arminianism in England', in G. O. McCulloh (ed.), *Man's Faith and Freedom: The Theological Influence of Jacobus Arminius* (New York, 1962), pp. 60 f.
69 Wesley to Newton, 14 May 1765, *Letters*, ed. Telford, Vol. 4, p. 298.
70 Nuttall, 'Influence', pp. 56 f.
71 Wesley on T. Vivian to Wesley, 10 October 1748, in Davies, *Cornish Evangelicals*, p. 85.
72 R. Davies, 'The people called Methodists: 1: "Our doctrines"', in Davies and Rupp (eds), *Methodist Church*, Vol. 1, pp. 167 f.
73 For example, Tyerman, *Wesley*, Vol. 1, p. 551. *WV*, Vol. 7, pp. 24 ff., 39, 66.
74 Davies, '"Our doctrines"', pp. 176–9.
75 F. Baker, *John Wesley and the Church of England* (London, 1970), esp. chs 10, 17.
76 Lackington, *Memoirs*, p. 179.
77 Hempton, *Methodism and Politics*, ch. 3.
78 W. R. Ward, *Religion and Society in England, 1790–1850* (London, 1972), chs 4, 6. W. R. Ward (ed.), *The Early Correspondence of Jabez Bunting, 1820–1829*, Camden Fourth Series, vol. 11 (London, 1972). W. R. Ward, *Early Victorian Methodism: The Correspondence of Jabez Bunting, 1830–1858* (Oxford, 1976).
79 Baker, 'Polity', p. 232.
80 Valenze, *Prophetic Sons and Daughters*, p. 20. See also J. C. Bowmer, *Pastor and People: A Study of Church and Ministry in Wesleyan Methodism from the Death of John Wesley (1791) to the Death of Jabez Bunting (1858)* (London, 1975).
81 E. Welch (ed.), *Two Calvinistic Methodist Chapels, 1743–1811* (London, 1975), pp. xiii f.
82 C. E. Watson, 'Whitefield and Congregationalism', *Transactions of the Congregational Historical Society*, vol. 8, no. 4 (1922), p. 175.
83 Welch (ed.), *Calvinistic Methodist Chapels*, pp. xi f., xvi. G. F. Nuttall, *The Significance of Trevecca College, 1768–91* (London, 1969), pp. 4 ff.
84 J. Walsh, 'Methodism at the end of the eighteenth century', in Davies and Rupp (eds), *Methodist Church*, Vol. 1, p. 292.
85 ibid. Welch (ed.), *Calvinistic Methodist Chapels*, p. xvii.
86 Dallimore, *Whitefield*, Vol. 2, pp. 157 f.
87 Welch (ed.), *Calvinistic Methodist Chapels*, pp. x f., xiv, 22, 45.
88 ibid., p. 18.
89 C. E. Watson, 'Whitefield and Congregationalism', p. 242.
90 Welch (ed.), *Calvinistic Methodist Chapels*, p. xi.
91 T. Beynon (ed.), *Howell Harris, Reformer and Soldier (1714–1773)* (Caernarvon, 1958), e.g. p. 168 (19 April 1763).
92 T. Scott, *The Force of Truth* [1779] (Edinburgh, 1984), pp. 27, 33, 44–8, 51, 52, 61, 66.
93 ibid., pp. 75, 100, 102 f.
94 Davies, *Cornish Evangelicals*, pp. 31 f.
95 Walsh, 'Yorkshire Evangelicals', pp. 117 ff.
96 T. Haweis, *The Life of William Romaine, M.A.* (London, 1797), p. 27.
97 Tyerman, *Wesley*, Vol. 3, p. 49.

98   Walker to Thomas Adam, 11 October 1759, in Davies, *Cornish Evangelicals*, p. 176.

99   Berridge to [Mrs Blackwell], n.d., in C. Smyth, *Simeon and Church Order* (Cambridge, 1940), p. 169.

100   F. Baker, *William Grimshaw, 1708–1763* (London, 1963), esp. ch. 17.

101   A. S. Wood, *Thomas Haweis, 1734–1820* (London, 1957), pp. 149 ff.

102   J. Venn, in H. Venn (ed.), *The Life and a Selection from the Letters of the Rev. Henry Venn, M.A.* (London, 1834), p. 171.

103   A. W. Brown, *Recollections of the Conversation Parties of the Rev. Charles Simeon, M.A.* (London, 1863), p. 107. See also Smyth, *Simeon and Church Order*, ch. 6.

104   Wood, *Haweis*, p. 115.

105   Smith, *Simeon and Church Order*, pp. 240–3. Davies, *Cornish Evangelicals*, pp. 212 f.

106   W. D. Balda, '"Spheres of influence": Simeon's Trust and its implications for Evangelical patronage', PhD thesis, University of Cambridge, 1981, esp. ch. 3.

107   M. R. Watts, *The Dissenters: From the Reformation to the French Revolution* (Oxford, 1978), pp. 436 ff.

108   G. F. Nuttall, 'Methodism and the older Dissent: some perspectives', *Journal of the United Reformed Church Historical Society*, vol. 2, no. 8 (1981), pp. 272 f.

109   Letter of 22 February 1765, National Library of Wales MS 5453C, in R. T. Jones, *Congregationalism in England, 1662–1962* (London, 1962), p. 161.

110   Davies, *Cornish Evangelicals*, pp. 75, 171 ff. 198.

111   Nuttall, *Correspondence of Philip Doddridge*, p. xxxv.

112   Nuttall, 'Methodism and the older Dissent', pp. 271 f.

113   Preface to *The Experience of Mr. R. Cruttenden* (London, 1744), p. vii.

114   K. R. Manley, 'The making of an Evangelical Baptist leader', *Baptist Quarterly*, vol. 26, no. 6 (1976), p. 259.

115   Brown, *Baptists*, pp. 79, 81.

116   Watts, *Dissenters*, pp. 451 f.

117   Brown, *Baptists*, pp. 67–70, 109–12.

118   J. Gillies, 'Memoir', in Goold (ed.), *Works of Maclaurin*, pp. xv ff.

119   Sir H. W. Moncrieff Wellwood, *Account of the Life and Writings of John Erskine, D.D.* (Edinburgh, 1818), pp. 144, 113, 134, 225.

120   J. Erskine, 'Memoir', in *Extracts from an Exhortation to the Inhabitants of the South Parish of Glasgow by the late Rev. Dr John Gillies* (Glasgow, 1819), pp. 9, 17, 14.

121   Sher and Murdoch, 'Patronage and party'.

122   G. Struthers, *The History of the Rise, Progress and Principles of the Relief Church* (Glasgow, 1843), p. 254.

123   Dallimore, *Whitefield*, Vol. 2, pp. 86–90.

124   Brown, *Religion in Scotland*, p. 31.

125   Especially in G. F. Nuttall, *Richard Baxter and Philip Doddridge: A Study in a Tradition*, Friends of Dr Williams's Library Fifth Lecture (London, 1951), p. 19. See also Nuttall, *Richard Baxter* (London, 1965); Nuttall (ed.), *Philip Doddridge, 1702–51: His Contribution to English Religion* (London, 1951); Nuttall, *Correspondence of Philip Doddridge*.

126 Whitefield to Doddridge, 21 December 1748, in J. Gillies (ed.), *The Works of the Reverend George Whitefield, M.A.*, Vol. 2 (London, 1771), p. 216.

127 Nuttall, 'George Whitefield's "Curate": Gloucestershire Dissent and the revival', *JEH*, vol. 27, no. 4 (1976).

128 Nuttall, 'Methodism and the older Dissent', p. 261.

129 Nuttall, 'Questions and answers: an eighteenth-century correspondence', *Baptist Quarterly*, vol. 27, no. 2 (1977). Manley, 'An Evangelical Baptist leader', pp. 260–9.

130 R. Wodrow, *Analecta*, Vol. 3 (Edinburgh, 1843), pp. 342, 379. Wodrow to Mrs Wodrow, 12 May 1727, *The Correspondence*, ed. T. M'Crie, Vol. 3 (Edinburgh, 1843), pp. 302 f.

131 G. H. Jenkins, *Literature, Religion and Society in Wales, 1660–1730* (Cardiff, 1978), esp. pp. 306–9. Jones, *Modern Wales*, pp. 128 ff.

132 J. A. Newton, *Susanna Wesley and the Puritan Tradition in Methodism* (London, 1968), pp. 138 f.

133 F. Baker, 'Wesley's Puritan ancestry', *London Quarterly and Holborn Review*, vol. 187, no. 3 (1962). R. C. Monk, *John Wesley: His Puritan Heritage* (London, 1966), pp. 245 f.

134 Monk, *Wesley*, pp. 36–41.

135 Lackington, *Memoirs*, pp. 94 f.

136 *WV*, Vol. 1, pp. 16, 212; Vol. 2, p. 22; Vol. 4, pp. 9, 242; Vol. 7, pp. 14, 17. See also I. Rivers, '"Strangers and pilgrims": sources and patterns of Methodist narrative', in J. C. Hilson *et al.* (ed.), *Augustan Worlds* (Leicester, 1978), p. 195.

137 *WV*, Vol. 2, p. 54.

138 Professor J. H. Liden of Uppsala in his journal, 2 November 1769, quoted by R. P. Heitzenrater, *The Elusive Mr Wesley: 2: John Wesley as seen by Contemporaries and Biographers* (Nashville, Tenn., 1984), p. 89.

139 J. A. Newton, *Methodism and the Puritans*, Friends of Dr Williams's Library Eighteenth Lecture (London, 1964), pp. 9–17.

140 Baker, *Wesley and the Church of England*, p. 52. Monk, *Wesley*, pp. 216, 182–5. P. Collinson, 'The English conventicle', in *Voluntary Religion*, Studies in Church History, vol. 23, ed. W. J. Sheils and D. Wood (Oxford, 1986). J. Lawson, 'The people called Methodists: 2: "Our discipline"', in Davies and Rupp (eds), *Methodist Church*, Vol. 1.

141 G. Rupp. *Religion in England (1688–1791)* (Oxford, 1986), pp. 111, 326.

142 C. J. Abbey, *The English Church and its Bishops, 1700–1800*, Vol. 1 (London, 1887), pp. 151 ff.

143 J. Walsh, 'Origins of the Evangelical Revival', in G. V. Bennett and J. D. Walsh (eds), *Essays in Modern English Church History in Memory of Norman Sykes* (London, 1966), p. 156. Walsh, 'Yorkshire Evangelicals', p. 53 n.

144 ibid. Brown, *Simeon*, p. 70.

145 Hervey, Letter of 12 January 1748, *The Works of the late Reverend James Hervey, A.M.*, Vol. 6 (London, 1807), p. 11.

146 [Bean], *Zeal without Innovation*, ch. 3, sect. V.

147 *WV*, Vol. 4, p. 38.

148 E. Duffy, 'Primitive Christianity revived: religious renewal in Augustan England', in *Renaissance and Renewal in Christian History*, Studies in Church History, vol. 14, ed. D. Baker (Oxford, 1977), p. 291. See

also J. S. Simon, *John Wesley and the Religious Societies* (London, 1921), ch. 1.

149 M. Schmidt, *John Wesley: A Theological Biography*, Vol. 1 (London 1962), p. 99.

150 R. P. Heitzenrater (ed.), *Diary of an Oxford Methodist: Benjamin Ingham, 1733–1734* (Durham, NC, 1985), pp. 8 f., 37 f.

151 R. P. Heitzenrater, *The Elusive Mr Wesley: 1: John Wesley his own Biographer* (Nashville, Tenn., 1984), p. 58.

152 Lawson, '"Our discipline"', pp. 190–6.

153 ibid., p. 194 n. Lackington, *Memoirs*, p. 67.

154 Walsh, 'Origins', pp. 146 ff. See also H. D. Rack, 'Religious societies and the origins of Methodism', *JEH*, vol. 38, no. 4 (1987), which points out the inconsistent relationship between Methodism and the older societies.

155 Wesley, 'A plain account of Christian perfection', in F. Whaling (ed.), *John and Charles Wesley*, The Classics of Western Spirituality (London, 1981), p. 299.

156 H. T. Hughes, 'Jeremy Taylor and John Wesley', *London Quarterly and Holborn Review*, vol. 174, no. 4 (1949), pp. 303 f. Schmidt, *Wesley*, Vol. 1, pp. 73–81.

157 Wesley, 'Christian perfection', p. 299; cf. Schmidt, *Wesley*, Vol. 1, pp. 82–5.

158 Wesley, 'Christian perfection', p. 299; cf. J. G. Green, *John Wesley and William Law* (London, 1945); E. W. Baker, *A Herald of the Evangelical Revival* (London, 1948).

159 Schmidt, *Wesley*, Vol. 1, pp. 48–57.

160 R. P. Heitzenrater, 'John Wesley and the Oxford Methodists, 1725–35', PhD thesis, Duke University, NC, 1972, pp. 513 f. See also J. Hoyles, *The Waning of the Renaissance, 1640–1740: Studies in the Thought and Poetry of Henry More, John Norris and Isaac Watts* (The Hague, 1971), pt 2.

161 Schmidt, *Wesley*, Vol. 1, pp. 213–17. J. Orcibal, 'The theological originality of John Wesley and continental spirituality', in Davies and Rupp (eds), *Methodist Church*, Vol. 1, p. 90.

162 ibid., pp. 90 f.

163 J. Walsh, 'The Cambridge Methodists', in Peter Brooks (ed.), *Christian Spirituality: Essays in Honour of Gordon Rupp* (London, 1975), pp. 278–82.

164 A. C. Outler (ed.), *John Wesley* (New York, 1964), pp. 9 f. Baker, *Wesley and the Church of England*, pp. 32–50.

165 G. Rupp, 'Introductory essay', in Davies and Rupp (eds), *Methodist Church*, Vol. 1, p. xxxiv.

166 W. R. Ward, 'Power and piety: the origins of the religious revival in the early eighteenth century', *Bulletin of the John Rylands University Library of Manchester*, vol. 63, no. 1 (1980), pp. 237–48.

167 P. C. Erb (ed.), *Pietists: Selected Writings*, The Classics of Western Spirituality (London, 1983), pp. 1–96.

168 Ward, 'Power and piety', pp. 232–7.

169 Nuttall, 'Continental pietism', pp. 209–19; cf. W. M. Williams, *The Friends of Griffith Jones*, Y Cymmrodor, vol. 46 (London, 1939).

170 W. G. Addison, *The Renewed Church of the United Brethren, 1722–1930* (London, 1932).

171 Erb (ed.), *Pietists*, pp. 291–330.

172   C. W. Towlson, *Moravian and Methodist* (London, 1957), chs 3–6.

173   *WV*, Vol. 3, p. 31.

174   R. T. Jenkins, *The Moravian Brethren in North Wales*, Y Cymmrodor, vol. 45 (London, 1938), p. 9.

175   Walsh, 'Cambridge Methodists', pp. 263 f.

176   Towlson, *Moravian and Methodist*, ch. 7.

177   Nuttall, *Baxter and Doddridge*, p. 19; 'Influence of Arminianism', p. 60.

178   C. Hill, 'Puritans and "the dark corners of the land"', in *Change and Continuity in Seventeenth-Century England* (London, 1974). G. F. Nuttall, 'Northamptonshire and *The Modern Question*: a turning-point in eighteenth-century Dissent', *Journal of Theological Studies*, n.s., vol. 16, no. 1 (1965), pp. 104 f. B. R. White, *The English Baptists of the Seventeenth Century* (London, 1983), p. 74.

179   S. Neill, *A History of Christian Missions*, 2nd edn (Harmondsworth, Middlesex, 1986), pp. 187–92.

180   W. T. Whitley, *Calvinism and Evangelism in England especially in Baptist Circles* (London, [1933]), p. 4.

181   E. Benz, 'The Pietist and Puritan sources of early Protestant world mission (Cotton Mather and A. H. Francke)', *Church History*, vol. 20, no. 2 (1951), p. 43.

182   Edwards, 'God's sovereignty in the salvation of men'. *Select Works*, Vol. 1, p. 233.

183   Edwards, 'The distinguishing marks of a work of the true Spirit', *Select Works*, Vol. 1, p. 98.

184   Booth, *Reign of Grace*, pp. 59 ff.

185   Carey, *Enquiry* (London, 1961), sect. 1.

186   Edwards, *An Account of the Life of the late Rev. Mr. David Brainerd . . .* (Boston, Mass., 1749). R. T. Handy, *A History of the Churches in the United States and Canada* (Oxford, 1976), pp. 89, 92.

187   E. D. Potts, *British Baptist Missionaries in India, 1793–1837: The History of Serampore and its Missions* (Cambridge, 1967), p. 13.

188   James Hutton to Zinzendorf, 14 March 1740, in Heitzenrater, *Wesley*, Vol. 2, pp. 69 f.

189   *WV*, vol. 4, p. 228.

190   Walker to Thomas Adam, 2 October 1755, in Davies, *Cornish Evangelicals*, p. 134.

191   Lovegrove, 'Itinerant evangelism'.

192   D. E. Meek, 'Evangelical missionaries in the early nineteenth-century Highlands', *Scottish Studies*, 28 (1987), esp. p. 20.

193   Walsh, 'Methodism at the end of the eighteenth century', pp. 299 f.

194   R. H. Martin, *Evangelicals United: Ecumenical Stirrings in Pre-Victorian Britain, 1795–1830* (Metuchen, NJ, 1983), pt 2. A. L. Drummond and J. Bulloch, *The Scottish Church, 1688–1843* (Edinburgh, 1973), pp. 151 f. E. Stock, *The History of the Church Missionary Society*, Vol. 1 (London, 1899), pt. 2.

195   Although this view is at variance with that expressed by C. W. Towlson (*Moravian and Methodist*, p. 175), it is partly indicated by his ch. 3. See below, pp. 45, 49–50.

196   Rupp, *Religion in England*, p. 422.

197   R. T. Kendall, *Calvin and English Calvinism to 1649* (Oxford, 1979), pt 2.

198 M. M. Knappen (ed.), *Two Elizabethan Puritan Diaries* (Chicago, 1933), pp. 14 f.

199 Kendall, *Calvin and English Calvinism*, ch. 3. M. C. Bell, *Calvin and Scottish Theology: The Doctrine of Assurance* (Edinburgh, 1985), pp. 45 ff.

200 S. Petto, *The Voyce of the Spirit*, 1654, epistle dedicatory, quoted by G. F. Nuttall, *The Holy Spirit in Puritan Faith and Experience* (Oxford, 1946), p. 58.

201 Guthrie, *The Christian's Great Interest* (London, 1901), pp. 195 f.

202 Perkins, 'A treatise tending unto a declaration whether a man be in the estate of damnation or in the estate of grace' [1589], *The Works of . . . W. Perkins*, Vol. 1 (Cambridge, 1608), p. 367.

203 For example, Bell, *Calvin and Scottish Theology*, p. 81.

204 *The Confession of Faith* (Edinburgh, 1810), ch. 18/3, p. 106.

205 Brooks, *Precious Remedies* (Evesham, 1792), pp. 189, 211 f., 213–22.

206 Baker, *Grimshaw*, p. 43.

207 O. C. Watkins, *The Puritan Experience* (London, 1972), p. 11. Baxter nevertheless treats the evidence of works as inconclusive. N. H. Keeble, *Richard Baxter: Puritan Man of Letters* (Oxford, 1982), pp. 134 ff.

208 For example, Bell, *Calvin and Scottish Theology*, p. 82.

209 Weber, *The Protestant Ethic and the Spirit of Capitalism* (London, 1930), ch. 4A.

210 P. G. Lake, *Moderate Puritans and the Elizabethan Church* (Cambridge, 1982), p. 159.

211 Willison, 'A sacramental directory' [1716] in W. M. Hetherington (ed.), *The Practical Works of the Rev. John Willison* (Glasgow, [1844]), pp. 166 f. Willison was later to support the revival. Henderson, 'Edwards and Scotland', p. 154.

212 Hughes, *Harris*, p. 12.

213 'Collection of hymns', ed. Hildebrandt *et al.*, p. 517.

214 *Journal of John Wesley*, Vol. 2, pp. 13 (12 July 1738), 37 (August 1738). Schmidt, *Wesley*, Vol. 1, pp. 286–96, discusses the Moravian testimonies without pointing out that Wesley's concern was with the relation of justification to assurance, not with justification only. See also A. S. Yates, *The Doctrine of Assurance with Special Reference to John Wesley* (London, 1952), ch. 4.

215 Wesley to Rev. Arthur Bedford, 28 September 1738, *Works of John Wesley*, Vol. 25, ed. F. Baker (Oxford, 1980), pp. 562 ff.

216 Yates's suggestion (*Doctrine of Assurance*, p. 72) that there is gradual development away from regarding assurance as essential to salvation is belied by his own evidence, not least the letter to Bedford (cf. n. 215).

217 Yates, *Doctrine of Assurance*, pp. 63 ff.

218 R. Southey, *The Life of Wesley* (London, 1820), Vol. 1, p. 295.

219 Brown, *Simeon*, p. 320. W. Myles, *The Life and Writings of the late Reverend William Grimshaw*, 2nd edn (London, 1813), pp. 109 f.

220 Davies, *Cornish Evangelicals*, pp. 153 f.

221 Venn, *Complete Duty*, p. 126.

222 [Bean], *Zeal without Innovation*, p. 158.

223 Milner, *The Essentials of Christianity Theoretically and Practically Considered* (London, 1855), p. 189.

224 Edwards, 'Narrative', p. 42.

225 Booth, *Reign of Grace*, pp. 55 f., 239 f.
226 *WV*, Vol. 2, p. 145; Vol. 3, p. 125.
227 *WV*, Vol. 6, p. 22.
228 *WV*, Vol. 3, p. 173; vol. 6, p. 41. Edwards, 'Distinguishing marks', *Select Works*, Vol. 1.
229 Venn, *Complete Duty*, p. 127.
230 *WV*, Vol. 3, pp. 97 f.
231 T. Jackson (ed.), *The Lives of Early Methodist Preachers*, 5th edn, Vol. 2 (London, n.d.), p. 283.
232 Whitefield, *Journals*, p. 57.
233 *WV*, Vol. 1, p. 33.
234 For example, 'The contrite heart', no. IX of the Olney hymns. M. F. Marshall and J. Todd, *English Congregational Hymns in the Eighteenth Century* (Lexington, Ky, 1982), p. 131.
235 Edwards, 'Narrative', p. 3.
236 ibid., pp. 8, 17.
237 ibid., pp. 38 ff.
238 ibid., p. 39.
239 Edwards, *Religious Affections* [1746] (*Works*, Vol. 2), ed. J. E. Smith (New Haven, Conn., 1959), p. 205.
240 R. I. Aaron, *John Locke*, 3rd edn (Oxford, 1971).
241 Hutcheson, *Illustrations on the Moral Sense* [1728], ed. B. Peach (Cambridge, Mass., 1971).
242 Especially by Perry Miller in *Jonathan Edwards* (n.p., 1949).
243 N. Fiering, *Jonathan Edwards's Moral Thought in its British Context* (Chapel Hill, NC, 1981), pp. 35–40.
244 Edwards, *Freedom of the Will* [1754] (*Works*, Vol. 1), ed. P. Ramsey (New Haven, Conn., 1957), ch. 4.
245 ibid., p. 43.
246 Edwards, *Religious Affections*, p. 205.
247 Hughes, 'Taylor and Wesley', pp. 298 f.
248 Wesley to Samuel Wesley, 10 December 1734, *Works of John Wesley*, Vol. 25, p. 407.
249 Hoyles, *Waning of the Renaissance*, pp. 101, 105.
250 Heitzenrater, 'Wesley and the Oxford Methodists', p. 511. V. H. H. Green, *Young Mr Wesley: A Study of John Wesley and Oxford* (London, 1961), pp. 116 n., 315.
251 R. E. Brantley, *Locke, Wesley, and the Method of English Romanticism* (Gainesville, Fla, 1984), pp. 68, 113, 83 f.
252 E. H. Sugden (ed.), *Wesley's Standard Sermons*, Vol. 2 (London, 1921), pp. 216 f.
253 A. R. Winnett, *Peter Browne: Provost, Bishop, Metaphysician* (London, 1974), pp. 108 f. See also Brantley, *Locke, Wesley*, ch. 1; J. C. Hindley, 'The philosophy of enthusiasm', *London Quarterly and Holborn Review*, vol. 182, no. 2 (1957).
254 *Journal of John Wesley*, Vol. 1, p. 424 (29 January 1738).
255 ibid., Vol. 1, p. 151 (8 February 1736).
256 Hindley, 'Philosophy of enthusiasm', p. 106.
257 1744 Methodist Conference minutes, quoted by Simon, *Wesley and the Methodist Societies*, p. 207.

258 Wesley, 'An earnest appeal to men of reason and religion' [1743], *Works of John Wesley*, Vol. 11, ed. G. R. Cragg (Oxford, 1975), pp. 46, 56.

259 Wesley, 'On conscience', *Works* (London, 1872), Vol. 7, pp. 188 f.

260 Hindley, 'Philosophy of enthusiasm', *London Quarterly and Holborn Review*, vol. 182, no. 3 (1957), pp. 204–7.

261 *WV*, Vol. 3, p. 65.

262 ibid., Vol. 1, p. 177.

263 P. Gay, *The Enlightenment: An Interpretation* (London, 1967), is a classic statement of this view. Donald Davie is an honourable exception in contending for the alignment of Methodism and the orthodox Old Dissent with the Enlightenment: see especially his *Dissentient Voice* (Notre Dame, Ind., 1982), chs 1 and 2.

264 Toland, *Christianity not Mysterious* (London, 1695); cf. R. E. Sullivan, *John Toland and the Deist Controversy* (Cambridge, Mass., 1982).

265 R. N. Stromberg, *Religious Liberalism in Eighteenth-Century England* (London, 1954), p. 43.

266 ibid., pp. 44 ff.; cf. J. P. Ferguson, *An Eighteenth Century Heretic: Dr Samuel Clarke* (Kineton, Warwickshire, 1976).

267 Drummond and Bulloch, *Scottish Church*, pp. 31–4.

268 R. B. Sher, *Church and University in the Scottish Enlightenment: The Moderate Literati of Edinburgh* (Edinburgh, 1985).

269 Watts, *Dissenters*, pp. 464–78.

270 L. Stephen, *History of English Thought in the Eighteenth Century*, 2nd edn (London, 1881), Vol. 2, ch. 12, pts 5 and 6.

271 Booth, *Reign of Grace*, p. 9.

272 Wellwood, *Erskine*, pp. 55, 59.

273 *WV*, Vol. 2, p. 116.

274 *WV*, Vol. 2, p. 247.

275 *WV*, Vol. 2, p. 168. Lackington, *Memoirs*, p. 50.

276 Lockington, *Memoirs*, p. 51.

277 *Works of John Wesley*, Vol. 1, ed. A. C. Outler (Abingdon, Tenn., 1984), p. 104.

278 Lackington, *Memoirs*, p. 179.

279 Wesley, *Primitive Physic* [1747], ed. A. W. Hill (London, 1960), p. 94.

280 *Journal of John Wesley*, Vol. 7, p. 13 (26 August 1784).

281 Wesley to Dr Thomas Rutherforth, 28 March 1768, *Letters*, ed. Telford, Vol. 5, p. 364.

282 Schmidt, *Wesley*, Vol. 1, p. 272.

283 F. Dreyer, 'Faith and experience in the thought of John Wesley', *American Historical Review*, vol. 88, no. 1 (1983). Brantley, *Locke, Wesley*, esp. chs 1 and 2.

284 B. Semmel, *The Methodist Revolution* (London, 1974), pp. 87–96.

285 Wesley to Maxfield in T. Coke and H. Moore, *The Life of the Rev. John Wesley, A.M.* (London, 1792), p. 337.

286 *WV*, Vol. 1, pp. 123, 210; Vol. 3, p. 69; Vol. 4, p. 239.

287 Milner, 'The treatment which Methodism, so called, has received from the critical and monthly reviewers', *Works*, Vol. 8, p. 214. Davies, *Cornish Evangelicals*, p. 140.

288 Nuttall, 'Methodism and the older Dissent', p. 271. Booth, *Reign of Grace*, p. 271.

289 S. Mews, 'Reason and emotion in working-class religion, 1794–1824', *Schism, Heresy and Religious Protest*, Studies in Church History, vol. 9, ed. D. Baker (Cambridge, 1972).

290 H. McLachlan, *The Methodist Unitarian Movement* (Manchester, 1919).

291 Walsh, 'Origins', pp. 148–53. Dr Walsh tells me that he has altered his view to that expressed in the text.

292 E. Halévy, *The Birth of Methodism in England*, ed. B. Semmel (Chicago, 1971).

293 K. MacLean, *John Locke and English Literature of the Eighteenth Century* (New Haven, Conn., 1936), pp. 2 f, 11.

294 J. C. D. Clark, *English Society, 1688–1832* (Cambridge, 1985), esp. ch. 2, pt 1.

295 Edwards, *The Great Awakening* (*Works*, Vol. 4), ed. C. C. Goen (New Haven, Conn., 1972), p. 38. Davies, *Cornish Evangelicals*, p. 32.

296 Watts, *Philosophical Essays* (1733), Essay 6 introductory paragraph, and preface, quoted by MacLean, *Locke and Literature*, pp. 1, 15.

297 ibid., pp. 15, 23, 124.

298 Watts, *Logick* (London, 1725), p. 505, quoted by W. S. Howell, *Eighteenth-Century British Logic and Rhetoric* (Princeton, NJ, 1971), p. 336.

299 Hoyles, *Waning of the Renaissance*, p. 176.

300 ibid., p. 162, and pt 3 generally.

301 Doddridge, *A Course of Lectures on the Principal Subjects in Pneumatology, Ethics and Divinity* (London, 1763).

302 M. Deacon, *Philip Doddridge of Northampton* (Northampton, 1980), p. 99.

303 Doddridge to John Nettleton, [February] 1721, in Nuttall, *Correspondence of Philip Doddridge*, p. 2.

304 Wellwood, *Erskine*, p. 20. V. L. Collins, *President Witherspoon: A Biography* (Princeton, NJ, 1925), Vol. 1, p. 16.

305 Handy, *United States and Canada*, p. 83.

306 Dallimore, *Whitefield*, Vol. 2, pp. 88 ff.

307 D. Scott, *Annals and Statistics of the Original Secession Church* (Edinburgh, [1886]), p. 16.

308 *Narrative and Testimony* (1804) of the Anti-Burghers quoted by J. M'Kerrow, *History of the Secession Church* (Glasgow, 1841), p. 443.

309 J. McL. Campbell, *Reminiscences and Reflections*, ed. D. Campbell (London, 1873), chs 2–4.

310 J. Kennedy, *The Days of the Fathers in Ross-shire* (Inverness, 1897), p. 114.

311 ibid., p. 116.

312 W. Wilson, *The History and Antiquities of Dissenting Churches and Meeting Houses in London, Westminster and Southwark*, Vol. 4 (London, 1814), p. 550.

313 Lovegrove, 'Itinerant evangelism', p. 184.

314 T. M. Bassett, *The Welsh Baptists* (Swansea, 1977), pp. 95 ff.

315 Brown, *Baptists*, pp. 129 f.

316 Handy, *United States and Canada*, p. 179.

317 Whitley, *Calvinism and Evangelism*, p. 38.

318 Warburton, *Mercies*, 2nd pt, 4th edn (London, 1859), p. 41.

319 R. C. Chambers and R. W. Olver, *The Strict Baptist Chapels of England*, 5 vols (London, 1952–68).

320 T. Scott in J. H. Pratt (ed.), *The Thought of the Evangelical Leaders: Notes of the Discussions of The Eclectic Society, London, during the years 1798–1814* (Edinburgh, 1978), p. 231. Milner, 'Scriptural proof of the influence of the Holy Spirit on the understanding', *Works*, Vol. 8, p. 258.

321 Scott, *Force of Truth*, p. 26. Venn, *Complete Duty*, pp. 48, 152.

322 Miller, *Edwards*, p. 45.

323 *Arminian Magazine*, May 1786, p. 253.

324 Venn, *Complete Duty*, p. 48.

325 L. P. Fox, 'The work of the Rev. Thomas Tregenna Biddulph, with special reference to his influence on the Evangelical movement in the west of England', PhD thesis, University of Cambridge, 1953, pp. 67–73. Haweis, *Romaine*, pp. 18, 27, 46, 61, 54. Davies, *Cornish Evangelicals*, p. 207.

326 Milner, 'The trial of prophets', *Works*, Vol. 8, p. 285.

327 W. J. Turrell, *John Wesley, Physician and Electrotherapist* (Oxford, 1938), pp. 18–24.

328 Wesley, *Primitive Physic*, p. 25.

329 'Collection of hymns', ed. Hildebrandt *et al.*, p. 74.

330 Edwards, *Religious Affections*, p. 452.

331 'Account of the life of the Rev. John Witherspoon, D.D., LL.D.', *The Works of John Witherspoon, D.D.* (Edinburgh, 1804), Vol. 1, p. xvii.

332 Venn, *Complete Duty*, p. 2.

333 Conder to Rev. H. March, 2 July 1824, in E. R. Conder, *Josiah Conder: A Memoir* (London, 1857), pp. 246 f.

334 Pratt (ed.), *Evangelical Leaders,* p 231.

335 Brown, *Simeon*, p. 269.

336 Fox, 'Biddulph', p. 66.

337 Wesley, Preface to Bishop Hall, 'Meditations and vows, divine and moral', in J. Wesley (ed.), *A Christian Library*, Vol. 4 (London, 1819), p. 106.

338 *WV*, Vol. 5, p. 249.

339 Walsh, 'Methodism at the end of the eighteenth century', p. 287.

340 D. Newsome, *The Parting of Friends: A Study of the Wilberforces and Henry Manning* (London, 1966), p. 51.

341 Pratt (ed.), *Evangelical Leaders*, pp. 230 ff; cf. M. L. Clarke, *Paley: The Evidence for the Man* (London, 1974); D. L. LeMahieu, *The Mind of William Paley* (Lincoln, Neb., 1976).

342 Lackington, *Confessions*, p. 35.

343 D. F. Rice, 'Natural theology and the Scottish philosophy in the thought of Thomas Chalmers', *Scottish Journal of Theology*, vol. 24, no. 1 (1971).

344 S. A. Grave, *The Scottish Philosophy of Common Sense* (Oxford, 1960).

345 J. Walker, *The Theology and Theologians of Scotland, chiefly of the Seventeenth and Eighteenth Centuries* (Edinburgh, 1872), p. 73.

346 Collins, *Witherspoon*, Vol. 1, p. 41.

347 Witherspoon, 'Lectures on moral philosophy', *Works*, Vol. 7 (Edinburgh, 1805), p. 47.

348 ibid., pp. 25, 46.

349 The legacy in American Evangelical thought is well documented: T. D. Bozeman, *Protestants in an Age of Science: The Baconian Ideal and Antebellum Religious Thought* (Chapel Hill, NC, 1977); G. M. Marsden, *Fundamentalism and American Culture: The Shaping of Twentieth-Century Evangelicalism,*

1870–1925 (New York, 1980), pp. 14–17. On Britain, cf. R. Anstey, *The Atlantic Slave Trade and British Abolition, 1760–1810* (London, 1975), pp. 177 f.

350   A. C. Chitnis, *The Scottish Enlightenment and Early Victorian English Society* (London, 1986).

351   D. W. Bebbington, *Patterns in History* (Leicester, 1979), ch. 4.

352   Semmel, *Methodist Revolution*, takes up this theme.

353   J. Bellamy, 'The millennium', *Sermons*, ed. J. Sutcliff (Northampton, 1783), p. 51, cited by W. R. Ward, 'The Baptists and the transformation of the church, 1780–1830', *Baptist Quarterly*, vol. 25, no. 4 (1973), p. 171.

354   Schmidt, *Wesley*, Vol. 1, p. 101 n.

355   *WV*, Vol. 1, p. 76.

356   Goold (ed.), *Works of Maclaurin*, Vol. 2. Venn, *Complete Duty*, p. 423. Wilberforce, *Practical View*, p. 402.

357   Lackington, *Memoirs*, p. 70.

358   Wesley, 'A plain account of Christian perfection', in Outler (ed.), *John and Charles Wesley*, p. 359. See also pp. 153–5, 171–4.

359   Newton, *Wesley and the Puritans*, p. 11.

360   Davies, *Cornish Evangelicals*, p. 158; cf. Booth, *Reign of Grace*, pp. 213 f.

361   Fox, 'Biddulph', p. 54.

362   Marshall and Todd, *Congregational Hymns*, pp. 102–13. Pratt (ed.), *Evangelical Leaders*, p. 77.

363   *WV*, Vol. 5, pp. 217 f.

364   Anstey, *Atlantic Slave Trade*, pp. 193–8.

365   Pratt (ed.), *Evangelical Leaders*, p. 77.

366   *WV*, Vol. 1, pp. 113, 96; Vol. 4, pp. 203 ff.

367   Pratt (ed.), *Evangelical Leaders*, pp. 236 f.

368   ibid., p. 468.

369   Wilberforce, *Practical View*, p. 48.

370   Anstey, *Atlantic Slave Trade*, pp. 128–39, 159. B. Hilton, 'The role of providence in Evangelical social thought', in D. Beales and G. Best (eds) *History, Society and the Churches* (Cambridge, 1985), esp. pp. 223 f.

371   E. L. Tuveson, *Millennium and Utopia* (Berkeley, Calif., 1949).

372   I. H. Murray, *The Puritan Hope* (Edinburgh, 1971).

373   Wellwood, *Erskine*, pp. 125 f.

374   Edwards, 'Some thoughts concerning the present revival of religion in New England' [1743], *Great Awakening*, p. 354; cf. E. L. Tuveson, *Redeemer Nation: The Idea of America's Millennial Role* (Chicago, 1968).

375   Edwards, 'An humble attempt to promote explicit agreement and visible union of God's people in extraordinary prayer', *Apocalyptic Writings (Works*, Vol. 5), ed. S. S. Steen (New Haven, Conn., 1977).

376   ibid., p. 88.

377   Doddridge, *Lectures*, p. 584. Wellwood, *Erskine*, pp. 126 f., 501. J. Conder, *An Analytical and Comparative View of All Religions* (London, 1838), pp. 584–92.

378   Carey, *Enquiry*, p. 12. Carey's endorsement of Edwards is mistaken for disagreement by the editor (pp. xii f.).

379   W. H. Oliver, *Prophets and Millennialists: The Uses of Biblical Prophecy in England from the 1790s to the 1840s* (Auckland, 1978), pp. 86 f.

380 Pratt (ed.), *Evangelical Leaders*, pp. 256 ff.
381 Stirling General Associate (Anti-Burgher) Presbytery Minutes, 9 January 1781, Central Regional Archives, CH 3/286/1, quoted by Brown, *Religion in Scotland*, p. 35.
382 Chalmers, *The Christian and Civic Economy of Large Towns*, Vol. 1 (Glasgow, 1821), p. 168.
383 [Bean], *Zeal without Innovation*, ch. 3, sect. I. See also p. 78.
384 Edwards, *Freedom of the Will*, p. 131.
385 A. G. Fuller, 'Memoirs of the Rev. Andrew Fuller', in *The Complete Works of the Rev. Andrew Fuller*, Vol. 1 (London, 1831), p. cxv. Fuller disclaimed 'moderate Calvinism', which he identified with Richard Baxter's position. He called his own system 'strict Calvinism'.
386 Wellwood, *Erskine*, p. 380.
387 [Bean], *Zeal without Innovation*, p. 56.
388 J. Scott, *The Life of the Rev. Thomas Scott*, 6th edn (London, 1824), p. 446.
389 The classic exposition of moderate Calvinism remains Walsh, 'Yorkshire Evangelicals', ch. 1; cf. Davies, *Cornish Evangelicals*, pp. 154 ff.
390 [Bean], *Zeal without Innovation*, p. 53.
391 R. I. and S. Wilberforce, *The Life of William Wilberforce*, 2nd edn, Vol. 2 (London, 1839), p. 136.
392 Venn, *Complete Duty*, p. xiii.
393 ibid., ch. 10.
394 Wellwood, *Erskine*, p. 381.
395 Scott, *Scott*, p. 664.
396 Edwards, *Freedom of the Will*, esp. pp. 35–40, 360.
397 Scott, *Force of Truth*, p. 78.
398 Scott, *Scott*, p. 664.
399 For example, Fuller in 1783, quoted by Whitley, *Calvinism and Evangelism*, p. 33.
400 Pratt (ed.), *Evangelical Leaders*, p. 223.
401 Nuttall, 'Northamptonshire and *The Modern Question*'.
402 J. Gadsby, *A Memoir of William Gadsby* (Manchester, 1842), p. 50.
403 Pratt (ed.), *Evangelical Leaders*, pp. 222 ff.
404 E. F. Clipsham, 'Andrew Fuller and Fullerism: a study in Evangelical Calvinism', *Baptist Quarterly*, vol. 20, no. 3 (1963), pp. 110–13.
405 W. T. Owen, *Edward Williams, D.D., 1750–1813: His Life, Thought and Influence* (Cardiff, 1963), p. 97 n. J. Milner, *The History of the Church of Christ*, 2nd edn, Vol. 2 (London, 1810), p. 386 n. Henderson, 'Jonathan Edwards and Scotland', p. 159.
406 Tyerman, *Wesley*, Vol. 2, p. 339.
407 G. Lawton, *John Wesley's English: A Study of his Literary Style* (London, 1962), p. 291.
408 Simeon to G. A. Underwood, 2 October 1817, Cheltenham File, Simeon Trust MSS, quoted by Balda, '"Spheres of influence"', pp. 76 f.
409 Davies, *Cornish Evangelicals*, ch. 5.
410 Chadwick, *Victorian Church*, Vol. 1, pp. 449 f.
411 S. J. Brown, *Thomas Chalmers and the Godly Commonwealth in Scotland* (Oxford, 1982), pp. 132 f.
412 Lovegrove, 'Itinerant evangelism', ch. 2.

413 J. Walford, *Memoirs of the Life and Labours of the Late Venerable Hugh Bourne* (London, 1855), Vol. 1, p. 173. See also p. 26.
414 For example, Jabez Bunting as cited by J. H. S. Kent, 'The doctrine of the ministry', *The Age of Disunity* (London, 1966), p. 85.
415 *The Works of the Rev. John Wesley, A.M.*, 3rd edn, Vol. 7 (London, 1829), p. 207.
416 Baker, *Wesley and the Church of England*, ch. 15.
417 Walsh, 'Methodism at the end of the eighteenth century', p. 288.
418 *WV*, Vol. 1, p. 150.
419 Brown, *Baptists*, p. 105.
420 W. R. Ward, 'Baptists and the transformation of the church'.
421 Sher, *Church and University*, pp. 50–6.
422 Davies, *Cornish Evangelicals*, p. 71.
423 D. M. Thompson, *Denominationalism and Dissent, 1795–1835: A Question of Identity*, Friends of Dr Williams's Library 39th Lecture (London, 1985), esp. p. 13.
424 Dallimore, *Whitefield*, Vol. 2, p. 92.
425 Martin, *Evangelicals United*, pts II and III.
426 D. M. Rosman, *Evangelicals and Culture* (London, 1984), ch. 8. T. W. Herbert, *John Wesley as Editor and Author* (Princeton, NJ, 1940), pp. 88–97.
427 C. Binfield, *So Down to Prayers: Studies in English nonconformity, 1780–1920* (London, 1977), ch. 3.
428 J. Erskine, 'Memoir', in *Extracts from an Exhortation to the Inhabitants of the South Parish of Glasgow by the late Rev. Dr John Gillies* (Glasgow, 1819), p. 6.
429 ibid., p. 7. Herbert, *Wesley*, p. 47.
430 Hall, 'Review of Foster's Essays', *The Miscellaneous Works and Remains of the Rev. Robert Hall* (London, 1846), p. 446.
431 Wesley to Samuel Furly, 15 July 1764, *Letters*, ed. Telford, Vol. 4, p. 256.
432 ibid., p. 290.
433 Sher, *Church and University*, pp. 57 f.
434 J. Dale, 'The theological and literary qualities of the poetry of Charles Wesley in relation to the standards of his age', PhD thesis, University of Cambridge, 1961, ch. 7.
435 *Arminian Magazine*, March 1785, p. 151.
436 Jones, *Congregationalism*, p. 166.
437 Marshall and Todd, *Congregational Hymns*, pp. 53 f., 71. Hoyles, *Waning*, p. 228.
438 Binfield, *So Down to Prayers*, p. 45. In *A Gathered Church: The Literature of the English Dissenting Interest, 1700–1930* (London, 1978), Donald Davie points out the classicism of Watts's Calvinism (pp. 25–8, 35), but mistakenly denies it to Charles Wesley or the early Evangelicals of the Church of England (chs 3 and 4); cf. Rosman, *Evangelicals and Culture*.
439 Marshall and Todd, *Congregational Hymns*, pp. 156 ff.
440 Dale, 'Poetry of Charles Wesley', ch. 5.
441 ibid., pp. 104, 108, 127, 146.
442 'Invitation to sinners', in G. Osborn (ed.), *The Poetical Works of John and Charles Wesley* (London, 1868), Vol. 4, p. 371. This paragraph is based on Dale, 'Poetry of Charles Wesley', ch. 6.
443 'Collection of hymns', ed. Hildebrandt *et al.*, p. 74.

444 Wesley to Richard Boardman (?), 12 January 1776, *Letters*, ed. Telford, Vol. 6, p. 201.

445 *Arminian Magazine*, 1781, p. iv.

446 For example, *WV*, vol. 4, p. 228. T. Jackson, *Recollections of My Own Life and Times* (London, 1873), p. 216.

447 E. Martin, 'Sale of Wesley's publications', *Proceedings of the Wesley Historical Society*, vol. 1 (1897), p. 90.

448 Jackson, *Recollections*, pp. 25 f.

449 Herbert, *Wesley*, p. 1.

450 Lackington, *Memoirs*, p. 73.

451 H. F. Mathews, *Methodism and the Education of the People, 1791–1851* (London, 1949), pp. 31 f., 184.

452 ibid., p. 182.

453 Lackington, *Confessions*, p. 184.

454 Nuttall, *Trevecca College*.

455 P. B. Cliff, *The Rise and Development of the Sunday School Movement in England, 1780–1980* (Nutfield, Surrey, 1986), p. 25.

456 Martin, *Evangelicals United*, ch. 8.

457 Mathews, *Methodism and Education*, p. 172.

458 V. Kiernan, 'Evangelicalism and the French Revolution', *Past & Present*, no. 1 (1952).

459 Brown, *Fathers of the Victorians*, esp. foreword.

460 J. Pollock, *Wilberforce* (London, 1977), ch. 7. R. J. Hind, 'William Wilberforce and the perceptions of the British people', *Historical Research*, vol. 60, no. 143 (1987). For Evangelical attacks on popular culture, see p. 132.

461 Jones, *More*, pp. 134 ff, 104–7.

462 L. and J. C. F. Stone, *An Open Elite? England, 1540–1880* (Oxford, 1984), p. 327.

463 Wellwood, *Erskine*, p. 72. A. Russell, *The Clerical Profession* (London, 1980), p. 114.

464 R. F. Wearmouth, *Methodism and the Common People of the Eighteenth Century* (London, 1945), pp. 202–11.

465 F. K. Prochaska, *Women and Philanthropy in Nineteenth-Century England* (Oxford, 1980), pp. 8 f.

466 Heitzenrater, *Wesley*, Vol. 1, p. 135.

467 Welch (ed.), *Calvinistic Methodist Chapels*, pp. xiv f.

468 *George Whitefield's Journals* (n.p., 1960), p. 395.

469 See pp. 121 ff.

470 W. Myles, *A Chronological History of the People called Methodists*, 3rd edn (London, 1803), p. 183.

471 D. G. Mathews, *Religion in the Old South* (Chicago, 1977), ch. 4.

472 Anstey, *Atlantic Slave Trade*, chs 4–8.

473 S. Drescher, *Econocide: Economic Development and the Abolition of the British Slave Trade* (Pittsburgh, 1977).

474 Anstey, *Atlantic Slave Trade*, ch. 9.

475 S. Drescher, 'Public opinion and the destruction of British colonial slavery', in James Walvin (ed.), *Slavery and British Society, 1776–1846* (London, 1982), pp. 37–40.

476 M. Craton, *Testing the Chains: Resistance to Slavery in the British West Indies* (Ithaca, NY, 1982).

477 Pollock, *Wilberforce*. Anstey, *Atlantic Slave Trade*, chs 10, 11, 14. C. D. Rice, 'The missionary context of the British anti-slavery movement', in Walvin (ed.), *Slavery and British Society*. R. Anstey, 'Religion and British slave emancipation', in D. Eltis and J. Walvin (eds), *The Abolition of the Atlantic Slave Trade* (Madison, Wis., 1981).

478 S. Drescher, 'Two variants of anti-slavery: religious organization and social mobilization in Britain and France, 1780–1870', in C. Bolt and S. Drescher (eds), *Anti-Slavery, Religion and Reform: Essays in Memory of Roger Anstey* (Folkestone, 1980), p. 48.

479 S. Drescher, *Capitalism and Antislavery: British Mobilization in Comparative Perspective* (London, 1986), ch. 6, esp. p. 131. G. Stephen, *Anti-Slavery Recollections in a Series of Letters addressed to Mrs Beecher Stowe* [1854] (London, 1971), p. 248.

480 J. Owen, *Memoir of the Rev. T. Jones, late of Creaton* (London, 1851), p. 160.

481 Witherspoon, *The Charge of Sedition and Faction against Good Men, especially Faithful Ministers, considered and accounted for* (Glasgow, 1758), p. 31.

482 R. Hall, 'An apology for the freedom of the press' [1793], in O. Gregory (ed.), *The Works of Robert Hall, A.M.* (London, 1839), Vol. 4, pp. 45–144. *The Trial of Wm. Winterbotham . . . for Seditious Words* (London, 1794).

483 Lovegrove, 'Itinerant evangelism', p. 224.

484 Gregory (ed.), *Works of Hall*, Vol. 4, p. 146.

485 A. Fuller, 'Thoughts on civil polity' [1808], *Complete Works*, Vol. 5 (London, 1832), p. 532.

486 Hempton, *Methodism and Politics*, pp. 47 f.

487 Kent, 'Wesleyan membership', pp. 111 f.

488 Newton to Mrs P—, August. 1775, in *The Works of the Rev. John Newton* (Edinburgh, 1837), p. 250.

489 Lawson, '"Our discipline"', p. 195.

490 Hempton, *Methodism and Politics*, ch. 2. Walsh, 'Methodism at the end of the eighteenth century', pp. 304 ff.

491 Wilberforce, *Practical View*, p. 403.

492 I. Bradley, 'The politics of godliness: Evangelicals in parliament, 1784–1832', DPhil thesis, University of Oxford, 1974.

493 Walsh, 'Methodism at the end of the eighteenth century', p. 303.

494 Evans, *A Letter to the Rev. Mr John Wesley occasioned by his Calm Address* (Bristol, 1775), p. 11, quoted by E. A. Payne, 'Nonconformists and the American Revolution', *Journal of the United Reformed Church History Society*, vol. 1, no. 8 (1976), p. 220.

495 John Rippon cited in ibid., p. 210.

496 Sher, *Church and University*, pp. 267 ff.

497 Handy, *United States and Canada*, p. 140.

498 For example, Hall, 'On toleration', in Gregory (ed.), *Works of Hall*, Vol. 6, pp. 370–96.

499 Scott, *Force of Truth*, p. 44 n.

500 Clarke, 'The origin and end of civil government', *The Miscellaneous Works of Adam Clarke, LL.D., F.A.S.*, Vol. 7 (London, 1836), p. 249.

501 Hempton, *Methodism and Politics*, pp. 30–43. Semmel, *Methodist Revolution*, pp. 88 ff.
502 Sher, *Church and University*, pp. 281–6.
503 Shaftesbury, *Characteristicks of Men, Manners, Opinions, Times in Three Volumes*, 6th edn (London, 1737), Vol. 3, p. 400, cited by J. Hook, *The Baroque Age in England* (London, 1976), p. 48. See also J. Steegman, *The Rule of Taste from George I to George IV* (London, 1968).
504 M'Kerrow, *Secession Church*, pp. 845–9.
505 Edwards, 'Narrative', p. 57.

CHAPTER 3: A TROUBLING OF THE WATER

1 D. M. Rosman, *Evangelicals and Culture* (London, 1984), pp. 35 f.
2 F. K. Brown, *Fathers of the Victorians: The Age of Wilberforce* (Cambridge, 1961), pp. 518 ff.
3 I. Bradley, *The Call to Seriousness: The Evangelical Impact on the Victorians* (London, 1976), pp. 194 f.
4 A. R. Vidler, *The Church in an Age of Revolution* (Harmondsworth, Middlesex, 1961), p. 49.
5 M. Hennell, *Sons of the Prophets: Evangelical Leaders of the Victorian Church* (London, 1979), pp. 9–15. Rosman, *Evangelicals and Culture*, pp. 24–37. See also E. R. Sandeen, *The Roots of Fundamentalism: British and American Millenarianism, 1800–1930* (Chicago, 1970), ch. 1; H. Willmer, 'Evangelicalism, 1785 to 1835', Hulsean Prize Essay, University of Cambridge, 1962; I. S. Rennie, 'Evangelicalism and English public life, 1823–1850', PhD thesis, University of Toronto, 1962.
6 R. Currie et al., *Churches and Churchgoers: Patterns of Church Growth in the British Isles since 1700* (Oxford, 1977), pp. 21–5.
7 E. R. Norman, *Church and Society in England, 1770–1970* (Oxford, 1976), pp. 52–5.
8 S. J. Brown, *Thomas Chalmers and the Godly Commonwealth in Scotland* (Oxford, 1982), ch. 3. R. A. Cage and E. O. A. Checkland, 'Thomas Chalmers and urban poverty: the St John's Parish experiment in Glasgow, 1819–1837', *Philosophical Journal*, vol. 13, no. 1 (1976).
9 J. H. Stewart, *Thoughts on the Importance of Special Prayer for the General Outpouring of the Holy Spirit* (London, 1821), p. 9; cf. D. D. Stewart, *Memoir of the Life of the Rev. James Haldane Stewart, M.A.*, 2nd edn (London, 1857), pp. 91–102.
10 R. Carwardine, *Transatlantic Revivalism: Popular Evangelicalism in Britain and America, 1790–1865* (Westport, Conn., 1978), p. 63.
11 E. Irving, *For Missionaries after the Apostolical School: A Series of Orations* (London, 1825), p. 18.
12 W. T. Gidney, *The History of the London Society for Promoting Christianity among the Jews from 1809 to 1908* (London, 1908), p. 70.
13 A. L. Drummond, 'Robert Haldane at Geneva, 1816–17', *Records of Scottish Church History Society*, vol. 9, no. 2 (1946). T. Stunt, 'Geneva and British Evangelicals in the early nineteenth century', *JEH*, vol. 32, no. 1 (1981), esp. p. 40.

14 A. Haldane, *The Lives of Robert Haldane of Airthrey, and his Brother, James Alexander Haldane*, 5th edn (Edinburgh, 1855), pp. 429 f., 454.
15 *Dialogues on Prophecy*, vol. 1 (London, 1827), p. 212.
16 J. Williams, 'Memoirs of the Rev. Robert Hawker, D.D.', in *The Works of the Rev. Robert Hawker, D.D.*, Vol. 1 (London, 1831).
17 *The Sinner Saved: or Memoirs of the Life of William Huntington* (London, [1813]).
18 W. Carus, *Memoirs of the Life of the Rev. Charles Simeon, M.A.*, 2nd edn (London, 1857), p. 417.
19 J. J. Evans, *Memoir and Remains of the Rev. James Harington Evans, M.A.*, 2nd edn (London, 1855), pp. 31–37, 30.
20 Carus, *Simeon*, pp. 566 f.
21 Evans, *Evans*, p. 27.
22 H. H. Rowdon, *The Origins of the Brethren, 1825–1850* (London, 1967), pp. 61 ff., 67 f. See also T. C. F. Stunt, 'John Henry Newman and the Evangelicals', *JEH*, vol. 21, no. 1 (1970).
23 E. Irving, *The Last Days: A Discourse on the Evil Character of these our Times, proving them to be the "Perilous Times" of the "Last Days"*, 2nd edn (London, 1850), pp. 451–6.
24 H. L. Alexander, *Life of Joseph Addison Alexander*, Vol. 1 (1870), p. 290, quoted by P. E. Shaw, *The Catholic Apostolic Church sometimes called Irvingite* (Morningside Heights, NY, 1946), p. 50.
25 A. L. Drummond, *Edward Irving and his Circle* (London, n.d.) is still the most useful general analysis of Irving.
26 Irving, *For the Oracles of God: Four Orations. For Judgment to Come: An Argument in Nine Parts* (London, 1823), p. 104.
27 Carlyle, *Reminiscences* [1887], ed. C. E. Norton (London, 1972), p. 195.
28 M. O. W. Oliphant, *The Life of Edward Irving*, 4th edn (London, n.d.), p. 96.
29 Carlyle, *Reminiscences*, p. 240. Irving, *Judgment to Come*, p. 307.
30 Irving, *Babylon and Infidelity Foredoomed of God*, Vol. 1 (Glasgow, 1826), pp. 308 f.
31 S. T. Coleridge to Daniel Stuart, [8?] July 1825, in E. L. Griggs (ed.), *Collected Letters of Samuel Taylor Coleridge*, Vol. 5 (Oxford, 1971), p. 474.
32 Irving, *Babylon and Infidelity*, p. 309; *Judgment to Come*, p. 138.
33 Coleridge to Edward Coleridge, 23 July 1823, in Griggs (ed.), *Letters of Coleridge*, Vol. 5, p. 286.
34 Irving, *Missionaries*, pp. vii f.
35 W. Hanna, *Memoirs of the Life and Writings of Thomas Chalmers, D.D., LL.D.*, Vol. 3 (Edinburgh, 1851), p. 160.
36 For example, Irving, *Missionaries*, p. xiv. R. J. White (ed.), *The Political Thought of Samuel Taylor Coleridge* (London, 1938).
37 Irving, *Missionaries*, pp. vii, 84, 85.
38 M. H. Abrams, *Natural Supernaturalism: Tradition and Revolution in Romantic Literature* (London, 1971), p. 32.
39 C. R. Sanders, *Coleridge and the Broad Church Movement* (Durham, NC, 1942). M. H. Bright, 'English literary Romanticism and the Oxford Movement', *Journal of the History of Ideas*, vol. 40, no. 3 (1979).

40 G. S. R. Kitson Clark, 'The Romantic element: 1830 to 1850', in J. H. Plumb (ed.), *Studies in Social History: A Tribute to G. M. Trevelyan* (London, 1955), pp. 230, 214–17.

41 See pp. 62 f.

42 *Morning Watch*, March 1830, p. 34. See also S. C. Orchard, 'English Evangelical eschatology, 1790–1850', PhD thesis, University of Cambridge, 1969; W. H. Oliver, *Prophets and Millennialists: The Uses of Biblical Prophecy in England from the 1790s to the 1840s* (Auckland, NZ, 1978); D. Hempton, 'Evangelicals and eschatology', *JEH*, vol. 31, no. 2 (1980); D. W. Bebbington, 'The advent hope in British Evangelicalism since 1800', *Scottish Journal of Religious Studies* (forthcoming).

43 Rather confusingly, Harrison calls the premillennialists 'millenarian' and the postmillennialists 'millennialist'. J. F. C. Harrison, *The Second Coming: Popular Millenarianism, 1780–1850* (London, 1979), pp. 5, 208.

44 Cuninghame, *A Dissertation on the Seals and Trumpets of the Apocalypse* (London, 1813). T. R. Birks, *A Memoir of the Rev. Edward Bickersteth*, Vol. 2 (London, 1856 edn), p. 45.

45 Frere, *A Combined View of the Prophecies of Daniel, Esdras, and St. John*, 2nd edn (London, 1815), pp. iv f, 210–16, esp. p. 212.

46 Irving, *Babylon and Infidelity*, Vol. 1, pp. v–viii; Vol. 2, pp. 23 n., 243.

47 J. J. Ben-Ezra, *The Coming of Messiah in Glory and Majesty*, trans. Irving (London, 1827), p. xlix.

48 R. H. Martin, *Evangelicals United: Ecumenical Stirrings in Pre-Victorian Britain, 1795–1830* (Metuchen, NJ, 1983), chs 8 and 9. M. Vrete, 'The restoration of the Jews in English Protestant thought, 1790–1840', *Middle Eastern Studies*, vol. 8, no. 1 (1972).

49 Sandeen, *Roots of Fundamentalism*, p. 12.

50 *Dialogues*, vol. 1, p. 208.

51 Carlyle, *Reminiscences*, p. 287.

52 E. Miller, *The History and Doctrines of Irvingism, or the So-Called Catholic and Apostolic Church*, Vol. 1 (London, 1878), pp. 35–46.

53 *Dialogues*, vol. 3, p. 2.

54 R. Wallis (ed.), *Millenialism and Charisma* (Belfast, 1982), p. 1.

55 Ben-Ezra, *Coming of Messiah*, pp. vi, xlix.

56 J. H. Pratt (ed.), *The Thought of the Evangelical Leaders: Notes of the Discussions of The Eclectic Society, London, during the Years 1798–1814* [1856] (Edinburgh, 1978), p. 256. Simeon to Miss E. Elliott, 19 February 1830, in Carus, *Simeon*, pp. 658 f.

57 H. McNeile, *A Sermon preached at the Parish Church of St Paul, Covent Garden, on Thursday Evening, May 5, 1826, before the London Society for Promoting Christianity amongst the Jews* (London, n.d.), pp. 8, 23, 25; G. T. Noel, *A Brief Enquiry into the Prospects of the Church of Christ, in Connexion with the Second Advent of Our Lord Jesus Christ* (London, 1828), pp. 28, 37.

58 J. H. Stewart, *A Practical View of the Redeemer's Advent, in a Series of Discourses*, 2nd edn (London, 1826), p. ix.

59 Harris, *The Great Commission* (London, 1842), p. 122.

60 D. Brown, *Christ's Second Coming: Will it be Premillennial?* (Edinburgh, 1846), pp. 13 ff.

61 ibid., 3rd edn (Edinburgh, 1853), pp. 10, 8.

62 E. Hodder, *The Life and Work of the Seventh Earl of Shaftesbury, K.G.* (London, 1888 edn), pp. 385, 524, 735.
63 Brown, *Christ's Second Coming*, 3rd edn, p. 10.
64 Blaikie, *Brown*, pp. 333, 44.
65 Brown, *Christ's Second Coming*, 3rd edn, p. 455.
66 T. R. Birks, *First Elements of Sacred Prophecy* (London, 1843), p. 3.
67 Elliott, *Horae Apocalypticae: Or, a Commentary on the Apocalypse* . . . [1844], 2nd edn, Vol. 1 (London, 1846), preceding p. 117.
68 S. Garratt, *Signs of the Times*, 2nd edn (London, 1869), pp. ix ff.
69 Cumming, *Apocalyptic Sketches* (London, 1848), p. 3; cf. R. Buick Knox, 'Dr John Cumming and Crown Court Church, London', *Records of Scottish Church History Society*, vol. 22, no. 1 (1984).
70 Stewart, *Stewart*, p. 307. R. Braithwaite, *The Life and Letters of Rev. William Pennefather, B.A.* (London, 1878), p. 253.
71 The first was *The Second Coming, the Judgement, and the Kingdom of Christ* (London, 1843). An annual volume was published up to 1858.
72 Waldegrave, *New Testament Millennarianism [sic]* (London, 1855).
73 *British and Foreign Evangelical Review*, vol. 4, no. 14 (1855), p. 698.
74 Maitland, *An Enquiry into the Grounds on which the Prophetic Period of Daniel and St. John has been supposed to consist of 1260 years* (London, 1826).
75 *Dialogues*, vol. 1, p. 366. Birks, *Sacred Prophecy*, p. 2.
76 Miller, *Irvingism*, Vol. 2, pp. 266 f.
77 Rowdon, *Origins of the Brethren*, ch. 1 and ch. 9, sect. 2. Sandeen, *Roots of Fundamentalism*, ch. 3. See also W. G. Turner, *John Nelson Darby* (London, 1926).
78 J. Sargent, *Memoir of the Rev. Henry Martyn, B.D.*, 8th edn (London, 1825), p. 426.
79 A. W. Brown, *Recollections of the Conversation Parties of the Rev. Charles Simeon* (London, 1863), p. 100.
80 Wilson, *Lectures on the Evidences of Christianity*, Vol. 1 (London, 1828), p. 455.
81 Horne, *An Introduction to the Critical Study and Knowledge of the Holy Scriptures*, Vol. 1 (London, 1818), pp. 435 f.
82 Rosman, *Evangelicals and Culture*, p. 40. T. R. Preston, 'Biblical criticism, literature and the eighteenth-century reader', in I. Rivers (ed.), *Books and their Readers in Eighteenth-Century England* (Leicester, 1982), pp. 105 f.
83 R. Hawker, *The Evidences of a Plenary Inspiration* (Plymouth, [c.1794]), pp. 21 f., 31, 50 ff.
84 Pratt (ed.), *Evangelical Leaders*, pp. 152 f., 2.
85 Haldane, *Haldanes*, ch. 18, esp. p. 412.
86 Haldane, *The Evidence and Authority of Divine Revelation* (Edinburgh, 1816), pp. 134 f.
87 Martin, *Evangelicals United*, pp. 123–31. Rennie, 'Evangelicalism and public life', pp. 42–9.
88 Haldane, *Haldanes*, p. 505.
89 Haldane, *Haldanes*, pp. 511–15. J. Medway, *Memoirs of the Life and Writings of John Pye Smith, D.D., LL.D., F.R.S., F.G.S.* (London, 1853), ch. 17.
90 H[enry] D[rummond], *A Defence of the Students of Prophecy* (London, 1828), p. 23.
91 Way, *The Latter Rain*, 2nd edn (London, 1821), p. v.

92   *CO*, 1843, p. 806.
93   'Modern millenarianism', *Eclectic Review*, March 1829, p. 214.
94   Bonar, *Prophetical Landmarks* (London, 1847), p. 274.
95   Rowdon, *Origins of the Brethren*, p. 52.
96   Sandeen, *Roots of Fundamentalism*, pp. 107 ff.
97   Haldane, *Haldanes*, p. 515.
98   Gaussen, *Theopneustia: The Plenary Inspiration of the Holy Scriptures* (London, 1841), pp. 27 f.
99   For example, J. Conder, *An Analytical and Comparative View of All Religions* (London, 1838), p. 514.
100 Gaussen, *Theopneustia*, ch. 3, p. 37.
101 W. J. Abraham, *The Divine Inspiration of Holy Scripture* (Oxford, 1981), p. 33.
102 Gaussen, *Theopneustia*, p. 25.
103 Haldane, *Divine Revelation*, p. 138.
104 Gaussen, *Theopneustia*, pp. ii, 27.
105 *CO*, September 1854, p. 625, Medway, *Pye Smith*, p. 285.
106 Abraham, *Divine Inspiration*, pp. 16 f.
107 Medway, *Pye Smith*, pp. 307 f. Harris in *New College, London: The Introductory Lectures Delivered at the Opening of the College* (London, 1851), p. 33. T. R. Birks, *Modern Rationalism and the Inspiration of the Scriptures* (London, 1853), pp. 101–12.
108 Haldane, *Haldanes*, p. 516.
109 A. C. Cheyne, *The Transforming of the Kirk: Victorian Scotland's Religious Revolution* (Edinburgh, 1983), pp. 7 f. Professor Cheyne, however, characterises these opinions as symptomatic of 'Scotland's religious conservatism', not recognising their novelty.
110 *R*, 24 October 1850.
111 *CO*, April 1861, p. 256.
112 *Dialogues*, vol. 1, p. 368.
113 Drummond, *Irving*, pp. 138 f., 153, 167 f. See also G. Strachan, *The Pentecostal Theology of Edward Irving* (London, 1973).
114 Miller, *Irvingism*, Vol. 1, pp. 64, 346; cf. Shaw, *Catholic Apostolic Church*.
115 See pp. 58 f.
116 Noel, *Prospects of the Church*, pp. 155 f.
117 *Dialogues*, vol. 1, pp. 346, 40.
118 Harris, *Great Commission*, pp. 11, 124.
119 See 142, 143 f.
120 W. Hanna (ed.), *Letters of Thomas Erskine of Linlathen from 1800 till 1840* (Edinburgh, 1877), pp. 66.
121 Erskine, *The Unconditional Freeness of the Gospel*, 4th edn (Edinburgh, 1831), p. 88, quoted in Hanna (ed.), *Erskine*, p. 376. See also D. Finlayson, 'Aspects of the life and influence of Thomas Erskine of Linlathen, 1788–1870', *Records of Scottish Church History Society*, vol. 20, no. 1 (1978).
122 [Drummond], *Defence*, p. 39. Hanna (ed.), *Erskine*, p. 127.
123 D. Campbell, *Memorials of John McLeod Campbell, D.D.*, Vol. 1 (London, 1877), pp. 51–4; cf. G. M. Tuttle, *So Rich a Soil: John McLeod Campbell on Christian Atonement* (Edinburgh, 1986).
124 Irving, *Last Days*, p. 451.

125 J. P. Newell, 'A nestor of Nonconformist heretics: A. J. Scott (1805–1866)', *Journal of the United Reformed Church History Society*, vol. 3, no. 1 (1983). Hanna (ed.), *Erskine*, pp. 127 ff. F. Maurice, *The Life of Frederick Denison Maurice*, 2nd edn, Vol. 2 (London, 1884), pp. 406 ff.

126 Irving, *Sermons, Lectures, and Occasional Discourses* (London, 1828), p. v.

127 Irving, *The Orthodox and Catholic Doctrine of Our Lord's Human Nature* (London, 1830), p. vii.

128 D. Newsome, *Two Classes of Men: Platonism and English Romantic Thought* (London, 1973), ch. 5.

129 F. Irving, *Missionaries*, pp. 28, 18.

130 F. R. Coad, *A History of the Brethren Movement* (Exeter, 1968), ch. 1.

131 *Autobiography of George Müller*, ed. G. F. Bergin (London, 1905), pp. 223, 16. See also p. 39.

132 H. and G. Taylor, *Hudson Taylor*, 2 vols (London, 1911 and 1918). See also B. Stanley, 'Home support for overseas missions in early Victorian England, c. 1838–1873', PhD thesis, University of Cambridge, 1979, chs 7 and 8.

133 J. Hudson Taylor, *A Retrospect*, 2nd edn (London, 1898), p. 41.

134 *Dialogues*, vol. 3, p. vii; vol. 2, p. 4.

135 Irving, *Last Days*, p. 447.

136 Thelwall, *Sermons, chiefly on Subjects connected with the Present State and Circumstances of the Church and the World* (London, 1833).

137 *A Memoir of the Rev. Henry Budd* (London, 1855), p. 449.

138 Irving, *Last Days*, p. xxxviii.

139 *Budd*, p. 449.

140 *Dialogues*, vol. 3, p. 472. H. Budd, *Infant-Baptism the Means of National Reformation according to the Doctrines and Discipline of the Established Church* (London, 1827), p. 235.

141 Irving, *Babylon and Infidelity*, Vol. 2, p. 264.

142 *Dialogues*, vol. 1, p. 349.

143 Drummond, *Defence*, p. 58.

144 R. L. Lively, 'The Catholic Apostolic Church and the Church of Jesus Christ of Latter-Day Saints: a comparative study of two minority millenarian groups in nineteenth-century England', DPhil thesis, University of Oxford, 1978, p. 108.

145 Drummond, *Defence*, pp. 57 f.

146 Griggs (ed.), *Letters of Coleridge*, Vol. 6, p. 976 n.

147 Irving, *Last Days*, pp. 121, 124–30.

148 T. Hill (ed.), *Letters and Memoir of the late Walter Augustus Shirley* (London, 1849), p. 177.

149 Coad, *Brethren Movement*, pp. 29 f.

150 Irving, *Last Days*, pp. 122 f.

151 Irving, *Homilies on the Sacraments: Vol. 1: On Baptism* (London, 1828), p. 434.

152 Oliphant, *Irving*, p. 216.

153 Irving, *Last Days*, p. 121.

154 Budd, *Infant-Baptism*, p. vii.

155 Hill (ed.), *Shirley*, p. 130. *Dialogues*, vol. 3, p. 472. F. D. Maurice, *The Kingdom of Christ*, Vol. 1 (London, 1838), pp. 104 ff.

156 Newsome, *Two Classes of Men*, p. 30.

157 *Dialogues*, vol. 2, pp. 4 f.

158 Irving, *Missionaries*, p. 83.
159 *Dialogues*, vol. 2, p. 242.
160 Irving, *Last Days*, p. 132.
161 *Dialogues*, vol. 3, p. 472.
162 Drummond, *Defence*, pp. 61–4.
163 *Dialogues*, vol. 1, pp. 373 f.
164 S. W. Gilley, 'Newman and prophecy, Evangelical and Catholic', *Journal of the United Reformed Church History Society*, vol. 3, no. 5 (1985). Stunt, 'Newman and the Evangelicals', p. 71. See also D. Newsome, 'Justification and sanctification: Newman and the Evangelicals', *Journal of Theological Studies*, vol. 15, pt 1 (1964); and 'The Evangelical Sources of Newman's Power', in J. Coulson and A. M. Allchin (eds), *The Rediscovery of Newman* (London, 1967).
165 H. Tristram (ed.), *John Henry Newman: Autobiographical Writings* (New York, 1957), pp. 202–6, 208.
166 E. A. Knox, *The Tractarian Movement, 1833–1845* (London, 1933), pp. 124 ff.
167 D. Newsome, *The Parting of Friends: A Study of the Wilberforces and Henry Manning* (London, 1966).
168 P. Toon, *Evangelical Theology, 1833–1856: A Response to Tractarianism* (London, 1979), ch. 1.
169 *Budd*, p. 602.
170 See pp. 147 ff.
171 Bickersteth, *Christian Hearer*, 2nd edn (London, 1826), pp. 128–42.
172 J. E. Gordon, *Original Reflections and Conversational Remarks chiefly on Theological Subjects* (London, 1854), p. 315.
173 G. F. A. Best, 'Evangelicals and the Established Church in the early nineteenth century', *Journal of Theological Studies*, vol. 10, pt 1 (1959).
174 Lord Henley, *A Plan of Church Reform* (London, 1832).
175 *Dialogues*, vol. 2, p. 252.
176 O. Chadwick, *The Victorian Church*, Vol. 1, 2nd edn (London, 1970), pp. 36 f.
177 [R. B. Seeley], *Essays on the Church* (London, 1834).
178 Rennie, 'Evangelicalism and public life', pp. 300–3.
179 Chalmers, *Lectures on the Establishment and Extension of National Churches* (London, 1838).
180 D. W. Bebbington in *Baptist Quarterly*, vol. 27, no. 8 (1978), pp. 376 ff. R. W. Davis, 'The Strategy of "Dissent" in the repeal campaign, 1820–1828', *Journal of Modern History*, vol. 36, no. 4 (1966).
181 Chadwick, *Victorian Church*, Vol. 1, pp. 60 ff.
182 H. S. Skeats and C. S. Miall, *History of the Free Churches of England, 1688–1891* (London, 1891), pp. 479 f.
183 D. M. Lewis, *Lighten their Darkness: The Evangelical Mission to Working-Class London, 1828-1860* (Westport, Conn., 1986), ch. 3. J. Wolffe, 'The Evangelical Alliance in the 1840s: an attempt to institutionalise Christian Unity', in *Voluntary Religion*, Studies in Church History, vol. 23, ed. W. J. Sheils and D. Wood (Oxford, 1986).
184 *CO*, 1843, pp. iii f. See also pp. 136 f.
185 J. H. Newman, *Apologia pro Vita Sua, being a History of his Religious Opinions* [1864] (London, 1946 edn), p. 197.

186 Irving, *Babylon and Infidelity*, p. 400.
187 *Random Recollections of Exeter Hall in 1834–1837* (London, 1838), p. 135.
188 J. C. Colquhoun, *William Wilberforce: His Friends and His Times* (London, 1867), p. 7.
189 *Dialogues*, vol. 2, p. 251.
190 B. Hilton, 'The role of providence in Evangelical social thought', in D. Beales and G. Best (eds), *History, Society and the Churches* (Cambridge, 1985), pp. 225–8.
191 *Dialogues*, vol. 2, p. 258.
192 Rennie, 'Evangelicals and public life', p. 158. *Random Recollections*, p. 144.
193 *Dialogues*, vol. 1, pp. 5 f.
194 ibid., vol. 1, p. 211; vol. 3, p. 423.
195 I. McCalman, 'Unrespectable radicalism: infidels and pornography in early nineteenth-century Britain', *Past & Present*, 104 (1984), pp. 84 ff.
196 *Dialogues*, vol. 1, p. 39.
197 Drummond, *Defence*, p. 110.
198 R. W. Davis, *Dissent in Politics, 1780–1830: The Political Life of William Smith, M.P.* (London, 1971), esp. ch. 11.
199 Irving, *Sermons, Lectures . . .*, p. ix.
200 Martin, *Evangelicals United*, pp. 131–40.
201 K. R. M. Short, 'London's General Body of Protestant Ministers: its disruption in 1836', *JEH*, vol. 24, no. 4 (1973).
202 E. Norman, *The English Catholic Church in the Nineteenth Century* (Oxford, 1984), ch. 1.
203 D. Bowen, *The Protestant Crusade in Ireland, 1800–70* (Dublin, 1978), esp. pp. 89, 99.
204 D. Hempton, *Methodism and Politics in British Society, 1750–1850* (London, 1984), ch. 5.
205 G. I. T. Machin, *The Catholic Question in English Politics, 1820 to 1830* (Oxford, 1964).
206 Davis, 'Strategy of "Dissent"'.
207 G. F. A. Best, 'The Protestant constitution and its supporters', *Transactions of the Royal Historical Society*, 5th series, vol. 8 (1958), p. 108. Marsh, *Marsh*, pp. 126 ff.
208 Irving, *Babylon and Infidelity*, pp. x f.; *Last Days*, pp. 489–508.
209 *Protestant Churchman*, October 1871, p. 493. I am grateful for this reference to Dr J. R. Wolffe.
210 L. H. Lees, *Exiles of Erin: Irish Immigrants in Victorian London* (Manchester, 1979), p. 15.
211 S. Gilley, 'English attitudes to the Irish in England, 1780–1900', in C. Holmes (ed.), *Immigrants and Minorities in British Society* (London, 1978).
212 G. F. A. Best, 'Popular Protestantism in Victorian Britain', in R. Robson (ed.), *Ideas and Institutions of Victorian Britain* (London, 1967). E. R. Norman, *Anti-Catholicism in Victorian England* (London, 1967). W. L. Arnstein, *Protestant versus Catholic in Mid-Victorian England: Mr Newdegate and the Nuns* (Columbia, Mo., 1982). J. R. Wolffe, 'Anti-Catholicism in mid-nineteenth-century Britain', DPhil thesis, University of Oxford, 1985.
213 Elliott, *Horae Apocalypticae*, Vol. 4, p. 279.
214 *Witness*, 9 January 1850.

215 G. I. T. Machin, *Politics and the Churches in Great Britain, 1832 to 1868* (Oxford, 1977), pp. 94–9.

216 McNeile, *Nationalism in Religion: A Speech delivered at the Annual Meeting of the Protestant Association, held in the Exeter Hall, on Wednesday, May 8, 1839* (n.p., n.d.), pp. 2, 4.

217 Norman, *Anti-Catholicism*, ch. 2. Machin, *Politics and the Churches*, ch. 5, pt 5.

218 W. Ralls, 'The Papal Aggression of 1850: a study in Victorian anti-Catholicism', *Church History*, vol. 43, no. 2 (1974). Norman, *Anti-Catholicism*, ch. 3.

219 Ben-Ezra, *Coming of Messiah*, pp. viii f.

220 Rowdon, *Origins of the Brethren*, p. 17.

221 *CO*, January 1844, p. 128.

222 Brooks, *Advent and Kingdom*, p. 340.

223 Waldegrave, *New Testament Millenarianism*, p. 424.

224 Harris, *Great Commission*, ch. 3.

225 *CO*, January 1844, p. 128.

226 G. F. Berwick, 'Life of Francis Close', vol. 8 (1938), p. 25, quoted by Hennell, *Sons of the Prophets*, p. 107.

227 P. Fairbairn, *The Interpretation of Prophecy* [1864] (London, 1964 edn), p. vii.

228 Lively, 'Catholic Apostolic Church', p. 258. Although the sample includes some twentieth-century members, they are relatively few.

229 Rowdon, *Origins of the Brethren*, pp. 302 ff.

CHAPTER 4: THE GROWTH OF THE WORD

1 T. Hardy, *Jude the Obscure* [1896] (London, 1978), p. 93.

2 I. Bradley, *The Call to Seriousness: The Evangelical Impact on the Victorians* (London, 1976), p. 38.

3 O. Anderson, 'The reactions of Church and Dissent towards the Crimean War', *JEH*, vol. 16, no. 4 (1965), p. 215.

4 J. Wigley, *The Rise and Fall of the Victorian Sunday* (Manchester, 1980), pt 3.

5 G. M. Young, *Victorian England: Portrait of an Age* [1936], 2nd edn (London, 1953), p. 5.

6 J. S. Mill, 'Essay on Liberty' [1859], *On Liberty and Considerations on Representative Government*, ed. R. B. McCallum (Oxford, 1946), p. 61.

7 ibid., chs 3 and 4, esp. pp. 62, 78.

8 W. E. Gladstone, 'The Evangelical movement: its parentage, progress and issue', *British Quarterly Review*, July 1879, p. 6.

9 Paper by J. Coates at the Elland Society, 14 April 1803, cited by J. D. Walsh, 'The Yorkshire Evangelicals in the eighteenth century: with especial reference to Methodism', PhD thesis, University of Cambridge, 1956, p. 327.

10 J. Jerram (ed.), *The Memoirs and a Selection from the Letters of the Late Rev. Charles Jerram, M.A.* (London, 1855), p. 295.

11 W. J. Conybeare, 'Church parties', *Edinburgh Review*, no. 200 (1853), p. 338. The figure is doubted by O. Chadwick (*The Victorian Church*, Vol. 1, 2nd edn (London, 1970), p. 446), but on inadequate grounds.

12   A. Haig, *The Victorian Clergy* (London, 1984), p. 2.
13   R. Brent, *Liberal Anglican Politics: Whiggery, Religion and Reform, 1830–1841* (Oxford, 1987), p. 119.
14   T. Hill (ed.), *Letters and Memoir of the late Walter Augustus Shirley, D.D.* (London, 1849). *R*, 16 March 1848.
15   B. E. Hardman, 'The Evangelical party in the Church of England, 1855–1865', PhD thesis, University of Cambridge, 1964, ch. 2.
16   W. S. F. Pickering, 'The 1851 religious census: a useless experiment?', *British Journal of Sociology*, vol. 18, no. 4 (1967), pp. 393 f.
17   K. S. Inglis, 'Patterns of religious worship in 1851', *JEH*, vol. 11, no. 1 (1960), pp. 80 ff.
18   *Prospects for the Eighties* (London, 1980), p. 23.
19   R. Currie *et al.*, *Churches and Churchgoers: Patterns of Church Growth in the British Isles since 1700* (Oxford, 1977), p. 22. R. B. Walker, 'Religious changes in Cheshire, 1750–1850', *JEH*, vol. 17, no. 1 (1966), pp. 80 ff.
20   A. D. Gilbert, *Religion and Society in Industrial England: Church, Chapel and Social Change, 1740–1914* (London, 1976), p. 32.
21   Currie *et al.*, *Churches and Churchgoers*, pp. 147 f.
22   C. G. Brown, *The Social History of Religion in Scotland since 1730* (London, 1987), p. 61.
23   W. D. Balda, '"Spheres of influence": Simeon's Trust and its implications for Evangelical patronage', PhD thesis, University of Cambridge, 1981, p. 187.
24   B. I. Coleman, *The Church of England in the Mid-Nineteenth Century: A Social Geography* (London, 1980), pp. 8–25. See also A. Everitt, *The Pattern of Rural Dissent: The Nineteenth Century* (Leicester, 1973); and pp. 26 f.
25   H. McLeod, 'Class, community and region; the religious geography of nineteenth-century England' in *A Sociological Yearbook of Religion in Britain*, vol. 6, ed. M. Hill (London, 1973).
26   Coleman, *Church of England*, pp. 40 f.
27   B. Stanley, 'Home support for overseas missions in early Victorian England, c.1838–1873' PhD thesis, University of Cambridge, 1979, p. 201.
28   For example, R. M. Goodridge, 'Nineteenth-century urbanization and religion: Bristol and Marseilles, 1830–1880', in *A Sociological Yearbook of Religion in Britain*, vol. 2, ed. D. Martin (London, 1969), pp. 126 f.
29   H. McLeod, *Religion and the Working Class in Nineteenth-Century Britain* (London, 1984), p. 13.
30   H. McLeod, *Class and Religion in the Late Victorian City* (London, 1974), pp. 299 f.
31   C. Booth, *Life and Labour of the People in London: Third Series: Religious Influences*, Vol. 7 (London, 1902), p. 396.
32   J. Cox, *The English Churches in a Secular Society: Lambeth, 1870–1930* (New York, 1982), p. 32.
33   Booth, *Life and Labour*, Vol. 7, p. 112.
34   G. Crossick, 'The emergence of the lower middle class in Britain: a discussion', in G. Crossick (ed.), *The Lower Middle Class in Britain, 1870–1914* (London, 1977), p. 19.
35   McLeod, *Class and Religion*, p. 33.
36   C. D. Field, 'The social structure of English Methodism: eighteenth–twentieth centuries', *British Journal of Sociology*, vol. 28, no. 2 (1977), p. 209.

37 E. R. Wickham, *Church and People in an Industrial City* (London, 1957), p. 107.
38 Gilbert, *Religion and Society*, p. 63.
39 P. Hillis, 'Presbyterianism and social class in mid-nineteenth-century Glasgow: a study of nine churches', *JEH*, vol. 32, no. 1 (1981), pp. 55, 63.
40 Stanley, 'Home support', p. 198.
41 J. Obelkevich, *Religion and Rural Society: South Lindsey, 1825–1875* (Oxford, 1976), p. 239.
42 Gilbert, *Religion and Society*, p. 63.
43 Field, 'English Methodism', p. 216.
44 S. Yeo, *Religion and Voluntary Organisations in Crisis* (London, 1976), pp. 118 ff. Hillis, 'Presbyterianism and social class', pp. 57, 62.
45 C. Kemble, *Suggestive Hints on Parochial Machinery* (London, 1859), p. 29. On pew rents, cf. C. G. Brown, 'The costs of pew-renting: church management, church-going and social class in nineteenth-century Glasgow', *JEH*, vol. 38, no. 3 (1987).
46 R. F. Horton, in G. Haw (ed.), *Christianity and the Working Classes* (London, 1906), p. 87.
47 A. A. MacLaren, *Religion and Social Class: The Disruption Years in Aberdeen* (London, 1974), pp. 128–31.
48 B. and F. Bowers, 'Bloomsbury Chapel and mercantile morality: the case of Sir Morton Peto', *Baptist Quarterly*, vol. 30, no. 5 (1984), pp. 210–20.
49 The decline of church discipline can be traced in C. Binfield, *Pastors and People: The Biography of a Baptist Church: Queen's Road, Coventry* (Coventry, 1984), pp. 35, 74, 93, 105, 156.
50 For example, *Labour Leader*, 19 May 1894, p. 2.
51 M. C. Bickersteth, *A Sketch of the Life and Episcopate of the Right Reverend Robert Bickersteth, D.D., Bishop of Ripon, 1857–1884* (London, 1887), p. 70.
52 Haw (ed.), *Christianity and the Working Classes*, p. 16.
53 Horton in ibid., p. 87.
54 A. E. Dingle, 'Drink and working-class living standards in Britain, 1870–1914', *Economic History Review*, 2nd series, vol. 25, no. 4 (1972), pp. 608–12.
55 W. R. Lambert, *Drink and Sobriety in Victorian Wales, c.1820–c.1895* (Cardiff, 1983), p. 32.
56 P. Bailey, *Leisure and Class in Victorian England* (London, 1978), p. 137. T. Mason, *Association Football and English Society, 1863–1915* (Brighton, 1980), p. 26.
57 E. Royle, *Victorian Infidels: The Origins of the British Secularist Movement, 1791–1866* (Manchester, 1974), p. 237.
58 Cox, *English Churches*, pp. 102 f. On rural folk religion: Obelkevich, *Religion and Rural Society*, ch. 6; D. Clark, *Between Pulpit and Pew: Folk Religion in a North Yorkshire Fishing Village* (Cambridge, 1982).
59 H. Pelling, 'Popular attitudes to religion', *Popular Politics and Society in Late Victorian Britain* (London, 1968), p. 19.
60 R. Carwardine, 'The Welsh Evangelical community and "Finney's Revival"'. *JEH*, vol. 29, no. 4 (1978), p. 467.
61 Currie *et al.*, *Churches and Churchgoers*, p. 106.
62 R. B. Walker, 'The growth of Wesleyan Methodism in Victorian England and Wales', *JEH*, vol. 24, no. 3 (1973), p. 270.

63 E. P. Thompson, *The Making of the English Working Class* (Harmondsworth, 1968 edn), pp. 427–30, 919–23.

64 E. J. Hobsbawm and G. Rudé, *Captain Swing* (Harmondsworth, 1973 edn), pp. 248–51.

65 P. Stigant, 'Wesleyan Methodism and working-class radicalism in the North, 1792–1821', *Northern History*, vol. 6 (1971). J. Rule, 'Methodism and Chartism among the Cornish miners', *Bulletin of the Society for the Study of Labour History*, vol. 22 (1971).

66 Currie *et al.. Churches and Churchgoers*, pp. 107–13.

67 S. E. Koss, '1906: revival and revivalism', in A. J. A. Mason (ed.), *Edwardian Radicalism, 1900–1914* (London, 1974).

68 Gilbert, *Religion and Society*, p. 195; cf. Currie *et al.*, *Churches and Churchgoers*, p. 111.

69 J. Kendall, *Rambles of an Evangelist*, pp. 42 f., quoted by Carwardine, 'Welsh Evangelical community', p. 470.

70 Walker, 'Growth of Wesleyan Methodism', pp. 268, 271.

71 See J. S. Werner, *The Primitive Methodist Connexion: Its Background and Early History* (Madison, Wis., 1984), pp. 44, 171–4.

72 W. Leach to J. Bunting, 22 October 1832, in W. R. Ward (ed.), *Early Victorian Methodism: The Correspondence of Jabez Bunting, 1830–1858* (Oxford, 1976), pp. 20 f.

73 Werner, *Primitive Methodist Connexion*, chs 2 and 3.

74 J. Kent, *Holding the Fort: Studies in Victorian Revivalism* (London, 1978), pp. 49 f.

75 Carwardine, 'Welsh Evangelical community'.

76 R. Carwardine, *Transatlantic Revivalism: Popular Evangelicalism in Britain and America, 1790–1865* (Westport, Conn., 1978), pp. 97–133.

77 A. Bennett, *Anna of the Five Towns* [1902] (Harmondsworth, 1963), ch. 5.

78 *Elgin Courier*, quoted by *Revival*, 31 March 1860, p. 103.

79 J. E. Orr, *The Second Evangelical Revival* (London, 1949).

80 *Revival*, 21 January 1860, p. 22.

81 ibid., 25 February 1860, p. 61.

82 ibid., 18 February 1860, p. 53; 28 January 1860, p. 30.

83 ibid., 25 February 1860, p. 61; 31 March 1860, p. 102.

84 *Revival*, 28 April 1860, p. 133. Carwardine, *Transatlantic Revival*, p. 133.

85 Hardman, 'Evangelical party', pp. 319 ff.

86 *Revival* for the first half of 1860.

87 O. Anderson, 'Women preachers in mid-Victorian Britain: some reflexions on feminism, popular religion and social change', *Historical Journal*, vol. 12, no. 3 (1969).

88 F. R. Coad, *A History of the Brethren Movement* (Exeter, 1968), pp. 167–74.

89 See pp. 162 ff.

90 H. James, *The Country Clergyman and his Work* (London, 1890), pp. 154 f.

91 Kemble, *Parochial Machinery*, p. 23.

92 C. Bridges, *The Christian Ministry*, 3rd edn (London, 1830), p. 471.

93 F. K. Prochaska, *Women and Philanthropy in Nineteenth-Century England* (Oxford, 1980), p. 99; cf. H. D. Rack, 'Domestic visitation: a chapter in early nineteenth-century evangelism', *JEH*, vol. 24, no. 4 (1973).

94 The scheme was in large measure evangelistic, even though it is often discussed as an exercise in poor relief. R. A. Cage and E. O. A. Checkland, 'Thomas Chalmers and urban poverty: the St John's parish experiment in Glasgow, 1819-1837', *Philosophical Journal*, vol. 13, no. 1 (1976).

95 Lord Henley, *A Plan of Church Reform*, 2nd edn (London, 1832), p. 14 n.

96 James, *Country Clergyman*, p. 148.

97 F. K. Prochaska, 'Body and Soul: Bible nurses and the poor in Victorian London', *Historical Research*, Vol. 60, no. 143 (1987).

98 L. E. Shelford, *A Memorial of the Rev. William Cadman, M.A.* (London, 1899), p. 44.

99 G. H. Sumner, *Life of Charles Richard Sumner, D.D.* (London, 1876), p. 248.

100 Hardman, 'Evangelical party', pp. 268 f.

101 E. Hodder, *Life of Samuel Morley* (London, 1888 edn), pp. 94–100. R. Carwardine, 'The evangelist system: Charles Roe, Thomas Pulford and the Baptist Home Missionary Society', *Baptist Quarterly*, vol. 28, no. 5 (1980).

102 S. J. Price, *A Popular History of the Baptist Building Fund* (London, 1927).

103 W. Hanna, *Memoirs of the Life and Writings of Thomas Chalmers, D.D., LL.D.*, Vol. 4 (Edinburgh, 1852), ch. 19.

104 A. Peel, *These Hundred Years: A History of the Congregational Union of England and Wales, 1831–1931* (London, 1931), pp. 302–16. E. A. Payne, *The Baptist Union: A Short History* (London, 1958), pp. 104 f.

105 James, *Country Clergyman*, p. 156.

106 *Occasional Paper* (Church Pastoral-Aid Society), no. 53 (1858), p. 6.

107 W. Cuff, *Fifty Years' Ministry, 1865–1915* (London, 1915), pp. 40 f., 45 f.

108 *Occasional Paper* (CPAS), no. 53 (1858), p. 8.

109 D. M. Lewis, *Lighten their Darkness: The Evangelical Mission to Working-Class London, 1828-1860* (Westport, Conn., 1986), ch. 5.

110 J. M. Weylland, *These Fifty Years: Being the Jubilee Volume of the London City Mission* (London, 1884), esp. p. 334. C. Binfield, *George Williams and the Y.M.C.A.* (London, 1973), pp. 151–5, chs 6, 13, 14.

111 J. Wood, *The Story of the Evangelization Society* (London, n.d.). H. D. Brown, *By Voice and Book: The Story of the Christian Colportage Association* (London, n.d.). L. A. G. Strong, *Flying Angel: The Story of the Missions to Seamen* (London, 1956).

112 Hodder, *Morley*, p. 218.

113 *C*, 8 January 1880, p. 13.

114 Address of 1858 in *Speeches of the Earl of Shaftesbury, K.G.* [1868] (Shannon, 1971), p. 308, quoted by G. B. A. M. Finlayson, *The Seventh Earl of Shaftesbury, 1801–1885* (London, 1981), p. 410.

115 For example, G. Kitson Clark, *Churchmen and the Condition of England, 1832–1885* (London, 1973), pp. 71–4.

116 See pp. 213–17.

117 K. Heasman, *Evangelicals in Action: An Appraisal of their Social Work in the Victorian Era* (London, 1962), p. 14.

118 J. Rose, *Elizabeth Fry* (London, 1980).

119 G. Wagner, *Barnardo* (London, 1979).

120 E. R. Norman, *Church and Society in England, 1770–1970* (Oxford, 1976), esp. pp. 62–7. C. M. Elliott, 'The Political Economy of English Dissent, 1780–1840', in R. M. Hartwell (ed.), *The Industrial Revolution* (Oxford, 1970).

121 Cage and Checkland, 'Chalmers and urban poverty', pp. 37 ff.
122 J. B. Sumner, *Christian Charity* (London, 1841), pp. vii f., xii.
123 B. W. Noel, *The State of the Metropolis Considered* (London, 1835), p. 21.
124 J. Clifford, *Jesus Christ and Modern Social Life* (London, [1872]), p. 35.
125 Bridges, *Christian Ministry*, p. 472.
126 Bickersteth, *Bickersteth*, pp. 68 f.
127 J. Stoughton, *Congregationalism in the Court Suburb* (London, 1883), pp. 60 f.
128 Kemble, *Parochial Machinery*, pp. 24–7.
129 Yeo, *Religion and Voluntary Organisations*, p. 58.
130 Bradley, *Call to Seriousness*, p. 122.
131 *Nottingham Athenaeum*, vol. 1 (1860), pp. 16–20, 43 ff., 64 ff.
132 J. Venn, 'Charity Schools', *CO*, September. 1804, p. 542, quoted by M.
     Hennell, *John Venn and the Clapham Sect* (London, 1958), p. 137.
133 T. W. Laqueur, 'The cultural origins of popular literacy in England, 1500–
     1850', *Oxford Review of Education*, vol. 2, no. 3 (1976), p. 255. R. Houston,
     'The literacy myth?: illiteracy in Scotland, 1630–1760', *Past & Present*, no.
     96 (1982), pp. 98 f.
134 T. C. Smout, 'Born again at Cambuslang: new evidence on popular religion
     and literacy in eighteenth-century Scotland', *Past & Present*, no. 97 (1982),
     p. 122.
135 R. S. Schofield, 'Dimensions of illiteracy, 1750–1850', *Explorations in Economic
     History*, vol. 10, no. 4 (1973).
136 W. W. Champneys, *Parish Work: A Brief Manual for the Younger Clergy*
     (London, 1866), pp. 19 f.
137 T. W. Laqueur, *Religion and Respectability: Sunday Schools and Working Class
     Culture, 1780–1850* (New Haven, Conn., 1976). P. B. Cliff, *The Rise and
     Development of the Sunday School Movement in England, 1780–1980* (Nutfield,
     Redhill, Surrey, 1986).
138 Kemble, *Parochial Machinery*, p. 21 n.
139 Laqueur, *Religion and Respectability*, p. 89.
140 Cox, *English Churches*, p. 80 n.
141 H. C. Colman, *Jeremiah James Colman* (London, 1905), p. 126.
142 Bickersteth, *Bickersteth*, p. 231.
143 Finlayson, *Shaftesbury*, pp. 251 f.
144 H. J. Burgess, *Enterprise in Education: The Story of the Work of the Established
     Church in the Education of the People prior to 1870* (London, 1958), pp.
     224, 142 ff., 160.
145 M. Sturt, *The Education of the People: A History of Primary Education in England
     and Wales in the Nineteenth Century* (London, 1967), pp. 21–7. Stoughton,
     Congregationalism, p. 63.
146 Burgess, *Enterprise in Education*, p. 224. The Wesleyan figure is for 1847:
     D. Hempton, *Methodism and Politics in British Society, 1750–1850* (London,
     1984), p. 171.
147 J. M. Goldstrom, *The Social Content of Education, 1808–1870: A Study of
     the Working-Class School Reader in England and Ireland* (Shannon, Ireland,
     1972), p. 19. Cox, *English Churches*, pp. 96 f. See also W. M. Humes
     and H. M. Paterson (eds), *Scottish Culture and Scottish Education, 1800–1980*
     (Edinburgh, 1983).
148 James, *Country Clergyman*, p. 118.

149 For example, O. Chadwick, *Victorian Miniature* (London, 1960).
150 Obelkevich, *Religion and Rural Society*, p. 35.
151 D. W. Bebbington, *The Nonconformist Conscience: Chapel and Politics, 1870-1914* (London, 1982), p. 31. *Witness*, 30 May 1854.
152 F. M. L. Thompson, 'Landowners and the rural community', in G. E. Mingay (ed.), *The Victorian Countryside*, Vol. 2 (London, 1981), p. 469.
153 P. Joyce, *Work, Society and Politics: The Culture of the Factory in Later Victorian England* (Hassocks, Sussex, 1980).
154 A. Howe, *The Cotton Masters, 1830–1860* (Oxford, 1984), pp. 61 f.
155 T. R. Blumer: G. E. Milburn, *Piety, Profit and Paternalism: Methodists in Business in the North-East of England, c.1760–1920* (Bunbury, Cheshire, 1983), p. 22.
156 R. Balgarnie, *Sir Titus Salt, Baronet* (London, 1877), pp. 142 f. Viscount Leverhulme, *Viscount Leverhulme* (London, 1927), pp. 95 f.
157 T. H. W. Idris: *Baptist Times*, 12 January 1906, p. 22.
158 J. B. Johnson: R. Moore, *Pit-Men, Preachers and Politics: The Effects of Methodism in a Durham Mining Community* (London, 1974), p. 83.
159 G. Stephen, *Anti-Slavery Recollections in a Series of Letters addressed to Mrs Beecher Stowe* [1854] (London, 1971), p. 161.
160 C. Binfield, '"Self-harnessed to the Car of Progress." Baines of Leeds and East Parade: a church and a dynasty', *So Down to Prayers: Studies in English Nonconformity, 1780–1920* (London, 1977), p. 79.
161 G. and W. Grossmith, *The Diary of a Nobody* [1892], (Harmondsworth, Middlesex, 1965 edn), p. 24.
162 B. Harrison and P. Hollis, 'Chartism, Liberalism and the life of Robert Lowery', *English Historical Review*, vol. 82, no. 3 (1967).
163 G. Crossick, *An Artisan Elite in Victorian Society: Kentish London, 1840–1880* (London, 1978), p. 142.
164 Moore, *Pit-Men*, pp. 142 ff.
165 Booth, *Life and Labour*, Vol. 7, p. 399.
166 Binney, *Is it Possible to make the Best of Both Worlds?*, 9th edn (London, 1855), pp. 94 f.
167 Coleman, *Church of England*, p. 7; cf. O. Anderson, 'The incidence of civil marriage in Victorian England and Wales', *Past & Present*, no. 69 (1975). In Scotland, however, marriage was a civil contract, and so ecclesiastical involvement was purely voluntary.
168 Cox, *English Churches*, pp. 97–100.
169 Gilbert, *Religion and Society*, pp. 89 f. Obelkevich, *Religion and Rural Society*, chs 4 and 5.
170 Moore, *Pit-Men*, pp. 124–32. Werner, *Primitive Methodist Connexion*, pp. 157–61.
171 C. Binfield, *So Down to Prayers*, pp. 26 f.
172 J. Lea, 'The growth of the Baptist denomination in mid-Victorian Lancashire and Cheshire', *Transactions of the Historic Society of Lancashire and Cheshire*, vol. 124 (1972), p. 143.
173 James, *Country Clergyman*, pp. 163 ff.
174 A. L. Drummond and J. Bulloch, *The Church in Late Victorian Scotland, 1874–1900* (Edinburgh, 1978), pp. 168 ff.
175 J. Burgess, *The Lake Counties and Christianity: The Religious History of Cumbria, 1780–1920* (Carlisle, 1984), p. 96.

176   Chadwick, *Victorian Church*, Vol. 2, p. 223.

177   Cox, *English Churches*, pp. 26 f., 282 f., 290 ff.

178   B. Harrison, *Separate Spheres: The Opposition to Women's Suffrage in Britain* (London, 1978). B. Heeney, 'The beginnings of church feminism: women and the councils of the Church of England, 1897–1919', *JEH*, vol. 33, no. 1 (1982), esp. p. 108 (Dean Wace).

179   Anderson, 'Women preachers', p. 468 n. Heeney, 'Church feminism', p. 90 n.

180   A. T. Pierson, *Forward Movements of the Last Half Century* (New York, 1900), ch. 13.

181   Z. Fairfield, *Some Aspects of the Woman's Movement* (London, 1915), appendix. See pp. 174 f.

182   Anderson, 'Women preachers'. Prochaska, *Women and Philanthropy*.

183   R. A. Knox, *A Spiritual Aeneid* (London, 1918), pp. 5 f.

184   H. Thornton, *Family Prayers* (London, 1834).

185   S. Butler, *The Way of All Flesh* (London, 1903). E. Gosse, *Father and Son* (London, 1907).

186   L. Hoare, *Hints for the Improvement of Early Education and Nursery Discipline* (London, 1819); *Friendly Advice on the Management and Education of Children* (London, 1824). J. H. Townsend (ed.), *Edward Hoare, M.A.*, 2nd edn (London, 1896), p. 7. See also Rosman, *Evangelicals and Culture*, ch. 4.

187   Shaftesbury's diary, 5 September 1840, quoted by Finlayson, *Shaftesbury*, p. 131.

188   *R*, 18 January 1855, p. 2, citing the *Leader*, as quoted by Hardman, 'Evangelical party', p. 133.

189   On Dickens: V. Cunningham, *Everywhere Spoken Against: Dissent in the Victorian Novel* (Oxford, 1975), ch. 8. On Eliot: E. Jay, *The Religion of the Heart: Anglican Evangelicalism and the Nineteenth-Century Novel* (Oxford, 1979), ch. 4.

190   G. Best, 'Evangelicalism and the Victorians', in A. Symondson (ed.), *The Victorian Crisis of Faith* (London, 1970), p. 48 f.

191   *The World of Cant* (London, 1880), p. 143; cf. A. Mursell, *Memories of My Life* (London, 1913), pp. 185 ff.

192   W. Wilberforce, *A Practical View of the Prevailing Religious Systems of Professed Christians in the Higher and Middle Classes in this Country Contrasted with Real Christianity*, 4th edn (London, 1797), p. 453.

193   M. Hennell, 'Evangelicalism and worldliness, 1770–1870', in G. J. Cuming and D. Baker (eds), *Popular Belief and Practice*, Studies in Church History, vol. 8 (Cambridge, 1972), p. 230.

194   J. H. Pratt (ed.), *The Thought of the Evangelical Leaders: Notes of the Discussions of The Eclectic Society, London, during the Years 1798–1814* (Edinburgh, 1978), pp. 157–62; cf. Rosman, *Evangelicals and Culture*, pp. 75–8.

195   A.W., 'The Theatre; and can it be improved?', *CO*, May 1851, p. 300.

196   J. Kay, *A Defence of the Legitimate Drama* (Edinburgh, 1883), p. 18.

197   G. S. Barrett, 'The secularisation of the church', in *Congregational Yearbook*, 1895, p. 47.

198   Rosman, *Evangelicals and Culture*, ch. 6, esp. p. 137.

199   M. Raleigh (ed.), *Alexander Raleigh: Records of his Life* (Edinburgh, 1881), p. 22.

200   P. Horn, *Education in Rural England, 1800–1914* (Dublin, 1978), p. 193.

201 C. Binfield, '"Old fashioned Dissenting narrowness": Crabb Robinson and the Patissons', *So Down to Prayers*, ch. 3. T. S. James, 'Home life', in R. W. Dale, *Life and Letters of John Angell James* (London, 1862 edn), p. 382, quoted by Cunningham, *Everywhere Spoken Against*, p. 48.

202 Rosman, *Evangelicals and Culture*, ch. 8, sect. C; cf. Jay, *Religion of the Heart*, pp. 195–202.

203 Cunningham, *Everywhere Spoken Against*, p. 59. J. Briggs and I. Sellers (eds), *Victorian Nonconformity* (London, 1973), pp. 117 f.

204 Cunningham, *Everywhere Spoken Against*, p. 62.

205 *CO*, September 1845, p. 522.

206 Hardman, 'Evangelical party', p. 377.

207 *T*, 27 December 1860, p. 8, cited by Hardman, 'Evangelical party', p. 79.

208 Bradley, *Call to Seriousness*, p. 28. G. Unwin and J. Telford, *Mark Guy Pearse: Preacher, Author, Artist* (London, 1930), p. 29.

209 J. B. B. Clarke (ed.), *An Account of the Infancy, Religious and Literary Life of Adam Clarke, LL.D., F.A.S.*, Vol. 2 (London, 1833), p. 38.

210 H. A. Thomas (ed.), *Memorials of the Rev. David Thomas, B.A.* (London, 1876), p. 4.

211 A. Delves, 'Popular recreation and social conflict in Derby, 1800–1850', in E. and S. Yeo (eds), *Popular Culture and Class Conflict* (Brighton, 1981). Hennell, *Sons of the Prophets*, p. 106. P. Bailey, *Leisure and Class in Victorian England: Rational Recreation and the Contest for Control, 1830–1885* (London, 1978), pp. 18 f.

212 G. Eliot, *Middlemarch* [1871–72] (Harmondsworth, Middlesex, 1965), p. 191.

213 S. K. Phillips, 'Primitive Methodist confrontation with popular sports: case study of early nineteenth century Staffordshire', in R. Cashman and M. McKernan (eds), *Sport: Money, Morality and the Media* (Sydney, NSW, n.d.).

214 B. Harrison, 'Animals and the state in nineteenth-century England', *Peaceable Kingdom: Stability and Change in Modern Britain* (Oxford, 1982), pp. 115 f., 118. A. Lloyd, *The Great Prize Fight* (New York, 1977), esp. ch. 16.

215 See p. 113 f.

216 Colman, *Colman*, p. 354.

217 See pp. 71 f.

218 Stephen, *Anti-Slavery Recollections*, p. 248.

219 For example, F. J. Klingberg, *The Anti-Slavery Movement in England* (New Haven, Conn., 1926).

220 G. A. Catherall, *William Knibb: Freedom Fighter* (n.p., 1972), p. 66; cf. K. R. M. Short, 'Jamaican Christian missions and the Great Slave Rebellion of 1831–2', *JEH*, vol. 27, no. 1 (1976).

221 J. C. Gill, *The Ten Hours Parson: Christian Social Action in the 1830s* (London, 1959).

222 For example, D. Bowen, *The Protestant Crusade in Ireland, 1800–70* (Dublin, 1978), p. 221 (A.R.C. Dallas).

223 G. I. T. Machin, *Politics and the Churches in Great Britain, 1832–1868* (Oxford, 1977), pp. 169–77.

224 K. Ingham, 'The English Evangelicals and the Pilgrim Tax in India, 1800–1862', *JEH*, vol. 3, no. 2 (1952).

225   S. E. Maltby, *Manchester and the Movement for National Elementary Education,*
      1800–1870 (Manchester, 1918), p. 67.
226   Binfield, *Pastors and People*, ch. 7. Bebbington, *Nonconformist Conscience*, ch. 7.
227   P. McHugh, *Prostitution and Victorian Social Reform* (London, 1980), ch. 7.
228   G. Battiscombe, *Shaftesbury: A Biography of the Seventh Earl* (London, 1974),
      p. 147.
229   A. Mearns, *The Bitter Cry of Outcast London* [1883] (Leicester, 1970), pp. 16 f.
230   *Occasional Paper* (CPAS), no. 133 (1884), p. 5.
231   A. E. Dingle, *The Campaign for Prohibition in Victorian England: The United*
      Kingdom Alliance, 1872–1895 (London, 1980). L. L. Shiman, *The Crusade*
      against Drink in Victorian England (London, 1986).
232   Sargent, *Martyn*, p. 67.
233   Wigley, *Victorian Sunday*, pp. 53–7, 64–7. Finlayson, *Shaftesbury*, pp. 313–16.
234   J. G. Bowran, *The Life of Arthur Thomas Guttery, D.D.* (London, n.d.), p. 63.
235   T. W. Moody, 'The Irish university question of the nineteenth century',
      History, vol. 43, no. 2 (1958).
236   P. Wright, *Knibb 'the Notorious': Slaves' Missionary, 1803–1845* (London,
      1973), p. 126.
237   Bebbington, *Nonconformist Conscience*, pp. 52 f.
238   B. Harrison, *Drink and the Victorians: The Temperance Question in England,*
      1815–1872 (London, 1971), pp. 269, 273.
239   D. B. Davis, 'The emergence of immediatism in British and American
      antislavery thought', *Mississippi Valley Historical Review*, vol. 49, no.
      2 (1962).
240   A. Miall, *Life of Edward Miall* (London, 1884), pp. 29 ff.
241   M. J. D. Roberts, 'Pressure-group politics and the Church of England: the
      Church Defence Institution, 1859–1896', *JEH*, vol. 35, no. 4 (1984).
242   W. H. Mackintosh, *Disestablishment and Liberation: The Movement for the Sepa-*
      ration of the Anglican Church from State Control (London, 1972). D. M.
      Thompson, 'The Liberation Society, 1844–1868', in P. Hollis (ed.), *Pressure*
      from Without in Early Victorian England (London, 1974).
243   Hardman, 'Evangelical party', ch. 7. P. M. H. Bell, *Disestablishment in Ireland and*
      Wales (London, 1969), pp. 96–109.
244   D. W. Bebbington, 'Nonconformity and electoral sociology, 1867–1918',
      Historical Journal, vol. 27, no. 3 (1984). K. O. Morgan, *Wales in British*
      Politics, 1868–1922 (London, 1963).
245   J. G. Kellas, 'The Liberal Party and the Scottish church disestablishment
      crisis', *English Historical Review*, vol. 79, no. 1 (1974).
246   I. G. C. Hutchison, *A Political History of Scotland, 1832–1924: Parties, Elections*
      and Issues (Edinburgh, 1986), pp. 84, 116 f.
247   D. E. H. Mole, 'The Church of England and society in Birmingham c.1830–
      1866', PhD thesis, University of Cambridge, 1961, p. 266. Bickersteth,
      Bickersteth, pp. 32, 189.
248   Bebbington, 'Nonconformity and electoral sociology'.
249   J. H. Newman, *Apologia pro Vita Sua* [1864] (London, 1946), p. 193.
250   J. Foster, 'On some of the causes . . .', *Essays in a Series of Letters to a Friend*
      (London, 1805); cf. Rosman, *Evangelicals and Culture*, pp. 203 f.
251   H. Crooke, *The Spirit No Respecter of Persons in His Gifts and Graces* (London,
      1755), p. 15, quoted by Walsh, 'Yorkshire Evangelicals', p. 147 n.

252 Finlayson, *Shaftesbury*, p. 336.

253 J. G. Breay, 'The pastor's obligations to the church of God', *The Faithful Pastor Delineated* (London, 1844), quoted by Mole, 'Church and society in Birmingham', p. 75.

254 E. Stock, *The History of the Church Missionary Society*, Vol. 2 (London, 1899), pp. 63, 550.

255 W. B. Brash, *The Story of Our Colleges, 1835–1935* (London, 1935), p. 72.

256 A. de Q. Robin, *Charles Perry, Bishop of Melbourne* (Nedlands, Western Australia, 1967), p. 15. Hardman, 'Evangelical party', pp. 396, 409.

257 See above, p. 123.

258 W. Robertson Nicoll, *My Father: An Aberdeenshire Minister, 1812–1891* (London, 1908), pp. 62, 72.

259 N. G. Brett-James, *The History of Mill Hill School, 1807–1923* (Reigate, [1925]), p. 219.

260 A. S. Wilkins, *Our National Universities* (London, 1871), p. 342 n.

261 They are unsympathetically portrayed by Butler, *Way of All Flesh*, pp. 231–4.

262 J. D. Walsh, 'The Magdalene Evangelicals', *Church Quarterly Review*, no. 159 (1958). J. A. Venn, *A Statistical Chart to Illustrate the Entries at the Various Colleges in the University of Cambridge, 1544–1907: Descriptive Text* (Cambridge, 1908), p. 10.

263 D. Rosman, 'Evangelicals and culture in England, 1790–1833', PhD thesis, University of Keele, 1979, p. 365.

264 Hardman, 'Evangelical party', pp. 402, 409.

265 A. C. Downer, *A Century of Evangelical Religion in Oxford* (London, 1938), pp. 70 f., 66 f.

266 J. B. McCaul, *A Memorial Sketch of the Rev. Alexander McCaul, D.D.* (London, 1863), p. 15. Stoughton, *Congregationalism*, p. 65.

267 J. S. Black and G. Chrystal, *The Life of William Robertson Smith*, (London, 1912). See pp. 184 f.

268 Mole, 'Church and society in Birmingham', p. 89.

269 Pfleiderer, *The Development of Theology in Germany since Kant and its Progress in Great Britain since 1825* (London, 1890), ch. 2 (Samuel Davidson and Robertson Smith qualify as biblical critics). B. M. G. Reardon, *Religious Thought in the Victorian Age* (London, 1980), ch. 12, pp. 456 f.

270 R. A. Soloway, *Prelates and People: Ecclesiastical Social Thought in England, 1783–1852* (London, 1969), pp. 107–16.

271 S. Waldegrave, *New Testament Millennnarianism* (London, 1855).

272 C. H. Davis to editor, *R*, 4 January 1861, p. 4.

273 Horne, *An Introduction to the Critical Study and Knowledge of the Holy Scriptures*, 4 Vols (London, 1818); ct. p. 87. McCaul, *The Old Paths* (London, 1837). L. Sergeant, 'Christopher Benson', *DNB*.

274 T. Cooper, 'Joseph Baylee', *DNB*. G. Goodwin, 'John Buxton Marsden'. *DNB*.

275 G. B. Smith, 'Thomas Rawson Birks', *DNB*.

276 *Obituary: The Very Rev. William Goode, D.D., Dean of Ripon* (London, 1883), reprinted from *Clerical Journal*, p. 4; cf. P. Toon, *Evangelical Theology, 1833–1856: A Response to Tractarianism* (London, 1979), pp. 117 ff.

277 F. Boase, *Modern English Biography*, Vol. 6 (Truro, 1921), col. 64.

278   Garbett, *The Bible and its Critics* (London, 1861); *The Dogmatic Faith* (London, 1867); cf. R. W. Macan, *Religious Changes in Oxford during the Last Fifty Years* (London, 1918), p. 12.

279   D. S. Margoliouth, 'Robert Payne Smith', *DNB*.

280   W. G. D. Fletcher, 'Nathaniel Dimock', *DNB, 1901–1911*.

281   P. Fairbairn, *The Interpretation of Prophecy* (London, 1964), pp. xvii–xxii. W. G. Blaikie, 'Patrick Fairbairn', *DNB*.

282   A. P. F. Sell, *Defending and Declaring the Faith: Some Scottish Examples, 1860–1920* (Exeter, 1987), chs 7 and 9.

283   R. S. Franks, 'The theology of A. M. Fairbairn', *Transactions of the Congregational Historical Society*, vol. 13, no. 3 (1939).

284   A. W. W. Dale, *The Life of R. W. Dale of Birmingham* (London, 1898), pp. 324 f., 710–17.

285   The ablest analysis of Forsyth remains W. L. Bradley, *P. T. Forsyth: The Man and his Work* (London, 1952).

286   Finlayson, *Shaftesbury*, p. 349.

287   A. Haig, *The Victorian Clergy* (London, 1984), p. 49.

288   L. Stephen, *Life of Henry Fawcett* (London, 1885), p. 94.

289   G. S. Spinks, *Religion in Britain since 1900* (London, 1952), p. 10 n; cf. Chadwick, *Victorian Church*, Vol. 2, ch. 8.

290   J. W. Burrow, *Evolution and Society* (Cambridge, 1966), esp. ch. 6.

291   Lecky, *A History of the Rise and Influence of Rationalism in Europe* (London, 1865). Chadwick, *Victorian Church*, Vol. 2, pp. 114 f., 11–23.

292   N. Barlow (ed.), *The Autobiography of Charles Darwin, 1809–1882* (London, 1958), p. 87.

293   Birks, *Supernatural Revelation* (London, 1879), p. 136. See also J. R. Moore, *The Post-Darwinian Controversies* (Cambridge, 1979).

294   J. Kent, *From Darwin to Blatchford: The Role of Darwinism in Christian Apologetic, 1875–1910* (London, 1966), pp. 20–8.

295   P. Mathias, *The First Industrial Nation: An Economic History of Britain, 1700–1914* (London, 1969), p. 378.

296   Cox, *English Churches*, ch. 6.

297   Yeo, *Religion and Voluntary Organisations*, esp. pp. 105 ff. Joyce, *Work, Society and Politics*, pp. 339 f.

298   S. Meacham, *A Life Apart: The English Working Class, 1890–1914* (London, 1977).

299   K. Hardie, 'Socialism' in *Labour Leader*, February 1894, p. 5.

300   J. H. Harley in *Labour Leader*, 8 February 1907, p. 595.

301   McLeod, *Class and Religion*, p. 25.

302   *R*, 2 January 1863, p. 2.

303   Birks, *Supernatural Revelation*, p. vi.

304   *R*, 2 January 1867; cf. R. Ferguson and A. M. Brown, *Life and Labours of John Campbell, D.D.* (London, 1867).

305   A. P. F. Sell, 'Henry Rogers and *The Eclipse of Faith*', *Journal of the United Reformed Church History Society*, vol. 2, no. 5 (1980).

306   Justus to editor, *CO*, September 1847, p. 519.

307   'Theological liberalism', *British Quarterly Review*, April 1861, p. 488.

308   J. Angus, *Theology an Inductive and a Progressive Science* (London, n.d.), pp. 20 f.

309 N. Goodman, *The Established Church a Hindrance to Progressive Thought* (Manchester, 1873).

310 Raleigh (ed.), *Raleigh*, p. 282.

311 Finlayson, *Shaftesbury*, p. 575.

312 D. A. Johnson, 'The end of the "evidences": a study in Nonconformist theological transition', *Journal of the United Reformed Church History Society*, vol. 2, no. 3 (1979).

313 Thomas, *Thomas*, p. 49.

314 C. S. Horne, *A Popular History of the Free Churches* (London, 1903), p. 421.

315 H. C. G. Moule, 'The Evangelical School III' in *R*, 18 January 1901, p. 79. J. Scott Lidgett, *My Guided Life* (London, 1936), p. 73. I. E. Page (ed.), *John Brash: Memorials and Correspondence* (London, 1912), p. 48. Bradley, *Forsyth*, pp. 94–7.

316 M. D. Johnson, 'Thomas Gasquoine and the origins of the Leicester conference', *Journal of the United Reformed Church History Society*, vol. 2, no. 10 (1982).

317 Binfield, '"No quest, no conquest." Baldwin Brown and Silvester Horne', *So Down to Prayers*, pp. 189–99.

318 Raleigh (ed.), *Raleigh*, p. 283.

319 T. Waugh, *Twenty-Three Years a Missioner* (London, n.d.), p. 33. Birks, *The Victory of Divine Goodness*, 2nd edn (London, 1870), pp. 42–8. E. R. Garratt, *Life and Personal Recollections of Samuel Garratt* (London, 1908), p. 79. See G. Rowell, *Hell and the Victorians* (Oxford, 1974), pp. 123–9.

320 R. T. Jones, *Congregationalism in England, 1662–1962* (London, 1962), p. 265.

321 R. W. Dale, *The Old Evangelicalism and the New* (London, 1889), pp. 38 ff.

322 Booth, *Life and Labour*, Vol. 7, p. 119.

323 *Sword and the Trowel*, July 1876, p. 306.

324 *Baptist*, 4 November 1881, quoted by P. S. Kruppa, *Charles Haddon Spurgeon: A Preacher's Progress* (New York, 1982), p. 416.

325 Payne, *Baptist Union*, ch. 7, supplemented by E. A. Payne, 'The Down Grade controversy: a postscript', *Baptist Quarterly*, vol. 28, no. 4 (1979) and by Kruppa, *Spurgeon*, ch. 8.

326 Spurgeon, *An All-Round Ministry* (London, 1900), p. 17, quoted by Kruppa, *Spurgeon*, p. 374.

327 Kruppa, *Spurgeon*, p. 424.

328 Payne, 'Down Grade controversy', p. 149.

329 A. Bentley, 'The transformation of the Evangelical party in the Church of England in the later nineteenth century', PhD thesis, University of Durham, 1971, p. 202.

330 N. Yates, *The Oxford Movement and Anglican Ritualism* (London, 1983), pp. 25 ff.

331 R. Braithwaite, *The Life and Letters of Rev. William Pennefather, B.A.* (London, 1878), p. 454.

332 Finlayson, *Shaftesbury*, p. 519.

333 O. Chadwick, *The Victorian Church*, 2nd edn, Vol. 1 (London, 1970), pp. 495–501.

334 J. Bentley, *Ritualism and Politics in Victorian Britain* (Oxford, 1978).

335 One of the knuckle-dusters is displayed at Clevedon Court, Somerset.

336	P. Toon and M. Smout, *John Charles Ryle: Evangelical Bishop* (Cambridge, 1976), p. 67.

337	Garratt, *What Shall We Do? Or, True Evangelical Policy* (London, 1881), pp. 15, 24.

338	S. Butler, *The Way of All Flesh* [1903] (Harmondsworth, Middlesex, 1966), pp. 402–5. The changes, however, are antedated by Butler (Jay, *Religion of the Heart*, p. 268).

339	*R*, 19 January 1883, p. 59 (Talbot Greaves).

340	J. Bateman, *The Life of the Right Rev. Daniel Wilson, D.D.*, Vol. 1 (London, 1860), p. 182.

341	Bickersteth, *Bickersteth*, pp. 28 f.

342	Shelford, *Cadman*, p. 61.

343	D. Voll, *Catholic Evangelicalism* (London, 1963), esp. pt 2, ch. 2. Kent, *Holding the Fort*, ch. 7.

344	Garbett, *Is Union Desirable?* (London, 1871).

345	Garbett, *Religious Thought in the Nineteenth Century* (Southport, [1877]), p. 4.

346	J. Morley, *Death, Heaven and the Victorians* (London, 1971), p. 30. J. F. White, *The Cambridge Movement: The Ecclesiologists and the Gothic Revival* (Cambridge, 1962), p. 188.

347	J. Bateman, *The Church Association: Its Policy and Prospects considered in a Letter to the Chairman*, 2nd edn (London, 1880), p. 86.

348	Waldegrave to the Rev. Henry Ware, 7 July 1868, Waldegrave MS Letter Book 4, quoted by Burgess, *Lake Counties and Christianity*, p. 57.

349	Shelford, *Cadman*, p. 62.

350	D. M. Murray, 'From Disruption to Union', in D. B. Forrester and D. M. Murray (eds), *Studies in the History of Worship in Scotland* (Edinburgh, 1984).

351	W. H. Harwood, *Henry Allon, D.D.* (London, 1894), p. 35. M. J. Street, *F. B. Meyer: His Life and Work* (London, 1902), pp. 83, 92. *CW*, 12 July 1906, p. 3 (Bernard Snell).

352	Binfield, 'Dissenting Gothic', *So Down to Prayers*.

353	Spurgeon, *Lectures to My Students*, Vol. 2 (London, 1887), p. 77.

354	Ward, *Religion and Society*, pp. 144–7.

355	J. Inglis, 'The Scottish churches and the organ in the nineteenth century', PhD thesis, University of Glasgow, 1987.

356	Chadwick, *Victorian Church*, Vol. 1, pp. 218 ff.

357	Waldegrave to the Rev. G. H. Ainger, Waldegrave MS Letter Book 2, quoted by Burgess, *Lake Counties and Christianity*, p. 56.

358	Garratt, *Garratt*, p. 252.

359	*R*, 10 June 1887, p. 561.

360	*R*, 18 September 1876.

361	N. G. Annan, *Leslie Stephen* (London 1951), ch. 3.

362	Strachey to Woolf, October 1904, quoted by M. Holroyd, *Lytton Strachey: A Critical Biography*, Vol. 1 (London, 1967), p. 198.

363	Holroyd, *Strachey*, Vol. 1, p. 267.

CHAPTER 5: HOLINESS UNTO THE LORD

1	I. E. Page, *A Long Pilgrimage with Some Guides and Fellow Travellers* (London, 1914), p. 162. On the holiness tradition, see R. Brown, 'Evangelical ideas of perfection: a comparative study of the spirituality of men and movements in nineteenth-century England', PhD thesis, University of Cambridge, 1965.

2   D. B. Hankin, in *Account of the Union Meeting for the Promotion of Scriptural Holiness, held at Oxford,' August 29 to September 7, 1874* (London, n.d.), p. 84.

3   M. E. Dieter, *The Holiness Revival of the Nineteenth Century* (Metuchen, NJ, 1980), p. 178. See p. 94 f.

4   *C*, 15 July 1875, p. 17; 12 August 1886, p. 6. *LF*, September 1880, p. 163. See pp. 81–6.

5   Mr Grane from Shanklin. *Meeting . . . at Oxford*, p. 210.

6   P. Brown, 'The holy man in late antiquity', *Society and the Holy in Late Antiquity* (London, 1982), p. 121.

7   *Meeting . . . at Oxford*, p. iv.

8   Wesley, 'A plain account of Christian perfection', in *John and Charles Wesley*, ed. F. Whaling, The Classics of Western Spirituality (London, 1981), p. 334.

9   ibid., p. 329.

10   ibid., pp. 335, 326. The standard monograph in this field is H. Lindström, *Wesley and Sanctification* (Stockholm, 1946).

11   Alexander, *Christian Holiness Illustrated and Enforced in Three Discourses* (Ewood Hall, near Halifax, 1800), p. 14.

12   Arthur, *The Tongue of Fire*, 10th edn (London, 1857), p. 48.

13   *KH*, January 1873, pp. 5 f. (W. Waters); September 1874, p. 295 (C. W. L. Christian); December 1872, p. 413 (W. G. Pascoe).

14   *KH*, January 1872, p. 34; September 1874, p. 295.

15   *KH*, January 1872, p. 5; June 1872, p. 203; April 1874, p. 112.

16   Page, *Long Pilgrimage*, p. 140.

17   J. A. Beet, *Holiness as Understood by the Writers of the Bible* (London, 1880), p. 53. Pope, *A Compendium of Christian Theology*, Vol. 3 (2nd edn, London, 1880), pp. 44–61. Pope, however, held (unlike Wesley) that genuine holiness must be unconscious: cf. W. Strawson, 'Methodist theology, 1850–1950', in R. Davies *et al.* (eds), *A History of the Methodist Church in Great Britain* Vol. 3 (London, 1983), pp. 225 f.

18   Page, *Long Pilgrimage*, p. 145.

19   I. E. Page (ed.), *John Brash: Memorials and Correspondence* (London, 1912), p. 36. F. H. Cumbers (ed.), *Richmond College, 1843–1943* (London, 1944), pp. 101 f.

20   H. T. Smart, *The Life of Thomas Cook* (London, 1913), p. 34. *KH*, October 1873, p. 347.

21   *KH*, October 1872, p. 338. T. H. Bainbridge, *Reminiscences*, ed. G. France (London, 1913), p. 87.

22   *KH*, October 1872, p. 338; December 1872, p. 414. Page, *Long Pilgrimage*, pp. 160, 196. Page, *Brash*, pp. 2 f., 26. R. M. Pope, *The Life of Henry J. Pope* (London, 1913), p. 88.

23   Bainbridge, *Reminiscences*, pp. 55 f. *KH*, October 1873, p. 346. Page (ed.), *Brash*, pp. 144, 147.

24   *KH*, June 1872, p. 186.

25   Page, *Brash*, p. 214.

26   *KH*, March 1873, p. 99.

27   *KH*, April 1874, p. 144.
28   Crewdson, *A Beacon to the Society of Friends* (London, 1835), p. 77.
29   E. Isichei, *Victorian Quakers* (London, 1970), pp. 7, 9.
30   D. E. Swift, *Joseph John Gurney: Banker, Reformer and Quaker* (Middletown, Conn., 1962), p. 175.
31   Isichei, *Victorian Quakers*, p. 12.
32   George Fox to Lady Claypole, *Journal of George Fox* (London, 1908), Vol. 1, p. 432, quoted by G. F. Nuttall, 'George Fox and his Journal', *The Puritan Spirit* (London, 1967), p. 185.
33   Robert Barclay, *An Apology for the True Christian Divinity*, 14th edn (Glasgow, 1886), p. 171.
34   *Book of Christian Discipline of the Religious Society of Friends in Great Britain* (London, 1883), pp. 98 (baptism with the Holy Ghost), 101 (rest). *Journal of the Life, Travels and Gospel Labours of William Williams* (Dublin, 1839), p. 13 (full surrender), quoted by H. H. Brinton, 'Stages in spiritual development as exemplified in Quaker journals', in H. H. Brinton (ed.), *Children of Light: In Honor of Rufus M. Jones* (New York, 1938), p. 395.
35   H. Pearsall Smith, *The Unselfishness of God and How I Discovered It* (London, 1903), ch. 29.
36   *Book of Christian Discipline*, p. 99.
37   Isichei, *Victorian Quakers*, p. 17. H. Pearsall Smith, *Unselfishness*, pp. 232 f. M. N. Garrard, *Mrs. Penn-Lewis: A Memoir* (London, 1930), pp. 34, 177.
38   H. Pearsall Smith, *Unselfishness*, pp. 119, 225. R. A. Parker, *A Family of Friends: The Story of the Transatlantic Smiths* (London, 1959), pp. 36 f.
39   *Meeting . . . at Oxford*, pp. 59, 202, 228, 38.
40   *Record of the Convention for the Promotion of Scriptural Holiness held at Brighton, May 29th to June 7th, 1875* (Brighton, n.d.), p. 335.
41   *Memoir of T. D. Harford-Battersby* (London, 1890), pp. 110 f. J. E. Cumming, 'The founder and some of the leaders', in C. F. Harford (ed.), *The Keswick Convention: Its Message, its Method and its Men* (London, 1907), pp. 60–3.
42   F. R. Coad, *A History of the Brethren Movement* (Exeter, 1968), pp. 262 f.
43   C. H. Mackintosh, *The Assembly of God*, pp. 35 f., quoted by W. Reid, *Plymouth Brethrenism Unveiled and Refuted* (Edinburgh, 1875), pp. 105 f.
44   C. H. Mackintosh, *Sanctification: what is it?*, 2nd edn, pp. 10, 19, quoted by Reid, *Plymouth Brethrenism*, pp. 272 f., 290.
45   George Goodman in *W*, October 1919, p. 160.
46   *C*, 17 September 1874, p. 11.
47   J. E. Orr, *The Second Evangelical Awakening in Britain* (London, 1949), p. 220. H. Pickering (ed.), *Chief Men among the Brethren*, 2nd edn (London, 1931), pp. 102 ff. Orr calls him 'Hambledon'.
48   *R*, 18 February 1874.
49   R. Pearsall Smith to editor, *R*, 24 April 1874.
50   H. Pearsall Smith, *Unselfishness*, pp. 190, 234 f.
51   Coad, *Brethren Movement*, pp. 168 f.
52   C. H. Mackintosh, *The Three Appearings*, p. 31, quoted by Reid, *Plymouth Brethrenism*, p. 290.
53   *Revival*, 4 November 1869, p. 3.
54   R. Braithwaite, *The Life and Letters of Rev. William Pennefather, B.A.* (London, 1878), pp. 290, 336, 305, 297.

55 ibid., pp. 325, 12, 316, 360 f.
56 *Harford-Battersby*, pp. 152 f. J. S. Reynolds, *Canon Christopher of St. Aldate's' Oxford* (Abingdon, 1967), p. 180. See p. 6.
57 Braithwaite, *Pennefather*, pp. 303, 379, 261.
58 *Revival*, 5 November 1868, p. 620.
59 Braithwaite, *Pennefather*, p. 271.
60 *C*, 5 February 1874, pp. 3 f.; 1 July 1875, p. 1.
61 *Some Records of the Life of Stevenson Arthur Blackwood, K.C.B.*, compiled by a friend and edited by his widow (London, 1896), p. 347.
62 A. Smellie, *Evan Henry Hopkins: A Memoir* (London, 1920), pp. 53 f. *Revival*, 4 November 1869, p. 6. Mrs Boardman, *Life and Labours of the Rev. W. E. Boardman* (London, 1886), pp. 156 ff. *Stevenson Blackwood*, p. 133. *C*, 17 September 1874, p. 10. Reynolds, *Christopher*, pp. 131 f. *Harford-Battersby*, p. 156. Braithwaite, *Pennefather*, pp. 431, 291. *R*, 24 May 1875.
63 *Revival*, 4 November 1869, p. 3.
64 H. Bonar, *Life of the Rev. John Milne of Perth*, 5th edn (London, 1868), pp. 337–40.
65 *C*, 15 October 1874, p. 8.
66 Boardman, *Boardman*, p. 161. *C*, 30 April 1874, p. 13; 21 October 1875, p. 14; 23 April 1874, p. 18; 17 May 1874, p. 8; 4 November 1875, p. 17.
67 O. Anderson, 'Women preachers in mid-Victorian Britain: some reflexions on feminism, popular religion and social change', *Historical Journal*, vol. 12, no. 3 (1969), esp. pp. 470–4. See also pp. 116 f.
68 J. Radcliffe, *Recollections of Reginald Radcliffe* (London, n.d.), p. 107.
69 H.W.S., *The Way to be Holy* (London, 1867), consists of articles reprinted from *The Revival*.
70 Dieter, *Holiness Revival*, p. 109, n. 51. 'D. Morgan Esq.', an English publisher, must in fact be R. C. Morgan.
71 *Revival*, 11 November 1869, p. 1; 4 November 1869, p. 15; 30 December 1869, p. 13; 20 January 1870, p. 13.
72 G. E. Morgan, *A Veteran in Revival: R. C. Morgan: His Life and Times* (London, 1909), pp. 126 f. D. W. Whittle and W. Guest (eds), *P. P. Bliss, Joint Author of "Sacred Songs and Solos": His Life and his Work* (London, 1877), p. 55.
73 Braithwaite, *Braithwaite*, pp. 280 f.
74 Radcliffe, *Radcliffe*, p. 118.
75 ibid.
76 Morgan, *Morgan*, p. 85.
77 *Meeting . . . at Oxford*, p. 58.
78 *Revival*, 14 January 1860, p. 22. Radcliffe, *Radcliffe*, p. 118 (Baptist Noel).
79 *Revival*, 28 January 1860, pp. 26, 27.
80 J. F. Findlay, *Dwight L. Moody: American Evangelist, 1837–1899* (Chicago, 1969), pp. 127 ff., 130 f., 149–55, 165 f.
81 J. Kent, *Holding the Fort: Studies in Victorian Revivalism* (London, 1978), p. 136.
82 W. H. Daniels, *D. L. Moody and his Work* (London, 1875), p. 249. Kent, *Holding the Fort*, pp. 143 f., 146. J. C. Ryle to editor, *R*, 28 May 1875. Dean Close to editor, *R*, 21 June 1875.
83 Daniels, *Moody*, pp. 425, 431, 432. On Moody's preaching, cf. Kent, *Holding the Fort*, pp. 169–204.

84   Kent, *Holding the Fort*, ch. 6. See also p. 174.
85   *KH*, June 1874, p. 213.
86   *C*, 22 January 1874, p. 5.
87   Findlay, *Moody*, p. 132.
88   Kent, *Holding the Fort*, p. 186.
89   *C*, 7 May 1874, p. 6. *R*, 24 May 1875. *C*, 19 May 1875, p. 9.
90   Findlay, *Moody*, pp. 342 n.6, 407 n.37, 408, 412 n.46. *C*, 4 August 1892, p. 23.
91   W. B. Sloan, *These Sixty Years: The Story of the Keswick Convention* (London, n.d.), p. 19.
92   Ryle to editor, *R*, 28 May 1875. Close to editor, *R*, 21 June 1875.
93   Page, *Brash*, p. 146.
94   Dieter, *Holiness Revival*, ch. 2. T. L. Smith, *Revivalism and Social Reform* (New York, 1965 edn).
95   Dieter, *Holiness Revival*, pp. 22 f. Page, *Long Pilgrimage*, p. 193. *KH*, September 1874, p. 295.
96   *Convention . . . at Brighton*, p. 217. Boardman, *Boardman*, pp. 253 f. J. B. Figgis, *Keswick from Within* (London, 1914), p. 17.
97   *Revival*, 4 November 1869, pp. 1 f. Boardman, *Boardman*, pp. 155–76. *Meeting at Oxford*, p. 73. *Convention . . . at Brighton*, pp. 383 f.
98   Dieter, *Holiness Revival*, pp. 27–32. Kent, *Holding the Fort*, ch. 8, pt 2.
99   Kent, *Holding the Fort*, pp. 342–7. *Meeting . . . at Oxford*, p. 52 ('the altar Christ').
100 Kent, *Holding the Fort*, ch. 8, pt 3.
101 Dieter, *Holiness Revival*, pp. 96–106. V. Synan, *The Holiness-Pentecostal Movement in the United States* (Grand Rapids, Mich., 1971).
102 *KH*, March 1872, pp. 74 f.; November 1872, pp. 364–72.
103 W. G. Pascoe quoted by Dieter, *Holiness Revival*, p. 167.
104 H. Pearsall Smith, *Unselfishness*, pp. 239–88.
105 For example, Anderson, 'Women preachers', p. 477.
106 Smiles, *Self-Help*, new edn (London, 1860), pp. 253, 293.
107 *Revival*, 9 January 1868, p. 17.
108 *Meeting . . . at Oxford*, p. 45.
109 *R*, 22 January 1875.
110 Smiles, *Self-Help*, p. 52.
111 T. R. Tholfsen, *Working Class Radicalism in Mid-Victorian England* (London, 1976), pp. 26–34, 61–5, 72 ff.
112 See p. 169.
113 J. W. Burrow, *Evolution and Society* (London, 1966), chs 5 and 6. A. W. Coats, 'The historist reaction in English political economy, 1870–90', *Economica*, new series, vol. 21, no. 4 (1954). A. Porter, 'Cambridge, Keswick and late nineteenth-century attitudes to Africa', *Journal of Imperial and Commonwealth History*, vol. 5, no. 1 (1976), p. 16.
114 M. J. Wiener, *English Culture and the Decline of the Industrial Spirit, 1850–1980* (Cambridge, 1981), ch. 3.
115 Arnold, *Culture and Anarchy*, ed. J. D. Wilson (Cambridge, 1971), p. 49.
116 Smith, *Revivalism and Social Reform*, pp. 113, 142.
117 *R*, 24 May 1875. C. Jerdan, 'Recent holiness teaching', *United Presbyterian Magazine*, vol. 9 (1892), p. 50. G. Jackson, 'Some Evangelical shortcomings', *A Parson's Log* (London, 1927), p. 143.

118 Fox to Dr Elder Cumming, in S. M. Nugent, *Charles Armstrong Fox: Memorials* (London, n.d.), p. 210.

119 C. Binfield, '"Old-fashioned Dissenting narrowness": Crabb Robinson and the Pattissons', *So Down to Prayers: Studies in English Nonconformity, 1780–1920* (London, 1977), p. 46.

120 J. Westbury-Jones, *Figgis of Brighton: A Memoir of a Modern Saint* (London, 1917), p. 213.

121 *C*, 25 July 1895, p. 14.

122 Wiener, *Decline of the Industrial Spirit*, pp. 46–65.

123 *Meeting . . . at Oxford*, p. 134.

124 E. H. Hopkins, *The Law of Liberty in the Spiritual Life* (London, 1884), p. 15.

125 *Meeting . . . at Oxford*, pp. 78 f.

126 Pearsall Smith to editor, *R*, 24 April 1874.

127 *Revival*, 10 December 1868, p. 683.

128 *R*, 18 January 1889, p. 56.

129 F. Meinecke, *Historism: The Rise of a New Historical Outlook* [1923], trans. J. E. Anderson (London, 1973). D. W. Bebbington, *Patterns in History* (Leicester, 1979), ch. 5.

130 *Meeting . . . at Oxford*, p. 42.

131 More, *Practical Piety* (London, 1830), pp. 2 f.

132 Bonar to G. T. Fox, quoted by Fox to editor, *R*, 18 June 1875.

133 Jerdan, 'Holiness teaching', p. 49.

134 D. D. Sceats, 'Perfectionism and the Keswick Convention, 1875–1900', MA thesis, University of Bristol, 1970, esp. p. 72.

135 Smart, *Cook*, p. 175.

136 Wesley, 'Christian perfection', p. 314.

137 For example, *Meeting . . . at Oxford*, p. 228.

138 *R*, 18 January 1882; cf. *R*, 22 January 1875, 21 January 1876.

139 Ryle to editor, *R*, 28 May 1875. Ryle, *A Letter on Mr Pearsall Smith's Brighton Convention by the Rev. John C. Ryle* (Stradbroke, Suffolk, 1875). Ryle, *Holiness* (London, 1877, and still in print); cf. Kent, *Holding the Fort*, pp. 351–4.

140 For example, Jerdan, 'Holiness teaching', p. 52.

141 J. C. Pollock, *The Keswick Story* (London, 1964), pp. 35 f.

142 J. B. Harford and F. C. Macdonald, *Handley Carr Glyn Moule, Bishop of Durham* (London, 1922), pp. 118 f. R. Matthews, *English Messiahs: Studies of Six English Religious Pretenders, 1656–1927* (London, 1936), ch. 5.

143 W. H. Aldis and W. M. Smith (introd.), *The Message of Keswick and its Meaning* (London, 1957), pp. 67, 70, 100.

144 *R*, 21 January 1878.

145 *Meeting . . . at Oxford*, p. 59.

146 Ryle, *Letter on . . . Brighton Convention*, p. 1.

147 A. T. Pierson, *Forward Movements of the Last Half Century* (New York, 1900), p. 21.

148 E. V. Jackson, *The Life that is Life Indeed: Reminiscences of the Broadlands Conference* (London, 1910), p. 19.

149 Smellie, *Hopkins*, p. 63.

150 *C*, 1 April 1886, p. 19.

151 H. Pearsall Smith, *Unselfishness*, pp. 205–25. Boardman, *Boardman*, p. 29. Page, *Brash*, pp. 10, 48. H. D. Rawnsley, *Literary Associations of the English Lakes*, Vol. 1 (Glasgow, 1894), pp. 135 f.
152 Battersby to editor, *R*, 14 June 1875.
153 *R*, 24 May 1875.
154 Bonar to G. T. Fox, quoted by Fox to editor, *R*, 18 June 1875.
155 *R*, 24 May 1875.
156 See p. 219.
157 See p. 28.
158 Page, *Brash*, pp. 35, 110.
159 Harford–Battersby to editor, *R*, 14 June 1875.
160 'The Brighton Convention and its opponents', *London Quarterly Review*, October 1875, p. 98.
161 Page, *Brash*, pp. 37 f.
162 Wesley, 'Christian perfection', pp. 335 f.
163 F. de L. Booth-Tucker, *The Life of Catherine Booth the Mother of the Salvation Army*, 3rd edn (London, 1924), Vol. 1, p. 208.
164 *Meeting . . . at Oxford*, p. 54.
165 Wesley, 'Christian perfection', p. 323.
166 *C*, 22 January 1874, p. 14. H. W. Webb-Peploe, *The Life of Privilege, Possession, Peace and Power* (London, 1896), pp. 28 f.
167 Wesley, 'Christian perfection', pp. 374, 320.
168 Pearsall Smith to editor, *R*, 24 April 1874.
169 *C*, 15 July 1880, p. 12; 29 July 1880, p. 12; 12 August 1880, p. 10. Smellie, *Hopkins*, p. 81.
170 *C*, 14 November 1895, p. 9; 21 November 1895, p. 21.
171 N. Frye, 'The drunken boat: the revolutionary element in Romanticism', in N. Frye (ed.), *Romanticism Reconsidered* (New York, 1963), pp. 8 ff.
172 Aldis and Smith (introd.), *Message of Keswick*, p. 43.
173 R. Sandall, *The History of the Salvation Army*, Vol. 2 (London, 1950), chs 18–21.
174 E. A. Wood, *Memorials of James Wood, LL.D., J.P., of Grove House, Southport* (London, 1902), p. 257.
175 *Convention . . . at Brighton*, pp. 10, 18 f. F. S. Webster, 'Keswick hymns', in Harford (ed.), *Keswick Convention*.
176 Morgan, *Veteran in Revival*, p. 174 n.
177 V. Gammon, '"Babylonian performances": the rise and suppression of popular church music, 1660–1870', in E. Yeo and S. Yeo (eds), *Popular Culture and Class Conflict* (Brighton, 1981), esp. p. 78.
178 R. W. Dale in G. Jackson, *Collier of Manchester: A Friend's Tribute* (London, 1923), p. 152 n.
179 Morgan, *Veteran in Revival*, pp. 172 f; cf. Kent, *Holding the Fort*, ch. 6.
180 J. M. Crane (ed.), *The Autobiography of Maria Vernon Graham Havergal* (London, 1888), p. 190.
181 Smellie, *Hopkins*, p. 178.
182 S. M. Nugent, 'Women at Keswick', in Harford (ed.), *Keswick Convention*, p. 195.
183 Anderson, 'Women preachers'. Braithwaite, *Pennefather*, p. 362.
184 Garrard, *Mrs Penn-Lewis*, pp. 194 f.

185 Z. Fairfield, *Some Aspects of the Woman's Movement* (London, 1915), p. 229.
186 Nugent, 'Women at Keswick', pp. 199 f.
187 *KH*, November 1874, p. 380.
188 H. Lockyer, *Keswick: The Place and the Power* (Stirling, [1936]), pp. 33 f.
189 M. V. G. Havergal, *Memorials of Frances Ridley Havergal* (London, 1880), pp. 138, 350. Garrard, *Penn-Lewis*, p. 29.
190 E.T.A. to editor, *C*, 18 July 1895, p. 16.
191 A. T. Pierson, 'The message: its practical application', in Harford (ed.), *Keswick Convention*, p. 93.
192 For example, H. F. Bowker in *C*, 4 November 1875, p. 9. I. E. Page in *KH*, June 1872, p. 196.
193 Pierson, *Forward Movements*, p. 34. T. Waugh, *Twenty-Three Years a Missioner* (London, n.d.), p. 142.
194 Charles Hollis to editor, *C*, 19 March 1885, p. 22.
195 *C*, 12 August 1880, p. 10.
196 *KH*, June 1872, p. 197.
197 D. W. Bebbington, *The Nonconformist Conscience: Chapel and Politics, 1870-1914* (London, 1982), pp. 47 f.
198 *Convention . . . at Brighton*, p. 289.
199 For example, *C*, 9 September 1875, p. 9.
200 Pierson, 'The message', p. 93.
201 Boardman, *Boardman*, ch. 16.
202 Pierson, 'The message', p. 94. *C*, 11 August 1892, p. 19.
203 P. S. Kruppa, *Charles Haddon Spurgeon: A Preacher's Progress* (New York, 1982), pp. 219 f. *LF*, 11 August 1926, p. 899.
204 Kent, *Holding the Fort*, p. 317, reaches the same conclusion.
205 Braithwaite, *Pennefather*, p. 303.
206 *Meeting . . . at Oxford*, p. 181.
207 P. Bailey, '"A mingled mass of perfectly legitimate pleasures": the Victorian middle class and the problem of leisure', *Victorian Studies*, vol. 21, no. 1 (1977).
208 J. D. Marshall and J. K. Walton, *The Lake Counties from 1830 to the Mid-Twentieth Century* (Manchester, 1981), pp. 188 ff.
209 J. S. Holden, 'Young men at Keswick', in Harford (ed.), *Keswick Convention*, p. 209. J. B. Figgis, *Keswick from Within* (London, 1914), p. 163.
210 Pollock, *Keswick Story*, p. 111.
211 *R*, 18 January 1892, p. 71. *C*, 4 August 1892, p. 23.
212 *R*, 18 January 1901, pp. 88 f.; 17 January 1902, pp. 67 f.
213 *C*, 2 August 1900, p. 11. Smellie, *Hopkins*, p. 124.
214 *Convention . . . at Brighton*, p. 456.
215 *C*, 24 September 1874, p. 12.
216 Page (ed.), *Brash*, pp. 106, 109, 185.
217 Page (ed.), *Brash*, p. 214. Page, *Long Pilgrimage*, p. 249.
218 *To the Uttermost: Commemorating the Diamond Jubilee of the Southport Methodist Holiness Convention, 1885–1945* (London, 1945), esp. pp. 63, 75.
219 Page (ed.), *Brash*, p. 146.
220 *KH*, November 1874, p. 391.
221 Page, *Long Pilgrimage*, p. 46.

222   Govan, *Spirit of Revival*, pp. 22, 24, 31, 33, 40. J. Rendel Harris (ed.), *The Life of Francis William Crossley* (London, 1900), ch. 5.
223   Ford, *Steps of John Wesley*, pp. 90 ff. Garrard, *Penn-Lewis*, p. 235.
224   R. M. Anderson, *Vision of the Disinherited: The Making of American Pentecostalism* (New York, 1979), p. 37.
225   Ford, *Steps of John Wesley*, p. 29.
226   An illuminating analysis of the first three is the substance of Ford, *Steps of John Wesley*. The fourth is discussed in T. R. Warburton, 'Organisation and change in a British Holiness Movement', in B. R. Wilson (ed.), *Patterns of Sectarianism* (London, 1967).
227   See pp. 196.
228   Ford, *Steps of John Wesley*, p. 130 n.
229   T. H. Darlow, in W. Y. Fullerton, *F. B. Meyer: A Biography* (London, n.d.), p. 36.
230   *R*, 2 August 1907, p. 679.
231   On CICCU: J. C. Pollock, *A Cambridge Movement* (London, 1953). On the creation of BTI: *C*, 16 June 1892, p. 8.
232   This is evident in C. H. Hopkins, *John R. Mott, 1865–1955: A Biography* (Grand Rapids, Mich., 1979).
233   Morgan, *Veteran in Revival*, p. 190.
234   Wilson (ed.), *Patterns of Sectarianism*, pp. 23 f., 27.
235   Smellie, *Hopkins*, p. 83.

CHAPTER 6: WALKING APART

1   Letter of December 1923 in E. N. Gowing, *John Edwin Watts-Ditchfield: First Bishop of Chelmsford* (London, 1926), p. 229.
2   H. A. H. Lea to editor, *R*, 12 January 1934, p. 18.
3   G. M. Marsden, *Fundamentalism and American Culture: The Shaping of Twentieth-Century Evangelicalism, 1870–1925* (New York, 1980), pp. 118–23, 159.
4   *LW*, June 1924, p. 122 (J. N. Ogilvie).
5   *JWBU*, August 1927.
6   *BW*, 29 May 1913, p. 226 (P. Watchurst).
7   J. A. Chapman, *The Bible and its Inspiration* (n.p., n.d. [*c.*1930]), pp. 14, 5.
8   *R*, 7 July 1933, p. 397.
9   K. H. Boynes, *Our Catholic Heritage* (n.p., n.d. [*c.*1927]), p. 8.
10   P. Austin, *Letters to a Fundamentalist* (London, 1930), pp. 26 f.
11   W. A. Challacombe to editor, *R*, 10 March 1911, p. 236. See pp. 90 f.
12   H. Cockayne to editor, *R*, 30 March 1922, p. 213.
13   I. Ellis, *Seven against Christ: A Study of 'Essays and Reviews'* (Leiden, 1980), p. 115.
14   J. Rogerson, *Old Testament Criticism in the Nineteenth Century* (London, 1984).
15   *Free Church of Scotland Special Report of the College Committee on Professor Smith's Article Bible* (Edinburgh, 1877), pp. 20, 16, 8 f.
16   J. S. Black and G. W. Chrystal, *The Life of William Robertson Smith* (London, 1912).
17   *Special Report*, p. 22.

18 W. B. Glover, *Evangelical Nonconformists and Higher Criticism in the Nineteenth Century* (London, 1954), pp. 128 f., 186–93.
19 R. A. Riesen, *Criticism and Faith in Late Victorian Scotland: A. B. Davidson, William Robertson Smith and George Adam Smith* (Lanham, Md, 1985).
20 *LW*, May 1912, p. 134.
21 S. Neill, *The Interpretation of the New Testament, 1861–1961* (Oxford, 1964), pp. 33–97.
22 A. M. Ramsey, *From Gore to Temple* (London, 1960), pp. 5–8.
23 Driver, *An Introduction to the Literature of the Old Testament* (Edinburgh, 1891).
24 Forsyth, 'Revelation and the Person of Christ', in *Faith and Criticism* (2nd edn, London, 1893), p. 109.
25 R. T. Jones, *Congregationalism in England, 1662–1962* (London, 1962), p. 258.
26 Glover, *Nonconformists and Higher Criticism*, pp. 205–11. J. T. Wilkinson, *Arthur Samuel Peake: A Biography* (London, 1971), pp. 24 f.
27 I. E. Page (ed.), *John Brash: Memorials and Correspondence* (London, 1912), p. 74.
28 See pp. 145 f.
29 *C*, 1 June 1893, p. 11. The author is identified at 8 June 1893, p. 19.
30 *Newness of Life*, January 1898, p. 1.
31 R. F. Horton, *An Autobiography* (London, 1917), pp. 84–98.
32 For example, H. Wace in *R*, 16 January 1903, p. 63.
33 *R*, 18 January 1878.
34 *R*, 25 June 1909, p. 673.
35 *C*, 12 May 1892, p. 7; 14 July 1892, p. 8.
36 *Baptist Handbook*, 1918, p. 133. *LF*, 7 March 1923, p. 269. G. E. Morgan, *A Veteran in Revival: R. C. Morgan: His Life and Times* (London, 1909), pp. 157 f.
37 *C*, 13 February 1896, p. 26.
38 *R*, 25 June 1909, p. 673. *C*, 4 January 1906, p. 12. *JWBU*, March 1915, p. 61.
39 *JWBU*, March 1915, pp. 60–3.
40 A. G. Wilkinson, *Christ or the Higher Critics* (London, 1917).
41 *JWBU*, April 1915, p. 79.
42 D. Johnson, *Contending for the Faith: A History of the Evangelical Movement in the Universities and Colleges* (Leicester, 1979), p. 70.
43 J. C. Pollock, *Cambridge Movement* (London, 1953), p. 178.
44 *JWBU*, May 1921, pp. 115 f. *LF*, 18 June 1924, p. 714.
45 *C*, 1 June 1893, p. 11.
46 *W*, September 1921, pp. 99 f.
47 *Expository Thoughts on St John's Gospel*, Vol. 1, p. vii, quoted by M. L. Loane, *John Charles Ryle, 1816–1900* (London, 1983), p. 60.
48 For example, H. D. Brown, *The Bible: The Word of God* (London, n.d.), p. 44.
49 *BC*, December 1922, p. 95 (W. R. Rowlatt-Jones).
50 *AW*, April 1921, pp. 187 f; cf. F. W. Pitt, *Windows on the World: A Record of the Life of Alfred H. Burton, B.A., M.D.* (London, n.d.), pp. 16 f. 27, 35.
51 D. F. Wright, 'Soundings in the doctrine of scripture in British Evangelicalism in the first half of the twentieth century', *Tyndale Bulletin*, vol. 31 (1980), pp. 100 ff.
52 *R*, 13 January 1911, p. 50.

53 Wace, 'Science and the Bible', in H. Wace *et al.*, *Creative Christianity* (London, 1921), p. 17.
54 *JWBU*, March 1922, p. 56.
55 *R*, 10 January 1924, p. 19.
56 Wace, *The Bible and Modern Investigation* (London, 1903). *R*, 14 October 1920, p. 790.
57 *LF*, 12 December 1923, p. 1535.
58 *R*, 5 October 1922, p. 650. For the contrast with a deductive approach to inspiration, see pp. 89 f.
59 Marsden, *Fundamentalism and American Culture*.
60 *R*, 27 April 1922, p. 279 (W. Young).
61 *C*, 11 March 1886, p. 24. See also pp. 88 f.
62 *AW*, October 1922, p. 113.
63 E. Morton and D. Dewar, *A Voice Crying in the Wilderness: A Memoir of Harold Christopherson Morton* (London, 1937), pp. 34 f.
64 For example, Lover of Keswick to editor, *LF*, 25 August 1926, p. 960.
65 Page (ed.), *Brash*, p. 176.
66 F. Ballard, *Christian Reality in Modern Light* (London, 1916), p. 383.
67 *LW*, November 1918, p. 164; May 1919, p. 69.
68 *R*, 3 July 1931, p. 441.
69 *C*, 22 June 1893, p. 20; 10 July 1884, p. 16.
70 See p. 152.
71 A. T. Pierson, *Forward Movements of the Last Half Century* (New York, 1900), p. 159 n.
72 A. Porter, 'Evangelical enthusiasm, missionary motivation and West Africa in the late nineteenth century: the career of G. W. Brooke', *Journal of Imperial and Commonwealth History*, vol. 6, no. 1 (1977), pp. 38 ff.
73 *R*, 18 January 1901, p. 99 (Prebendary Webb-Peploe).
74 Page (ed.), *Brash*, p. 186. For dispensationalism, see p. 86.
75 *C*, 21 July 1892, p. 8.
76 *C*, 26 June 1913, p. 14.
77 For historicism, see pp. 85.
78 Garratt to C. R. M'Clenaghan, 8 March 1906, in E. R. Garratt, *Life and Personal Recollections of Samuel Garratt* (London 1908), p. 165.
79 *R*, 29 November 1917, p. 805.
80 *MBAPPU*, June 1919, pp. 1 f.; *AW*, December 1923, pp. 134 f.; May–June 1947, pp. 232 f.
81 *LF*, 8 September 1926, p. 1021. *R*, 11 November 1926, p. 786.
82 *C*, 28 April 1921, p. 11.
83 E. Luff to editor, *C*, 14 July 1921, p. 27; cf. J. W. Newton, *The Story of the Pilgrim Preachers* (London, n.d.).
84 J. Cox, *The English Churches in a Secular Society: Lambeth, 1870–1930* (New York, 1982), p. 257.
85 *C*, 11 March 1886, p. 18 (Grattan Guinness).
86 *MBAPPU*, August 1919, p. 19 (A. H. Burton).
87 Page (ed.), Brash, p. 68.
88 *C*, 13 February 1919, p. 22 (G. E. Morgan).
89 *LF*, 26 May 1926, p. 547 (G. H. Lancaster).
90 See p. 171 and pp. 218 ff.

91 A. Close to editor, *LF*, 13 May 1925, p. 535.
92 G. Jackson, 'Some Evangelical shortcomings', *A Parson's Log* (London, 1927), p. 143.
93 *MR*, 1 August 1912, p. 22.
94 Page (ed.), *Brash*, p. 74.
95 *JWBU*, July 1915, p. 148; March 1917, pp. 53–60.
96 *R*, 13 July 1922, p. 482.
97 *JWBU*, August 1919, p. 177; February 1920, p. 25.
98 H. Murray, *Dinsdale Young: The Preacher* (London, 1938), pp. 108 f.
99 J. I. Brice, *The Crowd for Christ* (London, 1934), esp. pp. 150 f.
100 Mrs Boardman, *Life and Labours of the Rev. W. E. Boardman* (London, 1886), ch. 16. Pierson, *Forward Movements*, ch. 30.
101 *LF*, 22 June 1921, p. 689.
102 *LF*, 29 July 1921, p. 849.
103 *LF*, 7 December 1921, p. 1409. Victory to editor, *LF*, 31 August 1921, p. 1006.
104 *Oswald Chambers: His Life and Work* (London, 1959 edn), p. 48. For the Pentecostal League, see pp. 173 f., 178.
105 E. W. Gosden, *Thank You, Lord! The Eightieth Anniversary of the Japan Evangelistic Band, 1903–1983* (London, 1982), p. 82.
106 E. Evans, *The Welsh Revival of 1904* (London, 1969), p. 146.
107 *War on the Saints* (Leicester, 2nd edn, 1916), pp. 284–95.
108 M. N. Garrard, *Mrs Penn-Lewis: A Memoir* (London, 1930), ch. 10.
109 *LF*, December 1881, p. 236.
110 Evans, *Welsh Revival*, pp. 192 ff.
111 R. M. Anderson, *Vision of the Disinherited: The Making of American Pentecostalism* (New York, 1979), ch. 4.
112 D. Gee, *Wind and Flame* (n.p., 1967), chs 3–5. See also P. Lavin, *Alexander Boddy, Pastor and Prophet* (London, 1986).
113 A. F. Missen, *The Sound of a Going* (Nottingham, 1973), pp. 7 f.
114 Anderson, *Vision*, pp. 159 f. Evans, *Welsh Revival*, p. 194.
115 B. R. Wilson, *Sects and Society* (London, 1961), ch. 2; cf. E. C. W. Boulton, *George Jeffreys: A Ministry of the Miraculous* (London, 1928) and D. W. Cartwright, *The Great Evangelists: The Lives of George and Stephen Jeffreys* (Basingstoke, 1986).
116 Gee, *Wind and Flame*, pp. 126–30.
117 Wilson, *Sects and Society*, p. 22 n.
118 *Labourers with God: Being a Brief Account of the Activities of the Elim Movement* (London, [*c.*1943]), p. 30.
119 *LF*, 14 June 1922, p. 732.
120 Anderson, *Vision*, p. 6.
121 See pp. 143 f.
122 G. F. Nuttall, 'A. D. Martin', *The Puritan Spirit* (London, 1967), p. 328.
123 G. S. Wakefield, *Robert Newton Flew, 1886–1962* (London, 1971), p. 44.
124 I. Sellers, *Salute to Pembroke* (n.p., 1960), ch. 4. *CW*, 14 June 1906, p. 4.
125 Campbell, *The New Theology* (London, 1907), p. 74; cf. K. Robbins, 'The spiritual pilgrimage of the Rev. R. J. Campbell', *JEH*, vol. 30, no. 2 (1979).
126 Campbell, *Christianity and the Social Order* (London, 1907), pp. vii, 182.
127 *C*, 27 September 1906, p. 10.

128 *JWBU*, July 1915, p. 157.
129 R. J. Campbell, *A Spiritual Pilgrimage* (London, 1916), chs 10, 11.
130 Cox, *English Churches*, pp. 245 f. T. Rhondda Williams, *How I found my Faith* (London, 1938).
131 *R*, 13 January 1905, p. 38.
132 L. Elliott Binns to editor, *R*, 21 April 1921, p. 253.
133 *Ridley Hall, Cambridge: Annual Letter and Report of Triennial Reunion, 1912* (n.p., n.d.), pp. 22–33.
134 *MR*, 29 February 1912, p. 5 (Dinsdale Young). *C*, 14 August 1913, p. 8.
135 A. Wilkinson, *The Church of England and the First World War* (London, 1978), pp. 176 ff.
136 *JWBU*, April 1917, pp. 80 f. (W. T. Kitching).
137 *R*, 11 December 1914, p. 1125.
138 *JWBU*, November 1915, p. 246.
139 *W*, March 1920, p. 233. *If a Man die* (London, 1917).
140 *JWBU*, March 1915, p. 56.
141 For example, S. E. Burrows to editor, *C*, 29 January 1920, p. 18.
142 For example, *LCMM*, February 1919, p. 13 (Sir C. E. Tritton).
143 *R*, 15 January 1904, p. 97.
144 *R*, 18 September 1924, p. 591.
145 D. H. C. Bartlett to editor, *R*, 17 August 1922, p. 549.
146 K. Weatherhead, *Leslie Weatherhead: A Personal Portrait* (London, 1975), p. 61.
147 G. W. Bromiley, *Daniel Henry Charles Bartlett, M.A., D.D.: A Memoir* (Burnham-on-Sea, Somerset, 1959), p. 30. A. Mitchell to editor, *R*, 28 January 1922, p. 632.
148 G. Jackson, *The Preacher and the Modern Mind* (London, 1912), p. 166.
149 *R*, 26 May 1933, p. 311.
150 Jones, *Congregationalism*, p. 447.
151 Weatherhead, *Jesus and Ourselves* (London, 1930), p. 261.
152 *C*, 25 October 1906, p. 11; 29 November 1906, p. 9.
153 *JWBU*, May 1935, p. 94; September 1935, p. 200.
154 *R*, 24 December 1925, p. 918 (T. J. Pulvertaft).
155 *R*, 3 March 1933, p. 117 (E. A. Knox).
156 G. Rogers, *A Rebel at Heart: The Autobiography of a Nonconforming Clergyman* (London, 1950), p. 170.
157 G. H. Harris, *Vernon Faithfull Storr: A Memoir* (London, 1943), pp. 50 ff.
158 *Liberal Evangelicalism: An Interpretation* (London, [1923]), pp. vi f.
159 Harris, *Storr*, pp. 54 f.
160 *R*, 21 April 1933, p. 215.
161 Harris, *Storr*, pp. 50, 53.
162 Rogers, *Rebel*, p. 172.
163 *LF*, 20 January 1926, p. 61.
164 K. H. Boynes, *The Fellowship of the Kingdom* (London, [1922]).
165 J. A. Chapman, *Our Methodist Heritage* (London, [1919?]), p. 4.
166 H. G. Tunnicliff, *The Group* (London, [1920?]), p. 5.
167 J. M. Turner, 'Methodism in England, 1900–1932', in R. Davies *et al. A History of the Methodist Church in Great Britain*, Vol. 3 (London, 1983), pp. 319 f.
168 Chapman, *Methodist Heritage*, p. 2. Boynes, *Our Catholic Heritage*, p. 4.

169 Harris, *Storr*, p. 56.
170 W. Strawson, 'Methodist theology, 1850–1950', in Davies *et al.* (eds), *Methodist Church*, vol. 3, p. 206.
171 *R*, 19 January 1883, p. 56.
172 For example, *R*, 15 January 1904, pp. 100 ff. (W. H. Griffith Thomas).
173 *R*, 27 November 1924, p. 763.
174 *R*, 17 December 1909, p. 1278.
175 *R*, 21 January 1926, p. 55.
176 F. Courtenay Burroughs to editor, *R*, 9 September 1904, p. 898.
177 C. H. Tomkins to editor, *R*, 19 August 1904, p. 839.
178 Mary E. Burstow to editor, *R*, 26 August 1904, p. 858.
179 *R*, 3 March 1921, p. 149.
180 *R*, 8 October 1937, p. 627.
181 *R*, 10 March 1933, p. 127.
182 A. Mitchell to editor, *R*, 30 September 1904, p. 967.
183 *R*, 12 July 1917, p. 489.
184 *R*, 5 July 1935, p. 418.
185 T. A. Ballard and T. C. Chapman to editor, *R*, 27 September 1917, p. 649. *R*, 27 September 1935, p. 578. *R*, 27 June 1941, p. 235. *R*, 4 July 1941, p. 242.
186 *R*, 18 January 1907, p. 61.
187 *R*, 15 January 1904, pp. 99 f.
188 Garratt to editor, *R*, 11 November 1904, p. 1142; 9 December 1904, p. 1246; cf. Garratt, *Garratt*, ch. 9.
189 *R*, 3 February 1905, p. 99.
190 G. Denyer to editor, *R*, 1 December 1927, p. 854.
191 *R*, 23 June 1927, p. 466.
192 *R*, 21 July 1927, p. 542.
193 *R*, 1 December 1927, p. 852.
194 Boynes, *Our Catholic Heritage*, p. 11.
195 G. S. Wakefield, *Methodist Devotion: The Spiritual Life in the Methodist Tradition* (London, 1966), pp. 103 f.
196 D. Murray, 'Disruption to Union', in D. B. Forrester and D. M. Murray *Studies in the History of Worship in Scotland* (Edinburgh, 1984), pp. 90–3.
197 L. S. Hunter, *John Hunter, D.D.: A Life* (London, 1922), ch. 10.
198 *LF*, 27 May 1925, p. 600.
199 *BW*, 19 February 1920, p. 456.
200 Orchard, *From Faith to Faith* (London, 1933).
201 C. Binfield, 'Freedom through discipline: the concept of little church', in *Monks, Hermits and the Ascetic Tradition*, Studies in Church History, vol. 23, ed. W. J. Sheils (Oxford, 1985), pp. 441 f.
202 *LF*, 28 July 1926, p. 838. G. T. Brake, *Policy and Politics in British Methodism, 1932–1982* (London, 1984), pp. 314–28.
203 B. Heeney, 'The beginnings of church feminism: women and the councils of the Church of England, 1897–1919', *JEH*, vol. 33, no. 1 (1982), pp. 105, 108.
204 C. M. Coltman, 'Post-Reformation: the Free Churches', in A. Maud Royden, *The Church and Woman* (London, 1925), p. 116.

205 Baker, *Women in the Ministry* (London, 1911), pp. 13, 48 f., 55, 43.
206 *R*, 10 February 1933, p. 80; 13 April 1933, p. 208.
207 *R*, 18 September 1936, p. 569.
208 Strawson, 'Methodist theology', pp. 185 f. *R*, 13 January 1905, p. 38.
209 *C*, 17 September 1885, p. 8. *LF*, December 1887, p. 260.
210 H. H. Evans to editor, *C*, 23 September 1887, p. 16; 2 May 1895, p. 22.
211 *R*, 23 October 1924, p. 689. For Dixon, cf. *C*, 9 February 1893, p. 17.
212 C. L. Drawbridge to editor, *R*, 30 July 1915, p. 540.
213 *C*, 11 February 1926, p. 4.
214 *Church Family Newspaper*, 10 September 1920, pp. 8, 10.
215 J. Barnes, *Ahead of his Age: Bishop Barnes of Birmingham* (London, 1979), pp. 125–32. B. Booth, *These Fifty Years* (London, 1929), ch. 21.
216 *R*, 2 September 1920, p. 692; 9 September 1920, p. 708. *C*, 9 September 1920, p. 3.
217 *C*, 23 September 1920, pp. 1 f.
218 Barnes, 'The future of the Evangelical movement', in *Liberal Evangelicalism*. Barnes, *Barnes*, p. 175.
219 *LF*, 8 October 1924, p. 1192.
220 *F*, November 1927, p. 200.
221 *JWBU*, November 1923, p. 248. Morton and Dewar, *A Voice crying*, pt IV.
222 *R*, 29 September 1933, p. 549 (H. E. Boultbee).
223 B. Atkinson, *Is the Bible True?* (London, 1933), p. 49.
224 *R*, 24 June 1926, p. 427.
225 *R*, 9 October 1924, p. 658 (H. C. Morton). *LCMM*, October 1927, p. 156.
226 *F*, January 1935, p. 9; May 1941, p. 97; March/April 1943, pp. 24–9. *C*, 21 February 1935, p. 8.
227 *R*, 18 July 1930, p. 474 (H. Earnshaw Smith).
228 J. Forbes Moncreiff to editor, *LF*, 14 July 1926, p. 748. Sister L. Holt to editor, *LF*, 25 August 1926, p. 954. Winifred M. Gould to editor, *LF*, 1 September 1926, p. 983.
229 *BW*, 18 August 1921, p. 357.
230 *JWBU*, January 1918, p. 20. J. Lingard to editor, *LF*, 9 April 1924, p. 408. *LCMM*, July 1924, p. 102.
231 *W*, August 1919, p. 128 (D. Hewines).
232 See pp. 113, 127 f.
233 *C*, 5 February 1920, pp. 3 f.
234 *LW*, March 1922, p. 52.
235 Cox, *English Churches*, p. 219.
236 *BW*, 11 March 1920, p. 535.
237 *LF*, 16 May 1923, p. 556.
238 Morton to editor, *MR*, 21 March 1912, p. 6.
239 R. E. Jones to editor, *MR*, 8 August 1935, p. 18.
240 Wilson, *Sects and Society*, pp. 82, 84 (Elim).
241 *AW*, May 1922, p. 51 (A. H. Burton).
242 R. H. A. Morton to editor, *MR*, 10 November 1932, p. 20.
243 *LF*, 6 October 1926, pp. 1131 f.
244 *BC*, January 1925, p. 16.
245 R. E. A. Lloyd to editor, *R*, 12 June 1936, p. 375, and succeeding correspondence. *R*, 18 November 1938, p. 739.

246 *LW*, June 1919, p. 88.

247 H to editor, *LF*, 16 July 1924, p. 815.

248 *BW*, 13 July 1922, p. 309.

249 *R*, 25 January 1935, p. 57; 11 January 1935, p. 26.

250 *R*, 7 April 1932, p. 9; 6 March 1931, p. 143.

251 *R*, 20 February 1931, p. 117. J. Wigley, *The Rise and Fall of the Victorian Sunday* (Manchester, 1980), p. 193.

252 *C*, 3 November 1932, p. 5. *R*, 17 November 1933, p. 651.

253 *BW*, 27 November 1919, p. 206.

254 For example, Dean Wace in *R*, 17 March 1921, pp. 182 f.

255 *CW*, 6 June 1889, p. 65.

256 A. Scott Matheson, *The Church and Social Problems* (London, 1893), p. v.

257 *BW*, 6 March 1919, p. 401.

258 *MT*, 1 January 1885, p. 1.

259 Mudie-Smith (ed.), *The Religious Life of London* (London, 1904), p. 13.

260 Grant, *Free Churchmanship*, pp. 173 ff.

261 For example, D. P. Hughes, *The Life of Hugh Price Hughes* (London, 1905), p. 134.

262 K. S. Inglis, 'English Nonconformity and social reform, 1880–1900', *Past & Present*, no. 13 (1958). J. H. S. Kent, 'Hugh Price Hughes and the Nonconformist conscience', in G. V. Bennett and J. D. Walsh (eds), *Essays in Modern English Church History in Memory of Norman Sykes* (London, 1966). D. W. Bebbington, 'The city, the countryside and the social gospel in late Victorian Nonconformity', in *The Church in Town and Countryside*, Studies in Church History, vol. 16, ed. D. Baker (Oxford, 1979).

263 Hughes, *Social Christianity: Sermons delivered in St James's Hall, London*, 3rd edn (London, 1890), p. 15.

264 *CW*, 4 October 1888, pp. 758 f; cf. K. Marx and F. Engels, *The Communist Manifesto* (Harmondsworth, Middlesex, 1967), p. 116. See also D. Thompson, 'John Clifford's social gospel', *Baptist Quarterly*, vol. 21, no. 5 (1986).

265 *R*, 6 December 1907, p. 1066.

266 *R*, 1 January 1904, p. 8.

267 *R*, 21 January 1910, p. 72.

268 *R*, 17 January 1913, pp. 67 f.

269 *R*, 17 January 1918, pp. 37 f. Watts-Ditchfield, 'The Church and the Labour Movement', *Churchman*, January 1908.

270 Gowing, *Watts-Ditchfield*, pp. 10 f.

271 *R*, 17 January 1908, pp. 63, 67.

272 A country incumbent to editor, *R*, 31 January 1908, p. 106. F. D. Stammers to editor, *R*, 7 February 1908, p. 125.

273 *R*, 3 March 1921, p. 149.

274 A. E. Garvie, *Memories and Meanings of my Life* (London, 1938), pp. 241 ff.

275 Brake, *Policy and Politics*, chs 10 and 11.

276 *LW*, April 1934, pp. 161–4.

277 Jackson, 'The church and the social gospel', *Reasonable Religion* (London 1922), p. 139.

278 G. Studdert-Kennedy, *Dog-Collar Democracy: The Industrial Christian Fellowship* (London, 1982), esp. p. 40.

279 F. Coutts, *The History of the Salvation Army*, Vol. 6, *The Better Fight*, (London, 1973).
280 *JWBU*, May 1924, pp. 106 f. *LF*, 16 April 1924, p. 415.
281 *JWBU*, July 1917, p. 161.
282 D. W. Bebbington, 'Baptists and politics since 1914', in K. W. Clements (ed.), *Baptists in the Twentieth Century* (London, 1983), p. 86.
283 *W*, September 1920, pp. 323 ff.
284 Bebbington, 'Baptists and politics', p. 87.
285 ibid., p. 85. *C*, 3 March 1932, p. 5.
286 D. Moberg, *The Great Reversal: Evangelism versus Social Concern* (Philadelphia, 1972).
287 A Nonconformist Minister, *Nonconformity and Politics* (London, 1909), p. 130, quoted by D. W. Bebbington, *The Nonconformist Conscience: Chapel and Politics, 1870–1914* (London, 1982), p. 158.
288 D. W. Bebbington, 'Nonconformity and electoral sociology, 1867–1918', *Historical Journal*, vol. 27, no. 3 (1984).
289 *R*, 3 December 1909, p. 1224; 18 August 1911, p. 750.
290 *MR*, 4 January 1912, p. 3.
291 *LW*, July 1912, p. 197.
292 A. G. James, *The Spirit of the Crusade* (London, 1927), p. 16.
293 H. P. Hughes, 'The problem of London pauperism', *The Philanthropy of God* (London, 1892), p. 195.
294 *Labour Leader*, 9 February 1895, p. 2; cf. P. d'A. Jones, *The Christian Socialist Revival, 1877–1914: Religion, Class and Social Conscience in Late-Victorian England* (Princeton, NJ, 1968).
295 Rattenbury, *Six Sermons on Social Subjects* (London, [1908]).
296 M. Edwards, *S. E. Keeble: Pioneer and Prophet* (London, 1949), pp. 67 f.
297 *CW*, 8 April 1909, p. 13; 28 April 1910, p. 4.
298 *R*, 6 December 1907, p. 1066; 3 January 1908, p. 11.
299 *BW*, 7 April 1921, p. 9 (S. W. Hughes).
300 G. P. Thomas to editor, *BW*, 28 April 1921, p. 66.
301 Hughes, 'The Christian hope', *Ethical Christianity* (London, 1892), p. 76; cf. J. G. Mantle *Hugh Price Hughes* (London, 1901), pp. 49 f.
302 Clifford, *God's Greater Britain* (London, 1899), p. 164.
303 Page (ed.), *Brash*, p. 66.
304 *R*, 26 March 1925, p. 214.
305 *R*, 3 September 1925, p. 609 (London City Mission advertisement).
306 *LF*, 16 April 1924, p. 445.
307 *CW*, 14 May 1891, p. 395.
308 Thompson, 'John Clifford's social gospel', p. 214.
309 *R*, 8 November 1917, p. 750.
310 *R*, 18 September 1924, p. 591.
311 *AW*, November 1923, p. 123.
312 *MT*, 19 June 1913, p. 3.
313 D. W. Bebbington, 'The persecution of George Jackson: a British Fundamentalist controversy', in *Persecution and Toleration*, Studies in Church History, vol. 21, ed. W. J. Sheils (Oxford, 1984).
314 H. Cockayne to editor, *R*, 30 March 1922, p. 213.
315 *R*, 18 January 1907, p. 70.

316 Bromiley, *Bartlett*, p. 22. W. S. Hooton and J. S. Wright, *The First Twenty-Five Years of the Bible Churchmen's Missionary Society (1922–47)* (London, 1947), pp. 5 f.

317 D. H. C. Bartlett to editor, *R*, 6 April 1922, p. 224. Fox to editor, *C*, 28 July 1921, p. 22. Fox to Bartlett, April 1921, in Bromiley, *Bartlett*, pp. 26 f.

318 Bromiley, *Bartlett*, pp. 24–7.

319 *R*, 15 December 1921, p. 829.

320 G. Hewitt, *The Problems of Success: A History of the Church Missionary Society, 1910–1942*, Vol. 1 (London, 1972), pp. 467–71. Bromiley, *Bartlett*, pp. 27–36.

321 *R*, 11 November 1926, p. 786.

322 *R*, 31 July 1919, p. 646.

323 *W*, March 1920, p. 234. J. B. Figgis, *Keswick from Within* (London, 1914), p. 160.

324 *Church Family Newspaper*, 30 July 1920, p. 10. *JWBU*, October 1920, p. 223. J. Mountain, *The Keswick Convention and the Dangers which threaten it* (n.p., 1920), p. 8.

325 *C*, 6 July 1933, p. 12.

326 Mountain, *Keswick Convention*, p. 14.

327 Mountain, *What Keswick needs* (n.p., 1921). Mountain, *The Bible Vindicated* (n.p., 1921). Mountain, *Rev. F. C. Spurr and Keswick* (n.p., 1921). Mountain, *Rev. F. C. Spurr and his Bible* (n.p., 1922). Charles Brown to editor, *BW*, 14 July 1921, p. 276.

328 Battersby Harford to editor, *R*, 6 January 1921, p. 4. Douglas-Jones to editor, *R*, 13 January 1921, p. 32.

329 *C*, 17 February 1921, pp. 1 f. *JWBU*, July 1921, p. 159.

330 *R*, 28 April 1921, p. 282.

331 J. C. Pollock, *The Keswick Story* (London, 1964), pp. 154 ff.

332 *R*, 21 July 1933, p. 425.

333 *HC*, July–September 1919, p. 1; October–December 1919, p. 4.

334 Marsden, *Fundamentalism and American Culture*, p. 172.

335 *BC*, October 1923, p. 152.

336 *R*, 14 June 1923, p. 387; cf. H. G. Wood, *T. R. Glover: A Biography* (Cambridge, 1953), p. 155.

337 *BC*, July 1925, pp. 100 f.; November 1925, p. 147.

338 *BC*, January 1923, p. 8; February 1925, p. 30.

339 D. G. Fountain, *E. J. Poole-Connor (1872–1962): Contender for the Faith* (Worthing, 1966), pp. 122–8.

340 D. M. Thompson, *Let Sects and Parties Fall: A Short History of the Association of Churches of Christ in Great Britain and Ireland* (Birmingham, 1980), pp. 131 ff. K. O. Morgan, *Rebirth of a Nation: Wales, 1880–1980* (Oxford, 1981), pp. 199 f.

341 Wood, *Glover*, pp. 159–63.

342 *LF*, 20 May 1925, p. 573.

343 *F*, April 1929, p. 84.

344 *R*, 30 December 1925, p. 1607.

345 *R*, 20 September 1917, p. 637; 12 April 1929, p. 237.

346 H. Wace *et al.*, *Creative Christianity* (London, 1921); cf. *R*, 7 June 1923, p. 367; 14 June 1923, p. 391.

347 E. A. Payne, *The Baptist Union: A Short History* (London, 1958), p. 211.
348 J. T. Carson, *Frazer of Tain* (Glasgow, 1966), p. 49.
349 *R*, 30 October 1924, p. 708.
350 S. Bruce, *No Pope of Rome* (Edinburgh, 1985).
351 Cadoux, *Catholicism and Christianity* (London, 1928), p. 55; cf. E. Kaye, 'C. J. Cadoux and Mansfield College, Oxford', *Journal of the United Reformed Church History Society*, vol. 3, no. 8 (1986).
352 G. K. A. Bell, *Randall Davidson, Archbishop of Canterbury*, 3rd edn (London, 1952), p. 1326.
353 *R*, 24 March 1932, p. 184 (Exeter); 6 May 1932, p. 285 (Salisbury); 24 February 1933, p. 103 (London).
354 *R*, 31 July 1924, pp. 504 f.
355 *R*, 19 February 1925, p. 117.
356 *F*, October 1931, p. 226.
357 *LCMM*, February 1927, pp. 29–32.
358 N. G. Dunning, *Samuel Chadwick* (London, 1933), p. 193.
359 *LF*, 17 September 1924, p. 1116 (Holden); 20 October 1926, p. 1189 (Meyer); 30 July 1924, p. 895 (Scroggie). J. Morgan, *This was his Faith: The Expository Letters of G. Campbell Morgan* (n.p., [1954]), p. 245.
360 *LF*, 30 July 1924, pp. 895 f.
361 *C*, 1 November 1934, p. 43. *LF*, 16 June 1926, p. 647 (A. H. Carter).
362 *LF*, 16 January 1924, p. 61.
363 F. F. Bruce, *In Retrospect: Remembrance of Things Past* (London, 1980), p. 300.
364 Carter, *Modernism: The Peril of Great Britain and America* (Hounslow, [1923]); cf. *LF*, 5 December 1923, p. 1447.
365 *LF*, 20 January 1924, p. 122.
366 Cook to editor, *LF*, 3 February 1926, p. 120.
367 *LF*, 12 December 1923, p. 1535; 16 June 1926, p. 647.
368 *JWBU*, December 1920, p. 270; October 1923, p. 220. *LF*, 4 November 1925, p. 1270. *R*, 3 November 1927, p. 777; 24 December 1931, p. 833; 29 July 1932. p. 879.
369 *MBAPPU*, September 1919, p. 32.
370 *MBAPPU*, March 1920, p. 80; April 1920, p. 88; May 1920, p. 96.
371 *AW*, April 1922, p. 48.
372 D. H. C. Bartlett to editor, *R*, 17 August 1922, p. 549; 3 August 1934, p. 464; 16 October 1924, p. 666.
373 *R*, 12 June 1924, p. 395. Runs of the League's publications, the *Bible Witness* and the *Bible League Quarterly*, have not been discovered.
374 *F*, February 1931, p. 36; February 1928, p. 43.
375 *F*, December 1929, p. 268.
376 *C*, 27 October 1921, p. 21.
377 *BC*, July–September 1928, p. 34. *R*, 20 May 1926, p. 321.
378 *JWBU*, May 1920, p. 98. The first figure is presented as though it were also for 1918–19, but that must be a misprint.
379 Insertion in copy of *JWBU*, December 1920, at John Rylands University Library of Manchester; cf. D. Crane, *The Life-Story of Sir Robert W. Perks Baronet, M.P.* (London, 1909).
380 *LCMM*, August 1925, p. 113.
381 *BC*, April 1925, p. 65. *JWBU*, February 1926, p. 34.

382 *JWBU*, April 1926, p. 82.
383 E. Pritchard, *For Such a Time* (Eastbourne, 1973). G. Swan, *Lacked Ye Anything?* (London, 1913). J. L. Maxwell, *Half a Century of Grace: A Jubilee History of the Sudan United Mission* (London, n.d.). R. and E. Dewhurst, *God Gave the Increase* (London, 1979).
384 *LF*, 5 August 1925, p. 913; cf. N. Grubb, *Rees Howells, Intercessor* (London, 1952).
385 *BC*, November–December 1921, p. 15.
386 *BC*, October 1926, p. 103. Murray, *Young*, pp. 105–8. Wilson, *Sects and Society*, pp. 46 f., 51 f. See also J. Wilson, 'British Israelism: the ideological restraints on sect organisation', in B. R. Wilson (ed.), *Patterns of Sectarianism* (London, 1967).
387 *R*, 5 May 1933, p. 257. Armitage to editor, *R*, 2 June 1933, p. 321.
388 Woods to editor, *F*, September 1933, pp. 211 f.
389 S. Schor and A. P. Gold Levin to editor, *LF*, 30 June 1926, p. 691; 7 July 1926, p. 715. *C*, 7 December 1933, p. 64.
390 A. L. Glegg, *Four Score . . . and More* (London, 1962), p. 60.
391 W. K. Chaplin and M. J. Strect, *Fifty Years of Christian Endeavour* (London, 1931).
392 *C*, 27 October 1921, p. 14; cf. F. P. and M. S. Wood, *Youth Advancing* (London, 1961).
393 J. C. Pollock, *The Good Seed: The Story of the Children's Special Service Mission and the Scripture Union* (London, 1959).
394 J. Eddison (ed.), *'Bash': A Study in Spiritual Power* (Basingstoke, 1983), esp. p. 18.
395 R. Manwaring, *From Controversy to Co-Existence: Evangelicals in the Church of England, 1914–1980* (Cambridge, 1985), pp. 57, 59 f. 'Covenanters' Golden Jubilee: a special supplement', *Harvester*, February 1980. J. Kerr, *A Midnight Vision: The Story of Colin Kerr and the Campaigners* (Worthing, 1981). J. Springhall et al., *Sure and Stedfast: A History of the Boys' Brigade, 1883 to 1983* (London, 1983), pp. 70 f.
396 S. to editor, *LF*, 21 March 1923, p. 322.
397 *R*, 12 October 1934, p. 604 (W. H. Aldis).
398 For example, *JWBU*, October 1933, p. 224. *R*, 11 December 1924, p. 824 (Dinsdale Young and Russell Howden).
399 *R*, 27 January 1933, p. 57.
400 A. D. Gilbert, *The Making of Post-Christian Britain* (London, 1980), pt 3.
401 For example, *AW*, July 1922, p. 75. *JWBU*, January 1926, p. 11.

CHAPTER 7: THE SPIRIT POURED OUT

1 *CEN*, 15 November 1963, p. 1; C. H. May to editor, 22 November 1963, p. 6.
2 Quoted by P. Hocken, *Streams of Renewal: The Origins and Early Development of the Charismatic Movement in Great Britain* (Exeter, 1986), p. 96.
3 K. McDougall quoted by E. England, *The Spirit of Renewal* (Eastbourne, 1982), p. 17.
4 Hocken, *Streams of Renewal*, p. 184.

5   ibid., chs 10, 11, 14. M. Harper, *None Can Guess* (London, 1971).
6   Hocken, *Streams of Renewal*, chs 12, 21.
7   Harper, *None Can Guess*, p. 64. England, *Spirit of Renewal*, pp. 153 f.
8   W. Davies, *Rocking the Boat: The Challenge of the House Church* (Basingstoke, 1986), pp. 25 f.
9   Hocken, *Streams of Renewal*, sect. 1.
10 Wallis, *The Radical Christian* (Eastbourne, 1981), p. 10.
11 A. Walker, *Restoring the Kingdom* (London, 1985). Walker has popularised the use of the term 'Restorationism' for all the connexions together, but it should be noted that others would wish to confine the term to Bryn Jones's movement.
12 R. Trudinger, *Built to Last* (Eastbourne, 1982), ch. 2. P. Greenslade, 'The King's Church, Aldershot', in R. Forster (ed.), *Ten New Churches* (Bromley, 1986).
13 J. V. Thurman, *New Wineskins: A Study of the House Church Movement* (Frankfurt am Main, 1982), chs 2, 4. Walker, *Restoring the Kingdom*, pp. 25–9.
14 R. Forster, 'Icthus Christian Fellowship, Forest Hill, London', in Forster (ed.), *Ten New Churches*.
15 J. Gunstone, *Pentecostal Anglicans* (London, 1982), p. 46.
16 Hocken, *Streams of Renewal*, ch. 1, pp. 63–5, 68 f., 72, 128 ff.
17 J. Ford, *In the Steps of John Wesley: The Church of the Nazarene in Britain* (Kansas City, Mo., 1968), pp. 168–72. Hocken, *Streams of Renewal*, p. 64.
18 Hocken, *Streams of Renewal*, p. 76.
19 W. J. Hollenweger, *The Pentecostals* (London, 1971), p. 6. Hocken, *Streams of Renewal*, pp. 147 ff.
20 Walker, *Restoring the Kingdom*, p. 242. See p. 197.
21 Hocken, *Streams of Renewal*, pp. 144 f.
22 J. Ward, 'Pentecostal theology and the charismatic movement', in D. Martin and P. Mullen (eds), *Strange Gifts? A Guide to Charismatic Renewal* (Oxford, 1984).
23 For example, M. Harper, *Walk in the Spirit* (London, 1968), pp. 20 f.
24 Harper, *None Can Guess*, p. 9.
25 Hocken, *Streams of Renewal*, pp. 146 f.
26 D. J. Bennett, *Nine O'Clock in the Morning* (Plainfield, NJ, 1970).
27 Hocken, *Streams of Renewal*, ch. 17.
28 *The Charismatic Movement in the Church of England* (London, 1981), p. 12.
29 Walker, *Restoring the Kingdom*, pp. 77–85.
30 *AFR*, Spring 1985, pp. 3, 6, 7; Winter 1985, pp. 2 f.; Summer/Autumn 1986, pp. 3 f.
31 T. Roszak, *The Making of a Counter Culture* (London, 1970), esp. ch. 4. B. Martin, *A Sociology of Contemporary Cultural Change* (Oxford, 1981).
32 *Charismatic Movement in the Church of England*, pp. 41 f.
33 Martin, *Contemporary Cultural Change*, p. 225.
34 M. Harper, *As at the Beginning* (London, 1965), p. 84.
35 M. Bradbury and J. McFarlane (eds), *Modernism, 1890–1930* (Harmondsworth, Middlesex, 1976).
36 V. Woolf, 'Mr Bennett and Mrs Brown' [1924], *Collected Essays*, Vol. 1 (London, 1966), p. 321.

37 M. Bradbury and J. McFarlane, 'Movements, magazines and manifestos', in Bradbury and McFarlane (eds), *Modernism*, p. 202.
38 'The Layman with a Notebook', *What is the Oxford Group?* (London, 1933). Apart from works cited below, cf. A. W. Eister, *Drawing-Room Conversion* (Durham, NC, 1950) and D. W. Bebbington, 'The Oxford Group Movement between the wars', in *Voluntary Religion*, Studies in Church History, vol. 23, ed. W. J. Sheils and D. Wood (Oxford, 1986).
39 H. Begbie, *Life Changers* (London, 1923), p. 34.
40 T. Driberg, *The Mystery of Moral Re-Armament* (London, 1964), p. 16.
41 A. J. Russell, *For Sinners Only* (London, 1932), p. 160.
42 Begbie, *Life Changers*, 4th edn (London, 1929), p. 21.
43 R, 30 September 1932, p. 581; 18 November 1932, p. 689; 30 December 1932, p. 790.
44 G. Lean, *Frank Buchman: A Life* (London, 1985), pp. 132, 156.
45 M. Linton Smith and F. Underhill, *The Group Movement* (London, 1934), p. 36.
46 R, 27 January 1933, p. 55.
47 'Layman', *Oxford Group*, p. 50.
48 R, 7 October 1932, p. 601.
49 L. W. Grensted, 'Conclusion', in R. H. S. Crossman (ed.), *Oxford and the Groups* (Oxford, 1934), p. 198.
50 R, 14 October 1932, p. 617.
51 M. Harrison, *Saints Run Mad* (London, 1934), pp. 93, 81.
52 L. W. H. Bertie, 'Some aspects of the Oxford Group as seen by a medical practitioner', in F. A. M. Spencer (ed.), *The Meaning of the Groups* (London, 1934), p. 39.
53 R, 4 December 1931, p. 769.
54 Smith and Underhill, *Group Movement*, p. 42.
55 Bertie, 'Aspects', p. 43.
56 Russell, *Sinners*, p. 279.
57 S. A. King, *The Challenge of the Oxford Groups* (London, 1933), p. 61. B. Nichols, *All I Could Never Be* (London, 1949), pp. 249 f.
58 Smith and Underhill, *Group Movement*, pp. 23 f.
59 G. Allen, 'The Groups in Oxford', in Crossman (ed.), *Oxford*, p. 33.
60 R. Thomson, *The Pelican History of Psychology* (Harmondsworth, Middlesex, 1968), pp. 421 f.
61 *Groups*, May 1934, pp. 641–4.
62 F. C. Raynor, *The Finger of God* (London, 1934), p. 96.
63 *Groups*, June 1934, p. 2.
64 ibid., August 1934, p. 109.
65 Grensted, 'Conclusion'. *BW*, 27 July 1933, p. 340.
66 C. M. Chavasse in *R*, 18 November 1932, p. 689.
67 R, 27 October 1933, p. 610.
68 'Layman', *Oxford Group*, p. 70.
69 M. D. Biddiss, *The Age of the Masses: Ideas and Society in Europe since 1870* (Hassocks, Sussex, 1977), pp. 83–91.
70 'Layman', *Oxford Group*, p. 69.
71 H. H. Henson, *The Oxford Groups* (London, 1933), p. 70.
72 Quoted by Smith and Underhill, *Group Movement*, p. 34.

73 Russell, *Sinners*, p. 291. I. Thomas, *The Buchman Group* (London, [1933]), p. 3.
74 W. F. Brown to editor, *MR*, 3 November 1932, p. 20.
75 W. H. Clark, *The Oxford Group: Its History and Significance* (New York, 1951), p. 110.
76 Moore, *Brensham Village* [1946] (London, 1966 edn), pp. 162, 171.
77 H. R. Hammond to editor, *MR*, 28 January 1932, p. 17. *R*, 17 June 1932, p. 388.
78 Grensted, 'Conclusion', p. 199. Henson, *Oxford Groups*, p. 48.
79 Oldham to editor, *T*, 6 October 1933, p. 13.
80 *Groups*, April 1934, pp. 545 f.
81 'Layman', *Oxford Group*, p. 81.
82 *R*, 14 October 1932, p. 617. 'Observer' to editor, *R*, 16 December 1932, p. 766.
83 Harrison, *Saints Run Mad*, p. 99.
84 *R*, 14 October 1932, p. 617.
85 *T*, 27 July 1936, p. 9. Driberg, *Mystery*, p. 143.
86 *T*, 9 March 1939, p. 4.
87 *T*, 10 March 1939, p. 4.
88 *MR*, 17 October 1933, p. 4.
89 Harrison, *Saints Run Mad*, pp. 107 f.
90 Allen, *He that Cometh*, p. 212.
91 Henson, *Oxford Groups*, p. 48.
92 J. W. C. Wand, 'The Groups and the churches', in Crossman (ed.), *Oxford*, p. 168.
93 E. Brunner, *The Church and the Oxford Group* (London, 1937), p. 93.
94 Sir Francis Fremantle, MP, to editor, *T*, 9 December 1933, p. 8.
95 Bishop of Durham to editor, *T*, 19 September 1933, p. 8.
96 Russell, *Sinners*, p. 44.
97 Raynor, *Finger of God*, pp. 108–11, 170 f.
98 Henson, *Oxford Groups*, p. 48. L. P. Jacks, 'Group unity and the sense of sin', in Crossman (ed.), *Oxford*, pp. 117 f.
99 *BW*, 13 July 1933, p. 295. Driberg, *Mystery*, ch. 4.
100 F. N. D. Buchman, *Remaking the World* (London, 1958 edn), pp. 14 f. *T*, 15 July 1935, p. 12.
101 *T*, 27 July 1936, p. 9.
102 *T*, 8 August 1938, p. 8; 27 July 1936, p. 9.
103 Buchman, *Remaking*, pp. 45–8.
104 *R*, 3 August 1934, p. 465.
105 *R*, 29 April 1932, p. 261.
106 *R*, 20 November 1931, p. 729.
107 M. Harper, *A New Way of Living* (London, 1973), pp. 7 f.
108 Talcott Parsons quoted by Martin, *Cultural Change*, p. 15.
109 Harper, *Walk*, p. 43.
110 D. Bridge and D. Phypers, *More than Tongues Can Tell* (London, 1982), pp. 61, 74 f.
111 England, *Spirit of Renewal*, p. 111.
112 Walker, *Restoring the Kingdom*, p. 52.
113 *Renewal*, February/March 1979, p. 11.
114 P. Beall, *The Folk Arts in God's Family* (London, 1984), p. 33.
115 Hocken, *Streams of Renewal*, chs 4, 9, pp. 158 f.
116 *CEN*, 28 June 1974, p. 7.

117 *Charismatic Movement in the Church of England*, p. 16. Walker, *Restoring the Kingdom*, pp. 123 f., 191.

118 R. Peart and W. R. Davies, *What about the Charismatic Movement?* (London, 1980), p. 39.

119 I. Savile, 'Canford Magna Parish Church', in E. Gibbs (ed.), *Ten Growing Churches* (n.p., 1984), p. 181. S. Bruce, *Firm in the Faith* (Aldershot, 1984), p. 143. *AFR*, Autumn 1981, p. [7].

120 Harper, *Beginning*, p. 10. M. Israel, 'The Spirit of truth', in Martin and Mullen (eds), *Strange Gifts?*, pp. 131, 133.

121 England, *Spirit of Renewal*, p. 159.

122 Harper, *Beginning*, p. 105.

123 Thurman, *New Wineskins*, p. 43.

124 A. Mather, 'Talking points: the charismatic movement', *Themelios*, vol. 9, no. 3 (1984), p. 21.

125 Hocken, *Streams of Renewal*, p. 172.

126 V. Budgen, *The Charismatics and the Word of God* (Welwyn, 1985), p. 60.

127 J. Graham, *The Giant Awakes* (London, 1982), p. 112.

128 Harper, *None Can Guess*, p. 150.

129 Harper, *Beginning*, p. 110.

130 *Charismatic Movement in the Church of England*, p. 20.

131 Harper, *Beginning*, p. 94.

132 *Renewal*, February/March 1979, p. 5.

133 Harper, *None Can Guess*, p. 8.

134 'Gospel and Spirit: a joint statement', *Churchman*, vol. 91, no. 2 (1977), p. 103.

135 Budgen, *Charismatics and the Word of God*, pp. 206 f.

136 Harper, *None Can Guess*, p. 8.

137 'Gospel and Spirit', p. 106. Walker, *Restoring the Kingdom*, pp. 154 f.

138 Harper, *None Can Guess*, p. 142.

139 A. Kane, *Let There be Life* (Basingstoke, 1983), p. 88. Savile, 'Canford Magna', p. 180. Thurman, *New Wineskins*, pp. 43, 95.

140 *AFR*, Winter 1985, p. 26.

141 Gunstone, *Pentecostal Anglicans*, ch. 9. R. Trudinger, *Cells for Life* (Basingstoke, 1979).

142 F. Lees, *Love Is Our Home* (London, 1978).

143 Kane, *Let There be Life*, p. 67. Peart and Davies, *Charismatic Movement*, pp. 38 f.

144 Watson, *I Believe in the Church* (London, 1982 edn), pp. 85 ff.

145 J. Hardwidge, 'The Isca Christian Fellowship', in Forster (ed.), *Ten New Churches*, p. 125.

146 Martin, *Cultural Change*, p. 17.

147 Harper, *None Can Guess*, p. 13.

148 Wallis, *Radical Christian*, p. 165.

149 Thurman, *New Wineskins*, p. 61.

150 Walker, *Restoring the Kingdom*, pp. 88 f., 105.

151 P. Beall, *The Folk Arts in God's Family* (London, 1984). A. Long, *Praise Him in the Dance* (London, 1976).

152 For example, Hardwidge, 'Isca Christian Fellowship', p. 128.

153 G. Kendrick (ed.), *Ten Worshipping Churches* (n.p., 1986), pp. 11 f., 76.

154 *Charismatic Movement in the Church of England*, p. 25.

155 *Renewal*, April/May 1979, p. 28.
156 *Charismatic Movement in the Church of England*, p. 37.
157 Beall, *Folk Arts*, p. 55.
158 Harper, *None Can Guess*, p. 143.
159 Wallis, *Radical Christian*, pp. 88, 23.
160 A. Munden, 'Encountering the House Church Movement', *Anvil*, vol. 1, no. 3 (1984), p. 202.
161 Kane, *Let There be Life*, p. 160.
162 *Renewal*, April/May 1979, p. 12.
163 Wallis, *Radical Christian*, p. 171.
164 Walker, *Restoring the Kingdom*, p. 74.
165 Harper, *None Can Guess*, pp. 75, 26 f., 36.
166 Greenslade, 'King's Church', p. 147.
167 Wallis, *Radical Christian*, p. 184.
168 Harper, *None Can Guess*, p. 82.
169 *Charismatic Movement in the Church of England*, p. 37. Peart and Davies, *Charismatic Movement*, p. 13. Kane, *Let There be Life*, p. 127.
170 Thurman, *New Wineskins*, p. 71.
171 'Gospel and Spirit', p. 110.
172 Ern Baxter, quoted by Walker, *Restoring the Kingdom*, p. 145.
173 Walker, *Restoring the Kingdom*, ch. 13.
174 *Charismatic Movement in the Church of England*, p. 14.
175 Walker, *Restoring the Kingdom*, p. 188. D. Halls, 'Community Church in Tottenham, Waltham Forest and Ilford', in Gibbs (ed.), *Ten Growing Churches*, p. 114.
176 *Charismatic Movement in the Church of England*, p. 26.
177 P. Mullen, 'Confusion worse confounded', in Martin and Mullen (eds), *Strange Gifts?*, p. 105.
178 Walker, *Restoring the Kingdom*, p. 188.
179 B. R. Wilson, *Sects and Society* (London, 1961), pp. 106 f.
180 D. McBain, quoted by England, *Spirit of Renewal*, p. 128.
181 Hocken, *Streams of Renewal*, p. 112.
182 *AFR*, Summer/Autumn 1986, p. 4.
183 Harper, *Beginning*, p. 88.
184 Gunstone, *Pentecostal Anglicans*, p. 31.
185 *AFR*, Autumn 1982, p. [7]. England, *Spirit of Renewal*, p. 148.
186 *Charismatic Movement in the Church of England*, p. 9. *AFR*, Spring 1986, p. 3; Spring 1985, p. 8.
187 Peart and Davies, *Charismatic Movement*, p. 1.
188 Gunstone, *Pentecostal Anglicans*, p. 25. P. Beasley-Murray and A. Wilkinson, *Turning the Tide* (London, 1981), p. 37.
189 Walker, *Restoring the Kingdom*, p. 102.
190 Savile, 'Canford Magna', p. 185.
191 *CEN*, 10 January 1964, p. 1.
192 *CEN*, 14 June 1968, p. 1.
193 *CEN*, 22 April 1977, p. 7.
194 'Gospel and Spirit', pp. 102, 105.
195 C. Calver, *He Brings us Together* (London, 1987), pp. 66 f.
196 Walker, *Restoring the Kingdom*, p. 121.

197 England, *Spirit of Renewal*, p. 98.
198 Wallis, *Radical Christian*, p. 53.
199 Peart and Davies, *Charismatic Movement*, p. 36.
200 B. Hopkinson, 'Changes in the emphases of Evangelical belief, 1970–1980: evidence from new hymnody', *Churchman*, vol. 95, no. 2 (1981), pp. 130, 134.
201 R. Shaw, quoted by Hocken, *Streams of Renewal*, p. 156.
202 Harper, *Beginning*, p. 119.
203 ibid., p. 125.
204 Hopkinson, 'Evangelical belief', pp. 131, 134.
205 Carey, *The Gates of Glory* (London, 1986), p. 205.
206 Peart and Davies, *Charismatic Movement*, pp. 9 f.

CHAPTER 8: INTO A BROAD PLACE

1 Canon D. M. Paton in P. Crowe (ed.), *Keele '67: The National Evangelical Anglican Congress Statement* (London, 1967), p. 16.
2 J. C. King, in *CEN*, 14 April 1967, p. 6.
3 Sect. 83 in Crowe (ed.), *Keele '67*, p. 37. Letters to editor, *CEN*, 19 May 1967, p. 6.
4 Sects 20 and 37 in Crowe (ed.), *Keele '67*, pp. 23, 26.
5 C. Buchanan in *CEN*, 11 March 1977, p. 6.
6 *CEN*, 11 January 1957, p. 3.
7 M. Saward, *Evangelicals on the Move*, The Anglican Church Today (London, 1987), pp. 32 f.
8 G. E. Duffield, 'Evangelical involvement: the doctrine of the church', in J. C. King, *Evangelicals Today* (Guildford, 1973).
9 Stott, 'World-wide Evangelical Anglicanism', in ibid., p. 181.
10 R. Currie *et al.*, *Churches and Churchgoers* (Oxford, 1977), p. 30.
11 *Prospects for the Eighties* (London, 1980), p. 5. P. Brierley and B. Evans, *Prospects for Wales* (London, 1983), p. 5. P. Brierley and F. Macdonald, *Prospects for Scotland* (Bromley, 1985), p. 5.
12 *Social Trends*, 1982 edn (London, 1981), p. 193.
13 P. A. Welsby, *A History of the Church of England, 1945–1980* (Oxford, 1984), pp. 19 f.
14 P. B. Cliff, *The Rise and Development of the Sunday School Movement in England, 1780–1980* (Nutfield, Redhill, Surrey, 1986), pp. 318 f.
15 A. Marwick, *British Society since 1945* (Harmondsworth, Middlesex, 1982), ch. 9.
16 See pp. 201 f.
17 F. W. Dillistone, *Into all the World: A Biography of Max Warren* (London, 1980), pp. 60, 154.
18 ibid., pp. 50 f. S. Gummer, *The Chavasse Twins* (London, 1963).
19 R. T. Jones, *Congregationalism in England, 1662–1962* (London, 1962), pp. 450 f., 453–7.
20 W. M. S. West, *To Be a Pilgrim: A Memoir of Ernest A. Payne* (Guildford, 1983).
21 See p. 204.
22 D. M. Thompson, 'The older Free Churches', in R. Davies (ed.), *The Testing of the Churches, 1932–1982* (London, 1982), p. 93. G. W. Kirby to

editor, *CG*, September 1948, p. 11. S. Bruce, *Firm in the Faith* (Aldershot, 1984), p. 45.

23 Stott, in *Fundamentalism: A Religious Problem: Letters to the Editor of The Times and a Leading Article* (London, 1955), pp. 15 f.

24 P. Sangster, *Doctor Sangster* (London, 1962). For general trends, see A. Hastings, *A History of English Christianity, 1920–1985* (London, 1986).

25 Bishop J. W. Hunkin, in *LE*, May 1947, p. 9.

26 *LE*, September 1947, p. 33; September 1948, p. 153.

27 *CEN*, 31 July 1953, p. 6.

28 *LE*, November 1950, pp. 335, 351. *CEN*, 17 April 1964, p. 1.

29 *Modern Free Churchman*.

30 *LE*, May 1947, pp. 11, 13.

31 C. O. Rhodes in *LE*, February 1950, p. 289. *CEN*, 28 May 1954, p. 7.

32 *CEN*, 29 January 1960, p. 3.

33 L. Hickin, 'The revival of Evangelical scholarship', *Churchman*, vol. 92, no. 2 (1978). M. Warren, *Crowded Canvas* (London, 1974), pp. 223 f. *Evangelical Fellowship for Theological Literature: Annual Register*, no. 7 (1950).

34 *Evangelicals Affirm* (London, 1948), p. xi. *LE*, May 1948, p. 114. Warren, *Crowded Canvas*, pp. 167, 224.

35 *LE*, December 1951, p. 403.

36 R. Nixon in *Churchman*, vol. 92, no. 2 (1978), pp. 99 f.

37 Bruce, *Firm in the Faith*, pp. 75 ff.

38 J. Highet, *The Scottish Churches* (London, 1960), ch. 3. D. P. Thomson, *Personal Encounters* (Crieff, Perthshire, 1967), p. 70.

39 K. Robbins, 'Britain, 1940 and "Christian Civilization"', in D. Beales and G. Best (eds), *History, Society and the Churches: Essays in Honour of Owen Chadwick* (Cambridge, 1985).

40 A. W. Smith in *AW*, July–August 1945, p. 51.

41 *CEN*, 19 January 1951, p. 3.

42 Welsby, *Church of England*, pp. 45–8. Gummer, *Chavasse Twins*, ch. 12.

43 *CEN*, 11 January 1952, p. 3.

44 *CEN*, 16 January 1953, p. 3.

45 A. A. Woolsey, *Channel of Revival: A Biography of Duncan Campbell* (Edinburgh, 1974), chs 13–16.

46 G. T. Brake, *Policy and Politics in British Methodism, 1932–1982* (London, 1984), pp. 390 f. Thompson, 'Older Free Churches', p. 93.

47 J. E. Tuck (ed.), *This is My Story* (London, 1955), ch. 1.

48 Jones, *Congregationalism*, p. 450.

49 R. R. Williams in *LE*, May 1947, p. 12.

50 *CEN*, 21 June 1957, p. 7.

51 *CEN*, 27 November 1953, p. 3; 1 January 1954, p. 6; J. W. Roxburgh to editor, 8 January 1954, p. 10; R. A. Finlayson to editor, 22 January 1954, p. 10.

52 *CEN*, 3 May 1963, p. 10.

53 *Baptist Union Directory*, 1973–4, pp. 40 f.

54 Dr C. W. Hale Amos to editor, *R*, 20 August 1937, p. 536.

55 *AW*, September–October 1949, p. 459.

56 I. L. S. Balfour, 'The twentieth century (since 1914)', in D. W. Bebbington (ed.), *The Baptists in Scotland: A History* (Glasgow, 1988), pp. 75 f. *Baptists and Unity* (London, 1967), pp. 36 f.

57 See p. 267f.
58 *CEN*, 16 November 1974, p. 2.
59 R. Davies, 'Since 1932', in R. Davies *et al.* (eds), *A History of the Methodist Church in Great Britain*, Vol. 3 (London, 1983), pp. 374–9.
60 J. I. Packer (ed.), *All in Each Place: Towards Reunion in England* (Appleford, Abingdon, Berks., 1965), esp. pp. 9 f., 15 f. *CEN*, 7 February 1969, pp. 8 f.
61 Sect. 96 in Crowe (ed.), *Keele '67*, p. 39. *CEN*, 22 April 1977, p. 8.
62 J. King in *CEN*, 11 February 1977, p. 6.
63 *CEN*, 7 March 1986, p. 1.
64 C. O. Buchanan *et al.*, *Growing into Union* (London, 1970).
65 *English Churchman*, 9 January. 1953, pp. 14, 15 f., 17, 18; 6 February. 1953, p. 62.
66 *CEN*, 13 January 1961, p. 3.
67 C. Buchanan, 'Liturgy', in King (ed.), *Evangelicals Today*.
68 Sect. 76 in Crowe (ed.), *Keele '67*, p. 35. H. J. Burgess to editor, *CEN*, 21 April 1967, p. 6. P. Crowe to editor, *CEN*, 5 May 1967, p. 7.
69 N. Anderson, *An Adopted Son: The Story of my Life* (Leicester, 1985), pp. 239 ff.
70 *CEN*, 22 July 1949, p. 3.
71 Anderson, *Adopted Son*, p. 142.
72 Packer, '"Keswick" and the Reformed doctrine of sanctification', *Evangelical Quarterly*, vol. 27, no. 3 (1955), p. 158.
73 D. Winter in *CEN*, 29 July 1960, p. 2.
74 *CEN*, 14 July 1972, p. 6.
75 Bruce, *Firm in the Faith*, p. 50.
76 J. Eddison (ed.), *'Bash': A Study in Spiritual Power* (Basingstoke, 1983).
77 J. C. Pollock, *The Good Seed: The Story of the Children's Special Service Mission and the Scripture Union* (London, 1959), pp. 187–92.
78 R. Manwaring, *From Controversy to Co-Existence: Evangelicals in the Church of England, 1914–1980* (Cambridge, 1985), pp. 108 f.
79 A. L. Glegg, *Four Score . . . and More* (London, 1962), pp. 60–3.
80 *Operation Mobilisation: The History* (n.p., n.d.).
81 *CEN*, 8 October 1965, pp. 1, 16; 28 October 1966, pp. 3, 14.
82 *CEN*, 12 March 1954, p. 5; cf. F. Colquhoun, *Harringay Story* (London, 1955); J. Pollock, *Billy Graham: The Authorised Biography* (London, 1966); P. Back, *Mission England – What Really Happened?* (Bromley, 1986).
83 *CEN*, 26 February 1954, p. 5.
84 *CEN*, 28 May 1954, p. 6; 8 July 1966, p. 1.
85 *CEN*, 4 June 1954, p. 2. W. Sargant, *Battle for the Mind* (London, 1957), esp. ch. 6. But cf. Bruce, *Firm in the Faith*, pp. 104–12.
86 W. G. McLoughlin, *Modern Revivalism: Charles Grandison Finney to Billy Graham* (New York, 1959), p. 517. But cf. Highet, *Scottish Churches*, ch. 3.
87 *CEN*, 27 May 1955, p. 2.
88 *CEN*, 30 December 1966, p. 1.
89 G. Carr to editor, *CEN*, 27 May 1955, p. 14.
90 D. Johnson, *Contending for the Faith: A History of the Evangelical Movement in the Universities and Colleges* (Leicester, 1979), p. 359. For CICCU, see p. 188.

91   F. D. Coggan (ed.), *Christ and the Colleges: A History of the Inter-Varsity Fellowship of Evangelical Unions* (London, 1934), pp. 212, 214. F. F. Bruce, *In Retrospect: Remembrance of Things Past* (London, 1980), p. 68.
92   See also correspondence following review of *Is Evolution a Myth?* in *C*, 11 November 1949, p. 12, esp. Bible student to editor, 3 February 1950, p. 10.
93   *CG*, June 1948, p. 32.
94   Bruce, *In Retrospect*, p. 128.
95   F. F. Bruce, 'The Tyndale Fellowship for Biblical Research', *Evangelical Quarterly*, vol. 19, no. 1 (1947), p. 52.
96   Bruce, *In Retrospect*, pp. 127, 110 f.
97   *CG*, March 1948, p. 16.
98   H. H. Rowdon, *London Bible College: The First Twenty-Five Years* (Worthing, 1968). R. Coad, *Laing: The Biography of Sir John W. Laing, C.B.E. (1879–1978)* (London, 1979), pp. 189–92.
99   *CG*, March 1948, p. 8. 'A London graduate' is almost certainly Johnson.
100 D. Williams, *IVP: The First Fifty Years* (Leicester, 1986), p. 7.
101 Crowe (ed.), *Keele '67*, pp. 48–60.
102 *C.B.R.F.* (The Journal of the Christian Brethren Research Fellowship).
103 Bruce, *In Retrospect*, pp. 184–8, 182.
104 J. I. Packer, 'Expository preaching', in *CEN*, 15 January 1960, p. 3.
105 'Introduction', in D. M. Lloyd-Jones, *The Puritans: Their Origins and Successors* (Edinburgh, 1987).
106 E. Davies, 'God's gift to a nation', in C. Catherwood (ed.), *Martyn Lloyd-Jones: Chosen by God* (Crowborough, East Sussex, 1986), p. 185. See also I. H. Murray, *David Martyn Lloyd-Jones: The First Forty Years, 1899–1939* (Edinburgh, 1982) and J. Peters, *Martyn Lloyd-Jones: Preacher* (Exeter, 1986).
107 D. M. Lloyd-Jones, *Preaching and Preachers* (London, 1971), p. 120.
108 *CEN*, 4 January 1963, p. 3.
109 R. Horn, 'His place in Evangelicalism', in Catherwood (ed.), *Lloyd-Jones*, p. 16.
110 *Evangelical Library Bulletin*.
111 'Introduction', in Lloyd-Jones, *Puritans*, p. ix.
112 Maurice Wood in *CEN*, 15 January 1960, p. 3.
113 J. E. Davies, *Striving Together: A Statement of the Principles that Have Governed the Aims and Policies of the Evangelical Movement of Wales* (Bryntirion, Bridgend, 1984), pp. 5, 45.
114 S. B. Ferguson, 'William Still: a biographical introduction', in N. M. de S. Cameron and S. B. Ferguson (eds), *Pulpit & People: Essays in Honour of William Still on his Seventy-Fifth Birthday* (Edinburgh, 1986). Bruce, *Firm in the Faith*, p. 45.
115 *Prospects for the Eighties*, p. 41.
116 W. J. Hollenweger, *The Pentecostals* (London, 1972), p. 191.
117 Tychicus to editor, *LF*, October 1963, quoted by D. Gee, *Wind and Flame* (Croydon, 1967), p. 299.
118 M. J. C. Calley, *God's People: West Indian Pentecostal Sects in England* (London, 1965), pp. 118, 128, 39.
119 G. E. Vandeman to editor, *CEN*, 12 February 1954, p. 10.
120 J. Ford, *In the Steps of John Wesley: The Church of the Nazarene in Britain* (Kansas City, Mo., 1968), p. 274.

121 B. R. Wilson, 'The Exclusive Brethren: a case study in the evolution of a sectarian ideology', in B. R. Wilson (ed.), *Patterns of Sectarianism* (London, 1967).
122 Bruce, *In Retrospect*, p. 289. G. Brown and B. Mills, *'The Brethren': A Factual Survey* (Exeter, 1980), p. 46.
123 J. King in *CEN*, 11 February 1977, p. 6.
124 *CEN*, 14 April 1967, p. 6; 27 January 1978, p. 4. *Third Way*, 29 December 1977, pp. 7 ff.
125 F. Coutts, *The History of the Salvation Army*, Vol. 7, *The Weapons of Goodwill* (London, 1986), pp. 168 ff.
126 D. B. Winter, *New Singer, New Song* (London, 1967).
127 Bruce, *Firm in the Faith*, pp. 129–35, spec. p. 133; p. 50.
128 *CEN*, 20 February 1976, p. 3.
129 *CEN*, 6 February 1976, p. 4.
130 *CEN*, 28 October 1966, p. 14.
131 Coutts, *Salvation Army*, Vol. 7, esp. pp. 18, 180, 326 f.
132 *LCMM*, July 1929, p. 109.
133 T. C. Hammond, *Perfect Freedom* (London, 1938); cf. D. J. Tidball, *Contemporary Evangelical Social Thinking – A Review* (Nottingham, 1977), pp. 5 f.
134 *CG*, June 1948, p. 4.
135 Channon, 'Why I believe Christ is coming', *AW*, May–June 1949, p. 422.
136 M. Whitehouse, *Who Does She Think She Is?* (London, 1971). M. Caulfield, *Mary Whitehouse* (London, 1975).
137 *CEN*, 15 January 1965, p. 16. J. Capon, . . . *and There Was Light: The Story of the Nationwide Festival of Light* (London, 1972), p. 10.
138 *Pornography: The Longford Report* (London, 1972).
139 R. Wallis and R. Bland, *Five Years On: Report of a Survey of Participants in the Nationwide Festival of Light Rally in Trafalgar Square, London, on 25 September 1976* (n.p., n.d.), p. 45.
140 *T*, 16 April 1986, p. 1.
141 *CEN*, 13 January 1960, p. 3.
142 *CEN*, 22 April 1977, p. 10.
143 Tidball, *Social Thinking*, pp. 9 f.
144 *CEN*, 26 July 1974, p. 3; 2 August 1974, pp. 1 f. See also C. R. Padilla (ed.), *The New Face of Evangelicalism* (London, 1976).
145 *Evangelicalism and Social Responsibility: An Evangelical Commitment* (Exeter, 1982), p. 23.
146 *Third Way*, December 1982/January 1983, p. 5.
147 *Third Way*, January 1987, p. 19. *CEN*, 22 April 1977, p. 8.
148 Packer, 'A kind of Puritan', p. 44.
149 Horn, 'His place in Evangelicalism', p. 21.
150 L. Samuel, 'A man under the Word', in Catherwood (ed.), *Lloyd-Jones*, pp. 199 ff.
151 Lloyd-Jones, *Puritans*, pp. 73–100.
152 Horn, 'His place in Evangelicalism', pp. 22 ff. Stott, 'An appreciation', in Catherwood (ed.), *Lloyd-Jones*, p. 207.
153 *CEN*, 28 October 1966, p. 5.
154 Davies, *Striving Together*, pp. 5–8.
155 *British Evangelical Council Newsletter*, Summer 1981.

156 See pp. 230 f.

157 Sect. 14 in Crowe (ed.), *Keele '67*, p. 22.

158 J. Capon, *Evangelicals Tomorrow* (Glasgow, 1977), ch. 4. J. King in *CEN*, 11 February 1977, p. 6.

159 H. L. McBeth, *The Baptist Heritage* (Nashville, Tenn., 1987), p. 525.

160 R. J. Sheehan (ed.), *The Baptism of the Spirit and Charismatic Gifts* (St Albans, [1979]), esp. pp. 2 f. *Evangelical Times*, March 1978, p. 7; May 1985, p. 9; December 1985, p. 3; May 1986, pp. 12 ff.; June 1986, p. 3.

161 *CEN*, 24 July 1970, p. 3.

162 J. Drane, 'Bible use in Scottish churches', in Brierley and Macdonald, *Prospects for Scotland*, pp. 26–9.

163 *CEN*, 11 January 1974, p. 8.

164 *CEN*, 23 November 1966, p. 1; 27 January 1978, p. 4.

165 Capon, *Evangelicals Tomorrow*, ch. 3; cf. T. Thiselton, 'Understanding God's word today', in J. Stott (ed.), *Obeying Christ in a Changing World: 1: The Lord Christ* (London, 1977).

166 *CEN*, 26 January 1979, p. 3.

167 J. Dunn, 'The authority of scripture according to scripture', *Churchman*, vol. 96, no. 2, and vol. 96, no. 3 (1982).

168 *CEN*, 10 January 1986, p. 1.

169 Capon, *Evangelicals Tomorrow*, pp. 32, 34.

170 *CEN*, 25 January 1974, p. 5.

171 Capon, *Evangelicals Tomorrow*, p. 49.

172 J. I. Packer, *The Evangelical Anglican Identity Problem* (Oxford, 1978) p. 30.

173 K. N. Medhurst and G. Moyser, *Church and Politics in a Secular Age* (Oxford, 1988), ch. 11, sect. 6.

174 *CEN*, 11 March 1977, p. 6.

175 J. R. W. Stott, *What Is an Evangelical?* (London, 1977).

176 *CEN*, 27 January 1978, p. 1; 26 January 1979, p. 3; 2 February 1979, p. 2.

177 Stott, 'World-wide Evangelical Anglicanism', p. 180. *CEN*, 9 January 1980, p. 3.

178 Saward, *Evangelicals on the Move*, p. 45.

179 *CEN*, 8 October 1965, p. 16; cf. A. D. Gilbert, *The Making of Post-Christian Britain: A History of the Secularization of Modern Society* (London, 1980), ch. 6.

180 *CEN*, 28 October 1966, p. 3.

181 *Third Way*, January 1987, p. 19.

182 Wallis and Bland, *Five Years On*, p. 30.

183 Brake, *Policy and Politics*, p. 369.

184 Saward, *Evangelicals on the Move*, p. 34.

185 *Baptist Times*, 31 December 1987, p. 7.

CHAPTER 9: TIME AND CHANCE

1 *Hansard*, 3rd series, vol. 110 (1850), col. 713.

2 S. Bruce, *Firm in the Faith* (Aldershot, 1984), p. 79.

3 Dale, *The Old Evangelicalism and the New* (London, 1889).

4   W. M. Groser quoted by P. B. Cliff, *The Rise and Development of the Sunday School Movement in England, 1780–1980* (Nutfield, Redhill, Surrey, 1986), p. 197.

5   J. Stott, in J. Stott and R. T. Coote (eds), *Down to Earth: Studies in Christianity and Culture* (London, 1981), p. vii.

6   B. M. G. Reardon, *Religious Thought in the Victorian Age* (London, 1981), chs 5 and 6.

7   For example, T. Cauter and J. S. Downham, *The Communication of Ideas: A Study of Contemporary Influences on Urban Life* (London, 1954). The process has been described as 'stratified diffusion': J. Cox, *The English Churches in a Secular Society: Lambeth, 1870–1930* (New York, 1982), p. 8.

8   W. Wilberforce, *A Practical View of the Prevailing Religious System of Professed Christians in the Higher and Middle Classes in this Country Contrasted with Real Christianity*, 4th edn (London, 1797), pp. 9 f.

9   D. E. Allen, *British Tastes: An Enquiry into the Likes and Dislikes of the Regional Consumer* (London, 1968). A. P. Cohen (ed.), *Belonging: Identity and Social Organisation in British Rural Cultures*, Anthropological Studies of Britain, 1 (Manchester, 1982).

10 The pattern is comparable to that described in the classic study of the spread of telephones in Sweden by T. Hägerstrand, *Innovation Diffusion as a Spatial Process* (Chicago, 1967 edn), esp. pp. 7 f.

11 For an earlier case-study, cf. G. Donaldson, 'Scotland's conservative north in the sixteenth and seventeenth centuries', *Scottish Church History* (Edinburgh, 1985), pp. 201 f.

12 Barr, *Fundamentalism* (London, 1977), pp. 2–6, 61 f.

13 M. Saward, *Evangelicals on the Move*, The Anglican Church Today (London, 1987), p. 83. N. M. de S. Cameron to editor, *LW*, January 1987, p. 38.

14 J. I. Packer, *'Fundamentalism' and the Word of God* (London, 1958). I. H. Marshall, *Biblical Inspiration* (London, 1982), ch. 3.

15 M. Cowling, *Religion and Public Doctrine in Modern England*, Vol. 1 (Cambridge, 1980), pp. 375 f.

Index

For Richard
the Lion-Hearted —

with pleasure,
Van Allen Bradley

(His Knight)

THE
BOOK COLLECTOR'S
HANDBOOK
OF VALUES

THE
BOOK COLLECTOR'S
HANDBOOK
OF VALUES

❧ BY ☙

VAN ALLEN BRADLEY

G. P. Putnam's Sons
New York

This is for Sharon and
Gremlyn Angelica

ACKNOWLEDGMENTS

Since the compilation of this book not only has occupied a large part of my life for the last half dozen years but is also the cumulative result of many earlier years' experiences as a book lover and collector, it is difficult to know where to begin to acknowledge all the help and encouragement given me by associates and friends. In the dedication I have already acknowledged my indebtedness to my wife for understanding and help. Aside from this, my greatest thanks for continuing inspiration and goodwill throughout the long and sometimes agonizing effort to get the job done must go to William Targ, a great book collector and my wise and experienced editor, and to Walter J. Minton, Putnam's patient president, who never abandoned hope of getting the manuscript into the house.

Beyond this, there is a long list of other individuals to whom I wish to give credit for assistance of various kinds, both direct and indirect. These include the late Ben Abramson, one of the all-time great Chicago bookmen; Milton Altman, who shared with me the joys of his great Faulkner, Hemingway, Wolfe, and Steinbeck collections; John E. Baker, Jr., a D. H. Lawrence collector of wisdom, method, and discrimination; the late Frances Brewer, rare book specialist with the Detroit Public Library; Andreas Brown of the Gotham Book Mart, who has read this manuscript in parts and assisted in many ways; Richard Brown, who edited my first book about books many years ago; Joseph Camardo, my former partner in bookselling and a steadfast friend; the English bookman John Carter, who has given of his wit and wisdom; Leland D. Case, a Black Hills specialist and longtime friend; George Charney of Santa Barbara, artist, antiquarian, and onetime newspaper colleague, who provided valuable technical aid; Richard Christiansen, editor of *Panorama,* the Chicago *Daily News* weekend magazine in which my writings about books appeared for many years; Marguerite Cohn, a specialist in modern literature, who never failed to have the right answers when I needed them; Arnold H. Crane, in whose incomparable private library on photography I have always been welcome; Alice and Robert Cromie, longtime friends on the Chicago literary beat; Jeff C. Dykes, good friend and an outstanding authority on books of the cattle trade; the Eberstadt brothers of the New York firm of Americanists; Ralph D. Gardner, who owns the finest private Horatio Alger collection in the world; Dr. John T. Gernon, whose private library is a place of unending delight; the late Everett D. Graff, who let me roam at will among the Americana treasures in his Kenilworth (Illinois) home long before that great collection became a part of the Newberry Library's holdings;

Lawrence Gutter, whose collection of Chicagoana would be impossible for anyone to duplicate; Jane Faul, whose able secretarial staff helped make a readable manuscript out of mountains of handwritten notes, and especially to Peggy Halda, who typed most of the final manuscript with uncanny skill and accuracy in reading both my handwriting and my mind; Charles Feinberg, the Whitman collector who helped to make one of my Detroit visits a memorable experience; Lew D. Feldman (House of El Dieff), a foremost dealer in books and manuscripts; William Hanzel, Chicago book auctioneer and steadfast friend; Nancy Harris, who not only managed my own bookshop with charm and skill for some years, but also aided me in research; Richard Harwell, who first interested me in the rare books of the Confederacy; W. R. Hasbrouck, a Frank Lloyd Wright specialist, who offered invaluable aid on certain matters; Irwin Holtzman, who specializes in collecting the modern writers and is indefatigable when it comes to talking about books; Peter B. Howard of Berkeley, California, who has generously given of his sophisticated knowledge of modern literature; Warren R. Howell, San Francisco bookseller, who also has shared his special knowledge; Wright Howes, the compiler of the still-indispensable Americana guidebook *U. S.-iana,* a valued friend and mentor; the late Joseph Haas, my associate on the Chicago *Daily News* book pages, who had so wanted to see this book in print that he volunteered many kinds of help unasked (he died only five weeks after succeeding me upon my retirement in March, 1971); Thomas Joyce, collector and friend; Marilew and Herman Kogan, Chicago newspaper colleagues who have demonstrated a steady interest in my work; Adolph Kroch, pioneer Chicago bookseller, and his son Carl, who also encouraged me all the way; Lawrence Kunetka, a newcomer to the Chicago rare book scene, who has never hesitated to help me run down vital information in his formidable bibliographical library; Donald La Chance, a onetime Chicagoan now dealing in rare books on the West Coast; Richard Leekley, bookseller and friend, who has many times gone out of his way to help; Robert Liska, first a customer and later a cataloguer of my books, who has moved on to greater challenges; Mary Ann and Sol M. Malkin of The Antiquarian Bookman, who have been invariably sympathetic and helpful; Richard Mohr of Beverly Hills, California, and Howard S. Mott of Sheffield, Massachusetts, both distinguished bookmen, who have contributed substantially toward whatever merits this book may have; Harry T. Moore, the D. H. Lawrence specialist and biographer of that highly collectible Englishman; Kenneth Nebenzahl, the Chicago Americanist, who has always been ready with a helpful answer when I had a question; the Lincoln and Civil War specialist Ralph Newman, one of my earliest tutors; Edna and Hoke Norris, colleagues, collectors, and friends; Carl Petersen, whose monumental collection of Faulkner has always been open to my scrutiny; David A. Randall, curator of the Lilly Library at Indiana University, whose knowledge of modern literature is well-nigh incomparable; Esther Ratz, who volunteered for endless hours of typing in the early draft of the book; Vincent Starrett, Chicago bookman of almost legendary fame, always a source of generous counsel; the late Arthur

Swann, book auction specialist and a collector of impeccable taste, who befriended me when I first began to write about rare books; Terence Tanner, a knowledgeable specialist in books and publishing of the Chicago Renaissance period; Lawrence W. Towner, the Newberry librarian, valued friend; Robert Wilson, the Greenwich Village specialist in the literature of the moderns; Ernest J. Wessen, the Ohio bookman who has become a legend and who gave me valued advice at the start of my rare book columning; and, finally, James M. Wells, associate director of the Newberry Library, friend and mentor of many years' standing.

From all the others to whom I may be indebted but have failed or forgotten to mention here I beg indulgence, while at the same time expressing gratitude.

The catalogues of booksellers throughout the world have been freely consulted and drawn upon for much of the information contained herein, and I can only begin to list them all. Among the dealers whose catalogues have proved most helpful are the following:

American: Alta California Bookstore, Argosy Book Store, Bennett & Marshall, J. S. Canner & Co., Inc., Philip C. Duschnes, Dawson's Book Shop, Jeff Dykes, Peter Decker, Goodspeed's Book Shop, Gotham Book Mart and Gallery, Guidon Books, Lathrop C. Harper, Inc., Robert G. Hayman, Heritage Book Shop (of Hollywood), Holmes Book Co., House of Books, Ltd., House of El Dieff, John Howell—Books, International Bookfinders, J. & S. Graphics, the Jenkins Company, Literary Heritage, T. N. Luther, Midland Rare Book Company, Edward Morrill & Son, Inc., Howard S. Mott, Kenneth Nebenzahl, Inc., Phoenix Book Shop, Henry Schuman Rare Books, Scribner Rare Book Shop, Serendipity Books, Seven Gables Bookshop, Henry W. Wenning, Leo Weitz, Inc., Herbert West, Western Hemisphere, Inc., and Zeitlin & Ver Brugge. English: Deighton Bell & Co., Bow Windows Book Shop, Francis Edwards, Ltd., W. & G. Foyle, Ltd., Frank Hammond, Maggs Brothers, Ltd., Stanley Noble, Bernard Quaritch, Ltd., Bertram Rota, Ltd., Chas. J. Sawyer, Henry Sotheran, Ltd., Henry Stevens, Son & Stiles, and Charles W. Traylen.

Obviously a compilation of this kind must draw upon innumerable other bibliographic sources—far too many to be enumerated fully here. These include, of course, the annual and cumulative index volumes of *American Book-Prices Current* and its English equivalent series, *Book-Auction Records*. They include also the individual sales catalogues of the major English and American galleries where book auctions are conducted: Christie, Manson & Woods, Ltd., Hodgson & Company and Sotheby & Company, all of London; and the Parke-Bernet Galleries, Inc., and the Swann Galleries, Inc., both of New York City.

Basic bibliographical works I have consulted range upwards into the thousands of books, but the two most valuable series perhaps have been the first five volumes of Jacob Blanck's *Bibliography of American Literature* (Yale University Press) and the eight-volume (including the index volume) catalogue of *The Celebrated Collection of Americana Formed by the Late Thomas Winthrop Streeter* (Parke-Bernet). A few of the individual works that have served me well include Whitman Bennett's *A Practical Guide to American Book Collecting* (Bennett Book Studios); William Targ's 1932 book *Modern English First Editions and Their Prices* (Black Archer Press) and his 1931 publication *American First Editions and Their Prices* (Black Archer); Percy H. Muir's *Points, 1874-1930* (Constable); Robert W. Henderson's *Early American Sport* (Barnes); John C. Eckel's *The First Editions of the Writings of Charles Dickens* (Inman); T. W. Field's *An Essay Towards an Indian Bibliography* (Scribner, Armstrong); Ramon F. Adams' two fine compilations, *The Rampaging Herd* and *Six-Guns and Saddle Leather* (Oklahoma): Ralph D. Gardner's *Road to Success: The Bibliography of the Works of Horatio Alger* (Wayside); Percy Muir's *English Children's Books, 1600-1900* (Praeger); Jacob S. Blanck's *Peter Parley to Penrod* (Bowker); Henry S. Boutell's *First Editions of Today and How to Tell Them* (Peacock Press); Merle Johnson's *American First Editions* (Mark Press); Wright Howes' *U.S.-iana* (Bowker); Henry R. Wagner's *The Plains and the Rockies,* revised by Charles L. Camp (Grabhorn Press); Lyle H. Wright's two volumes, *American Fiction, 1774-1850,* and *American Fiction, 1851-1875* (Huntington Library); the Lilly Library exhibition catalogue *Three Centuries of American Poetry;* Solon J. Buck's *Travel and Description, 1765-1865* (Illinois State Historical Society); Cecil J. Byrd's *A Bibliography of Illinois Imprints, 1814-58* (University of Chicago Press); Colton J. Storm's *A Catalogue of the Everett D. Graff Collection of Western Americana* (Chicago); Peter Decker's catalogue of the library of George W. Soliday (Antiquarian Press); the fourth edition of *The Oxford Companion to English Literature,* edited by Sir Paul Harvey, and its counterpart, *The Oxford Companion to American Literature,* edited by James D. Hart (both published by Oxford University Press). As I look around at my bookshelves now, I see that this list could go on endlessly. Indeed, as a bookseller friend of mine remarked recently, "About $50,000 worth of reference books is a good beginning for anyone contemplating running a rare book shop." The truth is that all the biographical tools an ardent booklover can acquire in a lifetime can only lead him on relentlessly.

Beyond his little corner there are vast libraries where, if one looks long enough and hard enough, he may perhaps find all the answers.

INTRODUCTION

WHAT THIS BOOK IS ALL ABOUT: From December, 1957, until mid-May, 1971, I wrote for the Chicago *Daily News* and other newspapers in the United States and Canada a weekly syndicated column about rare books and their prices under the title "Gold in Your Attic" (in some newspapers "Rare Book Hunter"). So far as I know, it was the longest sustained series of its kind ever published anywhere, and the response from readers eager for information on the little-known rare book trade was enormous—a warning of which was given to me in advance by the distinguished English bookman John Carter and others with whom I had discussed the project. The mail was far greater than it was physically possible for me to respond to with personal answers, although I did try to reply to as many readers as possible, by personal letter, by notes in the column, or by means of various kinds of form letters which I designed to cover information of a generalized nature. The inadequacy of these means of communication prompted me to publish in 1958 my first book on the subject, *Gold in Your Attic* (Fleet), which reappeared ten years later in a revised edition as *The New Gold in Your Attic*. One story on that first book, by Hal Boyle of the Associated Press, brought countless letters to add to my communications problem. A sequel, *More Gold in Your Attic,* appeared in 1961 and will shortly reappear in a new revised edition. Each of these books, much smaller than the present volume, was designed primarily for the general public and bore alphabetical indexes to roughly 2,500 American books and pamphlets (with minimal detail and with no mention of English books). Despite their limited scope, they continue to have wide general use.

It was on the basis of my experiences with the column and these books that I began to prepare some six or seven years ago a much larger index, with the intention of including not only a great deal of additional information about individual books (binding data, bibliographical points, etc.), but a cross section not only of American books and pamphlets but also English books, for which my mail had indicated a heavy reader demand. I have also included a few books published elsewhere in Europe by English and American authors. So far as I know, the only comparable books of the kind I contemplated have been Seymour de Ricci's 1921 *The Book Collector's Guide* (Rosenbach) and *10,000 Rare Books and Their Prices,* by William Targ, published in 1936.

My aim was to prepare a comprehensive work that would be of use not only to the general reader, but also to the serious and sophisticated collector and to libraries, scholars, and booksellers as well. It was obvious almost from the start that in order to keep the project from becoming too formidable, I must establish a set of ground rules, which I have more or less followed.

THE SCOPE AND METHOD OF THE BOOK: My first decision was to limit the entries primarily to nineteenth- and twentieth-century books—*i.e.,* to use the year 1800 as a starting point. Since a compilation of this kind is not a bibliography in the true sense, I decided, as with the *Attic* series, to discard orthodox bibliographical form and list books simply in an author-title alphabetical form as an expedient method of making the book useful to the largest number of readers. In other words, if a book has an author named on the title page, it will be found, if included here, under the author's name as published, even though that may be a pseudonym. Thus, while most bibliographical works list Mark Twain's books under his real name, Samuel Langhorne Clemens, you will find him here under Twain. Another example: Mary Baker Eddy is widely known, but *Science and Health* is listed here under the name she used on the title page of that famous book, Mary Baker Glover. If an author's book is anonymous, it will be found listed here under its title, even though its authorship may be generally well known. An example is T. S. Eliot's anonymous *Ezra Pound His Metric and Poetry,* which is listed here under the title rather than under Eliot's name. In most cases in which this unorthodox method has been used, I have provided cross-references for the quick use of anyone who may be trying to locate a book.

A third ground rule I established was to exclude, with some exceptions, books with a retail value in the current market of less than $25, because to have included lower-priced books would have made necessary an index running into the hundreds of thousands of entries—an obviously impossible work without the cooperation of a large research staff and one that no commercial publishing house could possibly price within the means of the readers I wanted to reach.

A fourth ground rule was to limit the inclusions wherever possible to books *in fine condition and in their original binding* and to describe both the bindings and the editions (including bibliographical points of identification). Thus, with the exception of limited or signed editions issued as a regular part of publishing procedure, I have eliminated in most cases signed copies, unique or presentation copies, books annotated in the author's hand, etc. The reasons for these decisions are, first, that *in most cases rebound copies are worth less than copies in original binding* and, second, that an author's signature or other writing by the author may greatly enhance the value of the book. In other words, my chief aim was to include only books in their original condition—*i.e.,* as issued by the publisher and unaffected by anything that may have been done with or to them after publication.

The final ground rule was to provide as accurately as possible through examining the catalogues (and often the stocks) of leading booksellers in both England and America, as well as the book auction records of the major galleries, an up-to-date range of prices within which a scarce or rare book might be expected to be available at retail. (The auction prices are indicated with a capital

A, followed by the auction season concerned; example: "$150 (A, 1971).") The decision to include some auction records was intended as both a support and a background for the use of experienced collectors, librarians, and booksellers, as well as an aid to the general reader in understanding and interpreting the book market. In many cases—especially with rare and very expensive books—the only price information available to layman or professional is in the auction records. Parenthetically, I should add that in general, as I have pointed out in my column and my other books, auction prices in the case of the majority of books that appear on the market in America and England are in most cases at what should be considered the "wholesale" level—prices paid by dealers—since it is the dealers who make up most of the audience at rare book auctions. Thus, a book that brings $25 at auction will generally wind up in some dealer's catalogue at half again or twice that price, and often more. An example I have witnessed within the month was the purchase by a dealer at auction for $50 of a copy of an art book containing two original lithographs; it was later priced by the purchaser at $225. I should add, however, that auction prices in the case of books in the higher brackets—in the retail range of roughly $500 and upward—quite frequently are fairly close to retail values. The reason for this is that collectors, libraries, and institutions commonly authorize major booksellers to bid for them at auctions on a 10 percent fee arrangement. In other words, a library may authorize a dealer to pay $1,000 for a book for which, if obtained, it will pay the dealer $1,100 (plus travel or other allowances), the extra $100 representing the dealer's 10 percent commission for acting as representative. One other point to be made about the auction records is that they often present problems confusing even to the most experienced bookman, such as wide variations in the prices on the same book in the same year—for example, $15 to $85. In general there are reasons for these variations (usually a matter of condition), which one can solve only by consulting the auction catalogue (or through the happenstance of having attended the sale). From these comments then, it should be obvious that the book auction records, as accurate as their compilers try to make them, are not an absolute guide to values and must be used with caution and interpreted with a fairly sophisticated knowledge of the book trade in general.

CONDITION IS THE KEY: Let me underscore the fact that the price ranges indicated herein are for books *in original binding and in fine condition.* The price spreads are included because the book market is a free market in which each dealer is at liberty to price a book as he personally values it in relation to his own knowledge of scarcity and demand and basic value. Thus a New York dealer may have a book priced at $75, a London dealer at $110, and a San Francisco dealer at $65. From this, it should be obvious that shopping around may sometimes be advisable. In general, however, the international rare book trade is a vast, loose network of independent dealers in which there is, with certain limits, a general unanimity of opinion concerning the values of books.

By and large it is *condition* that determines the price asked for a scarce or rare book. In recent years I have noted a very strong trend among collectors (and sometimes libraries) to accept only the finest copies available—regardless of price. Thus I observed in one shop a customer who was offered a fine first edition copy of John Steinbeck's *The Grapes of Wrath* without dust jacket for $10 and turned it down for an absolutely mint copy in dust jacket at $75.

In considering the prices included in this compilation, it should always be kept in mind that inferior copies—poor, average, or even good to very good copies—may be worth less than the prices I have noted, as will be rebound copies. Obviously, books with defects—lacking dust jackets (if originally included, as with most books published since 1900) or having torn pages, soiled covers, or pages written on or underlined—are going to be worth less than the prices I have shown. Additionally, it should be kept in mind that the book market is steadily changing and that quite often the value of a book will rise sharply within a short space of time, so that even before this book is in your hands, the prices on some items listed herein may be considered low. This will be true despite the fact that every effort has been made to include catalogue prices and, where useful, auction records into the 1972 season.

POINTS: Bibliography is not an exact science, and no library, least of all my own, could possibly contain a complete bibliographical guide to the 15,000 to 18,000 separate items I have listed herein. Wherever possible, I have included the most reliable data I could find in order to assist the reader in identifying the first editions, as well as first issues, first states, etc. More detailed information on many of the major works listed may be consulted in bibliographies.

HOW DOES ONE TELL A FIRST EDITION?   This is the question asked most frequently, and it is one of the more difficult questions to answer. There is, in fact, no single statement that will serve as an adequate answer. In general, it can be said that if the date on the title page of a book agrees with the date on the verso, or back, of the title page, the book may be assumed to be a first edition, provided there are no indications to the contrary. The question is, however, much more complicated than that; this is one of the reasons why it is necessary to include in many of the entries herein the bibliographical points of identification.

There is unfortunately no unanimity of method among either English or American publishers of identifying their first editions. Henry S. Boutell's *First Editions of Today and How to Tell Them* (Peacock Press), in its 1965 fourth edition, revised, contains a relatively up-to-date list of American and English publisher statements concerning their various methods of identifying their books. For example, Atheneum, Bobbs-Merrill, Doubleday, Dutton, Farrar, Straus & Giroux, Harcourt Brace Jovanovich, Harper & Row, Holt, Rinehart & Winston, Houghton Mifflin, Alfred A. Knopf, Lippincott, Little, Brown, Macmillan, W. W. Norton, Prentice-Hall, Random House, and the University of Oklahoma Press are among the larger American publishers who in general currently indicate on the copyright page (or elsewhere) the first appearances of their books with the words "First edition," "First printing," or other equivalent terminology. (In the case of some of these publishers these conditions have not always applied.) Other publishers use different methods, such as, for example, Putnam's, which reports that it does not indicate on its first editions that they are such (meaning they are) and adds, "When a book is reprinted, we as a rule print under the copyright notice the words 'Second Impression,' or whatever number the printing may be." Many publishers frankly state that they have no means of identifying their first editions. Indeed, New Directions, the publishers of some of the more collectible of modern authors, including Dylan Thomas, have been the despair of collectors who have been unable to untangle their various printings. (I have seen one New Directions book exactly identical with another copy except that the binding was of an entirely different color and style. The company itself told the Boutell editors in 1964 that "we are trying to remember to mark First Edition on copyright pages," but I have seen few so marked.) The situation with English publishers is just as chaotic, with practices varying from publisher to publisher. Most of the English trade houses, such as Faber & Faber and Andre Deutsch, seem to favor a simple line "First Published 1972" (or some similar equivalent) on the copyright page, with notations of later printings or "impressions" being made on subsequent issues.

In the case of nineteenth-century books, the practices of publishers were equally various, so that, in summary, I must say that aside from the rule of thumb about title page and copyright page agreement, every book must be considered as an individual problem. Unless the book itself is somehow identifiable as a first edition, it may be necessary to consult author bibliographies (and other library or bookseller resources, including catalogues) for exact information unless I have included it herein.

ABOUT SELLING YOUR BOOKS: The rare book trade, like most antiquarian businesses, is a relatively small market operated by dealers of varying degrees of competence, style, and temperament. The prices given in this handbook are prices at the retail level and are *not* prices that a dealer can be expected to pay for them. Whether you sell at retail to collectors or at wholesale to dealers is your own choice. In my experience, most dealers are willing to pay about 50 percent of retail value (and sometimes more) for books for which they have immediate customers or a relatively steady demand. In general, they incline to pay less, 20 percent to, say, 35 percent—for books for stock. This, I think, is what one must expect when it is considered that they often must sit with books for years before finding a customer for them. Meanwhile, rent and salaries and all the other items of overhead, including the frightfully high present cost of printing catalogues, goes on and on. The net profit in the rare book trade is not noticeably large.

One final word: *Never be guilty of asking a dealer to price your books for you* (asking for a free appraisal). Most dealers will make appraisals—but probably they will expect to be paid a fee. One dealer I know charges $500 a day for appraising large collections. Another has a flat fee of $25 for appraising a single book. The best thing to do is to prepare your own list of books, identifying them as best you can, and decide what you want for them. *Do not* take a large lot of books to a dealer and ask him to look at them. He simply doesn't have the time. It is far better to list them first and show him the list, asking if he has a possible interest in them. Your list should include the following information: author's name; title of book (from the title page); place and date of publication (from the title page); copyright date (from the back of the title page); a statement of the edition (if shown or known); a description of the binding (leather, cloth, paper, etc.); a description of the condition, noting all defects such as binding wear, torn pages, writing in the book, etc. If your books are right for the dealer, he will be glad to examine and buy them. In the event, finally, that you cannot price your own books, you may wish to ask him to make an offer, but do this only if you have confidence in the dealer and are willing to accept his judgment. *Do not* put him in a competitive position by taking a list around to his competitors to angle for the best price you can find.

BOOKS AS TREASURES: I have prepared this book, I hope, for readers who are interested in scarce and rare books as items to buy and treasure rather than to sell, although selling for profit is certainly an honorable practice! Whatever emphasis I have placed on price in all my writing about books has been with the hope of helping readers to identify scarce and rare items and of encouraging the collector to use caution in his buying and to obtain the finest possible copy within his means. I think it is wholly right for the booklover to cherish his prizes while at the same time conducting his search for fine books in such manner that they will always be worth at least as much as he pays for them. In fact, the whole history of book collecting shows that the really good books *always* increase in value as the years pass. There is a certain comfort, I think, in knowing that one has bought wisely and well.

VAN ALLEN BRADLEY

Barrington, Illinois
November 16, 1971

THE
BOOK COLLECTOR'S
HANDBOOK
OF VALUES

A

A. *Empedocles on Etna and Other Poems.* By A. Green cloth. London, 1852. (By Matthew Arnold.) First edition. $250-$300.

A. *Strayed Reveller (The), and Other Poems.* By A. Dark green cloth. London, 1849. (By Matthew Arnold.) First edition. $200-$300.

A., T. B. *The Bells: A Collection of Chimes.* By T. B. A. Brown cloth. New York, 1855. (By Thomas Bailey Aldrich.) First edition. $35-$50. (Note: Also supposed to exist with "Boston & New York & Cincinnati" imprint.)

ABBEY, James. *California. A Trip Across the Plains in the Spring of 1850.* 64 pp., printed wrappers. New Albany, Ind., 1850. First edition. $1,500-$2,000.

ABBEY, John Roland. *Scenery of Great Britain and Ireland in Aquatint and Lithography, 1770-1860.* Frontispiece in color, numerous other illustrations. Buckram. London, 1952. One of 500. $300-$400.

ABBOT (The). 3 vols., boards. Edinburgh, 1820. (By Sir Walter Scott.) First edition. $75-$100.

ABBOTSFORD, and Newstead Abbey. By the Author of "The Sketch-Book." Boards. London, 1835. (By Washington Irving.) First edition. $75-$100. Philadelphia, 1835. Blue or green cloth, paper labels. First edition, first printing, with copyright notices on both pages 2 and 4. $100-$150.

ABBOTT, Jacob. See *Rollo Learning to Talk.*

A'BECKETT, Gilbert Abbott. *The Comic History of England.* Illustrated in color by John Leech. 20 parts in 19, blue wrappers. London, 1846-48. First edition. $300-$400. London, 1847-48. 2 vols., cloth. First edition in book form. $150-$200.

AB-SA-RA-KA, Home of the Crows. Folding map. Cloth. Philadelphia, 1868. (By Mrs. Henry B. Carrington.) First edition. $85-$100. Philadelphia, 1869. Cloth. Second edition. $25-$35. Philadelphia, 1878. Cloth. Third edition. $25-$35. Philadelphia, 1879. Fifth edition. $19 (A, 1968). Philadelphia, 1890. $35 (A, 1966).

ACKERMANN, Rudolph. *A History of the University of Cambridge* [and] *A History of the University of Oxford.* Illustrated with color plates. 4 vols., red morocco. London, 1815-14. First editions. Together, $5,880. Separately: *Cambridge,* $3,000-$3,500. Also $1,680 (A, 1969). *Oxford,* $2,000-$2,500. Also, $1,200 (A, 1969).

ACKERMANN, Rudolph. *The Microcosm of London.* 104 colored aquatint plates by Pugin and Rowlandson. 3 vols., half morocco. London, no date (1808-10). First edition. $1,000-$2,000. London, 1904. 3 vols., parchment and boards. $75-$100.

ACKLEY, Mary E. *Crossing the Plains and Early Days in California.* Illustrated. Boards, printed label on spine. San Francisco, 1928. First edition. $75-$100.

ACT Incorporating the Town of Berkeley (The). 44 pp., wrappers. Berkeley, Calif., 1878. First edition. $50.

ACTIVE Anthology (The). See Pound, Ezra.

ACTON, Harold. *The Last of the Medici.* Introduction by Norman Douglas. Portrait. Boards. Florence, Italy, 1930. First edition. One of 365 signed. In dust jacket. $60-$80.

ACTS, Resolutions and Memorials, Adopted by the Second Legislative Assembly of the Territory of Arizona. Boards. Prescott, Ariz., 1865. $50. Prescott, 1867. *Acts,* etc., for 3d Assembly. Boards. $40.

ADAIR, James. *The History of the American Indians.* Edited by Samuel C. Williams. Folding map, facsimiles. Cloth. Johnson City, Tenn., 1930. One of 750. $50-$80. Also, $22 (A, 1963). Nashville, 1953. Folding maps. Cloth. $25.

ADAMS, Andy. *The Log of a Cowboy.* 6 plates. Brown pictorial cloth. Boston, 1903. First edition. $35-$50.

ADAMS, Charles F., Jr., and Henry Adams. *Chapters of Erie, and Other Essays.* Terra-cotta or green cloth. Boston, 1871. First edition. $20-$25.

ADAMS, Henry. See Adams, Charles F., Jr. Also see *Democracy; Mont Saint Michel and Chartres* .

ADAMS, Henry. *The Education of Henry Adams.* Blue cloth, leather spine label. Washington, 1907. First edition. One of 100. $500-$750. Boston, 1918. Revised and edited by Henry Cabot Lodge. Blue cloth. First trade edition. In dust jacket. $25. New York, 1942. Limited Editions Club. Etchings by Samuel Chamberlain. Cloth. Boxed. $25.

ADAMS, Henry. *A Letter to American Teachers of History.* Green or blue cloth. Washington, 1910. First edition. $50. Signed by the author (Blanck suggests that most copies were signed), $150-$200.

ADAMS, John Quincy. *Oration on the Life and Character of Gilbert Motier de Lafayette.* Wrappers. Washington, 1835. First edition. $15-$25. Another issue: One of a few on thick paper, specially bound in morocco. $65. (Note: Inscribed copies bring more, of course, as with all Presidential items.)

ADAMS, Leonie. *High Falcon and Other Poems.* Cloth. New York, no date (1929). First edition. In dust jacket. $35-$40.

ADAMS, Leonie. *Those Not Elect.* Gray boards. New York, 1925. First edition. $40-$50.

ADAMS, Will. *Errata: or, The Works of Will. Adams.* 2 vols., boards. New York, 1823. (By John Neal.) First edition. $100-$150.

ADAMS, William Taylor. See Ashton, Warren T.

ADE, George. *Artie.* Cloth. Chicago, 1896. First edition. $15-$25. Author's first book.

ADE, George. *Fables in Slang.* Tan decorated cloth. Chicago, 1900. First edition. $25-$30.

ADE, George. *The Old-Time Saloon.* Blue cloth. New York, 1931. First edition. $25.

ADE, George. *One Afternoon with Mark Twain.* Stiff wrappers. Chicago, 1939. First edition. One of 350. $25.

ADE, George. *Revived Remarks on Mark Twain.* 36 pp., wrappers. Chicago, 1936. First edition. One of 500 signed. $25-$35.

ADE, George. *Stories of the Streets and of the Town.* Edited by Franklin J. Meine. Cloth. Chicago, 1941. Caxton Club. One of 500. $25.

ADE, George. *The Sultan of Sulu.* Illustrated. Pictorial cream wrappers. New York, 1903. First edition, with "Published May, 1903" on copyright page. $25-$35.

ADELER, Max. *Out of the Hurly-Burly.* Illustrated by A. B. Frost and others. Decorated cloth. Philadelphia, 1874. (By Charles Heber Clark.) First edition. $50. Author's first book and first book illustrated by Frost.

ADMIRARI, Nil. *The Trollopiad; or, Travelling Gentlemen in America.* Half leather. New York, 1837. (By Frederick William Shelton.) First edition. $50-$75.

ADVENTURES of a Brownie (The), as Told to My Child. By the Author of "John Halifax, Gentleman." Cloth. London, 1872. (By Dinah Maria Mulock.) First edition. $75-$150.

ADVENTURES of a Post Captain (The). By a Naval Officer. 25 colored plates. Boards. London, no date (1817). (By Alfred Thornton.) First edition. $100-$150.

ADVENTURES of Robin Day (The). 2 vols., purple cloth, paper label on spine. Philadelphia, 1839. (By Robert Montgomery Bird.) First edition. $100-$150.

ADVENTURES of Timothy Peacock, Esquire (The). By a Member of the Vermont Bar. Cloth. Middlebury, Vt., 1835. (By Daniel Pierce Thompson.) First edition. $600. Author's first novel.

ADVENTURES of Ulysses (The). Frontispiece, engraved title page. Boards, paper label. London, 1808. (By Charles Lamb.) First edition. $150-$250.

ADVENTURES of a Yankee (The), or The Singular Life of John Ledyard. By a Yankee. Woodcuts. Boards and morocco. Boston, 1831. (By John Ledyard.) First edition. $150-$200.

ADVENTURES of a Younger Son (The). 3 vols., boards. London, 1831. (By Edward John Trelawny.) First edition. $150-$200. Lacking ad at end of Vol. 3, $125. Author's first book.

AESCHYLUS. *Agamemnon: A Tragedy.* Translated by Edward FitzGerald. Wrappers. No place, no date (London, 1865). First edition. $50-$75. London, 1876. Half leather. One of 250. $35-$50.

AESCHYLUS. *The Oresteia.* Illustrated. Cloth and leather. New York, 1961. Limited Editions Club. Boxed. $35.

AESOP. *Fables.* Sir Roger L'Estrange translation. Illustrated by Stephen Gooden. Vellum. London, 1936. One of 500 signed by Gooden. Boxed. $150-$250. New York, 1933. Limited Editions Club. Samuel Croxall translation. Illustrated by Bruce Rogers. Boards and vellum. Boxed. $75-$100.

AGAPIDA, Fray Antonio. *A Chronicle of the Conquest of Granada.* 2 vols., boards and cloth, paper labels. Philadelphia, 1829. (By Washington Irving.) First edition. $50-$100. Large paper issue: $150-$200. London, 1829. 2 vols., boards. First English edition. $35-$50. New York, 1893. 2 vols., half morocco. Agapida Edition. One of 150. $50-$75.

AGATE, James. *Ego: The Autobiography of James Agate.* Illustrated. Cloth. London, no date (1935). First edition. In dust jacket. $25-$35.

AGATE, James. *A Shorter Ego: The Autobiography of James Agate.* 2 vols., half morocco. London, no date (1945). One of 100 signed. $35-$45.

AGE of Bronze (The). Plain drab wrappers. London, 1823. (By George Gordon Noel, Lord Byron.) First edition. $300-$400.

AGED Wanderer (An); A Life Sketch of J. M. Parker, A Cowboy on the Western Plains in the Early Days. (Cover title.) Frontispiece (inside front cover). 32 pp., pictorial wrappers. San Angelo, Tex., no date (By J. M. Parker.) First edition. $40. (Note: Also published under the title *The Poor Orphan Boy.*)

AGEE, James. *Four Early Stories.* Boards and buckram. Cummington, Mass., 1964. One of 285. $65-$75.

AGEE, James. *Let Us Now Praise Famous Men.* Walker Evans photographs. Black cloth. Boston, 1941. First edition. In dust jacket. $50-$75. Boston, 1960. Black cloth. In dust jacket. $12.50-$15.

AGEE, James. *The Letters of James Agee to Father Flye.* Black cloth. New York, 1962. First edition. In dust jacket. $25.

AGEE, James. *The Morning Watch.* Boards. Boston, 1951. First edition. In dust jacket. $45-$50.

AGEE, James. *Permit Me Voyage.* Cloth. New Haven, 1934. First edition. In dust jacket. $100-$150. Author's first book. New York dealer offered copy in 1972 for $150.

AGEE, G. W. *Rube Burrows, King of Outlaws.* 194 pp., wrappers. No place, no date (Cincinnati, 1890). First edition. $50. Chicago, no date (1890). $35.

AGNES Tobin, Letters, Poems, with Some Account of Her Life. Illustrated. Boards, linen spine. San Francisco, 1958. First edition, first issue, with page 99 uncanceled. In dust jacket. $35. (Note: Contains a W. B. Yeats letter.)

AGRICOLA, Georgius. See Hoover, Herbert C. and Lou Henry.

AIKEN, Conrad. *The Coming Forth by Day of Osiris Jones.* Green cloth. New York, 1931. First edition, first issue, with Scribner "A" on copyright page and "The Music" incorrectly printed as section title on page 37. In dust jacket. $45-$65.

AIKEN, Conrad. *Earth Triumphant and Other Tales in Verse.* Cloth. New York, 1914. First edition. $50. Author's first book.

AIKEN, Conrad. *The Jig of Forslin: A Symphony.* Cloth. Boston, 1916. First edition. In dust jacket. $50-$100.

AIKEN, Conrad. *Preludes for Memnon.* Cloth. New York, 1931. First edition. In dust jacket. $25.

AIKEN, Conrad. *Priapus and the Pool.* Boards. Cambridge, Mass., 1922. First edition. Printed by Bruce Rogers. One of 425. $25. One of 50 (of the same edition) on handmade paper and signed. $50-$75. New York, 1925. New edition, with added poems. $25.

AIKEN, Conrad. *Punch: The Immortal Liar.* Cloth. New York, 1921. First edition. In dust jacket. $35-$50.

AIKEN, Conrad. *Selected Poems.* Cloth. New York, 1929. First edition. One of 210 on large paper, signed. $35-$50. Trade edition: In dust jacket. $10-$15.

AIKEN, Conrad. *Senlin: A Biography.* Boards, paper label. London, 1925. First separate edition, revised. $25.

AIKEN, Conrad. *Thee.* Illustrated by Leonard Baskin. Boards. New York, no date (1967). First edition. One of 100 signed by author and artist. Boxed. $60-$80.

AIKEN, Conrad. *Turns and Movies and Other Tales in Verse.* Printed wrappers over boards. Boston, 1916. First edition. $35-$50.

AINSWORTH, W. Harrison. *Jack Sheppard.* Portrait and illustrations by George Cruikshank. 3 vols., green cloth. London, 1838-39. First edition. $150-$200.

AINSWORTH, W. Harrison. *Merry England: or, Nobles and Serfs.* 3 vols., green cloth. London, 1874. First edition. $200-$225.

AINSWORTH, W. Harrison. *The Miser's Daughter.* Illustrated by George Cruikshank. 3 vols., black cloth. London, 1842. First edition. $75-$100.

AINSWORTH, W. Harrison. *Old Saint Paul's.* Illustrated by John Franklin and Phiz. 3 vols., cloth. London, 1841. First edition. $75-$100. (Also issued in 12 paperbound parts.) London, 1847. Red cloth. First octavo edition. $35.

AINSWORTH, W. Harrison. *The Tower of London.* Illustrated by George Cruikshank. 13 parts in 12, wrappers. London, 1840. First edition. $150-$200. London, 1840. Purple cloth. First book edition. $75-$100.

AKEN, David. *Pioneers of the Black Hills.* Pictorial wrappers. No place, no date (Milwaukee, 1920?). First edition. $50-$75.

ALARIC at Rome: A Prize Poem. Recited in Rugby School. June XII, MDCCCXL. 12 pp., pink pictorial and printed wrappers. Rugby, England, 1840. (By Matthew Arnold.) First edition. $400-$500 and up. Author's first book of verse.

ALBEE, Edward. *The Zoo Story. The Death of Bessie Smith. The Sandbox: Three Plays.* Blue cloth. New York, no date (1960). First edition. In dust jacket. $60-$75. Author's first book.

ALCEDAMA, a Place to Bury Strangers In. By a Gentleman of the University of Cambridge. Wrappers. London, 1898. (By Aleister Crowley.) First edition. $75. Author's first book.

ALCOTT, A. Bronson. *Sonnets and Canzonets.* Illustrated with photographs. Cloth. Boston, 1882. First edition. One of 50 signed. $100-$150. Cover soiled, $85. (Note: The trade edition, lacking photographs, is not especially valuable—about $10 in fine condition.)

ALCOTT, Louisa May. *Flower Fables.* Frontispiece and 5 plates. Cloth. Boston, 1855. First edition. $50-$75.

ALCOTT, Louisa May. *Hospital Sketches.* Printed green boards or cloth. Boston, 1863. First edition, first printing, in boards, with ad on back announcing Wendell Phillips' *Speeches* at $2.50 (not $2.25). $65. Later, "$2.25," $25. Cloth, also later, $25.

ALCOTT, Louisa May. *Jack and Jill: A Village Story.* Cloth. Boston, 1880. First edition. $25.

ALCOTT, Louisa May. *Kitty's Class Day.* 12 pp., printed buff wrappers. Boston, no date (1868). First edition. $200-$300. (Note: Issue points on this pamphlet are debatable; see Blanck's *Bibliography of American Literature.*)

ALCOTT, Louisa May. *Little Men.* Frontispiece. Blue cloth. London, 1871. First edition. $35. Boston, 1871. Green cloth. First American edition, first issue, with ads at front listing *Pink and White Tyranny* as nearly ready. $75-$100. Also, $40 (A, 1966).

ALCOTT, Louisa May. *Little Women.* Frontispiece and 3 plates. 2 vols., cloth. Boston, 1868-69. First edition, without "Part One" on spine of Vol. 1 and with Vol. 2 having no notice of *Little Women, Part First,* on page iv. $750. Vol. 1 alone. $500 (1965 dealer catalogue). Vol. 2 alone. $100 and up. New York, 1967. Limited Editions Club. Illustrated. Brocade cloth. Boxed. $25-$35. Also, $20 (A, 1968).

ALCOTT, Louisa May. *Morning-Glories, and Other Stories.* Frontispiece and 3 plates. Cloth. Boston, 1868. First edition. $75.

ALCOTT, Louisa May. *An Old-Fashioned Girl.* Double frontispiece and 2 plates. Cloth. Boston, 1870. First edition, first issue, no ads on copyright page. $50-$75. Second issue, with ads on copyright page, $20.

ALCOTT, Louisa May. *The Rose Family.* 47 pp., printed wrappers or cloth. Boston, 1864. First edition. Wrappers: $150-$200. Cloth: $100-$150.

ALDINGTON, Richard. *A. E. Housman and W. B. Yeats, Two Lectures.* Boards. No place (Hurst, England), 1955. Peacocks Press. One of 350. $25.

ALDINGTON, Richard. *All Men Are Enemies.* Boards and buckram. London, 1933. One of 110 signed. $35-$70.

MILITARY MEMOIRS OF A
CONFEDERATE

A CRITICAL NARRATIVE

BY

E. P. ALEXANDER

BRIGADIER-GENERAL IN THE CONFEDERATE ARMY, CHIEF OF
ARTILLERY, LONGSTREET'S CORPS

WITH SKETCH-MAPS BY THE
AUTHOR

NEW YORK
CHARLES SCRIBNER'S SONS
1907

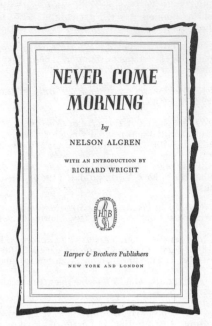

NEVER COME
MORNING

by

NELSON ALGREN

WITH AN INTRODUCTION BY
RICHARD WRIGHT

Harper & Brothers Publishers
NEW YORK AND LONDON

POEMS

BY
W. H. AUDEN

LONDON
FABER & FABER
24 RUSSELL SQUARE

EXPERIMENTS

AND

OBSERVATIONS

ON THE

GASTRIC JUICE,

AND THE

PHYSIOLOGY OF DIGESTION.

BY WILLIAM BEAUMONT, M. D.

Surgeon in the U. S. Army.

PLATTSBURGH,
PRINTED BY F. P. ALLEN.
1833.

ALDINGTON, Richard. *At All Costs.* Boards and buckram. London, 1930. First edition. One of 275 signed. $25-$35.

ALDINGTON, Richard. *Balls and Another Book for Suppression.* Wrappers. London, 1930. Blue Moon Booklets No. 7. First edition. $25. Also privately issued: No place (Westport), 1932. (Title: *Balls.*) Sewed, self-wrappers. One of "99 & a few others." $25.

ALDINGTON, Richard. *The Colonel's Daughter: A Novel.* Green cloth. London, 1931. First edition. One of 210 signed. $25.

ALDINGTON, Richard. *D. H. Lawrence.* Boards and buckram. London, 1930. First edition. One of 260 signed. In tissue dust jacket. $45-$50. Another issue: Orange wrappers. $10.

ALDINGTON, Richard. *Death of a Hero.* Cloth. London, 1929. First edition. In dust jacket. $25. Lacking jacket, $10. Paris, 1930. 2 vols., printed wrappers. Unexpurgated text. One of 300 signed. $100-$150.

ALDINGTON, Richard. *Ezra Pound and T. S. Eliot: A Lecture.* Boards. London, 1954. Peacocks Press. First edition. One of 350. $35. Another issue: Full morocco. One of 10. $50.

ALDINGTON, Richard. *Fifty Romance Lyric Poems.* Black cloth. New York, 1928. First edition. One of 9 on green paper, signed. $75. Another issue: One of 900. $15-$25.

ALDINGTON, Richard. *A Fool i' the Forest.* Cloth. London, 1925. First edition, limited, signed. In dust jacket. $60-$75.

ALDINGTON, Richard. *Images of War.* Boards and cloth. London, 1919. First edition. One of 200. $25-$30.

ALDINGTON, Richard. *Images—Old and New.* Stiff boards. Boston, 1916. First edition. In dust jacket. $35-$50. Author's first book.

ALDINGTON, Richard. *Love and the Luxembourg.* Red buckram. New York, 1930. First edition. One of 475 signed. Boxed. $25.

ALDINGTON, Richard. *The Love of Myrrhine and Konallis.* Cloth. Chicago, 1966. First edition. One of 150 signed. $35.

ALDINGTON, Richard. *Stepping Heavenward.* Boards and cloth. Florence, Italy, 1931. One of 808 signed. In dust jacket. $50-$75. London, 1931. Boards. $10-$15.

ALDRICH, Thomas Bailey. See A., T. B.

ALDRICH, Thomas Bailey. *The Ballad of Babie Bell and Other Poems.* Brown cloth. New York, 1859. First edition, first issue, with Broadway address for publisher. $50.

ALDRICH, Thomas Bailey. *Judith and Holofernes.* Cloth. Boston, 1896. First edition. One of 50 with paper labels. $100-$150. Trade edition: $25.

ALDRICH, Thomas Bailey. *Prudence Palfrey.* Cloth. Boston, 1874. First edition. $25.

ALDRICH, Thomas Bailey. *The Story of a Bad Boy.* Cloth. Boston, 1870. First edition, first issue, with line 20 on page 14 reading "scattered" and line 10 on page 197 reading "abroad." $250-$500. Boston, 1895. Illustrated by A. B. Frost. Decorated cloth. $25.

ALDRIDGE, Reginald. *Life on a Ranch.* Frontispiece and 3 plates. Stiff wrappers. New York, 1884. First edition. $75-$100. Rebound in cloth, paper covers bound in, $25-$30.

ALDRIDGE, Reginald. *Ranch Notes in Kansas.* 4 plates. Pictorial cloth. London, 1884. First English edition (of *Life on a Ranch*; see above). $50-$75.

ALEXANDER, E. P. *The American Civil War.* 2 portraits, map. Cloth. London, 1908. First English edition (of *Military Memoirs of a Confederate;* see below). $35-$50.

ALEXANDER, E. P. *Military Memoirs of a Confederate.* Maps, 3 plates. Cloth. New York, 1907. First edition. $35-$50.

ALEXANDER, Hartley B. (editor). *Sioux Indian Painting.* 50 color plates. 2 vols., large folio, loose in pictorial cloth portfolios, with ties. Nice, France, 1938. One of 400. $250-$350.

ALEXANDER, John H. *Mosby's Men.* Illustrated. Cloth. New York, 1907. First edition. In dust jacket. $30.

ALEXANDER, William. *Picturesque Representations of the Dress and Manners of the Austrians.* 50 color plates. Full contemporary morocco. London, no date (about 1813). $100. Also, similar volumes, various dates, covering the Chinese (50 color plates), Russians (64 plates), Turks (61), English (50), roughly $100 each.

ALEXANDRE, Arsène. *The Decorative Art of Leon Bakst.* Notes on the Ballets by Jean Cocteau. Translated by Harry Melvill. Portrait. 77 plates. 50 in color. Folio, half vellum. London, 1913. First edition. $350-$500.

ALGER, Horatio, Jr. See Putnam, Arthur Lee; Starr, Julian. Also see *Nothing to Do; Timothy Crump's Ward* .

ALGER, Horatio, Jr. *Abraham Lincoln, The Backwoods Boy.* Illustrated. Pictorial cloth. New York, 1883. First edition, first issue, with ads listing this book as No. 2 in "Boyhood and Manhood" series. $30-$35.

ALGER, Horatio, Jr. *Adrift in the City.* Illustrated. Tan cloth, stamped in blue and black. Philadelphia, no date (1895). First edition, with Porter & Coates imprint. $35-$50. Later issues, published by Henry T. Coates, $15-$20.

ALGER, Horatio, Jr. *Bertha's Christmas Vision: An Autumn Sheaf.* Blind-stamped cloth. Boston, 1856. First edition. $75. Author's first book. Offered by New York dealer in 1972 for $100.

ALGER, Horatio, Jr. *Dan, the Detective.* Illustrated. Cloth. New York, 1884. First edition. $150 and up.

ALGER, Horatio, Jr. *Dean Dunham.* Stiff tan pictorial wrappers. New York, 1890. First edition. (No. 32 in weekly series of "Leather-Clad Tales of Adventure and Romance.") $50.

ALGER, Horatio, Jr. *Digging for Gold.* Illustrated. Pictorial tan cloth. Philadelphia, no date (1892). First edition. $25-$35.

ALGER, Horatio, Jr. *The Errand Boy.* Red and black wrappers. New York, 1888. First edition. (Vol. 1, No. 14, of Boys' Home Library.) $35-$50.

ALGER, Horatio, Jr. *Fame and Fortune.* Illustrated. Cloth. Boston, no date (1868). First edition, first state, with no frontispiece and with damaged type in "By" on title page. $25-$35.

ALGER, Horatio, Jr. *Falling In with Fortune.* Illustrated. Pictorial green cloth. New York, no date (1900). (By Edward Stratemeyer.) First edition, with no Alger titles in ads at back. $25-$35.

ALGER, Horatio, Jr. *Finding a Fortune.* Illustrated. Pictorial tan cloth. Philadelphia, 1904. First edition, with interlocking script monogram on spine. $35-$50.

ALGER, Horatio, Jr. *The Five Hundred Dollar Check.* Pictorial tan cloth. New York, no date (1891). First book edition, first issue, with United States Book Co. imprint on title page and "Porter & Coates" on spine. $100-$125. Later issue, with "Lovell" on spine, $75-$100. (Note: This book had appeared earlier as a paperback Leather-Clad Tale under the title *$500; or Jacob Marlowe's Secret,* 1890. Value: $35-$50.)

ALGER, Horatio, Jr. *Forging Ahead.* Illustrated. Tan cloth. Philadelphia, 1903. First edition, with date in Roman numerals at foot of title page. $40-$50.

ALGER, Horatio, Jr. *Frank and Fearless.* Illustrated. Tan cloth. Philadelphia, 1897. First edition, with dated title page. $40-$50. Later, title undated, $20-$25.

ALGER, Horatio, Jr. *Frank Fowler, The Cash Boy.* Wrappers. New York, no date (1887). First edition, A. L. Burt imprint, Boys' Home Library. $35-$50. Another issue, same year: Cloth. $15-$20.

ALGER, Horatio, Jr. *Frank's Campaign.* Illustrated. Cloth. Boston, 1864. First edition, first state, with vertical lines on covers. $40. Second state, pebbled cloth. $27.50. (The second edition is so indicated on title page.)

ALGER, Horatio, Jr. *From Canal Boy to President.* Illustrated. Green cloth. New York, 1881. First edition, first issue, with pages 266 and 268 transposed and with erratum slip tipped to page 267. $35-$50. Later printings, about $15.

ALGER, Horatio, Jr. *Grand'ther Baldwin's Thanksgiving.* Purple cloth. Boston, no date (1875). First edition, published by Loring. $75.

ALGER, Horatio, Jr. *In a New World.* Cloth. Philadelphia, no date (1893). First edition, with *Digging for Gold* as last Alger title listed in ads at back. $25. (See *The Nugget Finders* for British reissue.)

ALGER, Horatio, Jr. *Joe's Luck.* Wrappers. New York, 1887. Boys' Home Library. $40-$50.

ALGER, Horatio, Jr. *Julius; or The Street Boy Out West.* Illustrated. Pictorial cloth. Boston, no date (1874) First edition, with no listing in ads of any volumes of the Brave and Bold series. $35.

ALGER, Horatio, Jr. *Luke Walton, or The Chicago Newsboy.* Cloth. Philadelphia, no date (1889). First edition. $25-$35.

ALGER, Horatio, Jr. *Making His Mark.* Illustrated. Dark blue cloth. Philadelphia, 1901. First edition, with only two Alger titles listed on last page of ads. $25-$35.

ALGER, Horatio, Jr. *Mark Stanton.* Wrappers. New York, 1890. (Leather-Clad paperback.) First edition. $.50

ALGER, Horatio, Jr. *The Nugget Finders.* Colored frontispiece. Green cloth. London, 1894. First English edition of *In a New World,* first state, with publisher's address as 48 Paternoster Row. $50. Later, with address as 3 Pilgrim Street. $25.

ALGER, Horatio, Jr. *Paul the Peddler.* Illustrated. Cloth. Boston, no date (1871). First edition, with book ads at front listing *Phil, the Fiddler* for April, 1872, *Slow and Sure* for November, and *Strive and Succeed* for October. $30-$35.

ALGER, Horatio, Jr. *Phil, The Fiddler.* Illustrated. Cloth. Boston, no date (1872). First edition, with ads at front listing *Slow and Sure* for November, 1872, and *Strive and Succeed* for October. $40-$50.

ALGER, Horatio, Jr. *Ragged Dick; or Street Life in New York with the Boot-Blacks.* Pictorial title page, 3 illustrations. Cloth. Boston, no date (1868). First edition, first issue, with *Fame and Fortune* listed in ads for publication "In December." $200-$250. Other Loring editions of this title bring as much as $35 to $50.

ALGER, Horatio, Jr. *Ralph Raymond's Heir.* Printed brown wrappers. New York, no date (1892). (Idle Hour Series paperback.) First edition. $35-$50.

ALGER, Horatio, Jr. *Robert Coverdale's Struggle.* Pictorial colored cover. New York, no date (1910). New Medal Library No. 555. First edition. Only one copy known. "Worth at least $350," according to the Alger bibliographer Ralph Gardner, who owns it.

ALGER, Horatio, Jr. *Tom Thatcher's Fortune.* Wrappers. New York, 1888. Boys' Home Library. First edition. $45.

ALGER, Horatio, Jr. *Tony, the Hero.* Cloth. New York, no date (1880). First edition, with J. S. Ogilvie imprint. $50-$60.

ALGER, Horatio, Jr. *The Train Boy.* 36 pp., wrappers. New York, no date (1882). First edition. $35. New York, 1883. Cloth. First complete edition. $25.

ALGER, Horatio, Jr. *The Western Boy.* Pictorial title. Cloth. No place, no date (New York, 1878). First edition, with G. W. Carleton ad at front of book. $150-$200.

ALGER, Horatio, Jr. *The Young Acrobat.* Orange wrappers. New York, 1888. First edition. No. 8 in Munsey's Popular Series for Boys and Girls. $50-$60.

ALGER, Horatio, Jr. *The Young Miner; or Tom Nelson in California.* Boards and cloth. San Francisco, 1965. Book Club of California. One of 450. $30-$50.

ALGER, Horatio, Jr. *The Young Musician.* Illustrated. Cloth. Philadelphia, 1906. First edition, with no book ads. $35-$50.

ALGER, Horatio, Jr., and Cheney, O. Augusta. *Seeking His Fortune and Other Dialogues.* Pictorial cloth. Boston, no date (1875). First edition. $400-$450. Also, $190 (A, 1969). New York, 1882. Boards. Reprint by Ward & Drummond. $35-$50.

ALGREN, Nelson. *Chicago: City on the Make.* Gray boards. Garden City, 1951. First edition. In dust jacket. $25-$35.

ALGREN, Nelson. *The Man with the Golden Arm.* Cloth. Garden City, 1949. First edition. In dust jacket. $25-$35.

ALGREN, Nelson. *The Neon Wilderness.* Green cloth. New York, 1947. First edition. In dust jacket. $35-$50.

ALGREN, Nelson. *Never Come Morning.* Introduction by Richard Wright. Blue cloth. New York, no date (1942). First edition (so stated). In dust jacket. $45-$50.

ALGREN, Nelson. *Somebody in Boots.* Brown cloth. New York, no date (1935). First edition. In dust jacket. $150-$200. Author's first book.

ALGREN, Nelson. *A Walk on the Wild Side.* Boards. New York, no date (1956). First edition. In dust jacket. $35-$50.

ALHAMBRA (The). See Crayon, Geoffrey.

ALKEN, Henry. *The National Sports of Great Britain.* 50 colored plates. Folio, boards (?) or morocco. London, 1820 (-21). First edition, first issue, with engraved 1820 title page and with watermarks dated 1816 and 1818. $1,600-$2,500. London, 1821. Second issue, without 1820 title page. $1,500-$2,500. London, 1823. Second edition. $1,500-$2,000. London, 1824. Morocco. $750-$1,000. London, 1825. Boards. First octavo edition. $250-$500. In morocco, $125-$450. Large paper issue: $250-$600. London, 1903. Boards and cloth. $150-$250. Another edition: No place (New York), 1904. Half morocco. $200-$300.

ALKEN, Henry. *Scraps from the Sketch-Book of Henry Alken.* 42 colored plates. Boards. London, 1821. First edition. $350-$500. Rebound in morocco, $200-$250. London, 1822. Contemporary half morocco. $168 (A, 1968). London, 1825. Morocco. $132 (A, 1968).

ALKEN, Henry. *Shooting, or One Day's Sport of Three Real Good Ones, However Ignorant of Sporting Rules.* 6 color plates. Buff printed wrappers (dated 1824). London, 1823. First edition. $225-$350.

ALLAHAKBARRIE Book of Broadway Cricket for 1899. Illustrated. Parchment wrappers. No place, no date (London, 1899). (By Sir James M. Barrie.) In cloth folder and slipcase. $200.

ALLAN, J. T. (compiler). *Central and Western Nebraska, and the Experiences of Its Stock Growers.* (Cover title.) 16 pp., pictorial wrappers. Omaha, 1883. $35-$75. (Note: A Union Pacific land department pamphlet.)

ALLAN, J. T. (compiler). *Western Nebraska and the Experiences of Its Actual Settlers.* 16 pp., wrappers. Omaha, 1882. $75.

ALLEN, Miss A. J. (compiler). *Ten Years in Oregon.* Portrait. Calf. Ithaca, N. Y., 1848. First edition. $50-$75. Second issue, same date, portrait omitted, pages added. Sheep. $30 (A, 1969). Ithaca, 1850. Pictorial cloth. $15 (A, 1969 and 1964).

ALLEN, Hervey. See Allen, William Hervy.

ALLEN, Hervey. *Anthony Adverse.* Blue cloth. New York, 1933. First trade edition, first printing, with publisher's monogram on copyright page and with numerous typographical errors, among them "Xaxier" for "Xavier" in line 6 of page 352, "ship" for "shop" in line 18 of page 1086, and the word "found" repeated in line 22 of page 397. In dust jacket. $35-$50. De luxe issue: 3 vols., suede boards. One of 105 signed. $75. New York, 1937. Limited Editions Club. 3 vols., orange cloth. One of 1,500. Boxed. $25-$35.

ALLEN, Hervey. *The Bride of Huitzil.* Boards and cloth. New York, 1922. First edition. One of 350 signed. $25.

ALLEN, Hervey. *Israfel: The Life and Times of Edgar Allan Poe.* 2 vols., cloth. New York, 1926. First edition, first state with wineglass on table in Longfellow portrait facing page 529. In dust jackets. $25-$35. De luxe issue: Three-quarters leather. One of 250. $35-$50.

ALLEN, Hervey. *Wampum and Old Gold.* Boards. New Haven, 1921. First edition. One of 500. $25-$30.

ALLEN, Hervey, and Mabbott, Thomas O. *Poe's Brother.* Boards. New York, 1926. First edition. $25.

ALLEN, Ira. *A Concise Summary of the Second Volume of the Olive Branch.* 24 pp., wrappers. Philadelphia, 1807. $100-$125.

ALLEN, J. A. *Notes on the Natural History of Portions of Montana and Dakota.* 61 pp., wrappers. Boston, 1874. $25-$30.

ALLEN, W. A. *The Sheep Eaters.* 6 plates. Cloth. New York, 1913. First edition. $25-$35.

ALLEN, William A. *Adventures with Indians and Game.* 25 plates. Cloth, or half leather. Chicago, 1903. First edition. $35-$50.

ALLEN, William Hervy. *Ballads of the Border.* Printed wrappers. No place (El Paso), 1916. (By Hervey Allen.) First edition, probable first state, with author's name misspelled "Hervy" on copyright page. $200-$300.(A copy signed twice by Allen brought $170 at auction in 1961.) There were many later printings. Author's first book.

ALLIES' Fairy Book (The). 12 colored plates, other illustrations by Arthur Rackham. Buckram. London, no date (1916). One of 525 signed by the artist. $150-$200. Trade edition: Cloth. First issue, with pictorial end papers. In dust jacket. $50-$60.

ALLINGHAM, William. *Sixteen Poems.* Selected by William Butler Yeats. Boards and linen. Dundrum, Ireland, 1905. Dun Emer Press. One of 200. $60-$100.

ALLISON, William. *The British Thoroughbred Horse.* Cloth. London, 1901. First edition. $35-$50. London, 1907. Second edition. $20.

ALLOM, Thomas. *Cornwall Illustrated.* Map, engraved title and 44 plates (on 22), hand-colored. Black morocco. London, 1831. Rebacked with brown morocco, $80.

ALMONTE, Juan Nepomuceno. *Noticia Estadistica sobre Tejas.* 3 folding tables. Boards or wrappers. Mexico, 1835. First edition. $450-$600.

ALNWICK Castle, with Other Poems. Printed tan wrappers. New York, 1827. (By Fitz-Greene Halleck.) First edition. $75-$100. New York, 1836. $35.

ALONZO and Melissa. Contemporary leather and boards. Brattleboro, Vt., 1824. (By Isaac Mitchell.) $25-$35. (Note: See author entry for first edition.)

ALTER, J. Cecil. *James Bridger: Trapper, Frontiersman, Scout, and Guide.* 18 plates. Cloth. Salt Lake City, no date (1925). First edition. One of 1,000 signed. $50-$75. Columbus, Ohio, 1951. Cloth. In dust jacket. $25-$35.

ALTISONANT, Lorenzo. *Letters to Esq. Pedant, in the East.* Boards. Cambridge City, Ind., 1844. (By Samuel Klinefelter Hoshour.) First edition. $75-$150. Cincinnati, 1850. Boards. $50.

ALTOWAN; Or Incidents of Life and Adventure in the Rocky Mountains. By an Amateur Traveller. Edited by J. Watson Webb. 2 vols., cloth. New York, 1846. (By Sir William Drummond Stewart.) First edition. $150-$200. (Note: Howes says this was "probably actually written by Webb.")

AMERICAN Arguments for British Rights. Wrappers. London, 1806. (By William Loughton Smith.) $35.

AMERICAN Caravan IV: A Yearbook of American Literature. Cloth. New York, 1931. First edition. In dust jacket. $35.

AMERICAN Church Silver of the 17th and 18th Centuries. Boards. Boston, 1911. Boston Museum of Fine Arts. $30-$40.

AMERICAN Cruiser (The). Cloth. Boston, 1846. (By Capt. George Little.) First edition. $65.

AMERICAN Shooter's Manual (The). By a Gentleman of Philadelphia County. Frontispiece, 2 plates, errata. Contemporary calf. Philadelphia, 1827. (By Dr. Jesse Y. Kester?) First edition. $150-$250.

AMERICANA–Beginnings: A Selection from the Library of Thomas W. Streeter. 97 pp., wrappers. Morristown, N. J., 1952. One of 325. $35-$50.

AMSDEN, Charles A. *Navaho Weaving.* 122 plates, many in color. Cloth. Santa Ana, 1934. First edition. $75-$100. Albuquerque, 1948 (actually 1949). Cloth. $45. Chicago, no date (1964). Cloth. $15.

ANALYSIS of the Hunting Field (The). 7 colored plates by Henry Alken, 43 woodcuts. Green or red cloth. London, 1846. (By Robert Smith Surtees.) First edition, first issue, green cloth (some copies with preface dated 1846, some dated 1847). $168-$400. Second issue, red cloth. (Some copies in red have two prefaces, dated 1846 and 1847.) $75-$150.

ANCIENT and Modern Michilimackinac. (Cover title.) 48 pp., wrappers. No place (St. James, Mich.), MDCCCLIV (1854). (By James Jesse Strang.) First edition, first issue. $1,000 and up. Another, dated 1854, but "obviously" (according to Howes) on later paper, $50 and up.

ANDERSEN, Hans Christian. *The Complete Andersen.* Translated by Jean Hersholt. Hand-colored illustrations by Fritz Kredel. 6 vols., buckram and boards. New York, 1949. Limited Editions Club. Boxed. $75.

ANDERSEN, Hans Christian. *Fairy Tales.* 12 colored plates and numerous black-and-white illustrations by Arthur Rackham. Vellum. London, no date (1932). De luxe edition. One of 525 signed by the artist. $150-$200. Another edition: London, no date (about 1920). Illustrated by Kay Nielsen. Full vellum. One of 500 signed by Nielsen. $175.

ANDERSEN, Hans. *Stories from Hans Andersen.* 28 color plates by Edmund Dulac. Vellum, silk ties. London, no date (1911). One of 750 signed by Dulac. $75 and $67.20. Another issue: Pigskin. One of 100 on Japan paper. $100-$150.

ANDERSON, Maxwell. *You Who Have Dreams.* Boards, paper labels. New York, 1925. First edition. One of 1,000. In dust jacket. $35-$50. Author's first book.

ANDERSON, Maxwell, and Stallings, Laurence. *Three American Plays.* Boards and cloth, paper label. New York, no date (1926). First edition. $35.

ANDERSON, Sherwood. *Alice and the Lost Novel.* Boards. London, 1929. First edition. One of 500 signed. In dust jacket. $35.

ANDERSON, Sherwood. *Beyond Desire.* Tan cloth. New York, no date (1932). First edition. One of 165 signed. $50. Trade edition: Cloth. In dust jacket. $25.

ANDERSON, Sherwood. *Dark Laughter.* Half vellum and boards. New York, 1925. First edition. One of 350 signed. Boxed. $35-$75. (There were also 20 copies lettered and signed by the author.) Trade edition: Black cloth. In dust jacket. $25. Lacking jacket, $10-$15.

ANDERSON, Sherwood. *Death in the Woods and Other Stories.* Boards. New York, no date (1933). First edition. In dust jacket. $50. Binding faded and worn, dust jacket frayed, $25.

ANDERSON, Sherwood. *Horses and Men.* Orange cloth. New York, 1923. First edition, first issue, with top edges stained orange. In dust jacket. $25.

ANDERSON, Sherwood. *Many Marriages.* Black cloth. New York, 1923. First edition, first issue, with top edges stained orange. In dust jacket. $35.

ANDERSON, Sherwood. *Marching Men.* Crimson cloth. New York, 1917. First edition. In dust jacket. $75-$100.

ANDERSON, Sherwood. *Mid-American Chants.* Yellow cloth. New York, 1918. First edition. In dust jacket. $50-$60.

ANDERSON, Sherwood. *Nearer the Grass Roots.* Half cloth. San Francisco, 1929. Grabhorn printing. First edition. One of 500 signed. $50-$60.

ANDERSON, Sherwood. *A New Testament.* Half vellum and boards. New York, 1927. First edition. One of 265 large paper copies, signed. In slipcase. $50-$75. Trade edition: Cloth. In dust jacket. $20-$25.

ANDERSON, Sherwood. *No Swank.* Cream-colored cloth. Philadelphia, 1934. First edition. One of 50 signed. $100-$150. (There were also 950 copies not signed.)

ANDERSON, Sherwood. *Poor White.* Blue cloth. New York, 1920. First edition, first issue, with top edges stained blue. In dust jacket. $25.

ANDERSON, Sherwood. *Tar: A Midwest Childhood.* Boards and vellum. New York, 1926. First edition. One of 350 large paper copies, signed. Boxed. $40-$50. Trade edition: Cloth. In dust jacket. $15-$20.

ANDERSON, Sherwood. *The Triumph of the Egg.* Plates. Green cloth. New York, 1921. First edition, first issue, with top edges stained yellow. In dust jacket. $25-$35.

ANDERSON, Sherwood. *Windy McPherson's Son.* Decorated brown cloth. New York, 1916. First edition. In dust jacket. $250-$300. Author's first book.

ANDERSON, Sherwood. *Winesburg, Ohio.* Yellow cloth, paper label on spine. New York, 1919. First edition, first issue, with top stained yellow and with perfect type in the word "the" in line 3 of page 251. In dust jacket. $75-$100.

ANDRÉ, John. *Major André's Journal.* Edited by Henry Cabot Lodge. Facsimile maps and plans and other illustrations. 2 vols., full vellum. Boston, 1903. First edition. One of 467. $100-$150. Another issue: One of 10 on Japan vellum. $150-$200.

ANDREAS, A. T. *History of Chicago.* Illustrated. 3 vols., morocco and cloth. Chicago, 1884-86. First edition. $50-$75. Another issue: Full morocco. $100-$150.

ANDREAS, A. T. *History of the State of Kansas.* Morocco. Folding map. Chicago, 1883. First edition. $50-$75.

ANDREAS, A. T. *Illustrated Historical Atlas of the State of Iowa.* Colored maps and views. Three-quarters morocco. Chicago, 1875. $100-$150.

ANDREWS, Alfred. *Genealogical History of Deacon Stephen Hart and His Descendants, 1632-1875.* Portraits. Cloth. New Britain, Conn., 1875. $35.

ANDREWS, Eliza Frances. *The War-Time Journal of a Georgia Girl, 1864-65.* 16 plates. Cloth. New York, 1908. First edition. $35.

ANDREWS, Jane. *Ten Boys Who Lived on the Road from Long Ago to Now.* Illustrated by Charles Copeland. Pictorial cloth. Boston, 1886. First edition. $40. London, 1886. Pictorial red cloth. First English edition. $50.

ANDREWS, William Loring. *An Essay on the Portraiture of the American Revolutionary War.* Green morocco. New York, 1896. First edition. One of 185. $35-$50. Spine faded, $25.

ANDREWS, William Loring. *A Choice Collection of Books from the Aldine Presses.* Wrappers. New York, 1885. First edition. One of 50. $35-$50. Author's first book.

ANGEL in the House (The). Cloth, paper label. London, 1854. (By Coventry Patmore.) First edition. $50-$75. London, 1863. 2 vols., cloth. $35-$50.

ANNE of Geierstein; or, The Maiden of the Mist. 3 vols., boards, paper labels. Edinburgh, 1829. (By Sir Walter Scott.) First edition. $75-$125.

ANNUAL Anthology (The). 2 vols., old mottled calf. Bristol, England, 1799 and 1800. First editions. With leaf C3 (page 37) of Vol. 2 uncanceled, printing the uncorrected version of line 3, stanza X, of Robert Southey's "Battle of Blenheim." $95.

ANNUAL Review: History of St. Louis, etc. Folding map. 47 pp., wrappers. St. Louis, 1854. $50-$75. Covers frayed, $25.

ANSTEY, F. *Vice Versa: or a Lesson to Fathers.* Cloth. London, 1882. (By Thomas Anstey Guthrie.) First edition. $75.

ANTHOLOGY of Younger Poets (An). Boards and linen. Philadelphia, 1932. First edition. One of 500. $30-$50. Trade edition: Boards. $10-$15. (Note: Contains five poems by William Faulkner.)

ANTIDOTE (An) to the Miseries of Human Life, in the History of the Widow Placid and Her Daughter Rachel. Marbled boards, leather spine. New Haven, 1809. (By Harriet Corp.) Third (first American) edition. $65.

ANTI-TEXASS Legion (The): Protest of Some Free Men, States, and Presses Against the Texass Rebellion. 72 pp., wrappers. New York, 1844. $50.

ANTIQUARY (The). 3 vols., boards. Edinburgh, 1816. (By Sir Walter Scott.) First edition, with pages 27-30 of Vol. 1 uncanceled. $100-$150.

ANTONINUS, Brother. *Novum Psalterium Pii XII.* Folio, cloth. Los Angeles, 1955. (By William Everson.) One of 20. $175.

APOCRYPHA (The). Authorized version. Full-page woodcuts by Stephen Gooden, Eric Jones, etc. Folio, black vellum. London, 1929. Cresset Press. One of 30 on handmade paper with an extra set of illustrations signed by the artists. Boxed. $400-$500. Another issue: Boards. One of 450. Boxed. $75-$100.

APPEAL by the Convention of Michigan . . . in Relation to the Boundary Question Between Michigan and Ohio. 176 pp., stitched. Detroit, 1835. $375 (A, 1967). (Note: Listed by a New York dealer a few years before at $75.)

APPEAL to the American People (An): Being an Account of the Persecutions of the Church of Latter Day Saints. 60 pp., wrappers. Cincinnati, 1840. Second edition. $375 (A, 1968). (Note: Listed by a New York dealer a few years before at $250.)

APPERLEY, C. J. See Nimrod. Also see *Memoirs of the Life of the Late John Mytton, Esq.*

APPLEGATE, Jesse. *A Day with the Cow Column in 1843.* Pictorial cloth. Chicago, 1934. Caxton Club. One of 300. $40-$50. Another edition: No place (Portland), 1952. One of 225. $45-$60. (Note: These are reprint editions of Applegate's *Recollections of My Boyhood;* see next entry.)

APPLEGATE, Jesse. *Recollections of My Boyhood.* 99 pp., pictorial wrappers. Roseburg, Ore., 1914. First edition. $200.

APPOLLONIUS RHODIUS. *Argonautica: Jason and the Quest for the Golden Fleece.* Illustrated. Cloth. New York, 1958. Limited Editions Club. Boxed. $25-$35.

APULEIUS, Lucius. *The XI Bookes of the Golden Asse.* Translated by William Adlington. Printed on handmade paper in an Italian semi-gothic type, initial letters in red and blue. Folio, decorated green boards, linen spine. Chelsea (London), 1924. Ashendene Press. One of 162. Boxed. $300-$400. Another issue: One of 3 on Japan paper (only one offered for sale). Morocco. $500 and up.

ARGYLE, Archie. *Cupid's Album.* Cloth. New York, 1866. (By Annie Argyle.) First edition. $45. Also, $25 (A, 1963).

ARIKARA Campaign. Documents Accompanying the Message of the President . . Relative to Hostilities of the Arickaree Indians. Folding tables. Unbound. Washington, 1832. First edition. $25-$30.

ARISTOPHANES. *Lysistrata.* 8 plates by Aubrey Beardsley. Boards. London, 1896. One of 100. $300-$400. London, no date (1926). Translated by Jack Lindsay. Illustrated by Norman Lindsay. Half morocco. One of 725 signed by the artist. $75-$100. New York, 1934. Limited Editions Club. Translated by Gilbert Seldes. Illustrated by Pablo Picasso. Boards. Boxed. $600-$750, possibly more. (Note: There is sometimes offered with this book a set of 6 proofs of the original Picasso etchings for the edition, each signed by Picasso. There were 150 issued in cloth portfolios. $1,250-$1,500.)

ARISTOTLE. *Politics and Poetics.* Illustrated by Leonard Baskin. Buckram. No place (New York), 1964. Limited Editions Club. Boxed. $75.

ARLEN, Michael. *The Green Hat.* Cloth. London, no date (1924). First edition. In dust jacket. $25. New York, 1925. (Acting version.) Boards. One of 175 signed. $75-$100. (Note: The typography is by Bruce Rogers.)

ARLEN, Michael. *May Fair.* Cloth. London, no date (1925). First edition. In dust jacket. $25.

ARMES, George A. *Ups and Downs of an Army Officer.* Illustrated. Pictorial cloth. Washington, 1900. First edition. $25-$35.

ARMORIAL Bindings from the Libraries of the Rulers of France. 41 lithograph plates in color, with text. Folio, half red morocco, gilt. London, 1903. $55.

ARMOUR, Samuel. *History of Orange County, California.* Illustrated. Cloth. Los Angeles, 1921. $40-$60.

ARMSMEAR: The Home, The Arm and the Armory of Col. Samuel Colt: A Memorial. Plates, map. Cloth. New York, 1866. First edition. Inscribed by Mrs. Colt. $150-$250.

ARMSTRONG, A. N. *Oregon: A Brief History and Description of Oregon and Washington.* Cloth. Chicago, 1857. First edition. $100-$150.

ARMSTRONG, Moses K. *History and Resources of Dakota, Montana and Idaho.* Map. Printed wrappers. Yanktown, Dakota Territory, 1866. First edition. $2,000 and up.

ARNOLD, Henry V. *The Early History of the Devil's Lake Country.* 105 pp., printed wrappers. Larimore, N. D., 1920. First edition. $75-$100.

ARNOLD, Henry V. *The History of Old Pembina, 1780-1872.* Wrappers. Larimore, N. D., 1917. First edition. $85-$100.

ARNOLD, Matthew. See: A. (pseudonym—first entry in this list). Also see *Alaric at Rome.*

ARNOLD, Matthew. *Cromwell: A Prize Poem.* Wrappers. Oxford, 1843. First edition. $200 and up.

ARNOLD, Matthew. *Culture and Anarchy.* Cloth. London, 1869. First edition. $50-$60.

ARNOLD, Matthew. *Discourses in America.* Cloth. London, 1885. First edition. $35-$40.

ARNOLD, Matthew. *Essays in Criticism.* Cloth. London, 1888. First edition. $25-$30.

ARNOLD, Matthew. *God and the Bible.* Cloth. London, 1875. First edition. $35.

ARNOLD, Matthew. *Last Essays on Church and Religion.* Cloth. London, 1877. First edition. $25-$30.

ARNOLD, Matthew. *Merope: A Tragedy.* Cloth. London, 1858. First edition. $40-$45.

ARNOLD, Matthew. *Mixed Essays.* Cloth. London, 1879. First edition. $25-$30.

ARNOLD, Matthew. *New Poems.* Green cloth. London, 1867. First edition. $50.

ARNOLD, Matthew. *Poems.* Cloth. London, 1853. First edition. $25-$50. Also, $33.60 (A, 1967). London, 1855. (Second Series.) Cloth. First edition. $30. Boston, 1856. Cloth. $35.

AROUND the Horn in '49. See *Journal of the Hartford Union Mining and Trading Company.*

ARRANGEMENT of Places. Will Each Gentleman Kindly Take in to Dinner the Lady Seated on His Right. 12 pp., wrappers. (Program of 70th birthday dinner for Mark Twain at Delmonico's.) No place (New York), 1905. $30-$35.

ARRIGHI, Ludovico. *The Calligraphic Models of Ludovico degli Arrighi.* 64 pp., facsimile. Marbled boards and vellum. Paris, 1926. One of 300. $75.

ARRINGTON, Alfred W. See Summerfield, Charles.

ART of Domestick Happiness and Other Poems (The). By the Recluse. Mottled calf. Pittsburgh, 1817. (By Aquilla M. Bolton.) First edition, with errata leaf. $25.

ARTHUR Mervyn; or Memoirs of the Year 1793. By the Author of Wieland. 2 vols., calf. Philadelphia, 1799-1800. (By Charles Brockden Brown.) First edition. $150-$200. (Note: The 1799 volume and the Second Part are usually listed separately in catalogues and bibliographies; relative values: $100 and up for the first, $50 and up for second. For first English edition, see author entry.)

ARTHUR, T. S. *Ten Nights in a Bar-Room, and What I Saw There.* Cloth. Philadelphia, 1854. First edition, first issue, with both Lippincott and Bradley named in imprint and woodcut frontispiece by Van Ingen. $50-$75.

ARTHUR, T. S. *True Riches.* Cloth. Boston, 1852. First edition. $35.

ARTHUR, T. S. *Words for the Wise.* Cloth. Philadelphia, 1851. First edition. $30.

ARTICLES of Religion, as Established by the Bishops, the Clergy, and Laity of the Protestant Episcopal Church in the United States of America, etc. 22 pp., half morocco. New York, 1802. $60.

ARTISTS and Tradesman's Guide (The). Boards, printed label. Utica, N.Y., 1827. (By John Shephard.) First edition. $35-$50.

ASHBERY, John. *Some Trees.* Cloth. New Haven, 1956. Foreword by W. H. Auden. First edition. Dust jacket. $35-$40.

ASHENDENE Press. See *Descriptive Bibliography, etc.*

ASHLEY, Clifford W. *The Yankee Whaler.* Plates, some in color. Half cloth and boards. Boston, 1926. First edition. One of 156 signed, with original drawing. Boxed. $125 and $85. Ordinary issue: $25-$50.

ASHLEY, William H. *The West of William H. Ashley.* Edited by Dale L. Morgan. Illustrated. Pictorial buckram. Denver, 1964. One of 750. $35-$50. De luxe issue: Half calf. One of 250 signed. $100-$150.

ASHTON, Warren T. *Hatchie, the Guardian Slave.* Illustrated. Black cloth. Boston, 1853. (By William Taylor Adams.) First edition. $75-$100.

"ASK Mamma;" or, The Richest Commoner in England. 13 full-page color plates and 69 woodcuts by John Leech. 13 parts, red wrappers. London, no date (1857) and 1858. (By Robert Smith Surtees.) First edition. $150-$250. London, 1858. Pictorial cloth. First book edition. $75-$100.

ASHBEE, Henry Spencer. *An Iconography of Don Quixote, 1605-1895.* Half cloth. London, 1895. First edition. $35-$50.

ATALANTIS. Cloth. New York, 1832. (By William Gilmore Simms.) First edition. $75-$100. Also, rebound in half morocco, $35 (A, 1960).

ATHERTON, Gertrude. See Lin, Frank.

ATHERTON, Gertrude. *Black Oxen.* Cloth. New York, no date (1923). First edition. One of 250 signed. In dust jacket. $25-$35.

ATHERTON, Gertrude. *The Conqueror.* Dark red cloth, gilt top. New York, 1902. First edition, first state, with page numerals on page 546 in upper left corner. $35-$50.

ATHERTON, Gertrude. *What Dreams May Come.* Cloth. London, 1889. First English edition (of author's first book, which was issued in America under the pseudonym Frank Lin, which see). $15-$20.

ATHERTON, William. *Narrative of the Suffering & Defeat of the North-Western Army,*

Under General Winchester. Leather-backed boards, printed paper label. Frankfort, Ky., 1842. First edition. $75-$100.

ATHLETIC Sports for Boys. Printed boards. New York, no date (1865). First edition. $25.

ATLAS of Jefferson County, Ohio. Folding maps in color. 36 pp., folio, cloth. New York, 1871. Published by Beers. $35-$50.

ATLAS of New York and Vicinity. Colored maps and plans. Folio, cloth. New York, 1867. Published by Beers. $50.

ATTACHE (The); or, Sam Slick in England, (Second Series.) 2 vols., ribbed plum-colored cloth. London, 1844. (By Thomas Chandler Haliburton.) First edition, with 48 pages of ads at end of Vol. 2. Spines faded, $60.

ATTERLEY, Joseph. *A Voyage to the Moon.* Boards. New York, 1827. (By George Tucker.) First edition. $300-$400.

ATWATER, Caleb. *A History of the State of Ohio.* Calf. Cincinnati, no date (1838). First edition. $50-$60.

ATWATER, Caleb. *Mysteries of Washington City.* Boards and leather. Washington, 1844. First edition. Bookplate, $30.

ATWATER, Caleb. *Remarks Made on a Tour to Prairie du Chien; Thence to Washington City.* Boards. Columbus, Ohio, 1831. First edition. $50-$75.

AUCHINCLOSS, Louis. See Lee, Andrew.

AUDEN, W. H. See Baudelaire, Charles; Rich, Adrienne Cecile. Also see *On the Frontier*.

AUDEN, W. H. *The Age of Anxiety.* Cloth. New York, no date (1947). First edition. In dust jacket. $25-$35.

AUDEN, W. H. *Another Time.* Cloth. London, 1940. First English edition. In dust jacket. $35-$50. Proof copy, in wrappers, $45 (A, 1966).

AUDEN, W. H. *Collected Shorter Poems.* Cloth. London, no date (1966). First edition. $20. Signed copy, $30 (A, 1968).

AUDEN, W. H. *The Dance of Death.* Boards. London, 1933. First edition. In dust jacket. $50-$75. Also, $38 (1971).

AUDEN, W. H. *Epithalamion.* Wrappers. Princeton, N.J., 1939. First edition. $35-$50.

AUDEN, W. H. *For the Time Being.* Boards and cloth. New York, 1944. First edition. In dust jacket. $25-$35. Inscribed, $50. London, 1945. First English edition. In dust jacket. $25.

AUDEN, W. H. *Goodbye to the Mezzogiorno.* Text in English and Italian. Wrappers and printed band. Milan, Italy, 1958. First edition. One of 1,000. $35.

AUDEN, W. H. *Homage to Clio.* Printed wrappers. London, 1960. Advance uncorrected proof copy. $25. London, 1960. Plum-colored cloth. First published English edition. In dust jacket. $15-$20.

AUDEN, W. H. *Look, Stranger!* Cloth. London, 1936. First edition. $50-$60. (For first American edition, see Auden, *On This Island.*)

AUDEN, W. H. *Louis MacNeice: A Memorial Address.* Printed wrappers. London, 1963. First edition. $75-$100.

AUDEN, W. H. *Marginalia.* Engravings by Laurence Scott. Oblong, printed wrappers. No place, no date (Cambridge, Mass., 1966). Ibex Press. First edition. One of 105 (150?) signed by author and artist. $100-$125.

AUDEN, W. H. *Nones*. Cloth. London, no date (1952). First edition. In dust jacket. Signed copy. $35-$50.

AUDEN, W. H. *On This Island*. Brown cloth. New York, 1937. First American edition. In dust jacket. $50. (Note: The first edition of this was published in London, 1936, as *Look, Stranger!*, which see.)

AUDEN, W. H. *The Orators: An English Study*. Cloth. London, 1932. First edition. In dust jacket. $75-$100.

AUDEN, W. H. *Our Hunting Fathers*. Wrappers. London, 1935. First edition. One of 25. $400-$500.

AUDEN, W. H. *The Platonic Blow*. Printed wrappers. New York, 1965. Fuck You Press. First edition. $50-$75. (Note: Appeared earlier in *Fuck You, A Magazine of the Arts*, Vol. 8, No. 5, which was catalogued in 1970 by a rare book shop at $50.)

AUDEN, W. H. *Poem*. Wrappers. No place (New Haven, Conn.), 1933. First edition. One of 5 on Fabriano paper. (Note: I can find no sales record for this except for the copy, inscribed to T. S. Eliot and with a presentation autograph letter, signed, sold at Sotheby's in 1966 to a New York dealer for $624.)

AUDEN, W. H. *Poems*. Printed blue-green wrappers. London, no date (1930). First edition. $150-$250. Author's first published book. New York, no date (1934). First American edition. In dust jacket. $50-$65. (Note: In 1928 Stephen Spender, the poet's friend, hand-printed "about 45" copies of a paperbound *Poems*. A copy inscribed to John Hayward was sold at Sotheby's in 1966 to a New York dealer for $1,560.)

AUDEN, W. H. *Selected Poems*. Cloth. London, 1938. First edition. In dust jacket. $50-$75.

AUDEN, W. H. *Sonnet*. Wrappers. London, 1935. First edition. One of 5 on Normandie paper. $400-$600.

AUDEN, W. H. *Spain*. Wrappers. London, no date (1937). First edition. $25-$35.

AUDEN, W. H. *Three Songs for St. Cecelia's Day*. Wrappers. No place (New York), 1941. First edition. $35.

AUDEN, W. H., and Isherwood, Christopher. *The Ascent of F6*. Cloth. London, 1936. First edition. In dust jacket. $35-$50.

AUDEN, W. H., and Isherwood, Christopher. *The Dog Beneath the Skin, or, Where Is Francis?* Cloth. London, no date (1935). First edition. In dust jacket. $35. New York, 1935. Cloth. First American edition. In dust jacket. $12.50-$15.

AUDEN, W. H., and Isherwood, Christopher. *A Melodrama in Three Acts*. Cloth. London, 1938. First edition, first issue, with first leaf and final two leaves blank. In dust jacket. $60-$80. Lacking jacket, $24. Also, inscribed, $110 (A, 1968).

AUDEN, W. H., and MacNeice, Louis. *Letters from Iceland*. Plates, folding map. Green cloth. London, 1937. First edition. In dust jacket. $35. Lacking jacket, signed by Auden, $50.

AUDUBON, John James. *The Birds of America from Original Drawings*. 435 double elephant folio hand-colored plates without text. 87 parts in wrappers, or 4 leatherbound double elephant folio volumes. London, 1827-38. First edition. (So rare in original parts it is pointless to speculate on what a fine and complete set might bring in the collector's market today; virtually unobtainable in complete form, fewer than 200 sets having been produced originally and most of these having been bound up or broken up, sold, or deposited in whole or in part in public or private libraries.) A new world record price for the 4 leatherbound volumes was established in November, 1969, with the sale at auction in London of the Baroness Burdett-Coutts copy for $216,000. The purchase was made by the Chicago bookseller Kenneth Nebenzahl for an unidentified Chicagoan. Another, rebound in modern cloth, 113 plates in first state, others repaired, foxed or creased, one loose, etc., $60,000 (A, 1966). Vol. 1 only, old calf, defective and repaired, with 100 plates, $14,400 at retail. Also, $11,480 (A, 1962). (A 15-page prospectus for the work, dated London, 1851, brought $110 at auction in 1956.) New York, 1840-44. 500 colored plates. 100 parts in wrappers, or 7 vols., octavo, full or half morocco; also half calf. First American and first octavo edition; also, first edition with all 500 plates and first edition with plates and text together (under the title *The Birds of America from Drawings Made in the United States and Their Territories)*; a reissue in smaller size of the plates from the original edition, with text, including changes, from the Edinburgh first edition of Audubon's *Ornithological Biography,* which see. Complete sets in wrappers are extremely rare, one such having brought $900 at auction in 1944. Another issue: New York and Philadelphia, no date(1840-41). First 42 parts (of 100) with 215 (of 500) colored plates. In wrappers, as issued. Worn, $170 (A, 1966). 7 vols., in bindings: $3,500 (A, 1970); $3,600 and $2,300 (A, 1969); $1,900 (A, 1968); some hinges cracked, $1,050 and $700 (A, 1965). New York, 1855. Third octavo edition. $1,150 at retail. New York, 1856. 7 vols., contemporary morocco. First edition issued with colored backgrounds for the plates. $616 (A, 1961). New York, 1858-60. Partial reissue of the folio edition by George R. Lockwood, publisher. 14 numbers of 10 plates each, plus supplement of 10 plates (150 in all). (All that were published.) Bound together in boards and morocco, lacking title page, spine torn, covers detached, "Wild Turkey" plate soiled and lacking portions of margin (accompanied by text from the 1870 edition), $10,000 (A, 1969). Another set of these plates, $2,500 (A, 1947). New York, 1861. 7 vols. in 5, contemporary half calf. Worn, $200 (A, 1966). New York, no date (1870). 8 vols., text and plates, half morocco. George R. Lockwood, publisher. Fine sets, $750 and up. New York, 1871. 8 vols. $750-$1,000 at retail. New York, 1937. Edited by William Vogt. 500 plates in color. One-volume edition. Buckram. Limited issue on all-rag paper. Boxed. $100-$125. Trade edition: Buckram. $75-$100.

AUDUBON, John James. *Delineations of American Scenery and Character.* Cloth. New York, 1926. First edition. One of 42 large paper copies. $35-$50. Trade edition, same date: $25. (500 copies with London imprint.)

AUDUBON, John James. *Journal of John James Audubon, Made During His Trip to New Orleans in 1820-21.* Edited by Howard Corning. 2 plates. Boards and cloth. Boston, 1929. One of 250. $150-$200. Also, $110 (A, 1967). (Note: This and the volume following, issued as a set by the Club of Odd Volumes, are most often offered together in the $200-$250 range. Also, $120 at auction, 1966.)

AUDUBON, John James. *Journal of John James Audubon, Made While Obtaining Subscriptions to His "Birds of America," 1840-1843.* Edited by Howard Corning. Plate. Boston, 1929. One of 250. $150-$200. (See note in preceding entry.)

AUDUBON, John James. *Ornithological Biography; or, An Account of the Habits of the Birds of the United States of America.* 5 vols., calf. Edinburgh, 1831-49 (actually 1839). First edition of the text volume to accompany the double elephant folios of *The Birds of America.* $100-$200.

AUDUBON, John James. *The Quadrupeds of North America.* See Audubon and Bachman, *The Viviparous Quadrupeds, etc.*

AUDUBON, John James. *A Synopsis of the Birds of America.* Cloth, paper label. Edinburgh, 1839. First edition. $100-$150. Rebound, $60.

AUDUBON, John James, and Bachman, John. *The Viviparous Quadrupeds of North America.* 150 colored plates without text. 30 parts in wrappers, or 3 vols. (Vol. 1, 1845; Vol. 2, 1846; Vol. 3, 1848), folio, half morocco. New York, 1845-48. (Text issued, New York, 1846-53. 31 parts in wrappers or 3 vols., cloth, dated 1846, 1851, and 1853, the 3 vols. sometimes bound in 2. A 93-page supplement, with 6 colored plates, was issued in 1854.) First edition (of the plates alone). 3 vols., folio, rebound in modern cloth, with 149 of the 150 plates, one repaired, $3,500 (A, 1966). (Note: The recent sharp rise of value in the Audubon animal plates is reflected in this sale, especially in comparison with the following.) First edition complete (consisting of the 3 plate volumes, the 3 text volumes, and the supplement). $1,456 (A, 1964); $850 (A, 1955)—for a set with the first text volume inscribed by Audubon. New York, 1849-54. Reissue under the title *The Quadrupeds of North America.* 155 colored plates (including all except one from the supplement to the original edition). 31 parts in wrappers, or 3 vols., morocco or half

morocco, dated 1849, 1851, and 1854. First octavo edition. Wrappers: $1,000 and up.
Also, $364 (A, 1961); $500 (A, 1956); spine chipped, $250 (A, 1964). In book form:
$500 and up. Also, $160 (A, 1966); $168 (A, 1965); worn, $90, and $190 (A, 1964);
$130 (A, 1961). New York, 1854. 3 vols., contemporary bindings (morocco, half
morocco, etc.). $500-$600. Also, binding broken, $400 (A, 1968). (Mixed sets from the
octavo and later editions are sometimes offered in the $250-$500 retail range.)

AUDUBON, John Woodhouse. *Audubon's Western Journal, 1849-50.* Edited by Maria R.
Audubon. Folding map, 6 plates. Cloth. Cleveland, 1906. Reprint of Audubon's
extremely rare and virtually unobtainable *Illustrated Notes of an Expedition Through
Mexico and California.* $50-$75.

AUDUBON, John Woodhouse. *The Drawings of John Woodhouse Audubon, Illustrating His
Adventures Through Mexico and California.* 34 full-page illustrations, including 2 in
color. Folio, boards and cloth. San Francisco, 1957. Grabhorn printing. One of 400.
$75-$100.

AUDUBON, Maria R. *Audubon and His Journals.* Edited by Elliot Coues. Plates. 2 vols.,
cloth. New York, 1897. First edition. $75-$100.

AUDSLEY, George Ashdown. *The Art of Organ-Building.* Illustrated. 2 vols., cloth. New
York, 1905. $150-$200.

AUDSLEY, George Ashdown. *The Ornamental Arts of Japan.* 70 plates in gold and colors,
31 in monochrome, loose in 5 cloth portfolios. 2 vols., folio. New York, 1882-84.
Artist's proofs edition. One of 50 signed. $175-$200. Another issue: 2 vols., morocco.
(Not signed.) $100. New York, 1883-84. Plates loose in 4 folders. One of 500 signed.
$100. New York, 1883-85. 2 vols. in 4 folders. One of 60. $75.

AUDSLEY, George Ashdown, and Bowes, J. L. *The Keramic Art of Japan.* 63 plates, 42 in
gold and colors; 4 plates of potters' marks, other illustrations. Morocco and cloth.
Liverpool, 1875. First edition. $80-$100. London, 1881. Cloth. $25-$50.

AUSCHER, Ernest Simon. *A History and Description of French Porcelain.* 24 plates in
color. Morocco. London, 1905. First edition, limited. $40-$50.

AUSTEN, Jane. See *Elizabeth Bennet; Emma; Mansfield Park; Northanger Abbey; Pride and
Prejudice; Sense and Sensibility.*

AUSTIN, Edward S. *The Housekeepers' Manual.* Wrappers. Chicago, 1869. First edition.
$50.

AUSTIN, Jane G. *Standish of Standish.* Tan cloth. Boston, 1889. First edition. $35. (Note:
Copies of the same date in gray-green cloth are of a later issue.)

AUSTIN, Mary. *The Land of Little Rain.* Illustrated. Pictorial cloth. Boston, 1903. First
edition. $50-$75. Author's first book.

AUSTIN, Mary. *What the Mexican Conference Really Means.* 14 pp., wrappers. New York,
no date (1915). First edition. $35.

AUSTIN, Mary, and Adams, Ansel. *Taos Pueblo.* Photographs by Adams and text by Mrs.
Austin. Folio, cloth, pigskin spine. San Francisco, 1930. Grabhorn printing. First
edition. One of 107 (Johnson says 108) signed by author and illustrator. $350-$500.

AUSTIN, Mary, and Martin, Ann. *Suffrage and Government.* 14 pp., printed wrappers. New
York, 1914. $25.

AUSTIN, Stephen F. *Esposicion al Publico sobre los Asuntos de Tejas.* 32 pp., stitched.
Mexico, 1835. First edition, with page 29 misnumbered 31. Bound in full red morocco,
$1,250. Also, in modern morocco, $900 (A, 1964).

*AUTHENTIC Narrative of the Seminole War (An), and of the Miraculous Escape of Mrs.
Mary Godfrey, and Her Four Female Children.* Folding frontispiece in color. 24 pp.,
plain wrappers. Providence, R.I., 1836. $400 and up. New York, 1836. $300-$400.

AUTHORS Take Sides on the Spanish War. Wrappers. London, no date (1937). Left Review. $150-$200. Also, $96 (A, 1970).

AUTHORSHIP: A Tale. Boards and cloth. Boston, 1930. (By John Neal.) First edition. $75-$100.

AUTOCRAT of the Breakfast Table (The). Illustrated. Cloth. Boston, 1858. (By Oliver Wendell Holmes.) First edition, first issue, with engraved half title, with period after word "Company" in imprint, and with left end paper at back headed "Poetry and the Drama" and right "School Books." (An unsolved controversy still exists over whether the first binding bore a five-ring or four-ring decoration on the spine.) In presumed second binding (Blanck is not certain) with five rings on spine, $175 (A, 1971), $270 (A, 1962). Four-ring binding, $50-$150 at retail. Boston, 1859. Illustrated. Cloth. Large paper edition. $150-$200. New York, 1955. Limited Editions Club. Cloth. Boxed. $35.

AVIRETT, James B. *The Memoirs of Gen. Turner Ashby and His Compeers.* Portrait. Cloth. Baltimore, 1867. First edition. $75.

AYESHA, The Maid of Kars. By the Author of "Zohrab," etc. 3 vols., boards. London, 1834. (By James Morier.) First edition. $100-$150.

B

B., A. *The Six Letters of A. B. on the Differences Between Great Britain and the United States of America.* Wrappers. London, 1807. First edition. $50.

B., E. B. *Sonnets.* By E. B. B. 47 pp., without wrappers. Reading, England, 1847 (actually printed about 1883-90). (By Elizabeth Barrett Browning.) Thomas J. Wise's forgery—the fake first edition of "Sonnets from the Portuguese," which actually appeared first in the second edition of *Poems,* 1850, which see under author entry; for later editions, see entry for *Sonnets from the Portuguese* under author's name. The Wise forgery, bound in morocco, sold for a record (at the time) $1,250 at auction in 1930. Following its exposure as a fake in 1934, the value declined, but in 1967 at a sale in London featuring Wise forgeries a New York City dealer paid $1,680 at auction for a copy in morocco.

B., F. *The Kasidah of Haji Abdu El-Yezdi.* Translated and annotated by his friend and pupil, F. B. (Sir Richard Burton is translator). Yellow wrappers. London, no date (1800). First edition, first issue, without Quaritch imprint. $500-$750.

B., H. *The Bad Child's Book of Beasts.* Pictorial boards. Oxford, no date (1896). First edition. $50.

B., J. K. *The Lorgnette.* By J, K, B Illustrated. Oblong, cloth. New York, no date (1886). (By John Kendrick Bangs.) First edition. $50. Author's first book. (Note: A cartoon book for which Bangs did the captions.)

BABB, James T. *A Bibliography of the Writings of William McFee.* Cloth. Garden City, 1931. First edition. One of 360 signed. Boxed. $35.

BABBITT, E. D. *The Principles of Light and Color.* Illustrated. Cloth. New York, 1878. Second edition. $100. East Orange, N.J., no date (1896). Cloth. $50-$75.

BABBITT, E. L. *The Allegheny Pilot.* 16 maps. 64 pp., wrappers. Freeport, Pa., 1855. First edition. $100. Rebound in three-quarters morocco, original covers bound in, $65.

BACA, Manuel Cabeza de. *Vincente Silva and His 40 Bandits.* Translated by Lane Kauffmann. Illustrated. Boards and cloth. Washington, 1947. First edition. One of 300 signed. $35-$50. Another issue: One of 25 bound in full goatskin, signed. $75-$100.

BACHELLER, Irving. *Eben Holden.* Cloth. Boston, no date (1900). First edition, first state, with line 13 on page 400 reading "go to fur," and with pine cones on spine with rounded top. $25-$35. (Later issue reads "go tew fur" and has flat-topped cones.)

BACHELLER, Irving. *The Story of a Passion.* Cloth. No place, no date (East Aurora, N.Y., 1899). One of 50. $25.

BACON, Sir Francis. *Bacon's Essays.* Edited by Sydney Humphries. Portrait and woodcut initial letters. Vellum. London, 1912. One of 30. $50-$60.

BACON, Francis. *The Essayes or Counsels Civill and Morall.* Folio, vellum. London, 1928. Shakespeare Head Press. $150. London, 1927 (or 1928). Cresset Press. Vellum. One of 250. $150-$200.

BACON, Francis. *Essays Moral, Economical and Political.* Boards, paper label. Boston, 1807. First American edition. $50-$75.

BAGE, Robert. See *Hermsprong; Man as He Is.*

BAHR, Jerome. *All Good Americans.* Preface by Ernest Hemingway. Cloth. New York, 1937. First edition. In dust jacket. $30-$40.

BAILEY, Washington. *A Trip to California in 1853.* Portrait. Printed wrappers. No place (LeRoy, Ill.), 1915. First edition, with errata slip. $150-$200.

BAILY, Francis. *Journal of a Tour in Unsettled Parts of North America in 1796 & 1797.* Decorated cloth. London, 1856. First edition. $300-$400. (Note: In the 1950's it was a $75-$100 book at retail in American dealer catalogues.)

BAINBRIDGE, George C. *The Fly-Fisher's Guide.* Colored frontispiece and 7 colored plates. Half leather. Liverpool, 1816. First edition. $100-$150. Another issue: Morocco. One of 12. $400-$500.

BAIRD, Spencer F.; Brewer, T. M.; and Ridgway, R. *The Water Birds of North America.* Hand-colored illustrations. 2 vols., cloth. Boston, 1884. First edition. $250-$300.

BAKER, B. *The Torn Book.* 24 color plates. Pictorial boards. New York, 1913. First edition. $37.50.

BAKER, Charles H. Collins, and Constable, W. G. *English Painting of the Sixteenth and Seventeenth Centuries.* 82 collotype plates. Half leather. London, 1930. $50-$75.

BAKER, C. H. Collins. *Lely and the Stuart Portrait Painters.* 240 reproductions, some in color. 2 vols., buckram. London, 1912. One of 375. $250-$350. Another issue: Vellum. One of 30, with an extra set of plates. $350-$500.

BAKER, D. W. C. (compiler). *A Texas Scrap-Book.* Cloth. New York, no date (1875). First edition. $75-$100.

BAKER, George P. *The Pilgrim Spirit: A Pageant . . . Landing of the Pilgrims.* Cloth. Boston, 1921. First edition, first issue, with the name "Brewster" on page 74. (Some with errata slip.) $35-$50. (Note: Contains contributions by Robert Frost and Edwin Arlington Robinson.)

BAKER, Hozial H. *Overland Journey to Carson Valley, Utah.* Woodcut frontispiece and other illustrations. 38 pp., yellow printed wrappers. Seneca Falls, N.Y., 1861. First edition. $2,500 and up. Also, rebacked, $2,250 (A, 1968).

BALDWIN, James. *A Story of the Golden Age.* Illustrated by Howard Pyle. Decorated brown cloth. New York, 1887. First edition. $60-$80.

BALDWIN, James. *The Story of Siegfried.* Illustrated by Howard Pyle. Pictorial cloth. New York, 1882. First edition. $50-$60.

BALDWIN, James. *Giovanni's Room.* Boards and cloth. New York, 1956. First edition. In dust jacket. $25-$35.

BALDWIN, James. *Go Tell It on the Mountain.* Cloth. New York, 1953. First edition. In dust jacket. $65-$75. Author's first book.

BALDWIN, Joseph G. *The Flush Times of Alabama and Mississippi.* Blue cloth. New York, 1853. First edition. $100-$150. Author's first book.

BALLADS and Songs of Love. Blue boards, paper label. No place, no date (Munich, 1930). Bremer Press. One of 280. Boxed. $100.

BALLOU, Hosea. *A Candid Review of a Pamphlet Entitled "A Candid Reply."* Calf. Portsmouth, N.H., no date (1809). First edition. $35-$40.

BALLOU, Hosea. *Treatise on Atonement.* Calf. Randolph, Vt., 1805. First edition. $25-$30.

BALME, J. R. *American States, Churches and Slavery.* Cloth. London, 1863. First edition. $25.

BALWHIDDER, The Rev. Micah. *Annals of the Parish; or The Chronicle of Dalmailing.* Boards, printed label. Edinburgh, 1821. (By John Galt.) First edition. $150-$200.

BANCROFT, George. *Poems.* Tan boards. Cambridge, Mass., 1823. First edition. $35-$50.

BANDELIER, Adolph F. A. *The Gilded Man.* Cloth. New York, 1893. First edition. $35-$50.

BANDINI, Joseph. *A Description of California in 1828.* Illustrated. Boards and cloth. Berkeley, Calif., 1951. One of 400. $25.

BANGS, John Kendrick. See B., J. K.

BANGS, John Kendrick. *A House-Boat on the Styx.* Illustrated. Cloth. New York, 1896. First edition. In dust jacket. $25-$30.

BANGS, John Kendrick. *Mr. Munchausen.* Cloth. Boston, 1901. First edition, first state, with Small, Maynard copyright. In dust jacket. $25.

BARBE-MARBOIS, François. *The History of Louisiana, Particularly the Cession of that Colony to the U.S.A.* Cloth. Philadelphia, 1830. First American edition. $100-$125.

BARHAM, Richard Harris. See Ingoldsby, Thomas.

BARING, Alexander. *An Inquiry into the Causes and Consequences of the Orders in Council; and An Examination of the Conduct of Great Britain Towards the Neutral Commerce of America.* Wrappers. London, 1808. First edition. $35-$50. Signed, $65.

BARING, Maurice. *Algae.* Wrappers, paper label. London, 1928. One of 100 signed. In dust jacket. Boxed. $30-$35.

BARKER, Eugene C. *The Life of Stephen F. Austin.* 2 maps, plan, 6 portraits. Boards and vellum. Nashville, 1925. First edition. One of 250 signed. $100. Trade edition: $30-$40.

BARKER, George. *Poems.* Cloth. London, no date (1935). First edition. In dust jacket. $30-$35.

BARKER, Matthew Henry. *The Old Sailor's Jolly Boat.* 24 full-page engravings by George and Robert Cruikshank. London, 1844. Rebound in half calf, $50.

BARLOW, Joel. *The Columbiad: A Poem.* Portrait and 11 plates. Contemporary or later morocco. Philadelphia, 1807. (New edition of *The Vision of Columbus,* which see in entry below.) $75-$100.

BARLOW, Joel. *Joel Barlow to His Fellow Citizens of the United States.* (Caption title.) Wrappers. No place, no date (Philadelphia, 1801). First American edition. $30-$35.

BARLOW, Joel. *The Vision of Columbus: A Poem in Nine Books.* Sheep. Hartford, 1787. First edition. $75-$100. Second edition. $50. Baltimore, 1814. Sheep. Rebacked, $30 (A, 1968). (Reprinted as *The Columbiad,* which see in entry above.)

BARNARD, George N. *Photographic View of Sherman's Campaign.* 61 gold-toned albumen prints, mounted, with lithographic captions. Oblong folio, morocco. New York, no date (1866). First edition, $5,000 and up. Also, $5,400 (A, 1970). (Note: In 1968 a copy had sold at auction for only $650. The sudden increase in value resulted from intense competition for photographic books.)

BARNES, Charles Merritt. *Combats and Conquest of Immortal Heroes.* Full morocco. San Antonio, 1910. First edition. $35-$50.

BARNES, David M. *The Draft Riots in New York, July, 1863.* 117 pp., wrappers, or cloth. New York, 1863. First edition. Wrappers: $100-$125. Cloth: $75-$100.

BARNES, Djuna. See *Ladies Almanack.*

BARNES, Djuna. *A Book.* 6 portraits. Black boards, paper label. New York, no date (1923). First edition. In dust jacket. $50-$60.

BARNES, Djuna. *The Book of Repulsive Women.* Illustrated. Wrappers. New York, 1915. First edition. $90-$120. Author's first book. New York, 1948. Stiff wrappers. One of 1,000. $25.

BARNES, Djuna. *A Night Among the Horses.* Boards, cloth spine. New York, 1929. First edition. In dust jacket. $40-$50.

BARNES, Djuna. *Nightwood.* Introduction by T. S. Eliot. Cloth. New York, no date (1937). First American edition. In dust jacket. $25-$35.

BARNES, Djuna. *Ryder.* New York, 1928. Cloth. First edition. In dust jacket. $20-$30.

BARNES, Will C. *Apaches and Longhorns.* Edited by Frank C. Lockwood. Illustrated. Cloth. Los Angeles, 1941. First edition. In dust jacket. $35-$50.

BARNEY, James M. *Tales of Apache Warfare.* 45 pp., wrappers. No place (Phoenix), 1933. $25.

BARNFIELD, Richard. *Complete Poems.* Edited by Alexander B. Grosart. Frontispiece, 7 facsimiles of title pages. Half morocco. London, 1876. Roxburghe Club. $125-$150.

BARNUM, H. L. *The Spy Unmasked; or, Memoirs of Enoch Crosby.* Map, 5 plates. Boards. New York, 1828. First edition. $50-$60. Foxed, stained, rubbed, $25.

BARREIRO, Antonio. *Ojeada sobre Nuevo-Mexico.* Illustrated, 3 tables. Marbled wrappers. Puebla, Mexico, 1832. First edition. $350, $450, and $500.

BARRETT, Elizabeth, and Browning, Robert. *Two Poems.* Printed wrappers. London, 1854. (By Elizabeth Barrett Browning, etc.) First edition. $50-$75.

BARRETT, Elizabeth B. *The Seraphim, and Other Poems.* Purple cloth. London, 1838. (By Elizabeth Barrett Browning.) First edition. $100-$125.

BARRETT, Elizabeth Barrett. *Poems.* 2 vols., dark green cloth, uncut. London, 1844. (By Elizabeth Barrett Browning.) First edition, with ads in Vol. 1 dated June 1. $400-$600. Later, 1844, no ads, $150-$300. London, 1850. 2 vols., cloth. Second edition. $200-$250. London, 1856. 3 vols., cloth. $250-$350. London, 1873. 5 vols., cloth. $75-$100. (See entry under Browning, Elizabeth Barrett.)

BARRETT, Ellen C. *Baja California, 1535-1956: A Bibliography.* Blue cloth. Los Angeles, 1957. First edition. One of 500. $35-$50.

BARRETT, Francis. *The Magus, or Celestial Intelligencer.* Illustrated. Boards and leather. London, 1801. First edition. $77.50 and $125.

BARRIE, Sir James M. See *The Allahakbarrie Book of Broadway Cricket for 1899.*

BARRIE, Sir James M. *The Admirable Crichton.* Illustrated by Hugh Thomson. Boards and cloth. London, no date (1914). $35-$50. Another issue: Vellum with ties. De Luxe edition, signed. $75-$100.

BARRIE, Sir James M. *Auld Licht Idylls.* Blue buckram. London, 1888. First edition, first issue, with black end papers. $35-$50. London, 1895. Illustrated by William Hole. Cloth. One of 550 signed. $50-$75.

BARRIE, Sir James M. *Better Dead.* Pictorial glazed yellow (or buff) wrappers. London, 1888 (actually 1887). First edition. $100-$150. Rebacked, $85. Author's first book.

BARRIE, Sir James M. *Courage: The Rectorial Address Delivered at St. Andrews University, May 3rd, 1922.* Cream cloth, gilt top. London, no date (1922). First edition. Limited issue on large paper. $25-$35. Also, inscribed, $27 (A, 1953), with ALS, $50 (A, 1957); with ALS about the speech, $90 (A, 1962).

BARRIE, Sir James M. *An Edinburgh Eleven.* Wrappers. London, 1889. First edition, first issue, with "Galvin Ogilvy" on front cover and "J. M. Barrie" on title page. $25-$35. Later issue, same date: Gray cloth. $10-$15.

BARRIE, Sir James M. *The Greenwood Hat: Being a Memoir of James Anon, 1885-1887.* 10 plates. Green leather, gilt top. London, 1930. First edition. One of 50. Boxed. $40-$50. With presentation inscriptions from Barrie, $70 and $80. Also, presentation copy inscribed, $50.40 (A, 1964).

BARRIE, Sir James M. *"The Ladies' Shakespeare."* 7 pp., dark-red printed wrappers. London, 1925. First edition. One of 25. $35-$50.

BARRIE, Sir James M. *The Little Minister.* 3 vols., brown cloth. London, 1891. First edition, first issue, with 16 pages of ads in Vol. 1 dated "5G. 9.91." $500-$750. Another set, unopened, with Barrie's autograph on front flyleaf of Vol. 1. $1,250. Also, "as new," $725 (A, 1957); "unopened," outer hinges rubbed, $300 (A, 1962); rebound, $130 (A, 1967). New York, no date (1891). Lovell, Coryell & Co. Wrappers. First American edition. $35-$50.

BARRIE, Sir James M. *The Little White Bird.* Cloth. London, 1902. First edition. In dust jacket. $35.

BARRIE, Sir James M. *My Lady Nicotine.* Blue buckram. London, 1890. First edition, first issue, with 6 pages of ads at back. $35-$50. Inscribed by the author, $90.

BARRIE, Sir James M. *Peter and Wendy.* Illustrated. Green cloth. London, 1911. First edition. $100-$125.

BARRIE, Sir James M. *Peter Pan in Kensington Gardens.* Illustrated in color and black and white by Arthur Rackham. Vellum. London, 1906. First edition. One of 500 signed by Rackham. $200-$300. Trade edition: Cloth. $75-$100. Inscribed by Rackham and with original sketch by him, $110 (A, 1962) and $79.60 (A, 1964). Paris, 1907. Text in French. Vellum. One of 20 on Japan paper. $100-$150. Also, $35 (A, 1961). Another issue: One of 270. $50-$75. Also, $16 (A, 1959). New York, 1910. $15-$20. London, no date (1912). Half blue morocco. $30-$40.

BARRIE, Sir James M. *Quality Street.* Illustrated by Hugh Thomson. Vellum with silk ties. London, no date (1901). First edition. One of 1,000. $35-$50.

BARRIE, Sir James M. *A Tillyloss Scandal.* Wrappers. New York, no date (1893). First edition, first issue, with publisher's address as "43, 45, 47 East 10th Street." $60-$100.

BARRIE, Sir James M. *Walker London.* Frontispiece. Green printed wrappers. New York, 1907. First edition. $35-$50.

BARRIE, Sir James M. *When a Man's Single: A Tale of Literary Life.* Blue buckram, gilt top. London, 1888. First edition, with ads at back. $40-$65. Presentation copy, signed, $100.

BARRIE, Sir James M. *A Window in Thrums.* Cloth. London, 1889. First edition. With 6 pages of ads at back. $35-$50. Also, inscribed by the author, $40 (A, 1952); with ALS, $53.20 (A, 1959). London, 1892. Illustrated by William Hole. Blue cloth. One of 50 signed. $75-$100. Another issue: One of 500. $25-$35.

BARROW, John. *A Chronological History of Voyages into the Arctic Regions.* Illustrated, folding map. Boards and cloth. London, 1818. First edition. $100-$150. Worn, $30. Also, old morocco, $98 (A, 1965).

BARROW, John. *A Voyage to Cochinchina, 1792-1793.* Folding map, 20 colored aquatint plates. Contemporary calf. London, 1806. First edition. $150-$250. Rebacked, $72 and $100.

BARRY, T. A., and Patten, B. A. *Men and Memories of San Francisco, in the "Spring of '50."* 2 plates. Flexible cloth. San Francisco, 1873. First edition. $25.

BARTH, John. *The End of the Road.* Cloth. New York, 1958. First edition. In dust jacket. $50-$60.

BARTH, John. *The Floating Opera.* Cloth. New York, no date (1956). First edition. In dust jacket. $50-$75.

BARTH, John. *Giles Goat-Boy.* Cloth. Garden City, 1966. First edition. One of 250 signed. Boxed. $45-$60.

BARTH, John. *Lost in the Fun House.* Cloth. Garden City, 1968. First edition. One of 250 signed. Boxed. $35-$40.

BARTH, John. *The Sot-Weed Factor.* Cloth. New York, 1960. First edition. In dust jacket. $35-$50.

BARTHELME, Donald. *Come Back, Dr. Caligari.* Cloth. Boston, no date (1964). First edition. In dust jacket. $25-$30.

BARTLETT, J. S., M.D. *The Physician's Pocket Synopsis.* Leather. Boston, 1822. First edition. $35.

BARTLETT, John. See *A Collection of Familiar Quotations.*

BARTLETT, John Russell. *Personal Narrative of Explorations and Incidents in Texas, New Mexico, California, etc.* Folding map, 44 plates. 2 vols., pictorial cloth. New York, 1854. First edition. $200-$250. Another issue (?): 2 vols. in one, cloth. $125 at retail. London, 1854. 2 vols., cloth. $100-$150.

BARTON, James L. *Commerce of the Lakes.* Folding table. 80 pp., wrappers. Buffalo, 1847. First edition. $50-$60.

BARTON, James L. *Lake Commerce.* 34 pp., wrappers. Buffalo, 1846. First edition. $25.

BASILE, Giambattista. *The Pentamerone, or The Story of Stories.* Illustrated by George Cruikshank. Cloth. London, 1850. Second edition. $25.

BASKIN, Leonard. *Figures of Dead Men.* Preface by Archibald MacLeish. Illustrated. Boards and cloth. No place (Boston), 1968. One of 100 signed by Baskin, with an original signed woodcut. $100-$150.

BASS, W. W. (editor). *Adventures in the Canyons of the Colorado by Two of Its Earliest Explorers, James White and H. W. Hawkins.* Frontispiece, plate, facsimiles. 38 pp., wrappers. Grand Canyon, 1920. First edition. $35-$50.

BATES, Ed. F. *History . . . of Denton County, Texas.* 5 plates. Denton, Tex., no date (1918). First edition. $50-$75.

BATES, H. E. *The Beauty of the Dead, and One Other Story.* Boards and cloth. London, 1941. Corvinus Press. One of 25. $75-$100.

BATES, H. E. *Flowers and Faces.* Engravings by John Nash. Boards. London, 1935. Golden Cockerel Press. One of 319. $35-$50. Another issue: Full morocco. One of 60 with an extra set of plates. $75-$100.

BATES, H. E. *A German Idyll.* Engravings. Morocco and cloth. Waltham Saint Lawrence, 1932. Golden Cockerel Press. $35.

BATES, H. E. *Sally Go Round the Moon.* Vellum. London, 1932. White Owl Press. One of 21 signed. Boxed. $35.

BATES, H. E. *Story Without an End.* Parchment. No place (London), 1932. White Owl Press. $40-$50.

BATES, J. H. *Notes of a Tour in Mexico and California.* Cloth. New York, 1887. First edition. $35-$50.

BAUDELAIRE, Charles. *Les Fleurs du Mal.* Illustrated by Auguste Rodin. Wrappers. New York, 1940. Limited Editions Club. Boxed. $35-$50.

BAUDELAIRE, Charles. *Flowers of Evil.* Edited by James Laver. Lithographs by Jacob Epstein. Buckram. New York, 1940. Limited Editions Club. Boxed. $35-$50.

BAUDELAIRE, Charles. *Intimate Journals.* Translated by Christopher Isherwood. Introduction by T. S. Eliot. Blue cloth, gilt top. London, 1930. First English edition. One of 650. Boxed. $25-$35. Hollywood, 1947. Cloth. Revised edition (with W. H. Auden introduction). Signed by Isherwood. In dust jacket. $35.

BAUER, Max. *Precious Stones.* Translated from the German by L. J. Spencer. Plates. Half morocco. London, 1903. $150-$250.

BAUM, L. Frank. See Stanton, Schuyler.

BAUM, L. Frank. *American Fairy Tales.* Illustrated. Pictorial cloth. Chicago, 1901. First edition. $75-$100.

BAUM, L. Frank. *The Army Alphabet.* Illustrated by Harry Kennedy. Pictorial boards. Chicago, 1900. First edition. $100-$150. Some pages soiled and torn, new cloth spine, $75.

BAUM, L. Frank. *Dorothy and the Wizard of Oz.* Illustrated by John R. Neill. Cloth. Chicago, no date (1908). First edition, first issue, with "Reilly & Britton Co." at bottom of spine. $35-$50.

BAUM, L. Frank. *The Enchanted Island of Yew.* Illustrated by Fanny Y. Cory. Pictorial cloth. Indianapolis, no date (1903). First edition. $50-$75.

BAUM, L. Frank. *The Life and Adventures of Santa Claus.* Cloth. Indianapolis, 1902. First edition. $50.

BAUM, L. Frank. *The Marvelous Land of Oz.* Illustrated by John R. Neill. Cloth. Chicago, 1904. First edition, first issue, without "Published July, 1904" on copyright page. In dust jacket. $200.

BAUM, L. Frank. *The Master Key.* Illustrated in color by Fanny Cory. Olive-green cloth. Indianapolis, no date (1901). First edition, first issue, with signatures of 8 pp. and with copyright line 1 21/32 inches wide. $75-$100. Second issue, signatures of 16 pp. $25. Third issue, copyright line 1 25/32 inches wide. $25.

BAUM, L. Frank. *Mother Goose in Prose.* Illustrated by Maxfield Parrish. Pictorial cloth. Chicago, no date (1897). First edition. $300-$350. Rebacked, covers and many leaves repaired, $150. Chicago, no date (1901). 12 plates. Pictorial cloth. $75.

BAUM, L. Frank. *A New Wonderland.* Illustrated by Frank Verbeck. Green cloth. New York, 1900. First edition. $50-$75.

BAUM, L. Frank. *The Patchwork Girl of Oz.* Illustrated. Pictorial cloth. Chicago, no date (1913). First edition. $40-$50.

BAUM, L. Frank. *Queen Zixi of Ix.* Illustrated in color. Pictorial cloth. New York, 1905. First edition. $35-$50.

BAUM, L. Frank. *The Road to Oz.* Illustrated by John R. Neill. Pictorial green cloth. Chicago, no date (1909). Reilly & Britton. First edition. $35.

BAUM, L. Frank. *Sea Fairies.* Illustrated. Light-green cloth. Chicago, no date (1911). First edition, first issue, with three heads on cover label. $50. Second issue, cover label showing girl on a sea horse. $25.

BAUM, L. Frank. *The Songs of Father Goose.* Illustrated by W. W. Denslow. Colored pictorial boards. Chicago, 1900. First edition. $30-$35.

BAUM, L. Frank. *The Songs of Father Goose for the Kindergarten.* 88 pp., pictorial boards and cloth. Indianapolis, no date (1909). $25.

BAUM, L. Frank. *The Wonderful Wizard of Oz.* Illustrated by W. W. Denslow. Green cloth. Chicago and New York, 1900. First edition, first issue, with 11-line colophon (not 13) on back end paper. $1,000-$1,250. Some catalogue prices of recent years: $650; copy with hinges broken, $550; hinges weak, two plates loose, $117.50; presentation copy signed by author, $600; leaf missing, binding shabby, $25. (Note: Several binding states make this a difficult book to evaluate properly. If you find a copy with title page date of 1900, seek a specialist dealer's help.)

BAX, Clifford (editor). *Florence Farr, Bernard Shaw and W. B. Yeats.* Boards, linen spine, paper label. Dublin, 1941. Cuala Press. First edition. One of 500. In tissue dust jacket. $55-$75.

BAXTER, William. *Pea Ridge and Prairie Grove.* Cloth. Cincinnati, 1864. First edition. $35-$50.

BAY, J. Christian. *The Fortune of Books.* Illustrated. Blue cloth. Chicago, no date (1941). In dust jacket. $40-$50.

BAY, J. Christian. *A Handful of Western Books *A Second Handful of Western Books* A Third Handful of Western Books.* Illustrated. 3 vols., boards and cloth. Cedar Rapids, Iowa, 1935-36-37. First editions. Limited to 350, 400, and 400 copies, respectively. Together, the three volumes, in tissue dust jackets, $75-$100 at retail. A set with two of the three bearing presentation inscriptions by the author, $135. Also, A-range, 1962-63: $15-$60. Odd volumes, in jackets, $25 to $40 at retail. (See following item.)

BAY, J. Christian. *Three Handfuls of Western Books.* (Combined one-volume edition of preceding items.) Boards. No place (Cedar Rapids), 1941. One of 35. $75.

BAYEUX Tapestry (The). Facsimile in color, by James Basire after C. A. Stothard. 17 double page plates in color. Folio, half calf. No place, no date (London, 1823). $50-$100.

BEAN, Edwin F. (compiler). *Bean's History and Directory of Nevada County, California.* Half leather and boards. Nevada, Calif., 1867. First edition. $200 and up.

BEAN, Ellis P. *Memoir.* Edited by W. P. Yoakum. No place (Houston), 1930. First edition. One of 200. $35-$50. (Howes lists place of publication as Dallas.)

BEARD, Charles R. *A Catalogue of the Collection of Martinware Formed by Frederick John Nettlefold.* 31 color plates, 46 in black and white. Half brown morocco. No place (London?), 1936. Privately printed. $75-$150.

BEARD, Daniel C. *What to Do and How to Do It.* Illustrated. Pictorial cloth. New York, 1882. First edition. $35-$65. "Corners bumped," $50.

BEARDSLEY, Aubrey. *A Book of Fifty Drawings.* Vellum. London, 1897. One of 50 on Japan paper. $50-$60.

BEARDSLEY, Aubrey. *Fifty Drawings.* Cloth. New York, 1920. First edition. One of 500. $25.

BEARDSLEY, Aubrey. *Last Letters.* Cloth. London, 1904. First edition. $30.

BEARDSLEY, Aubrey. *A Second Book of Fifty Drawings.* Vellum. London, 1899. One of 50 on Japan paper. $50-$60. Another issue: Cloth. $25.

BEARDSLEY, Aubrey. *Six Drawings Illustrating Theophile Gautier's Romance, "Mademoiselle de Maupin."* 6 plates, loose in half cloth portfolio, silk ties. London, 1898. One of 50. $125-$150. Also, $70 (A, 1971).

BEARDSLEY, Aubrey. *Some Unknown Drawings of Aubrey Beardsley.* Edited by R. A. Walker. 32 plates and facsimiles. Buckram. London, 1923. Signed. In dust jacket. $50-$60.

BEARDSLEY, Aubrey. *The Story of Venus and Tannhauser.* Green cloth, label on front cover. London, 1907. One of 50 on Japanese vellum. First complete edition. $85. New York, 1927. Boards and cloth. One of 750. $25-$35.

BEARDSLEY, Aubrey. *Under the Hill and Other Essays in Prose and Verse.* 16 illustrations by the author. Pictorial cloth. London, 1904. First edition. One of 50 on Japanese paper. $50-$75.

BEATTIE, George W. and Helen P. *Heritage of the Valley.* Cloth. Pasadena, 1939. First edition. In dust jacket. $25.

BEATTIE, William. *Switzerland Illustrated.* 107 plates by W. H. Bartlett, map. 2 vols., half calf. London, 1836. $100-$135.

BEAUCHAMPE; or, the Kentucky Tragedy. 2 vols., cloth. Philadelphia, 1842. (By William Gilmore Simms.) First edition. $50-$75.

BEAUMONT, Cyril W. *The History of Harlequin.* With a preface by Sacheverell Sitwell. 44 plates (5 colored), text decorations by Claudia Guercio. Decorated parchment boards, vellum spine. London, 1926. One of 325. $75-$100.

BEAUMONT, Cyril W. *Puppets and the Puppet Stage.* 110 pp. of illustrations. Cloth. London, 1938. In dust jacket. $25-$35.

BEAUMONT, Dr. Joseph. *Complete Poems.* Portrait frontispiece. 2 vols., half calf. London, 1880. Bookplates, $55.

BEAUMONT, William. *Experiments and Observations on the Gastric Juice, and the Physiology of Digestion.* Boards and cloth, paper label. Plattsburgh, N.Y., 1833. First edition. $1,000-$1,500. Also, presentation copy inscribed by the author, worn, $1,700 (A, 1969); "unbound," $576 (A, 1968); $800. Boston, 1834. Boards and cloth, paper label. Second issue (first edition copy with Boston title page). $500 and up. Edinburgh, 1838. Boards and calf. First English edition. $500-$750.

BEAUMONT, William. *The Physiology of Digestion.* Edited by Samuel Beaumont. Cloth. Burlington, Vt., 1847. Second edition of *Experiments and Observations on the Gastric Juice).* $400-$500. Also, worn, stained, foxed, $250 (A, 1969); $180 (A, 1968).

BEAUTY and the Beast. Boards, in printed paper case. London, no date (about 1811 or 1813?). (By Charles Lamb?) First edition. $500 and up.

BECK, Lewis C. *A Gazetteer of the States of Illinois and Missouri.* Folding map, 5 plates. Boards, paper label. Albany, 1823. First edition. $300-$500.

BECKETT, Samuel. (Note: Although Beckett has long been acknowledged by his contemporaries as one of our most significant writers, there exists as yet no reliable bibliographical guide to the immense complexities of his many published editions, French, English, American, and their sequences. The value of Beckett items has risen sharply since he was awarded the Nobel Prize, and the following listing, compiled from various reference works, including dealer catalogues and auction records, reflects the current collecting interest in his work.)

BECKETT, Samuel. *All That Fall: A Play.* 59 pp., stiff wrappers. New York, no date (1957). Special holiday greeting from Grove Press. First American edition. $100-$125. Also, $69 (A, 1970). Another issue?: Cloth. $25. London, 1957. Wrappers. First English edition. $15-$20.

BECKETT, Samuel. *Come and Go: Dramaticule.* Illustrated. Cloth. London, no date (1967). First edition. One of 100 signed. Boxed. $75-$100.

BECKETT, Samuel. *Comment C'est.* 177 pp., printed wrappers. No place, no date (Paris, 1961). Editions de Minuit. First edition. One of 100 for the Club de l'Edition Originale, signed. $125-$150.

BECKETT, Samuel. *Echo's Bones and Other Precipitates.* 30 pp., printed wrappers. Paris, 1935. Europa Press. First edition. One of 25 on Normandy vellum, signed. $125-$150. Another issue: One of 250 on Alfa paper, unsigned. $75-$100. Signed on title page by Beckett, $75 at retail. (Note: The total first edition printing is supposed to have been 327 copies.)

BECKETT, Samuel. *En Attendant Godot.* 163 pp., wrappers. Paris, 1952 (actually 1954 or later). Editions de Minuit. First edition in French (of *Waiting for Godot*). Exceedingly rare. Copy inscribed to Nancy Cunard, $720 (A, 1969). (Can locate no other retail or auction record.)

BECKETT, Samuel. *Endgame.* Translated by the author. Dark red cloth. London, no date (1958). First English edition. In dust jacket. $25. New York, 1958. Grove Press. First American edition. In dust jacket. $10-$15.

BECKETT, Samuel. *From an Abandoned Work.* Printed wrappers. London, no date (1958). First English edition. $20-$25.

BECKETT, Samuel. *How It Is.* Translated from the French by the author. Full brown morocco. London, no date (1964). First edition. One of 100 on handmade paper, signed, Series B. In glassine dust jacket. Boxed. $85-$125. Another issue: Full white vellum. One of 100 signed, Series B. Boxed. $85-$125.

BECKETT, Samuel. *Imagination Dead Image.* Brown buckram. London, no date (1965). First English edition. One of 100 signed. Boxed. $100-$125.

BECKETT, Samuel. *Imagination Morte Imaginez.* Wrappers. Paris, no date (1965). First edition. One of 450 numbered copies. $45-$60.

BECKETT, Samuel. *Krapp's Last Tape, and Embers.* Wrappers. London, 1959. First edition. $25-$35.

BECKETT, Samuel. *Malone Dies.* Translated by the author. 120 pp., cream-colored canvas. New York, no date (1956). First American edition. One of 500. In transparent dust jacket. $35-$50. London, 1958. Black cloth. First English edition. In dust jacket. $35.

BECKETT, Samuel. *Molloy.* Printed wrappers. Paris, 1955. Olympia Press. In dust jacket. $40-$50. (Note: The first edition in French appeared in Paris in 1955.)

BECKETT, Samuel. *Molloy. Malone Dies. The Unnamable: A Trilogy.* Wrappers. Paris, no date (1959). Olympia Press. First collected edition. $30-$35.

BECKETT, Samuel. *More Pricks Than Kicks.* Cloth. London, 1934. First edition. In dust jacket. $250-$350.

BECKETT, Samuel. *Murphy.* Cloth. London, no date (1938). First edition. In dust jacket. $50-$75. Paris, 1947. Wrappers. First edition in French. $75-$100. New York, no date (1957). Boards and cloth. First American edition. One of 100 signed. $75-$100.

BECKETT, Samuel. *No's Knife: Collected Shorter Prose, 1945-1966.* Full white calf, gilt. London, no date (1967). First edition. One of 100 signed. (Series A.) Boxed. $100-$110. Another issue: White calf and buckram. One of 100 signed. (Series B.) Boxed. $85-$100.

BECKETT, Samuel. *Nouvelles et Textes pour Rien.* Illustrated. Wrappers. Paris, no date (1958). Numbered edition. $35. (Note: The first edition appeared in Paris in 1955.)

BECKETT, Samuel. *Play and Two Short Pieces for Radio.* Red cloth. London, 1964. First English edition. In dust jacket. $20-$25.

BECKETT, Samuel. *Poems in English.* Mottled boards. London, no date (1961). One of 100 signed, "printed in advance of the first edition." $150-$250. Also, $84 and $96 (A, 1970). Also, a copy listed as "cloth, one of 100," inscribed to Nancy Cunard, $576 (A, 1969). Another issue: Cloth. One of 175 signed. In tissue dust jacket. $75-$125. First trade edition: Cloth. In dust jacket. $20-$25. New York, no date (1963). Green cloth. First American edition. In dust jacket. $20-$25.

BECKETT, Samuel. *Proust.* 72 pp., decorated boards. London, 1931. First edition. In dust jacket. $150-$250. Also, $264 (A, 1969).

BECKETT, Samuel. *The Unnamable.* Translated by the author. 179 pp., boards and cloth. New York, no date (1958). Grove Press. First American edition. One of 26 lettered copies, signed. $50. Another issue: Printed wrappers. Review copy. $25.

BECKETT, Samuel. *Waiting for Godot.* Translated by the author. New York, 1954. In dust jacket. $25-$35. London, no date (1956). Yellow cloth. First English edition. In dust jacket. $35-$50. London, 1957. Printed wrappers. Acting edition, first printing. $17.50.

BECKETT, Samuel. *Watt.* Printed wrappers. Paris, 1958 (actually 1953). Olympia Press. First edition. $50-$75. New York, no date (1959). First American edition. $25. Another issue: Boards. One of 26 signed. $75-$100. Paris, no date (1968). Printed wrappers. First edition in French. One of 90. $50-$75.

BECKETT, Samuel. *Whoroscope.* 6 pp., printed wrappers, with white (separate) band around the book. Paris, 1930. Hours Press First edition. One of 100 signed and numbered (of a total edition of 300). $700-$800. Another issue: One of 200, unsigned. $300-$500; inscribed to Nancy Cunard, publisher of the book, with an autograph letter, signed, $2,280 (A, 1969). Author's first separately published work.

BECKETT, Samuel, and others. *Our Exagmination Round His Factification for Incamination of Work in Progress.* Printed wrappers. Paris, 1929. Shakespeare and Company. First edition. One of 96 on verge d'Arches paper. $250-$350. Ordinary issue: $150-$200. Also, $124.80 (A, 1969).

BEDFORD, Hilory G. *Texas Indian Troubles.* Decorated cloth. Dallas, 1905. First edition. $150-$200.

BEEBE, Lucius. *Aspects of the Poetry of Edwin Arlington Robinson.* Cloth. Cambridge, Mass., 1928. First edition. One of 200. $25-$35.

BEEBE, Lucius, and Clegg, Charles M. *Mixed Train Daily.* Illustrated. Cloth. New York, 1947. First edition. In dust jacket. $35-$50.

BEEBE, William. *The Arcturus Adventure.* Boards and vellum. New York, 1926. Autograph (first) edition. One of 50 signed. $100-$150. First trade edition: Cloth. In dust jacket. $15-$20.

BEEBE, William. *Galapagos: World's End.* 9 color plates, 88 photogravures. Buckram. New York, 1924. Autograph (first) edition. One of 100 signed. In dust jacket. $100-$150. First trade edition: Cloth. In dust jacket. $15-$20.

BEEBE, William. *A Monograph of the Pheasants.* 90 color plates, 20 maps, other illustrations. 4 vols., folio, cloth. London, 1918-22. First edition. One of 600. $1,250-$1,500. Rebound in half morocco, $1,260. Also, cloth, $912 (A, 1969); $1,008 (A, 1968).

BEEBE, William. *Pheasants: Their Lives and Homes.* 64 plates (some in color). 2 vols., vellum. Garden City, 1926. First edition. One of 201 on large paper, signed. $150-$250. Trade edition: 2 vols., cloth. $75-$100. Also, $32 (A, 1969). Garden City, 1931. 2 vols. $35-$60. Garden City, 1936. 2 vols. in one. $35-$50. London, 1937. 2 vols. in one. In dust jacket. $84. London, 1938. 2 vols. in one. $35-$50.

BEECHER, Harriet Elizabeth. *Prize-Tale: A New England Sketch.* Plain wrappers, cloth spine. Lowell, Mass., 1834. First edition. $750. First book by Harriet Beecher Stowe.

BEECHEY, F. W. *An Account of a Visit to California.* Map, color plates. Half vellum. No place, no date (San Francisco, 1941). Grabhorn printing. One of 350. $50-$75.

BEECHEY, F. W. *Narrative of a Voyage to the Pacific and Beering's Strait.* 23 plates, 3 maps. 2 vols., brown cloth, or boards and cloth. London, 1831. First edition. $400-$500. London, 1831. 2 vols. Second edition. $100-$200. Philadelphia, 1832. Boards and cloth. First American edition. $50-$100.

BEECHEY, F. W. *A Voyage of Discovery Towards the North Pole.* Folding map, 6 plates. Cloth. London, 1843. First edition. $100-$150. Rebound in half morocco, $75. Also, half morocco, $55 (A, 1968).

BEE-HIVE Songster (The). 32 pp., self-wrappers. Salt Lake, 1868. (By John Davis.) $65 (A, 1968).

BEE-HUNTER (The); or, The Oak Openings. By the author of "The Pioneers." 3 vols., drab boards. London, 1848. (By James Fenimore Cooper.) First edition (of the novel published in America as *The Oak Openings*, which see as title entry). $75-$100.

BEERBOHM, Max. *A Book of Caricatures.* Frontispiece in color, 48 drawings. Folio, cloth, paper label, gilt top. London, no date (1907). First edition. $125-$150.

BEERBOHM, Max. *Caricatures of Twenty-Five Gentlemen.* 25 plates. Cloth. London, no date (1896). First edition. $75-$100.

BEERBOHM, Max. *Cartoons: "The Second Childhood of John Bull."* 15 full-page tinted plates. Cloth. London, no date (1901). First edition. $50-$75. Another issue: Second issue. Plates in cloth folder. $50. London, no date (1911). Folio, boards and linen. $50-$60.

BEERBOHM, Max. *A Christmas Garland.* Violet cloth, with gilt lettering and decorations. London, 1912. First edition. $25-$35.

BEERBOHM, Max. *Collected Works.* 10 vols., cloth. London, 1922-28. One of 780, first volume signed by the author. In dust jackets. $280 and $264. Also, $156 (A, 1970); $168 (A, 1967 and 1966). (See *The Works of Max Beerbohm.*)

BEERBOHM, Max. *Fifty Caricatures.* 50 plates. Pictorial green cloth. London, 1913. First edition. $50-$75.

BEERBOHM, Max. *The Happy Hypocrite: A Fairy Tale for Tired Men.* Printed green wrappers. New York, 1897. First edition. No. 1 of the Bodley Booklets. $150-$200. Part of spine missing, $90. London, 1915. Illustrated by George Sheringham. Pictorial cloth. $25-$35. Another issue: Boards. One of 50 on Japan paper. $75-$100.

BEERBOHM, Max. *More.* Green cloth, paper label (with extra label tipped in). London, 1899. First edition. $40-$50.

BEERBOHM, Max. *Observations.* Color frontispiece, 51 other illustrations. Cloth. London, 1925. First edition. In dust jacket. $50. Also, $24 (A, 1967). London, 1926. Buckram. One of 280 signed, and with an additional colored plate, signed. $100-$125.

BEERBOHM, Max. *The Poet's Corner.* 20 colored caricatures. Folio, pictorial boards. London, no date (1904). First edition, first issue. $75-$100. Second issue: Pictorial wrappers. $50-$75.

BEERBOHM, Max. *Rossetti and His Circle.* 23 colored caricatures. Blue cloth. London, no date (1922). First edition. One of 380 signed. In dust jacket. $100-$132.

BEERBOHM, Max. *Seven Men.* Blue cloth. London, 1919. First edition, first issue, in bright-blue cloth. In dust jacket. $25-$35. Second issue: Dark-blue cloth. In dust jacket. $15-$20.

BEERBOHM, Max. *A Survey.* 52 plates, including colored frontispiece. Purple cloth. London, 1921. First edition. One of 275 signed. In dust jacket. $75. Another, spine faded, lacking jacket, $52.50. Trade edition: Cloth. In dust jacket. $25 and $37.50. New York, 1921. Boards and cloth. First American edition. $25-$35.

BEERBOHM, Max. *Things New and Old.* Colored frontispiece, 49 other plates. White buckram. London, 1923. One of 380 signed and with extra signed plate. In dust jacket. $100-$150. Trade edition: Cloth. In dust jacket. $50-$60.

BEERBOHM, Max. *The Works of Max Beerbohm.* Cloth. London, 1896. First edition. $100-$150. (Also see Beerbohm, *Collected Works.*)

BEERBOHM, Max. *Zuleika Dobson.* Smooth brown cloth, or rough cloth. London, 1911. First edition. In dust jacket. $100-$150. (Note: Percy H. Muir says there is no priority of issue for smooth brown cloth over rough cloth; they were issued simultaneously, but rough cloth is scarcer.) New York, 1960. Limited Editions Club. Cloth. Boxed. $35.

BEERS, F. W., and Co. *Atlas of the Counties of Lamoille and Orleans, Vermont.* Maps in color. Half leather. New York, 1878. First edition. $45-$50.

BEETON, Mrs. Isabella. *The Book of Household Management.* Frontispiece and pictorial title in color, numerous other illustrations. 2 vols., cloth. London, 1861. First edition, first issue, with "18 Bouverie St." on title page. $300-$400. Rebound in calf, $185. In half morocco, $185. Another issue: "18 Strand" on title page. Rebound in modern leather, lacking frontispiece, $57.60 (A, 1968).

BEETON'S Christmas Annual. 28th Season. Illustrated. Wrappers. London, 1887. (Contains first appearance of A. Conan Doyle's *A Study in Scarlet.*) $1,500 and up. Also, "most of spine missing," $1,080 (A, 1968); rebound in cloth, lacking wrappers and ads, $1,152 (A, 1968).

BEHAN, Brendan. *The Hostage.* Boards and cloth. New York, no date (1958). First American edition. One of 26 signed. (Issued without dust jacket.) $25-$35.

BEHAN, Brendan. *The Quare Fellow.* Black cloth. London, no date (1956). First edition. In dust jacket. $25.

BEHN, Mrs. Aphra. *The Works of Mrs. Aphra Behn.* Edited by Montague Summers. Portrait. 6 vols., cloth-backed boards. London, 1915. One of 50 sets on handmade paper. $150-$250. Another issue: One of 760. $50-$75.

BELCHER, Sir Edward. *Narrative of a Voyage Round the World . . . 1836-1842.* 19 plates, 3 maps in pocket. 2 vols., cloth. London, 1843. First edition. $150-$250.

BELL, Acton. *Agnes Grey.* See Bell, Ellis and Acton, *Wuthering Heights.*

BELL, Acton. *The Tenant of Wildfell Hall.* 3 vols., dark claret-colored cloth. London, 1848. (By Anne Brontë.) First edition. $100-$150.

BELL, Currer (editor). *Jane Eyre: An Autobiography.* 3 vols., red, or claret, cloth. London, 1847. (By Charlotte Brontë.) First edition. $1,000 and up for a fine copy. Foxed, $826. Hinges repaired, $500. Also, "recased," $490 (A, 1966); "very good," $800 (A, 1962). Other copies at retail, fair to very good condition, $100-$840. Rebound in green cloth, $750. Rebound in three-quarters morocco, $350. London, 1847. Second edition. (Currer Bell as author instead of editor on title page.) $150-$250. London, 1848. Third edition. $100-$150. Paris, 1923. Illustrated by Ethel Gabain. Folio, wrappers. One of 460. $25-$35.

BELL, Currer. *The Professor.* 2 vols., plum-colored cloth. London, 1857. (By Charlotte Brontë.) First edition, with 2 pages of ads at end of Vol. 1 and 16 pages of ads at end of Vol. 2 dated June, 1857. $100-$150.

BELL, Currer. *Shirley: A Tale.* 3 vols., deep claret-colored cloth. London, 1849. (By Charlotte Brontë.) First edition, with 16 pages of ads dated October, 1849, at end of Vol. 1. $200-$250.

BELL, Currer. *Villette.* 3 vols., olive-brown cloth. London, 1853. (By Charlotte Brontë.) First edition, with ads dated January, 1853, in Vol. 1. $100-$350.

BELL, Currer, Ellis, and Acton. *Poems.* Dark-green cloth. London, 1846. (By Charlotte, Emily, and Anne Brontë.) First edition, first issue, published by Aylott and Jones. $1,000 and up. London, 1846 (actually 1848). Green cloth. Published by Smith, Elder & Co. Second issue, with 4-line errata slip. $150-$200. Philadelphia, 1848. Boards. First American edition. $150-$200.

BELL, Ellis (and Acton). *Wuthering Heights.* 3 vols., claret-colored cloth (third vol. titled *Agnes Grey,* by Acton Bell). London, 1847. (First two vols. by Emily Brontë, third by Anne Brontë.) First edition. (1,000 copies printed.) $2,000 and up.

BELL, Horace. *On the Old West Coast.* Edited by Lanier Bartlett. Plates and facsimiles. Half buckram and boards. New York, 1930. First edition. One of 210 signed by the editor. Boxed. $50-$75. Trade edition: Cloth. In dust jacket. $15-$20.

BELL, Horace. *Reminiscences of a Ranger.* Pictorial cloth. Los Angeles, 1881. First edition. $50-$60. Santa Barbara, Calif., 1927. Green cloth. $15.

BELL, John. *Discourses on the Nature and Cure of Wounds.* 2 plates. 2 vols. in one, leather. Walpole, N.H., 1807. First American edition. $100. Spine damaged, $85.

BELL, Solomon. *Tales of Travel West of the Mississippi.* Map, plates. Boards and cloth, leather label. Boston, 1830. (By William J. Snelling.) First edition. $150-$200.

BELL, William A. *New Tracks in North America.* Plates and maps, some in color. 2 vols., cloth. London, 1869. First English edition. $100-$144.

BELLAMY, Edward. *Equality.* Salmon-colored or blue cloth. New York, 1897. First edition. In dust jacket. $40-$50.

BELLAMY, Edward. *Looking Backward, 2000-1887.* Pea-green, orange-brown, or gray cloth. Boston, 1888. First edition, first state, with printer's imprint of "J. J. Arakelyan" on copyright page. $100-$150. Another (second) issue: Gray wrappers. $65-$75. New York, 1941. Limited Editions Club. Cloth. Boxed. $25-$35.

BELLAMY, Edward. *Miss Ludington's Sister.* Cloth. Boston, 1884. First edition. $25.

BELLAMY, Edward. *Six to One: A Nantucket Idyl.* Frontispiece. Printed wrappers or cloth. New York, 1878. First edition. Cloth. $50. Dust-soiled, $35. Author's first book.

BELLOC, Hilaire. See B., H.

BELLOC, Hilaire. *The Book of the Bayeux Tapestry.* 76 colored facsimiles. Cloth. New York, 1914. $25.

BELLOC, Hilaire. *Cautionary Tales for Children.* Pictorial boards. London, no date (1907). First edition. $75-$100. Presentation copy, inscribed, $125.

BELLOC, Hilaire. *The Highway and Its Vehicles.* Illustrated. Buckram. London, 1926. One of 1,250. $25-$40.

BELLOC, Hilaire. *New Cautionary Tales.* Cloth. London, 1930. First edition. One of 110 signed. $50-$60.

BELLOC, Hilaire. *The Praise of Wine.* Loose sheets in printed wrappers. No place, no date (London, 1931). First edition. $67.20 and $49.

BELLOC, Hilaire. *Verse.* Edited by W. H. Roughead. Buckram. London, 1954. Nonesuch Press. $25.

BELLOC, Hilaire. *Verses and Sonnets.* Green cloth. London, 1896. First edition. $75-$100. Author's first book.

BELLOW, Saul. *The Adventures of Augie March.* Cloth. New York, 1953. First edition. In dust jacket. $25-$30.

BELLOW, Saul. *Dangling Man.* Cloth. New York, no date (1944). First edition. In dust jacket. $130-$150.

BELLOW, Saul. *The Victim.* Cloth. New York, no date (1947). First edition. In dust jacket. $35-$50.

BELTRAMI, J. C. *A Pilgrimage in Europe and America.* Portrait, folding map, other engravings. 2 vols., boards and linen. London, 1828. First English edition. $100-$150.

BEMELMANS, Ludwig. *My War with the United States.* Illustrated by the author. Cloth. New York, 1937. First edition. In dust jacket. $25.

BENAVIDES, Alonso de. *The Memorial of Fray Alonso de Benavides, 1630.* Facsimile of Madrid edition of 1630. Boards. Chicago, 1916. One of 300. $125-$150.

BENDIRE, Charles. *Life Histories of North American Birds.* 19 color plates. 2 vols., folio, cloth. Washington, 1892-95. First edition. $75-$150. Also, rebound in half morocco, $100-$125.

BENEDICT, Almon H. *A "Wide Awake" Poem.* 16 pp., wrappers. Cortland Village, N.Y., 1860. First edition. $60.

BENÉT, Rosemary, and Benét, Stephen Vincent. *A Book of Americans.* Illustrated. Cloth. New York, 1933. First edition. One of 125 signed. Boxed. $55. Trade edition: Cloth. First issue, with publisher's monogram on copyright page. In dust jacket. $15-$20. Second issue, in dust jacket, $7.50.

BENÉT, Stephen Vincent. See Rinehart, Mary Roberts, and Hopwood, Avery; Benét, Rosemary. Also see *The Yale Book of Student Verse, 1910-1919.*

BENÉT, Stephen Vincent. *The Ballad of the Duke's Mercy.* Cloth. New York, 1939. One of 250 signed. $50-$75. Trade edition: Cloth. In dust jacket. $25.

BENÉT, Stephen Vincent. *The Ballad of William Sycamore, 1790-1880.* Boards, paper label. New York-New Haven-Princeton, no date (1923). First edition. One of 500 signed. $25.

BENÉT, Stephen Vincent. *Ballads and Poems: 1915-1930.* Pictorial boards. Garden City, 1931. First edition. One of 201 signed. Boxed. $100-$125. Trade edition (first edition so stated): Cloth. In dust jacket. $15-$20.

BENÉT, Stephen Vincent. *The Barefoot Saint.* Decorations by Valenti Angelo. Cloth. Garden City, 1929. First edition. One of 367. Boxed. $50.

BENÉT, Stephen Vincent. *Burning City.* Red fabrikoid. New York, no date (1936). First edition. One of 275 signed. In glassine dust jacket. Boxed. $75-$100. Trade edition: Cloth. In dust jacket. $25-$35.

BENÉT, Stephen Vincent. *The Devil and Daniel Webster.* Illustrated by Harold Denison. Buckram. Weston, Vt., no date (1937). First edition. One of 700 signed. Boxed. $50-$75. New York, no date (1937). Cloth. First trade edition. In dust jacket. $10-$15.

BENÉT, Stephen Vincent. *The Drug-Shop; or, Endymion in Edmonstoun.* 24 pp., printed wrappers. No place (New Haven), 1917. First edition. 100 copies only. $75-$100.

BENÉT, Stephen Vincent. *Five Men and Pompey.* Wrappers over boards. Boston, 1915. First edition. First state, purple wrappers. $100-$150. Second state, brown wrappers. $25-$50. (Note: Johnson says there were "a few copies" on handmade paper.) Author's first book.

BENÉT, Stephen Vincent. *James Shore's Daughter.* Parchment boards. Garden City, 1934. First edition (so stated). One of 307 signed. Boxed. $35-$65. Trade edition: Cloth. In dust jacket. $15-$20.

BENÉT, Stephen Vincent. *John Brown's Body.* Vellum boards. No place, no date (Garden City, 1928). First edition. One of 201 signed. Boxed. $250-$350. Trade edition (first edition so stated): Cloth. In dust jacket. Boxed. $25-$35. Inscribed copies, in dust jacket, $25, $35, and $50. New York, 1948. Limited Editions Club. John Steuart Curry illustrations. Cloth. One of 1,500. Boxed. $35-$50.

BENÉT, Stephen Vincent. *Johnny Pye and the Fool Killer.* Illustrated. Wrappers. Weston, Vt., no date (1938). First edition. One of 750 signed. In glassine dust jacket. Boxed. $50-$75. New York, no date (1938). Green cloth. First trade edition. In dust jacket. $10-$15.

BENÉT, Stephen Vincent. *Nightmare at Noon.* Printed wrappers. New York, no date (1940). First edition, first printing, with publisher's monogram on copyright page. $35.

BENÉT, Stephen Vincent. *A Portrait and a Poem.* Half morocco. Paris, 1934. First edition. One of 50. $100-$150.

BENÉT, Stephen Vincent. *Kind David.* Printed boards, paper label. New York, 1923. First edition. One of 350 signed. $50.

BENÉT, Stephen Vincent. *Tuesday, Nov. 5th, 1940.* 8 pp., wrappers. New York, 1941. First edition. One of 50. $100-$150.

BENÉT, William Rose. *Merchants from Cathay and Other Poems.* Green cloth. New York, 1913. First edition. $25-$35. Author's first book.

BENJAMIN, Asher. *The Architect, or Practical House Carpenter.* 64 plates. Sheep. Boston, 1845. $87.50-$150. Boston, 1848. Sheep. $87.50. Contemporary leather, $50. Boston, 1850. Sheep. $75-$100.

BENJAMIN, Asher. *The Builder's Guide.* Plates. Boards and calf. Boston, 1839. Worn, $100. Boston, 1850. Sheep. $100-$150.

BENJAMIN, Asher. *The Practical House Carpenter.* Illustrated. Contemporary calf. Boston, 1832. $75-$150.

BENJAMIN, Asher. *The Practice of Architecture.* 60 full-page plates. Sheep. Boston, 1833. First edition. $150-$250. Philadelphia, 1835. Sheep. Second edition. $85. Boston, 1835. Contemporary leather. $75.

BENJAMIN, Asher. *The Rudiments of Architecture.* 36 plates, one folding. Calf. Boston, 1814. First edition. $250. Boston, 1820. Second edition. $100.

BENJAMIN, Asher, and Reynard, Daniel. *The American Builder's Companion.* 44 plates. Calf, or boards. Boston, no date (1806). First edition. $250-$300. Boston, 1826. 63 plates. Contemporary calf. Fifth edition, enlarged. $45-$50. Boston, 1827. Leather. Sixth edition. $35-$40.

BENNETT, Arnold. See Wadsworth, Edward.

BENNETT, Arnold. *Anna of the Five Towns.* Cloth. London, 1902. First edition. $25.

BENNETT, Arnold. *Clayhanger.* Cloth. London, no date (1910). First edition. In dust jacket. $35-$50. Lacking jacket, $25-$35.

BENNETT, Arnold. *The Clayhanger Family.* Cloth. London, 1925. One of 200 signed. In dust jacket. $50.

BENNETT, Arnold. *Don Juan de Marana.* Frontispiece. Vellum and boards. London, 1923. One of 1,000 signed. In dust jacket. $35-$50.

BENNETT, Arnold. *Elsie and the Child.* Color illustrations. Cloth. London, 1929. One of 100 signed. $50-$60.

BENNETT, Arnold. *From the Log of the Velsa.* Illustrated. White cloth. London, 1920. One of 110 signed. $35.

BENNETT, Arnold. *Hilda Lessways.* Cloth. London, no date (1911). First edition. In dust jacket. $25-$35.

BENNETT, Arnold. *Imperial Palace.* 2 vols., vellum. London, no date (1930). First edition. One of 100 signed. $35-$50.

BENNETT, Arnold. *The Loot of Cities.* Wrappers. London, no date (1904). First edition. $150-$200.

BENNETT, Arnold. *A Man from the North.* Red cloth, stamped in white. London, no date (1898). First edition. $50-$60. Author's first book.

BENNETT, Arnold. *The Old Wives' Tale.* Lavender, or pink, cloth, white lettering. London, 1908. First edition. $200-$250. Spine faded, foxed, $175. London, 1927. 2 vols., parchment and cloth. Facsimile of the manuscript. One of 500. $75-$100. New York, 1941. Limited Editions Club. Illustrated by John Austen. 2 vols., cloth. Boxed. $30-$40.

BENNETT, Arnold. *Things That Interested Me, Being Leaves from a Journal.* Cloth. Burslem (England), 1906. One of 100. $35-$50. Also, $20 (A, 1968). London, 1921. Second Series. Cloth. In dust jacket. $35-$50. London, 1926. Third Series. Cloth. In dust jacket. $35-$50.

BENNETT, Arnold. *Things Which Have Interested Me.* Second Series. Parchment and boards. Burslem (England), 1907. One of 100. $35-$40.

BENNETT, Emerson. *The Bandits of the Osage.* Printed wrappers (?). Cincinnati, 1847. Published by Edwards & Goshorn. $100 and up. Also, disbound, $25 (A, 1962). (Note: Blanck lists the first edition, same date, as published by Robinson & Jones. Estimated value at retail: $200-$300.)

BENNETT, Emerson. *Clara Moreland; or, Adventures in the Far South-West.* Printed wrappers or cloth. Philadelphia, no date (1863). First edition. $100-$150.

BENNETT, Emerson. *Leni-Leoti; or, Adventures in the Far West.* Printed orange wrappers. Cincinnati, 1849. First edition. $300-$400. Also, disbound, foxed and with title leaf detached, $190 (A, 1968).

BENNETT, Emerson. *Mike Fink. A Legend of the Ohio.* Printed wrappers (?). Cincinnati, 1848. First edition. $400-$500. Also, disbound (lacking covers), $300 (A, 1963). Cincinnati, no date (1852). Printed wrappers. Revised edition. $100. Also, $37 (A, 1954).

BENNETT, Emerson. *The Mysterious Marksman; or, The Outlaws of New York.* Wrappers. Cincinnati, no date (about 1855). First edition (?). $150-$200. (Note: This title not in Blanck.)

BENNETT, Emerson. *The Prairie Flower; or, Adventures in the Far West.* 128 pp., printed wrappers. Cincinnati, 1849. First edition. $250-$350. Later issue: Cloth. $150. Cincinnati, 1850. Boards and cloth. New edition, revised. $150-$200.

BENNETT, George. *Gatherings of a Naturalist in Australasia.* 7 colored plates, one in sepia, numerous woodcuts. Cloth. London, 1860. $75-$100.

BENNETT, John. *Barnaby Lee.* Illustrated by Clyde O. De Land. Decorated cloth. New York, 1902. First edition. $75.

BENNETT, John. *Master Skylark: A Story of Shakspeare's Time.* Illustrated by Reginald Birch. Pictorial cloth. New York, 1897. First edition. $65-$75.

BENNETT, Melba Berry. *Robinson Jeffers and the Sea.* Decorated boards, morocco spine. San Francisco, 1936. Grabhorn printing. First edition. One of 300. In mustard-colored dust jacket. $60.

BENSON, Frank W. (illustrator). *Etchings and Drypoints.* 285 reproductions. Text by Adam E. M. Paff. 4 vols., boards. Boston, 1917-29. One of 275, with frontispiece signed by Benson. In dust jackets. $300-$350.

BENSON, Henry C. *Life Among the Choctaw Indians.* Cloth. Cincinnati, 1860. First edition. $75.

BENTON, Frank. *Cowboy Life on the Sidetrack.* Illustrated. Pictorial cloth. Denver, no date (1903). First edition. $35-$50.

BEPPO, a Venetian Story. Drab wrappers. London, 1818. (By George Gordon Noel, Lord Byron.) First edition. $400-$500. Also, $375 (A, 1970).

BERACHYA, Son of Rabbi Natronai Ha-Nakdan. *Ethical Treatises.* Translated by Hermann Gollancz. Cloth. London, 1902. $25.

BERENSON, Bernard. *The Drawings of the Florentine Painters.* 180 full-page tinted plates. 2 vols., folio, half morocco. London, 1903. One of 355. $200-$300. New York, 1903. 2 vols., folio, boards and morocco. $150. Chicago, 1938. 3 vols., small folio, boards, vellum spine. Amplified edition. $200-$300. Milan, Italy, 1961. Italian text. 3 vols., half morocco. $75-$100.

BERENSON, Bernard. *The Italian Painters of the Renaissance.* Illustrated. Cloth. London, no date (1952). Phaidon Press. $25-$40.

BERENSON, Bernard. *A Sienese Painter of the Franciscan Legend.* 26 color illustrations. Boards and cloth. London, 1909. First edition. $25-$30.

BERENSON, Bernard. *Studies in Medieval Painting.* Illustrated. Cloth. New Haven, 1930. First edition. $50-$75.

BERENSON, Bernard. *Three Essays in Method.* Illustrated. Cloth. Oxford, 1927. First edition. $50-$60.

BERNARD, Auguste. *Geofroy Tory: Peintre et Graveur.* Morocco, gilt. Paris, 1865. One of a few printed on vellum. (The Hoe copy.) $85 (A, 1963).

BERNARD, Auguste. *Geofroy Tory, Painter and Engraver.* Translated by George B. Ives. Boards. No place (Cambridge, Mass.), 1909. One of 370 designed by Bruce Rogers. $100-$125.

BERNERS, Dame Juliana. *The Treatyse of Fysshynge with an Angle.* Woodcuts. Full green morocco. London (Chelsea), 1903. Ashendene Press. One of 20 (25?) on vellum. Boxed. $500-$600. Another issue: Vellum. One of 150. Boxed. $150-$200.

BERNSTEIN, Aline. *Three Blue Suits.* Frontispiece. Tan-blue cloth, paper labels. New York, 1933. First edition. One of 600 signed. Boxed. $60-$80.

BERQUIN-DUVALLON. See *Travels in Louisiana and the Floridas.*

BERRY, Wendell. *November Twenty Six Nineteen Hundred Sixty Three.* Illustrated by Ben Shahn. Cloth. New York, no date (1964). First edition. Limited issue signed by Shahn and Berry. Boxed. $50. Trade edition, not signed: $10.

BERRYMAN, John. *The Dispossessed.* Cloth. New York, 1948. First edition. In dust jacket. $75.

BERRYMAN, John. *His Thoughts Made Pockets & the Plane Buckt.* Boards, leather spine. Pawlet, Vt., 1958. First edition. One of 26 lettered copies signed by the author. In original imprinted envelope. $50-$75. Another issue: Wrappers. One of 500. $25-$30.

BERRYMAN, John. *Poems.* Printed blue wrappers. Norfolk, Conn., no date (1942). New Directions. First edition. Poet of the Month series. $25-$35. Another issue: Boards. In dust jacket. $40-$50. Author's first book.

BERT, Edmund. *Treatise of Hawks and Hawking.* Illustrated. Boards, leather spine. London, 1891. Limited Edition. $72.

BESANT, Walter. *The Art of Fiction.* Yellow cloth. Boston, 1885. First edition. $25. (Note: Contains an essay on fiction by Henry James.)

BESTERMAN, Theodore. *A World Bibliography of Bibliographies.* 3 vols., buckram. London, 1947-49. Second edition. $100-$150.

BETJEMAN, John. See O'Betjeman, Deirdre.

BETJEMAN, John. *Antiquarian Prejudice.* Wrappers. London, 1939. Hogarth Press. First edition. In slipcase. $50-$75.

BETJEMAN, John. *John Betjeman's Collected Poems.* Compiled by the Earl of Birkenhead. Scarlet leather. London, 1958. First edition. One of 100 signed. In slipcase. $75-$100. Also, proof copy in printed wrappers, $33.60 (A, 1962). Trade edition: Cream-colored cloth. In dust jacket. $10-$15.

BETJEMAN, John. *Continual Dew.* Black cloth. London, no date (1937). First edition. In dust jacket. $60-$75. Inscribed, $100.

BETJEMAN, John. *English Cities and Small Towns.* 8 color plates, 31 black and white illustrations. Brown boards. London, 1943. First edition. In dust jacket. $15-$20. Signed, $30.

BETJEMAN, John. *A Few Late Chrysanthemums.* White buckram. London, 1954. First edition. One of 50 signed. $50-$75. Trade edition: Purple cloth. In dust jacket. $20-$25.

BETJEMAN, John. *First and Last Loves.* Illustrated. Cream-colored cloth. London, no date (1952). First edition. In dust jacket. $25-$35.

BETJEMAN, John. *Ghastly Good Taste.* Folding plate. Printed pink boards and cloth. London, 1933. First edition, first issue, with pages 119-120 not canceled. $50.

BETJEMAN, John. *High and Low.* Buckram. London, no date (1966). First edition. One of 100 signed. $100-$125. Second printing: Yellow cloth. In dust jacket. $10 at retail.

BETJEMAN, John. *Mount Zion, or In Touch with the Infinite.* Illustrated. Red, white and blue striped boards, pictorial label on front cover. London, no date (1931). James Press. First edition. $150-$200. Author's first book.

BETJEMAN, John. *New Bats in Old Belfries.* Red cloth, paper label. London, 1945. One of a few signed copies on special paper with colored title page. In dust jacket. $75-$100. Unsigned, in dust jacket, $25-$35.

BETJEMAN, John. *Old Lights for New Chancels.* Portrait frontispiece. Wrappers. London, no date (1940). In dust jacket. $35-$50.

BETJEMAN, John. *An Oxford University Chest.* Photographs by Moholy-Nagy. Illustrations by Osbert Lancaster, etc. Marbled boards, cloth spine, gilt top. London, no date (1938). First edition. $85-$125.

BETJEMAN, John. *Poems in the Porch.* Illustrated. Pictorial wrappers. London, 1954. Talbot Press. First edition. $25-$30.

BETJEMAN, John. *Selected Poems.* Buckram. London, 1948. First edition. One of 18 signed. $200-$250. Trade edition: Red cloth. In dust jacket. $25.

BETJEMAN, John. *Summoned by Bells.* Illustrated. Full green leather, gilt top. London, 1960. First edition. One of 125 signed. $100-$125. Proof copy: Decorated wrappers. $27.50. Trade edition: Green cloth. In dust jacket. $25.

BEVIER, Robert S. *History of the First and Second Missouri Confederate Brigades, 1861-1865.* 2 portraits. Cloth. St. Louis, 1879. First edition. $50.

BEWICK, Thomas. (Note: The various works of this famous engraver exist in innumerable editions and issues. I have chosen only a few representative items here, omitting Bewick's *General History of Quadrupeds*, first published in 1790 and therefore not within the scope of this compilation.)

BEWICK Gleanings. Edited by Julia Boyd. 53 plates. Green morocco. Newcastle-on-Tyne, England, 1886. Large paper edition, signed. $150-$200.

BEWICK, Thomas. *A History of British Land and Water Birds*. Woodcuts. 2 vols., contemporary leather. Newcastle, 1797-1804. First edition. $200-$250. Newcastle, 1821. 2 vols., green morocco. Each volume signed by Bewick, $165.

BEWICK, Thomas. *Select Fables*. Portraits and woodcuts. Boards. Newcastle, 1820. First edition. $200 and up. Also, $108 (A, 1969); rebound in morocco, $91.20 (A, 1968); half morocco, $45 (A, 1968). Rebacked, $50.40 at retail. Edinburgh, 1879. Vellum and white boards. Edition De Luxe on Whatman paper. One of 100. $100. London, no date (1878). Brown cloth and leather. $35.

BEWICK, Thomas. *The Water Colour Drawings of Thomas Bewick*. 40 illustrations in color. Half pigskin. London, 1930. Alcuin Press. $35-$50.

BEY, Pilaff. *Venus in the Kitchen*. Edited by Norman Douglas, with foreword by Graham Greene. Illustrated. Wrappers. London, no date (1952). "Proof Copy for Your Personal Reading" (so imprinted on front cover). $50.

BEYER, Edward. *Album of Virginia*. 40 tinted lithograph views, plus decorated text. 2 vols., cloth, or half cloth (oblong folio plate volume and octavo text volume). Richmond, Va., 1856. First edition. $2,000-$3,000, possibly more. (No copy of the first edition has appeared for public sale in modern times.) Richmond, 1857. $2,000 or more. Richmond, 1858. $1,820 (in a dealer's catalogue).

BIBLE. Illustrated by Marc Chagall. 2 vols., paper folder within gray board folder and in slipcase. Teriade, 1956. One of 275 on Montval wove paper, signed by Chagall. $6,000.

BICKERSTAFF, Isaac. *The Rhode-Island Almanac for 1842*. Stitched. Providence, R.I., no date (1841). $35-$50. (Note: Contains "Indian Barbarity," about Miss Fleming's captivity.)

BIDDLE, Owen. *The Young Carpenter's Assistant*. 44 (of 46) plates. Morocco. Philadelphia, 1805. First edition. Worn, foxed, etc., $300 (A, 1969).

BIDWELL, John. *Echoes of the Past About California*. 3 photographic views. Wrappers. Chico, Calif., no date (1914). First edition. $75-$100.

BIDWELL, John. *A Journey to California*. 48 pp., boards and cloth. San Francisco, 1937. $45 and $75. (Note: One copy is known of the 1842 original of this narrative.)

BIERCE, Ambrose. See Grile, Dod; Herman, William; and Bowers, Mrs. Dr. J. Milton.

BIERCE, Ambrose. *Battle Sketches*. 8 wood engravings. Vellum. London, 1930. Shakespeare Head Press. One of 350. Boxed. $75-$100.

BIERCE, Ambrose. *Black Beetles in Amber*. Frontispiece. Light-gray or red cloth. San Francisco, 1892. First edition, first issue, with imprint of Western Authors Publishing Company. $75-$125. Second issue: Printed gray wrappers. Published by Johnson & Emigh. $150-$200.

BIERCE, Ambrose. *Can Such Things Be?* Golden brown cloth, or printed yellow wrappers. New York, no date (1893). First edition. Cloth: $35-$50. Wrappers: $75-$100. Washington, 1903. Maroon cloth. $10-$15.

BIERCE, Ambrose. *The Cynic's Word Book*. Olive-green cloth. New York, 1906. First edition, presumed first issue, without frontispiece. $75-$100. Front inner hinge cracked, $50. Also, $45 (A, 1968). Another (later?) issue: Frontispiece inserted. $45 and $27.50.

(Note: Blanck had seen no such copy, although Vincent Starrett had reported the existence of a frontispiece in some copies. Priority unknown.)

BIERCE, Ambrose. *Fantastic Fables.* Pictorial brownish yellow cloth. New York, 1899. First edition, first printing, with ads at back headed by "By Anna Fuller." $50-$75. Later, blue cloth, with ads headed "New Fiction." $10-$15.

BIERCE, Ambrose. *A Horseman in the Sky.* Boards and cloth. San Francisco, 1920. John Henry Nash printing. One of 400. $35-$50.

BIERCE, Ambrose. *In the Midst of Life.* Blue cloth. London, 1892. First English edition (of *Tales of Soldiers and Civilians*). $25-$35. (Second issue appeared in colored boards.) New York, 1898. Cloth. (Reprint of the *Tales* with three added stories.) $25-$35.

BIERCE, Ambrose. *The Letters of Ambrose Bierce.* Edited by Bertha C. Pope. Frontispiece portrait. Boards and cloth. San Francisco, 1922. Book Club of California. Printed by John Henry Nash. One of 415. $50-$75.

BIERCE, Ambrose. *The Shadow on the Dial and Other Essays.* Edited by S. O. Howes. Green buckram. San Francisco, 1909. First edition. In dust jacket. $25-$50.

BIERCE, Ambrose. *Shapes of Clay.* Blue or red cloth. San Francisco, 1903. First edition, first issue, with transposed lines on page 71. $35-$50.

BIERCE, Ambrose. *A Son of the Gods and a Horseman in the Sky.* Frontispiece. Vellum and boards. San Francisco, no date (1907). First separate edition. One of 1,000. $35-$50.

BIERCE, Ambrose. *Tales of Soldiers and Civilians.* Brown, green, or gray cloth. San Francisco, 1891. First edition. $100-$150. Some copies imprinted "Compliments of" on preliminary leaf and signed by Bierce—the so-called "limited" edition, $150-$200. New York, 1943. Limited Editions Club. Boards and leather. Boxed. $30. (For first English edition see Bierce, *In the Midst of Life*.)

BIERCE, Ambrose. *Ten Tales.* Preface by A. J. A. Symons. Red cloth. London, 1925. First edition. In dust jacket. $25-$35.

BIERCE, Ambrose. *Write It Right: A Little Blacklist of Literary Faults.* Tan cloth. New York, 1909. First edition, first issue, 5¾ by 3 inches in size. In dust jacket. $35-$50.

BIERCE, Ambrose, and Danziger, Gustav Adolph. *The Monk and the Hangman's Daughter.* Illustrated by Theodore Hampe. Printed yellow wrappers, or gray cloth. Chicago, 1892. First edition. Wrappers: $75-$100. Cloth: $50-$75. (Note: Danziger was a pseudonym for Adolphe De Castro.) New York, 1907. Green cloth. $10. New York, 1926. $5. New York, 1967. Illustrated. Limited Editions Club. Boxed. $25-$35.

BIGELOW, Jacob. *American Medical Botany.* 60 color plates. Vols. 1-3 in 6 vols., cloth, paper labels, or 6 parts, printed boards. Boston, 1817-18-20. First edition. Cloth (6 vols.): $600 and up. Boards (6 parts): $750 and up.

BIGGERS, Don H. *From Cattle Range to Cotton Patch.* Illustrated. Stiff wrappers. Abilene, Tex., no date (about 1908). First edition. $200. Bandera, Tex., 1944. Second edition. $20-$25.

BIGMORE, E. C., and Wyman, C. W. H. *A Bibliography of Printing.* 3 vols., cloth, leather spine, London, 1880-86. First edition. One of 350. $100. New York, 1945. 3 vols. in 2, buckram. Facsimile reprint, with type page enlarged. $100-$150.

BINGHAM, Caleb. *An Astronomical and Geographical Catechism for the Use of Children.* Wallpaper wrappers. Boston, 1802. Sixth edition. $75.

BIOGRAPHICAL Dictionary (A) of the Living Authors of Great Britain and Ireland. Contemporary calf. London, 1816. (By John Watkins and Frederic Shoberl.) First edition. $125-$150.

BIOGRAPHICAL Note of Commodore Jesse D. Elliott (A). By a Citizen of New York. Printed boards. Philadelphia, 1835. (By Russell Jarvis.) First edition. $50-$60.

BIOGRAPHICAL Sketch, Words of the Songs, Ballads, etc., of the Composer and Vocalist, Stephen Massett, "Jeems Pipes, of Pipesville." Portrait. 52 pp., wrappers. New York, 1858. First edition. $40.

BIOGRAPHY of James Lawrence, Esq. Portrait. Printed paper boards. New-Brunswick, N.J., 1813. (By Washington Irving?) First edition. $150-$250. Rebound in calf, binding cracked, $150.

BINYON, Laurence. *The Art of Botticelli.* Muirhead Bone etching, 23 color plates. Folio, cloth, vellum spine, London, 1913. One of 275. $50-$75.

BINYON, Laurence. *A Catalogue of Japanese and Chinese Woodcuts.* 39 illustrations. Cloth. London, 1916. $50-$60.

BINYON, Laurence. *The Court Painters of the Grand Moguls.* 39 full-page plates, 9 colored. Cloth. Oxford, 1921. First edition. $75-$100.

BINYON, Laurence. *The Drawings and Engravings of William Blake.* Plates, some in color. Folio, vellum portfolio with ties. London, 1922. One of 200. $100-$125. Another issue: Vellum and boards. $50-$75.

BINYON, Laurence. *Dream-come-True.* Boards. London, 1905. One of 185. $75-$100.

BINYON, Laurence. *The Engraved Designs of William Blake.* Plates. Half cloth and boards. London, 1926. One of 100 with an extra set of plates. $100-$200. Without the extra plates, $50-$75.

BINYON, Laurence. *The Followers of William Blake.* 79 plates, 7 colored. Cloth. London, 1925. First edition. $50-$75.

BINYON, Laurence. *The George Eumorfopolous Collection.* (Catalogue of the Chinese Frescoes.) 50 full-page color plates. Folio, gold and black cloth. London, 1927. One of 560. $195.

BINYON, Laurence. *Little Poems from the Japanese Rendered into English Verse.* Wrappers. Leeds, England, 1925. Swan Press. First edition. One of 200. $25-$35.

BINYON, Laurence. *Lyric Poems.* Cloth. London, 1894. First edition. One of 300. $35.

BINYON, Laurence. *Painting in the Far East.* 30 plates. Cloth. London, 1908. First edition. $50-$60.

BINYON, Laurence. *Penthesilea.* Cloth. London, 1905. First edition. In dust jacket. $25.

BINYON, Laurence. *Poems.* Wrappers. Oxford, 1895. Daniel Press. First edition. One of 200. $75-$100.

BINYON, Laurence. *The Poems of Nizami.* Folio, cloth. London, 1928. $35-$50.

BINYON, Laurence. *Porphyron and Other Poems.* Cloth. London, 1898. First edition. $25.

BINYON, Laurence. *Western Flanders.* Illustrated by William Strang. Folio, cloth. London, 1899. One of 250. $35-$50.

BINYON, Laurence. *The Winnowing-Fan.* Printed blue-gray wrappers. London, 1914. First edition. $25-$35.

BINYON, Laurence, and Sexton, J. J. O'Brien. *Japanese Colour Prints.* 46 plates, some in color. Buckram. London, 1923. $50. Another issue: Pigskin. One of 100 signed, with an extra set of plates. $100-$125.

BINYON, Laurence; Wilkinson, J. V. S.; and Gray, Basil. *Persian Miniature Painting.* Illustrated, including color plates. Folio, cloth. London, 1923. $100-$150.

BIRD, Robert Montgomery. See *The Adventures of Robin Day; Calavar; The Infidel; Nick-of-the-Woods; Peter Pilgrim; Sheppard Lee.*

BIRDSONG, James C. *Brief Sketch of the North Carolina State Troops in the War Between the States.* Cloth. Raleigh, 1894. First edition. $50.

BIRKBECK, Morris. See *An Impartial Appeal; Remarks Addressed to the Citizens of Illinois.*

BIRKBECK, Morris. *An Appeal to the People of Illinois, on the Question of a Convention.* 25 pp., wrappers. Shawneetown, Ill., 1823. First edition. $425 (A, 1967).

BIRKBECK, Morris. *Extracts from a Supplementary Letter from the Illinois.* 29 pp., disbound. New York, 1819. First edition. Foxed, $400 (A, 1967).

BIRKBECK, Morris. *Letters from Illinois.* 2 folding maps. Boards and calf. Philadelphia, 1818. First edition. $75-$100.

BIRKBECK, Morris. *Notes on a Journey in America from the Coast of Virginia to the Territory of Illinois.* Boards. Philadelphia, 1817. First edition. $75-$100. Also, $50 (A, 1968); rebound in modern boards, $30 (A, 1964). London, 1818. Map. Boards and calf. First English edition. $50-$75. Issued also without map, same date: $35-$50. (There were three other English editions in 1818; all are valued in the $40-$50 range.) Philadelphia, 1819. $35.

BISHOP, John Peale. *Act of Darkness.* Cloth. New York, 1935. First edition. In dust jacket. $35-$50. Author's first and only novel.

BISHOP, John Peale. *Green Fruit.* Boards and cloth. Boston, 1917. First edition. In dust jacket. $40-$50.

BISHOP, John Peale. *Minute Particulars.* Wrappers. New York, 1935. First edition. One of 165 signed. In glassine dust jacket. $25-$35.

BISHOP, Richard E. *Bishop's Birds: Etchings of Waterfowl and Upland Game Birds.* 73 reproductions. Pictorial cloth. Philadelphia, 1936. Limited edition. $100. Also, $55 (A, 1967). Another issue: One of 135 signed, with signed Bishop etching tipped in. Boxed. $150-$200.

BISHOP, Richard E. *Bishop's Wildfowl . . . Etchings and Oil Painting Reproductions.* Text by E. Prestrud and R. Williams. Color plates. Full calf. No place, no date (St. Paul, Minn., 1948). First edition. $100-$150.

BISLAND, Elizabeth (editor). *The Life and Letters of Lafcadio Hearn.* Illustrated. 2 vols., cloth. Boston, 1906. First edition. One of 200, with a page of an original manuscript by Hearn. $150-$200.

BLACKBIRD, Andrew J. *History of the Ottawa and Chippewa Indians of Michigan.* Cloth. Ypsilanti, Mich., 1887. First edition. $35-$50.

BLACKMORE, Richard D. *Lorna Doone: A Romance of Exmoor.* 3 vols., blue watered cloth. London, 1869. First edition. $750-$1,000.

BLACKMUR, R. P. *The Expense of Greatness.* Cloth. New York, no date (1940). First edition. In dust jacket. $35.

BLACKMUR, R. P. *From Jordan's Delight.* Cloth. New York, 1937. First edition. In dust jacket. $35.

BLACKMUR, R. P. *The Good European & Other Poems.* Cloth, paper label. Cummington, Mass., 1947. First edition. One of 40 signed. $75-$100.

BLACKMUR, R. P. *The Second World*. Cloth. No place (Cummington), 1942. Cummington Press. First edition. One of 300. In glassine dust jacket. $30.

BLACKWATER Chronicle (The). By "The Clerke of Oxenforde." Illustrated. Cloth. New York, 1853. (By Pendleton Kennedy, or, as some suppose, by his brother John Pendleton Kennedy.) First edition. $200 and up.

BLAIR, Robert. *The Grave: A Poem.* Portrait and 12 etchings by Schiavonetti after designs by Blake. Boards. London, 1808. First edition. $150-$250. Another issue: Large Paper. $300-$400.

BLAKE, W. O. *The History of Slavery and the Slave Trade*. Illustrated. Roan. Columbus, Ohio, 1858. First edition. $35-$50.

BLAKE, William. See Binyon, Laurence; Thornton, R. J. (Note: There have been innumerable facsimile reproductions of the illuminated books of William Blake, poet, mystic, artist, and engraver [1757-1827], the originals of which are of the greatest rarity. A few of the more popular editions are listed here. For more complete listings, see *American Book-Prices Current* and the British publication *Book Auction Records*.)

BLAKE, William. *America, a Prophecy*. Facsimile by William Muir of the rare 1793 first edition. Wrappers. Edmonton, Alberta, Canada, 1887. One of 50. $75-$100. No place (New York), 1947. Cloth. $25.

BLAKE, William. *The Book of Thel*. Facsimile. 8 plates in color with a set of 30 hand-colored plates showing progressive stages in the platework. No place, no date (Paris, 1956). Trianon Press. One of 20 sets. $300.

BLAKE, William. *The Book of Urizen*. Facsimile of the 1794 first edition, with 27 plates reproduced by color-collotype and stencil. Half morocco. London, 1958. One of 480. In slipcase. $100-$125. Another issue: Full morocco. One of 20, with 27 plates and a set of progressive stages, guide sheet stencil proofs, and other material used in making one of the plates. In handmade case. $250-$300.

BLAKE, William. *Genesis.* Cummington, Mass., 1952. One of 170. $35-$50.

BLAKE, William. *Illustrations of the Book of Job*. Title page and 21 other plates engraved by Blake. Folio. London, 1825. First edition, with plate No. 1 misdated 1828. (In various bindings—cloth folders, wrappers, morocco, etc.) $2,000-$3,000. London, 1902. Facsimile. Wrappers. $75-$100. New York, 1935. 6 parts, folio, wrappers. One of 200. Boxed. $1,000-$1,500.

BLAKE, William. *Jerusalem.* Facsimile of the original illuminated book of 1804. 10 full-page and 45 half-page watercolors, 45 pp. with colored designs. 5 parts, folio, wrappers. London, no date (1951). Trianon Press. One of 516. Boxed. $300-$500.

BLAKE, William. *The Marriage of Heaven and Hell*. J. C. Hotten's facsimile of the 1790 original. 27 leaves, hand-colored. Boards. No place, no date (London, 1868). $75-$100. Other editions: No place, no date (Edmonton, Alberta, Canada, 1885). William Muir's facsimile. Wrappers. One of 50. $100-$150. London, 1960. Trianon Press facsimile. Folio, boards and morocco. One of 526. $150-$200. Another issue: One of 20 of the edition of 526 with a set of hand-colored plates (proofs, etc.). $250-$300.

BLAKE, William. *The Note-Book of William Blake Called the Rossetti Manuscript*. Edited by Geoffrey Keynes. 120 pp. in facsimile. Buckram. London, 1935. Nonesuch Press. One of 650. In dust jacket. $125-$150.

BLAKE, William. *Pencil Drawings*. Edited by Geoffrey Keynes. 82 facsimile plates. Half buckram. London, 1927. Nonesuch Press. Limited edition. In dust jacket. $150-$175. Second Series: London, 1956. Cloth. Limited. In dust jacket. $50.

BLAKE, William. *Songs of Innocence*. Frontispiece. Half cloth. San Francisco, 1924. Grabhorn printing. One of 100. $40.

BLAKE, William. *Songs of Innocence and of Experience.* Facsimile reproduction in collotype of the 54 plates from the 1794 original. Full morocco. London, 1955. Trianon Press. One of 526. In slipcase. $600.

BLAKE, William. *The Writings of William Blake.* Edited by Geoffrey Keynes. 3 vols., half vellum and marbled boards. London, 1925. Nonesuch Press. One of 1,500. Boxed. $150-$250. Thin paper issue: 3 vols. in one, morocco. One of 75. $540.

BLANCHARD, Rufus. *Discovery and Conquests of the North West.* 7 maps and plates. 6 parts, wrappers, or bound together in morocco or cloth. Wheaton, Ill., 1879. First edition. In parts: $250. Morocco or cloth: $50-$60. Wheaton (some copies say "Chicago"), 1880. (One 1880 copy noted with 1881 copyright.) Reprint edition. $40-$50. Chicago (some copies say "Wheaton"), 1881. Enlarged edition, with 11 maps and plates. $35-$50. Wheaton, 1898-1900 (actually 1903). 2 vols. $35-$50.

BLANCK, Jacob. *Peter Parley to Penrod.* Cloth. New York, 1938. One of 500. $50. New York, 1956. Second edition. $40-$50. Cambridge, Mass., 1961. $25.

BLAND, David. *History of Book Illustration.* Illustrated. Cloth. Cleveland, no date (1958). First edition. In dust jacket. $50-$60.

BLAND, Jane Cooper. *Currier & Ives: A Manual for Collectors.* 24 pages of color plates, other illustrations. Cloth. New York, no date (1931). $40-$60.

BLAVATSKY, H. P. *Isis Unveiled: A Master Key to the Mysteries of Ancient and Modern Theology.* 2 vols., cloth. New York, 1877. First edition. With inserted autograph slip of certification. $100. New York, 1923. 2 vols., cloth. $15. New York, no date (1950). 2 vols., cloth. $15.

BLAVATSKY, H. P. *The Secret Doctrine.* 2 vols., cloth. London, 1888. First edition. $40-$60. London, 1893-98. 4 vols. (3 vols. with index), cloth. $35-$50. London, no date (1928). 3 vols., cloth. $20-$25.

BLEDSOE, A. J. *History of Del Norte County, California.* Printed wrappers. Eureka, Calif., 1881. First edition. $2,000 and up.

BLEDSOE, A. J. *Indian Wars of the Northwest.* Cloth. San Francisco, 1885. First edition. $150-$200.

BLEW, William C. A. *The Quorn Hunt and Its Masters.* Map, 12 hand-colored plates. Cloth. London, 1899. First edition. $25-$35.

BLEW, William C. A. *A History of Steeple-Chasing.* 28 illustrations, 12 hand-colored. Half morocco. London, 1901. $75-$100.

BLEWITT, Mary. *Surveys of the Seas.* Plates. Folio, buckram. No place, no date (London, 1957). $25-$35.

BLOSSOMS of Morality (The). 51 wood engravings. Half calf and boards. Philadelphia, 1810. (By Richard Johnson.) $45-$50.

BLOWE, Daniel. *A Geographical, Commercial, and Agricultural View of the United States of America.* Portrait, 2 maps, 4 plans. Calf. Liverpool, no date (1820). $35.

BLUE Grotto (The) and Its Literature. 18 pp., printed red wrappers. London, 1904. (By Norman Douglas.) First edition. $50. Signed on title page by Douglas, $125.

BLUNDEN, Edmund. See Collins, William; Lloyd, Robert.

BLUNDEN, Edmund. *Dead Letters.* Decorated wrappers, paper label. London, 1923. Pelican Press. One of 50. $100-$150.

BLUNDEN, Edmund. *Japanese Garland.* Color plates. Boards and vellum. London, 1928. Beaumont Press. One of 80 signed. $50-$75.

BLUNDEN, Edmund. *Masks of Time.* Boards and vellum. London, 1925. Beaumont Press. One of 80 on vellum, signed. $60-$75.

BLUNDEN, Edmund. *Near and Far.* Cloth. London, 1929. One of 150 signed. In dust jacket. $40. Trade edition: In dust jacket. $10.

BLUNDEN, Edmund. *Pastorals: A Book of Verses.* Wrappers. London, 1916. First edition. $75-$100.

BLUNDEN, Edmund. *Poems, 1914-1930.* Buckram. London, 1930. First edition. One of 200 signed. In dust jacket. $50-$60.

BLUNDEN, Edmund. *Retreat: New Sonnets and Poems.* Cloth. No place, no date (London, 1928). One of 112 signed. In dust jacket. $45-$50.

BLUNDEN, Edmund. *A Summer's Fancy.* Illustrated. Cloth, vellum spine. London, 1930. Beaumont Press. First edition. One of 80 signed. $60-$75.

BLUNDEN, Edmund. *To Nature.* Illustrated by Randolph Schwabe. Patterned boards, vellum spine. No place, no date (London, 1923). Beaumont Press. One of 80 on vellum, signed. $48 and $45.

BLUNDEN, Edmund. *Undertones of War.* Cloth. London, 1928. First edition. In dust jacket. $40-$50.

BLUNDEN, Edmund. *Winter Nights.* Illustrated. Boards. London, 1928. First edition. One of 500 signed. $30-$40.

BLUNT, Edmund M. *Traveller's Guide to and Through the State of Ohio, with Sailing Directions for Lake Erie.* 16 pp., leather. New York, 1832. First edition. $300-$400. New York, 1833. Folding map in color. 28 pp., leather. $300-$400.

BLUNT, Wilfrid Scawen. See Proteus.

BLUNT, Wilfrid Scawen. *The Celebrated Romance of the Stealing of the Mare.* Translated from the Arabic by Lady Anne Blunt and done into verse by W. S. B. Boards and leather. Newtown, Wales, 1930. Gregynog Press. One of 275. $200-$225.

BLUNT, Wilfrid Scawen. *The Love-Lyrics and Songs of Proteus and the Love-Sonnets.* Woodcut borders and initials. Limp vellum with ties. London, 1892. Kelmscott Press. One of 300. $300-$375.

BOCCACCIO, Giovanni. *The Decameron.* 1620 translation. Woodcuts by Fritz Kredel. 2 vols., boards and calf. New York, 1940. Limited Editions Club. One of 530. Boxed. $85. Another Limited Editions Club edition: New York, 1930. Translated by Frances Winwar. 2 vols., cloth. Boxed. $30-$40. London, 1920. Ashendene Press. Folio, boards and linen. One of 105. $250-$350.

BOCCACCIO, Giovanni. *Life of Dante.* Translated by Philip Henry Wicksteed. Woodcut title portrait. Boards and vellum. No place, no date (Boston, 1904). One of 325 designed by Bruce Rogers. $25-$35.

BODE, Winston. *A Portrait of Pancho.* Illustrated. Full leather. Austin, Tex., 1965. First edition. One of 150 signed. Boxed. $50. Trade edition: Cloth. $10.

BODENHEIM, Maxwell. See Hecht, Ben, and Bodenheim, Maxwell.

BODENHEIM, Maxwell. *Minna and Myself.* Red cloth. New York, 1918. First edition, first issue, with "Master-Posner" for "Master-Poisoner" on page 67. In dust jacket. $75. Author's first book.

BOEHME, Jacob. *The Aurora.* Translated by John Sparrow. Cloth. London, 1914. $40.

BOEHME, Jacob. *Christosophia.* Leather. Ephrata, Pa., 1811-12. $37.50.

BOERSCHMANN, Ernst. *Chinesische Architektur.* 340 plates. 2 vols., cloth. New York, no date (1925). First American edition. $75-$100.

BOGAN, Louise. *Body of This Death: Poems.* Blue boards, linen spine, paper label. New York, 1923. First edition. In dust jacket. $35-$50. Author's first book.

BOGAN, Louise. *Dark Summer.* Cloth. New York, 1929. First edition. In dust jacket. $35-$40.

BOGGS, Mae Helene Bacon (compiler). *My Playhouse Was a Concord Coach.* Maps, illustrations. Cloth. No place, no date (Oakland, 1942). First edition. $175-$300. Also, $150 (A, 1968). (Note: Streeter reported "all extant copies" were gift copies from the editor to her friends.)

BOKE of Noblesse (The). Addressed to King Edward IV on his Invasion of France in 1475. Half morocco. London, 1860. Roxburghe Club. $50-$75.

BOKE (The) Off the Revelacion Off Sanct Jhon the Devine done into Englysshe by William Tyndale. Printed in black and red. Green vellum. London, 1900. Ashendene Press. One of 54. $400-$500.

BOKER, George Henry. *The Podesta's Daughter.* Purplish brown cloth. Philadelphia, 1852. First edition. $25-$30.

BOLDREWOOD [sic], Rolf (Bolderwood). *Robbery Under Arms: A Story of Life and Adventure in the Bush and in the Goldfields of Australia.* Decorated green cloth. London, 1888. (By Thomas A. Browne.) First edition. $400-$500.

BOLLER, Henry A. *Among the Indians.* Folding map, cloth, paper label. Philadelphia, 1868. First edition. $250-$350.

BOLTON, Herbert Eugene. *Anza's California Expeditions.* Folding map, illustrations. 5 vols., cloth. Berkeley, Calif., 1930. First edition. In dust jackets. $125.

BOLTON, Herbert Eugene. *Athanase de Mezieres and the Louisiana-Texas Frontier.* Map, 2 facsimiles. 2 vols., cloth. Cleveland, 1914. First edition. $75-$100.

BOLTON, Herbert Eugene. *Coronado on the Turquoise Trail.* Illustrated. Cloth. Albuquerque, 1949. $45-$50.

BOLTON, Herbert Eugene. *Guide to Materials for the History of the United States in the Principal Archives of Mexico.* Printed wrappers. Washington, 1913. First edition. $35-$40.

BOLTON, Herbert Eugene. *The Rim of Christendom.* 12 plates, 3 facsimiles. Cloth. New York, 1936. First edition. $35-$50.

BOLTON, Herbert Eugene (translator). *Font's Complete Diary of the Second Anza Expedition.* Maps, plates, facsimiles. Cloth. Berkeley, Calif., 1931. First edition. $50-$75. Berkeley, 1933. Cloth. Second edition. $35-$50.

BOLTWOOD, Lucius M. *History and Genealogy of the Family of Thomas Noble.* Illustrated. Cloth. Hartford, 1878. First edition. $25-$30.

BOND, Henry. *Family Memorials.* Vol. 1. Buckram. Boston, 1855. (Watertown, Mass., genealogies, including Waltham and Weston.) $25-$30.

BONFILS, Winifred B. *The Life and Personality of Phoebe Apperson Hearst.* Vellum. San Francisco, 1928. John Henry Nash printing. One of 1,000. In original tan flannel bag. $25-$35.

BONNELL, George W. *Topographical Description of Texas.* Boards. Austin, Tex., 1840. First edition. $500-$750. Also, worn, $675 (A, 1966). (Other copies earlier were catalogued in the $350-$450 range.)

BONNER, T. D. *The Life and Adventures of James P. Beckwourth, Mountaineer, Scout and Pioneer, etc.* Frontispiece and plates. Cloth. New York, 1856. First edition. $100-$150.

BOOK of Commandments (A), for the Government of the Church of Christ. Boards. Zion (Independence, Mo.), 1833. (By Joseph Smith.) First edition. $5,000 and up.

BONNEY, Edward. *Banditti of the Prairies; or, The Murderer's Doom!* Plates. Pictorial wrappers. Chicago, 1850. First edition, with imprint "Chicago, W. W. Davenport, 1850" on front cover. $1,500 and up. Also, $1,350 (A, 1963). Philadelphia, no date (1855). $75. Philadelphia, 1856. Third edition. $150. Chicago, 1856. $200. Chicago, 1858. 13 plates. Wrappers. $225.

BOOK of Job (The). Illustrated in color by Arthur Szyk. Boards. New York, 1946. Limited Editions Club. Boxed. $35-$45.

BOOK of Kells (The). 48 color plates, 625 in black and white. 2 vols. facsimile, plus text volume, 3 vols. in all, vellum. Olten and Berne, Switzerland, 1950-51. One of 500. $2,550 and $3,000 (one New York dealer, 1968-69).

BOOK of the Law of the Lord (The). Saint James, A. R. I. (Beaver Island, Lake Michigan), no date (1851). (By James Jesse Strang.) First edition. $1,000 and up (3 copies known). No place, no date (Beaver Island, 1856). Second edition, lacking title page (some supplied, and with preface, in modern type, circa 1920). $250-$450. For a later edition, see James J. Strang entry.

BOOK of Psalms (The). Illustrated by Valenti Angelo. Morocco. New York, 1961. Limited Editions Club. Boxed. $35-$45.

BOOK of Ruth (The). Boards. London, 1923. Nonesuch Press. One of 250. $50-75. Also, $40 (A, 1969). London, 1934. Morocco. One of 10 on vellum. $70. New York, 1948. Limited Editions Club. Introduction by Mary Ellen Chase. Illustrated by Arthur Szyk. Boards. Boxed. $75-$100.

BOOK of Tobit (The) and the History of Susanna. Color plates by W. Russell Flint. Vellum, silk ties. London, 1929. One of 13 on vellum, signed by the artist. With duplicate plates in folder. $200-$250.

BOOK-LOVER'S Almanac (The) for 1895. Wrappers. New York, 1894. First edition. One of 100 on Japan paper. $25.

BOOTH, Stephen. *The Book Called Holinshed's Chronicles.* Woodcut reproductions and an original leaf from the 1587 edition. Decorated boards and cloth. San Francisco, 1968. One of 500. $50-$75.

BORDEN, Gail, Jr. *Letters of . . . to Dr. Ashbel Smith.* 9 pp., wrappers. Galveston, 1850. First edition. $125.

BORDEN, Spencer. *The Arab Horse.* Cloth. New York, 1906. $35-$50.

BORDER Beagles: A Tale of Mississippi. 2 vols, boards and cloth, paper labels. Philadelphia, 1840. (By William Gilmore Simms.) First edition. $250-$350. Foxed, rubbed, $125.

BORDERERS (The): A Tale. By the Author of "The Spy." 3 vols., drab tan boards, paper labels. London, 1829. (By James Fenimore Cooper.) First edition (of the novel published in America as *The Wept of Wish-Ton-Wish.*) $75-$150.

BORNEMAN, Henry S. *Pennsylvania German Illuminated Manuscripts.* 38 colored reproductions. Oblong, cloth. Norristown, Pa., 1937. $100-$150.

BORROW, George. See Ewald, Johannes.

BORROW, George. *The Bible in Spain.* 3 vols., red cloth. London, 1843. First edition. $125-$150.

BORROW, George. *Lavengro; the Scholar—the Gypsy—the Priest.* 3 vols., blue cloth, paper labels. London, 1851. First edition. $75-$100. New York, 1936. Limited Editions Club. 2 vols., cloth. Boxed. $20-$25.

BORROW, George. *Proud Signild and Other Ballads.* Wrappers. London, 1913. First edition. One of 30. $60-$70.

BORROW, George. *Wild Wales: Its People, Language, and Scenery.* 3 vols., cloth, paper labels. London, 1862. First edition, with 32 pages of ads and without half titles in Vols. 2 and 3. $35-$50.

BORZOI 1920 (The). Half cloth. New York, 1920. (By Alfred A. Knopf.) First edition. One of 100 on San Marco paper. $35-$50. New York, 1925. Half cloth. One of 500. $25.

BOSCANA, Father Geronimo. *Chinigchinich.* Translated by Alfred Robinson. Color plates, maps. Folio, boards and cloth. Santa Ana, 1933. $75-$100.

BOSQUI, Edward. *Memoirs.* Half cloth. No place (Oakland), 1952. Grabhorn Press. One of 350. $35-$50.

BOSSCHERE, Jean de. *12 Occupations.* Illustrated. Decorated wrappers. London, 1916. First edition. $100-$150. Worn, $85. (Translated anonymously by Ezra Pound.)

BOSSERT, Helmuth T. *Peasant Art in Europe.* 130 full-color plates and 32 plates in black and white. Folio, cloth. London, 1927. First English edition. $50-$75. New York, 1927. First American edition. $75-$100.

BOSTON Prize Poems, and Other Specimens of Dramatic Poetry. Printed boards. Boston, 1824. First edition. $50-$100. Longfellow's first appearance in a book,

BOSWELL, James. *Boswell for the Defence.* Edited by W. K. Wimsatt and Frederick A. Pottle. Illustrated, folding maps. Blue buckram, gilt, calf spine, leather label. London, 1960. Yale de luxe edition. One of 350. Boxed. $35-$50.

BOSWELL, James. *Boswell in Holland, 1763-1764.* Edited by Frederick A. Pottle. Illustrated, folding map. Blue buckram and calf. London, 1952. Yale de luxe edition. One of 1,050. Boxed. $25-$35.

BOSWELL, James. *Boswell in Search of a Wife.* Edited by F. Brady and Frederick A. Pottle. Blue buckram and calf. London, 1957. Yale de luxe edition. One of 400. Boxed. $50-$75.

BOSWELL, James. *Boswell on the Grand Tour: Germany and Switzerland.* Edited by Frederick A. Pottle. Illustrated, folding map. Blue buckram and calf. London, 1953. Yale de luxe edition. One of 1,000. Boxed. $35-$50.

BOSWELL, James. *Boswell on the Grand Tour: Italy, Corsica, and France.* Edited by F. Brady and Frederick A. Pottle. Illustrated, folding maps. Blue buckram and calf. London, 1955. Yale de luxe edition. One of 400. Boxed. $35-$50.

BOSWELL, James. *Boswell's Journal of a Tour to the Hebrides with Samuel Johnson, LL.D.* Boards, cloth spine, paper label. New York, 1936. First complete edition. One of 816. Boxed. $35.

BOSWELL, James. *The Life of Samuel Johnson.* Portrait, 2 folding plates. Contemporary sheep. Boston, 1807. First American edition. $100-$150. New York, 1938. Limited Editions Club. 3 vols., cloth. Boxed. $50. New York, 1945. Illustrated by Gordon Ross. Cloth. One of 1,000 signed by Ross. $35-$50.

BOSWORTH, Newton. *Hochelaga Depicta: The Early History and Present State of the City and Island of Montreal.* Illustrated, including 2 folding maps. Cloth. Montreal, 1839. $75-$100. Lacking dedication leaf and one plate, $50.

BOUCHETTE, Joseph. *A Topographical Description of the Province of Lower Canada, with Remarks Upon Upper Canada.* Maps and illustrations. Boards and calf. London, 1815. First English edition. $200-$300. London, 1832. Boards. $75-$100.

BOURDILLON, Francis W. *Among the Flowers, and Other Poems.* Decorated white cloth. London, 1878. First edition. $50-$75. Author's first book.

BOURKE, John G. *An Apache Campaign in the Sierra Madre.* Illustrated. Printed wrappers, or pictorial cloth. New York, 1886. First edition. Wrappers: $100-$150. Cloth: $75-$100.

BOURKE, John G. *Mackenzie's Last Fight with the Cheyennes.* Portrait. 44 pp., printed wrappers. Governor's Island, N.Y., 1890. First edition. $400-$500.

BOURKE, John G. *On the Border with Crook.* Frontispiece portrait, other plates. Cloth. New York, 1891. First edition. $75-$100.

BOURKE, John G. *Scatologic Rites of All Nations.* Cloth. Washington, 1891. First edition. $75-$100.

BOURKE, John G. *The Snake-Dance of the Moquis of Arizona.* Plates, some in color. Pictorial cloth. New York, 1884. First edition. $75-$100. New York, 1891. Cloth. $50-$75.

BOWDITCH, Nathaniel. *The New American Practical Navigator.* Folding frontispiece map, 6 plates. Boards or full leather. Newburyport, Mass., 1802. First edition. $1,000-$1,500.

BOWEN, Abel. *The Naval Monument.* 25 woodcuts. Calf. Boston, 1816. First edition. With errata slip. $50-$75.

BOWEN, Elizabeth. *Seven Winters.* Boards and linen. Dublin, 1942. Cuala Press. One of 450. In tissue dust jacket. $50-$60. Lacking jacket, $40-$50.

BOWERS, Mrs. Dr. J. Milton. *The Dance of Life: An Answer to the "Dance of Death."* Red or green cloth. San Francisco, 1877. (By Ambrose Bierce?) First edition. $25-$35.

BOWLES, Jane. *Two Serious Ladies.* Cloth. New York, 1943. First edition. In dust jacket. $75-$100.

BOWLES, Paul. *The Sheltering Sky.* Cloth. New York, no date (1949). First edition. In dust jacket. $30-$35.

BOX, Capt. Michael James. *Capt. James Box's Adventures and Explorations in New and Old Mexico.* Cloth. New York, 1861. First edition. $250. New York, 1869. Cloth. Second edition. $50-$75.

BOYD, Belle. *Belle Boyd in Camp and Prison, Written by Herself.* Cloth. New York, 1865. (By Belle B. Hardinge.) First American edition. $50. (There was a two-volume London first edition in 1865. No recent price data seen.) New York, 1866. Cloth. $35.

BOYD, Nancy. *Distressing Dialogues.* Cloth. New York, no date (1924). (By Edna St. Vincent Millay.) First edition (so stated). In dust jacket. $25-$35.

BOYD, James. *Drums.* Green cloth. New York-London, 1925. First edition. In dust jacket. $35. Author's first book. New York, no date (1928). Illustrated by N. C. Wyeth. Cloth. One of 525 signed by author and artist. Boxed. $35-$50.

BOYLE, Kay. *Short Stories.* Printed wrappers in gold or silver protective boards. Paris, 1929. Black Sun Press. First edition. One of 15 on Japan paper, signed. $75. Another issue: One of 150 on Van Gelder paper. Boxed. $50-$60. Author's first book. (See following entry.)

BOYLE, Kay. *Wedding Day and Other Stories.* Decorated boards, cloth spine. New York, no date (1930). First American edition (of the author's first book, retitled). In dust jacket. $25-$35.

BOYLE, Robert. See *The Martyrdom of Theodora.*

"BOZ." See Dickens, Charles. Also see *Sketches by "Boz."*

"BOZ." *Master Humphrey's Clock.* 88 weekly parts, white wrappers. London, 1840-41. (By Charles Dickens.) First edition. $300-$500. Also, $214 (A, 1969). Second edition: 20 monthly parts in 19, green wrappers. $250-$300. Third edition: 3 vols., brown cloth. (First book edition, issued under Dickens' name, which see.)

"BOZ." *Memoirs of Joseph Grimaldi.* Edited by "Boz." Illustrated by George Cruikshank. 2 vols., pink cloth. London, 1838. (Edited and written in part by Charles Dickens.) First edition, first issue, with no border around last plate. $150-$200. Second issue, crude border around plate. $75-$100.

"BOZ." *Oliver Twist; or, The Parish Boy's Progress.* Illustrated by George Cruikshank. 3 vols., brown cloth. London, 1838. (By Charles Dickens.) First edition, first issue, with "Fireside" plate, Vol. 3. $350-$450. Also, worn and foxed, $160 (A, 1970); $120 (A, 1968); $250 (A, 1967). (Eckel reports one copy that sold for $650.) Second issue, with "Rose Maylie and Oliver" replacing "Fireside" plate. $100-$150. (For second edition, sometimes called third issue, 1839, with Dickens on title page, and for first octavo edition, in parts and in book form, see author entries under *Oliver Twist* and *The Adventures of Oliver Twist.*)

"BOZ." *The Strange Gentleman: A Comic Burletta.* Printed buff wrappers. London, 1837. (By Charles Dickens.) First edition. $250 and up. Facsimile edition. No place, no date (London, 1871). $50.

BRACE, Jack. *Marie; or the Gambler of the Mississippi.* Boards. New York, 1861. (By Justin Jones.) First edition. $25-$35.

BRACKENRIDGE, H. M. See *Strictures on a Voyage to South America, etc.*

BRACKENRIDGE, H. M. *A Eulogy, on the Lives and Characters of John Adams & Thomas Jefferson.* 18 pp., plain wrappers. Pensacola, Fla., 1826. First edition. $350.

BRACKENRIDGE, H. M. *Journal of a Voyage up the Missouri River.* Printed boards. Baltimore, 1815. First edition (actually second appearance of the journal, which first appeared in author's *Views of Louisiana,* which see). $150-$200. Baltimore, 1816 (cover date 1815). Boards. Second edition. $150-$200.

BRACKENRIDGE, H. M. *Views of Louisiana; Together with a Journal of a Voyage up the Missouri River, in 1814.* Boards, or leather. Pittsburgh, 1814. First edition. $500-$750. Baltimore, 1817. Boards. (Containing only *Views* and not the *Journal.*) $50. (For separate publication of the *Journal,* see preceding entry.)

BRACKENRIDGE, Hugh Henry. *Gazette Publications.* Leather. Carlisle, Pa., 1806. First edition. $200-$250. Also, rebound, rubbed, stained, $90 (A, 1967).

BRADBURY, Ray. *Dark Carnival.* Black cloth. Sauk City, Wis., 1947. Arkham House. First edition. In dust jacket. $40-$50. Author's first book.

BRADBURY, Ray. *Fahrenheit 451.* Cloth. New York, no date (1953). First edition. In dust jacket. $30-$40. (Note: Also issued in a Ballantine paperback. $20-$25.)

BRADLEY, James. *The Confederate Mail Carrier.* 15 plates. Cloth. Mexico, Mo., 1894. First edition. $50-$60.

BRADLEY, Joshua. *Accounts of Religious Revivals in Many Parts of the United States from 1815 to 1818.* Calf. Albany, N.Y., 1819. First edition. $32.50.

BRADLEY, William Aspenwall. *The Etching of Figures.* Half vellum. Marlborough-on-Hudson, N.Y., 1915. Dard Hunter paper and printing. One of 250. $100-$150.

BRADY, William. *Glimpses of Texas.* Folding map in color. Stiff wrappers. Houston, 1871. First edition. $50-$75.

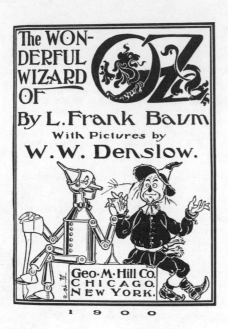

BRAITHWAITE, William (editor). *Anthology of Magazine Verse for 1923.* Boards and cloth. Boston, 1923. First edition. One of 245 signed by Braithwaite. $40-$50.

BRAMAH, Ernest. *English Farming and Why I Turned It Up.* Cloth. London, 1894. (By Ernest Bramah Smith.) First edition. $30-$50. Author's first book.

BRAMAH, Ernest. *The Wallet of Kai Lung.* Light-green cloth. London, no date (1900). (By Ernest Bramah Smith.) First English edition, first issue, measuring 1½ inches thick. $35-$50. Boston, 1900. Green cloth, gilt top. First American edition, with American ads at end. $25-$35.

BRAMAN, D. E. E. *Information About Texas.* Cloth. Philadelphia, 1857. First edition. $90. Philadelphia, 1858. Cloth. $25-$35.

BRATT, John. *Trails of Yesterday.* Portrait frontispiece and plates. Pictorial cloth. Lincoln, Neb., 1921. First edition. $60-$80.

BRAUTIGAN, Richard. *Four New Poets.* Wrappers. San Francisco, no date (1957). Inferno Press. First edition. $20-$25. First book appearance of Brautigan, with three other poets.

BRAUTIGAN, Richard. *Lay the Marble Tea.* Printed wrappers. San Francisco, 1959. First edition. $30-$35.

BRAUTIGAN, Richard. *The Octopus Frontier.* Printed wrappers. San Francisco, 1960. First edition. $15-$20.

BRAUTIGAN, Richard. *The Pill Versus the Springhill Mine Disaster.* Tan boards, brown cloth spine. San Francisco, no date (1968). First edition. One of 50 signed. $15-$20.

BRAUTIGAN, Richard. *In Watermelon Sugar.* Blue boards, black cloth spine. San Francisco, 1968. First edition. One of 50 signed. $15-$20.

BRAVO (The): A Venetian Story. 3 vols., boards, paper labels. London, 1831. (By James Fenimore Cooper.) First edition. $100-$150. Philadelphia, 1831. 2 vols., boards, paper labels. First American edition. $75-$100, possibly more.

BRAVO of Perth (The): or, Voorn the Robber. Colored frontispiece. 68 pp., boards. Boston, 1814. Second edition. $45-$50.

BRAY, William (editor). *Memoirs, Illustrative of the Life and Writings of John Evelyn.* 2 vols., contemporary calf. Bath, England, 1818. First edition. Bookplates, $65.

BRAYTON, Matthew. *The Indian Captive.* 68 pp., printed green wrappers, or boards. Cleveland, 1860. First edition. Wrappers: $450-$650. Boards: $250-$400. Also, $225 (A, 1954). Fostoria, Ohio, 1896. Boards. Second edition. $75-$100.

BRAZER, Esther Stevens. *Early American Decoration.* 34 color plates. Cloth. Springfield, Mass., no date (1947). $35. Springfield, no date (1950). $25-$35.

BREAD-WINNERS (The). Cloth. New York, 1884. (By John Hay.) First edition. $35-$50.

BRETON, Nicholas. *The Twelve Months and Christmas Day.* New York, 1951. One of 100, signed by Bruce Rogers. $35.

BRICE, Wallace A. *History of Fort Wayne.* 7 plates. Cloth. Fort Wayne, Ind., 1868. First edition. $30-$50.

BRIDGENS, Richard. *Furniture, with Candelabra and Interior Decoration.* 60 full-page color plates. Folio, boards. London, 1838. $150 and up.

BRIDGES, Robert. *Eros and Psyche, a Poem.* Woodcuts from drawings by Edward Burne-Jones. White pigskin. Newtown, Wales, 1935. Gregynog Press. One of 300. In buckram case. $150-$250. Another issue: One of 15 specially bound by George Fisher. $500-$600.

BRIDGES, Robert. *The Growth of Love.* Boards and parchment. Oxford, 1890. Daniel Press. One of 100. $150-$200. Also, $91 (A, 1971).

BRIDGES, Robert. *Poems.* Cloth. London, 1873. First edition. $150-$200. Author's first book (suppressed by him in 1878).

BRIDGES, Robert. *Poems Written in the Year MCMXIII.* Blue printed boards and cloth. Chelsea (London), 1914. Ashendene Press. First edition. One of 85 with initials in red and blue. Boxed. $500-$600. (Note: A remarkable example of how the prices of fine books have risen sharply in recent years. In the 1950's this book was listed by three leading dealers in London and New York at $80, $95, and $100, respectively.)

BRIDGES, Robert. *The Tapestry.* Boards. No place (London), 1925. First edition. One of 150. Boxed. $100-$150. Also, $72 (A, 1971).

BRIDGES, Robert. *The Testament of Beauty.* Buckram. Oxford, 1929. First published edition. One of 50 signed. In dust jacket. $50-$100. Another issue: One of 200, unsigned. $35-$50. Trade edition: Boards. $10-$25. New York, 1929. One of 250. $25. (Note: In 1961 a privately printed, 1927-29, "trial issue" of 5 unbound parts was sold at auction in London for $252.)

BRIDWELL, J. W. (compiler). *The Life and Adventures of Robert McKimie.* 56 pp., pictorial wrappers. Hillsboro, Ohio, 1878. First edition. $500-$750, possibly more. Rebound in cloth-backed wrappers with original front cover mounted, some leaves repaired, stains throughout, $600.

BRIEF History of Christ's Hospital (A). Boards, paper label. London, 1820. (By Charles Lamb.) First edition. $100-$150.

BRIGGS, L. Vernon. *Arizona and New Mexico, 1882; California, 1886; Mexico, 1891.* Portraits. Cloth. No place, no date (Boston, 1932). First edition. $40-$50.

BRIGGS, L. Vernon. *History of Shipbuilding on North River, Plymouth County, Massachusetts.* 57 illustrations. Cloth. Boston, 1889. First edition. $80-$100.

BRIGHAM, Clarence S. *Paul Revere's Engravings.* 77 plates (some in color). Cloth. Worcester, Mass., 1954. First edition. In dust jacket. $75-$100.

BRILLAT-SAVARIN, J. A. *The Physiology of Taste.* Introduction by Arthur Machen. Portrait, other illustrations. Boards. London, 1925. One of 750. $43.20-$75. Also, $33.60 (A, 1969). New York, 1949. Limited Editions Club. Translated by M. F. K. Fisher. Half leather. Boxed. $35-$50.

BRINNIN, John Malcolm. *The Garden Is Political.* Cloth. New York, 1942. First edition. In dust jacket. $25. Author's first book.

BRISBIN, James S. *The Beef Bonanza.* 8 plates. Pictorial cloth. Philadelphia, 1881. First edition. $50-$60.

BRITISH Military Library (The). 47 maps, plans and plates, 29 color plates of military costume, 10 leaves of music. 2 vols., morocco. London, 1799-1801. $275-$300.

BRITTON, Wiley. *Memoirs of the Rebellion on the Border, 1863.* Cloth. Chicago, 1882. First edition. $25-$35.

BRODIE, Walter. *Pitcairn's Island and The Islanders in 1850.* 4 plates. Cloth, paper label. London, 1851. First edition. $100-$150. London, 1851. Second edition. $50-$60.

BROMFIELD, Louis. *Awake and Rehearse.* Boards. New York, no date (1929). First edition. One of 500 signed. In dust jacket. Boxed. $20-$25.

BROMFIELD, Louis. *The Green Bay Tree.* Cloth. New York, 1924. First edition. In dust jacket. $25. Author's first book.

BRONTË, Anne. See Bell, Acton; Bell, Currer.

BRONTË, Anne. *Self-Communion.* 2 facsimiles. Boards. London, 1900. First edition. One of 30. $50-$60.

BRONTË, Charlotte. See Bell, Currer.

BRONTË, Emily. See Bell, Ellis.

BRONTË, The Rev. Patrick. *Cottage Poems.* Blue boards. Halifax, 1811. First edition. $50-$75.

BRONTË, The Rev. P(atrick). *The Rural Minstrel.* Blue-gray boards. Halifax, 1813. First edition. $50-$75.

BROOKE, Arthur De Capell. *Travels Through Sweden, Norway, and Finmark, to the North Cape.* Map, 21 plates (2 colored). Calf, or boards and calf. London, no date (1823). $150-$200. Worn, $75. London, 1831. Half calf. Second edition. $100-$150.

BROOKE, Arthur De Capell. *A Winter in Lapland and Sweden.* Calf, or boards and calf. London, 1826. $150-$200. London, 1827. $75-$100.

BROOKE, H. K. *Annals of the Revolution.* Boards. Philadelphia, no date (1848). First edition. $100-$125.

BROOKE, Rupert. *Collected Poems.* Portrait. Boards and cloth. New York, 1915. First edition. One of 100 specially bound for the Woodberry Society. $75.

BROOKE, Rupert. *Lithuania: A Drama in One Act.* Pictorial brown wrappers. Chicago, 1915. Chicago Little Theatre. First edition. $100-$150.

BROOKE, Rupert. *Poems.* Black cloth, paper label. London, 1911. First edition. $100-$150. Author's first book of verse.

BROOKE, Rupert. *1914, and Other Poems.* Portrait frontispiece. Dark-blue cloth, paper label. London, 1915. First edition. In dust jacket. $75-$100. New York, 1915. Morocco. First American edition. One of a few copies (out of an issue of 87) bound in morocco (others being in wrappers). $75-$100. Wrappers: $35-$50.

BROOKE, Rupert. *"1914": Five Sonnets.* Printed wrappers. London, 1915. First edition. $45-$50.

BROOKE, Rupert. *The Old Vicarage.* Woodcut. Gray wrappers. London, 1916. First edition. $25-$35.

BROOKS, Bryant B. *Memoirs of Bryant B. Brooks.* Plates. Cloth. Glendale, Calif., 1939. First edition. One of 150. $50-$75.

BROOKS, Gwendolyn. *Annie Allen.* Cloth. New York, no date (1949). First edition. In dust jacket. $20-$25.

BROOKS, Gwendolyn. *The Bean Eaters.* Cloth. New York, no date (1960). First edition. In dust jacket. $15-$20.

BROOKS, Gwendolyn. *A Street in Bronzeville.* Cloth. New York, 1945. First edition. In dust jacket. $25-$35.

BROTHERHEAD, William (editor). *The Book of the Signers: Facsimile Letters of the Signers of the Declaration of Independence.* Cloth. Philadelphia, 1861. First edition. One of 99 on large paper, with proof plates. $75-$100. Ordinary issue: $25-$35. Philadelphia, 1865. 60 plates. Second edition. One of 160. $25-$35. Philadelphia, no date (1875 or 1876?). New edition (published as *The Centennial Book of the Signers*). $35-$50.

BROTHERS (The): A Tale of the Fronde. 2 vols., cloth, paper labels. New York, 1835. (By Henry William Herbert.) First edition, first issue, in brown cloth. $150-$200. Author's first book.

BROUGHTON, William Robert. *A Voyage of Discovery to the North Pacific Ocean.* 9 plates and maps (7 folding). Half calf. London, 1804. First edition. $1,500-$2,000. Foxed, some plates with tears, $1,500. Also, original half calf, $1,100 (A, 1969).

BROUILLET, J. B. A. *Authentic Account of the Murder of Dr. Whitman and Other Missionaries.* 108 pp., wrappers. Portland, 1869. Second edition of *Protestantism in Oregon* (see item following). $500-$600.

BROUILLET, J. B. A. *Protestantism in Oregon: Account of the Murder of Dr. Whitman, and the Ungrateful Calumnies of H. H. Spalding, Protestant Missionary.* Wrappers. New York, 1853. First edition. Covers soiled, $1,750. Also, rebound in modern morocco, $700 (A, 1969).

BROWER, Jacob V. *Memoirs of Explorations in the Basin of the Mississippi.* Maps. 8 vols., cloth. St. Paul, Minn., 1898-1904. One of 300. Up to $250.

BROWN, Bob. *Demonics.* Wrappers. Cagnes-sur-Mer, France, 1931. First edition. $50-$60.

BROWN, Bob. *Readies for Bob Brown's Machine.* Wrappers. Cagnes-sur-Mer, France, 1931. First edition. $50.

BROWN, Charles Brockden. See *Monroe's Embassy.*

BROWN, Charles Brockden. *Arthur Mervyn: A Tale.* 3 vols., boards. London, 1803. First English edition. $50-$100. (Note: The first edition was issued anonymously in America in 1799-1800. See entry under *Arthur Mervyn.*)

BROWN, Charles Brockden. *Carwin, the Biloquist, and Other American Tales and Pieces.* Boards. London, 1822. First English edition (of "Memoirs of Carwin, etc.," from William Dunlap's *The Life of Charles Brockden Brown*, which see). $200 and up. Also, $106.40 (A, 1959).

BROWN, Isaac V. *Memoirs of the Rev. Robert Finley, D.D.* Calf. New Brunswick, N.J., 1819. First edition. $27.50.

BROWN, J. Cabell. *Calabazas, or Amusing Recollections of an Arizona "City."* Illustrated. Printed wrappers. San Francisco, 1892. First edition. $75-$100.

BROWN, J. Willard. *The Signal Corps, U.S.A., in the War of the Rebellion.* Cloth. Boston, 1896. $35-$50.

BROWN, James S. *California Gold: An Authentic History of the First Find.* Portrait frontispiece. 20 pp., printed wrappers. Oakland, 1894. First edition. One of 55. $100-$150. Also, $70 (A, 1968).

BROWN, James S. *Life of a Pioneer.* Portrait. 2 plates. Cloth. Salt Lake City, 1900. First edition. $100-$135. Also, $65 (A, 1966).

BROWN, Jesse, and Willard, A. M. *The Black Hills Trails.* 2 plates. Cloth. Rapid City, S.D., 1924. First edition. $75-$100.

BROWN, John. *Rab and His Friends.* Pictorial wrappers. Boston, 1859. First American edition. $35-$40.

BROWN, John Henry. *History of Dallas County from 1837 to 1887.* 114 pp., wrappers. Dallas, 1887. First edition. $110.

BROWN, John Henry. *History of Texas, 1685-1892.* 25 plates. 2 vols., cloth. St. Louis, no date (1892-93). First edition. $75-$100.

BROWN, John Henry. *Indian Wars and Pioneers of Texas.* Plates. Cloth. Austin, Tex., no date (1896). First edition. $150-$200.

BROWN, John Henry. *Political History of Oregon.* Vol. 1. (All published.) Illustrated, folding map. Cloth. Portland, Ore., 1892. First edition. $350-$400.

BROWN, John H(enry). *Reminiscences and Incidents, of "The Early Days" of San Francisco.* Folding frontispiece plan. 53 leaves, cloth. San Francisco, no date (1886). First edition. $400-$500. San Francisco, no date (1933). Grabhorn printing. Half cloth. One of 500. $35-$50. Another issue: One of 25 in morocco, with additional reproductions, etc. $150-$200.

BROWN, John Henry, and Speer, W. S. *The Encyclopedia of the New West.* Calf. Marshall, Tex., 1881. First edition. $75-$125.

BROWN, John P. *Old Frontiers: The Story of the Cherokee Indians.* Cloth. Kingsport, Tenn., 1938. First edition. $25-$35.

BROWN, Samuel J. *In Captivity: The Experience, Privations and Dangers of Sam'l J. Brown, etc.* Text in 2 columns. Illustrated. Full leather. Mankato, Minn., no date (1896). First edition. $250 (A, 1967).

BROWN, Samuel R. *The Western Gazetteer, or Emigrant's Directory.* Sheep. Auburn, N.Y., 1817. First edition, first issue, with 3-line errata slip. $75-$100. Also, $30 (A, 1966). Second issue, with 4-line errata. $50-$75. Third issue, with advertisements. $50.

BROWN, William C., *The Sheepeater Campaign in Idaho.* Folding map. 32 pp., wrappers. Boise, 1926. First edition. One of 50. $35-$50.

BROWN, William H. *The Early History of the State of Illinois.* 16 pp., printed wrappers. Chicago, 1840. First edition. $730-$1,000.

BROWN, William Robinson. *The Horse of the Desert.* Cloth. New York, 1929. Derrydale Press. One of 750. $60-$80.

BROWNE, J. Ross. *Adventures in the Apache Country.* Illustrated by the author. Cloth. New York, 1869. First edition. $75-$125.

BROWNE, J. Ross. *Report of the Debates in the Convention of California on the Formation of the State Constitution.* Cloth. Washington, 1850. First edition. $50-$75.

BROWNE, J. Ross. *Report . . . on the Late Indian War in Oregon and Washington Territory.* Half leather. Washington, 1858. First edition. $35-$50.

BROWNE, Thomas A. See Boldrewood, Rolf.

BROWNE, Sir Thomas. *Religio Medici.* Portrait and facsimile. Marbled boards and cloth. New York, 1939. Limited Editions Club. John Henry Nash printing. Boxed. $30.

BROWNE, Sir Thomas. *Urne Buriall and The Garden of Cyprus.* Edited by John Carter. 30 hand-colored drawings by Paul Nash. Folio, vellum and morocco. London, 1932. Curwen Press. One of 215. In slipcase. $250-$300.

BROWNE, William Bradford. *The Babbitt Family History.* Illustrated. Cloth. Taunton, Mass., 1912. $40-$50.

BROWNING, Elizabeth Barrett. See B., E. B.; Barrett, Elizabeth B.; Barrett, Elizabeth Barrett. Also see *An Essay on Mind; Prometheus Bound.*

BROWNING, Elizabeth Barrett. *Aurora Leigh.* Cloth. London, 1857. First edition. $100-$150.

BROWNING, Elizabeth Barrett. *Casa Guidi Windows: A Poem.* Green cloth. London, 1851. First edition. $75-$100.

BROWNING, Elizabeth Barrett. *The Enchantress and Other Poems.* Printed wrappers. London, 1913. First edition. One of 30. $80-$100.

BROWNING, Elizabeth Barrett. *Leila, A Tale.* Printed wrappers. London, 1913. First edition. One of 30. $80-$100.

BROWNING, Elizabeth Barrett. *Poems.* 2 vols., cloth. London, 1850. ("New edition.") Second edition (and containing first book appearance of "Sonnets from the Portuguese";' see B., E. B., entry and author-title entry below). $200-$250.

BROWNING, Elizabeth Barrett. *Poems Before Congress.* Red cloth. London, 1860. First edition, with 32-page publisher's catalogue. $75-$100.

BROWNING, Elizabeth Barrett. *Sonnets from the Portuguese.* (Note: For the first appearance of the sonnets, see *Poems* under author entry; for the faked Thomas J. Wise first edition, see B., E. B., entry. The following entries are all reprinted versions of the original work.) London, 1887 (date 1889 on cover). Ballantyne Press. Morocco. One of 8 on vellum. $200-$300. London, 1897. Illustrated. Wrappers. (No copies in original wrappers noted.) No place, no date (East Aurora, 1898). Roycrofters. Half cloth. One of 480. $25-$35. Chicago, no date (1899). One of 15. $25. New Rochelle, N.Y., 1900. Doves Press [*sic*]. One of 485. $25. No place (Boston), 1902. One of 250. $25. London, 1906. Vellum. One of a few printed in red and black on vellum. $25-$35. London, no date (1909). Buckram. One of 500. In dust jacket. $30. London, 1914. Riccardi Press. Calf. Limited edition. $12 (A, 1953). Montagnola, 1925. Morocco. One of 225. $50 (A, 1964). San Francisco, 1925-27. 2 vols., half vellum (including facsimile volume). One of 250. $50-$60. San Francisco, 1931. 2 vols. One of 250. $37.50. New York, 1948. Limited Editions Club. Cloth. Boxed. $50.

BROWNING, Robert. See Barrett, Elizabeth, and Browning, Robert. Also see *Pauline: A Fragment of a Confession.*

BROWNING, Robert. *Aristophanes' Apology.* Green cloth. London, 1875. First edition, with ad leaf at end. $25.

BROWNING, Robert. *Asolando.* Red cloth. London, 1890. First edition. $35-$50.

BROWNING, Robert. *Balaustion's Adventure.* Beveled red-brown cloth. London, 1871. First edition. $25.

BROWNING, Robert. *Bells and Pomegranates.* 8 parts, printed wrappers. London, 1841-46. First edition, with half title for second part. $500-$750 at retail, possibly more, for a perfect set. Also, $375 (A, 1945). (Note: This was Frank Hogan's set, slightly worn. Since then the only set noted at auction was one sold in the 1960 season; it included 5 presentation parts, inscribed, and brought $364.) First book edition (parts bound in one volume, cloth, with the half title to the second part). $300-$400.

BROWNING, Robert. *Dramatic Romances and Lyrics.* Illustrated. Morocco. London, 1899. Ballantyne Press. One of 10 on vellum. $500-$750. Another issue: Buckram. One of 210. $50.

BROWNING, Robert. *Dramatis Personae.* Red cloth. London, 1864. First edition. $125-$150. Lacking contents leaf, $91.20. Also, $70 (A, 1966). London, 1910. Doves Press. Vellum. One of 250 printed in red and black. $300.

BROWNING, Robert. *An Essay on Percy Bysshe Shelley.* Edited by W. T. Harden. Sheets printed on vellum, unbound, in buckram folder and slipcase. No place (London), 1888. One of 4 (3?) printed on vellum. $288.

BROWNING, Robert. *Fifine at the Fair.* Dark-brown cloth. London, 1872. First edition. $25-$35.

BROWNING, Robert. *La Saisiaz: The Two Poets of Croisic.* Blue-green cloth. London, 1878. First edition. $25-$35.

BROWNING, Robert. *Men and Women.* 2 vols., green cloth. London, 1855. First edition, first binding. $150-$200. London, 1908. Doves Press. 2 vols., vellum. One of 262 printed in red and black. $480.

BROWNING, Robert. *Pacchiarotto and How He Worked in Distemper: With Other Poems.* Beveled gray cloth. London, 1876. First edition, with ad leaf at end. $25-$35.

BROWNING, Robert. *Paracelsus.* Drab boards, paper label. London, 1835. First edition, first issue, with 8 pages of ads at front dated Dec. 1, 1842. $250-$500. Rebound in half calf, $100. Author's first acknowledged book.

BROWNING, Robert. *The Pied Piper of Hamelin.* 35 colored illustrations by Kate Greenaway. Pictorial boards. London, no date (1888). First edition. $150-$200. London, 1934. Illustrated by Arthur Rackham. Limp vellum. De luxe edition. $150.

BROWNING, Robert. *Prince Hohenstiel-Schwangau, Saviour of Society.* Cloth. London, 1871. First edition. $25-$35.

BROWNING, Robert. *The Ring and the Book.* 4 vols., green cloth. London, 1868-69. First edition, first issue, with Roman (not italic) figures on backs of all 4 volumes. $100-$125. New York, 1949. Limited Editions Club. 2 vols., boards and morocco. Boxed. $40.

BROWNING, Robert. *Some Poems.* Boards. London, 1904. Eragny Press. One of 226. $75-$100.

BROWNING, Robert. *Sordello.* Boards, paper label. London, 1840. First edition, first issue, in boards. $400-$500.

BROWNING, Robert. *Strafford: An Historical Tragedy.* Gray wrappers, paper label on front. London, 1837. First edition $125-$150.

BRUFF, J. Goldsborough. *Gold Rush: The Journals, Drawings and Other Papers of J. Goldsborough Bruff.* Edited by Georgia W. Read and Ruth Gaines. 21 plates. 2 vols., boards. New York, 1944. First edition. $75-$100. New York, 1949. Illustrated. 2 vols. in one, cloth. In dust jacket. $12.50-$15.

BRUFFEY, George A. *Eighty-one Years in the West.* Portrait. 152 pp., wrappers. Butte, Mont., 1925. First edition. $25.

BRUMBAUGH, Gaius Marcus. *Genealogy of the Brumbaugh Families.* Illustrated. Cloth. New York, no date (1913). One of 1,000. $25-$35.

BRUNSON, Alfred. *A Western Pioneer.* 2 vols., cloth. Cincinnati, 1872-79. First edition. $75-$100. (Note: A difficult set to bring together.)

BRUNSON, Edward. *Profits in Sheep and Cattle in Central and Western Kansas.* 16 pp., wrappers. Kansas City, 1883. First edition. $40-$50.

BRYANT, Edwin. *What I Saw in California.* Cloth. New York, 1848. First edition. $150-$200. Also, $120 (A, 1968). New York, 1848. Cloth. Second edition. $50. Santa Ana, Calif., 1936. Half morocco. $25-$35.

BRYANT, Gilbert Ernest. *The Chelsea Porcelain Toys.* 63 plates, 47 in color. Cloth. London, 1925. One of 650 signed. In dust jacket. $150-$200.

BRYANT, John Howard. *Poems.* Cloth. New York, 1855. First edition. $25-$30.

BRYANT, Wilbur F. *The Blood of Abel.* Cloth. Hastings, Neb., 1887. First edition. Lacking front free end paper, $100 (A, 1969).

BRYANT, William Cullen. *The Embargo; or, Sketches of the Times: A Satire.* (Cover title.) Self-wrappers (stitched); also plain slate blue or marbled paper wrappers. Boston, 1809. Second edition. Wrappers: $400-$500. Stitched: $200-$300. (For first edition, see title entry, *The Embargo.*)

BRYANT, William Cullen. *The Fountain and Other Poems.* Boards; or cloth, label on spine; or, cloth with gold stamping on front cover. New York, 1842. First edition. (No priority on bindings, according to Blanck.) $75-$100.

BRYANT, William Cullen. *Hymns.* Brown-orange or blue cloth. No place, no date (New York, 1864). First edition, first state, with reading "Dwells on Thy works in deep delight" in second line of fourth stanza on page 9. $50-$75.

BRYANT, William Cullen. *Poems.* Brown or grayish printed boards (375 copies?–Blanck) or printed brown wrappers (200 copies?–Blanck). Cambridge, Mass., 1821. First edition. $1,000-$1,500. New York, 1832. Second edition. Boards and blue cloth. $75-$100. New York, 1836. Third edition. $35-$50. New York, 1947. Limited Editions Club. Illustrated by Thomas Nason. Leather. Boxed. $20-$25.

BRYANT, William Cullen. *Thirty Poems.* Brown cloth. New York, 1864. First edition, first state, wove paper, line 5 from bottom of page 213 reading "veielo." $35-$50. Second state, laid paper, reading "vuielo" on page 213. $15-$20.

BRYANT, William Cullen. *Unpublished Poems.* Illustrated. Boards. Boston, 1907. Bibliophile Society. One of 470 on vellum. Boxed. $40-$50.

BRYCE, James. *The American Commonwealth.* 3 vols., cloth. London, 1888. First edition, first issue, with the chapter in Vol. 3 on the Tweed Ring, later suppressed. $200-$250. Second issue, with Tweed Ring matter omitted. $75-$125.

BUCHAN, John. *The Marquis of Montrose.* Plates, maps, plans. Cloth. London, 1913. First edition. $75-$100.

BUCHAN, John. *Pilgrim Fathers.* Wrappers. Oxford, 1898. First edition. $75-$100.

BUCHAN, John. *Poems–Scots and English.* Blue cloth and boards. London, 1917. One of 50 signed. $60.

BUCHAN, John. *Sir Quixote of the Moors.* Cloth. London, 1895. First edition, first issue, with full title on spine. $84. New York, 1895. Cloth. First American edition. $15-$25.

BUCHANAN, Margaret Gwen. *Du Vals of Kentucky from Virginia, 1794-1935.* Plates. Cloth. Lynchburg, Va., no date (about 1935). Limited edition. $35-$50.

BUCHANAN, Robert. *The Fleshly School of Poetry.* Violet pictorial wrappers. London, 1872. First edition. $75-$100.

BUCK, Irving A. *Cleburne and His Command.* Plates. Cloth. New York, 1908. First edition. $50-$75.

BUCK, Pearl S. (translator). *All Men Are Brothers.* Translated from the Chinese of Shui Hu Chuan. 2 vols. New York, no date (1933). First edition. $35-$50. New York, 1948. Limited Editions Club. Edited by Lin Yutang. Illustrated by Miguel Covarrubias. 2 vols., stiff wrappers, Chinese silk paper, tied with thongs. Boxed. $75-$100.

BUCK, Pearl S. *East Wind: West Wind.* Cloth. New York, no date (1930). First edition. In dust jacket. $35-$40.

BUCK, Pearl S. *The Good Earth.* Tan cloth. New York, no date (1931). First edition, first issue, with "flees" for "fleas" in line 17 of page 100, with "John Day Publishing Company" on copyright page, and with top edges stained brown. In brown dust jacket. $75-$100. Later issue, green top edges, in dust jacket. $10-$20. Advance issue, for review: Printed wrappers. $100.

BUCK, Pearl S. *Sons.* Cloth. New York, no date (1932). First edition (so stated). One of 371 de luxe copies, signed. In dust jacket. Boxed. $35-$50.

BUCKBEE, Edna Bryan. *The Saga of Old Tuolumne.* Plates. Cloth. New York, 1935. In dust jacket. $35-$50.

BUCKINGHAM, Nash. *De Shootinest Gent'man and Other Tales.* Edited by Col. Harold P. Sheldon. Illustrated. Cloth. New York, no date (1934). Derrydale Press. First edition. One of 950. $200-$250.

BUCKINGHAM, Nash. *Mark Right!* Illustrated. Cloth. New York, no date (1936). Derrydale Press. $60-$80.

BUCKINGHAM, Nash. *Ole Miss.* Edited by Paul A. Curtis. Illustrated. Leatherette. New York, no date (1937). Derrydale Press. $100-$125.

BUCKLEY, Francis. *English Baluster Stemmed Glasses of the 17th and 18th Centuries.* 18 plates. Buckram. Edinburgh, 1912. $75.

BUCKLEY, Francis. *Old London Drinking Glasses.* 14 plates. Buckram. Edinburgh, 1913. $75-$100.

BUCKLEY, Wilfred. *Diamond Engraved Glasses of the 16th Century.* 33 plates. Boards. London, 1929. One of 250. $35-$50.

BUDGE, Sir E. A. Wallis. *Amulets and Superstitions.* 22 plates, 300 other illustrations. Cloth. London, 1930. $35-$40.

BUDGE, Sir E. A. Wallis. *The Gods of the Egyptians, or Studies in Egyptian Mythology.* 98 color plates. 2 vols., pictorial cloth. London, 1904. $125. Also, $52.80 and $65 (A, 1969).

BUEL, J. W. *Life and Marvelous Adventures of Wild Bill, the Scout.* Frontispiece and plate. 93 pp., pictorial wrappers. Chicago, 1880. First edition, presumed first issue, with cover dated 1880. $400-$600.

BUFFUM, E. Gould. *Six Months in the Gold Mines.* Printed wrappers, or cloth. Philadelphia, 1850. First edition. Wrappers: $200. Also, $90 (A, 1960). Cloth: $100-$200. Also, $47 (A, 1969), $90 (A, 1968).

BUKOWSKI, Charles. *At Terror Street and Agony Way.* Cloth. Los Angeles, 1968. Black Sparrow Press. First edition. One of 75 signed by the author with an original illustration by the author. $75-$85.

BUKOWSKI, Charles. *Cold Dogs in the Courtyard.* Wrappers. Literary Times and Cyfoeth Publications, 1965. First edition. One of 500. $12-$15.

BUKOWSKI, Charles. *Crucifix in a Deathhand.* Pictorial wrappers. New Orleans, 1962. Loujon Press. First edition, limited and signed. $30-$35.

BULFINCH, Thomas. *The Age of Chivalry.* 6 illustrations. Brown cloth. Boston, 1859. First edition. $100-$125.

BULFINCH, Thomas. *The Age of Fable.* Brown cloth. Boston, 1855. First edition, first state, with names of both printer and stereotyper on copyright page. $75-$100. New York, 1956. Limited Editions Club. Illustrated by Joe Mugnaini. Cloth. Boxed. $25.

BULLEN, A. H. *A Collection of Old English Plays.* 7 vols., boards, parchment spines. London, 1882-90. One of 150. $250-$350.

BULLEN, Frank T. *The Cruise of the "Cachalot."* Folding map and plates. Blue cloth. London, 1898. First edition. $35-$75. Author's first book. (Note: Contains first publication of a Kipling letter.)

BULLER, Sir Walter Lawry. *A History of the Birds of New Zealand.* 35 hand-colored plates. Cloth. London, 1873. First edition. $400-$500. Also, $180 (A, 1969). Rebound in half morocco, $250-$300. London, 1887-88. 48 colored plates, 2 plain plates. 13 parts in 8, wrappers. $165.

BULLCOK, William. *Six Months Residence and Travels in Mexico.* 2 folding plans, folding view, 11 other views, 4 colored aquatint plates. Boards and cloth. 1824. First edition. $150-$200.

BULWER-LYTTON, Edward. See Caxton, Pisistratus. Also see *The Coming Race; Falkland; The Last Days of Pompeii; Pelham; Rienzi.*

BULWER-LYTTON, Edward. *Ismael; an Oriental Tale.* Boards. London, 1820. First edition. $100-$125. Author's first book.

BUNNER, H. C. *A Woman of Honor.* Cloth. Boston, 1883. First edition. $15-$25. Author's first book.

BUNTING, Basil. *Briggflatts.* Black cloth. London, no date (1966). One of 100 in cloth. In dust jacket. $25-$30.

BUNTING, Basil. *Descant on Rawthey's Madrigal: Conversations with Basil Bunting.* Boards. Kentucky, no date (1968). One of 25 signed by Bunting and Jonathan Williams. In dust jacket. $35-$40.

BUNTING, Basil. *First Book of Odes.* Boards. London, no date. One of 175 numbered copies (of an edition of 101). $25-$30.

BUNTING, Basil. *Loquitur.* Full morocco. London, no date (1965). First edition. One of 26 signed. In dust jacket. $75-$80.

BUNTING, Basil. *Redimiculum Matellarum.* Wrappers. Milan, 1930. First edition. $100-$125.

BUNTING, Basil. *Two Poems.* Wrappers. California, 1967. First edition. One of 30 signed (of an edition of 250). $35-$40.

BUNYAN, John. *The Pilgrim's Progress.* Portrait frontispiece. Full brown morocco, gilt. London, 1849. Chiswick Press. $75-$100. Bookplate, $50. New York, 1941. Limited Editions Club. 29 William Blake illustrations in color. One of 1,500. Boxed. $100-$125.

BURGESS, Gelett. *Are You a Bromide?* Boards, paper label on front cover. New York, 1906. First edition. $25-$30.

BURGESS, Gelett. *Goops and How to Be Them.* 90 drawings by the author. Red cloth. New York, no date (1900). First edition. $200-$250. London, 1900. Illustrated by the author. Pictorial cloth. First English edition. Lightly soiled, $200.

BURGESS, Gelett. *Le Petit Journal des Refusées: Number 1.* (All published.) Wrappers. San Francisco, 1896. First edition. (Printed on wallpaper.) $35-$50.

BURGESS, Gelett. *The Purple Cow!* Illustrated. 8 leaves. No place, no date (San Francisco, 1895). First edition, second state (printed on one side of leaf only), first printing (on rough China paper). (Only one known copy of first state printing on both sides of leaf.) $75-$100. Author's first book.

BURKE, Edmund. See *A Philosophical Enquiry, etc.*

BURKE, Edmund. *Correspondence of Edmund Burke and William Windham.* Edited by J. P. Gilson. Half morocco. Cambridge, England, 1910. Limited edition (fewer than 100 issued). $50.

BURKE, John. *Dreams and Derisions.* Illustrated by Rockwell Kent. Half morocco. No place (New York), 1927. (By Ralph Pulitzer.) First edition. One of 100 (of an edition of 300) signed by Kent. Boxed. $35-$40.

BURKE, Kenneth. *The White Oxen and Other Stories.* Cloth. New York, 1924. First edition. $35-$40. Author's first book.

BURKE, Thomas. *Limehouse Nights.* Terra-cotta cloth. London, 1916. First edition. $40-$50.

BURKE, W. S. (compiler). *Directory of the City of Council Bluffs and Emigrants' Guide to the Gold Regions of the West*. Folding map. 32 pp., plus ads, patterned cloth. Council Bluffs, Iowa, 1866. First edition. $950 (A, 1968). (Note: Previously the highest price noted was a copy offered at retail for $850.)

BURNETT, Frances Hodgson. *The Drury Lane Boys' Club*. 78 pp., blue wrappers. Washington, 1892. First edition. One of 800. $60-$100.

BURNETT, Frances Hodgson. *Editha's Burglar*. Illustrated by Henry Sandham. Pictorial brown cloth. Boston, 1888. First edition, first state, with "I thought I heard something" under frontispiece. $30. Second state, with name only under frontispiece, $10.

BURNETT, Frances Hodgson. *Little Lord Fauntleroy*. Illustrated by Reginald B. Birch. Pictorial gray-green (blue) or tan cloth. New York, 1886. First edition, first issue, with DeVinne Press imprint at end. $100-$200. London, 1886. Pictorial cloth. First English edition, with copyright page dated November 9, 1886. $75.

BURNETT, Peter H. *Recollections and Opinions of an Old Pioneer*. Cloth. New York, 1880. First edition. $75-$100.

BURNETT, W. R. *Little Caesar*. Cloth. New York, no date (1929). First edition. In dust jacket. $25-$30. Author's first book.

BURNEY, Fanny. *Evelina*. 16 full-page illustrations by Arthur Rackham. Cloth. London, 1898. $50-$100.

BURNEY, Frances. See D'Arblay, Madame.

BURNEY, James. *A Chronological History of the Discoveries in the South Sea or Pacific Ocean*. Maps, charts, plates. 5 vols., contemporary boards and leather. London, 1803-17. First edition. Large paper issue: $1,200-$1,500. Ordinary issue: $1,000 and up.

BURNEY, James. *History of the Buccaneers of America*. 3 maps (2 folding). Contemporary three-quarters morocco. London, 1816. First separate edition. Large paper issue: $250-$300. Ordinary issue: $100-$150.

BURNHAM, Daniel H., and Bennett, Edward H. *Plan of Chicago*. Illustrated. Three-quarters leather and cloth. Chicago, 1909. First edition. One of 1,500. $250-$300.

BURNS, John Horne. *The Gallery*. Cloth. New York, no date (1957). First edition. In dust jacket. $20-$25. Author's first book.

BURNS, Robert. *Poems Ascribed to Robert Burns*. Boards. Glasgow, 1801. First edition. $150-$200.

BURNS, Robert. *Poems*. Wood engravings by John Hassall. Boards and leather. New York, 1965. Limited Editions Club. Boxed. $35.

BURPEE, Lawrence J. *The Search for the Western Sea*. 6 maps, 51 plates. Cloth. London, 1908. First edition. $100. Also, $55 (A, 1969). New York, 1908. Cloth. First American edition. $50-$75. Toronto, no date (1908). Cloth. First Canadian edition. $55 and $45. New York, 1936. Maps and plates. 2 vols., cloth. In dust jackets. $50-$60.

BURR, Aaron. *The Private Journal of Aaron Burr*. Edited by W. K. Bixby. Portraits. 2 vols., half cloth. Rochester, N.Y., 1903. One of 250 signed by Bixby. $150-$200.

BURROUGHS, Edgar Rice. *At the Earth's Core*. Illustrated. Cloth. Chicago, 1922. First edition. In dust jacket. $20-$25.

BURROUGHS, Edgar Rice. *The Beasts of Tarzan*. Illustrated. Olive cloth. Chicago, 1916. First edition. $20-$25.

BURROUGHS, Edgar Rice. *The Chessmen of Mars*. Illustrated. Red cloth. Chicago, 1922. First edition. $20-$25.

BURROUGHS, Edgar Rice. *A Fighting Man of Mars.* Frontispiece. Red cloth. New York, no date (1931). First edition, with Metropolitan Books imprint. $20-$25.

BURROUGHS, Edgar Rice. *Jungle Tales of Tarzan.* Illustrated. Cloth. Chicago, 1919. First edition. In dust jacket. $35-$40.

BURROUGHS, Edgar Rice. *The Son of Tarzan.* Illustrated. Cloth. Chicago, 1917. First edition. In dust jacket. $40-$50. Lacking jacket, $25.

BURROUGHS, Edgar Rice. *Tarzan and the Golden Lion.* Illustrated. Gold cloth. Chicago, 1933. First edition. $25-$30.

BURROUGHS, Edgar Rice. *Tarzan and the Jewels of Opar.* Illustrated. Dark-green cloth. Chicago, 1918. First edition. In dust jacket. $25-$35.

BURROUGHS, Edgar Rice. *Tarzan of the Apes.* Frontispiece. Red cloth. Chicago, 1914. First edition, first issue, with acorn device at foot of spine. In dust jacket. $200-$300. Later, no acorn on spine. In dust jacket. $100-$125. Another issue: Advance review copy in pictorial wrappers. $200-$300. Author's first book. London, no date (1917). Orange-colored cloth. First English edition, with ads dated Autumn. In dust jacket. $150.

BURROUGHS, Edgar Rice. *Tarzan, Lord of the Jungle.* Illustrated. Cloth. Chicago, 1928. First edition. In dust jacket. $25-$30.

BURROUGHS, Edgar Rice. *Tarzan Triumphant.* Illustrated by Stanley Burroughs. Cloth. Tarzana, Calif., no date (1932). First edition. In dust jacket. $25-$30.

BURROUGHS, Edgar Rice. *Tarzan the Untamed.* Illustrated. Cloth. Chicago, 1920. First edition. In dust jacket. $40-$50.

BURROUGHS, Edgar Rice. *Thuvia, Maid of Mars.* Illustrated. Cloth. Chicago, 1920. First edition. In dust jacket. $25-$35.

BURROUGHS, Edgar Rice. *The Warlord of Mars.* Frontispiece. Red cloth. Chicago, 1919. First edition. In dust jacket. $25-$35.

BURROUGHS, John. *Notes on Walt Whitman as Poet and Person.* Cloth, or blue wrappers. New York, 1867. First edition, first issue, leaves trimmed to 6 9/16 inches tall. Cloth: $100-$150. Wrappers: $75-$150. Later, 1867, clothbound, leaves 7¼ inches tall: $35-$40.

BURROUGHS, John. *Wake-Robin.* Green or terra-cotta cloth. New York, 1871. First edition. $50-$60.

BURROUGHS, John. *Winter Sunshine.* Cloth. New York, 1876. First edition. $25-$35.

BURROUGHS, William. *The Naked Lunch.* Decorated wrappers. Paris, no date (1959). Olympia Press. First edition. $25-$35.

BURROUGHS, William. *Roosevelt After Inauguration.* Printed wrappers. New York, no date (1964). Fuck You Press. First edition. $35-$40.

BURROUGHS, William. *The Soft Machine.* Printed wrappers. Paris, no date (1961). Traveller's Companion. First edition. $25-$30.

BURROUGHS, William. *The Ticket That Exploded.* Wrappers. Paris, no date (1962). Olympia Press. First edition. $25-$35.

BURSON, William. *A Race for Liberty: or, My Capture, Imprisonment and Escape.* Cloth. Wellsville, 1867. $35-$40.

BURTON, Alfred. *The Adventures of Johnny Newcome in the Navy.* 16 colored plates by Rowlandson. Cloth. London, 1818. (By John Mitford.) First edition. $75-$100. (See John Mitford entry for third edition.)

BURTON, Harley True. *A History of the JA Ranch.* Portrait, map. Cloth. Austin, Tex., 1928. First edition. $100-$150.

BURTON, Maria Amparo. *The Squatter and the Don.* Cloth. San Francisco, 1885. First edition. $25-$30.

BURTON, Robert. *The Anatomy of Melancholy.* Illustrated by E. McKnight Kauffer. 2 vols., half vellum and boards. London, 1925. Nonesuch Press. One of 750. $150. Another issue: One of 40 on vellum. $250-$300.

BURTON, Sir Richard F. (translator). *The Kasidah.* Illustrated by Valenti Angelo. Full leather. New York, 1937. Limited Editions Club. Boxed. $35-$45. See B., F.

BURTON, Sir Richard F. (translator). *The Book of the Thousand Nights and a Night.* (Arabian Nights). Illustrated by Valenti Angelo. 6 vols., boards, cowhide spines. New York, 1934. Limited Editions Club. Boxed. $50-$100. Another Limited Editions Club edition: New York, 1954. Illustrated in color by Arthur Szyk. 4 vols. Boxed. $75-$100.

BURTON, Sir Richard F. *Vikram and the Vampire, or Tales of Hindu Devilry.* Illustrated. Pictorial cloth. London, 1870. First edition. $25-$35.

BURTON, Sir Richard F. *Falconry in the Valley of the Indus.* Frontispiece, other plates. Cloth. London, 1852. First edition. $150-$175.

BURTON, Sir Richard F. *First Footsteps in East Africa; or, an Exploration of Harar.* With 2 maps and 4 colored plates. Half calf. London, 1856. First edition, with 24 pp. of ads dated March, 1856. $100-$150.

BURTON, Sir Richard F. *The Gold-Mines of Midian and the Ruined Midianite Cities.* Folding map. Cloth. London, 1878. First edition. $100-$150.

BURTON, Sir Richard F. *The Lake Regions of Central Africa.* Folding map, 12 colored plates. 2 vols., cloth. London, 1860. First edition. $100-$150.

BURTON, Sir Richard F. *The Land of Midian (Revisited).* Folding map. 16 plates, 6 colored. 2 vols., cloth. London, 1879. First edition, with ads dated "9.78." $100-$150.

BURTON, Sir Richard F. *Personal Narrative of a Pilgrimage to El-Medinah and Meccah.* 16 plates (5 colored), 3 folding maps. 3 vols., cloth. London, 1855-56. First edition. $100-$125.

BURTON, W. *Josiah Wedgwood and His Pottery.* 32 color plates, 84 in black and white. Cloth. London, 1922. Limited Edition. In dust jacket. $65-$80.

BUTCHER, S. D. *S. D. Butcher's Pioneer History of Custer County.* Illustrated. Cloth, or leather. Broken Bow, Neb., 1901. First edition. $65-$75.

BUTLER, A. C. *Lepidoptera Exotica.* 64 plates, 63 colored and one plain. Cloth. London, 1874. $50-$60.

BUTLER, Arthur G. *Beautiful Foreign Finches and Their Treatment in Captivity.* 60 colored plates by F. W. Frohawk. Cloth. London, 1904. $50-$75.

BUTLER, Arthur G. *Foreign Finches in Captivity.* 60 hand-colored plates. Cloth. London, 1894. First edition. $250-$300. Binding split, $225. London, 1899. Illustrated with chromolithographs. Half cloth. Second edition. $50-$60.

BUTLER, Ellis Parker. See *Pigs Is Pigs.*

BUTLER, Mann. *A History of the Commonwealth of Kentucky.* Portrait. Leather. Louisville, 1834. First edition. $75-$100. Also, $50 (A, 1968).

BUTLER, Samuel. See *Erewhon; The Fair Haven.*

BUTLER, Samuel. *The Authoress of the Odyssey.* Maps and illustrations. Red cloth. London, 1897. First edition. $75-$100.

BUTLER, Samuel. *Erewhon Revisited Twenty Years Later.* Red cloth. London, 1901. First edition, with errata slip in preface. $75-$100. Lacking errata slip, $50.

BUTLER, Samuel. *A First Year in Canterbury Settlement.* Folding map. Red cloth. London, 1863. First edition, with 32 pages of ads and light-brown end papers. $250-$300. Author's first book.

BUTLER, Samuel. *Life and Habit.* Brown cloth. London, 1878. First edition, with brown end papers. $25-$30.

BUTLER, Samuel. *The Note-Books of Samuel Butler.* Edited by H. F. Jones. Cloth. London, 1912. First edition. $40-$50.

BUTLER, Samuel. *Seven Sonnets and A Psalm of Montreal.* Unbound, or printed wrappers. Cambridge, England, 1904. First edition. Unbound: $35-$50. (Note: Lord Esher's copy, in printed wrappers and with a specially made folding case with his bookplate, brought $420 at auction in 1967.)

BUTLER, Samuel. *The Way of All Flesh.* Red cloth, gilt, top edges gilt. London, 1903. First edition. $200-$300. New York, 1936. Limited Editions Club. 2 vols., leather. Boxed. $35-$50.

BUTLER, William Allen. See *Nothing to Wear.*

BUTTERFIELD, C. W. *An Historical Account of the Expedition Against Sandusky.* Portrait. Cloth. Cincinnati, 1873. First edition. $50-$60.

BUTTERFIELD, C. W. *History of the Discovery of the Northwest.* Cloth. Cincinnati, 1881. First edition. $75-$100.

BUTTERFIELD, C. W. *History of the Girtys.* Cloth. Cincinnati, 1890. First edition. $75-$125.

BUTTERFIELD, C. W. *History of Seneca County, Ohio.* Cloth. Sandusky, Ohio, 1848. First edition. $50-$60.

BUTTERWORTH, Benjamin J. *The Growth of Industrial Art.* 200 full-page plates. Cloth. Washington, 1892. First edition. $200-$300.

BUTTS, Harriet N. Greene. *Bertha and Willie.* Printed wrappers. Hopedale, Mass., no date (about 1858). $25-$30.

BUTTS, Harriet N. Greene. *The Little Angel.* Woodcuts. Printed wrappers. Hopedale, no date (about 1852-58). $25-$30.

BUTTS, Harriet N. Greene. *"Out of Work."* Printed wrappers. Hopedale, no date (about 1858). $25-$30.

BUTTS, Harriet N. Greene. *"Playing Soldier."* Illustrated. Printed wrappers. Hopedale, no date (about 1852-58). $25-$30.

BUTTS, Mary. *Ashe of Rings.* Wrappers. No place, no date (Paris, 1925). First edition. Contact Editions. $50-$60.

BUTTS, Mary. *Imaginary Letters.* Illustrated by Jean Cocteau. Cloth, paper label. Paris, 1928. $35-$40. Another issue: Boards. One of 250 numbered copies, with original copperplate engravings by Cocteau. $60-$70.

BUXTON FORMAN, H. *Elizabeth Barrett Browning and Her Scarcer Books.* White boards. London, 1896. One of 30. $60-$75.

BYERS, William N., and Kellom, John H. *A Hand Book to the Gold Fields of Nebraska and Kansas.* Map. Blue pictorial printed wrappers. Chicago, 1859. First edition. $3,700 (A, 1968).

BYNNER, Witter. See Morgan, Emanuel, and Knish, Anne.

BYNNER, Witter. *The New World.* Frontispiece. Decorated boards. San Francisco, 1919. One of 350. $35-$50.

BYNNER, Witter. *An Ode to Harvard and Other Poems.* Cloth, or leather. Boston, 1907. First edition. Cloth. $35-$50. Author's first book.

BYRD, William (of Westover). *The Writings of "Colonel William Byrd of Westover in Virginia, Esqr."* Edited by John Spencer Bassett. Half vellum. New York, 1901. One of 500. $75-$100.

BYRNE, B. M. *Florida and Texas: A Series of Letters Comparing the Soil, Climate, and Productions of These States.* 40 pp., wrappers. Ocala, Fla., 1866. Third edition (of *Letters on the Climate, etc.*; see below). $150.

BYRNE, B. M. *Letters on the Climate, Soils, and Productions of Florida.* 28 pp., wrappers. Jacksonville, 1851. Second edition. $200. (Note: The first edition, for which I locate no reliable price data, was published in Ralston, Pa., according to Howes, who gives no date.)

BYRNE, Donn. *Brother Saul.* Brown batik boards, vellum spine. New York, no date (1927). First American edition. One of 500 signed. $30-$35.

BYRNE, Donn. *Crusade.* Japan vellum and cloth. Boston, 1928. First American edition. One of 365 signed. Boxed. $35-$40.

BYRNE, Donn. *Destiny Bay.* Half vellum. Boston, 1928. First edition, with "Published September, 1928" on copyright page. $25-$30.

BYRNE, Donn. *Field of Honor.* Brown batik boards, vellum spine. New York, no date (1929). One of 500 large paper copies, signed by Dorothea Donn-Byrne (issued after the first trade edition). $25-$35.

BYRNE, Donn. *The Foolish Matrons.* Green cloth. New York, no date (1920). First edition, first issue, with "I-U" on copyright page. $45-$50.

BYRNE, Donn. *Messer Marco Polo.* Illustrated by C. B. Falls. Rust-colored cloth. New York, 1921. First edition, first printing, with conjugate of pages 145-146 used as terminal lining paper and with perfect type in the word "of" in the last line of page 10 and "forgetting" in the third line of page 39. In dust jacket. $50-$75.

BYRNE, Donn. *Stories Without Women.* Frontispiece. Red ribbed cloth. New York, 1915. First edition. $50-$100. Author's first book.

BYRNE, Donn. *The Strangers' Banquet.* Cloth. New York, no date (1919). First edition, with "M-T" on copyright page. In dust jacket. $35-$40.

BYRON, George Gordon Noel, Lord. See Hobhouse, J. C.; Hornem, Horace. Also see *The Age of Bronze; Beppo; The Curse of Minerva; Don Juan; English Bards and Scotch Reviewers; Fugitive Pieces; Lara, a Tale; Monody on the Death of the Right Honorable R. B. Sheridan; Ode to Napoleon Buonaparte; On John William Rizzo Hoppner; Poems on Various Occasions; The Siege of Corinth.*

BYRON, George Gordon Noel, Lord. *The Bride of Abydos.* 72 pp., drab wrappers. London, 1813. First edition, first issue, with errata slip and with only 20 lines on page 47. $250 and up. Second issue, without errata slip and with 22 lines on page 47. Rebound in calf, $115.20 (A, 1968).

BYRON, George Gordon Noel, Lord. *Childe Harold's Pilgrimage: A Romaunt.* (Containing Cantos I and II.) Drab boards, white spine label. London, 1812. First edition, first issue, with "Written beneath a Picture of J–V–D" on page 189. ("of J–V–D" omitted later). (Note: The three volumes of *Childe Harold's Pilgrimage* are almost always offered for sale as a set, although there are occasional exceptions. They are listed separately here for bibliographical identification. Fine sets in boards and wrappers as issued are rare, and the last major offerings were in the 1940's, when prices as high as $225 and $300 were realized at auction. The retail value of a complete set in original bindings and in fine condition has not been tested in today's market, so far as I have determined. My own estimate: $1,250 to $2,000. Rebound sets are worth $150 and up, depending on condition.)

BYRON, George Gordon Noel, Lord. *Childe Harold's Pilgrimage: Canto the Third.* 79 pp., plain wrappers. London, 1816. First edition. (See note in preceding entry.)

BYRON, George Gordon Noel, Lord. *Childe Harold's Pilgrimage: Canto the Fourth.* Drab boards, white label. London, 1818. First edition, first issue, with 6-line errata list on page 236 and with page 155 ending with "the impressions of," etc. Rebound in buckram, $32 (A, 1968). (See preceding entries.)

BYRON, George Gordon Noel, Lord. *The Corsair: A Tale.* Plain drab wrappers. London, 1814. First edition, first issue, with 100 pages. $250-$300. Second issue, 108 pages. $50-$100.

BYRON, George Gordon Noel, Lord. *The Deformed Transformed.* Drab wrappers. London, 1824. First edition. $75-$150. Also, $70 (A, 1970).

BYRON, George Gordon Noel, Lord. *Fare Thee Well! A Poem.* (No regular title page.) 4 pp. No place, no date (1814). First edition. (Only 4 copies known.) $1,000 and up?

BYRON, George Gordon Noel, Lord. *The Giaour: A Fragment of a Turkish Tale.* 41 pp., drab wrappers. London, 1813. First edition, on Whatman paper watermarked 1809-10. $100 and up.

BYRON, George Gordon Noel, Lord. *Hebrew Melodies.* Wrappers. London, 1815. First edition, first issue, with ad for *Jacqueline* on reverse of signature E4. $400-$500. Also, $225 (A, 1970); rebound in calf, $124.80 (A, 1969). Second issue, without *Jacqueline* ad. $100-$200.

BYRON, George Gordon Noel, Lord. *Hours of Idleness.* Drab boards. Newark, England, 1807. First edition, first issue, with line 2 of page 22 reading "Those tissues of fancy, etc." $500-$600. Second issue, with line 2 of page 22 reading "Those tissues of falsehood, etc." $100 and up.

BYRON, George Gordon Noel, Lord. *The Island, or Christian and His Comrades.* Plain drab boards. London, 1823. First edition, with paper watermarked 1822. $300-$400. Also, $190 (A, 1970).

BYRON, George Gordon Noel, Lord. *The Lament of Tasso.* 19 pp., stitched, without wrappers. London, 1817. First edition. $250 and up.

BYRON, George Gordon Noel, Lord. *Letter to **** ****** [John Murray] on the Rev. W. L. Bowles' Strictures on the Life of Pope.* 55 pp., drab wrappers. London, 1821. First edition, first issue, without 1819 watermark on 4 leaves before ads. $250 and up. Second issue, with the watermark. Rebound in morocco, original covers preserved, $168 (A, 1968).

BYRON, George Gordon Noel, Lord. *Manfred, a Dramatic Poem.* 80 pp., drab wrappers, without lettering or labels. London, 1817. First edition, first issue, without quotation on title page and with printer's imprint in 2 lines on back of title page. $250-$300. Second issue, with printer's imprint in one line. $100-$125. Third issue, with Hamlet quotation on title page. $75-$100. London, 1929. Fanfrolico Press. Full vellum. One of 30 on vellum. $75-$100. Another issue: Half parchment. One of 550. $25.

BYRON, George Gordon Noel, Lord. *Marino Faliero, Doge of Venice.* Drab boards. London, 1821. First edition, first issue, with speech on page 151 beginning "What crimes?" $150-$200. Worn and defective copies in original boards, $20-$55 at retail. Second issue, with speech on page 151 beginning "His Crimes!" $25-$50.

BYRON, George Gordon Noel, Lord. *Mazeppa: A Poem.* Plain drab wrappers. London, 1819. First edition, first issue, with imprint on page 70. $150-$200. Rebound in calf, $20 (A, 1968). Second issue, with imprint on back of page 71. $50-$100.

BYRON, George Gordon Noel, Lord. *The Parliamentary Speeches of Lord Byron.* Drab wrappers. London, 1824. First edition. $300-$400. Also, $250 (A, 1970).

BYRON, George Gordon Noel, Lord. *Poems.* Boards. London, 1816. First edition, first issue, with leaf of "Notes" and 2 ad leaves. $200-$300.

BYRON, George Gordon Noel, Lord. *The Prisoner of Chillon, and Other Poems.* Drab wrappers. London, 1816. First edition, first issue, with recto of signature E8 blank. $150-$250.

BYRON, George Gordon Noel, Lord. *Sardanapalus, The Two Foscari, Cain.* Boards, paper label on spine. London, 1821. First edition, with 10 pages of ads at front. $400-$500. Rubbed, $300.

BYRON, George Gordon Noel, Lord. *Werner: A Tragedy.* Plain drab wrappers. London, 1823. First edition, first issue, with ad for this book on page 188. $400-$500. Rebound in calf, $324. Second issue, without ad for this book. $200 and up. Also, $100 (A, 1971).

C

C. 3. 3. *The Ballad of Reading Gaol.* Cinnamon-colored cloth, vellum spine. London, no date (1898). (By Oscar Wilde.) First edition. One of 30 on Japanese vellum. $350-$500. Soiled, signature and book label on end papers, $238. Another issue: Cloth. One of 800. $50-$150. London, 1898. Cloth. Second edition. $35-$50. London, 1898. Cloth. Third edition (bearing Wilde's name). One of 99 signed. $200-$250. London, 1899. Cloth. Pirated edition. $25-$35. New York, 1937. Limited Editions Club. Calf. Boxed. $35-$50.

CABALLERIA Y COLLELL, Juan. *History of the City of Santa Barbara from Its Discovery to Our Own Days.* Translated by Edmund Burke. Plate, facsimile. 111 pp., wrappers. Santa Barbara, 1892. First edition. $100.

CABELL, James Branch. *Chivalry.* Illustrated by Howard Pyle and others. Red cloth. New York, 1909. First edition. In printed glassine dust jacket. Boxed. $35-$50. "Advance issue," no jacket: $50.

CABELL, James Branch. *The Eagle's Shadow.* Red cloth. New York, 1904. First edition, first state, with dedication "M. L. P. B." and frontispiece of seated figure. $60. Author's first book.

CABELL, James Branch *Gallantry.* Illustrated in color by Howard Pyle. Decorated cloth, gilt top. New York, 1907. First edition, first binding, silver-gray cloth, stamped with white, silver, and gold lettering. In printed glassine dust jacket. Boxed. $30-$35. Green cloth, $20 and $15.

CABELL, (James) Branch. *Jurgen.* Reddish-brown cloth. New York, 1919. First edition, first state, measuring about 1¼ inches across top of covers (second state about 1/4 inch more). In dust jacket. $100 and up. Lacking jacket. $50-$60. Also, $27 (A, 1969). London, 1921. Illustrated by Frank C. Pape. Cloth. First English edition. $25. London, 1949. Golden Cockerel Press. Half morocco. One of 500. $75-$100.

CABELL, James Branch. *The Line of Love.* Illustrated in color by Howard Pyle. Decorated green cloth, pictorial label. New York, 1905. First edition, first state, binding stamped with white and gold lettering. In glassine dust jacket. $50-$60.

CABELL, James Branch. *The Music from Behind the Moon.* 8 engravings. Boards. New York, 1926. First edition, first state, with spine label 3/8 inch wide (instead of later state of 1/2 inch). One of 3,000. In glassine dust jacket and slipcase. $25-$35. Later state, $15-$20.

CABELL, (James) Branch. *The Rivet in Grandfather's Neck.* Cloth. New York, 1915. First edition. In dust jacket. $25-$30.

CABELL, James Branch. *Some of Us: An Essay in Epitaphs.* Boards and cloth. New York, 1930. First edition. One of 1,295 signed. $25-$30.

CABELL, (James) Branch. *Sonnets from Antan.* Half cloth. New York, 1929. Grabhorn printing. First edition. One of 718 signed. $25-$35.

CABELL, James Branch. *The Way of Ecben.* Half vellum. New York, 1929. First edition. One of 850 signed. Boxed. $25-$35. Trade edition: Boards and cloth. $10-$15.

CABEZA DE VACA, Álvar Núñez. *The Narrative of Álvar Núñez Cabeza de Vaca.* Translated by Buckingham Smith. 8 maps. Cloth. Washington, 1851. One of 110. $300-$400. Also, rebound in new cloth, $250 (A, 1966). New York, 1871. Three-quarters morocco. One of 100. $100-$150. Also, $60 (A, 1965). (For another issue, under another title, see following entry.)

CABEZA DE VACA, Álvar Núñez. *Relation . . . of What Befel the Armament in the Indias Whither Pamphilo de Narvaez Went for Governor, etc.* Hand decorations in color by Valenti Angelo. Boards. San Francisco, 1929. Grabhorn printing. One of 300. Boxed. $150-$250.

CABINET of Natural History and American Rural Sports (The). 3 vols., half calf. Philadelphia, 1830-32-33. First book edition. (Published by J. and T. Doughty. Includes 29 monthly parts [dated 1830 to 1834] ; 57 plates, 54 colored.) $1,000-$1,500, possibly more. Also, 3 vols. in 2, $450 (A, 1962); incomplete set, Vols. 1 and 2 only, $130 (A, 1960). Philadelphia, 1832. Vol. 1 only. 24 colored plates. $110 (A, 1964). (Sets in parts are excessively rare.)

CABINET-MAKER'S Assistant (The); A Series of Original Designs for Modern Furniture. Plates. Folio, half calf. Glasgow, 1853. (By P. Thompson.) $100-$125.

CABLE, George W. *The Creoles of Louisiana.* Illustrated. Maroon pictorial cloth. New York, 1884. First edition. $40-$50.

CABLE, George W. *The Grandissimes.* Cloth. New York, 1880. First edition. $25-$30. New York, 1899. Illustrated. Vellum. One of 204. $25-$30.

CABLE, George W. *Old Creole Days.* Decorated red, brown, or blue cloth. New York, 1879. First edition, first state, with no ads at back. $100-$200. Second state, with ads. $50-$100. Rubbed and stained, $30. Author's first book. New York, 1897. Vellum. One of 204. $50-$75.

CABLE, George W. *The Southern Struggle for Pure Government.* Wrappers. Boston, 1890. First edition. $35-$50.

CABLE, George W. *Strange True Stories of Louisiana.* Illustrated. Pictorial cloth, paper label. New York, 1889. First edition. $35-$40.

CAESAR, Julius. *Commentaries.* Translated by Somerset de Chair. Woodcuts by Clifford Webb. Buckram. London, 1951. Golden Cockerel Press. One of 320. $125-$135.

CALAVAR; or, The Knight of the Conquest. 2 vols., purple cloth, printed paper labels. Philadelphia, 1834. (By Robert Montgomery Bird.) First edition. $100-$200. Author's first book. Philadelphia, 1847. 2 vols., printed wrappers. Revised edition. $25-$35.

CALDWELL, Erskine. *American Earth.* Brown cloth. New York, 1931. First edition, with code letter "A" on copyright page. In dust jacket. $20-$25.

CALDWELL, Erskine. *The Bastard.* Illustrated. Cloth. New York, no date (1929). First edition. One of 200 signed (in an edition of 1,100 numbered copies). $65-$85. Unsigned copies, about $25 at retail. Author's first book.

CALDWELL, Erskine. *God's Little Acre.* Black cloth. New York, 1933. First edition. In dust jacket. $35-$50.

CALDWELL, Erskine. *Journeyman.* Red buckram, paper band. New York, 1935. First edition. One of 1,475. In glassine dust jacket. Boxed. $35-$50. Box worn, $17.50.

CALDWELL, Erskine. *Kneel to the Rising Sun and Other Stories.* Reddish-brown buckram, labels, top edges gilt. New York, 1935. First edition. One of 300 signed. Boxed. $35-$50. Trade edition: Cloth. In dust jacket. $10-$15.

CALDWELL, Erskine. *Mama's Little Girl.* 2 drawings by Alfred Morang. Printed wrappers. Mount Vernon, Me., 1932. One of 75. $40-$60.

CALDWELL, Erskine. *A Message for Genevieve.* Drawing by Alfred Morang. Printed wrappers. Mount Vernon, Me., 1933. First edition. One of 100 signed. $50-$75.

CALDWELL, Erskine. *Poor Fool.* Blue cloth. New York, 1930. First edition. One of 1,000. $25-$30.

CALDWELL, Erskine. *The Sacrilege of Alan Kent.* Illustrated. Gray cloth. Portland, Me., 1936. First edition. In dust jacket. $15-$20. Revised edition, same date: Boards. One of 300 signed. $45. Also, $20 (A, 1969).

CALDWELL, Erskine. *Southways.* Gray-blue cloth. New York, 1938. First edition. In dust jacket. $25-$30.

CALDWELL, Erskine. *Tenant Farmer.* Green wrappers. New York, no date (1935). First edition. $20-$25.

CALDWELL, Erskine. *Tobacco Road.* Cloth. New York, 1932. First edition, with code letter "A" on copyright page. In dust jacket. $50-$75.

CALDWELL, Erskine. *We Are the Living.* Cloth. New York, 1933. One of 250 signed. In glassine dust jacket. Boxed. $35-$50.

CALDWELL, J. A. *History of Belmont and Jefferson Counties, Ohio.* Half leather. Wheeling, Ohio, 1880. $50-$60.

CALDWELL, J. F. J. *History of a Brigade of South Carolinians.* Cloth. Philadelphia, 1866. First edition. $50-$75.

CALHOUN, James S. *Official Correspondence of James S. Calhoun While Indian Agent at Santa Fe.* Illustrated, 4 maps. Cloth. Washington, 1915. First edition. $30-$35.

CALIFORNIA Illustrated. By a Returned Californian. 48 plates. Cloth. New York, 1852. (By J. M. Letts.) First edition, first issue, anonymous. $150-$200. Later issue, same year, author named: $75-$100.

CALL, Richard Ellsworth. *The Life and Writings of Rafinesque.* 2 plates, 3 facsimiles. 227 pp., wrappers. Louisville, Ky., 1895. First edition. $35-$50.

CALLAGHAN, Morley. *No Man's Meat.* Boards and cloth, paper label. Paris, 1931. First edition. One of 525 signed. $50-$60.

CALLAGHAN, Morley. *Strange Fugitive.* Cloth. New York, 1928. First edition. In dust jacket. $35-$45.

CALVERT, F. *The Isle of Wight Illustrated.* Sepia lithograph frontispiece, colored map, 20 colored aquatint plates. Cloth. London, 1846. $200.

CAMBRIDGE History of British Foreign Policy, 1783-1919. Edited by Sir A. W. Ward and G. P. Gooch. 3 vols., cloth. London, 1922-23. $125.

CAMERON, Julia M. *Victorian Photographs of Famous Men and Fair Women.* Boards and vellum. London, 1926. First edition. One of 450. $80-$95. (Note: Contains an introduction by Virginia Woolf.)

CAMPBELL, Alexander, and Rice, N. L. *A Debate . . . on the Action, Subject, Design and Administration of Christian Baptism.* Boards. Lexington, Ky., 1844. First edition. $50-$60.

CAMPBELL, Alexander, and Owen, Robert. *Debate on the Evidence of Christianity.* 2 vols. in one, calf. Bethany, Va., 1829. First edition. $60-$75.

CAMPBELL, Archibald. *A Voyage Around the World.* Illustrated, map in color. Boards. Edinburgh, 1816. First edition. $300-$400. In 2 vols., calf, $250 at retail.

CAMPBELL, Roy. *Adamastor: Poems.* Cloth. London, 1930. First edition. One of 90 signed. $75-$100. Trade edition: In dust jacket. $35-$40.

CAMPBELL, Roy. *Broken Record.* Cloth. London, 1934. First edition. In dust jacket. $25-$30.

CAMPBELL, Roy. *Choosing a Mast.* Illustrated by Barnett Freedman. Boards. London, 1931. First edition. One of 300 signed. $35-$50.

CAMPBELL, Roy. *The Flaming Terrapin.* Boards, cloth spine, paper label. London, 1924. First edition. In dust jacket. $50-$75. Author's first book.

CAMPBELL, Roy. *Flowering Reeds: Poems.* Cloth. London, 1933. First edition. One of 69 signed. $67.20. Trade edition: Cloth. In dust jacket. $10.

CAMPBELL, Roy. *The Georgiad.* Boards and cloth. London, 1931. Alcuin Press. One of 150 signed. $75-$100. Another issue: Vellum. One of 20 on goatskin parchment paper, signed. $100-$150.

CAMPBELL, Roy. *Poems.* Decorated boards and morocco. Paris, 1930. Hours Press. First edition. One of 200 signed. $100-$125.

CAMPBELL, Roy. *Pomegranates.* Illustrated by James Boswell. Cloth. London, 1932. First edition. One of 99 signed. In glassine dust jacket. $75-$100.

CAMPBELL, Roy. *The Wayzgoose: A South African Satire.* Brown cloth. London, 1928. First edition. $20-$25.

CAMPE, M. *Polar Scenes.* Woodcut illustrations. Contemporary boards and leather. New York, no date (before 1827). $35-$40.

CANFIELD, Chauncey L. (editor). *The Diary of a Forty-Niner.* Colored map. Pictorial boards. San Francisco, 1906. First edition. $35-$50.

CANFIELD, Dorothy. *Understood Betsy.* Illustrated. Pictorial green cloth. New York, 1917. First edition, with "Published August, 1917" on copyright page. In dust jacket. $35.

CANNON, George Q. *Writings from the "Western Standard," Published in San Francisco.* Full morocco. Liverpool, 1864. First edition. $25-$35.

CANNON, J. P. *Inside of Rebeldom: The Daily Life of a Private in the Confederate Army.* Cloth. Washington, 1900. $50-$75. Rebound in buckram, paper brittle, $50.

CANOVA, Andrew P. *Life and Adventures in South Florida.* 4 plates. Printed light-green wrappers. Palatka, Fla., 1885. First edition. $150. Unbound copy, $75.

CAPOTE, Truman. *A Christmas Memory.* Cloth. New York, no date (1966). First edition. One of 600 signed. Boxed. $45-$60.

CAPOTE, Truman. *Breakfast at Tiffany's.* Yellow cloth. New York, 1956. First edition. In dust jacket. $25-$30.

CAPOTE, Truman. *In Cold Blood.* Black cloth. New York, no date (1965). First edition, first printing. One of 500 signed. In glassine dust jacket. Boxed. $40-$60. Trade edition. Cloth. In dust jacket. $20-$25. Signed copy, $35. Advance copy, in wrappers: $50-$60. Another, signed, $75 (A, 1968).

CAPOTE, Truman. *The Grass Harp: A Play.* Boards. New York, no date (1952). First edition. In dust jacket. $40-$50.

CAPOTE, Truman. *Local Color.* Boards and cloth. New York, no date (1950). First edition. In dust jacket. $35-$50.

CAPOTE, Truman. *Other Voices, Other Rooms.* Cloth. New York, no date (1948). First edition. In dust jacket. $35-$50. Author's first book.

CAPOTE, Truman. *The Thanksgiving Visitor.* Cloth. New York, no date (1968). First edition. One of 300 signed. Boxed. $50-$60.

CAPRON, Elisha S. *History of California.* Colored map. Cloth. Boston, 1854. First edition. $50-$60.

CAPT. SMITH and Princess Pocahontas: An Indian Tale. Boards. Philadelphia, 1805. (By John Davis.) First edition, first issue, with undated copyright notice. Most of spine gone, $1,200.

CARELESS, John. *The Old English 'Squire: A Poem in Ten Cantos.* 24 colored plates. London, 1821. (By William A. Chatto.) First edition. $200. Another issue: Cloth. Large paper. $250-$300.

CAREW, Thomas. *Poems.* Portrait. Roxburghe binding. London, 1870. $20-$25.

CAREY, C. H. *History of Oregon.* Maps. Cloth. Chicago, 1922. Author's edition. $25-$35.

CARL Werner, An Imaginative Story. 2 vols., cloth. New York, 1838. (By William Gilmore Simms.) First edition. $200-$250.

CARLETON, William M. *Fax: A Campaign Poem.* Illustrated. Printed wrappers. Chicago, 1868. First edition. $500. Author's first book.

CARLTON, Robert. *The New Purchase: or, Seven and a Half Years in the Far West.* 2 vols., boards. New York, 1843. (By Baynard R. Hall.) First edition. $50-$60.

CARLISLE, Bill. *Bill Carlisle, Lone Bandit: An Autobiography.* Illustrated by Charles M. Russell. Fabrikoid. Pasadena, Calif., no date (1946). De luxe limited edition, signed. In dust jacket. $25-$35.

CARLYLE, Thomas. See *Sartor Resartus.*

CARLYLE, Thomas. *The French Revolution.* 3 vols., boards and cloth. London, 1837. First edition. $300-$350. London, 1910. Illustrated. Half cloth. One of 150. $75-$100.

CARLYLE, Thomas. *Lectures on the History of Literature.* Cloth. London, 1892. First English edition. $25-$30.

CARLYLE, Thomas. *On Heroes, Hero-Worship, & the Heroic in History: Six Lectures.* Purple cloth. London, 1841. First edition. $75-$100.

CARLYLE, Thomas. *Past and Present.* Cloth. London, 1843. First edition. $50-$60.

CARLYLE, Thomas. *Shooting Niagara: and After?* Printed green wrappers. London, 1867. First edition. $35.

CARMAN, Bliss. See Carmen [sic], Bliss; Lighthall, William D.

CARMAN, Bliss. *The Gate of Peace: A Poem.* Boards and cloth. New York, 1907. One of 112 signed. $75-$100. (Note: All except 24 destroyed by fire, says Johnson.)

CARMAN, Bliss. *Poems.* 2 vols., half leather. New York, 1904. One of 500. $50-$75. Boston, 1905. 2 vols., boards. One of 500. $25.

CARMAN, Bliss, and Hovey, Richard. *Songs from Vagabondia.* Boards. Boston, 1894. First edition. Limited Edition. $25-$30.

CARMEN, Bliss. *Low Tide on Grand Pre.* 13 pp., wrappers. Toronto, no date (1889? 1890?). (By Bliss Carman.) First edition (pirated). $75-$100. Author's first book, with his name misspelled. New York, 1893. Lavender cloth. First United States edition. $25-$35.

CARNEVALI, Emanuel. *A Hurried Man.* Wrappers. No place, no date (Paris, 1925). Contact Editions. First edition. $25-$35.

CAROLINE Tracy: The Spring Street Milliner's Apprentice. Illustrated. Half leather. New York, 1849. First edition. $45.

CAROLINE Westerley; or, The Young Traveller from Ohio. Boards. New York, no date (1833). (By Almira Phelps.) First edition. $25-$30.

CARR, John. *Early Times in Middle Tennessee.* Cloth. Nashville, 1857. First edition. $75-$100.

CARR, John. *Pioneer Days in California.* Portrait. Cloth. Eureka, Calif., 1891. First edition. $75-$100. Also, $40 (A, 1968).

CARR, Spencer. *A Brief Sketch of La Crosse, Wisconsin.* 28 pp., sewed. La Crosse, 1854. First edition. $150-$200. Also, $130 (A, 1967).

CARRINGTON, Mrs. Henry B. See *Ab-Sa-Ra-Ka, Home of the Crows.*

CARRINGTON, John Bodman, and Hughes, George Ravensworth. *The Plate of the Worshipful Company of Goldsmiths.* Illustrated. Red cloth. Oxford, 1926. $50-$65.

CARROLL, H. Bailey. *The Texan Santa Fe Trail.* Illustrated. Cloth. Canyon, Tex., 1951. Boxed. $75-$100.

CARROLL, H. Bailey, and Haggard, J. V. (translators). *Three New Mexico Chronicles.* Cloth. Albuquerque, 1942. $25-$35.

CARROLL, Lewis. See Dodgson, Charles L.

CARROLL, Lewis. *Alice's Adventures in Wonderland.* 42 illustrations by John Tenniel. Red cloth. London, 1865. (By Charles L. Dodgson.) First edition (suppressed by the author). Very rare in original binding. Modern sales records range from $2,464 for a copy "badly worn, leaves stained, etc.," sold at auction in 1961, to $11,760 (A, 1965) and $16,000 (A, 1962) for presentation copies inscribed by the author. The rebound Jerome Kern copy brought $10,000 in 1929. (Because of the extreme rarity of the original edition, the collecting fraternity in general has come to accept the New York edition of 1866—the first American edition—as the "first edition," which it, in fact, is, since it consists of the sheets of the suppressed London first edition with a new title page displaying the New York imprint of its publisher, Appleton.) New York, 1866. Red cloth. First American edition (and *second issue* of the first edition). $800-$1,000, possibly more. London, 1866. Red cloth. Second edition (and first published English edition). $300-$400. (Princess Beatrice's vellum-bound copy was sold for $784 at auction in 1959 and for $2,160 when reoffered in 1969.) Boston, 1869. Green cloth. First edition printed in America. $100-$150. London, 1907. Illustrated by Arthur Rackham. Cloth. One of 1,130. $200-$250. New York, 1932. Limited Editions Club. Cloth. Boxed. $75. Also, $35 (A, 1963). Signed by Alice Hargreaves, $200-$250.

CARROLL, Lewis. *Alice's Adventures Under Ground.* 37 illustrations by the author. Red cloth, gilt edges. London, 1886. (By Charles L. Dodgson.) First edition. $75-$150. (Note: This is a facsimile of the original manuscript from which *Alice's Adventures in Wonderland* was developed.)

CARROLL, Lewis. *Doublets: A Word-Puzzle.* Cloth. London, 1879. (By Charles L. Dodgson.) First edition. $50-$75.

CARROLL, Lewis. *Feeding the Mind.* Gray boards and cloth. London, 1907. (By Charles L. Dodgson.) First edition. $25-$30.

CARROLL, Lewis. *The Game of Logic.* With envelope containing 9 counters and board diagram. Cloth. London, 1886. (By Charles L. Dodgson.) First edition. $50-$75. London, 1887. $25.

CARROLL, Lewis. *The Hunting of the Snark.* Illustrated by Henry Holiday. Red pictorial cloth, gilt edges. London, 1876. (By Charles L. Dodgson.) First edition. $100-$150. Presentation copy: Red and gold cloth. With leaflet "An Easter Greeting to Every Child who Loves 'Alice.' " $300 at retail.

CARROLL, Lewis. *Phantasmagoria and Other Poems.* Blue cloth. London, 1869. (By Charles L. Dodgson.) First edition. $50-$60.

CARROLL, Lewis. *Rhyme? and Reason?* Illustrated by A. B. Frost and Henry Holiday. Green cloth. London, 1883. (By Charles L. Dodgson.) First edition. $25-$35.

CARROLL, Lewis. *Sylvie and Bruno.* Illustrated by Harry Furniss. Cloth. London, 1889. (By Charles L. Dodgson.) First edition. $35-$50.

CARROLL, Lewis. *Sylvie and Bruno Concluded.* Illustrated by Harry Furniss. Cloth. London, 1893. (By Charles L. Dodgson.) First edition. $25-$35.

CARROLL, Lewis. *A Tangled Tale.* Illustrated by A. B. Frost. Pictorial cloth. London, 1885. (By Charles L. Dodgson.) First edition. $50-$75.

CARROLL, Lewis. *Through the Looking-Glass, and What Alice Found There.* 50 illustrations by John Tenniel. Red cloth. London, 1872. (By Charles L. Dodgson.) First edition. $200-$250. Boston, 1872. Cloth. First American edition. $25-$50. New York, 1931. Cheshire House. Cloth. $25. New York, 1935. Limited Editions Club. Morocco. Boxed. $100-$125. Signed by Alice Hargreaves, $275 (A, 1969). Mount Vernon, N.Y., 1935. Illustrated. Leather. $50-$75.

CARROLL, Lewis. *The Vision of the Three T's.* Printed wrappers. Oxford, 1873. (By Charles L. Dodgson.) First edition. $50-$75.

CARRUTH, (Fred) Hayden. *The Voyage of the Rattletrap.* Illustrated by H. M. Wilder. Pictorial cloth. New York, 1897. First edition. $35-$50.

CARRYL, Charles E. *Davy and the Goblin.* Illustrated. Pictorial brown cloth. Boston, 1886. First edition, first issue, with "Korea" misspelled in terminal ad. $150-$200. Second issue, error corrected. $100.

CARSON, Christopher. See Grant, Blanche C.

CARSON, James H. *Early Recollections of the Mines, and a Description of the Great Tulare Valley.* Folding map. 64 pp., printed wrappers (with cover title reading "*Second Edition. Life in California, etc.*"). Stockton, Calif., 1852. First edition (in book form; earlier appearance was in the San Joaquin *Republican*). Spine repaired, $1,500 (A, 1968); part of map missing, $550 (A, 1954). Oakland, 1950. 2 maps. One of 750. Reprint edition. $25. (See next entry.)

CARSON, James H. *Life in California.* Map. Cloth. Tarrytown, N.Y., 1931. (Reprint of *Early Recollections of the Mines.*) $35.

CARSTARPHEN, J. E. *My Trip to California in '49.* 8 pp., wrappers. No place, no date (Louisiana, Mo., 1914). Limited edition. $35-$40.

CARTER, John, and Pollard, Graham. *An Enquiry into the Nature of Certain 19th Century Pamphlets.* 4 plates. Cloth. London, 1934. First edition. In dust jacket. $75-$100.

CARTER, Robert G. *The Old Sergeant's Story: Winning the West from the Indians and Badmen in 1870 to 1876.* Portrait, plates. Cloth. New York, 1926. First edition. $35-$50.

CARTER, Robert G. *On the Trail of Deserters.* Printed wrappers. Washington, 1920. One of 250. $35-$50.

CARTER, Robert G. *Pursuit of Kicking Bird: A Campaign in the Texas "Bad Lands."* 44 pp., wrappers. Washington, 1920. One of 100. $35-$40.

CARTER, Susannah. *The Frugal Housewife: or, Complete Woman Cook.* Illustrated. Boards. Philadelphia, 1802. $150-$200.

CARTER, Lieut.-Col. W. H. *From Yorktown to Santiago with the 6th U.S. Cavalry.* Cloth. Baltimore, 1900. $35-$50.

APRIL
TWILIGHTS

POEMS BY

Willa Sibert Cather

Boston: Richard G. Badger

The Gorham Press: 1903

MY ANTONIA

BY

WILLA SIBERT CATHER

Optima dies . . . prima fugit
VIRGIL

WITH ILLUSTRATIONS BY
W. T. BENDA

BOSTON AND NEW YORK
HOUGHTON MIFFLIN COMPANY
The Riverside Press Cambridge
1918

"Uncle Dick" Wootton

THE PIONEER FRONTIERSMAN OF THE ROCKY
MOUNTAIN REGION

AN ACCOUNT OF THE ADVENTURES AND THRILLING
EXPERIENCES OF THE MOST NOTED AMERICAN
HUNTER, TRAPPER, GUIDE, SCOUT, AND
INDIAN FIGHTER NOW LIVING

BY

HOWARD LOUIS CONARD

WITH AN INTRODUCTION
BY
MAJ. JOSEPH KIRKLAND

CHICAGO
W. E. DIBBLE & CO
1890

ALMAYER'S FOLLY

A Story of an
Eastern River

BY

Joseph Conrad

*Qui de nous n'a eu sa terre
promise, son jour d'extase et
sa fin en exil?*—AMIEL.

LONDON
T. FISHER UNWIN
PATERNOSTER SQUARE
MDCCCXCV

CARUTHERS, W. A. See *The Kentuckian in New-York.*

CARY, Joyce. *The Horse's Mouth.* Illustrated by the author. Edited by Andrew Wright. Marbled boards, vellum spine, leather label. No place (London), 1957. One of 1,500 special edition copies designed for the author and containing a discarded chapter from the novel. $35-$50.

CASEMENT, Roger. *Some Poems of Roger Casement.* Portrait. Gray printed wrappers. Dublin, 1918. First edition. $100.

CASENDER, Don Pedro. *The Lost Virgin of the South.* Cloth. Tallahassee, Fla., 1831. (By Michael Smith.) First edition. $500 and up. Courtland, Ala., 1833. Cloth. Second edition. $250 and up.

CASKODEN, Edwin. *When Knighthood Was in Flower.* Pictorial cloth. Indianapolis, 1898. (By Charles Major.) First edition, first issue, with 1897 copyright and no notice of reprints on copyright page. $60-$75.

CASLER, John. *Four Years in the Stonewall Brigade.* Folding facsimile. Cloth. Guthrie, Okla., 1893. First edition. $75-$100.

CASS, Lewis. *Address Delivered Before the New England Society of Michigan, Dec. 22, 1848.* 47 pp., sewed. Detroit, 1849. $35-$50.

CASS, Lewis. *Substance of a Speech Delivered by Hon. Lewis Cass, of Michigan . . . on the Ratification of the Oregon Treaty.* 16 pp., sewed. Detroit, 1846. $75-$100.

CASTLE Dismal; or, the Bachelor's Christmas. Boards. New York, 1844. (By William Gilmore Simms.) First edition. $75-$100.

CASTLE Rackrent; An Hibernian Tale. Boards. London, 1800. (By Maria Edgeworth.) First edition. $200-$300.

CASTLEMAN, Alfred L. *Army of the Potomac: Behind the Scenes.* Cloth. Milwaukee, 1863. First edition. $50.

CASTLEMAN, John B. *Active Service.* Plates. Cloth. Louisville, 1917. $35-$40.

CASTLEMON, H. C. (Harry). *Frank on the Lower Mississippi.* Illustrated. Cloth. Cincinnati, 1867. (By Charles Austin Fosdick.) First edition. $40-$45. Philadelphia, no date (1879). Pictorial cloth. $20.

CASTLEMON, Harry. *Guy Harris, the Runaway.* Printed wrappers. New York, 1887. (By Charles Austin Fosdick.) First edition, first issue. $25-$30.

CASTLEMON, Harry. *The Sportsman's Club Among the Trappers.* Plates. Cloth. Philadelphia, 1874. (By Charles Austin Fosdick.) First edition. $25-$30.

CATES, Cliff D. *Pioneer History of Wise County, Texas.* Illustrated. Stiff wrappers. Decatur, Tex., 1907. First edition. $100-$125. Rebound in cloth, $60.

CATHASAIGH, P. O. (editor). *The Story of the Irish Citizen Army.* Printed gray wrappers. Dublin, 1919. (By Sean O'Casey.) First edition. $75-$100. Author's first book.

CATHER, Willa. See McClure, S. S.; Milmine, Georgine. Also see *The Sombrero.*

CATHER, Willa. *Alexander's Bridge.* Blue, purple, and other colors of cloth. Boston, 1912. First edition, first issue, with "Willa S. Cather" on spine (later "Willa Cather") and with title and author's name in box on front cover and half title before title page. $75-$125. Another issue (?): "Willa S. Cather" on spine but title only in box on cover. $25-$35. Later issue, with half title after title page: $50.

CATHER, Willa. *April Twilights.* Brown boards, paper label. Boston, 1903. First edition. $200-$250. Author's first book. New York, 1923. Boards. First revised edition. One of 450 signed. Boxed. $75-$100. Trade edition: Cloth. $12.50-$15.

CATHER, Willa. *Death Comes for the Archbishop.* Green cloth. New York, 1927. First edition. In dust jacket. $35-$60. Another issue: One of 175 signed. Boxed. $75-$125. One of 50 on vellum, signed. Boxed. $175-$200. London, 1927. Black cloth. First English edition. In dust jacket. $50-$60. Lacking jacket, $30. New York, 1929. Illustrated by Harold von Schmidt. Vellum. One of 170 signed. $100-$125.

CATHER, Willa. *A Lost Lady.* Cloth. New York, 1923. First edition, first issue, in green cloth (later tan). In dust jacket. $25-$35. Another issue: Boards and cloth. One of 20 lettered A to T, signed. In glassine dust jacket. Boxed. $125-$150. One of 200 numbered copies (same issue). $75-$100. Advance issue: Printed wrappers. $100-$150.

CATHER, Willa. *Lucy Gayheart.* Cloth. New York, 1935. First edition, first printing (so stated). In dust jacket. $15-$25. Another issue: Buckram. One of 749 signed. In dust jacket. Boxed. $100-$125.

CATHER, Willa. *My Antonia.* Illustrated by W. T. Benda. Brown cloth. Boston, 1918. First edition, first issue, with illustrations on glazed paper inserted. $150-$200. Other copies, less than fine, have ranged at retail from $35 to $150. London, 1919. Cloth. First English edition. In dust jacket. $50-$60.

CATHER, Willa. *My Mortal Enemy.* Cloth. New York, 1926. First edition. In dust jacket. $15-$25. Another issue: Boards and cloth. One of 220 on vellum, signed. Boxed. $60-$75.

CATHER, Willa. *Not Under Forty.* Cloth. New York, 1936. First edition, first printing (so stated). In dust jacket. $12-$15. Another issue: One of 333 large paper copies on vellum, signed. Boxed. $60-$75.

CATHER, Willa. *The Novels and Stories of Willa Cather.* 13 vols., two-toned cloth. Boston, 1937-41. Autograph edition. One of 950 signed. $400-$500. Also, $325 (A, 1967).

CATHER, Willa. *O Pioneers!* Colored frontispiece by Clarence Underwood. Cloth. Boston, 1913. First edition, first issue, either tan or cream ribbed cloth (later, brown) and with last page of text on tipped-in leaf. In dust jacket. $100. Lacking jacket, $50-$75. Second issue (brown cloth). In dust jacket. $15-$20.

CATHER, Willa. *Obscure Destinies.* Green cloth. New York, 1932. First edition. In dust jacket. $20-$25. Another issue: Vellum and boards. One of 260 on vellum, signed. $50-$75.

CATHER, Willa. *One of Ours.* Cloth. New York, 1932. First edition. In dust jacket. $40-$50. Another issue: Boards. One of 35 on vellum, signed. Boxed. $100-$150. Another issue: One of 310 on handmade paper, signed. Boxed. $75-$100. Second printing (of trade edition): Boards. ("For bookseller friends.") $15-$25.

CATHER, Willa. *The Professor's House.* Orange and blue cloth. New York, 1925. First edition. In dust jacket. $25-$35. Another issue: Buckram and boards. One of 40 on vellum (of an issue of 225), signed. $150-$200. One of 185 (of this issue), signed. $100-$150.

CATHER, Willa. *Sapphira and the Slave Girl.* Cloth. New York, 1940. First edition (so stated). $10-$15. Another issue: Half buckram. One of 520 signed. $60-$75.

CATHER, Willa. *Shadows on the Rock.* Green cloth. New York, 1931. First edition, advance issue, mislabeled "Second edition" on copyright page. In dust jacket. $35-$50. Regular trade edition ("First edition" on copyright page): In dust jacket. $15-$25. Another issue: Marbled boards, leather label. One of 619 signed. In dust jacket. Boxed. $75-$100. Another issue: Full orange vellum. One of 199 on vellum, signed. In dust jacket. Boxed. $100-$150.

CATHER, Willa. *The Song of the Lark.* Blue cloth. Boston, 1915. First edition. In dust jacket. $50-$75.

CATHER, Willa. *The Troll Garden.* Crimson cloth. New York, 1905. First edition, first issue, with "McClure Phillips & Co." at foot of spine. $150-$250.

CATHER, Willa. *Youth and the Bright Medusa.* Cloth. New York, 1920. First edition. In dust jacket. $35-$50. Another issue: One of 25 signed. $75-$100.

CATHER, Willa, and Canfield, Dorothy. *The Fear That Walks by Noonday.* Boards, paper label. New York, 1931. First edition. One of 30. $90-$125.

CATHERWOOD, Frederick. *Views of Ancient Monuments in Central America, Chiapas, and Yucatan.* Colored title page, engraved map, 25 lithographs. Folio, half morocco. London, 1844. First edition. $1,500-$2,000. Also, $1,656 (A, 1967), $1,176 (A, 1965). New York, 1844. First American edition. Equally valuable. Barre, Mass., 1965. One of 500 facsimile copies. $275-$300. (Note: Still available in print at $275 in 1971.)

CATHERWOOD, Mrs. Mary Hartwell. *Spanish Peggy.* Red cloth. Chicago, 1899. First edition. $25-$35.

CATHOLIC Anthology, 1914-1915 (The). Edited by Ezra Pound. Gray boards. London, 1915. First edition. $200-$250. (Note: Includes T. S. Eliot's "The Love Song of J. Alfred Prufrock" and four other poems, marking his first appearance in a book.)

CATLIN, George. *Letters and Notes on the Manners, Customs, and Conditions of the North American Indians.* 2 maps (one folding), one chart, 309 illustrations. 2 vols., cloth, paper labels. London, 1841. First edition, first issue, with "Frederick" for "Zacharias" on page 104. $400-$500. London, 1841. 2 vols., cloth. Second edition. $200-$250. New York, 1841. 2 vols., cloth. First American edition. $200-$250. Also, half leatherette, $120 (A, 1969). (Note: Many other later editions, some with plates colored by hand, titles altered, etc. See American and British auction records.)

CATLIN, George. *O-Kee-Pa, a Religious Ceremony.* 13 colored lithographs. Cloth. London, 1867. First edition. $400-$500.

CATLIN, George. *North American Indian Portfolio.* 25 colored plates mounted on cardboard; text in cloth-backed wrappers. Large folio, morocco-backed cloth portfolio. London, 1844. First edition. $1,000-$1,500, probably more for fine copies. New York, 1845. 25 colored plates. Text badly damp-stained, $400 (A, 1961).

CATO. *Cato's Moral Distichs.* Facsimile of 1735 Philadelphia edition printed by Benjamin Franklin. Cloth. San Francisco, 1939. One of 250. $30-$40.

CATTLE Raising in South Dakota. 32 pp., wrappers. No place, no date (Forest City, 1904). $40.

CAVALCANTI, Guido. *Rime.* (In English and Italian.) Edited by Ezra Pound. 40 plates. Stiff red printed wrappers. Genova, Italy, no date (1932). First edition. $35-$40.

CAVENDISH, George. *Life of Thomas Wolsey, Cardinal Archbishop of York.* Edited by F. S. Ellis. Limp vellum with ties. London, 1893. Kelmscott Press. One of 250. $300-$350.

CAXTON, Pisistratus. *What Will He Do with It?* 4 vols., cloth. Edinburgh, no date (1859). (By Edward Bulwer-Lytton.) First edition. $150-$200.

CELEBRATION of the 73d Anniversary of the Declaration of Independence. . . on Board the Barque "Hannah Sprague," etc. 16 pp., wrappers. New York, 1849. First edition. $55.

CELIZ, Fray Francisco. *Diary of the Alarcon Expedition into Texas, 1718-1719.* Translated by Fritz L. Hoffman. 10 plates. Cloth. Los Angeles, 1935. One of 600. $35-$50.

CELLINI, Benvenuto. *The Autobiography of Benvenuto Cellini.* Translated by John Addington Symonds. Illustrated by Salvador Dali. Blue cloth, gilt top. Garden City, 1946. One of 1,000 signed by Dali. Boxed. $60-$80.

CENDRARS, Blaise. *Panama, or The Adventures of My Seven Uncles.* Translated from the French and illustrated by John Dos Passos. Pictorial wrappers. New York, 1931. First edition. One of 300 signed by Cendrars and Dos Passos. Boxed. $35-$40.

CERRUTI, Henry. *Ramblings in California.* Boards and cloth. Berkeley, Calif., 1954. One of 500. $25-$30.

CERVANTES, Miguel de. *Don Quixote.* (Note: Because this seventeenth-century classic has gone into innumerable editions, the following listings are limited to a few representative selections. See the British and American auction records for more extensive records.)

CERVANTES, Miguel de. *El Ingenioso Hidalgo Don Quixote de la Mancha.* Facsimile of the first and second parts, Madrid, 1605 and 1615. 2 vols., vellum with ties. No place (New York), no date. Hispanic Society of America. One of 100 on handmade paper. Boxed. $200-$300.

CERVANTES, Miguel de. *The History of Don Quixote of the Mancha.* P. A. Motteux's translation revised anew (1743). 21 illustrations by E. McKnight Kauffer. 2 vols., morocco. London, 1930. Nonesuch Press. $100-$150.

CERVANTES, Miguel de. *The History of the Valorous and Witty Knight-Errant, Don Quixote of the Mancha.* Thomas Shelton translation. Daniel Vierge illustrations. 4 vols., morocco. New York, 1906-07. One of 140 on Japan paper, with duplicate plates. $300-$350. Another issue: Cloth. One of 845. $100.

CERVANTES, Miguel de. *The History of the Valorous and Wittie Knight-Errant, Don Quixote of the Mancha.* Thomas Shelton translation. Woodcut initials and borders by Louise Powell. 2 vols., pigskin. London, 1927-28. Ashendene Press. One of 225. $500-$600. Another issue: 2 vols., boards, canvas backs. $200-$300.

CHADWICK, Henry. *The Game of Base Ball: How to Learn It, How to Play It, and How to Teach It.* Cloth. New York, no date (1868). First edition, with rules for 1868. $75-$100.

CHADWICK, Hector M. and N. K. *The Growth of Literature.* 3 vols., cloth. Cambridge, England, 1932-40. $95.

CHAGALL, Marc. *Illustrations for the Bible.* Edited by Jean Wahl. 29 lithographs (17 in color), 105 plates. Pictorial boards in color. New York, 1956. First edition. $750-$1,000. Paris, 1956. $616 (A, 1969).

CHAGALL, Marc. *The Story of the Exodus.* 24 colored lithographs, Bible text. Folio, unbound signatures, in stiff white wrappers. Paris-New York, 1966. First edition. One of 25 on Arches paper, signed by Chagall. Boxed. $3,900 (U.S. catalogue, 1970) and $5,290 (Swiss catalogue, 1970). Also, $4,133.33 (A, Switzerland, 1969).

CHAHTA-IMA. *La Nouvelle Atala ou La Fille de L'Esprit.* Printed wrappers. Nouvelle-Orléans (New Orleans), 1879. First edition. $100-$150. (Note: Contains a contribution by Lafcadio Hearn—his first book appearance.)

CHAINBEARER (The), or, The Littlepage Manuscripts. 3 vols., tan boards. London, 1845. (By James Fenimore Cooper.) First edition. $75-$100. New York, 1845. 2 vols., wrappers. $100. Also, $45 (A, 1960). (Note: Name is misspelled "Fennimore" on front cover.)

CHAMBERS, Andrew Jackson. *Recollections.* 40 pp., stapled. No place, no date (1947). First edition. $75-$100.

CHAMISSO, Adelbert von. *The Wonderful History of Peter Schlemihl.* 6 illustrations. Printed wrappers. London, 1843. First edition. $250-$300. Corner chipped from front wrapper, rebacked, $175.

CHAMISSO, Adelbert von. *A Sojourn at San Francisco Bay 1816.* Half cloth. San Francisco, 1936. One of 250. $75.

CHAMPNEY, Lizzie W. *Three Vassar Girls Abroad.* Illustrated by J. Wells Champney. Pictorial boards. Boston, 1883. First edition. $25-$35.

CHANDLER, Raymond. *The Big Sleep.* Cloth. New York, 1929. First edition. In dust jacket. $75-$125. Author's first book.

CHANDLER, Raymond. *Farewell, My Lovely.* Brown cloth. New York, 1940. First edition. In dust jacket. $35-$50.

CHANDLER, Raymond. *The Long Good-Bye.* Boards. London, 1953. First edition. In dust jacket. $35-$50.

CHANNING, William Ellery (1780-1842). *The Duties of Children.* Wrappers. Boston, 1807. First edition. $60.

CHANNING, William Ellery (1780-1842). *A Sermon Delivered at the Ordination of the Rev. Jared Sparks, etc.* Stitched. Boston, 1819. First edition. $50-$60.

CHANNING, William Ellery (1818-1901). *John Brown, and The Heroes of Harper's Ferry: A Poem.* Green cloth. Boston, 1886. First edition. $35-$50.

CHANUTE, Octave. *Progress in Flying Machines.* 85 illustrations. Cloth. New York, no date (1894). First edition. $50-$60.

CHAPELLE, Howard I. *The Baltimore Clipper.* 35 plates. Cloth (leatherette). Salem, Mass., 1930. $75-$100. Another issue: Marbled boards. One of 97. $125-$150.

CHAPMAN, George. *Captivity in Australia.* 38 pp., wrappers. Providence, R.I., 1871. First edition. $35-$50.

CHARSLEY, Fanny Anne, *The Wild Flowers Around Melbourne.* 13 color plates. Folio, blue cloth. London, 1867. $200-$225.

CHARTER of Dartmouth College (The). Stitched. Hanover, N.H., 1815. $35-$40.

CHARTERED Surveyor (The), His Training and His Work. Foreword by the Rt. Hon. Winston Churchill. Boards and cloth. London, no date (1932). First edition. $30-$35.

CHASE, Owen (and others). *Narratives of the Wreck of the Whale Ship "Esse."* 12 wood engravings by Robert Gibbings. Cloth. London, 1935. Golden Cockerel Press. One of 275. $100-$150.

CHATTERTON, E. Keble. *Ship-Models.* Edited by Geoffrey Holme. 142 plates, many in color. Buckram. London, 1923. One of 1,000. $75-$100.

CHATTERTON, E. Keble. *Steamship Models.* 128 plates, some in color. Buckram. London, 1924. One of 1,000 signed. $50-$75.

CHATTO, William A. See Careless, John.

CHAUCER, Geoffrey. (Note: The editions of Chaucer, like those of the Bible, Shakespeare, and other classic universal works, are too numerous to permit a complete listing here. Following are a few outstanding representative items.)

CHAUCER, Geoffrey. *The Canterbury Tales.* Colored plates by W. Russell Flint. 3 vols., limp vellum, silk ties. London, 1913. Riccardi Press. One of 500. $200-$250. Another issue: Boards. $150-$200. New York, 1930. Illustrated by Rockwell Kent. 2 vols., pigskin. One of 75 signed. $400-$450. Another issue: Cloth. One of 924. $100-$125. Also, $40 (A, 1969); $60 and $32 (A, 1968). Waltham Saint Lawrence, 1929-31. Golden Cockerel Press. Eric Gill engravings. 4 vols., folio, boards, morocco spine. One of 485. $1,000-$1,250. Also, $500, $528, $548, and $720 (A, 1969). New York, 1946. Limited Editions Club. Illustrated by Arthur Szyk. Half pigskin. Boxed. $100. Also, $22 and $52.80 (A, 1969).

CHAUCER, Geoffrey. *The Ellesmere Chaucer. (The Canterbury Tales.)*Facsimile, including 71 pages illuminated in gold and colors. 2 vols., folio, half morocco. Manchester, England, 1911. $500. Also, $168 (A, 1965).

CHAUCER, Geoffrey. *Troilus and Criseyde.* Edited by Arundell del Re. 5 full-page illustrations, 5 half-page decorations, and engraved title page by Eric Gill. Folio, boards and morocco. Waltham Saint Lawrence, 1927. Golden Cockerel Press. One of 225. $800-$1,000. Also, $480 (A, 1969), $384 (A, 1968), $288 (A, 1967).

CHAUCER, Geoffrey. *Works.* Woodcut illustrations, borders, and initials. Folio, boards. London, 1896. Kelmscott Press. One of 425. $2,500. Also, $1,104 (A, 1967); $2,000-$1,200 (A, 1966); $1,050 (A, 1965). Another issue: White blind-stamped pigskin, in wooden box with brass hinges and clasps, by the Doves Bindery. One of 46. $5,250 (A, 1969), $4,800 (A, 1967), $3,640 (A, 1966).

CHEEVER, John. *The Wapshot Chronicle.* Cloth. New York, no date (1957). First edition. In dust jacket. $25-$35.

CHEEVER, John. *The Way Some People Live.* Cloth. New York, no date (1943). First edition. In dust jacket. $60-$75.

CHESTERTON, G. K. *The Ballad of the White Horse.* Half cloth. London, no date (1928). First edition. One of 100. In dust jacket. $50-$60.

CHESTERTON, G. K. *Chaucer.* Cloth. London, 1932. First edition. In dust jacket. $25-$30.

CHESTERTON, G. K. *Collected Poems.* Boards and parchment. London, 1927. One of 350 signed. $30-$35.

CHESTERTON, G. K. *Grey-Beards at Play: Rhymes and Sketches.* Boards and buckram. London, 1900. First edition. $35-$50. Author's first book.

CHESTERTON, G. K. *The Innocence of Father Brown.* Illustrated by S. S. Lucas. Red cloth. London, 1911. First edition. $50-$60.

CHESTERTON, G. K. *The Sword of Wood.* Boards. London, 1928. First edition. One of 530 signed. In dust jacket. $25-$30.

CHESTERTON, G. K. *The Wild Knight and Other Poems.* Half vellum. London, 1900. First edition. $35-$40.

CHICAGO Illustrated. (Cover title.) 52 tinted lithograph views. Text by James W. Sheahan. Oblong folio, morocco. No place, no date (Chicago, 1866-67). Jevne and Almini, publishers. First edition, second issue (original issue was in 13 parts, of which no complete sets are known). $3,000 (A, 1966). New York, 1952. 12 plates. Portfolio. Reprint edition. $75-$150. (Note: The individual prints of the latter edition currently retail in the $25 range, unframed.)

CHILD, Andrew. *Overland Route to California.* Full leather. Milwaukee, 1852. First edition. $2,750 (A, 1968).

CHILD, Lydia Maria. See *Hobomok; The Frugal Housewife.*

CHILDREN in Prison and Other Cruelties of Prison Life. 16 pp., wired wrappers. London, no date (1898). (By Oscar Wilde.) First edition. $150-$200.

CHILDREN of the Chapel (The): A Tale. By the Author of "Mark Dennis." Red cloth. London, 1864. (By Algernon C. Swinburne.) First edition, first issue, with "Joseph Masters" in imprint (later, "J. Masters & Co."). $25-$35.

CHILDREN in the Wood: An Affecting Tale. 31 pp., printed wrappers. Cooperstown, N. Y., 1837. $35-$40.

CHILD'S Book About Whales (The). Woodcuts. 16 pp., printed wrappers. Concord, N.H., 1843. $25-$30.

CHILD'S Botany (The). Boards. Boston, 1828. (By Samuel Griswold Goodrich.) First edition. $45-$50.

CHILDS, C. G. (engraver). *Views in Philadelphia and Its Vicinity*. Engraved title page, plan, 24 engraved views. Boards. Philadelphia, 1827-(30). First edition. $100-$125.

CHITTENDEN, L. F. *The Emma Mine*. 76 pp., sewed. New York, 1876. $45-$50.

CHITTENDEN, Hiram M. *The American Fur Trade of the Far West*. Folding map, plan, 3 facsimiles, 6 plates. 3 vols., green cloth. New York, 1902. First edition. $200-$250. New York, 1936. Plates. 2 vols., cloth. Boxed. $75-$100.

CHITTENDEN, Hiram M. *History of Early Steamboat Navigation on the Missouri River*. 16 plates. 2 vols., cloth. New York, 1903. One of 950. $75-$100.

CHIVERS, Thomas Holley. *Conrad and Eudora*. Cloth, or leather (?). Philadelphia, 1834. First edition. $100-$150.

CHIVERS, Thomas Holley. *Eonchs of Ruby: A Gift of Love*. Printed white boards. New York, 1851. First edition. $125-$150.

CHIVERS, Thomas Holley. *The Lost Pleiad and Other Poems*. Printed tan wrappers. New York, 1845. First edition. $100-$150.

CHIVERS, Thomas Holley. *Memoralia*. Boards and cloth. Philadelphia, 1853. First edition. $50-$60.

CHIVERS, Thomas Holley. *Nacoochee: or, The Beautiful Star*. Cloth. New York, 1837. First edition. $150-$200.

CHIVERS, Thomas Holley. *The Path of Sorrow*. Blue boards, purple cloth, paper label. Franklin, T(enn.), 1832. First edition. $400-$500. Author's first book.

CHIVERS, Thomas Holley. *Search After Truth*. Printed tan wrappers. New York, 1848. First edition. $100-$150.

CHRISTMAS Gift from Fairy-Land (A). Cloth. New York, no date (1838). (By James Kirke Paulding.) First edition, second (?) issue. $150-$200. (Note: This was also published under the title *A Gift from Fairy-Land*.)

CHRONICLES of the City of Gotham. Half cloth. New York, 1830. (By James Kirke Paulding.) First edition. $100-$150.

CHRYSTAL, Peter. *A Voice from the Oppressed Spirits in Prison*. 11 pp., wrappers. No place, no date (New Orleans, 1848). $25-$30.

CHURCH, John A. *The Comstock Lode*. 6 plates. Cloth. New York, 1879. First edition. $35-$50.

CHURCHILL, Winston (American novelist). *The Celebrity*. Cloth. New York, 1898. First edition. $25-$30. Author's first book.

CHURCHILL, Sir Winston S. See *The Chartered Surveyor*.

CHURCHILL, Sir Winston S. *Arms and the Covenant: Speeches*. Compiled by Randolph S. Churchill. Frontispiece. Buckram. London, 1938. First edition. $75-$125.

CHURCHILL, Sir Winston S. *Beating the Invader*. 2 pp., unbound (as issued). No place, no date (London, 1941). $50-$75.

CHURCHILL, Sir Winston S. *Great Contemporaries.* Illustrated. Cloth. London, 1937. First edition. In dust jacket. $75-$100.

CHURCHILL, Sir Winston S. *Ian Hamilton's March.* Portrait, maps, plans. Red cloth. London, 1900. First edition. $200-$250.

CHURCHILL, Sir Winston S. *India: Speeches.* Orange wrappers. London, 1931. First edition. $200-$400. Second impression. Green wrappers: $75-$125.

CHURCHILL, Sir Winston S. *Liberalism and the Social Problem.* Cloth. London, 1909. First edition. $250-$300.

CHURCHILL, Sir Winston S. *London to Ladysmith via Pretoria.* Maps and plans. Faun-colored cloth. London, 1900. First edition. $100-$150.

CHURCHILL, Sir Winston S. *Lord Randolph Churchill.* Frontispieces, plates. 2 vols., cloth. London, 1906. First edition. $50-$100.

CHURCHILL, Sir Winston S. *Marlborough: His Life and Times.* Plates, facsimiles, maps, plans. 4 vols., morocco, gilt tops. London, no date (1933-38). First edition. One of 150 signed. $750-$1,000. Also, $600 (A, 1970), $576 (A, 1969), $528 (A, 1968). Trade edition: 4 vols., cloth. In dust jackets. $125-$150.

CHURCHILL, Sir Winston S. *My African Journey.* Maps and plates. Pictorial red cloth. London, 1908. First edition. $125-$192.

CHURCHILL, Sir Winston S. *My Early Life.* Portraits, maps, plates. Cloth. London, 1930. First edition. $100-$150. New York, 1930. Illustrated. Cloth. First American edition. $75-$100.

CHURCHILL, Sir Winston S. *The People's Rights.* Pictorial wrappers. London, no date (1909). First edition, first issue, with index. $300-$400. Also, rebound, $176 (A, 1966). Second issue. $100-$150.

CHURCHILL, Sir Winston S. *The River War.* Portraits, colored maps, folding illustrations. 2 vols., pictorial cloth. London, 1899. First edition. $400-$500. Also, $266 (A, 1968); $280 and $336 (A, 1966); $232 and $246 (A, 1965).

CHURCHILL, Sir Winston S. *Savrola: A Tale of the Revolution in Laurania.* Cloth. New York, 1900. First American edition. $300-$350. Also, $208 and $232 (A, 1965). London, 1900. Cloth. First English edition. $100-$200.

CHURCHILL, Sir Winston S. *Secret Session Speeches.* Cloth. London, no date (1946). First edition. In dust jacket. $25.

CHURCHILL, Sir Winston S. *Step by Step, 1936-1939.* Green cloth. London, 1939. First edition. $180.

CHURCHILL, Sir Winston S. *The Story of the Malakand Field Force.* Portrait and 5 maps and plans. Cloth. London, 1898. First edition, first issue, with errata slip preceding first map. $600-$800.

CHURCHILL, Sir Winston S. *Thoughts and Adventures.* Cloth. London, no date (1932). First edition. $100-$125.

CHURCHILL, Sir Winston S. *The World Crisis.* Maps, plans, other illustrations. 6 vols., cloth. London, 1923-31. First editions. $180.

CHURCHILL, Sir Winston S., and Martindale, C. C., S.J. *Charles IXth, Duke of Marlborough, K. G.* Wrappers. London, 1934. First edition. $50-$60.

CINCINNATUS. *Travels on the Western Slope of the Mexican Cordillera.* Engraved title page. Cloth. San Francisco, 1857. (By Marvin T. Wheat.) First edition. $150-$200.

CINDERELLA. Retold by C. S. Evans. Frontispiece in color and numerous silhouette illustrations by Arthur Rackham. Half cloth. London, 1919. One of 525 signed by the artist. In dust jacket. $75-$100. Another issue: One of 850. $35-$40.

CINDERELLA, or The Little Glass Slipper. 11 woodcuts. 30 pp., pictorial orange wrappers. Cooperstown, N. Y., 1839. (By Charles Perrault.) $25. New York, no date (about 1880). Illustrations, 10 pp., of text. Colored pictorial boards. McLoughlin toy book. $35-$50. Worn, $27.50.

CLAIBORNE, John Herbert. *Seventy-five Years in Old Virginia*. Cloth. New York, 1905. $25-$35.

CLARK, Charles E. *Prince and Boatswain: Sea Tales from the Recollection of Rear-Admiral Charles E. Clark*. Blue cloth. Greenfield, Mass., no date (about 1915). (Edited by John P. Marquand and James M. Morgan.) First edition. $35-$50. Marquand's first book appearance.

CLARK, Daniel M. *The Southern Calculator, or Compendious Arithmetic*. Boards. Lagrange, Ga., 1844. $35-$40.

CLARK, John A. *Gleanings by the Way*. Cloth. Philadephia, 1842. First edition. $100-$125.

CLARK, Walter (editor). *Histories of the Several Regiments and Battalions from North Carolina in the Great War, 1861-1865*. Plates. 5 vols., cloth. Raleigh, 1901. $150-$175.

CLARKE, Lewis. *Narrative of the Sufferings of Lewis Clarke During a Captivity of More Than Twenty-five Years*. Portrait. Wrappers. Boston, 1845. First edition. $50-$75.

CLARKE, Peyton Neale. *Old King William Homes and Families*. Illustrated. Cloth. Louisville, 1897. First edition. $30-$40.

CLARKE, Rebecca S. See May, Sophie.

CLASS Poem. Printed wrappers. No place (Cambridge, Mass.), 1838. (By James Russell Lowell.) First edition. $200-$300. Author's first published work.

CLAY, John. *My Life on the Range*. Illustrated. Cloth. Chicago, no date (1924). First edition. $100-$150.

CLAYTON, A. M. *Centennial Address on the History of Marshall County*. (Mississippi.) 32 pp., wrappers. Washington, 1880. $45-$50.

CLAYTON, W(illiam). *The Latter-Day Saints' Emigrants' Guide*. 24 pp., plain wrappers. St. Louis, 1848. First edition. $2,000 and up. Also, worn, pages stuck, back cover loose, $2,000 (A, 1968). Other auction records: $1,700 (A, 1959); $2,016 (A, 1958)— Brigham Young's copy.

CLELAND, Thomas. *Unitarianism Unmasked*. Cloth. Lexington, Ky., 1825. First edition. $60-$75.

CLEMENS, Samuel Langhorne. See Twain, Mark. Also see *What Is Man?; Date 1601*.

CLEMENT, Maud Carter. *The History of Pittsylvania County, Virginia*. Plates, maps, facsimiles. Cloth. Lynchburg, Va., 1929. $25-$30.

CLEVELAND, Richard J. *A Narrative of Voyages and Commercial Enterprises*. 2 vols., cloth. Cambridge, Mass., 1842. First edition. $200-$250.

CLOCKMAKER (The); or the Sayings and Doings of Samuel Slick of Slickville. Cloth, paper label. Halifax, 1836. (By Thomas Chandler Haliburton.) First edition. $150-$250. Also, $100 (A, 1968). Philadelphia, 1836. Boards. First United States edition. $35-$50.

CLUM, Woodworth. *Apache Agent: The Story of John P. Clum.* Illustrated, including frontispiece in color of Geronimo. Cloth. Boston, 1936. First edition. In dust jacket. $35-50.

CLUTTERBUCK, Captain. *The Monastery.* 3 vols., boards, paper labels. Edinburgh, 1820. (By Sir Walter Scott.) First edition. $75-$125.

CLYMER, W. B. S., and Green, Charles R. *Robert Frost: A Bibliography.* Cloth. Amherst, Mass., 1937. One of 500 (of an edition of 650). $50. Another issue: One of 150 signed. $100. Also, $55 (A, 1971).

COBB, Irvin S. *Back Home.* Illustrated. Cloth. New York, no date (1912). First edition, first printing, with "Plimpton Press" slug on copyright page, and first binding, with publisher's name in 3 lines on spine. $25-$35. Author's first book.

COBB, Irvin S. *Old Judge Priest.* Cloth. New York, no date (1916). First edition, first issue, with square-diamond insignia on title page. $25-$30.

COBB, Irvin S. *Piano Jim and the Impotent Pumpkin Vine, or "Charley Russell's Best Story—to My Way of Thinking."* 24 pp., wrappers. No place, 1947. One of 100. $35-$50.

COBBETT, William, *Rural Rides.* Woodcut map. Boards and cloth. London, 1830. First edition. $150-$200. Also, rebacked, $62.40 (A, 1968). London, 1930. Edited by G. D. H. and Margaret Cole. Illustrated. 3 vols., boards. $100-$150.

COBDEN-SANDERSON, T. J. *Amantium Irae: Letters to Two Friends, 1864-1867.* Frontispiece portrait. Limp vellum. Hammersmith (London), 1914. Doves Press. One of 150. $200-$250. Another issue: Morocco. $250-$400.

COCKERELL, S. C. (editor). *Laudes Beatae Mariae Virginis.* Printed in red, black, and blue. Boards and linen. London, 1896. Kelmscott Press. One of 250. $275-$300.

COCKERELL, S. C. (editor). *Some German Woodcuts of the 15th Century.* 35 reproductions. Boards and linen. London, 1898. Kelmscott Press. One of 225. $300-$350.

COFFIN, Charles C. *The Boys of '76.* Illustrated. Pictorial cloth. New York, 1887. First edition. $60-$75.

COFFIN, Joshua. *A Sketch of the History of Newbury, Newburyport, and West Newbury.* Map, tables. Cloth. Boston, 1845. $25-$35.

COHN, Albert M. *George Cruikshank: A Catalogue Raisonne.* Illustrated. Brown cloth. London, 1924. First edition. One of 500. $75-$100.

COHN, David L. *New Orleans and Its Living Past.* Illustrated. Cloth. Boston, 1941. Limited, signed edition. $25-$35.

COHN, Louis Henry. *A Bibliography of the Works of Ernest Hemingway.* Illustrated. Cloth. New York, 1931. First edition. One of 500. $75-$100.

COKE, Henry J. *A Ride over the Rocky Mountains to Oregon and California.* Portrait. Cloth. London, 1852. First edition. $50-$75.

COKE, Richard. *Inaugural Address.* 14 pp., wrappers. Austin, Tex., 1874. $50-$75.

COKE, Richard. *Message to the 14th Legislature.* 14 pp., sewed. Austin, Tex., 1874. $35-$50. Same, to 15th Legislature, 1st session: Houston, 1876. 68 pp., sewed. $35-$50.

COLE, Emma. *Life and Sufferings.* Plates. 36 pp., wrappers. Boston, 1844. $65-$75.

COLERIDGE, Samuel T. See *Lyrical Ballads.*

COLERIDGE, Samuel T. *Aids to Reflection.* Drab boards, paper label. London, 1825. First edition. $75-$100.

COLERIDGE, Samuel T. *Biographia Literaria.* 2 vols., green or blue boards, paper labels. London, 1817. First edition. $200-$300.

COLERIDGE, Samuel T. *Christabel: Kubla Khan, a Vision; The Pains of Sleep.* Plain drab wrappers. London, 1816. First edition, with 4 pages of ads in back. $750 and up. Also, $673 (A, 1968). London, 1904. Eragny Press. Boards. One of 236. $75-$100.

COLERIDGE, Samuel T. *Confessions of an Inquiring Spirit.* Cloth, paper label. London, 1840. First edition. $35-$50. Boston, 1841. Cloth, paper label. $25.

COLERIDGE, Samuel T. *Hints Towards the Formation of a More Comprehensive Theory of Life.* Boards. London, 1817. First edition. $100-$125.

COLERIDGE, Samuel T. *A Lay Sermon.* Printed wrappers. London, 1817. First edition. $150-$200.

COLERIDGE, Samuel T. *Notes, Theological, Political, and Miscellaneous.* Cloth. London, 1853. First edition. $35-$45.

COLERIDGE, Samuel T. *Osorio: A Tragedy.* Boards, paper label. London, 1873. First edition. One of 50 large paper copies. $150-$228.

COLERIDGE, Samuel T. *Poems Chosen Out of the Works of Samuel Taylor Coleridge.* Printed with "Golden" type in red and black. Woodcut borders and initial letters. Vellum. London, 1896. Kelmscott Press. One of 300. $200-$250.

COLERIDGE, Samuel T. *The Rime of the Ancient Mariner.* London, 1903. Essex House. Parchment boards. One of 150 on vellum. $75-$100. Also, $42 (A, 1966). London, 1910. Illustrated. Stiff vellum. One of 25 on vellum. In cloth wrapper and slipcase. $150-$250. Bristol, England, 1929. 10 engravings by David Jones. Canvas. One of 60 with extra set of engravings, signed by the artist. $75. Another issue: Boards and cloth. One of 400. $35. London, 1930. Boards. $35. London, 1944. Corvinus Press. Boards and cloth. One of 39. $100-$150. Los Angeles, no date (1964). Tamarind Workshop. Colored lithographs. Printed wrappers. One of 45. $600. (Note: For numerous other editions, see book auction records.)

COLERIDGE, Samuel T. *Selected Poems.* Vellum. London, 1935. Nonesuch Press. One of 500. $75-$100.

COLERIDGE, Samuel T. *Sibylline Leaves: A Collection of Poems.* Drab boards, paper label. London, 1817. First edition, with errata leaf. $250-$350.

COLERIDGE, Samuel T. *Specimens of the Table Talk of the Late Samuel Taylor Coleridge.* Frontispiece. 2 vols., boards with labels. London, 1835. First edition. $75-$100.

COLERIDGE, Samuel T. *The Statesman's Manual; or the Bible the Best Guide to Political Skill and Foresight.* Blue-green printed wrappers. London, 1816. First edition. $250 and up. Rebound in half morocco, $225.

COLERIDGE, Samuel T. *Zapolya.* Wrappers. London, 1817. First edition. $100-$125.

COLLECTION of Familiar Quotations (A). Brown cloth. Cambridge, Mass., 1855. (By John Bartlett.) First edition. $75-$100.

COLLIER, John Payne. *A Bibliographical and Critical Account of the Rarest Books in the English Language.* 2 vols., half cloth. London, 1865. First edition. $75-$100.

COLLIER, John Payne, *Memoirs of Edward Alleyn.* Cloth. London, 1841. First edition. $35-$50.

COLLINS, Charles. *Collins' History and Directory of the Black Hills.* 91 pp., printed yellow wrappers. Central City, Dakota Territory, 1878. First edition. $1,200 (A, 1968).

COLLINS, Charles (compiler). *Collins' Omaha Directory.* Printed boards. No place, no date (Omaha, 1866). First edition. $450. Also, $325 (A, 1968).

COLLINS, David. *An Account of the English Colony in New South Wales.* 2 maps, 32 plates. Leather or boards. London, 1804. Second edition. $100-$300.

COLLINS, Dennis. *The Indians' Last Fight; or, the Dull Knife Raid.* 8 plates. Cloth. No place, no date (Girard, Kan., about 1915). First edition. $100-$150.

COLLINS, John S. *Across the Plains in '64.* Pictorial cloth. Omaha, 1904. First edition. $75-$100.

COLLINS, Mrs. Nat. *The Cattle Queen of Montana.* Compiled by Charles Wallace. Illustrated. Stiff wrappers. St. James, Minn., 1894. First edition. $1,000 and up. Spokane, no date (*circa* 1898-1902). Edited by Alvin E. Dyer. Plates. Pictorial wrappers. Revised edition. $150-$200.

COLLINS, Lieut. R. M. *Chapters from the Unwritten History of the War Between the States.* Cloth. St. Louis, 1893. First edition. $75-$100. Rebound in buckram, $65.

COLLINS, Wilkie. *After Dark.* 2 vols., cloth. London, 1856. First edition. $100-$125.

COLLINS, Wilkie. *Antonina.* 3 vols., cloth. London, 1850. First edition. $150-$200. Also, signed copy, $156 (A, 1968). Author's first novel.

COLLINS, Wilkie. *Armadale.* Illustrated. 2 vols., decorated brown cloth. London, 1866. First edition. $75-$100. Rebound in calf, $40 (A, 1956).

COLLINS, Wilkie. *The Dead Secret.* 2 vols., cloth. London, 1857. First edition. $75-$100. Also, rebound in half morocco, $36.40 (A, 1965).

COLLINS, Wilkie. *The Evil Genius.* 3 vols., cloth. London, 1886. First edition. $100-$150.

COLLINGS, Wilkie. *The Frozen Deep: A Drama.* Printed wrappers. No place, 1866. First printing. One of a few copies privately printed. $50-$75. London, 1874. 2 vols., cloth. First published edition (*The Frozen Deep and Other Tales*). $50-$75.

COLLINS, Wilkie. *The Law and the Lady.* 3 vols., cloth. London, 1875. First edition. $75-$100.

COLLINS, Wilkie. *The Legacy of Cain.* 3 vols., cloth. London, 1889. First edition. $100-$125.

COLLINS, Wilkie. *Memoirs of the Life of William Collins, R.A.* 2 vols., cloth. London, 1848. First edition. $50-$75. Rebound in one vol., half cloth. $50. Author's first book.

COLLINS, Wilkie. *Miss Gwilt.* Wrappers. No place, 1869. First edition. $50-$75.

COLLINS, Wilkie. *Mr. Wray's Cash-Box.* Frontispiece. Cloth. London, 1852. First edition. $75-$100.

COLLINS, Wilkie. *The Moonstone: A Romance.* 3 vols., purple cloth. London, 1868. First edition, first issue, with misprint "treachesrouly" on page 129 of Vol. 2 and with ads in Vols. 2 and 3. $500-$750. Also, $288 (A, 1967); presentation copy, inscribed by Collins, $2,500 (A, 1963); half morocco, original covers bound in, $268.80 (A, 1965); rebound, no half titles, $78.40 (A, 1965). New York, 1868. Cloth. $50-$75. New York, 1959. Limited Editions Club. Cloth. Boxed. $25.

COLLINS, Wilkie. *No Name.* 3 vols., red cloth. London, 1862. First edition. $100-$150. London, 1870. Cloth. First edition of second dramatic version. $75-$100.

COLLINS, Wilkie. *The Woman in White.* Illustrated by John McLenan. Black cloth. New York, 1860. First edition, first issue, with the woman on spine in white. $125-$150. London, 1860. 3 vols., cloth. First English edition (published a month after the first

American edition), first issue, with ads at end of Vol. 3 dated August 1, 1860. $400-$500. Also, $350 (A, 1945), $225 (A, 1947). New York, 1964. Limited Editions Club. Boards. Boxed. $35-$40. Also, $20 (A, 1968).

COLLINS, William. *Poems of William Collins.* Edited by Edmund Blunden. Portrait frontispiece. Cloth. London, 1929. First edition. One of 500. In dust jacket. $25-$30.

COLMAN, George, the Younger. See Mathers, John.

COLMAN, Sir Jeremiah. *The Noble Game of Cricket.* 105 plates, 33 colored. Buckram. London, 1941. One of 150. In dust jacket. $150-$200.

COLT, Miriam Davis. *Went to Kansas.* Cloth. Watertown, N. Y., 1862. First edition. $100-$150.

COLTON, J. H. (publisher). See *The State of Indiana Delineated.*

COLTON, J. H. (publisher). *Particulars of Routes, Distances, Fares, etc.* (Caption title.) 12 pp. (11 of text). Accompanying Colton's *Map of the United States . . . and a Plan of the Gold Region.* Map folded into brown cloth covers, with printed paper label; text attached to inside of front cover. New York, 1849. First edition, first issue, with "longitude West from Greenwich" at top of map. $250-$350.

COLTON, Walter. *Three Years in California.* Map, 6 portraits, 6 plates, folding facsimile. Black cloth. New York, 1850. First edition. $75-$100.

COLUMBIA Verse: 1897-1924. Boards and cloth. New York, 1924. First edition. $45. (Note: Poems by Louis Zukofsky and others.)

COLUMBUS, Christopher. *The Voyage of Christopher Columbus: Being the Journals, etc.* Translated by Cecil Jane. 5 maps. Half vellum. London, 1930. One of 1,050. $75-$100.

COMBE, William. See: Doctor Syntax; Quiz. Also see *The English Dance of Death; The Dance of Life; The Tour of Doctor Prosody; A History of Madeira; Journal of Sentimental Travels, etc.; The History of Johnny Quae Genus.*

COMBS, Leslie. *Narrative of the Life of Gen. Leslie Combs.* (Cover title.) 23 pp., plus errata leaf. Wrappers. No place, no date (New York, 1852). First edition. $250. Another issue: No place (Washington), 1852. 20 pp., printed wrappers. Rebound in cloth, $130 (A, 1967)—the Streeter copy (with no mention of first edition).

COMING Race (The). Scarlet-orange cloth, blocked in black and gold. Edinburgh, no date (1871). (By Edward Bulwer-Lytton.) First edition. $30-$50.

COMMERCIAL Tourist (The); or, Gentleman Traveller: A Satirical Poem. 5 colored plates by I. R. Cruikshank. Boards with label. London, 1822. (By Charles William Hempel.) First edition. $50-$75.

CONARD, Howard Louis. *"Uncle Dick" Wootton, the Pioneer Frontiersman of the Rocky Mountain Region.* Portrait, 31 plates. Decorated cloth. Chicago, 1890. First edition. $150.

CONCLIN, George. *Conclin's New River Guide, or a Gazeteer of All the Towns on the Western Waters.* 44 full-page route maps. 128 pp., wrappers. Cincinnati, 1850. $50-$75. Cincinnati, 1853. $50-$75.

CONFEDERATE Receipt Book. Wrappers. Richmond, Va., 1863. First edition. $100-$150.

CONFESSION; or, The Blind Heart. 2 vols., cloth. Philadelphia, 1841. (By William Gilmore Simms.) First edition. $50-$75.

CONFESSIONS of an English Opium-Eater. Boards, paper label. London, 1822. (By Thomas De Quincey.) First edition, first issue, with ad leaf at end. $500-$600. Also, $200 [$210?] (A, 1963); in contemporary boards, repaired, $200 (A, 1966). Second issue, lacking ad leaf: Boards. $300-$400. Also, $100 (A, 1971), $200 (A, 1968), $110 (A, 1965), $160 (A, 1963). Philadelphia, 1823. Boards, paper label. First American edition. $75-$100. London, 1885. Morocco. One of 50 large paper copies. $100-$125. Also, $67.20 (A, 1968). New York, 1930. Limited Editions Club. Boards. Boxed. $35-$50. Also, $22 (A, 1968).

CONFESSIONS of Harry Lorrequer (The). Illustrated by Phiz. 11 parts, pictorial pink wrappers. Dublin, 1839. (By Charles Lever.) First edition. $200-$250. Another issue: Cloth. First edition in book form. $40-$50. Author's first book.

CONGREVE, William. *The Complete Works of William Congreve.* Edited by Montague Summers. 4 vols., boards and cloth. London, 1923. Nonesuch Press. One of 900. $150-$200. Another issue: Boards and vellum. One of 75 on handmade paper. $300-$400.

CONNELLEY, William E. *Quantrill and the Border Wars.* Illustrated. Buckram. Cedar Rapids, Iowa, 1910. First edition. $35-$50.

CONNELLEY, William E. *The War with Mexico, 1846-47: Doniphan's Expedition.* 2 maps, illustrations. Cloth. Topeka, 1907. First edition. $50-$60.

CONNELLEY, William E. *Wild Bill and His Era.* 12 plates. Cloth. New York, 1933. First edition. In dust jacket. $35-$50.

CONNELLY, Marc. *The Green Pastures.* Illustrated in color by Robert Edmond Jones. Half vellum and green boards. New York, 1930. One of 550 signed. Boxed. $50-$75. Some signed copies issued in morocco: $75-$125.

CONNICK, Charles J. *Adventures in Light and Color.* Color plates and collotype plates. Buckram. New York, no date (1937). First edition. De luxe issue, with 42 plates in color, 48 in collotype. $125-$150. Trade issue: 36 colored plates. Cloth. $75-$100. London, 1937. 36 color plates, 48 in collotype. Cloth. First English edition. $75-$100. (Note: The first edition contains the first printing of Robert Frost's poem "Unless I Call It a Pewter Tray.")

CONNOLLY, A. P. *A Thrilling Narrative of the Minnesota Massacre and the Sioux War of 1862-1863.* Illustrated. Cloth. Chicago, no date (1896). First edition. $35-$40.

CONNOLLY, Cyril. See Palinurus.

CONRAD, Joseph. *"Admiralty Paper."* Facsimile plate. Blue wrappers. No place, no date (New York, 1925). First edition. One of 93. $50.

CONRAD, Joseph. *Almayer's Folly: A Story of an Eastern River.* Dark-green cloth. London, 1895. First edition, first issue, with first "e" missing in "generosity" in the second line from last on page 110. $300-$400. Author's first book.

CONRAD, Joseph. *The Arrow of Gold: A Story Between Two Notes.* Dark-blue cloth. Garden City, 1919. First edition, first issue, with the reading "credentials and apparently" in the fifth line of page 16. In dust jacket. $150-$200. Second issue ("credentials and who"): In dust jacket. $75-$100. London, no date (1919). Dark-green cloth. First English edition, first issue, with running head intact on page 67. In dust jacket. $50-$75. Second issue, with "A" missing in "Arrow" in headline on page 67. In dust jacket. $25-$30.

CONRAD, Joseph. *The Black Mate.* Cloth. No place (Edinburgh), 1922. First edition. One of 50. $300-$400. Also, $210 (A, 1968).

CONRAD, Joseph. *Chance: A Tale in Two Parts.* Sage-green cloth. London, no date (1913). First edition, first issue, with "First published in 1913" on verso of title page. In dust jacket. $750-$1,000. Also, $600 (A, 1963), $280 (A, 1964). Second issue, with tipped in title page bearing 1914 date on verso: $50-$75. New York, 1913. First American edition. One of 150 issued for copyright purposes. $100-$150. New York, 1914. Cloth. First published American edition. In dust jacket. $25-$35.

CONRAD, Joseph. *The Children of the Sea.* Mottled blue-gray cloth. New York, 1897. First edition (of the book published in England as *The Nigger of the "Narcissus"*). $150-$250.

CONRAD, Joseph. *The Dover Patrol.* Light-blue wrappers. Canterbury, England, 1922. First edition. $75-$100.

CONRAD, Joseph. *Joseph Conrad's Letters to His Wife.* Limp imitation leather. London, 1927. First edition. one of 220 signed by Jessie Conrad. $60-$80.

CONRAD, Joseph. *Laughing Anne: A Play.* Full vellum, gilt top, uncut. London, 1923. First edition. One of 200 signed. Boxed. $100-$150.

CONRAD, Joseph. *Last Essays.* Green cloth. London, 1926. First edition. $20-$25.

CONRAD, Joseph. *Letters from Joseph Conrad to Richard Curle.* Boards and cloth. New York, 1928. First edition. One of 850. $35-$40.

CONRAD, Joseph. *Life and Letters.* Edited by G. Jean-Aubry. 13 plates, map, 4 facsimiles. 2 vols., cloth. London, 1927. $40-$50.

CONRAD, Joseph. *Lord Jim.* Gray-green cloth. Edinburgh, 1900. First edition. $100-$125.

CONRAD, Joseph. *The Mirror of the Sea: Memories and Impressions.* Dark-green cloth. London, no date (1906). First edition, with 40 pages of ads dated August, 1906. $50-$75. Spine creased, $35.

CONRAD, Joseph. *The Nigger of the "Narcissus."* Gray cloth. London, 1898. First published English edition (of *The Children of the Sea*). $150-$200. (A copyright issue of about 7 copies was published in London, 1897, in wrappers. An inscribed copy of this book sold for $4,900 in 1928.)

CONRAD, Joseph. *Nostromo: A Tale of the Seaboard.* Bright-blue cloth. London, 1904. First edition, first issue, with 7 preliminary leaves and 478 pages of text. $100-$150. Second issue, with 8 preliminary leaves and 480 pages of text: $35-$50. New York, 1904. Green cloth. First American edition. $25-$30.

CONRAD, Joseph. *Notes on My Books.* Boards, parchment spine. London, 1921. First edition. One of 250 signed. $100-$150.

CONRAD, Joseph. *Notes by Joseph Conrad in a Set of His First Editions in the Possession of Richard Curle.* Buckram, paper label. London, 1925. First edition. One of 100 signed by Curle. $75-$100.

CONRAD, Joseph. *Notes on Life and Letters.* Green cloth. London, 1921. First edition, first issue, with "S" and "A" missing from the word "Sea" in "Tales of the Sea" in table of contents. One of 33 privately printed. In dust jacket. $150-$200. Lacking jacket, $75. Also, presentation copy, $280 (A, 1968). First trade edition, with same errors in contents page: In dust jacket. $50-$75. Second issue, with "S" and "A" put in by hand press: In dust jacket. $35-$50. Third issue, page reprinted: In dust jacket. $25.

CONRAD, Joseph. *One Day More: A Play in One Act.* Buckram and boards. London, 1919. Beaumont Press. One of 274. $50-$75. Another issue: One of 24 on Japan vellum, signed. $350-$450. Also, $336 (A, 1969). Garden City, 1920. Boards and parchment. One of 377 signed. $100-$125.

CONRAD, Joseph. *An Outcast of the Islands.* Dark-green cloth, top edges gilt. London, 1896. First edition, first issue, with "this" for "there" in fourth line from last on page 26 and "absolution" for "ablution" in line 12 of page 110. $100-$125.

CONRAD, Joseph. *A Personal Record.* Cloth. New York, 1912. First American edition (of *Some Reminiscences*). In dust jacket. $20-$25.

CONRAD, Joseph. *The Point of Honor: A Military Tale.* Illustrated by Dan Sayre Groesbeck. Decorated cloth. New York, 1908. First edition. In dust jacket. $75-$100.

CONRAD, Joseph. *The Rescue: A Romance of the Shallows.* Dark-blue cloth. Garden City, 1920. First edition. In dust jacket. $50-$75. London, 1920. Flexible red cloth (text differing from other editions). First English edition, first issue. One of 40 privately printed advance copies. $150-$200. London, 1920. Green cloth. First published English edition. In dust jacket. $50-$60.

CONRAD, Joseph. *The Rover.* Boards. New York, 1923. First edition. One of 377 signed. $100-$150. Trade edition: Cloth. In dust jacket. $25-$35. London, no date (1923). Green cloth. First English edition. In dust jacket. $50-$75.

CONRAD, Joseph. *The Secret Agent: A Drama in Three Acts.* Portrait frontispiece. Boards and parchment. London, 1923. First edition. One of 1,000 signed. $75-$125. Trade edition: Cloth. First issue, with misprint on page 117 and with 40 pages of ads at end. In dust jacket. $50-$75.

CONRAD, Joseph. *The Secret Agent: A Simple Tale.* Red cloth. London, no date (1907). First edition, with September ads at end. $50-$100.

CONRAD, Joseph. *A Set of Six.* Blue cloth. London, no date (1908). First edition, first issue, with ads dated February, 1908. $50-$60. Second issue, with ads dated June, 1908: $25-$30.

CONRAD, Joseph. *The Shadow-Line: A Confession.* Pale-green cloth. London, no date (1917). First edition, with 18 pages of ads at end. In dust jacket. $75-$100.

CONRAD, Joseph. *Some Reminiscences.* Yellow wrappers. New York, 1908. First edition (advance issue for copyright purposes). One of about 6 copies. $400-$500. London, 1912. Dark-blue cloth. First published edition. In dust jacket. $35-$50. (For first published American edition, see Conrad, *A Personal Record.*)

CONRAD, Joseph. *Suspense.* Boards. Garden City, 1925. First edition. One of 377. In dust jacket. $50-$60. London, 1925. Dark-red cloth. First English edition. In dust jacket. $35-$50.

CONRAD, Joseph. *Tales of Hearsay.* Dark-green cloth. London, no date (1925). First edition. In dust jacket. $35-$50. Garden City, 1925. Dark-blue cloth. First American edition. In dust jacket. $25.

CONRAD, Joseph. *Tales of Unrest.* Dark-green cloth. London, 1898. First edition, first issue, with all edges untrimmed. $75 and $85. New York, 1898. Decorated brown cloth. First American edition. $75.

CONRAD, Joseph. *'Twixt Land and Sea: Tales.* Olive-green cloth. London, 1912. First edition, first issue, with misprint "Secret" instead of "Seven" on front cover. In dust jacket. $400-$600. Second issue, with "Seven" stamped over erased word "Secret": $100-$150.

CONRAD, Joseph, *Typhoon and Other Stories.* Illustrated. Dark-green cloth. New York, 1902. First edition, with 4 pages of ads. In dust jacket. $75-$100. London, 1903. Dark-gray cloth. First English edition, first issue, with windmill device and without "Reserved for the Colonies only" on verso of half title. In dust jacket. $50-$75.

CONRAD, Joseph. *Under Western Eyes.* Red cloth. London, 1911. First edition, with ads dated September, 1911. In dust jacket. $35-$50.

CONRAD, Joseph. *Victory: An Island Tale.* Cloth. New York, 1915. First edition. In dust jacket. $100-$150. London, no date (1915). Red cloth, with 35 pages of ads at back and "Author's Note," which is not in the American edition. First English edition. In dust jacket. $75-$100. Lacking jacket, $55 and $45.

CONRAD, Joseph. *Within the Tides: Tales.* Sage-green cloth. London, 1915. First edition. In dust jacket. $50-$75.

CONRAD, Joseph. *Youth: A Narrative and Two Other Stories.* Light-green cloth. Edinburgh, 1902. First edition, with ads dated "10/02" at end. In dust jacket. $75-$100.

CONRAD, Joseph, and Hueffer, Ford M. *The Inheritors: An Extravagant Story.* Pictorial yellow cloth. New York, 1901. First edition, first issue, with the dedication leaf reading "To Boys and Christina." Only a few copies known. Up to $1,000. Also, $425 (A, 1962). First published edition, with a corrected dedication, on a stub: "To Borys and Christina": $75-$100. London, 1901. Yellow cloth. First English edition, first issue, without dedication leaf. $50-$60.

CONRAD, Joseph, and Hueffer, Ford M. *Romance: A Novel.* Bright-blue cloth. London, 1903. First edition, with 8 pages of ads at end. $50-$75. New York, 1904. Cloth. First American edition. $15-$25.

CONRAD, Capt. Thomas Nelson. *The Rebel Scout.* Cloth. Washington, 1904. First edition. $75-$100.

CONSIDERANT, Victor. *European Colonization in Texas.* 38 pp., wrappers. New York, 1855. First edition. $75-$100.

CONSTABLE, Henry. *Poems and Sonnets.* Woodcut border, ornamental woodcut initials. White pigskin. London, 1897. One of 210. $40-$50.

CONSTITUTION and Laws of the Muskogee Nation. Sheep. St. Louis, 1880. $150-$250.

CONSTITUTION and Playing Rules of the International Baseball Association . . . and Championship Record for 1877. 77 pp., wrappers. Jamaica Plain, Mass., 1878. $25-$35.

CONSTITUTION and Rules of Business of the Essex Western Emigration Co. 8 pp., wrappers. Lawrence, 1856. $125-$150.

CONSTITUTION of the Republic of Mexico and the State of Coahuila and Texas (The). Half calf. New York, 1832. $150-$250.

CONSTITUTION of the U.S.A. . . . Also, an Act to Establish a Territorial Government for Utah. 48 pp., sewed. Salt Lake City, 1852. $300-$350.

CONTACT Collection of Contemporary Authors. Wrappers. No place, no date (Paris, 1925). Contact Editions. One of 300. $100. (Note: Contains work by Ernest Hemingway, James Joyce, Ezra Pound, Gertrude Stein, William Carlos Williams, and others.)

CONTESTACIONES Habidas entre el Supremo Gobierno Mexicano, etc. 36 pp., printed wrappers. Mexico, 1847. First edition, first issue, with horn of plenty at foot of last page. $75. Second issue, with Herrera letter on last page: $75.

CONVERSATIONS on the Mackinaw and Green-Bay Indian Missions. Boards, Boston, 1831. (By Elizabeth Sanders.) First edition. $35.

CONWAY, Moncure D. *Barons of the Potomack and Rappahannock.* Illustrated. Boards. New York, 1892. Grolier Club. First edition. One of 360. $40-$50.

COOK, David J. *Hands Up, or 20 Years of Detective Life in the Mountains and on the Plains.* 32 plates. Wrappers. Denver, 1882. First edition. $150 and up. Cloth, same date, later issue: $100 and up. Denver, 1897. Second edition, enlarged, with *20 Years* changed to *35 Years* in title. $50-$60.

COOK, James H. *Fifty Years on the Old Frontier.* Plates. Cloth. New Haven, 1923. First edition. In dust jacket. $35-$50.

COOK, Joel. *The Siege of Richmond.* Cloth. Philadelphia, 1862. $25-$35.

COOK, John R. *The Border and the Buffalo.* Plates. Pictorial cloth. Topeka, 1907. First edition. $25-$35.

COOKE, Giles B. *Just Before and After Lee Surrendered to Grant.* 8 pp., wrappers. No place, no date (Houston, 1922). First edition. $35-$50. With printing errors corrected in ink, $35.

COOKE, John (editor). *The Dublin Book of Irish Verse.* Dark-green limp leather. Dublin, 1909. First edition. $50. Another issue: Cloth. $25-$35. (Note: Contains three poems by James Joyce.)

COOKE, John Esten. See Effingham, C. Also see *Leather Stocking and Silk; The Life of Stonewall Jackson.*

COOKE, John Esten. *A Life of General Robert E. Lee.* Cloth. New York, 1871. First edition. $25-$35.

COOKE, John Esten. *Surry of Eagle's Nest.* Illustrated by Winslow Homer. Cloth. New York, 1866. First edition, with Bunce and Huntington imprint. $50-$75.

COOKE, Philip St. George. *The Conquest of New Mexico and California.* Folding map. Cloth. New York, 1878. First edition. $75-$100.

COON, James Churchill. *Log of the Cruise of 1889 D.T.S.C., New Smyrna to Lake Worth, East Coast of Florida.* 119 pp., printed wrappers. Lake Helen, Fla., 1889. First edition. $100.

COOPER, J. W. *Game Fowls, Their Origin and History.* Colored lithographs. Pictorial green cloth, gilt. West Chester, Pa., no date (1869). $50-$75. Damp-stained, $30.

COOPER, James Fenimore. See Morgan, Jane. Also see *The Bee-Hunter; The Bravo; The Borderers; The Chainbearer; The Deerslayer; The Headsman; The Heidenmauer; Home as Found; The Last of the Mohicans; Lionel Lincoln; The Monikins; The Pathfinder; The Pilot; The Pioneers; The Prairie; Precaution; Ravensnest; The Red Rover; The Redskins; Satanstoe; The Spy; The Two Admirals; The Water Witch; The Wept of Wish-Ton-Wish; The Wing-and-Wing; Wyandotte.*

COOPER, James Fenimore. *The Battle of Lake Erie.* Printed wrappers. Cooperstown, N.Y., 1843. First edition. $50-$75.

COOPER, James Fenimore. *The History of the Navy of the United States of America.* Map. 2 vols., cloth. Philadelphia, 1839. First edition. $50-$75. London, 1839. 2 vols., cloth. First English edition. $25. Paris, 1839. 2 vols. in one, half leather. $50.

COOPER, James Fenimore. *The Jack O'Lantern.* 3 vols., drab brown boards, purple cloth, paper spine labels. London, 1842. First edition (of the novel issued anonymously in America as *The Wing-and-Wing,* which see as title entry). $75-$100.

COOPER, James Fenimore. *Lives of Distinguished American Naval Officers.* 2 vols., cloth, or 2 vols., printed blue wrappers. Philadelphia, 1846. First edition. Cloth: $75-$100. Wrappers: $150-$200. Auburn, N.Y., 1846. Leather. Reprint edition. $60 (A, 1960).

COOPER, James Fenimore. *Notions of the Americans.* 2 vols., boards, paper labels. London, 1828. First edition. $75-$100. Philadelphia, 1828. 2 vols., boards, paper labels. First American edition. $50-$75.

COOPER, Lane (editor). *A Concordance to the Poems of William Wordsworth.* Cloth. London, 1911. First edition. $100-$125.

COOPER, Thomas. *On Irritation and Insanity.* 2 portraits. Boards. London, 1833. $35-$40.

COPLAND, Robert (translator). *The History of Helyas Knight of the Swan.* Illustrated. Pigskin. New York, 1901. Grolier Club. One of 325. $50.

COPPARD, A. E. *Adam and Eve and Pinch Me.* White buckram. No place (Waltham Saint Lawrence), 1921. Golden Cockerel Press. First edition. One of 160. $40-$50. Another issue: Orange boards. One of 340. $25-$30. New York, 1922. Boards and cloth. First American edition. $15-$20.

COPPARD, A. E. *The Black Dog.* Boards and cloth. London, 1923. First edition. $25. (Note: Forged title pages exist. Paper of title must be same texture and color as rest of book.)

COPPARD, A. E. *Cherry Ripe: Poems.* Illustrated. Full purple and green morocco. No place (Monmouthshire, England), 1935. Tintern Press. One of 10 signed. $50.

COPPARD, A. E. *Easter Day.* 4 pp., plus one holograph page, signed. Boards. No place, no date (London, 1931). First edition. $30.

COPPARD, A. E. *Fishmonger's Fiddle.* Boards. London, 1925. First edition. One of 60 signed. $25.

COPPARD, A. E. *Pink Furniture.* Illustrated. Vellum. London, 1930. First edition. One of 260 signed. In dust jacket. $35-$40.

COPPARD, A. E. *Silver Circus.* Full vellum. No place, no date (London, 1928). First edition. One of 125 signed. $35.

COPPARD, A. E. *Yokohama Garland and Other Poems.* Boards and buckram. Philadelphia, no date (1926). Centaur Press. First edition. One of 500 signed. Boxed. $25-$30.

CORELLI, Marie. *Jane: A Social Incident.* Frontispiece, 7 plates. Cloth. London, 1897. First edition. $25-$30.

CORELLI, Marie. *The Mighty Atom.* Cloth. London, 1896. First edition. $25-$30.

CORELLI, Marie. *Ziska: The Problem of a Wicked Soul.* Cloth. Bristol, England, 1897. First edition. $25-$30.

CORNER, William. *San Antonio de Bexar.* Map, 16 plates. Cloth. San Antonio, Tex., 1890. First edition. $35-$50.

CORNFORD, Frances. *Autumn Midnight.* Woodcuts by Eric Gill. Wrappers. London, 1923. First edition. $50-$60.

CORNWALL, Bruce. *Life Sketch of Pierre Barlow Cornwall.* 6 portraits. Boards. San Francisco, 1906. First edition. $35-$50.

CORSO, Gregory. *Bomb.* Wrappers. San Francisco, no date (1958). City Lights. First edition. $25-$30.

CORSO, Gregory. *Gasoline.* Wrappers. San Francisco, no date (1958). City Lights Books. First edition. $35-$50.

CORSO, Gregory. *The Vestal Lady on Brattle and Other Poems.* Printed wrappers. Cambridge, Mass., 1955. First edition. $75-$100. Author's first book.

CORVO, 1860-1960: A Collection of Essays by Various Hands. Edited by Cecil Woolf and Brocard Sewell. Aylesford, England, 1961. First edition. One of 300 signed. In glassine dust jacket. $35-$50.

CORVO, Baron (Frederick William Rolfe). See *Tarcissus.*

CORVO, Baron. *Chronicles of the House of Borgia.* 10 plates. Pictorial red buckram. London, 1901. (By Frederick William Rolfe.) First edition. $150-$200.

CORVO, Baron. *The Desire and Pursuit of the Whole.* Green cloth. London, 1905. (By Frederick William Rolfe.) First edition. In dust jacket. $35-$50.

CORVO, Baron. *Hadrian the Seventh.* Cloth. London, 1904. (By Frederick William Rolfe.) First edition, first issue, purple cloth; title and drawing stamped in white. $150-$200. Second issue, with title and drawing blind-stamped: $75-$100.

CORVO, Baron. *In His Own Image.* Blue-gray cloth. London, 1901. (By Frederick William Rolfe.) First edition, with ad leaf. In dust jacket. $50-$75. London, 1924. Second impression. $25-$30.

CORVO, Baron. *Letters to Grant Richards.* Boards. No place, no date (Hurst, England, 1952). (By Frederick William Rolfe.) Peacocks Press. First edition. One of 200. $35-$50.

CORVO, Baron. *Stories Toto Told Me.* Printed wrappers. London, 1898. (By Frederick William Rolfe.) First edition. No. 6 of the Bodley Booklets. $175-$200.

COSSLEY-BATT, Jill L. *The Last of the California Rangers.* Illustrated. Three-quarters green morocco. New York, 1928. First edition. One of 200 signed. $35-$50. Trade edition: Cloth. In dust jacket. $15-$20.

COSTANSO, Miguel. *The Spanish Occupation of California.* Portraits, folding maps. Boards. San Francisco, 1934. One of 550. In slipcase. $75-$100.

COSTUME of Turkey (The). 60 hand-colored engravings by Octavien Dalvimart. Full contemporary morocco. London, 1802. $75-$100.

COTTIN, Madame de. *Elizabeth; or The Exiles of Siberia.* Translated by Mrs. Meeke. Printed boards (dated 1816). London, 1817. First edition (of this translation). $35-$50.

COUES, Elliott (editor). *New Light on the Early History of the Greater Northwest.* Frontispiece, facsimile, 3 maps in pocket of Vol. 3. 3 vols., cloth. New York, 1897. One of 1,000. $75-$100. Another issue: Half vellum. One of 100 on large paper. $100-$150.

COULTER, E. Merton. *Travels in the Confederate States: A Bibliography.* Cloth. Norman, Okla., 1948. First edition. $35-$50.

COUNT Julian; or, the Last Days of the Goth. Cloth. Baltimore, 1845. (By William Gilmore Simms.) First edition. $50-$75.

COUNT Julian: A Tragedy. Boards, printed label. London, 1812. (By Walter Savage Landor.) First edition. $65-$80.

COURSEY, O. W. *"Wild Bill" (James Butler Hickok).* Illustrated. Cloth. Mitchell, S.D., no date (1924). First edition. $30-$50.

COUTS, Cave J. *From San Diego to the Colorado in 1849.* 3 maps on 2 sheets. Boards. Los Angeles, 1932. First edition. $35-$50.

COUTS, Joseph. *A Practical Guide for the Tailor's Cutting Room.* 13 colored plates, 14 uncolored. Half morocco. London, no date (1848). $80.

COWARD, Noel. *"I'll Leave It to You."* Wrappers. London, 1920. First edition. $50. Author's first book (?).

COWLEY, Malcolm. *Blue Juniata: Poems.* Cloth. New York, no date (1929). First edition. $50-$65. Author's first book.

COX, Isaac. *The Annals of Trinity County.* Half cloth. San Francisco, 1940. John Henry Nash printing. One of 350. Boxed. $35-$50.

COX, James. *Historical and Biographical Record of the Cattle Industry and the Cattlemen of Texas and Adjacent Territory.* Colored frontispiece, other illustrations. Decorated leather. St. Louis, 1895. First edition. $1,500 and up. Also, $1,050 (A, 1968); rebacked, $800 (A, 1966). New York, 1959. 2 vols., half leather. Boxed. One of 500. $150-$200.

COX, Palmer. *The Brownies Around the World.* Illustrated. Cloth. New York, no date (about 1894). $25-$35.

COX, Palmer. *The Brownies: Their Book.* Green glazed pictorial boards. New York, no date (1887). First edition, first issue, with DeVinne Press seal immediately below copyright notice. In dust jacket. $250-$300. Second issue, with seal about 2-1/2 inches from bottom of page. In dust jacket. $100-$150.

COX, Palmer. *Comic Yarns, in Verse, Prose and Picture.* Illustrated. Cloth. Philadelphia, 1889. First edition. $25-$30.

COX, Palmer. *Queer People with Wings and Stings and Their Kweer Kapers.* Pictorial boards. Philadelphia, no date (1888). First edition. $30-$35.

COX, Palmer. *Queerie Queers with Hands, Wings and Claws.* Pictorial boards. Buffalo, no date ("about 1887"). First edition. $35-$40.

COX, Sandford C. *Recollections of the Early Settlement of the Wabash Valley.* Cloth. Lafayette, Ind., 1860. First edition. $25-$35.

COXE, Louis O. *The Sea Faring and Other Poems.* Cloth. New York, no date (1947). First edition. In dust jacket. $25-$30. Author's first book.

COY, Owen C. *California County Boundaries.* Cloth. Berkeley, Calif., 1923. $40-$50.

COY, Owen C. *Pictorial History of California.* 261 photographs. Cloth. Berkeley, 1925. $40-$50.

COYNER, David H. *The Lost Trappers.* Cloth. Cincinnati, 1847. First edition. $300-$400. Cincinnati, 1850. Cloth. Second edition. $50.

COZZENS, Frederick S. *Acadia.* 2 plates. Cloth. New York, 1859. First edition. $50

COZZENS, James Gould. *Cock Pit.* Cloth. New York, 1928. First edition. In dust jacket. $25-$30.

COZZENS, James Gould. *Confusion.* Cloth. Boston, 1924. First edition. In dust jacket. $50-$75. Author's first book.

CRABBE, George. *The Borough: A Poem.* Boards, printed label. London, 1810. First edition. $100-$150.

CRABBE, George. *Tales of the Hall.* 2 vols., boards. London, 1819. First edition. $100-$150.

CRAIG, John R. *Ranching with Lords and Commons.* 17 plates. Pictorial cloth. Toronto, no date (1903). First edition. $100-$150.

CRAKES, Sylvester. *Five Years a Captive Among the Black-Feet Indians.* 6 plates. Cloth. Columbus, Ohio, 1858. First edition. $300-$350.

CRANCH, Christopher Pearse. *Giant Hunting; or, Little Jacket's Adventures.* Illustrated. Pictorial cloth. $75-$100.

CRANCH, Christopher Pearse. *The Last of the Huggermuggers.* Illustrated. Cloth. Boston, 1856. First edition. $50-$60.

CRANCH, Christopher Pearse. *Kobboltozo.* Illustrated. Cloth. Boston, 1857. First edition. $35-$50.

CRANE, Hart. *The Bridge.* 3 photographs. Stiff printed wrappers. Paris, 1930. Black Sun Press. First edition. One of 200. In glassine dust jacket. Boxed. $250-$400. Another issue: One of 50 on Japan vellum, signed. Boxed. $600-$1,000. New York, 1930. Cloth. First American edition. In dust jacket. $75-$100.

CRANE, Hart. *The Collected Poems of Hart Crane.* Edited by Waldo Frank. Portrait frontispiece. Red cloth. New York, no date (1933). First edition, first issue, with flat spine and imprint of "Liveright Inc., Publisher." In dust jacket. $50-$60. Second issue, with rounded spine and imprint of "Liveright Publishing Corporation": In dust jacket. $25-$35.

CRANE, Hart. *Voyages.* Illustrated. Oblong, wrappers in board folder. New York, 1957. First edition. Limited. $150-$200.

CRANE, Hart. *White Buildings.* Foreword by Allen Tate. Boards, cloth spine. No place (New York), 1926. First edition, first issue, with Tate's first name misspelled. In dust jacket. $600-$1,000. Second issue, with tipped-in title page, Tate's name spelled correctly: In dust jacket. $100-$150.

CRANE, Stephen. See Smith, Johnston. Also see *The Lanthorn Book; Pike County Puzzle.*

CRANE, Stephen. *Active Service.* Light-green cloth. New York, no date (1899). First edition. $25-$30.

CRANE, Stephen. *The Black Riders and Other Lines.* Yellow cloth or gray decorated boards. Boston, 1895. First trade edition. One of 500. $285-$350. Also, $125 and $230 (A, 1968). Another issue: Plain boards, paper label. One of 50 printed in green ink on vellum. No copies noted for sale in recent years. Estimated value: $600-$700. (Note: Johnson reports three copies of this issue were said to have been bound in full vellum. Value? $750 and up?)

CRANE, Stephen. *George's Mother.* Tan cloth. New York, 1896. First edition. $25-$35. London, 1896. Cloth. $20-$25.

CRANE, Stephen. *Great Battles of the World.* Illustrated by John Sloan. Red cloth. Philadelphia, 1901. First edition. $50-$60. London, 1901. Cloth. $25-$35.

CRANE, Stephen. *Last Words.* Red cloth. London, 1902. First edition. $100-$150.

CRANE, Stephen. *Legends.* 4 pp., printed buff wrappers. Ysleta, Tex., 1942. First edition. One of 45. $100-$125.

CRANE, Stephen. *The Little Regiment and Other Episodes of the American Civil War.* Cream-yellow buckram. New York, 1896. First edition, first state, with 6 pages of ads at the back, the first page headed "Gilbert Parker's Best Books." $75-$100.

CRANE, Stephen. *Maggie: A Girl of the Streets.* Cream-yellow buckram. New York, 1896. Second (revised) edition, first state, with title page printed in capital and lower case Roman type. (In later issues it is in Old English type.) $35-$50. Also, $25 (A, 1968). (For first edition, see Johnston Smith, *Maggie: A Girl of the Streets.)*

CRANE, Stephen. *The Monster and Other Stories.* Illustrated. Red cloth. New York, 1899. First edition. $30-$50. New York, 1901. Revised edition, with four stories added. $20-$25.

CRANE, Stephen. *The Open Boat and Other Tales of Adventure.* Dark-green pictorial cloth. New York, 1898. First American edition. $50-$60. London, 1898. First English edition, with nine added stories. $35-$50.

CRANE, Stephen. *The Red Badge of Courage.* Cream-yellow buckram. New York, 1895. First edition, first state, with perfect type in the last line on page 225. $500-$750. Also, $160 and $150 (A, 1968); "in very fine condition," $425 (A, 1965); $175 (A, 1966); $180 and, "in very fine condition," $325 (A, 1962); "in fine condition," $210 (A, 1965). New York, 1896. Cloth. $75-$100. Worn, $35. New York, no date (1931). Illustrated by Valenti Angelo. Grabhorn printing. Boards. $35-$50. Also, $25 and $35 (A, 1968). New York, 1944. Limited Editions Club. Illustrated. Embossed morocco. Boxed. $75. Also, $45 (A, 1968).

CRANE, Stephen. *The Third Violet.* Cream-yellow buckram. New York, 1897. First edition. $30-$50.

CRANE, Stephen. *War Is Kind.* Illustrated by Will Bradley. Pictorial gray boards. New York, 1899. First edition. $150-$175.

CRANE, Stephen. *Whilomville Stories.* Illustrated by Peter Newell. Light-green cloth. New York, 1900. First edition. $45-$75. London, 1910. Blue cloth. First English edition. $25-$35.

CRANE, Stephen. *Wounds in the Rain.* Cloth. London, 1900. First edition. $100-$150. New York, no date (1900). Cloth. First American edition. $75-$100.

CRANE, Walter. *The Baby's Own Aesop.* Illustrated. Colored lithograph covers. London, 1887. First edition. $25-$35.

CRANE, Walter. *The Bases of Design.* Blue-gray cloth. London, 1898. First edition. $35-$50.

CRANE, Walter. *Flora's Feast.* Illustrated by the author. Boards. London, 1889. First edition. $50-$75.

CRANE, Walter. *Queen Summer.* Illustrated by the author. Boards. London, 1891. First edition. $25-$35.

CRANE, Walter. *Slate and Pencil-Vania.* Illustrated. Pictorial covers. London, 1885. First edition. $25-$35.

CRANE, Walter. *Valentine and Orson.* 8 color illustrations. Printed wrappers. No place, no date (London, 1870). Sixpence Toy Book. $50-$75.

CRANFORD. By the author of "Mary Barton," "Ruth," etc. Green cloth. London, 1853. (By Elizabeth C. Gaskell.) First edition. $250-$350.

CRAWFORD, Lewis F. *Rekindling Camp Fires.* Illustrated. Half leather. Bismarck, N.D., 1926. First edition. One of 100 signed. Boxed. $90-$100.

CRAWFORD, Lucy. *The History of the White Mountains.* Cloth. Portland, Me., 1846. First edition. $50-60.

CRAWSHAY, Richard. *The Birds of Terra del Fuego.* 21 color plates by J. G. Keulemans, 23 photographic views, map. Half morocco. London, 1907. One of 300. $100-$125.

CRAYON, Geoffrey. *The Alhambra.* 2 vols., drab boards, printed spine label. London, 1832. (By Washington Irving.) First edition. $150-$200. Philadelphia, 1832. Anonymously published ("By the Author of 'The Sketch-Book' "). 2 vols., boards and cloth, paper spine label. First American edition. $150-$200. Boxed, two end papers torn, two bookplates, $60.

CRAYON, Geoffrey. *Bracebridge Hall, or The Humourists.* 2 vols., drab brown boards, paper label. New York, 1822. (By Washington Irving.) First edition. $100-$150. Spines defective, $36. London, 1822. Boards, paper label. First English edition (simultaneous with the American?), text ending on page 403, Vol. 2. $50-$75. New York, 1896. Surrey Edition. Arthur Rackham illustrations. 2 vols., pictorial cloth. $75.

CRAYON, Geoffrey. *The Sketch Book of Geoffrey Crayon, Gent.* 7 parts, wrappers. New York, 1819-20. (By Washington Irving.) First edition. Parts 1 through 5 dated 1819, parts 6 and 7 dated 1820. Rarely offered in original wrappers. Rebound in one volume, $150 and up. (Note: Second editions so identified on wrappers. Like *Salmagundi,* this is a complicated work to identify, and it exists in many variations. See Blanck, *A Bibliography of American Literature.*)

CRAYON, Geoffrey. *Tales of a Traveller.* 2 vols., boards and cloth, paper label. London, 1824. (By Washington Irving.) First edition. $75-$100. Philadelphia, 1824. 4 parts, wrappers. First American edition, first issue, with "H. C. Cary" (instead of Carey) on title page. $100-$150.

CREEK Treaty Correspondence Preliminary to the Treaty of Aug. 7, 1856. Boards. Washington, 1856. Spine broken, $50.

CREEK Treaty, Passed in Congress, Feb. 1901. 11 pp., wrappers. Muskogee, Okla., 1901. $45.

CREELEY, Robert. *About Women.* 5 pp., large square folio, unbound. Los Angeles, 1966. Limited extra issue of an introduction (3 poems) for a book of John Altoon lithographs. $50-$60.

CREELEY, Robert. *All That Is Lovely in Men.* Drawings by Dan Rice. Pictorial wrappers. Asheville, N.C., 1955. Jargon No. 10. First edition. One of 200 signed by Creeley and Rice. $50-$75.

CREELEY, Robert. *The Charm.* Marbled boards and cloth. San Francisco, 1969. First edition. One of 100 signed. $30-$35.

CREELEY, Robert. *5 Numbers.* Wrappers. No place, no date (New York, 1968). First edition. One of 150 manuscript facsimile copies, signed. $25-$30.

CREELEY, Robert. *For Love, Poems 1950-1960.* Cloth. New York, no date (1962). First edition. In dust jacket. $25-$30.

CREELEY, Robert. *The Gold Diggers.* Wrappers. No place, 1954. Divers Press. First edition. $40-$50.

CREELEY, Robert. *If You.* Illustrated by Fielding Dawson. 14 unsewn leaves in wrappers. San Francisco, 1956. One of 200. $40-$50.

CREELEY, Robert. *Le Fou.* Frontispiece. Decorated Wrappers. Columbus, Ohio, 1952. First edition. $125. Author's first book.

CREELEY, Robert. *Poems, 1950-1965.* Vellum and boards. London, no date (1966). First edition. One of 100 signed. In slipcase. $75-$100. New York, 1967. First American edition (with added poems). In dust jacket. $25-$30.

CREELEY, Robert. *A Sight.* Drawings by Ron Kitaj. Large portfolio, silk-screened facsimiles of handwritten poems. London, no date (1967). First edition. $100-$120.

CREELEY, Robert. *The Whip.* Wrappers. No place, no date (Mallorca,1957). First edition. $40-$50. Another issue: Boards. $80-$100.

CREUZBAUR, Robert (compiler). *Route from the Gulf of Mexico and the Lower Mississippi Valley to California and the Pacific Ocean.* 5 maps in pocket. 40 pp., cloth. New York, 1849. First edition. $2,000 and up. Also, $1,800 (A, 1968). Copy with maps missing, worn on covers, $150.

CREYTON, Paul. *Paul Creyton's Great Romance!! Kate the Accomplice; or, The Preacher and the Burglar.* Pictorial pink wrappers. Boston, no date (1849). (By John Townsend Trowbridge.) First edition, with 1849 cover date. $1,000 and up. Author's first book. (Note: A copy with an autographed letter, signed by Trowbridge, was offered in a 1970 catalogue of a Boston dealer at $1,500.)

CREYTON, Paul. *Martin Merivale; His X Mark.* Cloth. Boston, 1854. (By John Townsend Trowbridge.) First edition, first state, with Creyton, not Trowbridge, on spine and stereotyper's slug on copyright page. $25-$35. (Second state has Trowbridge on spine.)

CRITERION (The): A Quarterly Review. Vol. I, No. 1. Wrappers. London, October, 1922. First edition. This magazine contains the first appearance in print of T. S. Eliot's poem "The Waste Land." $60-$80.

CROAKER, Croaker & Co., and Croaker, Jun. *Poems.* 36 pp. Printed tan wrappers. New York, 1819. (By Joseph Rodman Drake and Fitz-Greene Halleck.) First edition. $500 and up. First book by each author. (Note: Reissued: *The Croakers.* Green cloth. New York, 1860. One of 250. $50.)

CROCKET, George L. *Two Centuries in East Texas.* Cloth. Dallas, no date (about 1932). First edition. $50-$75.

CROCKETT, David. *An Account of Col. Crockett's Tour to the North and Down East.* Cloth. Philadephia, 1835. (By Augustin S. Clayton?) First edition. $35-$50.

CROCKETT, David. *A Narrative of the Life of Col. David Crockett.* Written by Himself. Cloth. Philadephia, 1834. First edition, with 22 pages of ads at end. $100-$150.

CROMWELL: An Historical Novel. 2 vols., brown cloth, paper labels. New York, 1838. (By Henry William Herbert.) First edition, first issue, with 12 pages of ads. $75-$125.

CROSBY, Caresse. *Crosses of Gold: A Book of Verse.* Hand-colored illustrations. Green parchment. Paris, 1925. First edition. One of 100. $75-$100. Inscribed, spine cracked, $65. Author's first book.

CROSBY, Caresse. *Painted Shores.* Illustrated with 3 watercolors. Wrappers. Paris, 1927. First edition. One of 222 (244?). $75-$150.

CROSBY, Caresse. *Poems for Harry Crosby.* Frontispiece. Boards and cloth. Paris, 1931. Black Sun Press. First edition. One of 44. $50-$75.

CROSBY, Harry. *Transit of Venus.* Printed wrappers. Paris, 1928. Black Sun Press. First edition. One of 44. $35-$45.

CROSBY, Sylvester S. *The Early Coins of America.* 10 plates. Half morocco. Boston, 1878. $50-$60.

CROSLAND, Mrs. Camilla. *Lydia: A Woman's Book.* Brown cloth. London, 1852. First edition. $25-$30.

CROSLAND, T. W. H. *The First Stone.* Boards. London, 1912. First edition. $40-$50.

CROTCHET Castle. By the Author of *Headlong Hall.* Boards, paper label. London, 1831. (By Thomas Love Peacock.) First edition. $200 $250.

CROTHERS, Samuel McCord. *Miss Muffet's Christmas Party.* Pictorial vellum wrappers. St. Paul, Minn., no date (1892). First edition. $50-$60. Author's first book.

CROTTY, D. G. *Four Years Campaigning in the Army of the Potomac.* Half morocco. Grand Rapids, Mich., 1894. First edition. $35-$50.

CROWLEY, Aleister. See Therion, The Master. Also see *Alcedama.*

CROWLEY, Aleister. *Moonchild: A Prologue.* Cloth. London, 1929. First edition. $25-$30.

CROWLEY, Aleister. *Olla: An Anthology of Sixty Years of Song.* Cloth. London, no date (1946). First edition. One of 500. In dust jacket. $35-$50.

CROWLEY, Aleister. *Songs of the Spirit.* Cloth. London, 1898. First edition. $60-$75.

CROWLEY, Aleister. *The Soul of Osiris.* Boards, cloth spine, paper label. London, 1901. First edition. $50-$60.

CRUIKSHANK, George. See *The Humourist.*

CRUIKSHANK, Percy. *Hints to Emigrants, or, Incidents in the Emigration of John Smith.* 9 full-page etchings. Pictorial wrappers. London, no date (about 1830). $75.

CRYSTAL Age (A). Black cloth. London, 1887. (By W. H. Hudson). First edition, with 32 pages of ads at end. $100-$125.

CUFFE, Paul. *Narrative of the Life and Adventures of Paul Cuffe, a Pequot Indian.* Wrappers. New York, 1839. $32.50.

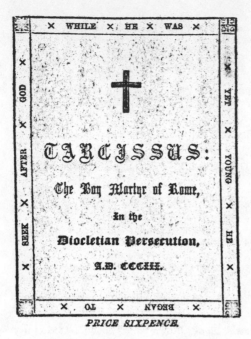

Baron Corvo's first book; see under
Tarcissus

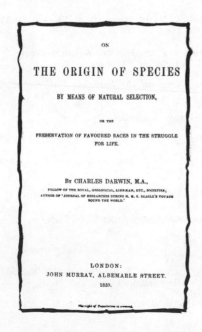

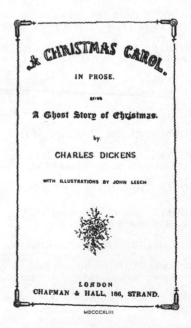

CUISINE Creole, La. Pictorial cloth. New York, no date (1885). (Compiled by Lafcadio Hearn.) First edition, first issue, brown cloth, with "Brùlot" (in the ninth line of introduction) instead of "Brûlot." $200-$250. New Orleans, 1922. Cloth. Second edition. $25-$35.

CULLEN, Countee. *The Ballad of the Brown Girl.* Cloth and boards, paper label. New York, 1927. First edition. $25-$30.

CULLEN, Countee. *Caroling Dusk.* Cloth. New York, 1927. First edition. In dust jacket. $25-$30.

CULPEPER, Nicholas. *Culpeper's Complete Herbal & English Physician Enlarged.* 40 color plates. Full brown calf. London, 1814. $75-$85.

CUMINGS, Samuel. *The Western Pilot.* Printed boards. Cincinnati, 1825. $125-$150. Cincinnati, 1829. $75.

CUMMINGS, E. E. See *Eight Harvard Poets.*

CUMMINGS, E. E. (No title.) Illustrated by the author. New York, 1930. First edition. One of 491 signed. $60-$80.

CUMMINGS, E. E. *Adventures in Value.* 50 photographs by Marion Morehouse. New York, no date (1962). First edition. In dust jacket. $25-$35.

CUMMINGS, E. E. *&.* Green gold-flecked boards. New York, 1925. First edition. One of 111 on Vidalon paper, signed. Boxed. $100-$150. Another issue: One of 222 on rag paper, signed. Boxed. $60-$80.

CUMMINGS, E. E. *Christmas Tree.* Green decorated boards. New York, 1928. First edition. $75-$100.

CUMMINGS, E. E. *Ciopw.* Cloth. New York, 1931. First edition. One of 391 signed. $100-$150, possibly more.

CUMMINGS, E. E. *Eimi.* Yellow cloth. No place, no date (New York, 1933). First edition. One of 1,381 signed. In dust jacket. $65-$90.

CUMMINGS, E. E. *The Enormous Room.* Tan buckram. New York, no date (1922). First edition. With or without fifth word ("shit") of last line on page 219 inked out. In dust jacket. $100-$150. Author's first book. Copy with author's signature offered by New York dealer in 1971 for $225.

CUMMINGS, E. E. *50 Poems.* Cloth. New York, no date (1940). First edition. One of 150 signed. In dust jacket. Boxed. $80-$120.

CUMMINGS, E. E. *Him.* Decorated boards, vellum spine and corners. New York, 1927. First edition. One of 160 signed. Boxed. $80-$125. First trade edition: $15-$20.

CUMMINGS, E. E. *Is 5.* Gold-flecked orange boards, cloth spine. New York, 1926. First edition. In dust jacket. $75-$100.

CUMMINGS, E. E. *A Miscellany.* Cloth. New York, 1958. First edition. One of 50 advance copies for review. $75. One of 75 signed. $75-$100.

CUMMINGS, E. E. *95 Poems.* Cloth. New York, no date (1958). First edition. One of 300 signed. In glassine dust jacket. Boxed. $60-$85.

CUMMINGS, E. E. *No Thanks.* Oblong, dark-blue cloth. No place, no date (New York, 1935). First edition. One of 90 on handmade paper, signed. In dust jacket. Boxed. $100-$125. Another issue: One of 9 on Japan vellum, signed. Boxed. $450-$650. Another issue: First trade edition. One of 900 on Ricardi Japan paper. $35-$50.

CUMMINGS, E. E. *Santa Claus.* Frontispiece. Cloth. New York, no date (1946). First edition. One of 250 signed. In glassine jacket. $75. Trade edition: $20-$30.

CUMMINGS, E. E. *Six Nonlectures.* Cloth. Cambridge, Mass., 1953. First edition. One of 350 signed. In dust jacket. $65-$75.

CUMMINGS, E. E. *Tom: A Ballet.* Frontispiece by Ben Shahn. Cloth. No place, no date (Santa Fe, N.M., 1935). Arrow Editions. First edition. In dust jacket. $40-$50.

CUMMINGS, E. E. *Tulips and Chimneys.* Boards and cloth. New York, 1923. First edition. In dust jacket. $80-$125. Mount Vernon, N.Y., 1937. Boards, vellum spine. One of 481. In dust jacket. $50-$60. (Of this edition, there were supposed to be 148 signed by the author, but the sheets were lost between printer and binder.)

CUMMINGS, E. E. *W (Viva: Seventy New Poems).* Folio, buckram and boards. New York, 1931. First edition. One of 95 signed. In glassine dust jacket. $150-$175.

CUMMINGS, E. E. *XLI Poems.* Cloth, gilt label. New York, 1925. First edition. $50-$75.

CUMMINS, Ella Sterling. *The Story of the Files: A Review of California Writers and Literature.* Illustrated. Decorated boards. No place, no date (San Francisco, 1893). $30-$50.

CUMMINS, Mrs. Sarah J. W. *Autobiography and Reminiscences.* Portrait. Printed wrappers. No place, no date (LaGrande, Ore., 1914). First edition. $35-$50. Reprint edition: No place, no date (Walla Walla, Wash., 1914). $25-$30.

CUNARD, Nancy. *Black Man and White Ladyship: An Anniversary.* 10 pp., red wrappers. No place (France), 1931. First edition. $50-$60.

CUNARD, Nancy. *Parallax.* Boards. London, 1925. First edition. $60-$75.

CUNDALL, Joseph. See Percy, Stephen.

CUNNINGHAM, Eugene. *Triggernometry: A Gallery of Gunfighters.* 21 plates. Pictorial cloth. New York, 1934. First edition. In dust jacket. $50-$75.

CUNYNGHAME, H. H. *European Enamels.* 63 plates. New York and London, 1906. $30-$35.

CUNNINGHAME GRAHAM, R. B. See Graham.

CURLEY, Edwin A. *Nebraska: Its Advantages, Resources and Drawbacks.* Illustrated. Cloth. London, 1875. First edition. $35-$50.

CURSE of Minerva (The). 25 pp., dark-brown glazed wrappers. London, 1812. (By George Gordon Noel, Lord Byron.) First edition. $2,500 and up.

CURTIS, Edward S. *The Apsaroke.* Edited by Frederick W. Hodge. (Vol. 4 of *The North American Indian.*) Text volume, morocco-bound, plus portfolio of 36 plates. New York, 1909. $60-$75.

CURTIS, George William. See *Nile Notes of a Howadji; The Potiphar Papers.*

CUSHMAN, H. B. *A History of the Choctaw, Chickasaw and Natchez Indians.* Greenville, Tex., 1899. First edition. $50-$75.

CUSHMAN, Henry Wyles. *A Historical and Biographical Genealogy of the Cushmans.* Illustrated. Cloth. Boston, 1855. $50-$60.

CURTISS, Daniel S. *Western Portraiture, and Emigrants' Guide.* Illustrated. Cloth. New York, 1852. First edition. $35-$50.

CUSTER, Elizabeth B. *"Boots and Saddles," or Life in Dakota with General Custer.* Portrait and map. Pictorial cloth. New York, 1885. First edition. $25-$35.

CUTBUSH, James. *The American Artist's Manual.* 39 plates. 2 vols., cloth. Philadelphia, 1814. $175-$200.

CUTTS, James M. *The Conquest of California and New Mexico.* Map, 3 plans. Cloth. Philadelphia, 1847. First edition. $75-$100.

CYNWAL, William. *In Defence of Woman.* 10 colored engravings. Full blue morocco. London, no date (1956). Golden Cockerel Press. One of 100. $75-$85.

D

D.,B., and M., W. G. *Rumpel Stiltskin.* By B. D. and W. G. M. Edited by Michael Sadleir. Boards. London, 1952. (By Benjamin Disraeli and [William] George Meredith.) Roxburghe Club. One of 66. $150-$250.

D., H. *Collected Poems of H. D.* Cloth. New York, 1925. (By Hilda Doolittle.) First edition. $25-$30.

D., H. *Hedylus.* By H. D. Decorated boards and cloth. Stratford-on-Avon (Oxford), 1928. (By Hilda Doolittle.) First edition. One of 775. In dust jacket. $37.50.

D., H. *Hippolytus Temporizes.* By H. D. Decorated boards and cloth. Boston, 1927. (By Hilda Doolittle.) First edition. One of 550. Boxed. $25. Presentation copy signed by author, in worn box, $35.

D., H. *Palimpsest.* By H. D. Wrappers. Paris, 1926. Contact Editions. First edition. $75-$100. Boston, 1926. Decorated boards and cloth. First American edition. One of 700. In dust jacket. $40-$50.

D., H. *Sea Garden: Imagist Poems.* By H. D. Printed wrappers. London, 1916. First edition $100-$150. Boston, 1917. Green wrappers. First American edition. $50-$75. Author's first book.

D., H. *The Tribute and Circe—Two Poems.* By H. D. Cloth. Cleveland, 1917. (By Hilda Doolittle.) First edition. One of 50. $35-$50.

D., H. *The Walls Do Not Fall.* By H. D. Cloth. New York, 1944. (By Hilda Doolittle.) First edition. In dust jacket. $25-$35.

DAFYDD ap Gwilym. *Selected Poems.* Boards and linen. Dublin, 1944. Cuala Press. One of 280. In tissue dust jacket. $75-$100.

DAHLBERG, Edward. *Bottom Dogs.* Introduction by D. H. Lawrence. Cloth. New York, 1930. First edition. $30-$35. Author's first book.

DAHLBERG, Edward. *The Confessions of Edward Dahlberg.* Illustrated. Cloth. New York, no date (1971). First edition. One of 200 signed. Boxed. $45-$50.

DAHLBERG, Edward. *Do These Bones Live?* Red cloth. New York, no date (1941). First edition. In dust jacket. $25-$30.

DAHLBERG, Edward. *The Sorrows of Priapus.* Illustrated by Ben Shahn. Printed white boards. No place, no date (New York, 1957). Thistle Press. First edition. One of 150 signed by author and artist. Extra signed lithographs laid in. In glassine dust jacket. Boxed. $100-$150.

DALCHO, Frederick. *An Historical Account of the Protestant Episcopal Church in South Carolina.* Cloth. Charleston, 1820. First edition. $100-$150. Rebound in cloth, $100.

DALE, Edward Everett. *The Range Cattle Industry.* Plates. Cloth. Norman, Okla., 1930. First edition. One of 500. $40-$60.

DALE, Harrison Clifford (editor). *The Ashley-Smith Explorations.* 2 maps, 3 plates. Cloth. Cleveland, 1918. First edition. One of 750. $50-$80. Glendale, Calif., 1941. Cloth. Revised edition. One of 750. $30-$35.

DALI, Salvador. *The Secret Life of Salvador Dali.* Cloth. New York, 1942. First edition. In dust jacket. $35-$50.

DALTON Brothers and Their Astounding Career of Crime (The). By an Eye Witness. Pictorial wrappers. Chicago, 1892. First edition. $50-$75.

DALTON, Emmett. *When the Daltons Rode.* Portrait and plates. Pictorial cloth. Garden City, 1931. First edition (so stated). In dust jacket. $35-$50.

DAMON, S. Foster. *William Blake: His Philosophy and Symbols.* Boards. Boston, 1924. First American edition. $35.

DAMON, Samuel C. *A Journey to Lower Oregon and Upper California, 1848-49.* Half cloth. San Francisco, 1927. Grabhorn printing. One of 250. $50-$60.

DAMPIER, William. *A New Voyage Round the World.* 4 maps, portrait. Half vellum. London, 1927. One of 975. $40-$60.

DAMSEL of Darien (The). 2 vols., boards or wrappers, paper spine labels. Philadelphia, 1839. (By William Gilmore Simms.) First edition, first issue, with errata slip before the first page of text in first volume. $75-$100.

DANA, Charles A. *The United States Illustrated.* (Prospectus.) Wrappers. New York, no date (1853). $30.

DANA, Edmund. *Geographical Sketches on the Western Country; Designed for Emigrants and Settlers.* Boards. Cincinnati, 1819. First edition. $150-$200.

DANA, J. G., and Thomas, R. S. *A Report of the Trial of Jereboam O. Beauchamp.* 153 pp., wrappers. Frankfort, Ky., no date (1826). First edition. $300-$400.

DANA, Richard Henry, Jr. See *Two Years Before the Mast.*

DANA, Richard Henry, Jr. *To Cuba and Back: A Vacation Voyage.* Brown cloth. Boston, 1859. First edition. $25-$35.

DANCE of Life (The). Frontispiece, engraved title, 24 plates by Thomas Rowlandson. Boards, or cloth. London, 1817. (By William Combe.) First edition. $200 and up. Also, $160 (A, 1948); half calf, gilt top, $84 (A, 1967); cloth, $52.80 (A, 1968). (An issue in parts is also recorded, but I have traced no copy for sale in recent years.)

DANIEL, John W. *Character of Stonewall Jackson.* Cloth. Lynchburg, Va., 1868. First edition. $35-$50.

DANIELS, Jonathan. *Thomas Wolfe: October Recollections.* Cloth. Columbia, S.C., no date (1961). First edition. One of 750 signed. In dust jacket. $25-$35.

DANIELS, William M. *A Correct Account of the Murder of Generals Joseph and Hyrum Smith, at Carthage, on the 27th Day of June, 1844.* 24 pp., wrappers. Nauvoo, Ill., 1845. First edition, first issue, without plates. $1,500-$2,000. Second issue, with two woodcut engravings added. Rebound in morocco, paper covers bound in, $1,100 (A, 1966).

DANTE ALIGHIERI. *La Divina Commedia, or The Divine Vision of Dante Alighieri.* In Italian and English. Illustrated. Orange vellum. London, 1928. Nonesuch Press. One of 1,475. $150-$200.

DA PONTE, Lorenzo. See *The Memoirs of Lorenzo Da Ponte.*

D'ARBLAY, Madame. *Memoirs of Doctor Burney.* (Arranged by his daughter, Madame D'Arblay.) 3 vols., boards. London, 1832. (By Frances Burney.) First edition. $50-$100.

DARBY, William. *The Emigrant's Guide to the Western and Southwestern States and Territories.* 3 maps, 2 tables. Leather. New York, 1818. First edition. $100-$150.

DARBY, William. *A Geographical Description of the State of Louisiana.* Map. Leather. Philadelphia, 1816. First edition. $75-$100. New York, 1817. Second edition, with 2 maps and large folding map in separate folder. $50-$75.

DARBY, William. *A Tour from the City of New-York, to Detroit, in the Michigan Territory.* 3 folding maps (one in some copies). Boards and calf. New York, 1819. First edition. $125-$150.

DARLINGTON, Mary Carson (editor). *Fort Pitt and Letters from the Frontier.* 3 maps, 3 plates. Cloth. Pittsburgh, 1892. First edition. One of 100 large paper copies. $50-$75. Ordinary issue: One of 200. $35-$50.

DARLINGTON, William M. (editor). *Christopher Gist's Journals.* 7 maps. Cloth. Pittsburgh, 1893. First edition. One of 100. $50-$60.

DARTMOUTH Verse, 1925. No place (Portland, Me.), 1925. Mosher Press. One of 500. (Note: Contains an introduction by Robert Frost.) $50-$60.

DARWIN, Bernard and Elinor. *The Tale of Mr. Tootleoo.* Color illustrations. Printed boards. London, no date. Nonesuch Press. $25-$30.

DARWIN, Charles. *The Descent of Man.* Illustrated. 2 vols., green cloth. London, 1871. First edition, first issue, with errata on back of title page in Vol. 2 and with ads in each volume dated January. $100-$150.

DARWIN, Charles. *The Expression of the Emotions in Man and Animals.* Plates. Cloth. London, 1872. First edition. $50-$75.

DARWIN, Charles. *On the Origin of Species by Means of Natural Selection.* Green cloth London, 1859. First edition, with ads at end dated June. $750-$1,250.

DARWIN, Charles. *The Voyage of H.M.S. Beagle.* Illustrated by Robert Gibbings. Folio, decorated sailcloth. New York, 1956. Limited Editions Club. One of 1,500 signed by Gibbings. Boxed. $50.

DATE 1601. Conversation, as It Was by the Social Fireside, in the Times of the Tudors. 7 single leaves, with title on front of first leaf, unbound. No place, no date (West Point, N.Y., 1882). (By Samuel Langhorne Clemens.) First authorized edition. $500-$750. Also, $380 (A, 1968). Another edition: No place, no date (Bangor, Me., 1894). Calf. $150-$200. Also, $70 (A, 1968). (Note: There have been numerous pirated printings of this *sub rosa* item, including at least two unauthorized 1880 printings. See BAL.)

DAUBENY, Charles. *Journal of a Tour Through the United States and Canada . . . 1837-1838.* Folding map. Cloth. Oxford, 1843. First edition. One of 100. $100-$150.

DAVENPORT, Cyril. *Royal English Bookbindings.* Frontispiece, 7 other color plates, 27 other illustrations. Cloth. London, 1896. $50-$75.

DAVENPORT, Homer. *My Quest of the Arab Horse.* Cloth. New York, 1909. First edition. $35-$60.

DAVIDSON, Alexander and Stuve, Bernard. *A Complete History of Illinois from 1673 to 1873.* Half leather. Springfield, 1874. First edition. $50-$60.

DAVIDSON, Donald. *Lee in the Mountains and Other Poems.* Cloth. Boston, 1938. First edition. In dust jacket. $35-$50.

DAVIDSON, Donald. *The Tall Men.* Boards, cloth spine, label. Boston, 1927. First edition. $30-$35.

DAVIDSON, Gordon Charles. *The North West Company.* 5 folding maps. Cloth. Berkeley, Calif., 1918. First edition. $75-$100.

DAVIDSON, James Wood. *The Living Writers of the South.* Cloth. New York, 1869. First edition. $45. (Note: Contains two poems constituting first book appearance of Joel Chandler Harris.)

DAVIES, W. H. *The Soul's Destroyer, and Other Poems.* Buff printed wrappers. No place, no date (London, 1905). First edition. $75-$125. Author's first book.

DAVIES, W.H. *Selected Poems.* Portrait. Green morocco. Newtown, Wales, 1928. Gregynog Press. One of a few (from an edition of 310) specially bound by the Gregynog Bindery. $400-$450. Also, $240 (A, 1968). Ordinary issue: Marbled boards and buckram. $75.

DAVIES, W. H. *The Lover's Song Book.* Marbled boards and cloth. Newtown, 1933. Gregynog Press. First edition. One of 250 signed. $75. Another issue: Morocco. One of a few bound by George Fisher. $400-$450. Also, $240 (A, 1968).

DA VINCI, Leonardo. *Thoughts on Art and Life.* Cloth. Boston, 1906. One of 303. $25-$30.

DAVIS, Duke. *Flashlights from Mountain and Plain.* Illustrated by Charles M. Russell. Cloth. Bound Brook, N.J., 1911. First edition. $35-$50.

DAVIS, Edmund W. *Salmon-Fishing on the Grand Cascapedia.* Half vellum. No place (New York), 1904. First edition. One of 100. $150-$200.

DAVIS, Ellis A. *Commercial Encyclopedia of the Pacific Southwest.* Cloth. Oakland, Calif., 1915. $100-$150.

DAVIS, H. S. (compiler). *Reminiscences of Gen. William Larimer.* Plates. Folding table. Morocco. Lancaster, Pa., 1918. First edition. $200-$300.

DAVIS, Hubert. *The Symbolic Drawings . . . for "An American Tragedy."* Foreword by Theodore Dreiser. 20 drawings. Folio, gold and silver boards, cloth spine. No place, no date (New York, 1930). Limited edition signed by Davis and Dreiser. $40-$50.

DAVIS, John. See *Walter Kennedy: An American Tale.*

DAVIS, M. *Report on the Petition of T. H. Perkins and His Contract with the British Northwest Fur Company.* 15 pp., sewed. Washington, 1837. $45.

DAVIS, Paris M. *An Authentick History of the Late War Between the United States and Great Britain.* Calf. Ithaca, N.Y., 1829. First edition. $35-$50.

DAVIS, Rebecca Harding. *Kent Hampden.* Cloth. New York, 1892. First edition. $20-$25.

DAVIS, Rebecca Harding. *Margret Howth: A Story of To-Day.* Cloth. Boston, 1862. First edition. $50-$75. Author's first book.

DAVIS, Richard Harding. *Adventures of My Freshman.* Wrappers. Bethlehem, Pa., no date (1883). First edition. $100-$150.

DAVIS, Richard Harding. *Dr. Jameson's Raiders vs. the Johannesburg Reformers.* Wrappers. New York, 1897. First edition. $25-$35.

DAVIS, Richard Harding. *The West From a Car-Window.* Illustrated by Frederic Remington. Cloth. New York, 1894. First edition. $25-$30.

DAVIS, William Heath. *Sixty Years in California.* Cloth. San Francisco, 1889. First edition. $40-$50. San Francisco, 1929. 44 maps and plates. Half morocco. Second edition. One of 2,000 (with title changed to *Seventy-five Years in California*). $50-$75. Another issue: Argonaut Edition. One of 100, with added plates and a page of the author's original manuscript. $75-$125. San Francisco, 1967. Illustrated. Cloth. $27.50.

DAVIS, William J. (editor). *The Partisan Rangers of the Confederate States Army.* 65 plates. Cloth. Louisville, 1904. (By Adam R. Johnson.) First edition. $50-$75.

DAVIS, William W. H. *El Gringo; or New Mexico and Her People.* Frontispiece. Cloth. New York, 1857. First edition. $50-$60.

DAVIS, William W. H. *The Fries Rebellion.* 10 plates. Cloth. Doylestown, Pa., 1899. First edition. $50.

DAVIS, William W. H. *The Spanish Conquest of New Mexico: 1527-1703.* Folding map, plate. Cloth. Doylestown, 1869. First edition. $75-$100.

DAVISON, Lawrence H. *Movements in European History.* Light-blue cloth. London, 1921. (By D. H. Lawrence.) First edition. In dust jacket. $35-$50. (Note: The pen name was abandoned in the second issue.)

DAVY Crockett; or, The Lion-Hearted Hunter. 96 pp., wrappers. New York, no date (about 1875). $45-$50.

DAVY Crockett's Almanac, of Wild Sports in the West. Pictorial wrappers. Nashville, no date. For 1835, $250 and up; for 1836, $250 and up; for 1837, $250 and up; also, $120 (A, 1966); for 1838, $250 and up; for 1839, $250 and up; for 1840, $250 and up; for 1841, $250 and up. Other Crockett almanacs: Boston imprint, for 1836, $200 and up; also, $110 (A, 1966). Philadelphia imprint, for 1854. $100. Also, at auction: Nashville, 1835-41, 7 vols., together with Boston edition for 1842, $2,450 (1962).

DAWSON, Charles C. *A Collection of Family Records.* Illustrated. Cloth. Albany, 1874. First edition. $45-$50.

DAWSON, Moses. *A Historical Narrative of the Civil and Military Services of Maj.-Gen. William Henry Harrison.* Boards. Cincinnati, 1824. First edition, first issue, with 15-line errata slip. $200-$300. Also, $150 (A, 1967); rebacked, $150 (A, 1963); lacking errata slip, $90 (A, 1962). Later issue, with 24-line errata slip: $65-$90 at retail.

DAWSON, Nicholas. *California in '41. Texas in '51. Memoirs.* Frontispiece. Cloth. No place, no date (Austin, Tex., about 1901). First edition. Inscribed copies, $375 (A, 1968), $310 (A, 1960).

DAWSON, Nicholas. *Narrative of Nicholas "Cheyenne" Dawson.* Half cloth. San Francisco, 1933. Grabhorn Press. One of 500. In dust jacket. $50-$60.

DAWSON, Simon J. *Report on the Exploration of the Country Between Lake Superior and the Red River Settlement and the Assiniboine and Saskatchewan.* Illustrated, 2 folding maps. 45 pp., half leather and cloth. Toronto, 1859. First edition. $100-$150.

DAWSON, Thomas F., and Skiff, F. J. V. *The Ute War: A History of the White River Massacre, etc.* 184 pp., printed wrappers. Denver, 1879. First edition. $750 and up. Also, $500 (A, 1968), $425 (A, 1966).

DAWSON, William Leon. *The Birds of California.* Illustrated. 4 vols., folio cloth. San Diego, 1923. "Format De Luxe." Signed. $100-$150. Another issue: Morocco. "Patron's Edition." One of 250. $200. Also, $100 (A, 1969). Another issue: 3 vols., cloth. Student's edition. $75.

DAWSON, William Leon. *The Birds of Ohio.* Illustrated. 2 vols., cloth. Columbus, Ohio, 1903. $50-$75.

DAWSON, William Leon, and Bowles, John H. *The Birds of Washington.* 2 vols., boards. Seattle, 1909. First edition. One of 200 signed. $50-$100. Another issue: "Edition De Luxe." One of 85. $150.

DAY, Sherman. *Report of the Committee on Internal Improvements, on the Use of the Camels on the Plains, May 30, 1855.* 11 pp., unbound. No place (Sacramento), 1885. $40-$45.

DAY LEWIS, C. *Beechen Vigil & Other Poems.* Wrappers. London, no date (1925). First edition. $150-$250. Author's first book. A New York dealer offered it at $225 in 1971.

DAY LEWIS, C. *Country Cornets.* Boards. London, 1928. First edition. Boxed. $35-$40.

DEAN, Bashford. *Catalogue of European Daggers.* 85 plates. Half cloth. New York, 1929. $75-$100.

DEAN, James. *An Alphabetical Atlas, or, Gazetteer of Vermont.* Stitched. Montpelier, Vt., 1808. First edition. $35-$50.

DEARBORN, Henry. *The Revolutionary War Journals of Henry Dearborn, 1775-1783.* 6 plates. Cloth. Chicago, 1939. Caxton Club. One of 350. Boxed. $50-$75.

DEBAR, J. H. *The West Virginia Handbook and Immigrant's Guide.* Folding map. Cloth. Parkersburg, W. Va., 1870. First edition. $100-$150.

DE BARTHE, Joe. *The Life and Adventures of Frank Grouard, Chief of Scouts.* Frontispiece, 67 plates. Pictorial cloth. St. Joseph, Mo., no date (1894). First edition. $150-$250.

DEBOUCHEL, Victor. *Histoire de la Louisiane.* Boards. Nouvelle-Orléans, 1841. First edition. $75-$100.

DECALVES, Don Alonso (pseudonym). *New Travels to the Westward.* 48 pp., sewed. Greenwich, Mass., 1805. $75-$85.

DE CHAIR, Somerset. *The Golden Carpet.* Frontispiece. Half morocco. London, 1943. Golden Cockerel Press. One of 500. $75-$85.

DE CHAIR, Somerset. *The Silver Crescent.* Photographs. Half morocco. London, 1943. Golden Cockerel Press. One of 500. $90-$100.

DE CHAIR, Somerset. *The Story of a Lifetime.* Engravings by Clifford Webb. Full sheep. Waltham Saint Lawrence, England, 1954. Golden Cockerel Press. One of 100. $150-$200.

DECLARATION of the Immediate Cause Which Induce and Justify the Secession of South Carolina from the Federal Union, and the Ordinance of Secession. Wrappers. Charleston, 1860. First edition, first issue, with misprinted "Cause" for "Causes." $125-$150.

DE CORDOVA, J. *Lecture on Texas.* 32 pp., wrappers. Philadelphia, 1858. First edition. $30-$50.

DE CORDOVA, J. *Texas: Her Resources and Her Public Men.* Tables. Cloth. Philadelphia, 1858. $175-$200.

DE CORDOVA, J. *The Texas Immigrant and Traveller's Guide Book.* Cloth. Austin, 1856. First edition. $125-$150.

DECREE of Star Chamber Concerning Printing (A). Full red levant. No place, no date (New York, 1884). Grolier Club. One of 150 inscribed by the 9 founders of the Grolier Club. $250 (A, 1964).

DEERSLAYER (The); or, The First War-Path. By the Author of "The Last of the Mohicans." 2 vols., purple cloth, paper labels on spine. Philadelphia, 1841. (By James Fenimore Cooper.) First edition. $200-$300.

DEFOE, Daniel. *The Life and Surprising Adventures of Robinson Crusoe.* 54 pp., wrappers. New York, no date (1864). First Beadle Dime Classic edition, first issue, with publisher's address as 118 William Street. $35-$45.

DEFOE, Daniel. *A Tour Thro' London About the Year 1725.* Edited by Sir Mayson Beeton and E. B. Chancellor. Folio, cloth. London, 1929. One of 350. $75-$100. Another issue: Paneled calf. $150-$200.

DE FOREST, John W. *Miss Ravenel's Conversion from Secession to Loyalty.* Cloth. New York, 1867. First edition. $35-$50.

DE FOREST, John W. *Playing the Mischief.* 185 pp., wrappers. New York, 1875. First edition. $35-$40. New York, 1876. Second printing. $25.

DE GIVRY, G. *Witchcraft, Magic, and Alchemy.* Translated by J. C. Locke. 366 illustrations, 10 color plates. Cloth. London, no date (1931). In dust jacket. $35-$40.

DE GOURMONT, Rémy. *The Natural Philosophy of Love.* Boards, cloth spine. London, 1926. First English edition. One of 1,500. In dust jacket. $35-$50. (Note: Contains a postscript by Ezra Pound.)

DE GRESS, J. O. *Regulations to Be Observed Under an Act to Establish and Maintain a System of Public Free Schools in Texas.* 7 pp., wrappers. Galveston, 1873. $25-$30.

DE HASS, Wills. *History of the Early Settlement and Indian Wars of Western Virginia.* 4 plates, folding facsimile. Decorated cloth. Wheeling, W. Va., 1851. First edition. $100-$200.

DELAFAYE-BREHIER, Julie. *New Tales for Girls.* Illustrated. Printed boards. Boston, 1825 (cover date). $25-$30.

DELAFIELD, John, Jr. *An Inquiry into the Origin of the Antiquities of America.* 11 plates, including 18-foot-long folding tissue-paper plate. Cloth. New York, 1839. First edition. $100-$125. Cincinnati, 1839. $25-$35.

DE LA MARE, Walter. See Ramal, Walter.

DE LA MARE, Walter. *Behold, This Dreamer.* Colored frontispiece. Parchment. London, 1939. First edition. One of 50 signed. $50-$75.

DE LA MARE, Walter. *Broomsticks and Other Tales.* Wood engravings. Half cloth, leather label on spine. London, 1925. First edition. One of 278 signed. In dust jacket. $55-$95.

DE LA MARE, Walter. *The Captive.* Boards. New York, 1928. Bowling Green Press. First edition. Limited and signed. $35-$50.

DE LA MARE, Walter. *The Connoisseur.* Boards. London, 1926. First edition. One of 250 signed. In dust jacket. $50-$75.

DE LA MARE, Walter. *Crossings: A Fairy Play.* Color vignette on title page. Decorated boards, cloth spine. No place (London), 1921. Beaumont Press. First edition. One of 264. Boxed. $35. Another issue: Vellum. One of 10 on vellum, signed. Boxed. $75-$100.

DE LA MARE, Walter. *Desert Islands and Robinson Crusoe.* Engravings by Rex Whistler. Cloth. London, 1930. One of 650 signed. In dust jacket. $100-$150. First trade edition: Cloth. In dust jacket. $10-$15.

DE LA MARE, Walter. *Ding Dong Bell.* Boards. London, 1924. First edition. One of 300 signed. In dust jacket. $65-$75.

DE LA MARE, Walter. *Down-Adown-Derry.* Illustrated by Dorothy P. Lathrop. Blue cloth. London, 1922. First edition. In dust jacket. $25-$30.

DE LA MARE, Walter. *Henry Brocken.* Cloth. London, 1904. First edition, first issue, without gilt on top edges. $25-$35.

DE LA MARE, Walter. *Lispet, Lispett and Vaine.* Woodcut decorations. Limp vellum. London, 1923. One of 175 signed. Boxed. $75-$100.

DE LA MARE, Walter. *The Listeners, and Other Poems.* Cloth. London, 1912. First edition. In dust jacket. $50-$60.

DE LA MARE, Walter. *The Lord Fish.* Illustrated by Rex Whistler. Parchment. London, no date (1933). First edition. One of 60 signed. In dust jacket. Boxed. $200-$250.

DE LA MARE, Walter. *Memoirs of a Midget.* Boards. London, no date (1921). First edition, first issue, with "Copyright 1921" on verso of title page. One of 210 signed. Boxed. $100-$150. Trade edition: Blue cloth. In dust jacket. $30.

DE LA MARE, Walter. *On the Edge: Short Stories.* Illustrated. Pink cloth. London, 1930. First edition. One of 300 signed. In dust jacket. $50-$85. Trade edition: Cloth. In dust jacket. $15-$20.

DE LA MARE, Walter. *Peacock Pie: A Book of Rhymes.* Illustrated in color. Boards and cloth. London, 1924. One of 250 signed. In dust jacket. $75.

DE LA MARE, Walter. *Poems.* Cloth. London, 1906. First edition. In dust jacket. $50-$60.

DE LA MARE, Walter. *Poems, 1901 to 1918.* 2 vols., boards. London, 1920. First edition. $40-$50.

DE LA MARE, Walter. *The Return.* Smooth cloth. London, 1910. First edition. In dust jacket. $50. New York, 1922. Brown cloth. First American edition. In dust jacket. $15-$20.

DE LA MARE, Walter. *The Riddle and Other Stories.* Cream cloth. London, no date (1923). First edition. One of 310. In dust jacket. $50-$60. Another issue: "Author's edition." One of 25 for presentation. $100-$125.

DE LA MARE, Walter. *Seven Short Stories.* Colored illustrations. Boards. London, 1931. First edition. One of 170 signed. Boxed. $75-$100.

DE LA MARE, Walter. *Stuff and Nonsense and So On.* Boards. London, 1927. First edition. One of 275 signed. Boxed. $35-$50.

DE LA MARE, Walter. *The Sunken Garden and Other Poems.* Boards and linen. No place (London), 1917. Beaumont Press. First edition. One of 230 signed. Boxed. $35-$50. Another issue: Vellum. One of 20 on Japan paper, signed. Boxed. $75-$100.

DE LA MARE, Walter. *This Year: Next Year.* Colored illustrations. Decorated cloth. London, 1937. First edition. One of 100 signed. In dust jacket. $100-$150.

DE LA MARE, Walter. *The Traveller.* Illustrated in color by John Piper. Gray cloth. London, 1946. First edition. In dust jacket. $25-$35.

DE LA MARE, Walter. *Two Tales.* Vellum and boards. London, 1925. First edition. One of 250 signed. Boxed. $50.

DE LA MARE, Walter. *The Veil and Other Poems.* Boards. London, 1921. First edition. One of 250 signed. In dust jacket. $50.

DELAND, Margaret. *Florida Days.* Pictorial tan cloth. Boston, 1889. First edition. $25-$30.

DELAND, Margaret. *Old Chester Tales.* Illustrated by Howard Pyle. Cloth. New York, 1889. First edition, first issue, with "Chelsea" for "Chester" on page 5. $25-$35.

DELAND, Margaret. *The Old Garden and Other Verses.* White cloth and flowered cloth. Boston, 1886. First edition. $25-$30. Author's first book.

DELANO, Alonzo. See *Pen Knife Sketches.*

DELANO, Alonzo. *Life on the Plains and Among the Diggings.* Frontispiece and 3 plates. Cloth. Auburn, N.Y., 1854. First edition, first issue, with page 219 misnumbered 119 and with no mention of number of thousands printed. $150-$250.

DELANO, Alonzo. *Pen-Knife Sketches, or Chips of the Old Block.* Colored illustrations. Decorated boards. San Francisco, 1934. Grabhorn Press. One of 550. $35-$50. (For anonymous edition, see title entry.)

DELANO, Amasa. *A Narrative of Voyages and Travels, in the Northern and Southern Hemispheres.* 2 portraits, folding map, errata leaf. Boards, paper label. Boston, 1817. First edition. $125-$150.

DELANO, Judah. *Washington (D.C.) Directory.* Calf. Washington, 1822. First edition. $150-$175.

DELANO, Reuben. *Wanderings and Adventures of Reuben Delano.* 3 plates. 102 pp., wrappers. Worcester, Mass., 1846. First edition. $50-$75.

DELAY, Peter J. *History of Yuba and Sutter Counties, California.* Illustrated. Three-quarters leather. Los Angeles, 1924. $50-$75.

DE LINCY, A. J. V. Le Roux. *Researches Concerning Jean Grolier, His Life and His Library.* Color plates. Full leather. New York, 1907. $200-$300.

DELL, Floyd. *Women as World Builders.* Cloth. Chicago, 1913. First edition. In dust jacket. $50. Author's first book.

DEMOCRACY: An American Novel. White cloth, printed red end papers. New York, 1880. (By Henry Adams.) First edition. No. 112 in "Leisure Hour Series." Probable first issue copies have date March 31, 1880, in last line on front pasted-down end paper. $150-$200.

DE MORGAN, William. *Joseph Vance.* Light-green cloth. London, 1906. First edition. $25-$35. Author's first book.

DE MORGAN, William. *It Never Can Happen Again.* Portrait. 2 vols., cloth. London, 1909. First edition. $25-$30.

DEMOS: A Story of English Socialism. 3 vols., brown cloth. London, 1886. (By George Gissing.) First edition. $150-$200.

DENISON, Jesse. *First Annual Report to the Stockholders of the Providence Western Land Company.* 8 pp., wrappers. Providence, 1857. $25-$30.

DENNY, Arthur A. *Pioneer Days on Puget Sound.* Cloth. Seattle, 1888. First edition, with errata slip. $75-$100. Seattle, 1908. One of 850. $25-$30.

DENTON, Sherman F. *As Nature Shows Them: Moths and Butterflies of the United States East of the Rocky Mountains.* 56 colored plates. 2 vols., half leather. Boston, no date (1900). One of 500. $100-$125.

DEPONS, François. *Travels in Parts of South America, During the Years 1801-1804.* Folding map and plan. Contemporary boards. London, 1806. $150-$200.

DEPONS, François. *A Voyage to the Eastern Part of Terra Firma.* Translated by an American Gentleman. 3 vols., boards (none located) or contemporary leather. New York, 1806. (Translated by Washington Irving, Peter Irving, and George Caines.) First American edition. In leather: $100-$125.

DEPREDATIONS and Massacre by the Snake River Indians. 16 pp., sewed. No place (Washington), 1861. $25-$35.

DE QUILLE, Dan. *History of the Big Bonanza.* Illustrated. Decorated cloth. Hartford, Conn., 1876. (By William Wright.) First edition, first issue, without plate No. 44. $75-$100.

DE QUILLE, Dan. *A History of the Comstock Silver Lode and Mines.* Printed wrappers. Virginia City, Nev., 1889. (By William Wright.) First edition. $50-$60.

DE QUINCEY, Thomas. See *Confessions of an English Opium Eater; Klosterhiem, or, The Masque.*

DE QUINCEY, Thomas. *The Logic of Political Economy.* Cloth, paper label. Edinburgh, 1844. First edition. $75-$100.

DE RICCI, Seymour. *A Bibliography of Shelley's Letters Published and Unpublished.* Cloth. London, 1927. $40-$50.

DE RICCI, Seymour. *The Book Collector's Guide.* Green cloth. Philadelphia, 1921. First edition. $40-$50.

DE ROOS, Fred F. *Personal Narrative of Travels in the United States and Canada in 1826.* 14 plates and plans. Boards. London, 1827. First edition, $150-$200. Second edition, same date. 14 lithographs, 2 maps. Boards. $100-$150.

DERRY, Derry down. *A Book of Nonsense.* Illustrated. Oblong, printed wrappers. London, no date (1846). (By Edward Lear.) First edition. One of 175. $300-$500. Author's first book for children.

DESCENDANT (The). Decorated cloth. New York, 1897. (By Ellen Glasgow.) First edition, first printing, with single imprint on title page, and first binding, with author's name omitted from spine. $50-$75. Author's first book.

DESCRIPTION of Central Iowa (A), With Especial Reference to Polk County and Des Moines, the State Capital. 32 pp., stitched. Des Moines, 1858. $100-$150.

DESCRIPTION of Tremont House (A), with Architectural Illustrations. Boards. Boston, 1830. (By William G. Eliot.) First edition. $35-$50.

DESCRIPTIVE Account of the City of Peoria (A). 32 pp., wrappers. Peoria, Ill., 1859. $50-$75.

DESCRIPTIVE and Priced Catalogue of Books, Pamphlets, and Maps (A), etc. (Thomas Wayne Norris catalogue.) Patterned boards and red cloth. Oakland, Calif., 1948. Holmes Book Co.–Grabhorn. One of 500. $45-$50.

DESCRIPTIVE Bibliography of the Books Printed at the Ashendene Press, 1895-1935. 15 collotype plates, 10 of bindings; 2 photogravures, and numerous specimen pages, initial letters, woodcuts, etc. Cowhide. London, no date (1935). Boxed. $600-$650.

DESCRIPTIVE Catalogue of the Marine Collection to Be Found at India House (A). 35 plates, 11 hand-colored. Half leather. New York, 1935. (By Carl C. Cutler.) One of 1,000. $100-$125.

DESCRIPTIVE, Historical, Commercial, Agricultural, and Other Important Information Relative to the City of San Diego, California. 22 photographs. 51 pp., wrappers. No place (San Diego), 1874. $250 and up.

DESCRIPTIVE Scenes for Children. 14 pp., sewed. Boston, no date (1828). $50-$60.

DE SHIELDS, J. T. *Border Wars of Texas.* Cloth. Tioga, Tex., 1912. First edition. $50-$75.

DE SHIELDS, J. T. *Cynthia Ann Parker.* Frontispiece, 3 portraits. Pictorial cloth. St. Louis, 1886. First edition. $75-$100.

DES IMAGISTES: An Anthology. Olive wrappers. New York, 1914. (Edited by Ezra Pound.) First edition. $150. London, 1914. Boards. $125. (Note: Includes poems by Pound and James Joyce.)

DE SMET, Pierre-Jean. *Letters and Sketches.* Illustrations, folding leaf, "The Catholic Ladder." Cloth. Philadephia, 1843. First edition, first issue, with 352 (not 344) pages. $200-$300.

DE SMET, Pierre-Jean. *Oregon Missions and Travels over the Rocky Mountains.* Folding map, 12 plates. Cloth. New York, 1847. First edition. $100-$150. Later issue, same date, plates omitted: About $35.

DE SOTO, Hernando. *The Discovery of Florida.* Translated by Buckingham Smith. Decorations in color by Mallete Dean. Folio, half cloth. San Francisco, 1946. Grabhorn Press. One of 280. $75-$100.

DESPERATE Remedies: A Novel. 3 vols., red cloth. London, 1871. (By Thomas Hardy.) First edition. $750-$1,000. (A copy sold for $7,800 at the peak of Hardy's popularity.) Author's first book (500 printed). New York, 1874. Yellow cloth. First American edition, with "Author's Edition" on copyright page. $75-$100.

DESTINY; or, The Chief's Daughter. 3 vols., boards. Edinburgh, 1831. (By Susan Edmonstone Ferrier.) First edition. $150-$200.

DEUTSCH, Babette. *A Brittle Heaven.* Blue cloth. New York, no date (1926). First edition. In dust jacket. $40-$50.

DEUTSCH, Babette. *Banners.* Boards, labels. New York, no date (1919). First edition. In dust jacket. $35-$50. Author's first book.

DE VINNE, Theodore L. *Aldus Pius Manutius.* Boards and cloth. With original leaf from *Hypnerotomachia Poliphili,* printed by Aldus in 1499. San Francisco, 1925. Grabhorn printing. One of 250. $35-$50.

DE VINNE, Theodore L. *The Invention of Printing.* Half morocco. New York, 1876. First edition. $35-$50.

DE VINNE, Theodore L. *Title-Pages as Seen by a Printer.* Illustrated. Half calf. New York, 1901. Grolier Club. One of 340. $25-$35.

DE VOTO, Bernard. *Across the Wide Missouri.* 81 plates, some in color. Cloth. Boston, 1947. First edition. One of 265. Boxed. $50-$75. Trade edition: Cloth. In dust jacket. $25.

DE VRIES, David P. *Voyages from Holland to America, 1632-1644.* Cloth. New York, 1853. One of 125. $35-$50.

DE WITT, David Miller. *The Judicial Murder of Mary E. Surratt.* Cloth. Baltimore, 1895. First edition. $40-$50.

DE WOLFF, J. H. *Pawnee Bill (Maj. Gordon W. Lillie): His Experience and Adventures on the Western Plains.* Illustrated. Pictorial boards. No place, 1902. First edition. $35-$40.

DEXTER, A. Hersey. *Early Days in California.* Pictorial cloth. No place (Denver), 1886. First edition. $200-$250.

DEXTER, F. Theodore. *Forty-Two Years' Scrapbook of Rare Ancient Firearms.* Cloth. Los Angeles, no date (1954). Limited edition. $35-$40.

DÍAZ DEL CASTILLO, Bernal. *The Discovery and Conquest of Mexico, 1517-1521.* Translated by A. P. Mandslay. Illustrated by Miguel Covarrubias. Leather. New York, 1942. Limited Editions Club. Boxed. $100-$125.

DÍAZ DEL CASTILLO, Bernal. *The True History of the Conquest of Mexico.* Translated by Maurice Keatinge. Map, errata leaf. Contemporary half leather. London, 1800. First English edition. $80-$100.

DIBDIN, Thomas Frognall. *Aedes Althorpianae.* Illustrated. 2 vols., boards. London, 1822. First edition. $80-$100. (Note: This work consists of the fifth and sixth volumes of a 7-volume set usually listed as *Bibliotheca Spenceriana,* which see in entry following.) Another issue: Large paper, bound in full leather. One of 55. $375.

DIBDIN, Thomas Frognall. *The Bibliomania; or Book Madness.* Contemporary calf. London, 1809. First edition. $75-$100. London, 1811. 2 vols., morocco. Second edition. $50-$75. Large paper issue: One of 18. $115. Other issues in 2 vols.-in-one format, half leather: $35-$50. London, 1842. Calf. Third edition. $50. London, 1876. Half cloth. Large paper edition, limited. $35. Boston, 1903. Bibliophile Society. 4 vols., boards. One of 483. $50-$60.

DIBDIN, Thomas Frognall. *The Bibliographical Decameron.* 3 vols., contemporary leather. London, 1817. First edition. Large paper issue: $150-$200. Ordinary issue: Contemporary leather or cloth. $75-$100.

DIBDIN, Thomas Frognall. *Bibliotheca Spenceriana.* 7 vols., contemporary leather. London, 1814-15, 1822, and 1823. (4 vols., 1814-15, *Books Printed in the XV Century;* 2 vols., 1822, *Aedes Althorpianae;* one vol., 1823, *Catalogue of Books . . . Formerly in the Library of the Duke de Cassano Serra.*) First editions. $500-$600.

DICKENS, Charles. See "Boz." Also see *Sketches by "Boz"; The Loving Ballad of Lord Bateman.*

DICKENS, Charles. *The Adventures of Oliver Twist.* 24 illustrations by George Cruikshank. 10 monthly parts, green wrappers. London, 1846. "New edition." (Actually third edition, as stated in preliminary pages, and sometimes called first octavo edition; for earlier editions see *Oliver Twist* under "Boz" and Dickens.) Recent price range at retail: $600-$800; in January, 1931, a set brought $1,400 at auction in New York. Also, some stains and repairs, $350 (A, 1970); A-range, including repaired sets, 1941-71: $20, worn, to $392. London, 1846. Slate-colored cloth. Third edition (in book form). $100-$200, possibly more.

DICKENS, Charles. *American Notes for General Circulation.* 2 vols., brown cloth. London, 1842. First edition, first issue, with second page of "Contents to Volume I" numbered XVI. $150-$200. Also, $96 and $84 (A, 1968).

DICKENS, Charles. *The Battle of Life: A Love Story.* Engraved title page and frontispiece by Maclise. Cloth. London, 1846. First edition, first issue, imprint on engraved title page in 3 lines, with "A Love Story" printed. $150-$300. Second issue, with imprint in 3 lines and "A Love Story" engraved on a scroll. $100-$150.

DICKENS, Charles. *Bleak House.* Illustrated by H. K. Browne. 20 parts in 19, blue pictorial wrappers. London, 1852-53. First edition. $200-$300. Also, $130 (A, 1970). Defective copies for less. London, 1853. Green cloth. First book edition. $25.

DICKENS, Charles. *Charles Dickens on Fechter's Acting.* 24 pp., green wrappers. Leeds, England, no date (1872). $75.

DICKENS, Charles. *A Child's History of England.* Frontispiece. 3 vols., reddish cloth. London, 1852-53-54. First edition, with title pages dated. $200-$300. Also, $150 (A, 1970), $140 (A, 1968).

DICKENS, Charles. *The Chimes.* 13 illustrations. Engraved title page. Bright-red cloth. London, 1845. First edition, first issue, with imprint as part of engraved title. $100-$150. Also, $84 (A, 1967). New York, 1931. Limited Editions Club. Illustrated by Arthur Rackham. Cloth. Boxed. $40-$50.

DICKENS, Charles. *A Christmas Carol.* 4 colored plates and 4 woodcuts by John Leech. Brown cloth. London, 1843. First published edition, first issue, with "Stave I" (not "Stave One") on first text page and with red and blue title page and green end papers. $400-$600. Worn copies, $100 and up. Second issue, with "Stave I," red and blue title page, and yellow end papers. $250-$350. Third issue, with "Stave One," red and blue title page, and yellow end papers. $150-$250. Trial issue: London, 1844. (Richard Gimbel's "first state.") Title page in red and green, with green or yellow end papers. $500-$750. Also, $375 (A, 1967), $322 (A, 1962). Philadelphia, 1844. Yellow cloth. First American edition. $50-$75. New York, 1844. Cloth. $25-$35. Leipzig, 1843. Brown cloth. Tauchnitz copyright edition, without illustrations. $50. London, no date (1915). Illustrated in color by Arthur Rackham. Pictorial vellum. Large paper edition. One of 525. $200-$300. Also, $130 (A, 1969); $192 and $168 (A, 1968). Boston, 1934. Limited Editions Club. Boards and cloth. Boxed. $20-$25.

DICKENS, Charles. *The Complete Works of Charles Dickens.* Edited by Arthur Waugh, Hugh Walpole, Walter Dexter, and Thomas Halton. Illustrated. 23 vols., buckram (each vol. a different color), leather labels, gilt, with an original engraved steel plate. London, 1937-38. Nonesuch Press. One of 877 sets. $2,280. Another set, fading on some volumes, $1,920. Also, other copies, some with Retrospectus and Prospectus volumes included, $816-$1,560 (A, 1967-69).

DICKENS, Charles. *The Cricket on the Hearth.* Illustrated. Crimson cloth. London, 1846. First edition. $50-$75. New York, 1846. Wrappers. First American edition. $35-$50. New York, 1933. Limited Editions Club. Cloth. Boxed. $25-$35.

DICKENS, Charles. *Dombey and Son.* Illustrated by H. K. Browne. 20 parts in 19, green pictorial wrappers. London, 1846-47-48. First edition, with 12-line errata slip in Part V. $200-$300. Also, repaired, $100 (A, 1970). London, 1848. Dark-green cloth. First book edition. $35-$50. New York, 1957. Limited Editions Club. 2 vols., buckram. Boxed. $25-$35.

DICKENS, Charles. *Great Expectations.* 3 vols., purple cloth. London, 1861. First edition, first issue, with ads dated May, 1861. Estimated retail value of a fine copy in today's market: $1,500 and up. Circulating library labels removed from cover and inside one cover, $750. Also, A-range, 1960-70: $175-$1,100. (The record auction price is $3,500 for the Jerome Kern copy, 1929.) Later issue, without ads, bindings rubbed, inner hinges cracked: $275 at retail. New York, 1937. Limited Editions Club. Cloth. Boxed. $25.

DICKENS, Charles. *Hard Times, for These Times.* Green cloth. London, 1854. First edition. $75-$100.

DICKENS, Charles. *The Haunted Man.* Illustrated. Cloth. London, 1848. First edition. $75-$100.

DICKENS, Charles. *The Life and Adventures of Martin Chuzzlewit.* Illustrated by Phiz. 20 parts in 19, green wrappers. London, 1844. First edition, first issue, with "£" sign after "100" in reward notice on engraved title page. $250-$300. Also, repaired, $140 (A, 1970). London, 1844. Prussian blue cloth (later, brown cloth). First edition, first issue. $100-$150.

DICKENS, Charles. *The Life and Adventures of Nicholas Nickleby.* Frontispiece portrait by Maclise, illustrations by Phiz. 20 parts in 19, green pictorial wrappers. London, 1838-39. First edition, first issue, with "vister" for "sister" in line 17, page 123, part IV. $250-$350. Also, $100 and $135 (A, 1970). London, 1839. Cloth. First book edition. $75-$100.

DICKENS, Charles. *Little Dorrit.* Illustrated by H. K. Browne. 20 parts in 19, blue wrappers, London, 1855-57. First edition, first issue, with errata slip in Part XVI and uncorrected errors in Part XV. $200-$300. Also, $150 (A, 1970). London, 1857. Green cloth. First book edition, first issue. $75-$100.

DICKENS, Charles. *Master Humphrey's Clock.* Illustrated by George Cattermole and H. K. Browne. 3 vols., brown cloth. London, 1840-41. First book edition. $50-$60. (See entry under "Boz" for editions in parts.)

DICKENS, Charles. *Mr. Nightingale's Diary.* Green or brown cloth, gilt. Boston, 1877. First American edition. $30-$50. (Note: This book was published originally as an anonymous pamphlet in London in 1851. The Dickens bibliographer John C. Eckel reports only "three known copies traceable." Estimated value: $1,000 and up.)

DICKENS, Charles. *The Mystery of Edwin Drood.* 12 illustrations by S. L. Fildes. 6 parts, green pictorial wrappers. London, 1870. First edition. $200-$250. Also, $125 (A, 1970). London, 1870. Green cloth. First book edition. (Issued in a tan dust jacket—the earliest known dust jacket, according to the London *Times Literary Supplement.* The only known copy with a jacket, owned by A. Edward Newton, brought $100 at auction in 1941.) Boston, 1870. Wrappers. First American edition. $50-$75. Brattleboro, Vt., 1873. Cloth. "Completed by the Spirit-Pen of Dickens, Through a Medium." (By Thomas P. James.) First edition in this form. $27.50-$50.

DICKENS, Charles. *Oliver Twist.* 3 vols., brown cloth. London, 1839. Second edition (or third issue of the 1838 original, which see under "Boz" entry). With Dickens on title page instead of "Boz." $50-$75. (For third, or first octavo, edition, see Dickens, *The Adventures of Oliver Twist.*)

DICKENS, Charles. *Our Mutual Friend.* Illustrations by Marcus Stone. 20 parts in 19, green pictorial wrappers. London, 1864-65. First edition. $200-$300. Also, $130 (A, 1970). London, 1865. 2 vols., brown cloth. First book edition. $50-$60.

DICKENS, Charles. *The Personal History of David Copperfield.* Illustrated by H. K. Browne. 20 parts in 19, green pictorial wrappers. London, 1849-50. First edition. $400-$600. Also, $350 (A, 1970); A-range, 1965-71: $140-$425 for fine copies. London, 1850. Dark-green cloth. First book edition. $100-$150.

DICKENS, Charles. *Pictures from Italy.* Illustrations on wood by Samuel Palmer. Dark-blue cloth. London, 1846. First edition, first issue, with pages 5 and 270 unnumbered and with 2 pages of ads. $50-$75.

DICKENS, Charles. *The Posthumous Papers of the Pickwick Club.* Illustrated by R. Seymour and Phiz. 20 parts in 19, green wrappers. London, 1836-37. First edition. The most difficult of all of Dickens' works to obtain in collector's condition and therefore impossible to evaluate without close examination. Literally hundreds of "points" must be met for a "perfect Pickwick," as is evidenced in John C. Eckel's bibliographical notes covering 42 pages in *The First Editions of Charles Dickens.* The Jerome Kern copy (once owned by Dr. R. T. Jupp) brought $28,000 at auction in 1939. The highest auction price (for an imperfect copy) in recent times was $2,800 for the Louis Silver copy in 1965. Defective copies in any kind of acceptable state begin at retail at around $200. London, 1837. Green cloth. First book edition. $100 and up. Presentation copy, bound for Dickens in green morocco. Inscribed. $1,850. Philadelphia, 1836-37. 5 vols., boards. First American edition. $300 and up. New York, 1933. Limited Editions Club. 2 vols., cloth. Boxed. $35-$50.

DICKENS, Charles. *The Story of Little Dombey.* Green wrappers. London, 1858. First edition. $100-$125.

DICKENS, Charles. *A Tale of Two Cities.* Illustrated by H. K. Browne. 8 parts in 7, blue wrappers. London, 1859. First edition, first issue, with page 213 misnumbered "113." $1,176 (1965 catalogue). Another copy, $616. Also, $850 (A, 1970). London, 1859. Red or green (scarcer) cloth. First book edition. $150-$250, possibly more.

DICKENS, Charles. *The Uncommercial Traveller.* Lilac cloth. London, 1861. First edition, with ads dated December, 1860, at end. $175-$200. Spine faded, $156.

DICKENS, Charles. *The Village Coquettes: A Comic Opera.* Gray boards, or unstitched, unopened sheets. London, 1836. First edition. Very rare in original boards. In sheets: $200-$300.

DICKENSON, Jonathan. See Dickinson, Jonathan.

DICKENSON, Luella. *Reminiscences of a Trip Across the Plains in 1846.* Pictorial cloth. San Francisco, 1904. First edition. $350-$400. Also, rubbed, hinges weak, $300 (A, 1966).

DICKERSON, Oliver M. *American Colonial Government, 1696-1765.* Cloth. Cleveland, 1912. First edition. $25-$35.

DICKERSON, Philip J. *History of the Osage Nation.* Illustrations and map. 144 pp., pictorial wrappers. No place, no date (Pawhuska, Okla., 1906). First edition. $75-$100.

DICKEY, James. *Buckdancer's Choice.* Cloth. Middletown, no date (1965). First edition. In dust jacket. $15-$25.

DICKEY, James. *Two Poems of the Air.* Decorated boards. Portland, no date (1964). Oblong, decorated boards. First edition. One of 300 signed. $35.

DICKEY, James. *The Suspect in Poetry.* Boards. No place. (Madison, Minn.), 1964. First edition. Dust jacket. $15-$20.

DICKINSON, Emily. *Further Poems of Emily Dickinson.* Edited by Martha Dickinson Bianchi and Alfred Leete Hampson. Green cloth. Boston, 1929. First edition. One of 465 on large paper. In dust jacket. $50-$75. Trade edition: Cloth. In dust jacket. $7.50-$10.

DICKINSON, Emily. *Letters of Emily Dickinson.* Edited by Mabel Loomis Todd. 2 vols., green cloth. Boston, 1894. First edition, first binding, with Roberts Brothers imprint on spine. In dust jacket. $125. Lacking jackets, $50-$75. Second printing: 2 vols., brown cloth. Lacking dust jackets, $20.

DICKINSON, Emily. *Poems.* Edited by Mabel Loomis Todd and T. W. Higginson. White and gray cloth. Boston, 1890. First edition. $250-$300. Author's first book. London, 1891. Cloth. First English edition. $40-$50. New York, 1952. Limited Editions Club. Morocco. Boxed. $50.

DICKINSON, Emily. *Poems: Second Series.* Edited by T. W. Higginson and Mabel Loomis Todd. Gray or gray-green cloth, or white cloth with green spine. Boston, 1891. First edition. $75-$100. Some special copies issued in decorated boards, calf spine: $100-$225.

DICKINSON, Emily. *Poems: Third Series.* Edited by Mabel Loomis Todd. Gray, green, or white and green cloth. Boston, 1896. First edition, first binding, with Roberts Brothers imprint on spine. $75-$100.

DICKINSON, Emily. *The Single Hound: Poems of a Lifetime.* Boards and cloth. Boston, 1914. First edition, with "Published, September, 1914" on copyright page. In dust jacket. $125-$175. Boston, 1915. Boards and cloth. Second edition. In dust jacket. $15-$25.

DICKINSON, Emily. *Unpublished Poems.* Edited by Martha Dickinson Bianchi and Alfred Leete Hampson. Green cloth, pink label on spine. Boston, 1935. First edition. One of 525 de luxe copies. Boxed. $35. Boston, 1936. Green cloth. First trade edition. In dust jacket. $10-$15.

DICKINSON, Henry C. *Diary of Henry C. Dickinson.* Plates. Cloth. Denver, no date (about 1889). First edition. One of 225. $50.

DICKINSON, Jonathan. *Narrative of a Shipwreck in the Gulf of Florida.* Leather. Stanford, N.Y., 1803. (By Jonathan Dickenson.) $150-$200. Burlington, N.J., 1811. Leather. $100-$150. Salem, Ohio, 1826. *(The Shipwreck and Dreadful Sufferings of Robert Barrow.)* Half calf. $150-$200. Also, worn, $130 (A, 1967). (Note: These are variant titles of reprintings of Dickenson's *God's Protecting Providence,* first published in Philadelphia in 1699, of which only 4 perfect copies are known.)

DIDIMUS, H. *New Orleans as I Found It.* Double columns, 125 pp., wrappers. New York, 1845. (By Edward H. Durrell.) First edition. $100-$150.

DIEHL, Edith. *Bookbinding: Its Background and Technique.* Illustrated. 2 vols., cloth. New York, 1946. First edition. $75-$100.

DIENST, Alex. *The Navy of the Republic of Texas, 1835-1845.* Blue leather. Temple, Tex., no date (1909). First edition. $60-$75.

DIETZ, August. *The Postal Service of the Confederate States of America.* 2 color plates. Half leather. Richmond, Va., 1929. First edition. $40-$50.

DIGBY, Sir Kenelm. *Poems from Sir Kenelm Digby's Papers, in the Possession of Henry A. Bright.* 2 portraits, facsimile. Half morocco. London, 1877. Roxburghe Club. One of 80. $150-$250.

DILLON, George. *The Flowering Stone.* Cloth. New York, 1931. First edition. In dust jacket. $15-$25.

DIMSDALE, Thomas J. *The Vigilantes of Montana.* 228 pp., printed wrappers. Virginia City, Mont., 1866. First edition. $750-$1,000. Also, half leather, original wrappers preserved, $750 (A, 1968); lacking back cover and spine, $475 (A, 1963); rebound in cloth, printed label, $250 (A, 1960); half morocco and lacking ads, $275 (A, 1959). Virginia City, 1882. 241 pp., printed wrappers. Second edition. $100-$150. Helena, Mont., no date (1915). 26 plates and 4 facsimiles. Third edition. $30. Helena, 1915. Fourth edition. $27.50.

DINKINS, James. *1861 to 1865, by an Old Johnnie: Personal Recollections and Experiences of the Confederate Army.* Cloth. Cincinnati, 1897. First edition. $75-$100.

DINSMOOR, Robert. *Incidental Poems.* Boards and cloth, paper label. Haverhill, Mass., 1828. First edition. $75. (Note: Contains first appearance of John G. Whittier's poems in a book.)

DIOMEDI, Alexander. *Sketches of Modern Indian Life.* 79 pp., wrappers. No place, no date (Woodstock, Md., 1894?). First edition. $75-$100.

DI PRIMA, Diane. *This Kind of Bird Flies Backward.* Introduction by Lawrence Ferlinghetti. Illustrated. Wrappers. No place, no date (New York, 1958). First edition. $15-$20. Author's first book.

DIRECTORY of the City of Mineral Point for the Year 1859. Map. 64 pp., sewed. Mineral Point, Wis., 1859. $35-$50.

DIRECTORY of Newark for 1835-6. Half leather. Newark, N.J., 1835. First edition. $50-$60.

DISCARDS (The). By Old Wolf. 22 pp., wrappers. No place (Yakima, Wash.?), 1920. (By Lucullus V. McWhorter.) $35-$50.

DISCOURSE on the Aborigines of the Valley of the Ohio (A). Folding map. 51 pp., sewed. Cincinnati, 1838. (By William Henry Harrison.) First edition. $25-$35.

DISIECTA Membra. 54 pp., red wrappers. London, 1915. (By Norman Douglas.) First edition. One of 100. $100.

DISNEY, Walt. *The Pop-Up Minnie Mouse.* Illustrated, with 3 double-page pop-up cutouts. Pictorial boards. New York, no date (1933). $35-$50.

DISRAELI, Benjamin. See D., B., and M. W. G. Also see *Henrietta Temple; The Letters of Runnymede; The Tragedy of Count Alarcos; Vivian Grey; The Young Duke.*

DISRAELI, Benjamin. *Sybil, or The Two Nations.* 3 vols., half cloth. London, 1845. First edition. $60-$75.

DISRAELI, Benjamin. *The Voyage of Capt. Popanilla.* Boards, printed label. London, 1828. First edition. $60-$90.

DISTURNELL, John. *The Influence of Climate in North and South America.* Cloth. New York, 1867. First edition. $25-$35.

DISTURNELL, John (publisher). *Disturnell's Guide Through the Middle, Northern, and Eastern States.* Map of New York City, folding map. Cloth. New York, June, 1847. First edition. $35-$50.

DISTURNELL, John (publisher). *The Emigrant's Guide to New Mexico, California, and Oregon.* Folding map. 46 pp., brown cloth. New York, 1849. First edition, first issue, with map published by Disturnell and dated 1849. $350-$400. Also, $325 (A, 1968). Second edition, same date: Wrappers. With 1849 Disturnell map including "Col. Hays' Route." $500 (A, 1968). New York, 1850. Cloth. Spine gone, covers detached, $250 (A, 1968). (Note: Howes cites an 1849 edition with "map published by Colton." Colton Storm's catalogue of the Graff collection calls the Disturnell map "preferable.")

DISTURNELL, John (publisher). *The Great Lakes or Inland Seas of America*. Cloth. New York, 1868. $50-$60.

DISTURNELL, John (publisher). *Mapa de los Estados Unidos de Mejico, California, etc.* Colored map, folded. New York, 1849. In cloth case. $60-$75.

DISTURNELL, John (publisher). *The Upper Lakes of North America: A Guide*. Cloth. New York, 1857. First edition. $25-$35.

DIX Ans sur la Côte du Pacifique par un Missionaire Canadien. 100 pp., wrappers. Quebec, 1873. (By François X. Blanchet.) First edition. $35-$50.

DIXON, Richard W. *Odes and Eclogues*. Wrappers. Oxford, 1884. Daniel Press. One of 100. $75-$100.

DIXON, Sam Houston. *The Heroes of San Jacinto*. Illustrated. Cloth. Houston, 1932. $35-$40.

DIXON, Sam Houston. *The Poets and Poetry of Texas*. Cloth. Austin, Tex., 1885. $25-$30.

DOBIE, J. Frank. *Apache Gold and Yaqui Silver*. Illustrated by Tom Lea. Buckram. Boston, 1939. First (Sierra Madre) edition. One of 265 signed by author and artist. Boxed. $350-$400. Trade edition: Cloth. In dust jacket. $25.

DOBIE, J. Frank. *Carl Sandburg and Saint Peter at the Gate*. Boards. Austin, Tex., 1966. One of 750. Boxed. $25-$30.

DOBIE, J. Frank. *Coronado's Children*. Maps, illustrated. Cloth. Dallas, no date (1930). First edition, first issue, without the word "clean" in dedication. In dust jacket. $50-$60. Second issue. In jacket. $25. New York, 1931. Illustrated. Cloth. In dust jacket. $15-$20.

DOBIE, J. Frank. *The First Cattle in Texas and the Southwest*. Stapled. Austin, 1939. First edition. $25-$35.

DOBIE, J. Frank. *The Flavor of Texas*. Illustrated. Cloth. Dallas, 1936. First edition. $25-$35.

DOBIE, J. Frank. *Folklore of the Southwest*. 16 pp., wrappers. No place, 1924. First edition. $25-$30.

DOBIE, J. Frank. *Guide to Life and Literature of the Southwest*. Illustrated. Wrappers. Austin, 1943. First edition. $25-$35.

DOBIE, J. Frank. *John C. Duval, First Texas Man of Letters*. Cloth. Dallas, 1939. First edition. One of 1,000. $35-$40.

DOBIE, J. Frank. *Legends of Texas*. Wrappers. Austin, 1924. First edition. $25-$35. Foxed, $20. Austin, 1924. Cloth. Second edition. $15.

DOBIE, J. Frank. *The Longhorns*. 16 plates by Tom Lea. Rawhide. Boston, 1941. First edition. One of 265 signed. Boxed. $500-$600. Also, $450 (A, 1968). Trade edition: Pictorial cloth. In dust jacket. $20. Advance pamphlet about the book: 20 pp., wrappers, Boston, 1941. $25.

DOBIE, J. Frank. *The Mustangs*. Illustrated. Leather. Boston, no date (1952). First edition. One of 100 with original drawing. Boxed. $500. Trade edition: Cloth. In dust jacket. $25-$35. Lacking jacket, $17.50.

DOBIE, J. Frank, and others (editors). *Mustangs and Cow Horses*. Cloth. Austin, 1940. First edition. $50-$75.

DOBIE, J. Frank. *Tales of the Mustang*. Morocco. Dallas, 1936. Book Club of Texas. Boxed. $150-$200.

DOBIE, J. Frank. *A Vaquero of the Brush Country.* Boards and cloth. Dallas, 1929. First edition. In dust jacket. $75-$100. Author's first book.

DOBIE, J. Frank. *The Voice of the Coyote.* Illustrated. Cloth. Boston, 1949. First edition (so stated). In dust jacket. $25-$30.

DOBSON, Austin. *Horace Walpole, A Memoir.* Illustrated by Percy and Leon Moran. Boards. New York, 1890. One of 50 on Japan paper. $45.

DOBSON, Austin. *Three Unpublished Poems.* 6 leaves, brown wrappers. Winchester, England, 1930. First edition. $38.40.

DOCTOR Bollus and His Patients. Illustrated. Cloth. Troy, N.Y., no date (about 1851-56). $35-$40.

DOCUMENTOS Relativos al Piadoso Fondo de Misiones para Conversión y Civilización de las Numerosas Tribus Barabaras de la Antiua y Nueva California. 60 pp., bound with 8 pp. *Esposición a la Comisión, etc.* Mexico, 1845. New paper covers, $250-$275.

DODDRIDGE, Joseph. *Notes, on the Settlement and Indian Wars, of the Western Parts of Virginia and Pennsylvania, etc.* Calf. Wellsburgh, Va., 1824. First edition. $100-$150. Also, $100 (A, 1967). Worn, $75.

DODGE, Grenville M. *Biographical Sketch of James Bridger, Mountaineer, Trapper and Guide.* 2 plates. 10 leaves, wrappers. Kansas City, Mo., no date (1905). First edition, without preface. $50-$75. New York, 1905. 3 plates, one folding. 27 pp., wrappers. $35-$50. Also, $25 (A, 1965).

DODGE, Grenville M. *How We Built the Union Pacific Railway.* 30 plates. Printed wrappers. Council Bluffs, Iowa, no date(1908?).First edition, first issue, without printer's name on page before title page. $35-$50. Second issue. $25. Another edition: No place, no date (New York, 1910 or 1908?). $25-$30.

DODGE, J. R. *Red Men of the Ohio Valley.* Illustrated. Cloth. Springfield, Ohio, 1859. First edition. $50-$75. Springfield, 1860. Second edition. $50.

DODGE, M. E. *The Irvington Stories.* Frontispiece, 4 plates. Cloth. New York, 1865. (By Mary Mapes Dodge.) First edition. $50-$75. Author's first book.

DODGE, M. E. *Hans Brinker; or, The Silver Skates.* Frontispiece, 3 plates. Cloth. New York, 1866. (By Mary Mapes Dodge.) First edition. $200-$250. New York, 1876. Cloth. With a new postscript by the author. $25.

DODGE, Mary Mapes. See Dodge, M. E.

DODGE, Mary Mapes. *Donald and Dorothy.* Illustrated. Cloth. Boston, 1883. First American edition. $40-$50.

DODGE, Orvil. *Heroes of Battle Rock.* 21 pp., printed wrappers. No place (Myrtle Point, Ore.?), 1904. First edition. $30 (A, 1968).

DODGE, Orvil. *Pioneer History of Coos and Curry Counties, Oregon.* Illustrated. Cloth. Salem, Ore., 1898. First edition. $50-$75. Binding stained and warped, $37.50.

DODGE, Richard Irving. See *A Living Issue.*

DODGE, Richard Irving. *Our Wild Indians.* Illustrated. Cloth. Hartford, 1882. First edition. $35-$50. (See *A Living Issue.*)

DODGE, Richard Irving. *The Plains of the Great West and Their Inhabitants.* Illustrated, folding map. Cloth. New York, 1877. First edition. $35-$50.

DODGE, Theodore A. *Riders of Many Lands.* 19 illustrations by Frederic Remington. Cloth. New York, 1894. First edition. $40-$65.

DODGE, William Sumner. *Oration: "Liberty, Her Struggles, Perils and Triumphs."* 30 pp., wrappers. San Francisco, 1868. First edition. $20-$25.

DODGE, William Sumner. *A Waif of the War; or, The History of the 75th Illinois Infantry.* Cloth. Chicago, 1866. $50.

DODGSON, Campbell (editor). *An Iconography of the Engravings of Stephen Gooden.* Illustrated. Buckram. London, 1944. One of 500. $30-$50. Another issue: Buckram, vellum spine, with original proof frontispiece (etching) signed by Gooden. One of 160. Boxed. $160.

DODGSON, Charles L. See Carroll, Lewis. Also see *An Index to "In Memoriam."*

DODGSON, Charles L. *Lawn Tennis Tournaments.* 10 pp., sewed, without wrappers. London, 1883. First edition. $100-$150.

DODGSON, Charles L. *Euclid and His Modern Rivals.* Charts and diagrams. Red cloth. London, 1879. First edition. $35-$50.

DODSON, W. C. (editor). *Campaigns of Wheeler and His Calvalry, 1862-1865.* Cloth. Atlanta, 1899. First edition. $40-$50.

DOLBEN, Digby Mackworth. *The Poems of Digby Mackworth Dolben.* Edited by Robert Bridges. Portrait, plates. Boards, cloth spine, paper label. London, 1911. First edition. $60-$75.

DOMESTIC Cookery: The Experienced American Housekeeper. Calf. New York, 1823. Worn at hinges, $25-35.

DOMESTIC Manners of the Americans. 24 plates. 2 vols., cloth, paper labels. London, 1832. (By Frances Trollope.) First edition. $100-$150. New York, 1832. Cloth. First American edition. $100-$150.

DONAN, P. *Gold Fields of Baker County, Eastern Oregon.* Folding map. 36 pp., wrappers. Portland, Ore., no date (1898). First edition. $35-$40.

DON Juan. 6 vols., boards, paper labels (*Don Juan,* 1819, followed by books of same title containing Cantos II, IV, and V; VI, VII, and VIII; IX, X, and XI; XII, XIII, and XIV; XV and XVI). London, 1819-21-23-23-23-24. (By George Gordon Noel, Lord Byron.) First editions. $1,000 and up. Rebound in three-quarters morocco, $200

DONLEAVY, J. P. *The Ginger Man.* Green wrappers. Paris, no date (1955). First edition. $45-$65. Author's first book.

DONNE, John. *Complete Poetry and Selected Prose.* Edited by John Hayward. Blue morocco. London, 1929. Nonesuch Press. One of 675. Boxed. $75-$100. Another issue: Thin paper edition. $150-$200.

DONNE, John. *Love Poems.* Portrait. Vellum. London, 1923. Nonesuch Press. Limited edition on handmade paper. $100-$150. Another issue: Boards, vellum spine. One of 1,250. $50-$75.

DONOHO, M. H. *Circle-dot, a True Story of Cowboy Life 40 Years Ago.* Frontispiece. Cloth. Topeka, 1907. First edition. $30-$35.

DOOLITTLE, Hilda. See D., H.; Helforth, John.

DOOMED City (The). Folding map. 54 pp., wrappers. Detroit, 1871. (By Charles H. Mackintosh.) $25-$35.

DORMAN, Caroline. *Wild Flowers of Louisiana.* Illustrated. Cloth. New York, 1934. $35-$50.

DORN, Edward. *Gunslinger.* Two volumes. Books I and II. Cloth. Los Angeles, 1968, 1969. Black Sparrow Press, Volume I limited to 100 numbered and signed copies; Volume II limited to 250 numbered and signed copies. Acetate jacket for Book II. $60-$75.

DORN, Edward. *The Shoshoneans.* Photographs. Oblong, cloth. New York, 1966. First edition. In dust jacket. $35.

DOS PASSOS, John. See Cendrars, Blaise.

DOS PASSOS, John. *Airways, Inc.* Blue boards and cloth. New York, no date (1928). First edition. In dust jacket. $40-$50.

DOS PASSOS, John. *The Bitter Drink.* No place, no date (San Francisco, 1939). Grabhorn Press. One of 35. $150-$200.

DOS PASSOS, John. *Facing the Chair: Story of the Americanization of Two Foreignborn Workmen.* Wrappers. Boston, 1927. First edition. $40-$50.

DOS PASSOS, John. *Ford and Hearst.* San Francisco, 1940. Grabhorn Press. One of 35. $100-$150.

DOS PASSOS, John. *The 42nd Parallel.* Decorated orange boards and cloth. New York, 1930. First edition (so stated). In dust jacket. $35-$50. Lacking jacket, $20.

DOS PASSOS, John. *Most Likely to Succeed.* Cloth. New York, no date (1951). First edition. One of 1,000 signed. In dust jacket. $25.

DOS PASSOS, John. *1919.* Orange cloth. New York, no date (1932). First edition (so stated). In dust jacket. $25.

DOS PASSOS, John. *Number One.* Gray and pink cloth. Boston, 1943. First edition. In dust jacket. $35-$40.

DOS PASSOS, John. *One Man's Initiation—1917.* Pale-blue cloth. London, no date (1920). First edition, with "First published in 1920" on copyright page. In dust jacket. $100-$135. Author's first book. New York, 1922. Red cloth, paper label. First American edition. One of 500 from English sheets. In dust jacket. $50-$75.

DOS PASSOS, John. *A Pushcart at the Curb.* Pictorial boards and cloth, paper label. New York, no date (1922). First edition, first state, with "GHD" insignia on copyright page. In dust jacket. $35-$50.

DOS PASSOS, John. *Rosinante to the Road Again.* Yellow boards and cloth, paper labels. New York, no date (1922). First edition, first state, with "GHD" on copyright page. In dust jacket. $35-$50.

DOS PASSOS, John. *Three Soldiers.* Black cloth. New York, no date (1921). First edition, first state, with "signing" for "singing" on page 213. In dust jacket. $40-$60.

DOS PASSOS, John. *U.S.A.* *(The 42nd Parallel, 1919, The Big Money).* Illustrated by Reginald Marsh. 3 vols., buckram. Boston, 1946. First illustrated edition. One of 365 signed. Boxed. $100-$125. Trade edition: 3 vols., cloth. $35-$50.

DOS PASSOS, John. *The Villages Are the Heart of Spain.* Cloth. Chicago, no date (1937). First edition, limited and numbered. $35-$50.

DOUGHTY, William. *The Physical Geography of the North Pacific Ocean and Peculiarities of Its Circulation.* 27 pp., wrappers. Augusta, Ga., 1867. First edition. $30-$40.

DOUGHTY, Charles M. *Travels in Arabia Deserta.* Illustrated, folding map in pocket. 2 vols., cloth. Cambridge, England, 1888. First edition. $200-$250. London, 1921. 2 vols., cloth. In dust jackets. $50-$75.

DOUGLAS, Lord Alfred. *In Excelsis.* Cloth. London, 1924. First edition. One of 100 signed. In dust jacket. $30-$40.

DOUGLAS, Lord Alfred. *My Friendship with Oscar Wilde.* Boards and cloth. New York, 1932. $25-$30.

DOUGLAS, Lord Alfred. *Oscar Wilde and Myself.* Cloth. London, 1914. First edition. In dust jacket. $25-$35.

DOUGLAS, Lord Alfred. *Poèmes.* Wrappers. Paris, 1896. First edition. One of 20 (25?) on Hollande paper. $50-$75. Ordinary issue: $25.

DOUGLAS, C. L. *Cattle Kings of Texas.* Illustrated. Cloth. Dallas, no date (1939). First edition. $25-$35. Second edition, same date: Rawhide. $50-$75.

DOUGLAS, C. L. *Famous Texas Feuds.* Illustrated. Decorated cloth and leather. Dallas, no date (1936). First edition. In dust jacket. $25-$35.

DOUGLAS, C. L. *The Gentlemen in White Hats.* Illustrated. Cloth. Dallas, no date (1934). First edition. In dust jacket. $25-$30.

DOUGLAS, David. *Journal Kept by David Douglas During His Travels in North America 1823-27.* Portrait. Cloth. London, 1914. First edition. One of 500. $95-$125.

DOUGLAS, George. *The House with the Green Shutters.* Cloth. London, 1901. (By George Douglas Brown.) First edition. $50-$60.

DOUGLAS, James. *The Gold Fields of Canada.* 18 pp., wrappers. Quebec, 1863. $100-$150.

DOUGLAS, Norman. See Bey, Pilaff; Douglass, G. Norman; McDonald, Edward D.; Normyx. Also see *The Blue Grotto and Its Literature; Disiecta Membra; Index; Some Antiquarian Notes; Three Monographs.*

DOUGLAS, Norman. *Alone.* Red cloth. London, 1921. First edition, first issue, with Postscript on page 140 and erratum slip facing page 156. In dust jacket, $35-$50.

DOUGLAS, Norman. *The Angel of Manfredonia.* Boards and cloth. San Francisco, 1929. One of 225 signed. $35-$40.

DOUGLAS, Norman. *Birds and Beasts of the Greek Anthology.* Frontispiece. Blue boards, paper label. No place (Florence, Italy), 1927. First edition. One of 500 signed. In dust jacket. $100-$125.

DOUGLAS, Norman. *Capri: Materials for a Description of the Island.* Illustrated. Boards and cloth, leather label. Florence, 1930. First edition. One of 525 (500?) signed. $100-$150. Another issue: Blue cloth. De luxe issue. One of 100 (103?) signed. $200-$250.

DOUGLAS, Norman. *D. H. Lawrence and Maurice Magnus.* Portrait frontispiece. Tan wrappers. No place (Florence), 1924 (actually, 1925). First edition, with pink printed price slip tipped in. $30-$50.

DOUGLAS, Norman. *Experiments.* Boards, paper label. No place (Florence), 1925. First edition. One of 300 signed. In dust jacket. $50-$75.

DOUGLAS, Norman. *Fountains in the Sand.* Illustrated. Blue cloth, blocked in white. London, no date (1912). First edition, first state of binding; first issue, with 16 plates. $35-$50.

DOUGLAS, Norman. *How About Europe?* Decorated boards. No place (Florence), 1929. First edition. One of 550 signed. In dust jacket. $50-$75. London, 1930. Orange cloth. In dust jacket. $10.

DOUGLAS, Norman. *In the Beginning.* Printed boards, leather label. No place (Florence), 1927. First edition. One of 700 signed. In dust jacket. $72. New York, no date (1928). Boards. First American edition. In dust jacket. $35.

DOUGLAS, Norman. *The Last of the Medici.* Frontispiece, other plates. Maroon boards, leather label. Florence, no date (1930). First edition. One of 365 signed. $25-$35.

DOUGLAS, Norman. *Late Harvest.* Brown cloth. London, 1946. First edition. In dust jacket. $35.

DOUGLAS, Norman. *London Street Games.* Buckram. London, no date (1916). St. Catherine Press. First edition. $75-$100. Also, $53 (A, 1971); $80 and $24 (A, 1968). London, no date (1931). Boards and cloth. Second edition. One of 110 signed. $120. Also, $72 (A, 1969). Trade issue: $15.

DOUGLAS, Norman. *Looking Back: An Autobiographical Excursion.* Illustrated. 2 vols., boards and buckram. London, 1933. First edition. One of 535 signed. In dust jacket. $100-$150. Also, $72 (A, 1969). New York, 1933. Brown cloth. First American edition. In dust jacket. $20-$25. Lacking jacket, $6 and $15.

DOUGLAS, Norman. *Nerinda (1901).* Orange boards. Florence, 1929. First edition. One of 475 signed. In dust jacket. Boxed. $35-$50.

DOUGLAS, Norman. *Old Calabria.* Brown buckram. London, no date (1915). First edition, first issue, with white end papers. In dust jacket. $50-$75. Boston, 1915. Light-green cloth. First American edition. In dust jacket. $50.

DOUGLAS, Norman. *One Day.* Portraits. Full scarlet leather. Chapelle-Beauville, France, 1929. Hours Press. First edition. One of 200 on Rives paper, signed. $75-$100. Another issue: Boards. One of 300. $35-$50.

DOUGLAS, Norman. *Paneros.* Gold cloth, leather label. Florence, no date (1931). First edition. One of 250 signed. In dust jacket. Boxed. $150-$200. London, 1931. Boards and cloth. First English edition. One of 630 (600? 650?). In dust jacket. $75-$100. New York, 1932. Illustrated. Vellum. First American edition. One of 750. Boxed. $25-$35.

DOUGLAS, Norman. *Siren Land.* Frontispiece portrait, plates and map. Cloth. London, 1911. First edition. $150-$200. New York, no date (1923). "New and revised edition." In dust jacket. $25.

DOUGLAS, Norman. *Some Limericks.* Gold-colored linen. No place (Florence), 1928. First edition. One of 110 signed. $225. Also, $132 (A, 1971). No place (Florence), 1929. Wrappers. $75-$100. Also, $43.20 (A, 1969). Another issue: Buckram. $75-$100. Also, $52.80 (A, 1969). No place, no date (Chicago, about 1928-30?). Buckram. First American edition. $35-$50. Second impression. $24 (A, 1969). Boston, 1942. Boards and leather. "4th Continental Edition." Boxed. $50.

DOUGLAS, Norman. *South Wind.* Brown cloth. London, no date (1917). First edition. $150-$200. London, 1922. Cloth. One of 150 on blue paper, signed. $100-$150. New York, 1928. Illustrated by Valenti Angelo. One of 250 signed by Douglas. Boxed. $35-$50. Chicago, 1929. Illustrated. 2 vols., buckram. In dust jacket. Boxed. $25-$35. Another issue: 2 vols., in one, half blue morocco. One of 40 signed. $50-$75. New York, 1932. Limited Editions Club. Cloth. Boxed. $15-$20.

DOUGLAS, Norman. *Summer Islands: Ischia and Ponza.* Blue cloth. London, no date (1931). First edition. One of 500. In dust jacket. $50-$60. First American edition: No place (New York), 1931. The Colophon. Illustrated. Cloth. One of 550 signed. Boxed. $35-$50.

DOUGLAS, Norman. *They Went.* Lavender cloth. London, 1920. First edition. In dust jacket. $25. New York, 1921. Cloth. $10.

DOUGLAS, Norman. *Together.* Illustrated. Cloth. London, 1923. First edition. One of 275 on handmade paper, signed. In dust jacket. Boxed. $50-$75. Trade edition: Cloth. In dust jacket. $35-$50.

DOUGLASS, G. Norman. *Contribution to an Avifauna of Baden.* 12 pp., without covers. No place, no date (London?, 1894). (By Norman Douglas.) First edition. $125.

DOUGLASS, G. Norman. *On the Darwinian Hypothesis of Sexual Selection.* 16 pp., wrappers. London, 1895. (By Norman Douglas.) First edition. $125.

DOUGLASS, G. Norman. *On the Herpetology of the Grand Duchy of Baden.* 64 pp., pale gray-blue wrappers. London, 1894. (By Norman Douglas.) First edition. $100.

DOUGLASS, G. Norman. *Report on the Pumice Stone Industry of the Lipari Islands.* 8 pp. London, 1895. (By Norman Douglas.) First edition. One of 125. $100.

DOW, George Francis. *The Arts and Crafts in New England.* Illustrated. Half cloth. Topsfield, Mass., 1927. First edition. $50-$60.

DOW, George Francis. *The Sailing Ships of New England:* Series Three. Illustrated. Cloth. Salem, Mass., 1928. First edition. In dust jacket. $30-$40.

DOW, George Francis. *Slave Ships and Slaving.* Illustrated. Buckram. Salem, 1923. $50-$60. Another issue: Half cloth. Large paper. One of 97. $150-$200.

DOW, George Francis. *Whale Ships and Whaling.* Illustrated. Buckram. Salem, 1925. First edition. One of 950. $100-$150. Another issue: Half cloth. Large paper. One of 97. $150-$250.

DOW, George Francis, and Edmonds, John H. *The Pirates of the New England Coast.* 29 plates. Cloth. Salem, 1923. First edition. In dust jacket. $50-$75. Another issue: Large paper. One of 84. $150.

DOW, Lorenzo. *The Life and Travels of Lorenzo Dow.* Half calf. Hartford, Conn., 1804. First edition. $250.

DOWDEN, Edward. *A Woman's Reliquary.* Boards, cloth spine. Dundrum, Ireland, 1913. Cuala Press. One of 300. $47.60.

DOWNEY, Fairfax. *Indian-Fighting Army.* Illustrated. Cloth. New York, 1941. First edition. In dust jacket. $50-$75. New York, 1944. Cloth. In dust jacket. $25-$35.

DOWNFALL and Death of King Oedipus (The). 2 parts, blue wrappers, or (later) bound together in blue wrappers. No place, no date (Guildford, England, 1880-81). (By Edward FitzGerald.) First edition. Bound together, $35-$50. (No copies noted singly in parts in many years.)

DOWNIE, William. *Hunting for Gold: Personal Experiences in the Early Days on the Pacific Coast.* Frontispiece. Half morocco or cloth. San Francisco, 1893. First edition. $50-$75.

DOWSON, Ernest. *Decorations: In Verse and Prose.* Vellum. London, 1899. First edition. $50-$75.

DOWSON, Ernest. *The Pierrot of the Minute.* Illustrated by Aubrey Beardsley. Cloth. London, 1897. First edition. One of 300 on handmade paper. $75-$100. Another issue: One of 30 on Japan paper. $125-$150.

DOWSON, Ernest. *The Poems of Ernest Dowson.* Illustrated by Aubrey Beardsley. Cloth. London, 1905. First edition. In dust jacket. $25-$35.

DOWSON, Ernest. *Verses.* Vellum. Cover decorations by Aubrey Beardsley. London, 1896. First edition. One of 30 on Japan paper. $250-$300. Another issue: One of 300 on handmade paper. $75-$100.

DOYLE, A. Conan. See *Beeton's Christmas Annual; Dreamland and Ghostland.*

DOYLE, A. Conan. *The Adventures of Sherlock Holmes.* Illustrated by Sidney Paget. Light-blue cloth. London, 1892. First edition, first binding, lacking lettering on street sign. $150-$300.

DOYLE, A. Conan. *The Case-Book of Sherlock Holmes.* Red cloth. London, no date (1927). First edition. $25-$30.

DOYLE, A. Conan. *The Doings of Raffles Haw.* Cloth. London, 1892. First edition, first binding, smooth blue cloth. $35-$40.

DOYLE, A. Conan. *The Firm of Girdlestone.* Dark red-brown cloth, black lettering. London, 1890. First edition. $35-$40.

DOYLE, A. Conan. *The Great Shadow.* Pictorial wrappers. Bristol, England, 1892. First edition. $100-$150. Also, in cloth. $50-$75.

DOYLE, A. Conan. *The Great Shadow and Beyond the City.* Illustrated. Tan cloth. Bristol, England, no date (1893). First edition. $35-$50.

DOYLE, A. Conan. *His Last Bow.* Red cloth. London, 1917. First edition. $25-$50. New York, 1917. Cloth. First American edition. $15-$20.

DOYLE, A. Conan. *The History of Spiritualism.* 2 vols., cloth. New York, no date (1926). $50-$60.

DOYLE, A. Conan. *The Hound of the Baskervilles.* Illustrated by Sidney Paget. Decorated red cloth. London, 1902. First edition. $100-$150.

DOYLE, A. Conan. *The Land of Mist.* Cloth. London, no date (1926). First edition. In dust jacket. $30-$35.

DOYLE, A. Conan. *The Maracot Deep and Other Stories.* Cloth. London, no date (1929). First edition. In dust jacket. $30-$40.

DOYLE, A. Conan. *The Memoirs of Sherlock Holmes.* Illustrated by Sidney Paget. Dark-blue cloth. London, 1894. First edition. $150-$200.

DOYLE, A. Conan. *Micah Clarke.* Blue cloth. London, 1889. First edition. $35-$50. New York, 1894. Cloth. First American edition. $25.

DOYLE, A. Conan. *The Refugees: A Tale of Two Continents.* 3 vols., green cloth. London, 1893. First edition. $200-$225. Stained, $45. New York, 1893. Illustrated. Cloth. First American edition. $10.

DOYLE, A. Conan. *The Return of Sherlock Holmes.* Cloth. London, 1905. First edition. $50-$60.

DOYLE, A. Conan. *Round the Red Lamp.* Red cloth. London, 1894. First edition. $30-$40.

DOYLE, A. Conan. *The Sign of Four.* Frontispiece. Dark-red cloth. London, 1890. First edition, first issue, with "Spencer Blackett's Standard Library" on spine. $200-$250. Second issue, dated 1890, with Griffith, Farren imprint on spine. $50-$75.

DOYLE, A. Conan. *The Speckled Band.* Stage diagrams. Printed brown wrappers. London, 1912. First edition. $50-$75.

DOYLE, A. Conan. *The Stark Munro Letters.* Frontispiece and vignette title page. Dark-green or blue cloth. London, 1895. First edition. $25-$35. New York, 1895. Red cloth. First American edition. $10-$15.

DOYLE, A. Conan. *A Study in Scarlet.* Illustrated. White wrappers. London, 1888. First edition in book form, first issue, with "younger" correctly spelled in preface. $350-$450. Second issue, "younger" misspelled "youuger." $200 (A, 1962). (For actual first edition, see *Beeton's Christmas Annual.*)

DOYLE, A. Conan. *Uncle Bernac.* Red cloth. London, 1897. First published edition. $25. New York, 1897. Red cloth. First American edition. $10.

DOYLE, A. Conan. *The Valley of Fear.* Frontispiece. Red cloth. London, 1915. First edition. $40.

DOYLE, A. Conan. *The White Company.* 3 vols., dark-red cloth. London, 1891. First edition. $250-$300.

DOYLE, John T. *In the International Arbitral Court of The Hague: The Case of the Pious Fund of California.* 106 pp., unbound. San Francisco, 1906. $75-$85.

DOYLE, John T. *On Behalf of the Roman Catholic Church of Upper California. Points in Reply Submitted by Messrs. Doyle and Doyle of Counsel for the Prelates.* 8 pp., self-wrappers. No place, no date (1902). $25-$35. Another edition: No place, no date (Menlo Park, Calif., 1902). 11 pp., wrappers. $35-$40.

DOYLE, John T. *The Pious Fund Case.* 67 pp., unbound. San Francisco, 1904 (?). $40-$50.

DRAFT of a Constitution Published Under the Direction of a Committee of Citizens of Colorado. Denver, 1875. $45-$50.

DRAGOON Campaigns to the Rocky Mountains. By a Dragoon. Blue cloth. New York, 1836. (By James Hildreth.) First edition. $100-$150.

DRAKE, Benjamin. *The Great Indian Chief of the West.* Illustrated. Cloth. Cincinnati, 1856. Reprint edition of *The Life and Adventures of Black Hawk.* $50-$60.

DRAKE, Benjamin. *The Life and Adventures of Black Hawk.* Portrait and plates. Cloth. Cincinnati, 1838. First edition. $150-$175.

DRAKE, Benjamin. *Life of Tecumseh, and His Brother the Prophet.* Cloth. Cincinnati, 1841. First edition. $35-$50. Cincinnati, 1852. Reprint edition. $25.

DRAKE, Benjamin. *Tales and Sketches of the Queen City.* Cloth. Cincinnati, 1838. First edition. $35-$50.

DRAKE, Benjamin, and Mansfield, E. D. *Cincinnati in 1826.* 2 plates. Leather. Cincinnati, 1827. First edition. $60-$80.

DRAKE, Daniel. *An Account of Epidemic Cholera, as It Appeared in Cincinnati.* 46 pp., wrappers. Cincinnati, 1832. First edition. $75-$100.

DRAKE, Daniel. *Natural and Statistical View, or Picture of Cincinnati and the Miami Country.* 2 folding maps. Printed boards. Cincinnati, 1815. First edition. $150-$250.

DRAKE, Daniel. *Pioneer Life in Kentucky: A Series of Reminiscential Letters from Daniel Drake, M.D., of Cincinnati to His Children.* Portrait. Cloth. Cincinnati, 1870. First edition. $35-$50.

DRAKE, Daniel. *A Practical Treatise on the History, Prevention, and Treatment of Epidemic Cholera.* Cloth, paper spine label. Cincinnati, 1832. First edition. $250-$300.

DRAKE, Daniel. *A Systematic Treatise, Historical, Etiological, and Practical, on the Principal Diseases of the Interior Valley of North America.* Maps and plates. Full leather. Cincinnati, 1850. First edition. $250-$350.

DRAKE, Daniel, and Wright, Guy W. (editors). *The Western Medical and Physical Journal, Original and Eclectic.* Vol. 1. Leatherbound. Cincinnati, 1827-28. $65-$75.

DRAKE, Joseph Rodman. See Croaker.

DRAKE, Joseph Rodman. *The Culprit Fay and Other Poems.* Frontispiece, vignette title page. Blue or purple cloth. New York, 1835. First edition. $100-$150. (Also bound in full morocco.)

DRAKE, Joseph Rodman, and Halleck, Fitz-Greene. *The Croakers.* Green cloth. New York, 1860. One of 250. $50-$60. (See Croaker for first edition.)

DRAKE, Morgan. *Lake Superior Railroad: Letter to the Hon. Lewis Cass.* 24 pp., wrappers. Pontiac, Mich., 1853. $100-$125.

DRANNAN, Capt. William F. *Thirty-one Years on the Plains and in the Mountains.*

Illustrated. Cloth. Chicago, 1899. First edition. $25-$35. Chicago, 1900. $10. Chicago, 1904. $6.

DRAPER, John William. *Human Physiology.* Illustrated. Cloth. New York, 1856. First edition. $75.

DRAPER, John William. *A Treatise on the Forces Which Produce the Organization of Plants.* 4 plates. Cloth. New York, 1844. First edition. $125.

DRAYSON, Capt. Alfred W. *Sporting Scenes Amongst the Kaffirs of South Africa.* 8 colored plates by Harrison Weir. Cloth. London, 1858. First edition. $50.

DRAYTON, John. *Memoirs of the American Revolution.* Portrait, 2 maps. 2 vols., cloth. Charleston, S.C., 1821. First edition. $75-$100.

DRAYTON, John. *A View of South-Carolina.* 2 maps, 2 tables, 3 plates. Boards. Charleston, 1802. First edition. $400-$500. Rebound in half leather, $300 at retail.

DRAYTON, Michael. *Poems.* Edited by J. Payne Collier. Half morocco. London, 1856. Roxburghe Club. $50.

DREAM Drops, or, Stories from Fairy Land. By a Dreamer. Wrappers or cloth. Boston, no date (1887). (By Amy Lowell.) First edition. Wrappers: $600 and up. Also, $220 (A, 1960). Cloth: $350 and up.

DREAM of Gerontius (The). Wrappers. London, 1866. (By John Henry, Cardinal Newman.) First edition, printed dedication "J. H. N. " $750-$1,000.

DREAMLAND and Ghostland: An Original Collection of Tales and Warnings. 3 vols., pictorial red cloth. London, no date (1887). First edition, first binding (red cloth). $200-$225. (Note: Contains 5 stories by A. Conan Doyle, marking his first appearance in book publication.)

DREISER, Theodore. See Davis, Hubert.

DREISER, Theodore. *An American Tragedy.* 2 vols., black cloth, white end papers. New York, 1925. First edition, first issue, with Boni & Liveright imprint. In dust jackets. Boxed. $25-$35. Another (later) issue: 2 vols., blue boards and cloth. First limited edition. One of 795 signed. In dust jackets. Boxed. $50-$75.

DREISER, Theodore. *A Book About Myself.* Ribbed red cloth, white end papers. New York, no date (1922). First edition. In dust jacket. $25-$35.

DREISER, Theodore. *The Carnegie Works at Pittsburgh.* Decorations by Martha Colley. Boards, paper label. Chelsea, no date (New York, 1927). First edition. One of 150. In dust jacket. $25-$30. Another issue: Cloth. One of 27 on Marlowe Antique paper with a manuscript sheet in a special pocket at back of the book. In dust jacket. $100.

DREISER, Theodore. *Chains: Lesser Novels and Stories.* Decorated boards and cloth. New York, 1927. First edition. One of 440 signed. Boxed. $50-$75. Trade edition: Dark-blue cloth. In dust jacket. $10-$15.

DREISER, Theodore. *The Color of a Great City.* Illustrated. Black cloth, white end papers. New York, no date (1923). First edition. In dust jacket. $25-$30.

DREISER, Theodore. *Dawn: A History of Myself.* Boards and cloth. New York, no date (1931). First edition. One of 275 signed. Boxed. $50-$60. Trade edition: Red and black cloth. In dust jacket. $25.

DREISER, Theodore. *Epitaph: A Poem.* Illustrated by Robert Fawcett. Full leather. New York, no date (1929). Heron Press. First edition. One of 200 on Van Gelder paper, signed. Boxed. $50-$75. Another issue: Silk. One of 200 on Keijyo Kami paper, signed. $50-$60. Another: Cloth. One of 700 on Keijyo Kami paper. $40.

DREISER, Theodore. *The Financier.* Mottled light-blue cloth. New York, 1912. First edition, first issue, with "Published October, 1912" and code letters "K-M" on copyright page. In dust jacket. $50-$75.

DREISER, Theodore. *Free, and Other Stories.* Slate-blue cloth. New York, 1918. First edition. In dust jacket. $25-$35.

DREISER, Theodore. *A Gallery of Women.* 2 vols., boards and vellum. New York, 1929. First edition. One of 560 signed. In dust jackets. Boxed. $50-$75. Trade edition: 2 vols., brown cloth. In dust jackets. Boxed. $15-$25.

DREISER, Theodore. *The "Genius."* Ribbed red cloth, white end papers. New York, 1915. First edition, first issue, 1¾ inches thick, and with page 497 so numbered. In dust jacket. $75-$100. Second issue, 1½ inches thick, no number on page 497. In dust jacket. $25-$35.

DREISER, Theodore. *The Hand of the Potter.* Light-green boards and cloth, paper label. New York, 1918. First edition, first issue, with natural linen spine (second issue is blue). In dust jacket. $25-$35.

DREISER, Theodore. *Hey, Rub-A-Dub-Dub!* Dark-blue cloth. New York, 1920. First edition. In dust jacket. $25-$30.

DREISER, Theodore. *A Hoosier Holiday.* Illustrated. Light-green boards and dark-green cloth. New York, 1916. First edition, first issue, with page 173 as an integral leaf. In dust jacket. $25-$35.

DREISER, Theodore. *Jennie Gerhardt.* Frontispiece. Mottled light-blue cloth. New York, 1911. First edition, first issue, with "is" for "it" in line 30 of page 22. In dust jacket. $25-$35. Second issue, text corrected. $20.

DREISER, Theodore. *Moods, Cadenced and Declaimed.* Marbled boards and cloth, white end papers. New York, 1926. First edition. One of 550 signed. Boxed. $35-$50. New York, 1928. Cloth. First trade edition (with new material). In dust jacket. $25.

DREISER, Theodore. *My City.* Colored etchings by Max Pollak. Folio, boards and cloth. New York, no date (1929). First edition. One of 275. $35-$50.

DREISER, Theodore. *Plays of the Natural and the Supernatural.* Light-green boards, linen spine, green end papers. New York, 1916. First edition. With 4-page note, "The Anaesthetic Revelation," tipped in at back. In dust jacket. $35-$50.

DREISER, Theodore. *The Seven Arts: Life, Art and America.* 28 pp., cream wrappers. New York, 1917. First edition. $25-$30.

DREISER, Theodore. *Sister Carrie.* Dark-red cloth, white end papers. New York 1900. First edition. $250-$350. Presentation copy, inscribed and signed, $500. Author's first book. New York, 1907. Colored frontispiece. Cloth. First illustrated edition. $50-$60. New York, 1939. Limited Editions Club. Cloth. Boxed. $30-$40.

DREISER, Theodore. *The Titan.* Mottled light-blue cloth. New York, 1914. First edition. In dust jacket. $25-$30.

DREISER, Theodore. *Tragic America.* Gray cloth. New York, no date (1931). First published edition. In dust jacket. $25. (Note: There also exist a few copies—6 or 12?—of a suppressed prepublication issue bound for the author's private use. Value: About $100 at retail.)

DREISER, Theodore. *A Traveler at Forty.* Illustrated by W. Glackens. Red cloth. New York, 1913. First edition. In dust jacket. $25-$30.

DREISER, Theodore. *Twelve Men.* Blue cloth. New York, 1919. First edition. In dust jacket. $25-$35.

DREW, C. S. *Communication . . . of the Origin and Early Prosecution of the Indian War in Oregon.* 48 pp., sewed. Washington, 1860. First edition. $35-$50.

DRIGGS, George W. *Opening of the Mississippi; or Two Years' Campaigning in the Southwest.* Cloth. Madison, Wis., 1864. First edition. $50-$75.

DRINKWATER, John. *Abraham Lincoln.* Scarlet or purple wrappers, printed label on spine. London, 1918. First edition, with pen-and-ink correction of misprint on page (5). In dust jacket. $35-$50. Another issue: Red boards. In dust jacket. $25.

DRINKWATER, John. *A Book for Bookmen.* Buckram. London, 1926. First edition. One of 50 signed. $25.

DRINKWATER, John. *Loyalties.* Illustrated. Vellum and boards. No place (London), 1918. Beaumont Press. First edition. One of 30 on Japan vellum, signed. $35-$50.

DRINKWATER, John. *Persephone.* Cloth. No place, no date (New York, 1926). First edition. One of 550 signed. $25.

DRINKWATER, John. *Persuasion: Twelve Sonnets.* Wrappers. London, 1921. First edition. One of 50 signed. $20-$25.

DRINKWATER, John. *Poems.* Cloth. Birmingham, England, 1903. First edition. $35-$50. Author's first book.

DRINKWATER, John. *Rupert Brooke: An Essay.* Boards. London, 1916. First edition. One of 115. $20-$25.

DRINKWATER, John. *Tides: A Book of Poems.* Boards and cloth. No place (London), 1917. Beaumont Press. First edition. One of 250. $20-$25. Another issue: One of 20 signed. $35-$50.

DRINKWATER, John, and Rutherston, Albert. *Claud Lovat Fraser: A Story of His Life.* Portrait frontispiece by Rutherston, 39 Fraser illustrations, 20 in color. Cloth. London, 1923. One of 450 signed. $50-$60.

DRIPS, Joseph H. *Three Years Among the Indians in Dakota.* 139 pp., wrappers. Kimball, S.D., 1894. First edition. $400-$500.

DRUMHELLER, "Uncle Dan." *"Uncle Dan" Drumheller Tells Thrills of Western Trails in 1854.* Portraits. Cloth. Spokane, 1925. First edition. $35-$50.

DRURY, Dru, and Westwood, J. O. *Illustrations of Exotic Entomology.* 150 hand-colored plates. 3 vols., half leather. London, 1837. $150-$250.

DRURY, the Rev. P. Shelden (editor). *The Startling and Thrilling Narrative of the Dark and Terrible Deeds of Henry Madison, and His Associate and Accomplice Miss Ellen Stevens, Who Was Executed by the Vigilance Committee of San Francisco, on the 20th September Last.* Illustrated. 36 pp., pictorial wrappers. Cincinnati, no date (1857). First edition. $150-$200. Philadelphia, 1865. $40-$50.

DRYDEN, John. See *Satyr to His Muse; The Works of Virgil.*

DRYDEN, John. *Alexander's Feast.* London, 1904. Essex House. One of 140. $50-$60.

DRYDEN, John. *All for Love.* 2 vols., folio, half vellum. San Francisco, 1929. John Henry Nash printing. One of 250. $50-$75.

DRYDEN, John. *Dramatic Works.* Edited by Montague Summers. 6 vols., buckram and marbled boards. London, 1931-32. Nonesuch Press. $250-$350. Another issue: One of 50 sets on Van Gelder paper. $350-$500.

DRYDEN, John. *Of Dramatick Poesie. Preceded by a Dialogue on Poetic Drama by T. S. Eliot.* Marbled boards, cloth spine. London, 1928. First edition. One of 580. Boxed. $75. Another issue: Boards and vellum. One of 55 signed by Eliot. In dust jacket. Boxed. $150-$200.

DRYDEN, John. *Songs and Poems.* Illustrated. Half cloth. Waltham Saint Lawrence, England, 1957. Golden Cockerel Press. One of 400 (of an edition of 500). $35. Another issue: Specially bound in morocco. One of 100, with a duplicate set of plates. $200-$250.

DRYSDALE, Isabel. *Scenes in Georgia.* Frontispiece. 83 pp., boards and cloth, paper label. Philadelphia, no date (1827). First edition. $50-$60.

DUBLIN Book of Irish Verse (The). See Cooke, John (editor).

DU BOIS, John. *Campaigns in the West, 1856-61: The Journal and Letters of Col. John Du Bois with Pencil Sketches by Joseph Heger.* Plates, folding map. Boards and leather. Tucson, Ariz., 1949. Grabhorn Press. First edition. One of 300 signed. $100-$150.

DU BOIS, John Witherspoon. *Life and Times of William Lowndes Yancey.* 9 plates. Cloth. Birmingham, Ala., 1892. First edition. $50-$60.

DU CHAILLU, Paul. *Stories of the Gorilla Country.* Woodcuts. Pictorial cloth. New York, 1868. First edition. $150-$175.

DUER, John K. (editor). *The Nautilus: A Collection of Select Nautical Tales and Sea Stories.* 48 pp., plain wrappers. New York, 1843. First edition. $25-$35.

DUFF, E. Gordon. *Early English Printing.* Illustrated. Folio, half morocco. London, 1896. One of 300. $75-$100.

DUFF, E. Gordon. *Fifteenth Century English Books.* Facsimile plates. Boards and cloth. Oxford, 1917. $75-$100.

DUFF, E. Gordon. *William Caxton.* Boards and cloth. Chicago, 1905. Caxton Club. One of 145 with an original leaf from Chaucer's *Canterbury Tales* of 1478. $300-$400. Another issue: One of 107 without the leaf. $25-$35.

DUFLOT DE MOFRAS, Eugene. *Travels on the Pacific Coast.* Translated by Marguerite E. Wilbur. 2 folding maps, 8 plates. 2 vols., half leather. Santa Ana, Calif., 1937. $75-$100.

DUFY, Raoul. *Madrigaux.* 25 hand-colored illustrations. Loose sheets in paper folder and slipcase. Paris, no date (1960). One of 200. $100-$150.

DU HAYS, Charles. *The Percheron Horse.* Full-page plates. Vellum. gilt. No place (Gillis Press), 1886. $50-$60.

DUKE, Basil W. *History of Morgan's Cavalry.* Portrait. Cloth. Cincinnati, 1867. First edition. $50-$65. New York, 1906. 9 maps, 4 portraits. Cloth. Revised edition. $35-$40.

DUKE, Basil W. *Reminiscences.* Cloth. Garden City, 1911. First edition. $20-$25.

DU MAURIER, George. *Peter Ibbetson.* Edited and illustrated by George Du Maurier. 2 vols., gray cloth. London, 1892. First English edition, probable first issue, with brown lettering. $25-$50. New York, 1963. Limited Editions Club. Boards. Boxed. $25.

DU MAURIER, George. *Trilby.* 3 vols., gray cloth. London, 1894. First edition. $75-$100. New York, 1894. Cloth. First American edition. $7.50-$10. London, 1895. Illustrated. Half vellum. One of 250 signed. $35-$50. New York, 1895. Vellum. One of 250 signed. $35-$50.

DUN COW (The): An Hyper-Satyrical Dialogue in Verse. 12 leaves, blue wrappers. London, 1808. (By Walter Savage Landor.) First edition. $1,000 and up (?). Also, half calf, $648 (A, 1969).

DUNBAR, Paul (Laurence). *Oak and Ivy.* Blue cloth. Dayton, Ohio, 1893. (By Paul Laurence Dunbar.) First edition. $75-$100. Author's first book.

DUNBAR, Paul Lawrence. *L'il Gal.* Photographs by Leigh Richmond Miner. Pictorial green cloth. New York, 1904. (By Paul Laurence Dunbar.) First edition $25.

DUNBAR, Paul Lawrence. *Majors and Minors: Poems.* Frontispiece portrait. Cloth. No place, no date (Toledo, 1895). (By Paul Laurence Dunbar.) First edition, probable first binding, with beveled edges. $60-$80.

DUNCAN, Andrew. *The Edinburgh New Dispensatory.* 6 plates. Contemporary calf. Edinburgh, 1803. First edition. $25-$35. Edinburgh, 1804. Calf. Second edition. $18. Worcester, Mass., 1805. Calf. $25.

DUNCAN, John M. *Travels Through Part of the United States and Canada in 1818 and 1819.* 14 maps and plates. 2 vols., calf. Glasgow, 1823. First edition. $125-$150. Also, $120 (A, 1969). New York, 1823. 2 vols., half calf. First American edition. $35-$50.

DUNCAN, L. Wallace. *History of Montgomery County, Kansas.* Half leather. Iola, Kan., 1903. First edition. $50-$60.

DUNCAN, L. Wallace. *History of Wilson and Neosho Counties, Kansas.* Half leather. Fort Scott, Kan., 1902. First edition. $50-$60.

DUNCAN, Robert. *A Book of Resemblances.* Illustrated by Jess. Cloth. New Haven, 1966. First edition. One of 203 signed. In dust jacket. $40-$60.

DUNCAN, Robert. *Derivations.* Cloth. Fulcrum Press, 1968. First edition. One of 150 signed. In dust jacket. $15-$20.

DUNCAN, Robert. *Faust Foutu.* Wrappers. No place, no date ("Stinson Beach," 1959). First edition. One of 50 signed and including a special color drawing by the author. $35-$45.

DUNCAN, Robert. *Heavenly City, Earthly City.* Illustrated by Mary Fabilli. White boards. Berkeley, Calif., no date (1947). First edition. In dust jacket. $35-$50. Author's first book.

DUNCAN, Robert. *Letters.* Illustrated. Decorated wrappers. Highlands, N.C., 1958. First edition. One of 510. $40-$50.

DUNCAN, Robert. *65 Drawings.* Cloth. Los Angeles, 1970. Black Sparrow Press. First edition. One of 300 signed. Boxed. $25-$30.

DUNDASS, Samuel. *Journal of Samuel Rutherford Dundass.* 60 pp., wrappers. Steubenville, Ohio, 1857. First edition. $1,000 and up.

DUNIWAY, Mrs. Abigail J. *Captain Gray's Company; or, Crossing the Plains and Living in Oregon.* Rose-colored cloth. Portland, Ore., 1859. First edition. $500-$750.

DUNLAP, William. *The Life of Charles Brockden Brown.* Frontispiece. 2 vols., blue-gray boards, gray-green spine. Philadelphia, 1815. First edition. $50-$100. (Note: Contains first printing of "Memoirs of Carwin" and other Brown items; see Brown entry.)

DUNLAP, William. *A History of the American Theatre.* Purple muslin, paper spine label. New York, 1832. First edition. $75-$100. London, 1833. 2 vols., half calf. First English edition. $50.

DUNLAP, William. *History of the New Netherlands.* Illustrated, including 2 folding maps. 2 vols., boards and cloth, or cloth. New York, 1839 (and 1840). First edition, with errata leaf. $75-$100.

DUNLAP, William. *History of the Rise and Progress of the Arts of Design in the United States.* 2 vols., green boards and cloth. New York, 1834. First edition. $100-$150. Boston, 1918. Plates. 3 vols., cloth. $75-$100.

DUNLAP, William. *Memoirs of the Life of George Frederick Cooke.* Frontispieces. 2 vols., boards. New York, 1813. First edition. $50.

DUNLAP, William. *A Narrative of the Events Which Followed Bonaparte's Campaign, etc.* Frontispiece. 5 plates. Leather. Hartford, 1814. First edition. $50-$100.

DUNLAP, William, and Clarke, Francis L. *The Life of the Most Noble Arthur, Marquis and Earl of Wellington.* Frontispiece and map. Boards. New York, 1814. First edition. $50-$60. Rebacked, $30.

DUNN, Jacob Piatt. *Massacres of the Mountains.* Folding map. Pictorial cloth. New York, 1886. First edition. $75-$100.

DUNN, John. *History of the Oregon Territory and British North-American Fur Trade.* Folding map. Cloth. London, 1844. First edition. $150-$250.

DUNN, John. *The Oregon Territory and the British North American Fur Trade.* Wrappers. Philadelphia, 1845. First American edition (of *History of the Oregon Territory, etc.*). $150-$175.

DUNNE, Finley Peter. See *Mr. Dooley in Peace and in War*.

DUNNE, Finley Peter. *Mr. Dooley at His Best.* Half cloth. New York, 1938. One of 520, with a page of the original manuscript. $20-$25.

DUNSANY, Lord. *The Chronicles of Rodriguez.* Frontispiece. Light-brown cloth, vellum spine, leather label. London, 1922. One of 500 signed. $35-$50.

DUNSANY, Lord. *The Compromise of the King of the Golden Isles.* Illustrated by T. M. Cleland. Boards and cloth. New York, 1924. Grolier Club. One of 300. $35-$50.

DUNSANY, Lord. *Five Plays.* Illustrated. Cloth. London, 1914. First edition. $35-$50.

DUNSANY, Lord. *The Gods of Pegana.* Boards and cloth. London, 1905. First edition. In dust jacket. $100-$125.

DUNSANY, Lord. *A Journey.* Dark-blue boards. London, no date (1944). First edition. One of 250 initialed by the author. Boxed. $50.

DUNSANY, Lord. *The King of Elfland's Daughter.* Frontispiece. Orange cloth, vellum spine, leather label. London, no date (1924). One of 250 signed. $35-$50.

DUNSANY, Lord. *Selections from the Writings of Lord Dunsany.* Edited and with introduction by William Butler Yeats. Boards and linen. Churchtown, Dundrum, Ireland, 1912. Cuala Press. One of 250. $100-$150.

DUNSANY, Lord. *Time and the Gods.* Illustrated. Orange cloth, vellum spine, leather label. London, no date (1922). One of 250 signed. In dust jacket. $50-$60.

DU PONCEAU, M. *Mémoire au Sujet des Prétentions du Gouvernement des États Unis sur l'Alluvion du Fleuve Mississippi, etc.* Nouvelle-Orléans, 1808. Half calf. First edition. $150.

DuPONT, Samuel F. *Extracts from Private Journal-Letters of Capt. S. F. DuPont.* Three-quarters morocco. Wilmington, Del., 1885. First edition. $500 and up. (Note: Fewer than 50 copies printed.)

DuPONT, Samuel F. *Official Dispatches and Letters of Rear Admiral DuPont, 1846-48; and 1861-63.* Half leather. Wilmington, Del., 1883. First edition. $200-$250.

DUNTHORNE, Gordon. *Flower and Fruit Prints of the 18th and Early 19th Centuries.* Illustrated. Folio, cloth. Washington, 1938. One of 750, with folidng plate listing subscribers. Boxed. $250-$350. Lacking the subscriber plate, $200-$250.

DUNTON, John. *Letters Written from New-England.* Half morocco. Boston, 1867. Prince Society. One of 150. $25-$35.

DURRELL, Lawrence. See Norden, Charles; Royidis, Emmanuel. Also see *The Fifth Antiquarian Book Fair.*

DURRELL, Lawrence. *The Alexandria Quartet.* Cloth. London, no date (1962). First edition. (First publication of original four books of the "Quartet" series under this title.) Limited to 500 numbered and signed copies. Boxed. $150-$200. Also, $67 and $100 (A, 1970). New York, no date (1962). Marbled boards. First American edition. One of 199 signed. Boxed. $75-$100. Also, $40 (A, 1967).

THE SIGN OF FOUR

BY
A. CONAN DOYLE

AUTHOR OF
MICAH CLARKE,' 'THE FIRM OF GIRDLESTONE,' 'THE CAPTAIN
OF THE POLESTAR,' ETC., ETC.

LONDON
SPENCER BLACKETT
MILTON HOUSE, 35, ST. BRIDE STREET, E.C
1890
[All rights reserved]

EZRA POUND
HIS METRIC AND POETRY

NEW YORK · ALFRED A. KNOPF · 1917

By T. S. Eliot

THE WASTE LAND

BY
T. S. ELIOT

"NAM Sibyllam quidem Cumis ego ipse oculis meis
vidi in ampulla pendere, et cum illi pueri dicerent:
Σίβυλλα τί θέλεις; respondebat illa: ἀποθανεῖν θέλω."

NEW YORK
BONI AND LIVERIGHT
1922

LAST RAID

OF THE

DALTONS

A RELIABLE RECITAL OF THE BATTLE
WITH THE BANDITS
...AT...

COFFEYVILLE, KANSAS
OCTOBER 5, 1892

By DAVID STEWART ELLIOTT
Editor Coffeyville Journal

FIRST EDITION
Illustrated by E. A. FILLEAU

1892
COFFEYVILLE JOURNAL PRINT,
COFFEYVILLE, KANSAS.

DURRELL, Lawrence. *Balthazar*. Cloth. London, 1958. First edition. In dust jacket. $25-$35.

DURRELL, Lawrence. *Beccafico*. Translated and edited by F. J. Temple. Wrappers. La Licorne, 1963. First edition. One of 150 signed. $75.

DURRELL, Lawrence. *Bitter Lemons*. Illustrated. Cloth. London, 1957. First edition. In dust jacket. $35-$40.

DURRELL, Lawrence. *The Black Book: An Agon*. Decorated wrappers. Paris, 1938. Obelisk Press. First edition, with erratum slip pasted to title page. $375-$450. Also, $228 (A, 1969), $240 (A, 1968).

DURRELL, Lawrence. *Bromo Bombastes, a Fragment from a Laconic Drama, by Gaffer Peeslake*. Boards. London, 1933. Caduceus Press. One of 100. $500-$600. Also, $392 (A, 1966).

DURRELL, Lawrence. *Clea*. Cloth. London, no date (1960). First edition. In dust jacket. $25-$35.

DURRELL, Lawrence. *Deus Loci*. Printed blue-gray wrappers. Ischia, Italy, 1950. First edition. One of 200 signed. $75-$100.

DURRELL, Lawrence. *In Arcadia*. Music by Wallace Southam. Wrappers. London, 1968. Turret Books. First edition. One of 100 signed. $50.

DURRELL, Lawrence. *Justine*. Cloth. London, 1957. First edition. In dust jacket. $35-$45.

DURRELL, Lawrence. *La Descente du Styx*. Translated by F. J. Temple. Wrappers. No place, no date (Paris, 1964). First edition. One of 250 signed. $50-$75.

DURRELL, Lawrence. *Mountolive*. Cloth. London, 1958. First edition. In dust jacket. $30-$35.

DURRELL, Lawrence. *Nothing Is Lost, Sweet Self*. Music by Wallace Southam. Pictorial wrappers. No place, no date (London, 1967). Turret Books. First edition. One of 100 signed. $35-$50.

DURRELL, Lawrence. *On Seeming to Presume*. Cloth. London, no date (1948). In dust jacket. $40-$60.

DURRELL, Lawrence. *Pied Piper of Lovers*. Cloth. London, 1935. First edition. $250 and up? Author's first novel; exceedingly scarce.

DURRELL, Lawrence. *A Private Country: Poems*. Gray cloth. London, no date (1943). First edition. $35-$50.

DURRELL, Lawrence. *Private Drafts*. Illustrated. Pictorial wrappers. Nicosia, Italy, 1955. Proodos Press. One of 100 signed. $30-$40.

DURRELL, Lawrence. *Prospero's Cell*. Illustrated. Cloth, London, no date (1945). First edition. In dust jacket. $25-$30.

DURRELL, Lawrence. *Quaint Fragment*. Portrait. Blue wrappers, or rose-red boards. No place (London), 1931. Cecil Press. First edition. Of two known published copies, the one in rose-red boards was catalogued by a New York bookseller (about 1963) at $750. Author's first book.

DURRELL, Lawrence. *Sappho: A Play in Verse*. Cloth. London, no date (1950). First edition. In dust jacket. $25-$30.

DURRELL, Lawrence. *Six Poems, from the Greek of Sekilianos and Seferis*. Printed wrappers. Rhodes, 1946. First edition. Limited (50?). $150-$250.

DURRELL, Lawrence. *Ten Poems*. Cloth. London, 1932. Caduceus Press. First edition. One of 12. $200 and up.

DURRELL, Lawrence. *Zero and Asylum in the Snow.* Wrappers. Rhodes, 1946. First edition. $60-$85. Berkeley, Calif., 1947. White boards. First American edition. In dust jacket. $25.

DUSTIN, Fred. *The Custer Tragedy.* Folding map in pocket. Cloth. Ann Arbor, Mich., 1939. First edition. One of 200. $200-$250.

DUTCHMAN'S Fireside (The). 2 vols., cloth. New York, 1831. (By James Kirke Paulding.) First edition, first issue, with date of May, 1831, in ad on back cover of Vol. 1. $150.

DUVAL, John C. *The Adventures of Big-Foot Wallace.* 8 plates. Green cloth. Philadelphia, 1871. First edition. $50-$75.

DUVAL, John C. *Early Times in Texas.* Cloth. Austin, Tex., 1892. First edition. $35-$50.

DUVAL, K. D., and Smith, Sydney Goodsir (editors). *Hugh MacDiarmid: A Festschrift.* Cloth. Edinburgh, no date (1962). First edition. One of 50 with holograph poem signed by MacDiarmid tipped in. In dust jacket. $40-$60.

DWIGGINS, W. A. *Towards a Reform of the Paper Currency.* Boards and cloth. New York, 1932. Limited Editions Club. One of 452 signed. $125-$150. Also, $80 (A, 1968).

DWIGHT, Timothy. *A Discourse on Some Events of the Last Century.* Printed gray-blue wrappers. New Haven, 1801. First edition. $150-$200.

DWIGHT, Timothy. *The Psalms of David, Imitated in the Language of the New Testament.* Leather. Hartford, 1801. First edition. $35-$50.

DWIGHT, Timothy. *Travels in New-England and New York.* 3 maps. 4 vols., boards. New Haven, 1821-22. First edition, with errata slip in last volume. $100-$150.

DWINELLE, John W. *The Colonial History of the City of San Francisco.* Map. Printed wrappers. San Francisco, 1863. First edition. $300-$400. Also, $300 (A, 1968). San Francisco, 1866. Map, 3 plates. Third edition, second issue, with inserted slip "No. CLXXI-Bis" and 7 pages of addenda. $500-$600. Also, $300 (A, 1968), $500 (A, 1960).

DYER, Mrs. D. B. *"Fort Reno," or Picturesque "Cheyenne and Arrapahoe Army Life," Before the Opening of Oklahoma.* 10 plates. Cloth. New York, 1896. First edition. $35-$50.

DYER, Frederick H. *A Compendium of the War of the Rebellion.* Cloth. Des Moines, 1908. First edition. $75-$100.

DYKES, W. R. *The Genus Iris.* Colored and plain plates. Folio, cloth. Cambridge, England, 1913. $100-$150. Another issue: Half morocco. $250-$300.

DYLLIA Nova Quinque Heroum atque Heroidum. 2 parts in one, boards. Oxford, 1815. (By Walter Savage Landor.) First edition. $300-$400. Also, $192 (A, 1968).

E

E., A. *By Still Waters, Lyrical Poems Old and New.* By A. E. Boards. Dundrum, Ireland, 1906. Dun Emer Press. (By George W. Russell.) First edition. One of 200. $75-$85. Also, $52.80 (A, 1969).

E., A. *Collected Poems.* By A. E. Cloth. London, 1913. (By George W. Russell.) First edition. In dust jacket. $25-$35.

E., A. *The Dublin Strike.* By A. E. 7 pp., pictorial wrappers. Dublin, no date (1913). (By George W. Russell.) First edition. $35-$40.

E., A. *Gods of War, with Other Poems.* By A. E. Sewed. Dublin, 1915. (By George W. Russell.) First edition. $25-$30.

E., A. *The Hero in Man.* By A. E. Printed wrappers. No place (Orpheus Press), no date (1909). (By George W. Russell.) First edition. $25-$30.

E., A. *Homeward: Songs by the Way.* By A. E. Wrappers. Dublin, 1894. (By George W. Russell.) First edition. $35-$50. Author's first book.

E., A. *Midsummer Eve.* By A. E. Boards. New York, 1928. (By George W Russell.) First edition. One of 450 signed. $30-$40.

E., A. *The Nuts of Knowledge.* By A. E. Boards, linen spine. Dundrum, Ireland, 1903. Dun Emer Press. (By George W. Russell.) First edition. One of 200. $80-$90.

E., A. *Salutations.* By A. E. Wrappers. London, 1917. (By George W. Russell.) First edition. One of 25 signed. $132 (A, 1970).

E., A. *Some Passages from the Letters of A. E. to W. B. Yeats.* Boards, linen spine. Dublin, 1936. Cuala Press. (By George W. Russell.) One of 300. In tissue dust jacket. $75-$100.

EARHART, John F. *The Color Printer.* Cloth. Cincinnati, 1892. $60-$100.

EARLE, Ferdinand (editor). *The Lyric Year.* Cloth. New York, 1912. First edition, first state, with "careful gentlemen" for "polite gentleman" in line 13 of page 25. In dust jacket. $35-$50. (Note: Contains first appearance of Edna St. Vincent Millay's "Renascence.")

EARLE, Swepson, and Skinner, Percy G. *Maryland's Colonial Eastern Shore.* Map. Cloth. Baltimore, 1916. First edition. $40-$50.

EARLE, Thomas (compiler). *The Life, Travels and Opinions of Benjamin Lundy.* Colored folding map. Cloth. Philadelphia, 1847. First edition. $75-$125.

EARLY, Gen. Jubal A. *Autobiographical Sketch and Narrative of the War Between the States.* Cloth. Philadelphia, 1912. $50-$60.

EARLY, Lieut. Gen. Jubal A. *A Memoir of the Last Year of the War for Independence in the Confederate States of America.* Wrappers. Lynchburg, Va., 1867. $50-$60. Rebound in buckram, $35.

EASTAWAY, Edward. *Poems.* Portrait frontispiece. Gray boards, paper label. London, 1917. (By Edward Thomas.) First edition. $75-$100.

EASTMAN, Mary H. *The American Aboriginal Portfolio.* Half leather. Philadelphia, no date (1853). First edition. $75-$100.

EASTON, John. *A Narrative of the Causes Which Led to Phillip's Indian War.* Map. Cloth. Albany, N.Y., 1858. First edition. $60-$75.

EATON, Daniel Cady. *The Ferns of North America.* 2 vols., half morocco. Salem, Mass., 1879-80. First edition. $40-$60.

EATON, Rachel Caroline. *John Ross and the Cherokee Indians.* Cloth. Menasha, Wis., 1914. First edition. $50-$60.

EBERHART, Richard. *A Bravery of Earth.* Cloth. London, 1930. First edition. $100-$125. Author's first book.

EBERHART, Richard. *Brotherhood of Men.* Wrappers. No place, no date (Pawlet, Vt., 1949.) Banyan Press. First edition. One of 26 signed. With printed card stating that this is a review copy. $60-$75.

EBERHART, Richard. *Collected Verse Plays.* Boards and cloth. Chapel Hill, N.C., no date (1962). First edition. One of 100 signed. In glassine dust jacket. $30-$40.

EBERHART, Richard. *Thirty-one Sonnets.* Cloth. New York, no date (1967). First edition. One of 99 signed. Boxed. $25-$35.

ECCLESIASTES-LLYFR y Pregeth-Wr. Woodcut vignette on title page, full page woodcut. Printed in red and black. Blue morocco, gilt. Newtown, Wales, 1927. Gregynog Press. One of 25 specially bound. In slipcase. $350-$400.

ECCLESIASTICUS. See *The Wisdom of Jesus, Son of Sirach.*

ECHO, The. Marbled boards and leather. No place, no date (New York, 1807). (By Richard Alsop, Lemuel Hopkins, Theodore Dwight, etc.) First edition. $35-$40.

ECHOES. By Two Writers. Printed wrappers. Lahore, India, no date (1884). (By Rudyard Kipling, with eight poems credited to his sister Beatrice.) First edition, printed at the Civil and Military Gazette Press. $250 and up. Also, $130 (A, 1948); $1,400 (A, 1930). (Note: A copy inscribed by Kipling and giving a history of the poems was sold at auction for $2,300 in 1971.)

ECKENRODE, Hamilton J. *The Revolution in Virginia.* Cloth. Boston, 1916. First edition. $25-$40.

ECKENRODE, Hamilton J., and Conrad, Bryan. *James Longstreet, Lee's War Horse.* Frontispiece. Cloth. Chapel Hill, N.C., 1936. In dust jacket. $25-$35.

ECKSTEIN, John. *Picturesque View of the Diamond Rock.* 16 plates, 14 hand-colored. Oblong, folio, half morocco. London, 1805. Rebound copy, $1,150.

EDDISON, E. R. *The Worm Ouroboros.* Illustrated by Keith Henderson. Cloth. London, no date (1922). First edition. In dust jacket. $50-$60. Author's first book. New York, 1926. Illustrated. Cloth. First American edition. In dust jacket. $25.

EDDY, Mary Baker. See Glover, Mary Baker.

EDE, Harold Stanley. *A Life of Gaudier-Brzeska.* 47 plates (some colored), other illustrations. Cloth. London, 1930. One of 350. In dust jacket. Boxed. $125-$150.

EDGAR, Patrick Nisbett. *The American Race-Turf Register.* Vol. 1. (All published.) New York, 1833. First edition. $75-$85.

EDGEWORTH, Maria. See *The Modern Griselda.*

EDGEWORTH, Maria. *Tomorrow, or The Dangers of Delay.* Woodcut on title page. Half calf and boards. New York, 1813. $40-$50.

EDMONDS, Walter D. *Rome Haul.* Cloth. Boston, 1929. First (presentation) edition, with "Published February, 1929" on copyright page. One of 1,001. In dust jacket. $25-$35. Trade edition: In dust jacket. $10-$12. Author's first book.

EDMONSTON, Catherine Devereux. *The Journal of Catherine Devereux Edmonston, 1860-1866.* Edited by Margaret Mackay Jones. Cloth. No place (Mebane, N.C.?), no date. $25-$30.

EDWARD Lear on My Shelves. Illustrated. Folio, boards, buckram spine, paper label. No place (Munich), 1933. (By William B. Osgood Field.) Bremer Press. First edition. One of 155. $85-$100.

EDWARD, David B. *The History of Texas.* Folding map in color. Cloth. Cincinnati, 1836. First edition. $100-$150. Also, $100 (A, 1966).

EDWARD VIII. *Farewell Speech of King Edward the Eighth Broadcast from Windsor Castle, December MCMXXXVI.* With 6-page note by William Saroyan. Large, decorated linen, white leather spine. San Francisco, 1938. Grabhorn Press. One of 200. $75-$100.

EDWARDS Chicago Directory (The). 40 pp., boards. Chicago, 1871. "Fire edition." $25-$30.

EDWARDS, Billy. *Gladiators of the Prize Ring, or Pugilists of America.* Folio, cloth. Chicago, no date (1895). $35-$50.

EDWARDS, E. I. *The Valley Whose Name Is Death.* Map. Cloth. Pasadena, 1940. First edition. $25-$35.

EDWARDS, Edward (editor). *The Napoleon Medals: A Complete Series of the Medals Struck in France, Italy, Great Britain and Germany.* Illustrated. Folio, cloth. London, 1837. In new binding, $30-$40.

EDWARDS, Frank S. *A Campaign in New Mexico with Col. Doniphan.* Folding map. 184 pp., wrappers (cover date 1848), and cloth. Philadelphia, 1847. First edition. Wrappers: $150-$250. Also, stained, $100 (A, 1966). Cloth: $100-$150.

EDWARDS, J. C. *Speech in Relation to the Territory in Dispute Between the State of Missouri and the United States, etc.* 20 pp., sewed. Washington, 1843. $35-$40.

EDWARDS, John N. *Noted Guerrillas.* Frontispiece, 15 plates. Cloth. St. Louis, 1877. First edition. $65-$75.

EDWARDS, John N. *Shelby and His Men, or The War in the West.* Portrait, folding map. Cloth. Cincinnati, 1867. First edition. $50-$60. Rebound, $25.

EDWARDS, John N. *Shelby's Expedition to Mexico.* Cloth. Kansas City, Mo., 1872. First edition. $75-$100.

EDWARDS, Jonathan. *Marcus Whitman.* Portraits. 48 pp. Spokane, 1892. First edition. $40-$50.

EDWARDS, Jonathan (1703-58). *Some Thoughts Concerning the Present Revival of Religion in New-England.* Calf. Lexington, Ky., 1803. $35-$50.

EDWARDS, Philip Leget. *The Diary of Philip Leget Edwards: The Great Cattle Drive from California to Oregon in 1837.* Boards. San Francisco, 1932. One of 500. $35-$50.

EDWARDS, Philip Leget. *Sketch of the Oregon Territory; or, Emigrant's Guide.* 20 pp. Liberty, Mo., 1842. First edition. $5,000 estimated value. (Only one copy known.)

EDWARDS, Samuel E. *The Ohio Hunter.* Portrait. Cloth. Battle Creek, Mich., 1866. First edition. $350-$500.

EDWARDS, W. F. (publisher). *W. F. Edwards' Tourists' Guide and Directory to the Truckee Basin.* 12 plates. Cloth. Truckee, Calif., 1883. First edition. $100-$150.

EDWARDS, Weldon. *Memoir of Nathaniel Macon, of North Carolina.* 22 pp., wrappers. Raleigh, 1862. $35-$40.

EDWARDS, William H. *The Butterflies of North America.* 101 color plates. 2 vols., half morocco. Boston, 1879-84. $150.

EFFINGHAM, C. *The Virginia Comedians.* 2 vols., wrappers, or cloth. New York, 1854. (By John Esten Cooke.) First edition, first issue, with "earsed" for "erased" in line 3, page 249, Vol. 2. Wrappers (cover date 1855): $75-$100. Also, $40 (A, 1964). Cloth: $35-$50.

EGAN, Pierce. See *Real Life in London*.

EGAN, Pierce. *Sporting Anecdotes.* 16 engraved plates, advertisement leaf at end. Morocco. London, 1804. First edition. $75-$100. London, 1825. 66 plates (3 in color, one folding). Morocco. $75-$100.

EGE, Ralph. *Pioneers of Old Hopewell.* Portrait. Cloth. Hopewell, N.J., 1908. $35-$50.

EGERTON, Hugh Edward (editor). *The Royal Commission on the Losses and Services of American Loyalists, 1783-1785.* Half morocco. Oxford, 1915. One of 25. $40-$45.

EGGLESTON, Edward. *Among the Elgin Watch-Makers.* 8 pp., wrappers. Chicago, 1872. First edition. $75.

EGGLESTON, Edward. *The Circuit Rider.* Decorated brown cloth. New York, 1874. First edition, first state, without the word "illustrated" on title page. $25.

EGGLESTON, Edward. *The Hoosier School-Boy.* Illustrated by George D. Bush. Pictorial cloth. New York, 1883. First edition, first issue, with "Cousin Sukey" frontispiece and first chapter ending on page 16. $60-$75.

EGGLESTON, Edward. *The Hoosier Schoolmaster.* Illustrated by Frank Beard. Brown or terra-cotta cloth. New York, no date (1871). First edition, first state, with line 3 of page 71 reading "was out" (not "is out"). $60-$80.

EGGLESTON, Edward. *Mr. Blake's Walking-Stick.* Light-gray wrappers. Chicago, 1870. First edition. $250-$300.

EGGLESTON, Edward. *The Manual: A Practical Guide to the Sunday-School Work.* Cloth. Chicago, 1869. First edition. $25. Author's first book.

EGGLESTON, George Cary. *How to Educate Yourself: With or Without Masters.* Cloth. New York, 1872. First edition, first issue, with "Ready in September" over ads at back. $75. Author's first book.

EGLE, William H. *History of Dauphine and Lebanon Counties (Pennsylvania).* Cloth. Philadelphia, 1883. $25-$40.

EGLINTON, John. *Irish Literary Portraits.* Boards and cloth. London, 1935. (By William C. Magee.) First edition. $25-$30.

EGLINTON, John. *Some Essays and Passages.* Selected by William Butler Yeats. Boards, linen spine. Dundrum, Ireland, 1905. (By William C. Magee.) Dun Emer Press. One of 200. $75.

EIGHT Harvard Poets. Boards and cloth. New York, 1917. First edition. In glassine dust jacket. $75. (Note: Contains poems by E. E. Cummings, John Dos Passos, and others.)

1862 Trip to the West (An). 10 plates. Full limp leather. Pawtucket, R.I., no date (1926). (By Lyman B. Goff.) First edition. $250-$300. Also, $250 (A, 1968).

EIGNER, Larry. *Air the Trees.* Illustrated by Bobbie Creeley. Decorated cloth, paper labels. Los Angeles, 1968. Black Sparrow Press. First edition. One of 100 signed. $35-$40.

EIGNER, Larry. *Look at the Park.* Mimeographed printed wrappers. No place, no date. First edition. $30. Author's first book.

EIGNER, Larry. *On My Eyes.* Oblong, wrappers. Highlands, N.C., no date (1960). Jargon. $25-$30.

ELIA: Essays Which Have Appeared Under That Signature in the London Magazine. Boards. London, 1823. (By Charles Lamb.) First edition, first issue, without Waterloo Place address in title page imprint. $350-$500. Rebound in leather, $150-$200. London, 1823. Boards. Second issue. $100-$150.

ELIA . . . Second Series. Boards, paper label. Philadelphia, 1828. First edition. (By Charles Lamb.) $100-$150.

ELIOT, George. See Strauss, Dr. David Friedrich.

ELIOT, George. *Adam Bede.* 3 vols., brown or salmon-colored (orange) cloth. Edinburgh, 1859. (By Mary Ann Evans.) First edition. $350-$400.

ELIOT, George. *Felix Holt, the Radical.* 3 vols., cloth. Edinburgh, 1866. First edition. (By Mary Ann Evans.) $100-$150.

ELIOT, George. *Middlemarch: A Study of Provincial Life.* 8 parts, pictorial wrappers. Edinburgh, 1871. (By Mary Ann Evans.) First edition. $300-$400. Edinburgh, 1871-72. 3 vols., cloth. First book edition. $100-$150.

ELIOT, George. *The Mill on the Floss.* 3 vols., salmon-colored cloth. Edinburgh, 1860. (By Mary Ann Evans.) First edition. $200-$250.

ELIOT, George. *Romola.* 3 vols., green cloth. London, 1863. (By Mary Ann Evans.) First edition, with 2 pages of ads at end of Vol. 2. $250-$350.

ELIOT, George. *Scenes of Clerical Life.* 2 vols., maroon cloth. Edinburgh, 1858. (By Mary Ann Evans.) First edition. $150-$250. Author's first book.

ELIOT, George. *Silas Marner: The Weaver of Raveloe.* Cloth. Edinburgh, 1861. (By Mary Ann Evans.) First edition. $150-$250.

ELIOT, T. S. See Ridler, Anne; Perse, St. John; Dryden, John. Also see *The Catholic Anthology; Ezra Pound His Metric and Poetry; Harvard Class Day 1910.*

ELIOT, T. S. *After Strange Gods: A Primer of Modern Heresy.* Black cloth. London, no date (1934). First edition. In dust jacket. $50-$75. New York, no date (1934). Red cloth. First American edition. In dust jacket. $35-$40.

ELIOT, T. S. *Animula.* Illustrated. Yellow wrappers. No place, no date (London, 1929). Ariel Poems, No. 23. First edition. $25-$35. London, 1929. Yellow boards. Large paper issue. One of 400 signed. $100-$150.

ELIOT, T. S. *Ara Vus Prec* (with spine reading *Ara Vos Prec*). Black boards and cloth. No place, no date (London, 1920). Ovid Press. First edition. One of 30 signed. $350-$450. Also, $336 (A, 1968). Another issue: One of 220 numbered (but not signed) copies. $150-$200. Also, $132 (A, 1966). (Note: There were also 4 presentation copies printed on Japan vellum.)

ELIOT, T. S. *Ash-Wednesday.* Blue cloth. New York, 1930. Fountain Press. First edition. One of 600 signed. In glassine dust jacket. Boxed. $100-$150. London, 1930. Brown cloth. First English trade edition. In dust jacket. $50-$60. New York, 1930. Black cloth. First American trade edition. In dust jacket. $25-$35.

ELIOT, T. S. *Charles Whibley: A Memoir.* Gray wrappers. No place (London), 1931. English Association Pamphlet No. 80. First edition. $25-$30. (Note: Of the edition of "probably" 4,000, says Donald Gallup in *T. S. Eliot: A Bibliography,* about 2,055 were issued without wrappers by the English Association and were reissued with other pamphlets for members.)

ELIOT, T. S. *The Classics and the Man of Letters.* Blue wrappers. London, 1942. First edition, first state, with "t" of "the" in line 6 of title page correctly printed. $25-$30.

ELIOT, T. S. *The Cocktail Party.* Green cloth. London, no date (1950). First edition, with or without misprint "here" for "her" in first line of page 29. (Gallup gives no priority to copies with the misprint.) In dust jacket. $25-$30.

ELIOT, T. S. *Collected Poems, 1909-1935.* Advance proof in printed paper covers. London, no date (1936). First edition. $110-$200. (Note: Text and typography differ from first published edition.) London, no date (1936). Blue cloth. First published edition. In dust jacket. $50-$60. New York, no date (1936). Blue cloth. First American edition. In dust jacket. $25.

ELIOT, T. S. *Dante.* Gray boards. London, no date (1929). First edition. In dust jacket. $50-$75. Another issue: Blue-green cloth. One of 125 signed. In glassine dust jacket. $144.

ELIOT, T. S. *The Dry Salvages.* Blue wrappers. London, no date (1941). First edition. $25-$30.

ELIOT, T. S. *East Coker: A Poem.* 8 pp., wire-stitched, unbound. No place (London), 1940. Reprint from the Easter number of *The New English Weekly.* 500 copies printed. "Second" edition. $25-$30. London, no date (1940). Yellow wrappers. First Faber & Faber edition. $25. (Note: The first appearance of this poem was in a 4-page supplement to *The New English Weekly,* Easter, 1940. A London dealer catalogued a copy at $24 in 1968.)

ELIOT, T. S. *El Canto de Amor de J. Alfred Prufrock.* Wrappers (with sheets laid in). Mexico, 1938. One of 50. $35.

ELIOT, T. S. *Elizabethan Essays.* Gray cloth. London, no date (1934). First edition, first issue, with misprint in series note on half title, "No. 21" (later copies have series note correctly printed "No. 24"). $75-$100.

ELIOT, T. S. *The Family Reunion.* Wrappers. London, no date (1939). "Proof copy," so imprinted on front cover. Signed on cover by Eliot. In dust jacket. $25-$35. London, no date (1939). Gray cloth. First edition. In dust jacket. $15-$20. New York, no date (1939). Black cloth. First American edition. In dust jacket. $7-$10.

ELIOT, T. S. *For Lancelot Andrewes.* Blue cloth, paper label. London, no date (1928). First edition. In dust jacket. $45-$50. Garden City, 1929. Purple-brown cloth. First American edition. In dust jacket. $25.

ELIOT, T. S. *Four Quartets.* Black cloth. New York, no date (1943). First edition, first impression, with "First American edition" on copyright page. One of only 788 copies of an original impression of 4,165, 3,377 of which were destroyed because of incorrect margins. In dust jacket with review slip tipped in. $150. Lacking review slip, $100-$125. Second impression, without the edition note on copyright page and without code designations in brackets used in subsequent impressions. In dust jacket. $45. London, no date (1944). Tan cloth. First English edition. $25-$35. London, no date (1960). Marbled boards and white parchment spine. One of 290 signed. Boxed. $175-$225.

ELIOT, T. S. *From Poe to Valéry.* Dark-blue boards. New York, no date (1948). First edition. One of 1,500. In original green paper mailing envelope. $50. Another, lacking envelope, $35. Washington, 1949. White wrappers with cover title. One of 1,000. $20-$25.

ELIOT, T. S. *Homage to John Dryden.* Stiff off-white wrappers. London, 1924. Hogarth Press. First edition. $50-$75.

ELIOT, T. S. *John Dryden: The Poet, the Dramatist, the Critic.* Frontispiece in color. Marbled boards and cloth. New York, 1932. First edition. One of 110 signed. In cellophane dust jacket. $300-$350. Trade edition: Mulberry boards. In white dust jacket. $35.

ELIOT, T. S. *Marina.* Illustrated. Blue wrappers. No place, no date (London, 1930). Ariel Poems No. 29. First edition. $35-$50. London, 1930. Blue boards. Large paper issue. One of 400 signed. $125-$150.

ELIOT, T. S. *Old Possum's Book of Practical Cats.* Yellow cloth. London, no date (1939). First edition. In dust jacket. $50-$75. New York, no date (1939). Gray cloth. First American edition. In dust jacket. $20-$25.

ELIOT, T. S. *Poems.* Decorated wrappers, white paper label. Richmond, England, 1919. Hogarth Press. First edition, first issue, with "capitaux" for "chapitaux" in line 12, etc. Spine chipped, $475. New York, 1920. Tan boards. First American edition (of *Ara Vus Prec*). (Note: This also includes the contents of the 1919 first edition of *Poems.*) In yellow dust jacket. $150-$200. Lacking dust jacket, $100-$150.

ELIOT, T. S. *Poems, 1909-1925.* Blue cloth, white paper spine label. London, 1925. First edition. In cream-colored dust jacket. $50-$75. Another issue: White linen, gilt. One of 85 signed (actually issued in 1926). In glassine dust jacket. $300-$350. New York, no date (1932). Blue cloth, gilt. First American edition. In cream-colored dust jacket. $25-$35.

ELIOT, T. S. *Prufrock and Other Observations.* 40 pp., buff printed wrappers. London, 1917. First edition. $750-$1,000. Also, $576 (A, 1971). Author's first book.

ELIOT, T. S. *Religious Drama: Medieval and Modern.* Red cloth. New York, 1954. First edition. One of 300 signed. In glassine dust jacket. $150-$200. (Note: There were also 26 lettered copies issued for presentation.)

ELIOT, T. S. *Ritratto Di Signora.* Illustrated with 2 signed etchings by Arnaldo Ciarrochi. Boards, leather spine and corners. Verona, Italy, 1966. First Italian edition (of *Portrait of a Lady*). One of 53. Boxed. $85.

ELIOT, T. S. *The Rock.* Heavy gray wrappers. London, no date (1934). First edition. (The paperbound issue was sold at the theatre in advance of the book's hardbound publication.) $35 and $21.60. Worn, $27.50.

ELIOT, T. S. *The Sacred Wood.* Blue cloth. London, no date (1920). First edition, first issue, with publisher's name at foot of spine measuring 3 mm. and without ads. $65-$75.

ELIOT, T. S. *Selected Essays, 1917-1932.* Blue vellum. London, no date (1932). First edition. One of 115 signed. In cellophane dust jacket. $250-$350. Also, $180 (A, 1969). First trade edition: Brown cloth. In dust jacket. $50.

ELIOT, T. S. *Shakespeare and the Stoicism of Seneca.* (Cover title.) Gray wrappers. London, 1927. First edition. $65-$75.

ELIOT, T. S. *A Song for Simeon.* Illustrated. White boards, gilt. London, 1928. Large paper signed edition. One of 500 signed. $150-$200. Also, $100 (A, 1971).

ELIOT, T. S. *Sweeney Agonistes.* Blue boards. London, no date (1932). First edition. In dust jacket. $75-$100.

ELIOT, T. S. *T. S. Eliot: The Complete Poems and Plays.* Blue-green cloth. New York, no date (1952). First edition (so stated). In dust jacket. $35-$50.

ELIOT, T. S. *Triumphal March.* Illustrated by E. McKnight Kauffer. Boards. London, 1931. First edition. One of 300 signed. $50-$65.

ELIOT, T. S. *The Undergraduate Poems of T. S. Eliot.* Printed gray wrappers. Cambridge, Mass., no date (1949). First edition. One of about 1,000. $100. Also, $45 (A, 1970).

ELIOT, T. S. *The Use of Poetry and the Use of Criticism.* Red cloth. London, no date (1933). First edition. In dust jacket. $50-$75.

ELIOT, T. S. *The Waste Land.* Flexible black cloth, gilt. New York, 1922. First edition, first issue, with the flexible binding, the word "mountain" correctly spelled in line 339 of page 41, and the limitation numbers stamped in type 5 mm. high. In salmon-colored dust jacket. $500-$750. Second state, flexible black cloth, with dropped "a" in "mountain." In dust jacket. $100-$150. New York, no date (1923). Black cloth. Second edition (so identified in colophon). In dust jacket. $100. Richmond, 1923. Hogarth Press. Blue marbled boards, paper label. First English edition, first issue, with border of asterisks on the label. $250-$350. Later, no asterisks, $200-$250. London, no date (1961). Marbled boards, white parchment spine. One of 300 signed. Boxed. $100-$150.

ELIOT, T. S. *What Is a Classic?* Green wrappers. London, no date (1945). First edition. One of 500. $100-$125. Slightly soiled, $95. First trade edition: Blue cloth. In dust jacket. $15-$20.

ELIOT, T. S. *Words for Music.* 4 pp., wrappers. No place (Bryn Mawr, Pa.), 1934 (actually 1935). First edition. One of 20 (?) copies. $302 (A, 1968).

ELIZABETH Bennet; or, Pride and Prejudice: A Novel. 2 vols., boards and linen, paper label. Philadelphia, 1832. (By Jane Austen.) First American edition of *Pride and Prejudice.* $100-$125. Also, $35 (A, 1967).

ELKUS, Richard J. *Alamos.* Foreword by Barnaby Conrad. Half suede and cloth. San Francisco, 1965. Grabhorn Press. One of 487. $100.

ELLICOTT, Andrew. *The Journal of Andrew Ellicott.* 14 maps and plates. Half calf. Philadelphia, 1803. First edition, with errata leaf. $400-$500. Also, $375 (A, 1967). Philadelphia, 1814. Half leather. Second edition. $75-$100.

ELLIOT, D. G. *A Monograph of the Tetraoninae, or Family of the Grouse.* 27 color plates. 5 parts in 4, boards. New York, 1864-65. First edition. $1,000-$1,500.

ELLIOT, D. G. *The New and Heretofore Unfigured Species of the Birds of North America.* Hand-colored plates. 2 vols., half morocco. New York, 1866-69. First edition. $2,000-$2,500. Also, $1,680 (A, 1965) and, 2 vols. in one, $1,800 (A, 1967).

ELLIOT, W. J. *The Spurs.* Plates and map. Cloth. No place, no date (Spur, Tex., 1939). First edition. $35-$50.

ELLIOTT, The Rev. Charles. *Indian Missionary Reminiscences.* Boards. New York, 1835. First edition. $50-$60.

ELLIOTT, David Stewart. *Last Raid of the Daltons.* Illustrated. 72 pp., wrappers. Coffeyville, Kan., 1892. First edition (so stated). $150. Coffeyville, 1892. (Actually 1954.) 60 pp. Second edition. (Facsimile, abridged.) $25-$50.

ELLIOTT, John, and Johnson, Samuel, Jr. *A Selected Pronouncing and Accented Dictionary.* Oblong, boards. Hartford, 1800. $35-$40.

ELLIOTT, W. W. *History of Arizona Territory.* Map and plates. Half cloth. San Francisco, 1884. First edition. $350-$500.

ELLIS, Edward S. See *On the Plains.*

ELLIS, Edward S. *The Life and Adventures of Col. David Crockett.* Half leather. New York, 1861. First edition. $35-$50.

ELLIS, Edward S. *The Life and Times of Christopher Carson.* Wrappers. New York, no date (1861). First edition. $50-$60.

ELLIS, Frederick S. *A Lexical Concordance to the Poetical Works of Percy Bysshe Shelley.* Half brown morocco, gilt. London, 1892. First edition. $100-$120.

ELLIS, Frederick S. (editor). *Psalmi Penitentiales.* Woodcut designs and initials. Boards and linen. London, 1894. Kelmscott Press. One of 300. $150-$200. Another issue: One of 12 on vellum. $400-$500.

ELLIS, Frederick S. (editor). *Syr Ysambrace.* Printed in black and red. Woodcut borders and designs by E. Burne-Jones. Boards and linen. London, 1897. Kelmscott Press. One of 350. $140-$175.

ELLIS, Frederick S. (editor), and Caxton, William, and Morris, William (translators). *The Book of the Order of Chivalry (L'Ordre de Chevalerie).* Printed in black and red. Woodcut by E. Burne-Jones. Vellum with ties. London, 1893. Kelmscott Press. One of 225. $400-$450.

ELLIS, Havelock. *Kanga Creek: An Australian Idyll.* Boards and cloth. Waltham Saint Lawrence, England, 1922. Golden Cockerel Press. First edition. In dust jacket. $25.

ELLIS, William. *The American Mission in the Sandwich Islands.* Boards. Honolulu, 1866. First edition. $100-$150.

ELLIS, William. *Polynesian Researches, During a Residence of Nearly Six Years in the South Sea Islands.* 10 plates and maps, 16 woodcuts. 2 vols., half calf and marbled boards. London, 1829. First edition. $100-$150.

ELLIS, William Turner. *Memories: My 72 Years in the Romantic County of Yuba, California.* Boards and cloth. Eugene, Ore., 1939. John Henry Nash printing. In dust jacket. $35-$50.

ELLSWORTH, Henry W. *Valley of the Upper Wabash, Indiana.* Folding map, 3 folding lithographs. Stiff wrappers. New York, 1838. First edition. $50-$75.

ELLSWORTH, Lincoln. *The Last Wild Buffalo Hunt.* 32 pp., cloth. New York, 1916. First edition. $50-$75.

ELMER, Jonathan. *An Eulogium on the Character of Gen. George Washington.* 25 pp., half leather. Trenton, N.J., 1800. $200-$400.

ELMORE, James B. *Love Among the Mistletoe, and Poems.* Cloth. Alamo, Ind., 1899. First edition. $25-$35.

ELMSLIE, Kenward. *Pavilions.* Wrappers. New York, 1961. First edition. One of 300. $20-$30.

ELTON, R. H. *Jackson Almanac, 1836.* 36 pp., wrappers. No place, no date (New York, 1835). $25-$30.

ÉLUARD, Paul. *Le Dur Désir de Dürer.* Frontispiece in color and 25 designs by Marc Chagall. Text in French. Folio, sheets in printed wrappers and board slipcase. Paris, no date (1946). Trianon Press. One of 330 on Rives paper, signed by author and artist. $450. Philadelphia and London, no date (1950). Trianon Press. Translated by Stephen Spender and Frances Cornford. Colored frontispiece and black and white illustrations. Printed wrappers. First edition of the English translation. One of 1,500. $50-$60.

ELZAS, Barnett A. *The Jews of South Carolina from the Earliest Period to the Present Day.* 11 plates. Cloth. Philadelphia, 1905. $35-$50.

EMBARGO (The), or Sketches of the Times; A Satire. By a Youth of Thirteen. (Cover title.) 12 pp., self-wrappers (stitched). Boston, 1808. (By William Cullen Bryant.) First edition. $500 and up. (For second edition, see author and title.)

EMERSON, Charles L. *Rise and Progress of Minnesota Territory.* 64 pp., pictorial printed wrappers. St. Paul, Minn., 1855. First edition. $375-$400.

EMERSON, Joseph. *Female Education.* 40 pp., plain wrappers. Boston, 1822. First edition. $20-$30.

EMERSON, Lucy. *The New-England Cookery.* Boards. Montpelier, Vt., 1808. First edition. $150-$200. Also, $117.60 (A, 1965).

EMERSON, Ralph Waldo. See *Nature*.

EMERSON, Ralph Waldo. *An Address Delivered Before the Senior Class in Divinity College, Cambridge . . . 15 July, 1838.* 31 pp., blue wrappers. Boston, 1838. First edition. $50-$75.

EMERSON, Ralph Waldo. *An Address Delivered in the Court-House in Concord, Massachusetts, on 1st August, 1844, on the Anniversary of the Emancipation of the Negroes in the British West Indies.* 34 pp., tan wrappers. Boston, 1844. First edition. $100-$150.

EMERSON, Ralph Waldo. *The American Scholar.* ("An Oration Delivered Before the Phi Beta Kappa Society.") 26 pp., wrappers or unlettered cloth. Boston, 1837. First edition. Wrappers: $75-$100. Cloth: $45 (A, 1968).

EMERSON, Ralph Waldo. *The Conduct of Life.* Cloth. Boston, 1860. First edition, first issue, without signature mark "1" and with ads dated December, 1860. $75-$100.

EMERSON, Ralph Waldo. *English Traits.* Cloth. Boston, 1856. First edition. $75-$100.

EMERSON, Ralph Waldo. *Essays.* Cloth. Boston, 1841. First edition, first binding, without "First Series" on spine. $225 and $250. London, 1906. Vellum. Doves Press. One of 300. $200-$300. Another issue: One of 25 printed on vellum. $500-$600. New York, 1934. Limited Editions Club. Boards. Boxed. $40.

EMERSON, Ralph Waldo. *Essays: Second Series.* Cloth. Boston, 1844. First edition, probable first binding, with "2D Series" on spine. $100-$150.

EMERSON, Ralph Waldo. *A Historical Discourse, Delivered Before the Citizens of Concord, 12th September, 1835.* 52 pp., blue wrappers. Concord, 1835. First edition. $150-$250.

EMERSON, Ralph Waldo. *The Journals of Ralph Waldo Emerson.* 10 vols., green cloth. Boston, 1909-1914. First edition. $100. Another issue: Tan linen. One of 600 on large paper. $300-$400.

EMERSON, Ralph Waldo. *Lectures and Biographical Sketches.* Cloth. Boston, 1884. First edition. $35-$50.

EMERSON, Ralph Waldo. *Letters and Social Aims.* Cloth. Boston, 1876. First edition. $35-$50. Inner hinges cracked, $25-$30.

EMERSON, Ralph Waldo. *May-Day and Other Pieces.* White cloth. Boston, 1867. First edition, first issue, with "flowers" for "hours" on page 184. $50-$75. (Also issued in other colors of cloth.) London, 1867. Cloth. First English edition. $50-$75.

EMERSON, Ralph Waldo. *The Method of Nature.* 30 pp., printed tan wrappers. Boston, 1841. First edition. $50-$80.

EMERSON, Ralph Waldo. *An Oration Delivered Before the Literary Societies of Dartmouth College, July 24, 1838.* Wrappers. Boston, 1838. First edition. $50-$75.

EMERSON, Ralph Waldo. *Poems.* Green cloth. London, 1847. First edition, first issue, with "Chapman Brothers" on foot of spine and ads dated Nov. 16, 1846. $100-$125. Boston, 1847. Yellow boards, paper label. First American edition, with 4 pages of ads dated Jan. 1, 1847. $500-$600. Also, $425 (A, 1968). New York, 1945. Limited Editions Club. Full leather. Boxed. $35-$50.

EMERSON, Ralph Waldo. *Representative Men.* Black or brown cloth. Boston, 1850. First edition, first issue, with hourglass design on front and back cover. $35-$50. London, 1850. Dark-brown cloth. First English edition (possibly issued simultaneously with the American edition, according to Blanck). $25.

EMERSON, Ralph Waldo. *Society and Solitude.* Green cloth. Boston, 1870. First edition. $75-$100.

EMILY Parker, or Impulse, Not Principle. Frontispiece. Buff boards. Boston, 1827. (By Lydia Maria Child.) First edition. $150-$175.

EMMA. By the Author of "Pride and Prejudice," etc. 3 vols., blue or brown paper boards, drab paper spine, paper labels. London, 1816. (By Jane Austen.) First edition. $1,250-$1,500. New York, 1964. Limited Editions Club. Illustrated in color by Fritz Kredel. Buckram. Boxed. $25-$35.

EMMART, Emily Walcott (translator). *The Badianus Manuscript.* By Martinus de la Cruz. 118 colored plates. Cloth. Baltimore, 1940. $100-$150.

EMMONS, George T. *The Emmons Journal.* 11 pp., wrappers. Eugene, Ore., no date (1925). $35-$40.

EMMONS, Dr. (Richard). *Tecumseh: Or, The Battle of the Thames.* 36 pp., wrappers. New York, 1836. $50-$60.

EMMONS, Samuel Franklin. *Atlas to Accompany a Monograph on the Geology and Mining Industry of Leadville, Colorado.* 35 single and double leaves, charts, etc., some in color. Large atlas, paper covers, unbound. Washington, 1883. $30-$40.

EMORY, William H. *Notes of a Military Reconnaissance.* 68 plates, 6 maps and plans. Cloth. Washington, 1848. House version. First edition. $50-$100. Another issue: Same place and date, Senate version. $50-$100.

ENGLEHARDT, Zephyrin. *The Franciscans in Arizona.* Map, plates. 236 pp., wrappers. Harbor Springs, Mich., 1899. First edition. $50-$60.

ENGELHARDT, Zephyrin. *The Franciscans in California.* Illustrated. Wrappers. Harbor Springs, 1897. First edition. $50-$60.

ENGLE, Paul. *Worn Earth.* Boards. New Haven, Conn., 1932. First edition. In dust jacket. $25-$35. Author's first book.

ENGLISH Bards and Scotch Reviewers. 54 pp., drab printed boards. London, no date (1809). (By George Gordon Noel, Lord Byron.) First edition, first issue, without preface. $600-$800. Also, calf, $312 (A, 1969). Later issue, with preface: $200-$300.

ENGLISH Bible (The). 5 vols., folio, vellum. London, 1903-05. Doves Press. One of 500. $1,500-$2,000. Also, $720, $1,080, and $1,750 (A, 1969).

ENGLISH Dance of Death (The). Frontispiece, engraved title and 72 color plates by Thomas Rowlandson. 24 parts, wrappers. London, 1814-16. (By William Combe.) First edition. $500 and up. London, 1814 (or 1815)-16. 2 vols., cloth. First book edition. $150-$300.

ENGLISH, William B. *Rosina Meadows, the Village Maid.* Wrappers. Boston, 1863. First edition. $50.

ENSIGN and Thayer's Traveller's Guide Through the States of Ohio, Michigan, Indiana, Illinois, Missouri, Iowa and Wisconsin. (Variant titles.) Folding colored map. Leather. New York, 1850. $75-$100. New York, 1850. $50-$75. Buffalo, 1853. $35-$50. New York, 1853. $40-$50. New York, 1854, $45.

EPIPSYCHIDION: Verses, etc. Drab wrappers. London, 1821. (By Percy Bysshe Shelley.) First edition. $2,000 and up. Auction record: spine missing, "only known copy in wrappers," $1,400 (1945). Rebound in morocco, $950 (A, 1962). Montagnola, Italy, 1923. Vellum. One of 222. $250-$350.

EPITOME of Electricity and Galvanism (An). By Two Gentlemen of Philadelphia. Boards. Philadelphia, 1809. (By Jacob Green and Ebenezer Hazard.) First edition. $75-$85.

EPPES, Susan Bradford. *Through Some Eventful Years.* Cloth. Macon, Ga., 1926. $35-$50. Spine worn, $30-$40.

EPSTEIN, Jacob. *Epstein: An Autobiography.* Illustrated. Leatherette. London, 1955. One of 195 signed. In dust jacket. $75-$80.

EPSTEIN, Jacob. *Let There Be Sculpture.* Frontispiece, 47 illustrations. Vellum. London, 1940. One of 100 signed. $125-$135.

EREWHON, or Over the Range. Brown cloth. London, 1872. First edition. (By Samuel Butler.) $75-$125. Newtown, Wales, 1932. Gregynog Press. Illustrated. Sheep. One of 275 on Japan vellum. $75-$100. Another issue: One of 25 specially bound in morocco by George Fisher. $400-$500. New York, 1934. Limited Editions Club. Introduction by Aldous Huxley. Illustrated by Rockwell Kent. Cloth. Boxed. $25-$50.

ESCANDON, Manuel, and Rascon, José. *Observaciónes que los Actuales Terceros Possedores de los Bienes que Pertenecieron al Fondo Piadoso de Californias, etc.* 12 pp., wrappers. Mexico, 1845. $75.

ESPEJO, Antonio de. *New Mexico: Otherwise the Voiage of Anthony Espeio, Who in the Yeare 1583, With His Company, Discovered a Lande of 15 Provinces, etc.* Boards. No place, no date (Lancaster, 1928). First edition. One of 200. $35-$45.

ESSAY on Mind (An), With Other Poems. Blue-gray boards, white label on spine. London, 1826. (By Elizabeth Barrett Browning.) First edition. $500-$600.

ESSAYS from Poor Robert the Scribe. Boards, leather spine. Doylestown, Pa., 1815. (By Charles Miner.) First edition. $150-$200.

ESSAYS of Howard on Domestic Economy. Contemporary calf. New York, 1820. (By Mordecai Manuel Noah.) First edition. $35-$40.

ESSE, James. *Hunger: A Dublin Story.* Printed wrappers. Dublin, 1918. (By James Stephens.) First edition. $25-$30.

ESSHOM, Frank. *Pioneers and Prominent Men of Utah.* Cloth. Salt Lake City, 1913. $25-$50.

ESTAVA, José María. *La Campaña de la Mision.* Boards and cloth. Xalapa-Enriquez, Mexico, 1894. First edition. $50-$75.

ETHELL, Henry C. *The Rise and Progress of Civilization in the Hairy Nation and the History of Davis County.* Cloth. Bloomfield, Iowa, 1883. $50-$75.

ETHNOLOGIC Dictionary of the Navajo Language (An). By the Franciscan Fathers. 536 pp., wrappers. St. Michaels, Ariz., 1910. One of 200 on Japan vellum. $150-$200.

EUGENE Aram: A Tale. 3 vols., boards, paper labels. London, 1832. (By Edward Bulwer-Lytton.) First edition. $50-$75.

EULOGY on the Life of Gen. George Washington (An). Wrappers. Newburyport, Mass., 1800. (By Robert Treat Paine, Jr.) First edition. $30-$35.

EUPHRANOR: A Dialogue on Youth. Green cloth. London, 1851. (By Edward FitzGerald.) $75-$100. London, 1885. Green cloth, or stitched, without ads at end. Second edition. $75-$100. (Note: A few copies were bound for presentation, appendix canceled, corrections made in FitzGerald's hand.) Another edition: No place, no date (Guildford, 1882). (With subtitle *A May-Day Conversation at Cambridge* instead of *A Dialogue on Youth.*) Half leather and green boards. Third edition. One of 50 (not so stated). $50-$75.

EURIPIDES. *The Plays of Euripides.* Translated by Gilbert Murray. Illustrated. 2 vols., folio, red buckram. Newtown, Wales, 1931. Gregynog Press. One of 500. $250-$300.

EVANGELICAL Hymns. 24 pp., stitched. Greenwich, Mass., 1807. First edition. $25.

EVANS, Augusta Jane. *St. Elmo.* Cloth. New York, 1867. (By Augusta Jane Evans Wilson.) First edition. $35-$50.

EVANS, Elwood. *Puget Sound: Its Past, Present and Future.* 16 pp., wrappers. Olympia, Wash., 1869. First edition. $100-$125. Rebound in half morocco, $75.

EVANS, Elwood. *Washington Territory.* 51 pp., wrappers. Olympia, 1877. First edition. $75-$100.

EVANS, Estwick. *A Pedestrious Tour, of 4,000 Miles, Through the Western States and Territories.* Portrait. Boards. Concord, N.H., 1819. First edition. $300 and up.

EVANS, John. *A Narrative of the Proceedings of the Religious Society of the People Called Quakers, in Philadelphia, Against John Evans.* Wrappers (cloth spine). Philadelphia, 1811. First edition. $35-$50.

EVANS, Capt. S. B. (compiler). *History of Wapello County, Iowa.* Morocco and cloth. Chicago, 1901. $50-$60.

EVELYN, John. *Memoirs, Illustrative of the Life and Writings of John Evelyn, Esq., F.R.S.* Edited by William Bray. Folding pedigree, 8 plates. 2 vols., calf. Bath, England, 1818. First edition. $100-$200.

EVENINGS in New England. By an American Lady. Brown boards. Boston, 1824. (By Lydia Maria Child.) First edition. $50-$60.

EVENTFUL Lives of Helen and Charlotte Lenoxa (The), the Twin Sisters of Philadelphia. Wrappers. Memphis, 1853. First edition, first issue, with date 1852 on cover. $100.

EVENTS in Indian History, Beginning with an Account of the Origin of the American Indians, etc. 8 plates. Lancaster, Pa., 1843. (By James Wimer). $45.

EVERETT, Edward. *A Defence of Christianity.* Boards, paper label. Boston, 1814. First edition. $35. Author's first book.

EVERETT, Horace. *Regulating the Indian Department.* Folding map. 133 pp., sewed. No place, no date (Washington, 1934). $50-$75.

EVERSON, William. See Antoninus, Brother.

EVERSON, William. *The Residual Years.* Batik boards and cloth. No place, no date (New York, 1948). First edition. One of 1,000. In dust jacket. $25-$30.

EVERSON, William. *The Blowing of the Seed.* Boards, leather spine. New Haven, 1966. First edition. One of 215 signed. $60-$75.

EVERSON, William. *Poems: MCMXLII.* Self-wrappers. Waldport, Ore., 1944-45. One of 500. $40-$50.

EVERSON, William. *Single Source: The Early Poems of William Everson.* Introduction by Robert Duncan. Boards. Berkeley, Calif., no date (1966). First edition. One of 25 signed. $50. Trade issue (1,000 copies): $15.

EVERSON, William (Brother Antoninus). *The Springing of the Blade.* Decorated cloth. No place, no date (Reno, Nev., 1968). First edition. One of 180 signed. $30-$35.

EVERSON, William. *There Will be a Harvest.* Woodcut on title page. 4 pp., on 8 pp. French fold. No place, no date (Berkeley, 1960). First edition. One of 200. $37.50.

EVERSON, William. *War Elegies.* Illustrated. Wrappers. Waldport, 1944. First printed edition. One of 975. $50-$60.

EVERSON, William. *The Year's Declension.* Boards. Berkeley, 1961. First edition. One of 100 signed. $40-$75.

EVERTS and Kirk. *The Official State Atlas of Nebraska.* Plates, 207 colored maps. Half calf. Philadelphia, 1885. $100-$150.

EVIDENCE Concerning Projected Railways Across the Sierra Nevada Mountains. Calf. Carson City, Nev., 1865. $500-$600.

EVIL of Intoxicating Liquor (The), and the Remedy. 24 pp., sewed. Park Hill, Okla., 1844. $27.50.

EVJEN, John O. *Scandinavian Immigrants in New York, 1630-1674.* Illustrated. Cloth. Minneapolis, 1916. First edition. $25-$30.

EWALD, Johannes. *The Death of Balder.* Translated by George Borrow. London, 1899. One of 250. $35-$40.

EWELL, Thomas T. *A History of Hood County, Texas.* Cloth. Grandbury, Tex., 1895. First edition. $60.

EXAMINATION and Review of a Pamphlet, etc. Stitched. Washington, 1837. $200.

EXAMINATION of the President's Reply to the New Haven Remonstrance (An). 69 pp., wrappers. New York, 1801. (By William Coleman.) First edition. $35-$50.

EXETER Book of Old English Poetry (The). Folio, buckram. London, 1933. $75-$80.

EXPOSICIÓN del Ministro de Hacienda. (Cover title.) 11 pp., wrappers. Mexico, 1836. $55-$60.

EXTRACTS from the Autobiography of Calvin Coolidge. Miniature book. Blue calf. Kingsport, Tenn., 1930. $25-$30.

EYE WITNESS (An). *Satan in Search of a Wife.* 4 full-page woodcuts and 2 vignettes by George Cruikshank. Pink wrappers. London, 1831. (By Charles Lamb.) First edition. $150-$250.

EZRA Pound His Metric and Poetry. Portrait frontispiece by Gaudier-Brzeska. Rose paper boards, lettered in gold on front cover. New York, 1917 (actually 1918). (By T. S. Eliot.) First edition. In plain buff dust jacket. $250-$300.

F

F., M. T. *My Chinese Marriage.* By M. T. F. Green boards and cloth. New York, 1921. (By Katherine Anne Porter.) First edition. $100-$125. Author's first book (a ghost-writing job).

FABLE for Critics (A). Cloth, or boards. New York, (18)48. (By James Russell Lowell.) First edition, first state, without "A Vocal and Musical Medley" on title page and with pages 63 and 64 misnumbered. $75-$100.

FABLES of Esope (The). Translated out of the Frensshe into Englysshe by William Caxton. 37 engravings on wood by Agnes Miller Parker. Sheepskin. Newtown, Wales, 1931. Gregynog Press. One of 250. $200-$250.

FACSIMILES of Royal, Historical, Literary, and Other Autographs in the Department of MSS., British Museum. Edited by George F. Warner. 150 plates. 5 parts, folio, sewed. London, 1899. $100.

FACTS Concerning the City of San Diego, the Great Southwestern Sea-port of the United States, with a Map Showing the City and Its Surroundings. 14 pp., wrappers. San Diego, no date (1888). $75-$100.

FACTS Respecting Indian Administration in the Northwest (The). 74 pp., wrappers. No place, no date (Victoria?, 1886). $40.

FAHEY, Herbert. *Early Printing in California.* Illustrated. Cloth. San Francisco, 1956. Grabhorn Press. One of 400. $125-$150.

FAIRBANKS, George R. *Early History of Florida.* 82 pp., sewed. St. Augustine, 1857. First edition. $100.

FAIRBANKS, George R. *The Spaniards in Florida.* 120 pp., wrappers. Jacksonville, 1868. First edition. $50.

FAIRCHILD, T. B. *A History of the Town of Cuyahoga Falls, Summit County.* 39 pp., cloth. Cleveland, 1876. $35.

FAIRFIELD, Asa Merrill. *Fairfield's Pioneer History of Lassen County, California.* 4 plates, folding map. Pictorial cloth. San Francisco, no date (1916). First edition. $50-$75.

FAIRY Book (The). Frontispiece and 81 woodcuts by Joseph A. Adams. Brown cloth. New York, 1837. First edition. $35-$50.

FAIRY Garland (A). 12 colored illustrations by Edmund Dulac. Half vellum. London, no date (1928). First edition. One of 1,000 signed by the artist. $75-$100.

FAITH Gartney's Girlhood. Cloth. Boston, 1863. (By Mrs. A. D. T. Whitney.) First edition. $40-$50.

FALCONER, Thomas. *Letters and Notes on the Texan Santa Fe Expedition, 1841-42.* Edited by F. W. Hodge. Portrait. Half cloth. New York, 1930. $35-$50.

FALCONER, Thomas. *On the Discovery of the Mississippi, and On the South-Western, Oregon, and North-Western Boundary of the United States.* Folding map, errata leaf. Half morocco. London, 1844. First edition, first issue, with the map (later absent). $150-$200.

FALCONER, William. *A New Universal Dictionary of the Marine.* 35 full-page and folding plates. Half calf, leather label. London, 1815. $250.

FALKLAND. Boards. London, 1827. (By Edward Bulwer-Lytton.) First edition. $150-$200. Author's first novel.

FALKNER: A Novel. 3 vols., cloth, paper labels. London, 1837. (By Mary Wollstonecraft Shelley.) First edition. $100-$150.

FANNIE, Cousin (translator). *Red Beard's Stories for Children.* Silhouette illustrations. Boards, yellow label. Boston, 1856. $25-$30.

FANNY. 49 pp., printed gray wrappers. New York, 1819. (By Fitz-Greene Halleck.) First edition. $100-$150. Author's first separate book. (Note: There also exists a pirated 1819 edition, 67 pp.)

FANSHAWE: A Tale. Brown or buff boards, purple cloth spine, paper labels. Boston, 1828. (By Nathaniel Hawthorne.) First edition. $3,000 and up. Also, $2,600 (A, 1958).

FARM Yard Story. 12 pp. with pull-out color illustrations. Glazed printed green boards. Boston, 1865. L. Prang & Co. $25-$30.

FARNHAM, S. B. *The New York and Idaho Gold Mining Co.* Folding map. 23 pp., wrappers. New York, 1864. $100.

FARNHAM, Thomas J. *History of Oregon Territory.* Frontispiece map. Cloth. New York, 1844. First edition. $150.

FARNHAM, Thomas J. *Travels in the Californias.* Map and plates. Cloth. New York, 1844. First edition, second (or clothbound) issue. $300-$400. Also, $300 (A, 1968). (Note: The first edition was issued first in 4 paperbound parts, which are rare in fine condition.)

FARNHAM, Thomas J. *Travels in the Great Western Prairies.* Cloth, leather label. Poughkeepsie, 1841. First edition. $300-$400. Also, $225 (A, 1969). Ploughkeepsie (sic), 1843. Tan boards, lavender cloth. $150-$200.

FARQUHARSON, Martha. *Elsie Dinsmore.* Red cloth. New York, 1867. (By Martha Finley.) First edition, with publisher's address misprinted "605" for 506 Broadway on title page. $150-$175.

FARRELL, James T. *Calico Shoes and Other Stories.* Blue cloth. New York, no date (1934). First edition. In dust jacket. $25-$35.

FARRELL, James T. *Gas-House McGinty.* Cloth. New York, 1933. First edition. In dust jacket. $25-$35.

FARRELL, James T. *Guillotine Party.* Green cloth. New York, no date (1935). First edition. In dust jacket. $25-$35.

FARRELL, James T. *Judgment Day.* Cloth. New York, 1935. First edition, with "thay" for "they" in third line of page 218. In dust jacket. $25-$30.

FARRELL, James T. *A Misunderstanding.* Cloth. New York, 1949. One of 300 signed. $35.

FARRELL, James T. *Young Lonigan: A Boyhood in Chicago Streets.* Cloth. New York, 1932. First edition. In dust jacket. $60-$80. Author's first book.

FARRELL, James T. *The Young Manhood of Studs Lonigan.* Brown cloth. New York, no date (1934). First edition, with errata slip listing eight typographical errors, among them "Connolly" for "Connell" in line 18 of page 88. In dust jacket. $35-$50.

FAST, Edward G. *Catalogue of Antiquities and Curiosities Collected in the Territory of Alaska.* 32 pp., wrappers. No place (New York), 1869. $45-$50.

FAULKNER, J. P. *Eighteen Months on a Greenland Whaler.* Portrait. Cloth. New York, 1878. $35-$50.

FAULKNER, William. *Absalom, Absalom!* Folding map at end. Printed paper boards, cloth spine. New York, 1936. First edition. One of 300 signed. $250-$350. First trade edition: Cloth. In dust jacket. $75-$100.

FAULKNER, William. *As I Lay Dying.* Beige cloth. New York, no date (1930). First edition, first state, with dropped "I" on page 11 and top edges stained brown. In dust jacket. $100-$150.

FAULKNER, William. *Big Woods.* Green cloth. New York, no date (1955). First edition. In dust jacket. $25-$35.

FAULKNER, William. *Descende, Moïse.* Wrappers. Paris, 1955. First French translation of *Go Down, Moses.* One of 76 on velin (paper). $35.

FAULKNER, William. *Doctor Martino and Other Stories.* Red and black cloth. New York, 1934. First edition. One of 360 signed. $150. Trade edition: Blue cloth. In dust jacket. $75-$100.

FAULKNER, William. *A Fable.* Blue buckram. No place, no date (New York, 1954). First edition, first printing (so stated). One of 1,000 signed. Boxed. $60-$125. Trade edition: Maroon cloth. In dust jacket. $35-$50.

FAULKNER, William. *Go Down, Moses and Other Stories.* Salmon-colored boards, red cloth spine. New York, no date (1942). First edition, first printing (so stated). One of 100 signed. $800-$900. Trade edition: Cloth (in various colors). In dust jacket. $75-$100. London, 1942. Cloth. First English edition. In dust jacket. $25.

FAULKNER, William. *A Green Bough.* Tan cloth, paper labels. New York, 1933. First edition. One of 360 signed. $200-$250. Trade edition: Green cloth. In dust jacket. $50-$75.

FAULKNER, William. *The Hamlet.* Green cloth and boards. New York, 1940. First edition, first printing (so stated). One of 250 signed. In glassine dust jacket. Boxed. $300. Trade edition: Black cloth. In dust jacket. $75-$125.

FAULKNER, William. *Histoires Diverses.* Wrappers. Paris, no date (1967). First French edition. One of 42. $25. (No corresponding title in English.)

FAULKNER, William. *Idyll in the Desert.* Red marbled boards, paper label. New York, 1931. First edition (so stated). One of 400 signed. In glassine dust jacket. $350-$480.

FAULKNER, William. *Intruder in the Dust.* Black cloth. New York, no date (1948). First edition, first printing (so stated). In dust jacket. $50-$75.

FAULKNER, William. *Jealousy and Episode.* Cloth. Minneapolis, 1955. First edition. One of 500. $60-$75.

FAULKNER, William. *La Ville.* Wrappers. Paris, no date (1962). First French translation of *The Town.* One of 66. $35.

FAULKNER, William. *Le Domaine.* Wrappers. Paris, no date (1962). First French translation of *The Mansion.* One of 66. $35.

FAULKNER, William. *Le Rameau Vert.* Wrappers. Paris, no date (1955). First French translation of *A Green Bough.* One of 80 with English and French on facing pages. $35.

FAULKNER, William. *Les Palmiers Sauvages.* Wrappers. Paris, no date (1952). First French edition of *The Wild Palms.* One of 100 on velin (paper). $40.

FAULKNER, William. *Light in August.* Coarse tan cloth. No place, no date (New York, 1932). First edition, first printing (so stated). In dust jacket. $75-$125.

FAULKNER, William. *The Mansion.* Black cloth. New York, no date (1959). First edition. One of 500 signed. In glassine dust jacket. $125-$150. Also, $90 (A, 1971). First trade edition: Blue cloth. In dust jacket. $25-$40.

FAULKNER, William. *The Marble Faun.* Mottled green boards, printed labels. Boston, no date (1924). First edition. One of about 500. In dust jacket. $1,250-$2,000, possibly more, especially if inscribed. Also, in dust jacket (torn), $1,700 (A, 1963). Author's first book.

FAULKNER, William. *Mirrors of Chartres Street.* Illustrated. Tan cloth. No place, no date (Minneapolis, 1953). First edition. One of 1,000. In dust jacket. $50-$60.

FAULKNER, William. *Miss Zilphia Gant.* Brownish red cloth. No place, no date (Dallas, 1932). Book Club of Texas. First edition. One of 300. $500-$750.

FAULKNER, William. *Mosquitoes.* Blue cloth. New York, 1927. First edition. In dust jacket. $150-$200.

FAULKNER, William. *Moustiques.* Wrappers. Paris, no date (1948). First French edition of *Mosquitoes.* One of 50 on velin (paper). $40.

FAULKNER, William. *New Orleans Sketches.* Edited by Carvel Collins. Brown boards. New Brunswick, N.J., 1958. First American edition, first printing (so stated). In dust jacket. $25-$35.

FAULKNER, William. *Notes on a Horsethief.* Decorations by Elizabeth Calvert. Illustrated green cloth. Greenville, Miss., 1950. First edition. One of 975 signed. $150-$200.

FAULKNER, William. *Pylon.* Folding facsimile. Half blue cloth and silver boards. New York, 1935. First edition. One of 310 signed. Boxed. $200-$250. Spine faded, $125. Trade edition: Blue cloth, with black band. In dust jacket. $75-$100.

FAULKNER, William. *The Reivers: A Reminiscence.* Maroon cloth. New York, no date (1962). First edition, first printing (so stated). One of 500 signed. $125-$150. Trade edition: Red cloth. In dust jacket. $25-$35.

FAULKNER, William. *Requiem for a Nun.* Half black cloth, marbled boards. New York, no date (1951). First edition. One of 750 signed. In acetate dust jacket. $100-$150. Trade edition: Green and black cloth. In dust jacket. $35-$50. Play version: New York, no date (1959). Adapted by Ruth Ford. Gray boards. First edition, first printing (so stated). In dust jacket. $15-$20.

FAULKNER, William. *Salmagundi.* Tan wrappers. Milwaukee, 1932. First edition. One of 525. Boxed. $350-$450. (Note: Includes a poem by Ernest Hemingway, listed on title page.)

FAULKNER, William. *Sanctuaire.* Preface by André Malraux. Wrappers. Paris, no date (1933). First French edition of *Sanctuary.* One of 150 on alfa paper. $35.

FAULKNER, William. *Sanctuary.* Magenta boards and gray cloth. New York, no date (1931). First edition, first printing, with "First Published 1931" on copyright page. In dust jacket. $150-$200. London, 1931. Cloth. First English edition. In dust jacket. $15-$25.

FAULKNER, William. *Sartoris.* Black cloth. New York, no date (1929). First edition. In dust jacket. $150-$200.

FAULKNER, William. *Scheckige Mustangs.* 44 lithographs. Folio, decorated boards. Stuttgart, Germany, 1965. Illustrated edition of "Spotted Horses." One of 50 with an extra set of plates signed by the artist, Gunter Böhmer. Boxed. $150.

FAULKNER, William. *Soldiers' Pay.* Blue cloth. New York, 1926. First edition. In dust jacket. $200-$300. London, 1930. Cloth. First English edition. In dust jacket. $40-$50. Author's first novel.

FAULKNER, William. *The Sound and the Fury.* Black, white, and gray patterned boards, white cloth spine. New York, no date (1929). First edition, first printing, with "First

Published 1929" on copyright page. In dust jacket. $150-$300. London, 1931. Black cloth. First English edition. In dust jacket. $50-$60.

FAULKNER, William. *These 13.* Tan and red cloth. New York, no date (1931). First edition. One of 299 signed. $150-$250. Trade edition: Blue and gray cloth. In dust jacket. $75-$100. Bookplate, smudge on spine, $60. London, 1933. Blue cloth. First English edition. In dust jacket. $25-$30.

FAULKNER, William. *This Earth.* Illustrated by Albert Heckman. 8 pp., stiff tan wrappers. New York, 1932. First edition. (1,000 copies.) $85-$100.

FAULKNER, William. *The Town.* Tan cloth, top edges red. New York, no date (1957). First edition, first printing (so stated). One of 450 signed. $100-$150. Trade edition: Red cloth. In dust jacket. $25-$40.

FAULKNER, William. *The Unvanquished.* Illustrated by Edward Shenton. Boards and red cloth. New York, no date (1938). First edition, first printing (so stated). One of 250 signed. $250. Trade edition: Gray cloth. In dust jacket. $75.

FAULKNER, William. *The Wild Palms.* Red cloth and boards. New York, no date (1939). First edition, first printing (so stated). One of 250 signed. $300-$400. Trade edition: Tan cloth. In dust jacket. $75.

FAULKNER, William. *William Faulkner's Speech of Acceptance Upon the Award of the Nobel Prize for Literature.* Beige wrappers. No place, no date (New York, 1951). First separate edition, first printing. One of 2,500 by the Spiral Press. $25-$35. Second printing. One of 2,500. $10.

FAULKNER, William (editor). *Sherwood Anderson and Other Famous Creoles.* Drawings by William Spratling. Green boards, green label. New Orleans, 1926. First edition. One of about 50 hand-tinted copies (of an issue of 250 numbered copies, from a 400-copy edition). With "W. Spratling" on front end paper. $550. Other copies, $400-$600. Unnumbered copies, $150-$250.

FAUSET, Jessie. *Comedy American Style.* Orange cloth. New York, 1933. First edition. In dust jacket. $45.

FEAST of the Poets (The). By the Editor of the Examiner. Boards, paper label. London, 1814. (By Leigh Hunt.) First edition. $150-$180.

FEDERALISM Triumphant in the Steady Habits of Connecticut Alone, etc. Stitched. No place (New Haven?), 1802. (By Leonard Chester.) First edition. $75-$100.

FELLOWS-JOHNSTON, Annie. *The Little Colonel.* Green cloth. Boston, 1896. First edition. $45.

FENLEY, Florence. *Oldtimers: Their Own Stories.* Illustrated. Cloth. Uvalde, Tex., 1939. First edition. In dust jacket. $25-$35. Not signed, $30.

FENOLLOSA, Ernest F. *Certain Noble Plays of Japan.* From manuscripts of Fenollosa, chosen and finished by Ezra Pound. Introduction by W. B. Yeats. Boards, linen spine. Churchtown, Dundrum, Ireland, 1916. Cuala Press. One of 350. $65-$95.

FENOLLOSA, Ernest F. *The Chinese Written Character as a Medium for Poetry.* Foreword by Ezra Pound. Green boards. New York, no date (1936). First American edition. In dust jacket. $35-$50.

FERBER, Edna. *American Beauty.* Cloth. Garden City, 1931. First edition. One of 200 signed. In dust jacket. $25.

FERBER, Edna. *Cimarron.* Printed wrappers (advance copies). Garden City, 1930. First edition. One of 1,000. $35.

FERBER, Edna. *A Peculiar Treasure.* Boards and cloth. New York, 1939. First edition. One of 351 signed. In dust jacket. Boxed. $25-$35.

FERBER, Edna. *Saratoga Trunk.* Blue buckram. New York, 1941. First edition. One of 526 signed. In dust jacket. $25-$35. Trade edition: Cloth. In dust jacket. $10.

FERBER, Edna. *Show Boat.* Green boards, white vellum spine. Garden City, 1926. First edition. One of 201 signed. Boxed. $50. Also, $30 (A, 1968). Another issue: Decorated boards (presentation copies, not signed). One of 1,000. $15-$20. Trade edition: Yellow cloth. In dust jacket. $10-$12.50.

FERLINGHETTI, Lawrence. *Pictures of the Gone World.* Stiff black printed wrappers. No place, no date (San Francisco, 1955). First edition. With wraparound label. $25-$35. Author's first book.

FERLINGHETTI, Lawrence. *The Secret Meaning of Things.* Cloth. New York, no date (1968). First edition. One of 150 signed. Boxed. $30-$35.

FERNÁNDEZ DE SAN SALVADOR, Augustín. *Los Jesuitas Quitados y Restituidos al Mundo. Historia de la Antigua California.* Cloth or leather. Mexico, 1861. First edition. $100-$200.

FERRIER, Susan Edmonstone. See *Destiny, or, The Chief's Daughter: Marriage.*

FERRINI, Vincent. *No Smoke.* Red cloth, cover and spine labels. Portland, Me., 1941. First edition. $25. Author's first book.

FERTILE and Beautiful Palouse Country in Eastern Washington and Northern Idaho (The). 32 pp., oblong, wrappers. St. Paul, 1889. $50-$60.

FEUCHTWANGER, Dr. Lewis. *A Treatise on Gems.* Cloth. New York, 1838. $50.

FICKE, Arthur Davison. See Morgan, Emanuel, and Knish, Anne.

FIDFADDY, Frederick Augustus. *The Adventures of Uncle Sam in Search After His Lost Honor.* Boards. Middletown, Conn., 1816. First edition. $75-$100.

FIELD, Eugene. *Culture's Garland.* Cloth, or printed gray wrappers. Boston, 1887. First edition. Wrappers: $35-$50. Another issue: Wrappers, leaves untrimmed. One of 6 (or 12?). Inscribed, $250. Blue cloth: $50.

FIELD, Eugene. *Florence Bardsley's Story.* Green cloth. Chicago, 1897. First edition. One of 25 on Japan vellum. $50-$75. Another issue: One of 150 on paper. $25-$35.

FIELD, Eugene. *The Holy Cross and Other Tales.* Vellum. Cambridge and Chicago, 1893. First edition. One of 20 on vellum, signed by the publisher. $100-$150. Another issue: Blue cloth. One of 110 on paper, signed by the publisher. $75-$100. Trade edition: Cloth, $40-$50.

FIELD, Eugene. *A Little Book of Tribune Verse.* Cloth. Denver, 1901. First edition. One of 750. $25.

FIELD, Eugene. *A Little Book of Western Verse.* Blue-gray boards and cloth. Chicago, 1889. First edition. One of 250 large paper copies. $75-$100. Also, $55 (A, 1960). New York, 1890. Cloth. First trade edition. $25. (Note: The first appearance of "Little Boy Blue.")

FIELD, Eugene. *The Love Affairs of a Bibliomaniac.* Frontispiece. Blue cloth. New York, 1896. First edition, first issue, with 8 titles listed. $25. Another issue: Half vellum. One of 150 on Holland paper. $50-$60.

FIELD, Eugene. *Love-Songs of Childhood.* Vellum. New York, 1894. First edition. One of 106 on Van Gelder paper. $50-$75. Another issue: One of 15 on Japan vellum. $100-$150. Trade edition: Blue cloth. $15-$25.

FIELD, Eugene. *Second Book of Tales.* Half vellum. Chicago, 1896. First edition. One of 150. $35-$50.

FIELD, Eugene. *Second Book of Verse.* Boards, leather label. Chicago, 1892. First edition. One of 300. In dust jacket. $25-$35.

FIELD, Eugene. *Sharps and Flats.* 2 vols., blue cloth. New York, 1900. First edition. $25. New York, 1901. 2 vols., half vellum. One of 150. $35.

FIELD, Eugene. *The Symbol and the Saint.* Wrappers. No place (Chicago), 1886. First edition. $300-$400.

FIELD, Eugene. *Tribune Primer.* Gray-blue wrappers. No place, no date (Denver, 1881). First edition. $2,000 (1970 catalogue). Also, rebound in leather, $260 (A, 1959). Author's first book.

FIELD, Eugene. *With Trumpet and Drum.* Boards. New York, 1892. First edition. One of 250. $35-$50. Another issue: One of 12 on vellum. $100. Trade edition: Cloth. $15-$20.

FIELD, Rachel. *Hitty: Her First Hundred Years.* Illustrated by Dorothy P. Lathrop. Decorated cloth, paper label. New York, 1929. First edition. In dust jacket. $25.

FIELD, Rachel. *Rise Up, Jennie Smith.* Wrappers. New York, no date (1918). First edition. $25. Author's first book.

FIELD, Stephen J. *Personal Reminiscences of Early Days in California.* Half calf. No place, no date (San Francisco, 1880?). First edition. $60-$80.

FIELD, William B. Osgood. See *Edward Lear on My Shelves; John Leech on My Shelves.*

FIELDING, T. H. *A Picturesque Description of the River Wye.* 12 colored aquatint plates. Boards. London, 1841. $75-$100.

FIELDING, T. H., and Walton, J. *A Picturesque Tour of the English Lakes.* Color vignette and 48 colored aquatint plates. Cloth. London, 1821. $250-$300.

FIFTH Antiquarian Book Fair (The): A Handlist of Exhibitors Introduced by Lawrence Durrell. 12 pp., stapled, wrappers. London, 1962. One of 10 on green paper, signed. $225-$300.

FIGUEROA, José. *The Manifesto.* (Translated from the original as published in Monterey in 1835.) Printed wrappers. San Francisco, 1855. $500-$750. Also, $350 (A, 1968), $500 (A, 1959). Rebound in leather, $350 at retail.

FILIPPI, Rosina. *Three Japanese Plays for Children.* Illustrated by Alfred Parsons. 57 pp., wrappers. Oxford, 1897. Daniel Press. One of 135. $25.

FILISOLA, Gen. Vicente. *Evacuation of Texas.* 68 pp., half leather. Columbia, Tex., 1837. First edition in English. $1,250 and up.

FILISOLA, Gen. Vicente. *Representación dirigida al Supremo Gobierno por el General Vicente Filisola, en Defensa de Su Honor y Aclaración de Sus Operaciones como General en Gefe del Ejército sobre Tejas.* 82 pp., wrappers. Mexico, 1836. First edition. $350-$500. Also, $325 (A, 1966).

FILLEY, William. *Life and Adventures of William Filley.* 7 plates and half-page cut. 96 pp., wrappers. Chicago, 1867. Printed by Fergus. First edition. $750 and up. Another edition, same place and date: 112 pp., wrappers. Printed by Filley & Ballard. Second edition. $250-$300. Rebound in half morocco, front cover bound in, $150.

FINDLAY, Alex G. *The British American Navigator.* 5 illustrations. Printed wrappers. London, 1847. $60-$70.

FINLAY, John. *Journal Kept by Hugh Finlay, Surveyor of Post Roads.* Leather and cloth. Brooklyn, 1867. One of 150. $50-$75.

FINLEY, Ernest L. (editor). *History of Sonoma County.* (California.) Morocco. Santa Rosa, 1937. First edition. $35-$50.

FINLEY, James B. *History of the Wyandott Mission at Upper Sandusky, Ohio.* Calf. Cincinnati, 1840. First edition. $50-$60.

FINN, Huck. See Twain, Mark, *Tom Sawyer Abroad.*

FINNEY, Charles G. *The Circus of Doctor Lao.* Cloth. New York, 1935. First edition. In dust jacket. $25-$30.

FINNEY & Davis (publishers). *Biographical and Statistical History of the City of Oshkosh.* 76 pp., half leather. Oshkosh, Wis., 1867. First edition. $75-$100.

FIRBANK, Ronald. *Concerning the Eccentricities of Cardinal Pirelli.* Cloth. London, 1926. First edition. In dust jacket. $30-$40.

FIRBANK, Ronald. *Odette D'Antrevernes, and A Study in Temperament.* Pink or blue-gray wrappers. London, 1905. First edition. $90-$100.

FIRBANK, Ronald. *Prancing Nigger.* Introduction by Carl Van Vechten. New York, no date (1924). First edition. In dust jacket. $35-$50.

FIRBANK, Ronald. *Sorrow in Sunlight.* Cloth. London, 1925. First English edition (of *Prancing Nigger*). One of 1,000. In dust jacket. $50.

FIRST Annual Review of Pierce County. (Wisconsin.) 48 pp., wrappers. Prescott, Wis., 1855. $75.

FIRST Annual Report of the Directors of the Central Mining Co. 13 pp., wrappers. Detroit, 1855. $35.

FIRST Catalogues and Circulars of the Botanical Garden of Transylvania University at Lexington in Kentucky, for the Year 1824. 24 pp., sewed. Lexington, 1824. (By C. S. Rafinesque.) $75.

FIRST Published Life of Abraham Lincoln (The). (Reprint of John Locke Scripps biography.) Half vellum. No place, no date (Detroit, 1900). Cranbrook Press. One of 245. $50-$75.

FIRST Settlement and Early History of Palmyra, Wayne County, New York (The). 10 pp., printed wrappers. Palmyra, 1858. $50-$75. Repaired, $45.

FIRST Settlers of New England (The), or, Conquest of the Pequods, Narragansets and Pokanokets. By a Lady of Massachusetts. Boards. Boston, no date (1829). (By Lydia Maria Child.) First edition, first issue, with undated title page. $50.

FISH, Daniel. *Lincoln Bibliography.* Red cloth. New York, no date (1906). One of 75 signed. Boxed. $35-$50.

FISH, H. C. *The Voice of Our Brother's Blood: Its Source and Its Summons.* 16 pp., sewed. Newark, 1856. First edition. $100-$150.

FISHER, George. *Memorials of George Fisher, etc.* Cloth. Houston, 1840. First edition. $100-$200.

FISHER, Harry C. *The Mutt and Jeff Cartoons.* Oblong folio, pictorial boards and cloth. Boston, 1910. First edition. $25. First Mutt and Jeff book.

FISHER, John, Bishop of Rochester. *A Mornynge Remembraunce.* Frontispiece by C. R. Ashbee. Vellum. London, 1906. One of 7 on vellum. $95.

FISHER, O. C. *It Occurred in Kimble.* Illustrated. Pictorial cloth. Houston, 1937. First edition. One of 500. $35-$50.

FISHER, Richard S. *Indiana: Its Geography, Statistics, County Topography.* Large folding map in color. Cloth. New York, 1852. $40-$50.

FISHER, Rudolph. *The Walls of Jericho.* Decorated cloth. New York, 1928. First edition. $25-$30.

FISHER, Vardis. *April: A Fable of Love.* Morocco. Caldwell, Idaho, and Garden City, 1937. First edition (so stated). One of 50 signed. $50-$75. Trade edition: Cloth. In dust jacket. $10-$15.

FISHER, Vardis. *Children of God, an American Epic.* Leather. Caldwell, 1939. First edition. One of 100 signed. $50-$75. New York, 1939. Cloth. First trade edition. In dust jacket. $25.

FISHER, Vardis. *City of Illusion.* Cloth. New York, no date. First edition. In dust jacket. $20-$25. Caldwell, 1941. One of 1,000. $35-$50. Another issue: Morocco. One of 100 signed. $75-$100.

FISHER, Vardis. *Dark Bridwell.* Cloth. Boston, 1931. First edition. In dust jacket. $25.

FISHER, Vardis. *Forgive Us Our Virtues.* Morocco. Caldwell, 1938. First edition. One of 75 signed. $75-$100. Also, $32 (A, 1969). Trade edition: Cloth. In dust jacket. $10-$15.

FISHER, Vardis. *A Goat for Azazel.* Cloth. Denver, no date (1956). First edition. One of 200 signed. $25-$35.

FISHER, Vardis. *In Tragic Life.* Cloth. Caldwell, 1932. First edition. In dust jacket. $35-$50. Another issue: Leather. One of 25 signed. $100. Garden City, 1932. Cloth. In dust jacket. $10-$15.

FISHER, Vardis. *Jesus Came Again.* Cloth. Denver, no date (1956). First edition. One of 200 signed. $25-$35.

FISHER, Vardis. *My Holy Satan.* Cloth. Denver, no date (1958). First edition. One of 200 signed. $25.

FISHER, Vardis. *The Neurotic Nightingale.* Cloth. No place, no date (Milwaukee, 1935). First edition. One of 300 signed. $50-$75. One of 25 unsigned (for review). $25.

FISHER, Vardis. *No Villain Need Be.* Cloth. Caldwell, 1936. First edition (so stated). In dust jacket. $25. Another issue: One of 75 in full leather, signed. $50-$75. Garden City, 1936. In dust jacket. $10-$15.

FISHER, Vardis. *Odyssey of a Hero.* Half cloth. Philadelphia, 1937. First edition. One of 50 signed. $75-$100. Trade edition: Cloth. $10-$15.

FISHER, Vardis. *Passions Spin the Plot.* Cloth. Caldwell, 1933. First edition, first state, with 1933 date (suppressed). In dust jacket. $100-$125. Also, $55 (A, 1963). Caldwell, 1934. Second state (dated 1934). In dust jacket. $25-$35. Another issue: Morocco. One of 75 signed. $50-$75.

FISHER, Vardis. *Peace Like a River.* Cloth. Denver, no date (1957). First edition. One of 200 signed. $25-$35.

FISHER, Vardis. *Sonnets to an Imaginary Madonna.* Boards, pink paper labels. New York, 1927. First edition. In dust jacket. $60-$75. Author's first book.

FISHER, Vardis. *Toilers of the Hills.* Cloth. Boston, 1928. First edition. In dust jacket. $25-$35.

FISHER, Vardis. *We Are Betrayed.* Cloth. Caldwell, no date (1935). First edition (so stated). In dust jacket. $25. Another issue: Morocco. One of 75 signed. $50-$75. Garden City, 1935. Cloth. In dust jacket. $10-$15.

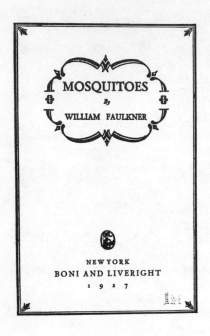

MOSQUITOES
By
WILLIAM FAULKNER

NEW YORK
BONI AND LIVERIGHT
1 9 2 7

SONNETS
TO AN
IMAGINARY
MADONNA

BY VARDIS FISHER

NEW YORK · HAROLD VINAL
MCMXXVII ·

Price 50 Cents.

MLISS.

AN IDYL OF RED·MOUNTAIN.

A STORY OF CALIFORNIA IN 1863.

BY BRET HARTE,

Author of "Condensed Novels," "Heathen Chinee," "Luck of Roaring Camp,"
"Mrs. Skaggs's Husbands," Etc., Etc.

NEW YORK:
ROBERT M. DE WITT, PUBLISHER,
No. 33 ROSE STREET,
(Between Duane and Frankfort Streets.)

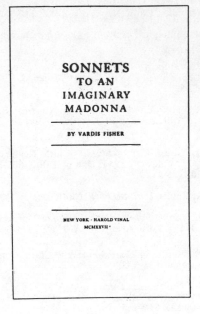

TEXAS.

OBSERVATIONS,

HISTORICAL, GEOGRAPHICAL AND DESCRIPTIVE,

In a Series of Letters,

Written during a Visit to Austin's Colony, with a view to a permanent
settlement in that country, in the Autumn of 1831.

BY MRS. MARY AUSTIN HOLLEY.

WITH AN APPENDIX,

Containing specific answers to certain questions, relative to Colonization in Texas, issued some time since by the London Geographical
Society. Also, some notice of the recent political events in that
quarter.

BALTIMORE:
ARMSTRONG & PLASKITT.
1833.

FISHER, William (compiler). *An Interesting Account of the Voyages and Travels of Captains Lewis and Clark.* 2 portraits. Calf. Baltimore, 1812. $50-$60. Baltimore, 1813. 2 portraits, 4 (sometimes 3) plates. Calf. $35-$50.

FISK, Capt. James L. *Expedition from Fort Abercrombie to Fort Benton.* (Caption title.) House Exec. Doc. No. 80. 36 pp., sewed. No place, no date (Washington, 1863). First edition. $35-$50.

FITCH, Samuel Sheldon. *A System of Dental Surgery.* Plates, folding tables. Calf. Philadelphia, 1835. Second edition. $35-$50.

FITE, Emerson D., and Freeman, Archibald (editors). *A Book of Old Maps Delineating American History.* 74 maps in facsimile, colored frontispiece. Folio, cloth. Cambridge, Mass., 1926. First edition. $150-$200.

FITHIAN, Philip Vickers. *Journal and Letters, 1767-1774.* 8 plates. Cloth. Princeton, N.J., 1900. First edition. $50-$75.

FITTS, Dudley. *Two Poems.* Wrappers. No place, no date (1932). First edition. $35.

FITZ GERALD, Edward. See Aeschylus. Also see *The Downfall and Death of King Oedipus; Euphranor; The Mighty Magician; Polonius; Readings in Crabbe's "Tales of the Hall"; Rubaiyat of Omar Khayyam; Salaman and Absal; The Two Generals.*

FITZ GERALD, Edward. *Letters and Literary Remains of Edward FitzGerald.* Edited by William Aldis Wright. Frontispiece plates. 3 vols., cloth. London, 1889. First edition. $25. London, 1902-03. 7 vols., cloth. One of 775. $100-$125.

FITZ GERALD, Edward. *Letters of Edward FitzGerald.* Frontispiece. 2 vols., cloth. London, 1894. First edition. $25.

FITZ GERALD, Edward. *Letters of Edward FitzGerald to Fanny Kemble, 1871-1883.* Edited by William Aldis Wright. Frontispiece portrait. Cloth. London, 1895. First edition. $25.

FITZ GERALD, Edward (translator). *Six Dramas of Calderon.* Watered crimson cloth. London, 1853. First edition. $50-$60.

FITZGERALD, F. Scott. See Van Dyke, Henry. Also see *Safety First.*

FITZGERALD, F. Scott. *All the Sad Young Men.* Dark-green cloth. New York, 1926. First edition, first printing, with Scribner seal on copyright page. In dust jacket. $150-$200.

FITZGERALD, F. Scott. *The Beautiful and Damned.* Dark-green cloth. New York, 1922. First edition, first issue, with no ads at back and with "Published March, 1922" on copyright page. In dust jacket. $100-$150. Dust jacket mended, $95. Lacking jacket, $65. Toronto, 1922. Cloth. First Canadian edition. In dust jacket. $75.

FITZGERALD, F. Scott. *The Crack-Up.* Edited by Edmund Wilson. Patterned boards and cloth, paper label. No place (Norfolk), 1945. New Directions. First edition, first printing, with title page in red and black. In dust jacket. $50.

FITZGERALD, F. Scott. *Flappers and Philosophers.* Cloth. New York, 1920. First edition, first printing, with "Published September, 1920" and publisher's seal on copyright page. In dust jacket. $100-$150.

FITZGERALD, F. Scott. *The Great Gatsby.* Dark-green cloth. New York, 1925. First edition, first issue, with "sick in tired" in line 9 of page 205. In dust jacket. $200-$350.

FITZGERALD, F. Scott. *Tales of the Jazz Age.* Dark-green cloth. New York, 1922. First edition, first issue, with "Published September, 1922" and Scribner seal on copyright page. In dust jacket. $100-$150.

FITZGERALD, F. Scott. *Taps at Reveille.* Green cloth. New York, 1935. First edition, with Scribner "A" on copyright page. In dust jacket. $135-$150.

FITZGERALD, F. Scott. *Tender Is the Night.* Dark-green cloth. New York, 1934. First edition, first issue, with Scribner "A" and seal on copyright page. In dust jacket. $100-$150. Advance review copy: Review slip and bookplate pasted in. In dust jacket. $175.

FITZGERALD, F. Scott. *This Side of Paradise.* Dark-green cloth. New York, 1920. First edition, first printing, with "Published April, 1920" and publisher's seal on copyright page. In dust jacket. $150-$250. Author's first book.

FITZGERALD, F. Scott. *The Vegetable.* Dark-green cloth. New York, 1923. First edition, first printing, with "Published April, 1923" and publisher's seal on copyright page. In dust jacket. $100-$150.

FITZGERALD, Zelda. *Save Me the Waltz.* Green cloth. New York, 1932. First edition. In dust jacket. $75-$100.

FIVE Years in a Lottery Office. Wrappers. Boston, 1841. (By John J. More.) First edition. $40-$50.

FIVE Young American Poets. Tan cloth. Norfolk, Conn., 1944. New Directions. First edition. In dust jacket. $35-$50. (Note: Contains work by Tennessee Williams and others.)

FLECKER, James Elroy. *The Golden Journey to Samarkand.* Dark-blue cloth. London, 1913. First edition. $25-$35. Another issue: Boards. One of 50 signed. $50.

FLEMING, C. B. *Early History of Hopkins County, Texas.* Cloth. No place, 1902. $50-$75.

FLEMING, Sanford. *Memorial of the People of Red River to the British and Canadian Governments.* 7 pp., printed front paper cover. Quebec, 1863. $200.

FLEMING, Walter L. *Documentary History of Reconstruction.* 9 facsimiles. 2 vols., half calf. Cleveland, 1906-07. First edition. $50-$60.

FLETCHER, Charles H. *Jefferson County, Iowa, Centennial History.* 35 pp., printed wrappers. Fairfield, Iowa, 1876. $75-$100. Also, rebound in cloth, $35 (A, 1966).

FLETCHER, John Gould. *Fire and Wine.* Cloth. London, no date (May, 1913). First edition. $150. (Offered by dealer in 1972.)

FLETCHER, John Gould. *Irradiations: Sand and Spray.* Green wrappers. Boston, 1915. First edition. $40-$50.

FLETCHER, John Gould. *Japanese Prints.* Cloth. Boston, 1918. Four Seas Press. First edition. $35-$50.

FLETCHER, John Gould. *Preludes and Symphonies.* Cloth, paper label. New York, 1930. First edition. In dust jacket. $35-$40.

FLETCHER, John Gould. *XXIV Elegies.* Cloth. Santa Fe, N.M., no date (1935). First edition. One of 400 signed. $25-$35.

FLETCHER, W. A. *A Rebel Private, Front and Rear.* Portrait. Cloth. Beaumont, Tex., 1908. First edition. $75.

FLEURY, Claude. *A Short Catechism, Containing a Summary of Sacred History, and Christian Doctrine.* Calf. Detroit, 1812. $725 (A, 1958).

FLICKINGER, Robert E. *Pioneer History of Pocahontas County, Iowa.* Cloth. Fonda, Iowa, 1904. $50-$60.

FLINT, James. *Letters from America.* Boards and calf. Edinburgh, 1822. First edition. Presentation copy. $35.

FLINT, Micah P. *The Hunter and Other Poems.* Boards. Boston, 1826. First edition. Worn, $50.

FLINT, Timothy. *A Condensed Geography and History of the Western States, or the Mississippi Valley.* 2 vols., tan boards, paper labels. Cincinnati, 1828. First edition. $75-$100.

FLINT, Timothy. *Indian Wars of the West.* Calf, or half leather. Cincinnati, 1833. $50-$75.

FLINT, Timothy. *Lectures Upon Natural History.* Cloth. Boston, 1833. First edition. $35.

FLINT, Timothy. *Recollections of the Last Ten Years.* Tan boards, paper label. Boston, 1826. First edition. $100-$150.

FLORENCE Farr, Bernard Shaw, and W. B. Yeats: Letters. Edited by Clifford Bax. Boards, cloth spine. Dublin, 1941. Cuala Press. One of 500. $35-$45.

FLOURE (The) and The Leafe, & the Boke of Cupide, God of Love, or the Cuckow and the Nightingale. 2 large woodcut initial words from the Kelmscott Chaucer. Printed in black and red. Boards and linen. London, 1896. Kelmscott Press. One of 300. $300-$325.

FLOWER, Richard. *Letters from Illinois, 1810-1821.* 76 pp., half morocco. London, 1822. First edition. $300-$500.

FLOWER, Robin (translator). *Love's Bitter-Sweet.* Boards and linen. Dublin, 1925. Cuala Press. One of 500. In dust jacket. $50-$75.

FOGGY Night at Newport (A). 39 pp., wrappers. St. Louis, 1860. (By Henry C. Brokmyer.) First edition. $50-$75.

FOLEY, P. K. *American Authors, 1795-1895: A Bibliography.* Cloth. Boston, 1897. One of 500. $50-$60. One of 75. $75-$100.

FOOTE, Henry Stuart. *Texas and the Texans.* 2 vols., cloth. Philadelphia, 1841. First edition. $100-$150.

FORBES, Alexander. *California: A History.* 10 lithographs, map colored in outline. Cloth. London, 1839. First edition, with errata slip. $200-$300. San Francisco, 1919. Map, 10 plates. One of 250 signed by the publisher. $80-$100. San Francisco, 1937. John Henry Nash printing. Marbled boards. One of 650. In dust jacket. $50-$60. San Francisco, 1939. $35-$50.

FORBES, Edwin. *Life Studies of the Great Army.* 40 plates. Half morocco. No place (New York), 1876. First edition. $150.

FORBES, Edwin. *Thirty Years After: An Artist's Story of the Great War.* 80 full-page plates, 20 portraits. 4 vols., folio, cloth. New York, no date (1890). First edition. $150. Another issue: 2 vols., cloth. $50.

FORBES, Sir James. *Oriental Memoirs.* 21 colored plates, other illustrations. 4 vols., contemporary full red morocco. London, 1813. First edition. $200-$300. London, 1834-35. 3 vols. (including atlas), half morocco. $100-$150.

FORBES, James Grant. *Sketches, Historical and Topographical, of the Floridas.* Map (not in all copies). Boards, paper label. New York, 1821. First edition. With the map. $150-$250.

FORBUSH, Edward Howe. *Birds of Massachusetts and Other New England States.* Color illustrations by L. A. Fuertes. 3 vols., cloth. No place (Boston), 1925-27-29. $125-$150.

FORBUSH, Edward Howe. *Our American Game Birds.* 18 color plates. Wilmington, Del., no date (1917). (Published by E. I. Du Pont de Nemours and Co.) $30-$35.

FORD, Charles Henri. *The Garden of Disorder and Other Poems.* Boards and cloth. London, no date (1938). First edition. One of 30 signed. In dust jacket. $50-$60.

FORD, Ford Madox. See Conrad, Joseph, and Hueffer, Ford Madox. (Note: Ford changed his name from Hueffer to Ford in 1919.) Also see *The Imagist Anthology.*

FORD, Ford Madox. *Mr. Bosphorus and the Muses.* Illustrated by Paul Nash. Cloth. London, no date (1923). First edition. One of 70. $75.

FORD, Ford Madox. *The Good Soldier.* Cloth. New York, 1927. First edition. In dust jacket. $100-$150.

FORD, Ford Madox. *Joseph Conrad: A Personal Remembrance.* Frontispiece, 2 other plates. Green cloth. London, 1924. First edition. In dust jacket. $25.

FORD, Ford Madox. *No More Parades.* Cloth. London, no date (1925). First edition. In dust jacket. $25-$30.

FORD, Ford Madox Hueffer. *Women & Men.* Wrappers. Paris, 1923. Three Mountains Press. First edition. One of 300. $250-$300.

FORD, James Everett. *A History of Grundy County, Missouri.* Illustrated. Cloth. Trenton, 1908. $40-$60.

FORD, Paul Leicester. *Franklin Bibliography.* Half leather. Brooklyn, 1889. First edition. One of 500. $40-$60.

FORD, Paul Leicester. *The Great K. & A. Train Robbery.* New York, 1897. First edition, first state, 7¼ inches tall, with top edges gilt, others untrimmed. $25-$35.

FORD, Paul Leicester. *The Honorable Peter Stirling and What People Thought of Him.* Red cloth. New York, 1894. First edition, first state, with "Sterling" for "Stirling" on front cover. $75-$100.

FORD, Thomas. *A History of Illinois.* Half leather. Chicago, 1854. First edition. $75.

FORD, Thomas. *Message of the Governor to the General Assembly, Dec. 2, 1844.* 12 pp., sewed. Springfield, Ill., 1844. $35-$50.

FORD, Webster. *Songs and Sonnets.* Cloth. Chicago, 1910. (By Edgar Lee Masters.) First edition. $50-$75.

FORE and Aft; or, Leaves from the Life of an Old Sailor. By "Webfoot." Illustrated. Cloth. Boston, 1871. (By W. D. Phelps). First edition. $100-$150.

FOREMAN, Grant. *Advancing the Frontier.* Maps. Cloth. Norman, Okla., 1933. First edition. In dust jacket. $35-$50.

FOREMAN, Grant. *Indian Removal.* Cloth. Norman, 1932. First edition. In dust jacket. $50-$75.

FOREMAN, Grant. *Indians and Pioneers.* Map, 8 plates. Cloth. New Haven, Conn., 1930. First edition. In dust jacket. $35-$50.

FOREMAN, Grant. *Pioneer Days in the Early Southwest.* Folding map. Cloth. Cleveland, 1926. First edition. $75-$100.

FOREMAN, Grant (editor). *Indian Justice.* Cloth. Harlow, Okla., 1934.-(By John Payne.) First edition. In dust jacket. $25.

FOREST and Stream Fables. Sewed. New York, no date (1886). (By Rowland Evans Robinson.) First edition. $150. Author's first published work.

FORESTER, Frank. See Forrester, Frank; Herbert, Henry William; Herbert, W. H.

FORESTER, Frank. *American Game in Its Seasons.* Illustrated by the author. Cloth. New York, 1853. (By Henry William Herbert.) First edition. $75-$100.

FORESTER, Frank. *The Complete Manual for Young Sportsmen.* Illustrated by the author. Cloth. New York, 1856. (By Henry William Herbert.) First edition. $35-$50.

FORESTER, Frank. *The Deerstalkers.* Printed wrappers. Philadelphia, 1849. (By Henry William Herbert.) First edition. $300-$400. Also, rebound in half cloth, $220 (A, 1962).

FORESTER, Frank. *Field Sports in the United States, and the British Provinces of America.* 2 vols., green cloth. London, 1848. (By Henry William Herbert.) First edition, first issue, with "Provinces of America" on title page (changed later to "Provinces of North America"). $100-$125. New York, 1849. 2 vols., green cloth. First American edition, first issue, with "Ruffed Grouse" frontispiece. (Issued as *Frank Forester's Field Sports of the United States, etc.)* $100-$125.

FORESTER, Frank. *Frank Forester and His Friends.* 3 vols., salmon cloth. London, 1849. (By Henry William Herbert.) First edition. $35-$50.

FORESTER, Frank. *Frank Forester's Fish and Fishing of the United States and British Provinces of North America.* Illustrated by the author. Blue cloth. London, 1849. (By Henry William Herbert.) First English edition. (Note: Possibly issued simultaneously with the American first edition, according to Blanck.) $35-$50. New York, 1850 (actually 1849). Blue cloth. First American edition. $35. New York, 1850. Second American edition, with bound sheets of the *Supplement* of 1850 bound in. (See Forester, *Supplement.*) $50.

FORESTER, Frank. *Frank Forester's Fugitive Sporting Sketches.* Edited by Will Wildwood (Fred E. Pond). Cloth or wrappers. Westfield, Wis., 1879. (By Henry William Herbert.) First edition. Wrappers: $50-$75. Cloth: $35-$50.

FORESTER, Frank. *Frank Forester's Horse and Horsemanship of the United States and British Provinces of North America.* Plates, pedigree tables. 2 vols., purple cloth. New York, 1857. (By Henry William Herbert.) First edition. $75-$100. Another issue: Half morocco. $50.

FORESTER, Frank. *Hints to Horse-Keepers.* Frontispiece, 23 plates. Cloth. New York, 1859. (By Henry William Herbert.) First edition. $35-$50.

FORESTER, Frank. *The Hitchcock Edition of Frank Forester.* 4 vols., cloth. New York, 1930. (By Henry William Herbert.) Derrydale Press. First edition. $150.

FORESTER, Frank. *My Shooting Box.* Frontispiece, 2 plates. Cloth. Philadelphia, 1846. (By Henry William Herbert.) First edition, first state, with ads dated May, 1845, on page 180 and "mattter" for "matter" in last line of page 35. $250-$350. Also, in new morocco, $220 (A, 1962).

FORESTER, Frank. *Supplement to Frank Forester's Fish and Fishing.* Frontispiece. Cloth. New York, 1850. (By Henry William Herbert.) First edition. $35-$50.

FORESTER, Frank. *Trouting Along the Catasauqua.* Boards. New York, 1927. (By Henry William Herbert.) First edition. One of 423. In dust jacket. $50-$60.

FORESTER, Frank. *The Warwick Woodlands.* Printed tan-yellow wrappers. Philadelphia, 1845. (By Henry William Herbert.) First edition. $1,000 and up. Rebound, $500 and up. Also, $275 (A, 1962). New York, 1851. Illustrated. Cloth, or printed wrappers. Second edition. Wrappers: $300-$500. Cloth: $75-$100. New York, 1934. Derrydale Press. Leatherette. $100-$150.

FORESTER, Harry. *Ocean Jottings from England to British Columbia.* Cloth. Vancouver, 1891. $45.

FORNEY, Col. John W. *What I Saw in Texas.* (Cover title.) Map and plates. 92 pp., pictorial wrappers. Philadelphia, no date (1872). First edition. $100-$150.

FORREST, Lieut. Col. Charles R. *A Picturesque Tour Along the Rivers Ganges and Jumna, in India.* 24 colored plates, map, colored vignettes. Cloth. London, 1824. First edition. $300-$400.

FORRESTER, Frank. *Fishing with Hook and Line.* Printed wrappers. New York, no date (1858). (By Henry William Herbert.) First edition, with Brother Jonathan imprint. $900 (A, 1962)—"one of two known copies."

FORSTER, E. M. *Abinger Harvest.* Plain brown printed wrappers. London, no date (1936). First edition. Advance proof copy, including "A Flood in the Office," later eliminated. $225. First published edition: Cloth. In dust jacket. $25-$35.

FORSTER, E. M. *Alexandria: A History and a Guide.* Folding map in pocket at rear. Boards. Alexandria, Egypt, 1922. First edition. $125-$150. Alexandria, 1938. Boards. Second edition. One of 250 signed. $200-$225. Also, $120 (A, 1969).

FORSTER, E. M. *Anonymity: An Enquiry.* Illustrated boards. No place (London), 1925. Hogarth Press. First edition. $50-$60.

FORSTER, E. M. *Aspects of the Novel.* Dark-red cloth. London, 1927. First edition. In dust jacket. $35-$50.

FORSTER, E. M. *The Celestial Omnibus and Other Stories.* Brown cloth. London, 1911. First edition. $75-$100.

FORSTER, E. M. *Egypt.* Wrappers, paper label. No place, no date (1920). (Official recommendations of a Labour committee, London, 1919.) First edition. $100-$125. Also, $62 (A, 1971).

FORSTER, E. M. *The Eternal Moment and Other Stories.* Red cloth. London, 1928. First edition. In dust jacket. $80-$100.

FORSTER, E. M. *Goldsworthy Lowes Dickinson.* Plain wrappers. London, 1934. First edition. Advance proof copy. $60. First published edition: Cloth. In dust jacket. $15-$25.

FORSTER, E. M. *Howard's End.* Cloth. London, 1910. First edition. In dust jacket. $50-$75.

FORSTER, E. M. *Le Legs de Mrs. Wilcox.* Wrappers. Paris, no date (1950). First French edition of *Howard's End.* One of 10 copies Hors Commerce. $45.

FORSTER, E. M. *Le Plus Long des Voyages.* Wrappers. Paris, no date (1952). First French translation of *The Longest Journey.* One of 10 copies Hors Commerce. $35.

FORSTER, E. M. *The Longest Journey.* Cloth. London, 1907. First edition. $75-$100. Also, $28 (A, 1965).

FORSTER, E. M. *Monteriano.* Wrappers. Paris, no date (1954). First French edition of *Where Angels Fear to Tread.* One of 12 copies Hors Commerce. $50.

FORSTER, E. M. *A Passage to India.* Red cloth. London, 1924. First edition. In dust jacket. $100-$150. Another issue: Boards and cloth. One of 200 signed. In slipcase. $400-$600.

FORSTER, E. M. *Pharos and Pharillon.* Boards. No place (Richmond, England), 1923. Hogarth Press. First edition, first issue, with horizontal pattern on boards. $60-$80. New York, 1923. Orange cloth. Find American edition. In dust jacket. $25-$35.

FORSTER, E. M. *The Story of the Siren.* Wrappers. Richmond, 1920. Hogarth Press. First edition. One of 500. $100-$125.

FORSTER, E. M. *Where Angels Fear to Tread.* Cloth. London, 1905. First edition, first issue, with this title not mentioned in ads at back. $150-$200. Author's first book. New York, 1920. Black cloth. First American edition. In dust jacket. $35-$50.

FORSYTH, James W., and Grant, F. D. *Report of an Expedition up the Yellowstone River, Made in 1875.* Folding map. 17 pp., wrappers. Washington, 1875. $35-$50.

FORT Braddock Letters. Boards and calf. Worcester, Mass., 1827. (By John G. C. Brainard.) $25-$35.

FORT, Charles. *The Book of the Damned.* Cloth. New York, 1919. First edition. In dust jacket. $40-$60.

FORT, Charles. *Lo!* Cloth. Illustrated by Alexander King. New York, no date (1931). First edition. In dust jacket. $35-$50.

FORT, Charles. *The Outcast Manufacturers.* Cloth. New York, 1909. First edition. $50. Author's first book.

FORTUNES of Colonel Torlogh O'Brien (The). 10 monthly parts, wrappers. Dublin, 1847. (By Joseph Sheridan Le Fanu.) First edition. $200-$250.

FORTUNES of Nigel (The). 3 vols., boards, paper labels. Edinburgh, 1822. (By Sir Walter Scott.) First edition. $150-$250.

FORTUNES of Perkin Warbeck (The). 3 vols., boards, cloth spine, printed labels. London, 1830. (By Mary Wollstonecraft Shelley.) First edition. $150-$250.

FOSS, Sam Walter. *The Song of the Library Staff.* Illustrated by Merle Johnson. Stapled. New York, 1906. First edition. $25.

FOSTER, Charles. *The Gold Placers of California.* Map. Printed wrappers. Akron, Ohio, 1849. First edition. $1,750 (A, 1968).

FOSTER, The Rev. G. L. *The Past of Ypsilanti.* 48 pp., printed wrappers. Detroit, 1857. First edition. $50-$60.

FOSTER, George G. (editor). *The Gold Regions of California.* Frontispiece map. Printed wrappers. New York, 1848. $100-$150. London, no date (1849). $75.

FOSTER, George G. *New-York by Gaslight.* Wrappers. New York, 1850. First edition. $35-$50.

FOSTER, Isaac. *The Foster Family, California Pioneers.* Illustrated. Cloth. No place, no date (Santa Barbara, Calif., 1925). $100.

FOSTER, James S. *Advantages of Dakota Territory.* 51 pp., wrappers. Yankton, 1873. First edition. $300-$400. Also, rebound in cloth, $225 (A, 1968).

FOSTER, James S. *Outlines of History of the Territory of Dakota and Emigrant's Guide to the Free Lands of the Northwest.* Folding map. 127 pp., wrappers. Yankton, 1870. First edition. $1,000 and up. Also, $950 (A, 1968).

FOUNTAIN, Albert J. *Bureau of Immigration of the Territory of New Mexico: Report of Dona Ana County.* 34 pp., wrappers. Santa Fe, N.M., 1882. $50-$75.

FOUQUÉ, F. H. K. de La Motte. *Undine.* Illustrated in color by Arthur Rackham. Vellum with ties. London, 1909. Limited edition, signed. $150-$200.

FOUR Gospels of the Lord Jesus Christ (The). Decorations by Eric Gill. Half pigskin. Waltham Saint Lawrence, England, 1931. Golden Cockerel Press. One of 500. In slipcase. $600-$850. Also, $448 and $476 (A, 1967).

FOURTEENTH Anniversary of the Society of California Pioneers. Wrappers. San Francisco, 1864. $75.

FOX, John, Jr. *The Little Shepherd of Kingdom Come.* Illustrated by F. C. Yohn. Smooth red cloth, paper label. New York, 1903. First edition, first issue, with "laugh" for "lap" in line 14, page 61. One of 100 signed by Fox and Yohn. $35-$50. Trade edition: Ribbed red cloth. $25. New York, 1931. Illustrated by N. C. Wyeth. Half vellum. One of 512 signed by Wyeth. $40-$60. Also, $45 (A, 1969).

FOX, John, Jr. *The Trail of the Lonesome Pine.* Red cloth. New York, 1908. First edition, first state, with Scribner seal on copyright page. $25-$30.

FOX, William F. *Regimental Losses in the American Civil War, 1861-1865.* Cloth. Albany, 1889. First edition. $35-$40.

FRAENKEL, Michael. *Werther's Younger Brother: The Story of an Attitude.* Printed wrappers. New York, no date (1931). Carrefour Editions. One of 400. In glassine dust jacket. $25-$35.

FRA Luca de Pacioli of Borge S. Sepolcro. Portrait, plates. Boards, vellum spine. New York, 1933. Grolier Club. One of 390. $40-$50.

FRANCE, Its King, Court, and Government. By an American. Cloth. New York, 1840. (By General Lewis Cass.) First edition. $50-$75.

FRANCHÈRE, Gabriel. *Narrative of a Voyage to the Northwest Coast 'of America, etc.* 3 plates. Cloth. New York, 1854. First edition in English. $75-$150.

FRANCHÈRE, Gabriel. *Relation d'un Voyage à la Côte du Nord-Ouest de l'Amérique Septentrionale, dans les Années 1810-1814.* Contemporary calf. Montreal, 1820. First edition. $750 and up. Also, $600 (A, 1969).

FRANCIS, Grant R. *Old English Drinking Glasses.* 71 plates. Buckram. London, 1926. $90-$100.

FRANCIS of Assisi, St. *I Fioretti del Glorioso Poverello di Cristo S. Francesco di Assisi.* 54 woodcuts. Vellum. London, 1922. Ashendene Press. One of 240. $300-$325.

FRANCIS of Assisi, St. *Un Mazzetto Scelto di Certi Fioretti del Glorioso Poverello di Cristo San Francesco di Assisi insieme col Cantico al sole del Medesimo.* 11 woodcuts. Folio, boards. London, 1904. Ashendene Press. One of 150. $300-$350. Another issue: One of 25 on vellum. $600-$800.

FRANCIS Parkman. 4 pp., leaflet. No place, no date (Boston, 1894). (By Oliver Wendell Holmes.) First edition. One of 50 (74?). $50-$60.

FRANK Fairleigh; or Scenes from the Life of a Private Pupil. Illustrated by George Cruikshank. 15 parts, blue-green wrappers. London, 1850. (By Frank E. Smedley.) First edition, first issue, with dated title page. $150-$200. Backs of three wrappers incorrect, two inserts lacking, $100. Another issue: Cloth. $35-$50.

FRANKENSTEIN; or The Modern Prometheus. 3 vols., boards, paper labels. London, 1818. (By Mary Wollstonecraft Shelley.) First edition. $1,000 and up. Spines defective, $750. Contemporary red leatherette backstrips, $650. New York, 1924. Limited Editions Club. Illustrated. Half leather. Boxed. $35-$50.

FRANKS, David. *The New-York Directory.* 82 pp., cloth. New York, 1786. First edition. $3,500. Also, $1,100 (A, 1969). (Note: There is an earlier auction record of $2,500.) New York, 1909. Folding map. Printed wrappers. Reprint. $35. Also, $16 (A, 1969).

FRAZER, Sir James George. *Totemism.* Cloth. Edinburgh, 1887. First edition. $50. Author's first book.

FREDERIC, Harold. *The Damnation of Theron Ware.* Dark-green cloth. Chicago, 1896. First edition. $50-$75.

FREDERIC, Harold. *The Deserter and Other Stories.* Cloth. Boston, no date (1898). First edition. $25-$30.

FREDERIC, Harold. *Seth's Brother's Wife.* Tan cloth. New York, 1887. First edition, first issue, with 1886 copyright and no ads. $25-$35.

FREDERICK, J. George (editor). *Artists' and Writers' Chap Book.* Wrappers. No place (New York), 1933. First edition. $30-$50.

FREDERICK, J. V. *Ben Holladay, the Stagecoach King.* Folding map. Cloth. Glendale, Calif., 1940. $50-$75. Also, $37 (A, 1969).

FREE-and-Easy Songbook (The). Plates. Davy Crockett portrait on title page. Cloth. Philadelphia, 1834. $45.

FREEMAN, George D. *Midnight and Noonday.* Printed boards and cloth. Caldwell, Kan., 1890. First edition. $150-$200. Also, $125 (A, 1968). Caldwell, 1892. Red cloth. Second edition. $50-$60.

FREEMAN, James W. See *Prose and Poetry of the Live Stock Industry.*

FREMAUX, Leon J. *New Orleans Characters.* 17 color plates. Folio, cloth and morocco. No place (New Orleans), 1876. First edition. $175-$200.

FRÉMONT, John Charles. *Geographical Memoir Upon Upper California.* Senate Misc. Doc. No. 148. Folding map (not in all copies). 67 pp., wrappers. Washington, 1848. First edition, with map. $75-$100. Lacking map, $35-$50.

FRÉMONT, John Charles. *Narrative of the Exploring Expedition to the Rocky Mountains, in the Year 1842, etc.* Folding map by Rufus B. Sage, 2 plates. Cloth. Syracuse, 1847. $300-$350. (First publication of the famous Sage map.)

FRÉMONT, John Charles. *Oregon and California: The Exploring Expedition to the Rocky Mountains, Oregon and California.* 2 portraits, 2 plates. Cloth. Buffalo, 1849. $75. (One of several reprints of *Report of the Exploring Expedition.*)

FRÉMONT, John Charles. *Report of the Exploring Expedition to the Rocky Mountains in the Year 1842.* Senate edition. 22 plates, 5 maps, one folding. Cloth. Washington, 1845. First edition. $100-$150. (House edition, same date.)

FRÉMONT, John Charles. *Report on an Exploration of the Country Lying Between the Missouri and the Rocky Mountains, etc.* Senate Doc. 243. 6 plates, folding map. Wrappers. Washington, 1843. First edition. $150-$200.

FRENCH, Capt. W. J. *Wild Jim, the Texas Cowboy and Saddle King.* Portrait. 76 pp., wrappers. Antioch, Ill., 1890. First edition. $250-$350.

FRENCH, William. *Some Recollections of a Western Ranchman.* Cloth. New York, no date (1928). First American edition. In dust jacket. $250-$300.

FREYTAS, Father Nicholas de. *The Expedition of Don Diego Dionisio de Penaloza, from Santa Fe to the River Mischipi and Quivira in 1662.* Edited by John G. Shea. Boards. No place (New York), 1882. $35-$40.

FRINK, F. W. *A Record of Rice County, Minnesota, in 1868.* 24 pp., wrappers. Faribault, Minn., 1868. First edition. $75-$100. Faribault, 1871. Second edition. $50.

FRINK, Margaret A. *Journal of the Adventures of a Party of California Gold-Seekers.* 2 frontispieces. Cloth. No place, no date (Oakland, 1897). First edition. $350-$500.

FROISSART, Sir John. *Chronicles of England, France, Spain, and the Adjoining Countries.* Translated by Thomas Johnes. Illustrations illuminated in gold and colors by H. Noel Humphreys. 2 vols., half red morocco. London, 1852. $150-$200.

FROM Ocean to Ocean in a Winton. Illustrated. 36 pp., wrappers. Cleveland, 1903. Winton Motor Carriage Co. $25-$30.

FROST, A. B. *Sports and Games in the Open.* 53 color plates. Folio, pictorial cloth portfolio. New York, 1899. First edition. $250. Covers spotted, $200.

FROST, John. *History of the State of California.* Contemporary morocco. Auburn, Calif., 1850. First edition. $50-$60.

FROST, Robert. See Robinson, Edwin Arlington. Also see *Dartmouth Verse, 1925; Poems of Child Labor.*

FROST, Robert. *Away!* Wood engravings by Stefan Martin. Pictorial wrappers. New York, 1958. First edition. One of 185 with Al Edwards imprint. $35-$50.

FROST, Robert. *A Boy's Will.* Bronze, or brown, pebbled cloth, lettered in gilt. London, 1913. First edition, first state, with all edges untrimmed. $750-$1,000. Also, $700 (A, 1968). Second state, white, or cream, parchment (vellum), stamped in red, $500-$600. Third state, buff (cream) printed wrappers, with horizontal rule at top of the "A" in title. $175-$300. Fourth state, wrappers, plain "A," $150-$200. Author's first book. New York, 1915. Cloth. First American edition, first issue, with "aind" for "and" in last line of page 14. In dust jacket. $100-$150. Second issue, spelling error corrected. In dust jacket. $35-$50.

FROST, Robert. *Collected Poems.* Tan buckram. New York, 1930. Random House. First collected edition. One of 1,000 signed. In dust jacket. $100-$125. Trade issue, later: New York, no date (1930). Holt. Portrait. Cloth. First edition (so stated). $50-$60. New York, 1939. Title page woodcut. Decorated cloth. In dust jacket. $35-$50. New York, 1949. Cloth. In dust jacket. $35-$50.

FROST, Robert. *Complete Poems.* Cloth. New York, 1949. Holt. First edition. One of 500 signed. In dust jacket. $150-$200.

FROST, Robert. *The Complete Poems of Robert Frost.* Illustrated. 2 vols., blue cloth. New York, 1950. Limited Editions Club. One of 1,500 signed. Boxed. $150-$200.

FROST, Robert. *The Cow's in the Corn.* Decorated boards. Gaylordsville, N.Y., 1929. Slide Mountain Press. First edition. One of 91 signed. $400-$500. Also, $275 (A, 1969), $325 (A, 1968).

FROST, Robert. *A Further Range.* Tan cloth. New York, no date (1936). First edition. One of 803 signed. In slipcase. $100-$150. Trade issue, later: Red cloth. First edition (so stated). (4,100 printed.) In dust jacket. $15-$20.

FROST, Robert. *The Gold Hesperidee.* 8 pp., wrappers. No place, no date (Cortland, N.Y., 1935). Bibliophile Press. First edition, first issue, with "A" on copyright page and with next to last line on page 7 unturned (second issue has the line turned and carried over). $100-$150. Second issue. $75-$100.

FROST, Robert. *Hard Not to Be King.* Cloth. New York, 1951. First edition. One of 300 signed. $100-$150.

FROST, Robert. *In the Clearing.* Buckram. New York, no date (1962). First edition. One of 1,500 signed. Boxed. $100-$150. Trade issue: Cloth. In dust jacket. $20-$25.

FROST, Robert. *The Lone Striker.* Printed wrappers in envelope. No place, no date (New York, 1933). First edition. No. 8 in the "Borzoi Chap Books." $30-$35.

FROST, Robert. *The Lovely Shall Be Choosers.* 6 pp., printed brown wrappers. New York, 1929. First edition. One of 475. $100-$125.

FROST, Robert. *A Masque of Mercy.* Half cloth. New York, no date (1947). First edition. One of 751 signed. Boxed. $75-$100. Trade issue: Blue cloth. In dust jacket. $15.

FROST, Robert. *A Masque of Reason.* Half cloth. New York, no date (1948). First edition. One of 800 signed. Boxed. $75-$100. Trade issue: Blue cloth. In dust jacket. $15.

FROST, Robert. *Mountain Interval.* Blue cloth. New York, no date (1916). First edition, first issue, with verses 6 and 7, page 88, repeated. In dust jacket. $75-$100. New York, 1921. Bust portrait. Boards. Second edition. In dust jacket. $20-$25.

FROST, Robert. *Neither Out Far nor in Deep.* Wrappers. (Christmas token.) No place (New York), 1935. First edition. Spiral Press. $35-$50.

FROST, Robert. *New Hampshire: A Poem with Notes and Grace Notes.* Woodcuts. Dark-green boards and cloth. New York, 1923. First trade edition. In dust jacket. $35-$50. Another issue: Boards. One of 350 signed. $200-$250. London, 1924. Boards. First English edition. $30-$40. Hanover, N.H., 1955. New Dresden Press. Buckram and boards. First separate edition of title poem. One of 750 signed. $50-$75.

FROST, Robert. *North of Boston.* Green buckram. London, no date (1914). First edition, first state, gold lettering on front cover and spine, blind-stamped rule all around front cover. In dust jacket. $800-$1,000 and up. Also, $400 (A, 1970); writing on flyleaf, $700 (A, 1969); $850 (A, 1968); inscribed, $1,050 (A, 1968). Second state, lettered in blind on front. $400-$500. Third state, blue cloth, black lettering. $300-$400. Also, $196 (A, 1964). Fourth state, green cloth, blind rule at top and bottom of front cover. $300-$400. Fifth state, leaves 5 3/8 by 7¾ inches. $200. Also, $140 (A, 1971). Other binding variants also noted, with A-range in the 1960's of $55 to $230. Also, inscribed copies in all bindings at higher prices than noted here. (Frost signed a great many books!) New York, 1914. Brown boards, cloth back. First American edition, made up of English sheets with a new title page tipped in on a stub. In dust jacket. $100-$150. New York, 1915. Linen. Second American edition (first to be printed in America). In dust jacket. $50-$75.

FROST, Robert. *Our Hold on the Planet.* Wrappers. (Christmas token.) No place, no date (various places, 1940). First edition. $30-$35.

FROST, Robert. *Selected Poems.* Green decorated boards and cloth. New York, 1923. First edition, with "March, 1923" on copyright page. In dust jacket. $75-$100. London, no date (1923). Cloth. First English edition. In dust jacket. $35.

FROST, Robert. *Steeple Bush.* Blue boards and cloth. New York, 1947. First edition. One of 751 signed. Boxed. $75-$100. Trade issue: Cloth. In dust jacket. $25-$35.

FROST, Robert. *Three Poems.* Wrappers. Hanover, N.H., no date (1935). First edition. (125 copies printed.) $150-$200.

FROST, Robert. *To a Young Wretch.* Wrappers. (Christman token.) No place, no date (various places, 1937). First edition. $50-$75. Also, $62.80 (A, 1968).

FROST, Robert. *Triple Plate.* Wrappers. (Christmas token.) No place, no date (eight varying places, 1939). First edition. $35-$50.

FROST, Robert. *Twilight.* (Cover title.) 20 pp., leather. No place, no date (Lawrence, Mass., 1894). First edition. Two copies known. Name your own price—starting at $1,000 (?).

FROST, Robert. *Two Letters Written on His Undergraduate Days at Dartmouth College in 1892.* Wrappers. Hanover, N.H., 1931. First edition. (10 copies printed.) $500 and up.

FROST, Robert. *Two Tramps in Mud Time.* Wrappers. (Christmas token.) No place, no date (various places, 1934). First edition. $35-$50.

FROST, Robert. *A Way Out.* Salmon-colored boards, cloth spine. New York, 1929. Harbor Press. First edition. One of 485 signed. In glassine dust jacket. $100-$150.

FROST, Robert. *West-Running Brook.* Green boards and cloth. New York, no date (1928). Printed by Plimpton Press. First (trade) edition (so stated). In dust jacket. $35-$50. Another issue: Merrymount Press. Boards. One of 980 (1,000 ?) signed. In glassine jacket. Boxed. $100-$150.

FROST, Robert. *A Witness Tree.* Portrait. Decorated boards and cloth. New York, 1942. First edition. One of 735 signed. Boxed. $100-$125. Trade issue: Blue cloth. In dust jacket. $25.

FRUGAL Housewife (The). By the Author of *Hobomok.* Boards. Boston, 1829. (By Lydia Maria Child.) First edition. $100-$150.

FRY, Frederick. *Fry's Traveler's Guide, and Descriptive Journal of the Great North Western Territories.* Cloth. Cincinnati, 1865. First edition. $200-$250. Rebound in half leather, $100. Also, $180 (A, 1968).

FRY, James B. *Army Sacrifices.* Cloth. New York, 1879. First edition. $60-$70.

FUGITIVE Pieces. 66 pp., green-gray wrappers. No place, no date (1806). (By George Gordon Noel, Lord Byron.) First edition. Price: In the thousands. All except four copies were destroyed, according to De Ricci. London, 1886. Vellum. Facsimile edition. One of 100. $35-$50. Another issue: One of 7 on Japan paper. $100-$125.

FUGITIVES, An Anthology of Verse. Decorated paper boards, cloth back. New York, no date (1928). First edition. $50-$75.

FULKERSON, H. S. *Random Recollections of Early Days in Mississippi.* Printed wrappers. Vicksburg, 1885. First edition. $250-$300.

FULLER, C. L. *Pocket Map and Descriptive Outline History of the Black Hills of Dakota and Wyoming.* Folding map. 56 pp., stiff wrappers. Rapid City, S.D., 1887. First edition. $450.

FULLER, Emeline. *Left by the Indians.* (Cover title.) Portrait. 41 pp., printed wrappers. No place, no date (Mt. Vernon, Iowa, 1892). First edition. $150-$200. New York, 1936. Facsimile reprint. $10-$15.

FULLER, Henry Blake. See Page, Stanton.

FULLER, Henry Blake. *The Cliff-Dwellers.* Cloth. New York, 1893. First edition. $25-$35.

FULLER, S. Margaret. *Woman in the 19th Century.* Wrappers. New York, 1845. First edition. $35-$40.

FULLMER, John S. *Assassination of Joseph and Hyrum Smith, the Prophet and the Patriarch of the Church of Jesus Christ of Latter-day Saints.* 40 pp., half leather. Liverpool, England, 1855. $75-$100.

FULMORE, Z. T. *The History and Geography of Texas as Told in County Names.* Cloth. No place, no date (Austin, Tex., 1915). First edition. $35-$50.

FULTON, A. R. *The Red Men of Iowa.* 26 plates. Cloth. Des Moines, Iowa, 1882. First edition. $50-$75.

FUNKHOUSER, W. D. *Wild Life in Kentucky.* Cloth. Frankfort, Ky., 1925. $35-$50.

G

GADDIS, William. *The Recognitions.* Cloth. New York, no date (1955). First edition. In dust jacket. $35-$40.

GAG, Wanda. *Millions of Cats.* Boards. New York, 1928. First edition. One of 250. $35-$40.

GAGE, Thomas. *The Correspondence of Thomas Gage.* Edited by Clarence Edwin Carter. 2 vols., boards. New Haven, 1931-33. First edition. $100.

GAINE, Hugh. *The Journals of Hugh Gaine, Printer.* Edited by Paul Leicester Ford. Plates. 2 vols., boards. New York, 1902. First edition. One of 350. $35-$50. Another issue: Cloth. One of 30 printed on Japan paper. $75.

GALE, George. *Upper Mississippi.* Frontispiece, maps, plates. Cloth. Chicago, 1867. First edition. $50-$60.

GALE, Norman. *A June Romance.* Portrait. Boards. Rugby, England, 1894. First edition. One of 40 signed. $35-$50.

GALLAHER, James. *The Western Sketch-Book.* Plates. Cloth. Boston, 1850. First edition. $40 $50.

GALLATIN, Albert. *Considerations on the Currency and Banking System of the United States.* Wrappers. Philadelphia, 1831. First edition. $35-$50.

GALLATIN, Albert. *Letters of Albert Gallatin on the Oregon Question.* Stitched. Washington, 1846. First edition. $30-$45.

GALLATIN, Albert Eugene. *Art and the Great War.* Illustrated. Folio, full morocco. New York, 1919. First edition. One of 100. Boxed. $35-$50.

GALLATIN, Albert Eugene. *Portraits of Whistler.* 40 illustrations. Boards. New York, 1918. First edition. One of 250. Boxed. $25-$30.

GALSWORTHY, John. See Sinjohn, John.

GALSWORTHY, John. *Caravan.* Green cloth. London, 1925. First edition. In dust jacket. $20-$25. Another (later) issue: Limp leather. One of 265 signed. $25-$35.

GALSWORTHY, John. *The Country House.* Green cloth. London, 1907. First edition, with publisher's windmill stamp in lower right corner of back cover. $35-$50.

GALSWORTHY, John. *The Dark Flower.* Dark-red cloth. London, 1913. First edition, first issue, with 22 pages of ads at end. In dust jacket. $50-$60.

GALSWORTHY, John. *The Forsyte Saga.* Folding genealogical table. Green cloth. London, 1922. First edition, first issue, with genealogical table pulling out to the right. In dust jacket. $100-$150. Another issue: Green limp leather. One of 275 signed. $100-$150.

GALSWORTHY, John. *The Freelands.* Green cloth. London, no date (1915). First edition, first issue, with gilt lettering. In dust jacket. $25.

GALSWORTHY, John. *The Full Moon: A Play in Three Acts.* Green wrappers. London, 1915. First edition, first issue, without the listing of cast on back leaf. $50.

GALSWORTHY, John. *The Inn of Tranquility.* Green buckram. London, 1912. First edition. In dust jacket. $20-$25.

GALSWORTHY, John. *The Island Pharisees.* Green cloth. London, 1904. First edition, first (unpublished) issue, with no mention of this title in publisher's list. $1,375 (A, 1930). (Note: This apparently is a freak among Galsworthy items; the only other copy noted is one of the first published edition, auctioned in 1942 for $45, and a presentation copy of the same edition to Ford M. Hueffer, auctioned in the 1963 season at $60. Ordinary copies of the first published edition should sell at $25-$35 in today's market.) New York, 1904. Blue cloth. First American edition (750 made from English sheets). $25-$35.

GALSWORTHY, John. *The Land: A Plea.* Woodcut. 24 pp., sewed. London, no date (1918). First edition. $25-$30.

GALSWORTHY, John. *The Man of Property.* Green cloth. London, 1906. First edition, first issue, with broken bar of music on page 200. $100-$150.

GALSWORTHY, John. *A Modern Comedy.* Folding table. Full limp vellum. London, 1929. First edition. One of 1,030 signed. $25-$35. Trade edition: Cloth. In dust jacket. $10.

GALSWORTHY, John. *The Plays of John Galsworthy.* Green cloth. London, 1939. First edition. One of 1,275 signed. $25-$35.

GALSWORTHY, John. *The Silver Spoon.* Cloth. London, no date (1926). First edition. One of 265 signed. $25-$35. Trade edition: Cloth. In dust jacket. $10.

GALSWORTHY, John. *Swan Song.* Blue buckram. London, no date (1928). First edition. One of 525 signed. $25-$35. Trade edition: Cloth. In dust jacket. $10.

GALSWORTHY, John. *The White Monkey.* Cloth. London, 1924. First edition. In dust jacket. $10. London, no date (1926). Buckram. One of 265 signed. $30-$40.

GALT, John. See Balwhidder, The Rev. Micah. Also see *The Provost; The Steam-Boat.*

GALT, John. *The Bachelor's Wife.* Boards. Edinburgh, 1824. First edition. $85.

GALT, John. *Lawrie Todd.* 3 vols., cloth. London, 1830. First edition. $100-$150. New York, 1830. 2 vols. in one, boards. First American edition. $50.

GALT, John. *Ringan Gilhaize.* Boards. London, 1823. First edition. $50-$75.

GAMEKEEPER at Home (The). Cloth. London, 1878. (By Richard Jefferies.) First edition. $25.

GANCONAGH. *John Sherman and Dhoya.* Gray cloth, lettered in blue; also in yellow wrappers, lettered in black. London, no date (1891). (By William Butler Yeats.) First edition. Cloth: $350-$500. Also, $312 (A, 1968). Wrappers: $250-$350. (Note: The cloth issue is scarcer than the one in wrappers.)

GANNET(T), William C. *The House Beautiful.* With designs by Frank Lloyd Wright. Folio, half leather. River Forest, Ill., Winter, 1896-97. One of 90 signed by Wright and William Winslow, the publisher (Auvergne Press). $2,000 and up. (Note: Gannett's text first appeared in a pamphlet of 24 pages in Boston in 1895. The original spelled his name correctly.)

GANOE, W. A. *History of the United States Army.* Cloth. New York, 1924. First edition. $25-$35.

GANTT, E. W. *Address to the People of Arkansas.* 24 pp., sewed. Little Rock, 1863. First edition. $50-$65.

GARCES, Francisco. *On the Trail of the Spanish Pioneer.* Translated by Elliott Coues. Illustrated. 2 vols., cloth. New York, 1900. First edition. One of 950. $60-$75.

GARCÍA y CUBAS, Antonio. *Atlas Geográfico, Estadístico e Histórico de la República Mexicana.* 33 double-page maps in color. Folio, boards. Mexico, 1858. One of 300. $200-$250.

GARD, Wayne. *Along the Early Trails of the Southwest.* Illustrated. Half leather. Austin, Tex., 1969. First edition. One of 250 signed and with an extra set of color plates. $50.

GARD, Wayne. *Sam Bass.* Illustrated. Cloth. Boston, 1936. First edition. In dust jacket. $35-$40.

GARDEN, Alexander. *Anecdotes of the Revolutionary War in America.* First Series. Boards. Charleston, S.C., 1822. First edition. $50-$60. Charleston, 1828. Second Series. First edition. $50.

GARDINER, Abigail. *History of the Spirit Lake Massacre and the Captivity of Miss Abbie Gardner.* Portrait. Cloth. Des Moines, Iowa, 1885. First edition. $35-$50.

GARDINER, G. A. *A Brief and Correct Account of an Earthquake.* Poughkeepsie, N.Y., 1820. $75.

GARDNER, Alexander: See *Photographic Sketch Book of the War.*

GARLAND, Hamlin. *The Book of the American Indian.* 35 plates by Frederic Remington. Folio, boards and cloth. New York, 1923. First edition (so stated). In dust jacket. $50-$75.

GARLAND, Hamlin. *Cavanagh, Forest Ranger.* Frontispiece. Cloth. New York, 1910. First edition, with "Published March, 1910" on copyright page. $25-$30.

GARLAND, Hamlin. *The Light of the Star.* Frontispiece. Cloth. New York, 1904. First edition, with "Published May, 1904" on copyright page. $25-$30.

GARLAND, Hamlin. *Main-Travelled Roads.* Gray printed wrappers. Boston, 1891. First edition, first issue, with "Arena Library" at top and "First Thousand" at bottom of front cover. $100-$125. Another issue: Blue or gray cloth. $50-$75.

GARLAND, Hamlin. *A Member of the Third House.* Wrappers. Chicago, no date (1892). First edition. $35-$50. Another issue: Cloth. $25.

GARLAND, Hamlin. *The Mystery of the Buried Crosses.* Cloth. New York, 1939. First edition (so indicated on copyright page). $25.

GARLAND, Hamlin. *A Pioneer Mother.* Wrappers. Chicago, 1922. First edition. One of 500. $25-$35. Another issue: Boards. One of 25. $35-$50.

GARLAND, Hamlin. *Under the Wheel: A Modern Play in Six Scenes.* Wrappers. Boston, 1890. First edition. $35-$50. Author's first book.

GARLAND, James. *Letter of James Garland to His Constituents.* 31 pp., sewed. No place, no date (Washington, 1840). $25.

GARMAN, K. E. *Moving-Picture Circus.* Illustrated. Movable book with 8 specially cut leaves on stiff cardboard. Chicago, 1909. $25.

GARNEAU, Joseph, Jr. *Nebraska: Her Resources, Advantages and Development.* (Cover title.) 24 pp., printed wrappers. Omaha, 1893. First edition. $35.

GARNER, James W. *Reconstruction in Mississippi.* Cloth. New York, 1901. First edition. $35-$40.

GARNETT, David. *The Grasshoppers Come.* Illustrated. Yellow buckram. London, 1931. First edition. One of 200 signed. $35.

GARNETT, Richard. *The Twilight of the Gods and Other Tales.* Cloth. London, 1888. First edition. $40-$50.

GARRARD, Lewis H. *Wah-To-Yah, and the Taos Trail.* Decorated cloth. Cincinnati, 1850. First edition, first issue, with page 269 misnumbered 26. $150-$250. San Francisco, 1936. Grabhorn Press. Boards. One of 550. $35-$50.

GARRETT, Edmund H. (editor). *Victorian Songs.* Illustrated by Garrett. Vellum, gilt. Boston, 1895. First edition. One of 225. In parchment dust jacket. $35-$50.

GARRETT, Pat F. *The Authentic Life of Billy, The Kid.* Frontispiece and 5 plates. 137 pp., pictorial blue wrappers. Santa Fe, N.M., 1882. First edition, with ad inside back wrapper. $500 and up. Also, $450 (A, 1969).

GARVIE, James. *Abraham Lincoln toni kin, qa Aesop tawoyake kin. (Life of Abraham Lincoln and Aesop's Fables.)* 17 pp., printed wrappers. Santee [Indian] Agency, Neb., 1893. $150.

GASCOYNE, David. *Poems 1937-1942.* Color illustrations. Pictorial boards. No place, no date (London, 1943). PL Editions. First edition. $50-$85.

GASKELL, Elizabeth C. See *Cranford; Mary Barton; North and South.*

GASKELL, Elizabeth C. *The Life of Charlotte Brontë.* 2 vols., cloth. London, 1857. First edition. $50-$75.

GASKELL, Elizabeth C. *Sylvia's Lovers.* 3 vols., cloth. London, 1863. First edition. $75-$100.

GASKELL, G. A. *A Dictionary of the Sacred Language of All Scriptures and Myths.* Cloth. New York, no date (1923). $35.

GASS, Patrick. *A Journal of the Voyages and Travels of a Corps of Discovery, Under the Command of Capt. Lewis and Capt. Clarke, etc.* Boards and leather. Pittsburgh, 1807. First edition. $300-$400. Also, $175 (A, 1968), $250 (A, 1966). Philadelphia, 1810. Calf. Second edition (without plates). $150-$300. Philadelphia, 1810. 6 plates added. Calf. Second illustrated edition (actually third edition). $300-$400. Philadelphia, 1812. 6 plates, folding map. Calf. Fourth edition. $350-$400.

GASS, Patrick. *Gass's Journal of the Lewis and Clark Expedition.* Edited by James K. Hosmer. Illustrated. Cloth. Chicago, 1904. $25-$30.

GAUGUIN, Paul. *Intimate Journals.* Translated by Van Wyck Brooks. 27 illustrations by Gauguin. Boards. New York, 1921. First edition in English. One of 999. $75-$100.

GAUGUIN, Paul. *Letters to Edouard Vollard and André Fontainas.* 10 woodcuts. Boards and cloth. San Francisco, 1943. Grabhorn Press. One of 250. $125-$200.

GAY, Frederick A. *For Gratuitous Distribution: Sketches of California.* (Cover title.) 16 pp., printed wrappers. No place, no date (New York, 1848). First edition. $250-$350.

GAYERRE (Gayarre?), Charles. *A Sketch of Gen. Jackson: By Himself.* 21 pp., printed wrappers. New Orleans, 1857. First edition. $40.

GEM (A): "The City of the Plains." Abilene: The Centre of the "Golden Belt." Woodcuts. 64 pp., printed wrappers. Burlington, Iowa, 1887. First edition. $45.

GEM of the Rockies! (The): Manitou Springs. Plates and tables. 23 pp., printed wrappers. Manitou Springs, Colo., no date (about 1885). First edition. $35-$40.

GENERAL and Statistical Description of Pierce County (Wisconsin). 8 pp., sewed. No place, no date (Prescott, Wis., 1854). First edition. $45.

GENERAL Instructions to Deputy Surveyors. Folding diagram. 25 pp., sewed. Little Rock, Ark., 1837. First edition. $75.

GENERAL Laws and Memorials and Resolutions of the Territory of Dakota, Passed at the 1st Session of the Legislative Assembly. Sewed. Yankton, 1862. $25-$30.

GENERAL Orders Affecting the Volunteer Force: Adjutant General's Office, 1863. Cloth. Washington, 1864. (Contains Lincoln Presidential orders, including Emancipation Proclamation.) $25-$35.

GENERAL Orders Affecting the Volunteer Force: Adjutant General's Office, 1864. Cloth. Washington, 1865. (Contains Lincoln presidential orders.) $30-$35.

GENÊT, Edmond Charles. *Memorial on the Upward Forces of Fluids.* Folding table, 6 plates. Printed brown boards. Albany, 1825. First edition. $500-$750, possibly more.

GENIUS of Oblivion (The), and Other Poems. By a Lady of New-Hampshire. Gray boards, paper label on spine. Concord, N.H., 1823. (By Sarah Josepha Hale.) First edition. $35-$50. Author's first book.

GEOLOGICAL Survey of Texas: First Annual Report. Austin, 1890. $35. Austin, 1891. Second report. $30. Austin, 1892. Third report. $25.

GEORGE, Alice. *The Story of My Childhood. Written for My Children.* Illustrated. Cloth. Whittier, Calif., 1923. First edition. $75.

GEORGE, Henry. *Our Land and Land Policy, National and State.* Folding map in black and red. 48 pp., printed wrappers. San Francisco, 1871. First edition. $250.

GEORGE, Henry. *Progress and Poverty.* Green or blue cloth. San Francisco, 1879. "Author's Edition." First edition, first issue, with the slip asking that no reviews be printed. $250-$350. Second issue, without the slip referring to reviews. $150-$200.

GEORGE Mason, The Young Backwoodsman. Tan boards, paper label. Boston, 1829. (By Timothy Flint.) First edition. $100-$150.

GEORGE Pierce Baker, A Memorial. Batik boards, paper label. New York, 1929. First edition. Large paper copy signed by all the contributors, including Eugene O'Neill. (A few copies only were issued.) $30-$50.

GEORGIA Scenes, Characters, Incidents, etc., in the First Half Century of the Republic. By a Native Georgian. Brown boards, cloth back, paper labels. Augusta, Ga., 1835. (By Augustus Baldwin Longstreet.) First edition. $400-$600. Author's first book. New York, 1840. Illustrated. Cloth. Second edition. $75.

GERARD Manley Hopkins. By the Kenyon Critics. Cloth. New York, no date (1945). First edition. In dust jacket. $35-$40.

GERNSBACK, Hugo. *Ralph 124C41: A Romance of the Year 2660.* Illustrated. Blue cloth. Boston, 1925. First edition. $35-$40.

GERSHWIN, George. *George Gershwin's Song-Book.* Illustrated by Alajolov. Portrait, song reproductions. Full blue morocco. New York, 1932. One of 300 signed by Gershwin and Alajolov. $150-$200.

GERSHWIN, George. *Porgy and Bess.* Frontispiece in color. Morocco. New York, 1935. First edition. One of 250 signed. $300-$350.

GERSTAECKER, Friedrich. *California Gold Mines.* Foreword by Joseph A. Sullivan. Folding map, illustrations. Pictorial boards. Oakland, 1946. One of 500 signed by Sullivan. $25-$30.

GESCHICHTE des Amerikanischen Krieges, von 1812, von Anfang bis zum Endichen Schluss vor New-Orleans. Portrait and plates. Calf. Reading, Pa., 1817. (By William McCarty.) First edition. $35-$50.

GETTING a Wrong Start: A Truthful Autobiography. Terra-cotta cloth. New York, 1915. (By Emerson Hough.) First edition, with "Published March, 1915" on copyright page. $25-$30.

GHOST in the Bank of England (The). Pictorial cloth. London, no date (1888?). (By Eden Phillpotts?) First edition (?). $25-$50. Author's first book?

GIBSON, Charles Dana. *Drawings.* Plates. Oblong folio, boards and cloth. New York, 1897. First edition. $35-$50.

GIBSON, Charles Dana. *Eighty Drawings, Including the Weaker Sex.* Oblong folio, cloth. New York, 1903. First edition. One of 250 signed. $35-$50.

GIBSON, Charles Dana. *The Gibson Book.* Illustrated. 2 vols., oblong folio, boards. New York, 1906. First edition. $50.

GIBSON, Wilfrid W. *Home: A Book of Poems.* Woodcut. Boards and vellum. London, 1920. Beaumont Press. First edition. One of 35 on vellum, signed. $35-$50.

GIDDINGS, Marsh. *First Annual Message to the Legislative Assembly of the Territory of New Mexico.* 54 pp., printed wrappers. Santa Fe, N.M., 1871. First edition. $45.

GIDE, André. *If It Die . . . An Autobiography.* Translated by Dorothy Bussy. Silk binding. New York, no date (1935). First edition. One of 100 signed. Boxed. $35-$50.

GIDE, André. *Montaigne: An Essay in Two Parts.* Cloth. London, 1929. One of 800 signed. In dust jacket. $50-$75.

GIDE, André. *Oscar Wilde.* Notes, etc., by Stuart Mason. 5 illustrations. Half parchment and cloth. Oxford, 1905. One of 50 signed by Mason. $40-$50.

GIDNEY, Eleazer. *A Treatise on the Structure, etc., of the Human Teeth.* Cloth. Utica, N.Y., 1824. First edition. $75-$100.

GILBERT, Ann (Taylor), and Taylor, Jane. *Hymns for Infant Minds.* Printed wrappers. Newburyport, Mass., 1814. $75.

GILBERT, Benjamin. *A Narrative of the Captivity and Sufferings of Benjamin Gilbert and His Family.* (Edited by William Walton.) Leather. Philadelphia, 1848. Third edition. $25.

GILBERT, Paul T., and Bryson, Charles L. *Chicago and Its Makers.* Illustrated. Buckram. Chicago, 1929. First edition. $35-$50. Another issue: Leather. $50-$75.

GILBERT, William. *On the Magnet, Magnetick Bodies, etc.* Woodcuts. Folio, limp vellum, silk ties. London, 1900. One of 250. $100-$125. (Note: Issued for the Gilbert Club along with S. P. Thompson's *Notes on the De Magnete of Dr. William Gilbert,* London, 1901. Together, $150-$200.)

GILBERT, W. S. *The "Bab" Ballads: Much Sound and Little Sense.* Illustrated by the author. Green cloth. London, 1869. First edition, first issue, with Hotten imprint on title page. $50-$75.

GILBERT, W. S. *Fifty "Bab" Ballads.* Green cloth. London, no date (1876). First edition. $25.

GILBERT, W. S. *More "Bab" Ballads.* Green cloth. London, no date (1873). First edition. $25.

GILBERT, W. S. *A New and Original Extravaganza Entitled Dulcamara; or, The Little Duck and the Great Quack.* Illustration. Orange-colored wrappers. London, 1866. First edition. $500. Author's first published work.

GILBERT, W. S. *Songs of a Savoyard.* Illustrated by the author. Cloth, edges gilt. London, no date (1890). First edition. $25-$30. (Note: Dated title page indicates second edition.)

GILCHRIST, Alexander. *Life of William Blake.* Illustrated. 2 vols., cloth. London, 1863. First edition. $50-$75. London, 1880. Blue cloth. Second edition. $100-$125.

GILDER, Richard Watson. *The New Day.* Cloth. New York, 1876. First edition. $15-$20.

GILES, William B. *Political Miscellanies.* Calf. No place, no date (Virginia, 1830). $65.

GILHAM, William. *Manual of Instruction for the Volunteers and Militia of the Confederate States.* Folding charts. Cloth. Richmond, Va., 1861. $150.

GILHESPY, F. Brayshaw. *Crown Derby Porcelain.* Plates. Cloth. Leigh-on-Sea, England, 1951. Limited signed edition. In dust jacket. $150-$250.

GILHESPY, F. Brayshaw. *Derby Porcelain.* 77 plates, 13 in color. Buckram. London, 1961. In dust jacket. $35-$50.

GILL, Eric. *Art-Nonsense and Other Essays.* Buckram. London, 1929. First edition. One of 100 signed. $100.

GILL, Eric. *Clothes.* 10 wood engravings by the author. Boards, leather spine. London, 1931. One of 160 signed. $79.20, $55, and $50.

GILL, Eric. *Clothing Without Cloth: An Essay on the Nude.* 4 wood engravings by the author. Cloth. London, 1931. One of 500. $60.

GILL, Eric. *An Essay on Typography.* Illustrated. Cloth. No place, no date (London, 1931). Limited edition of 500 copies, signed by author and René Hague, the artist. $25-$35.

GILL, Eric (illustrator). See: *The Four Gospels of the Lord Jesus Christ.*

GILLELAND, J. C. *The Ohio and Mississippi Pilot.* 16 maps. Calf, or boards and calf. Pittsburgh, 1820. First edition. $750 and up. Also, covers worn, text foxed and stained, $700 (A, 1967).

GILLELEN, F. M. L. *The Oil Regions of Pennsylvania.* 17 maps (one folding), frontispiece, 3 other plates. 67 pp., wrappers. Pittsburgh, no date (1865?). First edition. Rebound in half morocco, $175 (A, 1969).

GILLETT, James B. *Six Years with the Texas Rangers.* 8 plates. Cloth. Austin, Tex., no date (1921). First edition. $35-$50. Signed, $40 and $50. New Haven, Conn., 1925. Cloth. $15-$20.

GILMOR, Harry. *Four Years in the Saddle.* Cloth. New York, 1866. First American edition. $25-$30.

GINSBERG, Allen. *Empty Mirror: Early Poems.* Introduction by William Carlos Williams. Decorated wrappers. New York, no date (1961). Totem Press. First edition. $25-$35.

GINSBERG, Allen. *Howl and Other Poems.* Introduction by William Carlos Williams. Printed wrappers. San Francisco, no date (1956). First edition. $150-$200.

GINSBERG, Allen. *Kaddish: A Dramatic Mass.* Mimeographed, leatherette. New York, no date (about 1965). One of 18. $50-$75.

GINSBERG, Allen. *Siesta in Xbalha and Return to the States.* Self-wrappers, stapled. Near Icy Cape, Alaska, July, 1956. First edition. One of about 56 copies mimeographed. $500 and up. Author's first book.

GINSBERG, Allen. *T. V. Baby Poems.* Boards. No place, no date (London, 1967). Cape Goliard Press. First edition. One of 100 signed. $40-$50. Trade edition: Wrappers. $7.50.

GINSBERG, Allen. *Wales—A Visitation July 29, 1967.* Boards. London, no date (1968). Cape Goliard Press. First edition. One of 100 signed, with author's recording of poem. In dust jacket. $50-$60.

GINX'S Baby: His Birth and Other Misfortunes. Cloth. London, 1870. (By John Edward Jenkins.) First edition. $50. Author's first book.

GIRARD, Just. *Adventures of a French Captain, at Present a Planter in Texas.* Cloth. New York, 1878. (By Just Jean Étienne Roy.) $50-$65.

GIRARDEY, G. *The North American Compiler.* Boards. Rossville, Ohio, 1844. $35-$50.

GIRAUD, J. P., Jr. *The Birds of Long Island.* Plate. Cloth. New York, 1844. First edition. $25-$35.

GISSING, George. See *Demos: A Story of English Socialism.*

GISSING, George. *Born in Exile.* 3 vols., slate-gray cloth. London, 1892. First edition. $100-$150.

GISSING, George. *By the Ionian Sea: Notes of a Ramble in Southern Italy.* Illustrated in color and black and white. White cloth. London, 1901. First edition. $30-$40.

GISSING, George. *Charles Dickens: A Critical Study.* Dark-red cloth. London, 1898. First edition. $25-$35.

GISSING, George. *The Emancipated.* 3 vols., boards and cloth. London, 1890. First edition. $75-$100.

GISSING, George. *The House of Cobwebs and Other Stories.* Blue cloth. London, 1906. First edition. $25-$30.

GISSING, George. *In the Year of Jubilee.* 3 vols., blue cloth. London, 1894. First edition. $50-$75.

GISSING, George. *Isabel Clarendon.* 2 vols., green cloth. London, 1886. First edition. $100-$150.

GISSING, George. *A Life's Morning.* 3 vols., light-blue cloth. London, 1888. First edition. $100-$125.

GISSING, George. *The Nether World.* 3 vols., light-blue or green cloth. London, 1889. First edition. $125-$175.

GISSING, George. *New Grub Street.* 3 vols., dark-green cloth. London, 1891. First edition. $100-$150. Second edition, same date. $75-$100.

GISSING, George. *The Odd Women.* 3 vols., blue cloth. London, 1893. First edition. $75-$125.·

GISSING, George. *Our Friend the Charlatan.* Illustrated. Cloth. London, 1901. First edition. $25-$35.

GISSING, George. *The Private Papers of Henry Ryecroft.* Green cloth. Westminster, England, 1903. First edition. $50-$75. Portland, Me., 1921. Boards. One of 25 on Japan vellum. $35-$50. Another issue: One of 700. $10-$15. New York, no date (1927). Purple cloth. First authorized American edition. In dust jacket. $25.

GISSING, George. *Thyrza.* 3 vols., dark-red cloth. London, 1887. First edition. $100-$125.

GISSING, George. *The Town Traveller.* Light-red cloth. London, 1898. First edition, with ads dated April, 1898. $35-$50.

GISSING, George. *The Unclassed.* 3 vols., blue cloth. London, 1884. First edition. $75-$125.

GISSING, George. *Veranilda: A Romance.* Red cloth. London, 1904. First edition, with 16 pages of ads at back. In dust jacket. $30-$40.

GISSING, George. *Will Warburton: A Romance of Real Life.* Red cloth. London, 1905. First edition, with 16 pages of ads at back. $35.

GISSING, George. *Workers in the Dawn.* 3 vols., light-brown cloth. London, 1880. First edition, with black end papers. $750-$1,000. Author's first book. (Note: The auction record for this book is $1,550, established in 1928.)

GISSING, George. *A Yorkshire Lass.* Boards, paper label. New York, 1928. First edition. One of 93. $35-$50.

GIST, Christopher. *Christopher Gist's Journals.* 7 maps. Cloth. Pittsburgh, 1893. First edition. One of 10 on large paper. $45-$50.

GLASGOW, Ellen. See *The Descendant.*

GLEANINGS from the Inside History of the Bonanzas. 40 pp., printed wrappers. No place, no date (San Francisco, 1878). First edition. $125.

GLEANINGS of 50 Years: The Sisters of the Holy Names of Jesus and Mary in the Northwest, 1858-1909. Illustrated. Cloth. No place, no date (Portland, Ore., 1909). First edition. $25.

GLEANINGS, or Spirit of the Press. Edited by William Lyle Keys. Cloth. Cincinnati, 1841. First edition. $35.

GLEED, Charles S. (editor). *The Kansas Memorial.* Frontispiece. Cloth. Kansas City, Mo., 1880. First edition. $25.

GLEESON, William. *History of the Catholic Church in California.* 4 maps and plans, 9 plates. 2 vols., cloth. San Francisco, 1871-72. First edition. $300. San Francisco, 1872. 2 vols. in one. Second edition. $125.

GLEN, Duncan (editor). *Poems Addressed to Hugh MacDiarmid and Presented to Him on His 75th Birthday.* Frontispiece, other illustrations. Boards and leather. No place, no date (Preston, Lancashire, 1967). One of 50 signed by all the contributors, etc. $132. Another issue: One of 350 signed by editor and illustrator. $84. (Note: MacDiarmid is the pen name of C. M. Grieve.)

GLENN, Allen. *History of Cass County (Missouri).* Cloth. Topeka, 1917. First edition. $50. New spine, $30.

GLISAN, R. *Journal of Army Life.* Folding table, 21 plates. Cloth. San Francisco, 1874. First edition. $35-$50.

GLOVER, Mary Baker. *Science and Health, With Key to the Scriptures.* Black cloth. Boston, 1875. (By Mary Baker Eddy.) First edition, first issue, with errata slip and without index. $750 to $1,000 and up. Lynn, Mass., 1878. Second edition. $250-$300. Lynn, 1881. 2 vols., cloth. Third edition. $100-$150. Lynn, 1882. 2 vols., cloth. $100-$150. Boston, no date (1941). Folio, morocco. $350 (A, 1967).

GOBIERNO Independiente de Mexico. Wrappers. Mexico, 1882. $400.

GODDARD, Paul B., and Parker, Joseph E. *The Anatomy, Physiology and Pathology of the Human Teeth.* Illustrated. Half calf. Philadelphia, 1844. First edition. $65. New York, 1854. $30-$35.

GODWIN, William. *Deloraine.* 3 vols., boards. London, 1833. First edition. $100-$150. Another set, one cover loose, name cut from title of first volume, other defects, $60-$75.

GODWIN, William. *Essay on Sepulchres.* Engraved frontispiece. Boards, paper label. London, 1809. First edition. $100-$125.

GODWIN, William. *Fleetwood: or, The New Man of Feeling.* 3 vols., boards. London, 1805. First edition. $100-$150.

GODWIN, William. *Mandeville: A Tale of the 17th Century in England.* 3 vols., boards. London, 1817. First edition. $300-$350. Rebound in half morocco, $100.

GODWIN, William. *Of Population . . . An Answer to Mr. Malthus' Essay.* Boards. London, 1820. First edition. $150-$200.

GOETHE, Johann Wolfgang von. (Note: There are innumerable issues of Goethe's works in English and American reprint editions. The two following are typical.)

GOETHE, Johann Wolfgang von. *Faust.* Translated into English rhyme by Robert Talbot. Contemporary calf. London, 1835. First edition of this translation. $75-$80. Lowell, Mass. 1840. Translated by A. Hayward. Cloth. First American edition. $75. New York, no date (about 1925). Translated by John Anster. Illustrated by Harry Clarke. Half vellum. Large paper edition, signed by Clarke. In dust jacket. $125.

GOETHE, Johann Wolgang von. *Torquato Tasso: ein Schauspiel.* Printed in red and black. Vellum. London, 1913. Doves Press. One of 200. $100-$150.

GOGARTY, Oliver St. John. *Elbow Room.* Boards, linen spine. Dublin, 1939. Cuala Press. One of 450. In dust jacket. $75-$100.

GOGARTY, Oliver St. John. *An Offering of Swans.* Introduction by William Butler Yeats. Boards and cloth, paper label. Dublin, 1923. Cuala Press. First edition. One of 300. In dust jacket. $100-$125.

GOGARTY, Oliver St. John. *Wild Apples.* Preface by William Butler Yeats. Boards and linen. Dublin, 1930. Cuala Press. One of 250. In dust jacket. $100-$125.

GOLD, Silver, Lead, and Copper Mines of Arizona. 40 pp., printed wrappers. No place, no date (Philadelphia, 1867). $250.

GOLDEN Christmas (The): A Chronicle of St. John's, Berkeley. Cloth, or printed wrappers. Charleston, S.C., 1852. (By William Gilmore Simms.) First edition. Cloth: $15-$20. Wrappers: $25-$35.

GOLDER, Frank A. *Russian Expansion on the Pacific, 1641-1850.* Maps and plates. Cloth. Cleveland, 1914. First edition. $35-$50.

GOLDING, William. *Lord of the Flies.* Red cloth. London, no date (1954). First edition. In dust jacket. $55-$65. Author's first book.

GOLDSBOROUGH, Charles W. *The United States' Naval Chronicle.* Vol. 1. (All published.) Pictorial boards. Washington City, 1824. First edition, with errata slip pasted on last page. $100-$150. Rebound in boards and calf, $95.

GOLDSCHMIDT, E. P. *The Printed Book of the Renaissance.* 7 plates. Cloth. Cambridge, England, 1930. One of 750. $35-$40.

GOLDSMITH, Oliver. *The Vicar of Wakefield.* 12 color illustrations and some in black and white by Arthur Rackham. Parchment. London, 1929. One of 575 signed by the artist. $250-$300.

GOLL, Yvan. *Jean Sans Terre (Landless John).* Preface by Allen Tate. Translated by William Carlos Williams and others. Illustrated. Folio, boards. San Francisco, 1944. Grabhorn Press. One of 175. $75-$100.

GOOD, P. P. *A Materia Medica Botanica.* 48 colored plates. Cloth. New York, 1845. First edition. $75.

GOODE, William H. *Outposts of Zion.* Frontispiece. Cloth. Cincinnati, 1863. First edition. $35-$45.

GOODMAN, Paul. *Stop-light: 5 Dance Poems.* Harrington Park, N.Y., 1941. First edition. In dust jacket. $25-$30. Author's first book.

GOODRICH, Samuel G. See Parley, Peter. Also see *The Vagabond.*

GOODWIN, H. C. *Pioneer History; or Cortland County and the Border Wars of New York.* 3 portraits. Cloth. New York, 1859. First edition. $40-$50.

GOODWIN, Mrs. L. S. *The Gambler's Fate: A Story of California.* Woodcuts. 50 pp., pictorial wrappers. Boston, 1864. First edition. $35.

GOODYEAR, W. A. *The Coal Mines of the Western Coast of the United States.* Cloth. San Francisco, 1877. First edition. $25.

GOOKIN, Frederick W. *Daniel Gookin, 1612-1687.* 10 plates. Cloth. Chicago, 1912. First edition. One of 202. $35-$50.

GORDON, Alexander. *An Historical and Practical Treatise Upon Elemental Locomotion, by Means of Steam Carriages on Common Roads.* 14 plates. Gray boards. London, 1832. First edition. $100-$125.

GORDON, Caroline. *Alec Maury, Sportsman.* Cloth. New York, 1934. First edition. In dust jacket. $45-$50.

GORDON, Caroline. *The Forest of the South.* Cloth. New York, 1945. First edition. In dust jacket. $25.

GORDON, M. L. *Experiences in the Civil War.* Edited by Donald Gordon. Illustrated. Cloth. Boston, 1922. First edition. $25.

GORDON, Samuel. *Recollections of Old Milestown, Montana.* 19 plates. 42 pp., Miles City, Mont., 1918. First edition. $50.

GOREY, Edward. *The Curious Sofa.* Wrappers. New York, 1961. First edition. $20-$25.

GOREY, Edward. *The Gilded Bat.* Boards. New York, no date (1966). First edition. In dust jacket. $20-$25.

GOREY, Edward. *The Iron Tonic.* Decorated wrappers. New York, 1969. Albondocani Press. One of 200 numbered and signed copies. First edition. $15 $20.

GOREY, Edward. *The Object Lesson.* Boards. New York, 1958. First edition. In dust jacket. $40-$45.

GOREY, Edward. *The Sopping Thursday.* Cloth. New York, 1970. One of 26 copies, lettered, signed and in slipcase, with original unpublished drawing. $100-$125. Another issue: Wrappers, one of 300 copies, signed. $15-$20.

GOREY, Edward. *The Unstrung Harp.* Illustrated by the author. Decorated boards. New York, no date (1953). First edition. In dust jacket. $45-$50. Author's first book.

GOREY, Edward. *The Vinegar Works.* Three volumes comprising the following titles: *The Gashlycrumb Tinies; The Insect God; The West Wing.* Boards. New York, 1963. In decorated slipcase. $50-$60.

GORHAM, George C. *The Story of the Attempted Assassination of Justice Field.* Half leather. No place, no date (about 1893). First edition. $35-$40.

GORIN, Franklin. *The Times of Long Ago.* Cloth. Louisville, 1929. First edition. $35-$50.

GORMAN, Herbert. *James Joyce.* Cloth. New York, no date (1939). First edition. In dust jacket. $25-$35. (Note: Contains new material by Joyce.)

GORRELL, J. R. *A Trip to Alaska.* 40 pp., printed green wrappers. Newton, Iowa, 1905. First edition. $50-$75.

GOSNELL, Harpur Allen (editor). *Before the Mast in the Clippers.* Composed of the Diaries of Charles A. Abbey. Illustrated. Boards. New York, 1937. Derrydale Press. First edition. One of 950. $55.

GOTHEIN, M. L. *A History of Garden Art.* Illustrated. 2 vols., cloth. London, no date (1928). First edition. In dust jacket. $95.

GOUDY, Frederic W. *Typologia: Studies in Type Design and Type-Making.* Illustrated. Half morocco. Berkeley, Calif., 1940. First edition. One of 300 signed. Boxed. $50-$60. Trade edition: Cloth. $15.

GOUDY Gaudeamus: In Celebration of the Dinner Given Frederic W. Goudy, etc. Folding title page by Bruce Rogers. Marbled boards and cloth. No place (New York), 1939. One of 195. $30-$40.

GOUGE, William M. *The Fiscal History of Texas.* Cloth. Philadelphia, 1852. $50.

GOULD, A. C. *The Modern American Pistol and Revolver.* Illustrated. Cloth. Boston, 1888. $25-$30.

GOULD, E. W. *Fifty Years on the Mississippi.* Frontispiece. Pictorial cloth. St. Louis, 1889. First edition. $50-$75.

GOULD, John. *The Birds of Asia.* Edited by R. B. Sharpe. 530 hand-colored lithographed plates. 7 vols., folio, half (or full) morocco. London, 1850-83. $16,800 (A, 1968). (Note: Another set was listed in a London catalogue at $14,000 in 1967.)

GOULD, John. *The Birds of Australia.* 681 hand-colored lithographed plates. 8 vols., folio morocco (including supplement volume). London, 1840-69. $12,480 (A, 1968). (Note: A set of 7 vols., without supplement, was catalogued by a London dealer at $12,600 in 1967, and another set of 7 vols., London, 1848, was sold for $16,500, Australian dollars, in Melbourne in 1970.)

GOULD, John. *The Birds of Great Britain.* 367 hand-colored lithographed plates. 5 vols., half morocco. London, 1862-73. $3,600, $3,240, and $3,080 in London catalogues, 1966-67. Also, $2,640 and $3,600 (A, 1968).

GOULD, John. *Birds of New Guinea and the Adjacent Papuan Islands.* 320 hand-colored lithographed plates. 5 vols., folio half morocco. London, 1875-88. $6,600 and $7,000 (London catalogues, 1967 and 1965). Also, $6,720 (A, 1968).

GOULD, John. *Monographs.* (Note: There are also a number of scientific monographs by Gould which bring high prices because of the excellent plates. See the book auction records.)

GOULDING, F. R. *Marooner's Island.* Frontispiece. Cloth. Philadelphia, 1869. First edition. $35-$50.

GOULDING, F. R. *The Young Marooners on the Florida Coast.* 6 engraved plates. Decorated red cloth. London, 1853. First English edition (of *Robert and Harold; or, The Young Marooners on the Florida Coast*). $200 and up.

GOULDING, F. R. *Young Marooners of the Florida Coast; or, Robert and Harold,* 10 engraved plates. Decorated cloth. Philadelphia, 1867. New and enlarged edition (of *Robert and Harold*). First printing, with 1866 copyright. $50.

GOVE, Capt. Jesse A. *The Utah Expedition, 1857-58.* Edited by Otis G. Hammond. 5 plates. Half cloth. Concord, N.H., 1928. First edition. $25-$35. Another issue: One of 50 on large paper. $50-$75.

GRABHORN, Edwin. *The Fine Art of Printing.* Stiff wrappers. No place (San Francisco), 1933. First edition. One of 50. $60-$75.

GRABHORN, Edwin. *Figure Prints of Old Japan.* 52 reproductions. Boards. San Francisco, 1959. Book Club of California. One of 400. $175.

GRABHORN, Edwin. *Landscape Prints of Old Japan.* 52 full-color plates. Boards. San Francisco, 1960. Book Club of California. One of 450. $150.

GRABHORN, Jane Bissell (editor). *A California Gold Rush Miscellany.* Colored plates, folding map. Half leather. No place (San Francisco), 1934. First edition. One of 550. $35-$50.

GRACE Darling. 4 pp. (foolscap folded to form pamphlet). No place, no date (Carlisle, England, 1843). (By William Wordsworth.) First edition. Signed by Wordsworth. $150-$250. (Note: An unauthorized, undated reprint bearing a Newcastle imprint also exists.)

GRACIE, Archibald. *The Truth About Chickamauga.* Plates, folding maps. Cloth. Boston, 1911. First edition. $30-$40.

GRADUATION Lands: A Review of Sec. McClelland's Circular, by a Citizen of Central Michigan. 9 pp., half cloth. No place, no date (1856). $25-$30.

GRAHAM, Maria. *Journal of q Residence in Chile During the Year 1822 and a Voyage from Chile to Brazil in 1823.* 14 plates. Half calf. London, 1824. First edition. $150-$250.

GRAHAM, R. B. Cunninghame. *The District of Monteith.* Illustrated. Folio, half calf. Stirling, Scotland, 1930. One of 250 signed. $50-$60.

GRAHAM, R. B. Cunninghame. *The District of Monteith.* Illustrated. Folio, half calf. London, 1895. First edition. $50.

GRAHAM, Samuel. *Memoir of Gen. Samuel Graham.* 2 maps, 4 plates. Cloth. Edinburgh, 1862. First edition, with errata leaf. $65.

GRAHAM, Tom. *Hike and the Aeroplane.* Colored illustrations by Arthur Hutchins. Decorated cloth. New York, no date (1912). (By Sinclair Lewis.) First edition, first issue, with "August, 1912" on copyright page. In dust jacket. $400. Lacking jacket, $250-$350. Sinclair Lewis' first book.

GRAHAM, W. A. *The Custer Myth.* Cloth. Harrisburg, Pa., no date (1953). First edition. In dust jacket. $25.

GRAHAM, W. A. *Major Reno Vindicated.* 30 pp., wrappers. Hollywood, 1935. First edition. $25-$30.

GRAHAM, W. A. (editor). *The Official Record of a Court of Inquiry Convened . . . By Request of Major Marcus A. Reno to Investigate His Conduct at the Battle of the Little Big Horn, etc.* Multigraphed, 2 vols., folio, cloth. Pacific Palisades, Calif., 1951. One of 125. $200-$250.

GRAHAME, Kenneth. *Dream Days.* Cloth. New York, 1899 (actually 1898). First edition, first issue, with 15 pages of ads at end dated 1898. $35-$50. London, 1930. Illustrated by Ernest H. Shepard. Boards and vellum. Boxed. $50-$60.

GRAHAME, Kenneth. *The Golden Age.* Cloth. London, 1895. First edition. $25-$35. London, 1900. Illustrated by Maxfield Parrish. Cloth. $100. London, no date (1928). Illustrated by Ernest H. Shepard. Boards and vellum. One of 275 signed. $75-$100.

GRAHAME, Kenneth. *Pagan Papers.* Title page designed by Aubrey Beardsley. Cloth. London, 1894. First edition. One of 450. $50-$75. Author's first book.

GRAHAME, Kenneth. *The Wind in the Willows.* Frontispiece by Graham Robertson. Pictorial cloth. London, no date (1908). First edition. In dust jacket. $350-$400. New York, 1908. Cloth. First American edition. $50-$75. London, no date (1931). Illustrated by Ernest H. Shepard. Map. Gray boards and cloth. One of 200 signed. In dust jacket. Boxed. $400-$450. New York, 1940. Limited Editions Club. Edited by A. A. Milne. Illustrated by Arthur Rackham. Boards and cloth. Boxed. $200-$250. London, 1951. Illustrated by Rackham. Full white calf. One of 500. Boxed. $150-$200. London, no date (1964). Illustrated by Rackham. Calf. $100.

GRAND Jury Report, and the Evidence Taken by Them in Reference to the Great Riot in New Orleans, July 30, 1866. 17 pp., sewed. New Orleans, 1866. $35-$50.

GRANT, Arthur H. *A Genealogical History of the Descendants of Matthew Grant of Windsor, Conn., 1601-1898.* Cloth. Poughkeepsie, N.Y., 1898. $25-$35.

GRANT, Arthur H. *The Grant Family.* Cloth. Poughkeepsie, 1878. $25-$35.

GRANT, Blanche C. (editor). *Kit Carson's Own Story.* Plates. 138 pp., printed wrappers. Taos, N.M., 1926. First edition. $35-$50.

GRANT, Robert. *Jack Hall, or The School Days of an American Boy.* Illustrated by F. G. Attwood. Pictorial cloth. Boston, 1888. First edition. $35-$50.

GRANT, U. S. *General Orders, No. 67.* (Announcing the death of Lincoln and the succession of Johnson.) Sewed. Washington, 1865. $75.

GRANT, U. S. *General Orders, No. 74.* 43 pp., sewed. Washington, 1868. $75.

GRANT, U. S. *Message Communicating the Report and Journal of Proceedings of the Commission Appointed to Obtain Concessions from the Sioux Indians.* 90 pp., sewed. Washington, 1876. $35-$50.

GRANT, U. S. *Personal Memoirs.* 2 vols., three-quarters leather. New York, 1885-86. First edition. Large paper issue. $75-$100. Trade edition: Cloth. $10-$15.

GRAVES, H. A. *Andrew Jackson Potter, the Noted Parson of the Texan Frontier.* Portrait. Cloth. Nashville, 1881. First edition. $100-$150. Nashville, 1882. Second edition. $100. Nashville, 1883. Third edition. $75. Nashville, 1888. $30.

GRAVES, H. A. (compiler). *Reminiscences and Events of Rev. John Wesley DeVilbiss.* Cloth. Galveston, Tex., 1886. $50.

GRAVES, Richards. *Oklahoma Outlaws.* Illustrated. 131 pp., pictorial red wrappers. No place, no date (Oklahoma City, 1915). First edition. $25.

GRAVES, Robert. *Adam's Rib.* Wood engravings by James Metcalf. Brick-red cloth. No place, no date (1955). Trianon Press. First edition. One of 250 signed. In dust jacket. $125-$175. One of 26 (A to Z). $200-$250. Trade edition: Cloth. In dust jacket. $10.

GRAVES, Robert. *But It Still Goes On.* Bright-green cloth. London, no date (1930). First edition, first state, with reference to "The Child She Bare" on page 157. In dust jacket. $75-$100. Covers warped, $35. Second state, corrected page 157 tipped in. In dust jacket. $25.

GRAVES, Robert. *Colophon to Love Respelt.* Printed wrappers. No place (London), 1967. First edition. One of 350 signed. In dust jacket. $50-$75.

GRAVES, Robert. *Country Sentiment.* Light-blue boards. London, no date (1920). First edition. In dust jacket. $75-$100.

GRAVES, Robert. *Fairies and Fusiliers.* Wine-red cloth. London, no date (1917). First edition. In dust jacket, $100-$150. Second impression: No place, no date (London, 1919). Bright-red cloth. $75-$100.

GRAVES, Robert. *The Feather Bed.* Decorated pink boards. Richmond, England, 1923. Hogarth Press. One of 250 signed. $100-$125.

GRAVES, Robert. *Goliath and David.* Wrappers. No place, no date (London, 1916). First edition. One of 200. $375-$500.

GRAVES, Robert. *Good-bye to All That: An Autobiography.* Illustrated. Salmon-pink cloth. London, no date (1929). First edition, first state, with poem by Siegfried Sassoon on pages 341-43. In dust jacket. $150-$200. Second state, with Sassoon poem removed and erratum slip at 398-99. In dust jacket. $60. New York, no date (1930). Red cloth. First American edition. In dust jacket. $35.

GRAVES, Robert. *Impenetrability or the Proper Habit of English.* Light-blue boards. London, 1926. Hogarth Press. First edition. $50-$75.

GRAVES, Robert. *John Kemp's Wager: A Ballad Opera.* White boards. Oxford, 1925. First edition. $75-$85. Another issue: Boards, parchment spine. One of 100 signed. $100-$125.

GRAVES, Robert. *Lars Porsena, or The Future of Swearing and Improper Language.* Plum-colored boards, paper labels. London, no date (1927). First edition, with 16 pages of ads. $50. New York, no date (1927). Blue or olive-green cloth. First American edition. In dust jacket. $35.

GRAVES, Robert. *Lawrence and the Arabs.* Illustrated. Mustard-colored (orange) cloth. London, no date (1927). First edition. In dust jacket. $50-$60.

GRAVES, Robert. *Love Respelt.* Illuminated by Aemilia Laracuen. Cloth. London, no date (1965). First edition. One of 250 signed. In dust jacket. $25-$35.

GRAVES, Robert. *Mammon and the Black Goddess.* Wrappers. London, 1965. Proof copy (so imprinted on cover). $25. (Note: The published edition, bound in gray cloth, with dust jacket is not scarce and is of nominal value.)

GRAVES, Robert. *Man Does, Woman Is.* Buff linen, blue cloth spine. London, 1964. First edition. One of 175 signed. In glassine dust jacket. $100-$125. Another issue: One of 26 (A to Z). $200-$225. Trade edition: Cloth. In dust jacket. $10-$20.

GRAVES, Robert. *Mrs. Fisher, or The Future of Humour.* Plum-colored boards, paper labels. London, 1928. First edition. In dust jacket. $50-$75.

GRAVES, Robert. *Mock Beggar Hall.* Gray pictorial boards. London, 1924. Hogarth Press. First edition. $100-$125.

GRAVES, Robert. *The More Deserving Cases.* Portrait. Red morocco. No place (Marlborough, England), 1962. Marlborough College Press. First edition. One of 400 signed. $35-$50. Another issue: Blue buckram. One of 350 signed. $35-$50.

GRAVES, Robert. *My Head! My Head!* Decorated red cloth, black spine. London, 1925. First edition. $60-$80.

GRAVES, Robert. *On English Poetry.* Cream-colored boards. New York, 1922. First edition, first issue, with misprints "that" for "than that" on page 33 and "have" for "how" on page 145. In dust jacket. $75-$100. London, no date (1922). Bright yellow cloth. First English edition, first issue (with misprints), first binding. In dust jacket. $50-$75. Second state binding, buff boards. $40-$60.

GRAVES, Robert. *Over the Brazier.* Pictorial gray wrappers. London, 1916. Poetry Bookshop. First edition. $500-$600. Also, $432 (A, 1970). Author's first book. London, no date (1920). Gray boards, blue cloth spine. Second edition. In dust jacket. $200-$300.

GRAVES, Robert. *The Pier-Glass.* Portrait. Yellow decorated boards. London, no date (1921). First edition. One of 500. In dust jacket. $75-$100.

GRAVES, Robert. *Poems 1953.* Bright-green boards, white cloth spine. London, no date (1953). First edition. One of 250 signed. In dust jacket. $50. Trade edition: Sea-green cloth. In dust jacket. $10.

GRAVES, Robert. *Poems (1914-1927).* White boards, parchment spine. London, 1927. One of 115 signed. $75-$125.

GRAVES, Robert. *Poems (1914-1926).* Slick white cloth with black cobbled design. London, 1927. First edition. In dust jacket. $50-$75.

GRAVES, Robert. *Poems 1929.* Yellow-green cloth. London, 1929. Seizin Press. First edition. One of 225 signed. $100-$200.

GRÁVES, Robert. *Poems, 1926-1930.* Maroon cloth, paper labels. London, 1931. First edition. In dust jacket. $35-$50. Lacking jacket, $28.80.

GRAVES, Robert. *Poetic Unreason and Other Studies.* Dark-blue cloth, paper label. No place, no date (London, 1925). First edition. In dust jacket. $90.

GRAVES, Robert. *The Real David Copperfield.* Blue cloth. London, no date (1933). First edition. In dust jacket. $25.

GRAVES, Robert. *Seventeen Poems Missing from Love Respelt.* Wrappers over boards. No place (London), 1966. First edition. One of 330 signed. $35-$40.

GRAVES, Robert. *The Shout.* Decorated gray boards. London, 1929. First edition. One of 530 signed. In dust jacket. $75-$125. Also, $67 (A, 1970).

GRAVES, Robert. *T. E. Lawrence to His Biographer, Robert Graves.* Buff cloth. New York, 1938. First edition. One of 500 signed by Graves (issued with Liddell Hart's book of the same title) with Doubleday imprint. Boxed (with the Liddell Hart book). $250. Also, $150 (A, 1971). London, no date (1939). Red cloth. First English edition. One of 500 signed by Graves. In dust jacket. Issued boxed as a set with the Liddell Hart book. $250.

GRAVES, Robert. *Ten Poems More.* Boards and green morocco. Paris, 1930. Hours Press. First edition, with misprints on pages 7, 10, and 15. One of 200 signed. In transparent dust jacket. $100-$150.

GRAVES, Robert. *To Whom Else?* Pictorial boards and cloth. Deya, Majorca, 1931. Seizin Press. First edition. One of 200 signed. In dust jacket. $100-$125.

GRAVES, Robert. *Treasure Box.* Light-blue wrappers. No place, no date (London, 1919). First edition. One of 200. $300-$400.

GRAVES, Robert. *Welchman's Hose.* Wood engravings by Paul Nash. Decorated boards and cloth. London, 1925. First edition. One of 525. In transparent dust jacket. $100-$125.

GRAVES, Robert. *Whipperginny.* Decorated magenta boards. London, no date (1923). First edition. In dust jacket. $100-$125. New York, 1923. Boards. First American edition. In dust jacket. $50-$75.

GRAVES, Robert, and Lindsay, Jack (editors). *Loving Mad Tom: Bedlamite Verses of the 16th and 17th Centuries.* Illustrated. Boards and vellum. London, no date (1927). Fanfrolico Press. First edition. One of 375. $100.

GRAVES, W. W. *Annals of Osage Mission.* Illustrated. Cloth. St. Paul, Kan., 1935. First edition. $30.

GRAVES, W. W. *Life and Letters of Fathers Ponziglione, Schoenmakers, and Other Early Jesuits at Osage Mission.* Illustrated. Cloth. St. Paul, Kan., 1916. First edition. $25.

GRAY, Alonson. *Family Record of Edward Gray and His Wife, Mary Paddock, and Their Descendants.* Cloth. Rutland, Vt., 1889. $40-$45.

GRAY, Henry. *Anatomy, Descriptive and Surgical.* Cloth. London, 1858. First edition. $600-$800, possibly more. Philadelphia, 1859. Illustrated, including color. Calf. $45.

GRAY, John W. *The Life of Joseph Bishop.* Cloth. Nashville, 1858. First edition. $75.

GRAYDON, Alexander. *Memoirs of a Life, Chiefly Passed in Pennsylvania, Within the Last 60 Years.* Cloth. Harrisburg, Pa., 1811. First edition, with errata leaf. $35-$50. Edinburgh, 1822. Boards and cloth. First English edition. $35.

GREAT Eastern Gold Mining Co. (The). Map. 7 pp., wrappers. New York, 1880. $25-$35.

GREAT Steam-Duck (The) ... An Invention for Aerial Navigation. By a Member of the LLBB. 32 pp. Louisville, 1841. $750 and up.

GREAT Trans-Continental Railroad Guide. Wrappers. Chicago, 1869. First edition. $65.

GREAT Western Almanac for 1848. Wrappers. Philadelphia, no date (1847). First edition. $175.

GREAVES, Richard. *Brewster's Millions.* Red cloth. Chicago, 1903. (By George Barr McCutcheon.) First edition. $25-$30.

GRECE, Charles F. *Facts and Observations Respecting Canada, and the United States of America.* Contemporary leather. London, 1819. First edition. $175.

GREELEY, Horace. *An Overland Journey from New York to San Francisco.* Cloth. New York, 1860. First edition. $25-$35.

GREEN, Anna Katharine. *The Circular Study.* Red cloth. New York, 1900. First edition. In dust jacket. $35-$50.

GREEN, Anna Katharine. *The Leavenworth Case: A Lawyer's Story.* Plate. Terra-cotta cloth. New York, 1878. First edition. $150-$200.

GREEN, Jonathan S. *Journal of a Tour on the Northwest Coast of America in the Year 1829.* Edited by Edward Eberstadt. Boards, paper label. New York, 1915. First edition. One of 150. $50-$75. (Note: There were also 10 copies on Japan vellum, and they are of course more valuable.)

GREEN Mountain Boys (The). 2 vols., boards, paper labels. Montpelier, Vt., 1839. (By Daniel Pierce Thompson.) First edition, first issue, with publisher's name misspelled "Waltton" in copyright notices of Vol. 2. $100 and up. Another, spelling corrected, $50.

GREEN, Mowbray A. *The Eighteenth Century Architecture of Bath.* Plates and plans. Buckram. Bath, England, 1904. One of 500. $35.

GREEN, Thomas. *The Universal Herbal, or Botanical, Medical and Agricultural Dictionary.* Colored plates. 2 vols., contemporary half calf, gilt paneled spines. Liverpool, England, no date (1816-20). $200. Liverpool, no date (1820). 2 vols. $150-$175.

GREEN, Thomas J. *Journal of the Texian Expedition Against Mier.* 11 plates, 2 plans. Cloth. New York, 1845. First edition. $100-$125. Rebound in morocco, $75.

GREEN, Thomas M. *The Spanish Conspiracy.* Cloth. Cincinnati, 1891. First edition. $50-$60.

GREENAN, Edith. *Of Una Jeffers.* 5 photographic illustrations. Cloth. Los Angeles, 1939. One of 250. In dust jacket. $25.

GREENAWAY, Kate. See Harte, Bret; Mavor, William; Taylor, Jane and Ann.

GREENAWAY, Kate. *A Apple Pie.* Colored illustrations. Boards and cloth. London, no date (1886). First edition. $75-$100.

GREENAWAY, Kate. *Almanacks.* Illustrated in color by the author. Pictorial boards, wrappers, or cloth. London, no dates (1883-95 and 1897, with no *Almanack* issued in 1896). First editions. Complete sets in fine condition are worth $750 and up at retail. Auction records: $480 and $600 (1969). Individual years retail in the $35-$60 range.

GREENAWAY, Kate. *Kate Greenaway's Alphabet.* Colored illustrations. Pictorial colored wrappers. London, no date (1885?). First edition. $50.

GREENAWAY, Kate. *Kate Greenaway's Birthday Book for Children.* Verses by Mrs. Sale Barker. 382 illustrations (12 plates in color). Pictorial boards. London, no date (1880). First edition. $50-$60.

GREENAWAY, Kate. *Kate Greenaway's Book of Games.* Colored plates. Pictorial boards. London, no date (1889). $50-$60.

GREENAWAY, Kate. *Kate Greenaway Pictures.* Portrait frontispiece, 20 pictures in color. Cloth. London, 1921. In dust jacket. $75.

GREENAWAY, Kate. *Marigold Garden.* Illustrated in color by the author. Pictorial boards and cloth. No place, no date (London, 1885). First edition. $50-$60.

GREENAWAY, Kate. *Under the Window: Pictures and Rhymes for Children.* Colored illustrations. Pictorial boards. London, no date (1878). First edition, first issue, with printer's imprint on back of title page and with reading "End of Contents" at foot of page 14. In dust jacket. $75-$100.

GREENAWAY, Kate (illustrator). *Dame Wiggins of Lee and Her Seven Wonderful Cats.* Edited by John Ruskin. 22 woodcuts. Gray cloth. London, no date (1885). First edition with the Greenaway illustrations. $50-$60.

GREENAWAY, Kate (illustrator). *A Day in a Child's Life.* Music by Myles B. Foster. Color illustrations. Pictorial boards in color. London, no date (1881). First edition. $50-$75.

GREENAWAY, Kate (illustrator). *Language of Flowers.* Colored illustrations. Boards. London, no date (1884). First edition. $50-$60.

GREENAWAY, Kate (illustrator). *The "Little Folks" Painting Book.* Stories and verses by George Weatherly. Pictorial wrappers. London, no date (1879). First edition. $75-$100.

GREENAWAY, Kate (illustrator). *Mother Goose or The Old Nursery Rhymes.* Illustrated in color by Kate Greenaway. Pictorial blue cloth. London, no date (1881). First edition. In dust jacket. $50-$60. Inscribed copies, $75-$100.

GREENAWAY, Kate, and Crane, Walter. *The Quiver of Love.* Colored illustrations. Cloth. No place, no date (London, 1876). Marcus Ward & Co. First edition. $150.

GREENBURG, Dan W. *Sixty Years: A Brief Review. The Cattle Industry in Wyoming, etc.* Illustrated. 73 pp., pictorial wrappers. Cheyenne, 1932. First edition (so stated). $60-$75.

GREENE, Graham. See Bey, Pilaff.

GREENE, Graham. *Babbling April: Collected Poems.* Boards. Oxford, 1925. First edition. In dust jacket. $300-$400. Author's first book.

GREENE, Graham. *The Bear Fell Free.* Cloth. No place, no date (London, 1935). First edition. One of 285 signed. In dust jacket. $150-$200.

GREENE, Graham. *Brighton Rock.* Red cloth. London, no date (1938). First edition. In dust jacket. $100-$150.

GREENE, Graham. *Confidential Agent.* Cloth. London, 1939. First edition. In dust jacket. $50-$60.

GREENE, Graham. *A Gun for Sale.* Cloth. London, no date (1936). First edition. In dust jacket. $100-$150.

GREENE, Graham. *It's a Battlefield.* Black cloth. London, no date (1934). First edition. In dust jacket. $100-$150.

GREENE, Graham. *The Lawless Roads.* Cloth. London, 1939. First edition. In dust jacket. $35-$50.

GREENE, Graham. *L'Homme et Lui-Même.* Wrappers. Paris, no date (1947). First French translation of *The Man Within.* One of 10 copies marked "H. [ors] C. [ommerce]." $25-$30.

GREENE, Graham. *The Man Within.* Cloth. London, no date (1929). First edition. In dust jacket. $125-$150.

GREENE, Graham. *May We Borrow Your Husband?* Decorated boards. London, no date (1967). First edition. One of 500 signed. $35.

GREENE, Graham. *The Name of Action.* Cloth. London, no date (1930). First edition. In dust jacket. $75-$100.

GREENE, Graham. *The Power and the Glory.* Cloth. London, 1940. First edition. In dust jacket. $75-$100.

GREENE, Graham. *Rumour at Nightfall.* Red cloth. London, 1931. First edition. In dust jacket. $100-$125.

GREENE, Graham. *Stamboul Train.* Cloth. London, no date (1932). First edition. In dust jacket. $75.

GREENE, Max. *The Kanzas Region.* 2 maps. Printed wrappers. New York, 1856. First edition. $100-$150.

GREENE, Talbot. *American Nights' Entertainment.* Purple cloth. Jonesborough, Tenn., 1860. First edition. $60-$75.

GREENEWALT, Crawford H. *Hummingbirds.* Color plates. Boards. Garden City, no date (1960). First edition. One of 500. $150-$250. Trade edition: Cloth. In dust jacket. $50-$75.

GREENHOW, Robert. *The History of Oregon and California.* Map. Calf. Boston, 1844. Enlarged edition of his *Memoir.* $35-$50. Boston, 1845. Wrappers. "Second edition." $45 and $50.

GREENHOW, Robert. *Memoir, Historical and Political.* Folding map. Sewed. Washington, 1840. First edition. $100 $125.

GREENLEE, Ralph Stebbins, and Greenlee, Robert Lemuel. *Genealogy of the Greenlee Families in America.* Cloth. Chicago, 1908. $40-$45.

GREENLEE, Ralph Stebbins, and Greenlee, Robert Lemuel. *The Stebbins Genealogy.* 2 vols., cloth. Chicago, 1904. $50-$60.

GREER, James K. *Bois d'Arc to Barb'd Wire.* Plates, maps. Pictorial cloth. Dallas, 1936. First edition. In dust jacket. $50.

GREER, James K. (editor). *A Texas Ranger and Frontiersman.* Illustrated. Cloth. Dallas, 1932. First edition. In dust jacket. $50-$75.

GREGG, Alexander. *History of the Old Cheraws.* 4 maps, illustrated. Cloth. New York, 1867. First edition. $50-$75.

GREGG, Asa. *Personal Recollections of the Early Settlement of Wapsinonoc Township and the Murder of Atwood by the Indians.* Tables. Wrappers. West Liberty, Iowa, no date (about 1875-1880). First edition. $750-$1,000. Rebound, with original wrappers bound in, $600.

GREGG, Josiah. *Commerce of the Prairies.* 2 maps (one folding), 6 plates. 2 vols., brown pictorial cloth. New York, 1844. First edition, first issue, with only New York in imprint. $400-$550. Other sets, $350 and $225. Also, $375 (A, 1960). Second issue, with imprint "New York and London." $275. New York, 1845. 2 vols., cloth. Second edition. $150. Rebound in calf, $100.

GREGORY, Isabella Augusta Persse, Lady. *A Book of Saints and Wonders.* Boards and linen. Dundrum, Ireland, 1906. Dun Emer Press. One of 200. $80-$90.

GREGORY, Isabella Augusta Persse, Lady. *Coole.* Boards and linen. Dublin, 1931. Cuala Press. One of 250. In tissue dust jacket. $125-$150. (Note: Includes a poem by William Butler Yeats.)

GREGORY, Isabella Augusta Persse, Lady. *Gods and Fighting Men.* Cloth. London, 1904. $30-$35.

GREGORY, Isabella Augusta Persse, Lady. *Irish Folk-History Plays.* Cloth. London, 1912. $35-$40.

GREGORY, Isabella Augusta Persse, Lady. *The Kiltartan Poetry Book.* Boards and linen. Dundrum, Ireland, 1918. Cuala Press. One of 400. $85.

GREGORY, John. *Industrial Resources of Wisconsin.* Cloth. Milwaukee, 1855. First complete edition. $250.

GREGORY, Samuel. *History of Mexico; with An Account of the Texan Revolution.* 100 pp., pictorial wrappers. Boston, 1847. First edition. $75.

GREGORY, Thomas Jefferson, and others. *History of Solano and Napa Counties, California.* Illustrated. Maps. Three-quarters leather. Los Angeles, 1912. $50-$100.

GREVILLE, Charles C. F. *The Greville Memoirs.* Edited by Lytton Strachey and Roger Fulford. Frontispieces. 8 vols., buckram. London, 1938. One of 630. $335. (Also issued in cloth and in half leather.)

GREVILLE, Fulke, Lord Brooke. *Caelica.* Edited by Una Ellis-Fermor. Boards and leather. Newtown, Wales, 1936. Gregynog Press. One of 225. $35-$50. Another issue: Blue morocco, specially decorated by the Gregynog bindery. $170.

GREVILLE, Fulke, Lord Brooke. *The Life of the Renowned Sir Philip Sidney.* Portrait. Limp vellum, silk ties. London, 1907. One of 11 on vellum. $100-$125.

GREY, Zane. *Betty Zane.* Illustrated by the author. Cloth. New York, no date (1903). First edition. $75-$100. Author's first book.

GREY, Zane. *The Last of the Plainsmen.* Cloth. New York, 1908. First edition. In dust jacket. $25-$35.

GREYSLAER: A Romance of the Mohawk. 2 vols., cloth, paper labels on spines. New York, 1840. (By Charles Fenno Hoffman.) First edition, with errata slip in first volume. $75-$100.

GRIERSON, Gen. B. M. *Annual Report on the Department of Arizona, Bowie and Selden and the Point Loma and Navajo Reservations.* 32 pp., cloth. No place, 1889. $35-$40.

GRIEVE, C. M. See: Glen, Duncan; MacDiarmid, Hugh; Mc'Diarmid, Hugh.

GRIEVE, M. *A Modern Herbal.* Illustrated. 2 vols., cloth. London, no date (1931). First edition. In dust jackets. $75-$100. Ex-library, $50-$60.

GRIFFITH, Thomas. *Sketches of the Early History of Maryland.* Frontispiece. Calf. Baltimore, 1821. First edition. $75-$100.

GRIGGS, George B. *Norkoma.* Cloth. Houston, 1906. First edition. $25-$30.

GRILE, Dod. *Cobwebs: Being the Fables of Zambri, the Parsee.* Illustrated. Heavy pictorial printed wrappers, or boards. No place, no date (London, about 1884). "Fun" Office. (By Ambrose Bierce.) Reprint edition of *Cobwebs from an Empty Skull* (see entry following). $75-$100.

GRILE, Dod. *Cobwebs from an Empty Skull.* Illustrated. Blue cloth. London, 1874. (By Ambrose Bierce.) First edition. $50-$100. Presentation copy signed by Bierce, worn, $125. (For reprint, see foregoing entry.)

GRILE, Dod. *The Fiend's Delight.* Purple-brown cloth. London, no date (1872). (By Ambrose Bierce.) First edition. $75-$100. Author's first book. New York, 1873. Brown or purple-brown cloth. First American edition, without publisher's ads. $25-$35.

GRILE, Dod. *Nuggets and Dust Panned Out in California.* Yellow pictorial wrappers. London, no date (1873). (By Ambrose Bierce.) First edition. $50-$60.

GRIMALDI, Joseph. See "Boz."

GRIMM, Jacob L. K. and W. K. *The Fairy Tales of the Brothers Grimm.* Translated by Mrs. Edgar Lucas. Illustrated with color plates by Arthur Rackham. Vellum. London, 1909. One of 750 signed by Rackham. $250-$300. Trade edition: Cloth. $100-$125.

GRINNELL, George Bird. *American Game-Bird Shooting.* Illustrated. Cloth. New York, no date (1910). First edition. $40-$50.

GRINNELL, George Bird. *The Cheyenne Indians: Their History and Way of Life.* Illustrated. 2 vols., cloth. New Haven, 1923. First edition. $75-$100.

GRINNELL, George Bird. *The Fighting Cheyennes.* Maps. Cloth. New York, 1915. First edition. $25-$35.

GRINNELL, George Bird. *The Indians of Today.* Illustrated. Folio, pictorial cloth. Chicago, 1900. First edition. $50-$60.

GRINNELL, George Bird. *Two Great Scouts and Their Pawnee Battalion.* Map, illustrations. Cloth. Cleveland, 1928. First edition. $35-$50.

GRINNELL, Joseph. *Gold Hunting in Alaska.* Illustrated. Red boards and green cloth. Elgin, Ill., no date (1901). First edition. $50-$60.

GRINNELL, Joseph, and others. *Animal Life in the Yosemite.* Illustrations (some in color). Cloth. Berkeley, Calif., 1924. $35-$50.

GRINNELL, Joseph, and others. *The Game Birds of California.* 16 color plates, other illustrations. Cloth. Berkeley, 1918. $50.

GRINNELL, Joseph, and others. *Vertebrate Natural History of a Section of Northern California Through the Lassen Peak Region.* Folding colored map. Cloth. Berkeley, 1930. $35.

GRISWOLD, David D. *Statistics of Chicago, Ills., Together with a Business Advertiser, and Mercantile Directory for July, 1843.* 24 pp., printed wrappers. No place (Chicago), 1843. First edition. $500 and up. Also, $500 (A, 1967).

GRISWOLD, N. W. *Beauties of California.* 18 color plates. Wrappers. San Francisco, 1883. First edition. $35-$50.

GRISWOLD, W. M. *A Descriptive List of Novels and Tales Dealing with American Country Life.* 52 pp., stitched. Cambridge, Mass., 1890. First edition. $35.

GRISWOLD, Wayne. *Kansas Her Resources and Developments.* Illustrated. Printed wrappers. Cincinnati, 1871. First edition. $35-$50.

GRONOW, Rees Howell. *The Reminiscences and Recollections of Captain Gronow.* Illustrated. 2 vols., cloth. London, 1889. One of 875. $45-$50.

GROOS, J. J. *Report of the General Land Office.* 21 pp., wrappers. Houston, 1874. $25. Houston, 1876. 27 pp., wrappers. $25.

GROSART, A. B. (editor). *Occasional Issues of Unique and Very Rare Books.* 17 vols., half morocco. London, 1875-81. "Limited to a small number of copies." $800-$850.

GROSSMITH, George. *The Diary of a Nobody.* Illustrated by Weedon Grossmith. Light-brown cloth. Bristol, England, no date (1892). First edition. $50-$75.

GROUPED Thoughts and Scattered Fancies. Cloth. Richmond, Va., 1845. (By William Gilmore Simms.) First edition. $100-$150.

GROVER, La Fayette (editor). *The Oregon Archives.* Printed yellow wrappers. Salem, Ore., 1853 (actually 1854). First edition. $400-$500. Also, $400 (A, 1969).

GRYLL Grange. By the Author of *Headlong Hall.* Cloth. London, 1861. (By Thomas Love Peacock.) First edition, with 4 pages of ads at end. $100-$125. Rebound in leather, $30.

GUERIN, Maurice de. *The Centaur.* Translated by George B. Ives. Boards. No place (Montague, Mass.), 1915. One of 135. Bruce Rogers typography. $400-$500. Also, $400 (A, 1969).

GUERNSEY, Charles A. *Wyoming Cowboy Days.* Illustrated. Cloth. New York, 1936. First edition. In dust jacket. $25-$30.

GUIDE, Gazetteer and Directory of Nebraska Railroads. Folding map, 6 plates. 210 pp., wrappers. Omaha, 1872. (By J. M. Wolfe.) First edition. $100-$150.

GUIDE for Emigrants to Minnesota (A). By a Tourist. Map. 16 pp., printed blue wrappers. St. Paul, Minn., 1857. First edition. $100.

GUILD, Jo. C. *Old Times in Tennessee.* Green cloth. Nashville, 1878. First edition. $100-$150. Also, $100 (A, 1967).

GUINEY, Louise Imogen. *Songs at the Start.* Half morocco. Boston, 1884. First edition. $35-$40. (Also issued in cloth.) Author's first book.

GUNN, Donald. *History of Manitoba from the Earliest Settlement to 1835.* Portrait. Cloth. Ottawa, 1880. First edition. $75-$100.

GUNN, Otis B. *New Map and Hand-Book of Kansas and the Gold-Mines.* Large map in color, folding into black cloth covers, and accompanied by text pamphlet (*Gunn's Map and Hand-Book, etc.*), bound in salmon-colored printed wrappers. Pittsburgh, 1859. First edition. $1,500 and up. Also, $1,250 (A, 1966); lacking front cover for text, $1,300 (A, 1968).

GUNN, Thom. *The Explorers.* Printed wrappers. Devon, England, no date (1969). First edition. One of 20 (of an edition of 100) with a poem written out in author's hand and signed by him. $50. One of 64 numbered copies. $30.

GUNN, Thom. *A Geography.* Wrappers. Iowa City, 1966. First edition, signed. One of 220 copies. $20-$25.

GUNNISON, John W. *The Mormons; or, Latter-Day Saints, in the Valley of the Great Salt Lake.* Illustrated. Dark-blue cloth. Philadelphia, 1852. First edition. $60-$75.

GUNSAULUS, Helen C. *The Clarence Buckingham Collection of Japanese Prints: The Primitives.* Plates. Folio, cloth. Chicago, no date (1955). One of 500. $100.

GUNTER, Archibald Clavering. *Mr. Barnes of New York.* Cloth or wrappers. New York, 1887. First edition, first issue, with perfect type in copyright notice. Wrappers: $125. Cloth: $100.

GURNEY, Joseph John. *Familiar Letters to Henry Clay of Kentucky, Describing a Winter in the West Indies.* Cloth. New York, 1840. First edition. $35-$40.

GUY Mannering; or, The Astrologer. 3 vols., boards. Edinburgh, 1815. (By Sir Walter Scott.) First edition. $150-$200.

GUY Rivers: A Tale of Georgia. 2 vols., cloth, paper labels. New York, 1834. (By William Gilmore Simms.) First edition. $300-$400.

H

H., H. (translator). *Bathmendi: A Persian Tale.* Translated from the French of Florian. Printed wrappers. Boston, 1867. (Translated by Helen Hunt Jackson.) $150. First publication by the translator.

H., H. *Verses.* By H. H. Cloth. Boston, 1870. (By Helen Hunt Jackson.) First edition. $25-$30. Author's first book.

HABBERTON, John. See *Helen's Babies; Other People's Children* .

HABERLY, Loyd. *Almost a Minister: A Romance of the Oregon Hopyards.* Illustrated in color by the author. Patterned paper cover, leather spine. No place, no date (St. Louis, 1942). Mound City Press. One of 375. $35-$50.

HABERLY, Loyd. *Anne Boleyn, and Other Poems.* Printed in red and black on handmade paper. Niger morocco. Newtown, Wales, 1934. Gregynog Press. One of 300. $100-$150. Another issue: One of 15 (from the edition) elaborately bound. $420.

HABERLY, Loyd. *The Antiquary: A Poem.* Morocco. Long Crendon, England, 1933. Seven Acres Press. One of 100 signed. $100-$150.

HABERLY, Loyd. *Artemis: A Forest Tale.* Illustrated in color by Haberly. Full green morocco. No place, no date (St. Louis, 1942). Mound City Press. One of 240. $50-$75.

HABERLY, Loyd. *The Boy and the Bird: An Oregon Idyll.* Woodcuts. Full green morocco. Long Crendon, 1932. Seven Acres Press. One of 155 signed. $75.

HABERLY, Loyd. *The City of the Sainted King and Other Poems.* Full orange-red morocco. No place (Cambridge, Mass.), 1939. One of 200. $75.

HABERLY, Loyd. *The Copper-Coloured Cupid.* Morocco. Long Crendon, 1931. Seven Acres Press. One of 155. $50-$60.

HABERLY, Loyd. *The Keeper of the Doves.* Morocco. Long Crendon, 1933. Seven Acres Press. One of 100 signed. $100-$125.

HABERLY, Loyd. *Poems.* Dark-blue morocco. Long Crendon, 1930. Seven Acres Press. $65.

HACKETT, James. *Narrative of the Expedition Which Sailed from England in 1817, to Join the South American Patriots.* Boards. London, 1818. First edition. $150-$200.

HAEBLER, Konrad. *The Early Printers of Spain and Portugal.* Frontispiece and facsimiles. Wrappers. London, 1897 (actually 1896). $75-$100. (Also noted in cloth and half morocco.)

HAFEN, LeRoy R. *The Mountain Men and the Fur Trade of the Far West.* Illustrated. 6 vols., cloth. Glendale, Calif., 1965-68. $150-$200.

HAFEN, LeRoy R. *The Overland Mail, 1849-1869.* Map, 7 plates. Cloth. Cleveland, 1926. First edition. $60-$80.

HAFEN, LeRoy R. *Overland Routes to the Gold Fields.* 7 plates, folding map. Cloth. Glendale, 1942. First edition. $40-$50.

HAFEN, LeRoy R. and Ann W. *The Old Spanish Trail.* Plates and maps. Cloth. Glendale, 1954. First edition. $25-$35.

HAFEN, LeRoy R. and Ann W. (editors). *The Far West and the Rockies, 1820-75.* Illustrated. 15 vols., green cloth. Glendale, 1954-61. $300-$400. Also, $270 (A, 1968).

HAFEN, LeRoy R., and Young, Francis Marion. *Fort Laramie and the Pageant of the West, 1834-1890.* Illustrated. Cloth. Glendale, 1938. First edition. $50-$60.

HAFEN, LeRoy R., and Ghent, W. J. *Broken Hand: The Life Story of Thomas Fitzpatrick, Chief of the Mountain Men.* Map, 8 plates. Cloth-backed boards. Denver, 1931. First edition. One of 100 large paper copies, signed. $250-$300. Another issue: Cloth. One of 500. $150-$200.

HAFEN, Mary Ann. *Recollections of a Handcart Pioneer of 1860.* Plates. Cloth. Denver, 1938. First edition. $35-$50.

HAGGARD, H. Rider. *Allan Quatermain.* Frontispiece, 19 plates. Cloth. London, 1887. First edition. $90-$125. Another issue: Half brown morocco. One of 112 on large paper. $150-$200. Also, presentation copy, $100.80 (A, 1967).

HAGGARD, H. Rider. *Allan's Wife and Other Tales.* Illustrated. Half leather. London, 1889. First edition, first issue, with Spencer Blackett imprint on spine. One of 100 on large paper. $50. Trade edition: Cloth. $15-$25.

HAGGARD, H. Rider. *Ayesha: The Return of She.* Illustrated. Cloth. London, 1905. First edition. $25. New York, 1905. Red cloth. First American edition. $15.

HAGGARD, H. Rider. *Cetywayo and His White Neighbours.* Green cloth. London, 1882. First edition. $100-$150. Author's first book.

HAGGARD, H. Rider. *Cleopatra.* Illustrated. Half leather. London, 1889. First edition. One of 57 on large paper. $50-$75. Trade edition: Cloth. $25-$30.

HAGGARD, H. Rider. *Colonel Quaritch, V. C.: A Tale of Country Life.* 3 vols., red cloth. London, 1888. First edition. $100-$200. Soiled and shaken, presentation copy signed by the author, $288.

HAGGARD, H. Rider. *Dawn.* 3 vols., olive-green cloth. London, 1884. First edition. $400-$500. Presentation copies, signed by the author, $1,190 and $500 at retail. Also, another presentation copy, $168 (A, 1967). Author's first novel.

HAGGARD, H. Rider. *Heart of the World.* Dark-blue or black cloth. London, 1896. First edition. $25-$35.

HAGGARD, H. Rider. *King Solomon's Mines.* Folding colored frontispiece, map. Bright-red cloth. London, 1885. First edition, first issue, with the word "Bamamgwato" in line 14, page 10, and "wrod" for "word" in note on page 307. $100-$150.

HAGGARD, H. Rider. *Maiwa's Revenge.* Black cloth. London, 1888. First edition. $35-$40.

HAGGARD, H. Rider. *Mr. Meeson's Will.* Cloth. London, 1888. First edition. $25-$35.

HAGGARD, H. Rider. *Montezuma's Daughter.* Dark-blue cloth. London, 1893. First edition. $35.

HAGGARD, H. Rider. *She: A History of Adventure.* Printed wrappers. New York, 1886. First edition. $100-$150. London, 1887. Illustrated. Blue cloth. First English edition, first issue, with "Godness me" in line 38, page 269, etc. $100-$125.

HAGGARD, H. Rider. *Stella Fregelius: A Tale of Three Destinies.* Dark-blue cloth. London, 1904. First edition. $50. Worn and stained, presentation copy signed (to his brother). $204.

HAGGARD, H. Rider. *The Witch's Head.* 3 vols., cloth. London, 1885. First edition. $200-$300.

HAINES, Elijah M. *The American Indian.* Half morocco. Chicago, 1888. First edition. $25-$35.

HAINES, Elijah M. *Historical and Statistical Sketches of Lake County, State of Illinois.* Folding frontispiece. 112 pp., printed wrappers. Waukegan, Ill., 1852. First edition. $250-$300.

HAIR, James T. (publisher). *Gazetteer of Madison County, Illinois.* Cloth. Alton, Ill., 1866. First edition. $40-$60.

HAKES, Harlo. *Lundmarks of Steuben County, New York.* Cloth. Syracuse, 1896. First edition. $35.

HAKEWILL, James. *A Picturesque Tour of Italy.* 63 plates, 36 hand-colored. Folio, half morocco. London, 1820. $350.

HALBERT, Henry S., and Ball, Timothy H. *The Creek War of 1813 and 1814.* Portraits, folding map (not in all copies). Cloth. Chicago, 1895. First edition. $100-$125.

HALE, Edward Everett. See *The Man Without a Country.*

HALE, Edward Everett. *Kanzas and Nebraska.* Map. Blue or red cloth. Boston, 1854. First edition. $25-$35.

HALE, Edward Everett. *A Tract for the Day: How to Conquer Texas Before Texas Conquers Us.* 16 pp., self-wrappers. Boston, 1845. First edition. $25-$50.

HALE, John. *California as It Is.* Boards. San Francisco, 1954. Grabhorn Press. One of 150. $75.

HALE, Lucretia P. *Last of the Peterkins.* 4 plates. Red cloth. Boston, 1886. First edition. $50.

HALE, Lucretia P. *The Peterkin Papers.* Illustrated by F. G. Attwood. Green cloth. Boston, 1880. First edition. $250.

HALE, Sarah Josepha. See *The Genius of Oblivion.*

HALE, Sarah Josepha. *Northwood; A Tale of New England.* 2 vols., buff boards and rose-colored muslin. Boston, 1827. First edition. $75-$100. Also, rebound in one volume, half morocco, $50 (A, 1967).

HALE, Sarah Josepha (editor). *The Countries of Europe, and the Manners and Customs of Its Various Nations.* Illustrated. Printed wrappers. New York, no date (about 1842). First edition. $25-$35.

HALE, Sarah Josepha (editor). *The Good Little Boy's Book.* Printed flexible boards. New York, no date (about 1848). First edition. $40-$50.

HALE, Sarah Josepha Buell (editor). *Happy Changes; or Pride and Its Consequences.* Printed flexible boards. New York, no date (about 1842). First edition. $25-$35.

HALE, Will. *Twenty-four Years a Cowboy and Ranchman in Southern Texas and Old Mexico.* 268 pp., stiff wrappers. Hedrick, Oklahoma Territory, no date (1905). (By William Hale Stone.) First edition. $1,000 and up? (Note: A problem book. There are copies in the Library of Congress and at the University of Oklahoma, but none has been offered for sale in modern times, so far as I can find. Wright Howes, who gave this a rating in *U.S.-iana* of $25 to $100, once told me $5,000 might be the right price if another copy turned up. Ramon F. Adams, in *Six-Guns and Saddle Leather,* calls it "historically worthless," but concedes its rarity.)

HALEY, J. Evetts. *Charles Goodnight, Cowman and Plainsman.* Illustrated by Harold Bugbee. Cloth. Boston, 1936. First edition, with dated title page. In dust jacket. $35. Norman, Okla., 1949. Reprint edition. In dust jacket. $15-$20.

HALEY, J. Evetts. *Charles Schriener, General Merchandise: The Story of a Country Store.* Illustrated by Harold Bugbee. Cloth. Austin, Tex., 1944. First edition. $35-$50.

HALEY, J. Evetts. *Fort Concho on the Texas Frontier.* Cloth. San Angelo, Tex., 1952. First edition. One of 185 signed. $50-$60.

HALEY, J. Evetts. *The Heraldry of the Range.* Illustrated by Harold Bugbee. Cloth. Canyon, Tex., 1949. First edition. $25-$35.

HALEY, J. Evetts. *Life on the Texas Range.* Photographs by Erwin E. Smith. Pictorial cloth. Austin, 1952. First edition. Boxed. $35.

HALEY, J. Evetts. *The XIT Ranch of Texas.* 2 maps, 30 plates. Cloth. Chicago, 1929. First edition. $100-$125. Author's first book.

HALIBURTON, Thomas Chandler. See *The Clockmaker.*

HALL, Basil. *The Great Polyglot Bibles.* Folio, loose in wrappers. San Francisco, 1966. One of 400. Boxed. $100.

HALL, Capt. Basil. *Forty Etchings, from Sketches made with the Camera Lucida, in North America, in 1827 and 1828.* Folding map, 20 plates. Printed boards. Edinburgh, 1829. First edition. $200-$300. Edinburgh, 1830. Boards. Fourth edition. $100-$150.

HALL, Capt. Basil. *Travels in North America.* Colored folding map, folding table. 3 vols., half calf. Edinburgh, 1829. First edition. $100-$150. Philadelphia, 1829. Illustrated. 2 vols., boards. First American edition. $50-$100.

HALL, Bert L. *Roundup Years.* Illustrated. Pictorial cloth. No place, no date (Pierre, S.D., 1954). First edition. $50-$60.

HALL, Carroll D. *Heraldry of New Helvetia.* Half calf and boards. San Francisco, 1945. Book Club of California. One of 250. $35-$50.

HALL, Edward H. *The Great West.* Map. 89 pp., printed wrappers. New York, 1864. First edition. $150-$200. New York, 1865. Map. 198 pp., pictorial wrappers. $150-$200.

HALL, Francis. *Travels in Canada and the United States in 1816 and 1817.* Folding map. Boards and calf. London, 1818. First edition. $100-$125. Boston, 1818. Boards. First American edition. $50-$60. London, 1819. Second edition. $75-$100.

HALL, Frederic. *The History of San Jose and Surroundings.* Plates, map. Cloth. San Francisco, 1871. First edition. $50-$60.

HALL, Frederick. *Letters From the East and From the West.* Cloth. Washington, no date (1840). First edition. $50-$60. Baltimore, 1840. Cloth. $50.

HALL, George Eli. *A Balloon Ascension at Midnight.* Illustrated by Gordon Ross. Boards. San Francisco, 1902. One of 30 on vellum, signed. $25-$35.

HALL, Henry (editor). *The Tribune Book of Open-Air Sports.* Illustrated. Pictorial cloth. New York, 1887. First edition. $75-$150. (Note: The first book composed on the linotype machine.)

HALL, J. *Sonora: Travels and Adventures in Sonora.* Cloth. Chicago, 1881. First edition. $1,000 and up. Also, worn and shaken, $700 (A, 1966).

HALL, James. *The Harpe's Head; A Legend of Kentucky.* Wrappers. Philadelphia, 1833. First edition. $100-$150. Also, in cloth, $75 (A, 1967).

HALL, James. *Legends of the West.* Boards and muslin. Philadelphia, 1832. First edition. $50-$75. Philadelphia, 1833. Cloth. Second edition. $25-$35. Cincinnati, 1869. Cloth. $25.

HALL, James. *Letters from the West.* Boards. London, 1828. First edition. $50-$100.

HALL, James. *Notes on the Western States.* Cloth. Philadelphia, 1838. Later edition of *Statistics of the West.* $35.

HALL, James. *The Romance of Western History.* Frontispiece. Cloth. Cincinnati, 1857. First edition. $25-$35.

HALL, James. *Sketches of History, Life, and Manners in the West.* Vol. 1. (All published.) Brown cloth. Cincinnati, 1834. First edition. $35. Philadelphia, 1835. 2 vols., cloth. First complete edition. $50-$60.

HALL, James. *Statistics of the West.* Cloth. Cincinnati, 1836. First edition, first printing, purple cloth. $75-$100. Second printing, slate-colored cloth. $50-$75. Rebound in buckram, stained, $25. Cincinnati, 1837. Cloth. $35.

HALL, James (editor). *The Western Souvenir: A Christmas and New Year's Gift for 1839.* Illustrated. Silk. Cincinnati, no date (1828). First edition. $150-$300.

HALL, James Norman. *Kitchener's Mob.* Portrait. Cloth. Boston, 1916. First edition. In dust jacket. $25-$35. Author's first book.

HALL, James Norman, and Nordhoff, Charles B. *The Lafayette Flying Corps.* Illustrated, including colored plates. 2 vols., blue cloth. Boston, 1920. First edition. $250-$350.

HALL, Manly P. *An Encyclopedic Outline of Masonic, Cabbalistic and Rosicrucian Symbolical Philosophy.* Colored plates, text illustrations. Folio, boards and vellum. San Francisco, 1928. John Henry Nash printing. One of 800. $100-$200.

HALL, Marshall. *New Memoir on the Nervous System.* 5 plates. Boards. London, 1843. First edition. $200-$300.

HALL, Marshall. *Principles of the Theory and Practice of Medicine.* Sheep. Boston, 1839. First American edition. $25-$35. (Note: Contains new material by Oliver Wendell Holmes.)

HALL, Radclyffe. *The Master of the House.* Buckram, vellum spine. London, no date (1932). First edition. One of 172 signed. $60-$80. Trade edition: Cloth. In dust jacket. $15.

HALL, Radclyffe. *The Well of Loneliness.* Black cloth. London, 1928. First edition, first issue, with "whip" for "whips" on page 50. In dust jacket. $50-$60. Paris, 1928. Edited by Havelock Ellis. Three-quarters morocco. $35-$50. New York, 1928. Edited by Ellis. Half cloth. First authorized American edition. Boxed. $35-$50. New York, 1929. 2 vols., half cloth. Boxed. $35-$50.

HALL, Samuel R. *Lectures on School-Keeping.* Boards and cloth. Boston, 1829. First edition. $35.

HALLECK, Fitz-Greene. See Croaker. Also see *Alnwick Castle; Fanny.*

HALLEY, William. *Centennial Year Book of Description of the Contra Costa Under Spanish, Mexican, and American Rule.* Illustrated. Cloth. Oakland, Calif., 1876. $35-$50.

HALLIWELL, J. O. (editor). *Morte Arthure: The Alliterative Romance of the Death of King Arthur.* Half leather. London, 1847. One of 75. $35-$50.

HALLUM, John. *Biographical and Pictorial History of Arkansas.* Vol. 1. (All published.) Illustrated. Calf. Albany, 1887. First edition. $35-$50.

HALSEY, R. T. H. *Pictures of Early New York on Dark Blue Staffordshire Pottery.* 155 illustrations, mostly in color. Cloth. New York, 1899. First edition. One of 286 on handmade paper. $75-$100. Another issue: One of 30 on vellum. $100-$150.

HALSTEAD, Murat. *The Caucuses of 1860.* Cloth. Columbus, Ohio, 1860. First edition. $35-$50.

HAMERTON, Philip G. *Etching and Etchers.* Illustrated. Half morocco. London, 1868. First edition. $125-$200. London, 1880. Third edition. (With a Whistler etching.) $50-$100.

HAMILTON, Alexander. *Hamilton's Itinerarium.* Half leather. St. Louis, 1907. One of 487. Boxed. $35-$50.

HAMILTON, Alexander. *The Speeches at Full Length of Mr. Van Ness, Mr. Caines, the Attorney-General, Mr. Harrison and General Hamilton, etc.* 78 pp., wrappers. New York, 1804. $45-$50.

HAMILTON, Gail. *Gala-Days.* Cloth. Boston, 1863. (By Mary Abigail Dodge.) First edition. $45.

HAMILTON, H. W. *Rural Sketches of Minnesota.* 40 pp., printed wrappers. Milan, Ohio, 1850. First edition. $500 and up.

HAMILTON, John P. *Travels Through the Interior Provinces of Colombia.* Map, 7 plates. 2 vols., calf. London, 1827. First edition. $75-$100.

HAMILTON, W. T. *My Sixty Years on the Plains.* Edited by E. T. Sieber. 8 plates (6 by Charles M. Russell). Cloth. New York, 1905. First edition. $75-$100.

HAMILTON, The Rev. William, and Irvin, the Rev. S. M. *An Ioway Grammar.* Wrappers. No place (Wolf Creek, Neb.), 1848. Ioway and Sac Mission Press. First edition. $500-$750. Also, $450 (A, 1966), $625 (A, 1957).

HAMMETT, Dashiell. *The Dain Curse.* Cloth. New York, 1929. First edition. In dust jacket. $50-$75.

HAMMETT, Dashiell. *The Glass Key.* Light-green cloth. New York, 1931. First edition. In dust jacket. $50-$75.

HAMMETT, Dashiell. *The Maltese Falcon.* Gray cloth. New York, 1930. First edition. In dust jacket. $50-$75.

HAMMETT, Dashiell. *The Thin Man.* Green cloth. New York, 1934. First edition, first issue, with the misprint "seep" for "sleep." In dust jacket. $85-$125.

HAMMOND, George. *Campaigns in the West.* Cloth. Tucson, 1949. First edition. One of 300. $60-$75.

HAMMOND, J. H. *Two Letters on Slavery in the United States, Addressed to Thomas Clarkson.* 51 pp., sewed. Columbia, S.C., 1845. $25-$35.

HAMMOND, John Martin. *Colonial Mansions of Maryland and Delaware.* 65 plates. Cloth. Philadelphia, 1914. First edition. Limited. $35-$50.

HANCOCK, R. R. *Hancock's Diary: or, a History of the 2d Tennessee Confederate Cavalry.* 2 plates. Cloth. Nashville, 1887. First edition. $75-$100.

HANDBOOK for Scout Masters: Boy Scouts of America. Cloth. New York, no date (1914). First edition. In original khaki Scout case. $50. (Note: The first *Handbook for Scout Masters.*)

HAND Book of Monterey and Vicinity (The). 152 pp., printed wrappers. Monterey, Calif., 1875. $75-$100.

HAND-Book of Ness County, the Banner County of Western Kansas. 36 pp., wrappers. Chicago, 1887. $75-$100.

HANDLEY Cross: or, Mr. Jorrocks's Hunt. 17 color plates and numerous woodcuts by John Leech. 17 parts in pictorial wrappers. London, 1853-54. (By Robert Smith Surtees.) First illustrated edition. With all the ads and slips and with the words "with the aid of the illustrious Leech" in the preface. $300-$600. London, 1854. Cloth. First illustrated book edition. $50-$100. Rebound copies, $25 and up.

HANDLEY Cross; or, The Spa Hunt. 3 vols., boards and cloth. London, 1843. (By Robert Smith Surtees.) First edition. $50-$75.

HANNOVER, Emil. *Pottery and Porcelain: A Handbook for Collectors.* Illustrated. 3 vols., cloth. London, 1925. First edition. $150-$200.

HANSON, George A. *Old Kent: The Eastern Shore of Maryland.* Cloth. Baltimore, 1876. First edition. $50-$75.

HARBINGER (The): A May-Gift. Cloth, paper spine label. Boston, 1833. First edition. $25-$35. (Note: Contains 17 poems by Oliver Wendell Holmes.)

HARDEE, William J. *Rifle and Light Infantry Tactics.* 2 vols., or 2 vols. in one, half leather. Memphis, 1861. $50-$75. (Other editions in the same year in Richmond and Philadelphia.)

HARDIN, John Wesley. *The Life of John Wesley Hardin.* Portrait, other illustrations. 144 pp., printed wrappers. Seguin, Tex., 1896. First edition, first issue, with portrait of Hardin's brother mislabeled "John." $75-$100. Second issue, with the Hardin portrait tipped in. $35-$50.

HARDIN, Mrs. Philomelia Ann Maria Antoinette. *Everybody's Cook and Receipt Book.* Printed boards. Cleveland, 1842. First edition. $50-$75.

HARDING, George L. *Don Augustin V. Zamorano: Statesman, Soldier, Craftsman, and California's First Printer.* Illustrated. Cloth. Los Angeles, 1934. First edition. $75-$125.

HARDY, Joseph. *A Picturesque and Descriptive Tour in the Mountains of the High Pyrenees.* Map, 24 hand-colored plates. Cloth. London, 1825. First edition. $150-$200.

HARDY, Thomas. See Henniker, Florence. Also see *Desperate Remedies; Under the Greenwood Tree.*

HARDY, Thomas. *"And There Was a Great Calm."* Wrappers. London, 1920. Chiswick Press. First edition. One of 25 initialed by Florence Emily Hardy. $25-$35.

HARDY, Thomas. *Before Marching and After.* Wrappers. No place, no date (London, 1915). First edition. One of 25. $25.

HARDY, Thomas. *A Changed Man.* Green cloth. London, 1913. First edition. $25. New York, 1913. Blue cloth. First American edition. $15.

HARDY, Thomas. *Compassion: An Ode.* 6 pp., printed wrappers. No place, no date (Dorchester, England, 1924). First edition. One of 25 signed by Hardy. $35-$50. Another issue (?): 10 pp., printed wrappers. "Printed for A. J. A. Symons." One of 50 signed by Symons. $61.60 (A, 1966).

HARDY, Thomas. *The Convergence of the Twain.* Blue boards, paper label on front cover. London, 1912. First edition. One of 10 signed by the printers. $75-$100.

HARDY, Thomas. *A Defence of "Jude the Obscure."* Wrappers. Edinburgh, 1928. First edition. One of 30. $100.

HARDY, Thomas. *Domicilium.* Wrappers. No place, no date (London, 1916). First edition. One of 25. $50.

HARDY, Thomas. *The Duke's Reappearance.* Boards. New York, 1927. One of 89. $50-$75.

HARDY, Thomas. *The Dynasts: A Drama of the Napoleonic Wars.* 3 vols., green cloth. London, 1903-06-08. First edition, first issue (of Vol. 1, with date 1903 on title page). $350 and up. Presentation set (so blind-stamped on title pages). $450. Also, $175 (A, 1968). London, 1904-06-08. Second issue (of Vol. 1). $50-$100. London, 1910. Portrait. Cloth. First one-volume edition. In dust jacket. $25. London, 1927. Portrait etching, signed by Francis Dodd. 3 vols., half vellum. One of 525 signed by Hardy. In dust jackets. $135-$150.

HARDY, Thomas. *The Dynasts: Prologue and Epilogue.* Wrappers. No place, no date (London, 1914). First edition. One of 12. $25.

HARDY, Thomas. *The Famous Tragedy of the Queen of Cornwall at Tintagel in Lyonnesse.* Frontispiece. Green cloth. London, 1923. First edition. In dust jacket. $150-$200.

HARDY, Thomas. *Far from the Madding Crowd.* 12 illustrations by H. Patterson. 2 vols., pictorial green cloth. London, 1874. First English edition, first issue, with "Sacrament" in first line of page 2, Vol. 1. $150 and up. (At the peak of the collecting interest in Hardy, a copy of the first edition was sold for $1,000 at auction—Anderson Galleries, March, 1930.) New York, 1958. Limited Editions Club. Illustrated. Half leather. Boxed. $30.

HARDY, Thomas. *Fellow-Townsmen.* Wrappers. New York, no date (1880). First edition. George Munro, publisher. $100.

HARDY, Thomas. *A Group of Noble Dames.* Light-brown cloth. No place, no date (London, 1891). First edition, first issue, with yellow end papers. $35-$50. New York, 1891. Brown cloth. First American edition. $25.

HARDY, Thomas. *The Hand of Ethelberta.* 11 illustrations by George Du Maurier. 2 vols., terra-cotta cloth. London, 1876. First edition, first issue, with "two or three individuals" instead of "five or six individuals" in caption of illustration facing page 146 in Vol. 1. $75-$100.

HARDY, Thomas. *Human Shows: Far Phantasies; Songs and Trifles.* Green cloth. London, 1925. First edition. In dust jacket. $25-$35.

HARDY, Thomas. *An Indiscretion in the Life of an Heiress.* Vellum. No place (London), 1934. First edition. One of 100. $40-$50.

HARDY, Thomas. *Jezreel: The Master and the Leaves.* Wrappers. London, 1919. First edition. One of 25 initialed by Florence Emily Hardy. $25-$35.

HARDY, Thomas. *Jude the Obscure.* Map, etching by H. Macbeth-Raeburn. Green cloth. No place, no date (London, 1896). First edition. $75-$100.

HARDY, Thomas. *A Laodicean; or, The Castle of the De Stancys.* 3 vols., slate-colored cloth. London, 1881. First English edition, first issue, without the word "or" on half title of Vol. 1. $150-$200. Second issue, with the word "or" on half title of Vol. 1. $75.

HARDY, Thomas. *Late Lyrics and Earlier.* Green cloth. London, 1922. First edition. In dust jacket. $25-$35.

HARDY, Thomas. *Life's Little Ironies.* Green cloth. London, no date (1894). First edition. $50-$60. New York, 1894. Green cloth. First American edition. $25.

HARDY, Thomas. *The Mayor of Casterbridge.* 2 vols., blue cloth. London, 1886. First edition. $150-$200. New York, 1964. Limited Editions Club. Illustrated. Half morocco. Boxed. $40-$50.

HARDY, Thomas. *Moments of Vision and Miscellaneous Verses.* Green cloth. London, 1917. First edition. $25-$35.

HARDY, Thomas. *No Bell-Ringing.* Wrappers. Dorchester, England, 1925. First edition. One of 25. $35-$50.

HARDY, Thomas. *Notes on "The Dynasts."* Printed wrappers. Edinburgh, 1929. First edition. One of 20. $25.

HARDY, Thomas. *Old Mrs. Chundle.* Boards and cloth. New York, 1929. First edition. One of 742. $25.

HARDY, Thomas. *A Pair of Blue Eyes.* 3 vols., green or maroon cloth, yellow end papers. London, 1873. First edition, first issue, with "c" dropped or missing from the word "clouds" in last line on page 5 of Vol. 2. $200-$250.

HARDY, Thomas. *Poems of the Past and the Present.* White (cream) or dark-green cloth. No place, no date (London, 1902). First edition. $25-$35. Second edition, same date. $22.40.

HARDY, Thomas. *The Return of the Native.* Frontispiece map. 3 vols., brown cloth. London, 1878. First edition. $150-$200. New York, 1878. Cream-colored cloth. First American edition. $35. London, 1929. Illustrated by Clare Leighton. Batik boards, vellum spine. One of 1,500 signed by the artist. Boxed. $25-$35.

HARDY, Thomas. *Satires of Circumstances.* Green cloth. London, 1914. First edition. $25-$35.

HARDY, Thomas. *Selected Poems.* Photogravure portrait on title page. Blue cloth. London, 1916. First edition. $25. London, 1921. Riccardi Press. Woodcut engravings, including title page, by William Nicholson. Vellum. One of 100. In dust jacket. $75. Another issue: Limp vellum with ties. One of 14 on vellum, signed by author and artist. $400-$500. Another issue (?): Morocco. $336 (A, 1969).

HARDY, Thomas. *Some Romano-British Relics Found at Max Gate.* Printed wrappers. Dorchester, 1890. First edition. $50.

HARDY, Thomas. *Song of the Soldiers.* 4 pp., wrappers. Hove, England, 1914. First edition. $25.

HARDY, Thomas. *Souvenir Programme: Wessex Scenes from "The Dynasts."* Illustrated. Limp boards. No place, no date (Dorchester, 1916). One of 12 signed. $75-$100.

HARDY, Thomas. *Tess of the D'Urbervilles.* 3 vols., brownish-orange cloth. No place, no date (London, 1891). First edition, first issue, with "Chapter XXV" for "Chapter XXXV" and with "road" for "load" on page 198, Vol. 3. $400-$500. Second issue, with corrections (London, 1892). $150-$200. London, 1926. 41 wood engravings by Vivien Gribble, folding map. Marbled boards, vellum spine. One of 325 signed. In dust jacket. $150-$250.

HARDY, Thomas. *The Three Wayfarers.* Half cloth. New York, 1930. One of 542. $25.

HARDY, Thomas. *Time's Laughingstocks and Other Verses.* Green cloth. London, 1909. First edition. $25-$35.

HARDY, Thomas. *The Trumpet-Major.* 3 vols., decorated red cloth. London, 1880. First edition. $300-$400. Second issue, green cloth. $75-$150. New York, 1880. Pictorial cloth. First American edition. $50 (A, 1969).

HARDY, Thomas. *Two on a Tower: A Romance.* 3 vols., green cloth. London, 1882. First edition. $75-$100. New York, 1882. Decorated yellow cloth. First American edition. $35.

HARDY, Thomas. *The Two Hardys.* Unbound. No place (London?), 1927. One of 50. $50.

HARDY, Thomas. *The Well-Beloved.* Etching, map. Ribbed dark-green cloth. London, no date (1897). First edition. $75-$100.

HARDY, Thomas. *Wessex Poems and Other Verses.* 30 illustrations by the author. Dark green, blue, or white cloth. No place, no date (London, 1898). First edition. $75-$100. London, 1908. Illustrated. Cloth. $25.

HARDY, Thomas. *Wessex Tales, Strange, Lively and Commonplace.* 2 vols., green cloth. London, 1888. First edition. $100-$150.

HARDY, Thomas. *Winter Night in Woodland.* 6 pp., wrappers. No place, no date (London, 1925). First edition. One of 25 signed. $50-$75.

HARDY, Thomas. *Winter Words in Various Moods and Metres.* Olive-green cloth. London, 1928. First edition. In dust jacket. $40-$50. Also, $20 (A, 1963). New York, 1928. Green cloth. First American edition. In dust jacket. $25.

HARDY, Thomas. *The Woodlanders.* 3 vols., smooth dark-green cloth. London, 1887. First edition, first binding, first issue, with ad leaf at end of Vol. 1. $150-$200. Second binding, pebbled dark-green cloth. $75-$100.

HARDY, Thomas; Lorne, the Marquis of; and Alexander, Mrs. *Three Notable Stories.* Gray cloth. London, 1890. First edition. $25-$35.

HARE, George H. *Guide to San Jose and Vicinity.* 2 maps. 85 pp., wrappers. San Jose, Calif., 1872. First edition. $100.

HARFORD, Henry. *Fan: The Story of a Young Girl's Life.* 3 vols., sage-green cloth. London, 1892. (By W. H. Hudson.) First edition. $1,000 and up. (Note: No recent price noted; catalogued by a New York dealer in the 1940's at $550.)

HARGRAVE, Catherine Perry. *A History of Playing Cards.* Cloth. Boston, 1930. First edition. In dust jacket. $125-$150.

HARLAN, Jacob Wright. *California, '46 to '88.* Portrait frontispiece. Cloth. San Francisco, 1888. First edition. $50-$75.

HARLOW, Alvin F. *Old Towpaths.* Illustrated. Cloth. New York, 1926. First edition. $35-$50.

HARLOW, Alvin F. *Old Waybills.* Illustrated. Cloth. New York, 1934. First edition. In dust jacket. $35-$50.

HARLOW, Neal. *The Maps of San Francisco Bay.* Folio, half leather. San Francisco, 1950. Grabhorn Press. One of 375. $150-$250.

HARMAN, S. W. *Hell on the Border.* Portrait, map. Stiff printed green wrappers. Fort Smith, Ark., no date (1898). First edition. $200-$300.

HARMON, Daniel Williams. *A Journal of Voyages and Travels in the Interior of North America.* Portrait, folding map. Calf. Andover, Mass., 1820. First edition, first issue, with map placed opposite title page and with no errata slip. $250-$350.

HARPER, Henry H. *A Journey in Southeastern Mexico.* Boards. Boston, 1910. First edition. $35-$50.

HAROLD The Dauntless. Boards. Edinburgh, 1817. (By Sir Walter Scott.) First edition. $35-$50.

HARRINGTON, Kate. *In Memoriam: Maymie, April 6th, 1869.* 60 pp., cloth. Keokuk, Iowa, 1870. First edition. $75. Worn, $50.

HARRINGTON, Kate. *Old Settlers' Poem.* 17 pp., printed wrappers. Keokuk, 1874. $35-$50.

HARRIS, Albert W. *The Blood of the Arab.* Cloth. Chicago, 1941. First edition. $35-$50.

HARRIS, Chapin A. *The Dental Art.* Cloth. Baltimore, 1839. First edition. $100-$150.

HARRIS, Chapin A. *A Dictionary of Dental Science.* Calf. Philadelphia, 1849. First edition. $50.

HARRIS, Dean. *By Path and Trail.* Illustrated. Cloth. Chicago, 1908. $25.

HARRIS, Frank. *Elder Conklin and Other Stories.* Cloth. New York, 1894. First edition. $35-$50. Author's first book. London, 1895. Green cloth. First English edition. $25-$35.

HARRIS, Frank. *Joan La Romee: A Drama.* Cloth. London, no date (1926 or 1927). Fortune Press. First edition. One of 350 signed. In dust jacket. $25.

HARRIS, Frank. *La Vie d'Oscar Wilde.* 2 vols., printed wrappers. Paris, 1928. One of 110. $25.

HARRIS, Frank. *A Mad Love.* 70 pp., printed wrappers. New York, 1920. $25.

HARRIS, Frank. *The Man Shakespeare and His Tragic Life Story.* Boards and vellum. London, 1909. First edition. One of 150 on large paper, signed. $35-$50. Trade edition: Green cloth. $20-$25.

HARRIS, Frank. *Oscar Wilde: His Life and Confessions.* 2 vols., half morocco. New York, 1916. First edition. Japan paper issue. In dust jacket. $50-$75.

HARRIS, Frank. *Stories of Jesus the Christ.* Wrappers. New York, 1919. Pearson's 25¢ Library. First edition. $25. (Note: Includes a Shaw contribution.)

HARRIS, George Washington. See Spavery.

HARRIS, Henry. *California's Medical Story.* Half morocco. San Francisco, 1932. Grabhorn Press. One of 200. $35-$50.

HARRIS, Joel Chandler. See Davidson, James Wood.

HARRIS, Joel Chandler. *Daddy Jake the Runaway.* Illustrated. Pictorial cream-colored glazed boards. New York, no date (1889). First edition. $75-$100.

HARRIS, Joel Chandler. *Free Joe and Other Georgian Sketches.* Pictorial red cloth. New York, 1887. First edition. $40-$50

HARRIS, Joel Chandler. *Nights with Uncle Remus.* Illustrated. Pictorial gray cloth. Boston, 1883. First edition. $50-$60.

HARRIS, Joel Chandler. *Plantation Pageants.* Illustrated. Cloth. Boston, 1899. First edition. $40-$50.

HARRIS, Joel Chandler. *Tales of the Home Folks in Peace and War.* Illustrated. Cloth. Boston, 1898. First edition. In dust jacket. $35-$40.

HARRIS, Joel Chandler. *The Tar-Baby and Other Rhymes of Uncle Remus.* Cloth. New York, 1904. First edition. In dust jacket. $50-$75.

HARRIS, Joel Chandler. *Uncle Remus and His Legends of the Old Plantation.* Olive-green cloth. London, 1881. First English edition of *Uncle Remus: His Songs and His Sayings.* $150-$200.

HARRIS, Joel Chandler. *Uncle Remus: His Songs and His Sayings.* Illustrated by Frederick S. Church and James S. Moser. Pictorial blue cloth. New York, 1881. First edition, first issue, with "presumptive" for "presumptuous" in last line, page 9, and with no mention of this book in ads at back. $200-$300. Author's first book. Second issue, with "presumptuous" in last line, page 9. $50-$60. (For first English edition, see preceding entry.) New York, 1895. Illustrated by A. B. Frost. Vellum. One of 250 signed.

$50-$75. Trade edition: Red buckram. $15-$25. Mount Vernon, N.Y., no date (1937). Morocco. One of 50. $35-$50. New York, 1957. Limited Editions Club. Illustrated. Pictorial cloth. Boxed. $50-$60. Also, $55 (A, 1968).

HARRIS, Mark. *Trumpet to the World.* Yellow cloth. New York, no date (1946). First edition. In dust jacket. $35. Author's first book.

HARRIS, Sarah Hollister. *An Unwritten Chapter of Salt Lake, 1851-1901.* Cloth. New York, 1901. First edition. $200.

HARRIS, Thaddeus Mason. *The Journal of a Tour into the Territory Northwest of the Alleghany Mountains.* 4 maps (3 folding) and a folding plate. Marbled boards, paper spine and paper label. Boston, 1805. First edition. $150-$200.

HARRIS, Thomas M. *Assassination of Lincoln.* Illustrated. Pictorial cloth. Boston, no date (1892). First edition. $35-$50.

HARRIS, W. B. *Pioneer Life in California.* 98 pp., pictorial wrappers. Stockton, Calif., 1884. First edition. $250.

HARRIS, William Charles. *The Fishes of North America That Are Captured on Hook and Line.* Vol. 1. (All published.) Folio, half leather. New York, 1898. First edition. $75-$100.

HARRIS, William R. *The Catholic Church in Utah.* Map, 25 plates. Cloth. Salt Lake City, no date (1909). First edition. $50. (Also issued in 2 vols.)

HARRISON, E. J. *The Thrilling, Startling and Wonderful Narrative of Lieutenant Harrison.* Illustration in text. 30 pp., printed buff wrappers. Cincinnati, 1848. First edition. $1,000 and up. (Note: Three copies known.)

HARRISON, Fairfax. *Virginia Land Grants.* Cloth. Richmond, Va., 1925. First edition. $35-$50.

HARRISON, William Henry. *A Discourse on the Aborigines of the Valley of the Ohio.* Folding map. 51 pp., wrappers. Cincinnati, 1838. First edition. $75-$100.

HARRISON, William Welsh. *Harrison, Waples and Allied Families: Being the Ancestry of George Leib Harrison of Philadelphia and of His Wife Sarah Ann Waples.* Full morocco. Philadelphia, 1910. One of 100. $35-$50.

HART, Charles Henry, and Biddle, Edward. *Memoirs of the Life and Works of Jean Antoine Houdon.* 33 full-page plates. Cloth. Philadelphia, 1911. One of 250. $35-$50.

HART, George. *The Violin: Its Famous Makers and Their Imitators.* Illustrated. Cloth. London, 1875. First edition. $50-$60. Boston, 1884. Cloth. $35.

HART, John A., and others. *History of Pioneer Days in Texas and Oklahoma.* 12 plates. 249 pp., cloth. No place, no date (Guthrie, Okla., 1906). First edition. $50-$75. Second edition: (Guthrie, 1909?) 271 pp., cloth. $35-$50.

HART, John A., and others. *Pioneer Days in the Southwest.* 12 plates. 320 pp., cloth. Guthrie, 1909. Enlarged edition of *History of Pioneer Days, etc.* $25. Another issue: 16 plates. $20-$25.

HART, Joseph C. *The Romance of Yachting.* Cloth. New York, 1848. First edition. $50-$75.

HARTE, Bret. See *Oration, Poem, and Speeches; Outcroppings.*

HARTE, Bret. *The Argonauts of North Liberty.* Wrappers. Toronto, no date (1888). First Canadian edition. $19 (A, 1966). (Note: Possibly issued simultaneously with American and English first editions, Blanck suggests.)

HARTE, Bret. *Condensed Novels and Other Papers.* Illustrated by Frank Bellew. Violet cloth. New York, 1867. First edition. $50-$60. Spine faded, name on title page, etc., $22.50. Author's first book.

HARTE, Bret. *"Excelsior."* (Cover title.) 16 pp., oblong, blue wrappers. Five Points, N.Y., no date (1877). First edition, first issue, with Donaldson imprint. $75-$100. Later issue, without Donaldson imprint: $35-$50. (Also issued in cloth.)

HARTE, Bret. *Gabriel Conroy.* Illustrated. Mauve cloth. Hartford, 1876. First American edition, first binding, with small bear on spine. $75-$100.

HARTE, Bret. *The Lost Galleon and Other Tales.* Cloth. San Francisco, 1867. First edition. $100-$125. With a bookplate, $75. Author's first book of verse.

HARTE, Bret. *The Luck of Roaring Camp and Other Sketches.* Green or terra-cotta cloth. Boston, 1870. First edition, first issue, without the story "Brown of Calaveras." $300-$400. Worn, with bookplate, $125. Second issue: Brown cloth. $25. San Francisco, 1916. John Henry Nash printing. Half cloth. One of 260. $35-$50. San Francisco, 1948. Grabhorn Press. Folio, half cloth. One of 300. $35-$50.

HARTE, Bret. *Mliss: An Idyl of Red Mountain.* Printed wrappers. New York, no date (1873). (Pirated edition of the story, which originally appeared in *The Luck of Roaring Camp.* Contains 50 additional chapters by R. G. Densmore.) First edition, first issue, with Harte's name on title page and front cover. $1,000 and up. Part of spine missing, $500. Also, A-record: $900 (1945). Second issue, with Harte's name removed and with page 34 a cancel leaf. $400-$500. San Francisco, 1948. Grabhorn Press. Half cloth. One of 300. $50-$75.

HARTE, Bret. *The Pliocene Skull.* Illustrated by E. M. Schaeffer. 9 leaves, flexible purple boards and cloth. No place, no date (Washington, 1871?). First edition, presumed first issue. $100-$150. Presumed second issue: 10 leaves, flexible boards, with drawing of miner on front cover. $75-$100. Ink on cover, $75. (Note: Blanck questions this long-accepted sequence but doesn't say why. The first issue has an auction record of $170, set in 1944.)

HARTE, Bret. *Poems.* Green cloth. Boston, 1871. First edition, first issue, with Fields, Osgood monogram on title page and "S. T. K." for "T. S. K." on page 136. $35-$50.

HARTE, Bret. *The Queen of the Pirate Isle.* 28 color illustrations by Kate Greenaway. Decorated cloth. London, no date (1886). First edition, first issue, bound in unbleached linen, with green end papers, gilt edges. $75-$100. Boston, 1887. Illustrated. Cloth. First American edition. $50.

HARTE, Bret. *The Story of Enriquez.* Boards. San Francisco, 1924. Grabhorn Press. First edition. One of 100. $50-$75.

HARTE, Bret. *Tales of the Argonauts, and Other Sketches.* Cloth. Boston, 1875. First edition. $25-$30.

HARTE, Bret. *Tales of the Gold Rush.* Illustrated. Cloth. New York, 1944. Limited Editions Club. First edition. Boxed. $25-$35.

HARTE, Bret. *Tennessee's Partner.* Boards and vellum. San Francisco, 1907. First edition. $25-$35.

HARTE, Bret. *The Wild West.* Hand-colored illustrations. Buckram. No place, no date (London?, 1930). Harrison of Paris. First edition. One of 36 on vellum. $75-$100.

HARTE, Bret, and the Rev. Henry W. *Fourteenth Anniversary of the Society of California Pioneers: Oration: By Rev. Henry W. Bellows. Poem: By Frank Bret Harte, Esq.* Printed wrappers. San Francisco, 1864. First edition. $75-$100.

HARTE, Bret, and Twain, Mark. *Sketches of the Sixties.* Boards and cloth. San Francisco, 1926. First edition. One of 250. In dust jacket. $50-$60.

HARTLEY, Oliver C. *Digest of the Laws of Texas.* Buckram. Philadelphia, 1850. $50-$60.

HARTSHORNE, Albert. *Old English Glasses.* Color frontispiece, plates, numerous drawings. Folio, vellum and cloth. London, 1897. $75-$80.

HARTZENBUSCH, Juan Eugenio. *The Lovers of Teruel.* Translated by Henry Thomas. Morocco. Newtown, Wales, 1938. Gregynog Press. One of 175. $150. Another issue: One of 20 specially bound in morocco by George Fisher. $350-$400.

HARVARD Class Day 1910. (Cover title.) Illustrated. 17 leaves, stiff cream wrappers, red cord ties. No place, no date (Cambridge, Mass., 1910). $150-$200. (Note: Includes a class ode by T. S. Eliot.)

HARVEY BELDEN: or a True Narrative of Strange Adventures. Cloth. Cincinnati, 1848. (By Nathaniel A. Ware.) First edition. $50.

HARVEY, George. *Scenes of the Primitive Forest of America.* 4 hand-colored plates. Folio, boards. New York, 1841. With London imprint on binding. $750-$1,000.

HARVEY, Henry. *History of the Shawnee Indians.* Illustrated. Cloth. Cincinnati, 1855. First edition, first issue, without portrait. $35-$50.

HARVEY, William. *The Anatomical Exercises.* Edited by Geoffrey Keynes. Drawing by Stephen Gooden. Full morocco. London, no date (1928). Nonesuch Press. One of 450. $150-$175.

HASHEESH Eater (The). Cloth. New York, 1857. (By Fitz-Hugh Ludlow.) First edition. $25-$30. Author's first book.

HASKELL, Burnette G. *Kaweah, a Co-operative Commonwealth.* 16 pp., wrappers. San Francisco, 1887. $75.

HASKINS, C. W. *The Argonauts of California.* Cloth. New York, 1890. First edition. $50-$75.

HASTAIN, E. *Township Plats of the Creek Nation.* Full limp morocco. Muskogee, Okla., 1910. $45.

HASTINGS, Lansford W. *The Emigrants' Guide to Oregon and California.* 152 pp., wrappers, or printed boards. Cincinnati, 1845. First edition. $6,000-$7,000. Rebound in calf and boards, $6,500. Also, in boards, covers "cracked," $4,000 (A, 1968); rebound in leather, $4,700 (A, 1959); rebound in facsimile wrappers, $4,000 (A, 1963).

HASTINGS, Sally. *Poems, on Different Subjects. To Which Is Added a Descriptive Account of a Family Tour to the West, in the Year 1800.* Leather. Lancaster, Pa., 1808. First edition. $175-$200.

HASWELL, Anthony (editor). *Memoirs and Adventures of Capt. Matthew Phelps.* Leather. Bennington, Vt., 1802. First edition. $200-$300.

HATFIELD, Edwin F. *History of Elizabeth, New Jersey.* 8 plates. Morocco. New York, 1868. First edition. $35-$50.

HATTERAS, Owen. *Pistols for Two.* Pink wrappers. New York, 1917. (By H. L. Mencken and George Jean Nathan.) First edition. $55-$75.

HAUPT, Gen. Herman. *Reminiscences.* Cloth. Milwaukee, 1901. Limited, autographed. $35-$50.

HAVEN, Charles T., and Belden, Frank A. *History of the Colt Revolver.* Illustrated. Cloth. New York, 1940. First edition. Boxed. $50-$75. Another issue: Morocco. Signed. Boxed. $75-$125. New York, no date (about 1960). Cloth. $25-$35.

HAWBUCK Grange; or, The Sporting Adventures of Thomas Scott, Esq. 8 illustrations by Phiz. Blind-stamped pictorial red cloth. London, 1847. (By Robert Smith Surtees.) First edition, with 32-page catalogue dated April, 1847, bound in at end. $100-$150. Spine repaired, name and bookplate on end paper, $30-$35.

HAWES, Charles Boardman. *The Dark Frigate.* Illustrated by A. L. Ripley. Pictorial cloth. Boston, no date (1923). First edition. In dust jacket. $50.

HAWKER, Peter. *Instructions to Young Sportsmen.* Boards. London, 1814. First edition. $200-$300. London, 1816. Second edition. $100-$150. London, 1824. Third edition. $50-$100. Philadelphia, 1846. Cloth. First American edition. $50-$100.

HAWKER, The Rev. Robert S. *The Cornish Ballads and Other Poems.* Green cloth. London, 1869. First edition. $84-$150. Also, $67.20 (A, 1966).

HAWKER, The Rev. Robert S. *The Quest of the Sangraal: Chant the First.* Cloth. Exeter, England, 1864. First edition. Printed on vellum. $500. Also, $325 (A, 1970).

HAWKES, John. *The Cannibal.* Cloth. New York, no date (1949). First American edition. In dust jacket. $50-$60.

HAWKES, John. *Second Skin.* Cloth. New York, no date (1964). First edition. One of 100 signed copies. In slipcase. $35-$40.

HAWKINS, Alfred. *Hawkins's Picture of Quebec; with Historical Recollections.* 14 plates. Cloth. Quebec, 1834. First edition. $75.

HAWKS of Hawk-Hollow (The). 2 vols., purple cloth, paper labels. Philadelphia, 1835. (By Robert Montgomery Bird.) First edition. $100-$150.

HAWLEY, A. T. *The Climate, Resources, and Advantages of Humboldt County.* 42 pp., wrappers. Eureka, Calif., 1879. First edition. $450.

HAWLEY, A. T. *The Present Condition, Growth, Progress and Advantages of Los Angeles City and County, Southern California.* Map. 144 pp., printed wrappers. Los Angeles, 1876. First edition. $300 (A, 1968).

HAWLEY, R. D. *The Hawley Collection of Violins.* Half cloth. Chicago, 1904. Limited edition. $100-$150.

HAWLEY, W. A. *The Early Days of Santa Barbara.* 5 plates. 105 pp., printed wrappers. New York, 1910. First edition. $50-$75.

HAWLEY, Walter A. *Oriental Rugs: Antique and Modern.* Plates. Half morocco. New York, 1913. $50-$75. New York, 1922. $35-$50. New York, 1937. Cloth. $25-$35.

HAWLEY, Zerah. *A Journal of a Tour Through Connecticut, Massachusetts, New York, etc.* Boards. New Haven, 1822. First edition. $300-$400. Also, $250 (A, 1967); rebound in half morocco, $180 (A, 1966).

HAWTHORNE, Nathaniel. See *Fanshawe; Peter Parley's Universal History; The Sister Years.*

HAWTHORNE, Nathaniel. *The Blithedale Romance.* 2 vols., cloth. London, 1852. First edition. $100-$150. Boston, 1852. Tan cloth. First American edition, with 4 pages of ads at end. $75-$100.

HAWTHORNE, Nathaniel. *The Celestial Rail-Road.* 32 pp., buff wrappers. Boston, 1843. First edition, first issue, with Wilder & Co. imprint. $300-$400.

HAWTHORNE, Nathaniel. *Doctor Grimshawe's Secret.* Edited by Julian Hawthorne. Pictorial cloth. Boston, 1883. First edition. $25-$35. Large paper issue, same date but later: One of 250 signed by the editor. $75-$100.

HAWTHORNE, Nathaniel. *Famous Old People, Being the Second Epoch of Grandfather's Chair.* Cloth, paper label. Boston, 1841. First edition. $100-$150.

HAWTHORNE, Nathaniel. *Grandfather's Chair: A History.* Cloth, paper label. Boston, 1841. First edition. $75-$150.

HAWTHORNE, Nathaniel. *The House of the Seven Gables.* Brown cloth. Boston, 1851. First edition, presumed first printing, with line "TICKNOR & CO." on spine exactly 1¼ inches wide and ads dated March, 1851. $150-$200.

HAWTHORNE, Nathaniel. *Liberty Tree, with the Last Word of Grandfather's Chair.* Green cloth, paper label. Boston, 1841. First edition, first issue, with second line of page 24 ending "in a Con-". $50-$75.

HAWTHORNE, Nathaniel. *Life of Franklin Pierce.* Frontispiece. Printed wrappers, or cloth. Boston, 1852. First edition. Wrappers: $150-$200. Cloth: $100-$150.

HAWTHORNE, Nathaniel. *The Marble Faun: or, The Romance of Monte Beni.* 2 vols., brown cloth. Boston, 1860. First American edition, first issue, without "Conclusion" at end. $100-$150. Second issue, with "Conclusion." $75-$100. (For first English edition, which may have preceded the American, see Hawthorne, *Transformation.*)

HAWTHORNE, Nathaniel. *Mosses from an Old Manse.* 2 vols., wrappers, or one volume, cloth. New York, 1846. First edition, first state, with names of the printer (Craighead) and stereotyper (Smith) on versos of both title pages. Cloth: $100-$150. (No copies noted recently in wrappers.)

HAWTHORNE, Nathaniel. *Our Old Home.* Brown cloth. Boston, 1863. First edition, first state, with ad on page 399. $50. London, 1863. 2 vols., cloth. First English edition. $50. (Note: Blanck thinks this was issued simultaneously with the American first.)

HAWTHORNE, Nathaniel. *Passages from the American Note-Books.* 2 vols., green cloth. Boston, 1868. First edition, with spine reading "Ticknor & Co." (Later, "Fields, Osgood & Co.") $75.

HAWTHORNE, Nathaniel. *The Scarlet Letter.* Brown cloth. Boston, 1850. First edition, first issue, with "reduplicate" in line 20 of page 21; "characterss" in line 5 of page 41, and "catechism" in line 29 of page 132. $400-$600. Boston, 1850. Cloth. Second edition. $35-$50. New York, 1892. Cloth. Illustrated by F. O. C. Darley. $35-$50. New York, 1908. Grolier Club. Illustrated. Boards. One of 300. $35-$50. New York, no date (1915). Illustrated by Hugh Thomson. $35-$50. New York, 1928. Colored woodblocks by Valenti Angelo. Half morocco. One of 980. $50-$60. New York, 1941. Limited Editions Club. Illustrated by Henry Varnum Poor. Leather. Boxed. $35-$50.

HAWTHORNE, Nathaniel. *The Snow-Image and Other Twice-Told Tales.* Brown cloth. Boston, 1852. First edition. $50-$100. London, 1851. Cloth. First English edition. (Issued simultaneously with American first edition, Blanck suggests. Titled *The Snow-Image, and Other Tales.*) $25-$35.

HAWTHORNE, Nathaniel. *Tanglewood Tales, for Girls and Boys.* Decorated cloth. Boston, 1853. First American edition, first issue, with ads at page 2 reading "In press." $150-$200. London, 1853. Green cloth. First edition (preceding the American edition by a few days). $50-$75. London, no date (1915). Illustrated by Edmund Dulac. Half vellum. One of 500 signed by Dulac. $50.

HAWTHORNE, Nathaniel. *Transformation.* 3 vols., old rose cloth. London, 1860. First English edition of *The Marble Faun,* which see. $75-$100. (Note: Possibly preceded the American first edition, says Blanck.)

HAWTHORNE, Nathaniel. *True Stories from History and Biography.* Cloth. Boston, 1851. First edition, first issue, with verso of title page imprinted "Cambridge: Printed by Bolles and Houghton." $75-$100.

HAWTHORNE, Nathaniel. *Twice-Told Tales*. Brownish cloth. Boston, 1837. First edition. Auction record: $1,250 (1960) for a copy "in unusually fine condition . . . lettering on backstrip in brilliant gilt." Retail values for fine copies ordinarily range from $400 to $600. New York, 1966. Limited Editions Club. Colored illustrations by Valenti Angelo. Blue cloth. Boxed. $35.

HAWTHORNE, Nathaniel. *A Wonder-Book for Girls and Boys*. Frontispiece, 6 plates. Purple or green cloth. Boston, 1852. First edition, first issue, with gilt decorations covering only top third of spine and with no ads. $300-$400. London, 1852. 8 engravings. Decorated blue cloth. First English edition. $150-$200. London, 1892. Illustrated by Walter Crane. Decorated cloth. $35-$50. Cambridge, Mass., 1893. Crane illustrations. Boards. One of 250. $35-$50. London, no date (1922). Illustrated by Arthur Rackham. White buckram. One of 600 signed by the artist. Boxed. $200-$250. Also, $110 (A, 1969). "Another edition" (?) with Rackham plates: London, no date. $132 (A, 1969).

HAWTHORNE, Nathaniel (editor). *Journal of an African Cruiser*. Half leather. New York, 1845. (By Horatio Bridge.) First edition. $150.

HAY, John. See *The Bread-Winners*.

HAY, John. *Jim Bludso of the Prairie Belle, and Little Breeches*. Illustrated by S. Eytinge, Jr. 23 pp., printed orange wrappers. Boston, 1871. First edition. $40-$60. Author's first book.

HAY, John. *Letters of John Hay and Extracts from Diary*. 3 vols., cloth, paper labels. Washington, 1908. First edition. $250-$350.

HAYDEN, Ferdinand V. *Geological and Geographical Atlas of Colorado*. 20 double-page maps, mostly colored. Three-quarters morocco. No place (Washington), 1877. $35-$50. Washington, 1881. $50.

HAYDEN, Ferdinand V. *Sun Pictures of Rocky Mountain Scenery*. 30 mounted photographs. Half morocco. New York, 1870. First edition. $150-$200.

HAYDEN, Ferdinand V. *The Yellowstone National Park*. 2 maps. Illustrated in color by Thomas Moran. Three-quarters morocco. Boston, 1876. First edition. $1,000 and up.

HAYMOND, Creed. *The Central Pacific Railroad*. 181 pp., wrappers. Washington, no date (about 1888). First edition. $25-$35.

HAYMOND, Henry. *History of Harrison County, West Virginia*. Cloth. Morgantown, W. Va., no date (1910). $35-$50.

HAYWARD, John (compiler). *English Poetry: An Illustrated Catalogue of First and Early Editions Exhibited by the National Book League, 1947*. Facsimiles. Buckram. Cambridge, England, 1950. One of 550. In dust jacket. $100-$150.

HAYWOOD, John. *The Civil and Political History of the State of Tennessee*. Calf. Knoxville, 1823. First edition, with tipped-in copyright slip and inserted printed slip. $300 and up. Also, rebound in full green morocco, $275 (A, 1967).

HAYWOOD, John. *The Natural and Aboriginal History of Tennessee*. Calf. Nashville, 1823. First edition, with errata leaf. $400-$500. Also, rebound in blue morocco, $450 (A, 1967).

HAZEL, Harry. *The Flying Artillerist*. 3 full-page woodcuts. 92 pp., wrappers. New York, 1853. (By Justin Jones.) First edition. $75.

HAZEL, Harry. *Old Put; or, The Days of Seventy-Six*. 104 pp., sewed. New York, no date (1852). (By Justin Jones.) First edition. $35-$50.

HAZEL, Harry. *The Rebel and the Rover.* Wrappers. Philadelphia, no date (about 1855). (By Justin Jones.) $25-$35.

HAZEL, Harry. *The West Point Cadet.* Illustrated. 100 pp., printed wrappers. Boston, 1845. (By Justin Jones.) First edition. $50-$75.

HAZEN, Gen. W. B. *A Narrative of Military Service.* Map, illustrations. Cloth. Boston, 1885. $25-$35.

HAZEN, Gen. W. B. *Our Barren Lands.* 53 pp., printed blue wrappers. Cincinnati, 1875. First edition. $150-$250. Also, rebound in cloth, $225 (A, 1968).

HAZEN, Gen. W. B. *Some Corrections of "Life on the Plains."* (Cover title.) 18 pp., wrappers. St. Paul, 1875. First edition. $100-$150.

HAZLITT, William. *Characters of Shakespear's Plays.* Boards, paper label. London, 1817. First edition. $100. Also, rebound in calf, $47.60 (A, 1967).

HAZLITT, William. *Conversations of James Northcote, Esq., R.A.* Portrait. Boards, paper label. London, 1830. First edition. $25.

HAZLITT, William. *Lectures on the English Poets.* Boards, paper label. London, 1818. First edition, with 4 pages of ads at end dated May 1, 1818. $100-$125.

HAZLITT, William. *Political Essays, with Sketches of Public Characters.* Boards, paper label. London, 1819. First edition. $50. Rebound in cloth, $25.

HEADLEY, John W. *Confederate Operations in Canada and New York.* Portraits. Cloth. New York, 1906. First edition. $50. Cover discolored, $40.

HEADLONG Hall. Boards. London, 1816. (By Thomas Love Peacock.) First edition. $150.

HEADSMAN (The). 3 vols., tan boards, or rose-colored cloth. London, 1833. (By James Fenimore Cooper.) $200-$300. Also, in boards, worn, $100 (A, 1970). Philadelphia, 1833. 2 vols., blue boards. First American edition. $150-$200.

HEAP, Gwinn Harris. *Central Route to the Pacific.* Folding map (not in all copies), 13 tinted plates. Cloth. Philadelphia, 1854. First edition. $200-$250. Lacking map, $75-$100.

HEARN, Lafcadio. See Bisland, Elizabeth; Chahta-Ima.

HEARN, Lafcadio. *Chita: A Memory of Last Island.* Salmon-colored cloth. New York, 1889. First edition. $25-$35.

HEARN, Lafcadio. *Editorials from the Kobe Chronicle.* (Cover title.) Printed white wrappers. No place, no date (New York, 1913). First edition. One of 100. $100-$125.

HEARN, Lafcadio. *Gleanings in Buddha-Fields.* Blue cloth. Boston, 1897. First edition. $25-$35.

HEARN, Lafcadio. *Glimpses of Unfamiliar Japan.* Illustrated. 2 vols., black or olive cloth. Boston, 1894. First edition. $50-$60.

HEARN, Lafcadio. *"Gombo Zhebes": Little Dictionary of Creole Proverbs.* Pictorial cloth. New York, 1885. First edition. $50-$60.

HEARN, Lafcadio. *In Ghostly Japan.* Illustrated. Pictorial blue cloth. Boston, 1899. First edition. $25-$30.

HEARN, Lafcadio. *Insects and Greek Poetry.* Printed blue boards. New York, 1926. First edition. One of 550. In glassine dust jacket. $25.

HEARN, Lafcadio. *Japan: An Attempt at Interpretation.* Colored frontispiece. Tan cloth. New York, 1904. First edition. $25-$30.

HEARN, Lafcadio. *Japanese Fairy Tales.* 5 vols., wrappers. Tokyo, no dates (1898-1903). First editions. (*The Boy Who Drew Cats, The Goblin Spider, The Old Woman Who Lost Her Dumpling, The Fountain of Youth, Chin Chin Kobakama.*) $100 and up for complete sets. (Note: Blanck calls the bibliographical problems connected with these little woodblock books "insoluble." However, they have frequently been at auction in various forms, including large paper and crepe paper states.)

HEARN, Lafcadio. *The Japanese Letters of Lafcadio Hearn.* Green cloth. Boston, 1910. First edition. One of 200. $50.

HEARN, Lafcadio. *A Japanese Miscellany.* Illustrated. Pictorial green cloth. Boston, 1901. First edition. (Copies with or without "October, 1901" on copyright page are acceptable first editions, Blanck seems to suggest.) $35-$50.

HEARN, Lafcadio. *Kokoro.* Green cloth. Boston, 1896. First edition. $25.

HEARN, Lafcadio. *Kotto.* Illustrated. Pictorial olive cloth. New York, 1902. First edition, presumed first state, with background of title page upside down, artist's monogram in upper right corner. In dust jacket. $40-$50.

HEARN, Lafcadio. *Kwaidan.* Illustrated. Pictorial cloth. Boston, 1904. First edition. $50. New York, 1932. Limited Editions Club. Color plates. Printed silk binding. In silk wraparound case. $75-$100.

HEARN, Lafcadio. *Leaves from the Diary of an Impressionist.* Blue boards. Boston, 1911. First edition. One of 575. $25-$30.

HEARN, Lafcadio (translator). *One of Cleopatra's Nights.* By Théophile Gautier. Cloth. New York, 1892. First edition. $35-$40.

HEARN, Lafcadio. *Shadowings.* Illustrated. Pictorial blue cloth. Boston, 1900. First edition. In dust jacket. $35-$50.

HEARN, Lafcadio. *Some Chinese Ghosts.* Pictorial rose-colored cloth. Boston, 1887. First edition. $100-$125. (Also in red and other colors of cloth.)

HEARN, Lafcadio. *Stray Leaves from Strange Literature.* Blue cloth. Boston, 1884. First edition, first issue, with IR. O. &. CO. imprint on spine. $75-$100. Author's first book.

HEARN, Lafcadio. *Two Years in the French West Indies.* Illustrated. Decorated olive cloth. New York, 1890. First edition. $25-$35.

HEARN, Lafcadio. *Youma.* Frontispiece. Cloth, paper labels. New York, 1890. First edition, first binding, white calico with blue design. $25-$30.

HEART of the West (The): An American Story. By an Illinoian. Cloth. Chicago, 1871. First edition. $75.

HEART, Capt. Jonathan. *Journal.* Edited by C. W. Butterfield. 94 pp., tan printed wrappers. Albany, N.Y., 1885. First edition. One of 150. $35-$50.

HEARTMAN, Charles F. *The New-England Primer.* Facsimiles. Boards. New York, 1915. First edition. One of 265. $50-$60. New York, 1934. Cloth. One of 300. $25.

HEARTMAN, Charles F., and Canny, James R. *A Bibliography of the First Printings of Edgar Allan Poe.* Cloth. Hattiesburg, Miss., 1940. First edition. $50.

HEARTMAN, Charles F., and Rede, Kenneth. *A Bibliographical Checklist of the First Editions of Edgar Allan Poe.* 3 vols., boards. Metuchen, N.J., 1932. Limited to 240, 202, and 100. $50.

HEBARD, Grace R. *Sacajawea.* Plates and maps. Cloth. Glendale, Calif., 1933. First edition. One of 750. $75-$100.

HEBARD, Grace R. *Washakie.* 7 maps, 16 plates. Cloth. Cleveland, 1930. First edition. $50-$75.

HEBARD, Grace R., and Brininstool, E. A. *The Bozeman Trail.* Plates, 2 folding maps. 2 vols., cloth. Cleveland, 1922. First edition. $100-$150. Glendale, Calif., 1960. Cloth. $35.

HEBISON, W. C. *Early Days in Texas and Rains County.* 50 pp., wrappers. Emory, Tex., 1917. First edition. $50-$75.

HECHT, Anthony. *Seven Deadly Sins.* Illustrated. Oblong, stiff wrappers. Northampton, Mass., 1958. First edition. One of 300. $75-$100.

HECHT, Anthony. *A Summoning of Stones.* Cloth. New York, no date (1954). First edition. In dust jacket. $25-$35. Author's first book.

HECHT, Ben. *The Bewitched Tailor.* Drawing by George Grosz. 8 pp., printed wrappers. New York, 1941. First edition. $35-$50.

HECHT, Ben. *Christmas Eve: A Morality Play.* Vellum. No place, 1928. First edition. One of 111 signed. $25.

HECHT, Ben. *Fantazius Mallare.* Illustrated by Wallace Smith. Cloth. Chicago, 1922. First edition. One of 2,000. In dust jacket. $25-$35.

HECHT, Ben. *A Jew in Love.* Cloth. New York, no date (1931). First edition. One of 150 signed. $25-$35. Trade edition: First issue, with no indication of second printing. (Suppressed.) $50 and up. (Note: Only a small quantity issued.)

HECHT, Ben. *The Kingdom of Evil.* Illustrated. Black cloth. Chicago, 1924. One of 2,000. In dust jacket. $25.

HECHT, Ben. *A Thousand and One Afternoons in Chicago.* Illustrated. Boards. Chicago, no date (1922). First edition. In dust jacket. $30-$40.

HECHT, Ben, and Bodenheim, Maxwell. *Cutie, a Warm Mama.* Orange cloth. Chicago, 1924. (By Ben Hecht alone.) First edition. One of 200. In dust jacket. $30-$40.

HECHT, Ben, and Fowler, Gene. *The Great Magoo.* Illustrated. Cloth. New York, no date (1933). First edition. In dust jacket. $75-$100.

HECKENDORN & Wilson. *Miners and Business Men's Directory.* (For Tuolumne, Calif.) 104 pp., printed wrappers. Columbia, Calif., 1856. First edition. $950 (A, 1968), $1,100 (A, 1959).

HECKEWELDER, John. *An Account of the History, Manners, and Customs of the Indian Nations.* Calf. Philadelphia, 1818. First edition. $75-$100. Philadelphia, 1819. Second edition. $50.

HECKEWELDER, John. *A Narrative of the Mission of the United Brethren Among the Delaware and Mohegan Indians.* Portrait and errata slip. Boards. Philadelphia, 1820. First edition. $50-$75. Cleveland, 1907. 3 maps, 5 plates. Three-quarters leather. One of 160 on large paper. $125-$150.

HEGAN, Alice Caldwell. *Mrs. Wiggs of the Cabbage Patch.* Olive-green cloth. New York, 1901. First edition, first issue, with gold sky on cover. $40-$50.

HEIDENMAUER (The); or The Benedictines. By the Author of "The Pilot." 3 vols., green or tan boards. London, 1832. (By James Fenimore Cooper.) First edition. $150-$200. Philadelphia, 1832. 2 vols., gray-blue boards. First American edition. $100-$150.

HELEN'S Tower. Title page and 6 leaves. Pink wrappers. Clandeboye, Canada, 1861. First published edition. $50. (Note: Contains a leaf of verse by Alfred, Lord Tennyson.)

HELFORTH, John. *Nights.* Printed wrappers. No place, no date (Dijon, France, 1935). (By Hilda Doolittle). One of 100. $200.

HELLER, Elinor, and Magee, David. *Bibliography of the Grabhorn Press, 1915-1940.* Illustrated. Boards and calf. San Francisco, 1940. One of 210. $350. (Also, note: *Bibliography . . . from 1940 to 1956.* San Francisco, 1957. [By Dorothy and David Magee.] One of 225. Boards. $250.)

HELLER, Joseph. *Catch-22.* Cloth. New York, 1961. First edition. In dust jacket. $35-$50.

HELLMAN, Lillian. *Watch on the Rhine.* Leather. New York, 1942. One of 50. Boxed. $50.

HEMANS, Felicia. *The League of the Alps, The Siege of Valencia, The Vespers of Palermo, and Other Poems.* Boards, paper label. Boston, 1826. First edition. $50.

HEMINGWAY, Ernest. See Bahr, Jerome; Cohn, Louis Henry; Faulkner, William, *Salmagundi;* North, Joseph; Paul, Elliot. Also see *Kiki's Memoirs; Somebody Had to Do Something.*

HEMINGWAY, Ernest. *Across the River and into the Trees.* Cloth. New York, 1950. First edition, first issue, with "A" on copyright page. In dust jacket. $25. London, no date (1950). Green cloth. First English edition. In dust jacket. $15.

HEMINGWAY, Ernest. *Cinquante Mille Dollars.* Wrappers. Paris, 1928. First French translation of *Fifty Grand.* One of 110. $85-$100.

HEMINGWAY, Ernest. *Death in the Afternoon.* Frontispiece and photographs. Black cloth. New York, 1932. First edition, first issue, with "A" on copyright page. In dust jacket. $50-$75. London, no date (1932). Illustrated. Orange cloth. First English edition. In dust jacket. $50.

HEMINGWAY, Ernest. *A Farewell to Arms.* Black cloth, gold paper labels. New York, 1929. First edition, first state, without the notice that "none of the characters in this book is a living person." In dust jacket. $100-$150. Another issue: Light blue-green boards, vellum spine and corners, black leather label. One of 510 signed. Boxed. $400-$500. London, 1929. Cloth. First English edition. In dust jacket. $50. Leipzig, Germany, 1930. Printed wrappers. $25. New York, 1948. Illustrated by Daniel Rasmusson. Cloth. First illustrated edition. $75-$100.

HEMINGWAY, Ernest. *Fiesta.* Stiff printed wrappers. Buenos Aires, no date (1945). Spanish version of *The Sun Also Rises.* In dust jacket. $50.

HEMINGWAY, Ernest. *The Fifth Column and the First Forty-nine Stories.* Red cloth. New York, 1938. First edition, first printing, with "A" on copyright page. In dust jacket. $50-$75.

HEMINGWAY, Ernest. *For Whom the Bell Tolls.* Beige cloth. New York, 1940. First edition, first printing, with "A" on copyright page. In first state dust jacket without photographer's name ("Arnold") under author's picture. $75-$100. New York, 1942. Limited Editions Club. Cloth. Boxed. $50-$75.

HEMINGWAY, Ernest. *God Rest You Merry Gentlemen.* Red cloth. New York, 1933. First edition. One of 300. $125-$150.

HEMINGWAY, Ernest. *Green Hills of Africa.* Light green cloth. New York, 1935. First edition, first issue, with "A" on copyright page. In dust jacket. $75-$100.

HEMINGWAY, Ernest. *In Our Time.* Frontispiece portrait by Henry Strater. Decorated tan boards. Paris, 1924. Three Mountains Press. First edition. One of 170. $1,500-$2,000. New York, 1925. Black cloth. First American edition. In dust jacket. $400 and up. London, 1926. Cloth. First English edition. In dust jacket. $200 and up. New York, 1930. Introduction by Edmund Wilson. Cloth. In dust jacket. $75-$100.

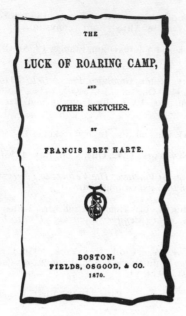

Nathaniel Hawthorne's first book

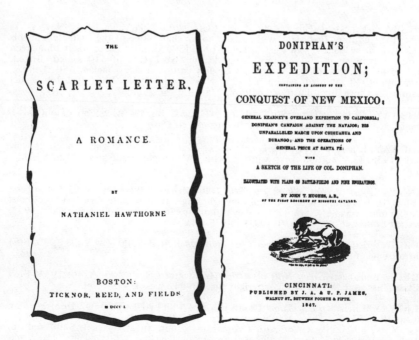

HEMINGWAY, Ernest. *Introduction to Kiki of Montparnasse*. (Cover title.) 8 pp., printed white wrappers. New York, 1929. First edition. One of 25 for copyright, published by Edward W. Titus. $950. Second issue, plain end papers. $50-$60.

HEMINGWAY, Ernest. *L'Adieu aux Armes*. Wrappers. Paris, 1931. First French translation of *A Farewell to Arms*. One of 180. $50-$75.

HEMINGWAY, Ernest. *Men Without Women*. Black cloth, gold labels. New York, 1927. First edition, first state, weighing 15 or 15½ ounces. In dust jacket. $150-$200.

HEMINGWAY, Ernest. *Nouvelles et Récits*. Colored plates. Decorated cloth. Paris, 1963. First edition. $50-$75.

HEMINGWAY, Ernest. *The Old Man and the Sea*. Folio, wrappers. *Life* magazine printing of the novel. First edition. Vol. 33, No. 9. Sept. 1, 1952. $10-$15. Uncorrected advance galley proofs of this printing, $75-$100. New York, 1952. Blue cloth. First edition. In dust jacket. $35-$50. New York, no date (1960). Illustrated by C. F. Tunnicliffe and R. Sheppard. Cloth. First illustrated edition. In dust jacket. $25-$35.

HEMINGWAY, Ernest. *Paris Est Une Fête*. Printed wrappers. Paris, 1964. First French translation of *A Moveable Feast*. One of 112 on velin. $30-$40.

HEMINGWAY, Ernest. *The Spanish Earth*. Illustrated. Pictorial tan cloth. Cleveland, 1938. First edition, first issue, with pictorial end papers showing a large FAI banner. One of 50 or 100 copies of a limited edition of 1,000. $150-$225.

HEMINGWAY, Ernest. *The Sun Also Rises*. Black cloth, gold labels. New York, 1926. First edition, first state, with "stoppped" for "stopped" on page 181, line 26. In dust jacket. $175-$275.

HEMINGWAY, Ernest. *Three Stories & Ten Poems*. Gray-blue wrappers. No place, no date (Paris, 1923). First edition. One of 300. $1,500-$2,000. Also, $1,400 (A, 1971); inscribed by Hemingway, $1,900 (A, 1968 and 1966). Author's first book.

HEMINGWAY, Ernest. *To Have and Have Not*. Black cloth. New York, 1937. First edition, first issue, with "A" on copyright page. In dust jacket. $50-$60.

HEMINGWAY, Ernest. *Today Is Friday*. (Caption title; no title page.) 8 pp., white wrappers (with Jean Cocteau drawing). No place, no date (Englewood, N.J., 1926). First edition. One of 300. In printed envelope. $200-$250.

HEMINGWAY, Ernest. *The Torrents of Spring*. Dark green cloth. New York, 1926. First edition. In dust jacket. $150-$200. Paris, 1932. White wrappers. In glassine dust jacket. $35-$50.

HEMINGWAY, Ernest. *Two Christmas Tales*. Blue wrappers. No place (Berkeley, Calif.), 1959. Hart Press. One of 150. $185.

HEMINGWAY, Ernest. *Winner Take Nothing*. Black cloth, gold paper labels. New York, 1933. First edition, with "A" on copyright page. In dust jacket. $75-$100.

HEMINGWAY, Ernest (editor). *Men at War: The Best War Stories of All Time*. Black cloth. New York, no date (1942). First edition. In dust jacket. $30-$40.

HENKLE, Moses. *Gospel of Nicodemus, the Believing Jew*. 40 pp., sewed. Columbus, Ohio, 1826. First edition. $35.

HENKLE, Moses. *Last Wills and Testaments of Thirteen Patriarchs, and Gospel of Nicodemus, the Believing Jew*. 67 pp., sewed. Urbana, Ohio, 1827. $35-$50.

HENLEY, William Ernest. *A Book of Verses*. Stiff printed wrappers. London, 1888. First edition. $35-$50.

HENLEY, William Ernest. *Hawthorn and Lavender with Other Verses.* Boards. London, 1901. One of 20. $25.

HENLEY, William Ernest. *Small Letters.* Frontispiece. Wrappers. No place (London), 1933. First edition. One of 60. $20-$25.

HENLEY, William Ernest. *A Song of Speed.* Printed wrappers, or cloth. London, 1903. First edition. $35-$50.

HENLEY, William Ernest. *The Song of the Sword and Other Verses.* Green cloth. London, 1892. First edition. $25.

HENLEY, William Ernest (editor). *Lyra Heroica: A Book of Verse for Boys.* Boards. London, 1892. One of 100 on large paper. $25.

HENNEPIN, Father Louis. *A Description of Louisiana.* Translated by John G. Shea. Cloth. New York, 1880. One of 250. $50-$100.

HENNIKER, Florence. *In Scarlet and Grey: Stories of Soldiers and Others.* Pictorial title page. Red cloth. London, 1896. First edition. $25-$50. (Note: Contains "The Spectre of the Real," by Thomas Hardy and Florence Henniker.)

HENRIETTA Temple: A Love Story. 3 vols., cloth. London, 1837. (By Benjamin Disraeli.) First edition. $100-$150.

HENRY, Alexander (the younger), and Thompson, David. *New Light on the Early History of the Greater Northwest.* Portrait, 4 maps in pocket. 3 vols., cloth. New York, 1897. First edition. One of 1,000. $100-$150. Also, $90 (A, 1967). Another issue: Boards, One of 100 on large paper. $150-$200.

HENRY, Alexander. *Travels and Adventures in Canada and the Indian Territories.* Boards. New York, 1809. First edition, first issue, without the portrait by Maverick. $300-$400. (Note: Howes says the second issue with the portrait is preferred by collectors, but recent sales do not indicate that this is the case.) Boston, 1901. Cloth. One of 700. $35.

HENRY, John Joseph. *An Accurate and Interesting Account of the Hardships and Sufferings of That Band of Heroes, Who Traversed the Wilderness in the Campaign Against Quebec in 1775.* Boards or leather. Lancaster, Pa., 1812. First edition. $200-$250.

HENRY, John Joseph. *Campaign Against Quebec.* Sheep. Watertown, N.Y., 1844. Revised edition of *An Accurate and Interesting Account, etc.* $25-$35.

HENRY, O. See *The O. Henry Calendar.*

HENRY, O. *Cabbages and Kings.* Pictorial black cloth. New York, 1904. (By William Sidney, later spelled Sydney, Porter.) First edition, first issue, with "McClure, Phillips & Co." on spine. In dust jacket. $200-$300. Also, $180 (A, 1963); lacking jacket, $110 (A, 1968). Author's first book.

HENRY, O. *The Four Million.* Cloth. New York, 1906. (By William Sidney Porter.) First edition. In dust jacket. $50-$75.

HENRY, O. *The Gentle Grafter.* Illustrated. Red cloth. New York, 1908. (By William Sidney Porter.) First edition. In dust jacket. $30-$35.

HENRY, O. *The Gift of the Magi.* Illustrated by Stephen Gooden. Half morocco. London, no date (1939). (By William Sidney Porter.) First edition. One of 105 signed. $75-$125. Another issue: Boards. In dust jacket. $35.

HENRY, O. *Heart of the West.* Pictorial cloth. New York, 1907. (By William Sidney Porter.) First edition. In dust jacket. $200-$300.

HENRY, O. *The Hiding of Black Bill.* Wrappers. New York, no date (1908). (By William Sidney Porter.) First edition. $35.

HENRY, O. *Let Me Feel Your Pulse.* Illustrated. Cloth. New York, 1910. (By William Sidney Porter.) First edition. In dust jacket. $35.

HENRY, O. *O. Henry Encore: Stories and Illustrations.* Edited by Mary Harrell. Leatherette. Dallas, no date (1936). (By William Sidney Porter.) First edition. (One of 5 issued for copyright purposes?) $100 (A, 1965).

HENRY, O. *O. Henryana.* Vellum and boards. Garden City, 1920. (By William Sidney Porter.) First edition. One of 377. $25.

HENRY, O. *Options.* Olive-green cloth. New York, 1909. (By William Sidney Porter.) First edition. In dust jacket. $35.

HENRY, O. *Roads of Destiny.* Red cloth. New York, 1909. (By William Sidney Porter.) First edition, first state, with "h" missing in line 6 on page 9. In dust jacket. $35. Lacking jacket, $25.

HENRY, O. *Rolling Stones.* Illustrated. Cloth. Garden City, 1912. (By William Sidney Porter.) First edition. In dust jacket. $40-$50.

HENRY, O. *Sixes and Sevens.* Red cloth. Garden City, 1911. (By William Sidney Porter.) First edition. In dust jacket. $35-$40.

HENRY, O. *Strictly Business.* Red cloth. New York, 1910. (By William Sidney Porter.) First edition. In dust jacket. $35.

HENRY, O. *The Trimmed Lamp.* Frontispiece by Alice Barber Stephens. Cloth. New York, 1907. (By William Sidney Porter.) First edition. In dust jacket. $25-$35.

HENRY, O. *The Voice of the City.* Cloth. New York, 1908. (By William Sidney Porter.) First edition. In dust jacket. $35-$50. New York, 1935. Limited Editions Club. Buckram. Boxed. $75-$100. Also, $65 (A, 1969).

HENRY, O. *Waifs and Strays: 12 Stories.* Cloth. Garden City, 1917. (By William Sidney Porter.) First edition. One of 200. $50.

HENRY, O. *Whirligigs.* Red cloth. New York, 1910. (By William Sidney Porter.) First edition, with "Published September, 1910" on copyright page. In dust jacket. $35-$60.

HENTY, G. A. *At Agincourt.* Illustrated. Cloth. London, 1897. First edition, first issue, with no mention of this title in ads at end. $25-$35.

HENTY, G. A. *In the Heart of the Rockies.* Pictorial green cloth. New York, 1894. First edition. $25.

HENTY, G. A. *The March to Coomassie.* Cloth. London, 1874. First edition. $75-$100.

HENTY, G. A. *The Tiger of Mysore.* Pictorial blue cloth. New York, 1895. First edition. $25.

HERBERT, A. P. *Poor Poems and Rotten Rhymes.* Wrappers. Winchester, England, 1910. First edition. $25. Author's first book.

HERBERT, Edward, Lord. *The Autobiography of Edward, Lord Herbert of Cherbury.* Wood engravings by H. W. Bray. Folio, buckram. Newtown, Wales, 1928. Gregynog Press. One of 300. $75-$125. Another issue: One of 25 specially bound in morocco. $400-$500.

HERBERT, George. *The Temple.* Portrait frontispiece. Cloth. London, 1927. Nonesuch Press. $40-$50.

HERBERT, George. *Poems.* Edited by H. W. Davies. Illustrated. Marbled boards and cloth. Newtown, 1923. Gregynog Press. One of 300. $75-$100. Another issue: One of 43 specially bound in morocco. $300-$400.

HERBERT, H. W. See Herbert, W. H.

HERBERT, Henry William. See Forester, Frank; Forrester, Frank; Herbert, W. H. Also see *The Brothers; Cromwell.*

HERBERT, Henry William. *Marmaduke Wyvil.* Drab boards, paper label. London, 1843. First edition. $200-$300. New York, no date (1843). Printed wrappers. First American edition. $200-$300.

HERBERT, Henry William. *The Quorndon Hounds.* Frontispiece, 3 plates. Cloth. Philadelphia, 1852. First edition. $250-$350.

HERBERT, Henry William. *Ruth Whalley; or, The Fair Puritan.* Printed wrappers (dated 1845 on front). Boston, no date (1844). First edition. $250 and up. Boston, 1845. (Cover title.) Pinkish tan wrappers. Second edition, first state of wrappers, with author's name as "Wm. Henry" instead of "Henry William." $100-$150.

HERBERT, Henry William. *The Village Inn.* Wrappers. New York, 1843. First edition. $250 and up.

HERBERT, J. A. *Illuminated Manuscripts.* Color frontispiece, 50 other plates. Cloth. London, 1911. First edition. $50-$100.

HERBERT, Sir William. *Croftus, sive de Hibernia Liber.* Printed from a manuscript at Powis castle. 2 genealogical tables. Half morocco. London, 1887. Roxburghe Club. $150-$200. Another issue: Printed on vellum. $250-$350.

HERBERT, W. H. *Ringwood the Rover: A Tale of Florida.* Printed wrappers. Philadelphia, 1843. (By Henry William Herbert.) First edition. $400-$500. Second edition, with "H. W. Herbert" as author. $150-$200.

HERFORD, Oliver. *Alphabet of Celebrities.* Illustrated. Cloth. Boston, 1899. First edition. $25.

HERGESHEIMER, Joseph. *Balisand.* Boards and cloth. New York, 1924. First edition. One of 175 signed. Boxed. $25.

HERGESHEIMER, Joseph. *The Bright Shawl.* Boards and vellum. New York, 1922. First edition, with "Published, October, 1922" on copyright page. One of 225 signed. $25.

HERGESHEIMER, Joseph. *Cytherea.* Red buckram. New York, 1922. First edition. One of 270 signed. In dust jacket. $25.

HERGESHEIMER, Joseph. *The Happy End.* Buckram. New York, 1919. First edition. One of 60 large paper copies, signed. In dust jacket. $25.

HERGESHEIMER, Joseph. *The Lay Anthony.* Cloth. New York, 1914. First edition. In dust jacket. $35-$50. Author's first book.

HERGESHEIMER, Joseph. *The Limestone Tree.* Buckram. New York, 1931. First edition. One of 225 signed. In dust jacket. Boxed. $25.

HERGESHEIMER, Joseph. *Mountain Blood.* Cloth. New York, 1915. First edition. In dust jacket. $25.

HERGESHEIMER, Joseph. *The Party Dress.* Limp orange vellum. New York, 1930. First edition. One of 60 on Japan vellum, signed. $35-$50.

HERGESHEIMER, Joseph. *Quiet Cities.* Cloth. New York, 1928. First edition. One of 210 signed. In dust jacket. $25.

HERGESHEIMER, Joseph. *San Cristóbal de la Habana.* Boards and cloth. New York, 1920. First edition. One of 100 signed. Boxed. $25.

HERGESHEIMER, Joseph. *Swords and Roses.* Decorated boards. New York, 1929. First edition. One of 225 signed. In dust jacket. $25. Trade edition: Gray cloth. In dust jacket. $10.

HERGESHEIMER, Joseph. *The Three Black Pennys.* Brown cloth. New York, 1917. First edition, first issue, with medallion on half title about 2 inches from bottom of page. In dust jacket. $25-$30. New York, 1930. Illustrated. Vellum. One of 170 signed. Boxed. $35-$50.

HERGESHEIMER, Joseph. *Tropical Winter.* Cloth. New York, 1933. First edition. One of 210 signed. In dust jacket. $36. Trade edition: Black cloth. In dust jacket. $10.

HERGESHEIMER, Joseph. *Wild Oranges.* Orange boards and cloth. New York, 1918. One of 85. In dust jacket. $25-$35.

HERMAN, William. *The Dance of Death.* Brown or green cloth. No place, no date (San Francisco, 1877). (By Ambrose Bierce.) First edition. $100 and up. San Francisco, 1877. Red or blue cloth. Second edition, with dated title page. $15-$20.

HERNDON, William H., and Weik, Jesse W. *Herndon's Lincoln: The True Story of a Great Life.* 63 plates. 3 vols., blue cloth. Chicago, no date (1889). First edition. $200-$300. Also, $150 (A, 1970); $425 [*sic*] (A, 1969). Chicago, 1890. 3 vols., cloth. Second edition. $50-$75.

HERNE, Peregrine (pseudonym). *Perils and Pleasures of a Hunter's Life; or the Romance of Hunting.* Colored frontispiece and plates. Cloth. Boston, 1854. First edition. $50-$75. Boston, 1856. 12 woodcut plates. Half leather. $35. New York, 1857. Plates. Cloth. $25.

HERRICK, Robert. *One Hundred and Eleven Poems.* Illustrated by W. Russell Flint. Sheepskin. London, 1955. Golden Cockerel Press. One of 105 copies issued with 8 extra plates signed by Flint. In slipcase. $250-$300. Another issue: Cloth, parchment spine. One of 550. Boxed. $100-$150.

HERRICK, Robert. *Poems.* Woodcut title page. Vellum. London, 1895. Kelmscott Press. $200-$350.

HERRING, John Frederick. *Portraits of the Winning Horses of the Great St. Leger Stakes.* 10 colored plates. Large folio, leather-backed boards. Doncaster, England, no date (1824). First edition, first state, with Sheardown & Son imprint on all plates. $2,660 (A, 1965). Another edition: No place, no date (London, 1829). 15 colored plates. Large folio, leather-backed boards. With a colored proof of "Tarrarre" plate. $1,456 (A, 1961).

HERRINGTON, W. D. *The Deserter's Daughter.* 27 pp., wrappers. Raleigh, 1865. First edition. $35-$50.

HERSCHEL, Sir John F. W. *Results of Astronomical Observations Made During the Years 1834-38 at the Cape of Good Hope.* 18 full-page and folding engraved plates. Cloth. London, 1847. $100-$150.

HERSEY, John. *The Wall.* Illustrated. Cloth. New York, 1957. Limited Editions Club. Boxed. $25.

HERTZ, John. *Racing Memoirs.* Mounted photographic plates, some in color. Half morocco. Chicago, 1954. $35.

HESTON, James Franklin. *Moral and Political Truth.* Calf. Philadelphia, 1811. First edition. $35.

HEWITSON, William. *Illustrations of New Species of Exotic Butterflies.* 250 hand-colored plates. 5 vols., half morocco. London, 1856-61. $150-$200.

HEWITT, Edward R. *Secrets of the Salmon.* Half cloth. New York, 1922. One of 780. $35-$50.

HEWITT, Graily. *Lettering for Students and Craftsmen.* Illustrated. White buckram. London, 1930. One of 380 signed. $85.

HEWITT, Graily. *The Pen and Type-Design.* Illustrated. Full red morocco. London, 1928. First Edition Club. One of 250. $75-$100. Another issue: Boards and cloth. $35. Inscribed, $56.40.

HEWITT, Randall H. *Across the Plains and over the Divide.* Folding map, portrait, 58 plates. Pictorial cloth. New York, no date (1906). First edition. $85-$125. Inscribed, $100.

HEWITT, Randall H. *Notes By the Way: Memoranda of a Journey Across the Plains, from Dundee, Ill., to Olympia, W. T. May 7 to November 3, 1862.* 58 pp., printed wrappers. Olympia, Wash., 1863. First edition. $2,000 and up.

HEWLETT, Maurice. *The Forest Lovers.* Pictorial cloth. London, 1898. First edition, first issue, with U. S. copyright notice on verso of half title. $25-$30.

HEWLETT, Maurice. *A Masque of Dead Florentines.* Illustrated. Oblong, tan buckram. London, 1895. First edition. $25-$35.

HEWLETT, Maurice. *Quattrocentisteria.* Illuminated by Valenti Angelo. Folio, half vellum. New York, 1927. One of 175. $35-$50.

HEWLETT, Maurice. *The Song of the Plow.* Frontispiece. Boards. London, no date (1916). First edition. One of 100 signed. $42.

HEYWARD, Du Bose. *The Half-Pint Flask.* Boards and cloth. New York, 1929. First edition. One of 175 signed. In dust jacket. $35.

HEYWARD, Du Bose. *Porgy.* Black cloth. New York, no date (1925). First edition, first issue, with gold-stamped binding and publisher's monogram on copyright page. In dust jacket. $25-$30.

HIGBEE, Elias, and Thompson, R. B. *The Petition of the Latter-Day Saints.* 13 pp., sewed. Washington, 1840. First edition. $35-$50.

HIGGINS, F. R. *Arable Holdings: Poems.* Boards and linen. Dublin, 1933. Cuala Press. One of 300. In tissue dust jacket. $60-$80.

HIGGINS, George. *"The King of Counties": Miami County.* 32 pp., wrappers. Paola, Kan., 1877. $60-$75.

HIGGINS, Godfrey. *Anacalypsis, an Attempt to Draw Aside the Veil of the Saitic Isis.* 6 engraved plates. 2 vols., cloth. London, 1836. First edition. $100-$150.

HIGGINSON, Thomas Wentworth. *The Birthday in Fairy-land: A Story for Children.* Printed wrappers. Boston, 1850. First edition. $50.

HILDEBRAND, Samuel S. *Autobiography.* Illustrated. Cloth. Jefferson City, Mo., 1870. First edition. $75. Worn, $50.

HILDRETH, Samuel P. *Biographical and Historical Memoirs of the Early Pioneer Settlers of Ohio.* 6 plates. Cloth. Cincinnati, 1852. First edition. $50.

HILDRETH, Samuel P. *Genealogical and Biographical Sketches of the Hildreth Family.* Cloth. Marietta, Ohio, 1840. $35-$50.

HILDRETH, Samuel P. *Memoirs of the Early Pioneer Settlers of Ohio.* Leather. Cincinnati, 1854. $35-$50.

HILDRETH, Samuel P. *Pioneer History.* Folding map. Half leather. Cincinnati, 1848. First edition. $50-$75.

HILL, George F. *A Corpus of Italian Medals of the Renaissance Before Cellini.* 201 full-page plates. 2 vols., folio, buckram. London, 1930. $250-$300.

HILL, W. H.; A. F.; and A. E. *Antonio Stradivari, His Life and Work.* Illustrated. Morocco. London, 1902. First edition. One of 100. $200-$250. London, 1909. Second edition. $75-$100.

HILL, W. H.; A. F.; and A. E. *Violin-Makers of the Guarneri Family.* Plates. Half vellum. London, 1931. $200-$250.

HILLARD, Elias B. *The Last Men of the Revolution.* 6 colored lithographs. Half morocco. Hartford, 1864. First edition. $50-$60.

HILLS, Chester. *The Builder's Guide.* 70 plates. 2 vols. in one, folio, boards. Hartford, Conn., 1834. First edition. $100-$150. Hartford, 1846. 50 plates. $75-$125.

HILLS, Sir John. *Points of a Racehorse.* Illustrated. Folio, cloth. London, 1903. $75-$100.

HILLS, John Waller. *History of Fly-Fishing for Trout.* Half cloth. London, 1921. One of 50 signed. $100-$125.

HILLS, John Waller. *A Summer on the Test.* 12 plates by N. Wilkinson. Calf. London, no date (1924). One of 300 signed. $75-$100. Another issue: 12 signed etchings by N. Wilkinson. Half parchment. London, no date (about 1925). $150-$200.

HILLYER, Robert. *Sonnets and Other Lyrics.* Boards. Cambridge, Mass., 1917. First edition. In dust jacket. $35-$40. Author's first book.

HILTON, A. *Oklahoma and Indian Territory Along the Frisco.* Illustrated, 2 folding maps. 91 pp., wrappers. St. Louis, 1905. $35-$50.

HIMSELF. See *Sheppard Lee.*

HIND, Henry Youle. *Narrative of the Canadian Red River Exploring Expedition of 1857, etc.* Plates (some colored), folding maps, charts. 2 vols., brown cloth. London, 1860. $200-$300.

HIND, Henry Youle. *North-West Territory.* Folding maps and plans. Cloth. Toronto, 1859. First edition. $150-$200.

HIND, Henry Youle. *A Sketch of an Overland Route to British Columbia.* Folding map. Dark-green flexible cloth, paper label on front cover. Toronto, 1862. First edition, with errata slip. $750 and up. Also, front hinge cracked, $600 (A, 1968).

HINKLE, James F. *Early Days of a Cowboy on the Pecos.* Illustrated. 35 pp., pictorial wrappers. Roswell, N. M., 1937. First edition. $200 and up.

HINMAN, Wilbur F. *The Story of the Sherman Brigade.* Morocco. No place (Alliance, Ohio), 1897. $35-$50. Worn at ends, inner hinges taped, $25.

HINTON, Richard J. *The Hand-Book of Arizona.* 4 maps, 16 plates. Cloth. San Francisco, 1878. First edition. $50-$60.

HINTS to My Countrymen. By an American. Boards. New York, 1826. (By Theodore Sedgwick.) First edition. $35-$50.

HINTS Towards Forming the Character of a Young Princess. 2 vols., contemporary (or original) boards. London, 1805. (By Hannah More.) First edition. $150-$165.

HIRSHBERG, Dr. L. K. *What You Ought to Know About Your Baby.* Cloth. New York, 1910. First edition. In dust jacket. $100. Also, $95 (A, 1967). (Note: Written in collaboration with H. L. Mencken.)

HISTORIA Cristiana de la California. Boards and calf. Mexico, 1864. (By El Domingo.) $75-$100.

HISTORICAL and Descriptive Review of the Industries of Tacoma, 1887. 108 pp., unbound. Los Angeles, 1887. $50-$75.

HISTORICAL and Descriptive Review of the Industries of Walla Walla. 112 pp., wrappers. No place, 1891. $75-$100.

HISTORICAL and Scientific Sketches of Michigan. Cloth. Detroit, 1834. First edition. $35-$50.

HISTORICAL Sketch Book and Guide to New Orleans and Environs. Plates, map. Pictorial wrappers. New York, 1885. (By Lafcadio Hearn and others.) First edition, first issue, with spelling "Bizoin" (instead of "Bisoin") at head of title page. $50.

HISTORICAL War Map (The). Folding maps, plus maps in text. 56 pp., printed boards. Indianapolis, 1862. Asher & Co. $50-$60.

HISTORY of Alameda County, California. Portraits. Cloth. Oakland, 1883. (By J. P. Munro-Fraser.) $100-$150.

HISTORY of Amador County, California. Full leather. Oakland, 1881. $150.

HISTORY of the Arkansas Valley, Colorado. Illustrated. Half leather. Chicago, 1881. $50-$60.

HISTORY of Beasts and Birds. 25 woodcuts. 30 pp., miniature book, 3 7/8 x 2½ inches. Orange wrappers. Cooperstown, N.Y., 1838. $25. Lacking cut for "Y," $20.

HISTORY of the Bible. Illustrated. 256 pp., miniature book (2 x 1 5/16 inches), sheep, gilt spine. Sandy-Hill, N.Y., 1825. $75-$100.

HISTORY of the Bible. Woodcuts. 192 pp., miniature book, 2 1/6 x 1¾ inches. Calf. Bridgeport, Conn., 1831. One woodcut damaged, $65.

HISTORY of Black Hawk County, Iowa. Illustrated. Half leather. Chicago, 1878. $50-$60.

HISTORY of the Brooklyn and Long Island Fair, Feb. 22, 1864. Leather. Brooklyn, 1864. $50.

HISTORY of the City of Denver, Arapahoe County, and Colorado. Illustrated. Half morocco. Chicago, 1880. First edition. $50.

HISTORY of the Counties of Woodbury and Plymouth, Iowa. Half leather. Chicago, 1890-91. $40-$50.

HISTORY of Crawford and Richland Counties, Wisconsin. Cloth. Springfield, Ill., 1884. (By C. W. Butterfield and George A. Ogle.) First edition. $50-$60.

HISTORY of Dearborn and Ohio Counties, Indiana, from Their Earliest Settlement, etc. Cloth. Chicago, 1885. First edition. $50-$60.

HISTORY of Floyd County, Iowa. Half leather. Chicago, 1882. $40-$50.

HISTORY of Franklin, Jefferson, Washington, Crawford and Gasconade Counties, Missouri. Illustrated. Half leather. Chicago, 1888. $50-$60.

HISTORY of Franklin and Pickaway Counties, Ohio. Illustrated. Half leather. No place, 1880. $50-$60.

HISTORY of Godefrey of Boloyne (The). Vellum with ties. London, 1893. Kelmscott Press. One of 300. $500-$600.

HISTORY of the Great Lakes. Plates, 5 double-page maps. 2 vols., cloth. Chicago, 1899. (Edited by John B. Mansfield.) First edition. $75-$100.

HISTORY of Henry Esmond (The). 3 vols., brown cloth, paper labels. London, 1852. (By William Makepeace Thackeray.) First edition, with 16 pages of ads dated September. $100-$150.

HISTORY of Herodotus of Halicarnassus (The). Translation of G. Rawlinson, revised by A. W. Lawrence. 9 wood engravings, maps. Vellum and cloth. London, 1935. Nonesuch Press. In dust jacket. $200-$250.

HISTORY of Howard and Cooper Counties, Missouri. Half leather. St. Louis, 1883. $40-$50.

HISTORY of Idaho Territory. 2 maps, 69 plates, 2 facsimiles. Half morocco. San Francisco, 1884. First edition. $100-$150.

HISTORY of the Indian Wars with the First White Settlers of the United States (A). Leather. Montpelier, Vt., 1812. (By Daniel C. Sanders.) First edition. $200-$250. Also, worn, $100 (A, 1967). Rochester, N.Y., 1828. Boards. Second edition. (Chapter 27 omitted.) $75-$100.

HISTORY of Jasper County, Missouri. Illustrated. Half leather. Des Moines, 1883. $40-$50.

HISTORY of Jo Daviess County, Illinois. Illustrated. Half leather. Chicago, 1878. $50-$60.

HISTORY of Johnny Quae Genus (The). 24 colored plates by Thomas Rowlandson. 8 parts, wrappers. London, 1822. First edition. $200-$300. London, 1822. Boards. First book edition. $100-$150.

HISTORY of the Late War in the Western Country. Leather. Lexington, Ky., 1816. (By Robert B. McAfee.) First edition, with the "extra" printed leaf (of Gen. Winchester's criticism) at end. $175-$200. Bowling Green, Ohio, no date (1919). Cloth. One of 300. $25-$35.

HISTORY of Lawrence County, Pennsylvania. Half morocco. Philadelphia, 1877. First edition. $50-$60.

HISTORY of Madeira (A). 27 colored plates. Boards or cloth. London, 1821. (By William Combe.) First edition. $100-$200.

HISTORY of Marin County, California. Full sheep. San Francisco, 1880. First edition. $200-$300.

HISTORY of Mercer County, Pennsylvania. Half morocco. Philadelphia, 1877. First edition. $40-$60.

HISTORY of Mendocino County, California. Portraits. Sheep. San Francisco, 1880. $150-$250.

HISTORY of Milam, Williamson, Bastrop, Travis, Lee and Burleson Counties, Texas. Half leather. Chicago, 1893. $100-$125.

HISTORY of Montana, 1739-1885. Folding map, plates. Half morocco. Chicago, 1885. (Edited by Michael A. Leeson.) First edition. $225. Others, $85-$150.

HISTORY of Napa and Lake Counties, California. Illustrated. Full sheep. San Francisco, 1881. First edition. $100.

HISTORY of Nevada. 116 plates. Half morocco. Oakland, 1881. (Edited by Myron Angel.) First edition. $100-$150. (Note: Although this book has a high auction record of $170, in 1959, it apparently is not as scarce as that would indicate. Copies have since sold for much less at auction—$60, in 1968, and $20, in 1966.)

HISTORY of Nevada County, California. Illustrated. Oblong folio, cloth, leather spine. Oakland, 1880. $200-$250.

HISTORY of Ontario County, New York. Half leather. Philadelphia, 1876. $75.

HISTORY of Pike County, Illinois. Half leather. Chicago, 1880. $50-$60.

HISTORY of Pike County, Missouri. Half leather. Des Moines, 1883. $50-$60.

HISTORY of Sangamon County, Illinois. Illustrated. Half leather. Chicago, 1881. $40-$60.

HISTORY of San Luis Obispo County, California. Portraits and scenes. Half leather. Oakland, 1883. (By Myron Angel.) First edition. $200-$250.

HISTORY of Santa Barbara and Ventura Counties, California. Half leather. Oakland, 1883. (By Jesse D. Mason.) $75-$100.

HISTORY of Sonoma County, California. Illustrated. Three-quarters leather. San Francisco, 1880. $75-$100. New spine, last page in facsimile, $65.

HISTORY of Southeastern Dakota. Cloth. Sioux City, 1881. $35-$50.

HISTORY of the Steam-Boat Case (A), Lately Discussed by Counsel Before the Legislature of New Jersey. 48 pp., unbound. Trenton, N.J., 1815. $50.

HISTORY of Texas (A), or The Emigrant's Guide to the New Republic, by a Resident Emigrant. Frontispiece. Cloth. New York, 1844. (Edited by A. B. Lawrence and C. J. Stille.) Third edition of *Texas in 1840.* $35-$50.

HISTORY of Wabasha County, Minnesota. Compiled by Franklyn Curtiss-Wedge and others. Cloth. Winona, Minn., 1920. $35.

HISTORY of Tioga County, Pennsylvania. Cloth. No place, 1897. $40-$50.

HISTORY of Walworth County, Wisconsin. Illustrated. Half leather. Chicago, 1882. $50-$60.

HISTORY of Waukesha County, Wisconsin. Illustrated. Half leather. Chicago, 1880. $50-$60.

HISTORY of Wayne County, New York. Illustrated. Half leather. Philadelphia, 1877. $50-$75.

HITTELL, John S. *A History of the City of San Francisco.* Cloth. San Francisco, 1878. First edition. $50-$75.

HITTELL, John S. *The Commerce and Industries of the Pacific Coast of North America.* Folding colored map, plates. Cloth. San Francisco, 1882. First edition. $35.

HITTELL, John S. *The Resources of Vallejo.* Folding map. Printed wrappers. No place, no date (Vallejo, Calif., 1869). First edition. $200 and up. Also, wrappers and map detached, $90 (A, 1968).

HITTELL, John S. *Yosemite: Its Wonders and Its Beauties.* 20 mounted photographic views by "Helios." Green cloth. San Francisco, 1868. First edition. $600. (Note: The plates are by the pioneer photographer Eadweard Muybridge, and the book is very scarce and much sought for by collectors in both the Americana and photographic fields.)

HITTELL, Theodore H. (editor). *The Adventures of James Capen Adams, Mountaineer and Grizzly Bear Hunter, of California.* 12 wood engravings. Cloth. San Francisco, 1860. First edition. $75-$100. Boston, 1861. 12 plates. Cloth. $50.

HOAR, A. W. *Lineage and Family Records of Alfred Wyman Hoar and His Wife Josephine Jackson.* Plates. Cloth. Delano, Minn., 1898. First edition. $50-$75.

HOARE, Sarah. *Poems on Conchology and Botany.* 5 hand-colored plates. Cloth, paper label. London, 1831. First edition. $50-$60.

HOBBS, James. *Wild Life in the Far West.* 20 plates, colored frontispiece. Cloth. Hartford, Conn., 1872. First edition. $100-$150. Hartford, 1873. Second edition. $80-$100. Hartford, 1874. $50. Hartford, 1875. $35.

HOBBS, G. A. *Bilbo, Brewer, and Bribery in Mississippi Politics.* Cloth. No place (Memphis), 1917. First edition. $50.

HOBHOUSE, J. C. (compiler). *Imitations and Translations from the Ancient and Modern Classics.* Pink boards. London, 1809. First edition. $50-$100. (Note: Contains nine new poems by Lord Byron.)

HOBOMOK, a Tale of Early Times. Boards. Boston, 1824. (By Lydia Maria Child.) First edition. $100. Rebound in modern leather, $50. Author's first book.

HOBSON, G. D. *English Binding Before 1500.* 55 plates, other illustrations. Folio, buckram. Cambridge, England, 1929. $75-$100.

HOBSON, G. D. *Maioli, Canevari and Others.* 6 plates in color, 58 in black and white. Brown morocco. London, 1926. One of 25. $424.80. Another issue: Cloth. $150-$175. Binding faded, $156.

HOBSON, G. D. *Thirty Bindings.* 30 plates (some in color). Folio, cloth. London, 1926. First Edition Club. One of 600. $76.80 and $60.

HOBSON, R. L. *A Catalogue of Chinese Pottery and Porcelain in the Collection of Sir Percival David.* 180 plates, mostly in color. Folio, linen. London, 1934. In portfolio box. $500-$600. Another issue: Silk boards. One of 30 on vellum, signed by Hobson. Boxed. $875-$1,000.

HOBSON, R. L. *Chinese Art.* 100 color plates. Cloth. New York, 1927. $50. London, 1954. In dust jacket. $35. London, no date (1964). $35.

HODGE, Frederick W. *Handbook of American Indians North of Mexico.* Map. 2 vols., cloth. Washington, 1907-10. First edition. $75-$100. Washington, 1912. $50 and $65. New York, 1959. $35-$50.

HODGE, Gene Meany. *The Kachinas Are Coming.* 18 color plates. Cloth. Los Angeles, 1936. $35-$50.

HODGES, M. C. *The Mestico; or, The War-path and Its Incidents.* 204 pp., printed wrappers. New York, 1850. First edition, with author identified on cover as "W. C. Hodges." $200 $250.

HODGSON, Adam. *Letters from North America.* Plates. Boards. London, 1824. First English edition of *Remarks During a Journey, etc.* $100-$125.

HODGSON, Adam. *Remarks During a Journey Through North America in the Years 1819-21.* Leather. New York, 1823. First (pirated) edition. $75-$100.

HODGSON, J. E. *The History of Aeronautics in Great Britain.* Colored frontispiece, 150 plates, of which 13 are colored. Buckram. Oxford, 1924. One of 1,000. $100-$125.

HODGSON, Joseph. *The Alabama Manual and Statistical Register for 1869.* Printed boards. Montgomery, 1869. First edition. $50-$75.

HODGSON, Joseph. *The Cradle of the Confederacy.* Cloth. Mobile, 1876. First edition. $35-$50.

HODGSON, Mrs. Willoughby. *Old English China.* 16 colored plates and 64 illustrations from photographs. Cloth. London, 1913. $40-$50.

HOELDERLIN, Friedrich. *Poèmes.* Translated by André du Bouchet. 7 etchings in color by Max Ernst. Loose sheets in blue cloth folder and slipcase. Paris, no date (1960). One of 90 (of an edition of 210, not all with etchings), signed. $400.

HOFER, A. F. *Grape Growing*. 32 pp., wrappers. McGregor, Iowa, 1878. First edition. $25.

HOFFMAN, Charles Fenno. See *Greyslaer; A Winter in the West*.

HOFFMAN, Charles Fenno. *The Pioneers of New York*. 55 pp., printed tan wrappers. New York, 1848. First edition, with seal on front cover 1 3/8 inches wide. $100-$125.

HOFFMAN, Charles Fenno. *Wild Scenes in the Forest and Prairie*. 2 vols., boards, paper label on spine. London, 1839. First edition. $150-$200. New York, 1843. 2 vols., boards. First American edition. $150-$200.

HOGG, Robert, and Bull, H. G. (editors). *The Herefordshire Pomona, Containing Original Figures and Descriptions of the Most Esteemed Kinds of Apples and Pears*. 77 colored plates. 2 vols., half morocco. Hereford, England, 1876-85. $250-$350.

HOGG, Thomas E. *The Fate of Marvin and Other Poems*. Cloth. Houston, 1873. $25-$30.

HOKUSAI: Master of the Japanese Ukiyo-Ye School of Painting. 6 color reproductions. Green half morocco. No place, no date (London?, 1904). $100-$110.

HOLBROOK, John Edwards. *Ichthyology of South Carolina*. Vol. 1. (All published.) 28 colored plates. Three-quarters morocco. Charleston, 1860. First edition. $500 and up.

HOLDEN, W. C. *Alkali Trails*. Maps, illustrations. Cloth. Dallas, no date (1930). First edition. $35-$50.

HOLDEN, W. C. *Rollie Burns; or, An Account of the Ranching Industry on the South Plains*. Maps, illustrations. Pictorial cloth. Dallas, no date (1932). First edition, first issue, tan cloth. $50. Second issue, green cloth, without frontispiece. $25-$35.

HOLDEN, W. C. *The Spur Ranch*. Cloth. Boston, no date (1934). First edition. $35-$50.

HOLDER, Charles F. *All About Pasadena and Its Vicinity*. Wrappers. Boston, 1889. First edition. $35.

HOLDER, Charles F. *The Channel Islands of California*. Cloth. Chicago, 1910. First edition. $50-$75. Second edition, same date. $40.

HOLDING, C. B. *Green Bluff: A Temperance Story*. Cloth. St. Louis, 1874. First edition. $50.

HOLE in the Wall; or a Peep at the Creed-Worshippers. 3 plates. 36 pp., wrappers. No place, 1828. First edition.

HOLKHAM Bible Picture Book (The). Facsimile of the fourteenth-century manuscript. Folio, half morocco. London, 1954. (Edited by W. O. Hassall.) One of 100. $75. Another issue: Specially bound in levant morocco. $150-$200.

HOLLEY, Mary Austin. *Texas: Observations, Historical, Geographical and Descriptive*. Folding map. Cloth. Baltimore, 1833. First edition. $250-$350. Lexington, Ky., 1836. Map in color. Cloth. Second edition. $400 and $250.

HOLLIDAY, George H. *On the Plains in '65*. Illustrated. 97 pp., printed wrappers. No place, 1883. First edition. $400-$500.

HOLLISTER, Ovando J. *History of the First Regiment of Colorado Volunteers*. 178 pp., printed wrappers. Denver, 1863. First edition. $1,750-$2,000.

HOLLISTER, Ovando J. *The Silver Mines of Colorado*. 87 pp., printed wrappers. Central City, Colo., 1867. First edition. $400-$500. Also, $350 (A, 1968). Springfield, Mass., 1867. Cloth. Enlarged edition (retitled *The Mines of Colorado*). $35-$50.

HOLLISTER, Uriah S. *The Navajo and His Blanket*. 10 color plates, other illustrations. Cloth. Denver, 1903. First edition. $50-$60.

HOLLOWAY, W. L. (editor). *Wild Life on the Plains.* Illustrated. Pictorial cloth. St. Louis, no date (1891). First edition. $50-$60.

HOLMES, Mrs. Mary J. *Cousin Maude, and Rosamond.* Cloth. New York, 1860. First edition. $40-$50.

HOLMES, Mary J. *Tempest and Sunshine; or, Life in Kentucky.* Gray cloth. New York, 1854. First edition. $40-$50.

HOLMES, Oliver Wendell. See Hall, Marshall. Also see *The Autocrat of the Breakfast-Table; Francis Parkman; The Harbinger; The Poet at the Breakfast-Table; Songs of the Class of MDCCCXXIX.*

HOLMES, Oliver Wendell. *Astraea: The Balance of Illusions. A Poem.* Yellow boards. Boston, 1850. First edition, first printing, with ampersand in printer's imprint on copyright page set above the line. $25-$50. (Also issued in rough reddish-brown cloth.)

HOLMES, Oliver Wendell. *The Benefactors of the Medical School of Harvard University.* Tan wrappers. Boston, 1850. First edition. $25-$35.

HOLMES, Oliver Wendell. *Border Lines of Knowledge in Some Provinces of Medical Science.* Cloth. Boston, 1862. First edition, with Ticknor & Co. imprint on spine. $25.

HOLMES, Oliver Wendell. *Boylston Prize Dissertations for the Years 1836 and 1837.* Folding colored map of New England. Cloth. Boston, 1838. First edition. $25.

HOLMES, Oliver Wendell. *The Claims of Dentistry.* Tan wrappers. Boston, 1872. First edition. $25.

HOLMES, Oliver Wendell. *The Contagiousness of Puerperal Fever.* (Caption title.) 28 pp., printed buff wrappers. No place, no date (Boston, 1843 or 1844?). First edition. $500 and up. (Note. No copy has appeared for sale in many years.)

HOLMES, Oliver Wendell. *Currents and Counter-Currents in Medical Science: An Address . . . Before the Massachusetts Medical Society.* Printed salmon-colored wrappers. Boston, 1860. First edition. $75-$100.

HOLMES, Oliver Wendell. *Currents and Counter-Currents in Medical Science. With Other Address and Essays.* Cloth. Boston, 1861. First edition, first issue, with triple-ruled blind-stamped frame enclosing "T & F" initials on cover. $25-$35.

HOLMES, Oliver Wendell. *Elsie Venner: A Romance of Destiny.* 2 vols., brown cloth. Boston, 1861. First edition, "probable" first printing, with ads dated January, 1861. $50-$75. With February ads, $40.

HOLMES, Oliver Wendell. *The Guardian Angel.* 2 vols., plum-colored cloth. London, 1867. First edition. $25. Boston, 1867. Cloth. First American edition. $15.

HOLMES, Oliver Wendell. *Homoeopathy, and Its Kindred Delusions.* Tan boards, paper label. Boston, 1842. First edition. $50-$75.

HOLMES, Oliver Wendell. *Humorous Poems.* Portrait frontispiece. Printed wrappers, or cloth. Boston, 1865. First edition. Wrappers: $75-$100. Cloth: $50-$75.

HOLMES, Oliver Wendell. *John Lothrop Motley: A Memoir.* Portrait. Cloth. Boston, 1879. First American edition. $25. Another issue: Beveled cloth, gilt top. One of 516 on large paper. $50. (Note: An English copyright edition, dated London, 1878, bound in brown cloth, preceded the American edition.)

HOLMES, Oliver Wendell. *Mechanism in Thought and Morals.* Cloth. Boston, 1871. First edition. $50.

HOLMES, Oliver Wendell. *A Mortal Antipathy.* Green cloth. Boston, 1885. First edition, first issue, with *Elsie Venner* listed at $1.50 in ad opposite title page. $25-$30.

HOLMES, Oliver Wendell. *Oration Delivered Before the City Authorities of Boston, on the Fourth of July, 1863.* Printed salmon-colored wrappers. Boston, 1863. First trade edition. $25. Another issue, "Private Copy": Boston, 1863. Leather or cloth. One of about 12. Inscribed by Holmes. $50.

HOLMES, Oliver Wendell. *Over the Teacups.* Olive-green cloth. Boston, 1891. First edition, first state, with no price for this book on ad leaf facing title page. $100-$125. Also, "later issue, no advts.," $45 (A, 1968).

HOLMES, Oliver Wendell. *A Poem... Delivered at the Dedication of the Pittsfield Cemetery, Sept. 9, 1850.* 8 pp., drab wrappers. No place, no date (Pittsfield, Mass., 1850). First edition. $25-$35.

HOLMES, Oliver Wendell. *Poem for the Dedication of the Fountain at Stratford-on-Avon.* Printed wrappers. No place, no date (Boston, 1887). First edition. One of 58 signed. $225.

HOLMES, Oliver Wendell. *Poems.* Decorated cloth, paper label. Boston, 1836. First edition, with Boston imprint only. $50-$75. Worn, lacking back end paper, hinges repaired, signed by Holmes, $70. Another issue: Boston and New York imprint. Foxed. $35. Boston, 1849. William D. Ticknor imprint. Boards or cloth. "New and Enlarged Edition." $25.

HOLMES, Oliver Wendell. *The Position and Prospects of the Medical Student.* Printed tan wrappers. Boston, 1844. First edition. $100-$125.

HOLMES, Oliver Wendell. *The Professor at the Breakfast-Table.* Cloth. Boston, 1860. First edition. $25. Another issue: Beveled cloth, edges gilt. Large paper. $50-$75. Edges trimmed, spine worn, $45. Also, $35 (A, 1968). London, 1860. Cloth. First English edition. $15.

HOLMES, Oliver Wendell. *Teaching from the Chair and at the Bedside.* Printed gray wrappers. Boston, 1867. First edition. $100-$150.

HOLMES, Oliver Wendell. *Urania: A Rhymed Lesson.* Printed blue wrappers. Boston, 1846. First edition. $50-$75.

HOLMES, Justice Oliver Wendell. *The Common Law.* Cloth. Boston, 1881. First edition. $75-$125. Author's first book.

HOLMES, Roberta E. *The Southern Mines of California.* Plates and maps. Boards. San Francisco, 1930. Grabhorn Press. One of 250. $50-$75.

HOLY BIBLE. Folio, red cloth. Cleveland, 1949. One of 975 designed by Bruce Rogers. $100-$150. Another issue: One of 20 with a decorative headpiece for each book. $300-$400.

HOME as Found. By the Author of *Homeward Bound.* 2 vols., cloth, or boards and cloth, with paper spine labels. Philadelphia, 1838. (By James Fenimore Cooper.) First edition, first printing, with a note in Vol. 1 about the paper used in the book. $100-$150.

HOME on a Furlough: A Sketch of Real Life. 16 pp., wrappers. Springfield, Mass., 1864. First edition. $75.

HOMER. *The Homeric Hymn to Aphrodite.* Translated by F. L. Lucas. 10 wood engravings. Full red morocco. London, 1948. Golden Cockerel Press. One of 100 (from an edition of 750) specially bound, signed by Lucas. Boxed. $250-$300. Another issue: Half morocco. One of 650. $75.

HOMER. *The Odyssey of Homer.* Translated by T. E. Shaw (T. E. Lawrence, of Arabia). With 25 large rondels in gold and black. Small folio, black morocco. No place (London), 1932. First edition. One of 530 designed by Bruce Rogers. Boxed. $500. (Note: A few copies were signed by Lawrence, "T. E. Shaw," and Rogers and bring higher prices.) Boston, 1929. Translated by George H. Palmer. Illustrated by N. C. Wyeth. Half leather. One of 550 signed. With an extra set of color plates. $85.

HOMES in Texas on the Line of the International and Great Northern Railroad. 79 pp., wrappers. No place, no date (Chicago, 1879). (By N. W. Hunter.) First edition. $35-$50.

HONIG, Louis O. *James Bridger.* Illustrated. Leatherette. Kansas City, Mo., 1951. Limited, signed edition. $25-$35.

HONIG, Louis O. *Westpoint, Gateway to the Early West.* Illustrated. Cloth. North Kansas City, 1950. One of 525 signed. $50-$75.

HONORED in Verse: The Tributes of a Galaxy of American Poets. (On the Death of President Garfield.) 8 pp., wrappers. Boston, 1881. $50.

HOOKER, W. A. *The Horn Silver Mine: Report.* (Cover title.) 5 tinted views, colored map. 32 pp., wrappers. New York, 1879. $75-$100.

HOOPER, Johnson J. *Dog and Gun: A Few Loose Chapters on Shooting.* 105 pp., printed wrappers (woodcut on front). New York, 1856. First edition, published by A. O. Moore, with dated title page. $75-$100.

HOOVER, Herbert C. *Fishing for Fun.* Illustrated. Cloth. New York, no date (1963). First edition. One of 200 signed. Boxed. $100.

HOOVER, Herbert C. *A Remedy for Disappearing Game Fish.* Woodcuts. Marbled boards and cloth. New York, 1930. First edition. One of 990 signed. Boxed. $50-$75.

HOOVER, Herbert C., and Hoover, Lou Henry (translators). *De Re Metallica.* From the Latin of Georgius Agricola. Illustrated. Parchment boards. London, 1912. First English edition. $200-$250. Signed by Hoover, $350.

HOPE, Anthony. *The Dolly Dialogues.* 4 plates by Arthur Rackham. Cloth. London, 1894. (By A. H. Hawkins.) First edition, first issue, with "Dolly" as running headband on left-hand pages. $75 $100. (Also issued in wrappers.)

HOPE, Anthony. *The Prisoner of Zenda.* Dark-red cloth. London, no date (1894). (By A. H. Hawkins.) First edition, first issue, with list of 17 (not 18) titles on page 311. $35-$50.

HOPKINS, Gerard Manley. *Poems.* Edited by Robert Bridges. 2 portraits, 2 double-page facsimiles. Gray boards and linen. London, 1918. First edition. In dust jacket. $175-$240.

HOPKINS, Gerard T. *A Mission to the Indians, from the Indian Committee of Baltimore Yearly Meeting, to Fort Wayne in 1804.* Edited by Martha E. Tyson. 198 pp., wrappers. Philadelphia, 1862. First edition. $100-$150.

HOPKINS, Harry C. *History of San Diego: Its Pueblo Lands and Water.* Cloth. San Diego, no date (1929). $30-$35.

HOPKINS, T. M. *Reminiscences of Col. John Ketcham, of Monroe County, Indiana, by His Pastor, Rev. T. M. Hopkins.* 22 pp., printed wrappers. Bloomington, Ind., 1866. First edition. $250-$300. Inner margins foxed, $200.

HOPKINS, Timothy. *The Kelloggs in the Old World and the New.* 3 vols., cloth. San Francisco, 1903. $75.

HOPWOOD, Avery. See Rinehart, Mary Roberts.

HORN, Hosea B. *Horn's Overland Guide.* Folding map. Cloth. New York, 1852. First edition, first issue, 78 pp. $350-$450. Second issue, same date, 83 pp. $250-$300. New York, no date (1853). Map (different from that in original edition). Cloth. $185.

HORN, Stanley F. *Invisible Empire.* Illustrated. Cloth. Boston, 1948. First edition. In dust jacket. $35-$50.

HORN, Tom. *Life of Tom Horn, Government Scout and Interpreter.* 13 illustrations. Cloth. Denver, no date (1904). First edition. $40-$60. Another issue: Printed wrappers ("less scarce," says Ramon F. Adams). $25-$30.

HORNEM, Horace, Esq. *Waltz: An Apostrophic Hymn.* 27 pp., wrappers. London, 1813. (By George Gordon Noel, Lord Byron.) First edition. $5,000 and up. Rebound in full morocco, $4,000. Also, unbound, uncut, some repairs to margins and corners, $3,920 (A, 1965)–the Louis H. Silver copy; rebound in half calf, $1,176 (A, 1960).

HORSE-SHOE Robinson. 2 vols., purple cloth, paper labels on spines. Philadelphia, 1835. (By John Pendleton Kennedy.) First edition. $200-$250.

HORT, Lieut. Col. *The Horse Guards.* 12 colored lithographs. Boards. London, 1850. (By John Josiah Hort.) $75.

HORT, Lieut. Col. *Penelope Wedgebone: The Supposed Heiress.* 8 colored etchings by Alfred Ashley. Calf. London, no date (about 1850). (By John Josiah Hort.) $35-$50.

HOSACK, David. *Essays on Various Subjects of Medical Science.* 3 vols., half leather. New York, 1824-30. First edition. $125. Another set, $60.

HOSHOUR, Samuel Klinefelter. See Altisonant, Lorenzo.

HOSMER, Hezekiah L. *Early History of the Maumee Valley.* 70 pp., printed wrappers. Toledo, Ohio, 1858. First edition. $250-$300.

HOSMER, Hezekiah L. *Montana: An Address . . . Before the Travellers' Club, New York City, January, 1866.* (Cover title.) 23 pp., printed wrappers. New York, 1866. First edition. $200.

HOSMER, Hezekiah L. *Report of the Committee on Foreign Correspondence of the Grand Lodge of Montana, at Its Seventh Annual Communication.* 55 pp., wrappers. Helena, Mont., 1872. $75-$100.

HOSMER, John Allen. *A Trip to the States, by the Way of the Yellowstone and Missouri.* Cloth, or tan printed boards. Virginia City, Mont., 1867. First edition. $1,000 and up. Also, last leaf torn away, $800 (A, 1968)–the Streeter copy, in cloth. (Note: The Graff copy at the Newberry Library is in boards.)

HOUDINI, Harry. *The Right Way to Do Wrong: An Exposé of Successful Criminals.* Wrappers. Boston, 1906. (By Ehrich Weiss.) First edition. $35. Author's first book.

HOUGH, Emerson. See *Getting a Wrong Start.*

HOUGH, Emerson. *The Covered Wagon.* Frontispiece. Cloth. New York, 1922. First edition, first issue, with "(1)" below last line of text. In dust jacket. $35-$50.

HOUGH, Emerson. *The Mississippi Bubble.* Cloth. Indianapolis, no date (1902). First edition, first issue, with "April" on copyright page and "Hough" on spine (not "Emerson Hough"). $25-$35.

HOUGH, Emerson. *The Singing Mouse Stories.* Cloth. New York, 1895. First edition. $40-$50. Author's first book.

HOUGH, Emerson. *The Story of the Cowboy.* Illustrated. Decorated cloth. New York, 1897. First edition. $25-$35.

HOUGH, Emerson. *The Story of the Outlaw.* Illustrated. Boards. New York, 1907. First edition, first state, with printer's rule at top of page v. $25-$35.

HOUGH, Franklin B. *History of Duryea's Brigade.* Cloth. Albany, N.Y., 1864. First edition. One of 300. $25.

HOUGH, Franklin B. *History of Jefferson County, New York.* Half leather. Albany, 1854. First edition. $50-$75.

HOUGH, Franklin B. *History of St. Lawrence and Franklin Counties, New York.* Illustrated. Half leather. Albany, 1853. $50-$75.

HOUGH, Franklin B. *Washingtonia.* Plates, folding map. 2 vols., half morocco. Roxbury, Mass., 1865. First edition. One of 91. $75-$100.

HOUGH, Romeyn B. *The American Woods.* Mounted specimens. 2 vols., leather-covered cases, silver clasps. Lowville, N.Y., 1888-91. $200 and up. Lowville, 1893-1910. 300 plates, 12 text pamphlets. In 12 cases. $300 and up.

HOUGHTON, Jacob. *The Mineral Region of Lake Superior.* 2 maps on one folding sheet. Cloth. Buffalo, 1846. First edition. $75-$100.

HOUSE, Homer D. *Wild Flowers of New York.* Illustrated in color. 2 vols., cloth. Albany, 1918. $50-$75. Rebound in half leather, $35. Albany, 1923. 2 vols., cloth. $50.

HOUSMAN, A. E. *Fragment of a Greek Tragedy.* Printed wrappers. Cambridge, England, 1921. First edition. $75-$100.

HOUSMAN, A. E. *Last Poems.* Dark-blue buckram. London, 1922. First edition, first issue, with comma and semicolon missing after "love" and "rain," respectively, on page 52. In dust jacket. $35-$50. Jacket worn, $25.

HOUSMAN, A. E. *More Poems.* Portrait. Morocco and cloth. London, no date (1936). First edition. One of 379. In dust jacket. $25-$35. Another issue: Cloth. First trade edition. In dust jacket. $12.50.

HOUSMAN, A. E. *A Shropshire Lad.* Gray boards, vellum spine, paper label. London, 1896. First edition, first state, with the word "Shropshire" on the label exactly 33 millimeters wide. $400-$600. (Only 500 printed.) New York, 1897. Boards, vellum spine. First American edition. $200-$250. Also, soiled and worn, $70 (A, 1970). (Only 150 copies.) Philadelphia, no date (1902). Henry Altemus, publisher. Cloth. First edition to be printed in America. $50-$75. New York, no date (1935). Heritage Press. Illustrated by Edward A. Wilson. Calf. Boxed. $75.

HOUSMAN, Laurence. *Articles of Faith in the Freedom of Women.* Printed wrappers. London, 1910. First edition. $25.

HOUSMAN, Laurence. *Followers of St. Francis.* Cloth. London, 1923. First edition. In dust jacket. $35-$50.

HOUSMAN, Laurence. *Stories from the Arabian Nights.* Mounted color plates by Edmund Dulac. Cloth. London, no date (1907). $50. Another issue: Vellum with silk ties. One of 350 signed. $125-$150. Lacking ties, $100.

HOUSTON, Sam. *Speech of . . . Exposing the Malfeasance and Corruption of John Charles Watrous, Judge of the Federal Court of Texas, and His Confederates.* Frontispiece. New York, 1860. $75.

HOUSTOUN, Mrs. Matilda C. *Texas and the Gulf of Mexico.* 10 plates. 2 vols., cloth. London, 1844. First edition. $75. Also, $32 (A, 1966). Philadelphia, 1845. Frontispiece of Santa Anna. Cloth. First American edition. $35.

HOVEY, Richard. *Poems.* Printed wrappers, or cloth. Washington, 1880. First edition. Wrappers: $200-$300. Cloth: $100-$150. Author's first book. Inscribed copy offered by dealer for $400 in 1972.

HOW the Buffalo Lost His Crown. Illustrated by Charles M. Russell. 44 pp., oblong, brown cloth. No place, no date (New York, 1894). (By John H. Beacom.) First edition. $600 and up.

HOW to Win in Wall Street. By a Successful Operator. Cloth. New York, 1881. (By Joaquin Miller.) First edition. $25.

HOW, George E. P., and Howe, Jane P. *English and Scottish Silver Spoons.* Photographs. 3 vols., cloth. London, 1952-57. First edition. One of 550. In dust jackets. $400-$500.

HOWARD, B. B. *The Charter and Ordinances of the City of Galena.* Half calf. Galena, Ill., 1853. $45.

HOWARD, Benjamin C. *A Report of the Decisions of the Supreme Court . . . in the Case of Dred Scott vs. John F. A. Sandford.* Wrappers. New York, 1857. $25-$35. (The Dred Scott Decision.)

HOWARD, H. R. See *The Life and Adventures of Joseph T. Hare.*

HOWARD, H. R. (editor). *The History of Virgil A. Stewart, and His Adventures in Capturing and Exposing the "Great Western Land Pirate" (John A. Murrell) and His Gang.* New York, no date (1836). First edition. $100-$150. Howard's first book. New York, 1837. Illustrated. Cloth. $75.

HOWARD, Henry Eliot. *British Warblers.* Illustrated, including maps and colored plates. Half morocco. London, 1907-14. $150. Also, $81.60 (A, 1968). (Also issued in parts in 10, or 11, volumes, bound in boards.)

HOWARD, James Q. *The Life of Abraham Lincoln.* 102 pp., wrappers. Columbus, Ohio, 1860. First edition, first issue, buff paper covers, 8 unnumbered pages of ads. $100-$150.

HOWARD, McHenry. *Recollections of a Maryland Confederate Soldier.* Folding map, 11 plates. Cloth. Baltimore, 1914. First edition. $50-$75.

HOWARD, Oliver Otis. *Account of Gen. Howard's Mission to the Apaches and Navajos.* 12 pp., wrappers. No place, no date. $35-$40.

HOWARD, Oliver Otis. *My Life and Experiences Among Our Hostile Indians.* 2 plates. Cloth. Hartford, no date (1907). First edition. $50-$75.

HOWARD, Oliver Otis. *Nez Perce Joseph.* 2 portraits. Cloth. Boston, 1881. First edition. $35-$50.

HOWARD, William. *Narrative of a Journey to the Summit of Mont Blanc.* Boards. Baltimore, 1821. First edition. $75.

HOWBERT, Irving. *The Indians of the Pike's Peak Region.* 4 plates. Cloth. New York, 1914. First edition. $35.

HOWBERT, Irving. *Memories of a Lifetime in the Pike's Peak Region.* Frontispiece. Cloth. New York, 1925. Enlarged edition of preceding title. $25.

HOWE, E. D. *History of Mormonism.* Frontispiece. Cloth. Painesville, Ohio, 1840. Second edition of *Mormonism Unvailed [sic].* $150-$200.

HOWE, E. D. *Mormonism Unvailed [sic].* Frontispiece. Cloth. Painesville, Ohio, 1834. First edition. $750 and up.

HOWE, E. W. *The Story of a Country Town.* Illustrated by W. L. Wells. Decorated cloth. Atchison, Kan., 1883. First edition, first issue, with "D. Caldwell, Manufacturer. Atchison, Kan." rubber-stamped inside front cover and no lettering at foot of spine. $50-$75. Author's first book.

HOWE, Henry. *Historical Collections of the Great West.* 2 vols. in one, cloth. Cincinnati, 1851. First edition. $35-$50. Cincinnati, 1852. $35. (Also bound in leather and half leather; numerous other later editions.)

HOWE, Henry. *Historical Collections of Ohio.* Map, woodcuts. Cloth. Cincinnati, 1847. First edition. $50. Cincinnati, 1848. $35. Cincinnati, 1875. $25. Columbus, 1889. 3 vols. in 2, cloth. $50. (Also bound in leather and half leather; numerous other editions, all of which range in the $25-$50 bracket.)

HOWE, Henry. *Historical Collections of Virginia.* Map, illustrations, engraved title page. Cloth. Charleston, S.C., 1845. First edition. $50-$75. (Also bound in leather and half leather; numerous other later editions, ranging at retail from about $25 to $50.)

HOWE, John. *Howe's Almanac for the Year of Our Lord, 1804.* Wrappers. Greenwich, Mass., no date (1803). $100.

HOWE, John. *A Journal Kept by Mr. John Howe, While He Was Employed as a British Spy, During the Revolutionary War.* 44 pp., wrappers. Concord, N.H., 1827. First edition. $200.

HOWE, Mark A. De Wolfe. *Rari Nantes: Being Verses and a Song.* Wrappers. Boston, 1893. First edition. One of 80. $50. Author's first book.

HOWE, Octavius T. *The Argonauts of '49.* Illustrated. Half cloth. Cambridge, Mass., 1923. First edition. In dust jacket. $35-$50.

HOWE, Octavius T., and Mathews, Frederick C. *American Clipper Ships, 1833-58.* 114 plates. 2 vols.: Vol. 1, marbled boards; Vol. 2, cloth. Salem, 1926-27. First edition. $100-$150.

HOWELL, William C. *Recollections of Life in Ohio.* Cloth. Cincinnati, 1895. First edition. $25.

HOWELLS, William Dean. See *Poems of Two Friends.*

HOWELLS, William Dean. *A Boy's Town.* Frontispiece and 22 plates. Cloth. New York, 1890. First edition, first state, without illustration on page 44. $40-$60.

HOWELLS, William Dean. *A Chance Acquaintance.* Cloth. Boston, 1873. First edition. $25.

HOWELLS, William Dean. *A Little Girl Among the Old Masters.* 54 plates. Oblong, cloth. Boston, 1884. First edition. $35.

HOWELLS, William Dean. *My Mark Twain.* Illustrated. Sage-colored cloth. New York, 1910. First edition. $25-$50.

HOWELLS, William Dean. *Niagara Revisited.* Colored illustrations, colored title page. 12 pp., decorated buff boards. Chicago, no date (about 1884). First edition, with or without 16 pages of ads at end. $150.

HOWELLS, William Dean. *Poems.* Cloth. Boston, 1873. First edition. $100.

HOWELLS, William Dean. *The Rise of Silas Lapham.* Blue or brown cloth. Boston, 1885. First edition, first issue, with "Mr. Howells' Latest Works" in boxed ad facing title page and with unbroken type in the word "sojourner" at bottom of page 176. $125-$150. New York, 1961. Limited Editions Club. Illustrated. Buckram. Boxed. $25-$35.

HOWELLS, William Dean. *Suburban Sketches.* Illustrated by A. Hoppin. Decorated brown cloth. Boston, 1872. New and enlarged edition. $25-$35.

HOWELLS, William Dean, and Hayes, J. L. *Lives and Speeches of Abraham Lincoln and Hannibal Hamlin.* 96 pp., printed buff wrappers. Columbus, Ohio, 1860. First edition, first issue, with pages 95-96 blank. $1,000 and up (?). Excessively rare: Blanck locates one copy, rebound. Second issue, engraving of Republican Wigwam, Chicago, on page 96. Howes locates two copies; Blanck reports two imperfect ones. Another issue: Wigwam on page 95. Howes locates five. Second edition, same date. 2 portraits. 74 pp., cloth. First issue, without period after "0" in imprint. $75-$100. Later issues, same date, with period. $25-$35.

HOWELLS, William Dean; Twain, Mark; and others. *The Niagara Book.* Cloth, or printed wrappers. Buffalo, 1893. First edition, first printing, with no ads at end, page 226 blank, and copyright notice in 3 lines. $150.

HOWES, Wright (compiler). *U.S.-iana.* Blue buckram. New York, 1954. First edition. $50-$75. New York, 1962. Buckram. Second edition. $50-$75.

HOWISON, John. *Sketches of Upper Canada.* Calf. Edinburgh, 1821. First edition. $150. Edinburgh, 1822. Second edition. $100-$125. Edinburgh, 1825. Third edition. $75-$100.

HOWITT, Samuel. *The British Sportsman.* Plates. Morocco and boards. London, 1812. First edition. $350-$450.

HOWITT, Samuel. *Foreign Field Sports.* Plates. Morocco. London, 1819. $300-$400. London, no date (1823). Plates. Folio, morocco. Large paper edition. $500-$600.

HOWLAND, S. A. *Steamboat Disasters and Railroad Accidents in the United States.* Illustrated. Sheep. Worcester, Mass., 1840. First edition. $35-$50.

HOWLEY, James P. *The Beothucks or Red Indians of Newfoundland.* Plates. Half leather. Cambridge, Mass., 1915. First edition. $150.

HRDLICKA, Ales. *The Anthropology of Florida.* Cloth. DeLand, Fla., 1922. First edition. $50-$60. Another, spine spotted, $35.

HUBBARD, Elbert. *A Message to Garcia.* Suede. East Aurora, N.Y., 1899. First edition. One of 1,000. $25. (Note: The limitation is listed variously as 1,000, 925, 928, which indicates special issues not traced in my researches.)

HUBBARD, Gurdon Saltonstall. *Incidents in the Life of Gurdon Saltonstall Hubbard.* Edited by Henry E. Hamilton. Frontispiece. Cloth. No place (Chicago), 1888. First edition. $100-$150.

HUBBARD, Jeremiah. *40 Years Among the Indians.* Cloth. Miami, Okla., 1913. First edition. $50-$60.

HUBBARD, John Niles. *Sketches of Border Adventures, in the Life and Times of Maj. Moses Van Campen.* Leather. Bath, N.Y., 1841. $150-$250. Bath, 1842. Half leather. $35-$50.

HUBBARD, Robert. *Historical Sketches of Roswell Franklin and Family.* Half leather. Dansville, N.Y., 1839. First edition. $325.

HUDSON, Charles. *History of the Town of Marlborough.* Cloth. Boston, 1862. First edition. $25-$30.

HUDSON, Derek. *Arthur Rackham: His Life and Work.* Color plates. Cloth. London, 1960. First edition. In dust jacket. $85-$100. New York, no date (1960). First American edition. In dust jacket. $60-$80.

HUDSON River Portfolio. See Wall, W. G.

HUDSON, W. H. See Harford, Henry; Sclater, P. L., and Hudson, W. H. Also see *A Crystal Age.*

HUDSON, W. H. *Birds in a Village.* Chocolate-colored buckram. London, 1893. First edition. $75-$100.

HUDSON, W. H. *El Ombu.* Light-green cloth. London, 1902. First edition. $40-$50.

HUDSON, W. H. *Far Away and Long Ago.* Dark-green cloth. London, 1918. First edition. In dust jacket. $35. London, 1931. Vellum. One of 110. $40-$50. New York, 1943. Limited Editions Club. Illustrated. Half leather. Boxed. $35-$50.

HUDSON, W. H. *Green Mansions.* Light-green cloth. London, 1904. First edition, first issue, without publisher's design on back cover. $150-$250. Second issue. $75-$100. London, 1926. Illustrated. One of 165. $25-$35. New York, 1935. Limited Editions Club. Illustrated. Boards. Boxed. $35-$50.

HUDSON, W. H. *Idle Days in Patagonia*. Illustrated. Crimson buckram. London, 1893. First edition, with 2 ad leaves at end and "Chapman & Hall" on cover. One of 1,750. $35-$50.

HUDSON, W. H. *A Little Boy Lost*. Illustrated. Dull yellow buckram. London, 1905. First edition. $25-$35.

HUDSON, W. H. *Lost British Birds*. Illustrated. 32 pp., light-green wrappers. No place, no date (London, 1894). First edition. $25. (Note: Reprints are dated 1894 on the cover.)

HUDSON, W. H. *The Naturalist in La Plata*. Illustrated. Dark-green cloth. London, 1892. First edition, with ads dated April, 1892, at end. $35-$50.

HUDSON, W. H. *The Purple Land That England Lost*. 2 vols., light-blue cloth. London, 1885. First edition, first issue, with October ads in second volume. $400-$500. Author's first book.

HUEFFER, Ford Madox. See Conrad, Joseph, and Hueffer, Ford Madox. Also see Ford, Ford Madox (for books published after 1919, when he changed his name).

HUEFFER, Ford Madox. *Between St. Dennis and St. George*. Cloth. London, 1915. (By Ford Madox Ford.) First edition. $40-$50.

HUEFFER, Ford Madox. *The Fifth Queen*. Cloth. London, 1906. (By Ford Madox Ford.) First edition. $35-$40.

HUEFFER, Ford Madox. *On Heaven*. Cloth. London, 1918. (By Ford Madox Ford.) First edition. $45-$50.

HUEFFER, Ford Madox. *The Queen Who Flew*. Illustrated. Vellum. London, 1894. (By Ford Madox Ford.) First edition. One of 25 signed. $200-$300. Trade issue: Decorated cloth. $50.

HUGHES, John T. *California: Its History, Population, Climate, Soil, Productions, and Harbors*. 105 pp., printed wrappers. Cincinnati, 1848. First edition. $200-$250.

HUGHES, John T. *Doniphan's Expedition, Containing an Account of the Conquest of New Mexico*. Frontispiece. 144 pp., printed wrappers (covers undated). Cincinnati, 1847. First edition, first issue, lacking words "cheap edition" on the covers. $1,300 (A, 1966)—the Streeter copy. (Note: Previously this book brought $200-$500 at retail, and this appears to be a realistic value range.) Cincinnati, 1848. Wrappers. Second edition. $100-$150. Cincinnati, 1848. Cloth. Third edition. With map. $75 $100. Cincinnati, no date. Fourth edition. $75-$100. Topeka, 1907. $25.

HUGHES, Langston. The *Weary Blues*. Boards. New York, 1926. First edition. In dust jacket. $50-$60. Author's first book.

HUGHES, Richard. *Gipsy-Night and Other Poems*. Portrait. Boards. No place (Waltham Saint Lawrence, England), 1922. Golden Cockerel Press. First edition. One of 750. $25-$35. Chicago, 1922. Portrait. Boards and cloth. One of 63 signed. $15-$20.

HUGHES, Richard. *A High Wind in Jamaica*. Boards and cloth. London, 1929. First complete English edition. One of 150. $50-$75. Trade edition: Green cloth. In dust jacket. $25. (Note: The first edition was published in New York as *The Innocent Voyage*. The actual first English appearance of this title was as a complete number of the periodical *Life and Letters,* August, 1929. Retail value around $10-$12.)

HUGHES, Richard. *The Innocent Voyage*. Decorated blue boards and blue linen. New York, 1929. First edition. In dust jacket. $25. New York, 1945. Limited Editions Club. Leather. Boxed. $25. (Published in England as *A High Wind in Jamaica*.)

HUGHES, Richard. *The Spider's Palace*. Illustrated. Boards and cloth. London, 1931. One of 110 signed. In dust jacket. $50-$60.

HUGHES, Richard B. *Pioneer Years in the Black Hills*. Edited by Agnes Wright Spring. Illustrated. Cloth. Glendale, Calif., 1957. First edition. $35-$50.

HUGHES, Ted. *The Burning of the Brothel.* Woodcuts in color. Printed wrappers. No place, no date (London, 1966). Turret Books. First edition. One of 300. $35-$45. One of 75 (of the edition of 300) signed by Hughes. $50.

HUGHES, Ted. *The Hawk in the Rain.* Cloth. London, no date (1957). First edition. In dust jacket. $15-$20. New York, no date (1957). In dust jacket. $15-$20.

HUGHES, Ted. *Pike.* Folio, broadside. Northampton, Mass., 1959. Gehenna Press. $35.

HUGHES, Ted. *Recklings.* Cloth. London, no date (1967). Turret Books. One of 150 signed. $100-$125.

HUGHES, Thomas. See *Tom Brown at Oxford; Tom Brown's School Days.*

HULME, F. Edward. *Suggestions in Floral Design.* 52 colored plates. Folio, cloth. London, no date (about 1880). $35-$50.

HULTON, Paul, and Quinn, David Beers. *The American Drawings of John White, 1577-1590.* Frontispiece, 160 plates, 76 in color. 2 vols., folio, red buckram. London, 1964. First edition. $375.

HUMANITAS (pseudonym). *Hints for the Consideration of the Friends of Slavery.* 32 pp., half leather. Lexington, Ky., 1805. First edition. $1,200 (A, 1967).

HUMFREVILLE, J. Lee. *Twenty Years Among Our Savage Indians.* 250 engravings. Cloth. Hartford, 1897. First edition. $40-$50.

HUMOURIST (The). 40 colored etchings, including vignette title pages by George Cruikshank. 4 vols., pink boards. London, 1819-20. (By George Cruikshank.) First edition, first issue, without "Vol. 1" on title page and with all plates dated 1819. $250-$350. Also, rebound in morocco, $204 (A, 1969).

HUMPHREYS, Arthur L. *Old Decorative Maps.* Illustrated. Buckram. London, 1926. Limited edition. $75-$100. Another issue: Half vellum. De luxe edition. One of 100 with separate mounted plates. $250-$300.

HUMPHREYS, Henry Noel. *The Illuminated Books of the Middle Ages.* Illustrated. Folio, half calf. London, 1849. First edition. $200-$300.

HUMPHRIES, Sydney. *Oriental Carpets, Runners and Rugs.* Illustrated. Folio, cloth. London, 1910. $35-$50.

HUNEKER, James. *Painted Veils.* Blue boards, vellum spine. New York, no date (1920). First edition, on watermarked paper. One of 1,200 signed. $40-$50.

HULANISKI, F. J. (editor). *History of Contra Costa County, California.* Illustrated. Half morocco. Berkeley, Calif., 1917. First edition. $75-$100.

HUNT, J. *An Adventure on a Frozen Lake: A Tale of the Canadian Rebellion of 1837-8.* 46 pp., wrappers. Cincinnati, 1853. $75.

HUNT, James H. *A History of the Mormon War.* Cloth. St. Louis, 1844. First edition. $150-$200.

HUNT, James H. *Mormonism: Embracing the Origin, Rise and Progress of the Sect.* Cloth. St. Louis, 1844. Expanded edition of the foregoing title. With errata leaf. $125-$150. Lacking the leaf, $75-$100.

HUNT, John. *Gazetteer of the Border and Southern States.* Folding map in color. Cloth. Pittsburgh, 1863. First edition. $75-$100.

HUNT, George M. *Early Days Upon the Plains of Texas.* Portrait. Cloth. Lubbock, Tex., no date (1919). $75-$100.

HUNT, George W. *A History of the Hunt Family*. Cloth. Boston, 1890. First edition. $40-$50.

HUNT, Leigh. See *The Feast of the Poets; Sir Ralph Esher*.

HUNT, Leigh. *The Autobiography of Leigh Hunt*. Portraits. 3 vols., cloth. London, 1850. First edition. $204. Westminster (London), 1903. 2 vols., blue buckram. Revised edition. $25.

HUNT, Leigh. *The Correspondence of Leigh Hunt*. Edited by His Eldest Son. Portrait. 2 vols., tan cloth. London, 1862. First edition. $125-$135.

HUNT, Leigh. *Captain Sword and Captain Pen: A Poem*. Illustrated. Cloth. London, 1835. First edition. $50.

HUNT, Leigh. *The Descent of Liberty: A Mask*. Boards. London, 1815. First edition. $100-$150.

HUNT, Leigh. *Foliage; or Poems Original and Translated*. Blue boards, label. London, 1818. First edition. $50.

HUNT, Leigh. *Imagination and Fancy*. Cloth. London, 1844. First edition. $50-$60.

HUNT, Leigh. *A Jar of Honey from Mount Hybla*. Engraved title page. Illustrated. Glazed boards. London, 1848. First edition. $35-$50.

HUNT, Leigh. *Juvenilia*. Engraved frontispiece. Boards. London, 1801. First edition. $150.

HUNT, Leigh. *Lord Byron and Some of His Contemporaries*. Illustrated. Boards and cloth. London, 1828. First edition. $100-$150.

HUNT, Leigh. *Men, Women and Books*. Portrait, 2 vols. Cloth. London, 1847. First edition. $50.

HUNT, Leigh. *The Poetical Works of Leigh Hunt*. Pink boards, printed label. London, 1832. First edition. $50-$75.

HUNT, Leigh. *Stories from the Italian Poets*. 2 vols., dark-blue cloth. London, 1846. First edition. $60.

HUNT, Leigh. *The Story of Rimini: A Poem*. Boards, white paper back label. London, 1816. First edition, with half title. $75-$100.

HUNT, Leigh. *The Town: Its Memorable Characters and Events*. 2 vols., orange cloth. London, 1848. First edition, with ads at end dated January. $50-$60.

HUNT, Leigh. *Ultra-Crepidarius: A Satire on William Gifford*. Wrappers. London, 1823. First edition. $250-$350. Rebound in morocco, $115.20 (A, 1968).

HUNT, Richard S., and Randel, Jesse F. *Guide to the Republic of Texas*. Folding map. 63 pp., cloth. New York, 1839. First edition. $350 and up.

HUNT, Richard S., and Randel, Jesse F. *A New Guide to Texas*. Folding map. 62 pp., cloth. New York, 1845. Second edition of preceding title. $250 and up.

HUNT, Rev. T. Dwight. *Address Delivered Before the New England Society of San Francisco, at the American Theatre*. 20 pp., sewed. San Francisco, 1853. $45.

HUNTER, Alexander. *Johnny Reb and Billy Yank*. Illustrated. Cloth. New York, 1905. First edition. $35-$50.

HUNTER, Dard. *Chinese Ceremonial Paper*. Photographs and paper specimens. Boards and morocco. Chillicothe, Ohio, 1937. First edition. One of 125 signed. Boxed. $1,000 and up.

HUNTER, Dard. *The Literature of Papermaking, 1390-1800.* Illustrated. Folio, folding sheets in half buckram folder. No place, no date (Chillicothe, 1925). One of 190 signed. $500 and up.

HUNTER, Dard. *Massachusetts Institute of Technology: Dard Hunter Paper Museum.* Frontispiece photograph. Printed wrappers with woodcut on front. No place, no date (Cambridge, Mass., 1939). $250.

HUNTER, Dard. *Old Papermaking in China and Japan.* 31 paper specimens, 11 wood engravings in color, other illustrations and photographs. Folio, linen portfolio. Chillicothe, 1932. One of 200 signed. $750.

HUNTER, Dard. *Papermaking by Hand in America.* Frontispiece in color, facsimiles tipped in. Boards and linen. No place, no date (Chillicothe, 1950). Mountain House Press. First edition. One of 210 signed. $2,500 and up.

HUNTER, Dard. *Papermaking by Hand in India.* 27 paper specimens, 85 photographs. India print cloth and calf. New York, 1939. One of 370 signed. In slipcase. $350-$400.

HUNTER, Dard. *Paper-Making in the Classroom.* 46 plates. Cloth. Peoria, Ill., no date (1931). $75-$150.

HUNTER, Dard. *Papermaking in Indo-China.* Reproductions. Decorated boards and morocco. No place (Chillicothe), 1947. Mountain House Press. One of 182 on handmade paper. $500 and up.

HUNTER, Dard. *A Papermaking Pilgrimage to Japan.* Photographs. Boards and morocco. New York, 1936. First edition. One of 370. $500 and up.

HUNTER, Dard. *Papermaking Through Eighteen Centuries.* Illustrated. Buckram. New York, 1930. First edition. In dust jacket. $100.

HUNTER, Dard. *Primitive Papermaking.* Illustrated. Folding sheets in buckram portfolio, with ties. Chillicothe, 1937. First edition. One of 200. $1,000 and up.

HUNTER, Dard, and others. *Five on Paper.* Illustrated, Morocco. North Hills, Pa., 1963. Bird & Bull Press. One of 169. $150-$200.

HUNTER, Dard, Jr. *A Specimen of Type.* Specimens and illustrations. 12 pp., folio, gray-blue wrappers, paper label. Cambridge, Mass., 1940. One of 100 signed. $100-$150.

HUNTER, George. *Reminiscences of an Old Timer.* 16 plates. Pictorial cloth. San Francisco, 1887. First edition. $80-$100. Battle Creek, Mich., 1888. Cloth. Third edition. $50.

HUNTER, George Leland. *Decorative Textiles.* Illustrated, including 17 color plates. Buckram. Philadelphia, 1918. First edition. $50-$75.

HUNTER, J. Marvin (compiler). *The Trail Drivers of Texas.* Illustrated. 2 vols., pictorial cloth. No place, no date (San Antonio, 1920-23). First edition. $125-$150. Also, $75 and $70 (A, 1968). Nashville, 1925. 2 vols. in one, cloth. In dust jacket. $50-$75. New York, 1963. 2 vols., half morocco. Boxed. $50-$75.

HUNTER, J. Marvin, and Rose, Noah H. *The Album of Gun-Fighters.* Illustrated. Pictorial cloth. No place, no date (Bandera, Tex., 1951). First edition. In dust jacket. $35.

HUNTER, John D. *Manners and Customs of Several Indian Tribes Located West of the Mississippi.* Plain boards, paper label. Philadelphia, 1823. First edition. $175-$200.

HUNTER, John D. *Memoirs of a Captivity Among Indians of North America.* Portrait. Boards. London, 1823. First English edition of *Manners and Customs* (see preceding entry). $175-$200. London, 1824. Boards. Third edition. $75-$100.

HUNTER, William S., Jr. *Hunter's Ottawa Scenery.* 14 plates. Folio, cloth. Ottawa, 1855. First edition. $250-$350.

HUNTER, William S., Jr. *Hunter's Panoramic Guide from Niagara Falls to Quebec.* Engraved title, folding panoramic chart. Pictorial cloth. Boston, 1857. $50-$100. Montreal, 1860. $40-$50.

HUNTERS of Kentucky (The). 100 pp., wrappers. New York, 1847. (By Benjamin Bilson.) First edition. $150-$200. (Piracy of James O. Pattie's *Personal Narrative.*)

HUNTINGTON, D. B. *Vocabulary of the Utah and Sho-Sho-Ne, or Snake Dialects, with Indian Legends and Traditions.* 32 pp., stitched. Salt Lake City, 1872. $125.

HURST, Samuel H. *Journal-History of the 73d Ohio Volunteer Infantry.* Cloth. Chillicothe, Ohio, 1866. First edition. $35. Cover faded, $25.

HUTCHINGS, James M. *Scenes of Wonder and Curiosity in California.* Illustrated. Decorated cloth. San Francisco, no date (1860). First edition. $50. Also, $25 (A, 1965). London, 1865. First English edition. $25.

HUTCHINS, Thomas. *A Topographical Description of Virginia, Pennsylvania, Maryland and North Carolina.* Folding map, 2 plans, 2 facsimiles. Cloth. Cleveland, 1904. One of 20 on handmade paper. $40-$60. One of 240 others. $25-$35.

HUTTON, Joseph. *The Wounded Hussar.* Unbound. New York, 1809. First edition. $45.

HUTTON, Laurence. *Plays and Players.* Cloth. New York, 1875. First edition. $25. Another issue: Unbound sheets in cloth case, as issued. One of 25. $50. Author's first book.

HUXLEY, Aldous. *Antic Hay.* Yellow cloth, yellow stained top. London, 1923. First edition. In dust jacket. $25.

HUXLEY, Aldous. *Apennine.* Boards and cloth, paper label. Gaylordsville, N.Y., 1930. First edition. One of 91 signed. In slipcase. $150.

HUXLEY, Aldous. *Arabia Infelix and Other Poems.* Boards and cloth. New York, 1929. Fountain Press. First edition. One of 692 signed. $125-$150.

HUXLEY, Aldous. *Beyond the Mexique Bay.* Illustrated. Boards and cloth. London, 1934. First edition. One of 210 signed. $75-$125. Also, $67.20 (A, 1969). Trade edition: Orange cloth. In dust jacket. $15.

HUXLEY, Aldous. *Brave New World.* Buckram, leather label. London, 1932. First edition. One of 324 signed. $125. Trade edition: Blue cloth. In dust jacket. $45-$50.

HUXLEY, Aldous. *Brief Candles.* Black cloth. New York, 1930. Fountain Press. First American edition. One of 842 signed. $75-$100. Trade edition: Cloth. In dust jacket. $25. London, 1930. Red cloth. First edition. In dust jacket. $35.

HUXLEY, Aldous. *The Burning Wheel.* Woodcut decorations. Yellow wrappers. Oxford, 1916. First edition. $300-$350. Also, $228 (A, 1970); copy with raised lettering "For Review," $150 (A, 1968). Author's first book.

HUXLEY, Aldous. *The Cicadas and Other Poems.* Boards and cloth. London, 1931. One of 160 signed. In dust jacket. $60-$80. Lacking jacket, with bookplate, $47.50. Trade edition: Brown cloth. In dust jacket. $35.

HUXLEY, Aldous. *Crome Yellow.* Yellow cloth, top stained green. London, 1921. First edition. In dust jacket. $35-$50.

HUXLEY, Aldous. *The Defeat of Youth and Other Poems.* Without title page. Decorated stiff wrappers. No place, no date (except in colophon) (Oxford, 1918). First edition. One of 500. $100-$125.

HUXLEY, Aldous. *Do What You Will.* Half cloth. London, 1929. First edition. One of 260 signed. $60-$80.

HUXLEY, Aldous. *Ends and Means.* Half cloth. London, 1937. First edition. One of 160 signed. $75-$100.

HUXLEY, Aldous. *Essays New and Old.* Boards and buckram. London, 1926. Florence Press. First edition. One of 650 signed. In dust jacket. $75-$100.

HUXLEY, Aldous. *Eyeless in Gaza.* Decorated boards and brown buckram. London, 1936. One of 200 signed. $100-$125. Trade edition: Tan cloth. In dust jacket. $35.

HUXLEY, Aldous. *Holy Face and Other Essays.* Colored illustrations. Buckram. London, 1929. First edition. One of 300. $75-$100.

HUXLEY, Aldous. *Jonah: Christmas, 1917.* Wrappers. Oxford, 1917. Holywell Press. First edition. One of about 50 for presentation, inscribed. $300-$400.

HUXLEY, Aldous. *Leda.* Half cloth. London, 1920. First edition. One of 160 signed. $100-$150. Trade edition: Red cloth, with top stained red. In dust jacket. $30-$50. Garden City, 1929. Cloth. One of 364 signed. Boxed. $75-$100.

HUXLEY, Aldous. *Little Mexican and Other Stories.* Red cloth, top stained red. London, 1924. First edition. In dust jacket. $25.

HUXLEY, Aldous. *Mortal Coils.* Blue cloth, top stained blue. London, 1922. First edition. In dust jacket. $25-$35.

HUXLEY, Aldous. *Music at Night and Other Essays.* Boards and buckram. New York, 1931. Fountain Press. First edition. One of 842 signed. $60-$80.

HUXLEY, Aldous. *The Olive Tree and Other Essays.* Green buckram. London, 1936. First edition. One of 160 signed. $100-$150.

HUXLEY, Aldous. *On the Margin.* Blue-green cloth, top stained blue. London, 1923. First edition, with page vi numbered v in error. In dust jacket. $35-$50.

HUXLEY, Aldous. *Point Counter Point.* Green buckram. London, 1928. First edition. One of 256 signed. $150-$200. Trade edition: Orange cloth. In dust jacket. $50-$75. Also, inscribed, $120 (A, 1970).

HUXLEY, Aldous. *Prisons.* Piranesi plates. Wrappers and cloth-backed board folder. No place (Paris), 1949. Trianon Press. One of 212 signed. $180-$200.

HUXLEY, Aldous. *Proper Studies.* Boards and cloth. London, 1927. First edition. One of 250 signed. $60-$80.

HUXLEY, Aldous. *Selected Poems.* Decorated boards. Oxford, 1925. First edition. $60-$80.

HUXLEY, Aldous. *Texts and Pretexts.* Decorated boards and buckram. London, 1932. First edition. One of 214 signed. $100-125.

HUXLEY, Aldous. *Vulgarity in Literature.* Boards and buckram. London, 1930. First edition. One of 260 signed. $60-$80. Trade edition: Decorated boards. $15-$25.

HUXLEY, Aldous. *Wheels.* Decorated boards and cloth. Oxford, 1917. First edition. $50-$75.

HUXLEY, Aldous. *The World of Light.* Boards and buckram. London, 1931. First edition. One of 160 signed. $100-$125.

HUXLEY, Aldous (editor). *An Encyclopedia of Pacifism.* Wrappers. London, no date (1937). First edition. $35-$50.

HUXLEY, T. H. *Evidence as to Man's Place in Nature.* Illustrated. Cloth. London, 1868. First edition. $75-$125.

HYDE, Douglas (translator). *The Love Songs of Connacht.* Boards and linen. Dundrum, Ireland, 1904. Dun Emer Press. One of 300. $80-$85.

HYDE, George E. *The Early Blackfeet and Their Neighbors.* 45 pp., wrappers. Denver, 1933. One of 75. $50.

HYDE, George E. *The Pawnee Indians.* 2 vols., printed wrappers. Denver, 1934. One of 100. $50.

HYDE, George E. *Red Cloud's Folk.* Cloth. Norman, Okla., 1937. First edition. $50-$60.

HYDE, George E. *Rangers and Regulars.* 47 pp., wrappers. Denver, 1933. $50.

HYDE, S. C. *Historical Sketch of Lyon County, Iowa.* Map. 40 pp., wrappers. Le Mars, Iowa, 1872. $40.

HYMNS and Prayers for Use at the Marriage of Michael Hornby and Nicolette Ward at St. Margaret's Church. 16 pp., blue wrappers. Westminster (London), 1928. Ashendene Press. $35-$50.

HYMNS for Infant Minds. Wrappers. Boston, 1814. (By Ann and Jane Taylor.) $35.

HYNE, C. J. Cutcliffe. *Honour of Thieves: A Novel.* Uncut. London, 1895. First edition. $35.

I

IBN KHALLIKAN. *Biographical Dictionary.* Translated from the Arabic by Baron Mac Guckin de Slane. 4 vols., cloth. New York, 1961. $150-$200.

IBSEN, Henrik. *Peer Gynt: A Dramatic Poem.* Illustrated in color by Arthur Rackham. Full white vellum. London, no date (1936). One of 460 signed by Rackham. Boxed. $200-$250. New York, 1955. Limited Editions Club. Illustrated. Pictorial boards. Boxed. $25-$35.

IDAHO: A Guide in Word and Picture. Illustrated. Pictorial cloth. Caldwell, 1937. First edition. In dust jacket. $50-$75. (Note: Edited by Vardis Fisher.)

IDE, Simeon. *The Conquest of California: A Biography of William B. Ide.* Illustrations, map. Boards and cloth. Oakland, Calif., 1944. Grabhorn Press. One of 500. $35-$50.

IDE, William Brown. *A Biographical Sketch of the Life of William B. Ide . . . And . . . Account of the Virtual Conquest of California, etc.* Half leather and cloth. No place, no date (Claremont, N.H., 1880). (By Simeon Ide.) First edition. One of 80. $250-$350. Another edition: Printed wrappers. No place, no date (Claremont, 1885 [?]). $200 and up.

IDE, William Brown. *Who Conquered California?* Printed boards and cloth. Claremont, N.H., no date (1880? 1885?). (By Simeon Ide.) First edition. $250 and up.

IDEAL Husband (An). By the Author of *Lady Windermere's Fan.* Lavender cloth. London, 1899. (By Oscar Wilde.) First edition. Large paper issue: One of 100. $300-$350. Signed issue: Vellum. One of 12 on vellum. $400-$500. Trade issue: Light brown-red linen. $50-$60.

IDLE Man (The). 6 parts, wrappers. New York, 1821-22. (Edited by Richard Henry Dana, Sr.) $50-$75. (Note: Contains new poems by William Cullen Bryant.)

IDLENESS and Industry Exemplified, in the History of James Preston and Ivy Lawrence. Boards and calf. Philadelphia, 1803. (By Maria Edgeworth.) First American edition. $100.

I KUNSTITUSHUN i Micha i nan vlhpisa Chickasha, Okla i nan apesa yvt apesa tokmak oke. ("Chickasaw People, Their Constitution and Their Law 1857-59. 1867-68. 1870-72.") Translated from English to Chickasaw by Allen Wright. Cloth. Chickasha, Okla., 1872. First edition. $100-$200.

ILLINOIS Central Railroad Company (The), Offers Over 2,000,000 Acres, etc. 64 pp., sewed. New York, 1856. (By John Wilson.) First edition. $35-$50.

ILLINOIS in 1837; A Sketch. Folding colored map. Boards and cloth. Philadelphia, 1837. (By S. Augustus Mitchell?) First edition, first issue, with "animals" misspelled "animalas" on title page. $50-$60. Second issue, error corrected. $35-$50. Philadelphia, 1838. (Title changed to *Illinois in 1837 & 8.*) $25-$35.

ILLUSTRATED Album of Biography of Pope and Stevens Counties, Minnesota. Half leather. Chicago, 1888. $50.

ILLUSTRATED Atlas and History of Yolo County, California (The). 50 plates, map in color. Atlas folio, cloth. San Francisco, 1879. First edition. $200 and up.

ILLUSTRATED Historical Atlas of the State of Indiana. Half leather. Chicago, 1876. $50-$60.

ILLUSTRATED History of Los Angeles County (An). Illustrated. Full morocco. Chicago, 1889. First edition. $150-$250.

ILLUSTRATED History of San Joaquin County (An). Full leather. Chicago, 1890. $100. Worn, $40.

IMAGINARY Conversations of Literary Men and Statesmen. 2 vols., boards, paper labels. London, 1824. (By Walter Savage Landor.) First edition. $150-$200. (Note: Three other volumes of the *Conversations* subsequently appeared.) New York, 1936. Limited Editions Club. Linen. Boxed. $25.

IMAGIST Anthology (The). Edited by Ford Madox Ford and Glenn Hughes. Cloth. New York, 1930. First edition. One of 1,000. $50-$60. London, 1930. Yellow cloth. First English edition. $50.

IMPARTIAL Appeal (An) to the Reason, Interest, and Patriotism of the People of Illinois, on the Injurious Effects of Slave Labour. 16 pp., disbound. No place (Philadelphia?), 1824. (By Morris Birkbeck.) $1,700 (A, 1967). (Note: Only four copies known.)

IMPARTIAL Inquirer (The). 96 pp., half leather. Boston, 1811. (By John Lowell.) First edition. $50-$60.

IMPORTANCE of Being Earnest (The). By the Author of *Lady Windermere's Fan.* Reddish-brown linen. London, 1899. (By Oscar Wilde.) First edition. $100-$150. Another issue: One of 100 on large paper, signed. $250-$350. Another issue: Vellum. One of 12 on Japan paper, signed. $400-$500. New York, 1956. 2 vols., decorated boards. Limited edition. Boxed. $35.

IN a Good Cause: A Collection of Stories, Poems, and Illustrations. Decorated vellum boards. London, 1885. First edition. $30-$35. (Note: Contains first appearance of an Oscar Wilde poem, "Le Jardin des Tuileries.")

INCHIQUIN, The Jesuit's Letters, During a Late Residence in the U.S.A. Leather. New York, 1810. (By Charles J. Ingersoll.) $35.

INCIDENTAL Numbers. Boards. London, 1912. (By Elinor Wylie.) First edition. One of 65. $200 and up.

INCIDENTS of Border Life. 5 plates. Half calf. Chambersburg, Pa., 1839. (By Joseph Pritts.) First edition, first issue, with only 491 pages. $75-$100. Second issue, 6 plates, 507 pages. $50-$75. Lancaster, Pa., 1841. $35-$50.

INDEX. 20 pp., red wrappers. London, 1915. (By Norman Douglas.) First edition. $75. (Note: The index is to nine Capri monographs by Douglas.)

INDEX to the Final Rolls of Citizens and Freedmen of the Five Civilized Tribes in Indian Territory. Cloth. No place, no date (Washington, 1907?). $50.

INDEX to "In Memoriam" (An). Dark-brown or purple cloth. London, 1862. (By Charles L. Dodgson.) First edition, first issue, without ads. $50.

INDIAN Council in the Valley of the Walla-Walla, 1855 (The). 32 pp., pale blue printed wrappers. San Francisco, 1855. (By Lawrence Kip.) First edition. $300-$350. Eugene, Ore., 1897. $35-$50.

INDIAN Summer. Stitched paper wrappers. No place, no date (Madison, Wis., 1912). (By William Ellery Leonard.) First edition. $35-$50.

INDIAN Treaties and Laws and Regulations Relating to Indian Affairs. Boards. Washington City, 1826. $50.

INDIANS (The): Or Narratives of Massacres and Depredations, etc. By a Descendant of the Huguenots. 79 pp., calf. Rondout, N.Y., 1846. (By Johannes H. Bevier.) First edition. $100.

INDUSTRIAL Prodigy of the New Southwest (The). Illustrated. 157 pp., wrappers. Muskogee, Indian Territory, no date (about 1902). $35-$50.

INFIDEL (The); or The Fall of Mexico. 2 vols., purple cloth, paper labels. Philadelphia, 1835. (By Robert Montgomery Bird.) First edition. $75.

INGELOW, Jean. *The High Tide.* Wrappers. Boston, 1864. First edition. $25.

INGERSOLL, Ernest. *An Island in the Air.* Cloth. New York, 1905. First edition. In dust jacket. $35.

INGERSOLL, Luther A. *Century Annals of San Bernardino County.* (1769 to 1904.) Portraits and views. Full morocco. Los Angeles, 1904. First edition. $50-$75.

INGERSOLL, Robert G. *The Gods and Other Lectures.* Cloth. Peoria, Ill., 1874. First edition, first binding, lettered title on spine. $35-$40.

INGERSOLL, Robert G. *An Oration Delivered . . . at Rouse's Hall, Peoria, Ill., at the Unveiling of a Statue of Humboldt, September 14th, 1869.* Wrappers. Peoria, 1869. First edition. Author's first published work. $35-$50.

INGOLDSBY, Thomas. *The Ingoldsby Legends, or Mirth and Marvels.* Etchings by George Cruikshank and John Leech. 3 vols., brown cloth. London, 1840-42-47. First edition, with misprint "topot" on page 350 of Vol. 3 and blank page 236 in Vol. 1. (By Richard Harris Barham.) $150-$250. London, 1898. Illustrated by Arthur Rackham. Green cloth. $50. London, 1907. Illustrated by Rackham. White vellum. One of 560 signed by Rackham. $200-$250. London, 1920. Illustrated by Rackham. Calf, $100

INGRAHAM, Joseph Holt. See *The South-West.*

INGRAHAM, Joseph Holt. *Pierce Fenning, or, The Lugger's Chase.* Illustrated, 95 pp., stitched. Boston, 1846. First edition. $75.

INGRAHAM, Joseph Holt (editor). *The Prince of the House of David.* Illustrated. Cloth. New York, 1855. First edition. $25-$35.

INHERITANCE (The). 3 vols., contemporary half calf. Edinburgh, 1831. (By Susan Edmonstone Ferrier.) First edition. $125-$135.

IN MEMORIAM. Dark-purple cloth. London, 1850. (By Alfred, Lord Tennyson.) First edition, first issue, with "baseness" for "bareness" in line 3, page 198. $100-$150. Spine faded, $45. London, 1914. Riccardi Press. Vellum with silk ties. One of 12 on vellum. $624 (A, 1971). London, 1933. Nonesuch Press. Limp vellum. $50-$75.

IN MEMORIAM: Harry Elkins Widener. Morocco. No place, 1912. (By Dr. A. S. W. Rosenbach.) $55.

IN PRINCIPIO. (The first chapter of Genesis.) Full dark-green crushed levant, gilt, by the Doves Bindery. London, no date (1911). Doves Press. One of 200. $200-$225.

INMAN, Col. Henry. *The Old Santa Fe Trail.* Frontispiece, 8 plates by Frederic Remington, folding map. Cloth. New York, 1897. First edition. $100-$125.

INMAN, Col. Henry. *Stories of the Old Santa Fe Trail.* Pictorial cloth. Kansas City, Mo., 1881. First edition. $50-$60. Author's first book.

INMAN, Col. Henry (editor). *Buffalo Jones' 40 Years of Adventure.* 43 plates. Pictorial cloth. Topeka, 1899. First edition. $60-$80.

INMAN, Col. Henry, and Cody, William F. *The Great Salt Lake Trail.* Map, 8 plates. Pictorial buckram. New York, 1898. First edition, first binding, blue (later brown). $50-$75.

INSTRUCTION for Heavy Artillery . . . for the Use of the Army of the United States. 39 plates, tables, charts. Cloth. Charleston, S.C., 1862. Binding a bit faded and frayed, $175.

IRENE the Missionary. Green or brown cloth. Boston, 1879. (By John W. DeForest.) First edition. $50-$60.

IRON, Ralph. *The Story of an African Farm.* 2 vols., cloth. London, 1883. (By Olive Schreiner.) First edition. $300-$350.

IRVING, John Treat, Jr. *The Hawk Chief: A Tale of the Indian Country.* 2 vols., cloth. Philadelphia, 1837. First edition. $100-$150.

IRVING, John Treat, Jr. *The Hunters of the Prairie, or The Hawk Chief.* 2 vols., half leather. London, 1837. First English edition of *The Hawk Chief.* $75-$100.

IRVING, John Treat, Jr. *Indian Sketches, Taken During an Expedition to the Pawnee Tribes.* 2 vols., boards. Philadelphia, 1835. First edition. $75-$100. London, 1835. 2 vols., boards. First English edition. $75.

IRVING, Washington. See Agapida, Fray Antonio; Crayon, Geoffrey; Depons, François; Knickerbocker, Diedrich; Oldstyle, Jonathan. Also see *Abbotsford: Biography of James Lawrence; Legends of the Conquest of Spain; A Tour of the Prairies.*

IRVING, Washington. *Adventures of Captain Bonneville.* 3 vols., boards, paper label. London, 1837. First edition. $75-$100. (For first American edition, see *The Rocky Mountains.*)

IRVING, Washington. *Astoria, or Anecdotes of an Enterprise Beyond the Rocky Mountains.* Folding map. 2 vols., blue cloth. Philadelphia, 1836. First edition, first state, with copyright notice on back of first title page and garbled footnote on page 239 of Vol. 2. $250-$350.

IRVING, Washington. *Biography and Poetical Remains of the Late Margaret Miller Davidson.* Black cloth. Philadelphia, 1841. First edition. $40-$60.

IRVING, Washington. *Chronicles of Wolfert's Roost.* Tan cloth. Edinburgh (London), 1855. First edition, first issue, with *Constable's Miscellany* listed as "In the Press . . . Volume V" (later reading, "Volume VII"). $75-$100. (For first American edition, see Irving, *Wolfert's Roost.*)

IRVING, Washington. *A History of the Life and Voyages of Christopher Columbus.* 2 folding maps. 4 vols., boards, paper labels. London, 1828. First edition. (Blanck thinks all copies issued by Murray under this date are acceptable first editions regardless of variations.) $150-$200. New York, 1828. Folding map. 3 vols., boards, paper labels. First American edition. $75-$100.

IRVING, Washington. *The Legend of Sleepy Hollow.* Illustrated in color by Arthur Rackham. Cloth. London, no date (1928). $50-$75. Another issue: Vellum. One of 375 signed by Rackham. $165-$250.

IRVING, Washington. *The Life of George Washington.* 5 vols., cloth. New York, 1855-59. First edition, with dates as follows: Vols. 1 and 2, 1855; 3, 1856; 4, 1857, and 5, 1859. $100. Another issue: Large paper edition (Vol. 2 dated 1856). One of 110 copies. $150-$250. (Note: See Blanck's detailed description for the complicated publishing history of this book.)

IRVING, Washington. *The Rocky Mountains.* "Digested from the Journal of Captain B. L. E. Bonneville . . . by Washington Irving." 2 folding maps. 2 vols., blue cloth, printed labels. Philadelphia, 1837. First American edition, first issue, with no ads and 2 blank flyleaves at each end. $150-$250. Maps torn, $110. (For first edition, see Irving, *Adventures of Captain Bonneville.*)

IRVING, Washington. *Voyages and Discoveries of the Companions of Columbus.* Cloth. London, 1831. First edition. $50-$75. Philadelphia, 1831. Boards and cloth, paper label. First American edition. $50-$75.

IRVING, Washington. *Wolfert's Roost and Other Papers.* Frontispiece. Slate-green cloth. New York, 1855. First American edition, first issue, with frontispiece and vignette title page on a stub. $25-$35. (For first edition, see Irving, *Chronicles of Wolfert's Roost.*)

ISELIN, Isaac. *Journal of a Trading Voyage Around the World, 1805-1808.* No place, no date (New York, about 1897). First edition. $80 and $125.

ISHERWOOD, Christopher. See Auden, W. H., and Isherwood, Christopher; Baudelaire, Charles. Also see *On the Frontier.*

ISHERWOOD, Christopher. *All the Conspirators.* Cloth. London, 1928. First edition. In dust jacket. $50. Author's first novel.

ISHERWOOD, Christopher. *The Berlin Stories: The Last of Mr. Norris. Goodbye to Berlin.* Cloth. No place (New York, or Norfolk, Conn.), 1945. New Directions. First edition. In dust jacket. $25. Another, signed, $35.

ISHERWOOD, Christopher. *Goodbye to Berlin.* Cloth. London, 1939. First edition. In dust jacket. $75-$100.

ISHERWOOD, Christopher. *Lions and Shadows: An Education in the Twenties.* Portrait frontispiece. Cloth. London, 1938. First edition, first issue. In dust jacket. $35. Norfolk, no date (1947). New Directions. Blue cloth. First American edition. In dust jacket. $15. Signed copy, $35.

ISHERWOOD, Christopher. *The Memorial: Portrait of a Family.* Cloth. London, 1932. Hogarth Press. First edition. In dust jacket. $50-$60. Norfolk, no date (about 1946). New Directions. Cloth. First American edition. In dust jacket. $20.

ISHERWOOD, Christopher. *Mr. Norris Changes Trains.* Cloth. London, 1935. Hogarth Press. In dust jacket. $75-$100.

ISHERWOOD, Christopher. *Prater Violet.* Gray cloth. New York, no date (1945). First edition. In dust jacket. $25. London, no date (1946). First English edition. In dust jacket. $15.

ISHERWOOD, Christopher. *Sally Bowles.* Cloth. London, 1937. First edition. In dust jacket. $40-$50.

ISHERWOOD, Christopher. *The World in the Evening.* Cloth. London, no date (1954). First edition. In dust jacket. $25. Another, signed, $35. New York, no date (1954). Cloth. First American edition. In dust jacket. $12.50.

IVANHOE: A Romance. 3 vols., boards. Edinburgh, 1820. (By Sir Walter Scott.) First edition. $200-$250. New York, 1951. Limited Editions Club. Illustrated. 2 vols., pictorial cloth. Boxed. $40-$50.

IVES, Joseph C. *Report Upon the Colorado River of the West.* 3 folding maps, 31 plates. Cloth. Washington, 1861. First edition, Senate issue. $100.

IVINS, Virginia W. *Pen Pictures of Early Western Days.* Plates. Cloth. No place (Keokuk, Iowa), 1905. First edition. $35-$50. Second edition: No place (Keokuk), 1908. $25.

J

JACKSON, A. W. *Barbariana: or Scenery, Climate, Soils and Social Conditions of Santa Barbara City and County.* 48 pp., printed wrappers. San Francisco, 1888. $60.

JACKSON, A. P., and Cole, E. C. *Oklahoma! Politically and Topographically Described.* Map (not in all copies). Kansas City, no date (1885). First edition. $75-$100. Map reinforced, $60.

JACKSON, Andrew. *Message from the President of the United States, in Compliance with a Resolution of the Senate Concerning the Fur Trade and Inland Trade to Mexico.* 86 pp., unbound. No place, no date (Washington, 1832). Senate Doc. 90. First edition. $50-$75.

JACKSON, Andrew. *To the Citizens of Pennsylvania.* 12 pp., wrappers. No place, no date (Washington, 1834). $50-$75.

JACKSON, Charles James. *An Illustrated History of English Plate, Ecclesiastical and Secular.* Colored frontispiece, 76 photogravure plates, 1,500 other illustrations. 2 vols., half morocco. London, 1911. $250-$350.

JACKSON, Mrs. F. Nevill. *Toys of Other Days.* 9 color plates, 273 plain illustrations. Full vellum. London, 1908. One of 50. $75-$100.

JACKSON, George. *Sixty Years in Texas.* Plates. Cloth. No place, no date (Dallas, 1908). First edition, first issue, with 322 pages. $75.

JACKSON, Helen Hunt. See H. H. Also see *Mercy Philbrick's Choice.*

JACKSON, Helen Hunt. *The Procession of Flowers in Colorado.* Illustrated. Cloth. Boston, 1886. First edition. One of 100. $50.

JACKSON, Helen Hunt. *Ramona.* Decorated olive-green cloth. Boston, 1884. First edition. $100-$150. Los Angeles, 1959. Illustrated. Buckram. $50.

JACKSON, Holbrook. *The Anatomy of Bibliomania.* 2 vols., cloth. London, 1930. Soncino Press. First edition. One of 1,000. $75-$125. Another issue: Morocco. One of 48 signed. $150. New York, 1931. 2 vols., cloth. First American edition. $25-$35. New York, 1950. Cloth. In dust jacket. $15.

JACKSON, Col. Oscar L. *The Colonel's Diary.* Cloth. No place, no date (Sharon, Pa., 1922?). First edition. $35.

JACKSON, Pearl Cashell. *Texas Governors' Wives.* Soft leather. Austin, Tex., no date (1905). First edition. $35-$50.

JACOB, J. G. *The Life and Times of Patrick Gass.* 4 plates. Cloth. Wellsburg, Va., 1859. First edition. $100-$150.

JAEGER, Benedict, and Preston, H. C. *The Life of North American Insects.* Cloth. Providence, 1854. First edition. $35.

JAMES, Edwin (editor). *Account of an Expedition from Pittsburgh to the Rocky Mountains.* 2 maps, 8 plates. 3 vols. (including atlas), boards and leather, paper labels. Philadelphia, 1822-23. First edition. $500-$600. Also, $550 (A, 1967). London, 1823. 3 vols., boards. First English edition. $250-$350.

JAMES, Edwin (editor). *A Narrative of the Captivity and Adventures of John Tanner.* Frontispiece portrait. Tan boards, purple cloth, paper label. New York, 1830. First edition. $300-$400.

JAMES, Frank. *The Only True History of the Life of Frank James, Written by Himself.* (Cover title.) Illustrated. 134 pp., wrappers. No place, no date (Pine Bluff, Ark., 1926). First edition. $50. (Note: Ramon F. Adams calls this a "brazen" and "worthless" fake.)

JAMES, Fred. *The Klondike Goldfields and How to Get There.* Map. 68 pp., tan wrappers. London, 1897. First edition. $180 (A, 1969).

JAMES, Henry. See Besant, Walter.

JAMES, Henry. *The Ambassadors.* Red cloth. London, 1903. First edition. $35-$50. New York, 1903. Gray-blue boards, with blue linen dust jacket. First American edition, first issue, with "Published November, 1903" on copyright page. $75-$125. New York, 1963. Limited Editions Club. Illustrated. Boards. Boxed. $35.

JAMES, Henry. *The American.* Cloth. Boston, 1877. First edition, first binding, with Osgood imprint on spine. $100.

JAMES, Henry. *The American Scene.* Maroon buckram. London, 1907. First edition. $50. Worn and faded, $30. New York, 1907. Blue cloth. First American edition. $25.

JAMES, Henry. *The Aspern Papers: Louisa Pallant: The Modern Warning.* 2 vols., blue cloth. London, 1888. First edition. $100-$125.

JAMES, Henry. *The Awkward Age.* Brown cloth. New York, 1899. First edition, first issue, with sans-serif "p" in spine imprint. $35. London, 1899. Light-blue cloth. First English edition (possibly simultaneous with the New York edition). $25.

JAMES, Henry. *The Better Sort.* Rose-colored cloth. New York, 1903. First edition, with "Published, February, 1903" on copyright page. $25. London, 1903. Red cloth. First English edition (simultaneous with the American first). $25.

JAMES, Henry. *The Bostonians.* 3 vols., blue cloth. London, 1886. First edition. $250 and up.

JAMES, Henry. *A Bundle of Letters.* Stiff printed wrappers. Boston, no date (1880). First edition, Blanck's state A, with comma after "Jr." on front cover. $50-$75.

JAMES, Henry. *Confidence.* 2 vols., cloth. London, 1880. First edition. $35. Boston, 1880. Brick-colored cloth (one volume). First American edition, first issue, with Houghton, Osgood imprint on spine. $35.

JAMES, Henry. *Daisy Miller: A Study.* Printed tan or gray wrappers, or green cloth. New York, 1879. First edition. Wrappers: $100-$150. Cloth: $100-$125.

JAMES, Henry. *Daisy Miller and An International Episode.* Vellum. New York, 1892. First edition. $25-$35. Trade edition: Cloth. $10-$15.

JAMES, Henry. *The Diary of a Man of Fifty, and a Bundle of Letters.* Tan wrappers, or green cloth. New York, 1880. First edition. Wrappers: $40. Cloth: $25-$30.

JAMES, Henry. *Embarrassments.* Blue cloth. London, 1896. First published edition, first issue, with 4 irises on front of binding. $25. New York, 1896. Maroon cloth. First American edition. $25.

JAMES, Henry. *English Hours.* Illustrated by Joseph Pennell. Gray cloth. London, 1905. First edition. $35. Second binding, half buckram. $15. Boston, 1905. Cloth, or half morocco. First edition. $10-$15. Another issue: Boards and linen. One of 421 on large paper. $15-$25.

JAMES, Henry. *Essays in London and Elsewhere.* Salmon-colored cloth. London, 1893. First edition. $25. New York, 1893. Blue cloth. First American edition. $15-$20.

JAMES, Henry. *The Europeans: A Sketch.* 2 vols., blue cloth. London, 1878. First edition. $35-$50. Boston, 1879. Cloth (in one volume). First American edition. $35.

JAMES, Henry. *The Golden Bowl.* 2 vols., tan cloth. New York, 1904. First edition, with "Published, November, 1904" on copyright page. $60-$80.

JAMES, Henry. *An International Episode.* Gray wrappers, or flexible green cloth. New York, 1879. First edition, first state, with "blue" for "beth" in first line of page 45. Wrappers: $50-$75. Cloth: $50.

JAMES, Henry. *Italian Hours.* Plates (some colored). Green buckram. London, 1909. First edition. In dust jacket. $35. Also, $19.20 (A, 1969). Boston, 1909. Terra-cotta cloth. First American edition, with "Published November 1909" on copyright page. In dust jacket. $25.

JAMES, Henry. *The Ivory Tower.* Edited by Percy Lubbock. Portrait. Blue cloth. London, no date (1917). First edition. In dust jacket. $25. New York, 1917. Greenish-brown cloth. First American edition, with "Published October, 1917" on copyright page. In dust jacket. $25.

JAMES, Henry. *The Letters of Henry James.* Edited by Percy Lubbock. 2 portrait frontispieces and facsimile. 2 vols., blue cloth. London, 1920. First edition. In dust jackets. $50 and $43.20. New York, 1920. 2 vols., greenish-black cloth. First American edition. In dust jackets. $25. Lacking jackets, $15.

JAMES, Henry. *Letters of Henry James to Walter Berry.* Printed vellum wrappers. Paris, 1928. Black Sun Press. First edition. One of 16 on Japan vellum, each with an original letter. $100 and up. Another issue: One of 100 on Van Gelder paper. $75-$100. (Note: There were also 4 copies not for sale.)

JAMES, Henry. *A Little Tour in France.* Cloth. Boston, 1885. First edition. $25-$35. Cambridge, Mass., 1900. Illustrated by Joseph Pennell. Boards and cloth. One of 250 large paper copies. $25. Another issue (?): Vellum (parchment). One of 150. $35-$50. Trade edition: Boston, 1900. Cloth. $10-$15.

JAMES, Henry. *The Madonna of the Future and Other Tales.* 2 vols., blue cloth. London, 1879. First edition. $25.

JAMES, Henry. *"A Most Unholy Trade."* Printed wrapper over flexible boards. No place (Cambridge, Mass.), 1923. Scarab Press. First edition. One of 100. $25-$35.

JAMES, Henry. *Notes and Reviews.* Tan boards. Cambridge, Mass., 1921. First edition. One of 30 on vellum. $50-$60. Trade edition: Boards and cloth. $7.50-$10.

JAMES, Henry. *Notes of a Son and Brother.* Frontispiece, 5 plates. Greenish-brown cloth. New York, 1914. First edition. In dust jacket. $25. London, 1914. Cloth. First English edition. In dust jacket. $35.

JAMES, Henry. *The Other House.* 2 vols., blue cloth. London, 1896. First English edition. $75-$100. Spines dull, $60. New York, 1896. Red cloth (one volume). First American edition (published simultaneously with the London edition?). $50-$60.

JAMES, Henry. *The Outcry.* Cloth. London, no date (1911). First edition. In dust jacket. $50. Lacking jacket, $35. New York, 1911. Greenish-brown cloth. First American edition, with "Published September, 1911" on copyright page. In dust jacket. $25-$30.

JAMES, Henry. *Partial Portraits.* Blue-green cloth. London, 1888. First edition. $25.

JAMES, Henry. *A Passionate Pilgrim, and Other Tales.* Cloth. Boston, 1875. First edition, first binding, with "J. R. Osgood & Co." on spine. $50-$75. Author's first book.

JAMES, Henry. *The Portrait of a Lady.* 3 vols., blue or dark-green cloth. London, 1881. First edition. $75-$100. Worn, $35. Boston, 1882. Cloth. First American edition. $25. Worn, $12.50. New York, 1967. Limited Editions Club. Colored plates. Marbled boards and cloth. Boxed. $35.

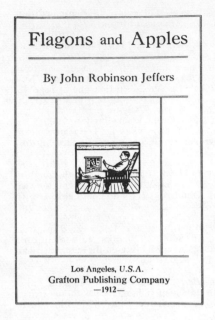

Flagons and Apples

By John Robinson Jeffers

Los Angeles, U.S.A.
Grafton Publishing Company
—1912—

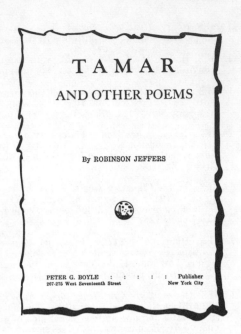

TAMAR
AND OTHER POEMS

By ROBINSON JEFFERS

PETER G. BOYLE : : : : : Publisher
267-275 West Seventeenth Street   New York City

POMES PENYEACH
BY
JAMES JOYCE

SHAKESPEARE AND COMPANY
PARIS
1927

WHY
ENGLAND
SLEPT

———

JOHN F. KENNEDY

NEW YORK · 1940

WILFRED FUNK, INC.

JAMES, Henry. *Portraits of Places.* Blue-green cloth. London, 1883. First edition, first binding, with "M" in Macmillan larger than other letters. $40-$50. Boston, 1884. Cloth. First American edition. $15-$20.

JAMES, Henry. *The Princess Casamassima.* 3 vols., blue cloth. London, 1886. First edition. $100-$150. Boston, 1886. Blue-green cloth (in one volume). First American edition. $50-$75. London, 1887. First British one-volume edition. $50.

JAMES, Henry. *Roderick Hudson.* Cloth. Boston, 1876. First edition, first binding, with Osgood imprint on spine. $50-$60. Later binding. Houghton Mifflin imprint on spine. $20. Author's first novel.

JAMES, Henry. *The Sense of the Past.* Edited by Percy Lubbock. Portrait. Blue cloth. London, no date (1917). First edition. In dust jacket. $35. New York, 1917. Greenish-brown cloth. First American edition, with "Published October, 1917" on copyright page. In dust jacket. $25.

JAMES, Henry. *A Small Boy and Others.* Greenish-brown cloth. New York, 1913. First edition, first issue, with 11-line publisher's ad. In dust jacket. $25. London, 1913. Blue cloth. First English edition (possibly simultaneous with New York edition). In dust jacket. $25.

JAMES, Henry. *The Soft Side.* Maroon buckram. New York, 1900. First edition. $25. London, 1900. Red cloth. First English edition (possibly simultaneous with the New York first). $25.

JAMES, Henry. *The Spoils of Poynton.* Blue cloth. London, 1897. First (?) edition. $25. Boston, 1897. Cloth. First American edition. (Blanck thinks this may have been simultaneous with the English first.) $10-$15.

JAMES, Henry. *Stories Revived.* 3 vols., cloth. London, 1885. First edition, first binding, blue cloth. $75-$100.

JAMES, Henry. *Transatlantic Sketches.* Brown cloth. Boston, 1875. First edition, first binding, with Osgood imprint on spine. $100-$150.

JAMES, Henry. *The Turn of the Screw.* Illustrated. Half morocco. London, 1940. Hand and Flower Press. One of 200. $100-$150. New York, 1949. Limited Editions Club. Illustrated. Buckram. Boxed. $15-$20.

JAMES, Henry. *Views and Reviews.* Vellum, leather spine. Boston, 1908. First edition. One of 160. $35-$50. Trade edition: Olive cloth. $20.

JAMES, Henry. *Washington Square.* Dark olive-green cloth. New York, 1881. First edition. $25-$30.

JAMES, Henry. *Washington Square: The Pension Beaurepas: A Bundle of Letters.* 2 vols., cloth. London, 1881. First edition. $25.

JAMES, Henry. *Watch and Ward.* Cloth. Boston, 1878. First edition, first printing, with blank leaf after page 219. $50.

JAMES, Henry. *What Maisie Knew.* Blue cloth. London, 1898 (actually 1897). First edition. $50-$75. Also, $28 (A, 1962). Chicago, 1897. Slate-colored cloth. First American edition. $35-$50.

JAMES, Henry. *The Wheel of Time.* Decorated gray-green cloth. New York, 1893. First edition. $25.

JAMES, Henry. *William Wetmore Story and His Friends.* Frontispiece. 2 vols., green cloth. Edinburgh, 1903. First British edition. $25. Spines faded, $12. Boston, 1903. 2 vols., green cloth. First American edition (issued simultaneously with the Edinburgh edition). $25.

JAMES, Henry. *The Wings of the Dove.* 2 vols., red cloth. New York, 1902. First edition, with "Published, August, 1902" on copyright page. $50-$75. Spines faded, hinges weak, $35.

JAMES, Jesse, Jr. *Jesse James, My Father.* 4 portraits. White printed wrappers. Kansas City, Mo., 1899. (Ghostwritten by A. B. Macdonald?) First edition. $150-$200. Cleveland, no date (1906). Reprint edition. $10-$15.

JAMES, Philip. *Children's Books of Yesterday.* Edited by G. Geoffrey Holme. Cloth. London, 1933. $25.

JAMES, Gen. Thomas. *Three Years Among the Indians and Mexicans.* 130 pp., plain wrappers. Waterloo, Ill., 1846. First edition. Waterstained and rebacked, $4,100 (A, 1963); rebound in boards, defective, $1,500 (A, 1968); new covers supplied, $2,600 (A, 1954). St. Louis, 1916. 12 plates. Half cloth. Second edition. One of 365. $85-$100.

JAMES, W. S. *Cow-boy Life in Texas.* 34 plates. Pictorial cloth. Chicago, no date (1893). First edition. $50-$75. Chicago, no date (1898). 27 plates. Cloth. $25.

JAMES, Will. *All in the Day's Riding.* New York, 1933. First edition. In dust jacket. $25.

JAMES, Will. *Cowboys North and South.* Illustrated by the author. Buckram. New York, 1924. First edition. In dust jacket. $25-$35. Author's first book.

JAMES, Will. *Lone Cowboy: My Life Story.* Illustrated. Cloth, leather label. New York, 1930. First edition. One of 250 with an original drawing. $37.50-$50. Trade edition: Green cloth. In dust jacket. $10.

JAMES, Will. *Smoky the Cowhorse.* Illustrated by the author. Cloth. New York, 1926. First edition. In dust jacket. $50-$60.

JAMES, William. *The Principles of Psychology.* 2 vols., green cloth. New York, 1890. First edition. $50-$75.

JAMES, William F., and McMurry, George H. *History of San Jose, California.* Cloth. San Jose, 1933. First edition. $25-$35.

JAMESON, Anna Brownell. *The Beauties of the Court of Charles II.* 21 hand-colored engraved portraits on India paper. Calf. London, 1833. $100.

JANSON, Charles William. *The Stranger in America.* Engraved title page, plan of Philadelphia, 9 aquatint plates. Boards and calf. London, 1807. First edition. $300-$400. Also, $302 (A, 1969). Philadelphia, 1807. Boards and calf. First American edition. $200-$300.

JANVIER, Thomas A. *The Aztec Treasure-House.* Illustrated by Frederic Remington. Decorated cloth. New York, 1890. First edition. $25-$45.

JARRELL, Randall. *Blood for a Stranger.* Cloth. New York, no date (1942). First edition. In dust jacket. $50-$65.

JEFFERIES, Richard. See *The Gamekeeper at Home.*

JEFFERIES, Richard. *Greene Ferne Farm.* Green cloth. London, 1880. First edition. $75-$100.

JEFFERIES, Richard. *The Open Air.* Printed cloth. London, 1885. First edition. $75-$100.

JEFFERS, Robinson. See Powell, Lawrence Clark; Sterling, George; *Continent's End.*

JEFFERS, Robinson. *Apology for Bad Dreams.* 16 pp., wrappers. Paris, 1930. First edition. One of 30 designed by Ward Ritchie. $200.

JEFFERS, Robinson. *An Artist.* Introduction by Benjamin De Casseres. 12 pp., wrappers. No place, no date (Austin, Tex., 1928). First edition. One of 96 (actually 196). $250. (Printed by John S. Mayfield; most copies destroyed or damaged by fire.)

JEFFERS, Robinson. *Be Angry at the Sun.* Marbled boards and cloth. New York, no date (1941). First edition. One of 100 signed. In glassine dust jacket. Boxed. $200. Jacket chipped, $175. Trade edition: Cloth. In dust jacket. $35.

JEFFERS, Robinson. *The Beaks of Eagles.* Folio, 3 leaves, printed yellow wrappers. San Francisco, 1936. Grabhorn Press. First edition. $200-$250.

JEFFERS, Robinson. *Californians.* Blue cloth. New York, 1916. First edition. In dust jacket. $250-$300. "Advance Copy, For Review Only" (perforation so stamped on title page), $350.

JEFFERS, Robinson, *Cawdor and Other Poems.* Buckram. New York, 1928. First edition. One of 375 on large paper, signed. Boxed. $150-$200. Trade edition: Boards and cloth. In dust jacket. $50-$75. London, 1929. Hogarth Press. First English edition. $25-$35.

JEFFERS, Robinson. *Dear Judas and Other Poems.* Boards and cloth. New York, 1929. First edition (preceding the limited edition). In dust jacket. $60-$80. Also, in dust jacket, $40 (A, 1970). Limited edition, same date: Boards, vellum spine. One of 375 signed. Boxed. $150. Another (?) issue: One of 25 lettered copies. $200-$250. London, 1930. Hogarth Press. Boards. First English edition. $25-$35.

JEFFERS, Robinson. *De Rerum Virtute.* Decorated boards, linen spine, leather label. No place, no date (San Francisco, 1953). Grabhorn Press. First edition. One of 30. In plain purple dust jacket. $650.

JEFFERS, Robinson. *Descent to the Dead.* Boards and vellum. New York, no date (1931). First edition. One of 500 signed. Boxed. $150-$200. (No trade edition issued.)

JEFFERS, Robinson. *The Double Axe and Other Poems.* Blue cloth. New York, 1948. First edition. In dust jacket. $35-$50.

JEFFERS, Robinson. *Flagons and Apples.* (By John Robinson Jeffers.) Cinnamon boards, linen spine, labels. Los Angeles, 1912. First edition. One of 500. $500-$600. Author's first book.

JEFFERS, Robinson. *Give Your Heart to the Hawks.* Marbled boards and calf. New York, 1933. First edition. One of 200 signed. $150-$200. Trade edition: Brown cloth. In dust jacket. $35-$45.

JEFFERS, Robinson. *Hope Is Not for the Wise.* Folio, 4 pp., printed wrappers. No place (San Mateo, Calif.), 1937. Quercus Press. First edition. One of 24. $250. Spot on upper cover, $225. Unnumbered copy, $200.

JEFFERS, Robinson. *The House-Dog's Grave—Haig's Grave.* Morocco. No place, no date (San Mateo, 1939). Quercus Press. One of 30. $125-$150.

JEFFERS, Robinson. *Hungerfield.* Foreword by Frederick Mortimer Clapp. 19 pp., boards, linen spine, morocco label. No place (San Francisco), 1952. Grabhorn Press. First edition. One of 30. $600. New York, no date (1954). Boards and cloth. First trade edition. In dust jacket. $25-$35.

JEFFERS, Robinson. *The Loving Shepherdess.* 9 etchings by Jean Kellogg. Boards. New York, 1956. First edition. One of 115. Boxed. $350.

JEFFERS, Robinson. *Medea.* Boards and cloth. New York, no date (1946). First edition, first issue, with word "least" omitted on page 99. In dust jacket. $50-$60. Second issue, corrected. $25. Lacking jacket, $15.

JEFFERS, Robinson. *Natural Music.* Folio, leaflet. San Mateo, 1947. Quercus Press. First edition. $50.

JEFFERS, Robinson. *The Ocean's Tribute.* 4 pp., folio broadside. San Francisco, 1958. Grabhorn Press. First edition. $35-$50.

JEFFERS, Robinson. *A Poem.* Single sheet, French-folded. No place (San Mateo), 1937. Quercus Press. First edition. One of 10. $275.

JEFFERS, Robinson. *Poems.* Portrait. Buckram. San Francisco, 1928. Book Club of California. First edition. One of 310 signed. Boxed. $150-$200.

JEFFERS, Robinson. *Return: An Unpublished Poem.* 4 pp., wrappers over flexible boards. San Francisco, 1934. Grabhorn Press. One of 250. $35-$50. Another issue: One of 3 on vellum. $100-$150.

JEFFERS, Robinson. *Poetry, Gongorism and a Thousand Years.* 12 pp., decorated boards. No place (Los Angeles), 1949. Ward Ritchie Press. First edition. One of 200. $50-$60.

JEFFERS, Robinson. *Roan Stallion, Tamar, and Other Poems.* Purple boards, black cloth spine. New York, no date (1925). First edition. In dust jacket. $60-$80. Another (later) issue, same date: Marbled boards. Author's Presentation Copy. One of 12. $150-$200. Also, $75 (A, 1966). New York, 1926. Second edition (or printing). $25. London, 1928. Hogarth Press. $25-$35. New York, no date (1935). First Modern Library Edition. Flexible cloth. In dust jacket. $25-$30. (Note: Contains a new introduction by Jeffers.)

JEFFERS, Robinson. *Rock and Hawk.* (Signed or inscribed as a Christmas token.) New Haven, 1934. First edition. One of 20. $100 and up.

JEFFERS, Robinson. *Solstice and Other Poems.* Patterned boards and buckram. New York, 1935. One of 320 signed. In gray dust jacket. $100-$150. Trade edition: Green cloth. In dust jacket. $35.

JEFFERS, Robinson. *Stars.* 3 leaves, boards, paper labels. No place (Pasadena), 1930. Flame Press. One of 80, with errata leaf. $200 and up. (There are said to be only 6 copies known.) Second edition, same date. Printed wrappers. One of 110. $150 and up.

JEFFERS, Robinson. *Such Counsels You Gave to Me.* Illustrated by Fritz Eichenberg. Patterned boards and morocco. New York, no date (1937). Spiral Press. First edition. One of 300 signed. In dust jacket. Boxed. $125-$150. Trade edition: Cloth. In dust jacket. $50.

JEFFERS, Robinson. *Tamar and Other Poems.* Cloth. New York, no date (1924). First edition. One of 500. $350. (Issued without a dust jacket.)

JEFFERS, Robinson. *Themes in My Poems.* Woodcuts by Mallette Dean. 46 pp., decorated boards, cloth spine, label. San Francisco, 1956. Book Club of California. First edition. One of 350. $55-$75.

JEFFERS, Robinson. *Thurso's Landing, and Other Poems.* Half cloth. New York, no date (1932). First edition. One of 200 signed. $250-$300. Trade edition: Boards and cloth. In dust jacket. $100.

JEFFERS, Robinson. *Two Consolations.* 6 leaves, rose or gray boards. No place (San Mateo), 1940. Quercus Press. First edition. One of 250. $350.

JEFFERS, Robinson. *The Women at Point Sur.* Cloth. New York, no date (1927). First edition (preceding the limited edition). In dust jacket. $50-$75. Limited edition, same date: Silver boards and vellum. One of 265 signed. $125-$150.

JEFFERS, Una. *Visits to Ireland: Travel Diaries of Una Jeffers.* Foreword by Robinson Jeffers. Boards and cloth. Los Angeles, 1954. Ward Ritchie Press. First edition. One of 300. Boxed. $27.50.

JEFFERSON, H. E. *Oklahoma: The Beautiful Land.* 202 pp., printed wrappers. Chicago, 1889. First edition. $500 and up.

JEFFERSON, Thomas. *An Appendix to the Notes on Virginia Relative to the Murder of Logan's Family.* 58 pp., sewed. Philadelphia, 1800. First edition. $100-$150.

JEFFERSON, Thomas. *A Manual of Parliamentary Practice for the Use of the Senate of the United States.* Calf. Washington, 1801. First edition. $200.

JEFFERSON, Thomas. *Message from the President of the United States, Communicating Discoveries Made in Exploring the Missouri, Red River, and Washita by Capts. Lewis and Clark, Dr. Sibley, and Mr. Dunbar, etc.* 2 folding tables. 171 pp., unbound. Washington, 1806. "Printed by Order of the Senate." First edition, first issue. $750-$1,000. Also, $650 (A, 1964).

JEFFERSON, Thomas. *Notes on the State of Virginia.* Leather. Baltimore, 1800. $25-$35. (For the first, anonymous publication, Paris, 1782—actually 1785—and other 18th-century editions, see the book auction records.)

JEFFREY, J. K. See *The Territory of Wyoming.*

JENKS, Ira C. *Trial of David F. Mayberry, for the Murder of Andrew Alger.* (Cover title.) 48 pp., wrappers. Janesville, Wis., 1855. First edition. $150.

JENKS, J. W. P. *(With the Compliments of J. W. P. Jenks:) Hunting in Florida in 1874.* (Cover title; caption title for text is *Hunting in Florida.*) Folding map of Everglades. 70 pp., printed buff wrappers. No place, no date (Providence, R.I., 1884?). First (?) edition. $175 (A, 1969).

JENNINGS, Al. *Through the Shadows with O. Henry.* Illustrated. Pictorial cloth. New York, no date (1921). First edition. In dust jacket. $25.

JENNINGS, N. A. *A Texas Ranger.* Colored pictorial cloth. New York, 1899. First edition. $50-$75.

JEPSON, Willis L. *The Silva of California.* Wrappers. Berkeley, Calif., 1910. $25.

JEREMIAH. See *The Lamentations of Jeremiah.*

JEROME, Chauncey. *History of the American Clock Business for the Past 60 Years.* Printed wrappers. New Haven, 1860. First edition. $50.

JEROME, Jerome K. *Three Men in a Boat.* Illustrated. Light-blue cloth. Bristol, England, 1889. First edition, first issue, with title page reading as follows: "Bristol / J. W. Arrowsmith, Quay Street / London / Simpkin, Marshall & Co., 4 Stationer's Hall Court / (rule) 1889 / All rights reserved / ." $35-$50.

JERROLD, Douglas. *A Man Made of Money.* 12 plates by John Leech. 6 parts, pictorial wrappers and in cloth. London, 1849. First edition. $25.

JERROLD, Douglas. *Mrs. Caudle's Curtain Lectures.* Cloth. London, 1866. First edition. $25.

JEWETT, Sarah Orne. *Betty Leicester.* Decorated cloth. Boston, 1890. First edition, early state, with this book last in ad opposite title page. $50.

JEWETT, Sarah Orne. *The Country of the Pointed Firs.* Cloth. Boston, 1896. First edition. $50-$75.

JEWETT, Sarah Orne. *Deephaven.* Cloth. Boston, 1877. First edition, first issue, with the reading "so" in line 16, page 65. $35-$50. Author's first book.

JEWITT, Charles. *Temperance Toy.* Hand-colored engravings. 16 pp., printed wrappers. Boston, 1840. $37.50.

JEWITT, John R. *Journal, Kept at Nootka Sound.* 48 pp., stitched. Boston, 1807. First edition. $2,200 (A, 1969). Boston, 1931. Frontispiece. Half cloth. $35-$50.

JEWITT, John R. *Narrative of the Sufferings and Adventures of John R. Jewitt.* Edited by Richard Alsop. 10 engravings and frontispiece. Boards. New York, no date (about 1815). $100-$150. Middletown, 1815. Calf. $185.

JOAQUIN (the Claude Duval of California); or The Marauder of the Mines. 160 pp., pictorial wrappers. New York, no date (1865—actually later, in the 1870's). (By Henry L. Williams.) First edition. $100-$150. New York, 1888. Decorated cloth. Second edition. $50-$75.

JOCKNICK, Sidney. *Early Days on the Western Slope of Colorado.* 25 plates. Cloth. Denver, 1913. First edition. $150-$200.

JOHL, Janet. *More About Dolls.* Illustrated. Cloth. New York, 1946. First edition. In dust jacket. $60-$80.

JOHL, Janet. *Still More About Dolls.* Illustrated. Cloth. New York, 1950. First edition. In dust jacket. $50-$60.

JOHL, Janet. *Your Dolls and Mine.* Illustrated. Cloth. New York, 1952. First edition. In dust jacket. $50-$60.

JOHN Bull in America; or, The New Munchausen. Boards, or cloth. New York, 1825. (By James Kirke Paulding.) First edition. $75-$100. Also, in boards, $70 (A, 1960).

JOHN Halifax, Gentleman. 3 vols., brown cloth. London, 1856. (By Dinah M. Craik.) First edition, first issue, with 3 pages of ads at end of Vol. 1, one page at end of Vol. 2, and 2 pages at end of Vol. 3. $200-$300.

JOHN Leech on My Shelves. Illustrated. Boards and buckram. No place (Munich), 1930. (By William B. Osgood Field.) Bremer Press. One of 155. Boxed. $75-$100.

JOHN Marr and Other Sailors. 103 pp., printed yellow wrappers. New York, 1888. (By Herman Melville.) First edition. One of 25. $850 (A, 1948)—"Believed to be Melville's copy, with some corrections in his hand." Princeton, N.J., 1922. Half cloth. One of 175. $35-$50.

JOHN, W. D. *Swansea Porcelain.* 20 color illustrations, others in black and white. Buckram. London, 1958. $85.

JOHN Woodvil: A Tragedy. Plain blue boards. London, 1802. (By Charles Lamb.) First edition. $250-$350.

JOHNSON, Benj. F. (of Boone). *"The Old Swimmin'-Hole" and 'Leven More Poems.* Wrappers. Indianapolis, 1883. (By James Whitcomb Riley.) First edition. $150-$250. (Note: There exists a 1909 facsimile, which lacks the "W" in "William" on page 41. Value: About $10.)

JOHNSON, Charles. *The History of the Pirates.* Sheepskin. Norwich, Conn., 1844. (By Daniel Defoe?) $50-$75.

JOHNSON, Crisfield (compiler). *History of Cuyahoga County, Ohio.* Double column pages. Half morocco. Cleveland, 1879. First edition. $50-$60.

JOHNSON, Don Carlos. *A Brief History of Springville, Utah.* Wrappers. Springville, 1900. First edition, with errata slip. $30.

JOHNSON, Edwin F. *Railroad to the Pacific, Northern Route.* 3 maps, 8 plates. Boards and calf. New York, 1854. Second (actually first) edition. $75-$100.

JOHNSON, Frank M. *Forest, Lake and River.* 2 vols., bound in suede. Boston, 1902. One of 350. $125-$150.

JOHNSON, Henry L. *Gutenberg and the Book of Books.* Illustrated. Folio, buckram. New York, 1932. One of 750. In slipcase. $35-$50.

JOHNSON, James Weldon. *Saint Peter Relates an Incident of the Resurrection Day.* Folio, black boards, gilt. New York, 1930. One of 200 signed. Boxed. $45-$50.

JOHNSON, Joseph. *The Memorial of the Chamber of Commerce and of the Citizens of Charleston, Against the Tariff on Woollen Goods.* 16 pp., half morocco. Charleston, S.C., 1827. $35.

JOHNSON, Lionel. *The Art of Thomas Hardy.* Portrait. Boards. London, 1894. First edition. One of 150. $50-$75.

JOHNSON, Lionel. *Twenty One Poems.* Selected by William Butler Yeats. Boards and linen. Dundrum, Ireland, 1904. Dun Emer Press. One of 220. $60-$70.

JOHNSON, Overton, and Winter, William H. *Route Across the Rocky Mountains, etc.* Cloth-backed boards. Lafayette, Ind., 1846. First edition. $1,250 and up. Also, $1,100 and $700 (A, 1968).

JOHNSON, Owen. *The Tennessee Shad.* 8 plates by F. R. Gruger. Pictorial cloth. New York, 1911. First edition. $75.

JOHNSON, Owen. *The Varmint.* Photographs, plus 6 drawings by F. R. Gruger. Black morocco. Boston, 1930. Special limited, signed edition. $40-$50.

JOHNSON, Rossiter. *Phaeton Rogers: A Novel of Boy Life.* Illustrated. Decorated cloth. New York, 1881. First edition. $150.

JOHNSON, Samuel. *A Diary of a Journey into North Wales.* Edited by R. Duppa. Plates. Boards. London, 1816. First edition. $100-$150.

JOHNSON, Samuel. *A Journey to the Western Islands of Scotland.* Half calf, marbled boards. Baltimore, 1810. First American edition. $35-$40.

JOHNSON, Sidney S. *Some Biographies of Old Settlers.* Cloth. Tyler, Tex., 1900. First edition. $35-$50.

JOHNSON, Sidney S. *Texans Who Wore the Gray.* Illustrated. Cloth. Tyler, Tex., no date (about 1907). $40.

JOHNSON, Mrs. Susannah. *A Narrative of the Captivity of Mrs. Johnson.* Boards and sheep. Windsor, Vt., 1807. Second edition. $125-$150.

JOHNSON, Theodore T. *Sights in the Gold Region, and Scenes by the Way.* Cloth. New York, 1849. First edition. $125-$150.

JOHNSTON, Carrier Polk, and McGlumphy, W. H. S. *History of Clinton and Caldwell Counties, Missouri.* Half leather. Topeka, 1923. $35-$50.

JOHNSTON, Charles. *A Narrative of the Incidents Attending the Capture, Detention, and Ransom of, etc.* Boards. New York, 1827. First edition. $100-$150.

JOHNSTON, George. *The History of Cecil County, Maryland.* Folding map. Cloth. Elkton, Md., 1881. First edition. $50-$60.

JOHNSTON, George. *The Poetry and Poets of Cecil County, Maryland.* Cloth. Elkton, 1887. First edition. $50.

JOHNSTON, Lieut. Col. J. E., and others. *Reports of the Secretary of War, with Reconnaissances of Routes from San Antonio to El Paso, etc.* 2 folding maps, 72 plates. Three-quarters morocco. Washington, 1850. First edition. $50-$75.

JOHNSTON, Mary. *To Have and to Hold.* Illustrated by Howard Pyle and others. Red buckram, paper label. Boston, 1900. First edition. One of 250. $35-$50.

JOHNSTON, William G. *Experiences of a Forty-niner.* Portrait, 13 plates. Cloth. Pittsburgh, 1892. First edition. (With later, separately issued, folding map and an extra portrait.) $250-$300.

JOHONNOT, Jackson. *The Remarkable Adventures of Jackson Johonnot.* 24 pp., stitched. Greenfield, Mass., 1816. First edition. $75-$100.

JOINVILLE, John, Lord of. *The History of Saint Louis, King Louis of France.* Illustrated. Dark maroon morocco. Newtown, Wales, 1937. Gregynog Press. One of 191. In slipcase. $400-$500.

JOLAS, Eugene. *Secession in Astropolis.* Wrappers. Paris, 1929. Black Sun Press. One of 110 (135?). In slipcase. $60-$80.

JOLAS, Maria (editor). *A James Joyce Yearbook.* Wrappers. Paris, 1949. Transition Press. First edition. In dust jacket. $35. (Note: Contains a section, "Ad Writer," attributed to Joyce.)

JONES, A. D. *Illinois and the West.* Folding map. Cloth. Boston, 1838. First edition. $100.

JONES, Anson B. *Memoranda and Official Correspondence Relating to the Republic of Texas, Its History and Annexation.* Portrait. Cloth. New York, 1859. First edition. $75-$100. Cloth faded, $35. Chicago, no date (1966). Map, facsimile letter. Leather. One of 150. Boxed. $75.

JONES, Charles Colcock. *The Religious Instruction of the Negroes in the United States.* Cloth. Savannah, Ga., 1842. First edition. $75-$100.

JONES, Charles C., Jr. *Biographical Sketches of the Delegates from Georgia to the Continental Congress.* Cloth. Boston, 1891. $25.

JONES, Charles C., Jr. *Antiquities of the Southern Indians.* 30 plates. Cloth. New York, 1873. First edition. $50-$60.

JONES, Charles C., Jr. *The Dead Towns of Georgia.* Maps. Cloth. Savannah, 1878. First edition. One of 250. $25.

JONES, Charles C., Jr. *Historical Sketch of the Chatham Artillery.* 3 maps. Half leather. Albany, Ga., 1867. First edition. $50.

JONES, Charles C., Jr. *The History of Savannah, Georgia.* 21 portraits. Half leather. Syracuse, 1890. First edition. $100-$125.

JONES, Charles C., Jr. *The Siege of Savannah in December, 1864.* 184 pp., wrappers. Albany, 1874. First edition. $35-$50. Another issue: One of 10 on large paper. $100.

JONES, Charles H. *Genealogy of the Rodman Family, 1620 to 1886.* Cloth. Philadelphia, 1886. $35-$50.

JONES, Charles Jesse. See Inman, Col. Henry.

JONES, D. W. *Forty Years Among the Indians.* Cloth. Salt Lake City, 1890. First edition, with portrait (not in all copies). $35-$50.

JONES, David. *A Journal of Two Visits Made to Some Nations of Indians on the West Side of the River Ohio, in the Years 1772 and 1773.* Wrappers. New York, 1865. Second edition. One of 50 on large paper. $100-$150. Rebound in half morocco, covers bound in, $37.50. (Note: Although this handbook is restricted to nineteenth- and twentieth-century titles, I must note that the first edition of David Jones' journal, Burlington, N.J., 1774, brought $5,250 at auction on May 4, 1966, and another copy has been catalogued by a Chicago bookseller at $6,000.)

JONES, Adj. Gen. R. *General Orders, No. 16, Reporting General Court Martial Convened at Fort Kearney, Oregon Route, for Offense Commited There.* 11 pp., sewed. Washington, 1851. $25.

JONES, E. Alfred. *The Old Silver of American Churches.* 145 plates. Folio, buckram. Letchworth, England, 1913. One of 506. $200-$250.

JONES, Edith Newbold. *Verses.* Wrappers. Newport, R. I., 1878. (By Edith Wharton.) First edition. $500. Also, half morocco, original front cover bound in, $165 (A, 1947). Author's first book.

JONES, Gwyn. *The Green Island.* Woodcuts by John Petts. Green and gray morocco. London, 1946. Golden Cockerel Press. One of 100. $50-$75.

JONES, James. *From Here to Eternity.* Black cloth. New York, 1951. First edition, with "A" on copyright page. Presentation edition, signed. In dust jacket. $45-$55. Trade edition: Cloth. In dust jacket. $10-$15. Author's first book.

JONES, Jonathan H. *A Condensed History of the Apache and Comanche Indian Tribes.* Illustrated. Cloth. San Antonio, 1899. First edition. $125.

JONES, Justin. See Brace, Jack; Hazel, Harry.

JONES, Owen. *The Grammar of Ornament.* 100 colored lithographs, engraved title page (illuminated), woodcuts. Half morocco. London, 1856. First edition. $150-$250. London, no date (1865). 112 plates. Cloth. $100-$125. London, 1868. 112 plates. Cloth. $100. London, 1910. Cloth. $100-$150.

JONES, Samuel. *Pittsburgh in the Year Eighteen-Hundred and Twenty-six.* Frontispiece. Boards. Pittsburgh, 1826. First edition. $1,000 and up.

JONES, T. Gwynn. *Detholiad o' Ganiadau: Collected Poems of T. Gwynn Jones.* Wood engravings by R. A. Maynard. Buckram. Newtown, Wales, 1926. Gregynog Press. One of 474. $25-$35. Another issue: Blue morocco. One of 26 specially bound. $350-$400.

JONES, Thomas A. *J. Wilkes Booth.* Illustrated. Cloth, Chicago, 1893. First edition. $50-$75.

JONES, U. J. *History of the Early Settlement of the Juniata Valley.* 14 plates. Cloth. Philadelphia, 1856. First edition. $35-$50.

JONES, William Carey. *Land Titles in California.* 55 pp., wrappers. San Francisco, 1852. First edition. $300 and up. Also, rebound in morocco, $275 (A, 1968).

JONES, William Carey. *Letters in Review of Attorney General Black's Report to the President of the U.S., on the Land Titles of California.* 31 pp., wrappers. San Francisco, 1860. $75-$100.

JONES, William Carey. *The "Pueblo Question" Solved.* 36 pp., sewed. San Francisco, 1860. First edition. $100.

JONES, William Carey. *Report on the Subject of Land Titles in California.* 60 pp., wrappers. Washington, 1850. First edition. $150-$200.

JONSON, Ben. *A Croppe of Kisses: Selected Lyrics.* Edited by John Wallis. Folio, morocco and buckram. London, 1937. Golden Cockerel Press. One of 250. $100-$150. Another issue: One of 50 specially bound in morocco. $150-$200.

JONSON, Ben. *The Masque of Queens.* Plates. Boards. London, 1930. $35-$50.

JONSON, Ben. *Poems.* Edited by B. H. Newdigate. Portrait, facsimiles. Linen. Oxford, 1936. Shakespeare Head Press. $75-$100.

JONSON, Ben. *Songs: A Selection.* Illustrated. Boards. London, 1906. Eragny Press. One of 185. $100-$150.

JONSON, Ben. *Volpone: or The Foxe.* Illustrated by Aubrey Beardsley. Decorated cloth. New York, 1898. One of 1,000. $75-$100. Another issue: Vellum. One of 100 on vellum. $150-$200. New York, 1952. Limited Editions Club. Illustrated. Cloth. Boxed. $35-$50.

JORDAN, Thomas, and Pryor, J. P.. *The Campaigns of Lieut.-Gen. N. B. Forrest.* 6 maps, 6 plates. Cloth. New Orleans, 1868. First edition. $50.

JORROCKS'S Jaunts and Jollities. 12 illustrations by Phiz. Decorated cloth. London, 1838. (By Robert Smith Surtees.) First edition. $150-$250. Philadelphia, 1838. 2 vols., half cloth. First American edition. $50. London, 1843. 15 color plates by Henry Alken. Green cloth. Second edition, first state, with 8 pages of ads and printer's imprint at end. $500-$600. Second edition, later state, with ads announcing a new edition of *The Life of John Mytton.* $400-$500. London, 1869. 16 colored Alken plates. Cloth. Third edition. $75-$150.

JOURNAL Historique de l'Éstablissement des Français à la Louisiane. Three-quarters morocco. Nouvelle-Orléans, 1831. (By Bernard de la Harpe). First edition. $75-$100.

JOURNAL of the Convention to Form a Constitution for the State of Wisconsin: Begun and Held at Madison on the 5th Day of October, 1846. Boards and calf. Madison, 1847. First edition. $75-$100.

JOURNAL of an Excursion Made by the Corps of Cadets. etc., Under Capt. Partridge. Marbled wrappers. Concord, N.H., 1822. $27.50.

JOURNAL of the Expedition of Dragoons Under the Command of Col. Henry Dodge to the Rocky Mountains During the Summer of 1835. 2 folding maps. Wrappers. No place, no date (Washington, 1836). (By Lt. G. P. Kingsbury.) First edition. $100. (See also Nolie Mumey entry.)

JOURNAL of the Hartford Union Mining and Trading Company. 88 pp., wrappers. On board the Henry Lee, 1849. (By George G. Webster, or John Linville Hall, who printed it?) First edition. $2,500-$3,000. Second edition (with title revised to *Around the Horn in '49: Journal, etc.*): No place, no date (Wethersfield, Conn., or Hartford, 1898). Cloth. $100-$150. San Francisco, 1928. Book Club of California. Half cloth. One of 250 printed by the Grabhorns. $60.

JOURNAL of the Proceedings of a Convention of Physicians, of Ohio, Held in Columbus, Jan. 5, 1835. Daniel Drake, Chairman. 30 pp., wrappers. Cincinnati, 1835. (Main report by Drake.) $75.

JOURNAL of the Senate of South Carolina, Being the Session of 1863. 190 pp., unbound. Columbia, 1863. $25.

JOURNAL of Sentimental Travels in the Southern Provinces of France. 18 colored plates by Thomas Rowlandson. Boards, morocco, or cloth (remainder). London, 1821. (By William Combe.) First edition. $150-$200.

JOURNAL of a Tour Around Hawaii, the Largest of the Sandwich Islands. 3 plates, folding map. Boards and cloth. Boston, 1825. (By William Ellis.) First edition. $250 and up.

JOURNAL of a Tour from Boston to Savannah, etc. (A). Cloth. Cambridge, Mass., 1849. (By Daniel Nason.) First edition. $35-$50.

JOUTEL'S Journal of LaSalle's Last Voyage. Folding map in pocket. Boards. Chicago, 1896. (By Henri Joutel.) Caxton Club. Boxed. $25-$35.

JOYCE, James. See Beckett, Samuel; Gorman, Herbert; Jolas, Maria; Skeffington, F. J. C., and Joyce, James A. Also see *Des Imagistes; The Dublin Book of Irish Verse.*

JOYCE, James. *Anna Livia Plurabelle.* Edited by Padraic Colum. Cloth. New York, 1928. First edition. One of 800 signed. $200-$225. Chicago, no date (1935). With music by Hazel Felman. Folio, printed wrappers. One of 350. $25.

JOYCE, James. *Chamber Music.* Cloth. London, 1907. First edition. $300-$400. Boston, no date (1918). Cloth. First (unauthorized) American edition. $75. New York, 1918. Cloth. First American edition. $100. London, 1918. Wrappers. Second English edition. $35-$50. New York, 1923. Black boards. $25.

JOYCE, James. *Collected Poems.* Frontispiece portrait. Decorated boards. New York, 1936. Black Sun Press. First edition. One of 750. In glassine dust jacket. $75-$100. Another issue: One of 50 on vellum, signed. Boxed. $250-$300. New York, 1937. Cloth. First trade edition. In dust jacket. $25-$35.

JOYCE, James. *Dublin.* Cloth. Basel, Switzerland, no date (1928). First German translation of *Dubliners.* $35-$50.

JOYCE, James. *Dubliners.* Red cloth. London, no date (1914). First edition. $450-$550. New York, 1917. Cloth. First American edition. In dust jacket. $100-$125. Also, $50 (A, 1967). London, 1917. Cloth. $160 (A, 1968).

JOYCE, James. *Epiphanies.* Boards and cloth. No place (Buffalo), 1956. First edition. One of 550. In plain white dust jacket. $50.

JOYCE, James. *Exiles.* Green boards and cloth. London, 1918. First edition. $150-$200. New York, 1918. Boards and buckram. First American edition. In dust jacket. $150.

JOYCE, James. *Finnegans Wake.* Buckram. London, 1939. First edition. One of 425 on large paper, signed. Boxed. $1,000-$1,250. Bookplate removed, some soiling, $700. Also, $1,000 and $400 (A, 1970). London, no date (1939). Cloth. First trade edition. In dust jacket. $100-$125. Dust jacket worn, $85. New York, 1939. Black cloth. First American edition. In dust jacket. $75-$100. Paris, 1962. Wrappers. First French translation. One of 67 on velin. $75-$100.

JOYCE, James. *Gas from a Burner.* Single sheet. Dublin, 1912. $728 (A, 1966).

JOYCE, James. *Haveth Childers Everywhere: Fragment from Work in Progress.* Stiff printed wrappers. Paris, 1930. First edition. One of 500 on Vidalon paper. Boxed. $150-$200. Another issue: One of 100 on vellum, signed. Boxed. $450-$550. Another issue: One of 10 signed. $1,000 and up. Also, spine torn, $850 (A, 1967). London, no date (1931). Yellow wrappers printed in red. First English edition. $50.

JOYCE, James. *The Holy Office.* Broadside. No place, no date (Pola, Austria-Hungary, 1904 or 1905?). First edition. $900-$1,000.

JOYCE, James. *Ibsen's New Drama.* Foolscap, boards, paper label. London, no date (1930). First edition. One of 40. $250 and up. Also, $190 (A, 1968).

JOYCE, James. *James Clarence Mangan.* Foolscap, boards, paper label. London, no date (1930). First edition. One of 40. $250 and up.

JOYCE, James. *Lettres.* Wrappers. Paris, no date (1961). First French translation. One of 47. $250-$300.

JOYCE, James. *The Mime of Mick, Nick and the Maggies.* Designs in color by Lucia Joyce. Stiff white wrappers. Boxed. The Hague, Netherlands, 1934. First edition. One of 1,000 $125-$150.

JOYCE, James. *Pomes Penyeach.* Boards. Paris, 1927. First edition, with errata slip. $60-$80. Also, covers broken and discolored, $25 (A, 1970). Another issue: One of 13 on handmade paper. $350-$400. Paris, 1932. Oblong folio sheets on Japan paper, illuminated by Lucia Joyce. Green silk folder. One of 25 signed. $500 and up. London, no date (1933). Printed wrappers. First English edition. $100-$125. Also, $55 (A, 1967).

JOYCE, James. *A Portrait of the Artist as a Young Man.* Blue cloth. New York, 1916. First edition. In dust jacket. $150-$200. London, no date (1917). Green cloth. First English edition. In dust jacket. $75-$100. Lacking jacket, name on end paper, $60.

JOYCE, James. *Stephen Hero.* Cloth. London, 1944. First edition. In dust jacket. $75-$100. New York, no date (1944). New Directions. Green boards and cloth. First American edition. In dust jacket. $50-$75.

JOYCE, James. *Storiella as She Is Syung.* Flexible orange vellum. No place (London), 1937. Corvinus Press. One of 150. Boxed. $400-$600 and up. Another issue: One of 25 signed. $750 and up.

JOYCE, James. *Tales Told of Shem and Shaun: Three Fragments from Work in Progress.* Portrait by Brancusi. Wrappers. Paris, 1929. Black Sun Press. First edition. One of 500 on Van Gelder paper. Boxed. $150-$200. Another issue: One of 100 on vellum, signed. Boxed. $400-$500. London, 1932. Boards. First English edition. In dust jacket. Inscribed by Joyce, $750 (A, 1967).

JOYCE, James. *Two Essays.* See Skeffington.

JOYCE, James. *Two Songs.* In *The Venture. An Annual of Art and Literature.* 23 plates. Pictorial cloth. London, 1905 (published November, 1904). First edition. First appearance of Joyce in clothbound book. $125-$150.

JOYCE, James. *Ulysses.* Printed blue wrappers. Paris, 1922. First edition. One of 100 on Dutch handmade paper, signed. $4,000-$5,000. Also, $4,000 (A, 1970). Another issue: One of 150 on Verge d'Arches paper. $1,500 and up. Also, $1,300 (A, 1968). Another issue: One of 740 on handmade paper. $1,500 and up. Also, spine torn, $750, $768, $720, and $800 (A, 1970). (Various later printings of the original edition through the 1920's retail in the $150-$250 range.) Paris, 1922. Egoist Press. Wrappers. First English edition (printed in France), with errata slip and 4-page leaflet of press notices. One of 2,000. $1,000 and up. Also, $864 (A, 1970). Paris, 1929. Wrappers. First French translation (as *Ulysse*). One of 10 on Van Gelder paper. $2,000 and up. Also, $1,600 (A, 1968). Another issue: One of 25 on Holland paper. $500 and up. Also, $450 (A, 1968). Another issue: One of 875 on Alfa paper. $250 and up. Hamburg, no date (1932). Odyssey Press. 2 vols., printed wrappers. First Odyssey Press edition. (One of 25 signed?) $1,750 and up. Also, $1,500 (A, 1968). First (authorized) American edition: No place, no date (New York, 1934). Cream-colored cloth. In dust jacket. $75-$100. Also, signed by Joyce, $130 (A, 1968). New York, 1935. Limited Editions Club. Illustrated by Henri Matisse. Pictorial buckram. One of 250 signed by Joyce and Matisse. $1,500-$2,100. Another issue: One of 1,250 signed only by Matisse. $800-$1,000. (Also, 6 signed proofs of the Matisse etchings for this book were issued in an edition of 150 in canvas portfolios. Value: $1,500-$2,000; $1,152 at auction, 1968.) London, 1936. Green buckram. First English edition to be printed in England. One of 900 on vellum. In dust jacket. $250-$350. Also, $100.80 (A, 1966). Another issue: Vellum. One of 100 signed. Boxed. $1,500-$2,000. Also, $800 (A, 1970), $1,500 (A, 1968).

JUDD, A. N. *Campaigning Against the Sioux.* Plate, other illustrations. 45 pp., pictorial wrappers. Watsonville, Calif., 1906. First edition. $350 and up. Rebound in cloth, covers bound in, $325. Watsonville, 1909. Wrappers. Second edition. $250 (A, 1968).

JUDD, Silas. *A Sketch of the Life and Voyages of Capt. Alvah Judd Dewey.* Boards and cloth. Chittenango, N.Y., 1838. First edition. $250.

JUDGES and Criminals: Shadows of the Past. 100 pp. San Francisco, 1858. (By Dr. Henry M. Gray?) First edition. $300-$500 (or more). (Note: Only 2 copies known, says Howes.)

JUDSON, Phoebe Goodell. *A Pioneer's Search for an Ideal Home.* Frontispiece. Cloth. Bellingham, Wash., 1925. First edition. $100-$150.

JUVENILE Lyre. Boards and leather. Boston, 1836. (By Lowell Mason and E. Ives, Jr.) $35.

JUSTICE and Expediency; or Slavery Considered with a View to Its Rightful and Effectual Remedy, Abolition. Stiched without covers. Haverhill, Mass., 1833. (By John Greenleaf Whittier.) First edition. $300 and up.

K

KA Euanelio a Mataio. (Together with *Marako and Ioane.*) Gospels of Matthew, Mark, and John in Hawaiian. 3 vols., sewed. Rochester, N.Y., 1828-29. $75.

KABOTIE, Fred. *Designs from the Ancient Mimbrenos, with Hopi Interpretation.* Illustrated, including color. Half cloth. San Francisco, 1949. One of 250. $100.

KAIN, Saul. *The Daffodil Murderer.* Yellow (orange) wrappers printed in red. No place (London), 1913. (By Siegfried Sassoon.) First edition. $150-$200.

KANE, Elisha Kent. *Arctic Explorations.* Plates, 2 folding maps. 2 vols., pictorial cloth. Philadelphia, 1856. First edition. $40-$50.

KANE, Paul. *Wanderings of an Artist Among the Indians of North America.* Folding map, 8 colored plates, woodcuts. Cloth. London, 1859. First edition. $400-$500. Also, $200 (A, 1969), $350 (A, 1968); rebound, $288 (A, 1968).

KANE, Thomas Leiper. *A Friend of the Mormons.* Portrait. Boards and cloth. San Francisco, 1957. Grabhorn Press. $35.

KANE, Thomas Leiper. *The Mormons.* 84 pp., printed wrappers. Philadelphia, 1850. First edition. $200-$250. Second edition, same date, 92 pp., wrappers. $100.

KANSAS City und sein Deutschthum im 19 Jahrhundert. Cloth. Cleveland, 1900. $50.

KATHERINE Walton; or, The Rebel of Dorchester. Cloth. Philadelphia, 1851. (By William Gilmore Simms.) First edition. $35-$50.

KAVANAGH, Patrick. *The Great Hunger.* Boards and linen. Dublin, 1942. Cuala Press. One of 250. In dust jacket. $30-$35.

KAYE-SMITH, Sheila. *Little England.* Cloth. London, no date (1918). First edition. In dust jacket. $35.

KAYE-SMITH, Sheila. *The Tramping Methodist.* Cloth. London, 1908. First edition. In dust jacket. $50. Author's first book.

KEATING, William H. (compiler). *Narrative of an Expedition to the Source of St. Peter's River, Lake Winnepeek, etc.* Map. 15 plates. 2 vols., boards. Philadelphia, 1824. First edition. $150-$200. Another, rebacked, $100. London, 1825. Maps, plates, tables. 2 vols., boards. First English edition. $150.

KEATS, John. *Endymion: A Poetic Romance.* Drab buff boards, printed paper label on spine. London, 1818. First edition, first issue, with one line of errata (not 5) and 2 (not 5) ad leaves at end. $1,500-$2,500. Also, rebound in morocco, $1,008 (A, 1967). Second issue, with 5-line errata. $750-$1,000. London, no date (1947). Golden Cockerel Press. Wood engravings. Buckram and vellum. One of 400. $100-$150. Another issue: Vellum. One of 100 specially bound. $250-$300.

KEATS, John. *John Keats' Unpublished Poem to His Sister Fanny April, 1818.* Facsimile. Vellum-backed cloth. Boston, 1909. Bibliophile Society. First edition. One of 489 on vellum. $25.

KEATS, John. *Lamia, Isabella, The Eve of St. Agnes, and Other Poems.* Boards, paper label; or calf. London, 1820. First edition, with half title and 8 pages of ads at end. Boards:

$2,500-$3,500. Also, lacking label, joint torn, $1,400 (A, 1970); rebacked, $1,680 (A, 1965); $2,500 and, rebound in contemporary boards, $1,000 (A, 1962). Calf: Without ads. $900. Waltham Saint Lawrence, England, 1928. Golden Cockerel Press. Woodcuts by Robert Gibbings. Sharkskin and cloth. One of 500. $150-$200.

KEATS, John. *Letters of John Keats to Fanny Brawne, Written in the Years 1819 and 1820.* Edited by Harry Buxton Forman. Etched frontispiece and facsimile. Cloth. London, 1878. First edition. One of 50. $125-$150.

KEATS, John. *Life, Letters, and Literary Remains of John Keats.* Edited by Richard Monckton Milnes. Engraved portrait and facsimile. 2 vols., cloth. London, 1848. First edition. $100-$150.

KEATS, John. *Odes, Sonnets and Lyrics.* Portrait frontispiece. Wrappers. Oxford, 1895. Daniel Press. One of 250. $50-$75.

KEATS, John. *Poems.* Woodcut vignette of Spenser on title page. Boards, paper label on spine. London, 1817. First edition. $5,000 and up. Also, some leaves loose, $4,320 (A, 1965); rebound in calf, lacking blank leaf, half title loose, $1,540 (A, 1965). London, 1894. Kelmscott Press. Vellum. One of 300. $500-$750. London, 1898. Ballantyne Press. Cloth. One of 217. $100. Another issue(?): Morocco. $192 (A, 1967). London, 1914. Doves Press. Edited by T. J. Cobden-Sanderson. Vellum. One of 200. $400-$500. London, 1915. Florence Press. 2 vols., limp vellum with ties. One of 250. $60 and $96. New York, 1966. Limited Editions Club. Boards and leather. Boxed. $25-$35.

KEATS, John. *Poetical Works.* Printed in double columns within ruled borders. Yellow wrappers. London, 1840. First complete collected edition. $300-$400.

KEEP Cool. 2 vols., boards. Baltimore, 1817. (By John Neal.) First edition. $200-$250. Author's first book.

KEES, Weldon. *Collected Poems.* Boards and leather. Iowa City, 1960. First edition. One of 180 (200?). $30-$40.

KEET, Alfred Ernest. *Stephen Crane: In Memoriam.* Light orange wrappers. New York, no date. First edition. One of 50. $35.

KEITH, G. M. *A Voyage to South America and the Cape of Good Hope.* Boards. London, 1819. First edition, first issue, printed by Phillips. $125-$150. London, 1819. Revised edition, printed by Vogel. With list of subscribers. $250-$300.

KELEHER, William A. *The Fabulous Frontier.* 11 plates. Cloth. Santa Fe, N.M., no date (1945). First edition. One of 500. In dust jacket. $50-$75.

KELEHER, William A. *The Maxwell Land Grant.* Illustrated. Pictorial cloth. Santa Fe, no date (1942). First edition. In dust jacket. $50-$75.

KELLER, George. *A Trip Across the Plains.* 58 pp., printed wrappers. No place, no date (Masillon, Ohio, 1851). First edition. $2,500 (A, 1968).

KELLEY, Hall J. *General Circular to All Persons of Good Character Who Wish to Emigrate to the Oregon Territory.* 28 pp., printed wrappers. Charlestown, Mass., 1831. First edition. $325 (A, 1969).

KELLEY, Hall J. *A Geographical Sketch of That Part of North America Called Oregon.* Folding map. 80 pp., printed wrappers. Boston, 1830. First edition. $1,000 and up. Also, $700 (A, 1969).

KELLEY, Hall J. *History of Colonization of the Oregon Territory.* 12 pp., sewed. Worcester, Mass., 1850. First edition. $500 and up. Also, leaves pinned together with a contemporary straight pin, $550 (A, 1969).

KELLEY, Hall J. *A History of the Settlement of Oregon and the Interior of Upper California.* 128 pp., printed wrappers. Springfield, Mass., 1868. First edition. $3,000 and up. Another edition (date and place unknown) in facsimile: $50 (A, 1969).

KELLEY, Hall J. *A Narrative of Events and Difficulties in the Colonization of Oregon and the Settlement of California.* 92 pp., printed wrappers. Boston, 1852. First edition. $750-$1,000. Also, inscribed by the author, $1000 (A, 1969).

KELLEY, Joseph (Bunco). *Thirteen Years in the Oregon Penitentiary.* Illustrated. 142 pp., stiff wrappers. Portland, Ore., 1908. First edition. $25.

KELLOGG, H. S. *Life of Mrs. Fmily J. Harwood.* Illustrated. Decorated cloth. Albuquerque, 1903. First edition. $125. (Note: Yes, "Fmily" is what it says.)

KELLY, Charles. *Old Greenwood: The Story of Caleb Greenwood, Trapper, Pathfinder and Early Pioneer of the West.* Illustrated. Cloth. Salt Lake City, 1936. First edition. One of 350. In dust jacket. $50-$60.

KELLY, Charles. *The Outlaw Trail: A History of Butch Cassidy and His Wild Bunch.* Illustrated. Pictorial cloth (leatherette). Salt Lake City, 1938. First edition. $60-$75. New York, 1959. Pictorial cloth. In dust jacket. $15-$20.

KELLY, Charles. *Salt Desert Trails.* Illustrated. Cloth (leatherette). Salt Lake City, 1930. First edition. $35.

KELLY, Charles (editor). See Lee, John D.

KELLY, Charles, and Birney, Hoffman. *Holy Murder.* Illustrated. Cloth. New York, no date (1934). First edition. In dust jacket. $35.

KELLY, Charles, and Howe, Maurice L. *Miles Goodyear, First Citizen of Utah.* Illustrated. Cloth. Salt Lake City, 1937. First edition. One of 350. In dust jacket. $60-$75.

KELLY, Ebenezer B. *Autobiography.* Cloth. Norwich, Conn., 1856. First edition. $35.

KELLY, George Fox. *Land Frauds of California.* 37 pp., wrappers. No place (Santa Clara?), 1864. First edition. In plain wrappers, defective, $350 (A, 1968).

KELLY, Jonathan F. *The Humors of Falconbridge.* Cloth. Philadelphia, no date (1856). First edition. $25.

KELLY, L. V. *The Range Men: The Story of the Ranchers and Indians of Alberta.* Illustrated. Pictorial cloth. Toronto, 1913. First edition. $150-$200.

KELLY, Robert. *Armed Descent.* No place, no date (New York, 1961). Hawk's Well Press. First edition. $25. Author's first book.

KELLY, Robert. *Her Body Against Time.* Wrappers. Mexico City, 1963. (Vol. 8 of *The Plumed Horn.*) $25.

KELLY, Robert. *Sonnets.* Illustrated in color by the author. Cloth, paper labels. Los Angeles, 1968. First edition. One of 75 signed. $35-$50.

KELLY, William. *An Excursion to California over the Prairie, Rocky Mountains, and Great Sierra Nevada.* 2 vols., cloth. London, 1851. First edition. $150-$200.

KEMPTON-Wace Letters (The). Green decorated cloth. New York, 1903. (By Jack London and Anna Strunsky.) First edition. $25-$35. Reprint edition, same date: Authors named on title page. $10.

KENDAL and Windermere Railway. Two Letters Reprinted from the Morning Post. Sewed. London, no date (1844). (By William Wordsworth.) First edition, with Whittaker imprint. $75-$100. Kendal, England, no date (1845). 24 pp., single sheet folded. Revised edition, with Branthwaite imprint. No recent sales noted; has a 1920 auction record of $105.

KENDALL, George Wilkins. *Narrative of the Texan Santa Fe Expedition.* 5 plates, folding map. 2 vols., cloth. New York, 1844. First edition. $150-$200. London, 1844. Map, 5 plates. 2 vols., cloth. First English edition. $75-$100.

KENDALL, George Wilkins. *The War Between the United States and Mexico.* Map, 12 colored plates. Folio, cloth. New York, 1851. First edition. $500-$600. Also, rebound in cloth, $350 (A, 1967).

KENDALL, Joseph. *A Landsman's Voyage to California.* Portrait. Marbled boards. San Francisco, 1935. One of 200. $35-$50.

KENDERDINE, T. S. *A California Tramp and Later Footprints.* 39 views. Pictorial cloth. Newtown, Pa., 1888. First edition. $60-$75.

KENILWORTH. 3 vols., boards. Edinburgh, 1821. (By Sir Walter Scott.) First edition. $100-$150.

KENNEDY, Edward G. *The Etched Work of Whistler.* 5 vols. (text vol. and 4 half cloth plate folders). New York, 1910. First edition. One of 400. $250 and up.

KENNEDY, James Harrison. *A History of the City of Cleveland.* Cloth. Cleveland, 1896. $40-$50.

KENNEDY, John F. *Inaugural Address.* Portrait. Vellum. Los Angeles, 1965. One of 1,000. $75-$100.

KENNEDY, John F. *Profiles in Courage.* Cloth. New York, no date (1956). First edition. In dust jacket. $75-$100.

KENNEDY, John F. *Why England Slept.* Cloth. New York, 1940. First edition. In dust jacket. $200-$300. London, no date (1940). Red cloth. First English edition, with ads dated 1940. In dust jacket. $150-$200.

KENNEDY, John F. (editor). *As We Remember Joe.* Portrait frontispiece, photographs. Red cloth. No place, no date (Cambridge, Mass., 1945). First edition. $1,500 and up. Also, rubbed, $1,000 (A, 1970); $550, $750, and $1,736 (A, 1965). Inscribed copies, up to $2,600 at auction (1965).

KENNEDY, John Pendleton. See Secondthoughts, Solomon. Also see *Horse-Shoe Robinson; Rob of the Bowl; Swallow Barn.*

KENNEDY, John Pendleton. *Memoirs of the Life of William Wirt.* Frontispiece. 2 vols., black cloth. Philadelphia, 1849. First edition. $50-$75.

KENNEDY, Margaret. *The Constant Nymph.* Cloth. London, 1924. First edition, first issue, with ads on verso of half title. In dust jacket. $35.

KENNEDY, Margaret. *The Ladies of Lyndon.* Cloth. London, no date (1923). First edition. In dust jacket. $35.

KENNEDY, Pendleton. See *The Blackwater Chronicle.*

KENNEDY, W. S. *The Plan of Union: or a History of the Churches of the Western Reserve.* Cloth. Hudson, Ohio, 1856. First edition. $35-$50.

KENNEDY, William. *Texas: Its Geography, Natural History, and Topography.* 118 pp., wrappers. New York, 1844. First edition. $75-$100. (Reprint in part of *Texas: The Rise, Progress, etc.)*

KENNEDY, William. *Texas: The Rise, Progress and Prospects of the Republic of Texas.* Maps, charts. 2 vols., cloth. London, 1841. First edition. $150-$250. Another issue: 2 vols. in one, cloth. $130 (A, 1965). Fort Worth, Tex., 1925. Maps. Cloth. $35.

KENT, Henry W. (compiler). *Bibliographical Notes on One Hundred Books Famous in English Literature.* Half vellum. New York, 1903. Grolier Club. One of 305. $75-$100.

KENT, Rockwell. *A Birthday Book.* Illustrated by the author. Pictorial cloth (silk). New York, 1931. First edition. One of 1,850 signed. $50-$60.

GEORGE WILKINS KENDALL 277

KENT, Rockwell. *The Bookplates and Marks of Rockwell Kent.* 85 plates. Decorated cloth. New York, 1929. First edition. One of 1,250 signed. $25.

KENT, Rockwell. *Forty Drawings . . . to Illustrate the Works of William Shakespeare.* Portfolio of drawings. No place, no date (Garden City, 1936). First edition. One of 1,000. Boxed. $150-$200.

KENT, Rockwell. *Greenland Journal.* Illustrated. Cloth. New York, no date (1962). First edition. With a set of 6 signed lithographs. Boxed. $100-$125. Worn, $75.

KENT, Rockwell. *How I Make a Wood Cut.* Illustrated. Cloth. Pasadena, 1934. First edition. One of 1,000. $35.

KENT, Rockwell. *It's Me O Lord.* Illustrated. Cloth. New York, no date (1955). In dust jacket. $35.

KENT, Rockwell. *Later Bookplates & Marks of Rockwell Kent.* Illustrated. Cloth. New York, 1937. First edition. One of 1,250 signed. $50-$60.

KENT, Rockwell. *N. by E.* Illustrated. Pictorial silvered blue buckram. New York, 1930. First edition. One of 900 signed. Boxed. $125-$150. Another issue: Linen, with an extra page, for presentation. Boxed. $200-$250. Also, $125 (A, 1969). Trade edition: Cloth. In dust jacket. $15-$25.

KENT, Rockwell. *Northern Christmas.* Illustrated. Pictorial boards. New York, no date (1941). First edition. $35.

KENT, Rockwell. *Salamina.* Illustrated. Blue cloth. New York, 1935. First edition (so stated). In dust jacket. $25.

KENT, Rockwell. *To Thee! A Toast in Celebration of a Century.* Boards. Manitowoc, Wis., no date (1946). First edition. $25.

KENT, Rockwell. *Voyaging Southward from the Strait of Magellan.* Tan buckram. New York, 1924. First edition. In dust jacket. $35. Another issue: Blue boards. One of 110 signed, with an extra signed woodcut. $150-$200.

KENT, Rockwell. *Wilderness: A Journal of Quiet Adventure in Alaska.* 69 illustrations. Gray linen. New York, 1920. First edition, first binding. $100-$150. Second binding, tan pictorial boards. $75-$100.

KENT, Rockwell (editor). *World-Famous Paintings.* 100 color plates. Brown cloth. New York, no date (1939). First edition. $35-$50.

KENTUCKIAN in New-York (The). By a Virginian. 2 vols., cloth. New York, 1834. (By W. A. Caruthers.) First edition. $55.

KENYON, Frederic G. *Ancient Books and Modern Discoveries.* Half vellum. Chicago, 1927. Caxton Club. First edition. One of 350. $80-$100.

KENYON, William Asbury. *Miscellaneous Poems.* Cloth. Chicago, 1845. First edition. $190 (A, 1967).

KER, Henry. *Travels Through the Western Interior of the United States.* Half leather. Elizabethtown, N.J., 1816. First edition. $40-$50.

KERCHEVAL, Samuel. *A History of the Valley of Virginia.* Leather. Winchester, Va., 1833. First edition. $100-$125. Woodstock, Va., 1850. $35.

KEROUAC, Jack. *Doctor Sax.* Boards and cloth. New York, no date (1959). First edition. One of 26 signed. $35-$50.

KEROUAC, Jack. *Excerpts from Visions of Cody.* Boards and cloth. No place, no date (New York, 1959). New Directions. First edition. One of 750 signed. $40-$60.

KEROUAC, Jack. *Mexico City Blues.* Boards and cloth. New York, no date (1959). First edition. One of 26 signed. $50-$75.

KEROUAC, Jack. *On the Road.* Cloth. New York, 1957. First edition. In dust jacket. $25-$35.

KEROUAC, Jack. *A Pun for Al Gelpi.* Broadside, oblong. First edition. One of 100 signed. $35-$50.

KEROUAC, John (Jack). *The Town and the City.* Cloth. New York, no date (1950). First edition. In dust jacket. $35-$50. Author's first book.

KERR, Hugh. *A Poetical Description of Texas, etc.* Cloth. New York, 1838. First edition. $300-$350.

KETTELL, Russell Hawes. *The Pine Furniture of Early New England.* 229 full-page reproductions and 55 working drawings. Linen. Garden City, 1929. First edition, limited. $35-$50.

KETTELL, Samuel. *Specimens of American Poetry, with Critical and Biographical Notices.* 3 vols., boards, paper labels. Boston, 1829. First edition. $100-$150.

KEWEN, Edward John Cage. *Idealina.* Cloth. San Francisco, 1853. First edition. $50-$60.

KEWEN, Edward John Cage. *Oration and Poem Before the Society of California Pioneers.* Wrappers. San Francisco, 1854. First edition. $45.

KEYNES, Geoffrey. *A Bibliography of Sir Thomas Browne.* Illustrated. Buckram. Cambridge, England, 1924. First edition. One of 750 signed. In dust jacket. $50-$75.

KEYNES, Geoffrey. *A Bibliography of William Blake.* Illustrated. Half blue leather. New York, 1921. Grolier Club. One of 250. $200-$250. New York, 1969. Boards. $45-$60.

KEYNES, Geoffrey. *A Bibliography of William Hazlitt.* Illustrated. Boards. London, 1931. Nonesuch Press. One of 750. $50-$70.

KEYNES, Geoffrey. *A Bibliography of the Works of Dr. John Donne.* Cloth. Cambridge, 1914. First edition. One of 300. $35. Cambridge, 1932. Second edition. One of 350. $50-$75. Cambridge, 1958. In dust jacket. $50.

KEYNES, Geoffrey. *A Bibliography of the Writings of William Harvey, M.D.* Illustrated. Buckram. Cambridge, 1928. First edition. One of 300. $84. Cambridge, 1953. Second edition. One of 750. $25.

KEYNES, Geoffrey. *Jane Austen: A Bibliography.* Illustrated. Boards. London, 1929. Nonesuch Press. One of 875. $60-$100.

KEYNES, Geoffrey. *John Evelyn: A Study in Bibliophily.* Illustrated. Cloth. Cambridge, 1937. First edition. One of 300. In dust jacket. $75-$100.

KEYNES, Geoffrey. *John Ray: A Bibliography.* Illustrated. Boards. London, 1951. First edition. One of 650. In dust jacket. $25.

KEYNES, Geoffrey. *Pencil Drawings by William Blake.* Illustrated. Half cloth. London, 1927. First edition. $75-$100.

KEYNES, Geoffrey. *William Pickering: Publisher.* Illustrated. Cloth. London, 1924. Chiswick Press. First edition. One of 350. $60-$75.

KEYNES, Geoffrey, and Wolfe, Edwin, II. *William Blake's Illuminated Books: A Census.* 8 plates. Cloth. New York, 1953. Grolier Club. First edition. One of 400. $75-$100.

KHERDIAN, David. *On the Death of My Father and Other Poems.* Introduction by William Saroyan. Cloth. Fresno, Calif., no date (1970). First edition. One of 26 signed by the poet and Saroyan. In dust jacket. $35.

KIDDER, A. V. *An Introduction to the Study of Southwestern Archaeology.* 50 plates. Cloth. New Haven, 1924. First edition. $35-$50.

KIKI'S Memoirs. Translated by Samuel Putnam. Introduction by Ernest Hemingway. Illustrated. Wrappers. Paris, 1930. First edition, with glassine wrapper and imprinted band around book. $100-$150.

KILBOURN, John. *Columbian Geography.* Leather. Chillicothe, Ohio, 1815. First edition. $200-$300.

KILBOURN, John. *The Ohio Gazetteer, or Topographical Dictionary.* Boards, or calf. Columbus, 1816. First edition. $100. Second edition, same date. $35-$50. (Note: There are numerous other later editions, ranging from $15 to $50 in price.)

KILBOURNE, D. W. *Strictures on Dr. I. Galland's Pamphlet, Entitled "Villainy Exposed," with Some Account of His Transactions in Lands of the Sac and Fox Reservation, etc., in Lee County, Iowa.* 24 pp., sewed. Fort Madison, Iowa, 1850. First edition. $100-$150.

KILBOURNE, Payne K. *History and Antiquities of the Name and Family of Kilbourne.* 3 plates. Cloth. New Haven, 1856. First edition. $40-$50.

KILMER, Joyce. *Summer of Love.* Cloth, gilt top. New York, 1911. First edition, first issue, with the Baker & Taylor imprint at foot of spine (later Doubleday, Page & Co.). In dust jacket. $35. Author's first book. Another (preliminary) issue: Trial binding of unlettered red cloth. $100. Second issue (Doubleday, Page). In dust jacket. $15-$20.

KILMER, Joyce. *Trees and Other Poems.* Boards, paper labels. New York, no date (1914). First edition, first state, without "Printed in U.S.A." on copyright page. In dust jacket. $75-$100.

KIMBALL, Fiske. *The Creation of the Rococo.* 274 illustrations. Buckram and boards. Philadelphia, 1943. In dust jacket. $75-$100.

KIMBALL, Fiske. *Domestic Architecture of the American Colonies and of the Early Republic.* Illustrated. Cloth. New York, 1922. First edition. In dust jacket. $100. Slightly rubbed, lacking jacket, $72.50.

KIMBALL, Fiske. *Mr. Samuel McIntire, Carver, the Architect of Salem.* Illustrated. Cloth. Portland, Me., 1940. One of 675. In dust jacket. $150-$200.

KIMBALL, Fiske. *Thomas Jefferson, Architect.* Illustrated. Cloth. Boston, 1916. First edition. One of 350. In dust jacket. $200-$300.

KIMBALL, Heber C. *The Journal of Heber C. Kimball.* Edited by R. B. Thompson. 60 pp., printed wrappers. Nauvoo, Ill., 1840. First edition. $400-$500.

KING and Queen of Hearts (The). 15 plain or colored illustrations. Printed wrappers. London, 1805. (By Charles Lamb.) First edition, early (earliest?) printing, undated cover, name of "Hodgkins" misspelled on cover. $1,150. Also, $1,000 (A, 1947; the Jerome Kern copy—"the only copy known" with wrapper dated 1805). Various cover dates have been noted on copies sold at auction over the years—1806, 1808, 1809, etc. A-prices, 1941-71: $250, $800, $700 (dated 1806, yellow wrappers, illustrations hand-colored), $182 (brown wrappers, spine defective).

KING, Alexander. *Gospel of the Goat.* Folio, boards and morocco. Chicago, 1928. One of 100. $50-$60.

KING, C. W. *Antique Gems and Rings.* Illustrated. 2 vols., cloth. London, 1872. $100-$150.

KING, C. W. *Handbook of Engraved Gems.* Illustrated. Cloth. London, 1866. First edition. $50-$75.

KING, Charles. *Cadet Days.* Illustrated. Pictorial cloth. New York, 1894. First edition. $25-$35.

KING, Charles. *Campaigning with Crook.* 9 plates. Cloth. New York, 1890. $35-$50.

KING, Charles. *The Fifth Cavalry in the Sioux War of 1876. Campaigning with Crook.* 134 pp., printed wrappers. Milwaukee, 1880. First edition. $250-$300.

KING, Frank M. *Longhorn Trail Drivers.* Illustrated. Cloth. No place, no date (Los Angeles, 1940). First edition. One of 400 signed. $50-$60.

KING, Frank M. *Wranglin' the Past.* Portrait. Leatherette. No place, no date (Los Angeles, 1935). First edition. One of 300 signed. $40-$50.

KING Glumpus: An Interlude in One Act. 3 hand-colored plates by William Makepeace Thackeray. Yellow wrappers. London, 1857. (By John Barrow.) First edition. $500 and up.

KING, Richard. *Narrative of a Journey to the Shores of the Arctic Ocean, in 1833, 1834, and 1835.* Plates, maps. 2 vols., boards. London, 1836. First edition. $150-$200.

KING, W. Ross. *The Sportsman and Naturalist in Canada.* 6 color plates, other illustrations. Cloth. London, 1866. $80-$85.

KING, William. *Chelsea Porcelain.* 171 illustrations (7 colored). Buckram. London, 1922. $43.20. Another issue: Vellum. One of 13 on vellum. $100-$125.

KINGLAKE, A. W. *Eothen, or Traces of Travel Brought Home from the East.* Frontispiece in color, colored plate. Cloth. London, 1844. First edition. $75-$100.

KINGMAN, John. *Letters, Written by John Kingman, While on a Tour to Illinois and Wisconsin, in the Summer of 1838.* 48 pp., printed wrappers. Hingham, Mass., 1842. First edition. $550 (A, 1967).

KINGSBURY, Jedidiah. *A New Improved Dictionary for Children.* Boards. Boston, 1822. First edition. $25.

KINGSLEY, Charles. *Andromeda and Other Poems.* Cloth. London, 1858. First edition. $40-$50.

KINGSLEY, Charles. *The Hermits.* 3 parts, printed wrappers. London, 1868. First edition. $125.

KINGSLEY, Charles. *The Heroes; or, Greek Fairy Tales for My Children.* 8 illustrations by the author. Pink decorated cloth. Cambridge, England, 1856. First edition. $75-$100. Also, foxed, worn, $25 (A, 1970). London, 1912. Riccardi Press. Illustrated by W. Russell Flint. Vellum. One of 500. In dust jacket. $50-$75. Another issue: One of 12 on vellum, with a duplicate set of plates. $200-$300.

KINGSLEY, Charles. *The Roman and the Teuton.* Purplish-brown cloth. Cambridge, 1864. First edition. $50-$60.

KINGSLEY, Charles. *Sermons for the Times.* Cloth, paper label on spine. London, 1855. First edition. $25.

KINGSLEY, Charles. *The Water-Babies.* Illustrated. Cloth. London, 1863. First edition, first issue, with "envoi" leaf. $75-$100.

KINGSLEY, Charles. *Westward Ho!* 3 vols., blue cloth. Cambridge, 1855. First edition, with 16 pages of ads at end of Vol. 3 dated February, 1855. $100-$150. New York, 1947. Limited Editions Club. Illustrated. 2 vols., boards. Boxed. $35.

KINGSLEY, Charles. *Yeast.* Cloth. London, 1851. First edition. $35.

KINGSLEY, Henry. *Austin Elliott.* 2 vols., blue cloth. London, 1863. First edition, with 2 ad leaves in Vol. 1 and 16 pages of ads in Vol. 2. $50-$60.

KINGSLEY, Henry. *The Recollections of Geoffrey Hamlyn.* 3 vols., blue cloth. Cambridge, 1859. First edition. $100-$150. Also, $76.80 (A, 1968). Worn, $60 at retail. Author's first book. Boston, 1859. Cloth. First American edition. $25.

KINGSLEY, Henry. *Valentin: A French Boy's Story of Sedan.* 2 vols., brick-red rough cloth. London, 1872. First edition. $65.

KINO, Eusebio F. *Historical Memoir of Primeria Alta.* Edited by Herbert Eugene Bolton. 7 maps, plates. 2 vols., cloth. Cleveland, 1919. One of 750. In dust jackets. $100-$125. Berkeley, Calif., 1948. Illustrated. 2 vols. in one, cloth. $60.

KINZIE, Mrs. Juliette A. See *Narrative of the Massacre at Chicago.*

KINZIE, Mrs. Juliette A. *Wau-Bun, the "Early Day" in the North-West.* 6 plates. Pictorial cloth. New York, 1856. First edition. $50-$75. London, 1856. First English edition. $50. Chicago, 1901. Caxton Club. Illustrated. Cloth. $30-$40.

KIP, Lawrence. See *The Indian Council in the Valley of the Walla Walla.*

KIP, Lawrence. *Army Life on the Pacific.* Cloth. New York, 1859. First edition. $50-$75.

KIPLING, Rudyard. See *Echoes; Quartette.*

KIPLING, Rudyard. *Barrack-Room Ballads and Other Verses.* Red cloth. London, 1892. First English edition. One of 225 on large paper. $100-$125. Another issue: Buckram and vellum. One of 30 on vellum. $150-$200. (For first American edition, see Kipling, *Departmental Ditties.*)

KIPLING, Rudyard. *"Captains Courageous:" A Story of the Grand Banks.* 22 illustrations. Blue cloth, gilt edges. London, 1897. First English edition. In dust jacket. $100-$150. (Note: A few copies were issued in paper covers in 1896 for copyright purposes.)

KIPLING, Rudyard. *The City of Dreadful Night and Other Places.* Gray-green pictorial wrappers. Allahabad, 1891. No. 14 of Wheeler's Indian Library. First published (and second Indian) edition. $500 and up. Also, $375 (A, 1970). Allahabad and London, no date (1891). Wrappers. First English edition. $100-$150.

KIPLING, Rudyard. *The City of Dreadful Night and Other Sketches.* Sewed, without cover. Allahabad, India, 1890. First (suppressed) edition. In contemporary brown cloth, $2,200 (A, 1942). (Note: The only known copy.)

KIPLING, Rudyard. *Collected Verse.* Red cloth. New York, 1907. First edition, first issue, without index. $25. New York, 1910. Color illustrations. Half vellum. First illustrated edition. One of 125 signed. $50. London, 1912. Limp vellum. One of 100 signed. $75-$100.

KIPLING, Rudyard. *The Courting of Dinah Shadd.* Blue wrappers. New York, 1890. First authorized edition. No. 680 in Harper's Franklin Square Library. $25-$35. (Note: The pirated Hurst clothbound edition, New York, 1890, is considered the genuine first edition. A copy brought $210 at auction in 1930.)

KIPLING, Rudyard. *Departmental Ditties and Other Verses.* Pictorial tan wrappers, with flap and red tape tie. Lahore, India, 1886. First edition. (Issued in the form of a government envelope.) $500 and up. Calcutta, India, 1886. Printed boards. Second edition. $25-$35. Spine defective, $15. New York, no date (1890). Red cloth. First American edition, first issue, with "Lovell" at foot of spine. $100-$125. (Note: This also constitutes the first American edition of *Barrack-Room Ballads.*) London, 1897. Illustrated. Vellum and cloth. First English (and first illustrated) edition. One of 150 on large paper. $50-$75.

KIPLING, Rudyard. *The Feet of the Young Men.* Illustrated with photographs. Brown boards and vellum. Garden City, 1920. First edition. One of 377 signed by the author. $150-$200.

KIPLING, Rudyard. *The Female of the Species.* Oblong, boards. Garden City, 1912. First edition. $25-$35. (Note: There also exists an earlier broadside printing, New York, about 1911. A copy brought $120 at auction in 1960.)

KIPLING, Rudyard. *In Black and White.* Gray-green pictorial wrappers. Allahabad, no date (1888). First edition. No. 3 of the Indian Railway Library. $300-$400. Allahabad and London, no date (1890). Gray-green wrappers. First English edition. $20-$25.

KIPLING, Rudyard. *The Five Nations.* Limp vellum. London, 1903. First edition. One of 30 on vellum. $35-$50. Another issue: Boards. One of 200. $10-$15.

KIPLING, Rudyard. *The Jungle Book* [and] *The Second Jungle Book.* Illustrated. Blue pictorial cloth. London, 1894-95. First editions. In dust jackets. $250 and up.

KIPLING, Rudyard. *Just So Stories for Little Children.* Illustrated by the author. Decorated red cloth. London, 1902. First edition. In dust jacket. $75-$100.

KIPLING, Rudyard. *Kim.* Illustrated by J. K. Kipling. Green cloth. New York, 1901. First edition, first issue, with rhymed chapter headings for Chapters 8 and 13 only. In dust jacket. $100-$125. London, 1901. Red cloth. First English edition. In dust jacket. $100. (Note: There also exists a single proof copy of the English first, dated 1900 on title page. It brought $800 at auction in 1942.) Paris, 1930. Illustrated. 2 vols., sheets in board folders. $75-$100. New York, 1962. Limited Editions Club. Cloth. Boxed. $35.

KIPLING, Rudyard. *Letters of Marque.* Red and blue cloth. Allahabad, 1891. First (suppressed) edition. $228. (Note: A "trial" copy, unbound, brought $260 at auction in 1942.) London, 1891. Gray-green pictorial wrappers. First English edition, with "Vol. I" notation. (One of only 3 known copies.) $1,000 (A, 1942).

KIPLING, Rudyard. *Letters to the Family.* Light-blue wrappers. Toronto, 1908. First edition. $50.

KIPLING, Rudyard. *The Light That Failed.* Blue cloth. London, 1891. First English edition. $25. (Note: A few paperbound copies dated 1890 were issued for copyright purposes.)

KIPLING, Rudyard. *On Dry-Cow Fishing as a Fine Art.* Vignette. Decorated boards. Cleveland, 1926. Rowfant Club. First edition. One of 176. Boxed. $125-$150.

KIPLING, Rudyard. *Pan in Vermont.* Stiff dark-gray wrappers. London, 1902. First edition. $125.

KIPLING, Rudyard. *The Phantom 'Rickshaw and Other Tales.* Gray-green pictorial wrappers. Allahabad, no date (1889). No. 5 of the Indian Railway Library. First edition, first binding, with apostrophe before the word "Rickshaw" on front cover. $100-$150. Second issue, without apostrophe. $75-$100. London, no date (1890). First English edition. $35-$50.

KIPLING, Rudyard. *Plain Tales from the Hills.* Olive-green pictorial cloth. Calcutta, 1888. First edition, first issue, with ads dated December, 1887. $150-$200. (Note: A few copies exist with front cover blank.)

KIPLING, Rudyard. *Poems, 1886-1929.* 3 vols., red morocco. London, 1929. First edition. One of 525 signed. $250.

KIPLING, Rudyard. *Puck of Pook's Hill.* Red cloth. London, 1906. First edition. $35. New York, 1906. Illustrated by Arthur Rackham. Pictorial cloth. First illustrated edition. $100-$125.

KIPLING, Rudyard. *Schoolboy Lyrics.* Brown printed or plain white wrappers. Lahore, 1881. First edition, first issue, plain white wrappers. $750-$1,000. (Note: The brown wrappered copies are worth only a little less.)

KIPLING, Rudyard. *Sea and Sussex from Rudyard Kipling's Verse.* 24 color plates by Donald Maxwell. Boards and vellum. London, 1926. One of 500 signed. In dust jacket. Boxed. $50-$75. Garden City, 1926. One of 150 signed. $50-$75.

KIPLING, Rudyard. *Soldier Tales.* Illustrated. Blue cloth. London, 1896. First edition. In dust jacket. $35-$50.

KIPLING, Rudyard. *Soldiers Three.* Pictorial wrappers. Allahabad, 1888. First edition, first state, without cross-hatching on barrack doors on the cover. $100-$150. Second issue, with the cross-hatching. $75-$100.

KIPLING, Rudyard. *A Song of the English.* Illustrated by W. Heath Robinson. Full white vellum. London, no date (1909). First edition. One of 500 signed by the artist. Boxed. $50.

KIPLING, Rudyard. *Stalky and Co.* Cloth. London, 1899. First edition. $25.

KIPLING, Rudyard. *The Story of the Gadsbys.* Gray-green pictorial wrappers. Allahabad, no date (1888). No. 2 of the Indian Railway Library. First edition. $75-$100.

KIPLING, Rudyard. *Under the Deodars.* Wrappers. Allahabad, no date (1888). No. 4 of the Indian Railway Library. First edition, first state of wrappers, without shading around "No. 4" and "One Rupee." $200-$250. Later, with shading on wrappers. $100-$150.

KIPLING, Rudyard. *Verse: Inclusive Edition, 1885-1918.* 3 vols., vellum. London, 1919. First edition. One of 100 signed. $100-$125. Trade issue: Red cloth. $50-$60. Garden City, 1919. Boards. One of 250 signed. $50-$60.

KIPLING, Rudyard. *Wee Willie Winkie and Other Child Stories.* Gray-green pictorial wrappers. Allahabad, no date (1888). No. 6 of the Indian Railway Library. First edition, first issue, with periods after "A" and "H" on cover. $300-$350.

KIPLING, Rudyard. *White Horses.* Lilac-colored printed wrappers. London, 1897. First edition (a Thomas J. Wise forgery). $90-$100.

KIPLING, Rudyard. *The White Man's Burden.* Lilac-colored printed wrappers. London, 1899. First English edition (a Thomas J. Wise forgery). $200-$300. (Note: There also exists a true first edition, for copyright, issued in 10 copies, gray wrappers, in New York in 1899. A copy inscribed by Kipling sold for $500 in 1942.)

KIT BOOK for Soldiers, Sailors, and Marines. Pictorial boards. Chicago, no date (1943). First edition. $50-$60. (Note: Contains J. D. Salinger's short story "The Hang of It," his first appearance in a book.)

KLONDYKE Mines and the Golden Valley of the Yukon (The). 24 pp., self-wrappers. No place, 1897. $60-$70.

KLOSTERHEIM: or the Masque. Boards, paper label. Edinburgh, 1832. (By Thomas De Quincey.) First edition. $75-$100.

KNEEDLER, H. S. *The Coast Country of Texas.* 76 pp., wrappers. Cincinnati, 1896. First edition. $35-$50.

KNICKERBOCKER, Diedrich. *A History of New York, from the Beginning of the World to the End of the Dutch Dynasty.* Engraved plate. 2 vols., blue boards, or calf. New York, 1809. (By Washington Irving.) First edition. $500 and up. Rebound copies, $200 and up. New York, 1867. 2 vols., full morocco. Author's revised edition. $50-$100. New York, 1900. Illustrated by Maxfield Parrish. Boards and cloth. $75-$100. New York, 1915. Illustrated by Parrish. Half cloth. $75-$100.

KNIGHT, Dr. (John), and Slover, John. *Indian Atrocities.* 96 pp., plain yellow boards, cloth spine. Nashville, 1843. First edition. $1,500 (A, 1967). Cincinnati, 1867. Printed wrappers. $50-$100.

KNIGHT, Sarah K., and Buckingham, The Rev. Mr. *The Journals of Madam Knight and Rev. Mr. Buckingham.* Boards. New York, 1819. First edition. $50-$75.

KNIGHT, William Allen. *The Song of Our Syrian Guest.* 14 pp., green leatherette. Boston, no date (1903). First edition, first issue, with announcement of *The Love Watch* for "early in 1904" on next to last page. $35.

KNISH, Anne. See Morgan, Emanuel, and Knish, Anne.

KNOEPFEL'S Schoharie Cave. 2 folding woodcuts. 16 pp., wrappers. New York, 1853. First edition. $50-$75.

KNOX, Dudley W. *Naval Sketches of the War in California.* 28 colored drawings by William H. Meyers. Introduction by Franklin D. Roosevelt. Boards, white leather spine. New York, 1939. Grabhorn printing. One of 1,000. $100-$125.

KOCH, Frederick H. (editor). *Carolina Folk-Plays, Second Series.* Cloth. New York, 1924. First edition, with dated title page. In dust jacket. $100-$150. Covers soiled, $55. (Note: Contains "The Return of Buck Gavin," Thomas Wolfe's first appearance in a book.)

KONINGSMARKE, the Long Finne: A Story of the New World. 2 vols., boards. New York, 1823. (By James Kirke Paulding.) First edition. $75-$100.

KOOP, Albert J. *Early Chinese Bronzes.* 110 plates (3 colored). Cloth. London, 1924. $60. Another issue: Calf. One of 40 on China paper, signed. $100-$125. New York, 1924. Cloth. First American edition. In dust jacket. $50-$60.

KOOPS, Matthias. *Historical Account of the Substances Which Have Been Used to Describe Events . . . from the Earliest Date to the Invention of Paper.* Printed on paper made of straw alone. Morocco. London, 1801. First edition. $250-$350. London, 1801. Boards and cloth. Second edition. $150-$200.

KOREN, Elizabeth. *Fra Pioneertiden.* Illustrated. Cloth. Decorah, Iowa, 1914. First edition. $75-$100.

KOSEWITZ, W. F. von. *Eccentric Tales, from the German.* 20 hand-colored etched plates by George Cruikshank from sketches by Alfred Crowquill. Cloth. London, 1827. First edition. $100-$150. Rebound in morocco, $75-$100.

KOTZEBUE, Otto Von. *A New Voyage Round the World, 1823-26.* 3 maps and 2 plates. 2 vols., boards, paper labels. London, 1830. First edition in English. $350-$500. Also, rebound in half calf, $312 (A, 1968).

KOTZEBUE, Otto Von. *A Voyage of Discovery, Into the South Sea and Beering's Straits.* Colored plates, engraved folding charts. 3 vols., brown boards, paper labels. London, 1821. First English edition. $500-$750.

KRAKEL, Dean F. *The Saga of Tom Horn.* Illustrated. Cloth. No place, no date (Laramie, Wyo., 1954). First edition (suppressed). $35-$50. Second edition, with text on page 13 and 54 revised. $25.

KRAKEL, Dean F. *South Platte Country.* Illustrated. Pictorial wrappers. Laramie, 1954. First edition. $35-$50.

KREYMBORG, Alfred. *Selected Poems, 1912-1944.* Cloth. New York, 1945. First edition. One of 250 signed. Boxed. $25-$30.

KREYMBORG, Alfred (editor). *Others: An Anthology of the New Verse.* Boards. New York, 1917. First edition. $60-$75.

KROEBER, Alfred L. *Handbook of the Indians of California.* Folding map, 10 other maps, 73 plates on 38 sheets. Cloth. Washington, 1925. First edition. $40-$50.

KRUSENTERN, A. J. von. *Voyage Round the World in the Years 1803, 1804, 1805, and 1806.* 2 color plates, folding map. 2 vols., calf. London, 1813. First edition in English. $850 (A, 1969). Another copy, in new half morocco, ex-library, $550.

KUNZ, George Frederick. *The Curious Lore of Precious Stones.* 86 illustrations (6 in color). Pictorial cloth. Philadelphia, no date (1913). First edition. $50-$75.

KUNZ, George Frederick. *Gems and Precious Stones of North America.* 8 colored plates, other illustrations. Cloth. New York, 1890. First edition, with errata slip. $50-$75.

KUNZ, George Frederick. *Ivory and the Elephant in Art, in Archaeology, and in Science.* Illustrated. Cloth. New York, 1916. First edition. $85.

KUNZ, George Frederick. *The Magic of Jewels and Charms.* Illustrated, including color. Pictorial cloth. Philadelphia, no date (1915). $45.

KUNZ, George Frederick. *Rings for the Finger.* Illustrated. Cloth. Philadelphia, 1917. First edition. $65.

KUNZ, George Frederick, and Stevenson, Charles Hugh. *The Book of the Pearl.* Illustrated, including color plates. Pale-blue cloth. New York, 1908. First edition. $100. Tear in spine, $85. London, 1908. First English edition. $100.

KUYKENDALL, Judge W. L. *Frontier Days.* Portrait. Cloth. No place (Denver?), 1917. First edition. In dust jacket. $35.

L

L., E. V. *Sparks from a Flint: Odd Rhymes for Odd Times.* By E. V. L. Cloth. London, 1890. (By E. V. Lucas?) First edition. $25. Lucas' first book?

LABOULAYE, Édouard. *Laboulaye's Fairy Book.* Translated by Mary L. Booth. Cloth. New York, 1867. First edition. $32.50.

LA BREE, Ben (editor). *The Confederate Soldier in the Civil War, 1861-1865.* Illustrated. Folio, cloth. Louisville, 1895. First edition. $100. Louisville, 1897. Cloth. $75. Spine fraying, $55. Rebound, $30.

LA CROIX, Arda. *Billy the Kid.* Illustrated. Wrappers. New York, 1907. First edition. $40-$50.

LADIES Almanack . . . Written and Illustrated by a Lady of Fashion. Pictorial wrappers. No place (Dijon, France), 1928. (By Djuna Barnes.) First edition. One of 1,000. $125-$150. Spine repaired, $100.

LADY Audley's Secret. 3 vols., blue cloth. London, 1862. (By Mary E. Braddon.) First edition. $3,000 and up. Also, $2,240 (A, 1965).

LADY'S Economical Assistant (The). 9 woodcuts in text and a separate atlas with 27 folding copper plates. 2 vols., gray boards, printed labels. London, 1808. $75-$100.

LAFITTE: The Pirate of the Gulf. 2 vols., cloth. New York, 1836. (By Joseph Holt Ingraham.) First edition. $150-$250. Also, rebound in half leather, $47 (A, 1967).

LA FONTAINE, Jean de. *The Fables of Jean de la Fontaine.* Translated into English verse by Edward Marsh. 26 engravings on copper by Stephen Gooden. 2 vols., vellum. London, 1931. One of 525 signed by the translator and artist. $150-$200. Soiled, $125 (Also, see Marianne Moore entry for her translation.)

LA FRENTZ, F. W. *Cowboy Stuff.* Illustrated. Boards. New York, 1927. First edition, first issue, with 49 plates. One of 500. $100-$125. Also, $50 (A, 1968). Second issue, 50 plates. $75.

LA GUERRA de Tejas sin Máscara. 20 pp., stitched. Mexico, 1845. In new paper covers, $125.

LAMANTIA, Philip. *Touch of the Marvelous.* Boards. No place (Berkeley, Calif.), 1966. First edition. One of 50 signed. $25.

LAMB, Charles. See An Eye Witness. Also see *The Adventures of Ulysses; Beauty and The Beast; Elia; John Woodvil; The King and Queen of Hearts; The Last Essays of Elia; Mr. H.; Mrs. Leicester's School; The New Year's Feast on His Coming of Age; Poetry for Children.*

LAMB, Charles. *Album Verses, with a Few Others.* Cloth-backed boards, paper label. London, 1830. First edition. $75-$125.

LAMB, Charles. *The Child Angel, a Dream.* Printed in red and black. Vellum. London, 1910. One of 12 on vellum. $50-$75.

LAMB, Charles. *Elia and the Last Essays of Elia.* Woodcut portrait. 2 vols., buckram. Newtown, Wales, 1929. Gregynog Press. One of 285. In slipcase. $200-$250. Another issue: One of 25 specially bound in morocco. $400-$450. (For first editions of the *Elia* books, see title entries.)

LAMB, Charles. *The Letters of Charles Lamb, to Which Are Added Those of His Sister Mary Lamb.* Edited by E. V. Lucas. 3 vols., cloth. No place, no date (London, 1935). First edition. In dust jackets. $50-$75.

LAMB, Charles. *Specimens of English Dramatic Poets, Who Lived About the Time of Shakespeare: with Notes.* Gray boards. London, 1808. First edition. $50-$75.

LAMB, Charles. *Tales from Shakespear.* 20 plates by William Mulready. 2 vols., boards. London, 1807. First edition, first issue, with imprint on back of page 235. $1,000-$1,500. Also, in contemporary calf, $575 (A, 1970). Second issue, back of page 235 blank. $500 and up. London, 1909. Illustrated by Arthur Rackham. Buckram with ties. Large paper edition, signed by Rackham. $250-$300. (Note: Mary Lamb collaborated in writing this book.)

LAMB, Charles. *The Works of Charles Lamb.* 2 vols., cloth-backed boards, paper labels. London, 1818. First edition, first issue, with ads at end dated "June, 1818." $300-$400.

LAMBOURNE, Alfred. *An Old Sketch-book. Dedicated to the Memory of My Father.* 18 plates. 78 pp., atlas folio, half morocco and tan cloth. Boston, no date (1892). First edition. $250-$350.

LAMBOURNE, Alfred. *The Old Journey: Reminiscences of Pioneer Days.* 18 plates. 53 pp., yellow and buff cloth. No place, no date (Salt Lake City, 1897). "Jubilee Edition" (of *An Old Sketch-book).* $35-$50.

LAMBOURNE, Alfred. *Scenic Utah: Pen and Pencil.* 20 plates. White cloth, black leather spine. New York, 1891. First edition. $35-$50.

L'ÂME PÉNITENTE, ou Le Nouveau Pensez-y-Bien; Considération sur les Vérités Éternelles, etc. Unbound, uncut. Detroit, 1809. (Barthelemi Baudrand, editor.) $1,100 (A, 1967). In calf binding, uncut, $750 (1956 catalogue).

LAMENTATIONS of Jeremiah (The). Folio, morocco. Newtown, Wales, 1933. Gregynog Press. One of 250. $200.

LAMON, Ward H. *The Life of Abraham Lincoln.* Plates and facsimiles. Green or rust-colored cloth. Boston, 1872. First edition. $25-$30.

LANCASTER, Joseph. *The British System of Education.* 5 plates, frontispiece. Cloth. Georgetown, 1812. First edition. $30-$35.

LANCASTER, Robert A., Jr. *Historic Virginia Homes and Churches.* Illustrated. Cloth. Philadelphia, 1915. First edition. $65-$75. Philadelphia, 1917. $45.

LANDOR, Walter Savage. See *Count Julian: A Tragedy; The Dun Cow; Idyllia Nova Quinque; Imaginary Conversations; Pericles and Aspasia; Poems from the Arabic and Persian; Poetry by the Author of Gebir; Popery, British and Foreign; Simonidea.*

LANDOR, Walter Savage. *Andrea of Hungary, and Giovanna of Naples.* Boards, paper label; or purple cloth. London, 1839. First edition. $35-$50.

LANDOR, Walter Savage. *Dry Sticks, Fagoted.* Dark-green cloth. Edinburgh, 1858. First edition. $50-$75.

LANDOR, Walter Savage. *Epicurus, Leontion, and Ternissa.* Woodcut border, initial, and ornaments. Pigskin. London, 1896. Vale Press. One of 210. $100-$125.

LANDOR, Walter Savage. *Gebir, Count Julian, and Other Poems.* Boards, cloth spine, label. London, 1831. First edition. $125-$150.

LANDOR, Walter Savage. *Heroic Idyls, with Additional Poems.* Cloth. London, 1863. First edition. $25-$35.

LANDOR, Walter Savage. *The Last Fruit Off an Old Tree.* Purple cloth. London, 1853. First edition, with 8 pages of ads. $35-$50.

LANDOR, Walter Savage. *A Modern Greek Idyl.* Green printed wrappers. London, 1917. First edition. One of 30. $50.

LANDOR, Walter Savage. *A Poet's Dream.* Orange-colored wrappers. Edinburgh, 1928. One of 35, with a manuscript note in Thomas J. Wise's hand. $50. Also, $36 (A, 1967).

LANDOR, Walter Savage. *To Elizabeth Barrett Browning and Other Verses.* Green printed wrappers. London, 1917. First edition. One of 30. $50.

LANE, Lydia Spencer. *I Married a Soldier.* Cloth. Philadelphia, 1893. First edition. $25.

LANE, Walter P. *Adventures and Recollections of Gen. Walter P. Lane.* Portrait. 114 pp., wrappers. Marshall, Tex., 1887. First edition. $200.

LANG, Andrew. *Ballads and Lyrics of Old France, with Other Poems.* White cloth. London, 1872. First edition. $35. Author's first book.

LANG, Andrew. *The Blue Fairy Book.* Illustrated. Boards. London, 1889. First edition. $50. New York, no date (about 1897). McLoughlin. Pictorial boards. $20-$25.

LANG, Andrew. *The Blue Poetry Book.* Illustrated. Boards. London, 1891. First edition. One of 150. $45. Trade edition: $10-$15.

LANG, Andrew. *The Gold of Fairnilee.* Cloth. Bristol, England, no date (1888). First edition. $50.

LANG, Andrew. *The Green Fairy Book.* Illustrated. Boards. London, 1892. First edition. One of 150. $50. Trade edition: $15-$20.

LANG, Andrew. *Letters on Literature.* Boards. London, 1889. One of 113. $35.

LANG, Andrew. *Old French Title Pages.* Boards and vellum. San Francisco, 1924. Grabhorn printing. One of 725. $25-$35.

LANG, Andrew. *The Olive Fairy Book.* Illustrated. Decorated cloth. London, 1907. First edition. $35. New York, 1907. Cloth. First American edition. $25.

LANG, Andrew. *Prince Charles Edward.* Illustrated. Half morocco. London, 1900. First edition. One of 350. $25. Another issue: Morocco, extra. $50-$75.

LANG, Andrew. *The Red Fairy Book.* Illustrated. Gray and white boards. London, 1890. First edition. One of 113 on large paper. $50.

LANG, Andrew. *The True Story Book.* Illustrated. Boards. London, 1893. First edition. One of 150 (100?). $40-$50. Trade edition: Cloth. $10.

LANG, Andrew. *XXII Ballades in Blue China.* Full vellum. London, 1880. First edition. $110. Another copy, morocco, $96 (A, 1968).

LANG, Andrew (translator). *Johnny Nut and the Golden Goose.* By Charles Denlin. Illustrated. Decorated cloth. London, 1887. First English edition. $30-$35.

LANG, H. O. (editor). *History of the Willamette Valley.* 6 plates, facsimile, errata leaf. Calf. Portland, Ore., 1885. First edition. $35-$50.

LANG, William W. *A Paper on the Resources and Capabilities of Texas.* 19 pp., wrappers. No place (New York), 1881. First edition. $50-$75. Second edition, same date, 31 pp. $35.

LANG, William W. *The Relative Increase of Population and Production.* 8 pp., sewed. New York, 1881. $35.

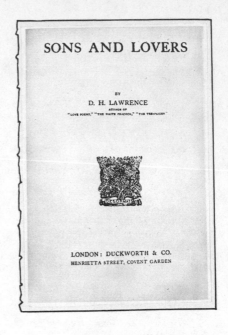

THE RAINBOW

BY
D. H. LAWRENCE
AUTHOR OF "SONS AND LOVERS"

NEW YORK
B. W. HUEBSCH
MCMXVI

SONS AND LOVERS

BY
D. H. LAWRENCE
AUTHOR OF
"LOVE POEMS," "THE WHITE PEACOCK," "THE TRESPASSER"

LONDON: DUCKWORTH & CO.
HENRIETTA STREET, COVENT GARDEN

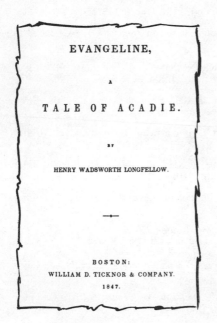

EVANGELINE,

A

TALE OF ACADIE.

BY

HENRY WADSWORTH LONGFELLOW.

BOSTON:
WILLIAM D. TICKNOR & COMPANY.
1847.

IN A GERMAN PENSION

BY
KATHERINE MANSFIELD

LONDON
STEPHEN SWIFT & CO. LTD
10   John Street,   Adelphi

LANGFORD, Nathaniel Pitt. *Vigilante Days and Ways.* 15 plates. 2 vols., pictorial cloth. Boston, 1890. First edition. $75-$125.

LANGLEY, Henry G. *The San Francisco Directory for the Year 1858.* Boards. San Francisco, 1858. $100-$150.

LANGSDORFF, George H. von. *Narrative of the Rezanov Voyage to Neuva California, 1806.* Map, plates. Half cloth. San Francisco, 1927. One of 260. $50-$60.

LANGSDORFF, George H. von. *Voyages and Travels in Various Parts of the World During 1803-7.* Maps and plates. 2 vols., boards, or cloth. London, 1813-14. First English edition. $750-$1,000. Also, $800 (A, 1968); rebacked, $500 (A, 1963). Carlisle, Pa., 1817. Sheep. First American edition (abridged). $75-$100.

LANGSTAFF, Launcelot, and others. *Salmagundi; or, The Whim-Whams and Opinions of Launcelot Langstaff, Esq., and Others.* 2 vols., wrappers, or 20 parts, wrappers. New York, 1807-08. (By Washington Irving, William Irving, and James Kirke Paulding.) First edition. No complete sets noted for sale in many years. Most items offered are mixed sets of the parts bound in one or two volumes. Example: 20 parts (16 of them first issue), bound in 2 vols., calf, $2,000 (A, 1963). Most sets sell at much lower prices. It should be noted that this is an extremely complicated work, existing in numerous states and difficult to identify. See Blanck, *A Bibliography of American Literature.*

LANGSTON, Mrs. George. *History of Eastland County, Texas.* Illustrated. Cloth. Dallas, 1904. First edition. $40-$50.

LANGWORTHY, Franklin. *Scenery of the Plains, Mountains and Mines.* Cloth. Ogdensburgh, N.Y., 1855. First edition. $100-$150. Also, $80 (A, 1968).

LANGWORTHY, Lucius H. *Dubuque: Its History, Mines, Indian Legends.* 82 pp., printed green wrappers. Dubuque, Iowa, no date (1855). First edition. $200 and up. Also, rebound in morocco, $120 (A, 1967); in cloth, $150 (A, 1966).

LANIER, Sidney. *The Boy's Mabinogion.* Illustrated by Alfred Fredericks. Decorated cloth. New York, 1881. First edition. $35-$50.

LANIER, Sidney. *Florida: Its Scenery, Climate, and History.* Illustrated. Cloth. Philadelphia, 1876. First edition, with dated title page. $50-$75. Later issues, lacking title page date, $10-$15.

LANIER, Sidney. *Tiger-Lilies.* Cloth. New York, 1867. First edition, first state, with title page on a stub. $75-$100. Second state, title page an integral leaf. $50. Author's first book.

LANMAN, Charles. *Adventures of an Angler in Canada.* Frontispiece. Half leather. London, 1848. First edition. $50-$75.

LANMAN, Charles. *A Summer in the Wilderness.* Cloth. New York, 1847. First edition. $35-$50.

LANMAN, Charles. *A Tour to the River Saguenay.* Cloth. Philadelphia, 1848. First edition. $50-$75.

LANMAN, James H. *History of Michigan.* Folding map. Cloth. New York, 1839. First edition. $50-$75.

LANTHORN Book (The). Half brown leather and green cloth. New York, no date (1898). (By Stephen Crane and others.) First edition. One of 125. $100. Another issue: One of 12 signed by Crane and others. $200-$250.

LAPHAM, I. A. *A Geographical and Topographical Description of Wisconsin.* Folding map. Cloth. Milwaukee, 1844. First edition. $150-$200. Also, $120 (A, 1967).

LARA, a Tale. Jacqueline, a Tale. Drab boards, paper label. London, 1814. (By George Gordon Noel, Lord Byron.) First edition, with 4 pages of ads. $75-$100.

LARAMIE, Hahn's Peak and Pacific Railway System: The Direct Gateway to Southern Wyoming, Northern Colorado, and Eastern Utah. 110 illustrations. Oblong folio, wrappers. No place, no date (about 1910). $35-$50.

LARCOM, Lucy. *Similitudes.* Cloth. Boston, 1854. First edition. $25-$30. Author's first book.

LARDNER, Ring W. *Bib Ballads.* Illustrated by Fontaine Fox. Decorated brown cloth. Chicago, no date (1915). First edition. Boxed. $75. Lacking box, $50. Also, $40 and $30 (A, 1967). Author's first book (500 printed).

LARDNER, Ring W. *The Big Town.* Green cloth. Indianapolis, no date (1921). First edition. In dust jacket. $35-$50.

LARDNER, Ring W. *Gullible's Travels.* Indianapolis, no date (1917). First edition. In dust jacket. $75-$100.

LARDNER, Ring W. *How to Write Short Stories (with Samples).* Green cloth. New York, 1924. First edition. In dust jacket. $25-$35. Also, inscribed, $75 (A, 1967).

LARDNER, Ring W. *The Love Nest and Other Stories.* Green cloth. New York, 1926. First edition. In dust jacket. $50.

LARDNER, Ring W. *My Four Weeks in France.* Cloth. Indianapolis, no date (1918). First edition. In dust jacket. $35.

LARDNER, Ring W. *Regular Fellows I Have Met.* Cloth. Chicago, 1919. First edition. In dust jacket. $25-$35.

LARDNER, Ring W. *Round Up.* Green cloth. New York, 1929. First edition. In dust jacket. $25.

LARDNER, Ring W. *Treat 'Em Rough: Letters from Jack the Kaiser Killer.* Illustrated. Green boards, paper labels. Indianapolis, no date (1918). First edition, first issue, with the poem to R. W. L., later omitted. In dust jacket. $50-$75. Second issue, without the poem. In dust jacket. $25-$35.

LARDNER, Ring W. *What of It?* Green cloth. New York, 1925. First edition, first issue, with pages 191, 201, 200. In dust jacket. $75. Second issue, pages 191 to 201 corrected by cancel leaf. In jacket. $35.

LARDNER, Ring W. *You Know Me, Al.* Brown cloth. New York, no date (1916). First edition. In dust jacket. $35-$50.

LARDNER, Ring W., and Kaufman, George S. *June Moon.* Mauve cloth. New York, 1930. First edition. In dust jacket. $25-$35.

LARDNER, W. B., and Brock, M. J. *History of Placer and Nevada Counties.* Illustrated. Three-quarters leather. Los Angeles, 1924. $50.

LARIMER, Mrs. Sarah L. *The Capture and Escape; or, Life Among the Sioux.* 5 plates. Cloth. Philadelphia, 1870. First edition. $50-$75. Philadelphia, 1871. $25-$35.

LARKIN, Thomas O., and others. *California in 1846.* Half cloth. San Francisco, 1934. Grabhorn Press. One of 550. $35-$50.

LAROQUE, François A. *Journal of François A. Laroque from the Assiniboine to the Yellowstone, 1805.* 82 pp., printed wrappers. Ottawa, 1910. First edition. $75-$100.

LARRANCE, Isaac. *Post Office Chart.* Maps (2 each) of 10 states. Printed in red and blue. 47 pp., cloth. Cincinnati, 1860. First edition. $60-$70.

LA SALLE, Charles E. *Colonel Crocket, the Texas Trailer.* 84 pp., pictorial wrappers. New York, no date (1871). $50-$60.

LA SHELLE, Kirke. *Poker Rubaiyat.* 12 full-page woodcuts in color by Frank Holme. Colored wrappers. No place, no date (Phoenix, Ariz., 1903). Bandar-Log Press. One of 254. $250-$350. Rebound in cloth, wrappers preserved, $75.

LASSEPAS, Ulises. *De la Colonización de la Baja California.* Calf. Mexico, 1859. $50-$75.

LAST Days of Pompeii (The). 3 vols., boards. London, 1834. (By Edward Bulwer-Lytton.) First edition, with errata slips in each volume. $150-$200. "Some spine defects," $100. New York, 1956. Limited Editions Club. Illustrated. Cloth. Boxed. $20.

LAST Essays of Elia (The). Boards, paper label. London, 1833. (By Charles Lamb.) First English edition (second edition of the Second Series of Elia essays, the first edition having been published in Philadelphia 5 years before; see *Elia* entry). $100-$150.

LAST Hours of Charles R. S. Boyington (The). 44 pp., plain wrappers. Mobile, Ala., 1835. $45-$50.

LAST Man (The). 3 vols., boards. London, 1826. (By Mary Wollstonecraft Shelley.) First edition, with ad leaf at end of Vol. 1. $150-$250.

LAST of the Mohicans (The). By the Author of "The Pioneers." 2 vols., tan boards, paper labels. Philadelphia, 1826. (By James Fenimore Cooper.) First edition, first issue, with page 89 misnumbered 93 in first volume. $3,000-$4,000. Also, $2,550 (A, 1952). London, 1826. 3 vols., boards. First English edition. $400-$600. Also, $350 (A, 1968). New York, 1932. Limited Editions Club. Illustrated. Half buckram. Boxed. $40-$50.

LATOUR, A. Lacarrière. *Historical Memoir of the War in West Florida and Louisiana in 1814-15.* With an atlas. 2 vols., boards. Philadelphia, 1816. First edition. $500-$750. Also, 2 vols., contemporary calf, rebacked, $425 (A, 1967); spine "perished," lacking atlas, $175 (A, 1968); atlas plates bound in, $160 (A, 1970).

LAUGHTON, L. D. Carr. *Old Ship Figure-Heads and Sterns.* 8 colored plates, 48 in monochrome. With 2 portfolios of plates, one a duplicate set of the colored plates and an unpublished plate, matted, the other a series of 8 engraved plates, matted, similar, and apparently unpublished. Three-quarters pigskin. London, 1925. One of 100. $250-$300.

LAURENS, Henry. *The Army Correspondence of Col. John Laurens in the Years 1777-8.* Three-quarters calf. New York, 1867. Bradford Club. One of 75. $50.

LAVATER, J. G. *Le Lavater Portatif, ou Précis de l'Art de Connaître les Hommes par les Traits du Visage.* 33 colored portraits. Wrappers. London, 1811. $50-$80.

LA VERDAD Desnuda sobre la Guerra de Tejas, O sea contestación al Folleto Titulado; La Guerra de Tejas sin Máscara. 42 pp., sewed. Mexico, 1845. $125.

LAW, John. *Address Delivered before the Vincennes Historical and Antiquarian Society.* Folding map. 48 pp., wrappers. Louisville, 1839. First edition. $100-$150. Also, $80 (A, 1967).

LAW, John. *Colonial History of Vincennes.* Cloth. Vincennes, Ind., 1858. $35-$50.

LAW of Descent and Distribution Governing Lands of the Creek Nation, as Held by C. W. Raymond, Judge of the U.S. Court for the Western District of the Indian Territory. 14 pp., printed wrappers. No place, 1903. Democrat Printing Co. $100.

LAWRENCE, D. H. See Davison, Lawrence H.; Verga, Giovanni.

LAWRENCE, D. H. *Amores: Poems.* Cloth. London, no date (1916). First edition, first issue, with 16 pages of ads at end. In dust jacket. $150-$175. Later issue, without the 16 ad pages. In dust jacket. $50-$75. (Also, a variant issue without ads, unknown to bibliographers, brought $132 at auction at Sotheby's in July, 1969.)

LAWRENCE, D. H. *Apocalypse.* Photographic frontispiece. Boards, leather label. Florence, Italy, 1931. First edition. One of 750. $125-$150. London, no date (1932). Frontispiece. Cloth. First English edition. In dust jacket. $25-$35. Back faded, lacking jacket, $14.40.

LAWRENCE, D. H. *Assorted Articles.* Red cloth. London, 1930. First edition. In dust jacket. $25.

LAWRENCE, D. H. *Bay: A Book of Poems.* Hand-colored illustrations. Decorated boards. No place, no date (Westminster, England, 1919). Beaumont Press. First edition. One of 30 on Japan vellum, signed. $750-$1,000. Also, $672 (A, 1969). Another issue: One of 50 on cartridge paper. $350-$500. Also, $216 (A, 1970). Another issue: One of 120 on handmade paper. $250-$300. Also, $132 (A, 1968).

LAWRENCE, D. H. *Birds, Beasts and Flowers.* Pink buckram, paper label. New York, 1923. First edition. In dust jacket. $75-$100. London, 1923. Boards and cloth. First English edition. In dust jacket. $50-$60. London, 1930. Cresset Press. 12 engravings. Vellum-backed boards. $100-$150. Another issue: Cloth-backed boards. $75-$100.

LAWRENCE, D. H. *Collected Poems.* 2 vols., boards, parchment spines. London, 1928. One of 100 signed. $500-$600. New York, 1929. 2 vols. First American edition. Boxed. $35.

LAWRENCE, D. H. *David: A Play.* Tan cloth. London, no date (1926). First edition. One of 500. In dust jacket. $75-$100.

LAWRENCE, D. H. *England, My England and Other Stories.* Blue-gray cloth. New York, 1922. First edition. In dust jacket. $50-$75. London, 1924. First English edition. In dust jacket. $35-$50.

LAWRENCE, D. H. *The Escaped Cock.* Color frontispiece by Lawrence. White wrappers. Paris, 1929. Black Sun Press. First edition. One of 450 on Van Gelder paper. In tissue dust jacket. Boxed. $200-$250. Another issue: One of 50 on vellum. $325-$400. (Note: Published later in England as *The Man Who Died.*)

LAWRENCE, D. H. *Etruscan Places.* 20 plates. Cloth. London, 1932. First edition. In dust jacket. $100-$125.

LAWRENCE, D. H. *Fantasia of the Unconscious.* Blue ribbed cloth. New York, 1922. First edition. In dust jacket. $25-$35. London, 1923. First English edition. In dust jacket. $25.

LAWRENCE, D. H. *Fire and Other Poems.* Introduction by Robinson Jeffers. Linen. San Francisco, 1930. Grabhorn Press. First edition. One of 300. In plain dust jacket. $125-$150.

LAWRENCE, D. H. *Glad Ghosts.* Wrappers. London, 1926. First edition. One of 500. $75-$100.

LAWRENCE, D. H. *Kangaroo.* Brown cloth. London, no date (1923). First edition. In dust jacket. $40-$50. Paris, no date (1933). Wrappers. One of 67. $25.

LAWRENCE, D. H. *Lady Chatterley's Lover.* Mulberry boards, paper spine label. No place (Florence, Italy), 1928. First edition. One of 1,000 signed. In plain dust jacket. $400-$500. Paris, no date (1950). Color plates, text drawings. Loose leaves in wrappers. One of 100 on velin. In cloth case. $75-$100. (A New York dealer offered a copy with an autograph letter, signed, laid in at $1,350 in 1971.)

LAWRENCE, D. H. *The Ladybird, etc.* Brown cloth. London, no date (1923). First edition (of a book published later in America as *The Captain's Doll*). In dust jacket. $50-$60.

LAWRENCE, D. H. *Last Poems.* Edited by Richard Aldington and G. Orioli. Frontispiece in color. Boards, paper label. Florence, 1932. First edition. One of 750. In dust jacket. $100-$150. London, 1933. Boards and cloth. First English edition. In dust jacket. $35-$50.

LAWRENCE, D. H. *The Letters of D. H. Lawrence.* Edited by Aldous Huxley. Plates. Vellum. London, no date (1932). First edition. One of 525. In slipcase. $90-$100. Trade issue: Cloth. In dust jacket. $24. Second edition, same date. Cloth. In dust jacket. $15.

LAWRENCE, D. H. *Look! We Have Come Through!* Bright-red cloth. London, 1917. First edition. In dust jacket. $75-$100. Lacking jacket, $56. New York, 1919. Cloth. First American edition. In dust jacket. $25.

LAWRENCE, D. H. *The Lost Girl.* Brown cloth. London, no date (1920). First edition, first issue, with pages 256 and 268 not tipped in and with page 268 reading "whether she noticed anything in the bed." In dust jacket. $200-$250. Second issue, pages 256 and 268 tipped in. In dust jacket. $75-$100. Third issue, text on page 268 changed. In dust jacket. $25. New York, 1921. Cloth. First American edition. In dust jacket. $50-$75.

LAWRENCE, D. H. *Love Among the Haystacks.* Boards. London, 1930. Nonesuch Press. One of 1,600. In dust jacket. $35-$50.

LAWRENCE, D. H. *Love Poems and Others.* Dark-blue cloth. London, 1913. First edition. In dust jacket. $200-$250.

LAWRENCE, D. H. *The Lovely Lady.* Cloth. London, 1933. First edition. In dust jacket. $35.

LAWRENCE, D. H. *The Man Who Died.* Buckram. London, 1931. First English edition (of a book first published in Paris, 1929, as *The Escaped Cock*). One of 2,000. In dust jacket. $50-$75. Trade edition: Cloth. In dust jacket. $20.

LAWRENCE, D. H. *My Skirmish with Jolly Roger.* Boards. New York, 1929. First edition. One of 600. In tissue dust jacket. $75-$100.

LAWRENCE, D. H. *New Poems.* Gray wrappers. London, 1918. First edition. One of 500. $150-$200. New York, 1920. Boards, paper labels. First American edition. $25.

LAWRENCE, D. H. *The Paintings of D. H. Lawrence.* 26 colored plates. Folio, half morocco and green cloth. London, no date (1929). Mandrake Press. First edition. One of 500. $250-$300. Another issue: One of 10 on Japan paper. $500-$600.

LAWRENCE, D. H. *Pansies.* Portrait frontispiece. Boards and cloth. London, no date (1929). First edition. In dust jacket. $50-$60. Limited issue: One of 250 signed. $150-$200. Another (later) edition, same place and date: White wrappers. "Definitive and Complete Edition." One of 500 signed. In glassine dust jacket. Boxed. $125-$150. Another issue: Limp leather. One of 50 on vellum, signed. $400-$500. Another issue: Prepublication advance copy, pink wrappers. (Not signed.) $50. New York, 1929. First American edition. In dust jacket. $20.

LAWRENCE, D. H. *The Plumed Serpent.* Brown cloth. London, no date (1926). First edition. In dust jacket. $35-$50. New York, 1926. Cloth. In dust jacket. $25-$35. Dust jacket frayed, $18.

LAWRENCE, D. H. *A Prelude.* Cloth, leather spine. Surrey, England, 1949. Merle Press. First edition. One of 100. $50-$75.

LAWRENCE, D. H. *The Prussian Officer and Other Stories.* Blue cloth. London, no date (1914). First edition, first issue, with 20 pages of ads at back. In dust jacket. $100-$125. Second issue, with 16 pages of ads. In dust jacket. $75-$100. New York, 1914. Cloth. In dust jacket. $25.

LAWRENCE, D. H. *Psychoanalysis and the Unconscious.* Gray boards. New York, 1921. First edition. In dust jacket. $35-$50.

LAWRENCE, D. H. *The Rainbow.* Blue-green cloth. London, no date (1915). First edition, with ads dated "Autumn, 1915." In dust jacket. $500-$750. New York, 1916. Cloth. First American edition. In dust jacket. $100-$150. Stockholm, 1942. Printed yellow wrappers. Pirated edition. $35.

LAWRENCE, D. H. *Rawdon's Roof.* Decorated boards. London, 1928. First edition. One of 530 signed. In dust jacket. $100-$150.

LAWRENCE, D. H. *Reflections on the Death of a Porcupine and Other Essays.* Marbled boards, canvas spine. Philadelphia, 1925. Centaur Press. First edition. One of 475. $100-$125. (Another issue of 475 for sale in England: $48 at auction at Sotheby's in 1969.)

LAWRENCE, D. H. *St. Mawr.* (With "The Princess.") Brown cloth. London, no date (1925). First edition. In dust jacket. $35-$50. New York, 1925. Cloth. First separate edition (without "The Princess"). In dust jacket. $25.

LAWRENCE, D. H. *Sea and Sardinia.* 8 colored plates. Boards and cloth. New York, 1921. First edition. In dust jacket. $50-$75. Lacking jacket, $22.50. London, 1923. Cloth. First English edition. In dust jacket. $50-$75.

LAWRENCE, D. H. *Sons and Lovers.* Dark-blue cloth. London, no date (1913). First edition, first issue, without date on title page. In dust jacket. $750-$1,000. Second state, with dated title page tipped in. In dust jacket. $250-$300. New York, 1913. Cloth. First American edition. In dust jacket. $35-$50.

LAWRENCE, D. H. *Stories, Essays and Poems.* Wrappers. London, no date (1939). "Proof Copy" (so imprinted on covers) of the Everyman Edition. $100. Worn, $60.

LAWRENCE, D. H. *Studies in Classic American Literature.* Blue cloth. New York, 1923. First edition. In dust jacket. $75-$100.

LAWRENCE, D. H. *Sun.* Marbled wrappers. London, 1926. First edition. One of 100. $400-$600. Paris, 1928. Black Sun Press. Vellum. Limited and signed. In glassine dust jacket. Boxed. $200-$250. London, 1928. Boards and cloth. In dust jacket. $35-$50. (Note: There also exists a spurious edition, dated 1922, boards and cloth. $25-$35.)

LAWRENCE, D. H. *Tortoises.* Pictorial boards. New York, 1921. First edition. In dust jacket. $150-$200.

LAWRENCE, D. H. *Touch and Go.* Flexible orange boards, paper labels. London, 1920. First edition. In dust jacket. $60-$80. New York, 1920. Boards. First American edition. In dust jacket. $50-$60.

LAWRENCE, D. H. *The Trespasser.* Dark-blue cloth. London, 1912. First edition, with 20 pages of ads at end. In dust jacket. $250-$300.

LAWRENCE, D. H. *Twilight in Italy.* Blue cloth. London, no date (1916). First edition. In dust jacket. $150-$200.

LAWRENCE, D. H. *The Universe and Me.* Stiff black wrappers. No place, no date (1935). Powgen Press. First edition. One of 150. $40.

LAWRENCE, D. H. *The Virgin and the Gipsy.* White boards, paper label. Florence, 1930. First edition. One of 810. In dust jacket. Boxed. $75-$90. London, 1930. Cloth. First English edition. In dust jacket. $40-$60.

LAWRENCE, D. H. *The White Peacock.* Dark blue-green cloth. London, 1911. First English edition, first issue, with publisher's windmill device on back cover and with page 227 not tipped in. In dust jacket. $400-$500. Second issue, with page 227 tipped in. $275. Rubbed, hinges cracked, $75. New York, 1911. Blue cloth. First edition, first issue, with title page tipped in. In dust jacket. $500-$700. Lacking jacket, worn, $250. Copy with integral title page and with 1910 copyright date sold for $3,250 at Parke-Bernet in 1972. Author's first book.

LAWRENCE, D. H. *The Widowing of Mrs. Holroyd.* Red cloth. New York, 1914. First edition. In dust jacket. $75-$100. London, 1914. Cloth. First English edition. In dust jacket. $50-$75.

LAWRENCE, D. H. *The Woman Who Rode Away.* Brown cloth. London, no date (1928). First edition. In dust jacket. $50-$60.

LAWRENCE, D. H. *Women in Love.* Dark-blue cloth. New York, 1920. First edition. One of about 18 (or 25) (of an edition of 1,250) signed on the title page by Lawrence. In dust jacket. $500-$600. Unsigned copies of the limited issue: In dust jacket. $100-$150. Trade edition: Blue cloth. In dust jacket. $25-$35. Another issue: New York, 1920 (actually 1922). Brown boards. One of 50 signed. $200-$250. Also, $130 (A, 1968). (There were also 50 copies from the same sheets issued in England.) London, 1921. Brown cloth. First English trade edition. In dust jacket. $75-$100.

LAWRENCE, D. H. (translator). *The Story of Dr. Manente.* Frontispiece, 2 plates. Parchment boards. Florence, 1929. First edition. One of 200 signed by Lawrence. In dust jacket. $150-$200. Another issue: One of 1,000. In dust jacket. $35-$50.

LAWRENCE, Frieda. *"Not I, But the Wind."* Boards and cloth. Santa Fe, N.M., 1934. First edition. One of 1,000 signed. In dust jacket. $100-$110. London, 1935. Cloth. First English edition. In dust jacket. $40-$50.

LAWRENCE of Arabia. (Two essays: "The Artist in War and Letters," by B. H. Liddell Hart, and "Himself," by Ronald Storrs.) Boards and cloth. No place, no date (London, 1936). First edition. One of 25 on Barcham Green "Boswell" paper (of an edition of 128, signed). $250 and up. Ordinary issue: One of 103 signed. $75-$100.

LAWRENCE, Richard Hoe (compiler). *History of the Society of Iconophiles of the City of New York.* Reproductions of 119 plates. Boards and morocco. New York, 1930. First edition. One of 186. $50-$75.

LAWRENCE, T. E. See Graves, Robert; Shaw, T. E. Also see *The Seven Pillars of Wisdom.*

LAWRENCE, T. E. *Crusader Castles.* Portraits and facsimiles, 2 maps in envelopes. 2 vols., half red morocco. London, 1936. Golden Cockerel Press. First edition. One of 1,000. $450-$500. Also, $288 (A, 1970); $350 and $204 (A, 1969).

LAWRENCE, T. E. *The Diary of T. E. Lawrence.* Illustrated. Boards and morocco. London, 1937. Corvinus Press. First edition. One of 203. $400-$500.

LAWRENCE, T. E. *Eight Letters.* Edited by H. Granville-Barker. Wrappers. London, 1939. First edition. One of 50. $500 and up. Also, $360 and $384 (A, 1968).

LAWRENCE, T. E. *An Essay on Flecker.* Buckram. London, 1937. Corvinus Press. First edition. One of 30. $500 and up. Also, $384 (A, 1968).

LAWRENCE, T. E. *Letter to His Mother.* Plates. Boards. London, 1936. Corvinus Press. First edition. One of 24. $500 and up. Also, $408 (A, 1968).

LAWRENCE, T. E. *Letters.* Edited by David Garnett. Maps and plates. Buckram. London, 1938. First edition. In dust jacket. $25.

LAWRENCE, T. E. *Letters from T. E. Shaw to Bruce Rogers* [and] *More Letters to Bruce Rogers.* 2 vols., limp buckram. No place, 1933-36. First editions. Limited to 200 and 300, respectively. $200-$250.

LAWRENCE, T. E. *Men in Print.* Half morocco. London, 1940. Golden Cockerel Press. First edition. One of 500. $75-$100. Another issue: Morocco. One of 30 specially bound with supplement. $300-$400.

LAWRENCE, T. E. *The Mint: A Day-book of the R. A. F. Depot Between August and December, 1922.* Leather and blue cloth. London, no date (1955). First published edition. One of 2,000. Boxed. $40-$50. Trade edition: Cloth. In dust jacket. $10-$15.

LAWRENCE, T. E. *Revolt in the Desert.* Frontispiece, map, and portraits. Buckram. London, 1927. In dust jacket. $35-$50. Another issue: Half morocco. One of 315 on large paper. $125-$150. New York, 1927. Illustrated. Cloth. First American edition. In dust jacket. $15-$25. Another issue: Buckram. One of 250. $35-$50.

LAWRENCE, T. E. *Secret Despatches from Arabia.* Portrait frontispiece. Morocco and cloth. London, no date (1939). Golden Cockerel Press. First edition. One of 1,000. $250-$300. Another issue: White pigskin. One of 30 with part of the manuscript of *The Seven Pillars of Wisdom.* $660-$800.

LAWRENCE, T. E. *Seven Pillars of Wisdom.* 66 plates, other illustrations, 4 folding maps. Full leather. No place (London), 1926. First edition, inscribed "Complete" and signed "T. E. S." (for T. E. Shaw, Lawrence's adopted name). $4,320 (A, 1968)–J. M. Barrie's copy. Others at auction: $2,280 (1968); $2,100 and $1,968 (A, 1967); inscribed "Incomplete" by "T. E. S.," $840 (A, 1966). (For first American copyright edition, one of only two copies, with no author named, see title entry.) London, no date (1935). Buckram and leather. First published edition. One of 750. In dust jacket. Boxed. $200-$250. Also, rubbed, $132 (A, 1970). Trade edition: Buckram. In dust jacket. $35-$50. Garden City, 1935. Buckram and leather. First published American edition. Limited. In dust jacket. Boxed. $100. Trade edition: Cloth. In dust jacket. $25.

LAWRENCE, W. J. *The Elizabethan Playhouse and Other Studies.* 30 plates. 2 vols., boards and cloth. Stratford-on-Avon, England, 1912-13. Shakespeare Head Press. One of 760. $70-$100.

LAWS and Decrees of the State of Coahuila and Texas, in Spanish and English. Calf. Houston, 1839. $150.

LAWS and Regulations of Union District, Clear Creek County, C. T. 19 pp., printed wrappers. Central, C. T. (Colorado Territory), 1864. $350 (A, 1968).

LAWS for the Better Government of California. 68 pp. San Francisco, 1848. Only two copies known of this first English book printed in California. Estimated value: $5,000 or more (?).

LAWS of the Cherokee Nation. Cloth. Tahlequah, Indian Territory, 1852. $225.

LAWS of the Choctaw Nation, Made and Enacted by the General Council from 1886 to 1890. (In English and Choctaw.) Cloth. Atoka, Indian Territory, 1890. One of 250. $50-$75.

LAWS of Gregory District, February 18 & 20, 1860. (Cover title.) 12 pp., printed wrappers. Denver, 1860. $600 (A, 1968).

LAWS of the Territory of Kansas, Passed at the 2d Session of the General Legislative Assembly. Cloth. Lecompton, Kan., no date (1857). $50-$75.

LAWS of the Territory of Louisiana (The). Sheep. St. Louis, 1808 (actually 1809). $8,000 (A, 1967).

LAWS of the Territory of Michigan. Leather. Detroit, 1833. $50-$75. Hinges started, small piece torn from title page, not affecting text, $35.

LAWS of the Territory of New Mexico. 71 pp., wrappers. Santa Fe, N.M., 1862. $75-$100.

LAWS of the Town of San Francisco (The). 8 pp., wrappers (?). San Francisco, 1847. First edition. $1,000 and up. Also, an imperfect copy (lacking pages 5-8) in board binder, $1,000 (A, 1968). (Said to be "probably the first pamphlet printed in English in California.")

LAWS Relating to Internal Improvement in the State of Michigan. 16 pp., sewed. Detroit, 1837. $35-$50.

LAWYERS and Legislators, or Notes on the American Mining Companies. Half calf. London, 1825. (By Benjamin Disraeli.) First edition. $100-$125.

LAY, William, and Hussey, Cyrus M. *A Narrative of the Mutiny on Board the Ship Globe of Nantucket.* Calf. New-London, Conn., 1828. First American edition. $175.

LAYNE, J. Gregg. *Annals of Los Angeles.* Plates. Cloth. San Francisco, 1935. First edition. $35-$50.

LEA, Albert M. *Notes on the Wisconsin Territory.* Folding map. 53 pp., printed boards. Philadelphia, 1836. First edition. $500-$600. Also, $500 (A, 1967). Another issue: Wrappers. $750 and up. Also, repaired and rebacked, $525 (A, 1964).

LEA, Homer. *The Vermilion Pencil.* Cloth. New York, 1908. First edition. In dust jacket. $50.

LEA, Pryor. *An Outline of the Central Transit, in a Series of Six Letters to Hon. John Hemphill.* 32 pp., printed wrappers. Galveston, Tex., 1859. First edition. $75.

LEA, Tom. *Calendar of the Twelve Travelers Through the Pass of the North.* Illustrated. Folio, cloth. El Paso, Tex., 1946. Carl Hertzog printing. First edition. One of 365 signed. $100.

LEA, Tom. *The King Ranch.* Illustrated by the author. 2 vols., buckram. Boston, no date (1957). First edition. Boxed. $50. Another issue: Limited "Private Edition," printed on paper watermarked with running "W" brand. 2 vols., decorated crash linen. Boxed. $100-$150.

LEA, Tom. *Randado.* Illustrated. Stiff wrappers. No place, no date (El Paso, Tex., 1941). Carl Hertzog printing. First edition. One of 100 signed. $75-$100.

LEACH, A. J. *Early Day Stories: The Overland Trail, etc.* 7 plates. Brown cloth. No place, no date (Norfolk, Neb., 1916). First edition. In dust jacket. $50-$75.

LEACOCK, Stephen. *Canada: The Foundations of Its Future.* 31 full-page illustrations. Montreal, 1941. First edition. $20-$25.

LEACOCK, Stephen. *Literary Lapses: A Book of Sketches.* Half linen, green boards. Montreal, 1910. First edition. In dust jacket. $50. Author's first book.

LEACOCK, Stephen. *Nonsense Novels.* Cloth. London, 1911. First edition. In dust jacket. $25-$35. New York, 1911. Cloth. First American edition. In dust jacket. $25. Montreal, 1911. Green cloth. First Canadian edition. In dust jacket. $25. London, 1921. Illustrated by John Kettlewell, including 8 color plates. Cloth. First illustrated edition. In dust jacket. $15.

LEACOCK, Stephen. *Sunshine Sketches of a Little Town.* Colored frontispiece. Cloth. London, 1912. First edition. In dust jacket. $25.

LEADBEATER, Mary. *Cottage Dialogues Among the Irish Peasantry.* Edited by Maria Edgeworth. Illustrated. 2 vols., boards, paper labels. London, 1811, and Dublin, 1813. First editions. $180.

LEADVILLE Chronicle Annual. 40 pp., wrappers. Leadville, Colo., 1881. $75-$100.

LEADVILLE, Colorado: The Most Wonderful Mining Camp in the World. 48 pp., printed wrappers. Colorado Springs, 1879. (By John L. Loomis.) $175 (A, 1968).

LEAF, Munro. *The Story of Ferdinand.* Illustrated by Robert Lawson. Pink decorated boards, cloth spine. New York, 1936. First edition. In dust jacket. $150-$200.

LEAR, Edward. See Derry, Derry down.

LEAR, Edward. *A Book of Nonsense.* Illustrated. Oblong, stiff wrappers. London, 1861. Second (and enlarged) edition. $150-$200. London, 1862. Boards. Sixth edition. $25-$35. (For first edition, see entry under Lear's pen name Derry, Derry down.)

LEAR, Edward. *Calico Pie.* Illustrated by the author. Glazed boards. London, no date. First edition. $50-$100.

LEAR, Edward. *Illustrated Excursions in Italy.* 2 vols., folio, cloth. London, 1846. First edition. $400-$600. Also, $240 and $252 (A, 1969).

LEAR, Edward. *Illustrations of the Family of Psittacidae, or Parrots.* 42 hand-colored plates. Folio, half morocco. London, 1832. First edition. $3,500 and up. Ex-library copy, repaired, $2,660. Also, $2,800 (A, 1966).

LEAR, Edward. *Journal of a Landscape Painter in Corsica.* Illustrated. Cloth. London, 1870. First edition. $50-$100.

LEAR, Edward. *Journals of a Landscape Painter in Albania.* Map. Illustrated in color. Cloth. London, 1851. First edition. $150-$200.

LEAR, Edward. *Journals of a Landscape Painter in Southern Calabria.* 2 maps. Illustrated. Cloth. London, 1852. First edition. $150-$200.

LEAR, Edward. *Laughable Lyrics.* Illustrated. Cloth. London, 1877. First edition. $50-$75.

LEAR, Edward. *More Nonsense, Pictures, Rhymes, Botany, etc.* Illustrated. Boards and linen. London, 1872. First edition. $200. Foxed, with bookplate, $168.

LEAR, Edward. *Nonsense Songs, Stories, Botany, and Alphabets.* Illustrated. Boards and cloth. London, 1871. First edition. $150-$200. Boston, 1871. Illustrated. Boards. First American edition. $22.50.

LEAR, Edward. *Views in Rome and Its Environs.* Illustrated (plates in sepia). Folio, half morocco. London, 1841. First edition. $200-$300. Plates hand-colored, $500 and up.

LEAR, Edward. *Views in the Seven Ionian Islands.* Illustrated. Folio, cloth. London, 1863. First edition. $500 and up.

LEAR, P. G. and L. O. *The Strange and Striking Adventures of Four Authors in Search of a Character.* 24 pp., light-purple wrappers, purple label on front cover. London, 1926. (By Charles Kenneth Scott-Moncrief.) One of 350 signed. $40-$75.

LEATHER Stocking and Silk. Cloth. New York, 1854. (By John Esten Cooke.) First edition. $35-$50. Author's first book.

LEAVES from Margaret Smith's Journal. Cloth, or wrappers. Boston, 1849. (By John Greenleaf Whittier.) First edition. Cloth: $25-$35. (No copies noted recently in wrappers.)

LEAVES of Grass. Portrait frontispiece on plain paper. Dark-green cloth, gilt- and blind-stamped, marbled end papers. Brooklyn, 1855. (By Walt Whitman.) First edition, first issue, without ads or reviews; first binding, gilt lettering and borders on both covers. $3,500-$5,000 and up. Also, $9,000 (A, 1969). (Note: This exceptionally fine copy, owned by the late Thomas Winthrop Streeter, was the same copy, formerly the property of the late Arthur Swann, New York collector and auction gallery executive, sold for $3,700 in 1960 at the auction of the Swann library. Despite these records, it seems likely that the retail value of this work in acceptable collector's condition should stabilize roughly in the $3,500-$5,000 price range in the 1970's.) Worn copies at retail, $500-$1,000. Second issue, plain yellow end papers, no gold on back cover. $500-$1,000. Third issue, same as second but with ads or press notices bound in. $550 (A, 1970). Brooklyn, 1856. Second edition, with ad leaf of Fowler & Wells, the publisher, at back of the book. $300-$400. Boston, "Year '85 of the States" (1860-61). Third edition, first issue, with "George C. Rand & Avery" on copyright page, portrait on tinted paper, orange-colored (or brick-red) cloth. $50-$100. Second issue, same date, has portrait on white paper. Third issue (first pirated issue), without the Rand & Avery notice. $50-$100. New York, 1867. Half morocco or cloth. Fourth edition, with "Ed'n 1867" stamped on back in gold. (Several variant issues, for which see Wells and Goldsmith, *A Concise Bibliography of the Works of Whitman.*) $100-$150. Washington, 1871. Wrappers, or half morocco. Fifth edition. $200-$250. Also, half morocco, $85 (A, 1965). (For later issue, see *Leaves of Grass, Passage to India* under author entry.) Camden, 1876. Half cream-colored calf and marbled boards. Sixth edition. "Author's Edition," signed. $100-$150. (For variants, see Wells and Goldsmith, cited above.) Boston, 1881-82. Yellow cloth. Seventh edition, first issue (very rare), with "Third edition" on title page (suppressed). $100 and up. Second issue. $35-$50. (Note: A presentation copy to A. C. Swinburne sold for $1,200 in London in 1968.) Camden, 1882. Dark-green cloth. "Author's Edition," signed. $100-$150. Philadelphia, 1882. Yellow cloth. "First Philadelphia edition," with Whitman's name on cover. $50-$75. Philadelphia, 1889. Black morocco. One of 300 signed. $200-$250. Inscribed, $115.20 (A, 1968). Philadelphia, 1891-92. First issue, brown wrappers. $200 and up. Later issue: Dark-green cloth or gray wrappers. $100 and up. Portland, Me., 1919. Mosher Press. Cloth. One of 400. $35-$50. Other issues: Boards. One of 250. $35. One of 100. $50. One of 50 on Japan paper. $60. New York, 1930. Grabhorn printing. 37 woodcuts.

Leather-backed mahogany boards. One of 300. $385-$450. New York, no date (1933). Cloth. Introduction by Sherwood Anderson. $25. New York, 1942. Limited Editions Club. Edward Weston photographs. 2 vols., boards. $75-$150. Mount Vernon, N.Y., no date (1943). Peter Pauper Press. Half morocco. $50.

LEAVES of Grass Imprints: American and European Criticisms of "Leaves of Grass." 64 pp., printed brown wrappers. Boston, 1860. First edition. $100-$150.

LEAVITT, Emily W. *The Blair Family of New England.* Cloth. Boston, 1900. $25-$35.

LEBRIJA, Joaquin, and Berrera, Ignacio. *Análisis e Impugnación del Proyecto de le Sobre Arbitrios para la Guerra de Tejas.* 31 pp., sewed. Mexico, 1841. $45-$50.

LECKENBY, Charles H. (compiler). *The Tread of Pioneers.* Illustrated. Cloth. Steamboat Springs, Colo., no date (1945). First edition. $50-$75.

LE CONTE, Joseph. *A Journal of Ramblings Through the High Sierras of California.* 9 mounted photos. Cloth. San Francisco, 1875. First edition. $100-$150. (Only 20 copies printed.)

LE DUC, W. G. *Minnesota Year Book and Traveller's Guide for 1851.* Folding map. Boards, leather spine. St. Paul, Minn., no date (1851). First year of issue. $100-$200. Other issues: For 1852, with frontispiece plate. $75. For 1853, folding map. $35.

LEDYARD, John. See *The Adventures of a Yankee.*

LEE, Andrew. *The Indifferent Children.* Cloth. New York, no date (1947). (By Louis Auchincloss.) First edition. In dust jacket. $35-$40. Author's first book.

LEE, Harper. *To Kill a Mockingbird.* Wrappers. Philadelphia, no date (1960). First edition. Advance reading copy. $50. Trade edition: Cloth. In dust jacket. $15-$20.

LEE, Maj. Henry, Jr. *The Campaign of 1781 in the Carolinas.* Calf. Philadelphia, 1824. First edition. $75.

LEE, John D. *J. D. Lee's Bekjendelse.* 36 pp., wrappers. Salt Lake City, 1877. $40.

LEE, John D. *The Journals of John D. Lee, 1846-47 and 1859.* Edited by Charles Kelly. Cloth. Salt Lake City, 1938. First edition. One of 250. In dust jacket. $75-$100.

LEE, John D. *The Life and Confessions of John D. Lee.* Wrappers. Philadelphia, no date (1888). $50.

LEE, L. P. (editor). *History of the Spirit Lake Massacre!* (Cover title.) Illustrated. 48 pp., pictorial wrappers. New Britain, Conn., 1857. First edition. $35-$50.

LEE, Nelson. *Three Years Among the Camanches.* 2 plates (including portrait-title page). Wrappers, or cloth. Albany, N.Y., 1859. First edition. Wrappers: $500-$600. Also, covers frayed, $350 (A, 1966). Cloth: $400-$500. Also, worn, $230 (A, 1966); in half morocco, $160 (A, 1967).

LEE, Susan P. *Memoirs of William Nelson Pendleton.* Portrait. Cloth. Philadelphia, 1893. First edition. $50-$75.

LEE Trial (The)! An Exposé of the Mountain Meadows Massacre. 64 pp., printed wrappers. Salt Lake City, 1875. $400 (A, 1968).

LEECH, John. *Follies of the Year.* 21 hand-colored plates. Oblong, leather-backed cloth. London, no date (1864). First collected edition. $50-$100. London, no date (about 1865). $35-$50. London, no date (about 1866). $35-$50. (Also, in wrappers, scarcer.)

LEECH, John. *Hunting: Sports and Pastimes.* Illustrated. 2 vols., elephant folio, boards. London, 1865. First edition. $200-$250.

LEECH, John. *Mr. Briggs and His Doings: Fishing.* 12 color plates. Oblong, wrappers. London, no date (1860). First edition. $300-$400.

LEECH, John. *Portraits of Children of the Nobility.* Illustrated. Cloth. London, 1841. First edition. $35-$50.

LEECH, John. *The Rising Generation.* 12 color plates. Folio, boards and morocco. London, no date (1848). First edition. $100-$150.

LEEPER, David Rohrer. *The Argonauts of Forty-nine.* Illustrated. Cloth. South Bend, Ind., 1894. First edition. $50-$75.

LEESE, Jacob P. *Historical Outline of Lower California.* 46 pp., printed wrappers. New York, 1865. First edition. $50-$75.

LE FANU, Joseph Sheridan. See *The Fortunes of Colonel Torlogh O'Brien.*

LE FANU, Joseph Sheridan. *All in the Dark.* 2 vols., cloth. London, 1866. First edition. $150.

LE FANU, Joseph Sheridan. *Checkmate.* 3 vols., cloth. London, 1871. First edition. $200-$250.

LE FANU, Joseph Sheridan. *Chronicles of Golden Friars.* 3 vols., cloth. London, 1871. First edition. $150.

LE FANU, Joseph Sheridan. *The Evil Guest.* Illustrated. Cloth. London, no date (1894). First edition. $75-$100. London, no date (1895). Revised edition. $50.

LE FANU, Joseph Sheridan. *Ghost Stories and Tales of Mystery.* Illustrated by "Phiz." Cloth. Dublin, 1851. First edition. $250-$350.

LE FANU, Joseph Sheridan. *Green Tea and Other Ghost Stories.* Cloth. Sauk City, Wis., 1945. First edition. $35-$45.

LE FANU, Joseph Sheridan. *Guy Deverell.* 3 vols., cloth. London, 1865. First edition. $300-$400.

LE FANU, Joseph Sheridan. *Haunted Lives.* 3 vols., cloth. London, 1868. First edition. $250-$300.

LE FANU, Joseph Sheridan. *The House by the Churchyard.* 3 vols., cloth. London, 1863. First edition. $150. Second edition, same date. 3 vols. in one, cloth. $35.

LE FANU, Joseph Sheridan. *In a Glass Darkly.* 3 vols., cloth. London, 1872. First edition. $150-$200. Also, $117.60 (A, 1962).

LE FANU, Joseph Sheridan. *The Purcell Papers.* 3 vols., blue-black cloth. London, 1880. First edition. $75-$100.

LE FANU, Joseph Sheridan. *The Rose and the Key.* 3 vols., cloth. London, 1871. First edition. $100-$150.

LE FANU, Joseph Sheridan. *Wylder's Hand.* 3 vols., cloth. London, 1864. First edition. $150-$200.

LE FANU, Joseph Sheridan. *The Wyvern Mystery.* 3 vols., cloth. London, 1869. First edition. $200-$250.

LEFÈVRE, Raoul. *The Recuyell of the Historyes of Troye.* Translated by William Caxton. Edited by H. Halliday Sparling. Woodcut title, borders, and initials. 3 vols. in two, folio, limp vellum with ties. London, 1892. Kelmscott Press. One of 300. $450-$500. Dust-soiled set, $400.

LE GALLIENNE, Richard. *The Book-Bills of Narcissus.* Wrappers. Derby, England, 1891. First edition. One of 50 on large paper. $25. Another issue: Wrappers. $10.

LE GALLIENNE, Richard. *English Poems.* Boards. London, 1892. First edition. $25. Another issue: One of 25 on Japan paper. $35-$50.

LE GALLIENNE, Richard. *George Meredith: Some Characteristics.* Blue cloth. London, 1890. First edition. One of 75 on large paper. $25.

LE GALLIENNE, Richard. *My Ladies' Sonnets.* Boards. No place (Liverpool, England), 1887. First edition. One of 50 on large paper, signed. $50-$100. Ordinary issue: $10-$20. Author's first book.

LE GALLIENNE, Richard. *The Quest of the Golden Girl.* Green cloth. Cambridge, England, 1896. First edition. $25-$30.

LE GALLIENNE, Richard. *Robert Louis Stevenson: An Elegy, and Other Poems, Mostly Personal.* Cloth. London, 1895. First edition. One of 500. $25. Another issue: One of 75 on large paper. $35-$50.

LE GALLIENNE, Richard. *Volumes in Folio.* Blue boards, parchment spine. London, 1889. First edition. One of 50 on large paper. $25-$30.

LEGENDS of the Conquest of Spain. By the Author of "The Sketch-Book." Green cloth, paper label. Philadelphia, 1835. (By Washington Irving.) First edition. $50-$100.

LEGION Book (The). Edited by H. Cotton Minchin. Stephen Gooden copperplate of "Mounted Soldier" (self-portrait) on title page, numerous other illustrations, including 9 color plates. Full white pigskin, gilt- and blind-stamped. London, 1929. One of 100 signed by authors and artists, by Edward, Prince of Wales, and by 5 prime ministers. (Gift book published for the Prince of Wales.) $450.

LEIGH, William R. *The Western Pony.* 6 color plates, with an extra signed plate laid in. Cloth. New York, no date (1933). First edition. One of 100. In dust jacket. $150-$200.

LELAND, Charles Godfrey. *Meister Karl's Sketch-Book.* Cloth. Philadelphia, 1855. First edition. $25. Author's first book.

LELAND, Charles Godfrey. *The Union Pacific Railway.* 95 pp., printed wrappers. Philadelphia, 1867. First edition. $50-$75.

LEONARD, H. L. W. *Oregon Territory.* 88 pp., printed blue or buff wrappers. Cleveland, 1846. First edition. $1,500 and up. Also, $1,300 (A, 1969). (Note: Only 3 copies known.)

LEONARD, Irving (translator). *The Mercurio Volante of Don Carlos De Siguenza y Gongora.* Boards. Los Angeles, 1932. One of 665. In dust jacket. $25-$35.

LEONARD, William Ellery. See *Indian Summer.*

LEONARD, William Ellery. *Aesop and Hyssop.* Decorated gray cloth. Chicago, 1912. First edition. $25.

LEONARD, William Ellery. *Glory of the Morning.* Brown printed wrappers. Madison, Wis., 1912. First edition. $35-$50. Loose, spine torn, $25.

LEONARD, William Ellery. *The Lynching Bee and Other Poems.* Green cloth. New York, 1920. First edition. In dust jacket. $25.

LEONARD, William Ellery. *A Son of Earth: Collected Poems.* Portrait frontispiece. Cream boards, paper label. New York, 1928. First edition. One of 35 lettered copies, signed. $25.

LEONARD, William Ellery. *Two Lives.* Cloth. New York, 1925. First published edition. One of 150 signed. $35-$50. Spine darkened, $30-$35.

LEONARD, William Ellery (translator). *The Tale of Beowulf.* Illustrated by Rockwell Kent. Folio, cloth. New York, 1932. First edition. One of 950. $100.

LEONARD, Zenas. *Narrative of the Adventures of Zenas Leonard.* 87 pp., wrappers. Clearfield, Pa., 1839. First edition. Rebound in three-quarters leather and marbled boards, $6,250 (A, 1968); in morocco, tears in 5 leaves repaired, $5,500 (A, 1966); in half morocco, title page repaired, $5,000 (A, 1964). Cleveland, 1904. Illustrated. Cloth. $40-$60.

LES ORNEMENS de la Mémoire, ou les Traits Brillans des Poètes François les Plus Célèbres. Boards. Detroit, 1811. (By Pons Augustin Alletz.) First edition, first issue, with "k" instead of "x" in name of printer, A. Coxshaw. $350-$400.

LESSING, Doris. *The Grass Is Singing.* Cloth. London, no date (1950). First edition. In dust jacket. $25.

LESTER, John C., and Wilson, D. L. *Ku Klux Klan: Its Origin, Growth and Disbandment.* 117 pp., wrappers. Nashville, 1884. First edition. $150.

LETTER from the Secretary of State, Accompanying Certain Laws of the North-western and Indian Territories of the United States, etc. 53 pp., sewed. No place (Washington), 1802. $50-$75.

LETTER of Amerigo Vespucci (The), Describing His Four Voyages to the New World. Hand-colored map and illustrations by Valenti Angelo. Vellum. San Francisco, 1926. Grabhorn Press. One of 250. Boxed. $100-$125.

LETTER of J. C. Frémont to the Editors of the National Intelligencer, Communicating Some General Results of a Recent Winter Expedition Across the Rocky Mountains, etc. 7 pp., binder's cloth. No place, no date (Washington, 1854). $25.

LETTER to the Hon. Abraham Edwards, etc. (A). 16 pp., sewed. Detroit, 1827. (By William Woodbridge.) $25.

LETTERS from the South. 2 vols., printed boards. New York, 1817. (By James Kirke Paulding.) First edition. $100-$150.

LETTERS of Edward, Prince of Wales, 1304-1305. Edited by Hilda Johnstone. Frontispiece. Half leather. London, 1931. Roxburghe Club. $50.

LETTERS of Runnymede (The). Cloth. London, 1836. (By Benjamin Disraeli.) First edition. $40-$60.

LETTS, J. M. See *California Illustrated; A Pictorial View of California.*

LEVER, Charles. See Lorrequer, Harry. Also see *The Confessions of Harry Lorrequer.*

LEVER, Charles. *Davenport Dunn, or The Man of the Day.* Illustrated by H. K. Browne ("Phiz"). 22 parts in 21, wrappers. London, 1857-59. First edition. $75-$100.

LEVER, Charles. *The Knight of Gwynne: A Tale of the Time of the Union.* Frontispiece, title page and 38 plates by "Phiz." 20 parts in 19, wrappers. London, 1846-47. $50-$75.

LEVER, Charles. *Luttrell of Arran.* Illustrated. 16 parts in 15, pictorial wrappers. London, 1863-65. First edition. $50.

LEVER, Charles. *The O'Donoghue: A Tale of Ireland.* 13 parts in 11, wrappers. Dublin, 1845. First edition. $100.

LEVER, Charles. *One of Them.* Illustrated by "Phiz." 15 parts in 14, pictorial wrappers. London, 1861. First edition. $100.

LEVER, Charles. *Roland Cashel.* 20 parts in 19, wrappers. London, 1848-49. First edition. $100. London, 1850. Cloth. First book edition. $10-$15.

LEVER, Charles. *Sir Brook Fossbrooke.* 3 vols., blue cloth. Edinburgh, 1866. First edition, first binding, with publisher's imprint on spine. $150.

LEVERTOFF (LEVERTOV), Denise. *The Double Image.* Cloth. London, no date (1946). Cresset Press. First edition. In dust jacket. $40-$50. Author's first book.

LEVERTOV, Denise. *The Cold Spring and Other Poems.* Boards. New York, 1968. New Directions. First edition. One of 100 on Shagun paper, signed. In dust jacket. $35-$50.

LEVERTOV, Denise. *In the Night: A Story.* Wrappers. New York, 1968. Albondocani Press. One of 150 signed. $35.

LEVERTOV, Denise. *Overland to the Islands.* Decorated wrappers. Highlands, N.C., 1958. First edition. One of 450. In dust jacket. $35. Highlands, 1964. De luxe edition. One of 50 signed. $35.

LEVERTOV, Denise. *Three Poems.* Stiff wrappers. Mt. Horeb, Wis., 1968. Perishable Press. One of 250. $25.

LEVERTOV, Denise. *With Eyes at the Back of Our Heads.* No place, no date (New York, 1959). New Directions. First edition. In dust jacket. $25.

LEVY, Daniel. *Les Français en Californie.* 373 pp., wrappers. San Francisco, 1884. First edition. $50-$75.

LEVY, Julien. *Surrealism.* 64 illustrations. Pictorial boards. New York, 1936. Black Sun Press. First edition. In dust jacket. $85-$100.

LEWIS, Alfred Henry. *The Apaches of New York.* Frontispiece and 10 plates. Red cloth. New York, no date (1912). First edition. In dust jacket. $25.

LEWIS, Alfred Henry. *The Black Lion Inn.* Frontispiece and 15 plates by Frederic Remington and others. Tan cloth. New York, 1903. First edition, with "Published, May, 1903" on copyright page. In dust jacket. $75. Lacking jacket, $35-$50.

LEWIS, Alfred Henry. *Richard Croker.* Frontispiece and 15 plates. Green cloth. New York, 1901. First edition, first issue, with transposed lines in last paragraph of page 26. $25.

LEWIS, Alfred Henry. *Wolfville.* Frontispiece and 11 plates by Frederic Remington. Cloth. New York, no date (1897). First edition, first issue, with "Moore" in perfect type in line 18, page 19. $75-$100. Worn, $30. (Later printings so identified.) Author's first book.

LEWIS, Alfred Henry. *Wolfville Days.* Frontispiece by Frederic Remington. Red cloth. New York, no date (1902). First edition. $50-$60.

LEWIS, Elisha J. *The American Sportsman.* Illustrated. Cloth. Philadelphia, 1855. $50-$75. Philadelphia, 1857. $35-$50.

LEWIS, Elisha J. *Hints to Sportsmen.* Cloth. Philadelphia, 1851. First edition. $50-$60.

LEWIS, H. *Das Illustrirte Mississippithal.* Engraved title page, frontispiece, 78 other color plates (one folding). Half morocco. Düsseldorf, Germany, no date (1854-57). First edition. $6,250 (A, 1967).

LEWIS, J. O. *The Aboriginal Port Folio.* 72 colored portraits. 3 advertisement leaves (constituting, with title leaf, all the text). 10 parts, wrappers. Philadelphia, 1835. First edition. $1,000 and up. Rebound in decorated leather, front cover bound in and 3 ad leaves included. $750-$1,000. Also, $518 (A, 1964)—"12" numbers, 72 plates. (Note: Howes says that "ordinary" copies have 72 plates, while some have 77 and a few 80, which may account for the listing of 2 extra numbers. Twenty-two of the plates, in 3 parts, brought $360 at a London auction in 1969.)

LEWIS, John Frederick. *Sketches of Spain and Spanish Character.* Lithograph title page and 25 plates. Folio, half morocco. London, no date (1836). $150.

LEWIS, Matthew Gregory. See *Tales of Terror.*

LEWIS, Matthew Gregory. *The Isle of Devils.* Marbled boards and gray cloth. London, 1912. Second edition. One of 20 on large paper. $50.

LEWIS, Matthew Gregory. *Journal of a West Indian Proprietor in the Island of Jamaica.* Boards. London, 1834. $100-$150.

LEWIS, Matthew Gregory. *The Life and Correspondence of Matthew Gregory Lewis.* Illustrated. 2 vols., boards. London, 1839. First edition. $100.

LEWIS, Matthew Gregory. *The Monk.* Engraved title page, 5 color plates. Morocco. London, 1826. $200. Another edition: No place, no date (privately printed). Portrait. 2 vols., half morocco. One of 300. $100. Another edition: Cloth. (About 1880.) One of 60. $25-$35. (Note: Since this handbook is limited to nineteenth- and twentieth-century books, the anonymous 3-volume 1796 London first edition of Lewis' Gothic tale is not included in the detailed listings. A Chicago dealer has lately catalogued the 3-volume set in contemporary calf at $650, while a London dealer has offered another at $182. A worn set brought $154 at auction in 1964. A spurious 1796 edition sometimes appears for sale. It bears a Waterford, Ireland, imprint, but, as noted in the A. Edward Newton sale catalogue, "As usual with copies bearing the above imprint the paper is watermarked 1818.")

LEWIS, Matthew Gregory. *Poems.* Boards, paper label. London, 1812. First edition. $100-$150.

LEWIS, Matthew Gregory. *Romantic Tales.* 4 vols., boards. London, 1808. First edition. $250-$350.

LEWIS, Matthew Gregory. *Rosario, or The Female Monk.* Half calf. Chicago, 1891. $25-$30.

LEWIS, Matthew Gregory. *Tales of Wonder.* 2 vols., calf. London, 1801. First edition. $150-$250. Rebacked, $98. Also, in contemporary half calf, $72 (A, 1969). Another issue: 2 vols. in one, on large paper. $150-$200. Dublin, 1801. 2 vols., contemporary calf. $75-$100.

LEWIS, Matthew Gregory (translator). *The Bravo of Venice.* (From the German of J. D. Zschokke.) Boards. London, 1805. First edition. $100-$125.

LEWIS, Meriwether, and Clark, William. *History of the Expedition Under the Command of Captains Lewis and Clark, etc.* Prepared for the Press by Paul Allen (actually by Nicholas Biddle). Folding map and 5 charts. 2 vols., printed boards. Philadelphia, 1814. First edition. $35,000 (A, 1967)—the exceptionally fine Thomas Winthrop Streeter copy. Previously the highest auction price recorded for this book was $5,200 (1963), earlier prices having ranged from $1,000 to $3,500 (1966) for copies in original binding and up to $500 for copies rebound in leather. New York, 1842. Folding map. 2 vols., calf. Abridged edition. $50-$75. Dublin, 1817. 2 vols., half calf. First Irish edition. $350. New York, 1893. Edited by E. Coues. Map. 4 vols., boards and cloth. $150-$200. Chicago, 1902. Edited by James K. Hosmer. 2 vols., cloth. $50. Chicago, 1905. Edited by Hosmer. Cloth. $25-$35. (For first English edition, see Lewis and Clark, *Travels to the Source of the Missouri River etc.*)

LEWIS, Meriwether, and Clark, William. *Original Journals of the Lewis and Clark Expedition, 1804-1806.* Edited by Reuben Gold Thwaites. 8 vols., cloth, including atlas of maps and plates. New York, 1904-05. First edition. $600 and up. Another issue: Large paper. 15 vols. (7 vols. in 14, plus atlas vol.), cloth. $600-$800. Another issue: One of 50 sets on Japan paper. $1,500-$2,000. New York, 1959. 8 vols., cloth. Facsimile of 1904-05 edition. $150-$200.

LEWIS, Meriwether, and Clark, William. *Travels to the Source of the Missouri River and Across the American Continent to the Pacific Ocean.* Edited by Thomas Rees. Map and 5 charts. Boards. London, 1814. First English edition of *History of the Expedition, etc.* $350-$400. London, 1815. 6 maps. 3 vols., boards and calf. Second English edition. $150.

LEWIS, Oscar. *Hearn and His Biographers.* Facsimiles. Boards and cloth in portfolio. San Francisco, 1930. Westgate Press (Grabhorn printing). First edition. One of 350. $35-$40.

LEWIS, Oscar. *The Origin of the Celebrated Jumping Frog of Calaveras County.* Decorations by Valenti Angelo. Boards. San Francisco, 1931. Grabhorn Press. One of 250. $60-$75.

LEWIS, Sinclair. See Graham, Tom.

LEWIS, Sinclair. *Arrowsmith.* Blue boards and buckram. New York, no date (1925). First edition. One of 500 signed. In glassine dust jacket. Boxed. $100-$125. First trade edition: Cloth. Marked "Second printing" (first trade edition) on copyright page. In dust jacket. $25.

LEWIS, Sinclair. *Babbitt.* Blue cloth. New York, no date (1922). First edition, first state, with "Purdy" for "Lyte" in line 4, page 49. In dust jacket. $80-$100. London, no date. Purple cloth. First English edition. In dust jacket. $35-$50.

LEWIS, Sinclair. *Cheap and Contented Labor.* Illustrated. 32 pp., pictorial blue wrappers. New York, 1929. First edition, first state, without quotation marks in front of "Dodsworth" on title page. $50. Later, error corrected. $35.

LEWIS, Sinclair. *Elmer Gantry.* Blue cloth. New York, no date (1927). First edition, first binding (20,000 copies) with "G" on spine resembling "C" (reading "Elmer Cantry"). In dust jacket. $35-$50. Later binding, corrected. $15-$20.

LEWIS, Sinclair. *Free Air.* Decorated blue cloth. New York, 1919. First edition. In dust jacket. $35-$50.

LEWIS, Sinclair. *The Innocents.* Cloth. New York, no date (1917). First edition, with "F-R" on copyright page. In dust jacket. $150-$200. Also, lacking jacket, spine lettering tarnished, $100 (A, 1963).

LEWIS, Sinclair. *The Job.* Green cloth. New York, no date (1917). First edition, with "B-R" on copyright page. In dust jacket. $50-$60.

LEWIS, Sinclair. *Kingsblood Royal.* Reddish-brown buckram. New York, no date (1947). First edition. One of 1,050 signed. Boxed. $25-$35.

LEWIS, Sinclair. *Launcelot.* 4 pp., decorated wrappers. No place, no date (New York, 1932). First edition in book form. One of 100. $25. (First published in *The Yale Literary Review.*)

LEWIS, Sinclair. *Main Street.* Cloth. New York, 1920. First edition, first issue, with perfect folio on page 54. In dust jacket. $25-$35. New York, 1937. Limited Editions Club. Grant Wood illustrations. Cloth. Boxed. $75.

LEWIS, Sinclair. *The Man Who Knew Coolidge.* Blue cloth. New York, no date (1928). First edition. In dust jacket. $20-$25.

LEWIS, Sinclair. *Our Mr. Wrenn.* Cloth. New York, 1914. First edition, with "M-N" on copyright page. In dust jacket. $50-$75. Another issue: "Advance Copy—Not Published" stamped on title page. $35-$50. Author's second book and the first under his own name. (For actual first book, see entry under Graham, Tom.)

LEWIS, Sinclair. *The Trail of the Hawk.* Blue cloth. New York, no date (1915). First edition, with "H-P" on copyright page. In dust jacket. $50-$75. Also, title page stamped "Advance Copy." $85 (A, 1960).

LEWIS, W. S., and Phillips, P. C. (editors). *The Journal of John Work.* Map. Illustrations. Cloth. Cleveland, 1923. First edition. $25-$35.

LEWIS, Wyndham. *The Apes of God.* Illustrated by the author. Cream-colored buckram. London, 1930. First edition. One of 750 signed. In dust jacket. $50-$75.

LEWIS, Wyndham. *The Art of Being Ruled.* Cloth. London, 1926. First edition. $30-$35.

LEWIS, Wyndham. *Blasting and Bombardiering: Autobiography 1914-1926.* Illustrated. Cloth. London, 1937. First edition. In dust jacket. $30-$35.

LEWIS, Wyndham. *The Caliph's Design.* Stiff wrappers. London, 1919. The Egoist, Ltd. First edition. $35.

LEWIS, Wyndham. *The Childermass: Section I.* (All published.) Yellow buckram. London, 1928. First edition. One of 225 signed. In dust jacket. $50-$75.

LEWIS, Wyndham. *The Diabolical Principle and The Dithyrambic Spectator.* Cloth. London, 1931. First edition. In dust jacket. $35.

LEWIS, Wyndham. *Doom of Youth.* Cloth. London, 1932. First edition (withdrawn). In dust jacket. $35.

LEWIS, Wyndham. *The Enemy.* Nos. 1-3. (All published.) Illustrated. Pictorial wrappers. London, 1927-29. $150.

LEWIS, Wyndham. *Enemy Pamphlets: No. 1.* Wrappers. London, no date (1930). $25-$35.

LEWIS, Wyndham. *The Enemy of the Stars.* Illustrated by the author. Pictorial boards and cloth. London, 1932. First edition. In dust jacket. $35.

LEWIS, Wyndham. *The Ideal Giant.* Boards and cloth. London, no date (1917). First edition. One of 50. $150-$175. Author's first written work, a collection of stories. $30-$35.

LEWIS, Wyndham. *Left Wings Over Europe, or, How to Make a War About Nothing.* Cloth. London, 1936. First edition. In dust jacket. $25-$35.

LEWIS, Wyndham. *Tarr.* Cloth. London, 1918. The Egoist, Ltd. First edition. In dust jacket. $75-$100.

LEWIS, Wyndham. *Thirty Personalities and A Self-Portrait.* 31 plates, loose in buckram and board portfolio. London, 1932. First edition. One of 200 signed. $75-$150.

LEWIS, Wyndham. *Time and Western Man.* Cloth. London, 1927. First edition. In dust jacket. $27.50. Another, signed, $50. Also, signed, $36 (A, 1969).

LEWIS, Wyndham. *Timon of Athens.* 16 plates, loose in folio folder. London, no date (1914). First edition. $200-$250. Lewis' first book.

LEWIS, Wyndham. *The Tyro.* Nos. 1 and 2. (All published.) Illustrated. Wrappers. London, 1921-22. $150-$200.

LEWIS, Wyndham. *The Wild Body: A Soldier of Humour and Other Stories.* Decorated boards, cloth spine. London, 1927. First edition. One of 79 signed. In dust jacket. $100-$125.

LEWISOHN, Ludwig. *The Case of Mr. Crump.* Portrait frontispiece. Stiff printed white wrappers. Paris, 1926. First edition. One of 500 signed. $25-$35.

LEY y Reglamento Aprobado de la Junta Directiva y Económica del Fondo Piadoso de Californias. 20 pp., calf. Mexico, 1833. $250. Also, in marbled wrappers, $100 (A, 1968).

LHOMOND, M. *Elements of French Grammar.* Cloth, paper label. Portland (Brunswick), Me., 1830. (Translated anonymously by Henry Wadsworth Longfellow; Longfellow's first book.) First edition. The only copy noted for sale in many years was a repaired copy, rebound in morocco, sold at auction in 1960 for $200.

LHOMOND, M. *French Exercises.* Purple cloth, paper label. Portland (Brunswick), Me., 1830. (Translated anonymously by Henry Wadsworth Longfellow.) First edition. Rebound in morocco, $100 (A, 1960). (Note: Johnson says that this book and Lhomond's *Elements of French Grammar* were bound as one volume later in 1830 and that the combined book edition of 1831 was "the first book to bear Longfellow's name on the title page.")

LIBBY, Charles T. *The Libby Family in America, 1602-1881.* Portraits. Full sheep. Portland, Me., 1882. $25-$30.

LIBER Amoris: or, The New Pygmalion. Pink boards, green cloth spine, paper label on side. London, 1823. (By William Hazlitt.) First edition. $75-$100. London, 1894. Illustrated. Buckram. One of 500. $25.

LIBER Scriptorum: The First Book of the Authors Club. Full morocco. New York, 1893. First edition. One of 251 signed by contributors. $75-$100. *Liber Scriptorum: The Second Book, etc.* New York, 1921. Morocco. One of 251. $40-$50.

LIEBLING, A. J. *Back Where I Came From.* Orange-tan cloth. New York, no date (1938). First edition. In dust jacket. $30-$35. Author's first book.

LIEBLING, A. J. *The Telephone Booth Indian.* Gray cloth. Garden City, 1942. First edition. In dust jacket. $50-$75.

LIFE Among the Indians. Woodcut plates. 80 pp., colored pictorial wrappers. No place, no date (New Haven, about 1870). (By Healy & Bigelow.) Kickapoo Indian medicine promotion pamphlet. $25-$35.

LIFE and Adventures of Broncho John: His Second Trip up the Trail, by Himself. (Cover title.) Illustrated. 32 pp., pictorial wrappers. No place, no date (Valparaiso, Ind., 1908). (By John H. Sullivan.) $25-$30.

LIFE and Adventures of Calamity Jane. By Herself. Portrait. 8 pp., wrappers. Livingston, Mont., no date (1896). First edition. $300.

LIFE and Adventures of Charles Anderson Chester, the Notorious Leader of the Philadelphia "Killers." Wrappers. Philadelphia, 1850. First edition. $35.

LIFE and Adventures of John A. Murrell (The), the Great Western Land Pirate. Wrappers. New York, 1848. $85.

LIFE and Adventures of John Nicol, Mariner (The). Illustrated by Gordon Grant. White canvas, leather labels. New York, 1936. Limited edition. With an original signed drawing by Grant. $35-$50. London, no date (1937). Cloth. $35-$50,

LIFE and Adventures (The) of Joseph T. Hare, the Bold Robber and Highwayman. 16 engravings. Pictorial wrappers. New York, 1847. (By H. R. Howard.) First edition. $100.

LIFE, and Most Surprising Adventures of Robinson Crusoe of York, Mariner, etc. (The). Boards. Philadelphia, 1803. $35-$50.

LIFE and Scenes Among the Kickapoo Indians: Their Manners, Habits and Customs. Portrait, other illustrations. 175 pp., printed wrappers. New Haven, Conn., no date (1839). $35-$50.

LIFE and Travels of Josiah Mooso (The). Portrait. Cloth. Winfield, Kan., 1888. First edition. $75-$100.

LIFE and Writings of Maj. Jack Downing of Downingville (The), Away Down East in the State of Maine. Boston, 1833. (By Seba Smith.) First edition. $100. Rubbed, shaken, $50.

LIFE for a Life (A). By the Author of "John Halifax, Gentleman," etc. 3 vols., cloth. London, 1859. (By Dinah Maria Mulock.) First edition. $150-$200.

LIFE History of Mrs. Annie St. John: Containing Her Marriage, Seduction of Her Sister by Her Own Husband, Subsequent Divorce. Marbled boards and cloth. New York, 1872. $75.

LIFE in California, etc. By an American. 9 plates. Cloth. New York, 1846. (By Alfred Robinson.) First edition. $200-$250. San Francisco, 1897. Cloth. $35-$50. San Francisco, 1925. Cloth. One of 250. $50-$75.

LIFE in a Man-of-War, etc. By a Fore-Top-Man. Brown cloth. Philadelphia, 1841. (By Henry J. Mercier.) First edition. $75-$100.

LIFE in the New World; or Sketches of American Society. Cloth. New York, no date (1844). (By Karl Postl.) First edition. $50.

LIFE of Joaquin Murieta the Brigand Chief of California (The). 7 full-page plates. Pictorial wrappers (dated 1861). San Francisco, 1859. (By John R. Ridge.) Second ("spurious") edition. $1,400 (A, 1968).

LIFE of Major-General Harrison (The). Portrait, plates. Printed boards. Philadelphia, 1840. First edition. $35-$50.

LIFE of MA-KA-TAI-ME-SHE-KIA-KIAK or Black Hawk. Tan boards and cloth. Cincinnati, 1833. (J. B. Patterson, editor.) First edition. $150-$200. Boston, 1834. Pale-green boards. $50-$75. Oquawka, Ill., 1882. Cloth. $35-$50.

LIFE of Saint David (The). Edited by Ernest Rhys. Colored wood engravings. Red morocco. Newtown, Wales, 1927. Gregynog Press. One of 150. $360 and $400. Another issue: One of 25 specially bound by George Fisher. $400-$500.

LIFE of Saint George (The). Engraved frontispiece and title page by I. de B. Lockyer. Marbled boards. London, no date (modern). One of 21 on vellum. $35-$50.

LIFE of Stonewall Jackson (The). By a Virginian. Printed wrappers. Richmond, Va., 1863. (By John Esten Cooke.) First edition, with Ayres & Wade imprint. $50.

LIFE of Thomas W. Gamel (The). 32 pp., wrappers. No place, no date (1932). $35-$50.

LIFE, Speeches and Public Services of Abram [sic] Lincoln, Together with a Sketch of the Life of Hannibal Hamlin (The). Portrait. 117 pp., pictorial wrappers. New York, 1860. Wigwam Edition. $100-$150.

LIFE, Travels, Voyages, and Daring Engagements of Paul Jones (The). Calf. Albany, N.Y., 1809. Third American edition. $30-$35.

LIGHTHALL, William D. (editor). *Songs of the Great Dominion.* Cloth. London, 1889. (By Bliss Carman.) First edition. $25.

LILY and the Totem (The); or, the Huguenots in Florida. Cloth. New York, 1850. (By William Gilmore Simms.) First edition. $35-$50.

LIN, Frank. *What Dreams May Come.* Cloth, or wrappers. Chicago, no date (1888). (By Gertrude Atherton.) First edition. Cloth: $50-$60. Also, inscribed copy in wrappers, with slipcase, $125 (A, 1967). London, 1889. First English edition. $40-$50. Author's first book.

LINCOLN, Abraham. *The Life and Public Services of General Zachary Taylor.* Marbled boards. Boston, 1922. First edition. One of 435. $35-$50.

LINCOLN, Abraham, and Everett, Edward. *The Gettysburg Solemnities: Dedication of the National Cemetery at Gettysburg, Pennsylvania, November 19, 1863.* 16 pp., printed pamphlet. Washington, no date (1863). First known printing in pamphlet form of the Gettysburg Address. $15,000 (A, 1967).

LINCOLN, Abraham, and Douglas, Stephen A. *Political Debates.* Brown rippled, or tan, cloth. Columbus, Ohio, 1860. First edition, first issue, with no ads, no rule on copyright page, and with a "2" at foot of page 17. $75-$100. (Note: Second and later editions of this work differ in various minor details, the principal distinguishing point being the "2" at page 13, instead of 17. For a detailed discussion, see Ernest J. Wessen's pamphlet, *Debates of Lincoln and Douglas: A Bibliographical Discussion,* New York, 1946. The value range of these later editions, in various states, is roughly $30-$60.)

LINCOLN Centennial Medal (The). Presenting the Medal of Abraham Lincoln by Jules Edouard Roine Together with Papers on the Medal, etc. Portrait (silvered bronze medal). White cloth. New York, 1908. First edition, first issue. One of 100. Boxed. $25. Second issue, blue cloth, 5 pages of ads at end. $10.

LINCOLN, Mrs. D. A. *Frozen Dainties.* 32 pp., wrappers. Nashua, N.H., 1889. First edition. $50.

LINCOLN, Mrs. D. A. *Mrs. Lincoln's Boston Cook Book.* Marbled boards, cloth spine and corners. Boston, 1884. First edition. $500-$600.

LINCOLN, Joe. *Cape Cod Ballads and Other Verse.* Drawings by E. W. Kemble. Decorated yellow cloth. Trenton, N.J., 1902. (By Joseph C. Lincoln.) First edition. In dust jacket. $25-$35. Author's first book.

LINCOLN, Joseph C. *Cape Cod Yesterdays.* 12 mounted plates. Cloth. Boston, 1935. Large paper Chatham edition. One of 1,075 signed. $35.

LINCOLN, Joseph C. *Cap'n Eri.* Cloth. New York, 1904. First edition. $50-$75.

LINDBERGH, Charles A. *"We": The Famous Flier's Own Story of His Life and His Trans-Atlantic Flight.* Illustrated. Half vellum. New York, 1927. Author's autograph edition. One of 1,000 signed. Boxed. $100. Trade edition: Blue cloth. In dust jacket. $12.50-$15.

LINDLEY, John. *Rosarum Monographia: Or, a Botanical History of Roses.* One plain and 18 colored plates. Boards. London, 1820. First edition. $400-$500. London, 1830. Second edition. $300-$400.

LINDLEY, John. *Pomologia Britannica; or Figures and Descriptions of the Most Important Varieties of Fruit Cultivated in Great Britain.* 152 colored plates. 3 vols., half brown morocco. London, 1841. First edition. $600-$750.

LINDSAY, Jack. See Graves, Robert, and Lindsay, Jack.

LINDSAY, Jack. *Storm at Sea.* Engravings by John Fairleigh. Half morocco. London, 1935. One of 250 signed. $75.

LINDSAY, Jack, and Lindsay, Norman. *A Homage to Sappho.* Illustrated. Vellum. London, 1928. Fanfrolico Press. One of 70. $150-$200.

LINDSAY, Norman. *Etchings.* Cloth. London, 1927. One of 129. $75-$100.

LINDSAY, Vachel. *Collected Poems.* Half cloth. New York, 1923. First edition. One of 400 signed. $50. Also, $25 (A, 1969). Trade edition: Cloth. In dust jacket. $15-$20. New York, 1925. Illustrated by Lindsay. Pictorial boards. First illustrated edition. One of 350 signed. Boxed. $35-$50. Trade edition: Blue cloth. In dust jacket. $15-$20.

LINDSAY, Vachel. *The Congo and Other Poems.* Pictorial cloth. New York, 1914. First edition. In dust jacket. $35-$50.

LINDSAY, Vachel. *General William Booth Enters into Heaven and Other Poems.* Red cloth. New York, 1913. First edition. In dust jacket. $50-$60. Inscribed, $65.

LINDSAY, Vachel. *The Golden Whales of California, and Other Rhymes in the American Language.* Reddish-brown decorated cloth. New York, 1920. First edition. In dust jacket. $35.

LINDSAY, Vachel. *A Handy Guide for Beggars.* Cloth. New York, 1916. First edition. In dust jacket. $35-$50.

LINDSAY, Vachel. *Proclamation of the Gospel of Beauty.* Broadside. No place, no date (Springfield, 1912). First edition. $100.

LINDSAY, Vachel. *The Tramp's Excuse and Other Poems.* (Cover title.) Decorations by the author. Printed wrappers with cord tie. No place, no date (Springfield, Ill., 1909). First edition. $300-$400. Three inscribed copies noted at auction sold for $240 (1958), $180 (1952), and $200 (1949). Author's first book. (Note: Both Merle Johnson and the auction records incorrectly—and persistently—list the place of publication as Springfield, Ohio.)

LINDSAY, Vachel. *The Wedding of the Rose and the Lotus.* Illustrated stiff printed leaflet poem. 3 pp. No place, no date (Springfield, 1912). First edition. $150-$200.

LINDSAY, William S. *History of Merchant Shipping and Ancient Commerce.* 3 maps, 3 plates, numerous other illustrations. 4 vols., cloth. London, 1874-76. $200.

LINDSEY, Charles. *The Prairies of the Western States.* 100 pp., wrappers. Toronto, 1860. First edition. $150-$200.

LINDSLEY, John Berrien. *The Military Annals of Tennessee.* 2 plates. Cloth. Nashville, 1886. First edition. $75-$100.

LINES on Leaving the Bedford St. Schoolhouse. 4 pp., plain wrappers. No place, no date (Boston, 1880). (By George Santayana.) First edition. $600. Author's first published work.

LINFORTH, James (editor). *Route from Liverpool to Great Salt Valley.* Map and 30 full-page plates. 120 pp., plus "Notice to Subscribers." 15 paperbound parts. Liverpool, July, 1854, to September, 1855. In morocco case, one paper cover in facsimile, $2,000. Liverpool, 1855. Boards. First edition in book form. With map partly colored by hand. $500-$600. Also, rebound, $350 and $225 (A, 1968).

LINGUAL Exercises for Advanced Vocabularians. By the Author of "Recreations." Cloth. Cambridge, 1925. (By Siegfried Sassoon.) First edition. One of 90. $75.

LINKLATER, Eric. *Position at Noon.* Beige buckram. London, no date (1958). First edition. One of 250 signed. In dust jacket. $25-$35.

LINN, John Blair (1777-1804). *Valerian: A Narrative Poem.* Portrait and silhouette. Boards. Philadelphia, 1805. First edition. $75-$100. (Note: Contains Charles Brockden Brown's sketch of Linn, his brother-in-law.)

LINN, John Blair (1831-1899). *Annals of Buffalo Valley, Pennsylvania.* Illustrated. Cloth. Harrisburg, Pa., 1877. First edition. $40-$50.

LINN, John J. *Reminiscences of Fifty Years in Texas.* Illustrated. Cloth. New York, 1883. First edition, with errata slip. $100-$150.

LINSLEY, Daniel C. *Morgan Horses.* Illustrated. Cloth. New York, 1857. First edition. $50-$60. New York, 1860. Cloth. $35-$50.

LINTON, William James. *The Masters of Wood-Engraving.* Illustrated. Folio, cloth. New Haven, 1889. One of 500. $50-$75.

LIONEL Lincoln: or, The Leaguer of Boston. By the Author of *The Pioneers.* 2 vols., drab boards, paper labels. New York, 1825-24. (By James Fenimore Cooper.) First edition. (Vol. 2 is dated 1824.) $150-$200.

LIPSCOMB, George. *History and Antiquities of the County of Buckingham.* Numerous maps, plates and woodcuts. 4 vols., half leather. London, 1847. First edition. $200-$300. Another issue: Large paper. $400-$500.

L'ISLE-ADAM, Villiers de. *Axel.* Translated by H. P. R. Finberg. Preface by W. B. Yeats. Illustrated by T. Sturge Moore. White cloth. London, 1925. One of 500. $50-$60.

LIST of Persons to Whom Permits to Locate Mineral Lands on the South Shore of Lake Superior Have Been Granted and Leases Issued up to June 16, 1846. 16 pp., cloth. No place, no date (Detroit, 1846). $65.

LITCH, Josiah. *The Probability of the Second Coming of Christ About A.D. 1843.* Cloth. Boston, 1838. First edition. $100.

LITTELL, William. *Festoons of Fancy.* Mottled calf. Louisville, Ky., 1814. First edition. $2,000 (A, 1967).

LITTELL, William. *Principles of Law & Equity, etc.* 101 pp., plus errata page, half leather. No place (Frankfort, Ky.?), 1808. First edition, with errata slip. $50-$100.

LITTLE, David. *The Wanderer and Other Poems.* 32 pp., printed wrappers. Los Angeles, 1880. $45.

LITTLE, James A. *Biographical Sketch of Feramorz Little.* Morocco. Salt Lake City, 1890. First edition. $50-$60.

LITTLE, James A. *From Kirtland to Salt Lake City.* Illustrated. Cloth. Salt Lake City, 1890. First edition. $75-$100.

LITTLE, James A. *Jacob Hamblin: A Narrative of Personal Experiences as a Frontiersman, Missionary to the Indians, and Explorer.* Cloth. Salt Lake City, 1881. First edition. $40-$50.

LITTLE, James A. *What I Saw on the Old Santa Fe Trail.* Frontispiece. 127 pp., printed wrappers. Plainfield, Ind., no date (1904). First edition. $100-$150.

LITTLEHEART, Oleta. *The Lure of the Indian Country.* Moccasin-skin binding. Sulphur, Okla., 1908. First edition. Signed presentation copy, $40.

LITTLE Lucy: or, The Careless Child Reformed. 33 pp., printed wrappers. Cambridge, Mass., 1820. First edition. $65.

LIVE Boys; or Charley and Nasho in Texas. Cloth. Boston, 1879. (By Thomas Pilgrim.) First edition. $50. Author's first book.

LIVING Issue (A). 37 pp., wrappers. (Suppressed portion of Dodge's *Our Wild Indians.*) Washington, 1882. (By Richard Irving Dodge.) $150.

LIVINGSTON, Luther S. *Franklin and His Press at Passy.* Illustrated. Boards and cloth. New York, 1914. Grolier Club. First edition. One of 300. $100-$125.

LIVINGSTONE, David. *Missionary Travels and Researches in South Africa.* Portrait, other illustrations. Cloth. London, 1857. First edition $50-$75. Signed presentation copies, $100 and up.

LIVRE d'Esther (Le). Illustrated in color by Arthur Szyk. Wrappers. Paris, no date (1925). One of 175 on Japan vellum, with an extra set of plates in black and white. In slipcase. $200.

LIZARS, John. *A System of Anatomical Plates of the Body, with Descriptions and Observations.* Text volume, plus folio atlas of 101 colored plates. Leather. Edinburgh, no date (1822-1826). First edition. $200-$250.

LLEWELLYN, Richard. *How Green Was My Valley.* Yellow buckram, leather label. London, no date (1939). First edition. One of 200 signed. In slipcase. $35-$50.

LLOYD, James T. *Steamboat Directory, and Disasters on the Western Waters.* Cloth. Cincinnati, 1856. First edition, first issue, with 326 pp. $35-$50. (Second issue has 331 pp.; valued a little less by purists.)

LLOYD, Robert. *The Actor.* With an Essay by Edmund Blunden. Illustrated. Boards and vellum. London, 1926. First edition. One of 60 on vellum, signed by Blunden. $60-$70.

LOAN Exhibition of 18th and Early 19th Century Furniture, Glass, etc. Cloth. New York, 1929. (Girl Scouts' Loan Exhibition catalogue.) $100-$150.

LOCKWOOD, Frank C. *The Apache Indians.* Cloth. New York, 1938. First edition. In dust jacket. $35-$50.

LOCKWOOD, Frank C. *Arizona Characters.* Illustrated. Pictorial cloth. Los Angeles, 1928. First edition. In dust jacket. $35-$60.

LOCKWOOD, Frank C. *Pioneer Days in Arizona.* Illustrated. Cloth. New York, 1932. First edition. In dust jacket. $35-$50.

LOCKWOOD, Luke Vincent. *The Pendleton Collection.* 102 full-page plates. Morocco. Providence, 1904. One of 160 on Japan vellum, signed. $150-$225.

LOFTING, Hugh. *The Story of Doctor Dolittle.* Illustrated by the author. Decorated orange-colored cloth, pictorial paper label. New York, 1920. First American edition. In dust jacket. $50-$75.

LOG of the Cruise of Schooner Julius Webb, Which Sailed from Norwich, Ct., on July 23, 1858, etc. 40 pp., wrappers. Worcester, Mass., 1858. (By A. B. R. Sprague.) First edition. $50.

LOGAN, John. *Cycle for Mother Cabrini: Poems.* Boards and cloth. New York, no date (1955). First edition. One of 250 signed. In dust jacket. $25. Author's first book.

LOMAS, Thomas J. *Recollections of a Busy Life.* Portraits. Folded sheets, unbound. No place, no date (Cresco, Iowa, 1923). First edition. $100. Rebound in morocco, $85.

LONDON by Night: A Descriptive Novel. By the Author of "Anonyma," "Skittles," etc. Pictorial title page and 10 colored plates, one folding. Wrappers. London, no date (about 1860). First edition. $50. Also, cloth, original wrappers mounted on sides, $20-$25.

LONDON Cries for Children. 20 woodcuts. 40 pp., plain boards. Philadelphia, 1810. $50.

LONDON, Charmian. *The Book of Jack London.* Illustrated. 2 vols., blue cloth. London, 1921. First edition. In dust jackets. $35-$50. New York, 1921. 2 vols., cloth. First American edition. In dust jackets. $35-$50.

LONDON, Jack. See *The Kempton-Wace Letters.*

LONDON, Jack. *The Abysmal Brute.* Frontispiece. Olive-green cloth, stamped in yellow and dark green. New York, 1913. First edition, with "Published, May, 1913" on copyright page. In dust jacket. $100. Later, binding stamped in black. In dust jacket. $50-$75.

LONDON, Jack. *Adventure.* Dark-blue or red pictorial cloth. New York, 1911. First edition. In dust jacket. $35-$40.

LONDON, Jack. *Before Adam.* Illustrated by Charles Livingston Bull. Tan pictorial buckram. New York, 1907. First edition. In dust jacket. $25-$35.

LONDON, Jack. *Burning Daylight.* Frontispiece. Blue and yellow pictorial cloth. New York, 1910. First edition, first printing, with blank leaf after ads. In dust jacket. $35-$50. London, 1911. Cloth. $10.

LONDON, Jack. *The Call of the Wild.* Illustrated by Philip R. Goodwin and Charles Livingston Bull. Green pictorial cloth. New York, 1903. First edition, first issue, with vertically ribbed cloth. In dust jacket. $75-$100. London, 1903. Decorated blue cloth. First English edition. In dust jacket. $75-$100. New York, 1960. Limited Editions Club. Cloth. Boxed. $25-$30.

LONDON, Jack. *Children of the Frost.* Illustrated by Raphael M. Bray. Green pictorial cloth. New York, 1902. First edition. In dust jacket. $50-$60.

LONDON, Jack. *The Cruise of the Dazzler.* Frontispiece. Cream-colored cloth. New York, 1902. First edition, first issue, with "Published October, 1902" on copyright page. In dust jacket. $250-$350.

LONDON, Jack. *The Cruise of the Snark.* Frontispiece in color. Blue cloth, colored print on front cover. New York, 1911. First edition. In dust jacket. $25-$30.

LONDON, Jack. *A Daughter of the Snows.* Illustrated in color by F. C. Yohn. Red pictorial cloth. Philadelphia, 1902. First edition. In dust jacket. $50. London, 1904. Red cloth. First English edition. Lacking jacket, $25.

LONDON, Jack. *The God of His Fathers and Other Stories.* Dark-blue decorated cloth. New York, 1901. First edition. In dust jacket. $35-$50.

LONDON, Jack. *The House of Pride.* Pictorial light-green cloth. New York, 1912. First edition. In dust jacket. $35.

LONDON, Jack. *The Human Drift.* Frontispiece portrait of London. Reddish-brown cloth. New York, 1917. First edition. In dust jacket. $25. "Advance Copy" stamp on title page, $25-$30.

LONDON, Jack. *The Iron Heel.* Blue pictorial cloth. New York, 1908. First edition. In dust jacket. $35. Lacking jacket, $25. Another issue: New York, no date (1908). Wilshire imprint. $25.

LONDON, Jack. *John Barleycorn.* Illustrated by H. T. Dunn. Dark-green (black) cloth. New York, 1913. First edition, first printing, with one blank leaf following page 243. In dust jacket. $50. Lacking jacket, $25-$35.

LONDON, Jack. *The Little Lady of the Big House.* Frontispiece in color. Blue decorated cloth. New York, 1916. First edition. In dust jacket. $35.

LONDON, Jack. *Martin Eden.* Frontispiece. Dark-blue cloth. New York, 1909. First published edition. In dust jacket. $35-$40. (Note: There was a copyright edition deposited in September, 1908.)

LONDON, Jack. *On the Makaloa Mat.* Decorated light-blue cloth. New York, 1919. First edition. In dust jacket. $40-$45.

LONDON, Jack. *Revolution.* Printed wrappers. Chicago, no date (1909). First edition. $75. (Note: This pamphlet occurs in two states: Blanck's A-state, with ad "A Socialist Success," and B-state, with ad "Pocket Library of Socialism." Priority uncertain.)

LONDON, Jack. *Revolution and Other Essays.* Dark-blue or light-tan cloth. New York, 1910. First edition. In dust jacket. $35.

LONDON, Jack. *The Road.* Frontispiece. Gray cloth. New York, 1907. First edition. In dust jacket. $35. Lacking jacket, $25.

LONDON, Jack. *The Sea-Wolf.* Illustrated by W. J. Aylward. Blue cloth. New York, 1904. First edition, first issue, with spine lettered in gold. In dust jacket. $75. Later, spine lettered in white. In dust jacket. $50. New York, 1961. Limited Editions Club. Cloth. Boxed. $35-$50.

LONDON, Jack. *Smoke Bellew.* Illustrated by P. J. Monahan. Blue-gray pictorial cloth. New York, 1912. First edition. In dust jacket. $35.

LONDON, Jack. *The Son of the Sun.* Illustrated by A. O. Fischer. Light-blue pictorial cloth. Garden City, 1912. First edition. In dust jacket. $35-$50.

LONDON, Jack. *The Son of the Wolf.* Frontispiece. Slate-colored cloth, stamped in silver, or green cloth. Boston, 1900. First edition, first printing, with flyleaf at back; favored first binding in slate-colored cloth. In dust jacket. $100-$150. Author's first book. (Note: Hensley C. Woodbridge, John London, and George H. Tweney, in *Jack London: A Bibliography,* Georgetown, Calif., 1966, question the long-accepted slate-colored binding as the first. They also note two states of that binding and conclude that either of these as well as two varying green bindings must be considered as firsts; in other words, they say a collector must own all four to be sure he has a correct first edition. A fine bit of hairsplitting for the avid collector to chew over. See Blanck for further comments.)

LONDON, Jack. *The Star Rover.* Frontispiece in color. Blue cloth. New York, 1915. First edition. In dust jacket. $35.

LONDON, Jack. *The Strength of the Strong.* Pictorial wrappers. Chicago, no date (1911). First edition, first issue, with Kinzie Street address in ads. $100. Second issue, with Ohio Street in ads. $50.

LONDON, Jack. *The Strength of the Strong and Other Pieces.* Frontispiece. Light-blue decorated cloth. New York, 1914. First edition. In dust jacket. $35.

LONDON, Jack. *Tales of the Fish Patrol.* Illustrated by George Varian. New York, 1905. First edition. In dust jacket. $35.

LONDON, Jack. *War of the Classes.* Dark-red cloth. New York, 1905. First edition. In dust jacket. $35.

LONDON, Jack. *When God Laughs and Other Stories.* Illustrated. Dark olive-green pictorial cloth. New York, 1911. First edition. In dust jacket. $35-$50.

LONDON, Jack. *White Fang.* Illustrated, including colored frontispiece. Gray cloth. New York, 1906. First edition, first issue, without tipped-in title page and with no plates missing (they often are). In dust jacket. $50-$60. London, no date (1907). Dark-gray pictorial cloth. First English edition. Lacking dust jacket, $15-$25.

LONDON, Jack. *Wonder of Woman: A "Smoke Bellew" Story.* Printed wrappers. New York, no date (1912). First edition. $75-$100.

LONE Star Guide Descriptive of Countries on the Line of the International and Great Northern Railroad of Texas (The). Folding map and table, plates. 32 pp., wrappers. St. Louis, no date (about 1877). (By H. M. Hoxie.) $50-$75.

LONG Island Atlas. Cloth. New York, 1873. Published by Beers, Comstock & Cline. $50.

LONG, Stephen H. *Voyage in a Six-Oared Skiff to the Falls of St. Anthony in 1817.* Map. Half leather. Philadelphia, 1860. First edition. $75.

LONGFELLOW, Henry Wadsworth. See M. Lhomond's *Elements of French Grammar* (Longfellow's first book) and *French Exercises.* Also see *Manuel de Proverbes Dramatiques; Novelas Españolas; Outre-Mer.*

LONGFELLOW, Henry W. *Ballads and Other Poems.* Boards, paper label. Cambridge, Mass., 1842. First edition, first issue, with small "t" in "teacher" in last line of page 88 and with quotation marks at end of line 1, page 34. $250-$350.

LONGFELLOW, Henry W. *The Belfry of Bruges and Other Poems.* White wrappers. Cambridge, 1846. First edition, first state, with date 1845 on front cover and 1846 on title page. $250-$300. (Note: There were also some copies issued in boards.)

LONGFELLOW, Henry Wadsworth. *The Courtship of Miles Standish.* 135 pp., drab printed wrappers, imprinted "Author's Protected Edition." London, 1858. First edition, first printing. $400-$500. Later, cloth, 227 pp. Second printing. $350. Boston, 1858. Brown cloth. First American edition, first printing, with "treacherous" for "ruddy" in third line of page 124. $250-$300. Another issue: Purple "gift" binding. $250-$350.

LONGFELLOW, Henry Wadsworth. *Evangeline: A Tale of Acadie.* Brown or yellow boards, paper label. Boston, 1847. First edition, first printing, with line 1, page 61, reading "Long," not "Lo." $350-$400. Also, rebound, original boards preserved, $225 (A, 1968). "Lo" issue: $150-$200. Cambridge, 1893. Illustrated by F. O. C. Darley. Cloth (?). One of 150. $25.

LONGFELLOW, Henry Wadsworth. *From My Arm-Chair.* Leaflet, 2 leaves. No place, no date (Cambridge, 1879). First published edition, with reading "is wrought" in line 3 of 11th stanza. $150-$250. (Note: In a proof printing noted by Blanck the reading "are wrought" occurs.)

LONGFELLOW, Henry Wadsworth. *The Golden Legend.* Cloth. Boston, 1851. First edition. $25. London, 1851. Cloth. First English edition. $25.

LONGFELLOW, Henry Wadsworth. *Hyperion: A Romance.* 2 vols., tan boards, paper labels, white end papers. New York, 1839. First edition. $200. (Note: Also issued in a remainder binding of black cloth in 2 vols. and in 2 vols. bound as one. Fine copies in this binding retail in the $50 range and up.)

LONGFELLOW, Henry Wadsworth. *Poems on Slavery.* 31 pp., printed yellow wrappers. Cambridge, 1842. First edition. $150-$250. Cambridge, 1842. Second edition. $35-$50. Inscribed, $100.

LONGFELLOW, Henry Wadsworth. *The Seaside and the Fireside.* Cloth or boards. Boston, 1850. First edition. $35-$75. Another (later) issue: Large paper. $25-$35.

LONGFELLOW, Henry Wadsworth. *The Song of Hiawatha.* Green cloth, or printed tan wrappers. London, 1855. First edition, with ads dated March. $528. (No copies noted recently in wrappers.) Boston, 1855. Brown cloth. First American edition, first printing, with November ads and "dove" for "dived" in line 7 of page 96. $150-$200. Another issue: Blue or red "gift" bindings. $150-$200. Boston, 1856. Blue cloth. Large paper edition. $75-$100. Boston, 1891. Illustrated by Frederic Remington. Vellum. One of 250. $150-$200. Another issue: Cloth or suede. Unnumbered. $75-$100.

LONGFELLOW, Henry Wadsworth. *The Spanish Student: A Play in Three Acts.* Yellow boards, paper label. Cambridge, 1843. First edition. $25-$50.

LONGFELLOW, Henry Wadsworth. *Syllabus de la Grammaire Italienne.* Cloth. Boston, 1832. First edition, first state, with "la traite" for "le traite" in line 13 of advertisement and rule under "Bowdoin College" on title page. $100.

LONGFELLOW, Henry Wadsworth. *Tales of a Wayside Inn.* Cloth. Boston, 1863. First edition, first state of ads on page 11, with "Nearly ready" for this book, which is not priced. $75-$100.

LONGFELLOW, Henry Wadsworth. *"There Was a Little Girl."* Boards. New York, no date (1883). First edition. $30 (A, about 1945). (Note: Blanck and others have questioned Longfellow's authorship of this nursery poem.)

LONGFELLOW, Henry Wadsworth. *Voices of the Night.* Tan or drab boards, paper label. Cambridge, 1839. First edition, first state, with line 10 on page 78 reading "His, Hector's arm" instead of "The arm of Hector." $400-$500. (Note: Fewer than 10 copies known, says David A. Randall, curator of the Lilly Library at Indiana University.) Second state. $100-$150. Author's first book of poetry.

LONGFELLOW, Henry Wadsworth (translator). *Coplas de Don Jorge Manrique.* Cloth, paper spine label. Boston, 1833. First edition. $35.

LONGSTREET, Augustus Baldwin. See *Georgia Scenes, Characters, Incidents, etc.*

LONGSTREET, James. *From Manassas to Appomattox.* 44 maps and plates, 2 leaves of facsimiles. Cloth. Philadelphia, 1896. First edition. $35-$50.

LONGUS. *Les Amours Pastorales de Daphnis et Chloé.* Translated by J. Amyot. 151 lithographs by Pierre Bonnard. Morocco. Paris, 1902. One of 40 on Chine paper. $8,160 (A, 1969). London, 1933 (actually 1934). Ashendene Press. Woodcuts by Gwendolen Raverat. Half vellum. One of 290. $300-$350. Another issue: Morocco. One of 20 on vellum. $560 (A 1965). (Note: For numerous other editions of this classic, see the book auction records.)

LOOMIS, Chester A. *A Journey on Horseback Through the Great West, in 1825.* 27 pp., printed wrappers. Bath, N.Y., no date (1820's). First edition. $200.

LORANT, Stefan (editor). *The New World: The First Pictures of America.* Illustrated. Cloth. New York, no date (1946). In dust jacket. Boxed. $35-$50.

LORIMER, George Horace. *Letters from a Self-Made Merchant to His Son.* 36 pp., wrappers. Philadelphia, 1901. First edition. $25. Boston, 1902. Cloth. First (complete) edition. $25.

LORING, Rosamond B. *Decorated Book Papers.* Illustrated. Boards and cloth. Cambridge, 1942. In dust jacket. One of 250. $100.

LORREQUER, Harry (pseudonym for Charles Lever). See *The Confessions of Harry Lorrequer.*

LORREQUER, Harry. *Charles O'Malley, the Irish Dragoon.* Illustrated by H. K. Browne ("Phiz"). 22 parts in 21, printed pink pictorial wrappers. Dublin, 1841. (By Charles Lever.) First edition. $75-$100. Also, $40 (A, 1968).

LOST "Spade" (The); or The Grave Digger's Revenge. 16 pp., wrappers. New York, 1864. First edition. $100.

LOTHROP, Amy. *Dollars and Cents.* 2 vols., purple cloth. New York, 1852. (By Anna Bartlett Warner.) First edition. $50.

LOTHROP, Harriet M. S. See Sidney, Margaret.

LOUDON, Archibald. *A Selection of Some of the Most Interesting Narratives, of Outrages, Committed by the Indians, in Their Wars, with the White People.* 2 vols., leather. Carlisle, Pa., 1808-11. First edition. $1,000-$1,500. Also, $1,500 (A, 1967).

LOUDON, Mrs. Jane. *British Wild Flowers.* 60 hand-colored plates. Cloth. London, 1846. First edition. $150-$250. Rebound copies, $100-$150. (Note: A number of later editions—1847, 1849, 1855, 1859, etc.—are all worth in general about as much as the original.)

LOUDON, Mrs. Jane. *The Ladies' Flower Garden of Ornamental Annuals.* 48 colored plates. Cloth. London, 1840. First edition. $300-$350. (Note: Editions following in 1842, 1844, and 1849 are about as valuable as the original. Mrs. Loudon also produced four other books in this series: *Ornamental Bulbous Plants.* London, 1841. 58 colored plates. Cloth. $250-$350. *Ornamental Greenhouse Plants.* London, 1848. 75 colored plates. Cloth. $300-$400. *Ornamental Perennials.* 96 colored plates. 2 vols., cloth. London, 1843-44. $400-$500. As with Mrs. Loudon's wild flower book, the later editions of this color plate series sometimes bring almost as much as the originals. A complete set of the *Ornamentals* is currently worth about $1,250 and up at retail.)

LOUGHBOROUGH, John. *The Pacific Telegraph and Railway.* 2 folding maps. 80 pp., unbound. St. Louis, 1849. First edition. $500 and up. Another issue: Printed wrappers. $300 (A, 1966).

LOUGHEED, Victor. *Vehicles of the Air.* Illustrated. Cloth. Chicago, no date (1909). First edition. $35-$50.

LOVE, Nat. *The Life and Adventures of Nat Love.* Plates. Pictorial cloth. Los Angeles, 1907. First edition. $100-$125.

LOVE of Admiration, or Mary's Visit to B——: A Moral Tale. By a Lady. 160 pp., unbound. New Haven, Conn., 1828. First edition. $35.

LOVE, Robertus. *The Rise and Fall of Jesse James.* Frontispiece. Cloth. New York, 1926. First edition. $25-$35.

LOVECRAFT, H. P. *Beyond the Wall of Sleep.* Cloth. Sauk City, Wis., 1943. First edition. One of 1,217. In dust jacket. $125-$150.

LOVECRAFT, H. P. *The Cats of Ulthar.* 16 pp., wrappers. Cassia, Fla., 1935. First edition. One of 40. $75-$100.

LOVECRAFT, H. P. *Marginalia.* Illustrated. Black cloth. Sauk City, 1944. First edition. One of 2,035. In dust jacket. $50-$75.

LOVECRAFT, H. P. *The Outsider and Others.* Cloth. Sauk City, 1939. First edition. One of 1,268. In dust jacket. $100-$200. First book produced by Arkham House.

LOVECRAFT, H. P. *The Shadow Over Innsmouth.* Cloth. Everett, Pa., 1936. First edition, with errata sheet. In dust jacket. $75-$100.

LOVECRAFT, H. P. *The Shunned House.* 59 pp., unbound, folded signatures. Athol, Mass., 1928. First edition, first issue. $150-$200. Later, bound in wrappers: One of 10. $100-$150. Author's first (unpublished) book.

LOVECRAFT, H. P. *Something About Cats and Other Pieces.* Edited by August Derleth. Cloth. Sauk City, 1949. First edition. One of 2,995. In dust jacket. $35-$50.

LOVECRAFT, H. P., and Derleth, August. *The Lurker at the Threshold.* Cloth. Sauk City, 1945. First edition. One of 3,041. In dust jacket. $25.

LOVEDAY, John. *Diary of a Tour in 1732 Through Parts of England, Wales, Ireland and Scotland.* Half morocco. London, 1890. Roxburghe Club. $150-$200.

LOVER, Samuel. *Handy Andy: A Tale of Irish Life.* Illustrated by the author. 12 parts, printed wrappers. London, January-December, 1842. First edition. $200-$250. London, 1842. Green cloth. First edition in book form. $40-$50.

LOVING Ballad of Lord Bateman (The). Illustrated by George Cruikshank. Green cloth. London, 1839. (By William Makepeace Thackeray, though sometimes ascribed to Dickens, or to both Thackeray—for the ballad—and Dickens, or to Cruikshank.) First edition, first issue, with the word "wine" in fifth stanza. $100-$150.

LOWE, C. Bruce. *Breeding Racehorses by the Figure System.* Edited by William Allison. Illustrated. Cloth. London, 1895. First edition. $50-$60.

LOWE, Robert W. *A Bibliographical Account of English Theatrical Literature.* Buckram. London, 1888. One of 500. $50-$75.

LOWELL, Amy. See *Dream Drops; Some Imagist Poets.*

LOWELL, Amy. *A Dome of Many-Colored Glass.* Boards, cloth spine, paper labels. Boston, 1912. First edition. In dust jacket. $35.

LOWELL, Amy. *What's O'Clock.* Gray-blue boards and cloth. Boston, 1925. First edition. In dust jacket. $25. Another issue: Advance review copy (so indicated). $35.

LOWELL, James Russell. See Wilbur, Homer. Also see *Class Poem; A Fable for Critics.*

LOWELL, James Russell. *Among My Books.* Cloth. Boston, 1870. First edition. $25.

LOWELL, James Russell. *Among My Books: Second Series.* Cloth. Boston, 1876. First edition, first state, with 1875 copyright date and "Belles-Letters" on title page. $35-$50.

LOWELL, James Russell. *Anti-Slavery Papers.* Boards, paper label. Boston, 1902. First edition. One of 525. $25.

LOWELL, James Russell. *Conversations on Some of the Old Poets.* Cloth, wrappers, or boards. Cambridge, Mass., 1845. First edition. $35-$50. (Note: A copy in a white cloth "gift" binding sold at auction in the 1960 season for $30.)

LOWELL, James Russell. *Heartsease and Rue.* Boards and cloth. Boston, 1888. First edition. $75-$100.

LOWELL, James Russell. *Ode Recited at the Commemoration of the Living and Dead Soldiers of Harvard University, July 21, 1865.* Gray boards, paper label. Cambridge, 1865. First edition. One of 50. $300 and up. Also, inscribed, $550 (A, 1962).

LOWELL, James Russell. *On Democracy.* 15 pp., wrappers. Birmingham, England, no date (1884). First edition, first state, privately printed and without price at top of first leaf. $75-$100. Second state (first published edition), with price. $35-$50.

LOWELL, James Russell. *Poems.* Boards, paper label. Cambridge, 1844. First edition. $35-$50.

LOWELL, James Russell. *Poems.* 2 vols., boards or cloth. Boston, 1849. First edition. $25-$35. (Note: A "gift" binding in red cloth brought $40 at auction in the 1964 season.)

LOWELL, James Russell. *Poems: Second Series.* Boards or cloth. Cambridge, 1848. First edition. $35-$50.

LOWELL, James Russell. *The President's Policy.* Wrappers. No place, no date (Philadelphia, 1864). First edition, first state, with "crises" spelled "crisises" in first line of text. $75-$100.

LOWELL, James Russell. *Under the Willows and Other Poems.* Cloth. Boston, 1869. First edition, first issue, with errata slip at page 286 and first word in line 7 of page 224 reading "Thy." $100-$150.

LOWELL, James Russell. *The Vision of Sir Launfal.* Printed glazed yellow boards. Cambridge, 1848. First edition. $100-$150.

LOWELL, James Russell. *A Year's Life.* Boards, paper label. Boston, 1841. First edition, with errata slip. $50-$100. Another, lacking errata slip, $25. Author's first book (preceded by *Class Poem* pamphlet).

LOWELL, Robert. *Fall 1961.* Broadside. Milford, Conn., 1965. First edition. One of 115 signed. $75-$80.

LOWELL, Robert. *For the Union Dead.* Cloth. New York, 1964. First edition. In dust jacket. $20-$25.

LOWELL, Robert. *The Land of Unlikeness.* Printed boards. Cummington, Mass., 1944. First edition. One of 250. $900-$1,000. Author's first book.

LOWELL, Robert. *Life Studies.* Cloth. New York, 1959. First edition. In dust jacket. $25.

LOWELL, Robert. *The Mills of the Kavanaughs.* Cloth. New York, no date (1951). First edition. In dust jacket. $25-$35.

LOWELL, Robert. *Poesie di montale: Con uno studio di Alfredo Rizzardi e un acquerello di Georgio Morandi.* Stiff printed wrappers. Bologna, Italy, no date (1960). First edition. One of 550. $25-$35.

LOWELL, Robert. *R. F. K. 1925-1968.* Broadside. No place, 1969. One of 50 signed. $100.

LOWELL, Robert (translator). *The Voyage and Other Versions of Poems by Baudelaire.* Illustrated by Sidney Nolan. Folio, blue and purple beveled cloth. London, no date (1968). First edition. One of 200 signed by Lowell and the illustrator. Boxed. $100-$125.

LOY, Mina. *Lunar Baedeker.* Printed wrappers. Dijon, France, 1923. First edition. $50-$75.

LOY, Mina. *Lunar Baedeker & Time Tables.* Cloth. Highlands, N. C., 1958. First edition. Jargon 23. One of 50 signed "author's copies." In acetate dust jacket. $50-$55. (Note: Contains an introduction by William Carlos Williams and others.)

LUBBOCK, Basil. *Adventures by Sea from the Art of Old Time.* 115 plates, including 22 in color. Buckram. London, 1925. First edition. One of 1,750. $50-$60.

LUBBOCK, Basil, and Spurling, John. *Sail: The Romance of the Clipper Ship.* 78 full-page color plates. 3 vols., cloth. London, 1927-30-36. First edition. One of 1,000. $750-$1,000.

LUCAS, E. V. See L., E. V.

LUCAS, E. V. *The Book of Shops.* Illustrated in color. Oblong folio, boards and cloth. London, no date (1899). $25-$35.

LUCAS, E. V. *Playtime and Company.* Illustrated by Ernest H. Shepard. Vellum. London, no date (1925). One of 15 signed by author and artist. $100.

LUCAS, Capt. Thomas J. *Pen and Pencil Reminiscences of a Campaign in South Africa.* 21 colored plates. London, no date (1861). $100-$150.

LUCAS, Victoria. *The Bell Jar.* Cloth. London, 1963. First edition. (By Sylvia Plath.) In dust jacket. $75. London, 1964. Contemporary Fiction Edition. In dust jacket. $15.

LUCE, Edward S. *Keoghe, Comanche and Custer.* Illustrated. Cloth. No place (St. Louis), 1939. Limited, signed edition. In dust jacket. $50-$75.

LUCERNE: Its Homes, Climate, Mineral Resources, etc. 37 pp., printed wrappers. Los Angeles, 1888. (By Theron Nichols.) First edition. $35-$50.

LUCRETIUS CARUS, Titus. *De Rerum Natura Libri Sex.* Printed in red and black, with initial letters in blue and one in gold. Boards, vellum spine. London, 1913. Ashendene Press. One of 85 on handmade paper. $400-$500.

LUDLOW, Fitz-Hugh. See *The Hasheesh Eater.*

LUDLOW, N. M. *Dramatic Life as I Found It.* Cloth. St. Louis, 1880. First edition. $50-$60.

LUKE Darrell, the Chicago Newsboy. Cloth. Chicago, 1865. First edition. Bottom of spine frayed, $45-$50.

LUKE, L. D. *Adventures and Travels in the New Wonder Land of Yellowstone Park.* Cloth. Utica, N.Y., 1886. $35-$50.

LUMPKIN, Wilson. *The Removal of the Cherokee Indians from Georgia.* 2 portraits. 2 vols., cloth. Wormsloe, Ga., 1907. First edition. One of 500. $35-$50.

LUTTIG, John C. *Journal of a Fur-Trading Expedition on the Upper Missouri.* Map, 4 plates. Boards and cloth. St. Louis, 1920. First edition. One of 365. $50-$100.

LYELL, James P. R. *Early Book Illustrations in Spain.* Colored frontispiece, 247 other illustrations. Cloth. London, 1926. One of 500. $125-$150.

LYFORD, William G. *The Western Address Directory.* Cloth. Baltimore, 1837. First edition. $35-$50.

LYKKEJAEGER, Hans. *The Luck of a Wandering Dane.* Boards. Philadelphia, 1855. (By Andrew M. Smith.) First edition. $75-$100.

LYMAN, Albert. *Journal of a Voyage to California, and Life in the Gold Diggings.* Frontispiece. Pictorial wrappers or cloth. Hartford, 1852. First edition. Wrappers: $500-$750. Cloth: $200-$300.

LYMINGTON, Lord. *Spring Song of Iscariot.* Wrappers. Paris, 1929. Black Sun Press. One of 125 on Van Gelder paper. $25-$35. Another issue: One of 25 on Japan paper. $35-$50.

LYON, Irving Whitall. *The Colonial Furniture of New England.* Plates. Cloth. Boston, 1891. First edition. $35-$50. Boston, 1925. Cloth. Third edition. One of 515. $35.

LYRE, Pinchbeck. *Poems.* Boards. No place, no date (London, 1931). (By Siegfried Sassoon.) First edition. $75-$100.

LYRICAL Ballads with Other Poems. 2 vols., drab boards. London, 1800. (By William Wordsworth and Samuel Taylor Coleridge.) Second edition (so designated on the first volume alone). $1,000-$1,500. London, 1802. 2 vols., boards. Third edition. $100-$150. London, 1805. 2 vols., boards. Fourth edition. $75-$100. (Note: The first edition, first issue, 1798, with a Bristol—instead of London—imprint on the title page, is an extremely rare book, of which no complete copy in original pink boards has appeared in many years. A copy in contemporary marbled boards brought $2,700 at auction in 1945. Second issue 1798 copies, with London imprint, are more common. A copy in original boards brought $850 at auction in 1941; rebound copies at auction: $375 and $500 in 1970; $270 in 1969; $425 in 1968 and $200 in 1965.)

LYTLE, Andrew. *The Long Night.* Cloth. New York, no date (1936). First edition. In dust jacket. $50-$75. Author's first book.

LYTTON, Lord (Edward Bulwer). See Bulwer-Lytton, Edward.

M

MABIE, Hamilton Wright. *The Portrait Gallery of Eminent Lawyers.* Half morocco. New York, 1880. First edition. $25-$35.

MABINOGION (The): A New Translation from the White Book of Rhydderch and the Red Book of Hergest, by Gwyn Jones and Thomas Jones. Woodcut title page and other illustrations by Dorothea Braby. Folio, half morocco. London, 1948. Golden Cockerel Press. One of 500. $150-$200. Another issue: Full morocco. One of 75 signed. $300-$350.

McADAM, R. W. *Chickasaws and Choctaws.* Comprising the Treaties of 1855 and 1866. 67 pp., wrappers. Ardmore, Okla., 1891. First edition. $250.

McAFEE Brothers. *Tehama County: Geography, Topography, Soil, Climate, Productions, etc.* 32 pp., wrappers. No place, no date (San Francisco, 1881). $50-$100.

McAFEE, Robert B. See *History of the Late War in the Western Country.*

McALMON, Robert. *A Companion Volume.* Gray wrappers. No place, no date (Dijon, France, 1923). Contact Publishing Co. First edition. $95-$100.

McALMON, Robert. *Explorations.* Cloth. London, 1921. Egoist Press. First edition. $100-$150. Author's first book.

McALMON, Robert. *A Hasty Bunch.* Wrappers. No place, no date (Dijon, 1922?). First edition. $45. (Note: James Joyce suggested the title.)

McALMON, Robert. *North America, Continent of Conjecture.* Wrappers. No place, no date (Paris, 1929). First edition. One of 310. $85.

McALMON, Robert. *Not Alone Lost.* Cloth. Norfolk, Conn., no date (1937). New Directions. In dust jacket. $25.

McALMON, Robert. *Post-Adolescence.* Wrappers. No place, no date (Dijon, 1923). Contact Publishing Co. First edition. $85-$110.

McALMON, Robert. *The Portrait of a Generation.* Stiff wrappers. Paris, no date (1926). Contact Editions. First edition. One of 200. $100-$150.

McALMON, Robert. *Village: As It Happened Through a Fifteen-Year Period.* Wrappers. Dijon, 1924. First edition. $40-$50.

MACARIA: or, Altars of Sacrifice. 183 pp., wrappers. Richmond, Va., 1864. (By Augusta Jane Evans Wilson.) First edition. $350-$500.

MacARTHUR, Douglas. *Military Demolitions.* Printed wrappers. Fort Leavenworth, Kan., 1909. $75.

MACARTHUR, James. *New South Wales: Its Present State and Future Prospects.* Colored map. Cloth. London, 1837. (Written by Edward Edwards from Macarthur's notes.) $150-$200.

MACAULAY, Rose. *Catchwords and Claptrap.* Printed boards. London, 1926. Hogarth Press. First edition. $25-$35.

MACAULAY, Rose. *The Pleasure of Ruins.* 172 plates, 12 in color, 29 maps and plans. Cloth. London, 1964. Revised edition. In dust jacket. $25.

MACAULAY, Thomas Babington. *Evening: A Poem.* Wrappers. Cambridge, England, 1821. First edition. $100-$150.

MACAULAY, Thomas Babington. *Lays of Ancient Rome.* Brown cloth. London, 1842. First edition. $100.

MACAULAY, Thomas Babington. *Pompeii.* Contemporary blue morocco. No place, no date (Cambridge, 1819). First edition. $75. Author's first book.

MacCABE, Julius P. Bolivar. *Directory of the City of Detroit.* Printed boards. Detroit, 1837. First edition. $375 (A, 1967).

MacCABE, Julius P. Bolivar. *Directory of the City of Milwaukee.* Full leather. Milwaukee, 1847. First edition. $100 (A, 1967).

MacCABE, Julius P. Bolivar. *Directory of Cleveland and Ohio City, for the Years 1837-38.* Printed boards. Cleveland, 1837. First edition. $525 (A, 1967).

McCAIN, Charles W. *History of the S.S. "Beaver."* Illustrated. Blue cloth. Vancouver, Canada, 1894. First edition. $75-$100.

McCALL, George A. *Letters from the Frontiers.* Red cloth. Philadelphia, 1868. First edition. $100-$125.

McCALL, Hugh. *The History of Georgia.* 2 vols., boards. Savannah, Ga., 1811-16. First edition. $400-$500.

McCALLA, William L. *Adventures in Texas.* Black cloth. Philadelphia, 1841. First edition. $200-$250.

McCLELLAN, Henry B. *The Life and Campaigns of Maj. Gen. J. E. B. Stuart.* Portrait, 7 maps. Cloth. Boston, 1885. First edition. $50-$60.

McCLELLAND, Nancy. *Duncan Phyfe.* Illustrated. Cloth. New York, no date (1939). Limited, signed edition. Boxed. $80-$100.

McCLELLAND, Nancy. *Historic Wallpapers.* Illustrated, including color plates. Half cloth. Philadelphia, 1924. First edition, limited. $75-$125.

McCLINTOCK, John S. *Pioneer Days in the Black Hills.* Edited by Edward Senn. Illustrated. Cloth. Deadwood, S.D., no date (1939). First edition. $75-$100.

McCLINTOCK, Walter. *Old Indian Trails.* 28 plates, including 4 in color. Pictorial cloth. Boston, 1923. First edition. $35. London, 1923. First English edition. $25.

McCLINTOCK, Walter. *The Old North Trail.* Map, 9 plates. Cloth. London, 1910. First edition. $50-$60.

M'CLUNG, John A. *Sketches of Western Adventure.* Boards, linen spine. Maysville, Ky., 1832. First edition. $500-$750. Also, rebound in half calf, browned and foxed, $650 (A, 1967). Philadelphia, 1832. Second edition. $100-$150.

McCLURE, A. K. *Three Thousand Miles Through the Rocky Mountains.* Illustrated. Cloth. Philadelphia, 1869. First edition. $25-$35.

McCLURE, J. B. *Edison and His Inventions.* Illustrated. Cloth. Chicago, 1879. First edition, first state, with no reviews of this book in the ads and with "With copious illustrations" in one line on title page. $25. (Note: Contains Joel Chandler Harris' "Uncle Remus and the Phonograph.")

McCLURE, Michael. *The Beard.* Folio, pictorial wrappers. No place, no date (Berkeley, Calif., 1965). First edition. One of 350. $35-$40. Another edition: No place (San Francisco), 1967. Coyote Press. Wrappers. $10.

McCLURE, Michael. *The Cherub.* Full leather. Los Angeles, 1970. Black Sparrow Press. One of 26 signed, with an illustration by the author. $75. Another issue: Boards. One of 250 signed. $25.

McCLURE, Michael. *Dark Brown.* Boards and leather. San Francisco, 1961. One of 25 on Japan paper signed. $75.

McCLURE, Michael. *Ghost Tantras.* Cloth. San Francisco, 1964. First edition. One of 20 bound and signed. $30.

McCLURE, Michael. *Hail Thee Who Play.* Printed yellow boards and cloth. Los Angeles, 1968. Black Sparrow Press. First edition. One of 75 signed, with an original drawing by the author. In dust jacket. $50-$65. Another issue: Printed wrappers. One of 250 signed. $20.

McCLURE, Michael. *Hymns to St. Geryon and Other Poems.* Decorated wrappers. San Francisco, 1959. First edition. $25.

McCLURE, Michael. *Little Odes and The Raptors.* Blue linen. Los Angeles, 1969. First edition. One of 200 signed. $35.

McCLURE, Michael. *Love Lion Book.* Boards, cloth spine. San Francisco, 1966. First edition. One of 40 signed. $50.

McCLURE, Michael. *Muscled Apple Swift.* Decorated wrappers. Topango, Calif., 1968. First edition. One of 63 signed. $45-$50.

McCLURE, Michael. *Passage.* Wrappers. Big Sur, Calif., 1956. Jargon 20. First edition. One of 200. $45-$50. Author's first book.

McCLURE, Michael. *Plane Pomes.* Stiff wrappers. New York, 1969. One of 100 signed. $25.

McCLURE, Michael. *Poisoned Wheat.* Red cloth. San Francisco, 1965. First edition. One of 20 signed. $35.

McCLURE, Michael. *The Sermons of Jean Harlow and the Curses of Billy the Kid.* Boards. San Francisco, 1968. One of 50 signed. $35.

McCLURE, Michael. *Thirteen Mad Sonnets.* Illustrated. Stiff wrappers. Milano, Italy, no date (1964). One of 299. $25.

McCLURE, S. S. *My Autobiography.* Red cloth. New York, no date (1914). (Ghost-written by Willa Cather.) First edition, first issue, with "September, 1914" on copyright page. In dust jacket. $100-$125. (Note: A supposedly later issue, but with "May, 1914" on the copyright page, in dust jacket, was catalogued by one dealer recently at $75.)

McCONKEY, Mrs. Harriet E. (Bishop). *Dakota War Whoop; or, Indian Massacres and War in Minnesota.* 6 portraits. Cloth. St. Paul, Minn., 1863. First edition. $75-$100.

McCONNEL, Murray. *Claim to a Patent for a Tract of Land in Illinois.* 30 pp., stitched. Washington, 1857. $100.

McCONNELL, H. H. *Five Years a Cavalryman.* Text on pink paper. Cloth. Jacksboro, Tex., 1889. First edition. $35-$50.

McCONNELL, Joseph Carroll. *The West Texas Frontier.* Vol. 1. (All published.) No place, 1933. $35-$50.

McCOOK, Henry C. *American Spiders and Their Spinningwork.* Portrait, 35 hand-colored plates. 3 vols., cloth. Philadelphia, 1889-93. First edition. One of 750. $200-$250.

McCORKLE, John, and Barton, O. S. *Three Years with Quantrell.* 11 plates. Maroon wrappers. Armstrong, Mo., no date (1914). First edition. $150-$200.

McCORMICK, Richard C. *Arizona: Its Resources and Prospects.* Map. 22 pp., buff printed wrappers. New York, 1865. First edition. $100-$150.

McCORMICK, S. J. *Almanac for the Year 1864; Containing Useful Information Relative to the Population, Progress and Resources of Oregon, Washington and Idaho.* 56 pp., wrappers. Portland, no date (1863). $100-$125.

McCOY, Horace. *They Shoot Horses, Don't They?* Cloth. New York, 1935. First edition. In dust jacket. $25. Signed, $35. Author's first book.

McCOY, Isaac. *History of Baptist Indian Missions.* Cloth. Washington, 1840. First edition. $75-$100.

McCOY, Isaac. *Remarks on the Practicability of Indian Reform.* 47 pp., wrappers. Boston, 1827. First edition. $200. New York, 1829. Half leather. Second edition. $35-$50.

McCOY, Isaac. *Remove Indians Westward.* (Caption title.) 48 pp., sewed. No place (Washington), 1829. First edition. $75-$100.

McCOY, Joseph G. *Historic Sketches of the Cattle Trade of the West and Southwest.* Portraits and plates. Pictorial brown cloth. Kansas City, 1874. First edition. $400-$500.

McCRACKEN, Harold. *The Charles M. Russell Book.* Illustrated, including color plates. Leather. Garden City, 1957. First edition. One of 250 signed. Boxed. $300-$400. Trade edition: Buckram. In dust jacket. $35-$50.

McCRACKEN, Harold. *The Frederic Remington Book.* Illustrated. Leather. Garden City, 1966. First edition. In dust jacket. $150.

McCRACKEN, Harold. *Frederic Remington's Own West.* Illustrated. Calf. New York, 1960. First edition. One of 167 signed. Boxed. $150-$200.

McCRACKEN, Harold. *George Catlin and the Old Frontier.* Illustrated, including colored plates. Decorated leather. New York, 1959. One of 250, with extra color plate tipped in at front. Boxed. $200-$250. Trade edition: Cloth. In dust jacket. $25-$35.

M'CREERY, John. *A Selection, from the Ancient Music of Ireland, Arranged for the Flute or Violin.* Boards. Petersburgh, Va., 1824. (John Daly Burk collaborated.) First edition. $100.

McCULLERS, Carson. *The Heart Is a Lonely Hunter.* Cloth. Boston, 1940. First edition. In dust jacket. $50-$60. Author's first book.

McCULLERS, Carson. *Reflections in a Golden Eye.* Cloth. Boston, 1941. First edition. In dust jacket. $25-$30.

McCUTCHEON, George Barr. See Greaves, Richard.

McCUTCHEON, George Barr. *Brood House: A Play in Four Acts.* Boards. New York, 1910. First edition. One of 75. $50.

McCUTCHEON, George Barr. *A Fool and His Money.* Cloth. New York, 1913. First edition. One of 50 signed. In dust jacket. $35.

McCUTCHEON, George Barr. *Graustark.* Pictorial cloth. Chicago, 1901. First edition, first issue, with "Noble" instead of "Lorry" in line 6 of page 150. $35-$50.

McCUTCHEON, George Barr. *Kindling and Ashes.* Boards. New York, 1926. First edition. One of 25 signed. $50. Trade edition: Cloth. In dust jacket. $10.

McCUTCHEON, George Barr. *One Score and Ten.* Boards. New York, 1919. First edition. One of 30 signed. $50-$60.

McCUTCHEON, George Barr. *Viola Gwyn.* Boards and parchment. New York, 1922. First edition. One of 50 signed. $35-$50.

McCUTCHEON, John T. *Bird Center.* Illustrated. Pictorial boards and cloth. Chicago, 1904. First edition. $25-$35.

McDANIELD, H. F., and Taylor, N. A. *The Coming Empire.* Cloth. New York, no date (1877). First edition. $35.

MacDIARMID, Hugh. See Duval, K. D.; Glen, Duncan; Grieve, C. M. (Note: The following listings under MacDiarmid's name include books with title pages reading "M'Diarmid" and "Mc'Diarmid.")

MacDIARMID, Hugh. *Cunninghame Graham: A Centenary Study.* Cloth. Glasgow, no date (1952). (By C. M. Grieve.) First edition. In dust jacket. $25-$30.

MacDIARMID, Hugh. *A Drunk Man Looks at the Thistle.* Cloth. Edinburgh, 1926. (By C. M. Grieve.) First edition. In dust jacket. $65.

MacDIARMID, Hugh. *The Fire of the Spirit.* Blue wrappers. Glasgow, 1965. (By C. M. Grieve.) One of 50 signed. $90-$100. Another issue: Wrappers. One of 350. $25.

MacDIARMID, Hugh. *First Hymn to Lenin and Other Poems.* Portrait frontispiece. Half black morocco and boards. London, 1931. (By C. M. Grieve.) Unicorn Press. First edition. One of 50 signed. $80-$100. Another issue: Red and black buckram. One of 450. Boxed. $50.

MacDIARMID, Hugh. *The Kind of Poetry I Want.* Boards and vellum. Edinburgh, 1961. (By C. M. Grieve.) First edition. One of 300 signed. Boxed. $150-$160. Another issue: One of 500. Boxed. $60.

MacDIARMID, Hugh. *O Wha's Been Here Afore Me, Lass.* 4 pp., folded. No place, 1931. Blue Moon Press. (By C. M. Grieve.) First edition. One of 100 signed. $90-$100.

MacDIARMID, Hugh. *Penny Wheep.* Blue cloth. No place (Edinburgh), 1926. (By C. M. Grieve.) First edition. In dust jacket. $90-$100.

MacDIARMID, Hugh. *Poems to Paintings by William Johnstone, 1933.* Wrappers. Edinburgh, 1963. (By C. M. Grieve.) First edition. One of 100 signed. $120.

MacDIARMID, Hugh. *Poetry Like the Hawthorn. From In Memoriam James Joyce.* Stiff yellow wrappers. Hemel Hempstead, England, 1962. (By C. M. Grieve.) First edition. One of 25 signed (from an issue of 150). $50. Unsigned, $25.

MacDIARMID, Hugh. *Sangschaw.* Cloth. No place (Edinburgh), 1925. (By C. M. Grieve.) First edition. In dust jacket. $75. Poet's first book of verse.

MacDIARMID, Hugh. *Scots Unbound and Other Poems.* Frontispiece. Cloth. Stirling, Scotland, 1932. (By C. M. Grieve.) First edition. One of 350 signed. $100-$125.

MacDIARMID, Hugh. *Second Hymn to Lenin and Other Poems.* Frontispiece. Cloth. London, 1935. (By C. M. Grieve.) First edition. In dust jacket. $75-$100.

MacDIARMID, Hugh. *Stony Limits and Other Poems.* Cloth. London, 1934. (By C. M. Grieve.) First edition. $50-$60.

MacDIARMID, Hugh. *Sydney Goodsir Smith.* Buckram, leather label. Edinburgh, 1963. (By C. M. Grieve.) First edition. One of 35 specially bound and signed by the author. $120. Another issue: Wrappers. One of 100. $50.

MacDIARMID, Hugh. *To Circumjack Cencrastus, or The Curly Snake.* Wrappers. Edinburgh, 1930. (By C. M. Grieve.) First edition. $35. Another issue: Blue morocco extra. Binding signed by Arthur Currie. $100-$150.

MacDIARMID, Hugh. *The Uncanny Scot.* Edited by Kenneth Buthlay. Buckram. London, 1968. (By C. M. Grieve.) First edition. One of 40 signed by Grieve. In dust jacket. $90-$100.

MacDIARMID, Hugh. *When the Rat-Race Is Over.* Gray wrappers. London, 1962. (By C. M. Grieve.) First edition. One of 40 signed. $100.

MacDIARMID, Hugh. *Whuchulls: A Poem.* Wrappers. London, 1966. (By C. M. Grieve.) One of 100. $35-$40.

MacDIARMID, Hugh (editor). *The Voice of Scotland.* Vol. XIX, No. 3. Loose leaves, printed one side only, in cloth case. No place, no date (Edinburgh, 1961). (C. M. Grieve, editor.) Proof copies of an unpublished issue of this Scottish quarterly. (Only a few copies were run off for the editor.) $90-$100.

MacDONAGH, Donagh. *Veterans and Other Poems.* Boards and linen. Dublin, 1941. Cuala Press. First edition. One of 270. In dust jacket. $75.

MacDONALD, George. *Phantastes.* Cloth. London, 1858. First edition, with 16 pages of ads at end. $125-$150. London, 1912. Cloth. $10.

MacDONALD, George. *The Princess and the Goblin.* Illustrated by Arthur Hughes. Cloth. London, 1897. First edition. $100-$125.

MacDONALD, George. *Within and Without: A Dramatic Poem.* Cloth. London, 1855. First edition. $35-$50. Author's first book.

McDONALD, Archibald. *Peace River: A Canoe Voyage from Hudson's Bay to Pacific, by the Late George Simpson . . . in 1828.* Edited by Malcolm McLeod. Folding map. 119 pp., printed wrappers. Ottawa, 1872. First edition. $200-$300.

McDONALD, Edward D. *A Bibliography of the Writings of Norman Douglas.* Cloth. Philadelphia, 1927. First edition. In dust jacket. $25-$35.

McDONALD, Frank V. (editor). *Notes Preparatory to a Biography of Richard Hayes McDonald.* Vol. 1. (All published.) Illustrated. Brown cloth. Cambridge, Mass., 1881. First edition. One of 150. $200-$250.

MacDONALD, Hugh. *John Dryden: A Bibliography.* Portrait. Cloth. Oxford, 1939. First edition. In dust jacket. $75-$100.

MacDONALD, James. *Food from the Far West.* Decorated cloth. London, 1878. First edition. $35-$50. New York, no date (1878). Cloth. First American edition. $35.

McDONALD, John. *Biographical Sketches of Gen. Nathaniel Massie, Gen. Duncan McArthur, Capt. William Wells, and Gen. Simon Kenton.* Calf. Cincinnati, 1838. First edition. $100-$150.

M'DONELL, Alexander. *A Narrative of Transaction in the Red River Country.* Folding map. Boards. London, 1819. First edition. $750. Also, rebound in half morocco, $500 (A, 1969); in contemporary calf, $528 (A, 1969).

MACDOUGALL, William. *The Red River Rebellion.* 68 pp., wrappers. Toronto, 1870. First edition. $75-$100. Also, rebound in boards, $50 (A, 1969).

McEACHRAN, D. *Notes of a Trip to Bow River North-West Territories.* Cloth (not original). Montreal, 1881. First edition. $80 (A, 1969).

MacFALL, Haldane. *Aubrey Beardsley, the Man and His Work.* Illustrated. Cloth. New York, 1927. First edition. In dust jacket. $25-$35. Another issue: One of 300 signed. In dust jacket. $35-$50. New York, 1928. Cloth. In dust jacket. $25. London, no date (1928). Boards. First English edition. In dust jacket. $25. Another issue: One of 100, with 6 extra illustrations. In dust jacket. $50-$75.

MacFALL, Haldane. *The Book of Claude Lovat Fraser.* Half cloth. London, 1923. First edition. One of 150 signed. In dust jacket. $25-$35. Trade edition: Cloth. In dust jacket. $10.

MacFALL, Haldane. *The Wooings of Jezebel Pettyfer.* Pictorial cloth. London, 1898. First edition, first issue, with portrait of Jezebel on front cover. $45-$60.

McFADDEN, William S. *Corvallis to Crescent City, California, in 1874.* Mimeographed, 44 pp., wrappers. (WPA.) No place, no date (1937). $35-$50.

McFEE, William. *Aliens.* Cloth. London, 1914. First edition, first state, with ads dated 1915. In dust jacket. $25-$35. New York, 1916. Cloth. First American edition. In dust jacket. $25.

McFEE, William. *Casuals of the Sea.* Frontispiece in color. Cloth. London, 1916. First edition. In dust jacket. $75.

McFEE, William. *The Gates of the Caribbean.* Illustrated. Stiff printed wrappers. No place, no date (New York, 1922). First edition. $25.

McFEE, William. *The Harbourmaster.* Boards and cloth. Garden City, 1931. First edition. One of 377 signed. Boxed. $35. Garden City, 1932. Cloth. First trade edition. In dust jacket. $12.50-$15. Lacking jacket, spine faded, $8.50.

McFEE, William. *Letters from an Ocean Tramp.* Colored frontispiece. Blue cloth. London, 1908. First edition, first state, with "Cassell & Co." at foot of spine. $85-$100. Author's first book.

McFEE, William. *The Reflections of Marsyas.* Boards. Gaylordsville, N.Y., 1933. Slide Mountain Press. One of 300 signed. In glassine dust jacket. $25.

McFEE, William. *A Six-Hour Shift.* Boards, vellum spine. Garden City, 1920. First edition. One of 377 signed. In dust jacket. $25.

McGAW, James F. *Philip Seymour, or, Pioneer Life in Richland County, Ohio.* 2 plates. Cloth. Mansfield, Ohio, 1858. First edition. $100-$150.

McGEE, Joseph H. *Story of the Grand River Country, 1821-1905.* Portrait. Brown printed wrappers. No place, no date (Gallatin, Mo., 1909). First edition. $75-$100.

McGILLYCUDDY, Julia B. *McGillycuddy Agent: A Biography of Dr. Valentine T. McGillycuddy.* Illustrated. Pictorial cloth. Stanford, Calif., no date (1941). First edition. In dust jacket. $35.

McGLASHAN, C. F. *History of the Donner Party: A Tragedy of the Sierras.* Black cloth. Truckee, Calif., no date (1879). First edition. $300-$400. San Francisco, 1880. Illustrated. Cloth. Second edition. $300-$350. Third edition, same place and date. $75-$100.

McGOWAN, Edward. *Narrative of Edward McGowan.* Illustrated. Pictorial wrappers. San Francisco, 1857. First edition. $600-$800. Rebound in half morocco, $125 (A, 1963). San Francisco, 1917. (As *Narrative of Ned McGowan.*) Boards. One of 200. $35-$50.

McGREEVY, Thomas. *Poems.* Cloth. London, 1934. First edition. In dust jacket. $25. Author's first book (?).

McGUFFEY, William H. *The Eclectic Fourth Reader.* Three-quarters red morocco. Cincinnati, 1837. First edition. Rubbed, $45.

McGUFFEY, William H. *McGuffey's Rhetorical Guide; or, Fifth Reader of the Eclectic Series.* Cloth. Cincinnati, no date (1844). Slight breaks in hinges, $25.

McGUFFEY, William H. *Revised and Improved Third Reader.* Boards. Cincinnati, 1838. $45.

McGUSTY, H. *Sketches on My Plantation.* Oblong folio, pictorial wrappers. Enterprise, Miss., 1915. $25.

MACHEN, Arthur. See Siluriensis, Leolinus.

MACHEN, Arthur. *Bridles and Spurs.* Green boards and cloth. Cleveland, 1951. Grabhorn printing for the Rowfant Club. One of 178. Boxed. $50.

MACHEN, Arthur. *The Canning Wonder.* Boards and vellum. London, 1925. One of 130 signed. In dust jacket. $40. Trade edition: Cloth. In dust jacket. $10.

MACHEN, Arthur. *The Chronicle of Clemendy.* Frontispiece. Half vellum. Carbonnek, 1888. First edition. One of 250. Boxed. $40-$60. Carbonnek, 1923. (Printed in U.S.A.) Blue boards, parchment spine. One of 1,050 signed. $25.

MACHEN, Arthur. *Dog and Duck.* Illustrated. Batik boards and cloth. London, 1924. First edition. One of 150 (of an edition of 900) signed. In dust jacket. $25-$30.

MACHEN, Arthur. *Dreads and Drolls.* Boards, parchment spine. London. 1926. First edition. One of 100 signed. In dust jacket. $25.

MACHEN, Arthur. *Fantastic Tales.* Boards. Carbonnek, 1890. First edition. One of 500. $25. Carbonnek, 1923. (Printed in U.S.A.) One of 50 signed. In dust jacket. $35.

MACHEN, Arthur. *Far Off Things.* Boards. London, no date (1922). First edition. One of 1,000 signed. In dust jacket. $35. Trade edition, later: Green cloth. In dust jacket. $10.

MACHEN, Arthur. *The Great God Pan and the Inmost Light.* Pictorial blue cloth. London, 1894. First edition. $25-$30. (Note: The border on the book's cover was designed by Aubrey Beardsley.)

MACHEN, Arthur. *The Hill of Dreams.* Frontispiece. Dark-red buckram. London, 1907. First edition, with "E. Grant Richards" at bottom of spine. In dust jacket. $75. Lacking jacket, $50.

MACHEN, Arthur. *The House of Souls.* Frontispiece. Pictorial light-gray buckram. London, 1906. First edition. In dust jacket. $35.

MACHEN, Arthur. *Notes and Queries.* Green buckram, paper label. London, 1926. First edition. One of 265 signed. In dust jacket. $35. Trade edition: Cloth. In dust jacket. $10.

MACHEN, Arthur. *Ornaments in Jade.* Cloth. New York, 1924. First edition. One of 1,000 signed. In dust jacket. $40-$50.

MACHEN, Arthur. *The Shining Pyramid.* Edited by Vincent Starrett. Illustrated. Black cloth. Chicago, 1923. Limited first edition. In dust jacket. $25. London, 1925. Blue cloth. First English edition. One of 250 signed. In dust jacket. $25-$40. Trade edition: Cloth. In dust jacket. $10.

MACHEN, Arthur. *Strange Roads and With the Gods in Spring.* Cloth. London, 1923. First edition. In dust jacket. $25. London, 1924. Half vellum. One of 300 signed. $40-$50.

MACHEN, Arthur. *Things Near and Far.* Cloth. London, 1923. First edition. One of 100 signed. In dust jacket. $25-$30. Trade edition: Cloth. In dust jacket. $10.

MACHEN, Arthur. *The Three Impostors.* Blue cloth. London, 1895. First edition. $25. (Note: Border on cover designed by Aubrey Beardsley.)

MACHEN, Arthur (editor). *One Hundred Merrie and Delightsome Stories.* (Translated by Robert B. Douglas.) Illustrated. 2 vols., cloth. Carbonnek, 1924. (Printed in U.S.A.) First edition. In dust jacket. $75-$100.

McILVAINE, William, Jr. *Sketches of Scenery and Notes of Personal Adventure, in California and Mexico.* 16 plates, including engraved title page. Purplish cloth. Philadelphia, 1850. First edition. $500-$750. San Francisco, 1951. Folio, half cloth. One of 400. $35-$50.

McINTIRE, Jim. *Early Days in Texas: A Trip to Hell and Heaven.* 16 plates, pictorial cloth. Kansas City, Mo., no date (1902). First edition. $75-$125.

MACK, Effie. *Nevada: A History of the State.* Map, facsimiles. Glendale, Calif., 1936. First edition. One of 250 signed. $50-$75.

MACK, Solomon. *A Narraitive [sic] of the Life of Solomon Mack.* 48 pp., wrappers. Windsor (Conn.?), no date (1810-12?). First edition. $300-$400.

MACKAIL, J. W. *The Life of William Morris.* 22 illustrations. 2 vols., brown morocco. London, 1899. First edition. $350-$400. London, 1901. Half morocco. $25-$35.

MACKAIL, J. W. *William Morris: An Address.* Vellum. London, 1901. Doves Press. First edition. One of 300. $50. Another issue: Morocco. Specially bound by the Doves Bindery. Boxed. $672 (A, 1969).

MACKAY, Charles. *Memoirs of Extraordinary Popular Delusions and the Madness of Crowds.* 5 portraits. 3 vols., gray cloth. London, 1841. First edition. $50-$75.

MACKAY, Charles. *The Mormons: Their Progress and Present Condition.* 10 parts, wrappers. London, 1851. First edition. $150-$200. London, 1851. Cloth. First book edition. $25-$35.

McKAY, Claude. *Banjo.* Decorated boards and cloth. New York, 1929. First edition. In dust jacket. $35.

McKAY, Claude. *A Long Way from Home.* Green cloth. New York, no date (1937). First edition. In dust jacket. $35.

MACKAY, Malcolm S. *Cow-Range and Hunting Trail.* 38 illustrations. Cloth. New York, 1925. First edition. In dust jacket. $50-$60.

McKAY, Richard. *Some Famous Sailing Ships.* 10 color plates, 48 other illustrations. Cloth. New York, 1928. First edition. In dust jacket. $35-$50.

McKAY, Richard C. *South Street: A Maritime History of New York.* 48 illustrations. Two-tone cloth. New York, no date (1934). One of 200 signed. Boxed. $50.

McKAY, Robert H. *Little Pills.* 3 plates. Khaki cloth. Pittsburg, Kan., 1918. First edition. $35-$50.

McKAY, William, and Roberts, W. *John Hoppner, R.A.* Illustrated. Cloth. London, 1909. $75. London, 1909-14. 2 vols., buckram (including supplement). $100-$125.

MACKAYE, Percy. *Johnny Crimson: A Legend of Hollis Hall.* Cover design by Eric Pape. Wrappers. Boston, 1895. First edition. $75. Author's first book.

MACKAYE, Percy. *Saint Louis: A Civic Masque.* Boards, paper label. New York, 1914. First edition. One of 300 signed. $25-$30.

McKEE, James Cooper. *Narrative of the Surrender of a Command of U.S. Forces at Fort Fillmore, N.M., in July A.D. 1861.* (Cover title.) 30 pp., printed self-wrappers. New York, 1881. Second edition. $100-$125. (The very rare first edition appeared in Prescott, Arizona Territory, in 1878. Estimated value: $750-$1,000.)

McKEE, Dr. W. H. *The Territory of New Mexico, and Its Resources.* Map. 12 pp., printed wrappers. New York, 1866. First edition. $1,200 (A, 1966).

MACKENNA, F. Severne. *Worcester Porcelain.* Frontispiece in color, 80 plates. Buckram. London, 1950. One of 500 signed. In dust jacket. $150.

McKENNEY, Thomas L. *Sketches of a Tour to the Lakes.* 29 full-page engravings, some in color. Boards, paper label. Baltimore, 1827. First edition. $150-$200.

M'KENNEY, Thomas L., and Hall, James. *History of the Indian Tribes of North America.* Map. 120 colored plates and list of subscribers. 3 vols., folio, cloth, or half leather. Philadelphia, 1836-38-44. First edition. Up to $5,000 for fine sets. Philadelphia, 1837-42-44. 3 vols., folio. Second edition. Up to $3,000, possibly more. Philadelphia, 1838-42-44. 3 vols., folio. Third edition. Up to $3,000, possibly more. Also, $2,520 (A, 1967). Philadelphia, 1842-42-44. 3 vols., folio. Rice & Clark reprint. $775 (A, 1965). Philadelphia, no date (about 1845). 3 vols., folio. Rice & Clark reprint. $1,400 (A, 1965). Philadelphia, 1855. 3 vols., octavo, morocco. $1,250. Other editions, octavo, at auction: Philadelphia, 1855. 3 vols., $800 (1969); Philadelphia, 1858. 3 vols., $720 (1969). Edinburgh, 1933-34. 3 vols., blue cloth. Boxed. $300 at retail. Also, $210 (A, 1970).

MACKENZIE, Alexander. *Voyages from Montreal, on the River St. Lawrence, Through the Continent of North America.* Frontispiece, 3 folding maps. Boards and cloth. London, 1801. First edition. $500-$600. Also, $450 (A, 1969). London, 1802. 2 vols., boards. Second edition. $150. New York, 1802. Folding map. Boards. First American edition. $100-$150. Philadelphia, 1802. 2 vols., boards. $75-$100.

MACKENZIE, Compton. *Extraordinary Women.* Cloth. London, 1928. First edition. One of 100 signed. In dust jacket. $35.

McKIM, Randolph H. *A Soldier's Recollections: Leaves from the Diary of a Young Confederate.* Cloth. New York, 1911. First edition. $35.

McKINSTRY, George H., Jr. *Thrilling and Tragic Journal Written by George H. McKinstry, Jr., While on a Journey to California in 1846-47.* Broadside folded to book size, printed paper covers. West Hoboken, N.J., no date (1920). First edition. One of 65. $35-$50.

McKNIGHT, Charles. *Old Fort Duquesne: or, Captain Jack, the Scout.* Cloth. Pittsburgh, 1873. First edition. $35.

McKNIGHT, Geo. S. *California 49er: Travels from Perrysburg to California.* 27 pp., printed red wrappers. No place, no date (Perrysburg, Ohio, 1903). First edition. $150-$200.

McLAUGHLIN, James. *My Friend the Indian.* Illustrated. Cloth. Boston, 1910. First edition. $35.

McLEOD, Donald. *History of Wiskonsan, from Its First Discovery to the Present Period.* 4 plates, folding map. Cloth. Buffalo, N.Y., 1846. First edition. $250-$300. (Note: Wright Howes says some copies have plates and no map and others map and no plates.)

McLUHAN, Herbert Marshall. *The Mechanical Bride.* Cloth. New York, no date (1951). First edition. In dust jacket. $30-$35.

MacLEISH, Archibald. See Wells, Oliver.

MacLEISH, Archibald. *Conquistador.* Folding map. Cloth. Boston, 1932. First edition. In dust jacket. $35-$40.

MacLEISH, Archibald. *Einstein.* Printed wrappers. Paris, 1929. Black Sun Press. First edition. One of 100 on Van Gelder paper. Boxed. $35-$50. One of 50 on vellum, signed. Boxed. $100.

MacLEISH, Archibald. *The Happy Marriage and Other Poems.* Boards, paper label. Boston, 1924. First edition. In dust jacket. $35.

MacLEISH, Archibald. *Land of the Free.* Illustrated with photographs. Linen. New York, no date (1938). First edition. In dust jacket. $35.

MacLEISH, Archibald. *New Found Land.* Wrappers. Paris, 1930. Black Sun Press. First edition. One of 100 numbered copies (of an edition of 135). Boxed. $60 and $75. One of 35 on vellum, signed. Boxed. $100-$125. Boston, 1930. (Printed in Paris.) First American edition. $25.

MacLEISH, Archibald. *Nobodaddy.* Black cloth. Cambridge, Mass., 1926. First edition. One of 700. In dust jacket. $15-$20. Another issue: One of 50 on large paper. In dust jacket. $35-$50.

MacLEISH, Archibald. *Poems, 1924-1933.* Cloth. Boston, 1933. First edition. In dust jacket. $25.

MacLEISH, Archibald. *The Pot of Earth.* Gold decorated boards. Cambridge, 1925. First edition. One of 100 on handmade paper. In dust jacket. $35-$50. Boston, 1925. Boards. Trade edition. In dust jacket. $15-$25.

MacLEISH, Archibald. *Public Speech: Poems.* Full calf. New York, no date (1936). First edition. One of 275 signed. In glassine dust jacket. Boxed. $35. Spine faded, $25. Trade edition: Blue cloth. First issue, with F & R monogram on copyright page. In dust jacket. $15.

MacLEISH, Archibald. *Songs for a Summer Day.* Wrappers. No place (New Haven), 1915. First edition. $150-$250. Author's first book.

MacLEISH, Archibald. *Streets in the Moon.* Decorated boards and cloth. Boston, 1926. First edition. One of 60 on handmade paper, signed. Boxed. $50. Another issue: One of 540. $15.

MacLEISH, Archibald. *Tower of Ivory.* Boards, paper label. New Haven, 1917. First edition. In dust jacket. $35-$50. Author's first hardbound book.

MacLEISH, Archibald, and others. *"What Is America's Foreign Policy?"* 12 pp., mimeographed. State Dept. press release. No place (Washington), 1945. $45.

MacLOW, Jackson. *22 Light Poems.* Decorated cloth. Los Angeles, 1968. Black Sparrow Press. One of 125 signed. $25-$30. Another issue: Wrappers. One of 750. $10.

McMASTER, S. W. *Sixty Years on the Upper Mississippi.* 300 pp., flexible wrappers. Rock Island, Ill., 1893 (printer's foreword dated Galena, Ill., 1895). First edition. $75-$100.

McMURRAY, W. J. *History of the 20th Tennessee Regiment Volunteer Infantry, C.S.A.* Cloth. Nashville, 1904. First edition. $35.

McMURTRIE, Douglas C. *The Beginnings of Printing in Chicago.* Half cloth. Chicago, 1931. One of 160. $50.

McMURTRIE, Douglas C. *The Beginnings of Printing in Utah.* Half cloth. Chicago, 1931. One of 160. $50.

McMURTRIE, Douglas C. *Bibliography of Chicago Imprints, 1835-50.* Buckram. Chicago, 1944. One of 200. $50-$75.

McMURTRIE, Douglas C. *Early Printing in New Orleans, 1764-1810.* Illustrated. Half cloth. New Orleans, 1929. One of 410. $50-$75.

McMURTRIE, Douglas C. *Early Printing in Wisconsin.* Cloth. Seattle, 1931. $50-$75.

McMURTRIE, Douglas C. *Early Printing in Wyoming.* Cloth. Hattiesburg, Miss., 1943. $25.

McMURTRIE, Douglas C. *Eighteenth Century North Carolina Imprints, 1749-1800.* Facsimiles. Cloth. Chapel Hill, 1938. One of 200. In dust jacket. $25-$35.

McMURTRIE, Douglas C. *The First Printers of Chicago.* Half cloth. Chicago, 1927. One of 650. $25-$35. Another issue: One of 250. $50-$60.

McMURTRIE, Douglas C. *The Golden Book.* Illustrated. Half morocco. Chicago, 1927. First edition. One of 200 signed. $50-$60.

McMURTRIE, Douglas C. *A History of Printing in the United States.* Vol. II. (All published.) Cloth. New York, 1936. $50-$75.

McMURTRIE, Douglas C. *The Invention of Printing.* Printed wrappers. Chicago, 1942. $50.

McMURTRIE, Douglas C. *Jotham Meeker: Pioneer Printer of Kansas.* Portrait and facsimiles. Cloth. Chicago, 1930. One of 650. $25.

McMURTRIE, Douglas C., and Allen, Albert H. *Early Printing in Colorado.* Cloth. Denver, 1935. First edition. $50.

McMURTRIE, Douglas C., and Eames, Wilberforce. *New York Printing.* 78 illustrations. Cloth. Chicago, 1928. $50.

McMURTRIE, Henry. *Sketches of Louisville and Its Environs.* Map and table. Boards. Louisville, Ky., 1819. First edition. $150-$200.

MacNEICE, Louis. *Autumn Journal.* Cloth. London, 1939. First edition. In dust jacket. $50-$60.

MacNEICE, Louis. *Blind Fireworks.* Cloth. London, 1929. First edition. In dust jacket. $125-$150. Author's first book.

MacNEICE, Louis. *The Earth Compels.* Cloth. London, 1938. First edition. In dust jacket. $35-$50.

MacNEICE, Louis. *The Last Ditch.* Boards, linen spine, paper label. Dublin, 1940. Cuala Press. First edition. One of 450. In tissue dust jacket. $75-$100.

MacNEICE, Louis. *Poems.* Cloth. London, no date (1935). First edition. In dust jacket. $25. Signed, $35-$40.

MacNEICE, Louis. *Springboard.* Cloth. London, 1944. First edition. In dust jacket. $25.

McNEIL, Samuel. *McNeils [sic] Travels in 1849, to, Through and from the Gold Regions.* 40 pp., plain wrappers. Columbus, Ohio, 1850. First edition. $3,500 (A, 1968)–the Thomas W. Streeter copy, one of only 5 known.

MacNUTT, Francis A. *Bartholomew de Las Casas, His Life, Apostolate, and Writings.* Portrait. Half cloth. Cleveland, 1909. First edition. In dust jacket. $35-$50.

MACOMB, David B. *Answer to Enquiries Relative to Middle Florida.* 5 unnumbered leaves. Tallahassee, 1827. First edition. Bound in modern cloth, $800 (A, 1967).

MACON, T. J. *Reminiscences of the 1st Company of Richmond Howitzers.* Cloth. Richmond, Va., no date (about 1909). First edition. $50.

MACQUOID, Percy. *The History of English Furniture.* Illustrated, including color plates. 4 vols., buckram. London, 1904-08. First edition. $200-$250.

MACQUOID, Percy, and Edwards, Ralph. *The Dictionary of English Furniture.* 43 color plates, about 3,000 other illustrations. 3 vols., folio, buckram. London, 1924-27. First edition. $300-$400. London, 1954. 3 vols., folio, buckram. $400-$500.

McSHEEHY, H. J. *A Hunt in the Rockies.* Frontispiece and photographs. 135 pp., printed red wrappers. Logansport, Ind., 1893. First edition. $200 and up.

McWHORTER, Lucullus V. *The Border Settlers of Northwestern Virginia from 1768 to 1795.* Cloth. Hamilton, Ohio, 1915. First edition. $35-$50.

McWILLIAMS, John. *Recollections.* Portrait. Cloth. Princeton, N.J., no date (about 1919). First edition. $75-$100.

MACY, John (editor). *American Writers on American Literature.* Cloth. New York, 1931. First edition. In dust jacket. $25-$35.

MADDEN, Frederic W. *Coins of the Jews.* 279 woodcut illustrations and a folding plate of alphabets. London, 1903. Second edition. $45.

MADISON, James. *Communications from the American Ministers at Ghent.* 74 pp., sewed. Washington, 1814. First edition, with final signature "10." $35.

MADISON, James. *Communications from the Plenipotentiaries of the U. S. Negotiating Peace with Great Britain.* 28 pp., sewed. Washington, 1814. $25.

MADISON, James. *Message from the President of the United States.* 19 pp. Washington, 1813. $75-$100. (Note: Covers the captivity of Mrs. Crawley among the Creek Indians.)

MADISON, James. *Message from the President of the United States, Recommending an Immediate Declaration of War Against Great Britain.* 12 pp., sewed. Washington, 1812. $60.

MADRID Y ORMAECHEA, German. *Historia Christiana de la California.* 5 plates. 238 pp., wrappers. Mexico, 1864. $100.

MAGEE, David. *The Hundredth Book: A Bibliography of . . . the Book Club of California.* 18 reproductions, many in color. Folio, half cloth. San Francisco, 1958. Grabhorn printing. One of 400. $85.

MAGEE, Dorothy, and Magee, David. *Bibliography of the Grabhorn Press, 1940-1956.* Illustrated. Folio, half morocco. San Francisco, 1957. One of 225. $250. Also, $110 (A, 1967). See Heller, Elinor, and Magee, David.

MAGNA Carta and Other Charters of English Liberties. Tan pigskin. No place, no date (London, 1938). Guyon House Press. One of 250. $85.

MAGOFFIN, Susan Shelby. *Down the Santa Fe Trail and into Mexico.* Edited by Stella M. Drumm. Map, plates. Cloth. New Haven, 1926. First edition. In dust jacket. $50-$60.

MAGOUN, F. Alexander. *The Frigate Constitution and Other Historic Ships.* Illustrated, including 16 folding plates. Buckram. Salem, 1928. In dust jacket. $100-$150.

MAGRUDER, Allan B. *Political, Commercial and Moral Reflections, on the Late Cession of Louisiana, to the United States.* Boards. Lexington, Ky., 1803. First edition. $2,100 (A, 1967).

MAGUIRE, H. N. *The Coming Empire: A Complete and Reliable Treatise on the Black Hills, Yellowstone and Big Horn Regions.* 7 plates, folding map. Cloth. Sioux City, Iowa, 1878. First edition. $300-$400.

MAGUIRE, H. N. *The Lakeside Library: The People's Edition of the Black Hills and American Wonderland.* (Caption title.) Illustrations and map. 36 pp., stitched. Chicago, 1877. First edition. $150 (A, 1968).

MAHAN, A. T. *The Influence of Sea Power upon History.* Cloth. Boston, 1890. First American edition. $100.

MAHAN, D. H. *An Elementary Course of Civil Engineering.* 176 wood engravings. Cloth. New York, 1846. $40-$50.

MAHAN, D. H. *An Elementary Treatise on Advanced-Guard, Out-Post and Detachment Service of Troops in the Presence of an Enemy.* Cloth. New Orleans, 1861. $35-$50.

MAHAN, D. H. *Summary of the Course of Permanent Fortification.* Boards. West Point, 1850. First edition. $50.

MAHONEY, J. W. *The Cherokee Physician, or Indian Guide to Health.* Half calf. Asheville, N.C., 1849. Second edition. $75.

MAID Marian. Boards. London, 1822. (By Thomas Love Peacock.) First edition. $200-$250.

MAILER, Norman. *Barbary Shore.* Black cloth. New York, no date (1951). First edition. In dust jacket. $25.

MAILER, Norman. *Deaths for the Ladies and Other Disasters.* Printed wrappers. New York, 1962. First edition. $25. Another issue: Cloth. In dust jacket. $15-$20.

MAILER, Norman. *The Naked and the Dead.* Black boards. New York, 1948. First edition. In dust jacket. $35. Author's first book. London, no date (1949). Full wine-colored morocco. First English edition. One of 240 bound for the Collector's Book Club. $50. Another issue: One of 13. $162.40 (A, 1966).

MAILLARD, N. Doran. *The History of the Republic of Texas, from the Discovery of the Country to the Present Time.* Folding map. Dark-blue cloth. London, 1842. First edition. $250.

MAJOR, Charles. See Caskoden, Edwin.

MAJOR Jones's Courtship; or Adventures of a Christmas Eve. 61 pp., wrappers. Savannah, Ga., 1850. (By William Tappan Thompson.) Name on cover, $30.

MAJOR Jones's Sketches of Travel, Comprising the Scenes, Incidents, and Adventures in His Tour from Georgia to Canada. Illustrated by F. O. C. Darley. Philadelphia, 1848. (By William Tappan Thompson.) First edition. Rebound in modern boards and calf, $95.

MAJORS, Alexander. *Seventy Years on the Frontier.* Frontispiece and plates. Blue pictorial cloth, or wrappers. Chicago, 1893. First edition. Wrappers: $75. Cloth: $50. Another edition: Denver, no date. Wrappers, without illustrations. $15-$25.

MALET, Capt. H. E. *Annals of the Road.* 10 colored plates, woodcuts. Cloth. London, 1876. $50-$75.

MALKIN, B. H. *A Father's Memoirs of His Child.* Folding map, 3 plates. Boards. London, 1806. First edition. $100-$150.

MALLOCK, W. H. *The New Paul and Virginia, or Positivism on an Island.* Decorated cloth. London, 1878. First edition, with ads dated March. $25.

MALONE, James H. *The Chickasaw Nation.* Maps and plates. Cloth. Louisville, 1922. Enlarged edition. $35.

MALORY, Sir Thomas. *Le Morte D'Arthur.* Edited by H. O. Sommer and Andrew Lang. 3 vols., wrappers. London, 1889-91. $100. London, no date (1893-94). Illustrated by Aubrey Beardsley. 12 parts, printed wrappers. One of 300 on Dutch handmade paper. $350-$450. Another issue: 3 vols., pictorial cloth. One of 300. $250-$350. Another issue: 2 vols., cloth. One of 1,500. $100-$150. London, 1909. Cloth. Second Beardsley edition. $75-$100. London, 1910-11. Riccardi Press. Illustrated in color by W. Russell Flint. 4 vols., limp vellum. One of 500. $225-$250. Another issue: Boards and cloth. $100-$150. Rebound in full brown morocco, $400. London, 1913. Ashendene Press. Illustrated by Charles and Margaret Gore. Folio, full cowhide. One of 145. Boxed. $1,000. Also, $850 (A, 1969); $576 (A, 1967). Another issue: One of 8 on vellum. $2,700 (A, 1965). London, 1933. Shakespeare Head Press. Illustrated. 2 vols., morocco. $200-$300. New York, 1936. Limited Editions Club. Illustrated by Robert Gibbings. 3 vols., boards and cloth. Boxed. $50.

MALRAUX, André. *Days of Wrath.* Cloth. New York, 1936. First American edition. In dust jacket. $25-$30.

MALRAUX, André. *The Metamorphosis of the Gods.* Illustrated. Red morocco. Garden City, 1960. First American edition. One of 50 signed. Boxed. $100-$150. Trade edition: Cloth. In dust jacket. $20-$25.

MALRAUX, André. *The Psychology of Art.* Illustrated. 3 vols., cloth. No place, no date (New York, 1949-50). $150.

MALRAUX, André. *The Voices of Silence.* Cloth. Garden City, 1953. First American edition. Boxed. $50.

MALRAUX, André. *The Walnut Trees of Altenburg.* Translated by A. W. Fielding. Cloth. London, 1952. First English edition. In dust jacket. $40.

MALTHUS, Thomas Robert. *Definitions in Political Economy.* Boards. London, 1827. First edition. $150-$200.

MALTHUS, Thomas Robert. *An Essay on the Principle of Population.* Boards. London, 1803. Second edition. $100-$150. (Note: The anonymous first edition, London, 1798, boards, sells for $750-$1,000 if in fine condition.) Georgetown, 1809. 2 vols., contemporary marbled boards and calf. First American edition. $90 (A, 1968).

MALTHUS, Thomas Robert. *An Inquiry into the Nature and Progress of Rent.* Boards. London, 1815. First edition. $75-$100.

MALTHUS, Thomas Robert. *Principles of Political Economy.* Boards. London, 1820. First edition. $300-$400. Rebound in calf, $150, $175, and $225. Also, $210 (A, 1969). Boston, 1821. Boards. First American edition. $100-$150.

MAN *Without a Country (The).* 23 pp., terra-cotta wrappers. Boston, 1865. (By Edward Everett Hale.) First edition, first issue, without the publisher's printed yellow "Announcement" slip tipped in. $275-$350. Second issue, with the "Announcement" slip tipped in. $200. Another, bound in cloth with paper covers bound in, $50. New York, 1902. Vellum. "Birthday Edition." One of 80 on Japan paper. $35. New York, 1936. Limited Editions Club. Calf. Boxed. $25-$35.

MANIFIESTO *al Mundo. La Justicia y la Necesidad de la Independencia de la Nueva España.* 19 pp., sewed. Puebla, Mexico, 1821. (By Manuel Barcena.) First edition. $300-$500.

MANIFIESTO *del Congreso General en el Presente Ano.* 20 pp., printed wrappers. Mexico, 1836. (By Angel G. Quintanar.) $100-$150.

MANLY, William Lewis. *Death Valley in '49.* 4 plates. Cloth. San Jose, Calif., 1894. First edition. $65.

MANN, Thomas. *The Beloved Returns.* Boards. New York, 1940. First American edition. One of 395 signed. In dust jacket. Boxed. $50.

MANN, Thomas. *Buddenbrooks, Verfall einer Familie.* 2 vols., half morocco. Berlin, 1901. First edition. $150. Author's first book. London, 1924. Translated by H. T. Lowe-Porter. 2 vols., cloth. First edition in English. In dust jackets. $25-$35.

MANN, Thomas. *The Magic Mountain.* 2 vols., half vellum. New York, 1927. One of 200 signed. $100-$150. New York, 1962. Limited Editions Club. Illustrated. Half cloth. Boxed. $85-$100.

MANN, Thomas. *Nocturnes.* Lithographs by Lynd Ward. Pictorial cloth. New York, 1934. One of 1,000 signed. Boxed. $35-$50.

MANNING-SANDERS, Ruth. *Martha Wish-You-Ill.* 16 pp., wrappers. London, 1926. Hogarth Press. First edition. $25-$30.

MANNING, Wentworth. *Some History of Van Zandt County, Texas.* Vol. 1. (All published.) Illustrated. Maps. Cloth. Des Moines, Iowa, no date (1919). First edition. $35-$50.

MANSFIELD, Edward D. *Exposition of the Natural Position of Mackinaw City, and the Climate, Soil, and Commercial Elements of the Surrounding Country.* 2 maps. 47 pp., printed wrappers. Cincinnati, 1857. First edition. $100-$150.

MANSFIELD, Katherine. *The Aloe.* Buckram. London, 1930. First edition. One of 750. In dust jacket. $35-$50. Also, $20 (A, 1965). New York, 1930. Boards. First American edition. One of 975. In dust jacket. Boxed. $25.

MANSFIELD, Katherine. *Bliss and Other Stories.* Brick-red cloth. London, no date (1920). First edition, with page 13 numbered 3. In white dust jacket with author's portrait. $100-$150. Lacking jacket, $100. Also, $50 (A, 1965).

MANSFIELD, Katherine. *The Doves' Nest and Other Stories.* Blue-gray cloth, blue spine lettering. London, no date (1923). First edition, first issue, with verso of title page blank. One of 25. In dust jacket. $75-$100. Second issue, with "First published June, 1923" on back of title page. In dust jacket. $25-$35.

MANSFIELD, Katherine. *The Garden Party and Other Stories.* Light-blue cloth. London, 1922. First edition, first issue, with "sposition" for "position" in last line on page 103. In strawberry-colored dust jacket, with blue lettering. One of 25. $50-$100. Later issue, orange (ocher) lettering. In dust jacket. $25-$35. London, 1939. Verona Press. 16 color lithographs by Marie Laurencin. Decorated cloth. One of 1,200. Boxed. $125-$150.

MANSFIELD, Katherine. *In a German Pension.* Green cloth. London, no date (1911). First edition. In orange (ocher) dust jacket. $200-$250. Author's first book.

MANSFIELD, Katherine. *Je Ne Parle Pas Français.* Green wrappers. Hampstead, England, 1919 (actually 1918). Heron Press. First edition. One of 100. $350-$450.

MANSFIELD, Katherine. *The Journal of Katherine Mansfield.* Edited by J. Middleton Murry. Cloth. London, 1927. First edition. In dust jacket. $40-$50.

MANSFIELD, Katherine. *Poems.* Brown boards, red leather spine label. London, no date (1923). First edition. In cream-colored dust jacket. $75-$100. Lacking jacket, $35-$50.

MANSFIELD, Katherine. *Prelude.* Blue pictorial wrappers. Richmond, England, no date (1918). Hogarth Press. First edition, with or without design on covers by J. D. Fergusson. $200-$250.

MANSFIELD, Katherine. *Something Childish and Other Stories.* Gray buckram. London, no date (1924). First edition, first issue, without "First Published 1924" on verso of title page. In dust jacket. $100-$150. Second issue. In dust jacket. $35.

MANSFIELD, Katherine. *To Stanislaw Wyspianski*. Printed wrappers. London, 1938. One of 100 printed for Bertram Rota. $150-$200.

MANSFIELD Park: A Novel. By the Author of "Sense and Sensibility" and "Pride and Prejudice." 3 vols., blue boards, white paper labels. London, 1814. (By Jane Austen.) First edition, with Vols. 1 and 3 bearing Sidney imprint on back of half titles and Vol. 2 the Roworth imprint. $2,500 and up. Also, $960 (A, 1969), $1,300 (A, 1963). Rebound in full calf, $650 at retail.

MANUEL de Proverbes Dramatiques. 288 pp., cloth, printed spine label. Portland (Brunswick), Me., 1830. First edition, second issue, with last page misnumbered 188. (Edited anonymously by Henry Wadsworth Longfellow.) Rebound in morocco, $80 (A, 1960). (Note: Blanck's *BAL* also describes a preliminary issue of the same edition with only 156 pages.)

MAP of Texas with Parts of the Adjoining States. 30 sections, folded into red leather covers. Philadelphia, no date (1830). (Compiled by Stephen F. Austin.) First edition. $350-$500.

MARCH of the First (The). (First Regiment of Colorado Volunteers.) 36 pp., stitched, plus 4 pp. of ads. Denver, 1863. First edition. $2,000 (A, 1968).

MARCLIFFE, Theophilus. *The Looking-Glass: A True History of the Early Years of an Artist.* Boards. London, 1805. (By William Godwin.) First edition. $150-$250.

MARCUS Aurelius Antoninus. *The Thoughts of the Emperor Marcus Aurelius.* Translated by George Long. Wrappers. London, 1897. Ashendene Press. One of 30. $1,000. Also, $700 (A, 1969). London, 1909. Illustrated by W. Russell Flint. Limp vellum with ties. One of 17 on vellum. $250-$350. Another issue: Vellum or half cloth. One of 500. $100-$150.

MARCY, Randolph B. *Exploration of the Red River of Louisiana.* (Senate Exec. Doc. 54.) 65 plates, 2 maps. 2 vols., brown cloth and green cloth (atlas case). Washington, 1853. First edition. $100. Washington, 1854. Second edition, printed by Tucker. $50. Washington, 1854. House version, printed by Nicholson. $50.

MARCY, Randolph B. *The Prairie Traveler: A Hand-Book for Overland Expeditions.* Maps. 31 illustrations. Cloth. New York, 1859. First edition. $100-$125. London, 1863. Edited by R. F. Burton. Illustrated. Half morocco. $100.

MARDERSTEIG, Hans. *Pastonchi: A Specimen of a New Letter for Use on the "Monotype."* Illustrated with plates and booklet inserts. Marbled boards and vellum. No place, no date (London, 1928). One of 200 on Fabriano paper. $50.

MARIGNY, Bernard. *Réflexions sur la Campagne du Gen. Jackson en Louisiane en 1814-15.* 51 pp., wrappers. Nouvelle-Orléans, 1848. First edition. $50-$75.

MARK Twain's Sketches. See Twain, Mark.

MARKET Harborough; or, How Mr. Sawyer Went to the Shires. Cloth. London, 1861. (By George John Whyte-Melville.) First edition. $40-$50.

MARKHAM, Edwin. *The Man with the Hoe.* 4 pp., printed wrappers. San Francisco, 1899. First book edition. $85-$100. (Earlier, Jan. 15, 1899: Special supplement to San Francisco Sunday *Examiner,* containing first separate printing of the poem, 4 pp. $100.) New York, 1899. Green cloth. Second edition, first issue, with "fruitless" for "milkless" in line 5, page 35. $75-$100.

MARKHAM, Edwin. *New Poems: Eighty Songs at Eighty.* Portrait. Boards and leather. Garden City, 1932. First edition (so stated). One of 100 signed. Boxed. $50-$75. Trade edition: Cloth. In dust jacket. $10-$15.

MARKS, B. *Small-Scale Farming in Central California.* 48 pp., printed wrappers. San Francisco, no date (1888). $50.

MARKS, Elias, M.D. *The Aphorisms of Hipprocrates.* Boards, paper label. New York, 1818. First edition. $30-$35.

MARKS, M. R. *The Advantages and Resources of Orange County, Florida.* 2 maps. 16 pp., wrappers. Orlando, Fla., no date (1879). $50-$75.

MARLOWE, Christopher. *Edward the Second.* Illustrated. Vellum. London, 1929. Aquila Press. One of 500. $35-$50.

MARLOWE, Christopher. *The Famous Tragedy of the Rich Jew of Malta.* Engravings by Eric Ravilious. Three-quarters red calf and cloth. London, 1933. Golden Hours Press. One of 200. Boxed. $50. Another issue: Cloth. In dust jacket. $25.

MARLOWE, Christopher, and Chapman, George. *Hero and Leander.* Illustrated. Vellum. London, 1894. One of 220. $100-$150.

MARQUAND, John P. See Clark, Charles E.

MARQUAND, John P. *Four of a Kind.* Green cloth. New York, 1923. First edition. In dust jacket. $25-$35.

MARQUAND, John P. *The Late George Apley.* Cloth. Boston, 1937. First edition. In dust jacket. $25-$35.

MARQUAND, John P. *The Unspeakable Gentleman.* Cloth. New York, 1922. First edition. In dust jacket. $25-$35. Another issue: Boards and cloth. Limited, signed, for booksellers. $45-$60. Author's first book.

MARQUIS, Don. *Archy and Mehitabel.* Black cloth. Garden City, 1927. First edition, first printing (so indicated). In dust jacket. $35-$45.

MARQUIS, Don. *Danny's Own Story.* Illustrated by E. W. Kemble. Cloth. Garden City, N.Y., 1912. First edition. In dust jacket. $35. Author's first book.

MARQUIS, Don. *Dreams and Dust.* Cloth. New York, no date (1915). First edition. In dust jacket. $25.

MARQUIS, Don. *How Hank Signed the Pledge in a Cistern.* Wrappers. New York, no date (about 1912). First edition. $25.

MARQUIS, Don. *The Old Soak, and Hail and Farewell.* Boards and cloth. Garden City, 1921. First edition. In dust jacket. $25.

MARQUIS, Thomas B. *Memoirs of a White Crow Indian (Thomas H. LeForge).* Illustrated. Pictorial yellow cloth. New York, no date (1928). First edition. In dust jacket. $35-$50. Lacking jacket, $25-$30. London, 1928. Illustrated. Pictorial cloth. First English edition. In dust jacket. $25-$35.

MARQUIS, Thomas B. *A Warrior Who Fought Custer.* Illustrated. Cloth. Minneapolis, 1931. First edition. In dust jacket. $35.

MARRANT, John. *A Narrative of the Life of John Marrant.* 48 pp., wrappers. Halifax, 1812. (Edited by William Aldridge.) $50. (Note: One of innumerable nineteenth-century reprints of a book first published in London in 1785. Howes calls it "one of the earliest written by an American Negro.")

MARRIAGE: A Novel. 3 vols., boards. Edinburgh, 1818. (By Susan Edmonstone Ferrier.) First edition. $400-$500. Also, $360 (A, 1968).

MARRIOTT, William. *A Collection of English Miracle-Plays or Mysteries.* Boards, paper labels. Basel, Switzerland, 1838. First edition. $50.

MARRYAT, Frank. *Mountains and Molehills.* 18 woodcuts, 8 color plates. Salmon-colored cloth. London, 1855. (By Francis S. Marryat.) First edition. $250-$350. New York, 1855. Frontispiece. Pictorial cloth. First American edition. $50-$75.

MARRYAT, Frederick. See *Mr. Midshipman Easy; Olla Podrida; Percival Keene; Snarleyyow.*

MARRYAT, Frederick. *A Diary in America.* 6 vols., (Parts I and II, each 3 vols.), boards. London, 1839. First editions. $150-$200. Philadelphia, 1839-40. 3 vols., half cloth (2 vols., 1839, and 2d Series, 1 vol., 1840). First American editions. $50-$75. Paris, 1839-40. 2 folding maps. 2 vols., half leather. $65.

MARRYAT, Frederick. *Jacob Faithful.* 3 vols., half cloth. London, 1834. First edition. $100-$125.

MARRYAT, Frederick. *The Little Savage.* Illustrated. 2 vols., green cloth. London, 1848-49. First edition. $50.

MARRYAT, Frederick. *Masterman Ready.* Illustrated. 3 vols., cloth. London, 1841-42-42. First edition. $100-$150.

MARRYAT, Frederick. *The Mission.* Map, frontispiece. 2 vols., cloth. London, 1845. First edition, with 32 pages of ads in Vol. 1. $75.

MARRYAT, Frederick. *Narrative of the Travels and Adventures of Monsieur Violet, in California, Sonora and Western Texas.* Map. 3 vols., cloth. London, 1843. First edition. $50-$75. Second edition: London, 1843. Retitled: *The Travels and Romantic Adventures of Monsieur Violet, etc.* Map omitted. $25.

MARRYAT, Frederick. *Poor Jack.* Illustrated. 12 parts, pictorial wrappers. London, 1840. First edition. $75-$100. London, 1840. Pictorial cloth. First book edition. $35-$50.

MARRYAT, Frederick. *The Privateer's-Man.* 2 vols., cloth. London, 1846. First edition, with May ads in first volume. $75-$100.

MARRYAT, Frederick. *The Settlers in Canada.* 2 frontispieces. 2 vols., cloth. London, 1844. First edition. $100.

MARSH, James B. *Four Years in the Rockies.* Portrait. Blue cloth. New Castle, Pa., 1884. First edition. $200-$250.

MARSH, John. *Hannah Hawkins, the Reformed Drunkard's Daughter.* Cloth. New York, 1844. First edition. $50.

MARSH, W. Lockwood. *Aeronautical Prints and Drawings.* Illustrated, including color plates. Cloth. London, 1924. First edition. In dust jacket. $100-$150.

MARSHALL, Archibald. *The Honour of the Clintons.* Cloth. London, no date (1913). First edition. In dust jacket. $30-$35.

MARSHALL, Charles I. *History of Door County, Wisconsin.* Portrait. Boards and cloth. Sturgeon Bay, Wis., 1881. First edition. $35-$50.

MARSHALL, Humphrey. *The History of Kentucky.* Vol. 1. (All published.) Calf. Frankfort, Ky., 1812. First edition. $750-$1,000. Also, $900 (A, 1967). Frankfort, 1824. 2 vols., calf. Second edition. $100-$150.

MARSHALL, Jabez P. *Memoirs of the Late Rev. Abraham Marshall.* Boards. Mount Zion, Ga., 1824. First edition. $75.

MARSHALL, John. *Opinion of the Supreme Court, etc., in the Case of Samuel Worcester Versus the State of Georgia.* 39 pp., sewed. Washington, 1832. First edition. $75-$100. Second edition, same date. 20 pp., half calf. $75.

MARSHALL, L. G. *The Arabian Art of Taming and Training Wild and Vicious Horses.* 36 pp., wrappers. No place (Circleville, Ohio), 1857. $35-$50.

MARSHALL, O. S. *A History of the Descendants of William Marshall.* Cloth. Kittanning, Pa., 1884. $50-$60.

MARSHALL, William I. *Acquisition of Oregon, and the Long Suppressed Evidence About Marcus Whitman.* Portrait. 2 vols., green cloth. No place (Seattle), 1905. First edition. $100-$150. Portland, Ore., 1911. 2 vols., cloth. $50. Seattle, 1911. 2 vols., cloth. $50.

MARTELL, Martha. *Second Love.* Cloth. New York, 1851. (By Mrs. Tuthill?) First edition. $25-$30.

MARTIAL Achievements of Great Britain and Her Allies from 1799 to 1815 (The). 52 colored plates. Half morocco. London, no date (1814-15). $750-$1,000.

MARTIN, Aaron. *An Attempt to Show the Inconsistency of Slave-Holding, with the Religion of the Gospel.* 16 pp., stitched. Lexington, Ky., 1807. First edition. $1,200 (A, 1967).

MARTIN Faber: The Story of a Criminal. Cloth. New York, 1833. (By William Gilmore Simms.) First edition. $75-$100.

MARTIN, Fredrik R. *The History of Oriental Carpets.* Illustrated, including color plates. 3 vols., boards. Vienna, 1908. $500.

MARTIN, Fredrik R. *The Miniature Painting and Painters of Persia, India and Turkey from the 8th to the 18th Century.* 271 collotype plates, 48 text illustrations, 5 plates in gold and colors by W. Griggs. 2 vols., folio, buckram. London, 1912. $400-$500.

MARTINEAU, Harriet. *Feats on the Fjord.* Illustrated by Arthur Rackham. Cloth. London, 1899. $50-$60.

MARTINEAU, Harriet. *How to Observe Morals and Manners.* Cloth. London, 1848. First edition. $75-$100.

MARTINEAU, Harriet. *Retrospect of Western Travel.* 3 vols., cloth. London, 1838. First edition. $75-$100. New York, 1838. 2 vols., half linen. First American edition. $25-$35.

MARTINEAU, Harriet. *Society in America.* 3 vols., cloth. London, 1837. First edition. $150-$200.

MARTÍNEZ CARO, Ramón. *Verdadera Idea de la Primera Campaña de Tejas y Sucesos Ocurridos después de la acción de San Jacinto.* Printed wrappers. Mexico, 1837. First edition. $350-$400. Also, rebound in half leather, original front cover bound in, $200 (A, 1966).

MARVEL, Ik. *Dream Life.* Cloth. New York, 1851. (By Donald G. Mitchell.) First edition, first state, with stereotyper's slug on copyright page. $25.

MARVEL, Ik. *Fresh Gleanings.* 2 vols., printed wrappers, or one vol., cloth. New York, 1847. (By Donald G. Mitchell.) First edition. Wrappers: $75-$100. Cloth: $25.

MARVEL, Ik. *Looking Back at Boyhood.* 21 pp., wrappers. No place (Norwich, Conn.), June, 1906. (By Donald G. Mitchell.) First edition. $45.

MARVEL, Ik. *The Reveries of a Bachelor.* Dark-blue cloth, or leather. New York, 1850. (By Donald G. Mitchell.) First edition, first printing, with last word, "sleep," on page 29 in perfect type. $25-$50.

MARVIN, Frederic R. *The Yukon Overland.* Folding map. Printed orange wrappers. Cincinnati, 1898. First edition. $75-$100.

MARVY, Louis (and Thackeray, William Makepeace). *Sketches After English Landscape Painters.* With Short Notices by W. M. Thackeray. 20 color plates. Cloth. London, no date (1850). First edition. $100-$150.

MARY BARTON: A Tale of Manchester Life. 2 vols., mulberry cloth. London, 1848. (By Elizabeth C. Gaskell.) First edition. $200-$300. Author's first book.

MASEFIELD, John. *Ballads.* Printed wrappers. London, 1903. First edition. No. 13 of "The Vigo Cabinet Series." $35-$75.

MASEFIELD, John. *The Bird of Dawning.* 4 color plates. Buckram. London, 1933. First illustrated edition. One of 300 signed. Boxed. $25-$40.

MASEFIELD, John. *Collected Poems.* Portrait. Cream-colored cloth, leather label. London, 1923. First edition. One of 530 signed. Boxed. $25-$35. Inscribed by Masefield with two lines of verse, $55.

MASEFIELD, John. *The Coming of Christ.* Boards and vellum. London, 1928. First edition. One of 275 signed. In dust jacket. $25-$30.

MASEFIELD, John. *The Hawbucks.* Boards, vellum spine. London, 1929. First edition. One of 275 signed. In dust jacket. $30.

MASEFIELD, John. *John M. Synge: A Few Personal Recollections.* Boards and linen. Dundrum, Ireland, 1915. Cuala Press. First edition. One of 350. $75-$100.

MASEFIELD, John. *Salt Water Ballads.* Blue buckram. London, 1902. First edition, first issue, with Grant Richards imprint on title page. One of 500. $200-$250. Author's first book.

MASEFIELD, John. *Some Memories of W. B. Yeats.* Boards and linen. Dublin, 1940. Cuala Press. First edition. One of 370. In tissue dust jacket. $75-$100.

MASEFIELD, John. *Sonnets and Poems.* Blue cloth, paper labels. Lollingdon, 1916. First edition. In dust jacket. $35.

MASEFIELD, John. *South and East.* Color plates. Vellum. London, 1929. Limited and signed. Boxed. $25-$35.

MASEFIELD, John. *The Wanderer of Liverpool.* Colored frontispiece, 4 diagrams (3 folding), other plates. Black cloth. London, 1930. Limited, signed edition. Boxed. $35. New York, 1930. Illustrated. Boards and cloth. One of 350 signed. Boxed. $35.

MASON, Allen C. *Tacoma.* (Caption title.) 24 pp., wrappers. No place, no date (Portland, Ore., 1888). $25.

MASON, Emily V. (editor). *The Southern Poems of the War.* Cloth. Baltimore, 1867. First edition. $35-$50.

MASON, The Rev. George. *Ode on the Loss of the Steamship Pacific.* 4 pp., printed wrappers. Nanaimo, B.C., 1875. $25.

MASON, Otis T. *Indian Basketry.* Illustrated, including color plates. 2 vols., pictorial buckram. New York, 1904. First edition. $125-$150.

MASON, Dr. Philip. *A Legacy to My Children.* Portrait. Cloth. Connersville, Ind., 1868. $50.

MASON, Z. H. *A General Description of Orange County, Florida.* Map. 56 pp., wrappers. Orlando, Fla., no date (1881). First edition. $250.

MASQUE of Poets (A). Black cloth. Boston, 1878. First edition, first issue. $35-$50. Second issue, reddish brown or green cloth. In cloth "Red Line" box. One of 500. $75-$100. (Note: Contains work by Henry David Thoreau, as well as Emily Dickinson's first book appearance—the poem "Success"—and the only such appearance in her lifetime.)

MASSEY, Gerald. *A Book of Beginnings.* 2 vols., cloth. London, 1881. $50.

MASSEY, Gerald. *The Natural Genesis, or Second Part of a Book of Beginnings.* 2 vols., cloth. London, 1883. $60.

MASSEY, Linton R. (compiler). *William Faulkner: "Man Working," 1919-1962.* Illustrated. Cloth. Charlottesville, Va., 1968. First edition. Catalogue of the Faulkner collections at the University of Virginia. $25.

MASSIE, J. Cam. *A Treatise on the Eclectic Southern Practice of Medicine.* Sheepskin. Philadelphia, 1854. First edition. $75-$100.

MASSON, L. R. *Les Bourgeois de la Compagnie du Nord-Ouest.* Folding map. 2 vols., green and orange wrappers. Quebec, 1889-90. First edition. $200-$250.

MASTERS, Edgar Lee. See Ford, Webster; Wallace, Dexter.

MASTERS, Edgar Lee. *A Book of Verses.* Gray boards. Chicago, 1898. First edition. $100-$150. Author's first book.

MASTERS, Edgar Lee. *Gettysburg, Manila, Acoma.* Cloth. New York, 1930. First edition. One of 375 signed. $50-$60.

MASTERS, Edgar Lee. *Godbey: A Dramatic Poem.* Boards and cloth. New York, 1931. First edition. One of 347 signed. Boxed. $35-$50.

MASTERS, Edgar Lee. *The Golden Fleece of California.* Woodcut illustrations. Cloth. Weston, Vt., no date (1936). First edition. One of 550 signed. In glassine dust jacket. Boxed. $30-$40. New York, no date (1937). Cloth. First trade edition. In dust jacket. $10.

MASTERS, Edgar Lee. *The Leaves of the Tree.* Printed wrappers. Chicago, 1909. First edition. $25.

MASTERS, Edgar Lee. *Lee: A Dramatic Poem.* Cloth. New York, 1926. First edition. One of 250 signed. $30-$40. Trade edition: Cloth. In dust jacket. $10.

MASTERS, Edgar Lee. *Lincoln the Man.* Illustrated. Cloth. New York, 1931. First edition. One of 150 signed. $35-$50.

MASTERS, Edgar Lee. *Maximilian.* Boards. Boston, 1902. First edition. $35-$50.

MASTERS, Edgar Lee. *The New Spoon River.* Vellum and boards. New York, 1924. First edition. One of 360 signed. $50-$75.

MASTERS, Edgar Lee. *The New Star Chamber and Other Essays.* Boards. Chicago, 1904. First edition. $50-$75.

MASTERS, Edgar Lee. *The Serpent in the Wilderness.* Boards and cloth. New York, no date (1933). First edition. One of 400 signed. In glassine dust jacket. Boxed. $35-$50. Another copy, same issue, but one of 84 copies with a page of the manuscript inserted, $75-$100.

MASTERS, Edgar Lee. *Spoon River Anthology.* Blue cloth. New York, 1915. First edition, first issue, measuring exactly 7/8 inches across top. In dust jacket. $100-$125. New York, 1942. Limited Editions Club. Illustrated. Buckram. Boxed. $40-$60.

MATHERS, E. Powys. *Procreant Hymn.* Engravings by Eric Gill. Buckram. Waltham St. Lawrence, England, 1916. One of 200. $100-$125.

MATHERS, John, and A Solid Gentleman. *The History of Mr. John Decastro and His Brother Bat, Commonly Called Old Crab.* 4 vols., boards, paper labels. London, 1815. (By George Colman, the Younger.) First edition. $100. Pittsburgh, 1902. 2 vols., half morocco. Reprint edition. $25-$35.

MATHEWS, A. E. *Canyon City, Colorado, and Its Surroundings.* Map, 5 plates. Cloth. New York, 1870. First edition. Waterstained, $2,100 (A, 1968).

MATHEWS, A. E. *Pencil Sketches of Colorado.* 23 plates in color. Cloth. No place (New York), 1866. First edition. Worn, foxed, $2,350 (A, 1968). Facsimile reprint: No place, no date (Denver, 1961). Oblong folio, cloth. $50.

MATHEWS, A. E. *Pencil Sketches of Montana.* 31 plates (4 folding). Cloth. New York, 1868. First edition. $2,000 (A, 1968).

MATHEWS, Alfred E. *Gems of Rocky Mountain Scenery.* 20 plates. Cloth. New York, 1869. First edition. $750-$1,000.

MATHEWS, Alfred E. *Interesting Narrative; Being a Journal of the Flight of Alfred E. Mathews, of Stark Co., Ohio, from the State of Texas, etc.* 34 pp., sewed. No place (New Philadelphia, Ohio), 1861. First edition. $550 (A, 1968).

MATHEWS, Edward J. *Crossing the Plains . . . in '59.* Cloth. No place, no date (1903? 1930?). First edition. $150.

MATHEWS, Mrs. M. M. *Ten Years in Nevada.* Illustrated. Leather, or cloth. Buffalo, N.Y., 1880. First edition. $100-$125.

MATSELL, George W. *Vocabulum; or, The Rogue's Lexicon.* Cloth. New York, no date (1859). First edition. $50-$75.

MATURIN, Charles Robert. *Melmoth the Wanderer.* 4 vols., cloth. Edinburgh, 1820. First edition. $500-$600. Edinburgh, 1821. 4 vols., boards. Second edition. $150.

MATURIN, Charles Robert. *Women; Or, Pour et Contre: A Tale.* 3 vols., boards. Edinburgh, 1818. First edition. $350-$400.

MAUGHAM, W. Somerset. *Ah King: Six Stories.* Blue cloth. London, no date (1933). First edition. In dust jacket. $15-$20. Another issue: Buckram. One of 175 signed. Boxed. $75-$100. Garden City, 1933. Black cloth. First American edition. In dust jacket. $10.

MAUGHAM, W. Somerset. *Ashenden, or The British Agent.* Blue-gray cloth. London, 1928. First edition. In dust jacket. $50-$60.

MAUGHAM, W. Somerset. *The Bishop's Apron.* Cloth. London, 1906. First edition. $100-$150.

MAUGHAM, W. Somerset. *The Book-Bag.* Portrait frontispiece. Half cloth and blue and white boards. Florence, Italy, 1932. First edition. One of 725 signed. In dust jacket. $75 $100.

MAUGHAM, W. Somerset. *Cakes and Ale.* Blue cloth. London, no date (1930). First edition, first issue, with "won" instead of "won't" in line 14 of page 147. In dust jacket. $25. London, no date (1954). Decorations by Graham Sutherland. Boards and leather. One of 1,000 signed. Boxed. $100-$150.

MAUGHAM, W. Somerset. *The Casuarina Tree.* Cloth. London, 1926. First edition. In dust jacket. $25.

MAUGHAM, W. Somerset. *Christmas Holiday.* Blue cloth. London, no date (1939). First edition. In dust jacket. $25.

MAUGHAM, W. Somerset. *The Constant Wife.* Blue cloth. New York, 1926. First edition. In dust jacket. $25-$35. London, 1927. Black cloth. First English edition. In dust jacket. $25.

MAUGHAM, W. Somerset. *Cosmopolitans: Very Short Stories.* Blue cloth. London, 1936. First edition. In dust jacket. $10-$20. Another issue: Red buckram. One of 175 signed. $50-$75.

MAUGHAM, W. Somerset. *Don Fernando.* Cloth. London, 1935. First edition. In dust jacket. $10-$15. Another issue: Buckram. One of 175 signed. Boxed. $55-$60. Garden City, 1935. Black cloth. First American edition. In dust jacket. $10.

MAUGHAM, W. Somerset. *The Explorer.* Cloth. London, 1908. First edition. $50-$60.

MAUGHAM, W. Somerset. *The Hero.* Red cloth. London, 1901. First edition. $75-$100.

MAUGHAM, W. Somerset. *The Judgment Seat.* Frontispiece by Ulrica Hyde. Cloth. London, 1934. Centaur Press. First edition. One of 150 signed. In dust jacket. $50-$75.

MAUGHAM, W. Somerset. *The Land of the Blessed Virgin.* Boards. London, 1905. First edition. $50-$60.

MAUGHAM, W. Somerset. *The Letter: A Play in Three Acts.* Cloth. London, no date (1927). First edition. $100-$150. (Also issued in wrappers.)

MAUGHAM, W. Somerset. *Liza of Lambeth.* Decorated green cloth. London, 1897. First edition. $225-$300. Author's first novel. London, 1947. Vellum and boards. Jubilee Edition. One of 1,000 signed. In dust jacket. $60-$70.

MAUGHAM, W. Somerset. *The Magician.* Cloth. London, 1908. First edition. $50-$60.

MAUGHAM, W. Somerset. *The Making of a Saint.* Pictorial cloth. Boston, 1898. First edition, first issue, with "In Press" under this title in ads. $150-$200.

MAUGHAM, W. Somerset. *A Man of Honour.* Printed wrappers. London, 1903. Chapman & Hall. First edition. $750 and up. (Only 150 printed.)

MAUGHAN. W. Somerset. *The Merry-Go-Round.* Blue cloth. London, 1904. First edition. $25-$35.

MAUGHAM, W. Somerset. *Mrs. Craddock.* Cloth. London, 1902. First edition. $25-$35.

MAUGHAM, W. Somerset. *The Moon and Sixpence.* Sage-green cloth. London, no date (1919). First edition, first issue, with 4 pages of ads, including a list of 6 (not 7) novels by Eden Phillpotts. In dust jacket. $100-$150. Lacking jacket, $45-$75. Third issue, listing 7 Phillpotts novels. $25. New York, no date (1919). Tan cloth. First American edition, first state, with "Maughan" for "Maugham" on front cover and spine. In dust jacket. $100-$150.

MAUGHAM, W. Somerset. *My South Sea Island.* Wrappers. Chicago, 1936. First edition, first issue, with "Sommerset" on title page. $400-$500. Second issue, error corrected. One of 50. $200-$250.

MAUGHAM, W. Somerset. *The Narrow Corner.* Cloth. London, no date (1932). First edition. In dust jacket. $25.

MAUGHAM, W. Somerset. *Of Human Bondage.* Green cloth. New York, no date (1915). First edition, first issue, with Doran imprint and misprint in line 4 of page 257. In dust jacket. $300-$400. London, no date (1915). Blue cloth. First English edition, first state, with ads at end. In dust jacket. $285-$400. Garden City, N.Y. 1936. Illustrated by Schwabe. One of 751 signed. $50-$75. New York, 1938. Limited Editions Club. Edited by Theodore Dreiser. Illustrated by John Sloan. 2 vols., cloth. Boxed. $100-$150.

MAUGHAM, W. Somerset. *Of Human Bondage; With Digression on the Art of Fiction.* Printed boards. No place (Washington), 1946. Limited edition, signed. $75-$100.

MAUGHAM, W. Somerset. *On a Chinese Screen.* Black cloth. London, no date (1922). First edition. In dust jacket. $25.

MAUGHAM, W. Somerset. *Orientations.* Cloth. London, 1899. First edition, first issue, with two-color title page and gilt top. $35-$50.

MAUGHAM, W. Somerset. *The Painted Veil.* Cloth. New York, 1925. First edition. In dust jacket. $35. Another issue: Boards. One of 250 signed. In dust jacket. $75-$100. London, no date (1925). Blue cloth. First English edition, first issue, with "Hong-Kong" (not "Tching-Yen") in line 15, page 16, etc. $400-$500.

MAUGHAM, W. Somerset. *Penelope: A Comedy.* Printed wrappers. London, 1912. First edition. $35-$50.

MAUGHAM, W. Somerset. *The Razor's Edge.* Buckram. Garden City, 1944. One of 750 signed. Boxed. $75-$100.

MAUGHAM, W. Somerset. *The Sacred Flame.* Black cloth, paper labels. London, 1928. First edition, first issue, measuring 6 3/4 x 5 1/16 inches. In dust jacket. $35-$50. New York, 1928. Cloth. First American edition. In dust jacket. $35.

MAUGHAM, W. Somerset. *Sheppy: A Play in Three Acts.* Brown cloth. London, 1933. First edition. In dust jacket. $35. Another issue: Advance copy in plain brown wrappers. $75.

MAUGHAM, W. Somerset. *Strictly Personal.* Buckram. Garden City, N.Y., 1941. First edition. One of 515 signed. Boxed. $75-$100.

MAUGHAM, W. Somerset. *The Summing Up.* Black cloth. London, no date (1938). First edition. In dust jacket. $25-$35. Garden City, 1938. Black cloth. First American edition. In dust jacket. $15-$20. New York, 1954. Buckram. One of 391 signed. Boxed. $50-$75.

MAUGHAM, W. Somerset. *The Trembling of a Leaf.* Cloth. London, no date (1921). First English edition. In dust jacket. $40-$50.

MAUGHAM, W. Somerset. *The Unattainable.* Red cloth, or wrappers. London, 1923. First edition. Cloth: $35.

MAUGHAM, W. Somerset. *The Unconquered.* Cloth. New York, 1944. One of 300 signed. $50.

MAUGHAM, W. Somerset. *The Vagrant Mood: Six Essays.* Boards and calf. London, no date (1952). First edition. One of 500 signed. Boxed. $50. Worn, $30. Garden City, 1953. Black cloth. First American edition. In dust jacket. $10.

MAUGHAM, W. Somerset. *A Writer's Notebook.* Blue buckram, vellum spine. London, no date (1949). First edition. One of 1,000 signed. Boxed. $80-$100. Garden City, 1949. Cloth. First American edition. One of 1,000 signed. Boxed. $50-$75. Trade edition: Cloth. In dust jacket. $10-$15.

MAURELLE, Don Antonio. *Abstract of a Narrative of an Interesting Voyage from Manilla to San Blas, etc.* Calf. Boston, 1801. $125.

MAVERICK, Samuel Augustus. *Notes on the Storming of Bexar in the Close of 1835.* Edited by F. C. Chabot. Illustrated. Cloth. San Antonio, Tex., 1942. $50.

MAVOR, William. *The English Spelling-Book.* Illustrated by Kate Greenaway. Pictorial boards. London, 1885 (actually 1884). First edition. $75-$100.

MAW, Henry Lister. *Journal of a Passage from the Pacific to the Atlantic.* Folding map. Boards. London, 1829. $50-$75.

MAWE, John. *Travels in the Interior of Brazil.* Map, 8 plates. Boards. London, 1812. First edition. $150-$200. London, 1821. Map, 5 color plates. Boards. Second edition. $150. Philadelphia, 1816. Illustrated. Boards. $100-$150.

MAXIMILIAN, Prince of Wied. *Travels in Brazil.* 9 plates. Half leather. London, 1820. First English edition. $150-$200.

MAXIMILIAN, Prince of Wied. *Travels in the Interior of North America.* Translated by H. E. Lloyd. Folding map, 81 colored vignettes and plates. 2 vols., half morocco (text plus atlas folio volume). London, 1843-44. First edition. $12,500-$15,000. Also, $13,000 (A, 1967); atlas volume alone, $9,520 (A, 1966).

MAY, Sophie. *Dottie Dimple.* 3 woodcut plates by N. Brown. Decorated brown cloth. Boston, 1865. (By Rebecca S. Clarke.) First edition. $100-$125.

MAYER, Luigi. *Views in the Ottoman Dominions.* 70 colored plates. 2 vols., folio, boards. London, 1810. $200.

MAYER, Luigi. *Views in Palestine.* 48 full-page colored plates. 2 vols. in one, folio, half morocco. London, 1804-03. $300-$400.

MAYHEW, Augustus. *Paved with Gold.* Illustrated by Hablot K. Browne. 13 parts, wrappers. London, 1857-58. First edition. $100. London, 1858. Cloth. First book edition. $25.

MAYHEW, Henry. *London Characters.* Illustrated. Cloth. London, 1874. First edition. $100-$125.

MAYHEW, Henry. *London Labour and the London Poor.* 4 vols., cloth. London, 1861-62. $150-$200.

MAYNARD, Charles J. *Atlas of Plates from the Directory to the Birds of Eastern North America.* Wrappers. West Newton, Mass., 1905. Rebound in half morocco, $75 (A, 1956).

MAYNARD, Charles J. *The Birds of Eastern North America.* Wrappers. Newtonville, Mass., 1881. Revised edition. Rebound in half morocco, $100. Newtonville, 1896. Cloth. $125.

MAYNARD, Charles J. *The Butterflies of New England.* 8 hand-colored lithographs. Half morocco. Boston, 1886. First edition. $50-$75.

MAYNARD, Charles J. *The Eggs of North American Birds.* 9 parts, wrappers. Boston, no date (1890). $100-$150.

MAYNARD, G. W. *Report on the Property of the Alice Gold and Silver Mining Co., Butte.* Maps, plates. 28 pp., wrappers. New York, 1882. $50-$75.

MAYO, W. S. (editor). *Kaloolah, or Journeyings to the Djebel Kumri: An Autobiography of Jonathan Romer.* Frontispiece and engraved title page by F. O. C. Darley. Pictorial cloth. New York, 1849. First edition. $75-$100.

MEAD, Peter B. *An Elementary Treatise on American Grape Culture and Wine Making.* Cloth. No place (New York), 1867. First edition. $35.

MEAD, Spencer P. *Ye Historie of Ye Town of Greenwich.* Cloth. New York, 1911. $45.

MEADE, Gen. G. G. *Report of the Ashburn Murder.* 130 pp., printed wrappers. No place, no date (Atlanta, about 1868). With errata slip and leaf of explanation from Meade. $100.

MEANS, James. *Manflight.* 29 pp., printed wrappers. Boston, 1891. $35-$50.

MEANS, James. *The Problem of Manflight.* Diagrams. 20 pp., pictorial wrappers. Boston, 1894. $65.

MEANY, Edmond S. *Origins of Washington Geographic Names.* Cloth. Seattle, 1923. $50.

MEANY, Edmond S. *Washington from Life.* 9 plates. Cloth. Seattle, 1931. $35.

MEDFORD, Macall. *Oil Without Vinegar, and Dignity Without Pride.* With a chart and the concluding chapter. Wrappers. London, 1807. Second edition. (First complete edition.) $40.

MEEKE, Mrs. (Mary). *The Veiled Protectress; or, The Mysterious Mother.* 5 vols., contemporary half calf. London, 1819. First edition. $250.

MEEKER, Ezra. *Washington Territory West of the Cascade Mountains.* 52 pp., printed wrappers. Olympia, Wash., 1870. First edition. $150-$250.

MEIKLE, James. *Famous Clyde Yachts, 1880-87.* 31 colored aquatints, mounted as drawings, with tissue guards. Atlas folio, cloth. Glasgow, 1888. $50-$60.

MEINHOLD, William. *Sidonia the Sorceress.* Translated by Lady Wilde. Illustrated. Limp vellum with ties. London, 1893. Kelmscott Press. One of 300. $600-$700. London, 1926. Illustrated. Buckram. One of 225. $35.

MELINCOURT. By the Author of *Headlong Hall.* 3 vols., boards. London, 1817. (By Thomas Love Peacock.) First edition. $250-$300. Rebound in half leather, 3 vols. in one, $150.

MELINE, James F. *Two Thousand Miles on Horseback.* Map. Cloth. New York, 1867. First edition. $100-$150.

MELISH, John. *A Geographical Description of the United States.* 3 maps. Boards. Philadelphia, 1815. First edition. $150-$200. Philadelphia, 1816. 5 maps. Boards. $75-$100. Philadelphia, 1818. 3 maps. Boards. Third edition. $50. Philadelphia, 1822. 12 maps. Boards. $50.

MELISH, John. *A Military and Topographical Atlas of the United States.* 8 maps and plans, 5 folding. Half leather. Philadelphia, 1813. First edition. $500-$600. Also, $450 (A, 1966). Philadelphia, 1815. 12 maps and plans, 9 folding and colored in outline. Half leather. $500.

MELLICK, Andrew D. *The Story of an Old Farm.* Frontispiece. Cloth. Somerville, N.J., 1889. First edition. $50-$75.

MELTZER, David. *The Dark Continent.* No place (Berkeley, Calif.), 1967. First edition. One of 26 signed. $25.

MELTZER, David. *The Process.* Cloth. Berkeley, 1965. First edition. One of 25 signed. In dust jacket. $40-$45.

MELTZER, David. *Ragas.* Pictorial wrappers. No place, no date (San Francisco, 1959). First edition. $25.

MELTZER, David. *Round the Poem Box.* Leather. Los Angeles, 1969. Black Sparrow Press. One of 26 signed, with an original illustration by the author. $50. Another issue: Wrappers. One of 300 signed. $10.

MELTZER, David. *Yesod.* Cloth. London, no date (1969). One of 100 signed. $25.

MELTZER, David, and Schenker, Donald. *Poems.* Glazed white wrappers, taped spine (as issued). San Francisco, no date (1957). First edition. One of 500. $30. Meltzer's first book.

MELVILLE, Herman. See *John Marr and Other Sailors; Timoleon.*

MELVILLE, Herman. *The Apple-Tree Table and Other Sketches.* Boards and cloth. Princeton, N.J., 1922. First edition. One of 175 on handmade paper. $25-$35. Trade edition: Cloth. $10.

MELVILLE, Herman. *Battle-Pieces and Aspects of the War.* Blue, green, or salmon-colored cloth. New York, 1866. First edition, first issue, with "hundred" misspelled "hnndred" in copyright notice. $200-$300. Worn, $150. Covers stained, $135. Second issue, error corrected. $100-$150. (Note: There was no English edition.)

MELVILLE, Herman. *Benito Cereno.* Illustrated in color by E. McKnight Kauffer. Folio, buckram. London, 1926. Nonesuch Press. One of 1,650. $35-$50. (Note: See entry following under *Billy Budd.*)

MELVILLE, Herman. *Billy Budd and Other Prose Pieces.* Edited by Raymond W. Weaver. Cloth. London, 1924. First edition. One of 750. (Issued as part of the *Works.*) In dust jacket. $35-$40.

MELVILLE, Herman. *Billy Budd* [and] *Benito Cereno.* Illustrated. White sailcloth. New York, 1965. Limited Editions Club. Boxed. $35-$50.

MELVILLE, Herman. *Clarel: A Poem and Pilgrimage in the Holy Land.* 2 vols., brick-red or green cloth, chocolate end papers. New York, 1876. First edition. $400-$500. Stained and worn, $375.

MELVILLE, Herman. *The Confidence-Man.* Green or purple-brown cloth. New York, 1857. First edition, without half title. $100-$150. London, 1857. Yellow-brown cloth. First English edition, first issue, without "Roberts" in publisher's name below ads on recto of front free end paper. $125-$150.

MELVILLE, Herman. *The Encantadas (Las Encantadas)*. Edited by Victor W. Von Hagen. Colored woodcuts by Mallette Dean. Pictorial boards and cloth. Burlingame, Calif., 1940. Grabhorn printing. One of 550. $35-$50.

MELVILLE, Herman. *Israel Potter*. Purple-brown or green cloth, yellow end papers. New York, 1855. First edition, without half title; first state, with perfect type in first line of page 113. $200-$300. Second state, imperfect type on page 113. $150-$200. Spine faded, stained, $150. Signature on title page, foxed, $75. London, 1855. Cloth. First English edition. $75-$100.

MELVILLE, Herman. *A Journal up the Straits, October 11, 1856—May, 1857*. Edited by Raymond W. Weaver. Portrait frontispiece. Marbled cloth. New York, 1935. First edition. One of 650. $50-$60.

MELVILLE, Herman. *Mardi: and A Voyage Thither*. 3 vols., pale-green cloth, white end papers with blue designs. London, 1849. First edition, without half title in Vol. 1. $200-$250. New York, 1849. 2 vols., dark purple-brown or green muslin, or wrappers. First American edition, with 8 pages of ads at end of Vol. 2. Cloth: $300-$400. Foxed, bookplate, $200. Foxed, $100. Wrappers: $300-$400, possibly more.

MELVILLE, Herman. *Moby-Dick; or, The Whale*. Slate-blue, black, brown, or scarlet cloth, orange end papers. New York, 1851. First American edition, with publisher's name blind-stamped at center of sides, 6 blank leaves at front and back. $2,500 and up. Also, minor defects, $850 (A, 1970); $1,100 (A, 1968); $2,500 (A, 1967); $1,000 (A, 1963). Worn and defective copies at lower prices. Chicago, 1930. Lakeside Press. Illustrated by Rockwell Kent. 3 vols., silver-decorated cloth. One of 1,000. In aluminum slipcase. $300-$350. Also, $250 and $210 (A, 1969). New York, 1943. Limited Editions Club. Illustrated by Boardman Robinson. 2 vols., full morocco. Boxed. $125.

MELVILLE, Herman. *Narrative of a Four Months' Residence Among the Natives of a Valley of the Marquesas Islands; or, A Peep at Polynesian Life*. Map. 2 parts, wrappers. London, 1846. First edition (of the book published later that year in New York as *Typee*). $1,500-$2,000. Another issue: Map. Red cloth, yellow end papers (one volume). First book edition, with incorrect numeral XV for XX on spine. $375-$400. Author's first book. London, 1847. Cloth. $50.

MELVILLE, Herman. *Omoo: A Narrative of Adventures in the South Seas*. Map. 2 vols., printed gray or brown wrappers. London, 1847. First edition. $420-$600. Another issue: Map. Red cloth (one volume). First book edition. $150-$250. New York, 1847. Chart facing title page. Blue watered muslin, or 2 vols., fancy wrappers. First American edition, "probable" first binding, smooth pictorial cloth, with 16 pages of ads. $250-$300. Wrappers: $400-$500. New York, 1961. Limited Editions Club. Illustrated. White linen. Boxed. $45-$60.

MELVILLE, Herman. *The Piazza Tales*. Pale-blue cloth. New York, 1856. First edition, first issue, with yellow end papers. $300-$400. Later issue, blue end papers. $200-$300. London, 1856. Blue cloth. First English edition. $75-$125.

MELVILLE, Herman. *Pierre; or, The Ambiguities*. Gray cloth, or wrappers. New York, 1852. First edition, cloth, with 4 blank pages at front and back, no half title, gray-green end papers. $200-$300. Wrappers: $300-$400. London, 1852. Blue embossed cloth, yellow end papers. First English edition. $100-$150.

MELVILLE, Herman. *Poems*. Cloth. London, 1924. First edition. (Issued as part of the *Works*.) In dust jacket. $25-$35.

MELVILLE, Herman. *Redburn: His First Voyage*. 2 vols., dark-blue cloth, white end papers with blue pattern. London, 1849. First edition. $210-$300. New York, 1849. Purple-brown muslin, or wrappers. First American edition, first issue, with October ads. Cloth: $150-$250. Wrappers: $300 and up.

MELVILLE, Herman. *The Refugee*. Cloth. Philadelphia, no date (1865). First edition. $75. Rebound in half morocco, rubbed, $50. Also, cloth, $30-$40. (Pirated edition of *Israel Potter*.)

MELVILLE, Herman. *Some Personal Letters.* Edited by Meade Minnigerode. Portrait, 2 facsimiles. Half linen. New York, 1922. First edition. In dust jacket. $50.

MELVILLE, Herman. *Typee: A Peep at Polynesian Life.* Map frontispiece. 2 parts, thick fawn-colored printed wrappers. New York, 1846. First American edition (of *Narrative of a Four Months' Residence Among the Natives of a Valley of the Marquesas*). $500 and up. Another issue: Cloth (blue or brown), in one volume. First American book edition, with 4 pages of ads. $400-$500. Second issue, same date, with added story, "The Story of Toby." $150 and up. Author's first book. New York, 1847. Cloth. Revised edition, with 8 pages of ads. $50-$100. New York, 1935. Limited Editions Club. Illustrated. Printed boards. Boxed. $35-$50.

MELVILLE, Herman. *The Whale.* 3 vols., bright-blue and cream-colored cloth, pale-yellow end papers. London, 1851. First edition (of the book published later that year in New York as *Moby-Dick*). $4,000 and up. London, 1853. 3 vols., half morocco. $40 (A, 1960).

MELVILLE, Herman. *White-Jacket: or, The World in a Man-of-War.* 2 vols., light-blue cloth, yellow end papers. London, 1850. First edition. $300-$400. New York, 1850. 2 parts, yellow wrappers, or one vol., purple-brown or blue-gray cloth, with 6 pages of ads. First American edition. Wrappers: $500 and up. Cloth (one volume): $300-$400. Library label, $170 (A, 1970). London, 1853. 2 vols. in one, cloth. First English one-volume edition, $130 (A, 1960).

MELVILLE, Herman. *The Works of Herman Melville.* 16 vols., cloth. London, 1922-24. ("Standard Edition.") First edition. In dust jackets. $300-$400. Another issue: Full or half leather. "Standard Edition." One of 750. $600-$800.

MEMOIRS of a Fox-Hunting Man. Blue cloth. London, no date (1928). (By Siegfried Sassoon.) First edition, first issue, with rough trimmed fore-edges. In dust jacket. $35-$50. Another issue: Cloth. One of 260 signed. $50-$75. London, no date (1929). Illustrated by William Nicholson. Vellum. One of 300 signed. Boxed. $50-$75.

MEMOIRS of an Infantry Officer. Blue cloth. London, no date (1930). (By Siegfried Sassoon.) First edition, first issue, with untrimmed edges. In dust jacket. $15-$25. Another issue: Blue cloth. One of 750 signed. $50-$75. London, 1931. Illustrated by Barnett Freedman. Vellum. One of 12. In slipcase. $100-$125. Another issue: Boards. One of 300 signed. Boxed. $50-$75.

MEMOIRS of the Life of the Late John Mytton, Esq. 12 plates in color by John Alken. Cloth. London, 1835. (By C. J. Apperley.) First edition. $500-$750. London, 1837. 18 plates. Cloth. Second edition. $250-$300. London, 1851. 18 plates. Cloth. Third edition. $150-$200.

MEMOIRS of Lorenzo Da Ponte (The). 22 pp., stitched. New York, 1829. First American edition. $35-$40.

MEMORANDA: Democratic Vistas. See Whitman, Walt.

MEMORIA sobre las Proporciones Naturales de las Provincias Internas Occidentales, Causas de que Han Provenido sus Atrasos, etc. 62 pp., sewed. Mexico, 1822. $400.

MEMORIAL and Biographical History of McLennan, Falls, Bell and Coryell Counties, Texas. Half leather. Chicago, 1893. $75-$100.

MEMORIAL to the Legislature of New York (A), Upon the Effects of the Passage of the Trade of the Western States Through the Welland and Oswego Canals. 24 pp., sewed. Rochester, 1845. $35-$50.

MEMORIAL to the President and Congress for the Admission of Wyoming Territory to the Union. 75 pp., wrappers. Cheyenne, 1889. $50-$75.

MENCKEN, H. L. See Hatteras, Owen; Hirshberg, Dr. L. K.

MENCKEN, H. L. *The American Language*. Black cloth. New York, 1919. First edition. One of 1,500. In dust jacket. $25-$35. Another issue: One of 25 signed. In dust jacket. $75-$100.

MENCKEN, H. L. *Damn! A Book of Calumny*. Cloth. New York, 1918. First edition. In dust jacket. $100.

MENCKEN, H. L. *George Bernard Shaw: His Plays*. Cloth. Boston, 1905. First edition. In dust jacket. $50-$60.

MENCKEN, H. L. *In Defense of Women*. Cloth. New York, 1918. First edition, first issue, with publisher's name mispelled "Ppilip." In dust jacket. $50. Second issue, with name corrected. $25.

MENCKEN, H. L. *The Literary Capital of the United States*. Wrappers. Chicago, 1920. First edition. $25-$45.

MENCKEN, H. L. *A Little Book in C Major*. Cloth. New York, 1916. First edition. In dust jacket. $35-$50.

MENCKEN, H. L. *Menckeniana: A Schimpflexikon*. Vellum. New York, 1928. First edition. One of 80 signed. Boxed. $100-$125. Another issue: Red boards and cloth. One of 230 signed. Boxed. $35-$50. Trade edition: Cloth. In dust jacket. $10.

MENCKEN, H. L. *Notes on Democracy*. Cloth. New York, no date (1926). First edition. In dust jacket. $10-$15. Another issue: One of 200 signed. $35-$50. Another issue: One of 35 on vellum, signed. $100.

MENCKEN, H. L. *The Philosophy of Friedrich Nietzsche*. Red cloth. Boston, 1908. First edition, first state, with "Friedrich" omitted on spine. In dust jacket. $25-$35. Presentation copy, signed, $60.

MENCKEN, H. L. *Prejudices: First Series*. Cloth. New York, no date (1919). First edition. In dust jacket. $10-$15. Another issue: One of 50 signed. Boxed. $35-$50.

MENCKEN, H. L. *Prejudices: Second Series*. Cloth. New York, no date (1920). First edition. In dust jacket. $10-$15. Another issue: One of a few large paper copies, signed. $40-$50.

MENCKEN, H. L. *Prejudices: Third Series*. Cloth. New York, no date (1922). First edition. In dust jacket. $10-$15. Another issue: One of 25 signed. $40-$50.

MENCKEN, H. L. *Prejudices: Fourth Series*. Cloth. New York, no date (1924). First edition. In dust jacket. $10-$15. Another issue: One of 110 signed. Boxed. $37.50.

MENCKEN, H. L. *Prejudices: Fifth Series*. Cloth. New York, no date (1926). First edition. In dust jacket. $10-$15. Another issue: One of 200 signed. Boxed. $25.

MENCKEN, H. L. *Prejudices: Sixth Series*. Cloth. New York, no date (1927). First edition. In dust jacket. $10-$15. Another issue: One of 50 on vellum, signed. $40-$50. Another issue: One of 140 on rag paper, signed. $25.

MENCKEN, H. L. *A Treatise on the Gods*. Cloth. New York, 1930. First edition (so stated). In dust jacket. $15. Another issue: One of 375 signed. $50-$60.

MENCKEN, H. L. *Ventures into Verse*. Illustrated. Boards, or brown wrappers. Baltimore, 1903. First edition. (100 to 200 copies printed.) Wrappers: $300 and up. Also, inscribed by Mencken, $900 (A, 1969). Boards: $250 and up. Author's first book.

MENCKEN, H. L. (editor). *The Gist of Nietzsche*. Cloth. Boston, 1910. First edition. In dust jacket. $35-$40. Lacking jacket, $25.

MENCKEN, H. L., and Nathan, George Jean. *The American Credo*. Black cloth. New York, 1920. First edition. In dust jacket. $25.

MENCKEN, H. L., and Nathan, George Jean. *Heliogabalus: A Buffoonery in 3 Acts.* Black cloth. New York, 1920. First edition. One of 2,000. In dust jacket. $35. Lacking jacket, $25. Another issue: One of 60 signed by the authors. $100. Another issue: Wrappers. $25-$35.

MENCKEN, H. L; Nathan, George Jean; and Wright, Willard Huntington. *Europe After 8:15.* Decorated yellow cloth. New York, 1914. First edition, first binding, with blue stamping. In dust jacket. $50.

MERCEDES of Castile: Or, the Voyage to Cathay. By the Author of "The Bravo." 2 vols., cloth, paper labels. Philadelphia, 1840. (By James Fenimore Cooper.) First edition. $75-$100.

MERCER, A. S. *The Banditti of the Plains.* Illustrated. Map. Cloth. No place, no date (Cheyenne, Wyo., 1894). First edition. $750-$1,000. Another edition: No place, no date (Cheyenne, 1895). Wrappers. With Mercer's manuscript notes, $250 (A, 1968). Sheridan, Wyo., 1930. Wrappers. $35-$50. San Francisco, 1935. Grabhorn Press. Illustrated. Half cloth. One of 1,000. $35-$50.

MERCER, A. S. *Washington Territory: The Great North-West.* 38 pp., printed wrappers. Utica, N.Y., 1865. First edition. $500-$600.

MERCY Philbrick's Choice. Black cloth. Boston, 1876. (By Helen Hunt Jackson.) First edition. $50-$60.

MEREDITH, George. *The Amazing Marriage.* 2 vols., green cloth. Westminster (London), 1895. First edition. $35-$50.

MEREDITH, George. *Beauchamp's Career.* 3 vols., green cloth. London, 1876. First edition. $200-$225.

MEREDITH, George. *Diana of the Crossways.* 3 vols., cloth. London, 1885. First edition. $50-$75.

MEREDITH, George. *The Egoist.* 3 vols., cloth. London, 1879. First edition. $175-$200. London, 1920. One of 30. ("Arranged for the Stage.") $50-$75.

MEREDITH, George. *Emilia in England.* 3 vols., purple cloth. London, 1864. First edition. $100-$150.

MEREDITH, George. *An Essay on Comedy.* Cloth. London, 1897. First edition. $25.

MEREDITH, George. *Farina.* Cloth. London, 1857. First edition. $100-$110.

MEREDITH, George. *Letters to Edward Clodd and Clement K. Shorter.* 39 pp., wrappers. London, 1913. One of 30. $150.

MEREDITH, George. *Lord Ormont and His Aminta.* 3 vols., cloth. London, 1894. First edition. $50-$75.

MEREDITH, George. *Modern Love and Poems of the English Roadside.* Green cloth. London, 1862. First edition. $75-$100. Portland, Me., 1891. Heavy printed wrappers. First American edition. In dust jacket. $50-$75.

MEREDITH, George. *One of Our Conquerors.* 3 vols., blue cloth. London, 1891. First edition. $75.

MEREDITH, George. *The Ordeal of Richard Feverel.* 3 vols., brown cloth. London, 1859. First edition. $200-$300.

MEREDITH, George. *Poems.* Green cloth. London, no date (1851). First edition. With half title and with errata slip at end. $250-$300. Author's first book.

MEREDITH, George. *A Reading of Earth.* Boards. London, 1888. First edition. $35.

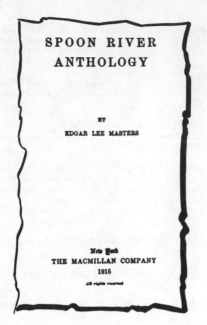

SPOON RIVER
ANTHOLOGY

BY
EDGAR LEE MASTERS

New York
THE MACMILLAN COMPANY
1915
All rights reserved

THE

Banditti of the Plains

— OR THE —

Cattlemen's Invasion of Wyoming in 1892

————

[THE CROWNING INFAMY OF THE AGES.]

————

By A. S. MERCER.

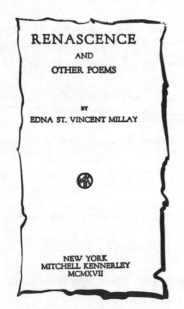

RENASCENCE
AND
OTHER POEMS

BY
EDNA ST. VINCENT MILLAY

NEW YORK
MITCHELL KENNERLEY
MCMXVII

American Dramatists Series

THIRST

And Other One Act Plays by

EUGENE G. O'NEILL

BOSTON: THE GORHAM PRESS
TORONTO: THE COPP CLARK CO., LIMITED

MEREDITH, George. *The Shaving of Shagpat*. Brown cloth. London, 1856. First edition. $200-$250. (Note: A copy in variant red cloth, with covers spotted, brought $80 at auction in 1965.) New York, 1955. Limited Editions Club. Illustrated. Boards and leather. Boxed. $20-$25.

MEREDITH, George. *The Tale of Chloe. The House on the Beach. The Case of General Ople and Lady Camper*. Boards and parchment. London, 1894. One of 250. $100-$150.

MEREDITH, George. *Vittoria*. 3 vols., purple or maroon cloth. London, 1867. First edition. $150-$200.

MERRICK, George B. *Old Times on the Upper Mississippi*. Illustrated. Blue cloth. Cleveland, 1909. First edition. $50-$75.

MERRICK, Leonard. *Conrad in Quest of His Youth: An Extravagance of Temperament*. Cloth. London, 1903. First edition. $75.

MERRILL, James. *First Poems*. Cloth. New York, 1951. First edition. One of 950. In dust jacket. $50-$60. Author's first book.

MERRILL, James. *Violent Pastoral*. Wrappers. Cambridge, Mass., no date (1965). First edition. One of 100 signed. $30.

MERRILL, Rufus. *Indian Ancedotes*. 7 wood engravings. 16 pp., wrappers. Concord, N.H., no date (about 1850). $25-$35.

MERRIMAN, Henry Seton. *From One Generation to Another*. 2 vols., pea-green cloth. London, 1892. (By Hugh Stowell Scott.) First edition. $100.

MERRITT, Abraham. *The Moon Pool*. Pictorial wrappers, or cloth. New York, 1919. First edition. Wrappers: $35. Cloth: In dust jacket. $25. Author's first book.

MERRY-MOUNT; a Romance of the Massachusetts Colony. 2 vols., cloth. Boston, 1849. (By John Lothrop Motley.) First edition. $75-$100. Second edition, same date. $50. (Also issued as 2 vols. in one, cloth.)

MERRY Tales of the Three Wise Men of Gotham (The). Boards and cloth. New York, 1826. (By James Kirke Paulding.) First edition. $50.

MERSEY, Clive Bigham. *The Roxburghe Club: Its History and Its Members, 1812-1927*. Portraits. Half morocco. Oxford, England, 1928. $75-$100.

MERTON, Thomas. *Original Child Bomb*. Boards. No place, no date (Norfolk, Conn., 1961). New Directions. One of 500 signed. $25. Trade edition: Boards. $10.

MERTON, Thomas. *The Tower of Babel*. Woodcut illustrations. Folio, boards and vellum. No place (Norfolk, Conn.), 1957. New Directions. First edition. One of 250 signed. Boxed. $40-$60.

MERVINE, William M. *Harris, Dunlop, Valentine and Allied Families*. Cloth. No place, 1920. One of 100. $75-$100.

MERWIN, W. S. *The Dancing Bears*. Cloth. New Haven, Conn., 1954. First edition. In dust jacket. $25.

MERWIN, W. S. *Green with Beasts*. Cloth. London, 1956. First English edition. In dust jacket. $25.

MERWIN, W. S. *Three Poems*. Stiff wrappers. New York, 1968. One of 100 signed. $25.

METCALF, Samuel L. *A Collection of Some of the Most Interesting Narratives of Indian Warfare in the West*. Portrait. Leather. Lexington, Ky., 1821. First edition. $250-$350.

MEW, Charlotte. *The Farmer's Bride*. Pictorial wrappers. London, 1916. First edition. $35-$50. Foxed, $25. Author's first book.

MEW, Charlotte. *The Rambling Sailor.* Boards. London, 1919. First edition. In dust jacket. $25-$35.

MEXICAN Treacheries and Cruelties. Illustrated. 32 pp., pictorial wrappers. Boston, 1847. First edition. (By Lieut. G. N. Allen.) $75-$100. Boston, 1848. Second edition. $50.

MEXICO and the United States: An American View of the Mexican Question. By a Citizen of California. 33 pp., printed wrappers. San Francisco, 1866. $45.

MEXICO in 1842 . . . to Which Is Added, An Account of Texas and Yucatan, and of the Santa Fe Expedition. Folding map. Cloth. New York, 1842. (By George F. Folsom or Charles J. Folsom?) First edition. $125-$150.

MEXICO, su Evolución Social. L. Justus Sierra, editor. 3 vols., folio, leather. Mexico, 1900-02. $100.

MEYER, George. *Autobiography of George Meyer: Across the Plains with an Ox Team in 1849.* 2 portraits. Printed tan wrappers. Shenandoah, Iowa, 1908. First edition. $100-$150.

MEYERS, William H. *Journal of a Cruise to California and the Sandwich Islands in the U.S. Sloop of War Cyane.* Frontispiece, 10 color plates. Folio, half leather. San Francisco, 1955. Grabhorn Press. One of 400 for the Book Club of California. $100.

MEYERS, William H. *Naval Sketches of the War in California, 1846-1847.* Descriptive text by Dudley Know. Introduction by Franklin D. Roosevelt. Folio, half white leather. San Francisco, 1939. Grabhorn Press. One of 1,000. $125-$150.

MEYNELL, Alice. See Thompson, A. C.

MEYNELL, Alice. *Essays.* Boards. London, 1914. First edition. One of 250 on large paper. $25. Presentation copy, $50. Trade edition: Blue buckram. $10.

MEYNELL, Alice. *Other Poems.* White wrappers. No place, no date (London, 1896). One of 50 printed for Christmas cards. $75-$100.

MEYNELL, Alice. *Poems.* Brown cloth. London, 1893. First edition (under this title). One of 50 signed. $100-$125. (For actual first edition, see Thompson, A. C., *Preludes.*) London, 1913. Portrait. Blue boards and cloth. One of 250 signed. $35. Trade edition: Blue buckram. $10.

MEYNELL, Alice. *The Rhythm of Life and Other Essays.* Cloth. London, 1893. First edition. One of 50 signed. $35-$50. Trade edition: $10.

MEYNELL, Alice. *Ten Poems, 1913-1915.* Boards. Westminster (London), 1915. First edition. One of 50. $100-$125.

MEYNELL, Francis. *Typography.* Illustrated, including color. Buckram. London, 1923. Pelican Press. $75-$100.

MEYRICK, Samuel R. *A Critical Inquiry into Antient Armour as It Existed in Europe, but Particularly in England from the Norman Conquest to the Reign of Charles II.* 80 plates, 71 hand-colored. 3 vols., folio, half morocco. London, 1824. First edition. $300-$500.

MEYRICK, Samuel R., and Skelton, J. *Engraved Illustrations of Antient Arms and Armour, from the Collection of Llewelyn Meyrick.* 2 frontispieces, 2 engraved titles, 2 vignettes and 151 engraved plates. 2 vols., half red morocco. London, 1830. $75-$100.

MICHAEL Bonham: or, the Fall of Bexar. By a Southron. Cloth. Richmond, Va., 1852. (By William Gilmore Simms.) First edition. $100-$150.

MICHAUX, F. A. *Travels to the Westward of the Allegany Mountains.* Translated by B. Lambert. Folding map. Boards. London, 1805. (Printed by Mawman.) First English edition. $250-$350. In contemporary boards, $175. London, 1805. (Printed by Crosby.) Boards. Second English edition. $200. London, 1805. (Printed by Phillips.) Another translation. Third English edition. $100-$150.

MIGHTY Magician (The). (Half title only): Bound with *Such Stuff as Dreams Are Made Of.* (Half title only.) The two plays apparently to have been published as *Two Dramas of Calderon* (but no title page known to exist). 132 pp., gray wrappers, with imprint at end: "John Childs & Son." Bungay, no date (1865). (By Edward Fitzgerald.) First edition. $60-$75.

MIKESELL, Thomas (editor). *The History of Fulton County, Ohio.* Leather. Madison, Wis., 1905. First edition. $50-$60.

MILES, Gen. Nelson A. *Personal Recollections and Observations.* Illustrated by Frederic Remington and others. Pictorial cloth, leather, or half leather. Chicago, 1896. First edition, first issue, with caption under frontispiece reading "General Miles." $75-$100. Second issue, with rank under portrait as "Maj. Gen." $50. Chicago, 1897. Second edition. With an added plate at end. $25-$35.

MILES, William. *Journal of the Sufferings and Hardships of Capt. Parker H. French's Overland Expedition to California.* 24 pp., printed wrappers. Chambersburg, Pa., 1851. First edition. $2,000 (A, 1968).

MILITARY Commanders and Designating Flags of the United States Army, 1861-1865. (Cover title.) Plates. Half leather. Philadelphia, 1887. $250.

MILLAY, Edna St. Vincent. See Boyd, Nancy; Earle, Ferdinand.

MILLAY, Edna St. Vincent. *Aria da Capo.* Cloth. New York, 1921. First edition. In dust jacket. $25. (Note: *The Chapbook,* No. 14, London, August, 1920, is composed entirely of this work. Auction price, 1968: $15.)

MILLAY, Edna St. Vincent. *The Ballad of the Harp-Weaver.* Illustrated. Decorated wrappers. New York, 1922. First edition (so stated). $100. Presentation copy, signed, $175. Also, signed copies, $150 and $160 (A, 1966). Another issue: One of 5 on Japan vellum. $250.

MILLAY, Edna St. Vincent. *The Buck in the Snow and Other Poems.* Boards and cloth. New York, 1928. First edition (so stated). $10-$12.50. Another issue: Full blue limp leather. $15. Another issue: One of 479 signed. In glassine dust jacket. Boxed. $50-$100. Another issue: Boards and vellum. One of 36 on vellum, signed. In glassine dust jacket. Boxed. $100-$125.

MILLAY, Edna St. Vincent. *Collected Sonnets.* Blue cloth. New York, 1941. In dust jacket. $10-$12.50. Another issue: Full red limp leather. $15.

MILLAY, Edna St. Vincent. *Conversation at Midnight.* Blue boards and cloth. New York, 1937. First edition (so stated). In dust jacket. $10-$15. Another issue: Full blue limp leather. Boxed. $15. Another issue: Boards and cloth. One of 579 signed. In glassine dust jacket. Boxed. $75-$100. Another issue: One of 36 on vellum, signed. In glassine dust jacket. Boxed. $75-$125.

MILLAY, Edna St. Vincent. *Fatal Interview: Sonnets.* Boards and cloth. New York, 1931. First edition (so stated), first issue, with top edges stained yellow. In dust jacket. $15. Another issue: One of 479 signed. In glassine dust jacket. Boxed. $50-$75. Another issue: One of 36 on vellum, signed. In glassine dust jacket. Boxed. $75-$100.

MILLAY, Edna St. Vincent. *A Few Figs from Thistles.* Wrappers. New York, 1920. First edition. $150. Signed, $175. New York, 1921. Green wrappers. Second edition, with added material. $25-$35.

MILLAY, Edna St. Vincent. *The Harp-Weaver and Other Poems.* Cloth. New York, 1923. First edition (so stated). In dust jacket. $50-$75. Also, inscribed, $120 (A, 1966).

MILLAY, Edna St. Vincent. *Huntsman, What Quarry?* Boards and cloth. New York, 1939. First edition (so stated). In dust jacket. $10-$12.50. Another issue: Full blue limp leather. Boxed. $15 and $25. Another issue: Boards and cloth. One of 551 signed. In glassine dust jacket. Boxed. $75-$100. Another issue: Boards and vellum. One of 36 on vellum. In glassine dust jacket. Boxed. $150-$200.

MILLAY, Edna St. Vincent. *The King's Henchman.* Boards and cloth. New York, 1927. First edition. In dust jacket. $25. Another issue: One of 158 signed. In glassine dust jacket. Boxed. $75-$100. Another issue: One of 31 on vellum, signed. $150-$200. Another issue: "Artist's Edition." One of 500 signed. $25.

MILLAY, Edna St. Vincent. *The Lamp and the Bell.* Printed green wrappers. New York, 1921. First edition. $100-$150. Also, in frayed wrappers, $45 (A, 1966). Another (later) issue, same date: Boards. In dust jacket. $15.

MILLAY, Edna St. Vincent. *Make Bright the Arrows.* Boards and cloth. New York, 1940. First edition (so stated). In dust jacket. $15. Another issue: Full blue limp leather. One of 1,550. Boxed. $20-$25.

MILLAY, Edna St. Vincent. *Poems Selected for Young People.* Boards and cloth. New York, 1929. First edition (so stated). One of 1,050 signed. Boxed. $75.

MILLAY, Edna St. Vincent. *Poems.* Cloth. London, 1923. First edition. In dust jacket. $150. Also, signed by the author, $100 (A, 1968).

MILLAY, Edna St. Vincent. *The Princess Marries the Page.* Decorations by J. Paget Fredericks. Full blue leather. New York, 1932. First edition (so stated). Boxed. $25. Another issue: Boards and cloth. In dust jacket. $15.

MILLAY, Edna St. Vincent. *Renascence and Other Poems.* Black cloth. New York, 1917. First edition, first issue, on Glaslan watermarked paper. In dust jacket. $300-$400. Another issue: Boards. One of 15 (17?) on Japan vellum, signed. $1,600 (A, 1969). Author's first book.

MILLAY, Edna St. Vincent. *Second April.* Black cloth. New York, 1921. First edition, first state, on Glaslan watermarked paper. In dust jacket. $75-$100. Signed, $125.

MILLAY, Edna St. Vincent. *Two Slatterns and a King.* Wrappers. Cincinnati, 1921. First edition. $35-$45.

MILLAY, Edna St. Vincent. *Wine from These Grapes.* Boards and cloth, or leather. New York, 1934. First edition (so stated). In dust jacket. $15. (Note: Also issued as part of a 2-vol. set with *Epitaph for the Race of Man.* One of 299 sets on paper, Vol. 1 of each set signed. $50-$75. Another issue: One of 36 on vellum, signed, $100-$150.)

MILLER, Andrew. *New States and Territories.* Folding map table. 32 pp., boards. No place, no date (Keene, N.H., 1818). First edition. Map table signed by author, $1,250. Also $1,200 (A, 1967). Another edition: No place (Keene), 1819. Folding table. 96 pp., boards. Second edition. $750-$1,000.

MILLER, Arthur. *After the Fall.* Light-brown buckram. New York, no date (1964). First edition. One of 499 signed. Boxed. $50. Trade edition: Boards and cloth. In dust jacket. $10.

MILLER, Arthur. *Death of a Salesman.* Pictorial orange cloth. New York, 1949. First edition. In dust jacket. $35-$45.

MILLER, Arthur. *Situation Normal.* Cloth. New York, 1944. First edition. In dust jacket. $35-$50.

MILLER, Arthur McQuiston. *The Geology of Kentucky.* Cloth. Frankfort, Ky., 1919. $35-$50.

MILLER, Benjamin S. *Ranch Life in Southern Kansas and the Indian Territory.* Frontispiece. 163 pp., printed wrappers. New York, 1896. First edition. $100-$150.

MILLER, E. *The History of Page County, from the Earliest Settlement in 1843 to 1876, etc.* Folding map. Limp black cloth. Clarinda, Iowa, 1876. First edition. $75-$100.

MILLER, Henry. *Account of a Tour of the California Missions, 1856.* Pencil drawings by Miller. 59 pp., boards. San Francisco, 1952. Grabhorn Press. One of 375. Boxed. $50-$60.

MILLER, Henry. *The Air-Conditioned Nightmare.* Gray cloth. No place, no date (Norfolk, Conn., 1945). New Directions. First edition. In dust jacket. $25.

MILLER, Henry. *Aller Retour New York.* Cloth. No place (Chicago), 1945. First American edition. One of 500. $35.

MILLER, Henry. *The Amazing and Invariable Beauford De Laney.* Printed wrappers. Yonkers, N. Y., 1945. Alicat Book Shop. First edition. $25.

MILLER, Henry. *Black Spring.* Wrappers. Paris, 1936. Obelisk Press. First edition. $200-$250. New York, 1963. Boards and cloth. First American edition. In dust jacket. $15.

MILLER, Henry. *The Books in My Life.* Cloth. Norfolk, no date (1952). (Printed in Ireland.) First edition. In dust jacket. $20-$25.

MILLER, Henry. *The Colossus of Maroussi.* Patterned blue boards and cloth. San Francisco, no date (1941). Colt Press. First edition. One of 100 signed. (Issued without dust jacket.) $75-$100. Worn, spine label faded, $25. Trade edition: Cloth, paper label. In dust jacket. $25.

MILLER, Henry. *The Cosmological Eye.* Tan cloth, with brown lettering and photograph of an eye inset on cover. Norfolk, 1939. New Directions. First edition. In dust jacket. First book under Miller's name to be published in the United States. $25.

MILLER, Henry. *Maurizius Forever.* Colored drawings by Miller. Green boards. San Francisco, 1946. Colt Press. First edition. One of 500. Printed at Grabhorn Press. In dust jacket. $45-$50.

MILLER, Henry. *Max and the White Phagocytes.* Thick tan wrappers. Paris, 1938. Obelisk Press. First edition. $150-$175.

MILLER, Henry. *Money and How It Gets That Way.* Wrappers. Paris, 1938. Booster Broadside No. 1. One of a few printed. $250.

MILLER, Henry. *Murder the Murderer.* Printed wrappers. No place, no date (Big Sur, Calif., 1944). First edition. $25.

MILLER, Henry. *Order and Chaos Chez Hans Reichel.* Introduction by Lawrence Durrell. Leather-backed cloth. New Orleans, no date (1966). First edition. "Green Oasis edition." One of 11 signed. In dust jacket, boxed. $150. Another issue: "Crimson Oasis edition." One of 26 signed. In jacket and box. $100. Another issue: "Cork edition." One of 99 signed. In dust jacket. Boxed. $75-$100.

MILLER, Henry. *Plexus.* 2 vols., wrappers. Paris, no date (1953). Olympia Press. One of 2,000 in advance of the first edition. $75-$100. First edition: Wrappers. $35.

MILLER, Henry. *Quiet Days in Clichy.* Photographs by Brassai. Printed wrappers. Paris, 1956. Olympia Press. First edition. $35.

MILLER, Henry. *Remember to Remember.* Cloth. No place, no date (Norfolk, 1947). New Directions. First edition. In dust jacket. $25-$35.

MILLER, Henry. *Scenario (A Film with Sound).* Double-page frontispiece. Loose in wrappers. Paris, 1937. Obelisk Press. First edition. One of 200 signed. $250.

MILLER, Henry. *Semblance of a Devoted Past.* Illustrated by Miller. Stiff wrappers. Berkeley, Calif., no date (1944). First edition. One of 1,150. $35-$50.

MILLER, Henry. *Sexus.* 2 vols. Paris, no date (1949). Obelisk Press. First edition, limited. $100.

MILLER, Henry. *The Smile at the Foot of the Ladder.* Pictorial boards and cloth. New York, no date (1948). First edition. In dust jacket. $50. Also, $20 (A, 1968). No place (San Francisco), 1955. Greenwood Press. Printed wrappers. One of 500. $10-$15.

MILLER, Henry. *Stand Still Like the Hummingbird.* Cloth. No place, no date (Norfolk, 1962). New Directions. First edition. In dust jacket. $25.

MILLER, Henry. *Sunday After the War.* Light tan cloth. Norfolk, no date (1944). New Directions. First edition, first binding. One of 2,000. In dust jacket. $25-$35.

MILLER, Henry. *The Time of the Assassins: A Study of Rimbaud.* Half cloth and cut-out boards. No place, no date (Norfolk, 1956). New Directions. $25-$30.

MILLER, Henry. *Tropic of Cancer.* Preface by Anaïs Nin. Decorated wrappers. Paris, 1934. Obelisk Press. First edition. (Exceedingly rare.) $400-$500. Author's first book. New York, 1940. Cloth. First American edition. $75. New York, no date (1961). Grove Press. Introduction by Anaïs Nin. Patterned boards and cloth. One of 100 signed. $45.

MILLER, Henry. *Tropic of Capricorn.* Decorated wrappers. Paris, 1939. Obelisk Press. With errata slip. $225-$250.

MILLER, Henry. *Tropique du Cancer.* Colored lithographs by Timar. Loose in pictorial wrappers. No place, no date (Paris, 1947). One of 51, with an extra set of plates and an original drawing. $200-$250. Another issue: One of 750. $75-$100.

MILLER, Henry. *Watercolors, Drawings and His Essay "The Angel Is My Watermark!"* Illustrated. Small folio, cloth. London, 1962. First edition. With each of the 12 reproductions signed by Miller. $150-$200. New York, no date (1962). First American edition. In glassine dust jacket. $50-$75.

MILLER, Henry. *The Waters Reglitterized.* Portrait and plates. Pictorial wrappers. No place (San Jose, Calif.), 1950. First edition. One of 1,000. $25.

MILLER, Henry. *What Are You Going to Do About Alf?* Printed wrappers. Paris, 1935. First edition. $135-$150. Berkeley, no date (1944). Printed self-wrappers. One of 738. $25-$30.

MILLER, Henry. *Wisdom of the Heart.* Brown cloth. Norfolk, no date (1941). New Directions. First edition. One of 1,500. In dust jacket. $25.

MILLER, Henry. *The World of Sex.* Blue cloth. No place, no date (New York, 1940). One of 250. Boxed. $25-$35.

MILLER, Henry, and Fraenkel, Michael. *Hamlet.* Vol. 1. Printed wrappers. No place, no date (Santurce, P.R., 1939). First edition. In tissue dust jacket. $25-$35. New York, 1941. Vol. 2. $25. London, 1963. Illustrated by A. E. Larking. Wrappers. First illustrated edition. $10.

MILLER, Henry, and Schatz, Bezalel. *Into the Night Life.* Illustrated. Folio, cloth. No place, no date (Berkeley, 1947). First edition. One of 800. $250-$300.

MILLER, Henry; Hiler, Hilaire; and Saroyan, William. *Why Abstract?* Cloth. New York, 1945. New Directions. First edition. In dust jacket. $25. London, no date (1948). Falcon Press. Cloth. Second edition. In dust jacket. $10.

MILLER, Cincinnatus H. *Joaquin, et al.* Cloth. Portland, Ore., 1869. (By Joaquin Miller.) First edition. $150.

MILLER, Joaquin. See Miller, Cincinnatus H. Also see *How to Win in Wall Street; Specimens.*

MILLER, Joaquin. *'49, The Gold-Seeker of the Sierras.* Printed wrappers. New York, 1884. First edition. $25-$35. (Also issued in cloth, and in boards and cloth.)

MILLER, Joaquin. *An Illustrated History of Montana.* Illustrated. 2 vols., morocco. Chicago, 1894. First edition. $100-$150.

MILLER, Joaquin. *Life Amongst the Modocs: Unwritten History.* Cloth. London, 1873. First edition. $35-$50.

MILLER, Joaquin. *Memorie and Rime.* Printed wrappers. New York, 1884. First edition. $25. Another issue: Cloth. $10.

MILLER, Joaquin. *Overland in a Covered Wagon.* Edited by Sidney A. Firman. Illustrated. Cloth. New York, 1930. First edition, first printing, with "(1)" below last line of text. In dust jacket. $25-$35.

MILLER, Joaquin. *Pacific Poems.* Green cloth, gilt. London, 1871. First edition. ("Suppressed by the author and extremely scarce." —De Ricci.) $500-$750. Also, rubbed, $475 (A, 1971).

MILLER, Joaquin. *A Royal Highway of the World.* Illustrated. Cloth. Portland, Ore., 1932. First edition. One of 245. $25.

MILLER, Joaquin. *Songs of the Mexican Seas.* Cloth. Boston, 1877. First edition. $25.

MILLER, Joaquin. *Songs of the Sierras.* Cloth. London, 1871. $25-$35. Boston, 1871. Cloth. First published American edition, first binding, with "R.B." at foot of spine. $25.

MILLER, Joaquin. *Songs of the Sun-Lands.* Cloth. London, 1873. First edition. $25. Another issue: Large paper. $35. Presentation copy, signed, $50.

MILLER, Joaquin. *Unwritten History: Life Among the Modocs.* Cloth. Hartford, 1874. First American edition (of *Life Amongst the Modocs*). $25.

MILLER, John C. *The Great Convention.* 40 pp., sewed. Columbus, 1840. $25.

MILLER, John F. *A Refutation of the Slander and Falsehoods Contained in a Pamphlet Entitled SALLY MILLER, etc.* 70 pp., wrappers. New Orleans, 1845. $30.

MILLER, J. P., and Patterson, John. *Nomination of President and Vice President of the United States.* (Caption title.) 12 pp., sewed. No place, no date (Steubenville, Ohio, 1823). $65.

MILLER, Lewis B. *Saddles and Lariats.* Illustrated. Pictorial cloth. Boston, 1912. First edition. $25-$35.

MILLER, Patrick. *The Green Ship.* 8 wood engravings by Eric Gill, with an extra set of the plates on Japan vellum. Full morocco. London, 1936. Golden Cockerel Press. One of 62 signed. $75-$100. Another issue: Half morocco and boards. One of 200 signed. $50.

MILLER, Patrick. *Woman in Detail.* 5 illustrations by Mark Severin, with a duplicate set of the 5 plates and with 3 additional ones in a pocket at the end. Half morocco and boards. London, 1947. Golden Cockerel Press. One of 100 signed. $40-$50.

MILLER, T. L. *History of Hereford Cattle.* Illustrated. Pictorial cloth. Chillicothe, Ohio, Mo., 1902. First edition. $75.

MILLER, Thomas. *Common Wayside Flowers.* Illustrated by Birket Foster. Decorated brown cloth. London, 1860. First edition. $30.

MILLER, William. *Evidence from Scripture and History of the Second Coming of Christ, About the Year 1843.* Boards. Troy, N. Y., 1838. First edition. $35-$40.

MILLS, Anson. *Big Horn Expedition.* Folding map. 15 pp., tan printed wrappers. No place, no date (1874?). First edition. $250 (A 1968).

MILLS, Robert. *Atlas of the State of South Carolina.* 29 double-page maps, colored by hand. Folio, half leather. Baltimore, no date (about 1826). First edition. (Issued to accompany Mills' *Statistics;* see item following.) $750-$1,000.

MILLS, Robert. *Statistics of South Carolina.* Map (not in all copies). Boards. Charleston, S.C., 1826. First edition. $100-$150.

MILLS, William W. *Forty Years at El Paso, 1858-1898.* Frontispiece. Cloth. No place, no date (Chicago, 1901). (Printed at El Paso, Tex.) First edition. $100-$125. El Paso, 1962. Mesquite Edition. $100.

MILMINE, Georgine. *The Life of Mary Baker G. Eddy and the History of Christian Science.* Edited by Willa S. Cather. Illustrated. Cloth. New York, 1909. (Largely written by Miss Cather.) First edition. $75-$125. London, 1909. Cloth. First English edition. $50.

MILNE, A. A. See Grahame, Kenneth; Shepard, Ernest H.

MILNE, A. A. *By Way of Introduction.* Cloth. London, no date (1929). First edition. In dust jacket. $25. New York, no date (1929). Decorated boards and cloth. First American edition. One of 166 on vellum. In dust jacket. $50. Trade edition: Boards and cloth. In dust jacket. $15.

MILNE, A. A. *The Christopher Robin Story Book.* Illustrated by Ernest H. Shepard. Pictorial cloth. London, no date (1926). First edition. In dust jacket. $25-$35. Signed, $75-$100. New York, no date (1929). Pictorial boards and cloth. One of 350 signed. $75-$100.

MILNE, A. A. *A Gallery of Children.* 12 full-page illustrations in color by Saida. White buckram. London, 1925. First edition. One of 500 signed. $35-$50.

MILNE, A. A. *The House at Pooh Corner.* Decorations by Ernest H. Shepard. Boards and buckram. London, 1928. First edition. One of 350 signed. In dust jacket. $175-$200. Another issue: Vellum. One of 20 on Japan paper, signed. $250-$300. Trade edition: Pink cloth. In dust jacket. $35-$50. New York, no date (1928). Illustrated. Cloth. First American edition. One of 250 signed. $75-$100. Trade edition: Cloth. In dust jacket. $10-$15.

MILNE, A. A. *Lovers in London.* Cloth. London, 1905. First edition. $50-$75. Covers dull, $37.50. Author's first book.

MILNE, A. A. *Michael and Mary: A Play.* Green cloth. London, 1930. First edition. One of 260 signed. $50-$75.

MILNE, A. A. *Now We Are Six.* Illustrated by Ernest H. Shepard. Boards and cloth. London, no date (1927). First edition. One of 200 signed. In dust jacket. $100-$150. Another issue: Vellum. One of 20 on Japan paper, signed. $200-$250. Trade edition: Red cloth. In dust jacket. $25-$35.

MILNE, A. A. *The Secret and Other Stories.* Red linen. New York, 1929. Fountain Press. First edition. One of 470 signed. In dust jacket. $35-$50.

MILNE, A. A. *Those Were the Days.* Decorated buckram. London, no date (1929). First edition. One of 250 signed. In dust jacket. $50-$75.

MILNE, A. A. *Toad of Toad Hall: A Play from Kenneth Grahame's Book "The Wind in the Willows."* Boards and buckram. London, no date (1929). First edition. One of 200 signed by Milne and Grahame. In dust jacket. $228. Also, $84 (A, 1970). Trade edition: Cloth. In dust jacket. $15.

MILNE, A. A. *When I Was Very Young.* Illustrated by Ernest H. Shepard. Cloth. New York, 1930. Fountain Press. First edition. One of 842 signed. Boxed. $50-$75.

MILNE, A. A. *When We Were Very Young.* Illustrated by Ernest H. Shepard. Boards and cloth. London, no date (1924). First edition. One of 100 signed. In dust jacket.

$300-$400. Trade edition: Cloth. In dust jacket. $50-$75. New York, no date (1924). Pictorial boards and cloth. First American edition. One of 100 signed. In dust jacket. $100-$150.

MILNE, A. A. *Winnie-the-Pooh.* Illustrated by Ernest H. Shepard. Boards and buckram. London, no date (1926). First edition. One of 350 signed. In dust jacket. $156-$200. Another issue: Vellum. One of 20 on vellum, signed. $300-$400. Trade edition: Cloth. In dust jacket. $35-$50. New York, no date (1926). Pictorial boards and cloth. First American edition. One of 200 signed. In dust jacket. $100-$150.

MILNE, A. A., and Fraser-Simon, H. *Fourteen Songs from "When We Were Very Young."* Decorations by Ernest H. Shepard. Folio, boards and cloth. New York, 1925. $25.

MILNE, A. A., and Fraser-Simon, H. *The Hums of Pooh.* Boards and cloth. London, 1929. First edition. One of 100 signed. $35-$50.

MILNE, A. A., and Fraser-Simon, H. *Songs from "Now We Are Six."* Boards and cloth. London, 1927. First edition. One of 100 signed. $35-$50.

MILNE, Ewart. *Time Stopped.* Cloth. London, 1967. One of 50 signed. $35.

MILTON, John. *Areopagitica.* Blue boards. No place, no date (London, 1903). Eragny Press. First issue of this edition. One of 40 saved from a fire (out of an edition of 226 copies). $300. London, 1907. Doves Press. Limp vellum. One of 300. $250-$300.

MILTON, John. *Comus.* Vellum. London, 1901. Essex House Press. One of 150 on vellum. $50. London, no date (1921). Illustrated in color by Arthur Rackham. Parchment. One of 550 signed by Rackham. $150-$200. Another issue: Boards and vellum. $100-$125. Newtown, Wales, 1931. Gregynog Press. Illustrated by Blair Hughes-Stanton. Boards and buckram. One of 250. $100-$125. Another issue: Morocco. One of 25 specially bound by George Fisher. $350-$400. Also, $288 (A, 1967). London, 1937. Nonesuch Press. Illustrated. Boards. $50. New York, 1954. Limited Editions Club. Illustrated by Edmund Dulac. Boards. Boxed. $20.

MILTON, John. *Four Poems: L'Allegro, Il Penseroso, Arcades, Lycidas.* Wood engravings by Blair Hughes-Stanton. Red morocco. Newtown, 1933. Gregynog Press. One of 250 on Japan vellum. $150-$200. Another issue: One of 14 specially bound by George Fisher. $350-$450.

MILTON, John. *Hymn on the Morning of Christ's Nativity.* Woodcut by Noel Rooke. 16 pp., folio, blue wrappers. No place (London), 1928. Ashendene Press. One of "about 220 copies." $100-$125.

MILTON, John. *Ode on the Morning of Christ's Nativity.* Wrappers. Oxford, 1894. Daniel Press. One of 200. $75-$100.

MILTON, John. *Paradise Lost and Miscellaneous Poems. Paradise Regain'd & Samson Agonistes.* Illustrated by William Blake. 2 vols., decorated boards and vellum-paper spine. London, 1926. Nonesuch Press. One of 1,450 on rag paper. $85.

MILTON, John. *Paradise Lost* [and] *Paradise Regain'd.* Printed in red and black. 2 vols., vellum. London, 1902-05. Doves Press. One of 300. $480. Another issue: 2 vols., vellum. One of 25 on vellum. $500-$750.

MILTON, John. *Paradise Lost* [and] *Paradise Regained.* Illustrated by D. Galanis. 2 vols., folio, pigskin. London, 1931. Cresset Press. One of 195. Boxed. $500.

MINNESOTA Guide (The). 94 pp., wrappers. St. Paul, 1869. (By J. F. Williams.) First edition. $50-$75.

MIROURE of Man's Salvacionne (The): a Fifteenth Century Translation into English of the "Speculum Salvationis." With a facsimile page. Half morocco. London, 1888. Rubbed, $70.

MIRROR of Olden Time Border Life. 13 plates (17 in some). Leather. Abingdon, Va., 1849. (By Joseph Pritts.) $75-$100.

MISCELLANIES. By the Author of "Letters on the Eastern States." Boards. Boston, 1821. (By William Tudor.) First edition. $75-$100.

MISFORTUNES of Elphin (The). Boards. London, 1829. (By Thomas Love Peacock.) First edition. $150-$200. Newtown, Wales, 1928. Gregynog Press. Woodcuts. Buckram-backed cloth. One of 225. $100-$125. Another issue: Morocco. One of 25 bound by George Fisher. $400-$500.

MR. DOOLEY in Peace and in War. Green cloth. Boston, 1898. (By Finley Peter Dunne.) First edition. In dust jacket. $35. Author's first book.

MR. FACEY Romford's Hounds. 24 color plates by John Leech and Phiz (H. K. Browne). 12 parts, pictorial wrappers. London, 1864-65. (By Robert Smith Surtees.) First edition, with first state wrappers of Part 1 reading "Mr. Facey Romford's Hounds" (second state and all subsequent parts read "Mr. Romford's Hounds"). $200-$300. London, 1865. Pictorial cloth. First book edition. $75-$100.

MR. H., or Beware a Bad Name. 36 pp., sewed. Philadelphia, 1813. (By Charles Lamb.) First edition. $1,150.

MR. MIDSHIPMAN Easy. 3 vols., boards and cloth. London, 1836. (By Frederick Marryat.) First edition. $150-$200.

MR. SPONGE'S Sporting Tour. 13 color plates and 84 woodcuts by John Leech. 13 parts in 12, pictorial wrappers. London, 1852-53. (By Robert Smith Surtees.) First edition, first issue, with the dedication to Lord Elcho (second issue reading "Earl Elcho"). $200-$300. Also, $132 and $96 (A, 1967). Second issue. $150-$200. London, 1853. Pictorial cloth. First edition, first issue, in book form. $100-$150.

MRS. LEICESTER'S School: or, The History of Several Young Ladies, Related by Themselves. Frontispiece by J. Hopwood. Boards. London, 1809. (By Charles and Mary Lamb.) First edition, first issue, with only one ad on last leaf. $250-$350.

MITCHEL, Martin. *History of the County of Fond du Lac, Wisconsin.* 96 pp., printed yellow wrappers. Fond du Lac, 1854. First edition. $100.

MITCHELL, Donald G. See Marvel, Ik.

MITCHELL, Donald G. *The Dignity of Learning: A Valedictory Oration.* Printed wrappers. New Haven, Conn., 1841. First edition. $45.

MITCHELL, G. R. *The Pacific Gold Company of Gilpin County, Colorado.* 19 pp., wrappers. Boston, 1866. $35-$50.

MITCHELL, Isaac. *The Asylum; or, Alonzo and Melissa.* Frontispiece. 2 vols., calf. Poughkeepsie, N.Y., 1811. First edition. $250. Author's first (and only) book. (Note: Many later editions appeared with Daniel Jackson, Jr., as the author.)

MITCHELL, John D. *Lost Mines of the Great Southwest.* Cloth. No place, no date (Phoenix, Ariz., 1933). First edition. $75-$100.

MITCHELL, Joseph. *The Missionary Pioneer.* Tan boards. New York, 1827. First edition. $200-$250.

MITCHELL, Margaret. *Gone with the Wind.* Gray cloth. New York, 1936. First edition, first issue, with "Published May, 1936" on copyright page. In dust jacket. $75-$125.

MITCHELL, S. Augustus. See *Illinois in 1837.*

MITCHELL, S. Augustus (publisher). *Accompaniment to Mitchell's New Map of Texas, Oregon and California, with the Regions Adjoining.* 46 pp., text and large colored map, folding into leather covers. Philadelphia, 1846. $200 and up.

MITCHELL, S. Augustus (publisher). *Description of Oregon and California, Embracing An*

Account of the Gold Regions. Folding map in color. Gold-stamped cloth. Philadelphia, 1849. First edition. $375-$400.

MITCHELL, S. Augustus. *Traveller's Guide Through the United States.* Folding map. 74 pp., leather. Philadelphia, no date (1836). First text edition under this title. $35-$50. New York, 1851. $25.

MITCHELL, S. Weir. See S., E. W., and M., S. W. Also see *The Wonderful Stories of Fuz-Buz the Fly.*

MITCHELL, S. Weir. *Hugh Wynne, Free Quaker.* Illustrated by Howard Pyle. 2 vols., gray or light brown cloth. New York, 1897. First edition, first issue, with last word on page 64, Vol. 1, being "in" and line 16 on page 260, Vol. 2, reading "before us." $75. Light-brown cloth, rubbed, $55. Later issue, text corrected: 2 vols., gray boards, white cloth spines, paper labels. One of 60 large paper copies, signed, with separate plates by Howard Pyle laid in. $75-$100. (Note: A few copies of the first edition, first issue, exist with an 1896 title page—not published. Value: Up to $500.)

MITCHELL, S. Weir. *Mr. Kris Kringle.* Boards and cloth. Philadelphia, 1893. First edition. $35-$50.

MITCHELL, S. Weir. *Researches upon the Venom of the Rattlesnake.* Folio, wrappers. Washington, 1861. $45 (A, 1965).

MITCHELL, S. Weir, and others. *Gunshot Wounds and Other Injuries of Nerves.* Unbound. Philadelphia, 1864. $117.60 (A, 1965).

MITCHELL, W. H. *Geographical and Statistical History of the County of Olmstead.* 121 pp., printed wrappers. Rochester, Minn., no date (1866). First edition. $75-$100.

MITCHELL, W. H. *Geographical and Statistical Sketch of the Past and Present of Goodhue County.* 191 pp., wrappers. Minneapolis, 1869. First edition. $75-$100.

MITFORD, John. *The Adventures of Johnny Newcome in the Navy.* 20 colored plates by Williams. Half calf. London, 1823. Third edition. $25-$50. (See Alfred Burton entry for first edition.)

MITFORD, Mary Russell. *Our Village.* Boards, paper label. London, 1824. First edition. $200-$250. London, 1910. Illustrated by Hugh Thomson. Half leather. $35-$50.

MITFORD, Mary Russell. *Poems.* Boards. London, 1810. First edition, with leaf of "Alterations." $200-$250. Also, $140 (A, 1966). Author's first book.

MIVART, St. George. *Dogs, Jackals, Wolves, and Foxes.* Illustrated, including 45 color plates. Cloth. London, 1890. First edition. $150-$200.

MIVART, St. George. *A Monograph of the Lories, or Brush-Tongued Parrots.* 61 colored plates and 4 maps. Cloth. London, 1896. First edition. $250-$300.

MODERN Griselda (The). Boards. London, 1805. (By Maria Edgeworth.) First edition. $75-$100. Rebound in half calf, lacking a blank leaf, $30.

MOELLHAUSEN, Baldwin. *Diary of a Journey from the Mississippi to the Coasts of the Pacific with a United States Government Expedition.* Translated by Mrs. Percy Sinnett. Illustrations, including color plates. Folding map. 2 vols., cloth. London, 1858. First edition. $300-$400.

MOFFETTE, Joseph F. *The Territories of Kansas and Nebraska.* 2 folding maps. Cloth. New York, 1855. First edition. $400-$600.

MOKLER, A. J. *History of Natrona County, Wyoming.* Illustrated. Buckram. Chicago, 1923. First edition. $50. Signed, $75.

MOLEVILLE, A. F. Bertrand de. *The Costume of the Hereditary States of the House of Austria.* 50 colored engravings. Full contemporary morocco. London, 1804. First English edition. $100-$150.

MOLL *Pitcher, a Poem.* Blue printed wrappers. Boston, 1832. (By John Greenleaf Whittier.) First edition. (Note: No copy in original wrappers has been noted at sale for many years. Estimated retail value: $500-$1,000.) Rebound copies at auction: $100 (1960), $225 (1955), $220 (1950). Philadelphia, 1840. (*Moll Pitcher, and the Minstrel Girl: Poems.*) Wrappers. $100-$150.

MONETTE, John W. *History of the Discovery and Settlement of the Valley of the Mississippi.* 3 maps, 4 plans, 2 plates. Cloth. New York, 1846. First edition. $100-$125.

MONIKINS (The): A Tale. By the Author of "The Spy." 3 vols., drab tan boards. London, 1835. (By James Fenimore Cooper.) First edition. $100-$150. Philadelphia, 1835. 2 vols., boards. First American edition. $75-$100.

MONKS, William. *History of Southern Missouri and Northern Arkansas.* Cloth. West Plains, Mo., 1907. First edition. $50-$75.

MONODY on the Death of the Right Honorable R. B. Sheridan. 12 pp., wrappers. London, 1816. (By George Gordon Noel, Lord Byron.) First edition, first issue, with first line on page 11 beginning "To weep," etc. Very rare; no copies in wrappers for sale in many years. In contemporary calf bindings, $84 (A, 1967). Second issue, line 1 on page 11 beginning "To mourn." In contemporary calf, $108 (A, 1969).

MONROE, Harriet. *Valeria and Other Poems.* Vellum and cloth. Chicago, 1891. First edition. $25-$35. Author's first book.

MONROE, James. *The Memoir of James Monroe, Esq., Relating to His Unsettled Claims Upon the People and Government of the U.S.* 60 pp., sewed. Charlottesville, Va., 1828. $80.

MONROE'S Embassy, or the Conduct of the Government, in Relation to Our Claims to the Navigation of the Missisippi [sic]. 57 pp., wrappers. Philadelphia, 1803. (By Charles Brockden Brown.) $250-$300. Also, disbound, $130 (A, 1967). (Note: Signed at the end with the pseudonym Poplicola.)

MONSIGNY, Madame. *Mythology: or, a History of the Fabulous Deities of the Ancients.* Leather. Randolph, N.H., 1809. First American edition. $25-$30.

MONT Saint Michel and Chartres. Blue cloth, leather label on spine. Washington, 1904. (By Henry Adams.) First edition. Privately printed. $400-$600. Inscribed by the author, $750. Washington, 1912. Revised and enlarged edition. $75-$125. Boston, 1913. Half brown cloth and tan boards. First published edition. $25. New York, 1957. Limited Editions Club. Cloth and leather. Boxed. $40-$50.

MONTAGUE, C. E. *A Hind Let Loose.* Cloth. London, no date (1910). First edition. In dust jacket. $35-$50. Author's first book.

MONTAGUE, C. E. *A Writer's Notes on His Trade.* Introduction by H. M. Tomlinson. Woodcut portrait. Buckram and boards. London, 1930. First edition. One of 700 signed by Tomlinson. $25-$30.

MONTAIGNE, Michel de. *Essays.* Translated by John Florio. 3 vols., folio, half cloth. Boston, 1902-04. One of 265 designed by Bruce Rogers and inscribed by him. In dust jackets and folding cases. $200-$250. London, 1931. Nonesuch Press. 2 vols., full morocco. Boxed. $75.

MONTANA, Its Climate, Industries and Resources. Illustrated. 74 pp., wrappers. Helena, Mont., 1884. First edition. $50-$60.

MONTANA Territory. History and Business Directory 1879. Map. 5 plates. Printed boards and leather. Helena, no date (1879). (By F. W. Warner.) First edition. $200-$250.

MONTGOMERY, Cora. *Eagle Pass; or, Life on the Border.* Stiff wrappers. New York, 1852. (By Mrs. William L. Cazneau.) First edition. $25-$35.

MONTULE, Eduard. *A Voyage to North America, and the West Indies, in 1821.* Folding and full-page plates. Printed wrappers. London, 1821. First edition in English. $50-$75.

MOODY, William Vaughn. *The Masque of Judgment.* Cloth. Boston, 1900. First edition. $35. Another issue: Boards. One of 150. $50. Author's first book.

MOORE, Sir Alan. *Sailing Ships of War, 1800-1860.* 90 full-page plates, 12 in color. Cloth. London, 1926. One of 1,500. $75-$100. Another issue: Half leather. One of 100. $150-$200.

MOORE, Brian. *The Lonely Passion of Judith Hearn.* Boards and cloth. Boston, no date (1955). First American edition. In dust jacket. $25. Author's first book.

MOORE, Clement C. See *A New Translation, etc.; The New York Book of Poetry; Observations upon Certain Passages in Mr. Jefferson's "Notes on Virginia."*

MOORE, Clement C. *Christmas Carol. The Visit of Saint Nicholas.* Broadside; text printed in blue. Philadelphia, no date (1842). $35-$50.

MOORE, Clement C. *The Night Before Christmas.* 4 color plates and text drawings by Arthur Rackham. Cloth. Philadelphia, no date (1931). $100. London, no date (1931). Vellum. One of 550. $100.

MOORE, Clement C. *Poems.* Brown boards. New York, 1844. First edition. $250-$300.

MOORE, Clement C. *A Visit from St. Nicholas.* Illustrated by F. O. C. Darley. Pictorial wrappers. New York, 1862. $25.

MOORE, Edward A. *The Story of a Cannoneer Under Stonewall Jackson.* Cloth. New York, 1907. First edition. $50.

MOORE, George. *Aphrodite in Aulis.* Parchment boards. London, 1930. First edition. One of 1,825 signed. Boxed. $25-$30.

MOORE, George. *The Brook Kerith.* Half brown cloth, marbled sides. Edinburgh, 1916. First edition. $25. Another issue: Parchment and boards. One of 250 signed. $50. London, 1929. Illustrated by Stephen Gooden. Vellum. One of 375 signed by Moore and Gooden. $40-$60. New York, 1929. Half vellum. $10-$15.

MOORE, George. *Esther Waters.* Dark olive-green cloth. London, 1894. First edition, first issue, without floral ornament on front cover. $40-$50.

MOORE, George. *Flowers of Passion.* Black cloth. London, 1878. First edition, with 1877 copyright and errata slip. $75-$100.

MOORE, George. *Heloise and Abelard.* 2 vols., half vellum. London, 1921. First edition. One of 1,000 signed. In dust jackets. $25-$35. New York, 1921. 2 vols., boards. First American edition. One of 1,250. In dust jackets. $15-$20.

MOORE, George. *The Making of an Immortal.* Cloth. New York, 1927. Bowling Green Press. One of 15 on green paper, signed. $35-$40. One of 1,240 on white paper, signed. $20.

MOORE, George. *Memoirs of My Dead Life.* Blue-gray cloth. London, 1906. First edition. $75-$85. London, 1921. Colored frontispiece and decorated title page. Boards and parchment. One of 1,030 signed. $25-$30.

MOORE, George. *A Modern Lover.* 3 vols., blue cloth. London, 1883. First edition. $450.

MOORE, George. *A Mummer's Wife.* Cloth. London, 1885. First edition. $50.

MOORE, George. *Pagan Poems.* Blue cloth. London, 1881. First edition. $250-$350. (Note: Moore removed the title page from most copies, and complete copies are rare.)

MOORE, George. *Parnell and His Island.* Wrappers. London, 1887. First edition. $100.

MOORE, George. *Peronnik the Fool.* Cloth. London, 1926. Bruce Rogers printing. $25-$35. Paris, 1928. Hours Press. Cloth. Revised edition. One of 200 signed. $50-$75. London, 1933. Engravings by Stephen Gooden. Full vellum. One of 525 signed by author and artist. $35-$50.

MOORE, George. *Spring Days.* Green cloth. London, 1888. First edition. $40-$50.

MOORE, George. *A Story-Teller's Holiday.* Half vellum. London, 1918. First edition. One of 1,000 signed. In dust jacket. $35-$50. New York, 1918. Cloth. First American edition. One of 1,250 signed. $25. New York, 1928. 2 vols., cloth. One of 1,250 signed. $15-$20.

MOORE, George. *Ulick and Soracha.* Engraved plate by Stephen Gooden. Buckram. London, 1926. Nonesuch Press. One of 1,250 on vellum, signed. In dust jacket. $35-$40.

MOORE, George. *Vain Fortune.* Illustrated. Buckram. London, no date (1890). First edition. One of 150. $35-$50. Trade edition: $15-$20.

MOORE, George, and Lopez, Bernard. *Martin Luther: A Tragedy in Five Acts.* Blue-gray cloth. London, 1879. First edition. $40.

MOORE, H. Judge. *Scott's Campaign in Mexico.* Cloth. Charleston, S.C., 1849. First edition. $75-$100.

MOORE, J. J. *The British Mariner's Vocabulary.* 9 copperplates. Calf. London, 1801. $40.

MOORE, Julia A. *The Sentimental Song Book.* 54 pp., wrappers. Grand Rapids, Mich., 1876. First edition. $100.

MOORE, Marianne. *The Absentee: A Comedy in Four Acts.* Blue cloth. New York, 1962. First edition. One of 300 signed. In glassine dust jacket. $75-$95.

MOORE, Marianne. *Collected Poems.* Cloth. London, no date (1951). First edition. In dust jacket. $25-$30.

MOORE, Marianne. *Complete Poems.* Half buckram. New York, no date (1967). First edition. In dust jacket. $25.

MOORE, Marianne. *Eight Poems.* 10 hand-colored drawings. Half cloth. New York, no date (1962). First edition. One of 195 signed. Boxed. $250.

MOORE, Marianne. *Le Mariage.* Translated by Jeffrey Kindley. Decorated wrappers. New York, 1965. First edition. One of 50. $35-$50.

MOORE, Marianne. *Marriage: Manikin No. 3.* 16 pp., light-blue pictorial wrappers. New York, no date (1923). First edition. $100-$150.

MOORE, Marianne. *Nevertheless.* Wrappers. New York, no date (1944). First edition. $25-$35.

MOORE, Marianne. *Observations.* Cloth-backed boards, paper label. New York, 1924. First edition. $25-$35.

MOORE, Marianne. *The Pangolin and Other Verse.* Drawings by George Plank. Decorated boards, paper label. London, no date (1936). First edition. One of 120. $175-$200.

MOORE, Marianne. *Poems.* Decorated wrappers, paper label. London, 1921. Egoist Press. First edition. $200-$300. Signed on title page, $350. Author's first book.

MOORE, Marianne. *Predilections.* Cloth. New York, 1955. First edition. In dust jacket. $25-$35.

MOORE, Marianne. *Selected Poems.* Introduction by T. S. Eliot. Cloth. New York, 1935. First edition. In dust jacket. $50-$60. London, 1935. Cloth. First English edition. In dust jacket. $35.

MOORE, Marianne. *Silence.* Wrappers. No place, no date (Cambridge, Mass., 1965). First edition. One of 25. $75-$100.

MOORE, Marianne. *The Student.* Broadside. New York, 1965. First edition (of this reprint from *What Are Years*). One of 25 signed. $30-$35.

MOORE, Marianne. *A Talisman.* Wrappers. No place, no date (Cambridge, 1965). First edition. One of 20. $75-$100.

MOORE, Marianne. *Tipoo's Tiger.* Printed wrappers. New York, 1967. First edition. One of 100 signed and with correction in line 24 in author's hand. $50-$75.

MOORE, Marianne. *What Are Years.* Cloth. New York, 1941. First edition. In dust jacket. $35-$50.

MOORE, Marianne (translator). *The Fables of La Fontaine.* Cloth. New York, 1954. One of 400 signed. Boxed. $100-$150. New York, no date (1964). Cloth. Revised edition. In dust jacket. $15. Another issue: Wrappers. $5.

MOORE, Marianne, and Wallace, David. *Letters from and to the Ford Motor Company.* Half cloth. New York, 1958. First edition. Boxed. $50-$75.

MOORE, Marinda B. (Mrs. M. B.). *The Dixie Speller.* Boards. Raleigh, N. C., 1864. $25.

MOORE, Marinda B. (Mrs. M. B.). *The Geographical Reader, for the Dixie Children.* 48 pp., boards. Raleigh, 1863. First edition. $45.

MOORE, S. S., and Jones, T. W. *The Traveller's Directory.* 38 maps on 22 leaves. 52 pp., contemporary calf. Philadelphia, 1802. First edition. $325 (A, 1969). Philadelphia, 1804. $300 (A, 1969).

MOORE, Thomas. See *M. P., or The Blue-Stocking.*

MOORE, Thomas. *The Epicurean: A Tale.* Boards. London, 1827. First edition. $35-$50.

MOORE, Thomas. *Epistles, Odes and Other Poems.* Edited by Joseph Dennie. Boards. Philadelphia, 1806. Second American edition. $30.

MOORE, Thomas. *Fables for the Holy Alliance.* Boards. London, 1823. First edition. $25.

MOORE, Thomas. *Irish Melodies.* Boards. Dublin, 1820. First edition. $25-$35. London, 1821. Boards. First authorized edition. $150-$200.

MOORE, Thomas. *Lalla Rookh, an Oriental Romance.* Boards. London, 1817. First edition. $100-$150.

MOORE, Thomas. *The Loves of the Angels: A Poem.* Boards. London, 1823. First edition. $75-$100.

MOORE, Thomas. *Lyrics and Satires.* Selected by Sean O'Faolain. 5 designs by Hilda Roberts. Boards and cloth. Dublin, 1929. Cuala Press. One of 130. In dust jacket. $75-$100.

MOORE, Thomas. *Paradise and the Peri.* Illuminated borders. Folio, morocco. No place, no date (London, about 1860). $35-$50.

MOORE, Thomas (translator). *The Odes of Anacreon.* Morocco. London, 1800. $35-$50.

MOORE, T. Sturge. *A Brief Account of the Origin of the Eragny Press.* Illustrated. Boards. London, 1903. Eragny Press. One of 235. $100-$125.

MOORE, T. Sturge. *The Little School: A Posy of Rhymes.* Woodcuts. Boards. London, 1905. Eragny Press. One of 185. $75. Also, $43.20 (A, 1968). Another issue: Morocco. One of 10 on vellum. $110-$200.

MOORE, T. Sturge. *The Vinedresser and Other Poems.* Cloth. London, 1899. Unicorn Press. First edition. $75-$100.

MORDECAI, Alfred. *A Digest of the Laws Relating to the Military Establishment of the United States.* Cloth. Washington, 1833. $75.

MORE, Hannah. See *Hints Towards Forming the Character of a Young Princess.*

MORE, Hannah. *Sacred Dramas, Chiefly Intended for Young Persons.* Calf. Boston, 1801. First American edition. $45-$50.

MORE, Sir Thomas. *Utopia.* Woodcut borders and initials, printed in black and red. Vellum with ties. London, 1893. Kelmscott Press. $300-$400. Also, $300 (A, 1969—two sales). London, 1906. Ashendene Press. Boards and linen. One of 100. $500-$600. Another issue: One of 20 on vellum. $750 and up. Waltham Saint Lawrence, England, 1929. Golden Cockerel Press. Decorations by Eric Gill. Buckram. $50-$60. New York, 1934. Limited Editions Club. Woodcuts by Bruce Rogers. Vellum and boards. Boxed. $35-$50.

MOREHEAD, James T. *Address in Commemoration of the First Settlement of Kentucky.* Printed wrappers. Frankfort, Ky., 1840. First edition. $75-$100.

MORES, Edward Rowe. *A Dissertation upon English Typographical Founders and Foundries.* Cloth. New York, 1924. Grolier Club. One of 250. $25.

MORGAN, Charles. *The Gunroom.* Cloth. London, 1919. First edition. $35. Author's first novel.

MORGAN, Charles. *Sparkenbroke.* Morocco. London, 1936. First edition. One of 210 signed. $80-$90. Trade edition: Green cloth. In dust jacket. $10.

MORGAN, Dale L. See Ashley, William H.

MORGAN, Dale L. *Jedediah Smith and the Opening of the West.* 20 plates. Cloth. Indianapolis, no date (1953). First edition. In dust jacket. $35-$50.

MORGAN, Dale L., and Wheat, Carl I. *Jedediah Smith and His Maps of the American West.* 7 folding maps. Cloth. San Francisco, 1954. First edition. One of 530. $150-$200.

MORGAN, Dick T. *Morgan's Manual of the U. S. Homestead and Townsite Laws.* Buff printed wrappers. Guthrie, Okla., 1893. First Edition. $75.

MORGAN, Emanuel, and Knish, Anne. *Spectra: A Book of Poetic Experiments.* Boards. New York, 1916. (By Witter Bynner [Morgan] and Arthur Davison Ficke [Knish].) First edition. $75-$100.

MORGAN, Jane. *Tales for Fifteen.* Printed tan boards. New York, 1823. (By James Fenimore Cooper.) First edition. Extremely rare; no sales noted in any records consulted. Value: $1,000 and up?

MORGAN, James Morris. *Recollections of a Rebel Reefer.* Half leather. Boston, 1917. First edition. $25.

MORGAN, John Hill, and Fielding, Mantle. *The Life Portraits of Washington and Their Replicas.* Illustrated. Folio, cloth. Philadelphia, no date (1931). First edition. One of 1,000. $75-$100. Another issue: Full morocco. One of 180 signed. $100-$150.

MORGAN, Lewis H. *The American Beaver and His Works.* Map, 23 plates. Cloth. Philadelphia, 1868. First edition. $35-$50.

MORGAN, Lewis H. *The Indian Journals of Lewis Henry Morgan.* Illustrated, including color plates and maps. Oblong, cloth. Ann Arbor, Mich., no date (1959). In dust jacket. $35-$50.

MORGAN, Lewis H. *The League of the Ho-De'-No-Sau-Nee, or Iroquois.* 21 plates, map, table. Cloth. Rochester, N. Y., 1851. First edition. $75-$100. Another issue: Maps and plates colored by hand. $150-$200. New York, 1922. Edited by H. M. Lloyd. 2 vols. in one, cloth. $50.

MORGAN, Martha M. (editor). *A Trip Across the Plains in the Year 1849.* 31 pp., printed wrappers. San Francisco, 1864. First edition. $2,750 (A, 1969).

MORIER, James. See *Ayesha.*

MORISON, Stanley. *The Art of the Printer.* Illustrated. Cloth. London, 1925. In dust jacket. $75-$100. Paris, no date (1925). $50.

MORISON, Stanley. *The English Newspaper.* Illustrated. Folio, cloth. Cambridge, England, 1932. First edition. $75-$125.

MORISON, Stanley. *Four Centuries of Fine Printing.* Illustrated with 625 facsimiles. Folio, cloth. London, no date (1924). One of 390 in English. $150-$200. Another issue: Morocco. One of 13 signed. $300-$400. Also, $240 (A, 1967). London, no date (1949). 272 facsimile title pages. Calf. One of 200. $75-$100.

MORISON, Stanley. *Fra Luca de Pacioli of Borgo S. Sepolcro.* Boards, vellum spine. New York, 1933. First edition. One of 390. $75-$100.

MORISON, Stanley. *Modern Fine Printing.* Facsimiles. Folio, half linen. London, 1925. One of 650 in English. $125.

MORISON, Stanley. *On Monotype Printers' Flowers.* Boards. London, 1924. $50-$75.

MORISON, Stanley. *On Type Faces.* Illustrated. Folio, half cloth. London, 1923. One of 750. In dust jacket. $75-$100.

MORISON, Stanley (editor). *A Newly Discovered Treatise on Classic Letter Design.* Facsimile reproduction. Vellum and boards. Paris, 1927. One of 350. $50.

MORISOT, Berthe. *The Correspondence of Berthe Morisot.* Illustrated. Cloth. London, 1957. First English edition. $25.

MORLAND, T. H. *The Genealogy of the English Race-Horse.* Frontispiece. Boards. London, 1810. $75-$100.

MORLEY, C. D. *The Eighth Sin.* Printed pale blue-gray wrappers. Oxford, England, 1912. (By Christopher Morley.) First edition. One of 250. $350-$500. Author's first book.

MORLEY, Christopher. *The Haunted Bookshop.* Cloth. New York, 1919. First edition, first state, with page number at bottom of page 76 and perfect "Burroughs" above it. In dust jacket. $25-$35.

MORLEY, Christopher. *The Palette Knife.* Illustrated in color. Pictorial cloth. Chelsea, N.Y., 1929. First edition. One of 450 signed. $35.

MORLEY, Christopher. *Parnassus on Wheels.* Gray boards, tan cloth spine. Garden City, N.Y., 1917. First edition, first state, with space between the "Y" and "e" in "Years" in line 8, page 4. In dust jacket. $125-$150.

MORLEY, Christopher. *Paumanok.* Boards. Garden City, 1926. First edition. One of 107 signed. In dust jacket. $35.

MORLEY, Christopher. *The Romany Stain.* Decorated boards and cloth. Garden City, 1926. One of 365 signed. $25.

MORLEY, Christopher. *Songs for a Little House.* Boards. New York, no date (1917). First edition, first state, with quotation from Southwell facing title page. $25.

MORLEY, Christopher. *Where the Blue Begins.* Pictorial cream and blue marbled boards, blue cloth spine. Garden City, 1922. First edition. In dust jacket. $10-$15. London and New York, no date (1924). Illustrated, including color plates, by Arthur Rackham. Light-blue decorated cloth. First large paper edition. In dust jacket. $50-$75. Another issue: Green and blue boards. One of 100 signed by author and artist. In tissue dust jacket. Boxed. $100-$150. London, no date (1924). Illustrated by Rackham. Deep-blue cloth. First English large paper edition. $50. Another issue: London, no date (1925). One of 175 signed. In dust jacket. Boxed. $100-$150.

MORPHIS, J. M. *History of Texas.* Plates, folding map in color. Cloth. New York, 1874. First edition. $50-$60.

MORRELL, Benjamin. *Narrative of Four Voyages to the South Seas, North and South Pacific Ocean.* Portrait. Boards and cloth. New York, 1832. First edition. $75-$100.

MORRELL, Z. N. *Flowers and Fruits from the Wilderness; or 36 Years in Texas.* Cloth. Boston, 1872. First edition. $50-$75.

MORRIS, Eastin. *The Tennessee Gazetteer.* Printed boards, leather spine. Nashville, 1834. First edition. $800-$1,000. Also, stained and worn, $650 (A, 1967).

MORRIS, William. *Child Christopher and Goldilind the Fair.* Woodcuts. 2 vols., decorated boards and cloth. London, 1895. Kelmscott Press. One of 600. $200-$225.

MORRIS, William. *The Defence of Guenevere, and Other Poems.* Printed in black and red. Woodcut borders. Vellum with ties. London, 1892. Kelmscott Press. One of 300. $225.

MORRIS, William. *A Dream of John Ball and A King's Lesson.* Woodcut borders and designs by Morris and E. Burne-Jones. Vellum with ties. London, 1892. Kelmscott Press. One of 300. $200-$300.

MORRIS, William. *The Earthly Paradise.* Woodcut title. 8 vols., vellum with ties. London, 1892. Kelmscott Press. One of 225. $400-$500. Also, $360 and $325 (A, 1969).

MORRIS, William. *In Praise of My Lady.* Half leather. New York, 1928. Aries Press. One of 31. $35.

MORRIS, William. *The Life and Death of Jason: A Poem.* Woodcut frontispiece, other decorations by E. Burne-Jones. Vellum with ties. London, 1895. Kelmscott Press. One of 200. $500-$600.

MORRIS, William. *Love Is Enough.* Woodcut borders and 2 illustrations by E. Burne-Jones. Vellum with ties. London, 1898. Kelmscott Press. One of 300. $300-$400.

MORRIS, William. *News from Nowhere.* Woodcut frontispiece, borders, and initials. Vellum with ties. London, 1892. Kelmscott Press. One of 300. $300-$350.

MORRIS, William. *Note by William Morris on His Aims in Gounding the Kelmscott Press.* Woodcuts. Boards and cloth. London, 1898. Kelmscott Press. With errata slip. One of 525. $150-$250. (Note: The last book printed at the Kelmscott Press.)

MORRIS, William. *Printing: An Essay.* Boards. Park Ridge, Ill., 1903. First edition. Limited, signed. $35-$50.

MORRIS, William. *The Roots of the Mountains.* Decorated cloth. London, 1890. One of 250. $100-$150.

MORRIS, William. *The Story of the Glittering Plain.* Woodcut title and borders. Illustrations by Walter Crane. Vellum with ties. London, 1894. Kelmscott Press. One of 250. Boxed. $600.

MORRIS, William. *The Story of Gunnlaug the Worm-tongue and Raven the Skald.* (All copies have spaces where initial capital letters were to have been printed at the beginning of each chapter.) Boards and cloth. London, 1891. Chiswick Press. One of 75. $175-$225.

MORRIS, William. *The Sundering Flood.* Woodcuts. Boards and cloth. London, 1897. Kelmscott Press. One of 300. $150-$250.

MORRIS, William. *The Water of the Wondrous Isles.* Woodcut borders and initials. Vellum with ties. London, 1897. Kelmscott Press. One of 250. $400-$500.

MORRIS, William. *The Well at the World's End.* 4 woodcuts and initial letters by E. Burne-Jones. Vellum with ties. London, 1896. Kelmscott Press. One of 350. $400-$500.

MORRIS, William. *The Wood Beyond the World.* Woodcut frontispiece, other illustrations. Vellum with ties. London, 1894. Kelmscott Press. First edition. One of 350. $300-$400.

MORRIS, William (translator). *Of the Friendship of Amis and Amile.* Woodcut title and borders. Full red morocco. London, 1894. Kelmscott Press. One of 500. $100-$150.

MORRIS, William (translator). *The Tale of the Emperor Coustans and of Over the Sea.* 2 woodcut titles and borders. Boards and linen. London, 1894. Kelmscott Press. One of 525. $100-$125.

MORRIS, William, and Wyatt, A. J. (translators). *The Tale of Beowulf.* Woodcut title and borders. Vellum with ties. London, 1895. Kelmscott Press. One of 300. $350-$400.

MORRIS, Wright. *The Deep Sleep.* Cloth. New York, 1953. First edition. In dust jacket. $25-$30.

MORRIS, Wright. *The Inhabitants.* Illustrated with author's photographs. Cloth. New York, 1946. First edition. In dust jacket. $25-$35.

MORRIS, Wright. *The World in the Attic.* Cloth. New York, 1949. First edition, with the Scribner "A" on copyright page. In dust jacket. $25-$30.

MORSE, Edward S. *Catalogue of the Morse Collection of Japanese Pottery.* Frontispiece, 68 plates. Boards. Cambridge, Mass., 1901. First edition. $100-$125.

MORSE, Jedidiah. *A Report to the Secretary of War . . . on Indian Affairs.* Colored folding map. Boards. New Haven, 1822. First edition. $50-$75.

MORSE, John F., and Colville, Samuel. *Illustrated Historical Sketches of California.* Frontispiece. Printed wrappers. Sacramento, 1854. First edition. $275 (A, 1968).

MORTON'S Hope; or, The Memoirs of a Provincial. 2 vols., cloth. New York, 1839. (By John Lothrop Motley.) First edition. $50.

MOTLEY, John Lothrop. *Peter the Great.* Wrappers. New York, 1878. First edition. $50.

MOTLEY, Willard. *Knock on Any Door.* Gray cloth. New York, no date (1947). First edition. In dust jacket. $25.

MOUNTAINEER (The). Harrisonburg, Va., 1812. (By Conrad Speece.) First edition. (But called second edition, after publication in Collet's *Republican Farmer.*) $75. Harrisonburg, 1818. $35-$40.

MOURELLE, Don Francisco Antonio. *Voyage of the Sonora in the Second Bucareli Expedition.* Translated by Daines Barrington. Portrait, 2 maps. Boards. San Francisco, 1920. First American edition. One of 230 signed by the translator. $50-$65.

MOWRY, Sylvester. *Memoir of the Proposed Territory of Arizona.* Map (not in all copies). 30 pp., printed wrappers. Washington, 1857. First edition. $1,100 (A, 1966).

MOXON, Joseph. *Moxon's Mechanick Exercises, or The Doctrine of Handy-Works Applied to the Art of Printing.* 2 vols., half leather. New York, 1896. Reprint of 1683 first edition. One of 450. $75.

M. P., or The Blue-Stocking, a Comic Opera. 94 pp., wrappers. London, 1811. (By Thomas Moore.) First edition. $35-$40.

MUIR, Edwin. *Latitudes.* Cloth. New York, 1924. First edition. In dust jacket. $25-$30. London, 1924. Cloth. First English edition. In dust jacket. $25.

MUIR, John. *The Mountains of California.* Cloth. New York, 1894. First edition. In dust jacket. $35-$50. Lacking jacket, $25. Author's first book.

MUIR, Percy H. *English Children's Books, 1600-1900.* Illustrated, including color plates. Cloth. London, 1954. First edition. In dust jacket. $50-$75. New York, 1954. Illustrated. Blue cloth. First American edition. In dust jacket. $50-$75.

MUIR, Percy H. *Points, 1874-1930.* Illustrated. Parchment and boards. London, 1931. First edition. $50-$75.

MUIR, Percy H. *Points, 1866-1934.* Illustrated. Parchment and boards. London, 1931. First edition. $50-$75.

MULFORD, Clarence E. *Bar-20.* Illustrated by N. C. Wyeth and F. E. Schoonover. Pictorial cloth. New York, 1907. First edition, first issue, with the reading "Blazing Star" in the list of illustrations. In dust jacket. $40-$50. Author's first book.

MULFORD, Clarence E. *Bar-20 Days.* Illustrated by Maynard Dixon. Brown cloth. Chicago, 1911. First edition. In dust jacket. $35.

MULLAN, John. *Miners' and Travelers' Guide to Oregon, etc.* Folding colored map. Cloth. New York, 1865. First edition. $150-$200.

MULLAN, John. *Report on the Construction of a Military Road from Fort Walla-Walla to Fort Benton.* 4 folding maps, 10 plates, 8 colored. Cloth. Washington, 1863. First edition. $150-$200.

MULLET, J. C. *A Five Years' Whaling Voyage.* 68 pp. Cleveland, 1859. First edition. $100-$150.

MULOCK, Dinah Maria (Mrs. Craik). See *The Adventures of a Brownie; John Halifax, Gentleman; A Life for a Life; The Ogilvies.*

MUMEY, Nolie. *Bloody Trails Along the Rio Grande.* Portrait, map. Cloth. Denver, 1938. Limited edition. In dust jacket. $35-$50.

MUMEY, Nolie. *Calamity Jane.* Folding map, illustrations, 2 pamphlets in envelope at end. Boards, pictorial label. Denver, 1950. One of 200 signed. $75.

MUMEY, Nolie. *Colorado Territorial Scrip.* Illustrated. Cloth. Boulder, Colo., 1966. One of 350 signed. $50-$75.

MUMEY, Nolie. *Creede: History of a Colorado Mining Town.* Illustrated. Half cloth. Denver, 1949. One of 500 signed. $50.

MUMEY, Nolie. *History of the Early Settlements of Denver.* Map, 2 folding plates. Boards and vellum. Glendale, Calif., 1942. First edition. One of 500 signed. $75.

MUMEY, Nolie. *James Pierson Beckwourth.* Folding map. Boards. Denver, 1957. First edition. One of 500. $75.

MUMEY, Nolie. *John Williams Gunnison.* Colored portrait, plates, folding map. Boards. Denver, 1955. First edition. One of 500 signed. $35-$50.

MUMEY, Nolie. *The Life of Jim Baker.* Frontispieces, other illustrations, map. Boards. Denver, 1931. First edition. One of 250 signed. $200-$250.

MUMEY, Nolie. *March of the First Dragoons to the Rocky Mountains in 1835.* Errata slip, plates, folding map. Boards. Denver, 1957. First edition. One of 350 signed. $40-$60.

MUMEY, Nolie. *Nathan Addison Baker: Pioneer Journalist.* Illustrated, 4 folding facsimiles in cover pocket. Cloth. Denver, 1965. $35.

MUMEY, Nolie. *Old Forts and Trading Posts of the West.* Vol. 1. Boards. Denver, 1956. First edition. One of 500. $35-$50.

MUMEY, Nolie. *Pioneer Denver, Including Scenes of Central City, Colorado City, and Nevada City.* Folding plate, other illustrations. Boards. Denver, 1948. First edition. One of 240 signed. $100.

MUMEY, Nolie. *Poker Alice.* Illustrated. Pictorial wrappers. Denver, 1951. One of 500. $40-$50.

MUMEY, Nolie. *Rocky Mountain Dick (Richard W. Rock): Stories of His Adventures.* Illustrated. Cloth. Denver, 1953. One of 500. $40-$50.

MUMEY, Nolie. *A Study of Rare Books.* Illustrated. Half cloth and boards. Denver, 1930. First edition. $60-$75.

MUMEY, Nolie. *The Teton Mountains.* Boards. Denver, 1947. First edition. One of 700. $50-$75.

MUMEY, Nolie (editor). *Edward Dunsha Steele: A Diary of His Journey from Lodi, Wisc., Across the Plains to Boulder, Colo., in 1859.* Half cloth. Boulder, 1960. One of 500. $35.

MUNDY, Talbot. *Rung Ho!* Cloth. New York, 1914. First edition. In dust jacket. $25-$35. Author's first book.

MUNRO, H. H. See Saki.

MUNRO, Robert. *A Description of the Genessee Country, in the State of New-York.* Map. 16 pp., boards. New York, 1804. (By Charles Williamson.) First edition. $50-$75.

MUNROE, Kirk. *The Fur-Seal's Tooth.* Illustrated by W. A. Rogers. Pictorial cloth. New York, 1894. First edition. $35.

MUNTHE, Axel. *The Story of San Michele.* Cloth. London, no date (1929). First edition. With printed slip about distribution of profits. Boxed. $25-$35.

MURDER by Deputy U.S. Marshal E. M. Thornton of E. M. Dalton Waylaid and Assassinated in Cold Blood. 16 pp., wrappers. Salt Lake, 1886. $35-$50.

MURDOCH, Iris. *Les Eaux du Péché.* Wrappers. Paris, no date (1958). First French translation of "The Bell." One of 10 Hors Commerce. $30-$35.

MURPHY, Jerre C. *The Comical History of Montana.* Wrappers. San Diego, 1912. $25.

MURRAY, Charles A. *Travels in North America.* 2 plates. 2 vols., cloth. London, 1839. First edition. $150. New York, 1839. 2 vols., cloth. First American edition. $75-$100.

MURRAY, Sir John, and Hjort, Dr. Johan. *The Depths of the Ocean.* 13 plates and folding maps, 575 text illustrations. Cloth. London, 1912. $35-$50.

MURRAY, Keith A. *The Modocs and Their War.* Unbound. Norman, Okla., no date (1959). First edition. Advance copies which escaped warehouse fire. $50. Second printing, bound in cloth, same date. In dust jacket. $10.

MURRAY, Lois L. *Incidents of Frontier Life.* 2 portraits. Cloth. Goshen, Ind., 1880. First edition. $75 and $50.

MUSAEUS, J. C. A. See *Popular Tales, etc.*

MUSICA Sacra. Leatherbound. Utica, N. Y., 1815. First edition. $45-$60.

MY Darling's A. B. C. Accordion sheet of 26 leaves with colored alphabet. Orange boards. Philadelphia, no date (about 1835-40). $75.

MYER, Isaac. *Qabbalah.* Illustrated. Cloth. Philadelphia, 1888. One of 350. $150-$200.

MYERS, Frank. *Soldiering in Dakota.* Wrappers. Huron, S.D., 1888. First edition. $450. Pierre, S.D., 1936. Wrappers. $25.

MYERS, J. C. *Sketches on a Tour Through the Northern and Eastern States.* Contemporary sheepskin. Harrisonburg, Va., 1849. First edition. $90.

MYRICK, Herbert. *Cache la Poudre: The Romance of a Tenderfoot in the Days of Custer.* Cloth. New York, 1905. First edition. In dust jacket. $35-$50. Another issue: Buckskin. One of 500 signed. $100.

MYSTERIES and Miseries of San Francisco (The). By a Californian. Cloth. New York, no date (1853). First edition. Rebound in morocco and marbled boards, internally waterstained, $750. (Note: This is the Thomas W. Streeter copy, purchased for $175 in 1959 from my friend the late Paul Schopflin, and sold at auction in 1968 for $425. Mr. Streeter notes, "No other copy seems to be recorded," but Wright's *American Fiction, 1871-1875* lists a copy in the Library of Congress. Author unknown.)

MYSTERIES of a Convent. By a Noted Methodist Preacher. 112 pp., wrappers. Philadelphia, no date (1854). First edition. $50.

MYSTERIES of Mormonism (The): A Full Exposure of Its Secret Practices and Hidden Crimes. By an Apostle's Wife. Wrappers. New York, 1882. $50-$75.

MYSTERIOUS Marksman (The): or The Outlaws of New York. Wrappers. Cincinnati, no date (about 1855). (By Emerson Bennett.) First edition. $150-$200.

N

NABOKOFF-SIRIN, Vladimir. *Camera Obscura.* Translated by Winifred Roy. Cloth. London, no date (1936). (By Vladimir Nabokov.) First edition. $75-$100. First novel by the author to be published in English.

NABOKOFF-SIRIN, Vladimir. *Despair.* Cloth. London, no date (1937). (By Vladimir Nabokov.) First edition. $125-$150.

NABOKOV, Vladimir. *Bend Sinister.* Cloth. New York, no date (1947). First edition. In dust jacket. $35.

NABOKOV, Vladimir. *Conclusive Evidence: A Memoir.* Cloth. New York, no date (1951). First edition. In dust jacket. $25-$30.

NABOKOV, Vladimir. *Invitation au Supplice.* Wrappers. Paris, no date (1960). First French translation (of *Invitation to a Beheading*). One of 60. $30-$40.

NABOKOV, Vladimir. *Lolita.* 2 vols., wrappers. Paris, no date (1955). Olympia Press. First edition. $150-$175.

NABOKOV, Vladimir. *Nine Stories.* Printed blue wrappers. New York, no date (1947). First edition. $25-$30.

NABOKOV, Vladimir. *Poems.* Cloth. New York, 1959. First edition. In dust jacket. $25-$30.

NABOKOV, Vladimir. *The Real Life of Sebastian Knight.* Rough cloth, paper labels. Norfolk, Conn., no date (1941). New Directions. First edition, first issue (with binding as described). In dust jacket. $50-$60. London, no date (1945). Cloth. First English edition. In dust jacket. $15-$20.

NABOKOV, Vladimir. *The Waltz Invention.* Cloth. No place (New York), 1966. Phaedra. First edition in English. In dust jacket. $25-$30.

NABOKOV, Vladimir (translator). *Three Russian Poets: Selections from Pushkin, Lermontov, and Tyutchev.* Stiff wrappers. Norfolk, no date (1944). New Directions. First edition. $25-$35.

NAPTON, William B. *Over the Santa Fe Trail, 1857.* 99 pp., pictorial wrappers. Kansas City, Mo., 1905. First edition. $35-$50.

NARRATIVE and Report of the Causes and Circumstances of the Deplorable Conflagration at Richmond. Sheepskin and oak boards. No place (Richmond, Va.?), 1812. First edition. $40.

NARRATIVE of the Adventures and Sufferings of Capt. Daniel D. Heustis (A). Frontispiece. 168 pp., printed wrappers. Boston, 1847. First edition. $600 (A, 1968).

NARRATIVE of Arthur Gordon Pym (The). Blue or gray cloth, paper label on spine. New York, 1838. (By Edgar Allan Poe.) First edition. $400-$500. Also, $250 (A, 1962). Rebound, $100 and up. London, 1838. Cloth. First English edition. $50-$100. Also, $25 (A, 1962). New York, 1930. Limited Editions Club. Boards. Boxed. $25.

NARRATIVE of the Captivity and Providential Escape of Mrs. Jane Lewis. (Cover title.) Woodcut plate. 24 pp., cloth. No place (New York), 1833. (By William P. Edwards?) First edition. $150. New York, 1834. Wrappers. $75.

NARRATIVE of the Captivity and Sufferings of Ebenezer Fletcher of New-Ipswich (A). 22 pp., stitched. Windsor, Vt., 1813. Second edition. $200. New-Ipswich, N.H., 1827. Fourth edition (so stated; it is actually the third edition). $150 and up. New-Ipswich, no date (about 1828). $75. (Note: There are only 3 known copies of the first edition, published in Amherst in 1798.)

NARRATIVE of the Captivity and Sufferings of Mrs. Hannah Lewis. 24 pp., including folding woodcut plate. Boston, 1817. (By William P. Edwards.) First edition. $150. Another edition: (Identical main title except "Harriet" for "Hannah.") Boston, 1821. Three-quarters morocco. Repaired copy, $90 (A, 1967).

NARRATIVE of the Capture and Burning of Fort Massachusetts. Boards. Albany, 1870. (By the Rev. John Norton.) One of 100. $35-$50. (Note: The first edition, Boston, 1748, is very rare.)

NARRATIVE of the Capture and Providential Escape of Misses Frances and Almira Hall, etc. Plate. 24 pp., printed wrappers. No place (St. Louis?), 1832. (By William P. Edwards?) First edition. $100.

NARRATIVE of Dr. Livingston's Discoveries in Central Africa, from 1849 to 1856. Folding woodcut map. Illustrated boards. London, 1857. First edition, with David Livingstone's name spelled "Livingston." $75.

NARRATIVE of the Extraordinary Life of John Conrad Shafford. Frontispiece. 24 pp., wrappers. New York, 1840. First edition. $50.

NARRATIVE of the Facts and Circumstances Relating to the Kidnapping and Presumed Murder of William Morgan (A). 36 pp., stitched. No place, no date (Batavia, N.Y., 1827). First edition. $35.

NARRATIVE of the Life and Adventures of Matthew Bunn. 55 pp., sewed. Batavia, N.Y., 1828. Seventh edition. $35.

NARRATIVE of the Massacre at Chicago, August 15, 1812, and of Some Preceding Events. Frontispiece map. 34 pp., printed wrappers. Chicago, 1844. (By Mrs. Juliette A. Kinzie.) First edition. $1,750-$2,000. Front cover mended, text stained, $1,500. Also, rebound in boards, $1,300 (A, 1967); in morocco, $1,400 (A, 1966).

NARRATIVE of Occurrences (A), in the Indian Countries of North America. Stiff printed wrappers. London, 1807. (By Samuel Hull Wilcocke?) $400-$500.

NARRATIVE of Some of the Adventures, Dangers, and Sufferings of a Revolutionary Soldier (A). Cloth. Hallowell, Me., 1830. (By James Sullivan Martin?) First edition. $50.

NARRATIVE of the Sufferings and Adventures of Capt. Charles H. Barnard (A). Folding map, 6 plates. Boards. New York, 1829. First edition. $100-$150.

NARRATIVE of the Sufferings of Massy Harbison. 66 pp., leather. Pittsburgh, 1825. First edition. $200-$300. Pittsburgh, 1828. 98 pp., boards and linen. Second edition. $100. Beaver, Pa., 1836. Half cloth. Fourth edition. $50-$75.

NARRATIVE of the Suppression by Col. Burr (A), of the "History of the Administration of John Adams." Stitched. New York, 1802. (By James Cheetham.) First edition. $35-$50.

NARRATIVE of the Tragical Death of Mr. Darius Barber and His Seven Children (A). Frontispiece. 24 pp., wrappers. Boston, no date (about 1818). First edition. Very rare; Howes says "4 perfect copies known." Value: Up to $500, possibly more?

NASBY, Petroleum V. *The Nasby Papers.* 64 pp., printed wrappers. Indianapolis, 1864. (By David Ross Locke.) First edition, first binding, with "Indianaolis" on front cover. $75-$100. Author's first book.

NASH, Ogden. *Hard Lines.* Illustrated by O. Soglow. Tan cloth. New York, 1931. First edition. In dust jacket. $35-$50. Author's first book.

NATHAN, George Jean. See Hatteras, Owen; Mencken, H. L., and Nathan, George Jean.

NATHAN, Robert. *One More Spring.* Illustrated. Decorated boards. Stamford, Conn., 1935. One of 750. Boxed. $25.

NATHAN, Robert. *Peter Kindred.* Cloth. New York, 1919. First edition. In dust jacket. $25-$35. Author's first book.

NATIONAL Elgin Watch Company's Illustrated Almanac for 1875 (The). Printed wrappers. Chicago, no date (1874). First edition. $25-$30. (Note: Includes "My Rococo Watch," by Louisa May Alcott.)

NATURE. Cloth. Boston, 1836. (By Ralph Waldo Emerson.) First edition, first state, with page 94 misnumbered 92. $250-$350. Second state, error corrected. $75-$100. New York, 1929. Boards. One of 250. $35.

NAUTICAL Reminiscences. By the Author of "A Mariner's Sketches." Boards and cloth. Providence, 1832. (By Nathaniel Ames.) First edition. $35-$50.

NAVAL Achievements of Great Britain and Her Allies from 1793 to 1817 (The). 55 hand-colored plates. Half morocco. London, no date (1817). $1,500-$2,000.

NAVAL Monument (The). 25 plates. Errata slip. Calf. Boston, 1816. (By Abel Bowen.) First edition. $75-$100.

NAVIGATOR (The). Boards or wrappers. Pittsburgh, 1804. (By Zadok Cramer.) Fourth edition (of *The Ohio and Mississippi Navigator,* which see) and first edition with this title. The two copies known are in institutional libraries. Pittsburgh, 1806. 14 charts. 94 pp., plain wrappers. Fifth edition. Worn, $1,700 (A, 1967). Pittsburgh, 1808. Boards. Sixth edition. $325 (A, 1967). Pittsburgh, 1811. Boards. Seventh edition. $175 (A, 1967). Pittsburgh, 1814. Boards. Eighth edition. $150-$200. Pittsburgh, 1814. Boards. Ninth edition. $150-$200. Pittsburgh, 1818. Boards. Tenth edition. $100-$150. Pittsburgh, 1821. Boards. Eleventh edition. $75-$100. Pittsburgh, 1824. Boards. Twelfth edition. $50-$100.

NEAGOE, Peter. *Storm.* Stiff wrappers. Paris, 1932. First edition. $35-$50. Author's first book.

NEAGOE, Peter (editor). *Americans Abroad.* Illustrated. Yellow cloth, tan cloth spine. The Hague, Netherlands, 1932. First edition. In dust jacket. $60-$75. (Note: This anthology contains Henry Miller's first book appearance, as well as new material by William Carlos Williams and others.)

NEAL, John. See Adams, Will. Also see *Authorship: A Tale; Keep Cool; Seventy-Six.*

NEAL, John. *The Moose-Hunter; or, Life in the Maine Woods.* Wrappers. New York, no date (1864). First edition, first issue, with No. 73 announced on the inside of the front cover. $75-$100.

NEAL, John. *Rachel Dyer: A North American Story.* Boards and cloth. Portland, Me., 1828. First edition. $200-$250.

NEAL, Joseph Clay. *Peter Ploddy, and Other Oddities.* Boards. Philadelphia, 1844. First edition. $35-$50.

NECESSITY of a Ship-Canal Between the East and West (The). 45 pp., sewed. Chicago, 1863. (By J. W. Foster.) First edition. $50-$75.

NEESE, George M. *Three Years in the Confederate Horse Artillery.* Cloth. New York, 1911. First edition. $40-$50.

NEIHARDT, John G. *Black Elk Speaks.* Illustrated, including color plates. Decorated cloth. New York, 1932. First edition. In dust jacket. $35-$50.

NEIHARDT, John G. *A Bundle of Myrrh.* Limp leather. No place (New York), MCMIII (1903). First edition. One of 5. $100 and up. New York, 1907. Boards and cloth. Revised edition. $10-$15.

NEIHARDT, John G. *Collected Poems.* 2 vols., cloth. New York, 1926. First edition. One of 250 signed. In dust jackets. $50.

NEIHARDT, John G. *The Divine Enchantment: A Mystical Poem.* Cloth. New York, 1900. First edition. $250. Author's first book.

NEIHARDT, John G. *The Lonesome Trail.* Frontispiece. Pictorial cloth. New York, 1907. First edition. $50.

NEIHARDT, John G. *The Song of Hugh Glass.* Cloth. New York, 1915. First edition. In dust jacket. $25.

NEIHARDT, John G. *The Song of the Indian Wars.* Cloth. New York, 1925. First edition. One of 500 signed. In dust jacket. $25-$35. Trade edition: Cloth. In dust jacket. $10.

NEIHARDT, John G. *The Song of Three Friends.* Cloth. New York, 1919. First edition. In dust jacket. $25.

NEIHARDT, John G. *The Splendid Wayfaring.* Cloth. New York, 1920. First edition. In dust jacket. $25.

NEIL, John B. *Biennial Message of the Governor of Idaho to the 11th Session of the Legislature of Idaho Territory.* 19 pp., wrappers. Boise City, Idaho, 1880. $35-$50.

NEMEROV, Howard. *The Image and the Law: Poems.* Cloth. New York, no date (1947). First edition. In dust jacket. $40-$50. Author's first book.

NEMEROV, Howard. *The Painter Dreaming in the Scholar's House.* Oblong, stiff wrappers. New York, 1968. One of 126 signed. In dust jacket. $25.

NERUDA, Pablo. *We Are Many.* Translated by Alastair Reid. Boards. London, no date (1967). First edition in English. One of 100 signed. In dust jacket. $25-$30.

NESBIT, Edith. *Ballads and Lyrics of Socialism, 1883-1908.* Cloth. London, 1908. First edition. $40-$50.

NEVE, John. *A Concordance to the Poetical Works of William Cowper.* Cloth. London, 1887. $50-$60.

NEVERS, William. *Memoir of Col. Samuel Nevers.* 80 pp., wrappers. Norway, Me., 1858. First edition. $35-$50.

NEVILL, Ralph. *British Military Prints.* Plates, including color. Pictorial cloth. London, 1909. $50.

NEVILL, Ralph. *Old English Sporting Books.* Plates, including color. Buckram. London, 1924. $75-$100.

NEVILL, Ralph. *Old English Sporting Prints and Their History.* 103 full-page plates, 47 in color. Buckram. London, 1923. $50-$75.

NEW BEDFORD and Fairhaven Signals. Boards. New Bedford, Mass., 1834. $90-$100.

NEW BRITAIN: A Narrative of a Journey, by Mr. Ellis, to a Country So Called by Its Inhabitants, Discovered in the Vast Plain of the Missouri, in America. Boards. London, 1820. (By G. A. Ellis.) $50.

NEW Conjuror's Museum, and Magical Magazine. Vol. 1. 5 folding plates. Old half calf. London, no date (1803). $35.

NEW Country: Prose and Poetry. Edited by Michael Roberts. Cloth. London, 1933. Hogarth Press. First edition. $25. (Note: Contains first appearance of three W. H. Auden poems.)

NEW Directions in Prose and Poetry. (Vol. 1) Edited by James Laughlin IV. Printed yellow and red wrappers. Norfolk, Conn., 1936. First edition. $60-$75. (Note: Includes new material by Ezra Pound, Wallace Stevens, E. E. Cummings, and others.) Other annuals in this series: 1937 edition (Vol. 2), boards, $50; 1938 (Vol. 3), boards, $35-$50; 1939 (Vol. 4), boards, $35-$50; 1940 (Vol. 5), cloth, $20-$25; 1941 (Vol. 6), cloth, $20-$25; 1942 (Vol. 7), cloth, $20-$25.

NEW Empire (The): Oregon, Washington, Idaho. Folding map. Wrappers. Portland, Ore., 1888. First edition. $35-$50.

NEW ENGLAND Primer (The). Illustrated. 63 pp., boards and leather. Boston, printed for G. Smith, no date (about 1815-30). Boards chipped and broken, $35. Other editions: New England (Boston ?), Printed for the Purchaser, no date (about 1800-12). Illustrated. 32 leaves, boards. $75. Walpole, N.H., 1814. Isaiah Thomas printing. 32 leaves, boards. $65. Middletown, Conn., 1820. Illustrated. 32 leaves, wallpaper wrappers. $65. Boston, no date (about 1815-30). Loring, publisher. 32 leaves, wrappers. $45. Another issue, same imprint: Boards and leather.

NEW Guide of the Conversation in Portuguese and English (The). Introduction by Mark Twain. Unbound sheets. Boston, 1883. First edition. $35-$50. (Note: Blanck does not list this but records a London paperback of 1884 by this title.)

NEW Poets. Spiral-bound stiff wrappers. Prairie City, Ill., 1941. Press of James A. Decker. $35-$50.

NEW Ritual for "Sam" (A): Written by One Connected with the Cincinnati Times, and Dedicated to "Sam's" Numerous Friends. Wrappers. Cincinnati, 1855. First edition. $50-$75.

NEW SPAIN and the Anglo-American West: Contributions Presented to Herbert E. Bolton. Portrait. 2 vols., cloth. No place, no date (Los Angeles, 1932). First edition. One of 500. Boxed. $75-$100.

NEW TESTAMENT of Our Lord and Saviour Jesus Christ. Translated into the Choctaw Language. Cloth. New York, 1854. Second edition. $35.

NEW Texas Spelling Book (The). Pictorial boards. Houston, 1863. (By E. H. Cushing.) $100-$200.

NEW Topographical Atlas of St. Lawrence County, New York. Colored maps and plans. Cloth. Philadelphia, 1865. First edition. $35-$50.

NEW Translation with Notes (A), of the Third Satire of Juvenal. Marbled boards. New York, 1806. (By Clement C. Moore and John Duer.) First edition, with "Additional Errata" leaf. $100. Moore's first book appearance.

NEW Year's Feast on His Coming of Age (The). 6 color plates. Stiff wrappers. London, 1824. (By Charles Lamb.) First edition. $350 and up.

NEW YORK Book of Poetry (The). Engraved half title. Cloth. New York, 1837. (Edited anonymously by Charles Fenno Hoffman.) $35-$50. (Note: Contains first book appearance of Clement C. Moore's "A Visit from St. Nicholas.")

NEW YORK and Oro-Fino Gold and Silver Mining Co. of Idaho. 31 pp., wrappers. New York, 1865. First edition. $50-$75.

NEW YORK Primer (The). Woodcuts. 33 pp., dark-blue pictorial wrappers. New York, 1818. $125.

NEW ZEALAND, Graphic and Descriptive. Edited by W. T. L. Travers. Map, 25 colored lithographic views, 19 other views on 6 plates, woodcuts in text. Folio, half cloth. London, 1877. $100.

NEWBERRY, J. S. *Report on the Properties of the Ramshorn Consolidated Silver Mining Company at Bay Horse, Idaho.* 16 pp., wrappers. New York, no date (1881). $75-$100.

NEWCOMB, Harvey. *The Wyandott Chief; or The History of Barnet, a Converted Indian.* Cloth. Boston, 1835. First edition. $35-$50.

NEWCOMB, Rexford. *Old Mission Churches.* Illustrated. Buckram. Philadelphia, 1925. $50.

NEWELL, Rev. Chester. *History of the Revolution in Texas.* Folding map. Half calf. New York, 1838. First edition. $125-$150.

NEWELL, Peter. See *Topsys & Turveys.*

NEWELL, Peter. *The Hole Book.* Illustrated in color by the author. Stapled blue cloth, pictorial cover label. New York, no date (1908). First edition, with "Published October 1908" below copyright notice. $35-$50.

NEWELL, Peter. *The Rocket Book.* 22 colored plates. Cloth. New York, no date (1912). First edition. $25-$35.

NEWHALL, J. B. *The British Emigrants' "Hand Book."* (Cover title.) 99 pp., printed yellow wrappers. London, 1844. First edition. $450 (A, 1967).

NEWHALL, John B. *Sketches of Iowa.* Map in color. Cloth. New York, 1841. First edition. $100-$150.

NEWMAN, John Henry, Cardinal. See *The Dream of Gerontius; Verses on Various Occasions.*

NEWMAN, John Henry, Cardinal. *Apologia Pro Vita Sua.* 8 parts, printed wrappers. London, 1864. First edition. $300-$400. London, 1864. Cloth. First book edition. $150-$200.

NEWMAN, John Henry, Cardinal. *Discourses Addressed to Mixed Congregations.* Cloth. London, 1949. First edition. $40-$50.

NEWMAN, John Henry, Cardinal. *Lectures.* Cloth. London, 1837. First edition. $50.

NEWMAN, John Henry, Cardinal. *Lectures on Justification.* Cloth, paper label. London, 1838. First edition. $40-$50.

NEWMAN, John Henry, Cardinal, and others (editors). *Lyra Apostolica.* Purple cloth. Derby, England, 1836. First edition. $250.

NEWMARK, Harris. *Sixty Years in Southern California, 1853-1913.* 33 plates. Cloth. New York, 1916. First edition. $30-$40. Boston, 1930. Edited by M. H. and M. R. Newmark. 182 illustrations. Cloth. $50-$75.

NEWTON, A. Edward. *The Amenities of Book Collecting and Kindred Affections.* Illustrated. Half cloth. Boston, 1918. First edition, without index. In dust jacket. $25-$35.

NEWTON, A. Edward. *Derby Day and Other Adventures.* Illustrated. Cloth. Boston, 1934. First edition. In dust jacket. $10. Another issue: Half cloth. One of 1,129 signed. Boxed. $15-$25.

NEWTON, A. Edward. *Doctor Johnson: A Play.* Illustrated. Boards. Boston, 1923. First edition. In dust jacket. $10. Another issue: One of 585 signed. $25-$30.

NEWTON, A. Edward. *End Papers.* Illustrated. Cloth. Boston, 1933. First edition. In dust jacket. $10. Another issue: Boards and cloth. One of 1,351 signed. Boxed. $25.

NEWTON, A. Edward. *The Format of the English Novel.* Illustrated, including colored frontispiece. Boards. Cleveland, 1928. First edition. One of 289. Boxed. $25.

NEWTON, A. Edward. *The Greatest Book in the World.* Boards. Boston, no date (1925). First edition. In dust jacket. $15. Another issue: One of 470 signed. $25.

NEWTON, A. Edward. *A Magnificent Farce and Other Diversions of a Book Collector.* Illustrated. Boards. Boston, no date (1921). First edition. In dust jacket. $10. Another issue: One of 265 signed. Boxed. $25-$35.

NEWTON, A. Edward. *Newton on Blackstone.* Cloth. Philadelphia, 1937. First edition. One of 2,000 signed. In dust jacket. $15-$25.

NEWTON, A. Edward. *On Books and Businesss.* Boards. No place (New York), 1930. First edition. One of 325 signed. $20-$25.

NEWTON, A. Edward. *Rare Books, etc.* (Sale catalogue.) Illustrated. 3 vols., printed gray boards. New York, 1941. In dust jackets. $50-$75.

NEWTON, A. Edward. *This Book Collecting Game.* Illustrated. Half cloth. Boston, 1928. First edition. In dust jacket. $10. Another issue: One of 990 signed. $25.

NEWTON, A. Edward. *A Tourist in Spite of Himself.* Cloth. Boston, 1930. First edition. In dust jacket. $10. Another issue: One of 525 signed. $25.

NEWTON, J. H. (editor). *History of the Pan-handle . . . West Virginia.* Maps and plates. Cloth. Wheeling, W. Va., 1879. First edition. $40-$50.

NEWTON, J. H. (editor). *History of . . . Venango County, Pennsylvania.* 47 plates. Half leather. Columbus, Ohio, 1879. $40-$60.

NEWTON, James. *A Compleat Herbal.* 176 copper plates. Boards, printed label. London, 1802. Reprint edition. $50.

NEWTON, John F. *The Return to Nature.* Boards. London, 1811. First edition. $85.

NICHOLLS, John Ashton. *In Memoriam: A Selection from the Letters of the Late John Ashton Nicholls.* Edited by his mother. Cloth. No place (Manchester, England), 1862. First edition. $100.

NICHOLLS, J. G. (editor). *The Legend of Sir Nicholas Throckmorton.* Half morocco. London, 1874. $40.

NICHOLS, Beach. *Atlas of Schuyler County, New York.* 21 maps in color, 31 leaves. Cloth. Philadelphia, 1874. $50-$75.

NICHOLS, Robert. *The Budded Branch.* Colored illustrations. Boards. London, 1918. First edition. One of 120. $30.

NICHOLSON, John. *The Martyrdom of Joseph Standing.* Cloth. Salt Lake City, 1886. First edition. $25-$35.

NICK of the Woods, or The Jibbenainosay. 2 vols., purple cloth, paper label. Philadelphia, 1837. (By Robert Montgomery Bird.) First edition. $400-$500. Also, $375 (A, 1962). New York, 1853. Cloth. Revised edition. $25.

NICOLL, Allardyce. *Stuart Masques and the Renaissance Stage.* 197 illustrations. Cloth. London, 1937. $40-$50.

NICOLLETT, Joseph Nicolas. *Report Intended to Illustrate a Map of the Hydrographical Basin of the Upper Missouri River.* Senate Doc. 237, 26th Congress, 2d session. Folding map. 170 pp., wrappers. Washington, 1843. First edition. $75-$100. Also, in half morocco, $90 (A, 1967). Washington, 1845. House Doc. 52. Smaller map. Sewed. $25-$30.

NIGHTINGALE, Florence. *Notes on Nursing.* Flexible cloth. London, no date (1859). First edition. $75-$100.

NIGHTMARE Abbey. Blue boards, paper spine, paper label. London, 1818. (By Thomas Love Peacock.) First edition. $200-$250.

NILE Notes of a Howadji. Cloth, or tan printed wrappers. New York, 1851. (By George William Curtis.) First edition. Wrappers: $100-$150. Cloth: $75. Author's first book.

NIMMO, Joseph, Jr. *Range and Ranch Cattle Traffic.* (Caption title.) 4 folding maps, 200 pp., wrappers. No place, no date (Washington, 1885). First edition. $50-$75.

NIMROD. *The Life of a Sportsman.* 36 colored plates by Alken. Cloth. London, 1842. (By C. J. Apperley.) First edition, first issue, in blue cloth. $600-$800. Second issue, red cloth. $200-$250.

NIMROD. *Remarks on the Condition of Hunters, the Choice of Horses, and Their Management.* Half calf, leather label. London, 1831. (By C. J. Apperley.) First collected edition. $40-$50.

NIMROD'S Hunting Tours. 18 hand-colored plates. Grained calf. London, 1903. (By C. J. Apperley.) One of 500. $75-$100.

NIN, Anaïs. *D. H. Lawrence: An Unprofessional Study.* Facsimiles. Black cloth. Paris, 1932. First edition. One of 550. In dust jacket. $75-$100. Author's first book. Denver, no date (1964). Wrappers. First American edition. $20.

NIN, Anaïs. *The House of Incest.* Covered wrappers. Paris, 1936. First edition. One of 249. $60-$75. No place, no date (New York, 1947). Gemor Press. Cloth. One of 50 signed. $50-$60.

NIN, Anaïs. *Nuances.* Cloth. No place, 1970. Sans Souci Press. One of 99 signed. $45-$75.

NIN, Anaïs. *This Hunger.* 5 hand-colored woodcuts by Ian Hugo. Decorated boards. No place, no date (New York, 1945). Gemor Press. First edition. One of 50 signed. $100. Trade edition: One of 1,000. $25-$30.

NIN, Anaïs. *Unpublished Selections from the Diary of Anaïs Nin.* Wrappers. Athens, Ohio, no date (1968). First edition. One of 140 signed. $25.

NIN, Anaïs. *Winter of Artifice.* Copper engravings by Ian Hugo. Pictorial boards. No place (New York?), no date. First edition. One of 500. $25-$35. Denver, no date (1948). Cloth. In dust jacket. $10.

NINA Balatka. 2 vols., cloth. Edinburgh, 1867. (By Anthony Trollope.) First edition, first issue, with ad leaf inset in Vol. 1. $300-$400. Also, $250 (A, 1970).

NOEL, Theophilus. *Autobiography and Reminiscences of Theophilus Noel.* Red cloth. Chicago, 1904. First edition. $35-$50.

NONESUCH Century (The): An Appraisal, a Personal Note and a Bibliography of the First Hundred Books Issued by the Press, 1923-1934. Illustrated. Buckram. London, 1936. One of 750. In dust jacket. $150-$200.

NORDEN, Charles. *Panic Spring.* Cloth. New York, no date (1937). (By Lawrence Durrell.) First edition. In dust jacket. $85-$100.

NORMYX. *Unprofessional Tales.* Pictorial white cloth. London, 1901. (By Norman Douglas and Elsa Fitzgibbon.) First edition. One of 750. $250-$300. Norman Douglas' first book, written in collaboration with his wife.

NORRIS, Frank. *Blix.* Tan pictorial cloth. New York, 1899. First edition. $25-$30.

NORRIS, Frank. *A Deal in Wheat and Other Stories of the New and Old West.* Illustrated by Frederic Remington and others. Red cloth. New York, 1903. First edition. $25-$35.

NORRIS, Frank. *A Man's Woman.* Red cloth. New York, 1900. First edition. $25.

NORRIS, Frank. *McTeague: A Story of San Francisco.* Red cloth. New York, 1899. First edition, first issue, with "moment" as last word on page 106. $125-$200. San Francisco, 1941. Colt Press. Illustrated. Buckram and boards. One of 500. $25-$35.

NORRIS, Frank. *Moran of the Lady Letty.* Green cloth. New York, 1898. First edition. $45-$50.

NORRIS, Frank. *The Octopus.* Red cloth. New York, 1901. First edition. $25-$35.

NORRIS, Frank. *The Pit.* Red cloth. New York, 1903. First edition (so stated on copyright page). $25. Another issue: Gray boards, paper label. Presentation edition. $50-$60.

NORRIS, Frank. *The Responsibilities of the Novelist and Other Literary Essays.* Green cloth. New York, 1903. First edition, first state, with untrimmed edges. $25.

NORRIS, Frank. *Yvernelle: A Legend of Feudal France.* Illustrated. Brown cloth, or leather. Philadelphia, 1892 (actually 1891). First edition. $500-$750. Author's first book.

NORRIS, J. W. *A Business Advertiser and General Directory of the City of Chicago for the Year 1845-6.* Folding plate. 156 pp., wrappers. Chicago, 1845. First edition. $1,000 and up. Also, rebound in cloth, $700 (A, 1967); in half morocco, $450 (A, 1966). (Note: The folding plate in this second Chicago city directory is believed to be the earliest view of Chicago as a city.)

NORRIS, J. W. *General Directory and Business Advertiser of the City of Chicago for the Year 1844.* 116 pp., printed wrappers. Chicago, 1844. First edition. $750-$1,000. Also, rebound in cloth, front cover preserved, $425 (A, 1967). Second issue, clothbound. $750 and up. (Note: This is the first Chicago city directory.)

NORRIS, Thomas Wayne (book collection). *A Descriptive and Priced Catalogue . . . of California and the Far West.* Illustrated. Boards and cloth. Oakland, Calif., 1948. $50-$60.

NORTH and South. 2 vols., cloth. London, 1855. (By Elizabeth C. Gaskell.) First edition. $50-$75.

NORTH, Joseph. *Men in the Ranks: The Story of 12 Americans in Spain.* Foreword by Ernest Hemingway. Wrappers. New York, 1939. First edition. $25-$35.

NORTH, Thomas. *Five Years in Texas; or, What You Did Not Hear During the War.* Cloth. Cincinnati, 1870. First edition. $35-$50.

NORTHANGER Abbey; and Persuasion. By the Author of "Pride and Prejudice," etc. 4 vols., blue-gray or pink boards and linen, white paper labels. London, 1818. (By Jane Austen.) First edition. $1,000 and up. Hinges cracked, three spines chipped, label of Vol. 1 defective, $800. Also, $550 (A, 1963).

NORTHERN Route to Idaho (The). Large folding map, 8 pp. of text. Cloth. St. Paul, Minn., no date (1864). (By D. D. Merrill.) $1,800. Also, $1,000 (A, 1968).

NORTHERN Traveller (The). 16 maps and 4 plates. Boards. New York, 1825. (By Theodore Dwight, Jr.) First edition. $50. New York, 1826. Second edition. $30.

NORTH-WEST Coast of America, Being Results of Recent Ethnological Researches from the Collections of the Royal Museum at Berlin. 15 plates, 5 in color. Half leather. New York, no date. $55.

NORTON, Harry J. *Wonder-Land Illustrated; or, Horseback Rides Through the Yellowstone National Park.* Map, 18 plates. Pictorial wrappers. Virginia City, Mont., no date (1873). First edition. $100-$125.

NOTES by Joseph Conrad, Written In a Set of His First Editions in the Possession of Richard Curle. Cloth, paper label. London, 1925. One of 100 signed by Curle. Boxed. $40-$60.

NOTES of a Journey Through France and Italy. Boards, paper label. London, 1826. (By William Hazlitt.) First edition, first issue, with author's name omitted on title page. $150-$250. Second issue (corrected). $100-$150. Also, $52.80 (A, 1969).

NOTES on California and the Placers. 2 plates (not in all copies). 128 pp., printed wrappers. New York, 1850. (By James Delavan.) First edition. $1,250. Also, copy with covers frayed, back cover loose, $600 (A, 1968).

NOTHING to Do. Frontispiece. Cloth. Boston, 1857. (By Horatio Alger, Jr.) First edition. $75-$150. (Note: Ralph D. Gardner's new bibliography—*Road to Success: The Bibliography of the Works of Horatio Alger*—lists a catalogue price of $145, with which he disagrees, concluding a proper price is probably between $80 and $85.)

NOTICE sur la Rivière Rouge dans le Territoire de la Baie-d'Hudson. 32 pp., wrappers. Montreal, 1843. (By Alexandre Taché?) First edition. $1,000. Rebound in cloth, part of original cover stuck to title page, $650.

NOTICES of Parkersburg, Virginia, As It Is in 1860. Folding map, colored plate. 12 pp., printed wrappers. Baltimore, 1860. First edition. $75-$100.

NOTICES of Sullivan's Campaign, or the Revolutionary Warfare in Western New-York. Colored frontispiece (not in all copies). Cloth. Rochester, N.Y., 1842. First edition. $75-$100.

NOTICIA breve de la Expedición Militar de Sonora y Cinoloa, su Éxito Feliz, y Ventajoso Estado en que por Consecuencia de ella se han Puesto Ambar Provincias. 12 pp., wrappers. Mexico, 1927. (By José de Galvez.) Reprint of Mexico, 1771, edition. $60.

NOTT, Stanley Charles. *Chinese Jade Throughout the Ages.* 39 color illustrations, 182 in black and white. Cloth. London, 1936. In dust jacket. $50-$60.

NOVELAS Españolas. Marbled boards. Portland, Me., 1830. First edition. (Edited anonymously by Henry Wadsworth Longfellow.) $100.

NOVUM TESTAMENTUM: Juxta Exemplar Joannis Millii Accuratissimi Impressum. Calf. Worcester, Mass., 1800. $35-$50.

NOWLIN, William. *The Bark Covered House.* 6 plates. Cloth. Detroit, 1876. First edition. $550-$1,000.

NOYES, Alva J. *In the Land of Chinook: or, The Story of Blaine County, Montana.* 24 plates. Cloth. Helena, Mont., no date (1917). First edition. $50-$75.

NUTTALL, Thomas. *The Genera of North American Plants.* 2 vols. in one, boards. Philadelphia, 1818. First edition. $150-$200.

NUTTALL, Thomas. *Journal of Travels into the Arkansa Territory, During the Year 1819.* Folding map, 5 plates. Boards. Philadelphia, 1821. First edition. $300-$350.

NUTTALL, Zelia. *The Book of the Life of the Ancient Mexicans.* Part I. 90 pp. of color plates. Oblong, leather. Berkeley, Calif., 1903. $35-$50.

NUTTING, Wallace. *The Clock Book.* Cloth. Framingham, Mass., 1924. First edition. In dust jacket. $50. Garden City, 1935. Cloth. In dust jacket. $25.

NYE-STARR, Kate. *A Self-Sustaining Woman; or, The Experience of Seventy-Two Years.* Portrait. Red cloth. Chicago, 1888. First edition. $1,500 and up. (Note: A little-known book. Apparently there are only three known copies of this narrative of Western travel—the Graff copy at the Newberry Library, one at Yale, and one recently found by one of my book scouts. Both Howes and Charles P. Everitt [in *Adventures of a Treasure Hunter*] give inaccurate titles; the latter reference also gives the date incorrectly as 1881.)

O

OAK Openings (The); or, The Bee-Hunter. By the Author of "The Pioneers." 2 vols., printed tan wrappers. New York, 1848. (By James Fenimore Cooper.) First American edition. $100-$150.

OAKES, William. Scenery of the White Mountains. 16 plates, sometimes colored, each with a leaf of text. Folio, cloth. Boston, no date (1848). First edition. Uncolored: $50-$75. Colored: $100-$150.

OAKLEY, Violet. The Holy Experiment . . . Murals in the Governor's Reception Room at Harrisburg. Elephant folio, full leather, copper clasps. No place, no date (Harrisburg, Pa., 1922). First edition. One of 500. $50-$75. Another issue: One of 250 signed. $100-$125.

OAKWOOD, Oliver. Village Tales, or Recollections of By-past Times. Cloth. Trenton, N.J., 1827. (By Stacy Gardner Potts.) First edition. $50-$75.

OATES, Joyce Carol. By the North Gate. Cloth. New York, no date (1963). First edition. In dust jacket. $25-$30. Author's first book.

OATES, Gen. William C. The War Between the Union and the Confederacy and Its Lost Opportunities. 13 plates. Cloth. New York, 1905. First edition. $35-$65.

O'BEIRNE, H. F. Leaders and Leading Men of the Indian Territory. Vol. 1, History of the Choctaws and Chickasaws. 7 plates. Cloth. Chicago, 1891. First edition. $50-$75.

O'BETJEMAN, Deirdre. Some Immortal Hours: A Rhapsody of the Celtic Twilight. 7 leaves, folio. London, 1962. (By John Betjeman.) One of 12 (of a total issue of 20) copies of a facsimile printing of the author's holograph manuscript, hand colored and signed by Betjeman. $150.

O'BRYAN, William. A Narrative of Travels in the United States, . . . and Advice to Emigrants and Travellers Going to That Interesting Country. Portrait. Dark-blue cloth. London, 1836. First edition. $50-$75.

OBSERVATIONS upon Certain Passages in Mr. Jefferson's "Notes on Virginia." 32 pp., plain gray wrappers. New York, 1804. (By Clement C. Moore?) First edition. $75. Rebound in half cloth, $35. If Moore wrote this, it is his first publication.

O'CASEY, Sean. Windfalls. Cloth. London, 1934. First edition. In dust jacket. $25-$30.

O'CASEY, Sean. The Plough and the Stars. Portrait. Boards and cloth. London, 1926. First edition. In dust jacket. $25-$35.

O'CASEY, Sean. The Silver Tassie. Portrait. Boards and cloth. London, 1928. First edition. $25-$30.

O CATHASAIGH, P. The Story of the Irish Citizen Army. Gray printed wrappers. Dublin, 1919. First edition. $60-$80. Sean O'Casey's first book.

OCCLEVE, Thomas. De Regimine Principum: a Poem. Edited by Thomas Wright. 2 engravings. Boards, roan spine. London, 1860. Roxburghe Club. $100.

O'CONNOR, Flannery. Wise Blood. Cloth. New York, no date (1952). First edition. In dust jacket. $45-$60. Author's first book.

O'CONNOR, Frank. *Lords and Commons.* Boards and linen. Dublin, 1938. Cuala Press. First edition. One of 250. In dust jacket. $75-$100.

O'CONNOR, Frank. *A Picture Book.* Illustrated by Elizabeth Rivers. Boards, linen spine. Dublin, 1943. Cuala Press. First edition. One of 480. In dust jacket. $75-$100.

O'CONNOR, Frank. *Three Tales.* Boards, linen spine. Dublin, 1941. Cuala Press. One of 250. In dust jacket. $75-$100. Also, $62 (A, 1971).

O'CONNOR, Frank. *The Wild Bird's Nest.* Boards and cloth. Dublin, 1932. Cuala Press. One of 250. $75-$100.

OCULUS. *The Home of the Badgers.* 36 pp., tan printed wrappers. Milwaukie [*sic*], 1845. (By Josiah B. Grinnell.) First edition. $750-$1,000. Also, $735 (A, 1959); rebound in modern morocco, $600 (A, 1967). (For second edition, see *Sketches of the West.*)

ODE Performed in the Senate-House, Cambridge, on the Sixth of July, MDCCCXLVII at the First Commencement After the Installation of His Royal Highness the Prince Albert, Chancellor of the University. 8 pp., printed wrappers. Cambridge, England, 1847. (By William Wordsworth.) First edition. $350-$500.

ODE to Napoleon Buonaparte. 16 pp., wrappers. London, 1814. (By George Gordon Noel, Lord Byron.) First edition. $500-$1,000.

ODES. Gray wrappers. No place, no date (London, 1868). (By Coventry Patmore.) First edition. $150-$200.

ODETS, Clifford. *Golden Boy.* Brown cloth. New York, no date (1937). First edition. In dust jacket. $25-$35.

ODETS, Clifford. *Three Plays.* Brown cloth. New York, no date (1935). First edition. In dust jacket. $25-$30.

OEHLER, Andrew. *The Life, Adventures, and Unparalleled Sufferings of Andrew Oehler.* Leather. No place (Trenton, N.J.), 1811. First edition. $50-$75.

OF the Just Shaping of Letters. From the Applied Geometry of Albrecht Dürer. Translated by R. T. Nichol. Decorations by Bruce Rogers. Marbled boards. New York, 1917. One of 215. $75-$100.

O'FAOLAIN, Sean. *The Born Genius.* Green buckram. Detroit, 1936. One of 250 signed. Boxed. $35-$50.

O'FAOLAIN, Sean. *There's a Birdie in the Cage.* Green cloth. London, 1935. First separate edition. One of 285 signed. In dust jacket. $35.

OFFICIAL Historical Atlas of Alameda County. Folding maps, full-page views. Atlas folio, half leather. Oakland, Calif., 1878. First edition. $200-$250.

OFFICIAL Record from the War Department of the Proceedings of the Court Martial Which Tried, and the Orders of Gen. Jackson for Shooting the Six Militia Men, etc. 32 pp., sewed. Washington, 1828. First edition. $75-$100.

OFFICIAL Report of the Trial of Laura D. Fair, for the Murder of Alex P. Crittenden. Frontispiece. Printed wrappers. San Francisco, 1871. First edition. $35-$50.

OFFICIAL Reports of the Debates and Proceedings in the Constitutional Convention of the State of Nevada . . . July 4,1864. Sheepskin. San Francisco, 1866. $25.

OFFUTT, Denton. *The Educated Horse.* Illustrated. Cloth. Washington, 1854. $50.

O'FLAHERTY, Liam. *The Ecstasy of Angus.* Green cloth. London, 1931. Chiswick Press. First edition. One of 365 signed. $35.

O'FLAHERTY, Liam. *The Informer.* Cloth. London, no date (1925). First edition. In dust jacket. $35-$50.

O'FLAHERTY, Liam. *The Puritan.* Orange cloth. London, 1932. First edition. In dust jacket. $25.

OGDEN, George W. *Letters from the West.* Boards. New Bedford, Mass., 1823. First edition. $400. Library stamp on title page, $350. Also, contemporary boards, recased, $325 (A, 1967).

OGILVIES (The). 3 vols., cloth. London, 1849. (By Dinah Maria Mulock.) First edition. $100. Author's first novel.

O'HARA, John. *And Other Stories.* Green cloth. New York, no date (1968). First edition. One of 300 signed. Boxed. $25-$35. Trade edition: Cloth. In dust jacket. $10.

O'HARA, John. *Appointment in Samarra.* Pictorial wrappers. New York, no date (1934). "Presentation Edition" (so imprinted on end paper), laid into dust jacket of published book. $150-$200. First trade edition: Black cloth. In dust jacket. $100-$150.

O'HARA, John. *Butterfield 8.* Black cloth. New York, no date (1935). First edition. In dust jacket. $35-$50.

O'HARA, John. *The Doctor's Son.* Black cloth. New York, no date (1935). First edition. In dust jacket. $25-$35.

O'HARA, John. *The Instrument.* Brown cloth. New York, no date (1967). First edition. One of 300 signed. Boxed. $35. Trade edition: Cloth. In dust jacket. $10.

O'HARA, John. *The Lockwood Concern.* Blue cloth. New York, no date (1965). First edition. One of 300 signed. Boxed. $35. Trade edition: Cloth. In dust jacket. $10.

O'HARA, John. *Pal Joey.* Black cloth. New York, no date (1940). First edition. In dust jacket. $35-$50.

O. HENRY Calendar, 1917 (The). Paper covers, cord tie. No place, no date (New York, 1916). $35.

OLD Age. 8 woodcuts. 16 pp., pictorial wrappers. Nerv-York (New York), 1815. (Children's toybook published by Samuel S. Wood.) $60.

OLD Fashioned Mother Goose' Melodies (The). Pictures in color. Cloth. No place (New York), 1879. First edition. $50. (Note: Contains "There Was a Little Girl," probably by Henry Wadsworth Longfellow.)

OLD Soldier's History (The). Written by Himself. 20 pp., printed wrappers. Haverhill, Mass., 1861. (By Charles Fairbanks?) First edition. $75.

OLDER, (Mr. and Mrs.) Fremont. *The Life of George Hearst, California Pioneer.* Vellum. San Francisco, 1923. John Henry Nash printing. First edition. $50-$75.

OLDHAM, Williamson S., and White, George W. *Digest of the General Statute Laws of the State of Texas.* Cloth. Austin, 1859. $50-$75.

OLDSTYLE, Jonathan. *Letters of Jonathan Oldstyle, Gent.* By the Author of "The Sketch-Book." Brown wrappers. New York, 1824. (By Washington Irving.) First edition. $75-$100.

OLIVER, John W. (publisher). *Guide to the New Gold Region of Western Kansas and Nebraska.* Folding map. 32 pp., printed wrappers. New York, 1859. First edition. $3,000 (A, 1968). Another copy, $2,800. (Note: I arranged the sale of the latter copy, discovered by one of my newspaper column readers in the late 1950's, to a Chicago dealer, who catalogued it at $2,800.)

OLLA Podrida. 3 vols., cloth. London, 1840. (By Frederick Marryat.) First edition. $75-$100.

OLLIVANT, Alfred. *Bob: Son of Battle.* Green decorated cloth. New York, 1898. First edition. $25-$35.

OLMSTEAD, Henry K. *Genealogy of the Olmstead Family in America, 1632-1912.* Cloth. New York, 1921. $35-$50.

OLNEY, J. (editor). *The Easy Reader; or Introduction to the National Preceptor.* Boards. New-Haven, Conn., 1833. First American edition. $25.

OLSON, Charles. *Call Me Ishmael.* Cloth. New York, no date (1947). First edition. In dust jacket. $60-$75. Author's first book.

OLSON, Charles. *Human Universe and Other Essays.* Edited by Donald Allen. Woodcut by Robert LaVigne, photography by Kenneth Irby. Decorated boards, vellum spine. San Francisco, 1965. First edition. One of 250. $35.

OLSON, Charles. *The Maximus Poems.* 1/10. Printed wrappers. Jonathan Williams: Stuttgart, 1953. Jargon 7. First edition. One of 50 copies. $125-$150.

OLSON, Charles. *Mayan Letters.* Printed wrappers. Mallorca, no date (1953). Divers Press. First edition. $30.

OLSON, Charles. *O'Ryan 12345678910.* Linen, vellum spine. San Francisco, no date (1965). First edition. One of 26 signed. $45.

OLSON, Charles. *Stocking Cap: A Story.* Printed white wrappers, tied. San Francisco, 1966. Grabhorn printing. First edition. One of 100. $35.

OLSON, Charles. *'West.'* Boards. London, 1966. First edition. One of 25 signed. $35-$50.

OLSON, Charles. *Y&X.* Illustrated by Corrado Cagli. Printed wrappers. No place (Paris), 1948. Black Sun Press. First edition. One of 100. Boxed. $50-$75.

OMAR Khayyam. See *The Rose Garden of Omar Khayyam; Rubaiyat of Omar Khayyam.*

ON the Frontier. Cloth. London, no date (1938). (By W. H. Auden and Christopher Isherwood.) First edition. In dust jacket. $35-$50.

ON the Plains; or, The Race for Life. 62 pp., pictorial yellow wrappers. New York, no date (1863). (By Edward S. Ellis.) $300-$400. Also, rebound in cloth, $200 (A, 1968).

ON the "White Pass" Pay-Roll. By the President of the White Pass & Yukon Route. 15 plates. Dark-blue cloth. Chicago, 1908. (By S. H. Graves.) First edition. $200.

ONDERDONK, James L. *Idaho: Facts and Statistics.* Wrappers. San Francisco, 1885. First edition. $100.

O'NEILL, Eugene. See Sanborn, Ralph; Shay, Frank. Also see *George Pierce Baker, a Memorial.*

O'NEILL, Eugene. *Ah, Wilderness!* Blue cloth. New York, 1933. First edition (so stated). In dust jacket. $25. Another (later) issue: Blue calf. One of 325 signed. In dust jacket. Boxed. $75-$100.

O'NEILL, Eugene. *All God's Chillun Got Wings, and Welded.* Buff boards and cloth. New York, no date (1924). First edition. In dust jacket. $35-$50.

O'NEILL, Eugene. *Anna Christie.* Yellow boards, or wrappers. London, no date (1923). First separate edition. Boards: In dust jacket. $75. Wrappers: $100. New York, 1930. 12 illustrations by Alexander King. Purple and red boards, black cloth spine. First illustrated (and first American) edition. One of 775. In dust jacket. Boxed. $75-$100.

O'NEILL, Eugene. *Before Breakfast.* Light blue-green wrappers. New York, 1916. First separate edition. $100-$125.

O'NEILL, Eugene. *Beyond the Horizon.* Brown boards and cloth. New York, no date (1920). First edition, probable first state, with capital letters on front cover 9/16 inch high. In dust jacket. $75-$100. Second issue. In dust jacket. $25.

O'NEILL, Eugene. *Days Without End*. Blue cloth. New York, no date (1934). First edition (so stated). In dust jacket. $25. Another (later) issue: Morocco. One of 325 signed. $75-$100.

O'NEILL, Eugene. *Desire Under the Elms*. Pictorial black cloth. New York, 1925. First separate edition. In dust jacket. $35.

O'NEILL, Eugene. *Dynamo*. Green cloth. New York, 1929. First edition. In dust jacket. $25. Another (later) issue: Purple vellum. One of 775 signed. Boxed. $60-$80. Covers faded, $50. (Note: Most copies I have seen are faded.)

O'NEILL, Eugene. *The Emperor Jones: Diff'rent: The Straw*. Buff boards and cloth. New York, no date (1921). First edition, first issue, with plain (not mottled) boards. $50. Cincinnati, no date (1921). White wrappers. $100. New York, 1928. 8 illustrations in color by Alexander King. Boards and cloth. Limited, signed edition. In dust jacket. Boxed. $75-$100.

O'NEILL, Eugene. *Gold*. Blue-green boards and cloth. New York, no date (1921). First edition (with 1920 copyright). In dust jacket. $25-$35.

O'NEILL, Eugene. *The Great God Brown: The Fountain: The Moon of the Caribbees and Other Plays*. Green cloth. New York, 1926. First edition. In dust jacket. $25-$35. London, no date (1926). (*The Great God Brown*.) Bright-blue cloth. First English edition. In dust jacket. $25.

O'NEILL, Eugene. *The Hairy Ape: Anna Christie: The First Man*. Buff boards and cloth. New York, no date (1922). First edition. In dust jacket. $100. London, no date (1923). (*The Hairy Ape and Other Plays*.) Bright-blue cloth. First English edition. In dust jacket. $25. New York, no date (1929). 9 illustrations in color by Alexander King. Boards. First separate and illustrated edition. One of 775 signed. In dust jacket. Boxed. $75-$100.

O'NEILL, Eugene. *The Iceman Cometh*. Blue cloth. New York, no date (1946). First edition. In dust jacket. $40-$50.

O'NEILL, Eugene. *Lazarus Laughed*. Green cloth. New York, 1927. First edition. In dust jacket. $25. Another (later) issue: Vellum and boards. One of 775 signed. In dust jacket. Boxed. $50-$60.

O'NEILL, Eugene. *Long Day's Journey into Night*. Black and gray cloth. New Haven, no date (1956). First edition. In dust jacket. $25-$30.

O'NEILL, Eugene. *Marco Millions*. Green cloth. New York, 1927. First edition. In dust jacket. $25. Another (later) issue: Vellum and boards. One of 450 signed. Boxed. $50-$75.

O'NEILL, Eugene. *The Moon of the Caribbees and Six Other Plays of the Sea*. Brown boards and cloth. New York, 1919. First edition, first state, 7/8 inch thick. In dust jacket. $75-$100. London, no date (1923). Bright-blue cloth. First English edition. In dust jacket. $20.

O'NEILL, Eugene. *Mourning Becomes Electra*. Cloth. New York, 1931. First edition. (Issued simultaneously with Theatre Guild edition.) In dust jacket. $25-$30. Another (later) issue: Japan vellum. One of 550 signed. Boxed. $75-$100. London, no date (1932). Blue cloth. First English edition. In dust jacket. $15.

O'NEILL, Eugene. *Strange Interlude*. Green cloth. New York, 1928. First edition. In dust jacket. $25-$35. Another (later) issue: Vellum. One of 775 signed. Boxed. $100-$125. London, no date (1928). Blue cloth. First English edition. In dust jacket. $20.

O'NEILL, Eugene. *Thirst and Other One Act Plays*. Dark gray boards, tan cloth spine, paper labels. Boston, no date (1914). First (and only) edition. In dust jacket. $150-$250. Author's first book.

O'NEILL, Eugene, and others. *The Provincetown Plays: First Series*. Printed light-blue wrappers. New York, 1916. First edition. $150-$175. (Note: Contains first book appearance of O'Neill's *Bound East for Cardiff*.)

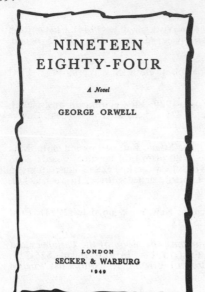

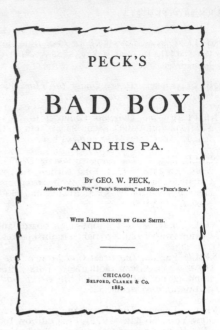

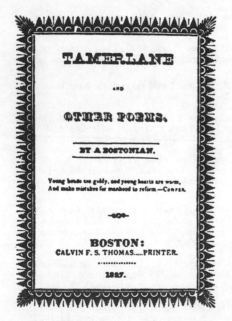

The most scarce of all American
works of literature, Poe's first book

O'NEILL, Eugene, and others. *The Provincetown Plays: Third Series.* Orange wrappers. New York, 1916. First edition. In green dust jacket. $100-$150. (Note: Contains first book appearance of O'Neill's *Before Breakfast.*)

ONKEN, Otto: See Wells, William, and Onken, Otto.

ONLY Authentic Life of Abraham Lincoln, Alias "Old Abe," a Son of the West. (Cover title.) Illustrated. 16 pp., printed wrappers. No place, no date (1864?). $75-$100. Another edition: New York, no date (1864). $60.

ONTWA, the Son of the Forest: A Poem. Boards. New York, 1832. (By Henry Whiting.) $45.

OPDYKE, Charles Wilson. *The OP Duck Genealogy.* Three-quarters morocco. New York, 1889. First edition. $35-$50.

OPPOSITION of the South to the Development of Oregon and Washington Territory. 8 pp., folded. No place, no date (Washington, 1859). $45.

OPTIC, Oliver. *The Boat Club; or, The Bunkers of Rippleton.* Frontispiece, 3 plates. Slate-purple pictorial cloth. Boston, 1855. (By William T. Adams.) First edition. $35-$50. Another issue: Pictorial presentation binding. $275. First Oliver Optic book.

ORANGE County History Series. 2 vols., folio, boards and cloth. No place, no date (Santa Ana, Calif., 1931-32). $100-$150.

ORATION, Poem, and Speeches . . . June 5th, 1867. Printed wrappers. San Francisco, 1867. $50. Also, $27 (A, 1961). (Note: Includes a poem by Bret Harte.)

ORBELIANI, Sulkhan-Saba. *The Book of Wisdom and Lies.* Translated by Oliver Waldorp. Woodcut title and borders. Vellum with ties. London, 1894. Kelmscott Press. One of 250. $200.

ORCUTT, William Dana. *The Book in Italy.* Plates, including color. Folio, boards. New York, 1928. One of 750. In dust jacket. $35-$50. Also, with prospectus laid in, $43.20 (A, 1968). Trade edition: Cloth. In dust jacket. $10. London, 1928. Half vellum. One of 750. In dust jacket. $50.

ORCUTT, William Dana. *In Quest of the Perfect Book.* Plates, including color. Half vellum. Boston, 1926. First edition. One of 365. In dust jacket. $35-$50. Trade edition: Cloth. In dust jacket. $10.

ORCUTT, William Dana. *The Kingdom of Books.* Plates, including color. Half vellum. Boston, 1927. One of 475. Boxed. $35-$50. Trade edition: Cloth. In dust jacket. $10.

ORCUTT, William Dana. *The Magic of the Book.* Illustrated. Half vellum. New York, 1930. First edition. One of 375. In dust jacket. $25-$35. Trade edition: Cloth. In dust jacket. $10.

ORD, John Walker. *England. A Historical Poem.* 2 vols., contemporary cloth, paper labels. London, 1834. First edition. Covers faded, $40-$50.

ORDEAL (The): A Critical Journal of Politicks and Literature. 26 numbers. Boards. Printed and edited by Joseph T. Buckingham. Boston, 1809. $45.

ORDER of the Governor in Council, for Further Regulating the Inland Navigation from the United States by the Port of St. Johns. No place, no date (Quebec, 1800). $35-$40.

ORDINANCES of the Town of Berkeley, Alameda County, California (The). 24 pp., wrappers. Berkeley, Calif., 1882. $45.

OREGON: Agricultural, Stock Raising, Mineral Resources, Climate, etc. (Published by U.P.R.R.) 68 pp., wrappers. Council Bluffs, Iowa, 1888. $30.

O'REILLY, Bernard. *Greenland, the Adjacent Seas, and the North-West Passage.* Maps and plates. Half cloth. London, 1818. First edition. $100-$150.

O'REILLY, Harrington. *Fifty Years on the Trail.* Illustrated by Paul Frenzeny. Pictorial cloth. London, 1889. First edition. $75. New York, 1889. Cloth. First American edition. $50.

ORIGIN and Traditional History of the Wyandotts. Cloth. Toronto, 1870. (By Peter D. Clarke.) First edition. $35-$50.

ORIGINAL Charades. Oblong, cloth. Cambridge, Mass., 1839. First edition. $30.

ORIOLI, G. *Adventures of a Bookseller.* Pictorial orange wrappers folded over blue paper. Florence, Italy, no date (1937). First edition. One of 2 on blue paper, signed. $250. Another issue: One of 300 signed. $50.

ORME, Edward. *Collection of British Field Sports.* Colored title page and 20 colored plates after Howitt. Oblong folio, half morocco. London, 1807-08. First edition. $4,000-$5,000. Also, $3,220 (A, 1967). Guildford, England, 1955. 20 color plates. Facsimile. Folio, full crimson morocco. One of 20 with an original plate included. $350-$500. Ordinary issue: Half morocco. $75-$100.

ORPHEUS in Diloeryum. Wrappers. London, 1908. (By Siegfried Sassoon.) First edition, first issue, anonymously issued. $100. Another (later) issue in the same year, bearing the author's name: Vellum and cloth. $35.

ORR, George. *The Possession of Louisiana by the French.* 44 pp., boards. London, 1803. First edition. $75-$100.

ORR, N. M. (compiler). *The City of Stockton.* 64 pp., printed wrappers. Stockton, Calif., 1874. First edition. $100.

ORR and Ruggles. *San Joaquin County.* Map, plates. 130 pp., wrappers. Stockton, 1887. First edition. $100-$150.

ORTEGA, José. *Historia del Nayarit, Sonora, Sinaloa y Ambas Californias.* Half leather. Mexico, 1887. $35-$50.

ORTEGA, Luis. *California Hackamore (La Jáquima).* 109 photographs, 20 sketches by Al Napoletano. Pictorial leather. No place, no date (Sacramento, Calif., 1948). First edition. $35-$50.

ORTON, Richard H. *Records of California Men in the War of the Rebellion, 1861-1867.* Cloth. Sacramento, 1890. First edition. $35-$50.

ORVIS, Charles F., and Cheney, A. Nelson (compilers). *Fishing with the Fly.* 15 color plates. Cloth. Manchester, Vt., 1883. First edition. $50-$60. Boston, 1892. Cloth. $25-$30.

ORWELL, George. *Animal Farm: A Fairy Story.* Green cloth. London, 1945. (By Eric Arthur Blair.) First edition. In dust jacket. $75-$100. New York, no date (1946). Green cloth. First American edition. In dust jacket. $25.

ORWELL, George. *Burmese Days.* Cloth. New York, 1934. (By Eric Arthur Blair.) First edition. In dust jacket. $50-$75. London, 1935. Cloth. First English edition. In dust jacket. $15-$25. Author's first novel.

ORWELL, George. *Down and Out in Paris and London.* Cloth. London, 1933. (By Eric Arthur Blair.) First edition. In dust jacket. $75-$100. Lacking jacket, $50. New York, 1933. Cloth. First American edition. In dust jacket. $27.50-$35. Author's first book.

ORWELL, George. *Homage to Catalonia.* Cloth. London, 1938. (By Eric Arthur Blair.) First edition. In dust jacket. $50. New York, 1952. Cloth. First American edition. In dust jacket. $10-$15.

ORWELL, George. *The Lion and the Unicorn.* Cloth. New York, 1941. (By Eric Arthur Blair.) First edition. In dust jacket. $25-$35. London, 1941. Cloth. First English edition. In dust jacket. $35-$50.

ORWELL, George. *Nineteen Eighty-four.* Green cloth. London, 1949. (By Eric Arthur Blair.) First edition. In dust jacket. $50-$75. New York, 1949. Gray cloth. First American edition. In red dust jacket. $25.

ORWELL, George. *The Road to Wigan Pier.* Foreword by Victor Gollancz. Illustrated. Limp orange cloth wrappers. London, 1937. (By Eric Arthur Blair.) First edition, wrappers lettered "Left Book Club Edition." $50-$75. Trade edition: Cloth. $25.

OSBORN, H. S. *Plants of the Holy Land.* Colored illustrations. Pictorial cloth. Philadelphia, 1860. $35-$50.

OSCEOLA; or, Fact and Fiction: A Tale of the Seminole War. By a Southerner. Illustrated. Cloth. New York, 1838. (By James Birchett Ransom.) First edition. $50-$75.

OSGOOD, Ernest Staples. *The Day of the Cattleman.* 14 plates and maps. Cloth. Minneapolis, 1929. First edition. In dust jacket. $50-$60.

OSGOOD, Frances S. *The Poetry of Flowers and Flowers of Poetry.* Half leather. New York, 1851. $50.

O'SHAUGHNESSY, Arthur W. E. *An Epic of Women and Other Poems.* Pictorial title page, 2 plates. Purple cloth. London, 1870. First edition. $100-$150.

O'SHAUGHNESSY, Arthur W. E. *Music and Moonlight.* Cloth. London, 1874. First edition. $35-$50.

O'SHAUGHNESSY, Arthur W. E. *Songs of a Worker.* Cloth. London, 1881. First edition. $40-$50.

OSLER, Sir William. *Aequanimitas.* 10 pp., printed wrappers. Philadelphia, 1889. First edition. $100. London, 1904. First English edition. $25-$35.

OSLER, Sir William. *An Alabama Student and Other Biographical Essays.* Cloth. Oxford, England, 1908. First edition. $35-$50. New York, 1909. Cloth. Second edition. $15-$20.

OSLER, Sir William. *Aphasia and Associated Speech Problems.* Illustrated. Cloth. New York, 1920. $25 $30.

OSLER, Sir William. *The Cerebral Palsies of Children.* Cloth. Philadelphia, 1889. $60.

OSLER, Sir William. *The Evolution of Modern Medicine.* Cloth. New Haven, Conn., 1921. First edition. $50.

OSLER, Sir William. *Incunabula Medica: A Study of the Earliest Printed Medical Books, 1467-1480.* Illustrated. Boards and cloth. London, 1923. First edition. $100-$150.

OSLER, Sir William. *Lectures on the Diagnosis of Abdominal Tumors.* Cloth. New York, 1894. $75-$100. New York, 1895. Wrappers. $35. London, 1898. Cloth. $35.

OSLER, Sir William. *The Master-Word in Medicine.* Wrappers. Baltimore, 1903. $30.

OSLER, Sir William. *On Chorea and Choreiform Affections.* Cloth. Philadelphia, 1894. $60-$75.

OSLER, Sir William. *The Principles and Practice of Medicine.* Cloth. New York, 1892. First edition. $60-$75. Edinburgh, 1894. Cloth. First English edition. $50-$75.

OSLER, Sir William. *Students' Notes.* Half cloth. Montreal, 1882. First edition. $100.

OSLER, Sir William (editor). *Bibliotheca Osleriana: A Catalogue of Books Illustrating the History of Medicine.* Cloth. Oxford, England, 1929. First edition. $500 and up. Montreal, 1969. Cloth. New edition. $55.

O'SULLIVAN, Timothy, and Bell, William. *Photographs Showing Landscapes, Geological, and Other Features.* (Wheeler Survey.) 60 mounted photos, printed title page. Folio, three-quarters leather. No place, no date (Washington, 1875). $6,000 (A, 1971).

OTERO, Miguel Antonio. *My Life on the Frontier.* Illustrated. 2 vols., cloth. New York, 1935, and Albuquerque, 1939. First editions. (Vol. 1 limited to 750 signed; Vol. 2 limited to 400.) $100-$125. Trade editions (illustrations omitted in each): Cloth. Each, in dust jackets, $20-$30.

OTERO, Miguel Antonio. *The Real Billy the Kid.* Illustrated. Cloth. New York, 1936. First edition. In dust jacket. $50-$75.

OTHER End of the Couch (The). Wrappers. Cambridge, Mass., 1964. One of 151. $80.

OTHER People's Children. Woodcuts. Cloth. London, no date (about 1878). (By John Habberton.) In binder's cloth, soiled, $45.

OTIS, James. *Jenny Wren's Boarding-House.* Illustrated. Pictorial brown or blue cloth. Boston, no date (1893). (By James Otis Kaler.) First edition. $35.

OTIS, James. *Toby Tyler or Ten Weeks with a Circus.* Illustrated by W. A. Rogers. Light-brown, green, or orange cloth. New York, 1881. (By James Otis Kaler.) First edition. $100.

OTWAY, Thomas. *The Complete Works of Thomas Otway.* Edited by Montague Summers. 3 vols., batik boards and vellum. London, 1926. Nonesuch Press. One of 90 on handmade paper. $150. Another issue: 3 vols., boards, paper label. One of 1,250. $60.

OUIDA. *Syrlin.* 3 vols., cloth. London, 1890. (By Marie Louise de la Ramée.) First edition. $150-$200.

OUIDA. *A Tale of a Toad.* Decorated cloth and morocco. London, 1939. Corvinus Press. (By Marie Louise de la Ramée.) One of 25. $150-$200.

OUIDA. *Under Two Flags.* 3 vols., cloth. London, 1867. (By Marie Louise de la Ramée.) First edition. $300.

OUR Friends the Coeur D'Aleine Indians. 21 pp., wrappers. St. Ignatius Print., Mont., 1886. (By Lawrence B. Palladino.) $75.

OUR Great Indian War: The Miraculous Lives of Mustang Bill (Mr. William Rhodes Decker) and Miss Marion Fannin. Illustrated. 78 pp., pictorial pale-green wrappers. Philadelphia, no date (1876?). $100-$150.

OUR Kith & Kin, or, a History of the Harris Family, 1754-1895. Cloth. No place, no date (Philadelphia, 1895). $30.

OUTCROPPINGS: Being Selections of California Verse. Cloth. San Francisco, 1866. First edition, probable first issue, with "Staining" spelled "Sraining" on page 70 and with no ornament on page 102. $150-$200. (Note: Edited anonymously by Bret Harte.)

OUTLINE Description of U. S. Military Posts and Stations in the Year 1871. Cloth. Washington, 1872. $75-$100.

OUTLINE Descriptions of the Posts in the Military Division of the Missouri. 121 maps, one folding. Three-quarters morocco and purple cloth. Chicago, 1876. $100-$150.

OUTRE-MER: A Pilgrimage Beyond the Sea. Nos. I and II. Marbled wrappers and blue wrappers. Boston, 1833 and 1834. (By Henry Wadsworth Longfellow.) First editions. $250 and up. (Note: A complicated title bibliographically; for example, there are at least three wrapper variants on No. I, while No. II may be in either wrappers or boards of various colors. For a full discussion, see BAL.) Also issued clothbound as 2 vols. in one. $200.

OVID. *The Amores of P. Ovidius Naso.* Translated by E. Powys Mathers. 5 engravings on copper by T. E. Laboureur. Half morocco. Waltham Saint Lawrence, England, 1932. Golden Cockerel Press. One of 350. $75-$100.

OVID. *L'Art d'Aimer.* 12 lithographs and 15 woodcuts by Aristide Maillol. Folio, loose sheets in printed wrappers and slipcase. No place, no date (Lausanne, Switzerland, 1935). One of 225 signed by the artist. $2,000.

OVID. *Shakespeare's Ovid: Being Arthur Golding's Translation of the Metamorphoses.* Edited by W. H. D. Rouse. With a type-facsimile of the original title page. Boards, linen spine. London, 1904. De La More Press. One of 350 copies. $25-$35. Another issue: Morocco. One of 12 on vellum. $350-$400.

OWEN, John Pickard. *The Fair Haven.* By the Late John Pickard Owen. Edited by William Bickersteth Owen. Green cloth. London, 1873. (By Samuel Butler, of *Erewhon.*) First edition. $50.

OWEN, Richard E., and Cox, E. T. *Report on the Mines of New Mexico.* (Cover title.) 59 pp., printed wrappers. Washington, 1865. First edition. $350 (A, 1966).

OWEN, Robert. See Campbell, Alexander.

OWEN, Robert Dale. *A Brief Practical Treatise on the Construction and Management of Plank Roads.* Plate. Cloth. New Albany, Ind., 1850. First edition. $50.

OWENS, Rochelle. *Not Be Essence That Cannot Be.* Stiff printed wrappers. New York, 1961. First edition. $25. Author's first book.

OWENS, Rochelle. *Salt and Core.* Decorated cloth. Los Angeles, 1968. Black Sparrow Press. One of 125 signed. $30.

P

PACKARD, Wellman, and Larison, G. *Early Emigration to California.* 2 portraits. 23 pp., printed wrappers. Bloomington, Ill., 1928. One of 30. $75-$100.

PAGE, Stanton. *The Chevalier of Pensieri-Vani.* Cloth, or wrappers. Boston, no date (1890). (By Henry Blake Fuller.) First edition. $25-$35. Author's first book.

PAGE, Thomas Nelson. *The Coast of Bohemia.* Cloth. New York, 1906. First edition. In dust jacket. $25.

PAGE, Thomas Nelson. *In Old Virginia.* Pictorial cloth. New York, 1887. First edition, first issue, with no advertisement for "Free Joe" on last page. $35-$50.

PAINE, Albert Bigelow. *Captain Bill McDonald, Texas Ranger.* Illustrated. Cloth. New York, 1909. First edition. $25. Another issue: Morocco. $35-$50.

PAINE, Albert Bigelow. *Thomas Nast: His Period and His Pictures.* Illustrated. Cloth. New York, 1904. First edition. $35-$50.

PAINE, R. D. *The Book of Buried Treasure.* Illustrated. Cloth. New York, 1911. $30.

PALINURUS. *The Unquiet Grave: A Word Cycle.* Frontispiece and 3 collotype plates. Gray wrappers. London, 1944. (By Cyril Connolly.) Curwen Press. First edition. One of 1,000. In dust jacket. $75.

PALLADINO, Lawrence B. See *Our Friends the Coeur D'Aleine Indians.*

PALLADINO, Lawrence B. *Indian and White in the Northwest.* Illustrated. Cloth. Baltimore, 1894. First edition. $50-$75. Lancaster, Pa., 1922. Fabrikoid. Revised edition. $25-$35.

PALLAS, P. S. *Travels Through the Southern Provinces of the Russian Empire.* Maps and plates. 2 vols., boards. London, 1802-03. First edition. $300-$400.

PALMER, H. E. *The Powder River Indian Expedition, 1865.* 59 pp., gray printed wrappers. Omaha, 1887. First edition. $75-$100.

PALMER, Harry. *Base Ball: The National Game of the Americans.* 69 pp., wrappers. Chicago, 1888. $35-$50.

PALMER, Joel. *Journal of Travels over the Rocky Mountains, to the Mouth of the Columbia River, etc.* Brown printed wrappers. Cincinnati, 1847. First edition, first issue, with date 1847 on paper cover not overprinted or changed, and with errata slip tipped in. $1,000-$1,500. Second issue, with corrections made. $1,000. Cincinnati, 1852. Half leather. Second edition. $100-$150.

PALMER, John. *Awful Shipwreck: An Affecting Narrative of the Unparalleled Sufferings of the Crew of the Ship Francis Spaight.* Sewed. Boston, 1836. $75-$100. Boston, 1837. Boards. $50-$75.

PALOU, Francisco. *The Expedition into California of the Venerable Padre Junipero Serra and His Companions in the Year 1769.* Translated by Douglas S. Watson. Half vellum. San Francisco, 1934. One of 400. $35-$50.

PALOU, Francisco. *Historical Memoirs of New California.* 4 vols., cloth. Translated by Herbert Eugene Bolton. Berkeley, Calif., 1926. $100-$150.

PALOU, Francisco. *The Life of the Venerable Padre Junipero Serra.* Translated by the Rev. J. Adam. Cloth. San Francisco, 1884. $50-$60.

PALOU, Francisco. *Noticias de la Nueva California.* Illustrated. 4 vols., printed wrappers. San Francisco, 1874. One of 100. $750-$1,000.

PAPWORTH, John B. *Hints on Ornamental Gardening.* 27 hand-colored plates, sepia plate, woodcut plans. Boards. London, 1823. First edition. $300-$400.

PAPWORTH, John B. *Rural Residences.* 27 full-page hand-colored aquatint plates. Three-quarters morocco. London, 1818. First edition. $200-$250. London, 1832. Cloth. Second edition. $200-$250.

PAPWORTH, John B. *Select Views of London.* 76 colored aquatint plates, 5 folding. Boards. London, 1816. First edition. $1,250 and up.

PAREDES Y ARRILLAGA, Mariano. *Manifiesto del Exmo. Sr. Presidente Interino de la República Mexicana.* (Cover title.) 19 pp., printed wrappers. No place, no date (Mexico, 1846). $75-$100.

PAREDES Y ARRILLAGA, Mariano. *Ultimas Communicaciones Entre el Gobierno Mexicano y el Enviada Estraordinario y Ministro Plenipotenciario Nombrado por el de los Estados Unidos.* 22 pp., wrappers. Mexico, 1846. $150.

PARK Hotel (The): Travelers' Guide for 1872, Containing a Brief History of the City of Madison and Its Attractions. Illustrated. 128 pp., wrappers. Madison, Wis., 1872. $50.

PARK, Robert Emory. *Sketch of the 12th Alabama Infantry.* Wrappers. Richmond, Va., 1906. First edition. $60-$75.

PARK, Roswell. *Selections of Juvenile and Miscellaneous Poems.* Cloth. Philadelphia, 1836. First edition. $35.

PARKER, A. A. *Trip to the West and Texas.* 2 plates. Cloth. Concord, N. H., 1835. First edition. $75-$100. Concord, 1836. Colored folding map and 3 plates. Cloth. Second edition. $75-$125. (Note: Howes reports 2 plates; my own copy came with 3. Howes says not all copies included the map.)

PARKER, Aaron. *Forgotten Tragedies of Indian Warfare in Idaho.* 10 pp., double-column, wrappers. Grangeville, Idaho, 1925. $35-$50.

PARKER, Alan. *James Joyce: A Bibliography.* Cloth. Boston, 1948. First edition. $100.

PARKER, Dorothy. *After Such Pleasures.* Buckram. New York, 1933. First edition. One of 250 signed. Boxed. $50-$75. Trade edition: Tan cloth. In dust jacket. $10-$15.

PARKER, Dorothy. *Death and Taxes.* Half cloth. New York, 1931. First edition. One of 250 signed. $50. Trade edition: Cloth. In dust jacket. $10.

PARKER, Dorothy. *Laments for the Living.* Cloth. New York, 1930. First edition. In dust jacket. $25. New York, 1932. Black Sun Press. Printed wrappers. $10-$15.

PARKER, Dorothy. *Men I'm Not Married To.* Boards. Garden City, 1922. First edition (so stated). (Bound in, inverted and with separate title, *Women I'm Not Married To,* by Franklin P. Adams.) In dust jacket. $50. Author's first book.

PARKER, Dorothy. *Not So Deep as a Well.* Illustrated by Valenti Angelo. Half buckram. New York, 1936. First edition. One of 485 signed. $75-$100. Trade edition: Cloth. In dust jacket. $15.

PARKER, Dorothy. *Sunset Gun.* Boards and cloth. New York, 1928. First edition. One of 250 signed. Boxed. $25-$35. Trade edition: Boards. $10.

PARKER, Frank J. (editor). *Washington Territory! The Present and Prospective Future of the Upper Columbia Country.* 17 pp., printed wrappers. Walla Walla, Wash., 1881. First edition. $240 (A, 1968).

PARKER, Henry W. *How Oregon Was Saved to the U.S.* 10 pp., wrappers. New York, 1901. $35-$50.

PARKER, John R. *The New Semaphoric Signal Book.* Hand-colored flags. Printed boards. Boston, 1836. $50-$75.

PARKER, John R. *The United States Telegraph Vocabulary.* 3 plates, one in color. Pictorial boards. Boston, 1832. First edition. $75-$100.

PARKER, Dr. M. *The Arcana of Arts and Sciences, or Farmers and Mechanics' Manual.* Leather. Washington, Pa., 1924. $35.

PARKER, Samuel. *Journal of an Exploring Tour Beyond the Rocky Mountains.* Folding map, plate. Cloth. Ithaca, N.Y., 1838. First edition. $350-$450. Edinburgh, 1841. Half leather. $100. Auburn, N.Y., 1846. Cloth. $35.

PARKER, Solomon. *Parker's American Citizen's Sure Guide.* Boards. Sag Harbor, N.Y., 1808. First edition. $75-$100.

PARKER, W. B. *Notes Taken During the Expedition Commanded by Capt. R. B. Marcy.* Cloth. Philadelphia, 1856. First edition. $75-$125.

PARKER & Huyett. *The Illustrated Miners' Hand-Book and Guide to Pike's Peak.* 6 plates, 2 folding maps. Cloth. St. Louis, 1859. (By Nathan H. Parker and D. H. Huyett.) First edition. $2,000 (A, 1968).

PARKMAN, Francis, Jr. *The California and Oregon Trail.* One vol. in cloth, or 2 vols. in printed wrappers. New York, 1849. First edition. Wrappers: $1,500-$2,000. New York, 1849. Frontispiece and engraved title page. Cloth. First clothbound edition. $400-$500. (Note: See the Thomas W. Streeter sale catalogue for a note on the inconclusive bibliographical data on this book.)

PARKMAN, Francis, Jr. *Count Frontenac and New France Under Louis XIV.* Map. Cloth. Boston, 1877. (Part 5 of *France and England in North America.*) First edition. One of 75 large paper copies. $25.

PARKMAN, Francis, Jr. *History of the Conspiracy of Pontiac and the War of the North American Tribes.* 4 maps. Gray cloth. Boston, 1851. First edition. $50-$75.

PARKMAN, Francis, Jr. *The Old Regime in Canada.* Cloth. Boston, 1874. First edition. One of 75 on large paper. $35-$50.

PARKMAN, Francis, Jr. *The Oregon Trail.* Illustrated by Frederic Remington. Leather, or pictorial tan cloth. Boston, 1892. First edition. Leather: $100-$125. Cloth: $85-$100.

PARLEY, Peter. *The Tales of Peter Parley About America.* 32 (30?) engravings. Blue boards, red leather spine. Boston, 1827. (By Samuel G. Goodrich.) First edition. $1,500 and up. Author's first book.

PARMLY, Levi Spear. *A Practical Guide to the Management of the Teeth.* Boards. Philadelphia, 1819. First edition. $100-$125.

PARNELL, Thomas. *Poems.* Selected by Lennox Robinson. Boards and linen. Dublin, 1927. Cuala Press. One of 200. In dust jacket. $85.

PARRY, William Edward. *Journal of a Second Voyage for the Discovery of a North-West Passage.* 39 plates, maps and charts. Cloth. London, 1824. First edition. $50-$75.

PARRY, William Edward. *Journal of a Voyage for the Discovery of a North-West Passage . . . in the Years, 1819-20.* 20 plates and maps. Boards. London, 1821. First edition, with errata slip. $100.

PARSONS, George Frederic. *The Life and Adventures of James W. Marshall.* Portrait frontispiece. Cloth. Sacramento, Calif., 1870. First edition. $100-$150. San Francisco, 1935. Grabhorn Press. Boards. $50.

PARTICULAR Account of the Dreadful Fire at Richmond, Dec. 26, 1811. 48 pp., sewed. Baltimore, 1812. $35.

PARTISAN (The); A Tale of the Revolution. 2 vols., cloth, paper labels. New York, 1835. (By William Gilmore Simms.) First edition. $50-$75.

PASADENA as It Is Today from a Business Standpoint. (Cover title.) 32 pp., printed wrappers. No place, no date (Pasadena, Calif., 1886). $80 (A, 1968).

PASADENA, California, Illustrated. Plates. 45 pp., pictorial wrappers. Pasadena, 1886. $70 (A, 1968).

PASADENA, Los Angeles County, Southern California. 36 pp., wrappers. Los Angeles, 1898. $35-$50.

PASQUIN, Peter. *A Day's Journal of a Sponge.* 6 plates. Wrappers. London, 1824. (By M. Egerton.) $100.

PASSION-Flowers. Cloth. Boston, 1854. (By Julia Ward Howe.) $25-$50. Author's first book.

PASTERNAK, Boris. *The Collected Prose Works of Boris Pasternak.* 10 illustrations. Cloth. London, no date (1945). First edition. In dust jacket. $25.

PASTERNAK, Boris. *Selected Poems.* Cloth. London, 1946. First edition. In dust jacket. $25.

PASTIME of Learning (The), with Sketches of Rural Scenes. 4 colored botanical plates. Boards. Boston, 1831. First edition. $35-$50.

PATCHEN, Kenneth. *Before the Brave.* Red cloth. New York, no date (1936). First edition. In dust jacket. $50-$75. Author's first book.

PATCHEN, Kenneth. *The Dark Kingdom.* Wrappers, painted by the author. New York, no date (1942). First edition. One of 75 signed. Boxed. $150. Trade edition: Cloth. In dust jacket. $25-$30.

PATCHEN, Kenneth. *Fables and Other Little Tales.* Boards and cloth, paper labels. Karlsruhe, Germany, 1953. First edition. One of 50 with covers hand-painted by Patchen, signed. $200-$300.

PATCHEN, Kenneth. *The Famous Boating Party.* Boards and cloth. No place, no date (New York, 1954). First edition. One of 50 with covers hand-painted by Patchen and with limitation in Patchen's hand, signed. $150-$200.

PATCHEN, Kenneth. *First Will.* Cloth. No place, no date (New York, 1948). First edition. One of 126 signed. In dust jacket. $60-$80.

PATCHEN, Kenneth. *Glory Never Guesses.* Silk-screened poems on Japanese papers, some leaves hand-colored by Patchen, in portfolio wrappers. No place, no date (1955). First edition. One of 200. $150-$200.

PATCHEN, Kenneth. *Hurrah for Anything.* Illustrated. Boards. Highlands, N.C., 1957. First edition. One of 100. $150.

PATCHEN, Kenneth. *The Journal of Albion Moonlight.* Boards and cloth. No place, no date (Mount Vernon, N.Y., 1941). First edition. One of 50 signed. Boxed. $100-$125.

PATCHEN, Kenneth. *The Moment.* Hand-painted and -lettered by the author. Woven boards, vellum spine. No place, no date (1955). First edition. One of 47. $50-$100. Another edition: No place, no date (Alhambra, Calif., 1960). Folio, vellum and cloth. One of 42 signed. $150.

PATCHEN, Kenneth. *Orchards, Thrones and Caravans.* Boards. No place, no date (San Francisco, 1952). First edition. "Vellum edition." One of 170 signed. $100-$150. Another issue: Boards. One of 90. "Engraver's edition," with cover engraving by David Ruff, signed by Patchen and Ruff. $150.

PATCHEN, Kenneth. *Panels for the Walls of Heaven.* Boards. No place (Berkeley, Calif.), 1946. First edition. One of 150 with covers hand-painted by author and with limitation notice in Patchen's hand, signed. $100-$150. Another issue: Boards, with different design. One of 150. $100-$150. Also, $50 (A, 1970). Another issue: Also different. One of 150. $100-$150.

PATCHEN, Kenneth. *Poem-Scapes.* Hand-painted boards. Highlands, 1958. First edition. One of 75 signed. $150. Another (?) issue: One of 42 signed and including a handwritten poem. $75-$150. Trade edition: Stiff wrappers. $7.50-$10.

PATCHEN, Kenneth. *Red Wine and Yellow Hair.* Boards and cloth. New York, no date (1949). First edition. One of 108 with covers hand-painted by author and with limitation notice in Patchen's hand, signed. $75-$125. Another issue: One of 108 with different design on cover. $75-$125. Trade edition: Cloth. In dust jacket. $25.

PATCHEN, Kenneth. *Sleepers Awake.* Red cloth. No place, no date (New York, 1946). First (black paper) edition. One of 148 signed. $50-$75. Another issue: White cloth, with original decoration on cover by the author. One of 75 signed. In dust jacket. $100-$125.

PATCHEN, Kenneth. *A Surprise for the Bagpipe Players.* Silk-screened poems on Japanese papers, some leaves hand-colored by Patchen, in portfolio wrappers. No place, no date (1955). First edition. One of 200. $100-$125.

PATCHEN, Kenneth. *When We Were Here Together.* Boards. No place, no date (New York, 1967). First edition. One of 75 with hand-painted covers by author, signed. $100-$125.

PATER, Walter. *Appreciations, with An Essay on Style.* Cloth. London, 1889. First edition. $25-$35.

PATER, Walter. *Essays from "The Guardian."* Boards. London, 1896. Chiswick Press. First edition. One of 100. $25-$35.

PATER, Walter. *An Imaginary Portrait.* Wrappers. London, 1894. Daniel Press. One of 250. $25.

PATER, Walter. *Imaginary Portraits.* Cloth. London, 1887. First edition. $25.

PATER, Walter. *Marius the Epicurean.* 2 vols., cloth. London, 1885. First edition. $50-$60. London, 1929. Illustrated. 2 vols., half vellum. One of 325. $25-$35.

PATER, Walter. *Plato and Platonism: A Series of Lectures.* Cloth. New York, 1893. First American edition. One of 100. $25-$35.

PATER, Walter. *Sebastian Van Storck.* 8 colored plates. Cloth. London, 1927. Limited edition. $35-$50.

PATER, Walter. *Studies in the History of the Renaissance.* Dark-green cloth. London, 1873. First edition. $50-$75. Author's first book.

PATHFINDER (The); or, The Inland Sea. By the Author of "The Pioneers." 3 vols., boards and cloth, paper labels. London, 1840. (By James Fenimore Cooper.) First edition. $200-$300. Philadelphia, 1840. 2 vols., green or purple cloth, paper labels. First American edition, first issue, without copyright notice in Vol. 1 and with printer's imprint at about center of page 2. $150-$250. New York, 1965. Limited Editions Club. Color plates. Buckram. Boxed. $25.

PATMORE, Coventry. See *The Angel in the House; Odes.*

PATMORE, Coventry. *Faithful For Ever.* Cloth. London, 1860. First edition. $25.

PATMORE, Coventry. *Poems.* Cloth. London, 1844. First edition. $50. Author's first book.

PATTERSON, A. W. *History of the Backwoods; or, The Region of the Ohio.* Folding map. Cloth. Pittsburgh, 1843. First edition. $350-$500.

PATTERSON, Lawson B. *Twelve Years in the Mines of California.* Cloth. Cambridge, Mass., 1862. First edition. $50-$75.

PATTERSON, Samuel. *Narrative of the Adventures and Sufferings of Samuel Patterson.* Boards. Rhode Island, 1817. First edition. $100-$150. Palmer, Mass., 1817. Contemporary sheep. Second edition. $110 (A, 1969). (Note: Ghostwritten by Ezekiel Terry.)

PATTIE, James O. *The Personal Narrative of James O. Pattie, of Kentucky.* Edited by Timothy Flint. 5 plates. Mottled calf. Cincinnati, 1831. First edition, first issue, published by John H. Wood. $3,900 (A, 1968), $2,300 (A, 1963). Cincinnati, 1833. Second issue (reissue of the 1831 sheets with new title page). $500-$800.

PATTON, The Rev. W. W., and Isham, R. N. *U. S. Sanitary Commission, No. 38: Report on the Condition of Camps and Hospitals at Cairo . . . Paducah and St. Louis.* 12 pp., stitched. Chicago, 1861. First edition. $50-$60.

PAUL, Elliott, and Allen, Jay. *All the Brave.* Illustrated by Luis Quintinalla. Preface by Ernest Hemingway. Pictorial wrappers. New York, no date (1939). First edition. $25-$35.

PAUL, William. *The Rose Garden.* 15 color plates. Cloth. London, 1848. First edition. $125-$150.

PAULDING, James Kirke. See Langstaff, Launcelot. Also see *A Christmas Gift from Fairy-Land; Chronicles of the City of Gotham; The Dutchman's Fireside; John Bull in America; Letters from the South; The Merry Tales of the Three Wise Men of Gotham; A Sketch of Old England.*

PAULDING, James Kirke. *The Backwoodsman: A Poem.* Boards. Philadelphia, 1818. First edition. $100-$125.

PAULINE: A Fragment of a Confession. Gray or brown boards, paper label. London, 1833. (By Robert Browning.) First edition. $16,000 (A, 1929–the Jerome Kern copy). Author's first book—and the rarest of them all. London, 1886. Edited by Thomas J. Wise. Boards. One of 400. $50. Another issue: One of 25 on large paper. $100-$150.

PAULISON, C. M. K. *Arizona: The Wonderful Country.* 31 pp., printed wrappers. Tucson, Ariz., 1881. First edition. $1,800 (A, 1966).

PAYNE, John Howard. *Clari; or, The Maid of Milan; An Opera, in Three Acts.* Stitched, old paper wrappers. London, 1823. First edition. $500 and up. (Note: This work contains on page 8 the first printing of Payne's "Home! Sweet Home!")

PAYNE, John Howard, and Bishop, Henry R. *Home! Sweet Home! Sung by Miss M. Tree, in Clari.* 4 pp., folio, sheet music. London, no date (1823). First separate edition. $200-$300.

PEABODY, Joel R. *A World of Wonders.* Cloth. Boston, 1838. First edition. $25.

PEACH Orchard (The). Woodcuts. 24 pp., self-wrappers. Northampton, Mass., 1839. $25.

PEACE River: A Canoe Voyage from Hudson's Bay to the Pacific. Folding map, errata slip. Printed wrappers. Ottawa, 1872. (By Archibald McDonald.) First edition. $225.

PEACOCK, Francis. *Sketches Relative to the History and Theory, but More Especially to the Practice of Dancing.* Boards. Aberdeen, Scotland, 1805. First edition. $100.

PEACOCK, Thomas Love. See *Crotchet Castle; Gryll Grange; Headlong Hall; Maid Marian; Melincourt; The Misfortunes of Elphin; Nightmare Abbey; Rhododaphne.*

PEACOCK, Thomas Love. *The Genius of the Thames.* Boards. London, 1810. First edition. $150-$200.

PEACOCK, Thomas Love. *Palmyra and Other Poems.* Frontispiece. Boards. London, 1806. First edition. $200-$250.

PEACOCK, Thomas Love. *The Philosophy of Melancholy: A Poem in Four Parts.* Boards. London, 1812. First edition. $200-$250.

PEALE, Rembrandt. *Peale's Court of Death.* Wrappers. New York, 1820. First edition. $30.

PEARCE, Dutee. *Explore the Pacific Ocean.* 43 pp., sewed. Washington, 1835. $35-$50.

PEARSE, James. *A Narrative of the Life of James Pearse.* Boards and Leather. Rutland, Vt., 1825. First edition. $125-$150.

PEARSON, Edmund L. *The Voyage of the Hoppergrass.* Illustrated by Thomas Fogarty. Pictorial cloth. New York, 1913. First edition. In dust jacket. $50-$75. Worn, lacking jacket, $40.

PEARSON, Jonathan, and others. *The History of the Schenectady Patent.* 28 maps and plates. Albany, N.Y., 1883. Second edition. One of 300. $50-$75. Another issue: One of 50 on large paper. $100-$125.

PEATTIE, Donald Culross. *An Almanac for Moderns.* Lynd Ward illustrations. Cloth. New York, no date (1935). First edition. In dust jacket. $25-$35. Lacking jacket, $10. New York, 1938. Limited Editions Club. Illustrated. Cloth. $25.

PEATTIE, Donald Culross. *Audubon's America.* Color plates and other illustrations. Cloth. Boston, 1940. First edition. In dust jacket. $25 and $15. Another issue: Limited edition, with an extra set of color plates. $50.

PEATTIE, Donald Culross. *A Book of Hours.* Decorations by Lynd Ward. Buckram. New York, 1937. First edition. Limited, signed issue on all-rag paper. $50. Trade edition: Cloth. In dust jacket. $10.

PEATTIE, Elia W. *How Jacques Came into the Forest of Arden.* Illustrated. Boards. Chicago, no date (1901). Blue Sky Press. One of 25 on vellum. $25. Another issue: Tan morocco. One of 3. Boxed. $85.

PECK, George Wilbur. *Peck's Bad Boy and His Pa.* Wrappers, or cloth. Chicago, 1883. First edition, first issue, with the text ending on page 196, the last word in perfect type, and with the printer's rules on the copyright page 7/8 inch apart. Wrappers: $100-$150. Cloth: $50-$75. Later issues, same date, wrappers or cloth. $20-$25.

PECK, John M. *A Discourse in Reference to the Decease of the Late Governor of Illinois, Ninian Edwards.* 20 pp., printed wrappers. Rock Spring, Ill., 1834. First edition. $650 (A, 1967).

PECK, John M. *A Gazetteer of Illinois.* Cloth. Jacksonville, Ill., 1834. First edition. $50-$75.

PECK, John M. *A Guide for Emigrants, Containing Sketches of Illinois, Missouri, and the Adjacent Parts.* Map. Cloth. Boston, 1831. First edition. $35.

PECK, John M. *A New Guide for Emigrants to the West.* Map. Cloth. Boston, 1836. Enlarged edition. $50-$60.

PEEK, Peter V. *Inklings of Adventure in the Campaigns of the Florida Indian War.* (Cover title.) 72 pp., double columns, printed yellow wrappers. Schenectady, N.Y., 1846. First edition. $2,300 (A, 1967). Schenectady, 1860. Pictorial wrappers. $350. (Note: Catalogued by a New York dealer in the 1950's as, "so far as we can trace, the only known copy." The same dealer had sold the first edition copy noted above in 1936.)

PEET, Frederick T. *Civil War Letters and Documents of Frederick T. Peet.* Boards. Newport, R.I., 1915. First edition. One of 50. $75.

PEET, Frederick T. *Personal Experiences in the Civil War.* Boards. New York, 1905. First edition. One of 50. $75. Another copy, signed, $35.

PELAYO: A Story of the Goth. 2 vols., cloth, paper labels. New York, 1838. (By William Gilmore Simms.) First edition. $50-$100.

PELHAM. 3 vols., boards. London, 1828. (By Edward Bulwer-Lytton.) First edition, with ad leaf in Vol. 3. $50-$60.

PEN Knife Sketches; Or, Chips of the Old Block. 24 full-page illustrations. Half leather. Sacramento, Calif., 1853. (By Alonzo Delano.) First edition. $250-$350. (For a modern reprint, see entry under author's name.)

PENDENNIS, Arthur (editor). *The Newcomes.* Illustrated by Richard Doyle. 23 parts in 24, yellow wrappers. London, 1853-55. (By William Makepeace Thackeray.) First edition. $150-$300. London, 1855. 2 vols., cloth. First book edition. $25-$35.

PENDLETON, Nathanial Greene. *Military Posts—Council Bluffs to the Pacific Ocean.* (Caption title.) Folding map. Three-quarters morocco. No place, no date (Washington, 1843). $50-$75.

PENN, William (pseudonym). *Essays on the Present Crisis in the Present Condition of the . . . Indians.* Stitched. Boston, 1829. (By Jeremiah Evarts.) First edition. $50. Philadelphia, 1830. Stitched. $25.

PENNELL, Joseph. *The Glory of New York.* 24 color reproductions. Boards. New York, 1926. One of 350 designed by Bruce Rogers. In dust jacket. Boxed. $50-$75.

PENROSE, Charles W. *"Mormon" Doctrine, Plain and Simple.* Cloth. Salt Lake City, 1882. First edition. $30.

PENTLAND Rising (The). Green wrappers. Edinburgh, 1866. (By Robert Louis Stevenson.) First edition. $200-$500. (Note: In the 1930's auction sales of $800 and $875 were recorded for this rare work, Stevenson's first book. The Jerome Kern copy brought $825 in 1929.)

"PEOPLE'S Reville" (The): Souvenir Hill City, Graham County, Kansas. (Cover title.) 112 pp., wrappers. Topeka, 1906. $30.

PEPPER, Capt. George W. *Personal Recollections of Sherman's Campaigns in Georgia and the Carolinas.* Cloth. Zanesville, Ohio, 1866. First edition. $100-$150.

PEPYS, Samuel. *Memoirs . . . Comprising His Diary from 1659 to 1669.* Edited by Richard, Lord Braybrooke. Portraits, views and facsimiles. 2 vols., boards, paper labels. London, 1825. First edition. $1,000 and up for fine sets. Others less fine in original binding bring appreciably less, as do rebound sets. The highest modern auction record for a fine set was recorded in the 1948 season, when an uncut and unopened copy brought $1,800. In recent years the top auction price has been $392, obtained in 1963 for a copy with one label defective. London, 1828. 5 vols., boards. Second (and first octavo) edition. $100-$150. New York, 1942. Limited Editions Club. Illustrated. 10 vols., pictorial boards and buckram. $100-$125. (Note: There have been numerous other editions of the Pepys diary, most of them multivolume versions. See the British and American book auction records for detailed listings.)

PERCIVAL Keene. 3 vols., boards. London, 1842. (By Frederic Marryat.) First edition. $100-$150.

PERCY, Stephen. *Robin Hood and His Merry Foresters.* 8 full-page hand-colored illustrations. Cloth. New York, 1855. (By Joseph Cundall.) $35-$50.

PERELMAN, S. J. *Dawn Ginsbergh's Revenge.* Apple-green "plush" binding. (Second issue had silver cloth.) New York, no date (1929). First edition. In dust jacket. $100-$125.

PEREZ DE LUXAN, Diego. *Expedition into New Mexico Made by Antonio de Espejo, 1582-1583.* Translated by George Peter Hammond and Agapito Rey. Half vellum. Los Angeles, 1929. One of 50. $100-$125. Another issue: Boards. One of 500. $50-$60.

PERICLES and Aspasia. 2 vols., drab boards, blue-green cloth, paper labels. London, 1836. (By Walter Savage Landor.) First edition. $100. London, 1903. Half pigskin. One of 220. $25-$35. New York, 1903. Folio, boards. One of 210. $30.

PERILS of the Oceans, or Disasters of the Sea. Woodcuts. 72 pp., pictorial boards. New York, no date (about 1840). $50.

PERKINS, Charles Elliott. *The Pinto Horse.* Illustrated by Edward Borein. Pictorial boards. Santa Barbara, Calif., 1927. First edition. In dust jacket. $35-$50.

PERKINS, P. D. and Ione. *Lafcadio Hearn.* 6 plates. Cloth. Boston, 1934. Boxed. $75-$100.

PERRY, Oliver Hazard. *Hunting Expeditions of Oliver Hazard Perry.* 3 plates. Cloth. Cleveland, 1899. First edition. One of 100. $300-$400.

PERRY, William S. *History of the American Episcopal Church, 1587-1883.* 2 vols., half calf. Boston, 1885. $50-$60.

PERSE, St. J. *Anabasis.* Translated by T. S. Eliot. Blue-green cloth. London, 1930. (By Alexis St. Leger Leger.) First edition in English. In white dust jacket. $35-$50. Another issue: Green cloth. One of 350 signed by Eliot. In cellophane dust jacket. Boxed. $200-$250. Second trade issue, 1930 (actually 1937): Green boards. In green dust jacket. $35-$50. New York, no date (1949). Gray boards. First American edition (so stated). In dust jacket. $35-$50. London, no date (1959). Plum cloth. Revised edition. In gray dust jacket. $25-$35.

PERSONAL Reminiscences of a Maryland Soldier. Cloth. Baltimore, 1898. (By G. W. Booth.) First edition. $50. Signed, $75.

PETER Parley's Tales About Great Britain, Including England, Wales, Scotland. Folding map. Cloth. Baltimore, 1832. (By Samuel G. Goodrich.) $35.

PETER Parley's Universal History. Maps and engravings. 2 vols., black cloth. Boston, 1837. (Compiled by Nathaniel Hawthorne and his sister Elizabeth.) First edition, with "Great Tree" design in gilt on covers. $1,560 and up.

PETER Pilgrim; or a Rambler's Recollections. 2 vols., green or purple muslin, paper labels. Philadelphia, 1838. (By Robert Montgomery Bird.) First edition. $100-$150.

PETERS, DeWitt C. *Kit Carson's Life.* Illustrated. Cloth. Hartford, 1874. $75-$100. Also, $50 (A, 1968). Hartford, 1875. Cloth. $25-$35. London, no date (about 1875). Cloth. $25-$35. (Note: This is an enlarged version of the title following.)

PETERS, DeWitt C. *The Life and Adventures of Kit Carson, the Nestor of the Rocky Mountains.* 10 plates. Cloth. New York, 1858. First edition. $75-$100. New York, 1859. Cloth. $25.

PETERS, Fred J. *Railroad, Indian and Pioneer Prints by N. Currier and Currier and Ives. Clipper Ship Prints. Sporting Prints.* Illustrated. 3 vols., cloth. New York, 1930. Limited editions. Boxed. Together, $75-$100.

PETERS, Harry T. *America on Stone: A Chronicle of American Lithography.* 154 plates (18 in color). Cloth. Garden City, N.Y. 1931. First edition. One of 751. Boxed. $300-$400.

PETERS, Harry T. *California on Stone.* 112 plates. Cloth. Garden City, 1935. First edition. One of 501. In dust jacket. Boxed. $150-$200.

PETERS, Harry T. *Currier and Ives, Printmakers to the American People.* 300 reproductions (including color). 2 vols., cloth. Garden City, 1929-31. First edition. One of 50l. Boxed. $300-$400. Garden City, 1942. Cloth. Special edition in one volume. In dust jacket. $35-$50.

PETERS, William E. *Ohio Lands and Their History.* Cloth. Athens, Ohio, 1930. Third edition. $25-$35.

PETERS, William E. *Ohio Lands and Their Subdivision.* Folding map in pocket. Cloth. No place (Athens, Ohio), 1918. Second edition. $35.

PETERSEN, William J. *Steamboating on the Upper Mississippi.* Decorated cloth. Iowa City, 1937. First edition. $60-$80.

PETIT, Veronique. *Plural Marriage: The Heart-History of Adele Hersch.* 99 pp., wrappers. Ithaca, N.Y., 1885. $35.

PETITION of the Latter-Day Saints, Commonly Known as Mormons (The). (Caption title.) 13 pp., sewed. Washington, 1840. (By Elias Higbee, Robert B. Thompson, and others.) $50-$75.

PETTER, Rodolphe. *English-Cheyenne Dictionary.* Folio, full black calf. Kettle Falls, Wash., 1913-15. First edition. One of 100. $150.

PHAIR, Charles. *Atlantic Salmon Fishing.* Edited by Richard C. Hunt. Illustrated. Folio, cloth. New York, no date (1937). Derrydale Press. One of 950. In dust jacket. $200-$250. Another issue: Half morocco. One of 40 signed, with examples of 200 flies. $1,000.

PHELPS and Ensign (publishers). *Traveller's Guide Through the United States, Containing Stage, Steamboat, Canal and Rail-road Routes, with the Distances from Place to Place.* Folding map. Leather. New York, 1838. First edition. $35-$50. Other similar *Traveller's Guides,* same publishers: 1840, $40; 1850, $30; 1851, $35.

PHELPS, Noah A. *A History of the Copper Mines and Newgate Prison, at Granby, Conn.* 34 pp., wrappers. Hartford, 1845. $75.

PHILBY, H. St. J. B. *A Pilgrim in Arabia.* Portrait. Buckram, leather spine. London, 1943. Golden Cockerel Press. One of 350. $100-$125.

PHILIP Dru, Administrator. Cloth. New York, 1919. (By Col. E. M. House.) First edition. In dust jacket. $75. Lacking jacket, $35-$50.

PHILLIPS, D. L. *Letters from California.* Cloth. Springfield, Ill., 1877. First edition. $25-$35.

PHILLIPS, J. V. *Report on the Geology of the Mineral Districts Contiguous to the Iron Mountain Railroad.* 14 pp., printed wrappers. St. Louis, 1859. $35.

PHILLIPS, Philip A. S. *Paul de Lamerie, Citizen and Goldsmith of London.* Illustrated. Folio, cloth. London, 1935. One of 250. $500-$600.

PHILLIPS, R. *Modern London.* Folding frontispiece, folding map, 31 colored "Cries of London" with gray borders. Half calf. London, 1804. $100-$150.

PHILLPOTTS, Eden. See *The Ghost in the Bank of England.*

PHILLPOTTS, Eden. *Children of the Mist.* Frontispiece. Blue cloth. London, 1898. First edition. $100-$150.

PHILLPOTTS, Eden. *A Dish of Apples.* Illustrations, including color, by Arthur Rackham. White cloth. London, no date (1921). One of 500 signed. $75-$100. Another issue: One of 55 on Batchelor's Kelmscott paper. $100-$150.

PHILLPOTTS, Eden. *The Girl and the Faun.* Illustrated by Frank Brangwyn. Half vellum. London, 1916. One of 350 signed. $25-$35.

PHILLPOTTS, Eden. *My Adventure in the Flying Scotsman.* Stiff wrappers (boards). London, 1888. First edition. $75-$100. Author's first book.

PHOTOGRAPHIC Sketch Book of the War. 100 gold-toned albumen prints, with leaf of text for each. 2 vols., oblong folio, morocco. Washington, no date (1865-66). (By Alexander Gardner.) First edition. $5,000 and up. Also, $5,200 (A, 1970); $850 and $1,350 (A, 1968); $525 (A, 1963). (Note: The dramatically sharp rise in value for this book reflects the recent upsurge of interest in all early photographic items.)

PHYLOS. *The Tibetan, an Earth Dweller's Return.* Cloth. Milwaukee, 1940. In dust jacket. $25.

PICKETT, Albert James. *History of Alabama, and Incidentally of Georgia and Mississippi.* Map, 3 plans, 8 plates. 2 vols., cloth. Charleston, S.C., 1851. First edition. $100-$150. Second edition, same place and date. $75-$100.

PICKETT, Albert James. *Invasion of the Territory of Alabama, by 1,000 Spaniards, Under Ferdinand de Soto, in 1540.* 41 pp., wrappers. Montgomery, Ala., 1849. First edition. $100-$150.

PICTORIAL View of California (A). By a Returned Californian. 48 plates. Cloth. New York, 1853. (By J. M. Letts.) Later edition of *California Illustrated.* $150-$200.

PICTURESQUE Tourist (The); Being a Guide Through the Northern and Eastern States and Canada. Edited by O. L. Holley. Maps, illustrations. New York, 1844. $25.

PIERCE, N. H., and Brown, Nugent E. (compilers). *The Free State of Menard.* Illustrated. Pictorial cloth. Menard, Tex., 1946. First edition. $35-$50.

PIERPOINT, John. *The Portrait: A Poem.* Printed wrappers. Boston, 1812. $25. Author's first book.

PIERSON, B. T. *Directory of the City of Newark for 1838-9.* Printed boards. Newark, N.J., 1838. One of 500. $50-$75.

PIGAFETTA, Antonio. *Magellan's Voyage Around the World.* Translated by James A. Robertson. Portrait, maps, facsimiles. 3 vols., cloth. Cleveland, 1906. One of 350. $100-$125.

PIGMAN, Walter Griffith. *Journal.* Edited by Ulla Staley Fawkes. Boards. Mexico, Mo., 1942. First edition. One of 200. $35-$50.

PIGS Is Pigs. Decorated oyster-white wrappers. Chicago, 1905. Railways Appliances Company. (By Ellis Parker Butler.) First edition. $150 and up. (Note: Author's name appears only on decoration at first text page.)

PIKE, Albert. *Prose Sketches and Poems, Written in the Western Country.* Brown cloth, leather label. Boston, 1834. First edition. $400- $500. Rebound in half leather, $350.

PIKE County Puzzle, Vol. 1, No. 1. 4 pp. (Burlesque of country newspaper.) Camp Interlaken, Pa., 1894. (By Stephen Crane.) $100-$150.

PIKE, James. *The Scout and Ranger.* Portrait, 24 plates. Black cloth. Cincinnati, 1865. First edition, first issue, with errata leaf and uncorrected errors. $350.

PIKE, Z. M. *An Account of Expeditions to the Sources of the Mississippi.* Portrait, 4 maps, 2 charts, 3 tables. 2 vols., boards. Philadelphia, 1810. First edition. $400-$500. Another issue: Maps in separate cloth atlas-folder. $500-$600.

PIKE, Z. M. *An Account of a Voyage up the Mississippi River.* Map. 68 pp., stitched, plain wrappers. No place, no date (Washington, 1807?). (By Nicholas King from Pike's notes?) First edition. $1,100 (A, 1967).

PIKE, Z. M. *Exploratory Travels Through the Western Territories of North America.* 2 maps. Boards. London, 1811. First English edition (of *An Account of Expeditions to the Sources of the Mississippi*). $300-$400. Also, rebound in half calf, cover frayed, $125.

PILCHER, Joshua. *Report on the Fur Trade and Inland Trade to Mexico.* Cloth. Washington, 1832. First edition. $75-$100.

PILGRIM, Thomas. See *Live Boys.*

PILKINGTON, Mary. *Mentorial Tales, for the Instruction of Young Ladies Just Leaving School and Entering upon the Theater of Life.* Contemporary calf. Philadelphia, 1811. $30.

PILOT (The): A Tale of the Sea. By the Author of *The Pioneers.* 2 vols., blue boards, paper labels. New York, 1823. (By James Fenimore Cooper.) First edition. $150-$250. London, 1824. 3 vols., boards. First English edition. $75-$100.

PILOT Knob. Mendota. Map, portrait, and plates. 23 pp., pictorial wrappers. No place, no date (St. Paul, Minn., 1887). (By Gen. H. H. Sibley.) First edition. $50-$75.

PINDAR. *Odes of Victory.* Translated by C. J. Billson. 90 wood engravings by John Farleigh. 2 vols., limp vellum with ties, lettered in gold on front covers and spines. Oxford, England, 1928-30. Shakespeare Head Press. One of 7 printed on vellum. Boxed. $400-$500. Another issue: 2 vols., half cloth. One of 250. $25.

PINKERTON, A. F. *Jim Cummins: or, The Great Adams Express Robbery.* Illustrated. Pictorial cloth. Chicago, 1887. First edition. $30-$35.

PINKERTON, Allan. *The Detective and the Somnambulist.* Frontispiece. Cloth. Chicago, 1875. First edition, first state, with no mention of this book in ads. $25.

PINKERTON, Allan. *The Expressman and the Detective.* Cloth. Chicago, 1874. First edition. $25-$35.

PINKERTON, Allan. *The Spy of the Rebellion.* Illustrated. Cloth. New York, 1883. First edition. $35-$50. Kansas City, 1883. Cloth. $25. Hartford, 1884. Cloth. $25. Hartford, 1885. Cloth. $25.

PINKERTON, Allan. *Tests on Passenger Conductors.* 35 pp., wrappers. Chicago, 1867. First edition. $150. Author's first book.

PINKERTON, William A. *Train Robberies, Train Robbers, and "Hold-up" Men.* Illustrated. Wrappers. Chicago, 1907. $65. (Note: Adams, in *Six-Guns and Saddle Leather,* lists an undated edition without locating place of publication.)

PINTER, Harold. *Five Screen Plays.* Cloth. London, 1971. One of 150 signed copies. $30-$35.

PINTER, Harold. *Old Times.* Cloth. London, 1971. One of 150 signed copies. $15-$20.

PIONEERING on the Plains. Journey to Mexico in 1848. The Overland Trip to California. (Cover title.) Illustrated. 119 pp., wrappers. No place, no date (Kaukauna, Wis., 1924). (By Alexander W. McCoy and others.) First edition. $100-$150.

PIONEERS (The): or, The Sources of the Susquehanna: A Descriptive Tale. By the Author of "Precaution." 2 vols., tan boards, paper labels. New York, 1823. (By James Fenimore Cooper.) First edition, first issue, with E. B. Clayton imprint in Vol. 1 and with folio 329 at left side of page in Vol. 2. $200-$300. Second issue. $100-$150. London, 1823. 3 vols., boards. First English edition. $100-$150.

PIOZZI, Hester Lynch. *Piozzi Marginalia.* Edited by Percival Merritt. Boards and cloth. Cambridge, England, 1925. One of 75. $30.

PITCHER, M. *Witchcraft, or The Act of Fortune-Telling.* Boards. Boston, 1805. $35-$40.

PITMAN, Benn (reporter). *The Assassination of President Lincoln and the Trial of the Conspirators.* Illustrated. Cloth. Cincinnati, 1865. First edition. $35-$50. Signed copy, $100.

PITMAN, Benn (reporter). *The Trials for Treason at Indianapolis.* Illustrated. Cloth. Cincinnati, 1865. First edition. $25-$35.

PITTSBURGH Business Directory. Cloth, paper label. Pittsburgh, 1837. (By Isaac Harris.) With errata leaf. $35-$50.

PIUS XI on Christian Marriage. Latin and English. Portrait frontispiece. Three-quarters red morocco and boards. New York, 1931. One of 1,000 printed by D. B. Updike. $35-$50.

"PLAIN or Ringlets? " 13 colored plates. Other illustrations by John Leech. 13 parts in 12, wrappers. London, 1859-60. (By Robert Smith Surtees.) First edition. $250-$350. London, 1860. John Leech illustrations, including pictorial title page. Pictorial cloth. First book edition. $75-$100.

PLAIN Speaker (The): Opinions on Books, Men, And Things. 2 vols., boards, paper labels. (By William Hazlitt.) First collected edition. $50-$75.

PLATH, Sylvia. See Lucas, Victoria.

PLATH, Sylvia. *Ariel.* Cloth. London, no date (1965). First edition. In dust jacket. $25-$30. New York, no date (1966). Cloth. First American edition. In dust jacket. $15-$20.

PLATH, Sylvia. *The Colossus and Other Poems.* Cloth. London, no date (1960). First edition. In dust jacket. $45. New York, 1962. Cloth. First American edition. In dust jacket. $15-$25.

PLATH, Sylvia. *Crystal Gazer and Other Poems.* Buckram and boards. London, 1971. Rainbow Press. Limited edition of 400 copies. In slipcase. $65-$75.

PLATH, Sylvia. *Lyonesse.* Leather and boards. London, 1971. Rainbow Press. Limited edition of 300 copies. In slipcase. $40-$50.

PLATH, Sylvia. *Three Women: A Monologue for Three Voices.* Illustrated. White cloth. London, 1968. First edition. One of 150 numbered copies (of an edition of 185). $50-$60. Another issue: One of 5 on handmade paper. $100.

PLATH, Sylvia. *Uncollected Poems.* Facsimile. Wrappers. London, no date (1965). Turret Books. First edition. One of 150. $75-$100.

PLATO. *The Phaedo of Plato.* Translated by William Jowett. Title and initials in red. Buckram. Waltham Saint Lawrence, England, 1930. Golden Cockerel Press. With letter laid in calling attention to error of translator's name as William instead of Benjamin. $50.

PLATO. *Plato's Symposium, or Supper Newly Translated into English.* Introduction by Shane Leslie. 4 etchings by Jean de Bosschere. Cloth. London, no date. Fortune Press. One of 500. In dust jacket. $25.

PLATT, P. L., and Slater, N. *The Travelers' Guide Across the Plains, upon the Overland Route to California.* Folding map. 64 pp., printed yellow wrappers. Chicago, 1852. First edition. $5,000 and up. (Note: Only one perfect copy is known—in the Newberry Library, Chicago—and the only other complete copy lacks part of the map. Both copies were found through my syndicated column "Gold in Your Attic," published from 1957 to 1971. The Streeter copy, the only one known prior to these discoveries, lacked the first 16 pages, including the title page, and the bibliographer Wright Howes had guessed—incorrectly in both instances—that it was published in "English Prairie, Ill.," as suggested by the map, in 1854.) San Francisco, 1963. Edited by Dale Morgan. Illustrated. Black boards, orange cloth spine. Second edition. In acetate dust jacket. $35-$40.

PLEASANTS, J. Hall, and Sill, Howard. *Maryland Silversmiths, 1715-1830.* Illustrated. Half cloth. Baltimore, 1930. One of 300. $150-$200.

PLEASANTS, W. J. *Twice Across the Plains, 1849-1856.* 10 plates, 2 portraits. Pictorial green cloth. San Francisco, 1906. First edition. $350-$500. Also, $300 (A, 1968), $375 (A, 1966).

PLIMPTON, Florus B. *The Lost Child.* (Cover title.) 79 pp., wrappers. Cleveland, 1852. First edition. $200-$300.

PLUMBE, John, Jr. *Sketches of Iowa and Wisconsin.* Folding map on thin paper. 103 pp., printed wrappers. St. Louis, 1839. First edition. $1,250- $1,500.

POCAHONTAS. By a Citizen of the West. Boards. New York, 1837. (By Robert Dale Owen.) $35-$50.

POE, Edgar Allan. See *The Narrative of Arthur Gordon Pym; Tamerlane and Other Poems.*

POE, Edgar Allan, *Al Aaraaf, Tamerlane, and Minor Poems.* Blue or reddish-tan boards, ivory paper spine. Baltimore, 1829. First edition. (Some copies misdated 1820 on title page; a few also stitched, without covers.) $10,000 and up. Also, boards, $1,600 (A, 1954); $1,100 and $1,250 (A, 1947); stitched, $2,000 (A, 1954) and same copy, $3,100 (A, 1939); "first edition, early issue, bound with 5 others, half roan on marbled boards of circa 1840," $10,000 (A, 1968).

POE, Edgar Allan. *The Bells and Other Poems.* Illustrated by Edmund Dulac. Folio, decorated vellum with silk ties. London, no date (about 1912). Large paper, limited edition, signed by Dulac. $100-$150.

POE, Edgar Allan. *The Conchologist's First Book.* Illustrated. Printed pictorial boards, leather spine. Philadelphia, 1839. First edition, first state, with snail plates in color. $75-$100.

POE, Edgar Allan. *Eureka: A Prose Poem.* Black cloth. New York, 1848. First edition, with 12 or 16 pages of ads at end. $150. Also, $75 (A, 1969).

POE, Edgar Allan. *Histoires Extraordinaires.* Par Edgar Poe. Translated by Charles Baudelaire. Wrappers. Paris, 1856. First edition in French of Poe's *Tales.* $200-$250. Paris, 1857. (As *Nouvelles Histoires Extraordinaires.*) Wrappers. $150-$200. Rebound in half leather, $100. Paris, 1927-28. Etchings. 4 vols., morocco. One of 10 on Hollande paper. $500 (A, 1968).

POE, Edgar Allan. *Histoires Grotesques et Sérieuses.* Translated by Charles Baudelaire. Half leather. Paris, 1865. $50-$75.

POE, Edgar Allan. *The Journal of Julius Rodman.* Colored illustrations. Half cloth and boards. San Francisco, 1947. Grabhorn printing. One of 500. $40-$50.

POE, Edgar Allan. *La Chute de la Maison Usher.* Translated by Charles Baudelaire. Illustrated. Three-quarters morocco. Paris, 1922. One of 72 on Japan paper. $35-$50.

POE, Edgar Allan. *Mesmerism: "In Articulo Mortis."* 16 pp., stitched, without covers. London, 1846. First edition. $100-$150.

POE, Edgar Allan. *Murders in the Rue Morgue.* Facsimile of Drexel Institute manuscript. 2 water colors. Folio, half morocco. Philadelphia, no date (1895). $50. Also see Poe, *The Prose Romances.*

POE, Edgar Allan. *Poems.* Pale-green cloth. New York, 1831. Second edition (so identified on title page, but actually the first edition). Up to $10,000. Also, stained, binding detached, $6,250 (A, 1966); rebound in morocco, $1,000 (A, 1955). Brussels, 1888. Translated by Mallarmé. Illustrated by Manet. Wrappers. $100-$200. Rebound in half morocco, $100. Paris, 1889. Wrappers. $100-$200. Rebound in half morocco, $100. Brussels, 1897. Wrappers. One of 500. $100-$150. Rebound in half morocco. $100. New York, 1943. Limited Editions Club. Morocco. Boxed. $50.

POE, Edgar Allan. *The Prose Romances of Edgar A. Poe, etc. Uniform Serial Edition . . . No. 1. Containing The Murders in the Rue Morgue, and The Man That Was Used Up.* 40 pp., wrappers. Philadelphia, 1843. First edition. $25,000. Also see Poe, *Murders in the Rue Morgue.*

POE, Edgar, Allan. *The Raven and Other Poems.* Printed wrappers, or cloth. New York, 1845. First edition, first issue, with "T. B. Smith, Stereotyper" on copyright page. $1,500 and up. Also, front cover detached, $1,250 (A, 1969); lacking wrappers, $425 (A, 1963). London, 1846. Cloth. First English edition, with new title page tipped in over sheets of the American first. $200-$250. New York, 1884. Edited by E. C. Stedman. 26 plates. Pictorial cloth. $50-$75. Also, $32 (A, 1968). London, 1901. Vellum with ties. One of 50 on vellum. $50-$60. New York, 1906. Illustrated by Galen J. Perrett. Morocco. One of 26. $200-$250.

POE, Edgar Allan. *Tales.* Printed buff wrappers, or cloth. New York, 1845. First edition, first state, with T. B. Smith and H. Ludwig slugs on copyright page, 12 pp. of ads at back. $3,300. Later state, without Smith and Ludwig lines, rebound in cloth, $120 (A, 1963) and $100 (A, 1959).

POE, Edgar Allan. *Tales of the Grotesque and Arabesque.* 2 vols., purplish cloth, paper labels. Philadelphia, 1840. First edition, first issue, with page 213 in Vol. 2 wrongly numbered 231. $5,000 and up. Second issue, page 213 correctly numbered. $500. Another, label off Vol. 1, $337.50. Another issue: 2 vols. in one. Page 213 correctly numbered, 4 pages of ads bound in at end. Contemporary morocco. $5,000 (A, 1967). Chicago, 1930. Lakeside Press. Full morocco. One of 1,000. $150-$200.

POE, Edgar Allan. *Tales of Mystery and Imagination.* Illustrated by Harry Clarke. Pictorial vellum. London, 1919. One of 170 signed by Clarke. $100. Also, $55 (A, 1969). London, no date (1935). Illustrated by Arthur Rackham. Full pictorial vellum. One of 460 signed by Rackham. $175-$225. New York, 1941. Limited Editions Club. Illustrated. Buckram. Boxed. $50.

POE, Sophie A. *Buckboard Days.* Illustrated. Cloth. Caldwell, Idaho, 1936. First edition. In dust jacket. $35.

POEMS. Wrappers. No place, no date (London, 1906). Chiswick Press. (By Siegfried Sassoon.) First edition. $100-$150. Author's first book. London, no date (1911). Wrappers. One of 25 signed. $50-$100.

POEMS and Ballads of Young Ireland. White cloth. Dublin, 1888. First edition. $250-$300. (Note: Contains four contributions by William Butler Yeats.)

POEMS: A Chapter from the Modern Pilgrim's Progress. Cloth. No place (Philadelphia), 1882. (By Clara Jessup Moore.) First edition. $35-$40.

POEMS. By a Collegian. Cloth. Richmond, 1833. (By William Gilmore Simms?) First edition. $35-$50. Charlottesville, Va., 1833. $25-$35. (Note: Simms' authorship of this is in question.)

POEMS by Two Brothers. Drab boards, paper label. London, no date (1827). (By Alfred, Charles and Frederick Tennyson.) First edition. $250-$350. Alfred Tennyson's first book.

POEMS Chiefly in the Scottish Dialect. By a Native of Scotland. Contemporary calf. Washington, Pa., 1801. (By David Bruce.) First edition. $225. (Note: Contains original material also by H. H. Brackenridge.)

POEMS from the Arabic and Persian. Sewed. Warwick, England, 1800. (By Walter Savage Landor.) First edition, first issue, with "Rivington" in imprint and 10 leaves only. $200-$250. Also, in half morocco, $80 (A, 1966). Second issue, without "Rivington" in imprint, 12 leaves. $150-$200.

POEMS of Child Labor. Wrappers. New York, 1924. First edition. $50. (Note: Published by the National Child Labor Committee; includes a poem by Robert Frost.)

POEMS of Two Friends. Cloth. Columbus, Ohio, 1860. (By William Dean Howells and John J. Piatt.) First edition. $50-$60. Howells' first book.

POEMS on Various Occasions. Gray-green boards, pink label lettered "Poems." Newark (England), 1807. (By George Gordon Noel, Lord Byron.) First edition. $1,000 and up.

POET at the Breakfast Table (The). Cloth. Boston, 1872. (By Oliver Wendell Holmes.) First edition, first state, with "Talle" for "Table" in the running head on page 9. $35-$50.

POETRY by the Author of "Gebir." 111 pp., sewed. Warwick, no date (1800). (By Walter Savage Landor.) First (suppressed) edition, with pages 65-111, later suppressed, intact. $300-$400. London, 1802. Blue wrappers. First published edition, first issue, with Sharpe's imprint stamped by hand on page 64, where the text ends. $75-$100.

POETRY for Children, Entirely Original. Illustrated. 2 vols., green boards, red leather spines. London, 1809. (By Charles and Mary Lamb.) First edition. $1,000 and up. (Note: A very rare book, with auction records of $2,200 in 1900, $3,300 in 1920, and $375 in 1941. No copies have appeared for sale in many years.) Boston, 1812. Marble-backed boards. First American edition. $250-$500.

POLK, James K. *Message of the President of the United States in Relation to the Indian Difficulties in Oregon . . . March 29, 1848.* (Caption title.) No place, no date (Washington, 1848). $50-$75.

POLLARD, Alfred W. *An Essay on Colophons.* Folio, half vellum. Chicago, 1905. Caxton Club. One of 252. $75-$100.

POLLARD, Alfred W. *Fine Books.* Plates. Cloth. London, 1912. First edition. In dust jacket. $75-$100. New York, 1912. Plates. Cloth. First American edition. In dust jacket. $75.

POLLARD, Alfred W. *Last Words on the History of the Title-Page.* Colored frontispiece and facsimiles. Cloth. London, 1891. One of 260. $50-$75.

POLLARD, Alfred W. *Records of the English Bible.* Cloth. London, 1911. $75-$100.

POLLARD, Alfred W. *Shakespeare Folios and Quartos.* Illustrated. Boards. London, 1909. $100-$150.

POLLARD, Edward A. *The First Year of the War.* 374 pp., printed wrappers. Richmond, Va., 1862. First edition. $75-$100.

POLLARD, Edward A. *Observations in the North.* 142 pp., wrappers. Richmond, 1865. First edition. $75-$100.

POLLARD, Edward A. *The Seven Days' Battles in Front of Richmond.* 45 pp., printed wrappers. Richmond, 1862. First edition. $300.

POLLARD, Hugh B. C. *A History of Firearms.* Illustrated. Cloth. London, 1926. $100-$150. London, 1930. $100-$125. London, 1933. $100-$125.

POLLARD, Hugh B. C., and Barclay-Smith, Phyllis. *British and American Game-Birds.* Illustrated. Half leather and buckram. New York, 1939. Derrydale Press. First edition. One of 125. $200. London, 1945. Half leather. $100-$125.

POLLEY, J. B. *Hood's Texas Brigade.* 25 plates. Cloth. New York, 1910. First edition. $50.

POLLEY, J. B. *A Soldier's Letters to Charming Nellie.* 16 plates. Cloth. New York, 1908. First edition. $50-$75.

POLONIUS: A Collection of Wise Saws and Modern Instances. Green cloth. London, 1852. (By Edward FitzGerald.) First edition. $25.

POOLE, Ernest. *The Harbor.* New York, 1915. First edition. In dust jacket. $35-$50.

POOR, M. C. *Denver, South Park and Pacific.* Illustrated, with map in pocket. Cloth. Denver, 1949. First edition. One of 1,000 signed. In dust jacket. $250.

POOR Sarah. 18 pp., sewed. No place (Park Hill, Indian Territory, Oklahoma), 1843. Park Hill Mission Press, $50-$75. (Note: Originally this story of "a pious Indian woman" was a publication of the American Tract Society of New York.)

POORE, Ben Perley. *A Descriptive Catalogue of the Government Publications of the United States.* Cloth. Washington, 1885. $75-$100. New York, 1962. 2 vols., cloth. $75.

POPERY, British and Foreign. Printed wrappers. London, 1851. (By Walter Savage Landor.) First edition. $25.

PORTALIS, Baron Roger (editor). *Researches Concerning Jean Grolier, His Life and His Library.* Illustrated. Three-quarters morocco. New York, 1907. One of 300. Boxed. $75-$100.

PORTER, Edwin H. *The Fall River Tragedy.* Plates. Cloth. Fall River, Mass., 1893. First edition. $25.

PORTER, Eleanor H. *Pollyanna.* Pink silk cloth. Boston, 1913. First edition. $50-$75. Also, $32 (A, 1960). Later, green cloth, $30-$50.

PORTER, Gene Stratton. *The Song of the Cardinal.* Illustrated by the author's camera studies. Buckram. Indianapolis, no date (1903). First edition. $25. Author's first book.

PORTER, Jane. *The Scottish Chiefs: A Romance.* 5 vols., boards. London, 1810. First edition, with errata leaf at end of Vol. 1. $150-$250. Contemporary half calf, worn, lacking half title in Vol. 3, $125.

PORTER, Katherine Anne. See F., M. T.

PORTER, Katherine Anne. *Flowering Judas.* Boards and cloth. New York, no date (1930). First edition. One of 600. In glassine dust jacket. $75-$100. New York, no date (1935). Cloth. First printing (so stated). In dust jacket. $35.

PORTER, Katherine Anne. *French Song Book.* Blue boards and cloth. No place, no date (Paris, 1933). First edition. One of 595 signed. In dust jacket. $100-$150. Another issue: One of 15 on Spanish paper, signed. $250-$300.

PORTER, Katherine Anne. *Hacienda.* Cloth. No place, no date (New York, 1934). First edition. One of 895. Boxed. $35.

PORTER, Katherine Anne. *The Leaning Tower and Other Stories.* Cloth. New York, no date (1944). First edition. In dust jacket. $25-$30.

PORTER, Katherine Anne. *Noon Wine.* Decorated boards, paper label. Detroit, 1937. First edition. One of 250 signed. Boxed. $100-$150.

PORTER, Katherine Anne. *Outline of Mexican Popular Arts and Crafts.* Cloth. No place (Los Angeles), 1922. First edition. $150-$200.

PORTER, Katherine Anne. *Pale Horse, Pale Rider.* Light-blue cloth. New York, no date (1939). First edition, first printing (so indicated). In dust jacket. $35-$50.

PORTER, Katherine Anne (translator). *The Itching Parrot.* By José Joaquín Fernández de Lizardi. Cloth. New York, 1942. First edition. In dust jacket. $30.

PORTER, Lavinia Honeyman. *By Ox Team to California.* Portrait. Cloth. Oakland, 1910. First edition. One of 50. $350.

PORTER, William Sidney (or, later, Sydney). See: Henry, O. Also see *The O. Henry Calendar.*

PORTRAIT and Biographical Album of Henry County, Iowa. Three-quarters leather. Chicago, 1888. $50-$60.

PORTRAIT and Biographical Album of Jo Daviess County, Illinois. Three-quarters leather. Chicago, 1889. $50-$60.

PORTRAIT and Biographical Album of Otoe and Cass Counties, Nebraska. Three-quarters leather. Chicago, 1889. $50-$60.

PORTRAIT and Biographical Album of Will County, Illinois. Three-quarters leather. Chicago, 1890. $50-$60.

PORTRAIT and Biographical Record of Dickinson, Saline, McPherson and Marion Counties, Kansas. Three-quarters leather. Chicago, 1893. $50-$60.

PORTRAIT and Biographical Record of Sheboygan County, Wisconsin. Three-quarters leather. Chicago, 1894. $40-$60.

PORTRAITS of the British Poets. Engraved title page, 138 engraved portraits. Red morocco. London, 1824. $25.

POSEY, Alex. *The Poems of Alex Posey. Creek Indian Poet.* Arranged by Mrs. Minnie L. Posey. Cloth. Topeka, 1910. First edition. $35-$50.

POSNER, David. *Love as Image.* Wrappers. London, 1952. First edition. One of 150. $30-$40.

POSNER, David. *S'un Casto Amor.* Wrappers. Oxford, 1953. First edition. One of 30. $45.

POSTON, Charles D. *Apache Land.* Portrait and views. Cloth. San Francisco, 1878. First edition. $100-$125.

POSTON, Charles D. *Speech of the Hon. Charles D. Poston, of Arizona, on Indian Affairs.* 20 pp., printed wrappers. New York, 1865. $400 (A, 1966).

POSTSCRIPT to the Statement Respecting the Earl of Selkirk's Settlement Upon the Red River, in North America. (Caption title.) 28 pp. (195-222), plain wrappers. No place, no date (Montreal, 1818). (By John Halkett.) $450 (A, 1969).

POTOCKI, Count Joseph. *Sport in Somaliland.* Translated by Jeremiah Curtin. Portrait, 58 colored plates, 18 photogravure plates, map. Buckram gilt. London, 1900. One of 200 signed. $75-$100.

POTT, J. S. *A Plain Statement of Fact, etc.* (Claims of Florida inhabitants against British forces.) 16 pp., half morocco. London, 1838. $150.

POTTER, Beatrix. *Ginger and Pickles.* Illustrated by the author. Pictorial boards. London, 1909. First edition. $75. New York, 1909. Boards. First American edition. $35.

POTTER, Beatrix. *The Pie and the Patty-Pan.* Illustrated in color by the author. Pictorial boards. London, 1905. First edition. $75-$100. New York, 1905. Illustrated. Boards. $10-$20.

POTTER, Beatrix. *The Roly-Poly Pudding.* Illustrated in color by the author. Cloth. London, no date (1908). First edition. $75-$100.

POTTER, Beatrix. *The Tailor of Gloucester.* Frontispiece, 15 color illustrations by the author. Pink boards, rounded spine. No place, no date (London, 1902). First edition, with misprints on pages 26 and 34. $200-$250.

POTTER, Beatrix. *The Tale of Benjamin Bunny.* Illustrated in color by the author. Boards. London, 1904. First edition. $35-$50.

POTTER, Beatrix. *The Tale of the Flopsy Bunnies.* Illustrated in color by the author. Boards. London, 1909. First edition. $35-$50.

POTTER, Beatrix. *The Tale of Peter Rabbit.* Colored frontispiece, illustrations in black and white. Boards, flat spine. London, no date (1901). First edition, with copyright undated. One of 250. $250-$350. London, 1902. Second edition. One of 250. $150-$250.

POTTER, Beatrix. *The Tale of Mrs. Tiggy-Winkle.* Frontispiece and 26 colored illustrations by the author. Boards. London, 1905. First edition. $50-$75.

POTTER, Beatrix. *The Tale of Pigling Bland.* Illustrated in color by the author. Boards. London, 1913. First edition. $25-$35.

POTTER, Beatrix. *Wag-by-Wall.* Cloth. London, 1944. One of 100. In dust jacket. $125.

POTTER, Jack. *Lead Steer and Other Tales.* Illustrated. Pictorial wrappers. Clayton, N. M., 1939. First edition. $30.

POTTER, Theodore Edgar. *Autobiography.* 3 portraits. Cloth. No place, no date (Concord, N.H., 1913). First edition. $50-$60.

POTTLE, Frederick A. *Boswell and the Girl from Botany Bay.* Boards and cloth. New York, 1937. One of 500. In dust jacket. $25.

POTTLE, Frederick A. *The Literary Career of James Boswell.* Cloth. Oxford, England, 1929. In dust jacket. $35.

POUND, Ezra. See Bosschere, Jean de; Cavalcanti, Guido; Fenollosa, Ernest. Also see *The Catholic Anthology; Des Imagistes.*

POUND, Ezra. *A Lume Spento.* Wrappers. No place (Venice, Italy), 1908. First edition. $3,000-$4,000. Author's first book. Milan, Italy, 1958. Stiff printed wrappers. One of 2,000. In dust jacket. $30.

POUND, Ezra. *ABC of Reading.* Red cloth. London, 1934. First edition. In dust jacket. $60-$75. New Haven, Conn., 1934. Cloth. First American edition. In dust jacket. $25. Norfolk, Conn., 1951. New Directions. Cloth. In dust jacket. $10.

POUND, Ezra. *Antheil: And the Treatise on Harmony.* Wrappers. Paris, 1924. Three Mountains Press. First edition. One of 600. $150. Chicago, 1927. Cloth. First American edition. In dust jacket. $25.

POUND, Ezra. *Antologia.* Wrappers. Rome, 1956. One of 100. $100-$150.

POUND, Ezra. *Canto CX.* Frontispiece drawing of Pound. Wrappers. No place, no date (Cambridge, 1965). First edition. One of 80. $75-$100.

POUND, Ezra. *Cantos LII-LXXI.* Cloth. London, no date (1940). First edition. In dust jacket. $35-$50. Norfolk, no date (1940). Black cloth. First American edition. One of 500. In dust jacket. With envelope and pamphlet, *Notes on Ezra Pound's Cantos, Structure and Rhetoric.* $35-$50.

POUND, Ezra. *The Cantos of Ezra Pound, CX-CXVI.* Wrappers. New York, 1967. Fuck You Press. First (pirated) edition. $10.

POUND, Ezra. *Canzoni.* Gray cloth. London, 1911. First edition, first binding. $200-$250.

POUND, Ezra. *Canzoni & Ripostes.* Brown boards. London, 1913. (First edition sheets of *Canzoni* and *Ripostes* bound with new title page and half titles.) $50-$75.

POUND, Ezra. *Carta da Visita.* Decorated wrappers. Rome, Italy, 1942. First edition. $35.

POUND, Ezra. *Diptych Rome-London.* Folio, boards. No place, no date (Norfolk, 1957). New Directions. One of 125 (150?) signed. Boxed. $150-$200. Also, $100 (A, 1971). London, 1957. Faber & Faber. One of 50 signed. $150-$200. (These books were issued simultaneously as part of a total edition of 200 produced at the Bodoni Press in Verona, Italy.)

POUND, Ezra. *A Draft of XVI Cantos.* Folio, red parchment. Paris, 1925. First edition. One of 70 on Roma paper (of an edition of 90). $350.

POUND, Ezra. *A Draft of Cantos XVII-XXVII.* Folio, red parchment. London, 1928. First edition. One of 70 on Roma paper. $350-$500.

POUND, Ezra. *A Draft of Cantos XXXI-XLI.* Cloth. London, no date (1935). First English edition. In dust jacket. $35-$50.

POUND, Ezra. *A Draft of XXX Cantos.* Initials by Dorothy Shakespear. Beige linen. Paris, 1930. Hours Press. One of 200. $750 and up. Also, $384 (A, 1971), $624 (A, 1969). Another issue: Red leather. One of 10 signed. $1,000 and up. Also, $1,080 (A, 1969). (Note: Of this issue, there were 2 on vellum for Pound.) New York, no date. First American edition. $35. London, 1933. Cloth. First English edition. In dust jacket. $35.

POUND, Ezra. *Drafts and Fragments of Cantos CX-CXVII.* Folio, red cloth, paper labels. New York, no date (1968). New Directions and Stone Wall Press. First edition. One of 200 signed with New Directions imprint. Boxed. $150-$200.

POUND, Ezra. *Eleven New Cantos: XXXI-XLI.* Cloth. New York, no date (1934). First edition. In dust jacket. $45.

POUND, Ezra. *Exultations.* Maroon boards. London, 1909. First edition. $100-$150.

POUND, Ezra. *The Fifth Decade of Cantos.* Cloth. London, no date (1937). First edition. In dust jacket. $35-$50.

POUND, Ezra. *Gaudier-Brzeska: A Memoir.* Illustrated. Cloth. London, 1916. First edition. $100-$150. London, no date (1939). Cloth. Reissue. $50-$75. Milan, no date (1957). Wrappers. First state, with "Epistein" uncorrected. $25.

POUND, Ezra. *Homage to Sextus Propertius.* Blue boards. London, no date (1934). First separate edition. In dust jacket. $30.

POUND, Ezra. *How to Read.* Cloth. London, no date (1931). First edition. In dust jacket. $35.

POUND, Ezra. *Hugh Selwyn Mauberley.* Boards and cloth. No place (London), 1920. Ovid Press. First edition. One of 165. $150. Milan, 1959. Wrappers. First Italian edition. $20.

POUND, Ezra. *Imaginary Letters.* Stiff printed white wrappers. Paris, 1930. Black Sun Press. First edition. One of 300. In glassine dust jacket. Boxed. $60-$75. Another issue: One of 50 copies on vellum, signed. Boxed. $150-$200.

POUND, Ezra. *Indiscretions; or, Une Revue de Deux Mondes.* Boards and cloth. Paris, 1923. Three Mountains Press. First edition. One of 300. $100-$150. Inscribed by Pound, $375. Also, proof copy, unbound, $308 (A, 1966).

POUND, Ezra. *Instigations.* Cloth. New York, no date (1920). First edition. In dust jacket. $100.

POUND, Ezra. *Lustra.* Frontispiece portrait. Gray cloth. London, no date (1916). First edition. One of 200. $300. Second edition, same date: One of 1,000, with altered text. $75-$100. New York, 1917. Printed boards. First American edition. One of 60 signed with initials. $85.

POUND, Ezra. *Make It New.* Cloth. New Haven, 1935. First American edition. In dust jacket. $25.

POUND, Ezra. *Patria Mia.* Brown cloth. Chicago, 1950. First edition. In dust jacket. $25.

POUND, Ezra. *Pavannes and Divagations.* Cloth. No place, no date (Norfolk, 1958). New Directions. First edition. In dust jacket. $25.

POUND, Ezra. *Pavannes and Divisions.* Frontispiece. Dark-blue cloth. New York, 1918. First edition, first binding. In dust jacket. $75. Later binding, same date. Gray cloth. In dust jacket. $50.

POUND, Ezra. *Personae.* Drab boards. London, 1909. First edition, first issue (with binding as described). $100-$150. New York, 1926. Cloth. First American edition. In dust jacket. $50-$75.

POUND, Ezra. *Personae and Exultations.* Boards. London, 1913. First (combined) edition. In glassine dust jacket. $100-$150.

POUND, Ezra. *The Pisan Cantos.* Cloth. New York, 1948. First edition. In dust jacket. $50. London, no date (1949). Cloth. First English edition. In dust jacket. $25.

POUND, Ezra. *Poems 1918-1921, Including Three Portraits and Four Cantos.* Boards and vellum. New York, no date (1921). First edition. In dust jacket. $75-$100.

POUND, Ezra. *Polite Essays.* Cloth. London, no date (1937). First edition. In dust jacket. $35.

POUND, Ezra. *Provenca: Poems Selected from "Personae," "Exultations" and "Canzoniere."* Tan boards. Boston, no date (1910). First edition, first issue, with "Landantes" on pages 53 and 55 with no type wear. In dust jacket. $150-$200. Dust jacket torn, $135.

POUND, Ezra. *Quia Pauper Amavi.* Boards and cloth, paper label. London, no date (1919). Egoist, Ltd. First edition. One of 100 on handmade paper, signed. $200-$300. First trade edition: One of 500. $125.

POUND, Ezra. *A Quinzaine for This Yule.* Wrappers. London, 1908. First edition. $400-$500. Second issue. One of 100. $308 (A, 1966).

POUND, Ezra. *Redondillas, or Something of That Sort.* Blue boards, linen spine, label. No place, no date (New York, 1967). New Directions. Grabhorn-Hoyem printing. One of 110 signed. In dust jacket. $135.

POUND, Ezra. *Ripostes.* Boards. London, 1912. First edition. $100-$150. Also, inscribed, $210 (A, 1969). London, 1915. Wrappers. One of 100. $50-$75. Also, $48 (A, 1971).

POUND, Ezra. *Section: Rock-Drill.* Boards. Milan, 1955. First edition. One of 500. $35-$50. New York, no date (1956). Black cloth. First American edition. In dust jacket. $15. London, 1957. Black cloth. First English edition. In dust jacket. $10.

POUND, Ezra. *Selected Poems.* Introduction by T. S. Eliot. Boards. London, no date (1928). First edition. One of 100 signed. $300-$400. Trade edition: Cloth. In dust jacket. $30-$35.

POUND, Ezra. *Seventy Cantos.* Cloth. London, 1950. First English collected edition. In dust jacket. $25.

POUND, Ezra. *The Spirit of Romance.* Green cloth. London, no date (1910). First edition. In dust jacket. $75-$100. Norfolk, no date (1952). New Directions. Cloth. In dust jacket. $15-$20. Second printing. In dust jacket. $10.

POUND, Ezra. *Ta S'eu Dai Gaku Studio Integrale.* Wrappers. Rappolo, Italy, 1942. First edition. $25.

POUND, Ezra. *Thrones.* Boards. Milan, 1959. First edition. One of 300. In glassine dust jacket. $50-$75. London, no date (1960). First English edition. In dust jacket. $15-$25. No place, no date (Norfolk, 1959). New Directions. Cloth. First American edition. In dust jacket. $10-$20.

POUND, Ezra. *Umbra.* Half cloth and boards. London, 1920. First edition. In dust jacket. $75-$100.

POUND, Ezra, and Kokoschka, Oskar. *The Seafarer.* Portrait. Large board portfolio. Frankfurt, Germany, no date (1965). First edition. One of 195 signed by Pound and Kokoschka. $200.

POUND, Ezra (editor). *Active Anthology.* Cloth. London, 1933. First edition. In dust jacket. $100.

POUND, Ezra (translator). *Cathay.* By Ernest Fenollosa. Translated by Ezra Pound. Printed wrappers. London, 1915. First edition. $125-$150.

POUND, Ezra (translator). *Confucius: The Great Digest and The Unwobbling Pivot.* Wrappers. Norfolk, 1947. New Directions. First edition, without Chinese text. $35. Norfolk, 1951. Cloth. In dust jacket. $10-$15.

POUND, Ezra (translator). *The Sonnets and Ballate of Guido Cavalcanti.* Cloth. London, 1912. First English edition. $75-$100. Boston, no date (1912). Boards, vellum paper spine. First American edition. $85-$100.

POUND, Ezra (translator). *Ta Hio: The Great Learning.* Translated from Confucius' works. Pink-purple printed wrappers. Seattle, 1928. First edition. $35. Norfolk, no date (1936). Wrappers. One of 196. $25.

POWELL, Anthony. *Afternoon Men.* Cloth. London, 1931. First edition. In dust jacket. $50-$75. Author's first novel.

POWELL, Anthony. *Caledonia: A Fragment.* Boards and cloth. London, no date. In dust jacket. $200-$250.

POWELL, Anthony. *From a View to a Death.* Cloth. London, 1933. First edition. In dust jacket. $75-$100.

POWELL, Anthony. *Venusberg.* Cloth. London, 1932. First edition. In dust jacket. $35-$50.

POWELL, H. M. T. *The Santa Fe Trail to California, 1849-1852.* Edited by Douglas S. Watson. Maps and other illustrations. Half morocco. San Francisco, no date (1931). Grabhorn Press. One of 300. $350-$400.

POWELL, J. W. *Canyons of the Colorado.* Illustrated, including 10 folding plates. Cloth. Meadville, Pa., 1895. First edition. $100-$150. Also, rebound in half morocco, rubbed, $110 (A, 1966).

POWELL, Lawrence Clark. *The Alchemy of Books.* Decorated boards. Los Angeles, no date (1954). Ward Ritchie Press. First edition. $20-$25.

POWELL, Lawrence Clark. *Robinson Jeffers, the Man and His Work.* Foreword by Robinson Jeffers. Decorations by Rockwell Kent. Cloth, paper label. Los Angeles, 1934. First edition. One of 750. In dust jacket. $45-$50.

POWELL, Willis J. *Tachyhippodamia, or, Art of Quieting Wild Horses in a Few Hours.* Half leather and marbled boards. New Orleans, 1838. First edition. $75.

POWER, Sister Mary James. *Poets at Prayer.* Cloth. New York, 1938. First edition. In dust jacket. $25.

POWER, Tyrone. *Impressions of America.* 2 plates. 2 vols., boards and linen. London, 1836. First edition. $75-$100.

POWERS, J. F. *Prince of Darkness and Other Stories.* Cloth. New York, 1947. First edition. In dust jacket. $25. Author's first book.

POWERS, Stephen. *Afoot and Alone: A Walk from Sea to Sea by the Southern Route.* 12 plates. Cloth. Hartford, 1872. First edition. $35-$50.

POWESHEIK County, Iowa: A Descriptive Account of Its Climate, Soil, etc. Woodcut township map. 36 pp., printed wrappers. Montezuma, Iowa, 1865. $250.

POWYS, John Cowper. *Autobiography.* Portrait frontispiece. Brown cloth. London, no date (1934). First edition. In dust jacket. $25.

POWYS, John Cowper. *Ballads and Other Poems.* Boards. London, 1893. First edition. $35-$50. Author's first book.

POWYS, John Cowper. *Confessions of Two Brothers.* Cloth. Rochester, N.Y., 1916. $25-$35.

POWYS, John Cowper. *Ducdame.* Cloth. London, 1925. First English edition. In dust jacket. $25.

POWYS, John Cowper. *In Defense of Sensuality.* Cloth. London, 1930. First edition. In dust jacket. $35. Lacking jacket, $25.

POWYS, John Cowper. *Odes and Other Poems.* Cloth. London, 1896. First edition. $150-$200. Also, $108 (A, 1971).

POWYS, John Cowper. *The Owl, The Duck, and—Miss Rowe! Miss Rowe!* Boards. Chicago, 1930. Black Archer Press. First edition. One of 250 signed. Boxed. $25.

POWYS, John Cowper. *Poems.* Boards. London, 1899. First edition. $75-$100.

POWYS, John Cowper. *Psychoanalysis and Morality.* Half vellum. San Francisco, 1923. One of 500 signed. $75.

POWYS, John Cowper. *Wolf Solent.* Flexible black cloth. New York, 1929. First American edition. In dust jacket. $25-$35.

POWYS, Llewellyn. *The Book of Days.* 12 etchings. Half green morocco. London, 1937. Golden Cockerel Press. One of 50 signed, with an extra set of plates. $100-$150.

POWYS, Llewellyn. *Glory of Life.* Woodcuts by Robert Gibbings. Vellum and cloth. No place, no date (London, 1934). Golden Cockerel Press. One of 277. $100-$150.

POWYS, T. F. *Fables.* 4 drawings by Gilbert Spencer. Buckram. London, 1929. One of 750 signed. $25.

POWYS, T. F. *Goat Green, or The Better Gift.* Half morocco. London, 1937. Golden Cockerel Press. One of 150 signed. $35.

POWYS, T. F. *An Interpretation of Genesis.* Boards. London, 1929. First edition. One of 490 signed. In dust jacket. Boxed. $35. New York, 1929. White boards. First American edition. One of 260 signed. In glassine dust jacket. Boxed. $25.

POWYS, T. F. *The Key of the Field.* Woodcut frontispiece. Buckram. London, 1930. First edition. One of 550 signed. $25.

POWYS, T. F. *Mr. Weston's Good Wine.* Illustrated. Cloth. London, 1927. One of 660 signed. In dust jacket. $25.

POWYS, T. F. *The Soliloquy of a Hermit.* Cloth. New York, 1916. First edition. In dust jacket. $25. Author's first book.

POWYS, T. F. *The Two Thieves.* Half cloth. London, 1932. First edition. One of 85 signed. Boxed. $25.

POWYS, T. F. *Unclay.* Half buckram. London, 1931. One of 160 signed. $30.

POWYS, T. F. *Uncle Dottery.* Illustrated by Eric Gill. Half vellum and green linen. Bristol, England, 1930. One of 50 with an extra print. $25.

POWYS, T. F. *Uriah on the Hill.* Buckram. Cambridge, England, 1930. First edition. In dust jacket. $35.

PRACTICAL Guide for Emigrants to North America (A). Folding map in color. 57 pp., printed wrappers. London, 1850. (By George Nettle.) First edition. $125.

PRAIRIE (The): A Tale. By the Author of *The Spy.* 3 vols., boards and cloth, paper labels. London, 1827. (By James Fenimore Cooper.) First edition. $550. Philadelphia, 1827. 2 vols., boards, paper labels. First American edition, with copyright notices corrected by slip pasted in. $400-$500. New York, 1940. Limited Editions Club. Illustrated. Half buckskin and cloth. $25.

PRAIRIEDOM: Rambles and Scrambles in Texas. By A. Suthron. Map. Cloth. New York, 1845. (By Frederick Benjamin Page.) First edition. $150-$200. New York, 1846. Second edition. $75-$100.

PRATT, Parley P. *Late Persecution of the Church of Jesus Christ, of Latter Day Saints.* Cloth. New York, 1840. $100-$125.

PRECAUTION: A Novel. 2 vols., boards, or leather. New York, 1820. (By James Fenimore Cooper.) First edition, with errata leaf. $1,000 and up.

PRÉCIS Touchant la Colonie du Lord Selkirk, sur La Rivière Rouge, sa Destruction en 1815 et 1816, et le Massacre du Gouverneur Semple et de Son Parti. Boards. Montreal, 1818. (By John Halkett.) First edition. $100-$150.

PRESCOTT, George B. *The Speaking Telephone.* Cloth. New York, 1878. First edition. $35.

PRESCOTT, William H. *The History of the Conquest of Mexico.* Maps, other illustrations. 3 vols., cloth. New York, 1843. First edition. $150-$200.

PRESCOTT, William H. *The History of the Conquest of Peru.* Illustrated. 2 vols., cloth. New York, 1847. First edition. $150-$200.

PRESIDENT Lincoln Campaign Songster (The). 72 pp., printed wrappers. New York, no date (1864). First edition. $75.

PRESTON, Lieut.-Col. William. *Journal in Mexico, 1 Nov. 1847 to 25 May 1848.* 48 pp., morocco. No place, no date (modern printing). $60-$65.

PRICE, George F. *Across the Continent with the 5th Cavalry.* 4 portraits. Pictorial cloth. New York, 1883. First edition. $75-$125.

PRICE, R. K. *Astbury, Whieldon, and Ralph Wood Figures, and Toby Jugs.* 68 plates, including 18 in color. Half buckram. London, 1922. One of 500. In dust jacket. $150-$200.

PRICHARD, G. W. *Bureau of Immigration of the Territory of New Mexico. Report of San Miguel County.* Folding view. 30 pp., wrappers. Las Vegas, 1882. $75.

PRICHARD, James C. *An Analysis of the Egyptian Mythology.* Boards. London, 1819. $75-$100.

PRIDE and Prejudice. By the Author of "Sense and Sensibility." 3 vols., blue boards, paper labels. London, 1813. (By Jane Austen.) First edition, with November ads and with ruled lines in half title of Vol. 3 1 2/5 inches (1 inch in second edition). $2,000-$3,000. London, 1813. Second edition. $500 and up. New York, 1940. Limited Editions Club. Sheepskin. $20.

PRIEST, Josiah. *Stories of the Revolution.* Folding plate. 32 pp., half calf. Albany, N.Y., 1836. $50-$75.

PRIEST, Josiah. *A True Narrative of the Capture of David Ogden.* (Cover title.) Woodcut. Self-wrappers. Lansingburgh, 1840. First edition. $75.

PRIESTLEY, J. B. *Brief Diversions.* Boards and cloth. Cambridge, 1922. First collected edition. $25-$35.

PRIMAVERA: Poems by Four Authors. Wrappers. Oxford, England, 1890. First edition. $25. (Note: Contains poems by Stephen Phillips, Laurence Binyon, and others.)

PRINCE Dorus; or, Flattery Put Out of Countenance. Colored plate. Stiff blue or yellow wrappers. London, 1811. (By Charles Lamb.) First edition. $1,000 and up. London, 1818. Yellow-brown wrappers. $200-$300. London, 1889. 9 hand-colored illustrations. Half vellum. $25-$35.

PRINDLE, Cyrus. *Memoir of the Rev. Daniel Meeker Chandler.* Cloth. Middlebury, 1842. $30-$45.

PRITTS, Joseph. *Mirror of Olden Time Border Life.* 13 plates. Cloth. Abingdon, Va., 1849. $35-$50.

PROCEEDINGS of the Board of Mayor and Aldermen of the City of Memphis, Tenn. 2 maps. 22 pp., sewed. Memphis, 1842. $35.

PROCEEDINGS of Congress, in 1796, on the Admission of Tennessee as a State, into the Union. 15 pp., sewed. Detroit, 1835. $35-$50.

PROCEEDINGS of a Convention to Consider the Opening of the Indian Territory, Held at Kansas City, Mo., Feb. 8, 1888. 80 pp., wrappers. Kansas City, 1888. $150-$200.

PROCEEDINGS of the First Annual Session of the Territorial Grange of Montana. Diamond City, 1875. $300.

PROCEEDINGS of a General Meeting Held at Chester Courthouse, Nov. 18, 1831. 16 pp., sewed. Columbia, S.C., 1832. $75-$100.

PROCEEDINGS of a Meeting, and Report of a Committee of Citizens in Relation to Steamboat Disasters in the Western Lakes. 22 pp., sewed. Cleveland, 1850. $75-$100.

PROCEEDINGS of the Republican National Convention, Held at Chicago, May 16, 17, and 18, 1860. 153 pp., wrappers. Albany, N.Y. 1860. Rebound in sheepskin, $200. Another edition: Chicago, 1860. 44 pp., sewed. $37.50.

PROCEEDINGS of the St. Louis Chamber of Commerce, in Relation to the Improvement of the Navigation of the Mississippi River. 40 pp., sewed. St. Louis, 1842. $75-$100.

PROCEEDINGS of Sundry Citizens of Baltimore, Convened for the Purpose of Devising the Most Efficient Means of Improving the Intercourse Between That City and the Western States. 38 pp., sewed. Baltimore, 1827. $35-$50.

PROCTOR, Robert. *An Index to the Early Printed Books in the British Museum.* Cloth. London, 1960. In dust jacket. $50-$60.

PROGRESSIVE Men of Southern Idaho. Leather. Chicago, 1904. First edition. $50-$60. Binding cracking, $35.

PROKOSCH, Frederic. *Age of Thunder.* Cloth. New York, no date (1945). First edition. One of 30 signed, sheet of original ms. bound in. $35.

PROKOSCH, Frederic. *Death at Sea: Poems.* Cloth. New York, 1940. First edition. One of 55 signed, sheet of original ms. bound in. Boxed. $25-$30.

PROKOSCH, Frederic. *Three Songs—Three Images.* 2 vols., wrappers. New Haven, Conn., 1932. One of 10 large paper copies. $150.

PROMETHEUS Bound. Translated from the Greek of Aeschylus. And Miscellaneous Poems by the Translator. Dark-blue cloth, paper label on spine. London, 1833. (By Elizabeth Barrett Browning.) First edition. $75-$100.

PROPERT, W. A. *The Russian Ballet in Western Europe, 1909-1920.* Illustrated, including color plates. Boards and cloth. London, 1921. Limited edition, $200. (Note: There were 150 copies issued for America.)

PROSCH, J. W. *McCarver and Tacoma.* 2 plates. Cloth. Seattle, no date (1906). First edition. $35-$50.

PROSE and Poetry of the Live Stock Industry of the United States. Vol. 1. (All published.) Leather. Denver and Kansas City, Mo., no date (1905). (Edited by James W. Freeman.) First edition. $1,000 and $1,050 (A, 1968). New York, 1959. One of 550. $85.

PROSPECTUS of Hope Gold Company. (Gold dirt lode in Gilpin County, Colorado.) 25 pp., wrappers. New York, 1864. $75.

PROSPECTUS of the Deadwood Gulch Hydraulic Mining Co. of Deadwood Gulch, Lawrence County, Black Hills, of the Territory of Dakota. Folding map. 12 pp., wrappers. Deadwood, 1882. $150.

PROSPECTUS of the Leadville & Ten Mile Narrow Gauge Railway Company of Leadville, Col. (Cover title.) 20 pp., printed wrappers. Leadville, Colo., 1880. $125 (A, 1968).

PROSPECTUS of the Port Folio (New Series), a Monthly Miscellany. 11 pp., stitched. Philadelphia, 1809. (By Joseph Dennie.) First edition. $45.

PROSPERO and Caliban. *The Weird of the Wanderer.* Cloth. London, 1912. (By Baron Corvo [Frederick William Rolfe] and C. H. C. Pirie-Gordon.) First edition. In dust jacket. $75-$100.

PROSSER, R. P. (compiler). *Choice Selections of Prose and Poetry.* Plain gray wrappers. Cincinnati, 1857. First edition. $75-$100. (Note: First edition material by Park Benjamin and Sarah T. Bolton.)

PROTEST of the Columbia Typographical Society . . . Against the Washington Institute. 21 pp., wrappers. Washington, 1834. First edition. $45.

PROTEUS. *Sonnets and Songs.* Cloth. London, 1875. (By Wilfrid Scawen Blunt.) First edition. $150-$250. Author's first book.

PROUST, Marcel. *47 Unpublished Letters from Marcel Proust to Walter Berry.* White wrappers. Paris, 1930. Black Sun Press. One of 200 on Arches paper. Boxed. $50. (Note: There was also another issue of 15, including an original autograph letter, but in most cases the original letter has been removed by autograph collectors. One of these plundered copies brought $35 at auction in 1967.)

PROVOST (The). Boards, marbled spine, paper label. Edinburgh, 1822. (By John Galt.) First edition. $25.

PRYOR, Abraham. *Interesting Description of British America.* Wrappers. Providence, R.I., 1819. $35.

PSALMAU Dafydd yn oe William Morgan. Decorated paper covers, morocco spine. No place, no date (Newtown, Wales, 1929). Gregynog Press. One of 225. $125-$150. (Note: *The Psalms of David* in Welsh.)

PULITZER, Ralph. See Burke, John

PUNKIN, Jonathan (pseudonym). *Downfall of Freemasonry.* No place (Harrisburg, Pa.), 1838. First edition. $100.

PURDY, James. *Don't Call Me by My Right Name and Other Stories.* Blue-gray printed wrappers. New York, 1956. First edition. $25-$35. Signed on title page, $50. Author's first book.

PURVIANCE, Levi. *The Biography of David Purviance.* Cloth. Dayton, 1848. First edition. $35-$50.

PUSS in Boots. Illustrated in color. 10 pp., pictorial boards. New York, no date (1880's). McLoughlin book with overlays on center spread. $45.

PUTNAM, Arthur Lee. *Ned Newton; or The Fortunes of a New York Bootblack.* Wrappers. New York, 1890. (By Horatio Alger, Jr.) Leather-clad paperback. First edition. $45. Another edition: Cloth (later). American Publishers Corp. $25.

PUTNAM, Arthur Lee. *A New York Boy.* Wrappers. New York, 1890. (By Horatio Alger, Jr.) Leather-clad paperback. First edition. $45. Another edition: Cloth (later). American Publishers Corp. $30.

PUTNAM, Arthur Lee. *Number 91; or, The Adventures of a New York Telegraph Boy.* Printed orange wrappers. New York, 1887. (By Horatio Alger, Jr.) First edition. $45. Another edition: Cloth (later). Lovell, publisher. $30.

PUTNAM, Arthur Lee. *Tom Tracy.* Wrappers. New York, 1888. (By Horatio Alger, Jr.) First edition, with Munsey imprint on title page. $45. Another edition (later): Wrappers. Leather-clad. $30. Another (later): Cloth. Lovell, publisher. $30-$50.

PUT'S Golden Songster. 64 pp., wrappers. San Francisco, no date (1858). $25.

PYLE, Howard. *The Garden Behind the Moon.* Illustrated by the author. Cloth. New York, 1895. First edition. $25.

PYLE, Howard. *Howard Pyle's Book of the American Spirit.* Edited by Merle Johnson and Francis J. O'Dowd. Illustrated, including color plates, by Pyle. Boards and cloth. New York, 1923. First edition, with "B-X" on copyright page. In dust jacket. $35-$50. Another issue: One of 50 signed by the editors. $100-$150.

PYLE, Howard. *Howard Pyle's Book of Pirates.* Edited by Merle Johnson. Illustrated, including color plates, by Pyle. Boards and cloth. New York, 1921. First edition, with "D-V" at foot of copyright page. In dust jacket. $35-$50. Another issue: One of 50 on vellum, signed by Johnson. $100-$150.

PYLE, Howard. *Men of Iron.* New York, 1892. Illustrated by Pyle. Cloth. First edition, first issue (1 1/16 inches across top of covers). $100-$125. Second issue. $50-$75.

PYLE, Howard. *The Merry Adventures of Robin Hood.* Illustrated, including color plates, by Pyle. Full leather. New York, 1883. First edition. $150-$200. Worn, $125. New York, 1942. Illustrated. Cloth. Brandywine Edition. In dust jacket. $100-$125. London, 1883. Cloth. First English edition. $50-$75.

PYLE, Howard. *A Modern Aladdin.* Illustrated by Pyle. Cloth. New York, 1892. First edition. $75-$100.

PYLE, Howard. *Otto of the Silver Hand.* Illustrated by the author. Half calf and cloth. New York, 1888. First edition. $100-$125. London, 1888. Pictorial cloth. First English edition. $100-$125.

PYLE, Howard. *Pepper and Salt.* Illustrated by the author. Pictorial buckram. New York, 1886. First edition. $75-$100.

PYLE, Howard. *The Price of Blood.* Colored illustrations by Pyle. Pictorial boards and cloth. Boston, 1899. First edition, first binding, with unlettered spine. $50-$60. Second binding, spine lettered, $25-$35.

PYLE, Howard. *Rejected of Men.* Illustrated by Pyle. Cloth. New York, 1903. First edition, with "Published June, 1903" on copyright page. In dust jacket. $35-$50.

PYLE, Howard. *The Rose of Paradise.* Illustrated by Pyle. Cloth. New York, 1888. First edition. $25-$35.

PYLE, Howard. *The Ruby of Kishmoor.* Illustrated. Cloth. New York, 1908. First edition. In dust jacket. $25-$35.

PYLE, Howard. *Sabbath Thoughts.* 2 Pyle illustrations. Wrappers. No place, no date (New York, 1928). First edition. One of 20. $25-$35. Another issue: One of 6 large paper copies. $75-$100.

PYLE, Howard. *Stolen Treasure.* Illustrated. Cloth. New York, 1907. First edition, first issue, with "Published May, 1907" on copyright page. In dust jacket. $50-$75.

PYLE, Howard. *The Story of the Champions of the Round Table.* Cloth. New York, 1905. First edition. In dust jacket. $35-$50.

PYLE, Howard. *The Story of the Grail and The Passing of Arthur.* Illustrated by the author. Cloth. New York, 1910. First edition. In dust jacket. $25-$35.

PYLE, Howard. *The Story of Jack Ballister's Fortunes.* Illustrated by Pyle. Cloth. New York, 1895. First edition. $35-$50.

PYLE, Howard. *The Story of King Arthur and His Knights.* Illustrated by Pyle. Cloth. New York, 1903. First edition. In dust jacket. $25-$35.

PYLE, Howard. *The Story of Sir Launcelot and His Companions.* Illustrated by Pyle. Cloth. New York, 1907. First edition. In dust jacket. $50-$75.

PYLE, Howard. *Twilight Land.* Illustrated by Pyle. Half leather. New York, 1895. First edition. $35.

PYLE, Howard. *Within the Capes.* Illustrated by Pyle. Cloth. New York, 1885. First edition, first issue (cloth). $50. Later issue: Wrappers: $25-$35.

PYLE, Howard. *The Wonder Clock.* Illustrated by Pyle. Half leather. New York, 1888. First edition. $100-$150.

PYLE, Howard. *Yankee Doodle.* Illustrated by Pyle. Pictorial boards. New York, 1881. First edition. $75-$100. First book illustrated by Pyle.

PYNCHON, Thomas. *V.* Cloth. Philadelphia, no date (1963). First edition. In dust jacket. $25. Author's first book.

PYNE, W. H. *The History of the Royal Residences of Windsor Castle, St. James's Palace, Carlton House, Kensington Palace, Hampton Court, Buckingham House, and Frogmore.* 100 colored engravings. 3 vols., morocco, gilt. London, 1819. First edition. $500-$800. Another issue: Large paper. Slightly more. Another issue: Plates uncolored. $150. Worn copies for less.

PYRNELLE, Louise-Clarke. *Diddie, Dumps, and Tot, or Plantation Child-Life.* Pictorial cloth. New York, 1882. First edition. $100-$150.

Q

QUAILE, Edward. *Illuminated Manuscripts.* Cloth. Liverpool, 1897. $25-$35.

QUAKER Partisans (The). Cloth. Philadelphia, 1869. (By William Gilmore Simms?) First edition. $35-$50.

QUARTETTE. By Four Anglo-Indian Writers. Wrappers. Lahore, India, 1885. (By Rudyard Kipling and his sister, mother, and father.) First edition. $400-$500.

QUEEN, Ellery. *The Chinese Orange Mystery.* Cloth. New York, 1934. (By Frederic Dannay and Manfred B. Lee.) First edition. In dust jacket. $25.

QUEEN, Ellery. *The Devil to Pay.* Cloth. New York, 1938. (By Frederic Dannay and Manfred B. Lee.) First edition. In dust jacket. $25.

QUEEN, Ellery. *The Egyptian Cross Mystery.* Cloth. New York, 1932. (By Frederic Dannay and Manfred B. Lee.) First edition. In dust jacket. $25.

QUEEN, Ellery. *The Spanish Cape Mystery.* Cloth. New York, 1935. (By Frederic Dannay and Manfred B. Lee.) First edition. In dust jacket. $25.

QUEENY, Edgar M. *Prairie Wings: Pen and Camera Flight Studies.* Illustrated. Cloth. New York, 1946. In dust jacket. $40-$50. Another issue: Morocco. One of 225 signed. $220 (A, 1968).

QUENTIN Durward. 3 vols., boards and cloth, paper labels. Edinburgh, 1823. (By Walter Scott.) First edition. $100-$150.

QUICKFALL, Bob Grantham (pseudonym?). *Western Life, and How I Became a Bronco Buster.* Portrait. 96 pp., pictorial wrappers. London, no date (1890). First edition. $300 (A, 1968).

QUILLER-COUCH, Sir Arthur. *The Golden Pomp.* Half morocco. London, 1895. $35.

QUILLER-COUCH, Sir Arthur. *In Powder and Crinoline.* Illustrated by Kay Nielsen, including color plates. Boards, buckram spine. London, no date (about 1914). $40. Another issue: Vellum. One of 500 signed. $75-$100.

QUILLER-COUCH, Sir Arthur. *The Sleeping Beauty and Other Fairy Tales.* 30 colored plates by Edmund Dulac. Morocco. London, no date (about 1910). One of 100 signed. $75-$125. Another issue: Half morocco. One of 150 signed. $50-$75. Trade edition: Bright-blue cloth. $25-$35.

QUIZ. *The Grand Master, or Adventures of Qui Hi? in Hindostan: A Hudibrastic Poem in Eight Cantos.* Folding frontispiece, 26 plates by Thomas Rowlandson. Half calf. London, 1816. (By William Combe.) First edition, with errata slip and leaf containing pages 31-32. $300-$400. Later issue, lacking the slip and the leaf: $100-$150.

R

RACING at Home and Abroad. Edited by Charles Richardson. Plates. 3 vols., folio, brown morocco. London, 1921-23. One of 475. With the lists of subscribers. $125-$150.

RACKHAM, Arthur. *Arthur Rackham's Book of Pictures.* Edited by A. Quiller-Couch. Illustrated in color and black and white. Buckram. London, 1913. Large paper limited edition, signed by Rackham. $200-$250. Another issue: One of 30 signed and inscribed with an original end leaf drawing. $400. London, no date (1915). Cloth. First trade edition. In dust jacket. $50. London, no date (1927). In dust jacket. $25-$35.

RACKHAM, Arthur (illustrator). *The Fairy Tales of the Brothers Grimm.* 40 color plates, numerous black-and-white illustrations. Decorated full white vellum with ties. London, 1909. De luxe edition, signed by Rackham. $288. Trade edition: Cloth. $75-$100.

RACKHAM, Bernard. *The Ancient Glass of Canterbury Cathedral.* 21 plates in color and 80 in monochrome. Buckram. London, 1949. $50-$75.

RADICAL Reconstruction on the Basis of One Sovereign Republic. 17 pp., sewed. Sacramento, Calif., 1867. $50-$75.

RAFINESQUE, C. S. *Circular Address on Botany and Zoology.* 36 pp., sewed. Philadelphia, 1816. $75-$100.

RAHT, Carlysle Graham. *The Romance of Davis Mountains and Big Bend Country.* Map, 13 plates. Cloth. El Paso, Tex., no date (1919). First edition. In dust jacket. $40-$60.

RAILROAD to San Francisco. (Caption title.) No place, no date (1849). (By P. P. F. DeGrand.) $65-$75.

RAINE, William MacLeod. *Cattle Brands: A Sketch of Bygone Days in the Cow-Country.* 8 pp., wrappers. Boston, no date (1920). First edition. $35-$50.

RAINES, C. W. *A Bibliography of Texas.* Cloth. Austin, Tex., 1896. First edition. $100-$200. Facsimile reprint: Houston, 1955. Cloth. One of 500. Boxed. $35-$50.

RALFE, J. *The Naval Chronology of Great Britain.* 60 colored plates. Boards. London, 1820. First edition. $750-$1,000. Also, $576 (A, 1969).

RALPH, Julian. *On Canada's Frontier.* Illustrated. Cloth. New York, 1892. First edition. $50-$60.

RAMAL, Walter. *Songs of Childhood.* Frontispiece. Half blue decorated cloth and vellum. London, 1902. (By Walter De La Mare.) First edition. In dust jacket. $300-$400. Author's first book. London, 1923. Boards and vellum. One of 310 signed. $75-$100.

RAMÍREZ, D. José F. *Memorias, Negociaciones y Documentos, etc.* Boards, or wrappers. Mexico City, 1853. $50-$75.

RAMSAY, David. *The History of South Carolina.* 2 folding maps. 2 vols., half leather. Charleston, S.C., 1809. First edition. $150-$200.

RAMSDELL, Charles W. *Reconstruction in Texas.* 324 pp., wrappers. New York, 1910. First edition. $100-$150.

RAMSEY, Alexander. *Message of the Governor, in Relation to a Memorial from Half-breeds of Pembina.* 4 pp., unbound. No place, no date (St. Paul, Minn., 1849). $250-$450.

RAMSEY, Alexander. *Message of Governor Ramsey.* (On the Sioux uprising.) Wrappers. St. Paul, 1862. First edition. $150-$250.

RAMSEY, J. G. M. *The Annals of Tennessee.* Map. Cloth. Charleston, S.C., 1853. First edition. $100-$150. Philadelphia, 1853. Cloth. Second edition. $75. Philadelphia, 1860. Cloth. $50. Chattanooga, Tenn., 1926. Cloth. $50.

RANCK, George W. *History of Lexington, Kentucky.* Illustrated. Cloth. Cincinnati, 1872. First edition. $50-$75.

RAND, Thomas. *The Voice of the Turtle.* 52 pp., unbound. No place (Wrentham, Mass.), 1802. First edition. $35-$40.

RANDALL, Thomas E. *History of the Chippewa Valley.* Cloth. Eau Claire, Wis., 1875. First edition. $35-$50.

RANDOLL, Gen. A. M. *Last Days of the Rebellion.* Sewed. San Francisco, 1883. $35-$50.

RANKIN, M. Wilson. *Reminiscences of Frontier Days.* Frontispiece. Boards. Denver, no date (1938). First edition. $75-$100.

RANSOM, John Crowe. *Chills and Fever.* Batik boards, cloth spine, paper label. New York, 1924. First edition. In dust jacket. $40-$50.

RANSOM, John Crowe. *Grace After Meat.* Boards, paper label. London, 1924. First edition. In dust jacket. $100-$125.

RANSOM, John Crowe. *Poems About God.* Brown boards, paper label. New York, 1919. First edition. $125-$150. Author's first book. Copy offered for $150 in 1972 by New York dealer.

RANSOM, John Crowe. *Two Gentlemen in Bonds.* Decorated boards, cloth spine, paper label. New York, 1927. First edition. In dust jacket. $35.

RANSOM, Will. *Private Presses and Their Books.* Illustrated. Cloth. New York, 1929. One of 1,200. $75-$100.

RAPPORT sur les Missions du Diocèse de Quebec, No. 7. Wrappers. Quebec, 1847. $50-$75.

RAREY, J. S. *The Modern Art of Taming Wild Horses.* Wrappers. Columbus, Ohio, 1856. First edition. $250-$500. Rebound in boards, $325. Austin, Tex., 1856. Third edition, revised and corrected. 62 pp., wrappers. $75.

RATCLIFFE, Eliza. *The Mysterious Baron.* Marbled boards, sheep spine. London, 1808. First edition. $50-$60.

RAUNICK, Selma M., and Schade, Margaret. *The Kothmanns of Texas, 1845-1931.* Cloth. Austin, Tex., 1931. $35.

RAVEN, Ralph. *Golden Dreams and Leaden Realities.* Cloth. New York, 1853. (By George Payson.) First edition. $50.

RAVENSNEST; or, The Redskins. 3 vols., boards, green or blue cloth spine. London, 1846. (By James Fenimore Cooper.) First English edition of *The Redskins.* $75-$100.

RAWSTORNE, Lawrence. *Gamonia: or the Art of Preserving Game.* 15 colored aquatints. Green morocco. London, 1837. First edition, with errata slip at end. $125-$150.

R. B. Adam Library Relating to Dr. Samuel Johnson and His Era (The). 4 vols., half cloth. Buffalo, N.Y., 1929-30. First edition. One of 500 (for first 3 vols.) and 225 (for Vol. 4). In dust jackets. $150-$200.

READ, C. Rudston. *What I Heard, Saw and Did at the Australian Gold Fields.* Large folding map, tinted lithograph plates. Cloth. London, 1853. $75-$100.

READ, Herbert. *Eclogues.* Illustrated. Boards and cloth. London, 1919. Beaumont Press. $25.

READ, Herbert. *English Stained Glass.* Colored frontispiece, 70 full-page plates. Cloth. London. 1926. $35-$50.

READ, Herbert. *Staffordshire Pottery Figures.* Plates (6 colored). Cloth. London, 1929. In dust jacket. $35-$50.

READ, Herbert, and others. *Surrealism.* Plates. Cloth. London, 1936. First edition. $50-$60.

READ, Opie. *An American in New York.* Red pictorial cloth. Chicago, 1905. Autographed edition. $25-$35.

READ, Opie. *An Arkansas Planter.* Illustrated by W. W. Denslow and Ike Morgan. Green pictorial cloth. Chicago, no date (1896). First edition. $25-$35.

READ, Thomas Buchanan. *A Summer Story: Sheridan's Ride and Other Poems.* Cloth. Philadelphia, 1865. First edition. $35.

READE, Charles. *The Cloister and the Hearth.* 4 vols., cloth. London, 1861. First edition. $250-$500. New York, 1861. Cloth. First American edition. $50. New York, 1932. Limited Editions Club. Cloth. In dust jacket. Boxed. $25-$35.

READE, Charles. *The Course of True Love Never Did Run Smooth.* Cloth. London, 1857. First edition. $35-$50.

READE, Charles. *"It Is Never Too Late to Mend."* 3 vols., cloth spine. London, 1856. First edition. $50.

READINGS in Crabbe's "Tales of the Hall." Red or green cloth. Guildford, England, 1879. (By Edward FitzGerald.) First edition. $50. London, 1882. $10-$25.

REAGAN, John H. *Memoirs, with Special Reference to Secession and the Civil War.* 4 plates. Cloth. New York, 1906. $35-$50.

REAL Life in Ireland. 19 hand-colored aquatints. Boards. London, 1821. (By Pierce Egan.) First edition. $300-$400. Also, in morocco, $120 (A, 1969). London, 1829. Calf. Fourth edition. $110 (A, 1971).

REAL Life in London. By an Amateur. 32 colored plates by Alken, Rowlandson, etc. 21 parts in wrappers. (2 vols.) London, 1821-22. (By Pierce Egan.) First edition. $400-$500. London, 1821-22. 32 colored plates. 2 vols., boards. First book edition. (Often with 2 extra plates.) $200-$300. Another issue: Morocco. Printed on large paper. $300-$400. (Note: There were numerous later editions.)

RECIO, Jesus T. *Tomochie! Episodios de la Compañía de Chihuahua, 1893.* Boards and leather. Rio Grande City, Tex., 1894. $100.

RÉCIT des Événements qui ont eu Lieu sur le Territoire des Sauvages. Boards. Montreal, 1818. (By Simon McGillivray.) $150.

RECREATIONS. Boards, parchment spine. No place (London), 1923. (By Siegfried Sassoon.) First edition. One of 75. $50-$75.

RED Rover (The): A Tale. By the Author of The Pilot. 3 vols., wrappers (?). Paris, 1827. (By James Fenimore Cooper.) First edition. (No copy in wrappers noted.) Half calf, $100-$150. London, 1827. 3 vols., boards (?). First English edition. (No copy in boards noted.) Half calf, $100-$125. Philadelphia, 1828. 2 vols., blue-gray boards, paper labels. First American edition. (Vol. 2 dated 1827.) $75-$100.

REDHEAD, H. W. *The Horseman.* Illustrated. Wrappers. Cleveland, 1855. $75-$100. (Note: I know of only 2 copies.)

REDMOND, Pat H. *History of Quincy (Ill.) and Its Men of Mark.* Cloth. Quincy, 1869. $35-$40.

REDPATH, James, and Hinton, Richard J. *Hand-book to Kansas Territory and the Rocky Mountains Gold Region.* 3 maps in color on 2 large folding sheets. Cloth. New York, 1859. First edition. $200.

REDSKINS (The). By the Author of "The Pathfinder." 2 vols., printed brown wrappers. New York, 1846. (By James Fenimore Cooper.) First edition. $75-$150. Another issue (?): 2 vols. in one, half calf. $50-$75. (For first English edition, see *Ravensnest.*)

REED, Andrew, and Matheson, James. *A Narrative of the Visit to the American Churches by the Deputation from the Congregational Union of England and Wales.* 4 plates, folding map. 2 vols., leather. London, 1835. First edition. $65.

REED, J. W. *Map of and Guide to the Kansas Gold Region.* Map. 24 pp., printed wrappers. New York, 1859. First edition. $1,750 (A, 1968).

REED, John. *The Day in Bohemia.* Printed wrappers. New York, 1919. First edition. $100.

REED, John. *Sangar: To Lincoln Steffens.* Boards. Riverside, Conn., 1919. First separate edition. Limited. Boxed. $75.

REED, John. *Ten Days That Shook the World.* Illustrated. Cloth. New York, 1919. First edition. In dust jacket. $25-$35.

REED, S. G. *A History of the Texas Railroads.* Blue cloth. Houston, no date (1941). Limited, signed edition. $50.

REED, Silas. *Report of . . . Surveyor General of Wyoming Territory, for the Year 1871.* Tables. 46 pp., wrappers. Washington, 1871. First edition. $200. Also, rebound in cloth, $175 (A, 1968).

REED, Talbot Baines. *History of the Old English Letter Foundries.* Illustrated. Buckram. London, no date (1952). New edition. In dust jacket. $35.

REED, Wallace P. *History of Atlanta, Georgia.* 46 portraits. 2 parts in one, cloth. Syracuse, N.Y., 1889. First edition. $50-$75.

REED, William. *Life on the Border, Sixty Years Ago.* 120 pp., wrappers. Fall River, Mass., 1882. First edition. $35-$50.

REES, William. *The Mississippi Bridge Cities: Davenport, Rock Island and Moline.* Woodcut frontispiece. 32 pp., sewed. No place (Rock Island, Ill.), 1854. First edition. $75-$100.

REES, William. *Description of Keokuk.* 24 pp., printed self-wrappers. Keokuk, Iowa, 1854. First edition. $100-$150. Keokuk, 1855. 22 pp., with wrapper title. Second edition. $75-$100.

REESE, Lizette Woodworth. *A Branch of May: Poems.* Cloth. Baltimore, 1887. First edition. $125-$150. Portland, Me., 1920. Mosher Press. Boards. $25-$35.

REESE, Lizette Woodworth. *A Handful of Lavender.* Decorated cloth and parchment. Boston, 1891. First edition. $25-$35.

REESE, Lizette Woodworth. *White April and Other Poems.* Cloth. New York, no date (about 1930). First edition. In dust jacket. $25.

REFLECTIONS on the Cause of the Louisianians, Respectfully Submitted to Their Agents. 77 pp., boards. No place, no date (1804). $50-$75.

REFORMED Practice of Medicine (The). 2 vols. in one, boards. Boston, 1831. $50-$60.

REGLAMENTO, e Instrucción para los Presidios que se han de Formar en la Linea de Frontera de la Nueva España. 132 pp., modern vellum. Mexico, 1773. $2,750. Another edition: 30 pp., wrappers. Mexico, 1834. $350.

REGULATIONS and List of Premiums of the Jerauld County Agricultural and Industrial Society for the First Fair to Be Held at Wessington Springs, D.T. 16 pp., wrappers. Wessington Springs, Dakota Territory, 1884. $75.

REGULATIONS for the Uniform and Dress of the Army of the United States. 25 chromolithographs. 13 pp., cloth. Philadelphia, 1851. $200. Frayed at edges, lacking most of spine, $125.

REICHEL, Anton. *The Chiaroscurists of the XVI-XVII-XVIII Centuries.* 111 full-color reproductions. Folio, boards. Cambridge, England, no date. $150.

REID, A. J. *The Resources and Manufacturing Capacity of the Lower Fox River Valley.* Folding map and panorama, plates. 56 pp., wrappers. Appleton, Wis., 1874. First edition. $35-$50.

REID, Forrest. *Apostate.* Cloth. London, no date (1926). First edition. One of 50 signed. $35-$50.

REID, Forrest. *Illustrators of the Sixties.* Illustrated. Cloth. London, no date (1927). In dust jacket. $75-$100. London, 1928. Chiswick Press. Illustrated. Buckram. Presentation copy, $84 (A, 1968).

REID, J. M. *Sketches and Anecdotes of the Old Settlers and New Comers.* 177 pp., wrappers. Keokuk, Iowa, 1876. First edition. $200-$250.

REID, John C. *Reid's Tramp, or A Journal of the Incidents of Ten Months Travel Through Texas, New Mexico, Arizona, Sonora, and California.* Cloth. Selma, Ala., 1858. First edition. $2,000-$3,000 in fine condition. Also, $2,100 (A, 1968); $1,900 (A, 1965); $2,000 (A, 1964).

REID, Mayne. *The Headless Horseman.* Illustrated. 2 vols., cloth. London, no date (1866). (By Thomas M. Reid.) First edition. $100-$125.

REID, Mayne. *Osceola the Seminole.* Cloth. New York, no date (1858). (By Thomas M. Reid.) First American edition. $75-$100.

REID, Mayne. *The Quadroon; or, A Lover's Adventures in Louisiana.* 3 vols., orange cloth. London, 1856. (By Thomas M. Reid.) First edition. $200.

REID, Mayne. *The Wild Huntress.* 3 vols., cloth. London, 1861. (By Thomas M. Reid.) First edition. $75-$125.

REID, Samuel C., Jr. *The Scouting Expeditions of McCulloch's Texas Rangers.* 12 plates and plan. Cloth. Philadelphia, 1847. First edition. $150. Philadelphia, 1859. Cloth. $35-$50. Philadelphia, 1860. Cloth. $35-$50.

REID, Thomas M. See Reid, Mayne.

REIGN of Reform (The). By a Lady. Baltimore, 1830. (By Mrs. Margaret Botsford.) First edition. $35.

REIGN of Terror in Kanzas (The). 34 pp., wrappers. Boston, 1856. (By Charles W. Briggs.) First edition. $350-$450.

RELIEF Business Directory. Names and New Locations in San Francisco, Oakland, Berkeley and Alameda of 4,000 San Francisco Firms and Business Men. 64 pp., wrappers. Berkeley, Calif., May, 1906. $75.

REMARKS Addressed to the Citizens of Illinois, in the Proposed Introduction of Slavery.
14 pp., disbound. No place, no date (Vandalia?, 1824?). (By Morris Birkbeck.) Stained,
$1,700 (A, 1967).

REMARQUE, Erich Maria. *All Quiet on the Western Front.* Buckram. London, no date
(1929). First edition in English. In dust jacket. $50-$75. Boston, 1929. Gray cloth. First
American edition. In dust jacket. $15-$20. (Note: The first edition in German, *Im
Westen Nichts Neues,* Berlin, 1929, wrappers, is worth roughly $25-$35 if in fine
condition.)

REMBRANDT VAN RIJN, H. *The Complete Works of Rembrandt.* Text by W. Bode,
assisted by C. Hofstede de Groot, from the German translation by Florence Simmonds.
595 large, 21 small reproductions, 4 facsimiles of letters. 8 vols., folio, half brown
morocco. Paris, 1897-1906. One of 75 on Holland paper. $600-$800. Also, $450 (A,
1969).

REMINGTON, Frederic. *Crooked Trails.* 49 plates. Pictorial tan cloth. New York, 1898.
First edition. In dust jacket. $150-$200.

REMINGTON, Frederic. *Done in the Open.* Introduction by Owen Wister. Illustrations by
Remington. 90 pp., folio, cream-colored pictorial boards. New York, 1902. First edition,
first issue, with Russell imprint and with "Frederick" instead of "Frederic" on front
cover. $150. Another issue: Suede leather. One of 250 signed. $150-$200. Later issue:
New York, 1902. Collier imprint. Half cloth. $50-$60. New York, 1903. Half cloth. $25.

REMINGTON, Frederic. *Drawings.* 61 plates. Oblong folio, pictorial boards and cloth. New
York, 1897. First edition. Boxed. $100-$200. Another issue: Suede leather. One of 250
signed. $200-$300.

REMINGTON, Frederic. *Frederic Remington's Own West.* Edited by Harold McCracken.
Colored frontispiece, other illustrations. Cowhide. New York, 1960. First edition. One
of 167 signed by McCracken. Boxed. $125-$150.

REMINGTON, Frederic. *Frontier Sketches.* Illustrated by the author. Oblong, pictorial
boards. Chicago, no date (1898). First edition. $200-$225.

REMINGTON, Frederic. *John Ermine of the Yellowstone.* Brown cloth. New York, 1902.
First edition. $50-$75. (Note: First edition copies, as well as reprints, misspell the
author's name "Reminigton" on the spine.)

REMINGTON, Frederic. *Men with the Bark On.* Illustrated by the author. Pictorial
orange-tan cloth. New York, 1900. First edition, first issue, 7/8 inch thick (later 1 1/8
inches). $75-$125.

REMINGTON, Frederic. *Pony Tracks.* Illustrated by the author. Brown decorated cloth, or
leather. New York, 1895. First edition. Cloth: $150-$250. Leather: $150-$250.
Author's first book.

REMINGTON, Frederic. *A Rogers Ranger in the French and Indian War.* Printed wrappers.
No place (New York), 1897. First edition. $35.

REMINGTON, Frederic. *Sundown Leflare.* Illustrated by the author. Brown pictorial cloth.
New York, 1899. First edition. $35-$50.

REMINGTON, Frederic. *The Way of an Indian.* Illustrated by the author. Cloth. New York,
1906. First edition, first issue, February, crimson cloth, yellow lettering with "Fox,
Duffield & Company" on spine and page 9 so numbered. $100-$125. Second issue
copies: $35-$50.

REMINISCENCES of a Campaign in Mexico. Map, frontispiece. Cloth. Nashville, 1849. (By
John B. Robertson.) First edition. $50-$75. Spine chipped, light foxing, stains,
autographed, $75.

REMSBURG, John E. and George J. *Charley Reynolds, Soldier, Hunter, Scout and Guide.*
Portrait. Cloth. Kansas City, Mo., 1931. First book edition. One of 175. $37.50-$50.

RENFROW, W. C. *Oklahoma and the Cherokee Strip.* Folding map. 16 pp., wrappers. Chicago, 1893. $35-$50.

REPLY to the Essay on Population, by the Rev. T. R. Malthus (A). Leather-backed gray boards. London, 1807. (By William Hazlitt.) First edition. $250-$300. Also, half calf, $145.60 (A, 1967).

RÉSPONSE à une Addresse de la Chambre des Communes, en date du 23 Avril 1869, Demandant un Rapport Indiquant le Progrès qui ont été faits dans L'Ouverture d'une Communication entre Fort William et l'Établissement de la Rivière Rouge . . . Par Ordre Hector L. Langevin, Secrétaire d'État. 88 pp., half morocco. Ottawa. 1869. $35-$50.

REPORT from a Select Committee of the House of Representatives, on the Overland Emigration Route from Minnesota to British Oregon. Printed wrappers, marbled spine. St. Paul, Minn., 1858. $350 (A, 1968). Another copy in a retail catalogue: Rebound in cloth, $450.

REPORT from the Select Committee on the Hudson's Bay Company. 3 elephant folio colored folding maps by Arrowsmith. Half morocco. London, 1857. First edition. $150-$200. (Note: There was also an advance issue in wrappers, 2 parts, same date, catalogued in the 1950's by a New York dealer at $250.)

REPORT of a Committee Appointed by the Trustees of the Town of Milwaukee, Relative to the Commerce of That Town and the Navigation of Lake Michigan. 12 pp., sewed. Milwaukee, 1842. (By I. A. Lapham and F. Randall.) $250. Also, rebound in cloth, $250 (A, 1967).

REPORT of the Board of Canal Commissioners, to the General Assembly of Ohio. Sewed. Columbus, Ohio, 1824. $75.

REPORT of the Board of Directors of Internal Improvements of the State of Massachusetts, on the Practicability and Expediency of a Rail-Road from Boston to the Hudson River, and from Boston to Providence. 6 folding plans. Boston, 1829. $85.

REPORT of the Board of Internal Improvements for the State of Kentucky, and Reports of the Engineers. 47 pp., sewed. No place, no date (Frankfort, Ky., 1836). $25-$35.

REPORT of the Canal Commissioners, to the General Assembly of Ohio. 54 pp., stitched. Columbus, 1825. $45. Another issue, 66 pp., sewed. $25.

REPORT of the Commissioner of Public Buildings, with the Documents Accompanying the Same. 36 pp., stitched. No place, no date (Madison, Wis., 1842). (By John Smith.) $50-$60.

REPORT of the Committee to Whom Was Referred, on the 26th Ultimo, the Consideration of the Expediency of Accepting from the State of Connecticut, a Cession of Jurisdiction of the Territory West of Pennsylvania, Commonly Called the Western Reserve of Connecticut. 31 pp., calf. No place (Philadelphia), 1800. $75.

REPORT of the General Assembly upon the Subject of the Proceedings of the Bank of the U.S., Against the Officers of State. 37 pp., sewed. Columbus, Ohio, 1820. $50-$75.

REPORT of the Proceedings Connected with the Disputes Between the Earl of Selkirk and the North-West Company. Half leather. London, 1819. (Samuel Hull Wilcocke, editor.) $450. Montreal, 1819. Calf. $225 (A, 1969).

REPORT of the Secretary of the Interior, Communicating . . . the Report of J. Ross Browne, on the Late Indian War in Oregon and Washington Territories. 66 pp., stitched. Washington, 1858. First edition. $50. New paper covers, $35.

REPORT of the Trial of Frederick P. Hill, etc. 60 pp., wrappers. Chicago, 1864. (Allan Pinkerton, editor.) First edition. $75.

REPORT on the Committee of the Society of Arts. Engraved folding plate and 5 engraved full-page reproductions. Boards. London, 1819. $50-$60.

REPORT on the Governor's Message, Relating to the "Political Situation," "Polygamy," and "Governmental Action." 13 pp., wrappers. Salt Lake, 1882. $35.

REPORT on [sic] the Secretary of the Navy, etc. (December, 1864.) Half morocco. Washington, 1864. Inscribed "Compliments of the Secretary of the Navy." $45.

REPORT on the Subject of a Communication between Canandaigua Lake and the Erie Canal, Made at a Meeting of the Citizens. 23 pp., sewed. Canandaigua, N.Y., 1821. $35-$50.

REPORT Relative to the Excitements, on the Part of British Subjects, of the Indians to Commit Hostility Against the U.S., and the Late Campaign on the Wabash. 43 pp., sewed. Washington City, 1812. $50-$75.

REPORTS and Resolutions of the General Assembly of the State of South Carolina. Gathered, not sewed, but punched for stitching. Columbia, S.C., 1863. $25.

REPORTS of the Committee of Investigation Sent in 1873, by the Mexican Government, to the Frontier of Texas. 3 folding maps. Boards and leather. New York, 1875. $75-$125.

REPORTS of Territorial Officers of the Territory of Colorado. Wrappers. Central City, Colo., 1871. $35-$50.

REPPLIER, Agnes. *Books and Men.* Boards and cloth. Boston, 1882. First edition. $25. Author's first book.

REPTON, Humphrey. *Observations on the Theory and Practice of Landscape Gardening.* Portrait frontispiece and 27 plates, 10 of them in full color. Many vignettes. Three-quarters morocco. London, 1803. First edition. $750-$1,000. Also, $720 (A, 1969).

RESIGNATION: An American Novel by a Lady. 2 vols., marbled boards and calf. Boston, 1825. (By Sarah Ann Evans.) First edition, with errata leaf in Vol. 1. $100-$150.

RESOURCES of Arizona (The). 71 pp., wrappers. No place, no date (Florence, Ariz., 1881). (By Patrick Hamilton.) First edition. $50-$75. Prescott, Ariz., 1881. 120 pp., printed wrappers. (Author named.) Second edition. $35-$50. (Note: There were later editions, including a San Francisco edition of 1883, which Howes calls a "second" edition.)

RESOURCES and Development of the Territory of Washington. Folding map. 72 pp., sewed. Seattle, 1886. $35-$50.

REVERE, Joseph W. *A Tour of Duty in California.* 6 plates, folding map. Cloth. New York, 1849. First edition. $150-$200.

REVIEW of the Opinion of the Supreme Court in the Case of Cohen vs. Virginia, etc. 78 pp., stitched. Steubenville, Ohio, 1821. (By Charles Hammond.) $35.

REYNARDSON, C. T. S. Birch. *'Down the Road' or Reminiscences of a Gentleman Coachman.* Colored lithographs. Cloth. London, 1875. First edition. $50-$75.

REYNOLDS, H. D. (editor). *Wells Cathedral.* Frontispiece, 4 plans (one folding), a folding table, 8 plates and text illustrations. Folio, morocco. London, no date (1881). $50-$75.

REYNOLDS, J. N. *Voyage of the United States Frigate Potomac.* Illustrated. Half leather. New York, 1835. First edition. $50-$75.

REYNOLDS, John. *My Own Times.* Portrait. Cloth. Illinois (Belleville), 1855. First edition. $250-$350.

REYNOLDS, John. *The Pioneer History of Illinois.* Cloth. Belleville, 1852. First edition. $150-$200.

REYNOLDS, John. *Sketches of the Country on the Northern Route from Belleville, Ill., to the City of New York, and back by the Ohio Valley.* Black cloth. Belleville, 1854. First edition. $300-$400.

REZANOV, Nicolai P. *The Rezanov Voyage to Nueva California in 1806.* Edited by Thomas C. Russell. 5 plates. Half cloth. San Francisco, 1926. One of 200. $40-$45.

REZNIKOFF, Charles. *Five Groups of Verse.* Cloth. New York, no date (1927). First edition. One of 375. In dust jacket. Boxed. $30.

REZNIKOFF, Charles. *Nine Plays.* Cloth. New York, no date (1927). First edition. One of 400. In dust jacket. $30.

RHODES, Eugene Manlove. *The Best Novels and Stories of Eugene Manlove Rhodes.* Cloth. Boston, 1949. First edition. In dust jacket. $25.

RHODES, Eugene Manlove. *Bransford in Arcadia.* Cloth. New York, 1914. First edition. In dust jacket. $35-$50.

RHODES, Eugene Manlove. *Good Men and True.* Cloth. New York, 1910. First edition. In dust jacket. $35.

RHODES, Eugene Manlove. *The Little World Waddies.* Cloth. Chico, Calif., no date (1946). First edition. $35-$50.

RHODES, Eugene Manlove. *The Proud Sheriff.* Cloth. Boston, 1935. First edition. In dust jacket. $25-$30.

RHODES, Eugene Manlove. *Say Now Shibboleth.* Cloth. Chicago, 1921. Book Fellows. First edition. One of 400. $50.

RHODES, Eugene Manlove. *Stepsons of Light.* Cloth. Boston, no date (1921). First edition. In dust jacket. $25-$35.

RHODES, Eugene Manlove. *The Trusty Knaves.* Cloth. Boston, 1933. First edition. In dust jacket. $25-$35.

RHODES, Eugene Manlove. *West Is West.* Frontispiece. Cloth. New York, 1917. First edition. In dust jacket. $25-$35.

RHODES, W. H. *The Indian Gallows and Other Poems.* Cloth. No place (New York), 1846. First edition. $50-$60.

RHODODAPHNE; or The Thessalian Spell: A Poem. Blue boards. London, 1818. (By Thomas Love Peacock.) First edition. $150.

RICARDO, David. *On the Principles of Political Economy, and Taxation.* Contemporary calf. London, 1817. First edition. One of 500. $200-$250. Georgetown, D.C., 1819. Half leather. First American edition. $75 $100.

RICE County: Its Resources. 20 pp., wrappers. Faribault, Minn., 1860. $125-$150.

RICE, Edward Le Roy. *Monarchs of Minstrelsy, from "Daddy" Rice to Date.* Illustrated. Cloth. New York, no date (about 1911). $50-$75.

RICH, Adrienne Cecile. *A Change of World.* Foreward by W. H. Auden. Boards. New Haven, Conn., 1951. First edition. In dust jacket. $35-$50. Author's first book.

RICH, Edward R. *Comrades Four.* Cloth. New York, 1907. $60-$75.

RICHARD Hurdis; or, the Avenger of Blood. 2 vols., cloth, paper labels. Philadelphia, 1838. (By William Gilmore Simms.) First edition. $35-$50.

RICHARDS, Laura E. *Captain January.* Gray boards, white cloth spine. Boston, 1891. First edition, first state, with typography and presswork note at foot of copyright page. $35-$50.

RICHARDS, Thomas Addison. *American Scenery.* Illustrated. Cloth. New York, no date (1854). $75-$100.

RICHARDS, Thomas Addison. *Georgia Illustrated.* Plates. 44 pp., leather. Penfield, Ga., 1842. First edition. $75-$100.

RICHARDS, Thomas Addison. *The Romance of American Landscape.* 16 engravings. Morocco. New York, no date (1854). First edition. $40-$60.

RICHARDSON, Ernest C. *An Alphabetical Subject Index and Index Encyclopedia to Periodical Articles on Religion, 1890-1899.* Cloth. New York, 1907. $50.

RICHARDSON, Maj. John. *Eight Years in Canada.* Cloth. Montreal, 1847. $100-$150.

RICHARDSON, Richard. *The Genealogy of the Richardson Family of the State of Delaware.* Cloth. No place, 1878. $30-$40.

RICHARDSON, Rupert N. *The Comanche Barrier to South Plains Settlement.* Illustrated. Cloth. Glendale, Calif., 1933. $50-$75.

RICHARDSON, Rupert N., and Rister, C. C. *The Greater Southwest.* Cloth. Glendale, 1934. First edition. $35-$50.

RICHARDSON, William H. *The Journal of William H. Richardson: A Private Soldier in Col. Doniphan's Command.* 84 pp., wrappers. Baltimore, 1847. First edition. $3,300 (A, 1966). New York, 1848. Third edition. $50.

RICHEY, James H. *A Trip Across the Plains in 1854.* 8 pp., wrappers. No place, no date (Richey, Calif., 1908). $25-$35.

RICHMOND During the War; Four Years of Personal Observation. Cloth. New York, 1867. (By Sally A. Brock.) First edition. $50-$75. Rebound in buckram, $35.

RICHTOFEN, Walter, Baron Von. *Cattle-Raising on the Plains of North America.* Cloth. New York, 1885. First edition. $100-$125.

RIDGE, John R. See *Yellow Bird.* Also see *The Life of Joaquin Murieta.*

RIDGE, John R. *Joaquin Murieta, the Brigand Chief of California.* Color plates, folding reward poster facsimile. Boards. San Francisco, 1932. Grabhorn printing. One of 400. $50-$60.

RIDGE, John R. *The Life and Adventures of Joaquin Murieta the Celebrated California Bandit.* Printed wrappers. San Francisco, no date (1874). Third (?) edition. $375 (A, 1968). (Note: This edition included a separate title page—*Career of Tiburcio Vasquez*—and is listed by Howes as a reprint of the third edition, which he records as published in 1871.)

RIDING, Laura. *Americans.* Boards and cloth. No place, 1934. Primavera Press. One of 200. $40-$50.

RIDING, Laura. *Collected Poems.* Cloth. New York, 1938. First American edition. In dust jacket. $35.

RIDING, Laura. *Four Unposted Letters to Catherine.* Boards and leather. Paris, no date (1930). Hours Press. First edition. One of 200 signed. In glassine dust jacket. $50-$60.

RIDING, Laura. *Laura and Francisca.* Decorated blue boards and cloth. Deya, Majorca, 1931. Seizin Press. First edition. One of 200 signed. In glassine dust jacket. $60-$80.

RIDING, Laura. *Love as Love, Death as Death.* Tan or gray cloth. London, 1928. Seizin Press (its first book). First edition. One of 175 signed. $50-$75.

RIDING, Laura. *The Second Leaf.* Wrappers (actually a broadside folded to make 4 leaves). Deya, 1935. Seizin Press. First edition. Limited (fewer than 100). $40-$60.

RIDING, Laura. *Though Gently.* Decorated boards and cloth. Deya, 1930. Seizin Press. First edition. One of 200 signed. In glassine dust jacket. $60-$80.

RIDING, Laura. *Twenty Poems Less.* Half leather and boards. Paris, 1930. Hours Press. First edition. One of 200 signed. In glassine dust jacket. $50-$60.

RIDINGS, Sam P. *The Chisholm Trail.* Folding map. Cloth. Guthrie, Okla., no date (1936). First edition. In dust jacket. $75-$100.

RIDLER, Anne (editor). *The Little Book of Modern Verse.* Preface by T. S. Eliot. Cloth. London, 1941. First edition. In dust jacket. $25-$35.

RIENZI, The Last of the Tribune. 3 vols., boards. London, 1835. (By Edward Bulwer-Lytton.) First edition, with errata slips for Vols. 2 and 3 tipped into Vol. 2. $80-$100.

RILEY, James Whitcomb. See Johnson, Benj. F. (of Boone).

RILEY, James Whitcomb. *Character Sketches, The Boss Girl, A Christmas Story, and Other Sketches.* Cloth, or printed wrappers. Indianapolis, 1886. First edition, first printing, with copyright notice in the name of Riley and an exclamation point after "sir" in line 5 of page 9. Cloth: $25. Wrappers: $35.

RILEY, James Whitcomb. *Poems Here at Home.* Cloth, or vellum. New York, 1893. First edition, first state, with "girls" spelled correctly in line 5 on page 50. In dust jacket. $35. Later, $20-$25.

RILEY, James Whitcomb. *Rhymes of Childhood.* Cloth. Indianapolis, 1891. First edition, first state, with child's head illustrated on front cover. $37.50.

RILEY, James Whitcomb, and Nye, Edgar W. (Bill). *Nye and Riley's Railway Guide.* Cloth. Chicago, 1888. First edition. $25.

RIMBAUD, Arthur. *Prose Poems from "Les Illuminations."* Translated by Helen Rootham. Introduction by Edith Sitwell. Orange-colored cloth. London, no date (1932). First English edition. In dust jacket. $25.

RIMMEL, Eugene. *The Book of Perfumes.* Cloth. London, 1865. $100. London, 1897. 250 illustrations. Cloth. $35-$50.

RINEHART, Mary Roberts, and Hopwood, Avery. *The Bat: A Novel from the Play by Mary Roberts Rinehart and Avery Hopwood.* Cloth. New York, no date (1926). First edition. In dust jacket. $35-$50. Lacking jacket, $25. (Note: Believed to have been written by Stephen Vincent Benét.)

RINGWALT, John Luther. *American Encyclopedia of Printing.* Cloth. Philadelphia, 1871. $40-$60.

RIORDAN, Joseph W. *The First Half Century of St. Ignatius Church and College.* Cloth. San Francisco, 1905. $25.

RIVER Dove (The); with Some Quiet Thoughts on the Happy Practice of Angling. 14 engravings. Half leather. No place, no date (London?, about 1845). (By John L. Anderdon.) One of 25 privately printed. $250-$300. (Note: One of 6 folio copies, extra-illustrated, was offered for sale in 1969 in a London catalogue at $540.)

RIVERS, Elizabeth. *Stranger in Arran.* Illustrations (4 in color) by author. Boards, linen spine. Dublin, 1946. In dust jacket. $35-$50.

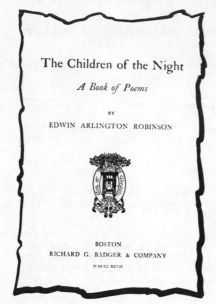

The Children of the Night

A Book of Poems

BY

EDWIN ARLINGTON ROBINSON

BOSTON
RICHARD G. BADGER & COMPANY
M DCCC XCVII

RUBÁIYÁT

OF

OMAR KHAYYÁM,

THE ASTRONOMER-POET OF PERSIA.

Translated into English Verse.

LONDON:
BERNARD QUARITCH,
CASTLE STREET, LEICESTER SQUARE.
1859.

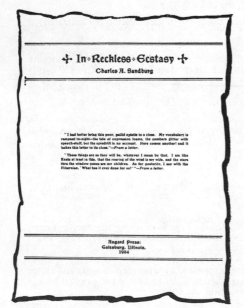

✠ In · Reckless · Ecstasy ✠
Charles A. Sandburg

"I had better bring this poor, pallid epistle to a close. My vocabulary is rampant to-night—the tide of expression foams, the combers glitter with speech-stuff, but the spindrift is no account. Here comes another! and it lashes this letter to its close."—*From a letter.*

"These things are as they will be, whatever I mean by that. I am like Keats at least in this, that the roaring of the wind is my wife, and the stars thru the window panes are my children. As for posterity, I say with the Hibernian, 'What has it ever done for us?' "—*From a letter.*

Asgard Press:
Galesburg, Illinois,
1904

CHICAGO POEMS

By

CARL SANDBURG

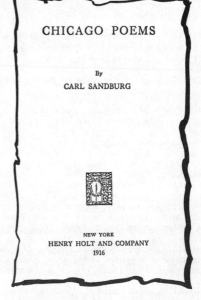

NEW YORK
HENRY HOLT AND COMPANY
1916

ROB of the Bowl. 2 vols., cloth, paper labels on spines. Philadelphia, 1838. (By John Pendleton Kennedy.) First edition. $100-$150.

ROB Roy. 3 vols., boards, paper labels. Edinburgh, 1818. (By Sir Walter Scott.) First edition. $150-$200.

ROBB, John S. See *Streaks of Squatter Life, etc.*

ROBB, John S. *Kaam, or Daylight.* Pictorial wrappers. Boston, 1847. $200 (A, 1968).

ROBBINS, Aurelia. *A True and Authentic Account of the Indian War, etc.* 28 pp., wrappers. New York, 1836. $150.

ROBERTS, Elizabeth Madox. *Black Is My Truelove's Hair.* Boards, green buckram spine. New York, 1938. First edition. One of 175 signed. Boxed. $35.

ROBERTS, Elizabeth Madox. *A Buried Treasure.* Green buckram. New York, 1931. First edition. One of 200 signed. Boxed. $25-$35.

ROBERTS, Elizabeth Madox. *The Great Meadow.* Green buckram. New York, 1930. First edition. One of 295 large paper copies, signed. Boxed. $25-$35.

ROBERTS, Elizabeth Madox. *In the Great Steep's Garden.* Cloth. No place, no date (Colorado Springs, Colo., 1915). First edition. $35-$50. Author's first book.

ROBERTS, Kenneth. *Arundel.* Dark-blue cloth. Garden City, N.Y., 1930. First edition (so indicated on copyright page). In dust jacket. $25.

ROBERTS, Kenneth. *Lydia Bailey.* Cloth. Garden City, 1947. First edition. Gray buckram. One of 1,050 signed with a page of the ms., with corrections in Roberts' hand, laid in. In dust jacket. Boxed. $50-$60.

ROBERTS, Kenneth. *Northwest Passage.* Dark-green cloth. Garden City, 1937. First edition (so indicated on copyright page). In dust jacket. $25-$35. Another issue: 2 vols., cloth. One of 1,050 signed. In dust jackets. Boxed. $75-$100.

ROBERTS, Kenneth. *Oliver Wiswell.* Cloth. New York, 1940. First edition (so indicated). 2 vols., cloth. One of 1,050 signed. $50-$60.

ROBERTS, Kenneth. *Rabble in Arms.* Cloth. Garden City, 1933. First edition (so indicated on copyright page). In dust jacket. $40-$50.

ROBERTS, Kenneth. *Sun Hunting.* Green cloth. Indianapolis, no date (1922). First edition. In dust jacket. $25.

ROBERTS, Kenneth. *Trending into Maine.* Illustrated by N. C. Wyeth. Tan buckram. First edition, with "Published June 1938" on copyright page. In dust jacket. $25. Another issue: Cloth. One of 1,075 signed. Boxed. $100-$125.

ROBERTS, Oran M. *A Description of Texas.* 8 colored plates, 5 double-page maps. Cloth. St. Louis, 1881. First edition. $75-$100.

ROBERTS, W. H. *Northwestern Washington.* Folding map. 52 pp., wrappers. Port Townsend, Wash., 1880. First edition. $150-$200.

ROBERTSON, John W. *Francis Drake and Other Early Explorers Along the Pacific Coast.* 28 maps. Illustrations by Valenti Angelo. Vellum and boards. San Francisco, 1927. Grabhorn Press. One of 1,000. $65-$75.

ROBERTSON, Wyndham, Jr. *Oregon, Our Right and Title.* Folding map. Boards and cloth, or printed wrappers. Washington, 1846. First edition. $750-$1,000. Also, original boards and cloth, $650 (A, 1969); original wrappers, $300 (A, 1959)

ROBIDOUX, Mrs. Orral M. *Memorial to the Robidoux Brothers.* Map. 16 plates. Cloth. Kansas City, Mo., 1924. First edition. $60-$80.

ROBINSON, Charles Edson. *A Concise History of the United Society of Believers Called Shakers.* Illustrated. Boards and calf. East Canterbury, N.H., no date (1893). $25.

ROBINSON, Charles N. *Old Naval Prints, Their Artists and Engravers.* 106 full-page plates, 24 in color. Cloth. London, 1924. In dust jacket. $125-$150.

ROBINSON, Edwin Arlington. *Amaranth.* Cloth. New York, 1934. First edition. Large paper issue, one of 226 signed. $35-$50. Trade edition: Green cloth. In dust jacket. $25.

ROBINSON, Edwin Arlington. *Avon's Harvest.* Light maroon boards and cloth. New York, 1921. First edition. In dust jacket. $25.

ROBINSON, Edwin Arlington. *Captain Craig: A Book of Poems.* Cloth, paper label. Boston, 1902. First edition, first issue, with copyright line and "Published October, 1902" on copyright page. One of 125 untrimmed. $100.

ROBINSON, Edwin Arlington. *Cavender's House.* Cloth. New York, 1929. First edition. One of 500 signed. In slipcase. $50. Trade edition: Cloth. In dust jacket. $6.

ROBINSON, Edwin Arlington. *The Children of the Night.* Muslin. Boston, 1897. First edition. One of 50 on Japan vellum. $250-$300. Another issue: Boards. One of 500 on Batchworth laid paper. In dust jacket. $150-$200.

ROBINSON, Edwin Arlington. *Dionysus in Doubt.* Cloth-backed boards. New York, 1925. First edition. One of 350 large paper copies, signed. $25-$35. Trade edition: Cloth. First issue, with gray (instead of white) labels. In dust jacket. $15-$25.

ROBINSON, Edwin Arlington. *Fortunatus.* Boards, paper label. Reno, 1928. Grabhorn printing. First edition. One of 171 signed. $100. Spine chipped, $30. One of 12 on brown paper, signed, for presentation. $300 and up.

ROBINSON, Edwin Arlington. *The Glory of the Nightingales.* Cloth. New York, 1930. First edition. One of 500 signed. $35-$50. Trade edition: Green cloth. In dust jacket. $10.

ROBINSON, Edwin Arlington. *King Jasper.* Introduction by Robert Frost. Cloth. New York, 1935. First edition. One of 250 large paper copies. $35-$50. Trade edition: Cloth. In dust jacket. $12.50 and $10.

ROBINSON, Edwin Arlington. *Lancelot.* Dark-maroon cloth. New York, 1920. First edition. One of 450 for the Lyric Society. $35-$50. Trade edition: Gray-green cloth (first binding; later red). In dust jacket. $25. Another, jacket torn, $15.

ROBINSON, Edwin Arlington. *The Man Against the Sky.* Dark-red cloth. New York, 1916. First edition, first state, with top edges gilt. In dust jacket. $35.

ROBINSON, Edwin Arlington. *The Man Who Died Twice.* Boards and cloth. New York, 1924. First edition. One of 500 signed. $25-$35. Trade edition: Red cloth. In dust jacket. $15.

ROBINSON, Edwin Arlington. *Matthias at the Door.* Green cloth. New York, 1931. First edition, first state, with no punctuation at end of fifth line from bottom of page 97. One of 500 signed. Boxed. $35-$45. Trade edition: Cloth. In dust jacket. $7.50.

ROBINSON, Edwin Arlington. *Merlin.* Red cloth. New York, 1917. First edition, first state, with "only philosophy" (instead of "one philosophy") in line 8 of page 79. In dust jacket. $15-$25.

ROBINSON, Edwin Arlington. *Modred: A Fragment.* Boards and cloth. New York, 1929. First edition. One of 250 signed. In slipcase. $25.

ROBINSON, Edwin Arlington. *Nicodemus.* Cloth. New York, 1932. First edition. One of 235 large paper copies, signed. $15-$25.

ROBINSON, Edwin Arlington. *The Porcupine.* Cloth. New York, 1915. First edition, first state, with top edges gilt and with rules and lettering on front cover in gold. Erratum slip. In dust jacket. $25. Lacking erratum slip, $17.50.

ROBINSON, Edwin Arlington. *The Prodigal Son.* Wrappers. New York, 1929. First edition. One of 475. $25.

ROBINSON, Edwin Arlington. *Roman Bartholow.* Boards and cloth. New York, 1923. First edition. One of 750 signed. $40-$60.

ROBINSON, Edwin Arlington. *Sonnets 1889-1927.* Boards and cloth. New York, 1928. First edition. One of 561. $25. Another issue: One of 9 on green paper. $50.

ROBINSON, Edwin Arlington. *Talifer.* Cloth. New York, 1933. First edition. One of 273 large paper copies, signed. $35. Trade edition: Cloth. In dust jacket. $15.

ROBINSON, Edwin Arlington. *Three Poems.* Cloth. Cambridge, Mass., 1928. First (pirated) edition. One of 15 (?) copies. $25-$50.

ROBINSON, Edwin Arlington. *The Three Taverns.* Maroon cloth. New York, 1920. First edition. In dust jacket. $25.

ROBINSON, Edwin Arlington. *The Torrent and the Night Before.* Blue wrappers. Gardiner, Me., 1896. First edition. $400-$600. Author's first book. New York, 1928. One of 110 signed. $75.

ROBINSON, Edwin Arlington. *The Town Down the River.* Dark-green silk. New York, 1910. First edition. In dust jacket. $50.

ROBINSON, Edwin Arlington. *Tristram.* Half cloth. New York, 1927. First edition, first state, with "rocks" for "rooks," line 2 on page 86. One of 350 large paper copies, signed. Boxed. $35-$50. Trade and Literary Guild editions (issued simultaneously): Cloth. In dust jacket. $15-$20.

ROBINSON, Edwin Arlington. *Van Zorn.* Dark-maroon cloth. New York, 1914. First edition, first state, with top edges gilt and with cover lettering in gold. In dust jacket. $30-$35.

ROBINSON, J. A. *The White Rover.* 100 pp., wrappers. New York, no date. $35-$50.

ROBINSON, Jacob. *Sketches of the Great West.* 71 pp., wrappers. Portsmouth, N.H., 1848. First edition. $3,500 and up.

ROBINSON, John, and Dow, George F. *The Sailing Ships of New England, 1607-1907.* 3 vols., cloth. Series I, II, and III. Salem, 1922-24-28. $75, $100, and $150. Separately: Series I, 1922, and Series II, 1924, each $47.50 in a recent catalogue.

ROBINSON, Lennox (editor). *A Little Anthology of Modern Irish Verse.* Blue boards, linen back, paper label. Dublin, 1928. Cuala Press. First edition. One of 300. In plain dust jacket. $75.

ROBINSON, Rowland Evans. See *Forest and Stream Fables.*

ROBINSON, Rowland Evans. *Uncle 'Lisha's Shop.* Cloth. New York, 1887. First edition. $30. Author's first book.

ROBINSON, William Davis. *Memoirs of the Mexican Revolution.* Half leather. Philadelphia, 1820. First edition. $100-$125. London, 1821. 2 vols., half morocco. $100-$125.

ROBSON, John S. *How a One Legged Rebel Lives, or a History of the 52nd Virginia Regiment.* Wrappers. Richmond, Va., 1876. $100.

ROCHESTER, John Wilmot, Earl of. *Collected Works.* Edited by John Hayward. Boards and buckram. London, 1926. Nonesuch Press. $100-$125. Another issue: Boards and vellum. One of 75. $200.

ROCK, Marion T. *Illustrated History of Oklahoma.* 90 plates. Cloth. Topeka, 1890. First edition. $100-$125.

RODD, Rennell. *Rose Leaf and Apple Leaf.* Introduction by Oscar Wilde. Vellum. Philadelphia, 1882. First edition. De luxe issue. $50.

RODENBOUGH, Theodore F. *Uncle Sam's Medal of Honor.* Cloth. New York, no date (1886). First edition. $25-$30.

RODRÍGUEZ DE SAN MIQUEL, Juan. *Documentos Relativos al Piadoso Fondo de Misiones para Conversión y Civilización de las Numerosas Tribus Barbaras de la Antigua y Nueva California.* 60 pp., calf. Mexico, 1845. First edition. $50 (A, 1968). (Note: Catalogued by one New York dealer at $350 a few years before.) Another edition, same date, 28 pp. added. Wrappers. $80 (A, 1968).

RODRIGUEZ DE SAN MIQUEL, Juan. *Rectificación de Graves Equivocaciones en que Inciden los Sonores Terceros Posedores de Bienes del Fondo Piadoso de Californias, etc.* 16 pp., stitched. Mexico, 1845. $200.

RODRÍGUEZ DE SAN MIQUEL, Juan. *Segundo Cuaderno de Interesantes Documentos Relativos a los Bienes del Fondo Piadoso de Misiones, para Conversión y Civilización de las Tribus Barbaras de las Californias.* 32 pp., wrappers. Mexico, 1845. $350.

ROE, Azel Stevens. *James Montjoy: or I've Been Thinking.* 2 parts, wrappers. New York, 1850. First edition. $50.

ROE, Edward Payson. *Barriers Burned Away.* Cloth. New York, 1872. First edition. $35-$50.

ROETHKE, Theodore. See *Ten Poets.*

ROETHKE, Theodore. *Open House.* Cloth. New York, 1941. First edition. One of 1,000. $100-$150.

ROETHKE, Theodore. *Sequence Sometimes Metaphysical.* Illustrated. Boards. Iowa City, no date (1963). First edition. One of 330. Boxed. $150-$200.

ROETHKE, Theodore. *Words for the Wind.* Cloth. London, 1957. First edition. In dust jacket. $35.

ROFF, Joe T. *A Brief History of Early Days in North Texas and the Indian Territory.* Wrappers. No place (Allen, Okla.), 1930. First edition. $35-$50.

ROGERS, A. N. *Communication Relative to the Location of the U.P.R.R. Across the Rocky Mountains Through Colorado Territory.* Wrappers. Central City, Colo., 1867. Lacking back cover, $325.

ROGERS, Robert. *Journals of Maj. Robert Rogers.* Edited by Franklin B. Hough. Map. Cloth. Albany, N.Y., 1883. $75-$100.

ROLFE, Frederick William. See Corvo, Baron. Also see *Prospero and Caliban.*

ROLLINS, Philip Ashton. *Jinglebob.* Illustrated in color by N. C. Wyeth. Cloth. New York, 1930. First edition. In dust jacket. $35.

ROLLINS, Philip Ashton (editor). *The Discovery of the Oregon Trail.* Cloth. New York, 1935. In dust jacket. $30-$40.

ROLLINSON, John K. *History of the Migration of Oregon-Raised Herds to Mid-Western Markets: Wyoming Cattle Trails.* Plates, maps, colored frontispiece by Frederic Remington. Cloth. Caldwell, Idaho, 1948. One of 1,000 signed. $50-$60.

ROLLINSON, John K. *Hoofprints of a Cowboy and a U.S. Ranger.* Cloth. Caldwell, Idaho, 1941. In dust jacket. $35-$50.

ROLLO Learning to Talk. Woodcut illustrations. Decorated cloth. Philadelphia, 1841. (By Jacob Abbott.) New edition (of *The Little Scholar Learning to Talk,* 1835). $50.

ROLPH, J. Alexander. *Dylan Thomas: A Bibliography.* 16 pp. of plates. Cloth. London, no date (1956). First edition. In dust jacket. $25-$35.

ROMANCE of Indian History: or, Thrilling Incidents in the Early Settlement of America. 24 pp., wrappers. New York, no date (185-?). (By Adam Poe.) $35-$50.

RONSARD, Pierre de. *Florilège des Amours.* 126 lithographs by Henri Matisse. Lithograph on paper cover, folio, in slipcase designed by Matisse. Paris, 1948. Albert Skira. One of 250 signed by the artist. $2,500 and up. Also, $2,400 (A, 1969).

ROOD, Hosea W. *Story of the Service of Co. E.* Cloth. Milwaukee, 1893. $50-$60.

ROOSEVELT, Eleanor. *This I Remember.* Frontispiece and plates. Buckram. New York, no date (1949). First edition. One of 1,000 on large paper, signed. Boxed. $40-$60.

ROOSEVELT, Eleanor. *This Is My Story.* Buckram. New York, 1937. First edition. One of 258 signed. $50-$75.

ROOSEVELT, Franklin D. *The Democratic Book, 1936.* Illustrated. Folio, wrappers. No place, 1936. Limited edition, signed by F. D. R. $150-$250.

ROOSEVELT, Franklin D. *The Happy Warrior: Alfred E. Smith.* 40 pp., black cloth, orange label. Boston, 1928. First edition. In dust jacket. $50-$60.

ROOSEVELT, Franklin D. *Inaugural Address of, March 4, 1933.* 9 pp., printed wrappers. Washington, 1933. $24. Same, for January 20, 1937. Printed wrappers. Washington, 1937. $35-$50. Other addresses: *Fourth Inaugural Address.* Printed wrappers. Washington, 1945. $110 (A, 1967). *Second Inaugural Address.* Printed wrappers. Washington, 1937. $25. *Third Inaugural Address.* Printed wrappers. Washington, 1941. $25.

ROOSEVELT, Franklin D. *Looking Forward.* Wrappers. New York, no date (1933). First edition. One of 100. $50-$75. Trade edition: Cloth. In dust jacket. $10-$15.

ROOSEVELT, Franklin D. *Whither Bound?* 34 pp., cloth. Boston, 1926. First edition. In dust jacket. $50.

ROOSEVELT, Franklin D. (editor). *Records of the Town of Hyde Park.* Cloth. No place, 1928. One of 100, with limitation notice written out and signed by F.D.R. $100-$125.

ROOSEVELT, Theodore. *American Ideals and Other Essays.* Cloth. New York, 1897. First edition. $25.

ROOSEVELT, Theodore. *Big Game Hunting in the Rockies.* 55 etchings. Signed frontispiece. Full tan buckram. First edition. $75-$100. (Note: Also issued in various types of leather binding.)

ROOSEVELT, Theodore. *Hunting Trips of a Ranchman.* 20 plates. Buckram. New York, 1885. First edition. Limited Medora Edition of 500. $50-$75. New York, 1886. Cloth. First trade edition. $25.

ROOSEVELT, Theodore. *Letter . . . Accepting the Republican Nomination for President of the United States.* 32 pp., self-wrappers. No place (New York), 1902. First edition. $50-$75.

ROOSEVELT, Theodore. *List of Birds Seen in the White House Grounds.* 4 pp., leaflet. No place (Washington), 1908. First edition. $50-$60.

ROOSEVELT, Theodore. *Naval War of 1812*. Cloth. New York, 1882. First edition. $35. (Note: Second edition so indicated on title page.)

ROOSEVELT, Theodore. *Ranch Life and the Hunting-Trail*. Illustrated by Frederic Remington. All edges gilt, light-colored, coarse weave, tan buckram, cover design in green and gold. New York, no date (1888). First edition. $75-$100. Later, bound in brown linen, cover design green and gold. $25-$35.

ROOSEVELT, Theodore. *The Rough Riders*. Cloth. New York, 1899. First edition. $25-$35.

ROOSEVELT, Theodore. *Some American Game*. Wrappers. New York, 1897. First edition. $50-$100.

ROOSEVELT, Theodore. *Theodore Roosevelt: An Autobiography*. Illustrated. Cloth. New York, 1913. First edition. In dust jacket. $25.

ROOSEVELT, Theodore. *Thomas Hart Benton*. Cloth. Boston, 1887. First edition. $25.

ROOSEVELT, Theodore. *The Value of an Athletic Training*. Edited by R. W. G. Vail. Wrappers. New York, 1929. First edition. One of 51. $50-$75.

ROOSEVELT, Theodore. *The Wilderness Hunter*. Tan or brown cloth. New York, no date (1893). First edition, with chapter headings in brown. $25. Another issue: Cloth. One of 200 signed. $75-$100.

ROOSEVELT, Theodore. *The Winning of the West*. 4 vols., cloth. New York, 1889-96. First edition. (Vol. 1: 1889; Vol. 2: 1889; Vol. 3: 1894; Vol. 4: 1896.) First edition, first issue, with "diame-" as last word on page 160 and "ter" as first word on page 161. $75-$125. New York, 1900. Illustrated. 4 vols. $35-$50. Another issue: Half morocco. One of 200 with a page of ms. $150-$200.

ROOSEVELT, Theodore, and Minot, H. D. *The Summer Birds of the Adirondacks*. 4 pp., leaflet. No place, no date (New York, 1877). First edition. $100-$125.

ROOT, Frank A., and Connelley, William E. *The Overland Stage to California*. Illustrated. Map. Pictorial cloth. Topeka, Kan., 1901. First edition. $125-$150.

ROOT, Henry. *Personal History and Reminiscences*. Cloth. San Francisco, 1921. One of 100 signed. $35-$50.

ROOT, Riley. *Musical Philosophy*. 20 pp., wrappers. Galesburg, Ill., 1866. First edition. $50-$75.

ROSE Garden of Omar Khayyam (The). Miniature book, magnifying glass, proof sheet and text "A Thimbleful of Books," contained in a case. Worcester, Mass., 1932. $100-$150.

ROSE, Mrs. S. E. F. *The Ku Klux Klan*. 8 pp., wrappers. West Point, Miss., 1909. $50-$75.

ROSEN, Peter. *Pa-Ha-Sa-Pah, or The Black Hills of South Dakota*. 27 plates. Pictorial cloth. St. Louis, 1895. First edition. $100-$150.

ROSENBACH, A. S. W. *Early American Children's Books*. Edited by A. Edward Newton. Hand-colored plates. Full blue morocco. Portland, Me., 1933. One of 88, signed. Boxed. $350. Another issue: Half morocco. One of 585 signed. Boxed. $200-$250.

ROSENTHAL, Leonard. *The Kingdom of the Pearl*. Illustrated in color by Edmund Dulac. Boards and vellum. New York, no date. One of 100 signed by Dulac. In dust jacket. $125.

ROSS, Harvey L. *The Early Pioneers and Pioneer Events of the State of Illinois*. Portrait. Cloth. Chicago, 1898. First edition. $75-$100.

ROSS, Mrs. William P. *The Life and Times of Hon. William P. Ross.* Portrait. Cloth. No place, no date (St. Louis, or Fort Smith, Ark., about 1893). First edition. $30-$40.

ROSSETTI, Christina. *Poems.* Chosen by Walter de la Mare. Wood-engraving portrait by R. A. Maynard. Printed on Japanese vellum. Red morocco, by the Gregynog bindery. Newtown, Wales, 1930. Gregynog Press. One of 300. Boxed. $600-$750. Also, $456 (A, 1968). Ordinary issue: Boards and calf. One of 300. $75-$100.

ROSSETTI, Christina. *Verses.* Edited by J. D. Symon. Boards. Hammersmith (London), 1906. Eragny Press. One of 175 on paper. $132.

ROSSETTI, Dante Gabriel. *Ballads and Sonnets.* Blue cloth. London, 1881. First edition. $60. London, 1893-94. Kelmscott Press. Woodcut title and initials. 2 vols., limp vellum with ties. One of 310. $150-$250.

ROSSETTI, Dante Gabriel. *Hand and Soul.* Woodcut title and borders. Vellum. London, 1895. Kelmscott Press. One of 225. $150-$200. London, 1899. Vale Press. Morocco. One of 210. $312 (A, 1967). Portland, Me., 1906. Mosher Press. Wrappers. $25.

ROSSETTI, Dante Gabriel. *Poems.* Cloth. London, 1870. First collected edition. $50-75. London, 1904. Plates. 2 vols., vellum. One of 30. $35-$50. Portland, Me., 1892. Mosher Press. One of 450. $25.

ROSSETTI, Dante Gabriel. *Sonnets and Lyrical Poems.* Woodcut title and borders by William Morris. Printed in black and red. Vellum with ties. London, 1893. Kelmscott Press. One of 310. $200-$250.

ROSSETTI, Dante Gabriel (translator). *The Early Italian Poets from Ciullo d'Alcamo to Dante Alighieri.* Cloth. London, 1861. First edition. $50-$60.

ROSSI, Filippo. *Italian Jewelled Arts.* Illustrated. Cloth. New York, 1954. $35-$50. London, 1957 (actually 1958). Illustrated. Cloth. $35-$50.

ROSSI, Mario M. *Pilgrimage in the West.* Boards and linen. Dublin, 1933. Cuala Press. One of 300. $75.

ROTH, Philip. *Goodbye Columbus.* Black cloth. Boston, 1959. First edition. In dust jacket. $25-$35. Author's first book. Paris, no date (1962). First French translation. One of 33 on velin. In glassine dust jacket. $25.

ROTHENSTEIN, William. *Twenty-four Portraits.* Cloth. London, 1923. First edition. One of 1,500. $25-$35.

ROTHERT, Otto A. *A History of Muhlenburg County.* Cloth. Louisville, 1913. First edition. $35-$50.

ROTHERT, Otto A. *The Outlaws of Cave-in-Rock.* 10 maps and plans. Cloth. Cleveland, 1924. First edition. In dust jacket. $50-$60.

ROUX, Antoine (illustrator). *Ships and Shipping: A Collection of Pictures Painted by Antoine Roux and His Sons.* Text by Bres and Gaubert, translated by Alfred Johnson. Folio, boards and cloth. Salem, Mass., 1925. One of 97 on large paper. Boxed. $200-$250. Ordinary issue: Cloth. $50-$60.

ROWLAND, Benjamin. *The Wall-Paintings of India.* Edited by A. K. Coomaraswamy. 30 colored plates, other illustrations. Printed wrappers. 1938. In cloth portfolio. $75-$100.

ROYAL Illuminated Book of Legends (The). 16 full-page color plates illuminated by Marcus Ward. Oblong, cloth. Edinburgh, no date (about 1890). $27.50.

ROYALL, Anne. See *Sketches of History, Life, and Manners, in the United States.*

ROYIDIS, Emmanuel. *Pope Joan.* Translated by Lawrence Durrell. Cloth. London, no date (1954). First edition. In dust jacket. $35.

RUBAIYAT of Omar Khayyam, The Astronomer-Poet of Persia. Translated into English verse. Brown wrappers. London, 1859. (Translated by Edward FitzGerald.) First edition. (250 copies printed.) $3,500-$4,000. Also, $2,600 (A, 1962); $1,500 (A, 1967); $500 (A, 1956); rebacked, $850 (A, 1952); $3,700, with pen correction by FitzGerald (A, 1963); rebound in vellum, $700 (A, 1961); in binder's cloth, $1,512 (A, 1963); in morocco, $800 (A, 1965); morocco, $800 (A, 1969); morocco, $550 (A, 1959); $400 (A, 1951); $325 (A, 1954). Madras, India, 1862. Limp green cloth. One of 50 reprinted from the London first edition with a note by M. Garcin de Tassy. $200-$300. Also, $106.40 (A, 1960). London, 1868. Wrappers. Second English edition. $300-$400. Also, $275 (A, 1962); rebacked, $110 (A, 1964); $80 (A, 1959); rebound in morocco, $15 (A, 1956); $40 and $42 (A, 1952); $260 (A, 1952); vellum boards, $130 (A, 1964); boards, $225 (A, 1962). London, 1872. Half dark-red cloth and leather. Third edition. $200-$250. Also, $45 (A, 1962); rebound in morocco, inlaid leathers, $1,000 (A, 1969). London, 1879. Frontispiece. Half cloth. Fourth edition. $150-$200. Also, $100 (A, 1962); rebound in morocco, with 8 original watercolors, $600 (A, 1969); Rebound with inlays of precious stone, $250 (A, 1956). London, 1896. Ashendene Press. Wrappers. One of 50. $1,000 and up. Also, $750 (A, 1969). No place (Cambridge, Mass.), 1900. Boards and buckram. One of 300 printed by Bruce Rogers. $75-$100. London, 1902. Vellum. Greek translation by E. Crawley. One of 25 on vellum. $150-$250. London, 1909. Illustrated by Edmund Dulac. Vellum. One of 750 signed by the artist. $100-$150. London, no date (1910). Edited by A. C. Benson. Pictorial vellum. $150-$250. London, 1920. Illustrated by Blanche McManus. Vellum. One of 21 on vellum. $100. Newtown, Wales, 1928. Gregynog Press. Translated into Welsh by J. Morris Jones. Woodcuts. Buckram. One of 310. $75-$100. London, 1930. Illustrated in color by Willy Pogany. Leather. One of 750 signed by the artist and with an extra proof etching, signed. $150-$200. London, 1938. Golden Cockerel Press. Illustrated. $150-$200. New York, 1940. Heritage Press. Color plates by Arthur Szyk. Pictorial padded calf and marbled boards. $50-$75. London, 1958. Golden Cockerel Press. Illustrated by J. Yunge Bateman. Pictorial morocco. One of 75 specially bound, with an extra set of plates. Boxed. $250-$300. Also, $157 (A, 1968). (Note: There have been numerous other editions of this classic work since its first appearance in 1859. Consult the British and American auction records for a more exhaustive survey.)

RUBEK, Sennoia. *The Burden of the South, in Verse.* Frontispiece. Printed wrappers. New York, no date (about 1864). (By John Burke.) $37.50-$50.

RUBESAM, Fred. *Grenzerleben, Bilder und Skizzen aus dem "Wilden Western."* Chicago, 1894. First edition. $50-$75.

RUDD, Dan A., and Bond, Theo. *From Slavery to Wealth: The Life of Scott Bond.* Illustrated. Cloth. Madison, Ark., 1917. First edition. $75-$100.

RUDO Ensayo, tentativa de nua Provencional Descripción, Geográphica de la Provincia de Sonora. Edited by Buckingham Smith. San Augustin (St. Augustine—printed in Albany), 1863. First edition. $200. Another issue: One of 10 on large paper. $250-$300.

RUINED Deacon (The): A True Story. By a Lady. Printed wrappers. Boston, 1834. (By Mary L. Fox.) First edition. $100-$125.

RULES and Orders of the House of Representatives of the Territory of Washington, 1864-5. 32 pp., wrappers. Olympia, Washington Territory, 1864. $50-$60.

RULES and Regulations of the Utah and Northern Railway, for the Government of Employees. Calf. Salt Lake City, 1879. $35-$50.

RULES for the Government of the Council of Wisconsin Territory. 10 pp., plain wrappers. Madison, Wis., 1843. $50-$60. Madison, 1845, 11 pp., plain wrappers. $40-$50.

RULES for the Government of the House of Representatives of Wisconsin Territory. 10 pp., plain wrappers. Madison, 1845. $75-$100.

RULES for Regulating the Practice of the District Court of the U.S. etc. 31 pp., stitched. Pittsburgh, 1824. First edition. $35-$50.

RULES, Regulations, and By-Laws of the Board of Commissioners to Manage the Yosemite Valley and Mariposa Big Tree Grove. 23 pp., wrappers. Sacramento, Calif., 1885. $50-$75.

RUPP, I. Daniel. *History of the Counties of Berks and Lebanon.* 3 plates. Sheep. Lancaster, Pa., 1844. First edition. $50-$75.

RUPP, I. Daniel. *History of Lancaster County, Pennsylvania.* Illustrated. Sheep. Lancaster, Pa., 1844. First edition. $75.

RUPPIUS, Otto. *Das Vermächtnis des Pedlars. Roman aus dem Amerikanischen Leben.* Half leather. St. Louis, 1859. $50.

RUPPIUS, Otto. *Der Prairie-Teufel. Roman aus dem Amerikanischen Leben.* Half leather. St. Louis, 1861. $75.

RUPPIUS, Otto. *Geld und Geist. Roman aus dem Amerikanischen Leben.* Leather. St. Louis, 1860. $50-$60.

RUSK, Fern H. *George Caleb Bingham.* Illustrated. Cloth. Jefferson City, Mo., 1917. One of 500. $50-$75.

RUSKIN, John. Special note: Many of the works once attributed to Ruskin have turned out to be Thomas J. Wise forgeries. The following brief list is representative of Ruskin's major endeavors.

RUSKIN, John. See Greenaway, Kate (illustrator), *Dame Wiggins of Lee.*

RUSKIN, John. *The Crown of Wild Olive.* Cloth. London, 1866. First edition. $25. Rebound in morocco by the Doves Bindery, $100.

RUSKIN, John. *The Elements of Drawing.* Cloth. London, 1857. First edition. $50-$75.

RUSKIN, John. *The King of the Golden River.* Boards. London, 1851. First edition. $100-$150. London, 1932. Illustrated by Arthur Rackham. Limp vellum. Boxed. $150.

RUSKIN, John. *The Nature of Gothic: A Chapter of the Stones of Venice.* Preface by William Morris. Illustrated. Vellum with ties. London, 1892. Kelmscott Press. One of 500. $150.

RUSKIN, John. *Poems.* Cloth. No place (London), 1850. First edition. $500-$600.

RUSKIN, John. *The Political Economy of Art.* Cloth. London, 1857. First edition. $30.

RUSKIN, John. *The Seven Lamps of Architecture.* Illustrated. Cloth. London, 1849. $100-$125.

RUSKIN, John. *Unto This Last: Four Essays on the First Principles of Political Economy.* Vellum. London, 1907. Doves Press. One of 300. $100-$125.

RUSSELL, Alex J. *The Red River Country, Hudson's Bay and North-west Territories, etc.* Folding map. Wrappers. Ottawa, 1869. First edition. $150. Montreal, 1870. Folding map, 7 folding plates. Wrappers. $150.

RUSSELL, Charles M. (illustrator). See *How the Buffalo Lost His Crown.*

RUSSELL, Charles M. *Back-trailing on the Old Frontiers.* 16 full-page drawings. 56 pp., pictorial wrappers. Great Falls, Mont., 1922. First edition. $75-$100.

RUSSELL, Charles M. *Good Medicine.* Introduction by Will Rogers. Illustrated by the author. Cloth. New York, 1930. First edition. In dust jacket. $75-$150. Another issue: Half buckram. One of 134 on large paper. $250-$300.

RUSSELL, Charles M. *More Rawhides*. Illustrated by the author. 60 pp., pictorial wrappers. Great Falls, 1925. First edition. $75-$150.

RUSSELL, Charles M. *Pen and Ink Drawings*. 2 vols., oblong boards and cloth. Pasadena, Calif., no date (1946). First edition. $50-$60.

RUSSELL, Charles M. *Pen Sketches*. 12 plates. Oblong, leatherette. Great Falls, no date (1898). First edition. $300-$400. (Note: Some copies with original drawings on flyleaves have brought much higher prices.)

RUSSELL, Charles M. *Rawhide Rawlins Stories*. Illustrated by the author. Pictorial wrappers. Great Falls, 1921. First edition. $75-$100. Another issue: Full limp leather. Presentation copy. $350-$400.

RUSSELL, Charles M. *Trails Plowed Under*. Cloth. New York, 1927. First edition. In dust jacket. $50-$60.

RUSSELL, George. See E., A.

RUSSELL, Osborne. *Journal of a Trapper*. 105 pp. No place, no date (Boise, Idaho, 1914). First edition. $200-$250. Boise, no date (1921). Second edition. 149 pp., cloth. $50-$75. Portland, no date. Champoeg Press. One of 750. $35-$50.

RUSSELL, Peter (editor). *A Collection of Essays . . . to Be Presented to Ezra Pound on His 65th Birthday*. Portrait frontispiece. Tan cloth. London, no date (1950). First edition. In dust jacket. $50-$60.

RUST, Margaret. *The Queen of the Fishes*. 16 woodcuts, 4 colored, by Lucien Pissarro. Vellum. Epping, England, 1894. Eragny Press. One of 150. $250-$275. (Note: The first book produced by this press.)

RUTH Whalley; or, The Fair Puritan. (Cover title.) 72 pp., pink wrappers. Boston, 1845. (By Henry William Herbert.) $75-$100. (Note: In some copies the author is listed as "William Henry Herbert." There is also said to be an 1844 edition.)

RUTTENBER, E. M. *History of the County of Orange: With a History of the Town and City of Newburgh*. Plates, maps. Newburgh, N.Y., 1875. First edition. $40-$60.

S

S., E. W., and M., S. W. *The Children's Hour.* Illustrated. Cloth. Philadelphia, 1864. (By Elizabeth W. Sherman and S. Weir Mitchell.) First edition. $100-$150.

S., P. B. *Zastrozzi: A Romance.* Dark blue-gray boards, drab cloth spine, paper label. London, 1810. (By Percy Bysshe Shelley.) First edition. $750-$1,000, possibly much more. London, 1955. Golden Cockerel Press. Plates. Morocco. One of 60 with duplicate set of plates. $150-$200.

S., S. H. *Nine Experiments.* Green wrappers. Hampstead, England, 1928. (By Stephen Spender.) First edition. One of about 18 copies issued. Bad presswork required filling in some letters by hand in ink. In cloth case, with leather label. $2,100. (This copy, catalogued by a New York dealer in 1968, belonged to Spender's sister-in-law. An inscribed copy offered by New York dealer in 1971 at $5,000.)

SABIN, Edwin L. *Kit Carson Days (1809-1868).* Maps, plates. Brown cloth. Chicago, 1914. First edition. $25-$50. Chicago, 1919. Second edition. $30. New York, 1935. 2 vols., cloth. Revised edition. One of 1,000. $35-$50. One of 200 signed. $75.

SABINE and Rio Grande Railroad Co. Memorial of Duff Green, President. 50 pp. Washington, 1860. $35.

SACRED Writings of the Apostles and Evangelists of Jesus Christ, etc. (The). New Testament translation by George Campbell, James McKnight, and Philip Doddridge. Preface by Alexander Campbell. Contemporary calf. Buffaloe, Brooke County, Va., 1826. First edition. $50-$75.

SACK and Destruction of the City of Columbia, S.C. Wrappers. Columbia, 1865. (By William Gilmore Simms.) First edition. Up to $500. Lacking wrappers, $300.

SACKVILLE-WEST, Victoria. *Sissinghurst.* Boards. London, 1931. One of 500 signed. $25-$35.

SADLEIR, Michael. *Hyssop.* Cloth. London, no date (1915). First edition. In dust jacket. $35. Lacking jacket, $25. Author's first novel.

SAFETY FIRST: A Musical Comedy in Two Acts. Decorated wrappers. Princeton, 1916-17. $350. (Note: Contains lyrics by F. Scott Fitzgerald.)

SAGE, Rufus B. *Scenes in the Rocky Mountains.* Half calf. Philadelphia, 1847. Second edition. $75-$100. (For first edition, see title entry.)

SAGE, Rufus B. *Wild Scenes in Kansas and Nebraska, the Rocky Mountains, etc.* Half leather. Philadelphia, 1855. Third ("revised") edition (of *Scenes in the Rocky Mountains,* which see under title entry). $35.

SAGRA, Ramón de la. *Historia Económica-Política y Estadística de la Isla de Cuba.* Wrappers. Havana, 1831. First edition. $50-$100.

ST. CLAIR, Maj. Gen. (Arthur). *A Narrative of the Manner in Which the Campaign Against the Indians, in the Year 1791, Was Conducted.* Boards. Philadelphia, 1812. First edition. $75-$100. Rebound, $35-$75.

ST. FRANCIS OF ASSISI. *I Fioretti del Glorioso Poverello di Cristo S. Francesco di Assisi.* 54 woodcuts. Vellum. London, 1922. Ashendene Press. One of 240. $100-$125.

ST. IRVYNE; or, The Rosicrucian: A Romance. By a Gentleman of the University of Oxford. Drab boards, green cloth spine. London, 1811. (By Percy Bysshe Shelley.) First edition. $1,000 and up.

ST. JOHN, James Augustus, and D'Avennes, Emile Prisse. *Oriental Album.* 30 full-page color plates. Elephant folio, half morocco. London, 1848. $100-$150.

ST. JOHN, John R. *A True Description of the Lake Superior Country.* 2 folding maps. Printed cloth. New York, 1846. First edition. $150-$250.

ST. LOUIS, Iron Mountain & Southern Railway Company vs. W. J. Newcom and J. F. Hudson. Brief for Plaintiff. 54 pp., wrappers. Little Rock, Ark., 1893. $25.

ST. RONAN'S Well. 3 vols., boards. Edinburgh, 1824. (By Sir Walter Scott.) First edition. $50-$75.

SAINTSBURY, George. *Notes on a Cellar-Book.* Parchment paper boards and cloth. London, 1921. First edition. One of 500 signed. $50.

SAISSY, Jean-Antoine. *An Essay on the Diseases of the Internal Ear.* Frontispiece. Sheep. Baltimore, 1829. First American edition. $50-$75.

SAKI. *Reginald.* Red cloth. London, no date (1904). (By H. H. Munro.) First edition. $25-$50. Author's first book.

SAKI. *The Westminster Alice.* Green wrappers. London, no date (about 1902). (By H. H. Munro.) First edition. $25.

SALAMAN and Absal: An Allegory. Translated from the Persian of Jami by Edward FitzGerald. Frontispiece. Blue cloth. London, 1856. First edition. $35-$50.

SALATHIEL: A Story of the Past, the Present, and the Future. 3 vols., half calf. London, 1828. (By the Rev. George Croly.) First edition. $50-$75.

SALAZAR Ylarregui, José. *Datos de los Trabajos Astronómicos y Topográficos, Dispuestos en Forma de Diario.* 2 folding maps. Blue wrappers. Mexico, 1850. First edition. $350-$500.

SALE, Edith Tunis. *Manors of Virginia in Colonial Times.* 49 plates. Cloth. Philadelphia, 1909. First edition. $25-$35.

SALINGER, J. D. See *The Kit Book for Soldiers, Sailors, and Marines.*

SALINGER, J. D. *The Catcher in the Rye.* Black cloth. Boston, 1951. First edition (so stated). In dust jacket. $75-$100. Also, $65 (A, 1970). Author's first novel. (Note: This book reached a peak of popularity within a decade after publication and has an auction record of $130 [1963].)

SALINGER, J. D. *Nine Stories.* Cloth. Boston, no date (1953). First edition (so stated). In dust jacket. $85-$100. Also, $80 (A, 1970).

SALINGER, J. D. *Raise High the Roof Beam, Carpenters, and Seymour: An Introduction.* Cloth. Boston, no date (1963). First edition, first issue, without dedication page. In dust jacket. $90-$100. Second issue, with dedication page tipped in in front of half title. $25-$35. Third issue, with dedication correctly placed. $15.

SALISBURY, Samuel. *A Descriptive, Historical, Chemical and Therapeutical Analysis of the Avon Sulphur Springs, Livingston County.* 95 pp., sewed. Rochester, N.Y., 1845. $35.

SALLEY, Alexander S., Jr. *The History of Orangeburg County.* Folding map, portrait. Cloth. Orangeburg, S.C., 1898. First edition. $35-$50.

SALMONY, Alfred. *Sculpture in Siam.* Collotype plates. Full morocco. London, 1925. One of 25. $75-$100. Trade edition: Cloth. $40-$60. Paris, 1925. Printed wrappers. $50. Also, $25 (A, 1968).

SALPOINTE, John B. *A Brief Sketch of the Mission of San Xavier del Bac with a Description of Its Church.* 20 pp., wrappers. San Francisco, 1880. First edition. $75.

SALPOINTE, J. B. *Soldiers of the Cross.* Portrait, 45 plates. Cloth. Banning, Calif., 1898. First edition. $50-$75.

SALT Lake City Directory and Business Guide (The). Folding map, folding view. 53-219 pp., as issued, boards. Salt Lake City, 1869. (By Edward L. Sloan.) First edition. $75.

SALTER, William. *Memoirs of Joseph W. Pickett.* Brown cloth. Burlington, Iowa, 1880. First edition. $35.

SALVERTE, Comte François de. *Les Ébénistes du XVIIIe Siècle.* 66 plates. Wrappers. Paris, 1927. $75.

SALZMANN, C. G. *Gymnastics for Youth.* 9 plates. Boards. London, 1800. First English edition. $150-$200. Philadelphia, 1802. First American edition. Leather. $75-$100. Philadelphia, 1803. 10 plates. Calf. $60-$70.

SAN BERNARDINO County, California. Illustrated Description of. 34 pp., printed wrappers. San Bernardino, 1881. $100-$150.

SAN BERNARDINO County, California. Ingersoll's Century Annals of San Bernardino County, 1769-1904. Full leather. Los Angeles, 1904. $35-$50.

SAN FRANCISCO Bay and California in 1776. Maps and facsimiles. 7 pp., boards. Providence, R.I., 1911. (By Pedro Font.) One of 125. $75.

SAN FRANCISCO Board of Engineers: Report upon the City Grades. 27 pp., wrappers. San Francisco, 1854. $60.

SANBORN, Ralph, and Clark, Barrett H. *A Bibliography of the Works of Eugene O'Neill.* Illustrated. Cloth. New York, 1931. First edition. One of 500. $35-$50. (Note: Contains previously unpublished work by O'Neill.)

SANDBURG, Carl. See Sandburg, Charles A.; Wright, Philip Green.

SANDBURG, Carl. *Abraham Lincoln: The Prairie Years.* Illustrated. 2 vols., blue cloth. New York, no date (1926). First edition, so stated on copyright page. In dust jackets. Boxed. $40. Large paper issue. 2 vols., boards and cloth. First state, with line 9 on page 175 of Vol. 1 reading "ears" instead of "eyes." One of 260 signed. Boxed. $250. Later, "ears" corrected, $200-$250.

SANDBURG, Carl. *Abraham Lincoln: The War Years.* Illustrated. 4 vols., blue cloth. New York, no date (1939-41). First edition, so stated. In dust jackets. Boxed. $50-$75. Large paper issue: Brown buckram. One of 525 sets on all rag paper, numbered and signed. In dust jackets. Boxed. $150-$250.

SANDBURG, Carl. *Always the Young Strangers.* Cloth. New York, no date (1953). First edition. $10-$15. Another issue. Cloth. One of 600 on large paper, signed. Boxed. $35-$50.

SANDBURG, Carl. *The American Songbag.* Red cloth. New York, no date (1927). First edition. In dust jacket. $25-$30.

SANDBURG, Carl. *Bronze Wood.* Frontispiece. 8 pp., orange boards. No place, no date (San Francisco, 1941). Grabhorn Press. First edition. One of 195. In dust jacket. $35-$50.

SANDBURG, Carl. *Chicago Poems.* Cloth. New York, 1916. First edition, with ads at back dated "3'16." In dust jacket. $75-$100.

SANDBURG, Carl. *The Chicago Race Riots.* Printed wrappers. New York, 1919. First edition. $50-$100.

SANDBURG, Carl. *Cornhuskers.* Boards. New York, 1918. First edition, first state, with page 3 so numbered at foot of page. In dust jacket. $35-$50.

SANDBURG, Carl. *Early Moon.* Cloth. New York, no date (1930). First edition, first printing, so indicated on copyright page. In dust jacket. $25-$35.

SANDBURG, Carl. *Good Morning, America.* Cloth. New York, 1928. First edition. In dust jacket. $10-$15. Limited issue. Cloth. One of 811 signed. $25-$35. (Note: A few were printed on blue paper.)

SANDBURG, Carl. *Lincoln Collector.* Illustrated. Cloth. New York, no date (1949). First edition. $10-$20. Large paper issue: Cloth. Signed. $25-$40.

SANDBURG, Carl. *A Lincoln and Whitman Miscellany.* Cloth. Chicago, 1938. First edition. One of 250. $50-$75.

SANDBURG, Carl. *Mary Lincoln, Wife and Widow.* Cloth. New York, no date (1932). First edition, first printing (so indicated on copyright page). $10-$15. Large paper issue: One of 260 signed. $35-$40.

SANDBURG, Carl. *The People, Yes.* Cloth. New York, no date (1936). First edition, first printing (so indicated on copyright page). In dust jacket. $15-$20. Large paper issue: One of 270 signed. In slipcase. $35-$50.

SANDBURG, Carl. *Potato Face.* Boards and cloth. New York, no date (1930). First edition (so stated). In dust jacket. $25-$35.

SANDBURG, Carl. *Remembrance Rock.* Cloth. New York, no date (1948). First edition. In dust jacket. $15-$20. Another issue: 2 vols., buckram. One of 1,000 signed. In tissue dust jackets. Boxed. $40-$60.

SANDBURG, Carl. *Rootabaga Pigeons.* Illustrated. Pictorial cloth. New York, no date (1923). First edition. In dust jacket. $50-$75.

SANDBURG, Carl. *Rootabaga Stories.* Illustrated by Maud and Miska Petersham. Pictorial cloth. New York, no date (1922). First edition. In dust jacket. $75-$100.

SANDBURG, Carl. *Slabs of the Sunburnt West.* Cloth. New York, no date (1922). First edition, first issue, with text ending at the foot of page 75. In dust jacket. $25-$35.

SANDBURG, Carl. *Smoke and Steel.* Green boards. New York, 1920. First edition. In dust jacket. $75-$100.

SANDBURG, Carl. *Steichen, the Photographer.* Illustrated. Cloth. New York, no date (1929). First edition. One of 925, signed by author and artist. $100-$150.

SANDBURG, Charles A. *In Reckless Ecstasy.* Wrappers. Galesburg, Ill., 1904. (By Carl Sandburg.) First edition. $1,000 and up. Author's first book. Copy offered by dealer for $1,250 in 1972.

SANDERS, Daniel C. *A History of the Indian Wars with the First Settlers of the United States.* Sheep. Montpelier, Vt., 1812. First edition. $100-$150.

SANDERS, Capt. John. *Memoir on the Military Resources of the Valley of the Ohio.* 19 pp., unbound. Pittsburgh, 1845. First edition. $75-$100. Washington, 1845. 24 pp., unbound. $50.

SANDOZ, Mari. *The Battle of the Little Bighorn.* Half morocco. New York, 1966. First edition. One of 249 signed. $50.

SANDOZ, Mari. *The Beaver Men.* Illustrated. Half leather. New York, 1964. First edition. One of 185 signed. $45-$50.

SANDOZ, Mari. *The Cattlemen.* Illustrated. Cloth. New York, no date (1958). First edition. Advance presentation copy, signed. $30-$35.

SANDOZ, Mari. *Crazy Horse.* Illustrated. Cloth. New York, 1942. First edition. In dust jacket. $35-$60.

SANDOZ, Maurice. *The Maze.* Illustrated by Salvador Dali. Cloth. Garden City, N.Y., 1945. First edition. In dust jacket. $50-$75.

SANDOZ, Maurice. *On the Verge.* Illustrated in color by Salvador Dali. Cloth. Garden City, 1950. First edition. In dust jacket. $25-$50.

SANDS, Frank. *A Pastoral Prince: The History and Reminiscences of Joseph Wright Cooper.* Illustrated. Pictorial cloth. Santa Barbara, Calif., 1893. First edition. $100-$125. Signed copy, $90.

SANFORD, Nettie. *Central Iowa Farms and Herds.* Cloth. Newton, 1873. First edition. $25-$30.

SANFORD, Nettie. *History of Marshall County, Iowa.* 5 plates. Cloth. Clinton, 1867. $45-$60.

SANSOM, Joseph. *Sketches of Lower Canada, Historical and Descriptive.* Frontispiece view of Quebec. Boards. New York, 1817. First edition. $50-$75.

SANTAYANA, George. See *Lines on Leaving the Bedford St. Schoolhouse.*

SANTAYANA, George. *Poems.* Cloth. London, no date (1922). First edition. One of 100 signed. $125-$150.

SANTAYANA, George. *Sonnets and Other Verses.* Buckram. Cambridge, Mass., 1894. First edition. $20-$40. Another issue: One of 50 on vellum. $100-$150.

SANTLEBEN, August. *A Texas Pioneer.* Cloth. New York, 1910. First edition. In dust jacket. $75.

SARA, Col. Delle. *Silver Sam; or, the Mystery of Deadwood City.* 166 pp., wrappers. New York, no date (1877). $35.

SARGENT, Charles Sprague. *The Silva of North America.* Illustrated. 14 vols., printed boards. Boston, 1890-1902. First edition. In dust jackets. $1,250. Also, $1,000 (A, 1969).

SARGENT, Charles Sprague (editor). *Plantae Wilsonianae: an Enumeration of the Woody Plants Collected in Western China by E. H. Wilson.* 3 vols., half morocco. Cambridge, Mass., 1913-17. $175.

SARGENT, George B. *Notes on Iowa.* Map. 74 pp., cloth. New York, 1848. First edition. $350-$500.

SAROYAN, William. See *Edward VIII.* Also see *The State of the Nation.*

SAROYAN, William. *A Christmas Psalm.* Rose boards, white cloth spine. San Francisco, 1935. Grabhorn Press. First edition, with greeting card and envelope, as issued, laid in. One of 200 signed. $50-$75.

SAROYAN, William. *Contes.* 8 colored woodcuts. Pictorial wrappers. No place, no date (Paris, 1953). One of 100 signed. $50-$75.

SAROYAN, William. *The Daring Young Man on the Flying Trapeze.* Gray cloth, paper label. New York, 1934. First edition. In dust jacket. $40-$50. Author's first book.

SAROYAN, William. *The Fiscal Hoboes.* Boards. New York, 1949. First edition. One of 250 signed. $35-$50.

SAROYAN, William. *Fragment.* Folio, wrappers. No place, no date (San Francisco, 1938). First edition. One of 150 signed. $30-$40.

SAROYAN, William. *Harlem as Seen by Hirschfeld.* Illustrated. Folio, cloth. New York, no date (1941). First edition. In slipcase. $75-$100.

SAROYAN, William. *Hilltop Russians in San Francisco.* 30 colored plates by Pauline Vinson. Boards and cloth. No place (San Francisco), 1941. Grabhorn Press. $35.

SAROYAN, William. *A Native American.* Cloth. San Francisco, 1938. First edition. One of 450. $40-$45.

SAROYAN, William. *Saroyan's Fables.* Illustrated by Warren Chappell. No place, no date (New York, 1941). One of 1,000 signed. Boxed. $35-$50.

SAROYAN, William. *A Special Announcement.* Cloth. New York, 1940. First edition. One of 250 signed. In tissue dust wrapper. $25-$35.

SAROYAN, William. *Those Who Write Them and Those Who Collect Them.* Printed wrappers. Chicago, 1936. Black Archer Press. One of 50. $35-$50. (Note: There are variant colored wrappers; no priority.)

SAROYAN, William. *Three Fragments and a Story.* Printed wrappers. Cincinnati, no date (1939). Little Man Press. First edition. $20-$25.

SAROYAN, William. *Three Times Three.* Cloth. No place (Los Angeles), 1936. First edition. One of 250 signed. In dust jacket. $35-$50.

SARTOR Resartus. (Reprinted from *Fraser's Magazine.*) Various bindings: calf, morocco, etc. No place (London), 1834. First edition. (By Thomas Carlyle.) One of about 48, 50, or 58 (bibliographers differ) privately printed for the author's friends. In full morocco, $750. Also, old calf, inscribed to the author's brother, $750 (A, 1969). London, 1907. Doves Press. Vellum. One of 300. $250-$300.

SASSOON, Siegfried. See Kain, Saul; Lyre, Pinchbeck. Also see *Lingual Exercises for Advanced Vocabularians; Memoirs of a Fox-Hunting Man; Memoirs of an Infantry Officer; Orpheus in Diloeryum; Poems; Recreations.*

SASSOON, Siegfried. *Counter-Attack and Other Poems.* Wrappers. London, 1918. First edition. $15-$50.

SASSOON, Siegfried. *Emblems of Experience.* Wrappers. Cambridge, 1951. First edition. One of 75 signed. $175.

SASSOON, Siegfried. *The Heart's Journey.* Boards and parchment. New York, 1927. First edition. One of 599. $100-$125. Another issue: One of 9 on green paper. $45.

SASSOON, Siegfried. *Memoirs of a Fox-Hunting Man.* Blue cloth. London, 1913. First edition. $75-$125.

SASSOON, Siegfried. *The Old Huntsman and Other Poems.* Boards. London, 1917. First edition, with errata slip. In dust jacket. $50-$100.

SASSOON, Siegfried. *The Path to Peace.* Boards and vellum. Worcester, 1960. One of 500. $25-$30.

SASSOON, Siegfried. *Picture Show.* Boards. No place (Cambridge, England), 1911. First edition. One of 200 signed. In plain dust jacket. $50-$60. Presentation copy to John Masefield, $240. New York, no date (1920). $15-$20. (Contains seven new poems.)

SASSOON, Siegfried. *The Redeemer.* Unnumbered leaves. Cambridge, 1916. One of about 250. $50-$75.

SASSOON, Siegfried. *Satirical Poems.* Cloth. London, 1926. First edition. In dust jacket. $85-$90.

SASSOON, Siegfried. *Something About Myself.* Wrappers. London, 1966. One of 250. $60-$75.

SASSOON, Siegfried. *The Tasking.* Morocco and buckram. Cambridge, 1964. One of 100. $35-$50.

SASSOON, Siegfried. *To the Red Rose.* Green boards. London, 1931. First edition. One of 400 signed. $25.

SASSOON, Siegfried. *Vigils.* Morocco. London, 1934. First edition. One of 272 signed. $35-$50. Another issue: One of 23 on large paper, signed. $100-$150.

SASSOON, Siegfried. *War Poems.* Red cloth. London, 1919. First edition. In dust jacket. $100-$150.

SATAN in Search of a Wife. By an Eye Witness. Pink wrappers. London, 1831. (By Charles Lamb.) First edition. $75-$150.

SATANSTOE; or, The Littlepage Manuscripts. By the Author of "Miles Wallingford." 2 vols., printed yellow wrappers. New York, 1845. (By James Fenimore Cooper.) First American edition. $75-$100. London, 1845. 3 vols., boards, paper label. First edition. $100. (Note: Cooper's name appeared on the title page of this edition.)

SATTERLEE, M. P. *A Detailed Account of the Massacre by the Dakota Indians of Minnesota in 1862.* Wrappers. Minneapolis, 1923. $35-$40.

SAUER, Martin. *An Account of a Geographical and Astronomical Expedition to the Northern Parts of Russia.* Folding map, 14 plates. Boards and calf. London, 1802. First edition. $250-$500. Spine cracked, $137.20. Also, $450 (A, 1969).

SAUNDERS, James E. *Early Settlers of Alabama.* Part I. (All published). Cloth. New Orleans, 1899. First edition. $35-$50.

SAUNDERS, Marshall. *Beautiful Joe: An Autobiography.* Mottled olive cloth. Philadelphia, 1894. First edition, first issue, with American Baptist Publication Society imprint. $75-$100.

SAUVAN, Jean-Baptiste-Balthazar. *Picturesque Tour of the Seine, from Paris to the Sea.* Map, colored vignette title and tailpiece, 24 colored aquatint plates. Half morocco. London, 1821. First edition. $600-$1,200. Large paper issue: $2,000 and up.

SAVAGE, Timothy. *The Amazonian Republic, Recently Discovered in the Interior of Peru.* Boards, paper label. New York, 1842. First edition. $75-$80.

SAVONAROLA, Hieronymus. *Epistola de Contemptu Mundi.* Illustrated. Red morocco. London, 1894. Kelmscott Press. One of 150. $100-$150. Another issue: One of 6 on vellum. $850.

SAVOY (The): An Illustrated Quarterly. Illustrations by Aubrey Beardsley. 8 parts. (All published.) Decorated boards and wrappers. London, 1896. $150-$300.

SAWYER, C. J., and Darton, F. J. Harvey. *English Books, 1475-1900: A Signpost for Collectors.* Illustrated. 2 vols., buckram. London, 1927. $50-$75.

SAWYER, Eugene T. *The Life and Career of Tiburcio Vasquez.* Printed wrappers. San Jose, Calif., 1875. First edition. $150-$250. Oakland, Calif., 1944. Grabhorn Press. Boards and cloth. One of 500. $30-$35.

SAWYER, Lorenzo. *Way Sketches.* Illustrated. Cloth. New York, 1926. One of 385. $25-$30. Large paper issue: Boards, parchment spine. One of 35. $50.

SAXE, John Godfrey. *Progress: A Satirical Poem.* Printed boards. New York, 1846. First edition. $35-$50. Author's first book.

SAXON, Lyle. *Lafitte the Pirate.* Colored frontispiece. Cloth. New York, no date (1930). First edition. $20-$25.

SCAMMON, Charles M. *The Marine Mammals of the North-Western Coast of North America, etc.* 27 plates. Cloth. San Francisco, 1874. First edition. $100.

SCENES in the Rocky Mountains, Oregon, California, New Mexico, Texas and Grand Prairies. By a New Englander. Folding map. Printed wrappers. Philadelphia, 1846. (By Rufus B. Sage.) First edition. $350-$650. (Note: For later editions, see Sage, Rufus B.)

SCHARF, John Thomas. *History of the Confederate States Navy.* 42 plates. Boards. New York, 1887. First edition. $35-$50.

SCHARF, John Thomas. *History of Delaware.* Illustrated. 2 vols., half morocco. Philadelphia, 1888. First edition. $75-$100.

SCHARF, John Thomas. *History of Western Maryland.* Map, 109 plates, table. 2 vols., cloth. Philadelphia, 1882. First edition. $35-$50.

SCHARMANN, H. B. *Overland Journey to California.* Portrait. Cloth. No place, no date (New York, 1918). First edition in English. $100-$150.

SCHATZ, A. H. *Opening a Cow Country.* Plates, maps. Wrappers. Ann Arbor, Mich., 1939. First edition. $50-$100.

SCHLEY, Frank. *American Partridge and Pheasant Shooting.* Illustrated. Cloth. Frederick, Md., 1877. First edition. $35-$50.

SCHMIDT, Gustavus. *The Civil Law of Spain and Mexico.* Cloth. New Orleans, 1851. First edition. $100.

SCHMITZ, Joseph M. *Texan Statecraft, 1836-1845.* Cloth. San Antonio, Tex., 1941. One of 200. $35-$50.

SCHOBERL, Frederic. *Picturesque Tour from Geneva to Milan, by Way of the Simplon.* Map, 36 color plates. Cloth or boards. London, 1820. $200-$250.

SCHOEPF, Johann David. *Travels in the Confederation.* Translated and edited by Alfred J. Morrison. Portrait, 2 facsimiles. 2 vols., cloth. Philadelphia, 1911. First American edition (and first in English). $50.

SCHOOLCRAFT, Henry R. *Algic Researches.* 2 vols., cloth. New York, 1839. First edition. $75-$100.

SCHOOLCRAFT, Henry R. *An Address Delivered Before the Was-ah Ho-de-no-son-ne, or New Confederacy of the Iroquois.* 48 pp., sewed. Rochester, N.Y., 1846. First edition. $55.

SCHOOLCRAFT, Henry R. *A Discourse Delivered on the Anniversary of the Historical Society of Michigan.* 44 pp., wrappers. Detroit, 1830. First edition. $75.

SCHOOLCRAFT, Henry R. *Historical and Statistical Information Respecting the . . . Indian Tribes, etc.* Numerous maps, plates, and tables. 6 vols., cloth. Philadelphia, 1851-57. First edition. $350-$500. (For reprint, see Schoolcraft, *Information Respecting the History, etc.*)

SCHOOLCRAFT, Henry R. *The Indian Tribes of the United States.* Edited by Francis S. Drake. Map, plates. 2 vols., buckram. Philadelphia, 1884. First edition. $100-$150. London, 1885. 2 vols., cloth. $50.

SCHOOLCRAFT, Henry R. *Information Respecting the History, Condition, and Prospects of the Indian Tribes of the United States.* Illustrated. 6 vols., cloth. Philadelphia, 1853-57. Reprint of *Historical and Statistical Information.* $250-$300. Rebound in half morocco, $150.

SCHOOLCRAFT, Henry R. *Inquiries Respecting the History . . . of the Indian Tribes of the United States.* (Caption title.) Printed wrappers. No place, no date (Washington, about 1847-50?). $300.

SCHOOLCRAFT, Henry R. *Journal of a Tour into the Interior of Missouri and Arkansaw.* Map. Leather. London, 1821. First edition. $75-$125.

SCHOOLCRAFT, Henry R. *The Myth of Hiawatha, and Other Oral Legends.* Cloth. Philadelphia, 1856. First edition. $35-$50.

SCHOOLCRAFT, Henry R. *Narrative of an Expedition Through the Upper Mississippi to Itasca Lake.* 5 maps. Cloth, paper label. New York, 1834. First edition. $35-$75. Rebound in three-quarters leather, $25.

SCHOOLCRAFT, Henry R. *Narrative Journal of Travels Through the Northwestern Regions of the U.S., etc.* Engraved title page, folding map, 7 plates. Boards. Albany, 1821. First edition, with errata slip. $100-$200.

SCHOOLCRAFT, Henry R. *Personal Memoirs of a Residence of 30 Years with the Indian Tribes.* Portrait (not in all copies). Cloth. Philadelphia, 1851. First edition. $40-$50.

SCHOOLCRAFT, Henry R. *Travels in the Central Portions of the Mississippi Valley.* 5 maps and plates. Boards. New York, 1825. First edition. $100-$125.

SCHOOLCRAFT, Henry R. *A View of the Lead Mines of Missouri.* 3 plates. Boards. New York, 1819. First edition. $100-$150.

SCHOOLCRAFT, Henry R., and Allen, James. *Expedition to North-West Indians.* (Caption title.) Map. 68 pp., modern wrappers. No place, no date (Washington, 1834). $150-$200.

SCHRANTZ, Ward L. *Jasper County, Missouri, in the Civil War.* Frontispiece, 9 plates. Cloth. Carthage, Mo., 1923. $25-$35.

SCHREINER, Olive. See Iron, Ralph.

SCHULTZ, Christian. *Travels on an Inland Voyage, etc.* Portrait, 2 plates, 4 (sometimes 5) maps. 2 vols., leather. New York, 1810. First edition. $100-$150.

SCHWAB, John Christopher. *The Confederate States of America, 1861-1865.* Cloth. New York, 1901. First edition. $50-$60.

SCHWERDT, C. F. G. R. *Hunting, Hawking, Shooting.* 382 full-page plates, including 54 in color. 4 vols., folio, half morocco. London, 1928-37. One of 300 signed. $800-$1,000.

SCHWETTMAN, Martin W. *Santa Rita, the University of Texas Oil Discovery.* 43 pp., wrappers. No place (Austin?), 1943. First edition. $35-$40.

SCLATER, P. L., and Hudson, W. H. *Argentine Ornithology.* 20 color plates. 2 vols., blue-gray boards. London, 1888-89. First edition. One of 200 signed. $500-$600.

SCORESBY, William, Jr. *Journal of a Voyage to the Northern Whale-Fishery.* 8 maps and plates. Boards, paper label. Edinburgh, 1823. First edition. $100-$150.

SCOT, Reginald. *The Discoverie of Witchcraft.* Edited by Montague Summers. Cloth or morocco and buckram. London, no date (1930). $75-$125.

SCOTFORD, John. *The Judd Family.* Cloth. Ann Arbor, Mich., 1869. First edition. $40-$50.

SCOTT, Evelyn. *On William Faulkner's "The Sound and the Fury."* Wrappers. New York, no date (1929). First edition. $35-$50.

SCOTT, James L. *A Journal of a Missionary Tour Through Pennsylvania.* Decorated cloth. Providence, R.I., 1843. First edition. $100-$165.

SCOTT, John. *Partisan Life with Col. John S. Mosby.* Illustrated. Cloth. New York, 1867. First edition. $35-$50. London, 1867. First English edition. $25-$35. Rebound in buckram, $25.

SCOTT, Michael. See *Tom Cringle's Log.*

SCOTT, Sir Walter. See Clutterbuck, Captain. Also see *The Abbot; Anne of Geierstein; The Antiquary; The Fortunes of Nigel; Guy Mannering; Harold the Dauntless; Ivanhoe; Kenilworth; Quentin Durward; Rob Roy; Saint Ronan's Well; Waverley.*

SCOTT, Sir Walter. *The Flowers of Scott.* Color plates. Cloth. London, 1858. $40-$50.

SCOTT, Sir Walter. *Halidon Hill: A Dramatic Sketch, from Scottish History.* 109 pp., drab wrappers. Edinburgh, 1822. First edition. $35-$50.

SCOTT, Sir Walter. *The Lady of the Lake.* Portrait. Boards. London, 1810. First edition. $150-$200. Large paper issue: $150-$200. Edinburgh, 1825. Contemporary morocco. $50.

SCOTT, Sir Walter. *The Lay of the Last Minstrel.* Boards, paper label. Edinburgh, 1805. First edition. $250-$500.

SCOTT, Sir Walter. *Marmion.* Boards. London, 1808. First edition. $50-$75.

SCOTT, William. *Lessons in Elocution.* 4 plates. Calf, leather label. Plymouth, England, 1825. First edition. $25-$35.

SCOTT-MONCRIEF, Charles Kenneth: See Lear, P. G. and L. O.

SCRIPPS, J. L. *The Undeveloped Northern Portion of the American Continent.* 20 pp., printed wrappers. Chicago, 1856. First edition. $200-$250. Another, plain wrappers, $150.

SCROPE, William. *The Art of Deer-Stalking.* 12 plates. Calf. London, 1838. First edition. $50-$75.

SCROPE, William. *Days and Nights of Salmon Fishing in the Tweed.* 13 plates. Cloth. London, 1843. First edition. $50-$75.

SEATON, William C. *A Manual of the Examinations of Masters and Mates . . . of Canada.* Folding diagram of compass deviations, double-page spread of signal flags. Cloth. Quebec, 1875. $20-$25.

SEAVER, James E. *A Narrative of the Life of Mrs. Mary Jemison, Who Was Taken by the Indians in the Year 1755, etc.* Boards. Canandaigua, N.Y., 1824. First edition. $350-$500.

SEBRIGHT, Sir John Saunders. *Observations upon Hawking.* Wrappers. London, 1828. First edition. $100-$150.

SECONDTHOUGHTS, Solomon. *Quodlibet.* Cloth. Philadelphia, 1840. (By John Pendleton Kennedy.) First edition. $50-$75.

SEDGWICK, Catharine M. *The Linwoods; or "Sixty Years Since" in America.* 2 vols., cloth, paper labels. New York, 1835. First edition. $50.

SEDGWICK, John. *Correspondence of John Sedgwick.* 2 vols., cloth. No place (New York), 1902-03. First edition. One of 300. $50-$75.

SEEGER, Alan. *Poems.* Dark-brown cloth. New York, 1916. First edition. In dust jacket. $35-$50. Author's first book.

SEELIGSON, Mrs. Leila. *A History of Indianola.* 16 pp., wrappers. Cuero, Tex., no date (1930-31). $25-$30.

SELBY, Julian A. *Memorabilia and Anecdotal Reminiscences of Columbia, S.C.* Portrait. Cloth. Columbia, S.C., 1905. First edition. $25-$35.

SELECT Collection of Valuable and Curious Arts, etc. (A). Boards. Concord, 1826. (By Rufus Porter.) First edition. $50-$60.

SELECT Translations and Imitations from the French of Marmontell and Gresset. By an Officer of the Army; Who Fought for America, Under Gen. Wolfe, at the Taking of Quebec. Half leather. New York, 1801. First edition. $100.

SELECT Views in Sicily. 36 full-page colored aquatint plates. Folio, half leather. London, 1825. (By Achille Etienne de la Salle Gigault.) $400-$500.

A SELECTION from the Papers of King George III. Edited by Sir John Fortescue. Portrait, facsimile. 2 vols., half morocco. London, 1927. $55-$60.

SELKIRK, (Thomas Douglas), Earl of. *A Sketch of the British Fur Trade in North America.* Boards. London, 1816. First edition. $750-$1,000. Also, in later calf, $500 (A, 1969). London, 1816. Second edition. $600-$750.

SENSE and Sensibility. By a Lady. 3 vols., blue or pink boards, paper labels. London, 1811. (By Jane Austen.) First edition, with ruled lines of half title in Vol. 1 measuring 4/5 inch (1 1/7 inches in second edition). $2,500 and up. Also, $1,700 (A, 1963). Rebound in full nineteenth-century calf, $1,000 at retail. Also, rebound in half calf, $525 (A, 1969), $532.80 (A, 1968), $840 (A, 1963). Another copy, in three-quarters leather, foxed, hinges repaired, several leaves torn, $475 at retail. London, 1813. 3 vols., boards. Second edition. $350-$500.

SERIES of Miscellaneous Letters (A), from a Father to His Children. 144 pp., wrappers. South Hanover, Iowa, 1835. $35.

SERVICE, Robert W. *Rhymes of a Red Cross Man.* Cloth. Toronto, 1916. First edition. $35-$50.

SETON, Ernest Thompson. *Life-Histories of Northern Animals.* Illustrated. Cloth. New York, 1909. First edition. $75. London, 1910. 2 vols., cloth. $30-$40.

SETON, Ernest Thompson. *Studies in the Art Anatomy of Animals.* Illustrated. Cloth. London, 1896. First edition. $100-$200.

SETON, Ernest Thompson. *Wild Animals I Have Known.* 200 drawings by the author. Pictorial cloth. New York, 1898. First edition, first issue, without the words "The Angel whispered don't go" in the last paragraph on page 265. $35-$50. New York, 1900. Illustrated. One of 1,000 signed. $35-$50.

SETON-THOMPSON, Ernest. *The Birch-Bark Roll of the Woodcraft Indians.* Illustrated. 71 pp., birchbark wrappers. New York, 1906. First separate edition. $35-$40.

SETON-THOMPSON, Ernest. *Boy Scouts of America: A Handbook of Woodcraft, Scouting, and Life-craft.* Pictorial wrappers. New York, 1910. First edition, "probable earlier state," with printer's slug on copyright page. $90-$100.

SEVEN Little Sisters Who Live on the Round Ball That Floats in the Air (The). Illustrated. Decorated blue cloth. Boston, 1861. (By Jane Andrews.) First edition. $75-$100.

SEVEN and Nine Years Among the Comanches and Apaches. Plates. Cloth. Jersey City, N.J., 1873. (By Edwin Eastman.) First edition. $75.

SEVEN Pillars of Wisdom (The). Specimen sheets. Half red buckram, vellum spine. New York, 1926. (By T. E. Lawrence.) First American (copyright) edition, with author's name accidentally omitted from title page. One of 22 (of which 10 were offered for sale at $10,000 each). $1,000. Also, $350 (A, 1963). Another issue: Out of series. One of 2 specially bound in three-quarters blue buckram for George H. Doran, the publisher, as presentation copies. $1,000. Also, $375 (A, 1964). (For first edition, see entry under Lawrence.)

SEVENTY-SIX . . . (A Novel). 2 vols., contemporary boards. Baltimore, 1823. (By John Neal.) First edition. $100-$150.

SEWALL, Rufus King. *Sketches of St. Augustine.* 6 plates. 69 pp., cloth. New York, 1848. First edition. Pages 39 and 40 removed, as with most copies. $50.

SEWARD, W. H. *Communication upon the Subject of an Intercontinental Telegraph, etc.* Folding map. 52 pp., wrappers. Washington, 1864. First edition. $300-$400.

SEWELL, Anna. *Black Beauty.* Blue, red, or brown cloth. London, no date (1877). First edition. $350-$400. Boston, no date (1890). Orange printed wrappers or buff boards. First American edition. Wrappers: $35-$75. Boards: $25-$50.

SEXTON, Lucy Ann (Foster), and Foster, Mrs. Roxana C. *The Foster Family: California Pioneers.* Cloth. No place, no date (Santa Barbara, Calif., 1925). Enlarged (first?) edition. $85-$100.

SEYD, Ernest. *California and Its Resources.* 22 plates (some tinted), 2 folding maps. Cloth. London, 1858. First edition. $100-$125.

SEYMOUR, E. S. *Emigrant's Guide to the Gold Mines of Upper California.* Folding map. 104 pp., wrappers. Chicago, 1849. First edition. $1,000 and, probably, much higher. (Two copies known.)

SEYMOUR, E. S. *Sketches of Minnesota.* Printed wrappers, or cloth. New York, 1850. First edition. Wrappers: $50-$75. Cloth: $35-$50.

SEYMOUR, Silas. *A Reminiscence of the Union Pacific Railroad.* Plates. Printed wrappers. Quebec, 1873. First edition. $175.

SEYMOUR, W. D. *The Isthmian Routes.* 27 pp., sewed. New York, 1863. First edition. $150.

SEYMOUR, William N. *Madison Directory and Business Advertiser.* Map. Leather. Madison, Wis., 1855. First edition. $75-$100.

SHAFFER, Ellen. *The Nuremberg Chronicle.* Illustrated. 61 pp., pictorial cloth. Los Angeles, 1950. $100.

SHAFFER, Ellen. *The Garden of Health.* Illustrated. Folio, boards and linen. San Francisco, 1957. Book Club of California. One of 300. $75.

SHAKESPEARE Rare Print Collection. Edited by Seymour Eaton. 146 plates, 12 parts, portfolio. No place (New York), 1900. Connoisseur Edition. $35-$60.

SHAKESPEARE, William. *Antony and Cleopatra.* Printed in red and black. Vellum. London, 1912. Doves Press. One of 200. $150-$200. Another issue: specially bound in morocco by the Doves Bindery. $1,000 and up. Also, $840 (A, 1967). San Francisco, 1960. Grabhorn Press. Illustrated in color by Mary Grabhorn. Folio, parchment. One of 185. $100.

SHAKESPEARE, William. *As You Like It.* Illustrated in color by Hugh Thomson. Morocco. London, no date. $50. Another issue: Vellum with ties. $50-$75.

SHAKESPEARE, William. *Comedies, Histories and Tragedies.* Facsimile from 4th Folio edition. Illustrated. Boards. London, 1904. $50-$60. London, 1910. Facsimile from the 1st Folio edition. Folio, boards and cloth. $100-$125.

SHAKESPEARE, William. *Coriolanus.* Vellum. London, 1914. Doves Press. One of 200. $125-$150. Rebound in morocco, $70. Another issue: specially bound in morocco by the Doves Bindery. $1,250 and up.

SHAKESPEARE, William. *Cymbeline.* Illustrated. Cloth. London, 1923. Shakespeare Head Press. One of 50. $75. Another issue: Morocco. One of 100. $100-$125.

SHAKESPEARE, William. *Hamlet, Prince of Denmark.* In Spanish and English. Illustrated in color by Anthony Salo. Printed on cork, bound in goatskin. Barcelona, no date (1930). One of 100. $250-$400. London, no date. 30 color plates by W. G. Simmonds. Vellum. Signed by the artist. $70. London, 1909. Doves Press. Printed in red and black. Vellum or white pigskin. One of 200. $200-$250. New York, 1933. Limited Editions Club. Engravings by Eric Gill. Pigskin. Boxed. Signed by Gill. $50-$60.

SHAKESPEARE, William. *Julius Caesar.* Morocco. London, 1913. One of 200. $78.40. London, 1925. 14 plates, 5 in color. Morocco and silk. One of 100. $98. San Francisco, 1954. Grabhorn Press. Illustrated by Mary Grabhorn. Folio, half leather. One of 180. $100.

SHAKESPEARE, William. *King Lear.* 16 plates. Folio, vellum. London, 1963. One of 275 signed by Kokoschka. $367.50. Also, with extra signed lithograph, $192 (A, 1968). San Francisco, no date (1930). Edited by G. K. Chesterton. 10 plates. Buckram. $35. San Francisco, 1959. Grabhorn Press. Illustrated in color by Mary Grabhorn. Cloth. One of 180. $100.

SHAKESPEARE, William. *Macbeth.* Illustrations in color by Mary Grabhorn. Boards, leather spine. No place, no date (San Francisco, 1952). One of 100. Boxed. $80-$100.

SHAKESPEARE, William. *The Merry Wives of Windsor.* Illustrated by Hugh Thomson. Pictorial vellum, silk ties. London, 1910. One of 350 signed by Thomson. $75-$100. Half morocco. $50-$60. London, no date. Illustrated by J. Finnemore and F. L. Emauel. Morocco. $100.

SHAKESPEARE, William. *A Midsummer-Night's Dream.* Illustrated by Arthur Rackham. Full white vellum with ties. London, 1908. One of 1,000 signed by Rackham. $250-$300. Trade edition. Boards: $50-$100. San Francisco, 1955. Illustrated in color by Mary Grabhorn. Parchment. One of 180. Boxed. $100.

SHAKESPEARE, William. *Othello.* Portraits in color by Mary Grabhorn. Boards, leather spine. San Francisco, 1956. One of 185. $100.

SHAKESPEARE, William. *The Poems of William Shakespeare.* Edited by F. S. Ellis. Limp vellum with ties. London, 1893. Kelmscott Press. $400-$500. London, 1899. Essex House. Limp vellum with ties. One of 450. $75-$100. Stamford, Conn., 1939. With initial letters designed by Bruce Rogers. One of 150. Boxed. $100-$150. New York, 1941. Limited Editions Club. 2 vols., pictorial boards. $50-$75.

SHAKESPEARE, William. *Poems and Sonnets.* Morocco. London, 1960. Golden Cockerel Press. One of 100. $200-$250.

SHAKESPEARE, William. *The Rape of Lucrece.* Printed in red and black. Text from the first edition. Vellum. London, 1915. Doves Press. One of 175. $65-$150. Another issue: Specially bound in morocco by the Doves Bindery. One of 175. $1,000 and up.

SHAKESPEARE, William. *Richard the Third.* Colored woodcuts by Mary Grabhorn. Vellum. San Francisco, 1953. Grabhorn Press. One of 180. Boxed. $100-$125.

SHAKESPEARE, William. *Romeo and Juliet.* Atlas folio, morocco. London, 1884. $150-$200.

SHAKESPEARE, William. *Sonnets.* Vellum. London, 1909. Doves Press. One of 250. $125-$200. London, 1913. Morocco. One of 12 on vellum. $200. London, 1929. Full morocco. One of 1,000. $50.

SHAKESPEARE, William. *The Taming of the Shrew.* 7 drawings in color by Valenti Angelo. Folio, cloth. San Francisco, 1967. $35-$50.

SHAKESPEARE, William. *The Tempest.* 40 color plates by Edmund Dulac. Vellum with ties. London, 1908. Edition de luxe, signed by Dulac. $100-$150. Another issue: Pictorial cloth. $40-$50. London, 1916. Illustrated by Arthur Rackham. Parchment sides, vellum spine. Signed by Rackham. $100. Montagnola (Paris), 1924. Vellum. One of 224. $250-$300. London, 1926. 21 color plates by Rackham. Limited and signed. $200-$300. San Francisco, 1951. Grabhorn Press. Illustrated by Mary Grabhorn. Half cloth. One of 160. $100.

SHAKESPEARE, William. *Twelfth Night.* 29 engravings. Folio, morocco and boards. London, 1932. Golden Cockerel Press. One of 275. $100-$200.

SHAKESPEARE, William. *Venus and Adonis.* Vellum. London, 1912. Doves Press. One of 200. $100-$150. Another issue: Specially bound in morocco by the Doves Bindery. $600-$800. Rochester, N.Y., 1931. Illustrated by Rockwell Kent. One of 75 (of an edition of 1,250) signed, together with 21 mounted illustrations. Boxed as a set. $100-$150. Without the extra plates, $40-$75.

SHALLY, Louis H. *The Book of Prices of the House Carpenters and Joiners of the City of Cincinnati.* Cloth. Cincinnati, 1844. Revised edition. $35-$50.

SHAPIRO, Karl. *Trial of a Poet.* Cloth. New York, no date (1947). One of 250 signed. Boxed. $35.

SHAPIRO, Karl. *V-Letter and Other Poems.* Tan cloth. New York, no date (1944). First edition. In dust jacket. $20-$25.

SHARON Against Terry. In the Circuit Court of the United States, 9th Circuit, District of California. Half morocco. San Francisco, no date. Worn, $75.

SHATTUCK, Lemuel. *A History of the Town of Concord.* Folding map. Half leather. Boston, 1835. First edition. $75-$100.

SHAW, Edward. *Civil Architecture.* 95 engravings. Calf. Boston, 1831. First edition. $50-$60. Rebound, $30. Boston, 1832. 97 plates. Second edition. $35-$50. Boston, 1836. 100 plates. Sheep. Fourth edition. $25-$35.

SHAW, Edward. *The Modern Architect.* 65 plates. Cloth. Boston, 1855. $50-$75.

SHAW, Edward. *Rural Architecture.* 52 plates. Calf. Boston, 1843. First edition. $35-$50.

SHAW, George Bernard. See Harris, Frank. Also see *This Is the Preachment on Going to Church.*

SHAW, George Bernard. *Androcles and the Lion.* Printed wrappers. London, 1913. First edition, with title page reading: "Rough Proof–Unpublished." $150-$200. London, 1916. Cloth. (With *Overruled* and *Pygmalion* added to title.) In dust jacket. $50-$60.

SHAW, George Bernard. *Augustus Does His Bit.* Wrappers. No place, no date (London, 1916). "Rough Proof–Unpublished." $75-$100.

SHAW, George Bernard. *Back to Methuselah: A Metabiological Pentateuch.* Green cloth. London, 1921. First edition. In dust jacket. $75-$100. New York, 1939. Limited Editions Club. Cloth. $25-$35.

SHAW, George Bernard. *Cashel Byron's Profession.* Blue printed wrappers. No place (London), 1886. First edition. $125-$150. Author's first book.

SHAW, George Bernard. *A Discarded Defence of Roger Casement.* Wrappers. London, 1922. First edition. One of 25. $150-$200.

SHAW, George Bernard. *The Doctor's Dilemma, Getting Married, and The Shewing Up of Blanco Posnet.* Cloth. London, 1911. First edition. In dust jacket. $75-$100.

SHAW, George Bernard. *Heartbreak House, Great Catherine, and Playlets of the War.* Cloth. London, 1919. First edition. In dust jacket. $35-$40.

SHAW, George Bernard. *How to Settle the Irish Question.* Blue printed wrappers. Dublin, no date (1917). First edition. $35-$50. Second issue: Green wrappers. $15-$30.

SHAW, George Bernard. *The Intelligent Woman's Guide to Socialism.* Green cloth. London, 1928. First edition. In dust jacket. $15-$25.

SHAW, George Bernard. *The Irrational Knot.* Blue cloth. London, 1905. First edition. $25. New York, 1905. First American edition. $15-$20.

SHAW, George Bernard. *John Bull's Other Island and Major Barbara.* Green cloth. London, 1907. First edition, first issue, with Archibald Constable & Co. imprint on title page. $15-$25.

SHAW, George Bernard. *Love Among the Artists.* Cloth. Chicago, 1900. First edition. $35-$50.

SHAW, George Bernard. *Man and Superman.* Green cloth. Westminster (London), 1903. First edition. $35-$50.

SHAW, George Bernard. *Mrs. Warren's Profession: A Play in Four Acts.* Cloth. London, 1902. First edition. $25-$30.

SHAW, George Bernard. *On the Rocks.* Printed wrappers. No place (London), 1933. "First Rough Proof—Unpublished." $75-$150. Another issue: "First Revise After Rehearsal—Unpublished." Printed wrappers. $75-$150.

SHAW, George Bernard. *Passion, Poison and Petrifaction.* Printed wrappers. New York, no date (1907). First edition. $50-$75. (Note: This first appeared in *Harry Furniss' Christmas Annual,* London, 1905.)

SHAW, George Bernard. *The Perfect Wagnerite.* Blue and tan cloth. London, 1898. First edition. $35-$50.

SHAW, George Bernard. *Plays: Pleasant and Unpleasant.* Portrait. 2 vols., green cloth. London, 1898. First edition. $40-$50. Chicago, 1898. 2 vols., cloth. First American edition. $25-$35.

SHAW, George Bernard. *The Political Madhouse in America and Nearer Home: A Lecture.* Wrappers. No place (London), 1933. Proof copy of the first English edition. $75-$90. London, 1933. Boards. First published English edition. $5-$10.

SHAW, George Bernard. *Press Cuttings.* Pink wrappers. London, 1909. First edition, first issue, with "Price One Shilling" at bottom of front cover. $15-$25.

SHAW, George Bernard. *Pygmalion: A Romance in Five Acts.* Printed wrappers. London, 1913. First edition, second (?) issue, with title page reading: "Rough Proof, Unpublished." $200-$300. (Note: In 1965 a similar "rough proof" copy, dated 1912 and with the subtitle reading "A Play in Five Acts," was sold at New York's Parke-Bernet Galleries for $350. It bore an inscription by Shaw identifying it as "the very first printing." Presumably this is the first issue of *Pygmalion.*)

SHAW, George Bernard. *The Quintessence of Ibsenism.* Dark-blue cloth. London, 1891. First edition. $25-$30.

SHAW, George Bernard. *Saint Joan: A Chronicle Play.* Blue-gray wrappers. London, 1923. First edition, first issue, with title page reading "Rough Proof, Unpublished." Presentation copies inscribed by Shaw have brought up to $260 at auction; also another "rough proof" presentation copy, dated 1924, has sold for $200. London, 1924. Cloth. First published edition. In dust jacket, $10-$15. London, no date (1924). Illustrated by Charles Ricketts. Folio, boards and cloth. First illustrated edition. One of 750. In dust jacket. $100. Jacket in tatters, $75.

SHAW, George Bernard. *The Sanity of Art.* Printed brown wrappers. London, 1908. First edition. $50-$75. Another issue: Boards and cloth. $25.

SHAW, George Bernard. *Shaw Gives Himself Away: An Autobiographical Miscellany.* Frontispiece woodcut portrait. Dark-green morocco, inlaid with red leather. Newtown,

Wales, 1939. Gregynog Press. One of 300. $250-$300. Another issue: One of 12 bound by George Fisher. $500-$600.

SHAW, George Bernard. *The Shewing Up of Blanco Posnet.* 36 pp., printed wrappers. New York, 1909. Copyright edition. $25-$35.

SHAW, George Bernard. *Three Plays for Puritans.* Plates. Green cloth. London, 1901. First edition. $25-$35. Chicago, 1901. Cloth. First American edition. $25-$35.

SHAW, George Bernard. *An Unsocial Socialist.* Scarlet cloth. London, 1887. First edition, first state, with title of Shaw's first novel incorrectly given on title page and with publisher's name spelled wrong on spine. $150-$200. Second state, with novel's title corrected and with publisher's name on spine stamped over. $125.

SHAW, George Bernard. *War Issues for Irishmen: An Open Letter to Col. Arthur Lynch from Bernard Shaw.* Gray wrappers. Dublin, 1918. First edition. $100-$200.

SHAW, George Bernard. *Widowers' Houses: A Comedy.* Blue-green cloth. London, 1893. First edition. $75-$100.

SHAW, Henry. *Details of Elizabethan Architecture.* 60 full-page plates, some in color. Boards. London, 1839. First edition. $75-$100.

SHAW, Henry. *Dresses and Decorations of the Middle Ages.* Hand-colored plates and other illustrations. 2 vols., folio, boards. London, 1843. First edition. $150-$250. Another issue: Three-quarters morocco. Large paper. $200-$300.

SHAW, Henry. *Examples of Ornamental Metal Work.* 50 plates. Boards. London, 1836. $50-$75.

SHAW, Henry, and Madden, Sir Frederic. *Illuminated Ornaments Selected from Manuscripts and Early Printed Books.* Illustrated. Boards. London, 1833. $75-$150. Large paper issue: Boards and leather. $175-$200.

SHAW, Joshua. *United States Directory for the Use of Travellers and Merchants, etc.* Leather. Philadelphia, no date (1822). First edition. $100-$150.

SHAW, R. C. *Across the Plains in Forty-nine.* Portrait. Cloth. Farmland, Ind., 1896. First edition. $45-$75.

SHAW, T. E. (adopted name). See Homer. Also see Lawrence, T. E.

SHAY, Frank (editor). *Contemporary One-Act Plays of 1921.* Green cloth. Cincinnati, no date (1922). First edition. $20-$25. (Note: Includes Eugene O'Neill's *The Dreamy Kid*—first book appearance of the play.)

SHEA, John Gilmary. *Early Voyages up and down the Mississippi.* Boards. Albany, N.Y., 1861. First edition. $25-$35. Large paper issue: $45-$75. Albany, no date (1902). Boards. Facsimile reprint. $50.

SHEA, John Gilmary. *A History of the Catholic Church Within . . . the United States.* Illustrated. 4 vols., cloth. New York, 1886-92. First edition. $100.

SHELDON, Charles M. *In His Steps: "What Would Jesus Do?"* Brown and white printed wrappers. Chicago, 1897. First edition. A curiosity among American novels, one of the greatest sellers in history, rare in wrappers but with uncertain value. My own estimate: $200-$250. A California dealer recently catalogued a copy, "browned and brittle," at $450, while a Boston dealer listed it at $25. A copy was sold at auction in New York for $15 in 1964.

SHELLEY, Mary W. See *Falkner; The Fortunes of Perkin Warbeck; Frankenstein; Lodore; Valperga; The Last Man.*

SHELLEY, Percy Bysshe. See S., P. B. Also see *St. Irvyne; Epipsychidon.*

SHELLEY, Percy Bysshe. *Adonais: An Elegy on the Death of John Keats.* 25 pp., blue ornamental wrappers. Pisa, Italy, 1821. First edition. Estimated value: Up to $5,000. Also, $3,250 and $3,000 (A, 1945); worn and repaired, $728 (A, 1960). Rebound in morocco, original covers bound in, $3,250 at retail. Also, rebound, $3,300 (A, 1970). Cambridge (London), 1829. Green wrappers. Second (first English) edition. $750-$1,000. Also, $525 (A, 1965). Rebound copies, $250-$500 at retail.

SHELLEY, Percy Bysshe. *Alastor; or, The Spirit of Solitude: and Other Poems.* Boards, paper label on spine. London, 1816. First edition. $1,250 and up. Lacking back end paper, with new spine, $1,000. Rebound, $250 and up.

SHELLEY, Percy Bysshe. *The Cenci.* Wrappers or boards. Italy, 1819. First edition. One of 250. $750-$1,000. Also, boards, worn and defective, $336 (A, 1966); boards, "heavy paper," $550 (A, 1965). In modern bindings, $350-$600. Also, $320 (A, 1966), $280 (A, 1965). London, 1821. Wrappers. First English edition. $350-$500.

SHELLEY, Percy Bysshe. *The Complete Works of Percy Bysshe Shelley.* 10 vols., cloth, vellum spines. London, 1927. One of 780. Boxed. $350.

SHELLEY, Percy Bysshe. *Hellas, A Lyrical Drama.* Stiff drab wrappers. London, 1822. First edition. $1,000 and up.

SHELLEY, Percy Bysshe. *History of a Six Weeks' Tour Through a Part of France, Switzerland, Germany, and Holland.* Boards, green spine, paper label. London, 1817. First edition. $150-$200.

SHELLEY, Percy Bysshe. *Laon and Cythna.* Boards. London, 1818. First edition, first issue, with four-line quotation from Pindar on half title. $300-$500. Second issue, same date, without Pindar lines. $200-$300.

SHELLEY, Percy Bysshe. *Letters from Percy Bysshe Shelley to J. H. Leigh Hunt.* Edited by Thomas J. Wise. 2 vols., cloth. London, 1894. First edition. $100-$125. Also, $60 (A, 1968). Another issue: Morocco. One of 6 on vellum. $150-$250.

SHELLEY, Percy Bysshe. *Letters of Percy Bysshe Shelley.* With an Introductory Essay by Robert Browning. Dark-red cloth. London, 1852. First edition. $200-$250. (Suppressed as forgeries.)

SHELLEY, Percy Bysshe. *The Masque of Anarchy: A Poem.* Preface by Leigh Hunt. Gray-blue boards. London, 1832. First edition, with white spine label lettered vertically "Shelley's Masque." $150-$200.

SHELLEY, Percy Bysshe. *On the Vegetable System of Diet.* Cloth. London, 1929. First edition. One of 12. $150-$200.

SHELLEY, Percy Bysshe. *Poems.* Decorations by Charles Ricketts. 3 vols., white buckram. No place, no date (London, 1901-02). Vale Press. $75-$100.

SHELLEY, Percy Bysshe. *Poems and Sonnets.* Edited by Charles Alfred Seymour. 74 pp., parchment wrappers. Philadelphia, 1887. (Thomas J. Wise piracy.) One of 30. $200-$250. Rebound in half morocco, original covers preserved, $224 (A, 1967).

SHELLEY, Percy Bysshe. *Posthumous Poems.* Boards, paper label on spine. London, 1824. First edition, first issue, without errata leaf. $300-$400.

SHELLEY, Percy Bysshe. *Prometheus Unbound.* Blue-gray boards, paper label. London, 1820. First edition, first issue, with "Miscellaneous" misprinted "misellaneous" in table of contents. Estimated value: $2,000-$2,500. Second issue, with misprint corrected. $500-$750.

SHELLEY, Percy Bysshe. *Queen Mab: a Philosophical Poem.* Boards. London, 1813. First edition. $3,500-$5,000. Also, $3,360 (A, 1965). Shelley removed the title, dedication, and imprint from many copies, and unmutilated copies rarely appear for sale. In 1959 one was sold at auction for $750 (bound in new morocco); in 1961, another rebound copy brought $600. London, 1821. Boards. $100-$200. New York, 1821. Boards. First American edition. $50. London, 1829. Contemporary calf.

SHELLEY, Percy Bysshe. *The Revolt of Islam.* Blue boards, white paper label on spine. London, 1817 (actually 1818). First edition, first issue, incorrectly dated on title page. Estimated retail value: up to $1,000. Also, $450 (A, 1946), $300 (A, 1945). London, 1818. Second issue, correctly dated. $250-$500.

SHELLEY, Percy Bysshe. *Rosalind and Helen.* Drab wrappers. London, 1819. First edition, with 2 ad leaves at end. $400-$600. Rebound, $150-$200.

SHELLEY-ROLLS, Sir John C. E. *Yachts of the Royal Yacht Squadron, 1815-1932.* Buckram. London, 1933. $55 and $75. Also, rebound in morocco extra, $50-$65.

SHELTON, Frederick William. See Admirari, Nil.

SHEPARD, A. K. *The Land of the Aztecs.* Cloth. Albany, N.Y., 1859. First edition. $40-$50.

SHEPARD, Ernest H. *Fun and Fantasy.* Introduction by A. A. Milne. Illustrated. Cloth. London, no date (1927). First edition. One of 150 signed. $50.

SHEPARD, Odell. *A Lonely Flute.* Boards. Boston, 1917. First edition. In dust jacket, $30-$50. Author's first book.

SHEPPARD Lee. Written by Himself. 2 vols., floral cloth. New York, 1836. (By Robert Montgomery Bird.) First edition. $100-$125.

SHERIDAN, Philip H. *Outline Descriptions of the Posts in the Military Division of the Missouri, etc.* Folding map. Cloth. Chicago, 1872. First edition. $75.

SHERMAN, Elizabeth Ware. See S., E. W., and M., S. W.

SHERWELL, Samuel. *Old Recollections of an Old Boy.* Portrait. Cloth. New York, 1923. First edition. $50-$60.

SHERWOOD, Mary Martha. *The History of Henry Milner, a Little Boy.* Calf. Princeton, N.J., 1827. $30.

SHIELDS, G. O. *The Battle of the Big Hole.* 8 plates. Cloth. New York, 1889. First edition. $25-$35.

SHILLIBEER, Lieut. J. *A Narrative of the Briton's Voyage to Pitcairn's Island.* 16 etchings (not 18 as title erroneously states). Contemporary boards. Taunton, 1817. First edition, with errata leaf and instructions to the binder. $150-$200. London, 1817. 11 plates. Boards. Second edition. $100. London, 1818. 12 plates. Half calf. Third edition. $100.

SHINN, Charles Howard. *Mining Camps.* Cloth. New York, 1885. First edition. $100-$125.

SHINN, Charles Howard. *Pacific Rural Handbook.* Cloth. San Francisco, 1879. First edition. $25.

SHIPMAN, Mrs. O. L. *Taming the Big Bend.* Folding map, 4 plates. Cloth. No place (Austin, Tex.?), no date (1926). First edition. $50-$60.

SHOBER, G. A. *A Choice Drop of Honey from the Rock Christ, or a Short Word of Advice to All Saints and Sinners.* 30 pp., wrappers. New Market, Va., 1811. $35-$40.

SHOEMAKER, James. *Directory of the City of Mankato, and Blue Earth County.* Printed boards. Mankato, Minn., 1888. $50-$75.

SHORT History of Gen. R. E. Lee (A). 15 pp., pictorial wrappers, miniature. New York, 1888. $25.

SHORT History of T. J. Jackson (A). 15 pp., pictorial wrappers, miniature. New York, 1888. $25.

SHOWMAN'S Series III (The): Theatre Picture Book. Pop-up book with colored folding scenes. Pictorial boards. New York, no date (about 1885). $30-$35.

SHUTE, Henry A. *The Real Diary of a Real Boy.* Cloth. Boston, 1902. First edition. $35-$50.

SIDNEY, Margaret. *Five Little Peppers and How They Grew.* Green, blue, or brown pictorial cloth. Boston, no date (1880). (By Harriet M. S. Lothrop.) First edition, first state, with 1880 copyright and with caption on page 231 reading "said Polly." $100-$200.

SIDNEY, Sir Philip. *The Defence of Poesie and Certain Sonnets.* Engraved portrait. Limp vellum, with ties. London, 1906. Caradoc Press. One of 14 (of an edition of 364) printed in red and black on vellum. $250-$275. Ordinary issue: Boards. One of 350. $75-$100.

SIEBERT, Wilbur Henry. *Loyalists in East Florida.* 6 maps and plates. 2 vols., cloth. DeLand, Fla., 1929. First edition. $80-$100.

SIEGE of Corinth (The). Drab wrappers. London, 1816. (By George Gordon Noel, Lord Byron.) First edition. $100-$150.

SILL, Edward Rowland. *The Venus of Milo and Other Poems.* Printed cream wrappers. Berkeley, Calif., 1883. First edition, with copyright stamp on title page. $35-$50.

SILLIMAN, Benjamin. *Report upon the Oil Property of the Philadelphia and California Petroleum Co.* 2 maps. 36 pp., wrappers. Philadelphia, 1865. First edition. $250-$300.

SILLITOE, Alan. *The Loneliness of the Long Distance Runner.* Cloth. London, 1959. First edition. In dust jacket. $25-$30.

SILURIENSIS, Leolinus. *The Anatomy of Tobacco.* White parchment boards. London, no date (1884). (By Arthur Machen.) First edition. $50-$75. Author's first book.

SILVER Mines of Virginia and Austin, Nevada. 19 pp., wrappers. Boston, 1865. $75-$85.

SIMMS, Jeptha R. *The American Spy, or Freedom's Early Sacrifice.* 63 pp., wrappers. Albany, N.Y., 1846. First edition. $50. Worn, $28.50. Albany, 1857. One of 28 large paper copies. $25-$30.

SIMMS, Jeptha R. *History of Schoharie County.* Plates. Cloth. Albany, 1845. First edition. $50-$60.

SIMMS, Jeptha R. *Trappers of New York.* 4 plates. Cloth. Albany, 1850. First edition. $50-$60. Albany, 1860. Red buckram. $35-$40.

SIMMS, William Gilmore. See *Atalantis; Beauchampe; Border Beagles; Carl Werner; The Damsel of Darien; Grouped Thoughts and Scattered Fancies; Guy Rivers; The Lily and the Totem; Martin Faber; The Partisan; Pelayo; Poems (By a Collegian); Richard Hurdis; Sack and Destruction of Columbia, S.C.; The Wigwam and the Cabin; The Yemasee.*

SIMMS, William Gilmore. *Areytos; or, Songs of the South.* Cloth. Charleston, S.C., 1846. First edition. $25-$30.

SIMMS, William Gilmore. *The Cassique of Accabee.* Boards. Charleston, 1849. First edition. $50-$75.

SIMMS, William Gilmore. *Egeria; or, Voices of Thought and Counsel for the Woods and Wayside.* Cloth. Philadelphia, 1853. First edition. $25-$30.

SIMMS, William Gilmore. *Father Abbott; or, The Home Tourist.* Cloth. Charleston, 1849. First edition. $50-$75.

SIMMS, William Gilmore. *The Forayers; or, The Raid of the Dog-Days.* Cloth. New York, 1855. First edition. $40-$50.

SIMMS, William Gilmore. *Helen Halsey; or, the Swamp State of Conelachita.* Cloth. New York, 1845. First edition. $35-$50.

SIMMS, William Gilmore. *The History of South Carolina.* Cloth. Charleston, 1840. First edition. $50-$60.

SIMMS, William Gilmore. *The Life of Chevalier Bayard.* Frontispiece, other illustrations. Cloth. New York, 1847. First edition. $40-$50.

SIMMS, William Gilmore. *The Life of Francis Marion.* Cloth. New York, 1844. First edition. $25-$35.

SIMMS, William Gilmore. *Lyrical and Other Poems.* Cloth. Charleston, 1827. First edition. $150-$250. Author's first book.

SIMMS, William Gilmore. *Marie De Berniere.* Cloth. Philadelphia, 1853. First edition. $25-$35.

SIMMS, William Gilmore. *Mellichampe: A Legend of the Santee.* 2 vols., cloth, paper labels. New York, 1836. First edition. $75-$100.

SIMMS, William Gilmore. *Norman Maurice; or, The Man of the People.* Cloth. Richmond, Va., 1851. First edition. $25-$35.

SIMMS, William Gilmore. *Poems: Descriptive, Dramatic, Legendary and Contemplative.* 2 vols., cloth. Charleston, 1853. First edition. $100-$150. New York, 1853. 2 vols., cloth. $75-$100.

SIMMS, William Gilmore. *Southward Ho! A Spell of Sunshine.* Cloth. New York, 1854. First edition. $25-$30.

SIMMS, William Gilmore. *The Spartanburg Female College Oration.* Wrappers (?). Spartanburg, S.C., 1855. First edition. $100 and up.

SIMMS, William Gilmore (editor). *War Poetry of the South.* Cloth. New York, 1866. First edition. $25-$30.

SIMON, Barbara Allan. *A Series of Allegorical Designs, Representing the Human Heart from Its Natural to Its Regenerated State.* Boards. New York, 1825. First edition. $75.

SIMONIDEA. Blue boards. Bath, England, no date (1806). (By Walter Savage Landor.) First edition. $150-$200.

SIMPLE Truths in Verse, for the Amusement and Instruction of Children, at an Early Age. Illustrated. Boards. Baltimore, no date (about 1820). (By Mary Belson Elliot.) First American edition. $25-$30.

SIMPSON, Elizabeth M. *Bluegrass Houses and Their Traditions.* Illustrated. Cloth. Lexington, Ky., 1932. $25-$40.

SIMPSON, George. *Journal of Occurrences in the Athabasca Department, etc.* Edited by E. E. Rich. Cloth. Toronto, 1938. One of 550. $35-$50.

SIMPSON, George. *Narrative of a Journey Round the World, During the Years 1841 and 1842.* Portrait, folding map. 2 vols., cloth. London, 1847. First edition. $150-$200.

SIMPSON, Harold B. *Gaines Mill to Appomattox.* Illustrated. Full leather. Waco, Tex., 1963. First edition. One of 50 signed. $35-$40.

SIMPSON, Gen. James H. *Coronado's March in Search of the Seven Cities of Cibola.* Map. 34 pp., wrappers. Washington, 1884. $45-$50.

SIMPSON, James H. *Journal of a Military Reconnaissance, from Santa Fe, N.M., to the Navajo Country.* Folding map, 75 plates (23 colored). Cloth. Philadelphia, 1852. First separate printing. $35-$50.

SIMPSON, James H. *Report from the Secretary of War . . . and Map of the Route from Fort Smith, Ark., to Santa Fe, N.M.* 4 folding maps. Stitched. No place, no date (Washington, 1850). First edition. $50-$75.

SIMPSON, Capt. James H. *Report of Explorations Across the Great Basin of the Territory of Utah, etc.* Folding map, plates, errata leaf. Half leather. Washington, 1876. First edition. $35-$50.

SIMSON, Frank B. *Letters on Sport in Eastern Bengal.* 10 lithograph plates. Half morocco. London, 1886. First edition. $25-$35.

SINCLAIR, Upton. *A Home Colony. A Prospectus.* 23 pp., wrappers. New York, no date (1906). First edition. $40-$50.

SINCLAIR, Upton. *The Jungle.* Green cloth. New York, 1906. First edition, first issue, with Doubleday imprint and with the "1" in date on copyright page in perfect type. $85-$100. Later issue: New York, 1906. Jungle Publishing Co. First state, with unbroken type on copyright page and with "Sustainers' Edition" note tipped in. $50-$60. Later state, type broken on copyright page, $10-$15.

SINCLAIR, Upton. *Oil!* Printed wrappers. Long Beach, Calif., no date (1927). First edition. $35-$50.

SINGLETON, Arthur. *Letters from the South and West.* Stiff wrappers or boards. Boston, 1824. (By Henry Cogswell Knight.) First edition. $200-$250.

SINGLETON, Esther. *Social New York Under the Georges.* Cloth. New York, 1902. First edition. $35-$50.

SINJOHN, John. *From the Four Winds.* Olive-green cloth. London, 1897. (By John Galsworthy.) First edition. One of 500. $200-$250. Author's first book.

SINJOHN, John. *Jocelyn.* Cloth. London, 1898. (By John Galsworthy.) First edition, first issue, with "you" for "my" on page 257, third line from bottom. $75-$150.

SINJOHN, John. *A Man of Devon.* Blue cloth. Edinburgh and London, 1901. (By John Galsworthy.) First edition, with ads dated "4/01." $125-$150.

SINJOHN, John. *Villa Rubein.* Cherry-red cloth. London, 1900. (By John Galsworthy.) First edition. $100-$125.

SIRINGO, Charles A. *A Cowboy Detective.* Illustrated. Pictorial cloth. Chicago, 1912. First edition, first issue, published by Conkey. $30-$50. Second issue, same date. Wrappers. Published by Ogilvie. $30.

SIRINGO, Charles A. *History of "Billy the Kid."* 142 pp., stiff pictorial wrappers. No place, no date (Santa Fe, N.M., 1920). First edition. $55-$60.

SIRINGO, Charles A. *A Lone Star Cowboy.* Illustrated. Pictorial cloth. Santa Fe, 1919. First edition. $35-$50.

SIRINGO, Charles A. *Riata and Spurs.* 16 plates. Pictorial cloth. Boston, 1927. First edition, first issue, with "1927" on title page. $35-$50. Boston, no date (1927). Pictorial cloth. Second issue, with many changes. $25-$30.

SIRINGO, Charles A. *A Texas Cowboy, or, Fifteen Years on the Hurricane Deck of a Spanish Pony.* Illustrated, including chromolithographic frontispiece in color. Black pictorial cloth. Chicago, 1885. First edition. $500-$750. Chicago, 1886. Siringo &

Dobson. 8 plates, 347 pp. Second edition. $75-$150. Another edition, same place and date: Rand McNally, same collation. Third edition. $75-$100. New York, no date (1886). Wrappers. $75-$100.

SIR Ralph Esher: or, Adventures of a Gentleman of the Court of Charles II. 3 vols., boards. London, 1832. (By Leigh Hunt.) First edition. $150-$200.

SISTER Years (The); Being the Carrier's Address, to the Patrons of the Salem Gazette, for the First of January, 1839. (Cover title.) 8 pp., printed self-wrappers. Salem, Mass., 1839. (By Nathaniel Hawthorne.) First edition. $350-$500.

SITGREAVES, Lorenzo. *Report of an Expedition down the Zuni and Colorado Rivers.* 79 plates, folding map. Cloth. Washington, 1853. First edition. $35-$50.

SITWELL, Edith. *Alexander Pope.* Illustrated. Yellow buckram. London, 1930. First edition. One of 250 (220?) signed. In dust jacket. Boxed. $75-$100.

SITWELL, Edith. *Clowns' Houses.* Decorated boards. Oxford, England, no date (1918). First edition. $35-$50.

SITWELL, Edith. *Collected Poems.* Cloth. London, 1930. One of 320 signed. In dust jacket. $50-$65.

SITWELL, Edith. *Façade.* Colored frontispiece. Boards. London, 1920. First edition. One of 150 signed. $125-$150.

SITWELL, Edith. *Five Poems.* Cloth. London, 1928. First edition. One of 275 signed. $50-$75.

SITWELL, Edith. *In Spring.* 3 wood engravings by Edward Carrick. Green boards, yellow label. London, 1931. First (special) edition. (10 copies signed by author and artist and one stanza in author's handwriting.) In dust jacket. $50-$75. Another issue: One of 350 signed. $35-$50.

SITWELL, Edith. *Jane Barston, 1719-1746.* Yellow boards. London, 1931. One of 250 signed. $25-$35.

SITWELL, Edith. *The Mother and Other Poems.* Wrappers. Oxford, 1915. First edition. $150-$250. Author's first book.

SITWELL, Edith. *The Pleasures of Poetry.* First, Second, and Third Series. 3 vols., cloth. London, 1930-31-32. First editions. In dust jackets. $200-$250.

SITWELL, Edith. *Street Songs.* Cloth. London, 1942. First edition. In dust jacket. $30-$40.

SITWELL, Edith. *The Wooden Pegasus.* Boards and cloth. Oxford, 1920. First edition. In dust jacket. $35-$50.

SITWELL, Edith, and Sitwell, Osbert. *Twentieth Century Harlequinade.* Cloth. Oxford, 1916. First edition. One of 500. $40-$50.

SITWELL, Osbert. *At the House of Mrs. Kinfoot.* Wrappers. London, 1921. First edition. One of 101 signed. $100-$125.

SITWELL, Osbert. *The Collected Satires and Poems of Osbert Sitwell.* Portrait frontispiece. Cloth. No place (London), 1931. First edition. Limited and signed. $40-$50.

SITWELL, Osbert. *Demos the Emperor.* Illustrated. Wrappers. London, 1949. $25-$30.

SITWELL, Osbert. *England Reclaimed.* Buckram. London, 1927. First edition. One of 165 signed. In dust jacket. $30-$40.

SITWELL, Osbert. *Miss Mew.* Half linen and boards. No place (London), 1929. First edition. One of 100. $75-$100.

SITWELL, Osbert. *Triple Fugue.* Boards and cloth. London, 1924. First edition. $35-$50.

SITWELL, Osbert. *Who Killed Cock-Robin?* Boards. London, 1921. First edition. In dust jacket. $35-$40.

SITWELL, Osbert. *The Winstonburg Line: 3 Satires.* Pictorial wrappers. London, 1919. First edition. $50-$75. Author's first book.

SITWELL, Sacheverell. *The Cyder Feast and Other Poems.* Yellow buckram. No place (London), 1927. One of 165 signed. $50.

SITWELL, Sacheverell. *Doctor Donne and Gargantua.* Wrappers. Kensington, 1921. First edition. One of 101 signed. $85. London, 1930. Boards. One of 200 signed. $35.

SITWELL, Sacheverell. *The People's Palace.* Frontispiece. Wrappers. Oxford, 1918. First edition. $25-$30.

SITWELL, Sacheverell. *Two Poems, Ten Songs.* Decorated boards. London, 1929. First edition. One of 275 signed. $35-$50.

SITWELL, Sacheverell, and Lambert, Constant. *The Rio Grande.* Boards. London, 1929. First edition. One of 75 signed. $75-$100. Unsigned (but numbered), $50-$60.

SITWELL, Sacheverell; Blunt, Wilfred; and Synge, Patrick M. *Great Flower Books, 1700-1900.* 36 plates, 20 in color. Folio, half morocco. London, 1956. First edition. One of 295 signed by the authors. Boxed. $150-$200.

SITWELL, Sacheverell; Buchanan, Handasyde; and Fisher, James. *Fine Bird Books, 1700-1900.* 38 plates in color, 36 in black and white. Folio, half morocco. London, 1953. One of 295 signed by the three authors. $200-$300. Another issue: Buckram and boards. $125-$225.

SIX to One; A Nantucket Idyl. Tan or gray cloth. New York, 1878. (By Edward Bellamy.) First edition, first state, cloth. $75-$100. Later state, printed wrappers. $50.

SIXTY Years of the Life of Jeremy Levis. 2 vols., boards, cloth spines, paper labels. New York, 1831. (By Laughton Osborn.) First edition. $65-$75.

SKEFFINGTON, F. J. C., and Joyce, James A. *Two Essays.* 4 leaves, pink printed wrappers. Dublin, no date (1901). First edition. Joyce's first published book, containing his essay "The Day of the Rabblement." $1,500 and up. A N.Y. dealer offered it at $1,850 in 1971.

SKETCH of the Geographical Rout [sic] of a Great Railway . . . Between the Atlantic States and the Great Valley of the Mississippi. Folding map. 16 pp., wrappers. New York, 1829. (By William C. Redfield.) First edition. $50-$75. Half cloth. $50.

SKETCH of the History of South Carolina, etc. (A). Cloth. Charleston, S.C., 1856. (By William James Rivers.) First edition. $50-$75.

SKETCH of Old England (A). By a New England Man. 2 vols., printed boards. New York, 1822. (By James Kirke Paulding.) First edition. $100-$150.

SKETCH of the Seminole War, and Sketches During the Campaign. Leather. Charleston, S.C., 1836. First edition. $100-$150.

SKETCHES by "Boz." Illustrated by George Cruikshank. 3 vols. (First Series, 1836, 2 vols., dark-green cloth; Second Series, 1837, pink cloth.) London, 1836-37. (By Charles Dickens.) First edition. $150-$350. Defective and rebound sets much less. Author's first printed book. London, 1837. 20 parts, pictorial pink wrappers. $1,000 and up. Also, $450 (A, 1963); $650 (A, 1954). Correct copies with all ads and wrappers in first state are very rare and bring highest prices. Imperfect copies bring much less than quoted here.

SKETCHES by a Traveller. Calf. Boston, 1830. (By Silas P. Holbrook.) First edition. $50.

SKETCHES, Historical and Descriptive of Louisiana. Boards and calf. Philadelphia, 1812. (By Amos Stoddard.) First edition. $100-$150.

SKETCHES of History, Life and Manners in the United States. By a Traveller. Woodcut frontispiece view. Boards. New-Haven, Conn., 1826. (By Anne Royall.) First edition. $150. Rebound in leather, $50-$100.

SKETCHES of Springfield. By a Citizen. 49 pp., plus 21 pp. of ads, wrappers. Springfield, Ohio, no date (1852). $60-$70.

SKETCHES of the West, or the Home of the Badgers. Folding map. 48 pp., wrappers. Milwaukee, 1847. (By Josiah B. Grinnell.) Second edition (of *The Home of the Badgers*, which see under Grinnell's pseudonym, Oculus). $200.

SLAUGHTER, Mrs. Linda W. *The New Northwest.* 24 pp., wrappers. Bismarck, 1874. First edition. $1,200 and up.

SLOAN, Edward L. (editor). *Salt Lake City: Gazetteer and Directory.* Cloth. Salt Lake City, 1874. $75-$100.

SLOAN, Robert S. *Utah Gazetteer and Directory of Logan, Ogden, Provo and Salt Lake Cities.* Cloth. Salt Lake City, 1884. $25-$35.

SLOCUM, Joshua. *Voyage of the Destroyer from New York to Brazil.* 47 pp., wrappers. Boston, 1894. First edition. $75.

SMART, Stephen F. *Leadville, Ten Mile . . . And All Other Noted Colorado Mining Camps.* 2 folding maps. 56 pp., printed wrappers. Kansas City, Mo., 1879. First edition. $300-$400. (For a similar work, see Willis Sweet entry.)

SMEDLEY, Frank E. See *Frank Fairleigh.*

SMEDLEY, William. *Across the Plains in '62.* Map and portrait. 56 pp., boards. No place, no date (Denver, 1916). First edition. $75-$100.

SMITH, Albert. *The Wassail-Bowl.* Illustrated. 2 vols., red cloth. London, 1843. First edition. $50-$75.

SMITH, Alexander. *Poems.* Cloth. London, 1853. First edition, with inserted ads dated November, 1852. $35. Author's first book.

SMITH, Alice R. H., and Smith, D. E. H. *The Dwelling Houses of Charleston.* Cloth. Philadelphia, 1917. First edition. $50-$75.

SMITH, Arthur D. Howden. *Porto Bello Gold.* Cloth. New York, no date (1924). First edition. $25.

SMITH, Buckingham (translator). *Narratives of the Career of Hernando de Soto in the Conquest of Florida.* Folding map. Boards. New York, 1866. One of 75. $50-$60. (See also De Soto, Hernando.)

SMITH, Buckingham (translator). *Rudo Ensayo, tentativa de una Provencional Descripción Geográfica de la Provincia de Sonora.* 208 pp., printed gray wrappers. San Agustin (St. Augustine, Fla.), 1863. (By Juan Nentuig?) First edition. One of 10 large paper copies. $350. Regular issue: One of 160. $200-$250. (Note: Actually printed in Albany, N.Y.)

SMITH, Charles H. *The History of Fuller's Ohio Brigade, 1861-1865.* Illustrated. Cloth. Cleveland, 1909. $30-$35.

SMITH, Charles Hamilton. *Orders of Knighthood.* Title and 74 watercolor drawings of knights, some with manuscript captions beneath. Folio, half red morocco. London, no date (about 1830). $800-$1,200.

SMITH, Charles Hamilton. *Selections of the Ancient Costume of Great Britain & Ireland.* 60 full-page color plates. Boards. London, 1814. First edition. $150-$250.

SMITH, Clark Ashton. *Odes and Sonnets*. Preface by George Sterling. Decorations by Florence Lundborg. Blue boards, tan cloth spine, paper label. San Francisco, 1918. First edition. One of 300. $50.

SMITH, Clark Ashton. *The Star-Treader and Other Poems*. Buff pictorial boards. San Francisco, 1912. First edition. In dust jacket. $25-$35.

SMITH, Emma (editor). *A Collection of Sacred Hymns for the Church of the Latter Day Saints*. Marbled boards and cloth. Kirtland, Ohio, 1835. First edition. $2,100 (A, 1968).

SMITH, F. Hopkinson. *American Illustrators*. Folio, 5 parts, printed wrappers in printed board folder. New York, 1892. First edition. One of 1,000. $75-$100.

SMITH, F. Hopkinson. *Colonel Carter of Cartersville*. Cloth. Boston, 1891. First edition, first issue, with no mention of the book in ads. $50-$60.

SMITH, F. Hopkinson, *Venice of Today*. Illustrated. Half morocco. New York, 1896. First book edition (?). $75-$100. (Note: This title first appeared the year before in 20 paperbound parts.)

SMITH, Frank Meriweather (editor). *San Francisco Vigilance Committee of '56*. 83 pp., wrappers. San Francisco, 1883. First edition. $35-$50.

SMITH, Harry B. *A Sentimental Library*. Half vellum. No place (New York), 1914. First edition. $40-$60.

SMITH, J. Calvin. *A New Guide for Travelers Through the United States*. Folding map in color. Cloth, or leather. New York, 1846. $50-$60. New York, 1848. $25-$30.

SMITH, J. Calvin. *The Western Tourist and Emigrant's Guide*. Colored folding map. Cloth, or leather. New York, 1839. First edition. $40-$75. New York, 1845. $35-$50.

SMITH, J. R. *A Key to the Art of Drawing the Human Figure*. 24 plates. Boards. Philadelphia, 1831. First edition. $50-$75.

SMITH, James E. *A Famous Battery and Its Campaigns, 1861-64*. Cloth. Washington, 1892. First edition. $35-$50.

SMITH, James F. *The Cherokee Land Lottery, etc.* Contemporary calf. New York, 1838. First edition. $75-$100.

SMITH, Jerome V. C. *Natural History of the Fishes of Massachusetts*. Engravings. Half cloth. Boston, 1833. First edition. $75-$100.

SMITH, Jodie (editor). *History of the Chisum War*. Illustrated. Stiff pictorial wrappers. No place, no date (Electra, Tex., 1927). (By Ike Fridge.) First edition. $50-$75.

SMITH, John Thomas. *Antiquities of Westminster*. 246 engravings, 13 pages of hand-colored plates. Boards. London, 1807. $100-$125.

SMITH, John Thomas. *Cries of London, Exhibiting Several of the Itinerant Traders of Antient and Modern Times*. Portrait and 30 hand-colored etchings. Half morocco. London, 1839. First edition. Large paper issue. $100-$150.

SMITH, Johnston. *Maggie: A Girl of the Streets*. Yellow printed wrappers. No place, no date (New York, 1893). (By Stephen Crane.) First edition. $1,500-$2,000. Also, $1,900 (A, 1968). (For the second edition, see the entry under Crane, Stephen.)

SMITH, Joseph, Jr. See *A Book of Commandments*.

SMITH, Joseph, Jr. *The Book of Mormon*. Calf or roan. Palmyra, N.Y., 1830. First edition, first issue, with 2 pp. preface and testimonial leaf at end and without index. $750-$1,000. Also, $750 (A, 1968); $775 (A, 1964). Second issue, without testimonials, etc., $500. Kirtland, Ohio, 1837. Second edition. $100-$200. Nauvoo, Ill., 1840. Third edition. $100-$150. Nauvoo, 1842. Fourth American edition. $100. New York, 1869. In Deseret (Mormon) alphabet. $100-$150. Plano, Ill., 1874. $25-$50.

SMITH, Joseph, Jr. *Te Buka A Mormona.* Translated by Frank Cutler and others. Cloth. Salt Lake City, 1904. First edition of *The Book of Mormon* in Tahitian. $35-$50.

SMITH, Joseph, Jr., and others (editors). *Doctrine and Covenants of the Church o, the Latter Day Saints.* Contemporary calf or sheep. Kirtland, Ohio, 1835. First edition. $250-$300. Worn, $140 and $75. New York, 1869. In Deseret alphabet. Printed boards, leather spine. $75-$100.

SMITH, Kate Douglas. *The Story of Patsy. A Reminiscence.* 27 pp., wrappers. San Francisco, 1883. (By Kate Douglas Wiggin.) Second edition. $25-$30.

SMITH, Mary E. *A Mother's Sacrifice; or, Who Was Guilty?* Cloth. New York, 1885. First edition. $35-$40.

SMITH, Michael. *A Geographical View, of the Province of Upper Canada, and Promiscuous Remarks upon the Government, etc.* 107 pp., wrappers. Hartford, Conn., 1813. First edition. $100-$150.

SMITH, Moses. *History of the Adventures and Sufferings of Moses Smith.* 2 plates. Boards. Brooklyn, N.Y., 1812. First edition. $45-$60.

SMITH, Nathan. *A Practical Essay on Typhous Fever.* Half calf. New York, 1824. First edition. $150-$200.

SMITH, Platt. *The Dubuque Claim Case; in the Supreme Court of the United States.* 20 pp., wrappers. Dubuque, Iowa, 1852. $75.

SMITH, Mrs. Sarah. *A Journal Kept by Mrs. Sarah Foote Smith While Journeying with Her People from Wellington, Ohio, to Footeville, Town of Nepeuskun, Winnebago County, Wis., April 15 to May 10, 1846.* Boards, paper label. No place, no date (Kilbourn, 1905). $35-$50.

SMITH, Thomas. *Extracts from the Diary of a Huntsman.* Illustrated. Cloth. London, 1838. First edition. $35-$40.

SMITH, Thorne. *Biltmore Oswald: The Diary of a Hapless Recruit.* Pictorial boards. New York, no date (1918). First edition. In dust jacket. $25-$35. Author's first book.

SMITH, Thorne. *Topper: An Improbable Adventure.* Red cloth. New York, 1926. First edition. In dust jacket. $25. Author's first novel.

SMITH, Wallace. *Garden of the Sun: A History of the San Joaquin Valley, 1772-1939.* Cloth. Los Angeles, no date (1939). First edition. $40-$50.

SMITH, William H. *History of Canada.* Folding table. 2 vols., boards, paper labels. Quebec, 1815 (actually 1826). First edition. $400-$500. Later edition: No place, no date (Quebec, 1827). 2 vols., half morocco. $400-$500.

SMITH, William H. *Smith's Canadian Gazeteer.* Map and plates. Cloth. Toronto, 1846. First edition, first issue, with numbers instead of place names on the map. $100. Later issue, same year, map with place-names. $75.

SMITH, William Rudolph. *Observations on the Wisconsin Territory.* Map. Cloth or boards. Philadelphia, 1838. First edition. $200-$250.

SMITH, William Russell. *Reminiscences of a Long Life.* Vol. 1. (All published.) 8 portraits. Cloth. Washington, no date (1889). First edition. $50-$75.

SMITHWICK, Noah. *The Evolution of a State.* Cloth. Austin, Tex., no date (1900). First edition. $35-$50.

SMOLLETT, Tobias. *The Adventures of Peregrine Pickle.* Illustrated by Alexander King. 2 vols., cloth. New York, no date (1929). $50-$75.

SNARLEYYOW, or The Dog Fiend. 3 vols., boards. London, 1837. (By Frederick Marryat.) First edition. $100-$150. Philadelphia, 1837. 2 vols., cloth. First American edition. (Published with by-line "F. Marryat.") $50-$75.

SNELLING, William J. See *Tales of the Northwest.*

SNELLING, William J. *The Polar Regions of the Western Continent Explored.* Contemporary calf. Boston, 1831. First edition. $100-$125.

SNOW, C. P. *Death Under Sail.* Cloth. London, no date (1932). First edition. In dust jacket. $45-$50.

SNYDER, Gary. *Riprap.* Japanese-style blue wrappers. Origin Press, 1959. First edition. $125-$175. Author's first book.

SNYDER, Gary. *Six Sections from Mountains and Rivers Without End.* Green cloth. London, no date (1967). Fulcrum Press. First edition. One of 100 on sage Glastonbury paper, signed. In dust jacket. $35.

SNYDER, Gary. *Three Worlds, Three Realms, Six Roads.* Illustrated. Wrappers. Marlboro, Vt., no date (1966). First edition. One of 200. $25-$35.

SOLDIER'S Story of the War (A). 9 plates (some copies without plates). Cloth. New Orleans, 1874. (By Napier Bartlett.) First edition, with plates. $75-$100.

SOMBRERO, The. Quarter-Centennial Number. Yearbook of the Class of 1895, University of Nebraska. White and red cloth. No place, no date (Lincoln, Neb., 1894). First edition. $325-$400. (Note: Contains Willa Cather's and Dorothy Canfield's prize story "The Fear That Walks by Noonday.")

SOME Account of the Work of Stephen J. Field. No place (New York?), no date (1881). (By Chauncey F. Black.) First edition. $40-$50. No place, 1895. Second edition. $25.

SOME Antiquarian Notes. 56 pp., red wrappers. Naples, 1907. (By Norman Douglas.) First edition. One of 250. Signed on title page. $100.

SOMEBODY Had to Do Something. Wrappers. Los Angeles, 1939. First edition. $150. (Contains tributes to James P. Lardner, killed in the Spanish Civil War, including material by Ernest Hemingway and Ring Lardner, Jr.)

SOME Imagist Poets. Printed wrappers. Boston, 1915. (Edited by Amy Lowell.) First edition. $75-$100. London, 1915. Pink printed wrappers. First English edition. $75-$100. Spine faded, $45. Other annual numbers: Boston, 1916. Boards. First edition. In dust jacket. $35-$50. Boston, 1917. Boards. First edition. In dust jacket. $35-$50.

SOME Southwestern Trails. Illustrated. Essays by J. Evetts Haley and others. Pictorial cloth. El Paso, Tex., 1948. Limited edition. $35-$50.

SONG of Roland (The). Translated by Isabel Butler. 7 hand-colored illustrations by Bruce Rogers. Boards, vellum spine. No place, no date (Cambridge, Mass., 1906). One of 220. First edition. $250-$350.

SONGS of the Class of MDCCCXXIX. Cream-yellow wrappers. Boston, 1854. First edition. (Contains 3 poems by Oliver Wendell Holmes.) About 6 copies are known to exist; none has appeared for sale in many years. Boston, 1859. Second edition, with 8 Holmes poems. $50-$75.

SOULE, Frank; Gihon, Frank; and Nisbet, James. *The Annals of San Francisco.* 6 plates, 2 maps. Morocco. New York, 1855. First edition. $100-$150.

SOUTH Carolina Jockey Club (The). Cloth. Charleston, S.C., 1857. (By John B. Irving.) First edition. $75-$100.

SOUTHERN Business Directory and General Commercial Advertiser (The). Vol. 1. (All published.) Illustrated. Charleston, S.C., 1854. $75-$100.

SOUTHERN Business Guide, 1881-82. Illustrated. Cloth. New York, 1882. $50-$75.

SOUTHERN History of the War. Illustrated. Cloth. New York, 1863. First edition. $25-$30.

SOUTHERN Primer (The). Illustrated. Wrappers. Richmond, Va., 1860. $25-$30.

SOUTHEY, Robert. *All for Love; and The Pilgrim to Compostella.* Cloth, paper label. London, 1829. First edition. $75-$100.

SOUTH-WEST (The). By a Yankee. 2 vols., cloth, paper labels. New York, 1835. (By Joseph Holt Ingraham.) First edition. $200-$250. Author's first book.

SOUTHWORTH, S. S. *California for Fruit-Growers and Consumptives.* Folding map, plates. 108 pp., wrappers. Sacramento, Calif., 1883. $35-$50.

SOUVENIRS of the Bal Costume, Given by . . . Queen Victoria, . . . May 12, 1842. Hand-colored plates. Large folio, contemporary half morocco. London, 1843. $100.

SOWELL, A. J. *Early Settlers and Indian Fighters of Southwest Texas.* 12 plates. Cloth. Austin, Tex., 1900. First edition. $150-$200.

SOWELL, A. J. *Rangers and Pioneers of Texas.* Illustrated. Pictorial cloth. San Antonio, Tex., 1884. First edition. $250-$300.

SPALDING, C. C. *Annals of the City of Kansas.* 7 plates. Cloth. Kansas City, Mo., 1858. First edition. $500 and up.

SPARGO, John. *Anthony Haswell: Printer, Patriot, Ballader.* 35 facsimiles. Half morocco. Rutland, Vt., 1925. First edition. One of 300. $35-$50.

SPARGO, John. *The Potters and Potteries of Bennington.* Boards. Boston, 1926. One of 800. $35-$40.

SPARROW, Walter Shaw. *A Book of Sporting Painters.* 138 illustrations, some in color. Buckram. London, no date (1931). One of 125 with 2 extra plates. $60-$80.

SPARROW, Walter Shaw. *British Sporting Artists, from Barlow to Herring.* 27 color plates, other illustrations. Cloth. London, no date (1922). First edition. $50-$100. Limited issue. Buckram. One of 95 signed. $250-$300.

SPAVERY (compiler). *The Harp of a Thousand Strings: or, Laughter for a Lifetime.* Illustrated. Cloth. New York, no date (1858). (By George Washington Harris.) First edition, first printing, with frontispiece in black and gray and with imprints of Craighead and Jenkins on copyright page. $150 and up. (The pen name Spavery in this case was used for Harris' pseudonym "Samuel Putnam Avery." The engravings are attributed on the title page to "S. P. Avery.")

SPEARS, John R. *Illustrated Sketches of Death Valley and Other Borax Deserts of the Pacific Coast.* Printed wrappers. Chicago, 1892. First edition. $35-$50.

SPECIFICATIONS of Steam Machinery and Building Directions of Hulls of U.S. Steamers Constructed 1861-1864. (Cover title.) No place, no date. $25-$30.

SPECIMENS. 54 pp., pink wrappers, stitched. No place, no date (Canyon City, Ore., 1868). (By Joaquin Miller—preface signed "C. H. Miller.") First edition. $1,000 and up. Made-up copy, with unsigned Miller inscription on cover, $850. Author's first book—rigorously suppressed by him.

SPECIMENS: A Stevens-Nelson Paper Catalogue. (Specimen sheets of fine papers, with text.) Half goatskin and boards. No place, no date (New York, about 1950-53). Boxed. $100-$150.

SPEED, Thomas. *The Wilderness Road.* Map. Cloth. Louisville, Ky., 1886. First edition. $35-$50.

SPEER, Emory. *The Banks County Ku-Klux.* 60 pp., wrappers. Atlanta, 1883. First edition. $75.

SPENCER, Herbert. *Education: Intellectual, Moral, and Physical.* Cloth. New York, 1861. First edition. In slipcase. $25-$30.

SPENCER, Herbert. *Social Statics.* Cloth. London, 1851. First edition. $35. Author's first book.

SPENCER, O. M. *Indian Captivity: A True Narrative of the Capture of, etc.* Gray wrappers. Washington, Pa., 1835. First edition (?). $250 and up. (Note: There was also a New York edition of 1835. Both these are rare.) New York, 1836. Third edition. $35-$50.

SPENDER, Stephen. See S., S. H.

SPENDER, Stephen. *The Burning Cactus.* Cloth. London, 1936. First edition, first issue, with first and final leaves blank. In dust jacket. $35-$50.

SPENDER, Stephen. *The Generous Days.* Boards and calf. Boston, 1969. One of 50 signed. $45.

SPENDER, Stephen. *Poems.* Black cloth. London, no date (1933). First edition. In dust jacket. $40-$50.

SPENDER, Stephen. *Returning to Vienna 1947.* Wrappers. No place, no date (London, 1947). Banyan Press. One of 500 signed. $35.

SPENDER, Stephen. *Ruins and Visions: Poems.* Blue-green cloth. London, no date (1942). First edition. In dust jacket. $75-$100. New York, no date (1942). Red cloth. First American edition. In dust jacket. $25.

SPENDER, Stephen. *Twenty Poems.* Wrappers. Oxford, England, no date (1930). First edition. One of 135. $200-$250. Signed copies (75 of the 135). $350-$450.

SPENDER, Stephen. *Vienna.* Cloth. London, 1934. First edition. In dust jacket. $35.

SPENSER, Edmund. *The Shepheardes Calender.* 12 woodcuts. Boards and linen. London, 1896. Kelmscott Press. One of 225. $450-$500.

SPEYER, Leonora. *Holy Night: A Yuletide Masque.* Designs by Eric Gill. Stiff blue decorated wrappers. New York, 1919. One of 500. $35-$50. Author's first book.

SPIELMANN, M. H., and Layard, G. S. *Kate Greenaway.* 53 colored plates, other illustrations. White cloth. London, 1905. One of 500 with an original pencil sketch by Kate Greenaway inserted. $300-$400. Trade edition: Purple cloth. $35-$50.

SPILMAN, The Rev. T. E. *Semi-Centenarians of Butler Grove Township, Montgomery County (Illinois).* Boards and cloth. No place (Butler), 1878. First edition. $35-$50.

SPIRIT of the Age (The). Boards, paper label. London, 1825. (By William Hazlitt.) First edition. $50-$75.

SPORTS and Amusements for the Juvenile Philosopher. Illustrated. Cloth. Middletown, 1835. First edition. $25-$30.

SPORTS of Childhood (The). 18 pp., wrappers. Northampton, Mass. no date (about 1830-40). First edition (?). $40-$45. (Henderson, in *Early American Sport,* also lists a New Haven edition of about 1839.)

SPORTSMAN'S Portfolio of American Field Sports (The). 20 full-page wood engravings, title page vignette, illustration at end. Oblong wrappers. Boston, 1855. First edition. $200-$250.

SPOTTS, David L. *Campaigning with Custer.* Map, 13 plates. Cloth. Los Angeles, 1928. First edition. One of 800 (Howes says all but about 300 burned). $75-$100.

SPRAGUE, Charles. *The Prize Ode . . . Recited at the Representation of the Shakespeare Jubilee.* (Caption title.) 8 pp., sewed. No place, no date (Boston, 1824). First edition. $25.

SPRAGUE, John T. *The Origin, Progress, and Conclusion of the Florida War.* Folding map, 8 plates. Cloth. New York, 1848. First edition. $75-$125.

SPRAGUE, John T. *The Treachery in Texas.* 35 pp., wrappers. New York, 1862. First edition. $35-$50.

SPRING: Infancy,—The Spring of Life. 8 woodcuts. 16 pp., pictorial wrappers. New York (New York), no date (about 1815-20). (Children's toybook published by Samuel S. Wood.) $75.

SPRING, Agnes Wright. *The Cheyenne and Black Hills Stage and Express Routes.* Map, 17 plates. Cloth. Glendale, Calif., 1949. First edition. $50-$60.

SPRING, Agnes Wright. *Seventy Years: A Panoramic History of the Wyoming Stock Growers Association.* Illustrated. Stiff pictorial wrappers. No place (Cheyenne, Wyo.), 1942. First edition. $35-$60.

SPRUNT, James. *Chronicles of the Cape Fear River.* Half leather. Raleigh, N.C., 1914. First edition. $60-$75.

SPY (The): A Tale of the Neutral Ground. By the Author of "Precaution." 2 vols., boards, paper labels. New York, 1821. (By James Fenimore Cooper.) First edition. $5,000 (1964 catalogue). Also, $7,600 (A, 1945). (There are said to be only 2 copies known in original boards.) New York, 1963. Limited Editions Club. Cloth. $40-$50.

SQUIER, E. G., and Davis, E. H. *Ancient Monuments of the Mississippi Valley.* 48 plates. Folio, cloth. New York, 1848. First edition, second issue. (First issue was in Washington.) $60-$65.

SQUIRE, Watson C. *Resources and Development of Washington Territory.* Folding map. 72 pp., wrappers. Seattle, 1886. First edition. $50-$60.

STALLINGS, Laurence. See Anderson, Maxwell.

STANLEY, David S. *Diary of a March from Fort Smith, Ark., to San Diego, Calif., Made in 1853.* 37 pp., multigraphed. No place, no date. In cloth case. $75.

STANLEY, F. *The Grant That Maxwell Bought.* Map, 15 plates. Cloth. No place, no date (Denver, 1952). (By Father Stanley Crocchiola.) First edition. One of 250 signed. $75-$100.

STANLEY, F. *The Las Vegas Story.* Illustrated. Cloth. No place, no date (Denver, 1951). (By Father Stanley Crocchiola.) First edition. $35.

STANLEY, F. *One Half Miles from Heaven, or, The Cimmaron Story.* 155 pp., wrappers. Denver, 1949. (By Father Stanley Crocchiola.) First edition. $35-$50.

STANSBURY, Phillip. *A Pedestrian Tour of 2,300 Miles, in North America, etc.* 9 plates. Boards. New York, 1822. First edition. $50-$75.

STANTON, Schuyler. *Daughters of Destiny.* Red cloth. Chicago, no date (1906). (By L. Frank Baum.) First edition. $25-$30.

STAPP, William P. *The Prisoners of Perote.* Wrappers, or cloth. Philadelphia, 1845. First edition. Wrappers: $300-$400.

STAR City of the West (The): Pueblo and Its Advantages. 24 pp., folded. Pueblo, Colo., 1889. $45.

STARBUCK, Alexander. *History of the American Whale Fishery, etc.* 6 plates. Half leather. Waltham, Mass., 1878. First edition. $75-$100. (Its first appearance was as Part IV, *Report of the U.S. Commissioner of Fish and Fishing,* Washington, 1878, catalogued in 1967 by a Boston dealer at $87.50.) New York, 1964. 2 vols., half leather. Boxed. One of 75 sets. $75. Trade edition: 2 vols., cloth. Boxed. $35.

STARKEY, James. *Reminiscences of Indian Depredations.* 25 pp., wrappers. St. Paul, Minn., 1891. First edition. $75-$125.

STARR, Julian. *The Disagreeable Woman.* Green cloth. New York, 1895. (By Horatio Alger, Jr.) First edition. $200 and up. (Note: Ralph D. Gardner's estimate: $175. Only known copy is in Library of Congress.)

STATE of Indiana Delineated (The). Boards, leather spine, printed label on cover. New York, 1838. First edition. (Published by J. H. Colton to accompany his separately published map, which is inserted in some copies.) $150-$200.

STATE of the Nation (The). Printed wrappers. Cincinnati, 1940. Little Man Press. First edition. One of 99 signed by contributors, including William Saroyan. $50-$60.

STATEMENT and Reports Concerning the Uncle Sam and Gold Canon Silver Lodes in Nevada. 2 colored maps. Wrappers. Boston, 1865. (By S. Chapin and J. Veatch.) $30.

STATEMENT of Payments on River Property in the City of Chicago, Belonging to John S. Wright, etc. 24 pp., wrappers. Chicago, 1849. $75.

STATEMENT Respecting the Earl of Selkirk's Settlement of Kildonan, upon the Red River, in North America. Folding map. 125 pp., boards. London, no date (about 1817). (By John Halkett.) First edition. $375. London, 1817. Second (enlarged) edition. 194 pp., boards. With title altered to *Statement Respecting the Earl of Selkirk's Settlement upon the Red River, in North America.* $250-$300.

STATISTICS of Dane County, with a Business Directory of the Village of Madison. 24 pp., wrappers. Madison, Wis., 1851. First edition. $35-$50.

STAUFFER, David McN., and Fielding, Mantle. *American Engravers upon Copper and Steel.* Illustrated. 3 vols., boards and cloth. New York and Philadelphia, 1907-17. Vols. 1 and 2, limited to 350 copies (1907); Vol. 3, limited to 220, signed by Fielding (1917). The 3 vols. complete. $200-$300. Incomplete set, Vols. 1 and 2 only, $150-$225. Vol. 3 only, $50-$75. (Note: T. H. Gage published an *Artist's Index to Stauffer,* Worcester, 1921, which is sometimes offered with the three-volume set.)

STEAD, William T. *If Christ Came to Chicago.* Pictorial wrappers. Chicago, 1894. First edition, first issue, with map of whorehouse and saloon areas in black and red. $50. Second issue, with map in black. $35-$40.

STEAM-BOAT (The). Boards, marbled spine. Edinburgh, 1822. (By John Galt.) First edition. $40-$50.

STEARNS, Charles. *Facts in the Life of Gen. Taylor.* 36 pp., unbound. Boston, 1848. First edition. $25-$30.

STEBBINS, Charles Livingstone (editor). *Harvard Lyrics and Other Verses.* Wine cloth, top edges gilt. Boston, 1890. First edition. $40-$45. (Note: Contains Wallace Stevens' "Vita Mea," his first book appearance.)

STEDMAN, Edmund C. *Songs and Ballads.* Morocco, with morocco slipcase. New York, 1884. First edition. One of 100 on Japan paper. $35-$40.

STEDMAN, John G. *Narrative of a Five Years' Expedition Against the Revolted Negroes of Surinam, in Guiana on the Wild Coast of America.* 80 full-page colored engravings, map. 2 vols., marbled boards and calf. London, 1813. Third edition. $225.

STEEDMAN, Charles J. *Bucking the Sagebrush.* 3 portraits, folding map, 9 Charles M. Russell plates. Pictorial cloth. New York, 1904. First edition. $50-$60.

STEEL, Flora A. *English Fairy Tales.* Illustrated in color by Arthur Rackham. London, 1918. One of 500 signed by Rackham. $200-$300.

STEELE, James W. *The Klondike.* Illustrated, 2 maps. 80 pp., pictorial gray wrappers. Chicago, 1897. First edition. $100-$125.

STEELE, John. *Across the Plains in 1850.* Cloth. Chicago, 1930. Caxton Club. First edition. $35-$50.

STEELE, John. *In Camp and Cabin: Mining Life and Adventure, in California, etc.* 81 pp., printed wrappers. Lodi, Wis., 1901. First edition. $130.

STEELE, Oliver G. *New and Corrected Map of Michigan.* Colored folding map, leatherbound. Buffalo, no date (1834). $75-$100.

STEELE, R. J., and others (compilers). *Directory of the County of Placer.* Boards and calf. San Francisco, 1861. $300-$400.

STEELE, Zadock. *The Indian Captive.* Calf. Montpelier, Vt., 1818. First edition. $200-$250.

STEFFENS, Lincoln. *The Shame of the Cities.* Cloth. New York, 1904. First edition. $25. Author's first book.

STEIN, Gertrude. *An Acquaintance with Description.* Oyster-white linen. London, 1929. Seizin Press. First edition. One of 225 signed. $95-$175.

STEIN, Gertrude. *Américains d'Amérique.* Wrappers. Paris, 1933. First edition. One of 50. $50.

STEIN, Gertrude. *The Autobiography of Alice B. Toklas.* Blue cloth. New York, 1933. First edition. In dust jacket. $35-$50.

STEIN, Gertrude. *Blood on the Dining Room Floor.* Half buckram and boards. No place, 1948. Banyan Press. One of 600. In glassine dust jacket. Boxed. $65.

STEIN, Gertrude. *Composition as Explanation.* Boards. London, 1926. $25-$35.

STEIN, Gertrude. *Dix Portraits.* Translated by G. Hugnet and Virgil Thomson. Illustrated by Picasso and others. Decorated wrappers. Paris, no date (1930). First edition. One of 25 on Holland paper, signed by author and translators. In glassine dust jacket. $200-$300. One of 65 on Velin d'Arches paper, signed. In dust jacket. $150-$210. One of 400 on Alfa paper without illustrations. $100-$150. Also, $22 (A, 1969), $90 (A, 1968).

STEIN, Gertrude. *An Elucidation.* Wrappers. No place, no date (Paris, 1927). First edition. $35-$50. (Issued as a supplement to *Transition* magazine after having been printed there with errors.)

STEIN, Gertrude. *First Reader & Three Plays.* Gray cloth. Boston, 1948. First edition. In dust jacket. $25.

STEIN, Gertrude. *The Geographical History of America or The Relation of Human Nature to the Human Mind.* Black and white cloth. New York, no date (1936). First edition. In dust jacket. $40-$50.

STEIN, Gertrude. *Geography and Plays.* Cloth and boards. Boston, no date (1922). First edition. In dust jacket. $50-$75.

STEIN, Gertrude. *Have They Attacked Mary. He Giggled.* (A Political Caricature.) Woodcut. Printed red wrappers. No place, no date (New York, 1917). First edition. One of 200. $250-$300.

STEIN, Gertrude. *How to Write.* Boards, paper label on spine. Paris, 1931. First edition. One of 1,000. $50-$75.

STEIN, Gertrude. *Ida.* Green cloth. New York, no date (1941). First edition. In dust jacket. $25.

STEIN, Gertrude. *In a Garden: An Opera in One Act.* Wrappers. New York, 1951. First edition. $30.

STEIN, Gertrude. *Lucy Church Amiably.* Boards. Paris, 1930. First edition. In plain brown paper dust jacket. $100-$1,35.

STEIN, Gertrude. *The Making of Americans.* Wrappers. Paris, no date (1925). First edition. $400-$500. Rebound in marbled boards, leather spine, original covers bound in, $275.

STEIN, Gertrude. *Morceaux Choisis de la Fabrication des Américains.* Translated by Georges Hugnet. Portrait frontispiece by Christian Bérard. Wrappers. Paris, no date (1929). First edition. One of 85 signed by author and illustrator. In glassine jacket. $150-$200. Another issue: One of 200. $100.

STEIN, Gertrude. *Narration: Four Lectures.* Introduction by Thornton Wilder. Blue, black, and gilt cloth. Chicago, no date (1935). First edition. One of 120 signed by Stein and Wilder. Boxed. $350-$400.

STEIN, Gertrude. *A Novel of Romantic Beauty and Nature and Which Looks Like an Engraving.* Boards. Paris, 1930. $25-$35.

STEIN, Gertrude. *Operas and Plays.* Wrappers. Paris, plain edition (1932). First edition. In slipcase. $100-$135.

STEIN, Gertrude. *Paris, France.* Blue cloth. New York, 1940. First edition, with Scribner "A" on copyright page. In dust jacket. $25-$30. Later, pink cloth. $10-$15.

STEIN, Gertrude. *Picasso.* Illustrated. Pictorial wrappers. Paris, 1938. First edition. $75. Front cover loose, lacking backstrip and back cover. $40.

STEIN, Gertrude. *Portraits and Prayers.* Pictorial cloth. New York, no date (1934). First edition. In dust jacket. $25.

STEIN, Gertrude. *Tender Buttons. Objects. Food. Rooms.* Boards, paper label. New York, 1914. First edition. $200-$250.

STEIN, Gertrude. *Things as They Are: A Novel in 3 Parts.* Cloth. No place, no date (Pawlet, Vt., 1950). First edition. One of 490 (of an edition of 516). $35-$50.

STEIN, Gertrude. *Three Lives.* Blue cloth. New York, 1909. First edition. $100-$125. Author's first book.

STEIN, Gertrude. *Two Poems.* Wrappers. New York, 1948. One of 415. $35.

STEIN, Gertrude. *A Village Are You Ready Yet Not Yet.* Illustrated by Élie Lascaux. Wrappers. Paris, no date (1928). First edition. One of 90 signed. In glassine dust jacket. $250 $350. One of 10 on Japan paper. $400-$500. Bethel, Conn., 1956. First American edition. $20.

STEIN, Gertrude. *What Are Masterpieces?* Portrait frontispiece. Blue cloth. Los Angeles, no date (1940). First edition. In dust jacket. $75-$100.

STEIN, Gertrude. *The World Is Round.* Illustrated by Clement Hurd. White boards. New York, no date (1939). One of 350 signed. Boxed. $100-$150. Copy sold for $200 at Parke-Bernet in 1972.

STEIN, Gertrude, and Toklas, Alice B. *On Our Way.* Wrappers. New York, 1959. First edition. One of 100. $35.

STEIN, Gertrude, and Thomson, Virgil. *Four Saints in Three Acts.* Purple cloth. New York, 1934. First edition. $50-$60. New York, no date (1948). Boards. One of 30 signed. $50.

STEINBECK, John. *Bombs Away.* Blue cloth. New York, 1942. First edition. In dust jacket. $25.

STEINBECK, John. *Cannery Row.* Yellow cloth. New York, 1945. First edition. In dust jacket. $25.

STEINBECK, John. *Cup of Gold: A Life of Henry Morgan, Buccaneer, with Occasional Reference to History.* Orange cloth. New York, 1929. First edition, first issue, with "First Published, August, 1929" on copyright page. In dust jacket. $250-$300. Author's first book. New York, no date (1936). Blue cloth. Second edition. In dust jacket. $25-$35.

STEINBECK, John. *East of Eden.* Green buckram. New York, 1952. First edition. One of 1,500 signed. Boxed. $100-$125. Trade edition: Cloth. In dust jacket. $25-$35.

STEINBECK, John. *The First Watch.* Wrappers. Los Angeles, no date (1947). First edition. One of 60. $150-$200.

STEINBECK, John. *The Forgotten Village.* Tan cloth. New York, 1941. First edition, first issue, with "First Published in May 1941" on copyright page. In dust jacket. $25.

STEINBECK, John. *The Grapes of Wrath.* Pictorial beige cloth. New York, no date (1939). First edition, with yellow top edges, with "First published in April, 1939" on copyright page, and with first edition notice on front flap of dust jacket. In dust jacket. $50-$75. London, no date (1939). First English edition. In dust jacket. $35. New York, 1940. Limited Editions Club. 2 vols., grass cloth and leather. Boxed. $100.

STEINBECK, John. *In Dubious Battle.* Orange cloth. New York, no date (1936). First edition. In dust jacket. $75-$100. Signed, $125 and $175. Another issue: Boards. One of 99 signed. Boxed. $200 and $185.

STEINBECK, John. *John Steinbeck Replies.* 4-page leaflet, unbound. (First page is letter to Steinbeck by L. M. Birkhead. Pages 2 and 3 are Steinbeck's reply.) No place, no date (New York, 1940). $50-$75. New York, 1940. Reprint by Overbrook Press. Boards. One of 350. $35-$50.

STEINBECK, John. *A Letter from John Steinbeck.* Printed wrappers. No place (San Francisco), 1964. First edition. One of 150. $60.

STEINBECK, John. *The Log from the Sea of Cortez.* Red cloth. New York, 1951. Revised edition of *Sea of Cortez,* with a new 67-page chapter, "About Ed Ricketts." In dust jacket. $35-$50. (See Steinbeck, *Sea of Cortez.*)

STEINBECK, John. *The Long Valley.* Rust-colored cloth, natural cloth spine. New York, 1938. First edition. In dust jacket. $35-$65.

STEINBECK, John. *Nothing So Monstrous: A Story.* Donald McKay drawings. Decorated boards, cloth spine. No place (New York), 1936. First edition. One of 370. $50-$75.

STEINBECK, John. *Nuits Noires.* Wrappers. Paris, 1944 (actually, 1945). (French translation of *The Moon Is Down.*) First openly published edition, issued by Editions de Minuit. In glassine dust jacket. $55. (Note: There was an earlier clandestine edition in French issued in 1944 during the Nazi occupation.)

STEINBECK, John. *Of Mice and Men.* Tan cloth. New York, no date (1937). First edition, first state, with "and only moved because the heavy hands were / pendula" at page 9, second and third lines from bottom of page. In dust jacket. $50-$60. Second state, lines 2 and 3 from bottom of page 9 corrected. $15-$20. London, no date (1937). "Proof copy" in printed wrappers. $60 (A, 1963).

STEINBECK, John. *The Pastures of Heaven.* Green cloth. New York, 1932. First edition, first issue, with Brewer, Warren & Putnam imprint. In dust jacket. $100-$150. Second issue, with Robert O. Ballou imprint. In dust jacket, with a 4-page Ballou brochure, *The Neatest Trick of the Year.* $75-$100. Another, no brochure, in dust jacket, $75. (Note: Johnson notes a third issue with Covici-Friede imprint.)

STEINBECK, John. *The Red Pony.* Pictorial tan cloth. New York, 1937. First edition. One of 699 signed. Boxed. $100-$150. New York, 1945. Gray cloth. First illustrated edition. In slipcase. $25-$35.

STEINBECK, John. *Rue de la Sardine.* Wrappers. Paris, no date (1947). (First French translation of *Cannery Row.*) One of 110. $50.

STEINBECK, John. *A Russian Journal.* Boards and cloth. New York, 1948. First edition. In dust jacket. $35.

STEINBECK, John. *Saint Katy the Virgin.* Printed boards, cloth spine. No place, no date (New York, 1936). First edition. One of 199 signed. (Issued as a Christmas greeting by Covici-Friede with greeting slip inserted.) In glassine dust jacket. $300-$500.

STEINBECK, John. *"Their Blood Is Strong."* Pictorial wrappers. San Francisco, 1938. First edition. $100-$150.

STEINBECK, John. *To a God Unknown.* Green cloth. New York, no date (1933). First edition, first issue, with Robert O. Ballou imprint. In dust jacket. $100-$150.

STEINBECK, John. *Tortilla Flat.* Tan cloth. New York, no date (1935). First edition. In dust jacket. $75-$100. Advance issue of 500, in wrappers. $100-$125.

STEINBECK, John. *The Wayward Bus.* Brown cloth. New York, 1947. First edition. In dust jacket. $25. Lacking jacket, $10. London, no date (1947). Red cloth. First English edition. In dust jacket. $15-$20.

STEINBECK, John. *The Winter of Our Discontent.* Cloth. New York, no date (1961). First edition. In dust jacket. $10-$15. Another issue: One of 500 signed. In dust jacket. $35-$50.

STEINBECK, John, and Ricketts, Edward F. *Sea of Cortez.* Cloth. New York, 1941. First edition. In dust jacket. $50-$100. Presentation copy, signed, in worn jacket, $150. Also, unrevised galley proofs, in wrappers, $100 (A, 1963). (See Steinbeck, *The Log from the Sea of Cortez.*)

STEP, Edward. *Hardy Bulbous Plants: Florilegium Harlemense.* 60 colored plates. Half white pigskin. London, 1908. One of 100. $75-$100.

STEPHENS, Alexander H. *A Constitutional View of the Late War Between the States.* Map, plates. 2 vols., cloth. Philadelphia, 1868-70. First edition. $50-$75.

STEPHENS, Alexander H. *Speech in January, 1861, Before the Georgia State Convention.* 12 pp., wrappers. Baltimore, 1864. $35-$40.

STEPHENS, Mrs. Ann S. *Malaeska: The Indian Wife of the White Hunter.* Printed orange wrappers. New York, no date (1860). First edition, first issue, with covers 6 5/8 x 4 1/2 inches, and without woodcut on cover. $300-$500.

STEPHENS, Ann Sophia. *The Portland Sketch Book.* Cloth. Portland, 1836. First edition. $35-$50.

STEPHENS, James. See Esse, James.

STEPHENS, James. *The Charwoman's Daughter.* Cloth. London, 1912. First edition. In dust jacket. $35-$50.

STEPHENS, James. *Collected Poems.* Boards and vellum. London, 1926. One of 500 large paper copies, signed. $35.

STEPHENS, James. *The Crock of Gold.* Green cloth. London, 1912. First edition. In dust jacket. $100-$150. London, 1926. Illustrated. Half vellum. Limited, signed edition. $75. New York, 1942. Limited Editions Club. Cloth. $40-$50.

STEPHENS, James. *Etched in Moonlight.* Light-blue cloth. London, 1928. First edition. In dust jacket. $35-$50. New York, 1928. Half cloth. First American edition. Limited, signed issue. $35-$50.

STEPHENS, James. *The Insurrection in Dublin.* Cloth. London, 1916. First edition. $25-$35.

STEPHENS, James. *Insurrections.* Brown boards. Dublin, 1909. First edition. In dust jacket. $35-$40.

STEPHENS, James. *Irish Fairy Tales.* Illustrated by Arthur Rackham. Vellum and boards. London, 1920. First edition. One of 520 signed. $250-$300. Trade issue: Cloth. $50-$60.

STEPHENS, James. *Julia Elizabeth.* Decorated boards. New York, 1929. First edition. One of 861 signed. $25.

STEPHENS, James. *Little Things.* Boards and cloth. Freelands, no date (1924). First edition. One of 25 signed. $50-$75. Another issue: Printed wrappers. One of 200 signed. $35-$50.

STEPHENS, James. *A Poetry Recital.* Boards. London, 1925. First edition. $25-$35.

STEPHENS, Lorenzo Dow. *Life Sketches of a Jayhawker of '49.* 6 plates. 68 pp., printed wrappers. No place (San Jose, Calif.), 1916. First edition. $65-$100.

STERLING, E. C. *First Biennial Report of the Territorial Treasurer, For the Years 1867-8.* 14 pp., sewed. Boise City, Idaho, 1868. $75.

STERLING, George. *The Caged Eagle and Other Poems.* Cloth. San Francisco, 1916. First edition. $75-$80.

STERLING, George. *Ode on the Opening of the Panama-Pacific International Exposition.* Boards and cloth. San Francisco, 1915. First edition. One of 525. $25-$30.

STERLING, George. *The Testimony of the Suns and Other Poems.* Black cloth. San Francisco, 1905. First edition. $35-$50. Author's first book. San Francisco, 1927. John Henry Nash printing. Folio, boards. One of 300. (Facsimile of title poem with comments by Ambrose Bierce.) $25-$35.

STERLING, George. *Truth.* Blue paper boards, cloth spine, two paper labels. Chicago, 1923. First edition. One of 285 signed. $35-$50.

STERLING, George; Taggard, Genevieve; and Rorty, James. *Continent's End: An Anthology of Contemporary California Poets.* Boards, pigskin spine. San Francisco, 1925. Book Club of California. First edition. One of 600. In half morocco slipcase. $35.

STERLING, R., and Campbell, J. *Our Own Second Reader: For the Use of Schools and Families.* Cloth. Greensboro, N.C., no date (1862). $30.

STEVENS, C. A. *Berdan's United States Sharpshooters in the Army of the Potomac.* Illustrated. Cloth. St. Paul, Minn., 1892. $50.

STEVENS, George W. *Adventures, American Anecdotes, Biographical, Historical and Descriptive.* Cloth, printed label. Dansville, 1845. First edition. $75.

STEVENS, Isaac I. *Campaigns of the Rio Grande and of Mexico.* 108 pp., wrappers. New York, 1851. First edition. $50-$75.

STEVENS, Isaac I. *A Circular Letter to Emigrants Desirous of Locating in Washington Territory.* 21 pp., sewed. Washington, 1858. First edition. $150-$200.

STEVENS, Wallace. See Stebbins, Charles Livingstone. Also see *Verses from the Harvard Advocate.*

STEVENS, Wallace. *The Auroras of Autumn.* Blue cloth. New York, 1950. First edition. In dust jacket. $35-$50.

STEVENS, Wallace. *The Collected Poems of Wallace Stevens.* Brown cloth. New York, 1954. First edition. One of 2,500. In dust jacket. $35.

STEVENS, Wallace. *Harmonium.* Striped boards or cloth. New York, no date (1923). First edition, first issue, striped boards. In dust jacket. $125-$175. Later, cloth. In dust jacket. $35. Author's first book.

STEVENS, Wallace. *Ideas of Order.* Yellow boards. New York, 1936. First edition. In dust jacket. $75-$100.

STEVENS, Wallace. *The Man with the Blue Guitar & Other Poems.* Cloth. New York, 1937. First edition. In dust jacket. $50-$75.

STEVENS, Wallace. *The Necessary Angel.* Green cloth. New York, 1951. First edition. In dust jacket. $25-$35.

STEVENS, Wallace. *Notes Toward a Supreme Fiction.* Cloth. Cummington, Mass., 1942. First edition. One of 190 signed. $350-$400.

STEVENS, Wallace. *Opus Posthumous.* Cloth. New York, 1957. First edition. In dust jacket. $35-$50.

STEVENS, Wallace. *A Primitive Like an Orb.* Illustrated by Kurt Seligmann. Printed wrappers. New York, 1948. First edition. One of 500. $35-$50.

STEVENS, Wallace. *Raoul Dufy: A Note.* 4 pp., wrappers. No place, no date (New York, 1953). First edition. One of 200. $50-$60.

STEVENS, Wallace. *Selected Poems.* Boards. London, no date (1952). First edition. $100. (Suppressed.)

STEVENS, Wallace. *Transport to Summer.* Green boards and cloth. New York, 1947. First edition. In dust jacket. $50-$60.

STEVENS, Walter B. *Through Texas: A Series of Interesting Letters.* Illustrated. Wrappers. No place (St. Louis), 1892. First edition. $45-$50.

STEVENS, William. See *The Unjust Judge.*

STEVENS & Conover. *Branch County Directory and Historical Record.* Cloth. Ann Arbor, Mich., 1871. $45.

STEVENSON, B. F. *Letters from the Army.* Cloth. Cincinnati, 1864. $35-$50.

STEVENSON, R. Randolph, M.D. *The Southern Side: or, Andersonville Prison.* Cloth. Baltimore, 1876. $35-$50.

STEVENSON, Robert Louis. See *The Pentland Rising.*

STEVENSON, Robert Louis. *Across the Plains.* Cream-colored cloth. London, 1892. First edition. One of 100 on large paper. $100-$150.

STEVENSON, Robert Louis. *An Appeal to the Clergy of the Church of Scotland.* 12 pp., stitched. Edinburgh, 1875. First edition. (About 3 copies known.) Auction record, $3,200 (1925).

STEVENSON, Robert Louis. *Ballads.* Portraits. Blue cloth. London, 1890. First edition. $20-$25. Another issue: White cloth. One of 100 on large paper. $35-$50.

STEVENSON, Robert Louis. *The Black Arrow.* Red cloth. London, 1888. First edition. $35-$50.

STEVENSON, Robert Louis. *Catriona, A Sequel to "Kidnapped."* Blue cloth. London, 1893. First edition. $35-$40.

STEVENSON, Robert Louis. *A Child's Garden of Verses.* Blue cloth. London, 1885. First edition. $175-$250.

STEVENSON, Robert Louis. *Edinburgh, Picturesque Notes.* Etchings and vignettes. Folio, cloth. London, 1879. First edition. $25-$30.

STEVENSON, Robert Louis. *Familiar Studies of Men and Books.* Pictorial green cloth. London, 1882. First edition. $75-$100. (Note: De Ricci notes a large paper reprint of 100 copies in 1888.)

STEVENSON, Robert Louis. *Father Damien.* Wrappers. Sydney, Australia, 1890. First edition. One of 25. $150-$200. Edinburgh, 1890. Unbound sheets in board portfolio. One of 30 on vellum. $50-$60. London, 1890. Wrappers. First English edition. $50-$75. Oxford, England, 1901. Printed wrappers. One of 299. $75-$100. San Francisco, 1930. John Henry Nash printing. 2 vols., half vellum. $35-$50.

STEVENSON, Robert Louis. *A Footnote to History: Eight Years of Trouble in Samoa.* Frontispiece. Blue or green cloth. London, 1892. First edition. $25-$35.

STEVENSON, Robert Louis. *The Graver & the Pen, or Scenes from Nature with Appropriate Verses.* Woodcuts. Gray wrappers. Edinburgh, no date (1882). First edition. $150-$200.

STEVENSON, Robert Louis. *An Inland Voyage.* Frontispiece by Walter Crane. Blue cloth. London, 1878. First edition. $75-$100. Author's first novel. Stamford, Conn., 1938. Overbrook Press. Boards. One of 150. $35-$50.

STEVENSON, Robert Louis. *Island Nights' Entertainments.* 28 illustrations. Cloth. London, 1893. First edition, first issue, with changes in ink in price list of Stevenson's works. $50-$75.

STEVENSON, Robert Louis. *Kidnapped.* Folding frontispiece map. Cloth. No place (London), 1886. First edition. (Issued in various colors of cloth—blue, red, brown, and green—with blue as first.) Blue cloth, first issue, with the reading "business" in line 11 of page 40, etc. $150-$200. Second issue, in bright red cloth, with the reading "pleasure" on line 11 of page 40, etc. $37.50. Another, green cloth, $35. New York, 1938. Limited Editions Club. Cloth. $20-$25. (Note: De Ricci records a "very scarce" London trial issue, undated, in advance of the first edition.)

STEVENSON, Robert Louis. *The Master of Ballantrae.* Red cloth. London, 1889. First edition. $35-$50. (There was also a "trial" edition of only 10 copies published in London in wrappers in 1888, according to De Ricci. A copy was sold at auction for $615 at Sotheby's in 1915.)

STEVENSON, Robert Louis. *Memoirs of Himself.* Boards. Philadelphia, 1912. First edition. One of 45 on Whatman paper. $75-$100.

STEVENSON, Robert Louis. *The Merry Men and Other Tales and Fables.* Decorated blue cloth. London, 1887. First edition, with 32 pages of ads at end dated September, 1886. $35-$50.

STEVENSON, Robert Louis. *A Mountain Town in France.* Gray wrappers. New York, 1896. First edition. One of 350. $75-$100.

STEVENSON, Robert Louis. *New Arabian Nights.* 2 vols., green cloth. London, 1882. First edition, first issue, with yellow end papers in Vol. 1. $150-$200.

STEVENSON, Robert Louis (Thomas J. Wise forgery). *On the Thermal Influence of Forests.* Blue wrappers. Edinburgh: Neill and Co., 1873. First edition. $100-$150.

STEVENSON, Robert Louis. *Pan's Pipes.* Glazed red boards. Boston, 1910. First separate edition. One of 550. Boxed. $50.

STEVENSON, Robert Louis. *Prince Otto, a Romance.* Decorated cloth. London, 1885. First edition, with ads dated January. $50-$75. Spine faded, name in ink on end paper, shaken, $25-$30.

STEVENSON, Robert Louis. *St. Ives.* Slate-colored cloth. London, 1898. First English edition. $25-$35.

STEVENSON, Robert Louis. *The Silverado Squatters.* Decorated green cloth. London, 1883. First edition, first issue, with 32-page catalogue dated 1883 at back. $50-$75. There was also a 10-copy trial issue of Chapter I, 14 pages, green wrappers, London, no date (1883), published for copyright: $725 (A, 1952); inscribed copy, $2,400 (A, 1946). San Francisco, 1952. Grabhorn Press. Boards and cloth. One of 900. In original plain wrapper. $30.

STEVENSON, Robert Louis. *The South Seas: A Record of Three Cruises.* Cloth. London, 1890. First edition. One of about 20 or 22 copies privately printed for copyright purposes. $400 (A, 1952). (Note: De Ricci noted this book in wrappers and in red cloth.)

STEVENSON, Robert Louis. *A Stevenson Medley.* Cloth. London, 1899. First edition. One of 300. $25-$35.

STEVENSON, Robert Louis (Thomas J. Wise forgery). *The Story of a Lie.* Folded sheets. London, 1882. First edition. (Withdrawn before publication.) $200-$250.

STEVENSON, Robert Louis. *The Strange Case of Dr. Jekyll and Mr. Hyde.* Printed wrappers, or pink cloth. London, 1886. First edition, first issue, in wrappers, with the date on front cover altered in ink from 1885 to 1886. $125-$150. Cloth: $75-$100. New York, 1952. Limited Editions Club. Marbled boards. Boxed. $40-$50.

STEVENSON, Robert Louis (Thomas J. Wise forgery). *Ticonderoga.* Vellum boards. Edinburgh, 1887. First edition. One of 50. $200-$350. Also, $312 (A, 1967).

STEVENSON, Robert Louis. *Travels with a Donkey in the Cevennes.* Frontispiece by Walter Crane. Green cloth. London, 1879. First edition. $50-$100. New York, 1957. Limited Editions Club. Monk's cloth. $40.

STEVENSON, Robert Louis. *Treasure Island.* Green, gray, blue, or rust-colored cloth. London, 1883. First edition, first state, with ads dated July, 1883. $300-$400. London, 1927. Illustrated by Edmund Dulac. Vellum. One of 50 signed. $75-$80. Philadelphia, 1930. Illustrated by Lyle Justis. Tan cloth. First printing. In dust jacket and slipcase. $25-$35. New York, 1941. Limited Editions Club. Cloth. $75-$100. Extra lithograph bound in, $125.

STEVENSON, Robert Louis. *Underwoods.* Green cloth. London, 1887. First edition, with ads at back. $25-$50. Large paper issue: White cloth. One of 50. $75-$100.

STEVENSON, Robert Louis. *Vailima Letters.* 2 vols., green buckram. Chicago, 1895. First edition. $50-$60. London, 1895. Terra-cotta cloth. First English edition. $25. Worn, $15. Large paper issue: Cloth. $35-$50.

STEVENSON, Robert Louis. *Virginibus Puerisque and Other Papers.* Orange cloth, beveled edges. London, 1881. First edition, with ads dated "8.80." $25-$100. London, 1910. Florence Press. Illustrated by Norman Wilkinson. Vellum. One of 10 (12?) on vellum. $75-$100. Another issue: One of 250. $35-$50.

STEVENSON, Robert Louis. *The Weir of Hermiston.* Blue buckram. London, 1896. First edition, with March ads. $25-$35.

STEVENSON, Robert Louis, and Henley, William Ernest. *Macaire: A Melodramatic Farce in Three Acts.* Printed wrappers. Edinburgh, 1885. First edition. $200-$250. Chicago, 1895. American copyright edition. $100-$150.

STEVENSON, Robert Louis, and Osbourne, Lloyd. *The Ebb Tide.* Cloth. Chicago, 1894. First edition. $25-$35. London, 1894. Reddish-brown cloth. First English edition, first issue, with 20 pages of ads at back. $25-$35.

STEVENSON, Robert Louis, and Osbourne, Lloyd. *The Wrecker.* Illustrated. Blue cloth. London, 1892. First edition. $25-$35.

STEVENSON, Robert Louis, and Van De Grift, Fanny. *More New Arabian Nights. The Dynamiter.* Cloth, or green pictorial wrappers. London, 1885. First edition. Cloth: $50-$100. Wrappers: $100-$150.

STEWART, Sir William Drummond. See *Altowan* .

STEWART, William F. *Last of the Filibusters.* 85 pp., pictorial wrappers. Sacramento, Calif., 1857. First edition. $400-$500.

STIFF, Col. Edward. *The Texan Emigrant.* Folding map. Cloth, Cincinnati, 1840. First edition. $150-$200.

STILL, James. *Hounds on the Mountain.* Cloth. New York, 1937. One of 700. $35-$40.

STILLMAN, Jacob D. B. B. *The Horse in Motion, as Shown by Instantaneous Photography.* 9 colored photographic plates, numerous other plates, by Eadweard Muybridge. Cloth. Boston, 1882. First edition. $100-$200. London, 1882. Cloth. $75-$100.

STILLMAN, Samuel. *Select Sermons on Doctrinal and Practical Subjects.* Illustrated. Calf. Boston, 1808. $25-$30.

STILLWELL, Margaret Bingham. *Gutenberg and the Catholicon of 1460.* Folio, cloth. New York, 1936. With an original leaf of the Catholicon printed by Gutenberg in 1460. In slipcase. $500-$600. Also, $468 (A, 1969).

STIPP, G. W. (compiler). *The Western Miscellany.* Calf. Xenia, Ohio, 1827. First edition. $2,000 and up. Also, $1,700 (A, 1967).

STOBO, Maj. Robert. *Memoirs of Maj. Robert Stobo.* 78 pp., boards. London, 1800. First edition. $100-$150. Pittsburgh, 1854. Folding frontispiece, map. Cloth. First American edition. $95-$150.

STOCKTON, Frank R. *The Casting Away of Mrs. Lecks and Mrs. Aleshine.* Cloth, or wrappers. New York, no date (1886). First edition, first issue, with signatures (divisions of paper) at pages 9, 25, 49, 57, 73, 81, 97, 105, 121, and 125. Wrappers, first state, with ads for *Century* and *St. Nicholas* magazines: $50-$75. Cloth, first state, half inch across top of covers: $35-$50.

STOCKTON, Frank R. *The Floating Prince and Other Fairy Tales.* Cloth. New York, 1881. First edition. $150.

STOCKTON, Frank R. *The Great War Syndicate.* Printed wrappers. New York, 1889. First edition, published by Collier. $35-$40.

STOCKTON, Frank R. *The Lady, or the Tiger? and Other Stories.* Pictorial gray and brown cloth. New York, 1884. First edition. $50-$75.

STOCKTON, Frank R. *Rudder Grange.* Pictorial red or green cloth. New York, 1879. First edition, first issue, with 18 chapters and no ads or reviews of this title. $35-$50.

STOCKTON, Frank R. *A Storyteller's Pack.* Green cloth. New York, 1897. First edition. $25-$30.

STOCKTON, Frank R. *Tales Out of School.* Illustrated. Cloth. New York, 1876. First edition. $25-$30.

STOCKTON, Frank R. *Ting-a-Ling.* Illustrated. Pictorial purple cloth. New York, 1870. First edition. $75-$100. Author's first book.

STOCKTON, Frank R. *What Might Have Been Expected.* Pictorial cloth. New York, 1874. First edition. $50-$60.

STODDARD, Maj. Amos. *Sketches, Historical and Descriptive of Louisiana.* Boards. Philadelphia, 1812. First edition. $75-$125.

STODDARD, Richard Henry. *Abraham Lincoln: An Horatian Ode.* Wrappers. New York, no date (1865). First edition. $35-$50.

STODDARD, William O. *Little Smoke: A Tale of the Sioux.* Illustrated by Frederick S. Dellenbaugh. Pictorial cloth. New York, 1891. First edition. $35-$50.

STOKER, Bram. *Dracula.* Yellow cloth. Westminster (London), 1897. First edition, first issue, without ads. $75-$125. New York, 1965. Limited Editions Club. Boxed. $40-$50.

STOKES, I. N. Phelps. *The Iconography of Manhattan Island.* Many plates, some in color. 6 vols., half vellum. New York, 1915-28. First edition. One of 360. In dust jackets. Boxed. $2,800. Another issue: One of 42 on Japan vellum. $3,000-$4,000.

STOKES, I. N. Phelps, and Haskell, Daniel C. *American Historical Prints: Early Views of American Cities.* Illustrated. Cloth. New York, 1932. $150-$200. New York, 1933. Cloth. $50.

STONE, Charles P. *Notes on the State of Sonora.* 28 pp., printed wrappers. Washington, 1861. First edition. $100. Presentation copy, $125.

STONE, George C. *A Glossary of the Construction, Decoration and Use of Arms and Armour.* Cloth. Portland, Me., 1934. First edition. $75-$100. De luxe issue: Leather. One of 35. $100-$150. New York, 1961. Facsimile edition. Buckram. One of 500. $40-$60.

STONE, Herbert Stuart. *First Editions of American Authors.* Cloth. Cambridge, Mass., 1893. First edition. One of 450 signed. $35. Another issue: One of 50 on large paper, signed. $50-$75.

STONG, Phil. *Horses and Americans.* Cloth. New York, 1939. First edition. In dust jacket. $25. Author's autograph edition: Buckram. $50-$60.

STOPFORD, Octaira. *Sketches in Verse, and Other Poems.* Boards, paper label. Hull, England, 1826. First edition. $50-$60.

STORIES *About Arnold, the Traitor, André, the Spy, and Champe, the Patriot, for the Children of the U.S.* Illustrated. Printed wrappers (dated 1836). New Haven, Conn., 1831. Second edition. $35-$40.

STORIES *from the Harvard Advocate.* Half morocco. Cambridge, Mass., 1896. First edition. $25-$30.

STORY *of Cripple Creek (A), the Greatest Gold Mining Camp on Earth.* Folding map. 28 pp., wrappers. No place, no date (Denver, 1896). First edition. $35-$50.

STORY *of Louis Riel, Rebel Chief (The).* Illustrated. Cloth. Toronto, 1885. (By J. E. Collins.) First edition. $35-$50.

STORY *of the Three Bears (The).* Illustrated by Harrison Weir and John Absolon. 12 leaves, yellow hand-colored wrappers. New York, no date (about 1870). $30.

STOTZ, Charles Morse. *The Early Architecture of Western Pennsylvania.* Cloth. Pittsburgh, 1936. First edition. $50-$75.

STOWE, Harriet Beecher. See Beecher, Harriet Elizabeth.

STOWE, Harriet Beecher. *A Key to Uncle Tom's Cabin.* Cloth, or wrappers. Boston, 1853. First edition. Wrappers: $35-$50. Cloth: $15-$25.

STOWE, Harriet Beecher. *Uncle Sam's Emancipation.* Cloth. Philadelphia, 1853. First edition. $40-$50.

STOWE, Harriet Beecher. *Uncle Tom's Cabin.* Title vignette, 6 plates. 2 vols., pictorial wrappers, or 2 vols., cloth. Boston, 1852. First edition, first issue, wrappers, with slug of Hobart and Robbins on copyright page. $2,000 and up. (The Paul Hyde Bonner copy, with the spines gauzed, brought $1,025 at auction in 1934. No comparably fine copy in wrappers seems to have been offered since.) Repaired copy, wrappers and spine mounted, $1,250. Second issue, cloth, with the Hobart and Robbins slug. $1,750. Others, $1,000-$1,500. Also, $325 (A, 1970); $110 and $408 (A, 1969); $1,400 (A, 1968)—the Feinberg copy; $1,200 (A, 1960)—"a brilliant copy." Others, $600 and up at retail. (For price ranges on numerous other copies—defective, rebound, and in various "gift" bindings—see the current auction records in *American Book-Prices Current.*) London, 1852. Cassell imprint. Illustrated by George Cruikshank. 13 parts, pictorial wrappers. First English edition. $200-$300. London, 1852. Cloth. First English book edition, with Cassell imprint. $75-$100. London, 1852. 40 plates. Cloth. C. H. Clarke, publisher. $25-$35. New York, 1937. Limited Editions Club. Marbled boards and leather. $25-$35.

STRACHEY, Lytton. *Books and Characters.* Portrait. Green cloth. London, 1922. First edition. In dust jacket. $25-$30.

STRAHORN, Mrs. Carrie A. *15,000 Miles by Stage.* 5 plates. Cloth. New York, 1911. First edition. $75-$100. New York, 1915. Second edition. $35-$50.

STRAHORN, Robert E. *The Handbook of Wyoming, and Guide to the Black Hills and Big Horn Regions.* 272 pp., printed wrappers. Cheyenne, Wyo., 1877. First edition. $100-$150. Also, in cloth: $75-$100.

STRAHORN, Robert E. *Montana and Yellowstone National Park.* 101 pp., flexible cloth wrappers, plus 14 pp. ads. Kansas City, Mo., 1881. First edition. $25-$35.

STRAHORN, Robert E. *To the Rockies and Beyond.* Maps and plates. 216 pp., printed wrappers. Omaha, Neb., 1878. First edition. $200-$300. Omaha, 1879. Second edition. $150-$200.

STRANG, James J. *The Book of the Law of the Lord.* 80 pp., cloth. No place, no date (Kansas City, Mo., 1927). $75. Pencil notes on front flyleaf, $50. (For earlier editions, see title entry.)

STRANGE, Edward F. *The Colour-Prints of Hiroshige.* 16 colored, 36 plain plates. Buckram. London, 1925. In dust jacket. $100-$125.

STRANGER in Lowell (The). Wrappers. Boston, 1845. (By John Greenleaf Whittier.) First edition. $50-$75.

STRANGER'S Guide to St. Louis, or What to See and How to See It. Folding map. Cloth. St. Louis, 1867. First edition. $35-$50.

STRATTON, R. B. *Captivity of the Oatman Girls, etc.* 231 pp., printed wrappers. San Francisco, 1857. Second edition of *Life Among the Indians* (entry following). $200-$250. Also, $100 (A, 1960). Chicago, 1857. (Reprint.) $75-$100. New York, 1858. 3 plates. Cloth. Third edition, enlarged. $35-$50.

STRATTON, R. B. *Life Among the Indians.* Illustrated. 183 pp., wrappers. San Francisco, 1857. First edition. $1,500 and up. San Francisco, 1935. Grabhorn Press. Plates. Half cloth. One of 550. $75-$100. (See preceding entry.)

STRAUSS, David Friedrich. *The Life of Jesus.* 3 vols., blue-green cloth. London, 1846. (By George Eliot.) First edition. $50-$100. Author's first book.

STREAKS of Squatter Life, and Far-West Scenes. Illustrated by F. O. C. Darley. Half calf. Philadelphia, 1847. (By John S. Robb.) First edition. $150-$200. Rebound in modern boards, $90.

STREETER, Edward. *Dere Mable: Love Letters of a Rookie.* Pictorial boards. New York, no date (1918). First edition. In dust jacket. $25. Author's first book.

STREETER, Floyd Benjamin. *Prairie Trails and Cow Towns.* 12 plates. Cloth. Boston, no date (1936). First edition. $50-$75. Also, $40 (A, 1968).

STREETER, Thomas W. See *Americana—Beginnings.*

STREETER, Thomas W. *Bibliography of Texas.* 5 vols. (Part I, 2 vols; Part II, one vol.; Part III, 2 vols.), cloth. Cambridge, Mass., 1955-56-60. First edition. One of 600. $400-$500. Parts I and II, 3 vols. $250 (A, 1969), $200 (A, 1968). Part III, 2 vols. $85 (A, 1969).

STRIBLING, T. S. *The Cruise of the Dry Dock.* Green cloth. Chicago, no date (1917). First edition. In dust jacket. $50-$75. Author's first book.

STRICKLAND, William. *Reports on Canals, Railways, Roads, and Other Subjects.* Plates. Oblong, boards and leather. Philadelphia, 1826. First edition. $250-$350.

STRICTURES Addressed to James Madison on the Celebrated Report of W. H. Crawford Recommending Intermarriage of Americans with the Indian Tribes. 22 pp., plain wrappers. Philadelphia, 1824. (By T. Cooper.) $35-$50.

STRICTURES on a Voyage to South America, as Indited by the "Secretary of the (Late) Mission" to La Plata, etc. By a Friend of Truth and Sound Policy. 108 pp., printed wrappers. Baltimore, 1820. (By H. M. Brackenridge.) $75.

STRONG, Sandford Arthur. *Reproductions of Drawings by Old Masters in the Collection of the Duke of Devonshire at Chatsworth.* 70 full-page facsimiles. Large folio, full morocco. London, 1902. One of 98 on Japan vellum. $125-$150.

STRONG, Gen. W. E. *A Trip to the Yellowstone National Park in July, August, and September, 1875.* 2 folding maps, 7 signed photos, 7 plates. Half morocco. Washington, 1876. First edition. $350-$500.

STRUTT, Joseph. *A Complete View of the Dress and Habits of the People of England.* 151 colored engravings. 2 vols., half morocco. London, 1842. $100-$150.

STRUTT, Joseph. *Glig-Gamena Angel-Deod, or The Sports and Pastimes of the English People.* 40 colored plates. Contemporary calf. London, 1801. $100-$125. London, 1810. Second edition. $75-$100.

STUART, Granville. *Forty Years on the Frontier.* Plates. 2 vols., cloth. Cleveland, 1925. First edition. $75-$100.

STUBBS, Charles H. *Historic Genealogy of the Kirk Family.* Cloth. Lancaster, Pa., 1872. $40-$50.

STUBBS, Robert. *Browne's Cincinnati Almanac, for . . . 1811.* 36 pp., wrappers. Cincinnati, no date (1810). $75-$100.

STUDER, Jacob H. *The Birds of North America.* 119 colored lithographs after Jasper. Cloth, or leather. Columbus, Ohio, 1878. First edition. $50-$75. New York, 1881. $25-$30. New York, 1895. Morocco. $35-$50. New York, 1903. Cloth. $40-$50.

STYRON, William. *The Confessions of Nat Turner.* Cloth. New York, no date (1967). First edition. One of 500 signed. Boxed. $35.

STYRON, William. *Les Confessions de Nat Turner.* Wrappers. Paris, no date (1969). First French translation. One of 46 on velin. $27.50.

STYRON, William. *Lie Down in Darkness.* Brown cloth. Indianapolis, no date (1951). First edition. In dust jacket. $25-$35. Author's first book.

STYRON, William. *This Quiet Dust.* Printed blue wrappers. No place, no date (New York, 1968). First edition. $25.

SUÁREZ Y Navarro, Juan. *Defensa que el Licenciado José G. P. Garay Hizo ante el Juez Primero de lo Civil, Don Gayetano Ibarra, etc.* 64 pp., sewed. Mexico, 1849. $100.

SUGDEN, Alan V. *A History of English Wallpaper, 1509-1914.* 70 color plates and 190 halftone illustrations. Folio, blue buckram. New York, no date (1925). In dust jacket. Boxed. $150.

SULLIVAN, Louis H. *A System of Architectural Ornament.* Illustrated. Folio, half cloth. New York, 1924. First edition. One of 1,000. $150.

SULLIVAN, Maurice S. *The Travels of Jedidiah Smith.* Map, 12 plates. Pictorial cloth. Santa Ana, Calif., 1934. First edition. $100-$150.

SULLIVAN, W. John L. *Twelve Years in the Saddle for Law and Order on the Frontiers of Texas.* 13 plates. Cloth. Austin, Tex., 1909. First edition. $35-$50.

SUMMERFIELD, Charles. *The Rangers and Regulators of the Tanaha.* Frontispiece, plates. Cloth. New York, no date (1856). (By Alfred W. Arrington.) First edition. $50-$60.

SUN Pictures of Rocky Mountain Scenery, etc. 30 plates. Three-quarters leather. New York, 1870. $75-$100.

SUNDERLAND, LaRoy. *Mormonism Exposed and Refuted.* 54 pp., printed wrappers. New York, 1838. First edition. $1,000-$1,250.

SUNDRY Documents Referring to the Niagara and Detroit River Railroad. 8 pp., wrappers. No place, no date (Albany, N.Y.?, 1845). (By W. H. Merritt.) $50.

SUPERIOR Court of the City and County of San Francisco (In the) . . . Sarah Althea Sharon, Plaintiff, vs. William Sharon, Defendant. Half morocco. San Francisco, no date (about 1884). $25.

SUPERNATURALISM of New England (The). Printed wrappers. New York, 1847. (By John Greenleaf Whittier—his name on cover but not on title page.) First edition. $50-$75.

SURTEES, Robert Smith. See *"Ask Mama"; The Analysis of the Hunting Field; Handley Cross; Hawbuck Grange; Mr. Facey Romford's Hounds; Mr. Sponge's Sporting Tour; Jorrocks's Jaunts and Jollities; "Plain or Ringlets?"*

SUTHERLAND, Thomas A. *Howard's Campaign Against the Nez Perce Indians.* 48 pp., wrappers. Portland, Ore., 1878. First edition. $450-$600.

SUTRO, Adolph. *The Mineral Resources of the United States.* Folding map, plates. Cloth. Baltimore, 1868. First edition. $40.

SUTRO, Adolph. *The Sutro Tunnel and Railway to the Comstock Lode in Nevada.* 2 folding maps. 37 pp., printed wrappers. London, 1873. $25.

SUTTER, Johann August. *Diary of Johann August Sutter.* Edited by Douglas S. Watson. 3 colored plates, 3 facsimiles. Boards. San Francisco, 1932. First edition. One of 500. $50-$60.

SUTTER, Johann August. *New Helvetia Diary.* 2 color plates, facsimile, map. Half cloth. San Francisco, 1939. Grabhorn Press. One of 950. $50-$75.

SUTTON, J. J. *History of the 2nd Regiment, West Virginia Cavalry Volunteers.* Cloth. Portsmouth, Ohio, 1892. $25-$35.

SWALLOW BARN, or A Sojourn in the Old Dominion. 2 vols., half cloth and boards, paper labels. Philadelphia, 1832. (By John Pendleton Kennedy.) First edition. $100-$150. Author's first book.

SWAMP Outlaws (The), or the Lowery Bandits of North Carolina. 84 pp., wrappers. New York, no date (1872). $50-$60.

SWAN, Alonzo M. *Canton: Its Pioneers and History.* Cloth. Canton, Ill., 1871. First edition. $50-$75.

SWAN, Alonzo M. *Life, Trial, Conviction, Confession and Execution of John Osborn, the Murderer of Mrs. Adelia Mathews, etc.* 85 pp., wrappers. Peoria, Ill., 1872. First edition. $100. Rebound in leather, original wrappers bound in, $75. Peoria, 1873. 95 pp., wrappers. Second edition. (Name of the murderer changed to John Marion Osborne.) $50 and up.

SWAN, James G. *The Northwest Coast.* Folding map, plates. Cloth. New York, 1857. First edition. $50-$75.

SWASEY, William F. *The Early Days and Men of California.* Portrait, 2 plates. Cloth. Oakland, Calif., no date (1891). First edition. $75-$100.

SWEET, Willis. *The Carbonate Camps, Leadville and Ten-Mile, of Colorado.* Maps and plates. 83 pp., pictorial wrappers. Kansas City, Mo., 1879. First edition. $125. (A 1956 catalogue price, with no other copy noted in some years. Probably rates a much higher price in today's market. For a similar work, see Stephen F. Smart entry.)

SWIFT, Jonathan. *Gulliver's Travels.* Illustrated by Arthur Rackham. Cloth. London, 1909. Signed by Rackham. $200-$250. New York, 1929. Limited Editions Club. Cloth and pigskin. $40-$60. London, 1930. 12 colored engravings by Rex Whistler. 2 vols., morocco and boards. One of 195. In slipcases. $350-$700. Unique issue: Engravings uncolored, $960 (A, 1969).

SWINBURNE, Algernon Charles. SPECIAL NOTE: So many of the books and pamphlets once attributed to Swinburne have turned out to be the forgeries of Thomas J. Wise that the listing of them in a brief reference work of this kind would constitute a bibliographical nightmare for both compiler and reader. For this reason, I have sought to eliminate here all except the better known items of legitimate Swinburniana.

SWINBURNE, Algernon Charles. See *The Children of the Chapel.*

SWINBURNE, Algernon C. *Astrophel and Other Poems.* Cloth. London, 1894. First edition. $35-$45.

SWINBURNE, Algernon C. *Atalanta in Calydon: A Tragedy.* White cloth. London, 1865. First edition, with only 111 pages. $200-$250. Rebound in morocco, original covers preserved, $168 (A, 1969). London, 1894. Kelmscott Press. Woodcut title, initials, etc. Vellum, silk ties. One of 250. $250-$300.

SWINBURNE, Algernon Charles. *Chastelard: A Tragedy.* Cloth. London, 1865. First edition. $50-$75.

SWINBURNE, Algernon Charles. *Erechtheus: A Tragedy.* Cloth. London, 1876. First edition. $25-$30.

SWINBURNE, Algernon Charles. *Letters . . . to Frederick Locker.* 16 pp., loose in printed wrappers. No place (New York), 1913. First edition. One of 20. $35-$50.

SWINBURNE, Algernon Charles. *Marino Faliero, A Tragedy.* Green cloth. London, 1885. First edition, with 32 pages of ads. $25-$35.

SWINBURNE, Algernon Charles. *Poems and Ballads.* Cloth. London, 1866. First edition, first issue, with E. Moxon imprint. $150-$250. Second issue with J. C. Hotten imprint. $75-$100.

SWINBURNE, Algernon Charles. *Poetical Fragments.* Wrappers. London, 1916. One of 25, signed by Clement Shorter. $50-$65.

SWINBURNE, Algernon Charles. *The Queen-Mother. Rosamond. Two Plays.* Slate-gray cloth, white spine label. London, 1860. First edition, first issue, with "A. G. Swinburne" on spine. $100 and up. Author's first book.

SWINBURNE, Algernon Charles. *Rosamond, Queen of the Lombards.* Boards. London, 1899. First edition. $25-$35.

SWINBURNE, Algernon Charles. *A Song of Italy.* Boards, green cloth, purple end papers. London, 1867. First edition, with 24 pages of ads at beginning and end. $50-$60. Portland, Me., 1904. Mosher Press. One of 10 on vellum. $35-$50.

SWINBURNE, Algernon Charles. *Songs Before Sunrise.* Blue-green cloth. London, 1871. First edition. $25-$35. Large paper issue: Morocco. One of 25. $250-$350. Portland, 1901. Mosher Press. One of 4 on vellum. $75-$100. London, 1909. Florence Press. Levant morocco extra. One of 12 on vellum. $300-$350. Half morocco. One of 650. $35-$50.

SWINBURNE, Algernon Charles. *The Springtide of Life: Poems of Childhood.* 9 color plates, numerous text illustrations by Arthur Rackham. Vellum. London, 1918. One of 765 signed by Rackham. $150-$175.

SWINBURNE, Algernon Charles. *William Blake: A Critical Essay.* Illustrated. Cloth. London, 1868. First edition, first issue, with the word "Zamiel" below woodcut on title page. $25-$35.

SWINBURNE, Algernon Charles. *A Word for the Navy.* Pictorial light-blue wrappers. London, 1887. First edition. One of 250. $35-$50.

SWISHER, James. *How I Know.* Plates. Cloth. Cincinnati, 1880. First edition. $50-$75. Cincinnati, 1881. Second edition. $35-$50.

SWISS Family Robinson (The). 2 vols., boards. New York, 1832. (By Johann David Wyss.) First American edition. $200-$300.

SYDENHAM, Thomas. *The Works of Thomas Sydenham, M.D.* Calf. Philadelphia, 1809. First American edition. $75-$100.

SYMONDS, A. J. A. *The Quest for Corvo.* Black cloth. London, no date (1934). First edition. In dust jacket. $40-$50.

SYMONDS, John Addington. *The Escorial: A Prize Poem.* Wrappers. Oxford, England, 1860. First edition. $75-$100. Author's first publication.

SYMONDS, John Addington. *Essays Speculative and Suggestive.* 2 vols., cloth. London, 1890. First edition. $50-$75.

SYMONDS, John Addington. *In the Key of Blue and Other Prose Essays.* Light-blue or cream cloth. London, 1893. First edition with 15 pages of ads at end. $35-$50. (The blue cloth binding is scarce.) Another issue: Vellum. One of 50 on large paper. $200-$250.

SYMONDS, John Addington. *The Life of Michael Angelo Buonarotti.* 2 vols., cloth. London, 1893. First edition. $35-$50.

SYMONDS, John Addington. *The Renaissance.* Wrappers. Oxford, 1863. First edition. $50-$60.

SYMONDS, John Addington. *Renaissance in Italy.* 7 vols., cloth. London, 1880-86. (First issue copies of *The Age of Despots, The Revival of Learning,* and *The Fine Arts* without stars on spines.) $75-$100.

SYMONDS, John Addington. *Wine, Women and Song: Mediaeval Latin Students' Songs.* Cloth. London, 1884. First edition. $25. Another issue: Vellum. One of 50 on large paper. $35-$50.

SYMONDS, Mary, and Preece, Louisa. *Needlework Through the Ages.* 8 color plates, 96 other plates. Half vellum. London, 1928. $100-$150.

SYMONS, Arthur. *An Introduction to the Study of Browning.* Green cloth. London, 1886. First edition. $50-$75. Author's first book.

SYMONS, Arthur. *Silhouettes.* London, 1892. Gray boards. First edition. One of 250. $25. Another issue: One of 25 on large paper, signed. $35-$50.

SYMONS, R. *The Rev. John Wesley's Ministerial Itineraries in Cornwall.* Folding map, 45 plates. Half red morocco. Truro, 1879. $50.

SYNGE, John M. *The Aran Islands.* Drawings. Cloth. Dublin, 1906. First edition. In dust jacket. $35-$50. Dublin, 1907. $25-$30. Another issue: One of 150 on large paper, signed. $75-$150.

SYNGE, John M. *Deirdre of the Sorrows: A Play.* Preface by W. B. Yeats. Boards, linen spine. Dundrum, Ireland, 1910. Cuala Press. First edition. One of 250. $100-$125. New York, 1910. Boards and cloth. One of 50. Very rare: $150 and up (all except five on vellum and five on handmade paper were reported destroyed by the publisher, John Quinn).

SYNGE, John M. *A Few Personal Recollections, with Biographical Notes by John Masefield.* Cloth. Dundrum, Ireland, 1913. Cuala Press. First edition. One of 350. $75-$85.

SYNGE, John M. *In the Shadow of the Glen.* Pale-gray printed wrappers. New York, 1904. First edition. One of 50 published for copyright purposes. $250-$350. Author's first book. (For first English edition, see *The Shadow of the Glen.*)

SYNGE, John M. *The Playboy of the Western World.* Portrait. Cloth. Dublin, 1907. First edition. $75-$125. Another issue: White linen. One of 25 on handmade paper. $300-$350.

SYNGE, John M. *Poems and Translations.* Blue boards, tan linen spine, paper label. Dundrum, 1909. Cuala Press. One of 250. $100-$125. New York, 1909. Boards and cloth. One of 50. $75-$85.

SYNGE, John M. *The Shadow of the Glen. Riders to the Sea.* Printed green wrappers. London, 1905. First English edition. $75-$100. (For first edition, see *In the Shadow of the Glen.*) Synge's first commercially published book.

SYNGE, John M. *The Tinker's Wedding.* Rust-colored cloth, beige spine. Dublin, 1907. First edition. In dust jacket. $35-$75.

SYNGE, John M. *The Well of the Saints.* Wrappers. London, 1905. First edition, first issue. $150-$200. London, 1905. Boards and cloth. Second issue, with introduction by William Butler Yeats. $100-$125. New York, 1905. One of 50. First American edition. $75-$100.

SYNGE, John M. *The Works of John Millington Synge.* Portraits. 4 vols., cloth. Dublin, 1910. First edition. $112-$154. Boston, 1912. 4 vols., cloth. $85-$100.

SYNTAX, Doctor. *Doctor Syntax in Paris.* 18 colored plates by Williams. Boards. London, 1820. (By William Combe?) First edition. $75-$100.

SYNTAX, Doctor. *The Life of Napoleon: a Hudibrastic Poem in 15 Cantos.* 30 color plates by George Cruikshank. Boards. London, 1815. (By William Combe.) First edition. $150-$200. Worn, $135. Rebound by Riviere in blue levant, gilt, $150.

SYNTAX, Doctor. *The Tour of Doctor Syntax Through London.* 19 colored plates. 8 parts, wrappers. London, 1820. (Sometimes attributed to William Combe, but not by him, says De Ricci.) First edition. $750-$1,000. London, 1820. Boards. First book edition. $75-$100.

SYNTAX, Doctor. *The Tours . . .* (1st, 2d, and 3d.) (By William Combe.) *The Tour of Doctor Syntax in Search of the Picturesque.* Frontispiece, title page, and 29 colored plates by Thomas Rowlandson. Boards. London, 1812. First edition. *The Tour of*

Doctor Syntax in Search of Consolation. 24 colored plates by Rowlandson. Boards. London, 1820. First edition. *The Tour of Doctor Syntax in Search of a Wife.* 24 colored plates by Rowlandson. Boards. London, no date (1821-22). First edition. Copies in original boards are rare, none having been at public sale since the 1940's. Estimated value today: $1,000 and up. Rebound copies of first edition sets ranged at auction in the 1960's from $90 to $180, and at retail up to $400. Many later editions and mixed sets at lower prices show the continuing popularity of the series. They include the 3-vol. *Tours of Doctor Syntax.* 80 color plates by Rowlandson. Pink boards, paper labels, uncut. London, 1823. First miniature edition, with printed title issued in Vol. 2 only. In half morocco cases. $75-$150.

SZYK, Arthur (artist). *Ink and Blood: A Book of Drawings.* Text by Struthers Burt. 74 plates. Morocco. New York, 1946. First edition. One of 1,000 signed by Szyk. Boxed. $175-$200.

T

TABB, John Banister. *Lyrics.* Boards. Boston, 1897. First edition. One of 5 on China paper. $60. Other issues: One of 50 on handmade paper. $25. One of 500. $10-$15.

TABB, John Banister. *Poems.* Cloth. No place, no date (Baltimore, 1882). First edition. $35-$50.

TACITUS, C. Cornelius. *De Vita et Moribus Julii Agricolae Liber.* Vellum. London, 1900. Doves Press. One of 225. $75-$100.

TAFT, Robert. *Artists and Illustrators of the Old West.* Illustrated. Cloth. New York, 1953. First edition. In dust jacket. $50-$60.

TAFT, Robert. *Photography and the American Scene: A Social History, 1839-89.* Cloth. New York, 1938. First edition. In dust jacket. $35. New York, 1942. Cloth. In dust jacket. $50.

TAGGARD, Genevieve. *For Eager Lovers.* Boards, paper labels, New York, no date (1922). First edition. $25-$30. Author's first book.

TAGGARD, Genevieve. *The Life and Mind of Emily Dickinson.* Boards. New York, 1930. One of 200, signed. $75-$80.

TAGGARD, Genevieve (editor). *An Anthology of Masses-Liberator Verse.* Cloth. New York, 1925. First edition. In dust jacket. $35-$40.

TAGORE, Rabindranath. *The Post Office: A Play.* Preface by William Butler Yeats. Boards and cloth. Dundrum, Ireland, 1914. Cuala Press. One of 400. $40-$60. New York, 1914. Blue cloth. First American edition. $20-$25. Signed and dated by Tagore, $35.

TALBOT, Eugene S. *Irregularities of the Teeth.* Illustrated. Cloth. Philadelphia, 1888. First edition. $25-$50.

TALBOT, Theodore. *The Journals of Theodore Talbot.* Edited by Charles H. Carey. Cloth. Portland, 1931. First edition. $25-$35.

TALES of the Northwest; or, Sketches of Indian Life and Character. By a Resident from Beyond the Frontier. Boards. Boston, 1830. (By William J. Snelling.) First edition. $200-$250. Title page torn, $112.50. Author's first book.

TALES of Terror; with an Introductory Dialogue. Engraved half title. Wrappers. London, 1801. (By Matthew G. Lewis?) First edition (?). $75-$100.

TALES of Travels West of the Mississippi. Map. Illustrated. Boards and cloth. Boston, 1830. (By William J. Snelling.) First edition. $250-$300.

TALLAHASSEE Girl (A). Cloth. Boston, 1882. (By Maurice Thompson.) First edition. $25.

TALLAPOOSA Land, Mining and Manufacturing Co., Haralson County. Map. 32 pp., wrappers. Tallapoosa, Ga., 1887. $25.

TALLENT, Annie D. *The Black Hills; or The Last Hunting Grounds of the Dakotahs.* 50 plates. Cloth, or half leather. St. Louis, 1899. First edition. $75-$100. Also, half leather, damaged, $50 (A, 1966); rebacked, $32 (A, 1969).

TAMERLANE and Other Poems. By a Bostonian. Printed wrappers. Boston, 1827. (By Edgar Allan Poe.) First edition. Last known price, $25,000. (Note: Exact facsimiles exist which require careful examination to distinguish from the original.) London, 1884. Vellum. One of 100. $50-$60.

TANNER, Henry S. *A Brief Description of the Canals and Railroads of the United States.* Maps. 31 pp., cloth. First edition. Philadelphia, 1834. $75-$100. Second edition, same place and date. 63 pp., 2 plates, map. $35-$50. New York, 1840. Enlarged edition. (*A Description, etc.*) 3 maps, 2 diagrams, 272 pp. $35-$50.

TARASCON, Louis A. *An Address to the Citizens of Philadelphia, on the Great Advantages Which Arise from the Trade of the Western Country, etc.* 13 pp., wrappers. Philadelphia, 1806. First edition. $500-$600. Also, rebound in cloth, title page stained, $400 (A, 1968).

TARASCON, Louis A., and others. *Petition . . . Praying the Opening of a Wagon Road from the River Missouri, North of the River Kansas, to the River Columbia.* 12 pp., sewed. Washington, 1824. $75-$100.

TARAVAL, Sigismundo. *The Indian Uprising in Lower California, 1734-1737.* Translated by Marguerite E. Wilbur. Boards. Los Angeles, 1931. One of 665. $35-$50.

TARCISSUS: The Boy Martyr of Rome, in the Diocletian Persecution, A.D.CCCIII. (By Baron Corvo [Frederick William Rolfe]). 4 leaves, printed gray boards. No place, no date (Saffron Walden, Essex, England, 1880). First edition. $1,000-$1,500. (Dealer catalogue, 1971, lists it at $1,000.) Also, £950 (A, 1971). Author's first book.

TARG, William (editor). *Bibliophile in the Nursery.* Illustrated. Cloth. Cleveland, no date (1957). First edition. In dust jacket. $25.

TARKINGTON, Booth. *Christmas This Year.* Manuscript facsimile and full-page plate. Wrappers. No place, no date (Los Angeles, 1945). First edition. One of 52. $35.

TARKINGTON, Booth. *The Gentleman from Indiana.* Pictorial green cloth, top stained green. New York, 1899. First edition, first issue, with "eye" as last word in line 12, page 245; with line 16 reading "so pretty"; and with ear of corn on spine pointing downward. $35-$50. Author's first published book.

TARKINGTON, Booth. *Monsieur Beaucaire.* Illustrated. Red cloth, gilt top. New York, 1900. First edition, first issue, with publisher's seal on page after end of text exactly ½ inch in diameter. $35-$50. Covers stained, $25. Worn, $10. Also, $37 and $16 (A, 1969).

TARKINGTON, Booth. *The Ohio Lady.* Wrappers. No place, no date (New York, 1916). First edition. $30.

TARKINGTON, Booth. *Penrod.* Illustrated by Gordon Grant. Cloth: first, blue mesh; second, blue ribbed cloth. Garden City, N.Y., 1914. First edition, first state, with page viii so numbered and with "sence" for "sense" in third line from bottom of page 19. In glassine dust jacket. $75-$100.

TARKINGTON, Booth. *Penrod and Sam.* Illustrated by Worth Brehm. Pictorial light-green cloth. Garden City, 1916. First edition, first issue, with perfect type on pages 86, 141, 144, 149, and 210. In dust jacket. $50. Lacking jacket, $25-$35.

TARKINGTON, Booth. *Seventeen.* Cloth or leather. New York, no date (1916). First edition, first issue, with letters "B-Q" beneath copyright notice. $25-$45.

TARKINGTON, Booth. *The Two Vanrevels.* Cloth. New York, 1902. First edition. In dust jacket. $10-$15. Another issue (later): White boards. One of 500 signed. $25-$35. Another issue: Brown boards (also with first edition notice). One of 500 signed. $20-$25.

TARRANT, Sgt. E. *The Wild Riders of the 1st Kentucky Cavalry.* Cloth. Louisville, Ky., no date (1894). $75-$100. Rebound in cloth, title page ragged, paper yellowed, corners off several pages, $40.

TATE, Allen. *Jefferson Davis, His Rise and Fall.* Cloth, paper label. New York, 1929. First edition. In dust jacket. $25.

TATE, Allen. *The Mediterranean and Other Poems.* Wrappers. New York, 1936. First edition. One of 165 on Strathmore all-rag paper, signed. $50-$60.

TATE, Allen. *Reason in Madness.* Green cloth. New York, 1941. First edition. In dust jacket. $35-$50.

TATE, Allen. *Two Conceits for the Eye to Sing, If Possible.* Wrappers, paper label. Cummington, Mass., 1950. First edition. One of 300. $25-$30.

TATE, Allen. *The Winter Sea: A Book of Poems.* Decorated cloth. Cummington, Mass., 1944. First edition. One of 300. In dust jacket. $25-$30.

TATTERSALL, C. E. C. *A History of British Carpets.* 116 plates (55 in color). Buckram. London, no date (1934). $75-$100. Also, $43 (A, 1971).

TATTERSALL, George. *The Pictorial Gallery of English Race Horses.* 90 plates. Cloth. London, 1850. $75-$100.

TAUNTON, Thomas Henry. *Portraits of Celebrated Racehorses.* 463 plates. 4 vols., half red morocco. London, 1887-88. $150-$200.

TAYLOR, Bayard. *Eldorado, or, Adventures in the Path of Empire, etc.* 8 lithograph views. 2 vols., cloth. New York, 1850. First edition, with list of illustrations in Vol. 2 giving Mazatlan at page 8 instead of page 80. $150-$250. New York, 1850. 2 vols., cloth. Second edition, with Mazatlan reference corrected. $50-$75. New York, 1850. 2 vols. in one, cloth, no plates. $15-$20. London, 1850. 2 vols., cloth. First English edition. $100-$150.

TAYLOR, F. *A Sketch of the Military Bounty Tract of Illinois.* 12 pp., boards and calf. Philadelphia, 1839. First edition. $125.

TAYLOR, James Wickes. *Northwest British America and Its Relations to the State of Minnesota.* Map. Cloth. St. Paul, Minn., 1860. First edition. $600-$800.

TAYLOR, Jane and Ann. *Little Ann and Other Poems.* Illustrated in color by Kate Greenaway. Pictorial boards and cloth. No place, no date (London, about 1883-84). Published by Warne. $80-$90.

TAYLOR, John W. *Iowa, the "Great Hunting Ground" of the Indian; and the "Beautiful Land" of the White Man.* 16 pp., printed wrappers. Dubuque, Iowa, 1860. $125.

TAYLOR, Joseph. *Curious Antiquities.* Frontispiece. Boards and cloth. New York, 1820. First American edition. $45.

TAYLOR, Joseph Henry. *Beavers — Their Ways and Other Sketches.* 20 plates. Cloth. Washburn, N.D., 1904. First edition. $40-$50.

TAYLOR, Joseph Henry. *Sketches of Frontier and Indian Life.* 12 plates. Half leather and boards. Pottstown, Pa., 1889. First edition. $150-$200.

TAYLOR, Joseph Henry. *Twenty Years on the Trap Line.* 8 plates. 154 pp., boards and calf. Bismarck, N.D., 1891. First edition. $100-$150. Also, boards, $55 (A, 1966). Second edition, same place and date. 173 pp., maroon cloth. $75-$100. Also, $70 (A, 1969).

TAYLOR, Lee M. *The Texan: A Tale of Texas.* Cloth. No place (Texas), 1908. With pages 171-174 removed (as in all copies noted). $50.

TAYLOR, Oliver I. *Directory of Wheeling and Ohio County.* 2 plates, including tinted frontispiece. Half leather. Wheeling, W. Va., 1851. First edition. $35-$50.

TAYLOR, Peter. *A Long Fourth and Other Stories.* Cloth. New York, no date (1948). First edition. In dust jacket. $35. Author's first book.

TAYLOR, Philip Meadows. *Confessions of a Thug.* 3 vols., half cloth, or boards. London, 1839. First edition. $150-$200. Author's first book.

TAYLOR, Thomas U. *Fifty Years on Forty Acres.* Illustrated. Cloth. Austin, Tex. (?), 1938. First edition. $25-$30.

TAYLOR, Thomas U. *Jesse Chisholm.* Illustrated. Cloth. Bandera, Tex., no date (1939). First edition. $25-$30.

TAYLOR and Tallmadge. *The Bill to Authorize the People of Missouri to Form a Constitution and State Government.* 16 pp., sewed. No place, no date (1819). $35-$45.

TAYLOR, Zachary. *Letters of Zachary Taylor from the Battle-Fields of the Mexican War.* Half cloth. Rochester, N.Y., 1908. One of 300. $25-$35.

TEASDALE, Sara. *Love Songs.* Cloth. New York, 1917. First edition. In dust jacket. $40-$50.

TEASDALE, Sara. *Sonnets to Duse and Other Poems.* Boards, paper labels. Boston, 1907. First edition. $100-$150. Author's first book.

TEHAUNTEPEC Railway: Its Location Features and Advantages Under the LaSere Grant of 1869. Folding map. Cloth. New York, 1869. $30.

TEMPLAR (The). To Which Is Added "Tales of the Passaic." By a Gentleman of New York. Half calf. Hackensack, N.J., 1822. First edition. $150.

TEN Poets. Oblong, decorated wrappers. Seattle, 1962. First edition. One of 37 (of an edition of 537) specially bound and signed by the ten poets, including Theodore Roethke. $25.

TEN Thousand a Year. 3 vols., dark-brown ribbed cloth. Edinburgh, 1841. (By Samuel Warren.) First English edition. $75-$85.

TENNYSON, Alfred, Lord. See *Helen's Tower; In Memoriam; Poems by Two Brothers.*

TENNYSON, Alfred, Lord. *The Antechamber.* Orange wrappers. London, 1906. First edition. $25-$30.

TENNYSON, Alfred, Lord (Thomas J. Wise forgery). *Carmen Saeculare: An Ode in Honour of the Jubilee of Queen Victoria.* Wrappers. London, 1887. $50-$75.

TENNYSON, Alfred, Lord. *Enoch Arden.* Green cloth. London, 1864. First edition, first issue, with ads dated August, 1864. $35-$50. Boston, 1864. Brown cloth. First American edition. $15.

TENNYSON, Alfred, Lord. *Idylls of the King.* Green cloth. London, 1859. First edition, first issue, with verso of title page a blank. $35-$50. London, 1868. Illustrations after Gustave Doré. Morocco. $50-$60. New York, 1952. Limited Editions Club. Illustrated by Lynd Ward. Half morocco. Boxed. $50.

TENNYSON, Alfred, Lord. *Maud, and Other Poems.* Green cloth. London, 1855. First edition, with yellow end papers and 8 pages of ads dated July, 1855, and a last leaf advertising Tennyson's books. $50-$75. (Note: Contains first printing of "The Charge of the Light Brigade.") London, 1893. Kelmscott Press. Morocco. One of 500. $300-$400. Another issue: Limp vellum. $55 and $84 (A, 1969).

TENNYSON, Alfred, Lord. *Poems.* Boards, white spine label. London, 1833 (actually 1832). First edition. $100-$150. London, 1842. 2 vols., boards. $100-$150. London, 1857. Cloth. First illustrated edition. $75. Rebound in morocco, $50 and $60. London, 1889. Illustrated by Lear. Folio, half morocco. One of 100 proof copies on Japan paper, signed by Tennyson. $50-$75.

TENNYSON, Alfred, Lord. *Poems, Chiefly Lyrical.* Drab or pink boards, white spine label. London, 1830. First edition, first issue, with page 91 misnumbered 19. $100-$200. Author's first separate book of poems.

TENNYSON, Alfred, Lord. *Poems MDCCCXXX. MDCCCXXXIII.* Printed blue wrappers. No place (Toronto), 1892. Pirated edition. $75.

TENNYSON, Alfred, Lord (Thomas J. Wise forgery). *The Sailor Boy.* Cream-colored printed wrappers. London, 1861. First edition. $100-$200.

TENNYSON, Alfred, Lord. *Seven Poems and Two Translations.* Vellum. London, 1902. Doves Press. One of 325. $75-$100.

TENNYSON, Charles. *Sonnets and Fugitive Pieces.* Boards. Cambridge, England, 1830. First edition. $35-$75.

TENNYSON, Frederick. *Days and Hours.* Cloth. London, 1854. First edition. $35-$50. Author's first book.

TENNYSON, Frederick. *Poems of the Day and Year.* Frontispiece portrait, woodcut title page. Red cloth. London, 1895. First edition. $25.

TERHUNE, Albert Payson. *Caleb Conover, Railroader.* Cloth. New York, 1907. First edition. In dust jacket. $25-$35. Author's first book.

TERRITORY of Wyoming (The); Its History, Soil, Climate, Resources, etc. 84 pp., printed wrappers. Laramie City, Wyoming Territory, 1874. (By J. K. Jeffrey.) First edition. $350-$400.

TEXAS, General Land Office. Abstract of Land Claims. Half sheep. Galveston, Tex., 1852. $150-$175.

TEXAS, the Home for the Emigrant, from Everywhere. Folding map. 43 pp., printed wrappers. Houston, 1875. (By J. B. Robertson.) First edition. $50-$75. St. Louis, 1876. $35-$50. Cover frayed, $25.

THACKER, J. B. *Christopher Columbus.* Plates. 3 vols., half vellum. New York, 1903. $75-$100. Also, $43 (A, 1971).

THACKERAY, William Makepeace. See Marvy, Louis; Pendennis, Arthur; Titmarsh, M. A.; Wagstaff, Theophile. Also see *King Glumpus; The Yellowplush Correspondence; The Loving Ballad of Lord Bateman; The History of Henry Esmond.*

THACKERAY, William Makepeace. *The Adventures of Philip on His Way Through the World.* 3 vols., brown cloth. London, 1862. First edition. $50-$100.

THACKERAY, William Makepeace. *The Book of Snobs.* Illustrated by the author. Green pictorial wrappers. London, 1848. First edition, first issue, with page 126 misnumbered 124. $75-$150. New York, 1852. Cloth. First American edition. $25-$30.

THACKERAY, William Makepeace. *The English Humourists of the Eighteenth Century.* Blue marbled cloth. London, 1853. First edition, first or second issues. $25-$35. New York, 1853. First American edition. $20-$25.

THACKERAY, William Makepeace. *The Four Georges.* Illustrated. Cloth. New York, 1860. First edition. $25-$35. London, 1861. First English edition. $25.

THACKERAY, William Makepeace. *The Great Hoggarty Diamond.* Vignette on title page. Cloth. New York, no date (1848). First edition, first issue, with "82 Cliff Street" on title page (later "306 Pearl Street"). $100-$150.

THACKERAY, William Makepeace. *The History of Henry Esmond, Esq.* 3 vols., cloth, paper labels. London, 1852. First edition. $100-$200.

THACKERAY, William Makepeace. *The History of Pendennis.* 46 full-page plates and other illustrations by the author. 24 parts in 23, printed yellow wrappers. London, 1848-50. First edition. $200-$250. London, 1849-50. 2 vols., cloth. First book edition. $50-$75.

THACKERAY, William Makepeace. *The Orphan of Pimlico, and Other Sketches.* Illustrated by Thackeray. Boards. London, 1876. First edition. $75-$100. (Note: There is much hairsplitting over the various states of the plates, and this picayunishness affects prices on this item.)

THACKERAY, William Makepeace. *Vanity Fair: A Novel Without a Hero.* Illustrated by the author. 20 parts in 19, yellow pictorial wrappers. London, 1847-48. First edition, first issue, with the heading in rustic type on page 1, woodcut of the Marquis of Steyne on page 336 (later omitted), and the reading "Mr. Pitt" on page 453 (later "Sir Pitt"). $2,000 and up. London, 1848. Cloth. First book edition, first issue, with engraved title page date of 1849. $250-$350. Also, plates stained, hinges broken, $90 (A, 1971); rebound in calf, $110.40 (A, 1968); rebound in green morocco, soiled, $90 (A, 1970). New York, 1931. Limited Editions Club. 2 vols., boards. $40.

THACKERAY, William Makepeace. *The Virginians: A Tale of the Last Century.* 24 parts, printed yellow wrappers. London, 1857-59. First edition. $150-$300. London, 1858-59. 2 vols., cloth. First book edition. $50-$100.

THADEUS Amat and Others Against Mexico: Argument for the Defense Before the Honorable Umpire. 50 pp., unbound. No place, no date (Washington, 1876). Original signatures, unbound, unopened. $25.

THAXTER, Celia. *Poems.* Brown cloth. New York, 1872. First edition. $25. Author's first book.

THAYER, Mrs. J. *The Drunkard's Daughter.* Cloth. Boston, 1842. First edition. $35.

THAYER, William N. *The Pioneer Boy, and How He Became President.* Illustrated. Cloth. Boston, 1863. First edition. $35.

THÉÂTRE Lyonnais de Guignol. Designs by Enas D'Orly. Half morocco. Lyon, France, 1890. (By Claudius Brouchoud.) One of 200. $50-$75.

THEOCRITUS. *The Idylls.* Translated by Andrew Lang. 20 color plates after drawings by W. Russell Flint. 2 vols., vellum. London, 1922. One of 12 printed on vellum. $100-$150. Another, with duplicate set of plates, $235. Another issue: 2 vols., half cloth. One of 500. $50-$75.

THERION, The Master. *The Book of Thoth.* 8 color plates, 78 other illustrations. Half morocco. No place (London), 1944. (By Aleister Crowley.) First edition. One of 200 signed. $125-$1500.

THIS Is the Preachment on Going to Church. Vellum. East Aurora, N.Y., 1896. (By George Bernard Shaw.) First edition. One of 26 on Japan paper. $50-$60. Another issue: Half cloth, $15-$25. (Note: These are pirated items.)

THISSELL, G. W. *Crossing the Plains in '49.* 11 plates. Cloth. Oakland, Calif., 1903. First edition. $75-$100.

THOM, Adam. *A Charge Delivered to the Grand Jury of Assiniboia, 20th February, 1845.* 44 pp., printed wrappers. London, 1848. $100-$175.

THOM, Adam. *The Claims to the Oregon Territory Considered.* 44 pp., sewed. London, 1844. First edition. $75-$100.

THOMAS, David. *Travels Through the Western Country in the Summer of 1816.* Folding map. Errata slip. Boards or cloth. Auburn, N.Y., 1819. First edition. $150-$200.

THOMAS, Dylan. *Adventures in the Skin Trade.* Black cloth. London, no date (1955). First separate edition, first issue, with "First published in Great Britain 1955" on verso of title page. In dust jacket. $60-$75.

THOMAS, Dylan. *Adventures in the Skin Trade and Other Stories.* Gray cloth. No place, no date (New York or Norfolk, Conn., 1955). New Directions. First edition. In dust jacket. $20-$35.

THOMAS, Dylan. *Caseg Broadsheet No. 5. From in Memory of Ann Jones.* (Caption title.) One sheet, quarto, printed one side only. Llanllechid (Llandyssul, South Wales), no date (1942). First edition. One of 500. $75-$125.

THOMAS, Dylan. *A Child's Christmas in Wales.* Pale-gray printed boards. Norfolk, no date (1954). First (separate) edition. (A Christmas token of New Directions, Thomas' American publisher, 1955.) In dust jacket. $35-$50.

THOMAS, Dylan. *Collected Poems 1934-1952.* Portrait. Dark-blue cloth. London, no date (1952). First English edition, "ordinary" issue, with "First published 1952" on verso of title page. In dust jacket. $50-$75. Proof copy, same place and date, pale-green wrappers printed in black, lacking dedication and without the poem "Paper and Sticks." 65 copies printed. $100-$200. Limited issue, same place and date: Full dark-blue morocco. One of 65 signed. $400-$500. London, 1954. Light-brown canvas. Reader's Union edition. $25-$35. Later issues are in finer brown cloth.

THOMAS, Dylan. *The Collected Poems of Dylan Thomas.* Blue cloth. No place, no date (New York, 1953). New Directions. First American edition (of *Collected Poems 1934-1952*), first issue, with "daughters" misprinted "daughers" in last line on page 199. In dust jacket. $35-$50.

THOMAS, Dylan. *Conversation About Christmas.* Wrappers (6 leaves stapled, including printed covers). No place (New York), 1954. First separate edition. $25.

THOMAS, Dylan. *Deaths and Entrances.* Orange cloth. London, no date (1946). First edition with "First published 1946" on verso of title page. In dust jacket. $150-$175.

THOMAS, Dylan. *The Doctor and the Devils.* Red cloth. London, no date (1953). First published edition, with "First published 1953" on verso of title page. $25-$50. New Directions imprint: No place, no date (New York, or Norfolk, 1953). Red cloth. First American edition, first issue, identical with English edition except for substitution of New Directions imprint for Dent, etc. In dust jacket. $25-$50. Second issue, gray cloth, with "Second printing" on dust jacket. $10-$20. Proof copies (unpublished): London, no date (1947). First edition, first issue, in cork-colored wrappers, with date on verso of title (35 printed). $160 (A, 1964). Also, with revisions in Thomas' hand, $960 (A, 1969). London, no date (1953). Green wrappers (97 printed). Second issue of the proofs. $110 (A, 1968).

THOMAS, Dylan. *18 Poems.* Black cloth. London, no date (1934). First edition, first issue, with flat spine and lacking leaf between half title and title page. In dust jacket. $350-$500. Also, inscribed, $950 (A, 1968). Same imprint, second issue, with rounded back and with leaf between half title and title (published 1936). In dust jacket. $150-$175. Author's first book. London, no date (about 1940). Second (?) edition (unrecorded by J. Alexander Rolph, *Dylan Thomas: A Bibliography,* but appearing in two binding variants in the Feinberg sale in 1968). Blue or green boards and cloth. In dust jacket. $25. Also, signed copies, $25 and $35 (A, 1968). London, no date (*circa* 1942). Fortune Press imprint. Red buckram. Rolph's second edition, first issue, with "First published in 1934" on verso of title page. $50-$75. Also, $25 (A, 1968); with a John Banting pencil sketch laid in, $62 (A, 1971). Later issue, green boards and cloth: In dust jacket. $35-$50. Dust jacket worn, $27.50.

THOMAS, Dylan. *The Hand.* Colored drawing by Frederic Prokosch as frontispiece. Wrappers. Venice, Italy, 1939. One of 3 (of an edition of 10) on Arches paper. $624 (A, 1971).

THOMAS, Dylan. *In Country Sleep and Other Poems.* Green boards. No place, no date (New York or Norfolk, 1952). New Directions. First edition. With picture of Thomas attached to title page. In dust jacket. $60-$75. Limited edition, same imprint: Buff-gray cloth. One of 100 signed. $200-$300.

THOMAS, Dylan. *The Map of Love: Verse and Prose.* Portrait frontispiece by Augustus John. Fine-grained mauve cloth, gilt, top edges purple. London, no date (1939). First edition, first issue (mauve cloth). In dust jacket. $100-$150. Second issue, plum-colored cloth (published 1947). Third issue, purple cloth (published 1948). Fourth issue, purple cloth, unstained top edges. (The second and third issues were 250 copies each as against 1,000 for the first issue and 500 for the fourth, according to Rolph.)

THOMAS, Dylan. *New Poems*. 32 pp., unnumbered, mauve boards, or mauve wrappers. Norfolk, no date (1943). First edition. Boards: $25-$35. Wrappers: $50-$75. (Note: This actually is a second printing, the entire first printing having been destroyed, according to Rolph.)

THOMAS, Dylan. *Portrait of the Artist as a Young Dog*. Cloth. London, no date (1940). First edition, first issue, with "First published 1940" on verso of title page. In dust jacket. $100-$125. Proof copy, printed wrappers. $225 (A, 1968). Norfolk, no date (1940). Brick-red cloth. First American edition. $35-$50. Norfolk, no date (1950). Yellow cloth. Second printing (so stated). $25. London, 1948. Guild Books. Wrappers. First printing. $25-$35.

THOMAS, Dylan. *A Prospect of the Sea*. Blue cloth. London, no date (1955). First edition with "First published July, 1955" on verso of title page. In dust jacket. $50-$60. "Proof copy," so imprinted, in wrappers, soiled. $75. Second edition, same date. In dust jacket. $25-$35.

THOMAS, Dylan. *Quite Early One Morning: Broadcasts*. Portrait frontispiece. Blue cloth. London, no date (1954). First edition, first issue, with full stop after "sailors" at end of verse 5 on pages 3 and 11. In dust jacket. $35-$50. New Directions imprint: No place, no date (New York, 1954). Gray cloth. First American edition, first issue, without note of later impression on dust jacket. $25-$35.

THOMAS, Dylan. *Selected Writings of Dylan Thomas*. Pinkish mauve cloth. No place, no date (Norfolk, 1946). First edition, without printing number on front flap of dust jacket. In dust jacket. $35-$50.

THOMAS, Dylan. *Twenty-five Poems*. Gray boards. London, no date (1936). First edition. In dust jacket. $200-$250.

THOMAS, Dylan. *Twenty-six Poems*. Decorated boards, canvas spine, paper label. No place, no date (New York or Norfolk, 1950). First edition. New Directions. One of 87 signed. Boxed. $300-$350. There were also 10 copies printed on Japan vellum (2 for Thomas; the rest for New Directions, his American publisher); no copies noted for sale. London, no date (1949). First English edition, identical (save for Dent imprint) with the American edition, which preceded it by three months. One of 50 signed. Boxed. $300-$350.

THOMAS, Dylan. *Under Milk Wood*. Light-brown cloth. London, no date (1954). First edition, with "First published 1954" on verso of title page. In dust jacket. $60-$100. New Directions imprint: No place, no date (New York, 1954). Mulberry-brown cloth. First American edition. In dust jacket. $35-$50.

THOMAS, Dylan. *The World I Breathe*. Light-brown buckram. Norfolk, no date (1939). First edition, first issue (according to the New York dealer Marguerite Cohn), with single star on either side of Thomas' name on title page and on spine (later copies having five stars on either side). Mrs. Cohn catalogued this at $75 in 1968. Rolph states: "*The World I Breathe* is perhaps, at least in Great Britain, the most scarce of Thomas's books." There were only 700 copies published, and no further printings were made. In view of this, and considering the prices of other Thomas items, the first issue of *The World I Breathe,* in dust jacket and in fine condition, should be worth at least $150-$250 at retail.

THOMAS, Edward. See Eastaway, Edward.

THOMAS, Edward. *Chosen Essays*. Wood engravings. Blue morocco. Newtown, Wales, 1926. Gregynog Press. One of 33 thus bound, in a limited edition of 350 copies. $500-$600. Another issue: Buckram. One of 317. $100-$150.

THOMAS, Edward. *Selected Poems*. Buckram. Newtown, 1930. Gregynog Press. One of 275 on vellum. $75-$100.

THOMAS, Henry W. *History of the Doles-Cook Brigade, Army of Northern Virginia*. Cloth. Atlanta, 1903. $50-$60. Rebound in buckram, $35.

THOMAS, Isaiah. *Isaiah Thomas's Catalogue of English, Scotch, Irish, and American Books.* Half leather. Worcester, Mass., 1801. First edition. Worn and chipped, some writing on title page. $160. (A, 1971).

THOMAS, Jerry. *The Bar-Tender's Guide.* Cloth. New York, 1862. First edition. $100.

THOMAS, Joseph B. *Hounds and Hunting Through the Ages.* Cloth. New York, 1928. First edition. Derrydale Press. One of 750. $75-$100. New York, 1929. Second edition. One of 250. $50-$75.

THOMAS, P. J. *Founding of the Missions.* Map, plates. Cloth. San Francisco, 1877. $75-$100.

THOMPSON, A. C. See Meynell, Alice.

THOMPSON, A. C. *Preludes.* Green cloth. London, 1875. (By Alice Meynell.) First edition, first issue, with brown end papers. $50-$75. Author's first book (republished later under the name Alice Meynell as *Poems,* which see under her name).

THOMPSON, Albert W. *The Story of Early Clayton, N.M.* Cloth. Clayton, 1933. First edition. $50-$75.

THOMPSON, Capt. B. F. *History of the 112th Regiment of Illinois Volunteer Infantry, 1862-1865.* Cloth. Toulon, Ill., 1885. $50-$75.

THOMPSON, C. Mildred. *Reconstruction in Georgia.* Wrappers. New York, 1915. First edition. $25.

THOMPSON, Daniel Pierce. See *The Adventures of Timothy Peacock, Esquire; The Green Mountain Boys.*

THOMPSON, Daniel Pierce. *May Martin.* Cloth. Montpelier, Vt., 1835. First edition. $50-$75.

THOMPSON, Daniel Pierce (editor). *The Laws of Vermont, 1824-34, Inclusive.* Calf. Montpelier, 1835. First edition. $50-$75. Author's first book.

THOMPSON, David. *David Thompson's Narrative of His Explorations in Western America: 1784-1812.* Edited by J. B. Tyrrell. 23 maps and plates. Cloth. Toronto, 1916. Champlain Society. First edition. One of 550. $400-$500.

THOMPSON, David. *History of the Late War, Between Great Britain and the U.S.A.* Boards or leather. Niagara, U.C. (Upper Canada), 1832. First edition. $110.

THOMPSON, Edwin P. *History of the First Kentucky Brigade.* 6 plates. Cloth. Cincinnati, 1868. First edition. $75-$100. Another issue (?): same place and date. 2 plates. Half calf. $30 (A, 1968).

THOMPSON, Francis. *Poems.* Decorated boards. London, 1893. First edition. With ads at back dated October. One of 500. $75-$100. Worn, $50. Another issue: Vellum. One of 12 signed. $150-$250. Author's first book.

THOMPSON, Francis. *Sister-Songs: An Offering to Two Sisters.* Green cloth. London, 1895. First edition, with ads at back dated 1895. (First published edition of *Songs Wing-to-Wing.*) $50-$75.

THOMPSON, Francis. *Songs Wing-to-Wing: An Offering to Two Sisters.* (Cover title.) Wrappers. London, no date (1895). First edition, first issue (of *Sister-Songs*), with no title page and no dedication leaf. $150-$250.

THOMPSON, Maurice. See *A Tallahassee Girl.*

THOMPSON, Maurice. *Alice of Old Vincennes.* Cloth. Indianapolis, no date (1900). First edition, first issue, with no page of "Acknowledgments" at end of text. $35-$50.

THOMPSON, Maurice. *Hoosier Mosaics.* Cloth. New York, 1875. First edition. $25-$50. Author's first book.

THOMPSON, Maurice. *The Story of Louisiana.* Cloth. Boston, no date (1888). First edition. $35.

THOMPSON, Maurice. *The Witchery of Archery.* Cloth. New York, 1878. First edition. $35-$50.

THOMPSON, R. A. *Central Sonoma: A Brief Description of the Township and Town of Santa Rosa, Sonoma County, California.* Printed wrappers. Santa Rosa, Calif., 1884. First edition. $75-$100.

THOMPSON, R. A. *Conquest of California.* Portrait, 3 plates. 33 pp., wrappers. Santa Rosa, 1896. First edition. $50-$100.

THOMPSON, R. A. *Historical and Descriptive Sketch of Sonoma County, California.* Map. Printed wrappers. Philadelphia, 1877. First edition. $100-$150.

THOMPSON, R. A. *The Russian Settlement in California Known as Fort Ross.* 2 plates, other illustrations. 34 pp., wrappers. Santa Rosa, 1896. First edition. $150-$200.

THOMPSON, Lieut. S. D. *Recollections with the 3rd Iowa Regiment.* Cloth. Cincinnati, 1864. $50-$60.

THOMPSON, William. *To the Committee on Election. Ought the Kanesville Vote in August, 1848, to Have Been Allowed?* 19 pp., boards and calf. No place (Iowa City?), 1850. $150.

THOMSON, James [1700-48]. *The Seasons.* Engravings by F. Bartolozzi and P. W. Tomkins. Contemporary calf. London, 1807. $100-$125.

THOMSON, James [1834-82]. See V., B. (for Bysshe Vanolis).

THOREAU, Henry David. *Autumn: From the Journal of Henry D. Thoreau.* Cloth. Boston, 1892. First edition. $25-$35.

THOREAU, Henry David. *Cape Cod.* Purple cloth. Boston, 1865 (actually 1864). First edition, with no pagination on title page and leaf following. $75-$100. Boston, 1896. Colored illustrations. 2 vols., decorated cloth. $35-$50.

THOREAU, Henry David. *Early Spring in Massachusetts: From the Journal of Henry D. Thoreau.* Cloth. Boston, 1881. First edition. $25-$35.

THOREAU, Henry David. *Excursions.* Engraved portrait. Green cloth. Boston, 1863. First edition. $50-$100.

THOREAU, Henry David. *Familiar Letters.* Edited by F. B. Sanborn. Green cloth. Boston, 1894. First edition. $25-$35. Another issue: One of 150 on large paper. $50-$60.

THOREAU, Henry David. *Letters to Various Persons.* Cloth. Boston, 1865. First edition. $50-$75.

THOREAU, Henry David. *The Maine Woods.* Green cloth, chocolate end papers. Boston, 1864. First edition, first issue, with one-leaf ad of *Atlantic Monthly* at end reading "The Thirteenth Volume." $150-$200. Spine faded, frayed, $90.

THOREAU, Henry David. *Poems of Nature.* Cloth. Boston, 1895. First edition. $50-$75.

THOREAU, Henry David. *Sir Walter Raleigh.* Half calf. Boston, 1905. First edition. One of 489. $35-$50.

THOREAU, Henry David. *Summer: From the Journal of Henry D. Thoreau.* Green cloth. Boston, 1884. First edition. $75-$100.

THOREAU, Henry David. *Walden or, Life in the Woods.* Cloth. Boston, 1854. First edition, with "post" for "port" on page 24, "single spruce" for "double spruce" on page 137, and "white spruce" for "black spruce" on page 217. (April ads presumably are earliest.)

$300-$600. Repaired copy, June ads, $200. London, 1884. Cloth, paper label. First English edition. $35-$50. Edinburgh, 1884. Cloth, paper label. $25. Boston, 1909. 2 vols., half vellum. One of 488. $75-$100. London, 1927. Illustrated. Half vellum. $50. Chicago, 1930. Lakeside Press. Illustrated. Half buckram. One of 1,000. $50-$75. New York, 1936. Limited Editions Club. Boards. Boxed. $40-$50.

THOREAU, Henry David. *A Week on the Concord and Merrimack Rivers.* Brown cloth, yellow end papers. Boston, 1849. First edition, with 3 lines dropped at bottom of page 396—usually written in with pencil by Thoreau. $1,000-$1,500. Also, spine defective, with Thoreau's writing, $900 (A, 1971); $600 (A, 1960). Second issue, with last 3 lines on page 396 present. $200-$300. Author's first book. Boston, 1862. Second edition. (Remaindered sheets of first edition with a new title page.) $35-$50.

THOREAU, Henry David. *Winter: From the Journal of Henry D. Thoreau.* Cloth. Boston, 1888 (actually 1887). First edition. $25-$35.

THOREAU, Henry David. *A Yankee in Canada, with Anti-Slavery and Reform Papers.* Cloth. Boston, 1866. First edition. $75-$100.

THORNTON, Alfred. See *The Adventures of a Post Captain.*

THORNTON, J. Quinn. *Oregon and California in 1848.* Folding map. 2 vols., cloth. New York, 1849. First edition. $150-$200. New York, 1855. 2 vols., cloth. $35-$50.

THORNTON, R. J. (editor). *The Pastorals of Virgil, with a Course of English Reading, Adapted for Schools.* 6 engravings by William Blake, 20 woodcuts designed by him, 3 maps, other illustrations. Contemporary calf. London, 1821. Third edition. $400-$500.

THORNTON, Robert John. *Botanical Extracts, or Philosophy of Botany.* 2 vols. of text, 2 vols. of copperplates, together, 4 vols., atlas folio, contemporary calf. London, 1810. $200-$250.

THORNTON, Robert John. *The Temple of Flora.* Engraved title with vignette, colored frontispiece, 28 colored and 2 uncolored plates. Contemporary morocco. London, 1812. $500-$750.

THOROUGHBRED Broodmare Records, 1935-1939. Morocco. No place (Lexington, Ky.), June, 1940. One of 250. $350.

THOROUGHBRED Mares' Records (The). Compiled by J. F. Mainwaring Sharp. Illustrated. London, 1930. One of 250. $125.

THOUGHTS on the Destiny of Man. 96 pp., wrappers. Harmony, Ind., 1824. (By Father George Rapp.) First edition. $75-$100.

THOUGHTS on the Proposed Annexation of Texas to the United States. 55 pp., wrappers. New York, 1844. (By Theodore Sedgwick.) First edition. $35-$50.

THOUSAND Miles in a Canoe from Denver to Leavenworth (A). Wrappers. Bushnell, Neb., 1880. (By W. A. Spencer.) First edition. $150.

THRALL, The Rev. Homer S. *A Pictorial History of Texas.* Folding map. Leather, or cloth. St. Louis, 1878. First edition. $75-$100. St. Louis, 1879. Cloth. Fourth edition. $50.

THRALL, The Rev. S. C. *The President's Death: A Sermon Delivered at Christ Church.* 12 pp., wrappers. New Orleans, 1865. First edition. $45.

THREE Monographs. 56 pp., light-brown printed wrappers. Naples, Italy, 1906. (By Norman Douglas.) First edition. One of 250. $100.

THWAITES, Reuben Gold. *Historic Waterways: Six Hundred Miles of Canoeing Down the Rock, Fox, and Wisconsin Rivers.* Cloth. Chicago, 1888. First edition. $25. Author's first book.

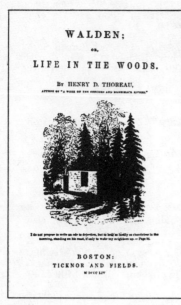

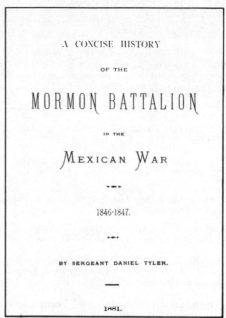

Title page of Tyler's *Mormon Battalion.* Published Salt Lake City, 1881.
—*Photo courtesy of Harold O. Wright.*

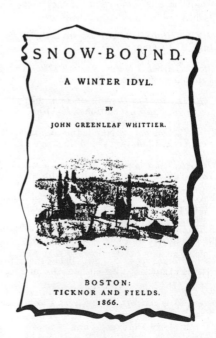

THUCYDIDES. *The History of the Peloponnesian War.* Translated by Benjamin Jowett. Folio, white pigskin. London, 1930. Ashendene Press. One of 260 printed on paper. $500-$750. Another issue: One of 20 on vellum. $1,000-$1,500; rebound in morocco by W. H. Smith, $1,232 (A, 1965).

TILLSON, Christina Holmes. *Reminiscences of Early Life in Illinois by Our Mother.* 4 plates. Cloth. No place, no date (Amherst, Mass., about 1872). First edition. $400-$500. Small gouge on cover, $350.

TIMBERLAKE, Lieut. Henry. *Memoirs, 1756-1765.* Portrait. Folding map. Plate. Cloth. Johnson City, Tenn., 1927. One of 35 on large paper. (Reprint of rare 1765 London edition.) $35-$50.

TIMOLEON. 70 pp., printed buff wrappers. New York, 1891. (By Herman Melville.) Caxton Press. First edition. One of 25. Copies with Melville's signature pasted in, $510 (A, 1944), $375 (A, 1945).

TIMOTHY Crump's Ward; or, The New Years Loan and What Came of It. Purple cloth, or wrappers. Boston, 1866. (By Horatio Alger, Jr.) First edition. Published by Loring. $1,000 and up. (According to the Alger bibliographer Ralph D. Gardner, there are only 3 copies known—2 in cloth and 1 in wrappers.)

TIPTON, R. B. *Directory of Marshalltown.* Printed boards. Marshalltown, Iowa, 1884. $35-$50.

TITMARSH, M. A. [Michael Angelo] (editor). *Comic Tales and Sketches.* 12 tinted plates. 2 vols., black or brown cloth. London, 1841. (By William Makepeace Thackeray.) First edition. $100-$150.

TITMARSH, M. A. *Doctor Birch and His Young Friends.* Illustrated in color by the author. Decorated boards. London, 1849. (By William Makepeace Thackeray.) First edition. $50-$75.

TITMARSH, M. A. *The Irish Sketch-Book.* Wood engravings. 2 vols., green cloth. London, 1843. (By William Makepeace Thackeray.) First edition. $100-$125. First book of which Thackeray acknowledged authorship.

TITMARSH, M. A. *Jeames's Diary; or, Sudden Riches.* Woodcuts. Wrappers. New York, 1846. (By William Makepeace Thackeray.) First edition. Up to $500. Very rare, with only 3 copies known to bibliographers.

TITMARSH, M. A. *The Knickleburys on the Rhine.* Illustrations in color by the author. Decorated boards. London, 1851. (By William Makepeace Thackeray.) Third edition. $25.

TITMARSH, M. A. *"Our Street."* Illustrated in color. Decorated boards. London, 1848. (By William Makepeace Thackeray.) Second edition. $35.

TITMARSH, M. A. *The Second Funeral of Napoleon: In Three Letters to Miss Smith, of London, and the Chronicle of the Drum.* Frontispiece, 3 plates, picture of Napoleon on front cover. Wrappers. London, 1841. (By William Makepeace Thackeray.) First edition, first issue, with six lines of shading on the cheek of Napoleon on front cover. $150-$350. (Note: A copy of this rarity was sold in 1914 for $825. The so-called "second issue" apparently is a reprint, done about 1880, according to De Ricci, and with the illustrations lithographed. Its value is nominal.)

TITTSWORTH, W. G. *Outskirt Episodes.* Portrait (tipped to title page). Red cloth. No place, no date (Avoca, Iowa, 1927). First edition. In dust jacket. $150.

TODD, The Rev. John. *The Lost Sister of Wyoming.* Frontispiece. Cloth. Northampton, Mass., 1842. First edition. $35-$50.

TOLSTOY, Leo. *Where God Is Love Is.* Wrappers. London, 1924. Ashendene Press. One of about 200 issued as a Christmas token. On the wrapper is printed "With all good Wishes for a Merry Christmass and a happy New Year from St. John and Cicely Hornby. Chantmarle, Dorset, 1924." $150-$250.

TOM Brown at Oxford. 3 vols., blue cloth. Cambridge, 1861. (By Thomas Hughes.) First edition. $300-$400.

TOM Brown's School Days. By an Old Boy. Blue cloth. Cambridge, England, 1857. (By Thomas Hughes.) First edition. $250-$350.

TOM Cringle's Log. 2 vols., cloth. London, 1833. (By Michael Scott.) First edition. $75-$100.

TOMKINSON, G. S. *A Select Bibliography of the Principal Modern Presses . . . in Great Britain and Ireland.* Illustrated. Boards and cloth. London, 1928. First edition. $75.

TOMLINSON, H. M. *All Our Yesterdays.* Boards and cloth. New York, 1930. First edition. One of 350. $25. Trade edition: Black cloth. In dust jacket. $10. London, no date (1930). Cloth. First English edition. One of 1,025 signed. $25. Trade edition: Cloth. First issue, with error in running head on page 67. $10-$15.

TOMLINSON, H. M. *Ports of Call.* Cloth. London, 1942. Corvinus Press. One of 30. $75-$100.

TOMLINSON, H. M. *The Sea and the Jungle.* Frontispiece. Green cloth. London, no date (1912). First edition, first issue, with 10 ad leaves at back. In dust jacket, $150-$200. Author's first book. London, or New York, 1930. Illustrated by Clare Leighton. Cloth. One of 515 signed by author. $25-$35. Trade edition: Boards and cloth. $10-$15.

TOMLINSON, H. M. *Under the Red Ensign.* Cloth. London, 1926. First edition. $25.

TOPOGRAPHICAL Description of the State of Ohio, Indian Territory, and Louisiana (A). 5 plates, errata slip. Calf, or sheep. Boston, 1812. (By Jervis Cutler.) First edition. $500-$600. Lacking errata slip, $425.

TOPONCE, Alexander. *Reminiscences of Alexander Toponce, Pioneer, 1839-1923.* 14 plates. Fabrikoid. No place, no date (Ogden, Utah, 1923). First edition. $50-$60.

TOPPING, E. S. *The Chronicles of the Yellowstone.* Folding map. Cloth. St. Paul, Minn., 1883. First edition. $50-$75.

TOPSYS & Turveys. 31 leaves with colored illustrations. Oblong folio, pictorial boards. New York, 1893. (By Peter Newell.) $50-$60. Author's first book.

TORNEL, José María (translator). *Diario Histórico del Último Viaje que Hizo M. de La Sale para Descubrir el Desembocadero y Curso del Missicipi.* Boards. New York, 1831. $75.

TORRENCE, Ridgely. *The House of a Hundred Lights.* Boards. Boston, 1900. First edition. $25. Author's first book.

TORY, Geoffroy. *Champ Fleury.* Translated by George B. Ives. Vellum and boards. New York, 1927. Grolier Club. Printed by Bruce Rogers. One of 7 on larger paper (of an edition of 397). $300-$400. Regular issue: One of 390. In dust jacket. Boxed. $150-$200.

TOTTEN, B. J. *Naval Text-Book.* Plates. Cloth. Boston, 1841. $35-$50.

TOUR of Doctor Prosody (The). 20 colored plates by C. Williams and W. Read. Boards. London, 1821. $100-$125. (Note: Sometimes attributed to William Combe, but not by him, according to De Ricci.)

TOUR on the Prairies (A). By the Author of "The Sketch-Book." Boards or cloth. London, 1835. (By Washington Irving.) First edition. $75-$100. Philadelphia, 1835. Blue or green cloth, paper label. First American edition, first state, without "No. 1" on the label. $75-$100. Second state. $35-$50.

TOUR Through Part of Virginia in the Summer of 1808 (A). 31 pp. New York, 1809. (By John E. Caldwell.) First edition. $50-$100.

TOWER, Col. Reuben. *An Appeal to the People of New York in Favor of the Construction of the Chenango Canal, etc.* 32 pp., sewed. Utica, 1830. First edition. $35-$50.

TOWLE, Mrs. C. W. *Stories for the American Freemason's Fireside.* Frontispiece. Cloth. Cincinnati, 1868. (By Catharine Webb Barber Towles.) First edition. $25. (Note: The by-line is spelled "Towle," without the "s" on title page.)

TOWNSEND, George Alfred. *The Real Life of Abraham Lincoln.* Frontispiece. 15 pp., printed wrappers. New York, 1867. First edition. $50-$75.

TOWNSEND, John K. *Narrative of a Journey Across the Rocky Mountains.* Cloth. Philadelphia, 1839. First edition. $150-$250.

TOWNSHIP Maps of the Cherokee Nation. 130 maps. Folio, cloth. Muskogee, Okla., no date. $150.

TRACY, J. L. *Guide to the Great West.* 2 maps. Cloth. St. Louis, 1870. First edition. $50.

TRAGEDY of Count Alarcos (The). Wrappers. London, 1839. (By Benjamin Disraeli.) First edition. $50. Also, $22 (A, 1951).

TRAHERNE, Thomas. *The Poetical Works of Thomas Traherne.* Frontispiece ms. facsimile. Cream-colored linen boards. London, 1903. First edition. One of 600. $60-$75.

TRAITS of American Indian Life and Character. By a Fur Trader. 6 plates. Half cloth. San Francisco, 1933. (By Peter Skene Ogden or Duncan Finlayson.) Grabhorn printing. One of 500. $35-$50.

TRANSACTIONS of the Chicago Academy of Sciences. Vol. 1, Part 1, and Vol. 1, Part 2. Plates, lithographs, folding map, separate title page for Part 2. Half leather. Chicago, 1867 and 1869. First edition. (All published.) $150-$200. Part 1 only, $40 (A, 1966).

TRANSCRIPT of Record of Proceedings Before the Mexican and American Mixed Claims Commission with Relation to the "Pious Fund of the Californias." Washington, 1902. $60.

TRANSITION Stories. Pictorial boards and cloth. New York, 1929. First edition. In dust jacket. $25.

TRAUBEL, Horace L. (editor). *At the Graveside of Walt Whitman: Harleigh, Camden, New Jersey, March 30th, and Sprigs of Lilac.* 37 pp., printed gray wrappers. No place (Philadelphia), 1892. First edition. $35-$50.

TRAUBEL, Horace L. (editor). *Camden's Compliment to Walt Whitman.* Cloth. Philadelphia, 1889. First edition. $25.

TRAVELLER'S Directory and Emigrant's Guide, etc. (The). Boards. Buffalo, N.Y., 1832. (By Oliver G. Steele.) First edition. $150. Other Buffalo editions, 1834, 1836, 1839, 1846, 1847, each $25-$50.

TRAVELS of Capts. Lewis and Clarke (The). Folding map and 5 portraits of Indians. Calf. Philadelphia, 1809. First edition. $200-$300. (Note: A spurious work. For authentic first edition see entry under Lewis' name..)

TRAVELS in Louisiana and the Floridas, in the Year, 1802. Translated from the French by John Davis. Boards, paper label. New York, 1806. (By Berquin-Duvallon.) First edition in English. $375. Also, rebound in half morocco, $350 (A, 1967).

TRAVEN, B. *The Bridge in the Jungle.* Green cloth. New York, 1938. First American edition. In dust jacket. $25-$35.

TRAVEN, B. *The Death Ship: The Story of an American Sailor.* Black cloth. New York, 1934. First American edition in English. In dust jacket. $35-$50. Author's first book.

TRAVEN, B. *Der Schatz der Sierra Madre.* Orange-colored pictorial cloth. Berlin, 1927. First edition (of *The Treasure of the Sierra Madre*). $150-$200. Soiled, $125.

TRAVEN, B. *The General from the Jungle.* Cloth. London, no date (1954). First edition. In dust jacket. $30.

TRAVEN, B. *The Rebellion of the Hanged.* Black cloth. New York, 1952. First edition. In dust jacket. $25-$35.

TRAVEN, B. *The Treasure of the Sierra Madre.* Black cloth. New York, 1935. First American edition. In dust jacket. $35-$50.

TREADWELL, Edward F. *The Cattle King.* 4 plates. Cloth. New York, 1931. First edition. In dust jacket. $35-$50. Boston, 1950. Cloth. $15-$20.

TREATISE on Tennis (A). By a Member of the Tennis Club. Folding engraved diagram of court. Boards. London, 1822. (By Robert Lukin.) First edition. $45.

TREATY Between the United States and the Chasta and Other Tribes of Indians. Wrappers. No place, no date (Washington, 1855). (By Joel Palmer.) $50.

TREATY Between the United States and the Comanche and Kiowa Tribes of Indians ... Proclaimed May 26, 1866. 8 pp., folio. No place, no date (Washington, 1866). $35.

TREATY Between the United States and the Creek and Seminole Tribes of Indians ... Ratified March 6, 1845. 6 pp., folio. No place, no date (Washington, 1845). $35.

TREATY Between the United States and the Klamath and Moadoc Tribes and Yahooskin Band of Snake Indians ... Proclaimed Feb. 17, 1870. 8 pp., folio. No place, no date (Washington, 1870). $35.

TREATY Between the United States and the Nez Perce Tribe of Indians ... Proclaimed April 20, 1867. 10 pp., folio. No place, no date (Washington, 1867). $25.

TRELAWNY, Edward John. See *The Adventures of a Younger Son.*

TRENT, William. *Journal of Captain William Trent from Logstown to Pickawillany, A. D. 1752.* Cloth. Cincinnati, 1871. First edition. $35-$50.

TRIAL of Impeachment of Levi Hubbell. Contemporary calf. Madison, Wis., 1853. First edition. $60.

TRIALS of A. Arbuthnot and R. C. Ambrister (The), Charged with Exciting the Seminole Indians to War Against the United States of America. 80 pp., morocco. London, 1819. First edition. $60.

TRIBES and Temples: A Record of the Expedition to Middle America Conducted by the Tulane University of Louisiana in 1925. 2 vols., cloth. New Orleans, 1926. $50.

TRIBUNE Book of Open Air Sports (The). Edited by Henry Hall. Illustrated. Pictorial cloth. New York, 1887. First edition. $100-$150. (Note: This is the first book composed by linotype.)

TRIBUNE Tracts No. 6, Life of Abraham Lincoln. 32 pp., sewed. New York, 1860. (By John Locke Scripps.) $35-$50. (Note: This book first appeared in an undated Chicago edition of 1860, 32 pp., under the caption title *Life of Abraham Lincoln.* That edition is rare, worth $1,000 and up.)

TRIGGS, J. H. *History and Directory of Laramie City, Wyoming Territory.* 91 pp., printed wrappers. Laramie City, 1875. First edition. $300-$400.

TRIGGS, J. H. *History of Cheyenne and Northern Wyoming, etc.* Folding map. 144 pp., printed wrappers. Omaha, Neb., 1876. First edition. $350-$500.•

TRIPLER, Eunice. *Some Notes of Her Personal Recollections.* Illustrated. Cloth. New York, 1910. First edition. $75.

TRIPLETT, Frank. *The Life, Times and Treacherous Death of Jesse James.* Plates. Pictorial cloth. Chicago, 1882. First edition. $150-$250.

TRIPP, C. E. *Ace High: The Frisco Detective.* Introduction by David Magee. Illustrated. Boards and cloth. San Francisco, 1948. Grabhorn Press. One of 500. $35-$50.

TRIP'S History of Beasts: A Trifle for a Good Boy. Illustrated. 31 pp., printed wrappers. Albany, N. Y., 1818. $50.

TRISTRAM, W. Outram. *Coaching Days and Coaching Ways.* Pictorial cloth. London, 1888. First edition. Large paper issue. $50-$75. Regular issue: $35-$50. Also, rebound in half calf, $31.20 (A, 1968). London, 1893. One of 250. $35-$50. London, 1924. Illustrated. Leather. $50-$60.

TROLLOPE, Anthony. See *Nina Balatka.*

TROLLOPE, Anthony. *The American Senator.* 3 vols., cloth. London, 1877. First edition. $100-$150. Detroit, 1877. Green cloth. "Craig & Taylor" on spine. $25. New York, no date (1940). One of 310. $25-$30.

TROLLOPE, Anthony. *Australia and New Zealand.* 8 colored maps. 2 vols., cloth. London, 1873. First edition. $50-$75. Melbourne, Australia, 1873. Cloth. $35-$50.

TROLLOPE, Anthony. *An Autobiography.* Portrait. 2 vols., cloth. Edinburgh, 1883. First edition, first issue, with smooth red cloth covers and dark-green end papers. $50-$75.

TROLLOPE, Anthony. *Ayala's Angel.* 3 vols., orange cloth. London, 1881. First edition. $300-$350.

TROLLOPE, Anthony. *Barchester Towers.* 3 vols., cloth. London, 1857. First edition, first binding, brown cloth. $250-$500. Second binding, tan cloth, with 24 pp. of ads dated October, 1860. $450. New York, no date (1859?). 2 vols. in one, purple-brown cloth. First American edition, without printer's imprint on back of title page. $200. Also, worn, $90 (A, 1971). New York, 1958. Limited Editions Club. Fritz Kredel illustrations in color. Boards and leather. Boxed. $25-$35.

TROLLOPE, Anthony. *The Belton Estate.* 3 vols., cloth. London, 1866. First book edition. $300-$400.

TROLLOPE, Anthony. *The Bertrams.* 3 vols., cloth. London, 1859. First edition. $100-$125.

TROLLOPE, Anthony. *Can You Forgive Her?* Illustrated. 20 parts, wrappers. London, 1864-65. First edition. $250-$350. London, 1864. 2 vols., cloth. First book edition. $100-$150.

TROLLOPE, Anthony. *Castle Richmond.* 3 vols., dark purple-gray cloth. London, 1860. First edition, first issue, without line under the author's name on spine. $100-$150. Second issue, with line under author's name on spine and ads in Vol. 3 dated May. $50-$75. Also, $70 (A, 1963). New York, 1860. Green cloth. First American edition. $150.

TROLLOPE, Anthony. *The Claverings.* Illustrated. 2 vols., green cloth. London, 1867. First edition. $75-$100.

TROLLOPE, Anthony. *Doctor Thorne.* 3 vols., cloth. London, 1858. First edition. $250-$300. Second edition, same date. $50-$75.

TROLLOPE, Anthony. *The Duke's Children.* 3 vols., cloth. London, 1880. First book edition. $75-$100.

TROLLOPE, Anthony. *An Editor's Tales.* Pinkish-brown cloth. London, 1870. First edition. $100-$150.

TROLLOPE, Anthony. *The Eustace Diamonds.* 3 vols., salmon-brown cloth. London, 1873. First book edition. $100-$150.

TROLLOPE, Anthony. *The Fixed Period.* 2 vols., cloth. Edinburgh, 1882. First edition. Publisher's embossed stamp on Vol. 1. $250-$350.

TROLLOPE, Anthony. *Framly Parsonage.* Millais illustrations. 3 vols., cloth. London, 1861. First edition. $50-$75.

TROLLOPE, Anthony. *The Golden Lion of Granpere.* Cloth. London, 1872. First edition. $35-$40.

TROLLOPE, Anthony. *He Knew He Was Right.* Illustrated by Marcus Stone. 32 parts, wrappers. London, 1868-69. First edition. $150-$200. London, 1869. 32 plates. 2 vols., green cloth. First book edition. $150-$238.

TROLLOPE, Anthony. *How the "Mastiffs" Went to Iceland.* Illustrated. Cloth. London, 1878. First edition. $150-$200.

TROLLOPE, Anthony. *Hunting Sketches.* Red cloth. London, 1865. First edition, with May ads. $100-$150.

TROLLOPE, Anthony. *John Caldigate.* 3 vols., cloth. London, 1879. First edition. First issue, lilac-gray cloth. $150-$200.

TROLLOPE, Anthony. *The Kellys and the O'Kellys.* 3 vols., boards. London, 1848. First edition. $300-$400.

TROLLOPE, Anthony. *Kept in the Dark.* 3 vols., cloth. London, 1882. First edition. $150-$200.

TROLLOPE, Anthony. *La Vendee: An Historical Romance.* 3 vols., cloth. London, 1850. First edition, first issue (issue points?). $250-$300.

TROLLOPE, Anthony. *Lady Anna.* 2 vols., cloth. London, 1874. First edition. $100-$150.

TROLLOPE, Anthony. *The Landleaguers.* 3 vols., cloth. London, 1883. First edition. $150-$200.

TROLLOPE, Anthony. *The Last Chronicle of Barset.* Illustrated. 32 parts, pictorial wrappers. London, 1866-67. First edition. $400-$500. Some wear and soiling, $375. London, 1867. 32 plates. 2 vols., blue cloth. First book edition. $100-$150. Also, "variant title page," same date, another issue: $57.60 (A, 1967).

TROLLOPE, Anthony. *The Life of Cicero.* 2 vols., dark-red cloth. London, 1880. First edition, first issue, with plain capitals on spine. $100-$125.

TROLLOPE, Anthony. *London Tradesmen.* Boards and cloth. London, 1927. First edition. One of 325 numbered copies for Great Britain. $25-$35.

TROLLOPE, Anthony. *Lotta Schmidt and Other Stories.* Cloth. London, 1867. First edition. $75-$100.

TROLLOPE, Anthony. *The Macdermots of Ballydoran.* 3 vols., cloth (?). London, 1847. First edition. No copy of the first issue has appeared at public sale for many years. London, 1848. Half calf. $350 (in Goodspeed's 1971 "First Books" catalogue). (Note: Evidently this is the copy, listed as "blue half morocco," sold at a London auction in 1968 for $139.20.) Author's first book.

TROLLOPE, Anthony. *Marion Fay.* 3 vols., cloth. London, 1882. First edition. $150-$200.

TROLLOPE, Anthony. *Miss Mackenzie.* 2 vols., dark-green cloth. London, 1865. First edition. $150-$200.

TROLLOPE, Anthony. *On English Prose Fiction as a Rational Amusement.* (Cover title.) 44 pp., sewed, uncut, title serving as top cover. No place, no date (London ?, 1869). First edition. $400-$500. (Note: Only three or four copies are believed to exist.)

TROLLOPE, Anthony. *Orley Farm.* Illustrated by J. E. Millais. 20 parts, wrappers. London, 1862 (and 1861). First edition. $300-$400. London, 1862. 2 vols., purple-brown cloth. First book edition. $200-$250.

TROLLOPE, Anthony. *The Prime Minister.* 8 parts, wrappers. London, 1876. First edition. $75-$100. London, 1876. 4 vols., cloth. First book edition. $50-$75.

TROLLOPE, Anthony. *Rachel Ray.* 2 vols., tan cloth. London, 1863. First edition. $100-$125.

TROLLOPE, Anthony. *Ralph the Heir.* Illustrated. 19 parts, wrappers. London, 1870. First edition. $3,000 (A, 1971). London, 1871. Partly illustrated. One-volume edition in cloth. $35-$50. London, 1871. 3 vols., cloth. $84.

TROLLOPE, Anthony. *Sir Harry Hotspur of Humblethwaite.* Scarlet-orange cloth. London, 1871. First book edition, with pages 201 and 318 perfectly paged and with small capitals at base of spine. $150-$200. New York, 1871. Plum-colored cloth. First American edition. $150-$200.

TROLLOPE, Anthony. *The Small House at Allington.* Illustrated by Millais. 2 vols., cloth. London, 1864. First book edition, first issue, with "hobbledehoya" on page 33. $100-$150.

TROLLOPE, Anthony. *South Africa.* Folding map in color. 2 vols., cloth. London, 1878. First edition. $150.

TROLLOPE, Anthony. *The Struggles of Brown, Jones, and Robinson.* Wrappers. New York, 1862. First edition. $200-$400. London, 1870. Illustrated. Brown cloth. First English and first illustrated edition. $200.

TROLLOPE, Anthony. *Tales of All Countries.* (First and Second series.) 2 vols., brown cloth. London, 1861 and 1863. First editions. $100-$150. (Individual volumes, $50-$75.)

TROLLOPE, Anthony. *Thompson Hall.* Illustrated. Pictorial boards. London, 1885. First English book edition. $75-$100.

TROLLOPE, Anthony. *The Three Clerks.* 3 vols., boards, blue cloth spine, labels. London, 1858. First edition. $200-$300. New York, 1860. Plum colored cloth. First American edition. $100-$150. Also, $100 (A, 1971).

TROLLOPE, Anthony. *Travelling Sketches.* Cloth. London, 1866. First edition. $75-$100.

TROLLOPE, Anthony. *The Vicar of Bulhampton.* Illustrated. 11 parts, decorated wrappers. London, 1870 (and 1869). First edition. $250-$300. London, 1870. Cloth. First book edition. $100-$125.

TROLLOPE, Anthony. *The Warden.* Brown cloth. London, 1855. First edition, first binding, with 24 pages of ads dated September, 1854. $500-$600.

TROLLOPE, Anthony. *The Way We Live Now.* Illustrated. 20 parts, pictorial wrappers. London, 1875 (and 1874). First edition. $150-$250. London, 1875. 2 vols., green cloth. First book edition. $100-$150.

TROLLOPE, Anthony. *Why Frau Frohmann Raised Her Prices, and Other Stories.* 2 vols., cloth. London, 1882. First edition. $75-$100.

TROLLOPE, Frances. See *Domestic Manners of the Americans.*

TROLLOPE, Frances. *Uncle Walter.* 3 vols., boards and cloth, paper labels. London, 1852. First edition. $75.

TROLLOPE, Frances. *The Vicar of Wrexhill.* 3 vols., boards, paper labels. London, 1837. First edition. $100-$150.

TROWBRIDGE, John Townsend. See Creyton, Paul.

TROWBRIDGE, John Townsend. *Cudjo's Cave.* Pictorial half title. Cloth. Boston, 1864. First edition, first printing, listing the "L'Envoy" as beginning on page 503 (later, page 501). $125-$150.

TROWBRIDGE, John Townsend. *Jack Hazard and His Fortunes.* Cloth. Boston, 1871. First edition. $50.

TROWBRIDGE, John Townsend. *The South: A Tour of Its Battlefields and Ruined Cities.* Cloth. Hartford, Conn., 1866. First edition. $35-$50.

TRUETT, Velma Stevens. *On the Hoof in Nevada.* Portraits, other illustrations. Oblong pictorial buckram. Los Angeles, 1950. First edition. $50-$60.

TRUMAN, Maj. Ben. C. *Life, Adventures and Capture of Tiburcio Vasquez, the Great California Bandit and Murderer.* Frontispiece map. 44 pp., pictorial wrappers. Los Angeles, 1874. First edition. $300-$400. Los Angeles, 1941. Cloth and leather. One of 100. $35-$50.

TRUMAN, Harry S. *Mr. Citizen.* Cloth. No place, no date (New York, 1960). First edition. One of 1,000 signed. Boxed. $35.

TRUMBO, Dalton. *Johnny Got His Gun.* Yellow cloth. Philadelphia, no date (1939). First edition. In dust jacket. $50-$75.

TUCKER, E. *History of Randolph County, Indiana.* Half leather and cloth. Chicago, 1882. First edition. $50-$75.

TUCKER, H. S. G. *Introductory Lecture Delivered by the Professor of Law in the University of Virginia, at the Opening of the Law School.* 24 pp., half leather. Charlottesville, Va., 1841. First edition. $35.

TUCKER, Dr. Joseph C. *To the Golden Goal, and Other Sketches.* Cloth. San Francisco, 1895. First edition. One of 50. $100-$125.

TUER, Andrew W. *History of the Horn-Book.* With 7 facsimile hornbooks in pockets. 2 vols., vellum. London, 1896. First edition. $350-$500. London, 1897. 2 vols., brown buckram. With 3 facsimile hornbooks. $150-$200.

TUER, Andrew. *Pages and Pictures from Forgotten Children's Books.* Illustrated. Cloth. London, 1898-99. $35-$50.

TUFTS, James. *A Tract Descriptive of Montana Territory.* Map. 15 pp., folded sheets. New York, 1865. First edition. One of 24 on fine paper. $150-$200. Another issue: Sewed. $100. Also, bound in morocco, $75.

TULLIDGE, Edward W. *The History of Salt Lake City and Its Founders.* 33 plates. Half morocco. Salt Lake City, no date (about 1886). $25. (Note: The first edition, with three plates, was published 1883-84, according to Howes.)

TURNER, Mary Honeyman Ten Eyck. *These High Plains.* Portrait and plates. Cloth, pictorial label. Amarillo, Tex., 1941. First edition. One of 150. $50.

TURNER, Orsamus. *History of the Pioneer Settlement of Phelps and Gorham's Purchase.* Boards and leather. Rochester, N. Y., 1851. First edition. $35-$50.

TURNER, T. G. *Gazetteer of the St. Joseph Valley.* Frontispiece and plate. Cloth. Chicago, 1867. First edition. $35-$50.

TURNER, T. G. *Turner's Guide from the Lakes to the Rocky Mountains.* Cloth. Chicago, 1868. First edition. $35-$50.

TURNLEY, Parmenas T. *Reminiscences of Parmenas T. Turnley, from the Cradle to Three-Score and Ten.* 6 plates. Cloth. Chicago, no date (1892). First edition. $90-$125.

TURRILL, H. B. *Historical Reminiscences of the City of Des Moines.* Double-page frontispiece plate and 7 other plates. 144 pp., printed dark-blue wrappers. Des Moines, 1857. First edition. $75-$100.

TUTTLE, C. R. *History of Grand Rapids.* Cloth. Grand Rapids, Mich., 1874. First edition. $50.

TWAIN, Mark. See Harte, Bret, and Twain, Mark. Also see *Date 1601; What is Man?*

TWAIN, Mark. *Adventures of Huckleberry Finn.* Illustrated. Pictorial red cloth. London, 1884. (By Samuel Langhorne Clemens.) First edition (preceding the American first). $75-$150. New York, 1885. Green or blue cloth (or various leathers), green cloth being most common. First American edition, first issue, with "was" for "saw" in line 23, page 57; with "Him and another man" given in list of illustrations as being on page 88, and with page 283 on a stub. Blue cloth: $1,000-$1,500. Also, blue cloth, $1,500 (A, 1960). (Note: This copy was called "perhaps the finest copy known." Another, in blue, brought $750 at auction in 1963. Another, with page 283 not on a stub, brought $325 at auction in 1964.) Green cloth: $500 and up. Average copies in the green or blue binding sell in the $150-$300 range at retail, with defective copies bringing less. (The prospectus for this work, with samples of text and binding, sells in the $150-$250 range.)

TWAIN, Mark. *The Adventures of Tom Sawyer.* Illustrated. Red cloth. London, 1876. (By Samuel Langhorne Clemens.) First edition (preceding the American first). $150 and up. Worn, $56 (A, 1965). Toronto, 1876. Illustrated. Decorated plum-colored cloth. First Canadian edition (also preceding the American). $150 and up. Hartford, Conn., 1876. Illustrated. Blue cloth (or various leathers). First American edition, first issue, printed on calendared paper, with versos of half title and preface blank. Up to $2,000. Auction prices, cloth copies, 1960-70: $1,500 (1960); $200 (worn, 1960); $1,400 (1962); $425 (1968). Publisher's leather, $450 (A, 1971)—for a copy inscribed as a first edition by the publisher. Second issue, lacking the two blank pages. Cloth. $150-$200. Also, worn, $80 (A, 1971). New York, 1939. Limited Editions Club. Cloth. Boxed. $30-$40.

TWAIN, Mark. *Be Good, Be Good: A Poem.* (Cover title.) 4 pp., French-folded, printed in green. New York, 1931. First edition. (By Samuel Langhorne Clemens.) $100-$150. (Also, 10 or 12 were printed in blue on vellum.)

TWAIN, Mark. *The Celebrated Jumping Frog of Calaveras County, and Other Sketches.* Edited by John Paul. Cloth, various colors. New York, 1867. (By Samuel Langhorne Clemens.) First edition, first issue, with perfect "i" in "this" in last line on page 198 and with page of yellow tinted ads preceding title page. $1,000-$1,500. (Note: The latter price, the highest I have noted, was for a copy with the gold-stamped frog in a vertical position, head pointing up, in the center of the front cover.) Second issue, with type in "this" on page 198 broken or worn, no ad leaf present. $50-$75. Author's first book.

TWAIN, Mark. *Christian Science.* Illustrated. Red cloth. New York, 1907. (By Samuel Langhorne Clemens.) First edition, first issue, with perfect "W" in "Why," line 14 on page 5. $35-$50.

TWAIN, Mark. *Concerning Cats: Two Tales.* Boards and cloth. San Francisco, 1959. (By Samuel Langhorne Clemens.) Grabhorn Press. One of 450. $35-$50.

TWAIN, Mark. *A Connecticut Yankee in King Arthur's Court.* Illustrated. Green cloth (or various leathers). New York, 1889. (By Samuel Langhorne Clemens.) First edition. $75-$100. New York, 1949. Limited Editions Club. Boards and cloth. Boxed. $35-$50.

TWAIN, Mark. *A Curious Dream.* Pictorial yellow boards. London, no date (1872). (By Samuel Langhorne Clemens.) First edition, first printing, with end paper blank. $50.

TWAIN, Mark. *The Curious Republic of Gondour.* Boards. New York, 1919. (By Samuel Langhorne Clemens.) First edition. $25.

TWAIN, Mark. *A Double-Barrelled Detective Story.* Illustrated by Lucius Hitchcock. Red cloth. New York, 1902. (By Samuel Langhorne Clemens.) First edition. $50.

TWAIN, Mark. *Eve's Diary.* Red cloth. New York, 1906. (By Samuel Langhorne Clemens.) First edition. $25.

TWAIN, Mark. *Extracts from Adam's Diary.* Red cloth. New York, 1904. (By Samuel Langhorne Clemens.) First edition. $25.

TWAIN, Mark. *Eye Openers.* Light yellow pictorial wrappers or cloth. London, no date (1871). (By Samuel Langhorne Clemens.) J. C. Hotten, publisher. First edition, with ads at end dated 1871. Wrappers: $100-$150. (Cloth copies less scarce.) London, no date ("after 1875"). Ward, Lock & Co., publishers. Cloth. $25.

TWAIN, Mark. *Following the Equator.* Illustrated. Blue cloth (or various leathers). Hartford, Conn., 1897. (By Samuel Langhorne Clemens.) First edition, first issue, with Hartford imprint only (New York added later). $50-$150.

TWAIN, Mark. *A Horse's Tale.* Red cloth. New York, 1907. (By Samuel Langhorne Clemens.) First edition. $25. London, 1907. Red cloth. First English edition. $15.

TWAIN, Mark. *The Innocents Abroad or, The New Pilgrim's Progress.* Black cloth (or various leathers). Hartford, 1869. (By Samuel Langhorne Clemens.) First edition, first issue, without page references on page xvii and xviii and lacking illustration on page 129. Cloth, $100-$150. Also, $90 (A, 1970). Leather copies bring less. Hartford, 1876. Illustrated. Decorated cloth. $150-$200.

TWAIN, Mark. *Letters from the Sandwich Islands.* Edited by G. Ezra Dane. Colored illustrations. Half cloth. San Francisco, 1937. (By Samuel Langhorne Clemens.) First edition. Grabhorn Press. One of 500. $75-$100.

TWAIN, Mark. *Life on the Mississippi.* Illustrated. Pictorial red cloth. London, 1883. (By Samuel Langhorne Clemens.) First edition. $75-$125. Also, $43.20 and $45 (A, 1968). Boston, 1883. Brown cloth (or various leathers.) First American edition, first issue, with drawing of author in flames on page 441 and with caption on page 443 reading "The St. Louis Hotel." $100-$200. Later, with the reading "St. Charles Hotel," $50-$75.

TWAIN, Mark. *The Love Letters of Mark Twain.* Edited by Dixon Wecter. Buckram. New York, 1949. First edition. One of 155 (signed as Clemens and Twain on limitation page). In dust jacket. Boxed. $300-$350.

TWAIN, Mark. *The Man That Corrupted Hadleyburg and Other Stories and Essays.* Illustrated. Red cloth. New York, 1900. (By Samuel Langhorne Clemens.) First edition, first state, with line reading "Page 2" on plate opposite page 2. $50-$75. Later, without "Page 2," $15-$20.

TWAIN, Mark. *Mark Twain's (Burlesque) Autobiography and First Romance.* Cloth or printed self-wrappers (with cover title). New York, no date (1871). (By Samuel Langhorne Clemens.) First edition, first issue, without Ball, Black & Co. ad on verso of title page. Wrappers: $50. Also, $25 (A, 1965). Cloth: $35-$50.

TWAIN, Mark. *Mark Twain's Sketches, New and Old.* Illustrated. Blue cloth (or various leathers). Hartford, 1875. (By Samuel Langhorne Clemens.) First collected edition, first state, with paragraph "From *Hospital Days*" at page 299 and (in some copies) erratum slip at that page. $150. Second issue, "From *Hospital Days*" not present. $10-$15.

TWAIN, Mark. *The £1,000,000 Bank-Note and Other New Stories.* Frontispiece. Pictorial tan cloth. New York, 1893. (By Samuel Langhorne Clemens.) First edition. $40-$60.

TWAIN, Mark. *A Murder, A Mystery, and A Marriage.* Printed gray wrappers. No place (New York), 1945. (By Samuel Langhorne Clemens.) First edition. One of 16. $300 and up.

TWAIN, Mark. *The Mysterious Stranger: A Romance.* Illustrated. Black cloth, with color illustration pasted on front cover. New York, no date (1916). (By Samuel Langhorne Clemens.) First edition, with "Published October, 1916" on copyright page and code letters "K-Q." $50-$60.

TWAIN, Mark. *Number One: Mark Twain's Sketches. Authorized Edition.* Illustrated. 32 pp., pictorial pale-blue or green wrappers. New York, no date (1874). (By Samuel Langhorne Clemens.) First edition, first state, with back cover blank. $125-$150. Wrappers frayed, loose, $100. (Second issue has Aetna Life ad on back.)

TWAIN, Mark. *Old Times on the Mississippi.* Gray wrappers. Toronto, 1876. (By Samuel Langhorne Clemens.) First edition, first issue, in wrappers (later, cloth). $100-$150. Cloth: $50.

TWAIN, Mark. *The Pains of Lowly Life.* (Cover title.) 8 pp., printed red or green wrappers (title in blue). No place (London), 1900. (By Samuel Langhorne Clemens.) First edition. $250-$300.

TWAIN, Mark (so designated on binding, but not on title page). *Personal Recollections of Joan of Arc.* Red buckram. New York, 1896. (By Samuel Langhorne Clemens.) First edition, first state, with ads listing third and fourth volumes of *Memoirs of Barras* as "just ready." $75-$100. London, 1896. Red cloth. First English edition, with Twain's name on title page. Issued simultaneously with American edition. $50-$75.

TWAIN, Mark. *The Prince and the Pauper.* Illustrated. Pictorial red cloth. London, 1881. (By Samuel Langhorne Clemens.) First edition, first issue, with ads dated November. $75-$100. Spine faded, some internal spotting, $45. Also, $33.60 (A, 1968). Montreal, 1881. Blue cloth. First (?) edition. (Blanck says, "Probably simultaneous with the London edition.") $50-$100. Boston, 1882. Green cloth (or various leathers). First American edition, first issue, with Franklin Press imprint on copyright page. $150-$250. Worn, $50 and up. Publisher's half morocco, $70 (A, 1969). (Note: This complicated book also exists in its American first edition in an issue of "6 or 8" copies—Twain was uncertain when he signed a copy for the New York Public Library on China paper, with white linen binding. Value: $600 and up? There was also supposed to be, Twain indicated, a Montreal issue in wrappers, but Blanck has not seen one. Value: $1,000 and up? Prospectuses for the American first edition, with samples of text and binding styles, are worth $25 and up.) New York, 1964. Limited Editions Club. Boxed. $50-$75.

TWAIN, Mark. *Pudd'nhead Wilson: A Tale.* Illustrated. Red cloth. London, 1894. (By Samuel Langhorne Clemens.) First English edition (of *The Tragedy of Pudd'nhead Wilson,* which see). $25-$35.

TWAIN, Mark. *Pudd'nhead Wilson's Calendar for 1894.* (Cover title.) 16 pp. (3 x 2½ inches), printed wrappers. No place, no date (Dawson's Landing, Mo., *i.e.,* New York, 1893). (By Samuel Langhorne Clemens.) First edition. $250-$450.

TWAIN, Mark. *Punch, Brothers, Punch!* Pictorial wrappers, or cloth. New York, no date (1878). (By Samuel Langhorne Clemens.) First edition, first issue, with Twain's name in Roman capitals on title page. Wrappers: $50-$100. Cloth: $60-$80.

TWAIN, Mark. *Queen Victoria's Jubilee.* Illustrated. Printed white boards. No place, no date (probably New York, 1910). (By Samuel Langhorne Clemens.) First edition. One of 195. $50-$75.

TWAIN, Mark. *Roughing It.* Illustrated. Black cloth (or various leathers). Hartford, 1872. (By Samuel Langhorne Clemens.) First American edition, first issue, with no words missing in lines 20 and 21 of page 242. $100-$150. Later issue, words missing on page 242. $40.

TWAIN, Mark. *To the Person Sitting in Darkness.* (Cover title.) 16 pp., self-wrappers. No place, no date (New York, 1901). (By Samuel Langhorne Clemens.) First edition. $50-$100.

TWAIN, Mark (editor). *Tom Sawyer Abroad.* By Huck Finn. Edited by Mark Twain. Illustrated. Tan cloth. New York, 1894. (By Samuel Langhorne Clemens.) First American edition. $150-$200. (Note: The English first edition of the same year, red cloth, preceded the American first but is worth much less—$15-$25).

TWAIN, Mark. *Tom Sawyer Abroad, Tom Sawyer, Detective, and Other Stories.* Illustrated by Dan Beard. Red cloth. New York, 1896. (By Samuel Langhorne Clemens.) First edition. $75-$100.

TWAIN, Mark. *The Tragedy of Pudd'nhead Wilson.* Illustrated. Brown cloth (or leather). Hartford, 1894. (By Samuel Langhorne Clemens.) First American edition. $200-$225. Also, $100 (A, 1970). (For English first edition, see Twain, *Pudd'nhead Wilson.*).

TWAIN, Mark. *A Tramp Abroad.* Illustrated. Black cloth (or various leathers). Hartford, 1880. (By Samuel Langhorne Clemens.) First edition, first state, with frontispiece entitled "Moses," not "Titian's Moses." $50-$75.

TWAIN, Mark. *A True Story.* Illustrated. Green or terra-cotta cloth. Boston, 1877. (By Samuel Langhorne Clemens.) First edition, first binding, with J R O monogram on front cover. $350-$400. Worn, $300. (Later issues have monogram H O.)

TWAIN, Mark. *What Is Man?* Cloth. London, 1910. (By Samuel Langhorne Clemens.) First English edition. $50. (For first edition, see title entry.)

TWAIN, Mark, and Warner, Charles Dudley. *The Gilded Age.* Illustrated. Black cloth (or various leathers). Hartford, 1873. (By Samuel Langhorne Clemens and Warner.) First edition, first issue, without an illustration on page 403. $300-$350. Later state, illustration on page 403. $100-$150.

TWEEDIE, William. *The Arabian Horse: His Country and People.* 10 color plates, 25 text illustrations, maps and tables. Green decorated cloth. London, 1894. $100-$150. Large paper issue: Half morocco. One of 100. $200-$250.

TWENTY Poems. White buckram. London, 1909. First edition. One of 25. $100. (Note: Supposedly contains four poems by George Meredith.)

TWIN Cities Directory and Business Mirror for the Year 1860, Including the Cities of Davenport, Iowa; Rock Island, Ill., and Moline, Ill. Vol. 1. Cloth. Davenport, 1859. (E. Coy & Co., publisher.) $100.

TWINING, Elizabeth. *Illustrations of the Natural Order of Plants, Arranged in Groups.* 160 colored lithograph plates. 2 vols., tall folio, half morocco. London, 1849. $3,500.

TWITCHELL, Ralph Emerson. *Old Santa Fe.* Illustrated. Cloth. No place, no date (Santa Fe, N.M., 1925). First edition. $35-$50.

TWO Admirals (The): A Tale. By the Author of "The Pilot." 2 vols., purple muslin, paper labels. Philadelphia, 1842. (By James Fenimore Cooper.) First American edition. $150-$200. Also, spine of Vol. 1 worn at top, $40 (A, 1970); covers spotted, $25 (A, 1968). London, 1842. 3 vols., boards and cloth, paper labels. First edition. (Issued under Cooper's name.) $75-$150.

TWO Generals (The). 8 pp., printed on a single sheet, unbound. No place, no date (1868?). (By Edward FitzGerald.) First edition. $50.

TWO Rivulets. See Whitman, Walt.

TWO Years Before the Mast. A Personal Narrative of Life at Sea. (Harpers' Family Library No. CVI.) Tan, black, or gray cloth. New York, 1840. (By Richard Henry Dana, Jr.) First edition, first issue, with perfect "i" in the word "in," first line of copyright notice. $1,000-$1,500. Fine copies at auction: $850 (1968), $800 (1965), $750 (1960). A previously unrecorded copy in brown cloth with calf spine was offered by an American dealer at $1,200 a few years ago. Second issue. $100 and up. Boston, 1869. Cloth. Revised edition. $25. Boston, 1911. Illustrated. 2 vols., boards. $100-$150. Chicago, 1930. Illustrated by Edward A. Wilson. Pictorial linen. One of 1,000. Boxed. $35-$50. New York, 1936. Grabhorn printing. Illustrated. Boards. One of 1,000. In dust jacket. $50-$60. New York, 1947. Limited Editions Club. Cloth. Boxed. $30-$40.

TYLER, Daniel. *A Concise History of the Mormon Battalion in the Mexican War.* Full leather. No place (Salt Lake City), 1881 (actually 1882). First edition. $150-$200.

TYLER, Parker (editor). *Modern Things.* Purple and white cloth. New York, no date (1934). First edition. $50.

TYNAN, Katherine. *Twenty One Poems.* Selected by W. B. Yeats. Blue boards and linen. Dundrum, Ireland, 1907. Dun Emer Press. One of 200. $45-$85.

TYNDALE, William (translator). *The Boke off the Revelacion off Sanct Jhon the Devine, Done into Englysshe.* Vellum. London, 1901. Ashendene Press. One of 54. $400-$500.

TYPES of Successful Men in Texas. Red leather. Austin, Tex., 1890. $50-$75.

TYSON, James L., M.D. *Diary of a Physician in California.* 92 pp., printed wrappers. New York, 1850. First edition. $150-$250. Oakland, Calif., 1955. One of 500. $15-$25.

TYSON, Philip T. *Geology and Industrial Resources of California.* Folding maps, charts, tables. Cloth. Baltimore, 1851. $50-$60.

TYSON, Robert A. *History of East St. Louis.* Folding map and folding view of stockyards. 152 pp., wrappers. East St. Louis, Mo., 1875. First edition. $100-$150.

U

UDELL, John. *Incidents of Travel to California, Across the Great Plains.* Portrait, errata leaf. Cloth. Jefferson, Ohio, 1856. First edition. $150-$250.

UDELL, John. *Journal of John Udell, Kept During a Trip Across the Plains.* Vignette portrait. 47 pp., printed wrappers. Jefferson, 1868. Second edition. Up to $1,000, possibly more. Also, $850 (A, 1968). Los Angeles, 1946. Edited by Lyle H. Wright. Half morocco. One of 35 signed by Wright. $35-$50. Another issue: Cloth. One of 750. $20-$25. (Note: The first edition of Udell's *Journal*, 45 pp., printed wrappers, including cover title, appeared in Suisun City, Calif., in 1859 and is known in only one surviving copy. The following facsimile was published by Yale University in 1952.) No place, no date (New Haven, Conn., 1952). Printed wrappers. One of 200. $35-$50.

ÚLTIMAS Communicaciones entre el Gobierno Mexicano y el Enviado Estraordinario y Ministro Plenipotenciario nombrado por el de los Estados Unidos, sobre la Cuestión de Tejas, etc. 22 pp., printed wrappers. Mexico, 1846. $150 and up.

UNCLE Abe's Republican Songster. Wrappers. San Francisco, 1860. $30.

UNDER the Greenwood Tree. 2 vols., green cloth. London, 1872. (By Thomas Hardy.) First edition. $250-$300.

UNIFORM and Dress of the Army of the Confederate States. 15 plates by Ernest Crehen. 5 pp., boards, paper label. Richmond, Va., 1861. First edition, first issue, with black-and-white plates. $250-$350. Second issue, same date, with 9 of the 15 plates in color, plus errata slip and tipped-in colored strip illustrating field caps. $1,000-$1,500.

UNITED States Enrollment Laws (The), for Calling Out the National Forces. Wrappers. New York, 1864. $25-$30.

UNITED States "History" as the Yankee Makes and Takes It. By a Confederate Soldier. 99 pp., yellow wrappers. Glen Allen, 1900. (By John Cussons.) $35-$50.

UNJUST Judge (The). By a Member of the Ohio Bar. Cloth. Mansfield, Ohio, 1854. (By William Stevens.) First edition. $30.

UPDIKE, John. *Bath After Sailing.* Wrappers, paper label. No place, no date (Monroe, Conn., 1968). First edition. One of 125 signed. $35.

UPDIKE, John. *The Carpentered Hen and Other Tame Creatures.* Cloth. New York, no date (1958). First edition. In dust jacket. $35-$50. Author's first book (poems).

UPDIKE, John. *Couples.* Wrappers. Paris, no date (1969). First French translation. One of 21 on velin. $35.

UPDIKE, John. *Dog's Death.* Broadside poem. No place (Cambridge, Mass.), 1965. First edition. One of 100 signed. $30-$40.

UPDIKE, John. *The Poorhouse Fair.* Boards and cloth. New York, 1959. First edition. In dust jacket. $25-$35. Author's first novel.

UPDIKE, John. *Rabbit, Run.* Boards and cloth. New York, 1960. First edition. In dust jacket. $25-$35.

UPDIKE, John. *Three Texts from Early Ipswich.* Wrappers. Ipswich, Mass., 1968. First edition. One of 50 signed. $65 and $50. Trade edition: $25.

UPHAM, Samuel C. *Notes from Sunland, on the Manatee River, Gulf Coast of South Florida.* Frontispiece. 83 pp., printed wrappers. Braidentown, Fla., 1881. First edition. $100-$125. Second edition (so stated), same date. $75.

UPS and Downs: A Book of Transformation Pictures. Illustrated in color. 16 pp., with pull slides to change pictures (a movable book). Boards. London, no date (about 1890). $45.

URREA, José. *Diario de las Operaciones Militares de la División que al Mando del Gen. José Urrea Hizo la Campana de Tejas.* Half leather. Victoria, Mexico, 1838. First edition. $750-$1,000. Also, $800 (A, 1966)—the Streeter copy. (Note: The last copy previously noted was in full calf and was catalogued by a New York dealer in the 1950's at $450.)

V

V., B. (for Bysshe Vanolis). *The City of Dreadful Night.* Cloth. London, 1880. (By James Thomson.) First edition. One of 40 on large paper. $200-$250. Ordinary issue: $50-$60.

V., B. *Vane's Story, Weddah, etc.* Cloth. London, 1881. (By James Thomson.) First edition. $25-$35.

VAGABOND (The): A New Story for Children. 16 pp., wrappers. Hartford, Conn., 1819. (By Samuel Griswold Goodrich.) First edition. $100-$150.

VAIL, Alfred. *Description of the American Electro Magnetic Telegraph.* 14 wood engravings. 24 pp., unbound. Washington, 1845. First edition. $35-$50.

VAIL, Isaac Newton. *Alaska: Land of the Nugget. Why?* 68 pp., wrappers. Pasadena, Calif., 1897. $35-$50.

VAIL, Isaac Newton. *Ophir's Golden Wedge.* 36 pp., wrappers. Pasadena, 1893. $35-$50.

VALENTIA, George, Viscount. *Voyages and Travels to India, Ceylon, the Red Sea, Abyssinia, and Egypt, 1802-6.* 69 engraved views and folding maps. 3 vols., boards. London, 1809. First edition. Large paper issue. $200.

VALENTINER, Wilhelm R. *Jacques Louis David and the French Revolution.* Illustrated. New York, 1929. One of 160. In dust jacket. Boxed. $25.

VALENTINER, Wilhelm R. *Rembrandt Paintings in America.* 175 plates. Half morocco. New York, 1931. First edition. $20-$25. Limited issue: Full morocco. One of 200 signed. $35-$50.

VALERY, Paul. *Eupalinos, or The Architect.* Translated by William M. Stewart. Buckram. London, 1932. One of 250 signed. $50.

VALERY, Paul. *Introduction to the Method of Leonardo Da Vinci.* Translated by Thomas McGreevey. Boards. London, 1929. One of 50. $60-$75. Binding worn, $50.

VALPERGA: Or, the Life and Adventures of Castruccio, Prince of Lucca. 3 vols., blue-gray boards. London, 1823. (By Mary Wollstonecraft Shelley.) First edition, without half titles. $150 and up.

VAN CLEVE, Mrs. Charlotte O. C. *"Three Score Years and Ten"; Life-Long Memories of Fort Snelling, Minn., and Other Parts of the West.* Portrait. Cloth. No place (Minneapolis), 1888. First edition. $35-$50.

VANDERBILT, William K. *Taking One's Own Ship Around the World.* 19 color plates, 112 photographs. Half (or full) morocco. New York, 1929. One of 200 (500?). Boxed. $65. (Note: *American Book-Prices Current* reports on this book and the one following appear to be thoroughly confused.)

VANDERBILT, William K. *To Galapagos on the Ara.* No place, no date (New York, 1926). Boards and leather. One of 900. $35-$50. Another issue, 1927: Boards and calf. One of 500. $100.

VANDERBILT, William K. *West Made East with the Loss of a Day.* 7 color plates, 13 charts. New York, 1933. One of 800. $50-$75.

VAN DE WATER, Frederic F. *Glory Hunter: A Life of Gen. Custer.* 2 maps, 13 plates. Cloth. Indianapolis, no date (1934). First edition. In dust jacket. $37.50-$50.

VAN DYKE, Henry (editor). *A Book of Princeton Verse II 1919.* Light-green cloth, top edges gilt. Princeton, no date (1919). First edition. $30-$40. (Note: Contains three poems by F. Scott Fitzgerald.)

VAN DYKE, T. S. *The Advantages of the Colony of El Cajon, San Diego County, and the Superiority of Its Fruit Lands.* Large folding map. 32 pp., wrappers. San Diego, Calif., 1883. $50-$75.

VAN LOON, Hendrik Willem. *The Story of Mankind.* Illustrated by the author. Cloth, pictorial label. No place (New York), 1921. First edition. In dust jacket. $75.

VAN TRAMP, John C. *Prairie and Rocky Mountain Adventures.* 61 plates. Leather. Columbus, Ohio, 1858. First edition. $75-$100. Columbus, 1867. Leather. $35. Columbus, 1870. Leather. $35.

VAN VECHTEN, Carl. *Firecrackers: A Realistic Novel.* Boards and cloth. New York, 1925. First edition. One of 205 signed. Boxed. $65.

VAN VECHTEN, Carl. *Music After the Great War.* Cloth, paper label. New York, 1915. First edition. In dust jacket. $45-$60. Author's first book.

VAN VECHTEN, Carl. *Nigger Heaven.* Boards, printed spine label. New York, 1926. First edition. One of 205 signed. Boxed. $75.

VAN VECHTEN, Carl. *Parties.* Lemon-yellow vellum, silver decorations. New York, 1930. One of 250 signed. In dust jacket. $55. Trade edition: Yellow cloth. In dust jacket. $10-$12.50.

VAN VECHTEN, Carl. *Spider Boy: A Scenario for a Moving Picture.* Half cloth. New York, 1928. First edition. One of 220. Boxed. $100. Margins of two pages torn, not affecting text, $75. Another issue: Red vellum. One of 75 on vellum. Boxed. $100-$150.

VAN VECHTEN, Carl. *The Tattooed Countess.* Boards and cloth. New York, 1924. First edition. One of 150 signed. Boxed. $40. Trade edition: Cloth. In dust jacket. $10.

VAN VECHTEN, Carl. *The Tiger in the House.* Half cloth. New York, 1920. First edition. In dust jacket. $25-$35.

VAN VLIET, Gen. S. *Table of Distances in the Department of the Missouri.* 3 folding maps, folding table. 20 pp., wrappers. Washington, 1874. $75.

VAN VOGT, A. E. *Slan: A Story of the Future.* Cloth. Sauk City, Wis., 1946. Arkham House. First edition. In dust jacket. $35-$50.

VAN WYCK, Frederick. *Keskachauge, or the First White Settlement on Long Island.* 6 maps, 55 plates. Cloth. New York, 1924. First edition. $35.

VAN ZANDT, Nicholas Biddle. *A Full Description of the Soil, Water, Timber, and Prairies of Each Lot, or Quarter Section of the Military Lands Between the Mississippi and Illinois River.* 127 pp., plus separately issued folding map. Boards and calf. Washington City, 1818. First edition. $1,500-$2,000. Also, $1,900 (A, 1967).

VARTHEMA, Ludovico de. *Itinerary in Southern Asia.* Maps, illustrations. Half vellum. London, 1928. Limited edition. $50-$75.

VAUGHAN, Dr. John. *A Concise History of the Autumnal Fever, Which Prevailed in the Borough of Wilmington, in the Year 1802.* 32 pp., wrappers. Wilmington, Del., 1803. First edition. $60-$100.

VAUGHN, Robert. *Then and Now, or 36 Years in the Rockies.* Illustrated. Pictorial cloth. Minneapolis, 1900. First edition. $75-$100.

VEBLEN, Thorstein. *The Theory of the Leisure Class.* Green cloth. New York, 1899. First edition. $35-$50.

VEGA CARPIO, Lope Félix de (attributed to). *The Star of Seville.* Translated by Henry Thomas. Full black morocco. Newtown, Wales, 1935. Gregynog Press. One of 175. $100-$200. (Note: A few special bindings recorded: Morocco, designed by B. Hughes-Stanton and bound by George Fisher, with a 1967 auction record of $288; another, maroon morocco, star in gilt and blind, inlaid with white and orange morocco, $210 in a London dealer's catalogue.

VELASCO, José Francisco. *Sonora: Its Extent, Population, Natural Productions, Indian Tribes, Mines, Mineral Lands, etc.* Translated by William F. Nye. Cloth. San Francisco, 1861. First American edition. $35-$50.

VENABLE, W. H. *Beginnings of Literary Culture in the Ohio Valley.* Cloth. Cincinnati, 1891. First edition. $35-$50.

VERGA, Giovanni. *Mastro—don Gesualdo.* Translated by D. H. Lawrence. Cloth. New York, 1923. First edition. In dust jacket. $25. London, 1925. Cloth. First English edition. In dust jacket. $12.

VERHAEREN, Émile. *Belle Chair: Onze Poèmes.* 12 lithographs and 3 wood engravings by Aristide Maillol. Printed wrappers. Paris, 1931. One of 50 on Montval paper (of an edition of 225). First edition of the text. $500.

VERINO, Ugolino. *Vita di Santa Chiara Vergine.* Printed in black and red. 4 facsimile pages. Limp vellum. London, 1921. Ashendene Press. One of 236. $150-$200.

VERNE, Jules. *Mistress Branican.* Illustrated, including 2 maps and 12 colored engravings. Pictorial red cloth. Paris, no date. First edition. $75.

VERSES from the Harvard Advocate. Cloth. Cambridge, Mass., 1906. First edition. $25. (Note: Contains five poems by Wallace Stevens.)

VERSES on Various Occasions. Cloth. London, 1868. (By John Henry Cardinal Newman.) First edition. $75-$100.

VESPUCCI, Amerigo. *Letter of Amerigo Vespucci Describing His Four Voyages to the New World.* Map in color, illustrations by Valenti Angelo. Vellum. San Francisco, 1926. One of 250. Boxed. $125.

VICENTINO, Ludovico. *The Calligraphic Models of Ludovico degli Arrighi, Surnamed Vicentino.* Edited by Stanley Morrison. 64 pp., facsimile. Montagnola (Paris), 1926. One of 300. $100. Also, $57.60 (A, 1968).

VIDAL, Gore. *Williwaw.* Cloth. New York, 1946. First edition. In dust jacket. $40-$50. Author's first book.

VILLAGRA, Gaspar Pérez de. *History of New Mexico.* Translated by Gilberto Espinosa. Boards. Los Angeles, 1933. One of 665 (650?). $55.

VILLON, François. *The Complete Works of François Villon.* 2 vols., cloth. New York, 1928. One of 960. $35-$50.

VINDICATION of the Recent and Prevailing Policy of Georgia in Its Internal Affairs, etc. (A). 90 pp., wrappers (?). Athens, Ga., 1827. (By Augustin S. Clayton.) First edition. $100-$150.

VINTON, John Adams. *The Vinton Memorial.* Cloth. Boston, 1858. $35-$50.

VIRGIL. *Les Georgiques.* In Latin and French. 122 woodcuts by Aristide Maillol. 2 vols., loose sheets, printed wrappers, in 2 slipcases, plus matching case with 2 extra sets of the woodcuts. Paris, 1937-50. One of 750. $750-$1,000. Also, $700 (A, 1969).

VIRGINIA Illustrated. Cloth. New York, 1857. (By David Hunter Strother.) First edition. $75-$100.

VISCHER, Edward. *Sketches of the Washoe Mining Region.* Cloth portfolio with 29 mounted plates (25 numbered) and 24 pp. of text, wrappers. San Francisco, 1862. First edition. $850-$1,250. Also, $1,100 (A, 1968)–the Streeter copy (catalogued "24 pp., 24 plates"). (Note: Another copy was offered in a Boston dealer's catalogue in 1957 as with 25 numbered plates and four other mounted plates at $850. Howes' *U.S.-iana* calls for 26 plates.)

VISIT to Texas (A). Folding map in color, 4 plates. Cloth. New York, 1834. (Attributed to Col. W. W. Morris and Dr. M. [or E.] Fisk[e]?) First edition. $300-$400. New York, 1836. Cloth. Second edition, with plates omitted. $150-$200.

VISSCHER, William Lightfoot. *"Black Mammy": A Song of the Sunny South.* Illustrated. Cloth. Cheyenne, Wyo., 1885. First edition. $35-$50. Author's first book.

VIVIAN, George. *Scenery of Portugal and Spain.* 29 pp. of hand-colored plates. Half morocco. London, 1839. First edition. $750 and up. Also, A-range, 1960-70: $490-$560.

VIVIAN, George. *Spanish Scenery.* Engraved title, 26 pp. of plates. Half cloth and morocco. London, 1838. First edition. $200-$300.

VIVIAN Grey. 5 vols., boards, paper labels. London, 1826. (By Benjamin Disraeli.) First edition. $150. Author's first novel.

VOIAGE and Travaile of Sir John Maundeville (The). Illuminated by Valenti Angelo. Red morocco. New York, 1928. Grabhorn Press (Random House). One of 150. $250.

VOICE of Scotland (The). See MacDiarmid, Hugh.

VOLTAIRE, Jean François Marie Arouet de. *Candide.* Translated by Richard Aldington. Illustrated by Rockwell Kent and colored by hand. Cloth, leather spine. New York, 1928. Limited edition. One of 95 signed. $350-$450. Ordinary issue (not hand-colored): Buckram. Signed by Kent. $50-$75.

VON OETTINGEN, B. *Horse Breeding in Theory and Practice.* Cloth. London, 1909. $50-$75.

VONNEGUT, Kurt, Jr. *Cat's Cradle.* Two-toned cloth. New York, no date (1963). First edition. In dust jacket. $25.

VONNEGUT, Kurt, Jr. *Player Piano.* Cloth. New York, no date (1952). First edition. In dust jacket. $35-$40. Author's first book.

VOORHEES, Luke. *Personal Recollections of Pioneer Life on the Mountains and Plains of the Great West.* Portrait. 75 pp., cloth. Cheyenne, Wyo., no date (1920). First edition. $50-$75.

VOYAGE to Mexico and Havanna (A); Including Some General Observations on the United States. By an Italian. Half calf. New York, 1841. (By Charles Barinetti.) First edition. $100-$150.

VOYNICH, E. L. *The Gadfly.* Red or brown cloth. New York, 1897. First American edition. $25.

W

WADDELL, Helen. *Mediaeval Latin Lyrics.* Half cloth. London, 1929. First edition. One of 100 signed. $25-$35.

WADSWORTH, Edward. *The Black Country.* Introduction by Arnold Bennett. 20 drawings and signed woodcut frontispiece. London, 1920. One of 50 on Japan vellum. $50.

WAGNER, Lieut. Col. A. L., and Kelley, Comm. J. D. *The United States Army and Navy: Their Histories, etc.* 43 colored plates. Oblong folio, leatherette. Akron, Ohio, 1899. First edition. $75-$100.

WAGNER, Henry R. *Bullion to Books.* Illustrated. Cloth. Los Angeles, 1942. First edition. $75-$100.

WAGNER, Henry R. *The Cartography of the Northwest Coast of America to the Year 1800.* 2 vols., folio, cloth. Berkeley, Calif., 1937. First edition. In dust jackets. Boxed. $150-$200.

WAGNER, Henry R. *The Plains and the Rockies.* Boards and cloth. San Francisco, 1920. First edition (suppressed). With 6-page pamphlet of corrections. $100-$150. San Francisco, 1921. Boards. First published edition. $35-$50. Another issue: Half vellum. 40 photostat reproductions. One of 50. $75-$100. San Francisco, 1937. Revised by C. L. Camp. Grabhorn Press. Cloth. Second edition. One of 600. $75-$100. Worn, $50. Columbus, Ohio, 1953. Cloth. Third edition. $50-$100. Another issue: Boards. De luxe edition. One of 50. $100-$150.

WAGNER, Henry R. *Sir Francis Drake's Voyage Around the World.* Maps, plates. Cloth. San Francisco, 1926. First edition. $50-$60. Another issue: Three-quarters morocco. One of 100 signed. $150.

WAGNER, Henry R. *Sixty Years of Book Collecting.* Portrait frontispiece. Boards. No place (Los Angeles), 1952. First edition. One of 200. $35-$50.

WAGNER, Henry R. *Spanish Explorations in the Strait of Juan de Fuca.* Maps, illustrations. Cloth. Santa Ana, Calif., 1933. First edition. One of 425. $150-$200.

WAGNER, Henry R. *The Spanish Southwest, 1542-1794.* Half morocco. Berkeley, Calif., 1924. First edition. One of 100. $300-$400. Albuquerque, 1937. 2 vols., half vellum. $150-$200.

WAGNER, Henry R. *The Spanish Voyages to the Northwest Coast of America.* Maps, plates. Cloth. San Francisco, 1929. First edition. $100-$150. Also, $65 (A, 1968), $60 (A, 1960). Another issue: Vellum. One of 25 signed. $150-$200.

WAGNER, Henry R. (editor). *California Voyages, 1539-1541.* Cloth. San Francisco, 1925. First edition. $50-$60.

WAGNER, Richard. *The Flying Dutchman.* Vellum. London, 1938. Corvinus Press. One of 130. $50-$75.

WAGNER, Richard. *The Rhinegold, and, The Valkyrie.* Color plates, other illustrations by Arthur Rackham. Vellum-backed brown boards. London, 1910. Limited edition, signed by the artist. $150-$200.

WAGNER, Richard. *Siegfried and the Twilight of the Gods.* Translated by Margaret Armour. Illustrated by Arthur Rackham. Pictorial vellum. London, 1911. One of 1,100 signed. In half morocco slipcase. $225.

WAGSTAFF, A. E. (editor). *Life of David S. Terry.* 5 plates. Cloth. San Francisco, 1892. First edition. $45.

WAGSTAFF, David; Sheldon, H. P.; Smith, Lawrence B.; and others. *Upland Game Bird Shooting in America.* Color plates, other illustrations. New York, 1930. One of 850. In dust jacket. $50-$75.

WAGSTAFF, Theophile. *Flore et Zephyr: Ballet Mythologique.* 9 tinted plates (including cover title) by the author. Wrappers. London, 1836. (By William Makepeace Thackeray.) First edition. $250-$350. Author's first separate publication.

WAITE, A. E. *The Book of Black Magic and of Pacts.* Buckram. London, 1898. First edition. $50-$75. Chicago, 1910. Cloth. $40.

WAITE, A. E. *The Hermetic and Alchemical Writings of Aureolus Philippus Theophrastus Bombast... Called Paracelsus the Great.* 2 vols., cloth. London, 1894. $150. Underlined, $100.

WAITE, A. E. *Lives of Alchemystical Philosophers.* Cloth. London, 1888. $35-$50.

WAKEFIELD, John A. *History of the War Between the United States and the Sac and Fox Nations of Indians, etc.* Cloth. Jacksonville, Ill., 1834. First edition. $300-$400. Worn, $200 and $275.

WAKEFIELD, Maj. Paul L. (compiler). *Campaigning Texas.* 156 pp., wrappers. Austin, Tex., 1932. One of 50. $50.

WAKEFIELD, Priscilla. *A Family Tour Through the British Empire.* Contemporary calf, leather label. Philadelphia, 1804. First American edition. $40.

WAKOSKI, Diane. *Coins and Coffins.* Printed wrappers. No place, no date (New York, 1962). First edition. $40-$50.

WAKOSKI, Diane. *The Magellanic Clouds.* Boards. Los Angeles, 1970. Black Sparrow Press. One of 250 signed. $25-$35.

WALGAMOTT, Charles S. *Reminiscences of Early Days.* Plates. 2 vols., cloth. No place, no date (Twin Falls, Idaho, 1926-27). First edition. $85-$125.

WALGAMOTT, Charles S. *"Six Decades Back."* Cloth. Caldwell, Idaho, 1936. Second edition (of *Reminiscences of Early Days*). $35.

WALKER, Charles D. *Biographical Sketches of the Graduates and Élèves of the Virginia Military Institute Who Fell During the War Between the States.* Cloth. Philadelphia, 1875. $75-$100. Spine worn, $30.

WALKER, George. *The Costume of Yorkshire.* Colored frontispiece and 40 colored aquatint plates. Folio, contemporary morocco. London, 1814. $200-$400. Large paper issue: Half morocco. $500. Another issue: 10 parts, wrappers. $750. Leeds, England, 1885. Half morocco. One of 600. $300. Also, $100.80 and $108 (A, 1969).

WALKER, Robert J. *American Slavery and Finances.* Cloth. London, 1864. $75-$100.

WALKER, Tacetta. *Stories of Early Days in Wyoming; Big Horn Basin.* Illustrated. Cloth. Casper, Wyo., no date (1936). First edition. $35-$50.

WALL, Bernhardt. *Ten Etched Poems: First Series.* Boards, paper label. New York, 1924. First edition. One of 50 signed. $35-$50.

WALL, W. G. *Wall's Hudson River Portfolio.* 21 color plates. Oblong atlas folio, boards and calf. New York, no date (about 1826). First edition. $4,000-$5,000, possibly more. (Note: The last two sales noted at auction were in 1948: copies without title page, $1,700 each.) New York, 1828. Second edition (or state), without title page. $4,000-$5,000, possibly more.

WALLA Walla County. Colored maps. Half leather. Chicago, 1909. $35-$50.

WALLACE, Dexter. *The Blood of the Prophets.* Cloth. Chicago, 1905. (By Edgar Lee Masters.) First edition. $35-$50.

WALLACE, Ed. R. *Parson Hanks.* Wrappers. Arlington, Tex., no date (1906?). First edition. $75-$100.

WALLACE, Edgar. *Writ in Barracks.* Cloth. London, 1900. First edition. $25. Author's first book.

WALLACE, J. H. *Wallace's American Stud-Book.* Vol. 1. Cloth. New York, 1867. $35-$50.

WALLACE, Lew. *Ben-Hur: A Tale of the Christ.* Light-blue floral cloth. New York, 1880. First edition, first issue, with dated title page, six-word dedication. $150-$200. Copies in brown cloth and other colors are considered later issues.

WALLACE, Lew. *The Fair God.* Cloth. Boston, 1873. First edition, first state on thin paper, bound in beveled boards. $25. Author's first book.

WALN, Robert. *American Bards: A Satire.* Half morocco. Philadelphia, 1820. $25.

WALTER Kennedy: An American Tale. Boards, leather spine label. London, 1805. (By John Davis.) First edition. $500-$600.

WALTERS, Henry. *Incunabula Typographica.* Calf. Baltimore, 1906. $35-$50.

WALTERS, Lorenzo D. *Tombstone's Yesterdays.* Illustrated. Cloth. Tucson, 1928. First edition. $60-$100.

WALTHER, C. F., and Taylor, I. N. *The Resources and Advantages of the State of Nebraska.* (Cover title.) Folding map. 27 pp., wrappers. No place, no date (Omaha, 1871). First edition. $50-$75.

WALTON, Izaak (or Isaac), and Cotton, Charles. *The Compleat* [or *Complete*] *Angler.* (Note: As with many classic works, there have been innumerable editions of this since its first publication in 1653. A representative group of nineteenth- and twentieth-century editions is listed here.) New York, 1847. Edited by George W. Bethune. 2 portraits, 2 plates, other illustrations. 2 parts bound in one vol., light-tan cloth, horizontal red stripes. First American edition. Large paper issue, with proof impressions of plates. $250-$350. Rebound in full morocco, $250. Ordinary issue: $150-$250. London, 1824-25. Proof impressions of plates on India paper. 2 vols., green morocco. $50. London, no date (1880). Vellum. Facsimile edition by Elliott Stock. One of 6 printed on vellum. $75-$100. New York, 1880. Half morocco. One of 100 large paper copies. Sixth Bethune edition. $25. London, 1888. Edited by R. B. Marston. Printed on India paper. 2 vols., green morocco. "Lea & Dove Edition." One of 250. $100-$150. London, 1902. Edited by G. A. B. Dewar. India paper. 2 vols., green vellum. "Winchester Edition." $100-$150. Cambridge, Mass., 1909. Boards. Designed by Bruce Rogers. One of 440. $37.50. London, 1929. Nonesuch Press. Full morocco. One of 1,100. $50-$100. London, no date (1931). Illustrated by Arthur Rackham. Vellum. One of 775 signed by Rackham. $200-$300. Trade edition: Cloth. $35-$50.

WALTON, W. M. *Life and Adventures of Ben Thompson, the Famous Texan.* 15 plates, 229 pp., pictorial wrappers. Austin, Tex., 1884. First edition. $400-$500.

WANDERER in Washington. Printed boards. Washington, 1827. (By George Watterston.) First edition. $35-$50.

WAR History of the National Rifles, Co. A, 3d Battalion, District of Columbia Volunteers, of 1861. Cloth. Wilmington, Del., 1887. First edition, with errata slip. $40-$50.

WAR in Florida (The). By a Late Staff Officer. Folding map, 2 plates. Green cloth. Baltimore, 1836. (By Woodburn Potter.) First edition. $100-$150.

WAR in Texas (The). By a Citizen of the United States. 57 pp., printed wrappers. Philadelphia, 1836. (By Benjamin Lundy.) First edition under this title (but second, enlarged edition of an earlier pamphlet of the same date, *The Origin and True Causes of the Texas Rebellion*). $75-$100. Philadelphia, 1837. 64 pp., wrappers (or sewed). $35-$50.

WARD, D. B. *Across the Plains in 1853*. (Cover title.) Portrait. 55 pp., printed wrappers. No place, no date (Seattle, 1911). First edition. $75-$100.

WARDER, T. B., and Catlett, J. M., *Battle of Young's Branch, or, Manassas Plain.* 2 folding maps. Wrappers, or half leather. Richmond, Va., 1862. First edition. Wrappers: $100-$150. Also, half leather, $70 (A, 1969).

WARE, Eugene F. *The Indian War of 1864*. Frontispiece. Cloth. Topeka, Kan., 1911. First edition. $100-$150.

WARE, Eugene F. *The Lyon Campaign in Missouri*. Cloth. Topeka, 1907. First edition. $50.

WARE, Joseph E. *The Emigrants' Guide to California*. Folding map. 56 pp., cloth. St. Louis, no date (1849). First edition. $1,500-$2,000. The last two copies to sell at auction lacked the map: $1,000 (1948); $500 (1968)—the Streeter copy.

WARNER, Charles Dudley. *Backlog Studies*. Illustrated. Boards. Cambridge, Mass., 1899. One of 250 signed. $25.

WARNER, Col. J. J.; Hayes, Benjamin; and Widney, Dr. J. P. *An Historical Sketch of Los Angeles County*. 88 pp., printed wrappers. Los Angeles, 1876. First edition. $100-$150. Also, rebound in half morocco, front cover preserved, $40 (A, 1966). Los Angeles, 1936. Boards and cloth. $50.

WARNER, M. M. *Warner's History of Dakota County, Nebraska*. Plates. Cloth. Lyons, Neb., 1893. First edition. $35-$50.

WARNER, Matt, and King, Murray E. *The Last of the Bandit Riders*. Illustrated. Pictorial cloth. Caldwell, Idaho, 1940. First edition. In dust jacket. $50.

WARNER, Susan B. See Wetherell, Elizabeth.

WARNER and Foote. *Directory of Carroll County (Iowa)*. 48 pp., wrappers. Minneapolis, 1884. $35-$50.

WARRE, Henry J. *Sketches in North America and the Oregon Territory*. Map, 20 colored views (on 16 sheets). Large folio, boards. London, no date (1848). First edition. $6,000. Also, $4,000 (A, 1969).

WARREN, Edward. *A Doctor's Experiences in Three Continents*. Cloth. Baltimore, 1855. $40-$50.

WARREN, Edward. *An Epitome of Practical Surgery for Field and Hospital*. Boards and cloth. Richmond, Va., 1863. First edition. $75-$100.

WARREN, Lieut. G. K. *The Report of the Secretary of War, etc*. Maps. Cloth. No place (Washington), 1855. $30-$40.

WARREN, John. *The Conchologist*. 34 plates, 17 colored. Morocco. Boston, 1834. First edition. $75-$100.

WARREN, John C. *Etherization: With Surgical Remarks*. Cloth. Boston, 1848. First edition. $100-$150.

WARREN, John C. *The Mastodon Giganteus of North America*. Cloth. Boston, 1852. First edition. $30-$40.

WARREN, Robert Penn. *Blackberry Winter*. Boards, paper label. Cummington, Mass., 1946. First edition. One of 280 (actually 230) on Arches paper. $55.

WARREN, Robert Penn. *Eleven Poems on the Same Theme.* Printed wrappers. New York, no date (1942). First edition. $25.

WARREN, Robert Penn. *Selected Poems: 1923-1943.* Cloth. New York, no date (1944). First edition. In dust jacket. $30.

WARREN, Robert Penn. *Selected Poems, 1923-1966.* Cloth. New York, no date (1966). First edition. One of 250 signed. Boxed. $35-$50.

WARREN, Samuel. See *Ten Thousand a Year.*

WASHBURNE, The Rev. Cephas. *Reminiscences of the Indians.* Cloth. Richmond, Va., no date (1869). First edition. $200-$300.

WASHINGTON, Booker T. *The Future of the American Negro.* Cloth. Boston, 1899. First edition. $25-$35. Author's first book.

WASSON, George S. *Sailing Days on the Penobscot.* Boards and cloth. Salem, Mass., 1932. One of 97 on rag paper. $50-$60. Trade edition: Cloth. $25-$35.

WASSON, Valentina Pavlova. *Mushrooms, Russia and History.* Color plates, folding maps and plates. 2 vols., folio, buckram. New York, 1957. First edition. One of 510. $950. Also, $625 (A, 1968).

WATER Witch (The), or The Skimmer of the Seas. By the Author of *Pilot.* 3 vols., boards, paper labels. Dresden, 1830. (By James Fenimore Cooper.) First edition. Up to $2,000. London, 1830. 3 vols., brown boards, paper labels. First English edition. $75-$100. Philadelphia, 1831. Blue or tan boards. First American edition. $50-$100.

WATERLOO, Stanley. *The Seekers.* Red cloth. Chicago, 1900. First edition. $25.

WATERLOO, Stanley. *The Wolf's Long Howl.* Pictorial cloth. Chicago, 1899. First edition. $25.

WATKINS, Lucy. *The History and Adventures of Little James and Mary.* 15 pp., wrappers. Philadelphia, no date (1810). $50-$60.

WATKINS, Lura W. *Early New England Potters and Their Wares.* Illustrated. Cloth. Cambridge, Mass., 1950. $25-$35.

WATSON, Douglas S. *West Wind: The Life Story of Joseph Reddeford Walker.* Plates, folding map. Boards. Los Angeles, 1934. First edition. One of 100. $200-$250.

WATSON, Douglas S. (editor). *California in the Fifties.* 50 views. Oblong folio, cloth. San Francisco, 1936. One of 850. In dust jacket. $50-$60.

WATSON, Douglas S. (editor). *The Spanish Occupation of California.* Illustrated. Boards and cloth. San Francisco, 1934. Grabhorn Press. One of 550. $75-$100.

WATSON, William. *The Eloping Angels.* Cloth. London, 1893. First edition. One of 250. $25-$35. Trade edition: Cloth. $15.

WATSON, William. *Epigrams of Art, Life and Nature.* Cloth. Liverpool, England, 1884. First edition. One of 50. $50-$60.

WATSON, William. *Excursions in Criticism.* Boards. London, 1893. First edition. One of 50. $35-$50. Trade edition: Cloth. $15-$20.

WATSON, William. *The Father of the Forest and Other Poems.* Frontispiece portrait. Cloth. London, 1895. First edition. One of 75. $35-$50.

WATSON, William. *Ode on the Day of the Coronation of King Edward VII.* Vellum. London, 1902. First edition. One of 175. $25.

WATSON, William. *Odes and Other Poems.* Cloth. London, 1894. First edition. One of 75. $35-$50.

WATSON, William. *The Purple East: A Series of Sonnets on England's Desertion of Armenia.* Frontispiece. Cloth. London, 1896. First edition. One of 75. $35-$50.

WATSON, William. *Wordsworth's Grave and Other Poems.* Frontispiece. Boards. London, 1890. First edition. $25-$30.

WATTS, W. J. *Cherokee Citizenship and a Brief History of Internal Affairs in the Cherokee Nation.* (Cover title.) Portrait. Wrappers. Muldrow, Indian Territory (Okla.), 1895. $100.

WATTS, W. W. *Old English Silver.* 307 plates. Cloth. New York, 1924. First American edition. $60-$80. London, 1924. Cloth. First English edition. $75-$100. One of 40 in leather binding. $100-$150.

WAUGH, Evelyn. *Basil Seal Rides Again.* Cloth. Boston, no date (1963). First separate edition. One of 1,000 large paper copies, signed. $50-$60. London, 1963. Cloth. One of 750. $35.

WAUGH, Evelyn. *Black Mischief.* Cloth. London, 1932. First trade edition. In dust jacket. $40-$60. Jacket worn, $37.50. Large paper issue: Purple cloth. One of 250 signed. In dust jacket. $75-$150.

WAUGH, Evelyn. *Decline and Fall.* Illustrated. Cloth. London, 1928. First edition. $100-$150.

WAUGH, Evelyn. *The Holy Places.* Woodcuts by Reynolds Stone. Morocco. London, 1952. First edition. Limited and signed. In dust jacket. $100.

WAUGH, Evelyn. *Labels: A Mediterranean Journal.* Illustrated. Light-blue cloth. No place (London), 1930. First edition. One of 110 signed and specially bound with a leaf of the original ms. $200-$250. Also, $132 (A, 1970). Trade edition: Cloth. $10-$15.

WAUGH, Evelyn. *Love Among the Ruins.* Illustrated. Decorated cloth. London, 1953. First edition. One of 300 signed. In glassine dust jacket. $35-$50.

WAUGH, Evelyn. *The Loved One.* Illustrated by Stuart Boyle. Buckram. London, no date (1948). First edition. One of 250 large paper copies, signed. $135. Boston, 1948. Gray cloth. First American edition. $25-$35.

WAUGH, Evelyn. *P. R. B.: An Essay on the Pre-Raphaelite Brotherhood.* Boards and linen. London, 1926. First edition, with errata slip. $750-$1,000.

WAUGH, Evelyn. *Vile Bodies.* Cloth. London, 1930. First edition. In dust jacket. $75-$100.

WAUGH, Evelyn. *Wine in Peace and War.* Decorations by Rex Whistler. Decorated boards. London, no date. First edition. $35-$50.

WAUGH, Lorenzo. *Autobiography of Lorenzo Waugh.* Illustrated. Cloth. Oakland, Calif., 1883. First edition. $35-$50.

WAVERLEY; or, 'Tis Sixty Years Since. 3 vols., boards, paper labels. Edinburgh, 1814. (By Sir Walter Scott.) First edition, first issue, with "our" instead of "your" in first line on page 136 in Vol. II. $3,500-$4,000. (Only a few copies known in original boards. One was catalogued by an English dealer early in 1970 at $3,600. The Frank Hogan copy, one hinge cracked, labels slightly defective, covers rubbed, sold at auction in 1945 for $1,950.) Other copies listed recently at retail: Contemporary calf, rebacked, $225; contemporary calf, defective, $125; contemporary russia, in slipcase, $210.

WAYLAND, John W. *History of Rockingham County.* Plates. Buckram. Dayton, Va., 1912. $50.

WAYLAND, John W. *Historic Homes of Northern Virginia and the Eastern Panhandle of Western Virginia.* Cloth. Staunton, Va., 1937. First edition. $45-$60.

WAYNE and Holmes Counties, Ohio (Commemorative Biographical Record of). Half leather. Chicago, 1889. $35-$50.

WEARY, Ogdred. *The Beastly Baby*. Illustrated. Wrappers. No place, no date (New York, 1962). Fantod Press. (By Edward Gorey.) First edition. One of 500. $35.

WEATHERLY, F. E. *Magic Pictures: A Book of Changing Scenes.* 16 pp., with pull slides to change pictures (a movable book). Pictorial cloth. London, no date (about 1890). $45.

WEBB, Mary. *The Chinese Lion.* Decorated boards, red cloth spine, red label on front cover. London, 1937. First edition. One of 350. Boxed. $50-$60.

WEBB, Mary. *The Golden Arrow.* Blue cloth. London, 1916. First edition. In dust jacket. $100-$150. Lacking jacket, $75-$100. Author's first book.

WEBB, Mary. *Gone to Earth.* Dark-red cloth. London, no date (1917). First edition. In dust jacket. $85-$125.

WEBB, Mary. *The House in Dormer Forest.* Green cloth. London, no date (1920). First edition. In dust jacket. $50-$75.

WEBB, Mary. *Precious Bane.* Green cloth. London, no date (1924). First edition. In dust jacket. $150-$250. Second edition, same date. Cloth. $25-$35.

WEBB, Mary. *Seven for a Secret: A Love Story.* Green cloth. London, no date (1922). First edition. In dust jacket. $100.

WEBB, Mary. *The Spring of Joy: A Little Book of Healing.* Cloth. London, 1917. First edition. In dust jacket. $35-$50.

WEBB, Walter Prescott. *The Texas Rangers.* Illustrated. Cloth. Boston, 1935. First edition. $25.

WEBBER, C. W. *The Hunter-Naturalist; Romance of Sporting, or Wild Scenes and Wild Hunters.* Engraved title page and 9 colored lithographs, other illustrations. Cloth, leather spine and corners. Philadelphia, no date (1851). First edition. $150-$200.

WEBBER, C. W. *Wild Scenes and Song Birds.* 20 colored plates. Morocco. New York, 1854. First edition. $100-$125. New York, 1855. Cloth. $40.

"WEBFOOT." *Fore and Aft; Or, Leaves from the Life of an Old Sailor.* Illustrated. Cloth. Boston, 1871. (By William D. Phelps.) First edition. $100-$150.

WEBSTER, Daniel. *A Discourse in Commemoration of the Lives and Services of John Adams and Thomas Jefferson.* 62 pp., brown printed wrappers. Boston, 1826. First edition. $35-$50.

WEBSTER, George G. See Hall, J. L.

WEBSTER, Jean. *Daddy-Long-Legs.* Illustrated by the author. Decorated cloth. New York, 1912. First edition. In dust jacket. $40-$50.

WEBSTER, Noah. *An American Dictionary of the English Language.* Portrait. 2 vols., light-brown boards, linen spines, paper labels. New York, 1828. First edition. With two-page ad leaf laid in. $750-$1,000. (Copies with the ad leaf are more valuable than those without.) Vol. 1 rebacked in leatherette, spine of Vol. 2 "eroded," $450. A presentation copy, with a 4-page letter in Webster's hand, brought $1,200 at auction in 1963. Also, rebound in calf, $260 (A, 1970); rebacked, $500 (A, 1969).

WEBSTER, Noah. *A Compendious Dictionary of the English Language.* Full leather, leather spine label. Hartford, Conn., 1806. First edition. $200 and up. Also, contemporary calf or sheep, $70 (A, 1970); $20 and $100 (A, 1968); $70 (A, 1963). Webster's first dictionary.

WEBSTER, Noah. *A Dictionary of the English Language Compiled for the Use of Common Schools in the United States.* Calf, red morocco label. New Haven, Conn., 1807. First edition. $50-$75.

WEBSTER, Noah. *Elements of Useful Knowledge.* Vol. 1. Boards and calf. Hartford, 1802. First edition. $35-$50.

WEBSTER, Noah. *History of Animals.* Boards and calf. New Haven, 1812. First edition. $50-$60.

WEEMS, M. L. *A History of the Life and Death, etc., of Gen. George Washington.* Contemporary calf. Philadelphia, no date (1800?). $150 and up. Margins shaved, $125. (Note: One of numerous editions, under various titles, based on Weems' original work, *The Life and Memorable Actions of George Washington,* Baltimore, 1800 [?], of which only 2 copies are known. Most editions to about 1810 are scarce and are valued in the $25-$100 range.)

WEGERSLEV, C. H., and Walpole, Thomas. *Past and Present of Buena Vista County, Iowa.* Cloth. Chicago, 1909. First edition. $35-$50.

WEIZMANN, Chaim. *Trial and Error.* 2 vols., cloth. New York, no date (1949). First edition. One of 500 signed. $100-$150.

WELLCOME, Isaac C. *History of the Second Advent Message and Mission, Doctrine and People.* Cloth. Yarmouth, Me., 1874. $27.50.

WELLMAN, Paul I. *The Callaghan, Yesterday and Today.* Map, plates. 82 pp., pictorial wrappers. Encinal, Tex., no date (about 1936-44?). First edition. $50-$60.

WELLS, Carolyn, and Goldsmith, A. F. *A Concise Bibliography of the Works of Walt Whitman.* Boards and cloth. Boston, 1922. First edition. One of 500. $50-$60.

WELLS, H. G. *The Country of the Blind.* Wood engravings. Orange vellum. London, 1939. Golden Cockerel Press. One of 30 signed. $200-$250.

WELLS, H. G. *The Door in the Wall.* Plates. Cloth. New York, 1911. First edition. One of 300. $50-$60. Worn, $25.

WELLS, H. G. *The First Men in the Moon.* Illustrated by Claude Shepperson. Dark-blue cloth. London, 1901. First edition, first issue, gilt lettering on cover. $75. Second issue, lettering in black. $25.

WELLS, H. G. *The Island of Doctor Moreau.* Brown cloth. London, 1896. First edition, with 32 pp. of ads at back. $35-$50.

WELLS, H. G. *The Outline of History.* 24 parts, pictorial wrappers. London, 1919-20. First edition. $100 and up. (One American dealer catalogued this at $220 in 1969.)

WELLS, H. G. *Select Conversations with an Uncle (Now Extinct) and Two Other Reminiscences.* Cloth. London, 1895. First edition. $25. Wells' first literary work.

WELLS, H. G. *Text-Book of Biology.* 2 vols., green cloth. London, no date (1893). First edition, first binding. $75-$100. (Note: Brown cloth is a later binding.) Author's first book.

WELLS, H. G. *The Time Machine.* Gray cloth. London, 1895. First edition, first issue, without ads at back and purple stamping on cloth. $90-$125.

WELLS, Oliver (editor). *An Anthology of the Younger Poets.* Preface by Archibald MacLeish. Buckram and boards. Philadelphia, 1932. First edition. In glassine dust jacket. $25-$30.

WELLS, William, and Onken, Otto. *Western Scenery; or, Land and River, Hill and Dale, in the Mississippi Valley.* Pictorial title page, 19 full-page lithographic views, 52 pp. of text. Boards and calf. Cincinnati, 1851. First edition. $1,500 and up. (Note: An extremely rare book. The price here is from a 1956 catalogue; I find no other records, and the current price for a copy might well be double this figure.)

WELTY, Eudora. *A Curtain of Green.* Brown cloth. Garden City, N.Y., 1941. First edition. In dust jacket. $50-$60. Author's first book.

WELTY, Eudora. *Delta Wedding.* Brown cloth. New York, no date (1946). First edition. In dust jacket. $30-$35.

WELTY, Eudora. *Golden Apples.* Cloth. New York, no date (1949). First edition. In dust jacket. $15-$20.

WELTY, Eudora. *Losing Battles.* Cloth. New York, 1970. Limited edition, signed. In slipcase. $30-$50.

WELTY, Eudora. *Music from Spain.* Decorated boards, paper spine label. Greenville, Miss., 1948. First edition. One of 750 signed. $35.

WELTY, Eudora. *Place in Fiction.* Cloth. New York, 1957. First edition. One of 300 signed. $25-$35.

WELTY, Eudora. *The Robber Bridegroom.* Blue cloth. Garden City, 1942. First edition. In dust jacket. $35-$40.

WENDTE, Charles H., and Perkins, H. S. *The Sunny Side: A Book of Religious Songs.* New York, no date (1875). First edition. $60.

WENTWORTH, Lady Judith Anne. *The Authentic Arabian Horse and His Descendants.* 26 color plates, numerous other illustrations. Blue cloth. London, no date (1945). First edition. In dust jacket. $75-$100. London, 1962. Second edition. In dust jacket. $35-$50. New York, 1962. Cloth. In dust jacket. $35-$50.

WENTWORTH, Lady Judith Anne. *Thoroughbred Racing Stock and Its Ancestors.* 21 color plates. Red buckram. London, 1938. First edition. In dust jacket. $75-$100. London, no date (1960). Second edition. In dust jacket. Boxed. $40-$60.

WEPT of Wish Ton-Wish (The): A Tale. By the Author of *The Pioneers.* 2 vols., boards, paper labels. Philadelphia, 1829. (By James Fenimore Cooper.) First American edition. $75-$100. Rebound in half leather, $35-$50. (For first edition, see *The Borderers.*)

WESCOTT, Glenway. *The Babe's Bed.* Cloth. Paris, 1920. First edition. One of 375 signed. $30-$40.

WESCOTT, Glenway. *The Bitterns: A Book of Twelve Poems.* Black wrappers with printed silver design. Evanston, Ill., no date (1920). First edition, signed. In cloth folding case. $200-$300. Also, $150 (A, 1970). Author's first book.

WESCOTT, Glenway. *A Calendar of Saints for Unbelievers.* Illustrated by Pavel Tchelitchew. Half morocco. Paris, 1932. First edition. One of 40 signed. Boxed. $250. Another issue: Cloth. One of 695. Boxed. $50-$75.

WESCOTT, Glenway. *Good-Bye, Wisconsin.* Boards and cloth. New York, 1928. First edition. One of 250 signed. $35-$50. Trade edition: Cloth. $15-$20.

WESCOTT, Glenway. *The Grandmothers.* Cloth-backed boards. New York, 1927. First edition. One of 250 signed. $25-$35. Trade edition: Cloth. $10-$15.

WESCOTT, Glenway. *Natives of Rock, XX Poems: 1921-1922.* Boards. New York, 1925. First edition. One of 25 on vellum (of an edition of 575). Boxed. $35-$50. Plain copies in glassine dust jacket. $20-$30.

WEST, John C. *A Texan in Search of a Fight.* 189 pp., wrappers. Waco, Tex., 1901. First edition. $50-$75. Rebound in buckram, $45.

WEST, Nathanael. *A Cool Million.* Cloth. New York, no date (1934). First edition. In dust jacket. $125-$150. Also, "probably an advance issue or trial binding in russet cloth without publisher's name at bottom of spine," $85 (A, 1970).

WEST, Nathanael. *The Day of the Locust.* Cloth, paper label. New York, no date (1939). First edition. In dust jacket. $100-$150.

WEST, Nathaniel. *The Dream Life of Balso Snell.* Printed wrappers. Paris and New York,

1931. Contact Editions. First edition. One of 500 numbered copies. $150-$200. Inscribed copy offered by dealer for $250 in 1972.

WEST, Nathanael. *Miss Lonelyhearts.* Cloth. New York, no date (1933). First edition. In dust jacket. $75-$150.

WESTCOTT, Edward Noyes. *David Harum.* Yellow cloth. New York, 1898. First edition, first state, with perfect "J" in "Julius" in next to last line of page 40. $40-$75. Author's first book. New York, no date (1900). First illustrated edition. One of 750. $25.

WESTERN Agriculturist (The) and Practical Farmer's Guide. Frontispiece, plates. Leather. Cincinnati, 1830. $35.

WESTERN Reserve Register for 1852, (The). Cloth. Hudson, Ohio. 1852. First issue. $25.

WESTERNERS Brand Books. Chicago, 1944-45, $35-$50; 1945-46, $35-$50. Denver, 1946, $75; 1947, $50; 1951, $35-$50; 1952, $35-$50; 1954-55, 2 vols., $89.60 (A, 1965). Los Angeles, 1947, $50-$60; 1948, $50; 1949, $125; 1950, $45; 1953, $45-$60; 1956, $40-$50; 1957, $50; 1959, $40; 1961, $50; 1963, $35; 1964, $50; 1966, $35; 1969, $25. New York, 1954-61, Vol. I, No. 1, to Vol. VIII, No. 4, bound in 4 vols., $40 (A, 1964).

WESTON, Silas. *Four Months in the Mines of California; or, Life in the Mountains.* 24 pp., printed wrappers. Providence, R.I., 1854. Second edition (of *Life in the Mountains*). $110-$150. (See below.)

WESTON, Silas. *Life in the Mountains: or Four Months in the Mines of California.* 36 pp., printed wrappers. Providence, 1854. First edition. $250-$350.

WESTROPP, M. S. Dudley. *Irish Glass.* 40 plates. Buckram. London, no date (about 1920-21?). $75.

WESTWARD Ho! 2 vols., cloth. New York, 1832. (By James Kirke Paulding.) First edition. $100-$125.

WETHERBEE, J., Jr. *A Brief Sketch of Colorado Territory and the Gold Mines of That Region.* 24 pp., printed wrappers. Boston, 1863. First edition. $350-$500.

WETHERELL, Elizabeth. *Queechy.* 2 vols., cloth. New York, 1852. (By Susan B. Warner.) First edition. $100-$150. London, 1852. 2 vols., cloth. First English edition. $75-$100.

WETHERELL, Elizabeth. *The Wide, Wide World.* 2 vols., cloth. New York, 1851. (By Susan Warner.) First edition, first issue, brown cloth. $35-$50. Later, blue cloth. $15-$20. London, 1853. 2 vols., red cloth. First English edition. $35-$50.

WETMORE, Alphonso (compiler). *Gazetteer of the State of Missouri.* Frontispiece and folding map. Cloth. St. Louis, 1837. First edition. $75-$100.

WEYMAN, Stanley J. *A Gentleman of France.* 3 vols., green cloth. London, 1893. First edition. $150.

WEYMAN, Stanley J. *The House of the Wolf.* Decorated gray cloth. London, 1890. First edition. $50. Author's first book.

WHALING Directory of the United States in 1869. Colored flags. Cloth. New Bedford, Mass., 1869. $30-$50.

WHARTON, Clarence. *Remember Goliad.* 61 pp., boards. Houston, 1931. One of 100. $75-$125.

WHARTON, Edith. See Jones, Edith Newbold.

WHARTON, Edith. *Ethan Frome.* Cloth. New York, 1911. First edition, first issue, with top edges gilt and perfect type in last line of page 135. $100-$150. No place (New York), 1939. Limited Editions Club. Cloth. Boxed. $25-$35.

WHARTON, Edith. *Twelve Poems.* Buckram and boards. No place, no date (London, 1926). Medici Society. First edition. One of 130 signed. $85-$125.

WHAT Is Man? Gray-blue boards, green-black leather label on spine. New York, 1906. (By Samuel Langhorne Clemens.) First edition, first issue, with "things about" as last line of page 131. One of 250. In tissue dust jacket. Boxed. $125-$150. (Note: The first English edition, London, 1910, cloth, identifies Twain as author. See Twain, *What Is Man?*)

WHEAT, Carl I. *Books of the California Gold Rush.* Illustrated. Pictorial boards and cloth. San Francisco, 1949. Grabhorn Press. First edition. One of 500. $40-$50.

WHEAT, Carl I. *Mapping the Trans-Mississippi West.* Illustrated. 5 vols. in 6 vols., folio, buckram, leatherette spine. San Francisco, 1957-63. Grabhorn Press. Limited edition. $300-$500.

WHEAT, Carl I. *The Maps of the California Gold Region, 1848-1857.* 26 maps. Folio, cloth. San Francisco, 1942. Grabhorn Press. First edition. One of 300. $400-$500. Another issue: Three-quarters calf. One of 22, with map by Gibbs added. $600-$800.

WHEAT, Carl I. *The Pioneer Press of California.* Boards and cloth. Oakland, Calif., 1948. One of 450. $40-$50.

WHEAT, Marvin T. See Cincinnatus.

WHEATLEY, Phillis. *Memoir and Poems of Phillis Wheatley, a Native African and a Slave.* Cloth, red paper label on front cover. Boston, 1834. $75-$100.

WHEELER, Edward L. *Deadwood Dick's Doom; or, Calamity Jane's Last Adventure.* 16 pp., self-wrappers. New York, 1881. Beadle's Half-Dime Library. First edition. $35. New York, 1887. Beadle's Pocket Library. Reprint. $25.

WHEELER, Ella. *Drops of Water: Poems.* Purple cloth. New York, 1872. (By Ella Wheeler Wilcox.) First edition. $35-$50. Author's first book.

WHEELER, William. *In Memoriam: Letters of William Wheeler.* Illustrated. Cloth. No place (Cambridge, Mass.), 1875. First edition. $25-$45.

WHEELER, William Ogden (compiler). *The Ogden Family in America.* 2 vols., cloth. Philadelphia, 1907. $50-$60.

WHERE Men Only Dare to Go, or, The Story of a Boy Company. By an Ex-Boy. Frontispiece. Cloth. Richmond, 1885. (By Royall W. Figg.) $40-$50.

WHILLDIN, M. *A Description of Western Texas.* 28 plates, folding map. 120 pp., pictorial wrappers. Galveston, Tex., 1876. First edition. $75-$100.

WHITAKER, Arthur Preston (editor). *Documents Relating to the Commercial Policy of Spain in the Floridas.* 7 maps and plates. Cloth. DeLand, Fla., 1931. First edition. One of 360. $50-$60.

WHITAKER, Fess. *History of Corporal Fess Whitaker.* Illustrated. Cloth. Louisville, Ky., 1918. First edition. $25.

WHITE, Diana. *The Descent of Ishtar.* Frontispiece. Boards, paper label. London, 1903. Eragny Press. One of 226. $85.

WHITE, E. B. *Stuart Little.* Cloth. New York, no date (1945). First edition. In dust jacket. $50-$70.

WHITE, The Rev. George. *Statistics of the State of Georgia.* Map. Cloth. Savannah, Ga., 1849. First edition, with errata leaf. $35-$50.

WHITE, Gilbert. *The Writings of Gilbert White of Selborne.* Wood engravings by Eric Ravilious. 2 vols., gray buckram. London, 1938. Nonesuch Press. One of 850. Boxed. $100-$200.

WHITE, John. *History of a Voyage to the China Sea.* Folding map, 6 plates. Half leather. Boston, 1823. First edition. $35-$50.

WHITE, John M. *The Newer Northwest.* 216 pp., wrappers. St. Louis, 1894. $75-$100.

WHITE, Joseph M. *A New Collection of the Laws . . . of Great Britain, France and Spain.* 2 vols., cloth. Philadelphia, 1839. $75-$100.

WHITE, Owen P. *Trigger Fingers.* Cloth. New York, 1926. First edition. In dust jacket. $50-$60.

WHITE, Philo. *Agricultural Statistics of Racine County.* 16 pp., wrappers. Racine, Wis., 1852. Presentation copy from author. $75.

WHITE, Stewart Edward. *The Claim Jumpers.* Cloth, printed wrappers, or marbled boards with leather spine. New York, 1901. First edition. Wrappers: $35-$50. Cloth or boards: $25-$35. Author's first book.

WHITE, William Allen. *The Court of Boyville.* Illustrated by Orson Lowell and Gustav Verbeek. Pictorial buckram. New York, 1899. First edition. $25-$35. '

WHITE, William Allen, and Paine, Albert Bigelow. *Rhymes by Two Friends.* Fort Scott, Kan., no date (1893). First edition. $35-$50. White's first book.

WHITEHEAD, Charles E. *Wild Sports in the South.* Illustrated. Cloth. New York, 1860. First edition. $50-$60.

WHITELY, Ike. *Rural Life in Texas.* 82 pp., wrappers. Atlanta, 1891. First edition. $50-$60.

WHITMAN, Walt. See Wells, Carolyn. Also see *Leaves of Grass; Leaves of Grass Imprints.*

WHITMAN, Walt. *After All, Not to Create Only.* 11 folio numbered sheets, printed on one side only, stitched. No place, no date (Washington, 1871). First edition, first (proof) issue. Very rare in proof state. Estimated value: $500 and up. The last copy at auction, along with a 4-line Whitman poem in author's hand, brought $200 (1951). Boston, 1871. Green or terra-cotta cloth. First book edition. $100-$150. "Almost loose in covers," $50. Erasure on end paper, $75.

WHITMAN, Walt. *An American Primer.* Edited by Horace Traubel. Boards, vellum spine. Boston, 1904. First edition. One of 500. $25-$35. (Also appears in white vellum, first binding, and blue cloth.)

WHITMAN, Walt. *As a Strong Bird on Pinions Free.* See entry following under *Leaves of Grass, As a Strong Bird, etc.*

WHITMAN, Walt. *Autobiographia, or Story of a Life.* Gray cloth. New York, 1892. First edition, with Charles L. Webster imprint. $25.

WHITMAN, Walt. *The Book of Heavenly Death.* Compiled from *Leaves of Grass* by Horace Traubel. Portrait. Portland, 1905. Mosher Press. One of 50 on Japan vellum. In dust jacket. Boxed. $40-$50. Another issue: One of 500. $15-$25.

WHITMAN, Walt. *Calamus: A Series of Letters Written During 1868-1880 . . . to a Young Friend (Peter Doyle).* Cloth. Boston, 1897. First edition. $25-$35. Another issue: Boards, cloth back, paper label. One of 35 on large paper. $50-$75.

WHITMAN, Walt. *Complete Poems and Prose, 1855-1888.* Half cloth and boards, paper label. No place, no date (Philadelphia, 1888-89). First edition. $35-$50. Another issue: Three-quarters buckram and boards, paper label on spine; or, half leather. One of 100 signed. $150-$250.

WHITMAN, Walt. *Criticism: An Essay.* Boards. Newark, 1913. First edition. One of 100. $75-$100.

WHITMAN, Walt. *Franklin Evans; or, The Inebriate.* 32 pp., reddish-brown wrappers. No place, no date (New York, 1842). First edition. (Supplement to *The New World,* November, 1842. Author's name as Walter Whitman.) $300-$400.

WHITMAN, Walt. *The Gathering of the Forces*. Edited by C. Rodgers and John Black. 2 vols., boards. New York, 1920. First edition. Limited. $25-$35.

WHITMAN, Walt. *Good-Bye, My Fancy. 2nd Annex to Leaves of Grass*. Phototype portrait. Green or maroon cloth. Philadelphia, 1891. First edition. $35-$50. Large paper issue: $50-$75.

WHITMAN, Walt. *The Half-Breed and Other Stories*. Edited by T. O. Mabbott. Illustrated. Half cloth. New York, 1927. First edition. $10-$15. Another issue: One of 155 on handmade paper, 30 with illustrations signed in proof by the artist, Allen Lewis. $35-$50.

WHITMAN, Walt. *Lafayette in Brooklyn*. Boards. New York, 1905. First edition. One of 235 numbered copies. $15-$25. Another issue: One of 15 on Japan vellum. $25-$35.

WHITMAN, Walt. *Leaves of Grass*. See title entry for first (anonymous) and later editions.

WHITMAN, Walt. *Leaves of Grass, As a Strong Bird on Pinions Free. And Other Poems*. Green cloth. Washington, 1872. First edition. $200-$250.

WHITMAN, Walt. *Leaves of Grass. Passage to India*. Light-green wrappers. Washington, 1871. First edition. $25-$35.

WHITMAN, Walt. *Leaves of Grass. With Sands at Seventy and A Backward Glance O'er Travel'd Roads*. Illustrated. Limp black morocco. No place, no date (Philadelphia, 1889). One of 300 signed. (70th Birthday Edition.) $500.

WHITMAN, Walt. *Letters Written by Walt Whitman to His Mother*. Greenish-gray wrappers. New York, 1902. First edition. Only 5 copies printed. $200-$300.

WHITMAN, Walt. *Memoranda: Democratic Vistas*. Light-green wrappers. Washington, 1871. First edition, later printing (the first did not have Whitman's name on title page but only in copyright notice). $75 $100. First printing, without Whitman's name on title page: $100-$150.

WHITMAN, Walt. *Memoranda During the War*. 2 portraits. Red-brown cloth, green end papers. Camden, 1875-76. First edition, first printed page beginning "Remembrance Copy" and with space below for autograph (all copies signed). $350-$500. Another issue, without the portraits and the leaf headed "Remembrance Copy": $100-$150 at retail.

WHITMAN, Walt. *New York Dissected: A Sheaf of Recently Discovered Newspaper Articles*. Cloth. New York, 1936. First edition. One of 750. $25-$35.

WHITMAN, Walt. *Notes & Fragments*. Edited by Richard Maurice Bucke. Blue pebbled cloth. No place, 1899. First edition. One of 225 (or 250) signed by Bucke. $50-$60.

WHITMAN, Walt. *November Boughs*. Frontispiece portrait. Maroon or green cloth. Philadelphia, 1888. First edition. $35-$50. Large paper issue: Limp red or green cloth. $37.50-$50. Inscribed by Whitman, $200.

WHITMAN, Walt. *Passage to India*. See Whitman, *Leaves of Grass. Passage to India*.

WHITMAN, Walt. *Pictures: An Unpublished Poem*. Cloth. New York, 1927. First edition. One of 700. $25.

WHITMAN, Walt. *Poems by Walt Whitman*. Edited by William Michael Rossetti. Frontispiece portrait. Ad leaf pasted in. Cloth, gilt panel on cover. London, 1868. First edition in England, first issue, without price on spine. $35-$50.

WHITMAN, Walt. *Rivulets of Prose*. Edited by Carolyn Wells and Alfred F. Goldsmith. Cloth. New York, 1928. First edition. One of 499. $35-$50.

WHITMAN, Walt. *Specimen Days & Collect*. Light-blue wrappers or yellow cloth. Philadelphia, 1882-83. First edition, first issue, with Rees Welsh & Co. imprint. $25-$35. Philadelphia, 1883. Cloth. David McKay imprint. First edition, second issue. $15-$20.

WHITMAN, Walt. *Six Poèmes*. Version Nouvelle de Léon Bazalgette; 13 compositions by Jean Lurcat. Sheets, uncut, in wrappers. Paris, 1919. One of 115. $50.

WHITMAN, Walt. *Two Rivulets.* Portrait frontispiece, signed "Walt Whitman." Half calf. Camden, 1876. First edition. $100-$150.

WHITMAN, Walt. *The Uncollected Poetry and Prose of Walt Whitman.* 2 vols., cloth. Garden City, N.Y., 1921. First edition. In dust jacket. $25.

WHITMAN, Walt. *Walt Whitman's Diary in Canada.* Edited by W. S. Kennedy. Vellum boards. Boston, 1904. First edition. One of 500. $35-$50. Later issue, blue cloth: $10-$15.

WHITMAN, Walt. *Walt Whitman's Drum-Taps.* Brown cloth. New York, 1865. First edition, first issue, with only 72 pages. $100-$150. New York, 1865-66. Second issue, with 24 more pages and separate title page, "Sequel, etc." $200-$300.

WHITMAN, Walt. *Walt Whitman's Workshop.* Cloth. Cambridge, Mass., 1928. First edition. $25-$35.

WHITMAN, Walt. *The Wound Dresser.* Edited by Richard Maurice Bucke. Red buckram. Boston, 1898. First edition, first printing, with 1897 copyright notice. $25-$35. Also, inscribed by Bucke, $50 (A, 1968). Large paper issue: One of 60 signed by Bucke. $75-$100.

WHITMER, David. *An Address to All Believers in Christ.* 77 pp., wrappers. Richmond, Mo., 1887. First edition. $50-$75.

WHITNEY, Henry C. *Life on the Circuit with Lincoln.* 67 plates. Cloth. Boston, no date (1892). First edition. $35-$50.

WHITNEY, J. D. *The Auriferous Gravels of the Sierra Nevada of California.* Folding maps and plates. Cloth. Cambridge, Mass., 1880. First edition. $50-$75.

WHITNEY, J. D. *The Yosemite Book.* Half leather. New York, 1868. First edition. One of 250. $100-$125.

WHITNEY, J. H. E. *The Hawkins Zouaves.* Cloth. New York, 1866. First edition. $35-$50.

WHITTIER, John Greenleaf. See Dinsmoor, Robert, *Incidental Poems.* Also see *Justice and Expediency; Leaves from Margaret Smith's Journal; Moll Pitcher; The Stranger in Lowell; The Supernaturalism of New England.* (Note: Whittier's numerous publications, with all the complicated [and sometimes confusing] bibliographical points, are exhaustively covered in Thomas F. Currier's *A Bibliography of John Greenleaf Whittier,* Cambridge, Mass., 1937. The list here includes only representative scarce and important items.)

WHITTIER, John Greenleaf. *At Sundown.* Pea-green cloth. Cambridge, Mass., 1890. First edition. One of 250, with facsimile autograph presentation slip. $25.

WHITTIER, John Greenleaf. *The Captain's Well.* Illustrated by Howard Pyle. 4 pp., leaflet, imitation alligator leather binding. Supplement to New York *Ledger,* January 11, 1890. First edition. $75-$100.

WHITTIER, John Greenleaf. *The Demon Lady.* 8 pp., wrappers. No place, 1894. One of 25. $75.

WHITTIER, John Greenleaf. *The King's Missive, and Other Poems.* Portrait. Reddish-brown cloth. Boston, 1881. First edition. $25.

WHITTIER, John Greenleaf. *Legends of New England.* Boards and cloth, paper label. Hartford, Conn., 1831. First edition, first state, with next to last line on page 98 reading "the go." $100-$150. Author's first book.

WHITTIER, John Greenleaf. *Miriam and Other Poems.* Frontispiece. Cloth. Boston, 1871. First edition, first issue, with publisher's monogram on spine. $50-$75.

WHITTIER, John Greenleaf. *Mogg Megone: A Poem.* Slate-colored cloth. Boston, 1836. First edition. $75-$100.

WHITTIER, John Greenleaf. *Moll Pitcher.* See title entry.

WHITTIER, John Greenleaf. *The Panorama, and Other Poems.* Cloth. Boston, 1856. First edition, without ads. $25.

WHITTIER, John Greenleaf. *Poems.* Leather or cloth. Philadelphia, 1838. First edition. $25-$50.

WHITTIER, John Greenleaf. *Poems Written During the Progress of the Abolition Question in the United States.* Frontispiece. Cloth. Boston, 1837. First edition, first issue, 96 pp. $35-$50. Second issue, 103 pp. $25 and $15.

WHITTIER, John Greenleaf. *A Sabbath Sane.* Printed wrappers. Boston, 1854. First edition. $25.

WHITTIER, John Greenleaf. *Snow-Bound.* Green, blue, or terra-cotta cloth. Boston, 1866. First edition, first issue, with last page of text numbered "52" below printer's slug. $200-$300. Large paper issue: White cloth. One of 50. $75-$100. New York, 1930. Limited Editions Club. Boards and cloth. Boxed. $25.

WHITTINGTON and His Cat. Illustrated. Printed wrappers. New York, no date (about 1836). $30.

WHITTINGTON, Sir Richard. *The Renowned History of Richard Whittington and His Cat.* Frontispiece. 8 woodcuts in text. 23 pp., wrappers. New Haven, Conn., 1826. $25.

WHITTOCK, Nathaniel. *The Decorative Painters' and Glaziers' Guide.* Plates, many colored. Leather. London, 1827. First edition. $150-$250. London, 1828. Second edition. $100-$200. London, 1832. Third edition. $75-$150. London, 1841. Half leather. $250 at retail.

WHO'S Who In America. Cloth. Chicago, 1899. First edition. $25-$35.

WHYTE-MELVILLE, George John. See *Market Harborough.*

WHYTE-MELVILLE, George John. *"Bones and I."* Brown cloth. London, 1868. First edition. $50-$75.

WHYTE-MELVILLE, George John. *Digby Grand: An Autobiography.* 2 vols., cloth. London, 1853. First edition. $75-$100. Worn, $50. Author's first novel.

WHYTE-MELVILLE, George John. *The Queen's Maries: A Romance of Holyrood.* 2 vols., lilac cloth. London, 1862. First edition. $60.

WHYTE-MELVILLE, George John. *Rosine.* Frontispiece, 7 plates. Cloth. London, 1877. First edition. $30.

WHYTE-MELVILLE, George John. *Sister Louise, or The Story of a Woman's Repentance.* Frontispiece, 7 plates. Cloth. London, 1876. First edition. $35.

WIAT (or Wyatt), Sir Thomas. *Poems.* Edited by A. K. Foxwell. Portrait, 10 facsimiles. 2 vols., cloth. London, 1913. $75-$100.

WICKERSHAM, James. *Is It Mt. Tacoma or Rainier. What Do History and Tradition Say?* 16 pp., wrappers. Tacoma, Wash., 1893. First edition. $35-$50.

WIENERS, John. *Youth.* Stiff wrappers. New York, 1970. First edition. One of 126 signed. $25.

WIERZBICKI, F. P. *California as It Is and as It May Be.* 60 pp., glazed lavender wrappers. San Francisco, 1849. First edition, with errata leaf. (The first book written and published in California.) $5,000 and up. (Note: The most recent sale of a copy in original wrappers was in 1945, when the C. G. Littell copy brought $475 at auction; it is now in the Everett D. Graff collection at the Newberry Library, Chicago. A Newberry duplicate, rebound in half morocco, with title page bearing part of the author's presentation inscription, brought $3,500 at auction in 1968.) San Francisco, 1849. 76

pp., errata, saffron wrappers. Second edition. $3,000 and up. Also, $2,600 (A, 1968)—the Streeter copy. San Francisco, 1933. Grabhorn Press. Boards and cloth. One of 500. In dust jacket. $35-$50.

WIGGIN, Kate Douglas. See Smith, Kate Douglas.

WIGGIN, Kate Douglas. *Rebecca of Sunnybrook Farm.* Green pictorial cloth. Boston, 1903. First edition, first issue, with publisher's imprint on spine in type only 1/16 inch high. $35-$75.

WIGWAM and the Cabin (The). First and Second Series. 2 vols. in one, cloth. New York, 1845. (By William Gilmore Simms.) First editions. $75-$100. (Note: The two books first appeared separately in printed wrappers, which are exceedingly rare. No copies have appeared at public sale for many years.)

WILBARGER, J. W. *Indian Depredations in Texas.* 38 plates (37 listed). Pictorial cloth. Austin, Tex., 1899. First edition. $50-$75. Austin, 1933. Facsimile. Pictorial cloth. $25.

WILBUR, Earl Morse. *Thomas Lamb Eliot, 1841-1936.* Frontispiece. Cloth. Portland, Ore., 1937. First edition. (About T. S. Eliot's family.) $25.

WILBUR, Homer (editor). *Meliboeus-Hipponax. The Biglow Papers.* Cloth, or glazed boards. Cambridge, Mass., 1848. (By James Russell Lowell.) First edition, first issue, with George Nichols only as publisher. $150 and up.

WILBUR, Richard. *The Beautiful Changes and Other Poems.* Cloth. New York, no date (1947). First edition. In dust jacket. $60-$80. Author's first book.

WILBUR, Richard (compiler). *A Bestiary.* Illustrated by Alexander Calder. Pictorial buckram. New York, no date (1955). First edition. One of 750 signed. Boxed. $50-$75. Another issue: Folio, half morocco. One of 50 signed by author and artist and with a signed pen-and-ink drawing by Calder. $250-$350.

WILCOX, Ella Wheeler. See Wheeler, Ella.

WILDE, Oscar. See C. 3.3.; Young, Dal. Also see *The Ballad of Reading Gaol; Children in Prison; An Ideal Husband; The Importance of Being Earnest.*

WILDE, Oscar. *De Profundis.* Blue buckram. London, no date (1905). First edition, first issue, with ads dated February. $35-$50. Later, ads dated March. $20-$25. Large paper issues: Cloth. One of 200 on handmade paper. $200-$250. One of 50 on Japan vellum. $300-$400.

WILDE, Oscar. *The Duchess of Padua.* Wrappers. New York, no date (1905). $50. London, no date (1908). Buckram. $35-$50.

WILDE, Oscar. *The Fisherman and His Soul.* Illustrations and initials in color, illuminated in gold. Boards and silk. No place, no date (San Francisco, 1939). Grabhorn Press. One of 200. $50.

WILDE, Oscar. *The Happy Prince and Other Tales.* Illustrated by Walter Crane and Jacomb Hood. Vellum boards. London, 1888. First edition. $135-$150. Another issue: One of 75 signed. $300-$400.

WILDE, Oscar. *The Harlot's House.* 5 plates. Gray wrappers. No place, 1905 (1904?). First edition. $25. New York, 1929. Illustrated. Boards. $5-$10.

WILDE, Oscar. *A House of Pomegranates.* Cream-colored linen boards, green cloth spine. London, 1891. First edition. $125-$150. London, 1915. Color plates by Jessie M. King. Decorated cloth. $35-$50.

WILDE, Oscar. *Impressions of America.* Stiff wrappers. Sunderland, 1906. First edition. One of 500. $35-$50. Another issue: One of 50 on handmade paper. $75-$100.

WILDE, Oscar. *Intentions.* Moss-green cloth. London, 1891. First edition. $50-$75. Worn, $35.

WILDE, Oscar. *Lady Windermere's Fan: A Play About a Good Woman.* Reddish-brown linen. London, 1893. First edition. $100-$150. Large paper issue: One of 50. $150-$250. Paris, 1903. Cloth. Pirated edition published by Leonard Smithers. One of 250. $50.

WILDE, Oscar. *Lord Arthur Savile's Crime & Other Stories.* Salmon-colored boards. London, 1891. First edition. $50-$75. Rebound in morocco, $25 at retail.

WILDE, Oscar. *Newdigate Prize Poem. Ravenna. Recited in the Theatre, Oxford, June 26, 1878.* 16 pp., printed wrappers. Oxford, England, 1878. First edition, with Oxford University on title page and cover. $200-$250. Author's first publication.

WILDE, Oscar. *Oscariana. Epigrams.* Printed wrappers. No place (London), 1895. First edition. $75-$100.

WILDE, Oscar. *The Picture of Dorian Gray.* Rough gray beveled boards, vellum spine. London, no date (1891). First edition, with letter "a" missing from "and" on page 208 in eighth line from bottom. $75-$100. Spine repaired, $60. Another issue: One of 250 signed. (Error corrected.) $300-$400.

WILDE, Oscar. *Poems.* White parchment boards. London, 1881. First edition, first issue, with the word "maid" in line 3, stanza 2, page 136. $100-$150. London, 1892. Violet cloth. One of 220 signed. $100-$150. Paris, 1903. Buckram. One of 250. $25.

WILDE, Oscar. *Salome: Drame en Un Acte.* Purple wrappers. Paris, 1893. First edition. $50-$75. Another issue: One of 50 on Van Gelder paper. $100 and up. London, 1894. Illustrated by Aubrey Beardsley. Decorated cloth. First English edition. One of 500. $75-$125. Large paper issue: One of 100. $100-$150. Also, $42 (A, 1964). San Francisco, 1927. Grabhorn Press. Illustrated. Boards. One of 195. Boxed. $35. New York, 1938. Limited Editions Club. 2 vols., cloth. Boxed. $35-$50.

WILDE, Oscar. *The Soul of Man.* Light-brown printed wrappers. London, 1895. First edition. One of 50. $200-$250.

WILDE, Oscar. *The Soul of Man Under Socialism.* Boards, green linen spine. Boston, 1910. First "authorized" American edition. $35-$50.

WILDE, Oscar. *The Sphinx.* Decorations by Charles Ricketts. Vellum. London, 1894. First edition. One of 150. $200-$250. Another issue: One of 50 signed by Ricketts. $350-$500.

WILDE, Oscar. *Vera; or, The Nihilists.* Gray wrappers. London, 1880. First edition. $500-$750. Very rare, with a $570 auction record, 1920. A presentation copy sold for $375 in the early 1950's and when reoffered in the 1959 auction season brought $650. London, 1882. Wrappers. Second edition. $100-$150. London, 1902. Wrappers. One of 200. $35-$50.

WILDE, Oscar. *A Woman of No Importance.* Red linen. London, 1894. First edition. $75-$100. Shaken, hinge broken, $25. De luxe edition: Cloth. One of 50. $150-$200.

WILDER, Thornton. *The Angel That Troubled the Waters.* Blue boards and cloth. New York, 1928. First edition. One of 775 signed. In dust jacket. $60-$75. Dust jacket soiled, $50. Lacking jacket, $35. London, 1928. Blue cloth. First English edition. One of 260 signed. In dust jacket. $75. Lacking jacket, $35.

WILDER, Thornton. *The Bridge of San Luis Rey.* Tan cloth. London, 1927. First edition (preceding American edition by a few days). $75. Also, signed copy, $50 (A, 1970). New York, 1927. Cloth. First American edition, "preliminary issue," with title page printed only in black. In dust jacket. $300-$400. Also, in dust jacket, $250 (A, 1960); lacking jacket, $120 (A, 1960). Regular trade issue, title page printed in green and black: In dust jacket. $50-$75. New York, 1929. Illustrated by Rockwell Kent. Pictorial cloth, leather label. One of 1,000 signed by Wilder and Kent. Boxed. $55. Worn box, $35.

WILDER, Thornton. *The Cabala.* Blue figured cloth or tan figured cloth. New York, 1926. First edition, first printing, with "conversation" for "conversion" in line 13, page 196. Blue (only a few copies issued): In dust jacket. $100-$150. Also, $60 (A, 1970). Tan: $50-$100. Spine faded, $75. Author's first book.

WILDER, Thornton. *The Ides of March.* Cloth. New York, 1948. First edition. One of 750 signed. In dust jacket. $50. Trade edition: Cloth. In dust jacket. $25.

WILDER, Thornton. *James Joyce, 1882-1941.* Wrappers. Aurora, N.Y., no date. First edition. One of 150. $40-$50.

WILDER, Thornton. *The Long Christmas Dinner and Other Plays in One Act.* Boards, imitation vellum spine. New Haven, Conn., 1931. First edition. One of 525 signed. In dust jacket. Boxed. $35-$50. Trade edition: Brick cloth. In dust jacket. $25.

WILDER, Thornton. *The Merchant of Yonkers.* Cloth, paper labels. New York, 1939. First edition, first printing (so indicated on copyright page). In dust jacket. $35-$50.

WILDER, Thornton. *The Woman of Andros.* Cloth. London, 1930. One of 260 signed. In dust jacket. $50. Trade edition: In dust jacket. $10.

WILKES, Charles. *Synopsis of the Cruise of the United States Exploring Expedition During the Years 1838-42.* Folding map. 56 pp., wrappers. Washington, 1842. First edition. $100-$150.

WILKES, Charles. *Western America, Including California and Oregon.* 3 folding maps. Tan printed wrappers. Philadelphia, 1849. First edition. $150-$250.

WILKES, George. *The History of Oregon, Geographical and Political.* Folding map. 127 pp., printed wrappers. New York, 1845. First edition. $750 and up.

WILKESON, Samuel. *Wilkeson's Notes on Puget Sound.* 47 pp., wrappers. No place, no date (New York, 1870?). First edition. $35-$50.

WILKINSON, Gen. James. *Memoirs of My Own Times.* 9 folding tables, 3 folding facsimiles. 4 vols., boards and calf. Philadelphia, 1814-16. First edition, including atlas of 19 maps and plans. $1,000 (A, 1967). (Note: This was Thomas W. Streeter's copy. The very high price obtained for this set is remarkable when compared with the previous price range of these items—$150 to $650 for the *Memoirs* at retail and $50 for the atlas. The identical set sold for $45 at retail in 1928.)

WILL, George F. *Notes on the Arikara Indians and Their Ceremonies.* 48 pp., wrappers. Denver, 1934. Old West Series. One of 75. $50-$75.

WILLARD, John Ware. *A History of Simon Willard, Inventor and Clockmaker.* Cloth. No place (Boston), 1911. One of 500. $200-$250.

WILLCOX, R. N. *Reminiscences of California Life.* Cloth. No place (Avery, Ohio), 1897. First edition. $40-$75.

WILLEY, S. H. *An Historical Paper Relating to Santa Cruz, California.* 37 pp., printed wrappers. San Francisco, 1876. $75-$100.

WILLIAMS, Alpheus F. *The Genesis of the Diamond.* 221 plates, 30 colored. 2 vols., buckram. London, 1932. First edition. $75.

WILLIAMS, Mrs. Ellen. *Three Years and a Half in the Army.* Cloth. New York, no date (1885). First edition. $50-$75.

WILLIAMS, G. T. *Receipts and Shipments of Livestock at Union Stock Yards for 1890.* 40 pp., wrappers. Chicago, 1891. $75-$125.

WILLIAMS, Jesse. *A Description of the United States Lands of Iowa.* Folding map in color. Green cloth. New York, 1840. First edition. $250-$350.

WILLIAMS, John G. *The Adventures of a Seventeen-Year-Old Lad.* Cloth. Boston, 1894. First edition. $35-$50.

WILLIAMS, John Lee. *The Territory of Florida.* Folding map, portrait, 2 plates. Cloth. New York, 1837. First edition. $150. New York, 1839. Cloth. $45.

WILLIAMS, John Lee. *A View of West Florida.* Folding map. Boards and leather. Philadelphia, 1827. First edition. $150.

WILLIAMS, John R. *Biographical Sketch of the Life of William G. Greene, of Menard County, Ill.* 18 pp., cloth. No place, 1874. $35.

WILLIAMS, Joseph. *Narrative of a Tour from the State of Indiana to the Oregon Territory.* 48 pp., plain blue wrappers. Cincinnati, 1843. First edition. Up to $3,500. Also, $3,000 (A, 1968)—the Streeter copy, with front wrapper only. New York, 1921. Cloth. One of 250. $35-$50.

WILLIAMS, O. W. *In Old New Mexico, 1879-1880: Reminiscences of Judge O. W. Williams.* 48 pp., wrappers. No place, no date. $35-$50.

WILLIAMS, R. H. *With the Border Ruffians.* Illustrated. Cloth. New York, 1907. First American edition. $35-$50. London, 1907. First English edition. $35-$50.

WILLIAMS, Tennessee. *American Blues.* Printed wrappers. New York, no date (1948). First edition, first issue, with author's name misspelled on cover. $50-$75. Second issue, name corrected. $35. Signed copy, $45.

WILLIAMS, Tennessee. *Battle of Angels.* Printed wrappers (comprising double number, Nos. 1 and 2, of *Pharos,* Spring, 1945). No place, no date (Murray, Utah, 1945). First edition. $200-$250. Also, $100 and $165 (A, 1970). Author's first book.

WILLIAMS, Tennessee. *Cat on a Hot Tin Roof.* Tan cloth. No place, no date (New York, 1955). First edition. In dust jacket. $25-$35.

WILLIAMS, Tennessee. *The Glass Menagerie.* Rust or blue cloth. New York, 1945. First edition. In dust jacket. $50-$75.

WILLIAMS, Tennessee. *Grand.* Cloth. New York, 1964. First edition. One of 300 signed. $35-$50.

WILLIAMS, Tennessee. *Hard Candy.* Patterned boards, cloth spine. No place, no date (Norfolk, Conn., 1954). First edition. Limited. Boxed. $25-$35.

WILLIAMS, Tennessee. *I Rise in Flames, Cried the Phoenix.* Boards and cloth. New York, no date (1951). First edition. One of 300 signed (of an edition of 310). Boxed. $125-$150. Another issue: One of 10 on Umbria paper, signed. $350-$450.

WILLIAMS, Tennessee. *In the Winter of Cities: Poems.* White parchment boards, gilt. No place, no date (New York, 1956). First edition. One of 100 signed. In slipcase. $150-$200. Trade edition: Patterned boards and cloth. In dust jacket. $35-$50.

WILLIAMS, Tennessee. *One Arm and Other Stories.* Boards, vellum spine. No place, no date (Norfolk, 1948). First edition. One of 50 signed. Boxed. $250-$350. Trade edition: Boards and cloth. Boxed. $100-$150. (Note: A catalogue of some years back from Mrs. Marguerite Cohn's House of Books, New York, states that first issue copies are copyrighted by New Directions, while later copies bear a tipped-in page with copyright in Williams' name. It lists such a copy, signed by Williams, at $110. Estimated value today: $250 or more.)

WILLIAMS, Tennessee. *The Roman Spring of Mrs. Stone.* Marbled boards, vellum spine. No place, no date (New York, 1950). First edition. One of 500 signed. Boxed. $50-$75. Trade edition: Black cloth. In dust jacket. $15-$20.

WILLIAMS, Tennessee. *A Streetcar Named Desire.* Pink decorated boards. No place, no date (Norfolk, 1947). First edition. In dust jacket. $75-$100. Same place and date: Fifth printing, with text revised. In dust jacket. $30-$50.

WILLIAMS, Tennessee. *Summer and Smoke.* Blue cloth. No place, no date (Norfolk, 1948). First edition. In dust jacket. $20-$25.

WILLIAMS, Tennessee. *27 Wagons Full of Cotton and Other One-Act Plays.* Light-gray cloth. No place, no date (Norfolk, 1945). First edition. In dust jacket. $75-$100. No place (Norfolk), 1953. Third edition. Buckram. (First appearance of two plays, *Something Unspoken* and *Talk to Me Like the Rain.*) In dust jacket. $25.

WILLIAMS, Tennessee. *The Two-Character Play.* Cloth. New York, no date (1969). First edition. One of 350 signed. Boxed. $40-$50. (There was no trade edition.)

WILLIAMS, Tennessee, and Windham, Donald. *You Touched Me: A Romantic Comedy.* Green boards. New York, no date (1947). First edition. In dust jacket. $50-$75. Same: In gray printed wrappers. $50-$75.

WILLIAMS, Thomas J. C. *A History of Washington County* (Maryland). 2 vols., cloth. No place (Hagerstown), 1906. First edition. $50-$60.

WILLIAMS, William Carlos. See Ginsberg, Allen; Loy, Mina.

WILLIAMS, William Carlos. *Al Que Quiere! A Book of Poems.* Yellow boards. Boston, 1917. First edition. In dust jacket. $150-$200.

WILLIAMS, William Carlos. *The Build-Up.* Boards and cloth. New York, no date (1952). First edition. In dust jacket. $25.

WILLIAMS, William Carlos. *The Clouds, Aigeltinger, Russia and Other Verse.* Cloth, paper label on spine. No place (Aurora, N.Y., and Cummington, Mass.), 1948. First edition. One of 310. $50-$75.

WILLIAMS, William Carlos. *Collected Poems, 1921-1931.* Cloth. New York, 1934. First edition. In dust jacket. $75-$85.

WILLIAMS, William Carlos. *The Desert Music and Other Poems.* Boards and cloth. New York, no date (1954). First edition. One of 100 signed. In dust jacket. $125-$150.

WILLIAMS, William Carlos. *An Early Martyr.* Wrappers. New York, 1935. First edition. One of 165 signed. $300-$350.

WILLIAMS, William Carlos. *Go Go. (Manikin No. 2).* New York, no date (1923). Stiff printed wrappers, in publisher's envelope. First edition, with "Shakespeare & Company" label on inner rear cover. $250-$300.

WILLIAMS, William Carlos. *The Great American Novel.* Boards and cloth, paper label. Paris, 1923. Three Mountains Press. One of 300. $200-$250.

WILLIAMS, William Carlos. *In the American Grain.* Buckram. New York, 1925. First edition. In dust jacket. $50-$75.

WILLIAMS, William Carlos. *In the Money.* Cloth. Norfolk, no date (1940). First edition. In dust jacket. $35-$50.

WILLIAMS, William Carlos. *The Knife of the Times and Other Stories.* Cloth, paper label. Ithaca, no date (1932). First edition. One of 500. In dust jacket. $75-$100.

WILLIAMS, William Carlos. *Kora in Hell: Improvisations.* Illustrated. Gray boards. Boston, 1920. First edition. In dust jacket. $100-$150.

WILLIAMS, William Carlos. *A Novelette and Other Prose.* Printed green wrappers. No place, no date (Paris, 1932). First edition. $100-$150.

WILLIAMS, William Carlos. *Paterson.* (Books 1, 2, 3, 4, and 5.) 5 vols., cloth. No place, no date (New York, 1946-48-49-51-58). First editions. In dust jackets. $200-$250. (Note: The first book is the scarcest and is worth $75-$100; the others were worth roughly $25-$35 each as of this writing.)

WILLIAMS, William Carlos. *The Pink Church.* Printed wrappers. Columbus, Ohio, 1949. First edition. One of 400. $50-$75.

WILLIAMS, William Carlos. *Poems.* 22 pp., printed brown wrappers. No place (Rutherford, N.J.), 1909. First edition. $2,000-$2,500. Author's first book. (100 printed.)

WILLIAMS, William Carlos. *Sour Grapes.* Boards, paper label. Boston, 1921. First edition. $100-$150.

WILLIAMS, William Carlos. *Spring and All.* Printed wrappers. No place, no date (Dijon, France, 1923). First edition. $100-$175.

WILLIAMS, William Carlos. *The Tempers.* Boards. London, 1913. First edition. In glassine dust jacket. $400-$500.

WILLIAMS, William Carlos. *A Voyage to Pagany.* Gray cloth. New York, 1928. First edition. In dust jacket. $50-$75.

WILLIAMS, William Carlos. *White Mule.* Buckram. Norfolk, 1923. First edition. In dust jacket. $50-$75.

WILLIAMSON, George C. *The History of Portrait Miniatures.* 107 plates. 2 vols., folio, white cloth. London, 1904. One of 500. $100-$150. One of 50 with hand-colored plates. $150-$200.

WILLIAMSON, Henry. *The Patriot's Progress.* Wood engravings by William Kermode. Half vellum. London, no date (1930). First edition. One of 350 signed. Boxed. $35.

WILLIAMSON, James J. *Mosby's Rangers.* Cloth. New York, 1896. First edition. $35-$50. New York, 1909. Cloth. Second edition. $25-$35.

WILLIS, Byrd C., and Willis, Richard H. *A Sketch of the Willis Family of Virginia.* Cloth. Richmond, Va., no date (1898). $30.

WILLIS, Nathaniel Parker. *American Scenery.* 117 views by W. H. Bartlett. 2 vols., contemporary leather. London, 1840. First edition. $250-$300.

WILLIS, Nathaniel Parker. *Sketches.* Glazed boards and cloth, paper label. Boston, 1827. First edition. $25. Author's first book.

WILLIS, William L. *History of Sacramento County.* Illustrated. Three-quarters leather. Los Angeles, 1913. $50-$60.

WILLMOTT, Ellen. *The Genus Rosa.* Colored and plain plates. 25 parts, gray wrappers. London, 1910-14. First edition. $300-$400.

WILLOUGHBY, Edwin Elliott. *The Making of the King James Bible.* 31 pp., folio, boards and cloth. Los Angeles, 1956. Plantin Press. One of 290. $50.

WILLYAMS, Cooper. *A Voyage up the Mediterranean in HMS "Swiftsure."* 40 (43?) plates, including folding map. Calf. London, 1802. Plates uncolored, $50-$75. Plates colored, $150-$200. Large paper issue: Plates colored. $250-$300.

WILSON, Edmund. *Axel's Castle.* Cloth. New York, 1931. First edition. In dust jacket. $45-$60.

WILSON, Edmund. *The Boys in the Back Room.* Boards and cloth, paper label. San Francisco, 1941. Colt Press. First edition. In dust jacket. $35.

WILSON, Edmund. *Memoirs of Hecate County.* Green cloth. Garden City, N.Y., 1946. First edition. In dust jacket. $25.

WILSON, Edmund. *Note-books of Night.* Cloth. San Francisco, 1942. First edition. In dust jacket. $35.

WILSON, Edmund, and Bishop, John Peale. *The Undertaker's Garland.* Cloth. New York, 1922. First edition. In dust jacket. $25-$35.

WILSON, Elijah N. *Among the Shoshones.* 8 plates. Red cloth. Salt Lake City, no date (about 1910). First (suppressed) edition, with 22 pages. $150-$200. Second edition, same place and date, 247 pages. $50-$75.

WILSON, Harry Leon. *Ruggles of Red Gap.* Illustrated. Cloth. Garden City, N.Y., 1915. First edition. $25-$35.

WILSON, Harry Leon. *Zigzag Tales from the East to the West.* Illustrated by C. Jay Taylor. Cloth. New York, 1894. First edition. $40. Author's first book.

WILSON, Sir John. *The Royal Philatelic Collection.* Edited by Clarence Winchester. 12 color facsimiles, 48 monochrome plates, other illustrations. Full red morocco. London, 1952. First edition. $160. Another issue (?): Buckram. Boxed. $50 (A, 1968).

WILSON, John A. *Adventures of Alf Wilson.* Cloth. Toledo, Ohio, 1880. $35.

WILSON, John Albert. *History of Los Angeles County, California.* Illustrated. Leather and cloth. Oakland, Calif., 1880. First edition. $300-$350.

WILSON, Obed G. *My Adventures in the Sierras.* Portrait. Cloth. Franklin, Ohio, 1902. First edition. $37.50-$75.

WILSON, Richard L. *Short Ravelings from a Long Yarn, or Camp and March Sketches of the Santa Fe Trail.* Edited by Benjamin F. Taylor. Illustrated. Printed boards. Chicago, 1847. First edition. $2,000 plus. Santa Ana, Calif., 1936. Cloth. $50-$75.

WILSON, Robert. *The Travels of Robert Wilson: Being a Relation of Facts.* Portrait, plates. Mottled calf. London, 1807. $200.

WILSON, Woodrow. *Congressional Government.* Cloth. Boston, 1885. First edition, first issue, with publisher's monogram on spine. $25-$35. Author's first book.

WILSON, Woodrow. *George Washington.* Illustrated. Cloth. New York, 1897. First edition. $35-$50.

WILSON'S History of Hickory County, Missouri. Cloth. Hermitage, Mo., no date. $50. Spine chipped, $30.

WILTSEE, Ernest A. *Gold Rush Steamers of the Pacific.* Illustrated. Cloth. San Francisco, 1938. Grabhorn Press. One of 500. $100-$125.

WINDELER, Bernard. *Sailing Ships and Barges of the Western Mediterranean and the Adriatic Seas.* Map, 17 hand-colored copperplate engravings by Edward Wadsworth. London, 1926. One of 450. $50-$75.

WING-and-Wing (The). By the Author of "The Pilot." 2 vols., printed terra-cotta wrappers. Philadelphia, 1842. (By James Fenimore Cooper.) First American edition (of the novel issued first in London under the title *The Jack O'Lantern* and under Cooper's name; see author entry). $75-$100. Later issue, wrappers dated 1843. $50.

WINKLER, A. V. *The Confederate Capital and Hood's Texas Brigade.* Illustrated. Cloth. Austin, Tex., 1894. First edition. $75.

WINSHIP, George Parker. *The First American Bible.* Cloth. Boston, 1929. Merrymount Press. One of 157 with a leaf from John Eliot's Indian Bible of 1663. $50-$75.

WINSHIP, George Parker (editor). *The Journey of Francisco Vazquez de Coronado, 1540-1542.* Cloth. San Francisco, 1933. One of 550. $50-$75.

WINTER in the West (A). By a New Yorker. 2 vols., cloth. New York; 1835. (By Charles Fenno Hoffman.) First edition. $75-$100.

WINTERS, Yvor. *Before Disaster.* Printed green wrappers. Tryon, N.C., 1934. First edition. $40.

WINTERS, Yvor. *Maule's Curse: Seven Studies in the History of American Obscurantism.* Blue cloth. Norfolk, Conn., no date (1938). First edition. In dust jacket. $25.

WINTERS, Yvor. *The Proof.* Decorated boards. New York, 1930. First edition. In dust jacket. $35.

WISDOM of Jesus (The), the Son of Sirach. Commonly called Ecclesiasticus. Orange vellum, silk ties. London, 1932. One of 328. Ashendene Press. $200-$250. Another issue: One of 25 printed on vellum. Morocco. Up to $1,500.

WISE, George. *Campaigns and Battles of the Army of Northern Virginia.* 2 portraits. Cloth. New York, 1916. First edition. $50-$60.

WISLIZENUS, Frederick A. *A Journey to the Rocky Mountains in the Year 1839.* Folding map. Boards and cloth. St. Louis, 1912. First edition. One of 500. $50-$75.

WISLIZENUS, Frederick A. *Memoir of a Tour to Northern Mexico.* 3 folding maps. Boards. Washington, 1848. First edition. $50-$75.

WISTAR, Casper. *A System of Anatomy for the Use of Students of Medicine.* 2 vols., boards. Philadelphia, 1811-1814. First edition. $75-$100.

WISTAR, Isaac Jones. *Autobiography of Isaac Jones Wistar, 1827-1905.* Folding map, portrait, plates. 2 vols., cloth, leather spine labels. Philadelphia, 1914. First edition. One of 250. $250-$350. Philadelphia, 1937. Illustrated. Buckram. $25.

WISTER, Owen. *The Virginian.* Illustrated. Yellow pictorial cloth. New York, 1902. First edition. $75-$100. Signed, $75 and $90 at auction. New York, 1911. Illustrated by Frederic Remington and Charles M. Russell. Boards. One of 100. $200-$300. New York, 1930. Limited Editions Club. Cowhide. $30-$40.

WITHERS, Alexander S. *Chronicles of Border Warfare.* Leather. Clarksburg, Va., 1831. First edition. $100-$150. Cincinnati, 1895. Cloth. $35-$50.

WODEHOUSE, P. G. *The Pothunters.* Cloth. London, 1902. First edition. In dust jacket. $35. Author's first book.

WOLCOTT, Samuel. *Memorial of Henry Wolcott, and of Some of His Descendants.* Cloth. New York, 1881. $35.

WOLFE, Humbert. *Cursory Rhymes.* Illustrated by Albert Rutherston. Cloth. London, 1927. One of 500 signed. $25-$35.

WOLFE, Humbert. *The Silver Cat and Other Poems.* Boards. New York, 1928. One of 780. $25.

WOLFE, Thomas. See Koch, Frederick H.

WOLFE, Thomas. *The Face of a Nation.* Cloth. New York, 1939. First edition. In dust jacket. $25-$35.

WOLFE, Thomas. *From Death to Morning.* Cloth. New York, 1935. First edition, with code letter "A" on copyright page. In dust jacket. $50.

WOLFE, Thomas. *Gentlemen of the Press.* Cloth, paper label. Chicago, no date (1942). First edition. One of 350. $50-$75.

WOLFE, Thomas. *The Hills Beyond.* Cloth. New York, no date (1941). First edition. In dust jacket. $50-$75.

WOLFE, Thomas. *Look Homeward, Angel.* Blue cloth, gilt. New York, 1929. First edition, first issue, with seal of Scribner Press on copyright page. Author's first novel. In first state dust jacket with Wolfe's picture on back. $385. Worn copy, inscribed, $425. Also, $150 (A, 1968), $140 (A, 1966). Later dust jacket, $100 and up at retail. New York, 1947. Illustrated by D. Gorsline. Cloth. First illustrated edition. In dust jacket. $35-$50. New York, no date (1963). Reprint of Gorsline edition. In dust jacket. $20-$25.

WOLFE, Thomas. *Mannerhouse: A Play in a Prologue and Three Acts.* Black cloth. New York, 1948. First edition. One of 500. In dust jacket. Boxed. $40. Trade edition: Cloth. $10.

WOLFE, Thomas. *A Note on Experts: Dexter Vespasian Joyner.* Cloth. New York, 1939. First edition. One of 300. $100-$150.

WOLFE, Thomas. *Of Time and the River.* Black cloth. New York, 1935. First edition, with "A" on copyright page. In dust jacket. $35-$75. Autographed copy, $50.

WOLFE, Thomas. *The Story of a Novel.* Cloth. New York, 1936. First edition, with "A" on copyright page. In dust jacket. $35-$50.

WOLFE, Thomas. *To Rupert Brooke.* 4 leaves, printed wrappers. No place (Paris), 1948. One of 100 used as a Christmas greeting. $150-$200.

WOLFE, Thomas. *The Web and The Rock.* Blue cloth. New York, 1939. First edition, first printing, so indicated on copyright page. In dust jacket. $50-$75.

WOLFE, Thomas. *You Can't Go Home Again.* Cloth. New York, no date (1940). First edition, first printing, so indicated on copyright page. In dust jacket. $35-$50.

WOMAN'S Daring; As Shown by the Testimony of the Rock. Recorded by an Exultant Woman and a Hugh-millerated Man. 24 pp., unbound (self-wrappers with cover title?). No place, no date (Annisguam, Mass.?, 1872). First edition. Last leaf crudely mended, $250. (Note: Contains a contribution by Thomas A. Janvier, his first book appearance.)

WONDERFUL Providence (A), in Many Incidents at Sea. 24 pp., wrappers. Buffalo, N.Y., 1848. (By Capt. Elijah Holcomb.) First edition. $35-$50.

WONDERFUL Stories of Fuz-Buz the Fly and Mother Grabem the Spider (The). 9 engraved plates. Half morocco. Philadelphia, 1867. (By S. Weir Mitchell.) First edition. One of 170 on large paper. $200-$300. First trade edition: Cloth. $100-$150. Faded and worn, $110.

WOOD, Arnold. *John Wood of Attercliffe, Yorkshire, England, and Falls, Bucks County, Pennsylvania, etc.* Plates. 85 pp., boards. New York, 1903. First edition. One of 50. $35-$50.

WOOD, Mrs. Henry. *East Lynne.* 3 vols., violet cloth. London, 1861. First edition. $400 and up.

WOOD, James H. *The War, Stonewall Jackson, His Campaigns and Battles, The Regiment, as I Saw Them.* Cloth. Cumberland, Md., no date (about 1910). $75-$100.

WOOD, John. *Journal of John Wood.* 76 pp., printed wrappers. Chillicothe, Ohio, 1852. First edition. $2,000 and up. Also, $1,700 (A, 1968). Columbus, Ohio, 1871. 112 pp., printed wrappers. Second edition. $400-$500. Also, same (?) copy, $225 (A, 1966).

WOOD, R. E. *Life and Confessions of James Gilbert Jenkins: the Murderer of 18 Men.* Illustrated. 56 pp., wrappers. Napa City, 1864. First edition. $75.

WOOD, W. D. *Reminiscences of Reconstruction in Texas.* 58 pp., wrappers. No place (San Marcos, Tex.), 1902. First edition. $50.

WOOD, William. *Zoography, or the Beauties of Nature Displayed.* Aquatint plates by William Daniell. 3 vols., diced calf. London, 1807. First edition. $75.

WOODMAN, David, Jr. *Guide to Texas Emigrants.* Map, plate. Light-blue cloth. First edition. $75-$100.

WOODRUFF, W. E. *With the Light Guns in '61-'65.* Cloth. Little Rock, Ark., 1903. First edition. $75-$100.

WOODS, Daniel B. *Sixteen Months at the Gold Diggings.* Cloth. New York, 1851. First edition. $100-$150.

WOODS, George. *Governor's Message to the Legislative Assembly of the Territory of Utah.* 16 pp., sewed. Salt Lake, 1874. $35-$50.

WOODSON, W. H. *History of Clay County, Missouri.* Cloth. Topeka, 1920. $35-$50.

WOODSTOCK. 3 vols., boards. Edinburgh, 1826. (By Sir Walter Scott.) First edition. $75-$100.

WOODWARD, Augustus B. *Considerations of the Executive Government on the United States of America*. 80 pp., unbound. Flatbush, N.Y., 1809. $35-$50.

WOODWARD, John, and Burnett, George. *A Treatise on Heraldry*. 56 plates, many colored, other illustrations. 2 vols., cloth or half morocco. Edinburgh, 1892. $75-$100. Edinburgh, 1896. 66 plates, many colored, etc. 2 vols., half leather. One of 325. $100-$150.

WOODWARD, W. E. *Bunk*. Cloth. New York, 1923. First edition. In dust jacket. $35. Author's first book.

WOODWORTH, Samuel. *The Champions of Freedom, or the Mysterious Chief*. 2 vols., boards. New York, 1816-18. $100-$150.

WOOLF, Virginia. See Cameron, Julia M.

WOOLF, Virginia. *Beau Brummel*. Boards and cloth. New York, 1930. First edition. One of 550 signed. $100-$125.

WOOLF, Virginia. *The Captain's Death Bed*. Brown cloth. London, 1950. First edition. In dust jacket. $35-$50. New York, 1950. Blue cloth. First American edition. In dust jacket. $25-$35.

WOOLF, Virginia. *The Common Reader*. White boards and cloth. No place (London), 1925. Hogarth Press. First edition. In dust jacket. $75-$100. London, 1932. Cloth. Second Series (same title). In dust jacket. $45. New York, 1948. Blue cloth. First and Second Series in one volume. First American edition thus. In dust jacket. $25.

WOOLF, Virginia. *Jacob's Room*. Cloth. No place (Richmond), 1922. Hogarth Press. First edition. In dust jacket. $100-$125.

WOOLF, Virginia. *Journal d'un Écrivain*. Wrappers. Monaco, no date (1965). First French translation of *A Writer's Diary*. One of 20 on velin. $55.

WOOLF, Virginia. *Kew Gardens*. Woodcuts. Wrappers. No place (Richmond), 1919. Hogarth Press. First edition, first issue, with correction slip pasted to imprint at end. $150-$200. Second issue, "Richard Madley for the Hogarth Press." $50-$75.

WOOLF, Virginia. *Les Vagues*. Wrappers. Paris, no date (1957). First French translation of *The Waves*. $30.

WOOLF, Virginia. *Mr. Bennett and Mrs. Brown*. Cloth. No place (London), 1924. Hogarth Press. First edition. In dust jacket. $35-$50.

WOOLF, Virginia. *Mrs. Dalloway*. Cloth. London, 1925. First edition. In dust jacket. $75-$100. Lacking jacket, $55. New York, 1925. Orange cloth. First American edition. In dust jacket. $35-$50.

WOOLF, Virginia. *Monday or Tuesday*. Woodcuts. Decorated boards and cloth. No place (Richmond), 1921. Hogarth Press. First edition. $75-$100.

WOOLF, Virginia. *Night and Day*. Cloth. London, no date (1919). First edition. In dust jacket. $175-$200.

WOOLF, Virginia. *On Being Ill*. Vellum and cloth. London, 1930. Hogarth Press. First edition. One of 250 signed. $200.

WOOLF, Virginia. *Orlando: A Biography*. Plates. Cloth. No place (London), 1928. Hogarth Press. First English edition, first issue, brown cloth. $25-$50. New York, 1928. Plates. Black cloth. First American edition. One of 861 large paper copies, signed. $75-$125.

WOOLF, Virginia. *A Room of One's Own*. Cloth. London, 1929. First English edition. One of 492 signed. In dust jacket. $75-$100. Trade edition: In dust jacket. $45. New York, 1929. Cloth. First American edition. One of 492 signed. In dust jacket. $75.

WOOLF, Virginia. *Street Haunting.* Boards and morocco. San Francisco, 1930. Westgate Press. One of 500 signed. Boxed. $200 and $150.

WOOLF, Virginia. *Three Guineas.* 5 plates. Yellow cloth. London, 1938. Hogarth Press. First edition. In dust jacket. $45.

WOOLF, Virginia. *To the Lighthouse.* Cloth. London, 1927. Hogarth Press. First edition. $75-$100. New York, no date (1927). Cloth. First American edition. $25-$35. "Advance Proof" copy in plain wrappers. $50.

WOOLF, Virginia. *The Voyage Out.* Cloth. London, 1915. First edition. In dust jacket. $100-$200. Author's first book.

WOOLF, Virginia. *The Waves.* Purple cloth. London, 1931. Hogarth Press. First edition. In dust jacket. $75. New York, 1931. Cloth. First American edition. In dust jacket. $25.

WOOLF, Virginia. *A Writer's Diary.* Orange cloth. London, 1953. First edition. In dust jacket. $35. New York, 1954. Pink cloth. First American edition. In dust jacket. $25.

WOOLF, Virginia. *The Years.* Green cloth. London, 1937. Hogarth Press. First edition. In dust jacket. $50-$60.

WOOLF, Virginia, and Woolf, L. S. *Two Stories.* Wrappers. Richmond, 1917. Hogarth Press. First edition. $200-$250. First book from the Hogarth Press.

WOOLWORTH, James M. *Nebraska in 1857.* Colored folding map. Printed cloth. Omaha, Neb., 1857. First edition. $250-$300.

WOOTEN, Dudley G. (editor). *A Comprehensive History of Texas, 1865 to 1897.* 23 plates. 2 vols., leather. Dallas, 1898. First edition. $100-$150.

WORDSWORTH, William. See *Grace Darling; Kendel and Windermere Railway, etc.; Lyrical Ballads; Ode Performed in the Senate-House.*

WORDSWORTH, William. *A Decade of Years: Poems, 1798-1807.* Printed in red and black. Limp vellum. London, 1911. Doves Press. One of 200. $300. Another issue: One of 12 on vellum. Morocco. $350-$500.

WORDSWORTH, William. *Ecclesiastical Sketches.* Blue-gray boards. London, 1822. First edition. $50-$75.

WORDSWORTH, William. *The Excursion, Being a Portion of the Recluse, a Poem.* Drab boards. London, 1814. First edition. $75-$100.

WORDSWORTH, William. *A Letter to a Friend of Robert Burns.* Wrappers. London, 1816. First edition. $75-$100.

WORDSWORTH, William. *Memorials of a Tour on the Continent, 1820.* Boards. London, 1822. First edition. $150-$200.

WORDSWORTH, William. *Peter Bell, a Tale in Verse.* Frontispiece. 88 pp., drab wrappers, paper label on back. London, 1819. First edition. $250-$300.

WORDSWORTH, William. *Poems.* 2 vols., boards, paper labels. London, 1807. First edition. $250-$350. London, 1815. 2 vols., boards, with frontispiece added to each volume. $100-$150.

WORDSWORTH, William. *The Prelude, or Growth of a Poet's Mind: An Autobiographical Poem.* Dark-red cloth. London, 1850. First edition. $75-$100. London, 1915. Doves Press. Vellum. One of 155. $100-$150. Another issue: One of 10 on vellum. Morocco. $750-$1,000.

WORDSWORTH, William. *The Recluse.* 56 pp., green cloth. London, 1888. First edition. $35-$50.

WORDSWORTH, William. *The River Duddon: A Series of Sonnets.* Boards and cloth. London, 1820. First edition. $100-$150.

WORDSWORTH, William. *Thanksgiving Ode, January 18, 1816.* Dark-green wrappers. London, 1816. First edition. $200-$250.

WORDSWORTH, William. *The Waggoner: A Poem, to Which Are Added, Sonnets.* Drab wrappers, label. London, 1819. First edition. $150-$200.

WORDSWORTH, William. *The White Doe of Rylstone.* Frontispiece, drab boards, paper label. London, 1815. First edition. $100-$150.

WORDSWORTH, William. *Yarrow Revisited, and Other Poems.* Drab boards, paper label on spine; also, in cloth. London, 1835. First edition, with inserted errata slip. $75-$100.

WORLD'S History of Cleveland" ("The). Cloth. Cleveland, 1896. Binding loose, $25.

WRECK of the "Grosvenor" (The). 3 vols., contemporary half calf and marbled boards, red and green labels. London, 1877. (By W. Clark Russell.) First edition. $150.

WRIGHT, Austin Tappan. *Islandia.* Beige buckram. New York, no date (1942). First edition, first issue, with Farrar & Rinehart monogram on copyright page. In dust jacket. $50. With Basil Davenport prospectus pamphlet *An Introduction to Islandia*, $75. Lacking jacket but with prospectus, $50. Lacking both jacket and pamphlet, $25.

WRIGHT, Crafts J. *Official Journal of the Conference Convention Held at Washington City, February, 1861.* Wrappers. Washington, 1861. $50.

WRIGHT, E. W. (editor). *Lewis and Dryden's Marine History of the Pacific Northwest.* Plates. Morocco. Portland, 1895. First edition. $200-$250.

WRIGHT, Frank Lloyd. See Gannett, William C., *The House Beautiful.*

WRIGHT, Frank Lloyd. *An Autobiography.* Illustrated. Cloth. New York, 1932. First edition. $35-$50.

WRIGHT, Frank Lloyd. *Buildings, Plans and Designs.* 100 plates, loose in portfolio. New York, 1963. Limited edition. $150-$200.

WRIGHT, Frank Lloyd. *Drawings for a Living Architecture.* 200 drawings by the author (75 colored). Oblong folio, cloth. New York, 1959. Signed by the author. In dust jacket. $400-$500.

WRIGHT, Frank Lloyd. *The Japanese Print.* Illustrated. Orange wrappers. Chicago, 1912. First edition (suppressed). $500-$600. (Note: All except about 50 burned by the publisher when Wright protested the binding.) First published edition: Printed boards. One of 35 on vellum. $300-$400. Also, $150 (A, 1969). Ordinary issue: $85-$100.

WRIGHT, Frank Lloyd. *On Architecture.* Edited by Frederick Gutheim. Cloth. New York, 1941. First edition. $50-$60.

WRIGHT, Harold Bell. *The Shepherd of the Hills.* Cloth. Chicago, 1897. First edition. $25.

WRIGHT, Harold Bell. *That Printer of Udell's: A Story of the Middle West.* Illustrated by John Clithero Gilbert. Pictorial cloth. Chicago, 1903. First edition. $25-$35. Author's first book.

WRIGHT, Harry. *Harry Wright's Pocket Base Ball Score Book, No. 1.* Cloth, paper label. Boston, 1876. $30.

WRIGHT, John Lloyd. *My Father Who Is on Earth.* Gray cloth. New York, no date (1946). First edition. In dust jacket. $35.

WRIGHT, Joseph (editor). *The English Dialect Dictionary.* 6 vols., half morocco. London, 1898-1905. $180. New York, 1962. 6 vols., cloth. Reprint. $100-$125.

WRIGHT, Philip Green. *The Dreamer.* Foreword by Charles A. Sandburg. White boards. Galesburg, Ill., no date (1906). First edition. $225. (Carl Sandburg's first prose writing—set, printed and bound, but not published, two years before his first book, *In Reckless Ecstasy.*)

WRIGHT, Richard. *How Bigger Was Born.* Printed wrappers. New York, no date (1940). First edition. $35.

WRIGHT, Richard. *Native Son.* Dark-blue cloth, stamped in red. New York, 1940. First edition, first binding. In dust jacket. $25.

WRIGHT, Richard. *Uncle Tom's Children.* Red cloth. New York, 1938. First edition. In dust jacket. $50. Author's first book.

WRIGHT, Robert M. *Dodge City, the Cowboy Capital.* Colored frontispiece, 40 plates. Cloth. No place, no date (Wichita, 1913). First edition, with 344 pp. $100-$125. Second edition, same place and date, 342 pp., black-and-white portrait. $15-$25.

WRIGHT, Capt. T. J. *History of the 8th Regiment, Kentucky Volunteer Infantry.* Cloth. St. Joseph, 1880. $50.

WRIGHT, William. See De Quille, Dan.

WRISTON, Jennie A. *A Pioneer's Odyssey.* 92 pp., cloth. No place (Menasha, Wis.), 1943. $35-$50.

WROTH, Lawrence C. *The Early Cartography of the Pacific.* Folding facsimile maps. Cloth. New York, 1934. First edition. One of 100. $75-$100.

WYANDOTTE; or, The Hutted Knoll. 3 vols., boards. London, 1843. (By James Fenimore Cooper.) First edition. $100-$150. Philadelphia, 1843. 2 vols., wrappers. First American edition. $75-$100.

WYATT, M. D. *The Art of Illuminating.* Illustrated. Decorated brown cloth. London, 1860. First edition. $75.

WYATT, Sir Thomas. See Wiat, Sir Thomas.

WYETH, John A. *Life of Gen. Nathan Bedford Forrest.* 55 plates, maps. Cloth. New York, 1899. First edition. $35-$50.

WYETH, John B. *Oregon; or A Short History of a Long Journey.* 87 pp., printed wrappers. Cambridge, Mass., 1833. First edition, first issue, with half title. (Very rare~with wrappers intact.) $1,000 and up. Rebound in full red morocco, $600. Cleveland, 1906. Cloth. Reprint (with John K. Townsend's *Journey Across the Rockies to the Columbia*). $35-$50.

WYLIE, Elinor. See *Incidental Numbers.*

WYLIE, Elinor. *Angels and Earthly Creatures: A Sequence of Sonnets.* Decorated wrappers. Henley-on-Thames, England, 1928. First edition. One of 51 numbered copies. About half of this edition were signed, the rest left unsigned at the author's death. In dust jacket, signed. $75-$100. Unsigned. $60. New York, 1929. Portrait. Black cloth. First American edition (and first commercially published). One of 200. Boxed. $35.

WYLIE, Elinor. *Mr. Hodge & Mr. Hazard.* Blue buckram. New York, 1928. First edition. One of 145 (actually 150) signed. Boxed. $35-$50.

WYLIE, Elinor. *Nets to Catch the Wind.* Cloth. New York, 1921. First edition, first issue, on unwatermarked paper. In dust jacket. $50-$75.

WYLIE, Elinor. *The Orphan Angel.* Boards and cloth. New York, 1926. One of 160 on rag paper, signed. Boxed. $50-$60. Spine faded, $25. Another issue: One of 30 on vellum, signed. $100.

WYLIE, Elinor. *Trivial Breath.* Boards. New York, 1928. First edition, with "In" for "An" in line 9 of page 13. One of 100 signed. $50-$75.

WYLIE, Elinor. *The Venetian Glass Nephew.* Boards. New York, 1925. First edition, first issue, without publisher's monogram on copyright page. One of 250 signed. $25-$35.

WYMAN, Capt. Thomas W., and others. *Tables of Allowances, etc.* (For Navy vessels.) Half leather. Washington, 1844. $35.

X

XENOPHON. *Cyrapaedia: The Institution and Life of Cyrus, the First of That Name, King of Persians.* Translated by Philemon Holland. (Reprint of 1632 edition.) Folio, goatskin. Newtown, Wales, 1936. Gregynog Press. One of 150. $350-$400. Special issue: One of 15 bound by George Fisher. Morocco. $1,000 and up. Also, $972 (A, 1968).

Y

YALE Book of Student Verse, 1910-1919 (The). Boards. New Haven, Conn., 1919. First edition. $25. (Note: Contains 14 poems by Stephen Vincent Benét.)

YANKEE Doodle. Illustrated by F. O. C. Darley. 8 pp., stiff printed wrappers. New York, no date (about 1860). $35.

YATES, Edmund Hodgson. *My Haunts and Their Frequenters.* Illustrated wrappers. London, 1854. First edition. $50. Author's first book.

YE Minutes of Ye CLXXVIIth Meeting of Ye Sette of Odd Volumes. Transcribed by John Todhunter. Printed wrappers. No place, no date (London, 1896). One of 154. $300-$400.

YE Preposterous Book of Brasse, Which Includes Divers Strange & Surprising Vituscan Voyages, etc. 55 pp., gold metallic covers. No place (San Francisco), 1937. $25.

YEARY, Mamie. *Reminiscences of the Boys in Gray, 1861-1865.* Cloth. Dallas, 1912. First edition. $100-$125.

YEATS, John Butler. *Early Memories.* Preface by W. B. Yeats. Boards and linen. Churchtown, Dundrum, Ireland, 1923. Cuala Press. One of 500. $100.

YEATS, John Butler. *Further Letters.* Selected by Lennox Robinson. Boards and linen. Churchtown, Dundrum, 1920. Cuala Press. One of 400. $85-$100.

YEATS, John Butler. *La la noo.* Boards and linen. Dublin, 1943. Cuala Press. One of 250. In dust jacket. $75-$100.

YEATS, John Butler. *Passages from the Letters of John Butler Yeats.* Selected by Ezra Pound. Boards and linen. Churchtown, Dundrum, 1917. Cuala Press. One of 400. $100-$125.

YEATS, William Butler. See Allingham, William; Bax, Clifford; Dunsany, Lord; Ganconagh; Gogarty, Oliver St. John; Gregory, Lady. Also see *Agnes Tobin.*

YEATS, William Butler. *The Bounty of Sweden.* Boards and linen. Dublin, 1925. Cuala Press. One of 400. In glassine dust jacket. $85.

YEATS, William Butler. *The Cat and the Moon and Certain Poems.* Boards and linen. Dublin, 1924. Cuala Press. First edition. One of 500. $100-$125.

YEATS, William Butler. *Cathleen ni Houlihan.* Vellum, silk ties. London, 1902. Caradoc Press. First edition. One of 8 on Japan vellum. $285. First regular edition: Cream-colored boards, leather spine. $125-$150.

YEATS, William Butler. *The Celtic Twilight.* Olive-green cloth. London, 1893. First edition, first binding, with publisher's name on back in capital letters. $125-$150. Also, worn, $67 (A, 1970), $67.20 (A, 1968). Later binding, capitals and lower case lettering, $50-$100.

YEATS, William Butler. *Collected Works.* Portraits. 8 vols., buckram. Stratford-on-Avon, England, 1908. $600-$750.

YEATS, William Butler. *The Countess Kathleen.* Frontispiece. Japan vellum boards. London, 1892. First edition. One of 30 signed by the publisher. $250-$350. Another issue: Dark-green boards, parchment spine. One of 500. $150-$200. London, 1919. Wrappers. Revised edition. $20-$25.

YEATS, William Butler. *The Cutting of an Agate.* Green boards. New York, 1912. First edition. In dust jacket. $75. Lacking jacket, $35-$50. London, 1919. Dark-blue cloth. First English edition. In dust jacket. $50-$60.

YEATS, William Butler. *The Death of Synge, and Other Passages from an Old Diary.* Boards and linen. Dublin, 1928. Cuala Press. First edition. One of 400. In dust jacket. $100-$150.

YEATS, William Butler. *De Gravin Catelene.* Vellum boards. The Hague, The Netherlands, 1941. First edition. One of 10. $85.

YEATS, William Butler. *Deirdre.* Gray boards, green cloth spine, paper label. London, 1907. First edition, with printer's imprint on page 48. $60-$75.

YEATS, William Butler. *Discoveries: A Volume of Essays.* Blue boards and linen. Dundrum, 1907. Dun Emer Press. First edition. One of 200. $100.

YEATS, William Butler. *Dramatis Personae.* Boards and linen. Dublin, 1935. Cuala Press. One of 400. In dust jacket. $125-$150.

YEATS, William Butler. *Early Memories.* Boards and linen. Churchtown, Dundrum, 1923. Cuala Press. First edition. One of 500. $35-$50.

YEATS, William Butler. *Enfance et Jeunesse Resongées.* Wrappers. Paris, no date (1965). First French translation of *Reveries over Childhood and Youth.* One of 10 on velin. $35.

YEATS, William Butler. *Essays.* Cloth. London, 1924. First edition. $200. New York, 1924. Boards and cloth. One of 250 signed. $150.

YEATS, William Butler. *Essays: 1931 to 1936.* Boards and linen. Dublin, 1937. Cuala Press. One of 300. In dust jacket. $75-$85.

YEATS, William Butler. *Estrangement: Being Some Fifty Thoughts from a Diary Kept by William Butler Yeats.* Boards and linen. Dublin, 1926. Cuala Press. First edition. One of 300. In dust jacket. $85-$100.

YEATS, William Butler. *Four Years.* Boards and linen. Churchtown, Dundrum, 1921. Cuala Press. First edition. One of 400. $100.

YEATS, William Butler. *A Full Moon in March.* Dark-green cloth. London, 1935. First edition. In dust jacket. $35.

YEATS, William Butler. *The Golden Helmet.* Gray boards. New York, 1908. First edition. One of 50. $200-$300.

YEATS, William Butler. *The Green Helmet and Other Poems.* Gray boards and linen. Churchtown, Dundrum, 1910. Cuala Press. One of 400. With erratum slip. $100-$150.

YEATS, William Butler. *The Hour Glass.* Unbound. London, 1903. First edition. 12 copies issued; without covers. $1,000, possibly more. (The scarcest of all Yeats items. An inscribed copy brought $170 at auction in 1941; no other sales noted.)

YEATS, William Butler. *The Hour Glass, Cathleen ni Houlihan, The Pot of Broth: Being Volume Two of Plays for an Irish Theatre.* Gray boards and green cloth. London, 1904. First English edition. $75-$100.

YEATS, William Butler. *Ideas of Good and Evil.* Green boards and cloth. London, 1903. First edition. $75-$100. London, 1913. Half cloth. Signed. $75.

YEATS, William Butler. *If I Were Four-and-Twenty.* Boards and linen. Dublin, 1940. Cuala Press. One of 450. In dust jacket. $75-$100.

YEATS, William Butler. *In the Seven Woods.* Printed in red and black. Linen. Dundrum, 1903. Dun Emer Press. First edition. One of 325. In plain dust jacket. $250-$350.

YEATS, William Butler. *John Sherman and Dhoya.* See Ganconagh.

YEATS, William Butler. *The King of the Great Clock Tower, Commentaries and Poems.* Boards and linen, paper label. Dublin, 1934. Cuala Press. One of 400. $100-$150.

YEATS, William Butler. *The Land of Heart's Desire.* Purple-pink wrappers. London, 1894. First edition. $100-$125. Chicago, 1814 (actually 1894). Gray boards. First American edition. One of 450. $75-$100.

YEATS, William Butler. *Last Poems and Plays.* Green cloth. London, 1940. First trade edition (after 500-copy Cuala Press edition of *Last Poems and Two Plays*). In dust jacket. $75-$100.

YEATS, William Butler. *Last Poems and Two Plays.* Boards and linen. Dublin, 1939. Cuala Press. One of 500. In dust jacket. $85-$100.

YEATS, William Butler. *Later Poems.* Light-green cloth. London, 1922. First edition. $85-$100. New York, 1924. Boards. First American edition. One of 250 signed. In glassine jacket. Boxed. $50-$75. Trade issue: Cloth. $15-$20.

YEATS, William Butler. *Michael Robartes and the Dancer.* Printed in red and black. Boards and linen. Churchtown, Dundrum, 1920. Cuala Press. First edition. One of 400. $85-$100.

YEATS, William Butler. *Modern Poetry.* Bright-green wrappers. London, 1936. First edition. One of 1,000. $50.

YEATS, William Butler. *Mosada. A Dramatic Poem.* Brown wrappers. Dublin, 1886. First edition. $3,000-$4,000. Also, $2,296 (A, 1962); inscribed by Yeats, $3,750 (A, 1963). Author's first book. Dublin, 1943. Cuala Press. Cream-colored parchment wrappers. One of 50. $150-$200. (Note: This poem was first published in the *Dublin University Review,* June, 1886, Vol. 2, No. 6, original decorated wrappers. A copy of the review was listed in 1971 in a New York dealer's catalogue at $750.)

YEATS, William Butler. *New Poems.* Boards and linen. Dublin, 1938. Cuala Press. One of 450. In glassine dust jacket. $100-$150.

YEATS, William Butler. *October Blast: Poems.* Boards and linen. Dublin, 1927. Cuala Press. One of 350. In dust jacket. $150-$200.

YEATS, William Butler. *On the Boiler.* Pictorial blue-green wrappers. Dublin, no date (1939). Cuala Press. Second edition. (Only about 4 copies of the first edition were printed, according to Mrs. Yeats.) $75-$100.

YEATS, William Butler. *A Packet for Ezra Pound.* Boards and linen. Dublin, 1929. Cuala Press. One of 425. In plain dust jacket. $200-$300.

YEATS, William Butler. *Pages from a Diary Written in Nineteen Hundred and Thirty.* Yellow boards and linen. Dublin, 1944. Cuala Press. One of 280. In dust jacket. $100-$150.

YEATS, William Butler. *Per Amica Silentia Lunae.* Dark-blue cloth. London, 1918. First edition. $75-$100.

YEATS, William Butler. *Plays and Controversies.* Boards and cloth. New York, 1924. One of 250 signed. Boxed. $150.

YEATS, William Butler. *Plays in Prose and Verse.* Boards and cloth. New York, 1924. One of 250 signed. $150.

YEATS, William Butler. *Poems.* Light-brown cloth. London, 1895. First edition. One of 25 printed on vellum, signed by Yeats. $400-$500. Trade edition: 750 copies. $75-$100. London, 1899. Dark-blue cloth. Second English edition. $100-$150. London, 1901. Dark-blue cloth. Third English edition. $65. London, 1908. Cloth. Fifth English edition. $50-$100. Dublin, 1935. Blue wrappers. Cuala Press. One of 30. $300-$350. London, 1949. 2 vols., olive-green cloth. Definitive Edition. One of 375 signed. Boxed. $500-$600.

YEATS, William Butler. *Poems, 1899-1905.* Blue cloth. London, 1906. First edition. $75-$150.

YEATS, William Butler. *Poems Written in Discouragement, 1912-1913.* Dark-gray wrappers. Dundrum, 1913. Cuala Press. One of 50. $300-$500.

YEATS, William Butler. *The Poetical Works of William Butler Yeats.* 2 vols., dark-blue cloth. New York, 1906-07. First edition. $50-$75.

YEATS, William Butler. *Responsibilities and Other Poems.* Dark-blue cloth. London, 1916. First edition. $50-$60. New York, 1916. Gray boards and cloth. First American edition. $40-$50.

YEATS, William Butler. *Responsibilities: Poems and a Play.* Gray boards and linen. Churchtown, Dundrum, 1914. Cuala Press. First edition. One of 400. $100-$125.

YEATS, William Butler. *Reveries over Childhood and Youth.* With a blue board portfolio containing a colored plate and 2 portraits. Gray boards and linen. Churchtown, Dundrum, 1915. Cuala Press. One of 425. $200. New York, 1916. Decorated boards, linen spine. First American edition. "Advance copy for Review Not for Sale." $35. (Note: This last price is from an American catalogue before the recent sharp advance in Yeats prices.) Regular issue: Buff cloth. $35-$50. London, 1916. Dark-blue cloth. First English edition. $75.

YEATS, William Butler. *The Secret Rose.* Illustrated by John Butler Yeats. Dark-blue cloth. London, 1897. First edition. $75-$100. Covers faded, signature of former owner on flyleaf, $50.

YEATS, William Butler. *A Selection from the Love Poetry of William Butler Yeats.* Gray boards and linen. Churchtown, Dundrum, 1913. Cuala Press. One of 300. $100.

YEATS, William Butler. *Seven Poems and a Fragment.* Gray boards and linen. Dundrum, 1922. Cuala Press. First edition. One of 500. $75-$100.

YEATS, William Butler. *The Shadowy Waters.* Dark-blue cloth. London, 1900. First edition. $75-$100. New York, 1901. Gray boards. First American edition. $50-$75.

YEATS, William Butler. *Stories of Michael Robartes and His Friends.* 2 woodcut illustrations. Boards and linen. Dublin, 1931. First edition. Cuala Press. One of 450. In dust jacket. $150-$200.

YEATS, William Butler. *Stories of Red Hanrahan.* Blue boards and linen. Dundrum, 1904. Dun Emer Press. First edition. One of 500. In dust jacket. $150-$200.

YEATS, William Butler. *Synge and the Ireland of His Time.* Gray boards and linen. Churchtown, Dundrum, 1911. Cuala Press. First edition. One of 350. $100.

YEATS, William Butler. *The Tables of the Law. The Adoration of the Magi.* Portrait frontispiece. Buckram. No place (London), 1897. First edition. One of 110. $360. London, 1904. Blue wrappers. First unlimited edition. $30-$50.

YEATS, W. B. *Three Things.* Blue boards. London, 1929. First edition. One of 500 large paper copies, signed. $75. Covers worn, $50. Trade issue (Ariel Poems): Blue wrappers. (Cover title only.) $25.

YEATS, William Butler. *The Tower.* Cloth. London, 1928. First edition. In dust jacket. $200.

YEATS, William Butler. *The Trembling of the Veil.* Portrait frontispiece. Blue boards and parchment. London, 1922. First edition. One of 1,000 signed. In dust jacket. $150-$200.

YEATS, William Butler. *Two Plays for Dancers.* Green boards and linen. No place (Dundrum), 1919. Cuala Press. First edition. One of 400. $85.

YEATS, William Butler. *The Wanderings of Oisin and Other Poems.* Dark-blue cloth. London, 1889. First edition. One of 500. $750.

YEATS, William Butler. *The Wild Swans at Coole, Other Verses, and a Play in Verse.* Dark-blue boards and linen. Churchtown, Dundrum, 1917. Cuala Press. First edition. One of 400. $100-$125. London, 1919. Dark-blue cloth. In dust jacket. $50-$60.

YEATS, William Butler. *The Wind Among the Reeds.* Dark-blue cloth. London, 1899. First edition, first issue, without correction slip. $150-$200. Second issue, same date, with correction slip. $35-$50.

YEATS, William Butler. *The Winding Stair.* Dark-blue cloth. New York, 1929. Fountain Press. First American edition. One of 642 signed. In dust jacket. $150-$200. (Note: Unbound folded sheets of another 1929 New York issue, unpublished, bearing Crosby Gaige's imprint and with Yeats' signature on limitation page, was sold at auction in New York in 1962 for $150.) London, 1933. Olive-green cloth. First English edition (with *And Other Poems* added to title). $50-$75.

YEATS, William Butler. *Words for Music Perhaps and Other Poems.* Blue boards and linen. Dublin, 1932. Cuala Press. One of 450. In dust jacket. $150-$200.

YEATS, W. B. *The Words upon the Window Pane: A Play in One Act.* Blue boards and linen. Dublin, 1934. Cuala Press. First edition. One of 350. In dust jacket. $150.

YEATS, William Butler, and Johnson, Lionel. *Poetry and Ireland: Essays.* Boards and linen. Churchtown, Dundrum, 1908. Cuala Press. First edition. One of 250. $100.

YELLOW BIRD. *The Life and Adventures of Joaquin Murieta.* 2 plates. 90 pp., wrappers. San Francisco, 1854. (By John R. Ridge.) First edition. Howes: "One copy known." $10,000 at auction (1967)—the Streeter copy. (Note: For later editions, see *The Life of Joaquin Murieta*; also see Ridge, John R.)

YELLOWPLUSH Correspondence (The). Boards and cloth, paper label. Philadelphia, 1838. (By William Makepeace Thackeray.) First edition. First publication in book form of any of Thackeray's works. $300-$350.

YEMASSEE (The): A Romance of Carolina. 2 vols., cloth, paper labels. New York, 1835. (By William Gilmore Simms.) First edition, first issue, with copyright notice pasted in in Vol. 1. $400-$600.

YOAKUM, Henderson K. *History of Texas.* Folding document, 4 maps, 5 plates. 2 vols., half calf. New York, 1855. First edition. $300-$400. New York, 1856. 2 vols., cloth. Second edition. $100-$200.

YOSY, A. *Switzerland.* 50 colored engravings. 2 vols., boards. London, 1815. $300-$400. London, 1816. 2 vols. $400-$500.

YOUNG, Andrew W. *History of Chautauqua County, New York.* Half morocco. Buffalo, N.Y., 1875. First edition. $35-$40.

YOUNG, Ansel. *The Western Reserve Almanac for the Year 1844.* 32 pp., wrappers. Cleveland, no date (1843). $35-$50.

YOUNG, Brigham. *Governor's Message to the First General Assembly of the State of Deseret.* 4 pp., folder. No place, no date (Great Salt Lake City, 1862). $100.

YOUNG, Dal. *Apologia pro Oscar Wilde.* Printed wrappers. London, no date (1895). First edition. $35-$50.

YOUNG Duke (The). By the Author of "Vivian Grey." 3 vols., boards, paper spines with labels. London, 1831. (By Benjamin Disraeli.) First edition, first issue, with half titles to Vols. 2 and 3 and advertisement leaf at end of Vol. 3. $100-$150.

YOUNG, Harry (Sam). *Hard Knocks: A Life Story of the Vanishing West.* 25 plates. Stiff wrappers. Portland, 1915. First edition. $50-$60. Chicago, no date (1915). Only 18 plates. Cloth. Reprint edition. $35-$50.

YOUNG, John. *An Address to the Senior Class, Delivered at the Commencement in Centre College, September 22, 1831.* 15 pp., sewed. Danville, Ky., 1831. $25.

YOUNG, John R. *Memoirs.* 4 portraits. Cloth. Salt Lake City, 1920. First edition. $100-$125.

YOUNG, Philip. *History of Mexico.* Sheep. Cincinnati, 1847. First edition. $75. Cincinnati, 1848. Cloth. Second edition. $60.

YOUNG, R. M. *Argument of Attorney for the Occupants of Portage City Against the State of Wisconsin.* 62 pp., wrappers. No place, no date (Washington, 1857). $45.

YOUNGBLOOD, Charles L. *Adventures of Chas. L. Youngblood During Ten Years on the Plains.* Portrait. Cloth. Boonville, Ind., 1882. First edition. $200-$250.

Z

ZACCARELLI, John. *Zaccarelli's Pictorial Souvenir Book of the Golden Northland.* Oblong, wrappers. Dawson, no date (1908). $35-$50.

ZAMACOIS, Niceto de. *El Buscador de Oro en California.* 81 pp., wrappers. Mexico, 1855. $40.

ZAMORANO 80 (The): A Selection of Distinguished California Books. Cloth. Los Angeles, 1945. First edition. One of 500. $55-$75.

ZAVALA, Lorenzo de. *Ensayo Histórico de las Revoluciones de Megico, etc.* 2 vols. (Vol. 1, Paris, 1831.) Vol. 2, New York, 1832. First edition. $200-$250.

ZONES of the Earth (The). 12 color plates. Oblong folio, cloth portfolio with pictorial cover. London, 1845. $25.

ZUCKER, E. *The Chinese Theatre.* Plates, 4 original paintings on silk. Pictorial cloth. Boston, 1925. One of 750. $50-$60.

ZUKOFSKY, Louis. See *Columbia Verse: 1897-1924.*

ZUKOFSKY, Louis. *"A" 1–12.* Cloth. No place (Ashland, Mass.), 1959. First edition. One of 200. Errata slip laid in. In glassine dust jacket. $25-$35.

ZUKOFSKY, Louis. *"A"–14.* Cloth. No place, no date (London, 1967). One of 250 signed. In dust jacket. $25-$35.

ZUKOFSKY, Louis. *Barely and Widely.* Oblong, wrappers. New York, 1958. First edition. One of 300 signed. $45.

ZUKOFSKY, Louis. *First Half of "A"–9.* Manila envelope. New York, privately printed, no date. "First Edition, Limited to 55 Autographed Copies." $200-$250. Author's first book.

ZUKOFSKY, Louis. *I Sent Thee Late.* No place, no date (Cambridge, Mass., 1965). First edition. One of 20 signed. $60.

ZUKOFSKY, Louis. *It Was.* Cloth. No place, no date (Kyoto, Japan, 1961). First edition. One of 50 signed. $45.

ZUKOFSKY, Louis. *Iyyob.* Oblong, wrappers. London, 1965. Turret Books. One of 100 signed. $40-$50.

ZUKOFSKY, Louis. *A Test of Poetry.* Cloth. Brooklyn, N.Y., 1948. First edition. In dust jacket. $35-$50.

ZUKOFSKY, Louis. *An Unearthing.* Wrappers. No place, no date (Cambridge, 1965). First edition. One of 77 signed. $35-$50.

ZUKOFSKY, Louis (editor). *An "Objectivist's" Anthology.* Wrappers. No place (Dijon, France), 1932. First edition. $50. (Contributors include T. S. Eliot, William Carlos Williams.)